FINANCIAL REPORTS

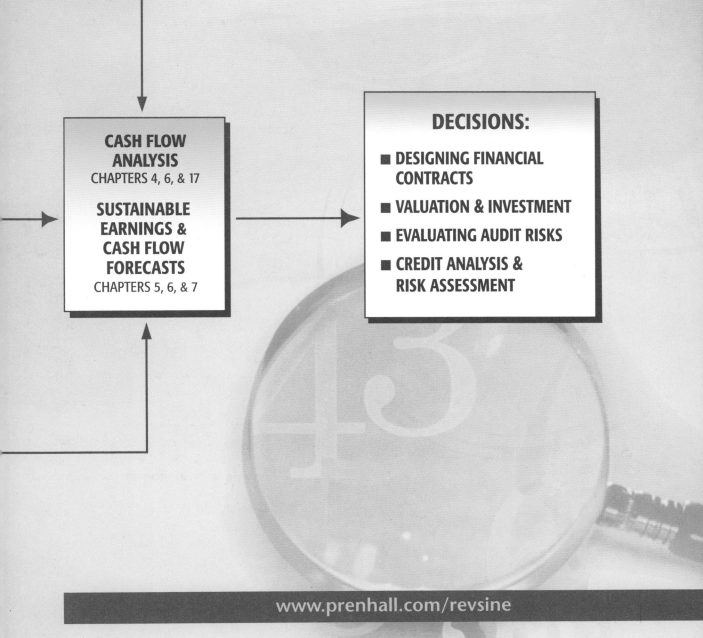

CASH FLOW ANALYSIS
CHAPTERS 4, 6, & 17

SUSTAINABLE EARNINGS & CASH FLOW FORECASTS
CHAPTERS 5, 6, & 7

DECISIONS:

- DESIGNING FINANCIAL CONTRACTS
- VALUATION & INVESTMENT
- EVALUATING AUDIT RISKS
- CREDIT ANALYSIS & RISK ASSESSMENT

www.prenhall.com/revsine

SECOND EDITION

Financial Reporting & Analysis

Lawrence Revsine

John and Norma Darling
Distinguished Professor of Financial Accounting
Kellogg Graduate School of Management Northwestern University

Daniel W. Collins

Henry B. Tippie Research Chair in Accounting
Tippie College of Business
The University of Iowa

W. Bruce Johnson

Arthur Andersen Professor of Accounting
Tippie College of Business
The University of Iowa

Prentice Hall

Prentice Hall, Upper Saddle River, NJ 07458

Library of Congress Cataloging-in-Publication Data

Revsine, Lawrence.
Financial reporting & analysis / Lawrence Revsine, Daniel W. Collins, W. Bruce Johnson.—2nd ed.
p. cm.
Includes index.
ISBN 0-13-032351-9
1. Financial statements. 2. Financial statements—Case studies. 3. Corporations—Accounting. I. Title: Financial reporting and analysis. II. Collins, Daniel W. III. Johnson, W. Bruce. IV. Title

HF5681.B2 R398 2001
657′.3—dc21 2001034035

Acquisitions Editor: Thomas Sigel
Editor-in-Chief: P.J. Boardman
Assistant Editor: Cheryl Clayton
Senior Editorial Assistant: Jane Avery
Senior Development Editor: Mike Elia
Media Project Manager: Nancy Welcher
Marketing Manager: Beth Toland
Managing Editor (Production): Cynthia Regan
Senior Production Editor: Anne Graydon
Page Production Assistance: Cindy Spreder
Production Assistant: Dianne Falcone
Associate Director, Manufacturing: Vincent Scelta
Production Manager: Arnold Vila
Interior Design: **TECH**BOOKS
Cover Design: Lorraine Castellano
Cover Illustration: Nancy D'Urso
Manager, Print Production: Christy Mahon
Composition: **TECH**BOOKS
Full-Service Project Management: **TECH**BOOKS
Printer/Binder: R.R. Donnelley/Willard

Credits and acknowledgments for material used from other sources and reproduced, with permission, in this textbook appear on appropriate pages within text.

Prentice Hall

10 9 8 7 6 5 4 3 2 1
ISBN 0-13-032351-9

Dedicated to our Families

Barbara, Pamela, David, and Michele (LR)

Mary, Melissa, and Theresa (DC)

Diane and Cory Elizabeth (WBJ)

About the Authors

Lawrence Revsine

John and Norma Darling Distinguished Professor of Financial Accounting. Kellogg Graduate School of Management, Northwestern University, BS 1963, MBA 1965, Ph.D. 1968, Northwestern University; CPA 1963

Lawrence Revsine joined the Kellogg faculty in 1971 and served as chair of the Accounting Information and Management Department for eight years.

The author of several books on various financial reporting issues, he has had approximately 50 articles published in leading academic journals.

His academic recognitions include participation in three American Accounting Association Doctoral Consortia. He has received both Ford Foundation and Peat Marwick Mitchell Foundation research grants. He was selected the American Accounting Association's Distinguished Overseas Lecturer, and the AAA named him the 1992 Outstanding Educator. The Illinois CPA Society designated Revsine its 1993 Outstanding Educator. Professor Revsine received the Alumni Choice Faculty Award from the 1995 Reunion Classes; this award is given to the Kellogg faculty member who has had the greatest impact on their professional and personal lives.

Professor Revsine has been a consultant to the American Institute of Certified Public Accountants, the Securities and Exchange Commission, and the Financial Accounting Standards Board and served on the Financial Accounting Standards Advisory Council.

He is a consultant to industry on external reporting issues and regulatory cases and has taught extensively in management development and continuing executive education programs in the United States and abroad. Professor Revsine has received numerous commendations for teaching excellence, including Teacher of the Year from the Kellogg Graduate Management Association student group, and the Sidney J. Levy Teaching Award, presented by the Kellogg Dean's Office.

Daniel W. Collins

Henry B. Tippie Research Chair in Accounting, Tippie College of Business, The University of Iowa. BBA 1968, Ph.D. 1973, The University of Iowa

Winner of the University of Iowa Board of Regents Award for Faculty Excellence in 2000 and the American Accounting Association's Outstanding Educator Award in 2001, Dan

Collins currently serves as the Chairman of the Accounting Department at The University of Iowa. Professor Collins' research focuses on the role of accounting numbers in equity valuation and the pricing implications of alternative accounting measurements.

A prolific writer and frequent contributor to the top academic accounting journals, Collins has been recognized as one of the top ten most highly cited authors in the accounting literature over the last 20 years.

Professor Collins is on the editorial review boards of the Journal of Accounting and Economics, Accounting Horizons, and Review of Quantitative Finance and Accounting. He has also served as Associate Editor of The Accounting Review and as Director of Publications for the American Accounting Association (AAA). Professor Collins has served on numerous AAA committees including the Financial Accounting Standards Committee and has chaired the Publications Committee, the National Program Committee, and the Doctoral Consortium Committee. He also served on the Financial Accounting Standards Advisory Council from 1994–1997.

A member of the American Accounting Association and an invited member of Accounting Researchers International Association, Collins is a frequent presenter at research colloquia, conferences, and doctoral consortia. He has also received outstanding teaching awards at both Michigan State University and The University of Iowa.

W. Bruce Johnson

Arthur Andersen Professor of Accounting, Tippie College of Business, The University of Iowa. BS 1970, University of Oregon, MS 1973, Ph.D. 1975, The Ohio State University

W. Bruce Johnson joined the University of Iowa faculty in 1988 and has served as director of its McGladrey Institute for Accounting Research, accounting group chairman, and associate dean for graduate programs, where he was responsible for Iowa's MBA and Executive MBA programs.

Professor Johnson has previously held faculty appointments at the University of Wisconsin, Northwestern University, and the University of Chicago.

His teaching and research interests include corporate financial reporting, financial analysis, value-driven management systems and investment strategies, and executive compensation practices. He has received the Gilbert P. Maynard Award for Excellence in Accounting Instruction, and the Chester A. Phillips Outstanding Professor Award.

A well-respected author, Professor Johnson's articles have appeared in numerous scholarly publications and in academic and professional journals. He has served on editorial boards of more than a dozen academic journals. Professor Johnson has also served as a research consultant to the Financial Accounting Standards Board, and on the Research Advisory, Professional Practice Quality and Outstanding Educator committees of the American Accounting Association. He is a member of the American Accounting Association, the Financial Executives Institute, and was formerly Senior Vice President for Equity Strategy at SCI Capital Management, a money management firm.

Brief Table of Contents

End-of-Chapter material includes Exercises, Problem/Discussion Questions, and Cases

Table of Contents

End-of-Chapter material includes Exercises, Problem/Discussion Questions, and Cases

Preface

Consistent with the mandates of the Accounting Education Change Commission (AECC), our objective in writing **Financial Reporting & Analysis,** Second Edition, is to change the way the second-level course in financial accounting is taught, both to graduate and undergraduate students. Typically this course—often called Intermediate Accounting—focuses on the details of GAAP with little emphasis on understanding the economics of transactions or how statement readers use the resultant numbers for decision making. Traditional intermediate texts are encyclopedic in nature and approach, emphasizing the accounting process and the myriad of arcane accounting rules and procedures that comprise GAAP.

In contrast, the goal of our book is to develop a "critical thinking" approach to financial accounting and reporting. We seek to develop students' understanding of the environment in which financial reporting choices are made, what the options are, how these data are used for various types of decisions, and—most importantly—how to avoid misusing financial statement data. We convey the exciting nature of financial reporting in two stages. First, we provide a framework for understanding management's accounting choices and how the accounting affects reported financial numbers. Business contracts—like debt covenant agreements and management compensation agreements—are usually linked to accounting numbers. We show how this often creates incentives for managers to exploit the flexibility in GAAP to "manage" reported accounting numbers to benefit themselves as well as shareholders. Second, we use real-world financial reports and events to illustrate vividly how GAAP alternatives and subjective accounting estimates give managers discretion in the timing of earnings and in reporting the components of financial position.

The approach adopted in this book integrates the perspectives of accounting, corporate finance, economics, and critical analysis to help students grasp how business transactions get reported and understand their decision implications. In this approach, we cover all of the core topics of intermediate accounting by first describing the business transactions that affect various accounts, the technical details of GAAP, how these rules are applied in practice, and what the financial statements look like. Then we go a step further and ask: What do the numbers mean? Does the accounting process yield numbers that accurately reflect the underlying economic situation of a company? And, if not, what can statement users do to overcome this limitation in order to make more informed decisions?

Our book is aimed not only at those charged with the responsibility of preparing financial statements, but also at those who will use financial statements for making decisions. Our definition of "users" is broad and includes lenders, equity analysts, investment bankers, boards of directors, and others charged with monitoring corporate performance and the behavior of management. As such, it includes auditors who establish audit scope and conduct analytical review procedures to spot problem areas in external financial statements. Statement of Auditing Procedures (SAS) 82, "Consideration of Fraud in a Financial Statement Audit," stresses that auditors must act as "financial detectives" to uncover financial reporting irregularities. To do this effectively requires an understanding of the incentives of managers, how the flexibility of GAAP can sometimes be exploited to conceal rather than reveal financial truth, and the potential danger signals that should be investigated. Our intent is to help readers learn how to conduct better audits, improve cash flow forecasts, undertake realistic valuations, conduct better comparative analysis and make more informed judgments about the performance of management.

Financial Reporting & Analysis, Second Edition, provides instructors with the teaching/learning approach for achieving many of the goals stressed by the Accounting Education Change Commission. Specifically, our book is designed to instill capacities for: 1) thinking in an abstract, logical manner, 2) solving unstructured problems, 3) understanding the determining forces behind management's accounting choices, and 4) encouraging an integrated, cross-disciplinary view of financial reporting. Text discussions were written, and exercises, problems, and cases were carefully chosen to help achieve these objectives. But the book achieves these AECC goals without sacrificing technical underpinnings. Throughout, we explain in detail where the numbers come from, what measurement rules are used, and how they are entered into the accounting records. We have strived to provide a comprehensive user-oriented focus while simultaneously helping students build a strong technical foundation.

Key Changes from the First Edition

The first edition of our book has been widely adopted in accounting departments at business schools throughout the United States, Canada, Europe, and the Pacific Rim. It has been used successfully at both the graduate and undergraduate levels as well as in investment banking, commercial lending, and other corporate training programs. Many of our colleagues who used the first edition have provided us with valuable feedback. Based on their input, we have made a number of changes in this edition of the book to achieve the objectives outlined above more effectively. Key changes include the following:

- More international examples and discussion of International Accounting Standards (IAS) are interspersed throughout the book.

- Special "Getting Behind the Numbers" icons are used to highlight and link discussions in later chapters back to the analysis, valuation, and contracting framework set forth in Chapters 5, 6, and 7.
- The examples and exhibits from actual company reports have been updated and expanded to illustrate alternative accounting treatments and new disclosures stemming from recent FASB pronouncements.

STRETCH

- Problems and cases in all chapters have been updated and expanded to provide a larger number of straight-forward application problems as well as "stretch" analysis problems that are designed to test students' reasoning and analytical thinking skills.
- A new appendix to Chapter 2 reviews the accounting equation, debit-credit procedures, journal entries, the adjusting and closing process, statement preparation, and T-account analysis.
- A new Chapter 3, "Additional Topics in Income Determination," has been added that contains a discussion of specialized areas of revenue recognition as well as issues covered in SEC Staff Accounting Bulletin (SAB) 101 on "Revenue Recognition." Prompted by recent concerns raised by former SEC Chairman Arthur Levitt, this chapter also provides an overview of techniques frequently used by firms to manage earnings.

- Chapter 4, "Structure of the Balance Sheet and Statement of Cash Flows," contains a new section on how financial statement "fingerprints" provide clues about unique industry characteristics (including dot.coms). The balance sheet of Cadbury Schweppes, plc, is used to illustrate international differences in statement format and account terminology.
- Chapter 5, "Essentials of Financial Statement Analysis," contains a new section on "Cash Earnings and EBITDA." Amazon.com is used as the focal point to illustrate the use—and misuse—of this earnings construct by Wall Street analysts.
- Chapter 6, "The Role of Financial Information in Valuation," features a new section on valuing "dot.com" companies and additional end-of-chapter problem material on valuation.
- Chapter 8, "Receivables," contains an expanded discussion of securitizations and a new Self-Study problem on this topic.
- Chapter 9, "Inventories," contains a new section on inventory errors and an expanded discussion of how earnings can be managed through inventory (production) decisions.
- Chapter 10, "Long-Lived Assets and Depreciation," has an expanded discussion of intangibles that explains how statement readers can overcome some of the limitations of GAAP reporting in this area. We have also expanded our discussion of capitalization of interest and how it affects interperiod analysis.
- Chapter 11, "Financial Instruments as Liabilities," has undergone extensive revision and now contains a thorough discussion of risk management, derivative securities, hedging transactions, and hedge accounting.
- Chapter 12, "Financial Reporting for Leases," contains an expanded discussion of leases with up-front payments and is one of the few texts that covers synthetic leases. The illustration of constructive capitalization of operating leases has been expanded and simplified.
- Chapter 13, "Income Tax Reporting," has been updated with new tax footnote disclosures from Merck. Tax footnote disclosures from Lubrizol and Cambrex are used to illustrate how adjustments can be made to reported earnings to compare firms that use different depreciation methods.
- Chapter 14, "Pensions and Postretirement Benefits," has been revised to illustrate real companies' SFAS No. 132 pension disclosure requirements and what they mean for informed analysis. We now include a discussion of the controversial "cash balance" pension plans.
- Chapter 15, "Financial Reporting for Owners' Equity," contains one of the most extensive discussions of employee stock option plans (ESOPs) and related accounting issues in any financial reporting text. We've also expanded our discussion of earnings per share calculations.
- Chapter 16, "Intercorporate Equity Investments," contains a discussion of the FASB's recently proposed changes for goodwill accounting and new criteria for determining control. Unlike most other texts, this chapter illustrates how purchase accounting for business combinations can distort year-to-year comparisons of sales and earnings growth.
- Chapter 17, "Statement of Cash Flows," contains an expanded discussion of why changes in working capital balance sheet accounts do not correspond to adjustments to accrual earnings to arrive at operating cash flows shown on the cash flow statement. It also contains a new "Analytical Insights" section that discusses "cash burn rates" and "time to burnout" measures for Internet stocks.

- Chapter 18, "Overview of International Financial Reporting Differences and Inflation," contains an expanded discussion of the International Accounting Standards Board's activities as well as the SEC's views on accepting IASC standards for Form 20-F filings.

Acknowledgments

Colleagues at Iowa and Northwestern have shared insights and provided many helpful comments. These individuals are Ronald Dye, Mark Finn, Robert Magee, Morton Pincus, Robert Hartman, and Elizabeth Keating. Former colleagues and doctoral students who provided feedback are Julia D'Souza (Cornell), Elizabeth Eccher (Analysis Group/Economics), Dan Givoly (Tel-Aviv University), Carla Hayn (U.C.L.A.), Rachel Hayes (University of Chicago), Bjorn Jorgensen (Harvard), Reuven Lehavy (University of California, Berkeley), Kin Lo (University of British Columbia), K. Ramesh (Analysis Group/Economics), Srinivasan Rangan (University of Colorado, Boulder), Leonard Soffer (University of Illinois, Chicago), Ramu Thiagarajan (Mellon Capital Management Corporation), and Charles Wasley (University of Rochester). We also wish to thank Ole-Kristian Hope, Emre Karaoglu, and the thousands of other M.B.A. and Ph.D. students who patiently raised issues and helped us communicate more straightforwardly.

Several colleagues at other universities have served as a sounding board on a wide range of issues over the past years and their input has helped us improve this book. In particular we thank Norman Bartczak (Columbia University), James Boatsman (Arizona State University), Thomas Linsmeier (Michigan State), and Stephen Zeff (Rice University). We also greatly appreciate the insight we received from the late Michael J. Murphy (First Chicago Bank) and Stephen Scheetz (Bank of America), which helped shape the financial-analytical focus of this book.

We are grateful to many users of the first edition of our book whose constructive comments and suggestions have contributed to an improved and expanded second edition. In particular, we wish to thank the following people for their valuable input:

Mark P. Bauman
University of Chicago-Illinois

Frank J. Beil
University of Minnesota

Robert Hartman
University of Iowa

Rachel Hayes
University of Chicago

Ole-Kristian Hope
Northwestern University

Elizabeth Keating
Northwestern University

Florence R. Kirk
SUNY-Oswego

Andrew J. Leone
University of Rochester

Brian Leventhal
University of Chicago-Illinois

Thomas Linsmeier
Michigan State University

Robert Lipe
University of Oklahoma

Kin Lo
University of British Columbia

The late Arijit Mukherji
University of Minnesota

Robert Magee
Northwestern University

Eric Press
Temple University

Thomas L. Stober
University of Notre Dame

Gary Taylor
University of Alabama

John Twombley
Illinois Institute of Technology

Paul Zarowin
New York University

Stephen A. Zeff
Rice University

We appreciate the contributions to the Problems and Cases made by Hollis Ashbaugh (University of Wisconsin), James Boatsman (Arizona State University), Robert Hartman (University of Iowa), Robert Magee (Northwestern University), K. Ramesh (Analysis Group/Economics), and Charles Wasley (University of Rochester). Cases contributed by these individuals are identified with their initials, (JB), (KR), and (CW).

We also thank the following students whose diligence and care in preparing various aspects of the book were most helpful: John Hoesley, Amanda Johnson, Imre Karaoglu, Kim O'Brien, Jacob Searingen, and Jason Wagner.

We wish to thank Linda Bostian for her administrative support, and Bonnie Lee, who patiently typed numerous drafts with unfailing good humor and kept the book on schedule.

Finally, we thank Thomas Sigel, our Pearson-Prentice Hall editor, for his help in making the second edition of this book a reality.

Our goal in writing this book was to improve the way financial reporting is taught and mastered. We would appreciate receiving your comments and suggestions.

—Lawrence Revsine *—Daniel W. Collins* *—W. Bruce Johnson*

The Textbook's Accessories

This edition offers instructors a greatly expanded and improved package of supplements. To learn more about these supplements, visit the Revsine/Collins/Johnson Accounting Web site at **www.prenhall.com/revsine,** contact your Prentice Hall sales representative, or call the Accounting and Tax Hotline at 1-800-227-1816.

Instructor Resources

Solutions Manual Prepared by the text authors, this extensive ancillary provides detailed solutions for every end-of-chapter assignment. The manual is designed in large font for easy conversion to overheads that can be used in the classroom.

Instructor's Resource Manual Written by Steven Henning of Southern Methodist University, this manual contains chapter overviews, outlines, and questions and answers. It also includes teaching tips and suggested readings to enhance your lectures and discussion groups.

Test Item File Completely revised by James Krause of University of Tampa, this new test bank includes a variety of examination questions to test students' grasp of chapter-by-chapter concepts and applications.

Prentice Hall Custom Test This is the computerized version of the Test Item File that enables you to create your own exams, as well as evaluate and track student results.

***NEW!* Transition Notes** Written by the author team, these notes provide faculty with suggested syllabi and extended teaching notes for transitioning from a competing text to Revsine, Collins, and Johnson's second-edition text. Sample syllabi are also available on the Web site at **www.prenhall.com/revsine.**

Student Resources

***NEW!* GAAP Guide** This valuable guide may be packaged with new copies of the text for only $15.00 net (a savings of over $50.00!).

NEW! Give your students 10 weeks of both the print AND online editions of the ***Wall Street Journal*** for only $10.00 net when they purchase a special version of the text (new texts

THE WALL prepare your students to succeed STREET JOURNAL.

only) with subscription card. All faculty requiring this version of the text for adoption receive complimentary print and online subscriptions. Or, students can receive 15 weeks of the ***Financial Times*** for only $10.00 net.

Study Guide Written by Charles Fazzi of Robert Morris College, this guide serves as the students' principle *reality check.* Do they really know the material? It provides detailed chapter summaries, a glossary of terms, and demonstration problems and solutions that will reinforce key principles and concepts and help students master the core material.

Technology Resources

Companion Web Site—Prentice Hall's new MyPHLIP www.prenhall.com/revsine This powerful Prentice Hall Web site offers chapter-specific current events, Internet exercises, sample syllabi, online study guide, and downloadable supplements. The Online Study Guide, written by David Baglia of Grove City College, includes multiple-choice, true/false, and essay questions so students can quiz themselves. Grading is done on the spot!

Go to the Faculty Resources for a complete list of supplements and tools available to all adopters. Please contact your Prentice Hall sales representative for password information to access protected areas.

Powerpoint Transparencies These slides, prepared by Brian Leventhal of University of Illinois-Chicago, include key lecture points as well as a variety of exhibits and graphics from the text. You can download these files from the text Web site at no charge.

Spreadsheet Templates Prepared by the authors, these templates provide students with text data in Excel format. These are also available at no charge from the Web site.

***Accounting Made Easy* Software** This supplemental software reviews accounting procedures using a vivid collection of animation, graphics, and quiz material. Available in two levels, this software can be packaged with the text at a nominal price.

1

The Economic and Institutional Setting for Financial Reporting

LEARNING OBJECTIVES:
After studying this chapter, you will understand:

1. Why financial statements are a valuable source of information about companies, their current health, and their prospects for the future.
2. How financial statements can be used by investors, creditors, securities analysts, and auditors.
3. Why accounting rules are established, and how management can still shape the financial information communicated to outsiders.
4. How the demand for financial information comes from its ability to improve decision making and to make it possible to monitor managers' activities.
5. How the supply of financial information is influenced by the costs of producing and disseminating it and by the benefits it provides.

"No one ever said accounting was an exact science."

It's the middle of June. Your brother called with a hot stock tip: Buy California Micro Devices.[1] It's been a rocket stock since he bought it last year at $5 per share. The company makes microchip components for computing, telecommunication, and aerospace customers. Its products are leading-edge, and its manufacturing facilities are state-of-the-art. What about company fundamentals? Your brother says they are solid! Last year Cal Micro had sales of $33 million and earned $4.7 million in pre-tax operating profit. That's a 45% increase in sales and a 400% increase in profits. This year is off to a great start as well—sales and earnings have increased more than 50% on a quarterly basis, and in March the company inked an alliance with Hitachi Ltd. that should fuel growth for the next several years. It's a great opportunity: Cal Micro has a solid management team and a strong financial track record, and it's an industry leader in an expanding market.

Your brother's enthusiasm for Cal Micro gets you thinking about it—but the stock is now trading at $21 per share. You're not sure how much higher it can go. On the other hand, all seven analysts following Cal Micro continue to rate the company as a "strong buy." The investment story is attractive, so you decide to take a closer look at the company's business model, its past financial performance, and its prospects for the future.

The financial statements confirm what your brother told you. Sales and earnings growth rates are at record levels and outpace the competition by a

[1] This publication is designed to provide accurate and authoritative information in regard to the subject matter. It is sold with the understanding that the Publishers and the Authors are not engaged in rendering legal, accounting, investment, or other professional services. If legal advice or other expert assistance is required, the services of a competent professional person should be sought.

wide margin. The Hitachi alliance looks promising as a catalyst for continued growth and expanded profitability. Operating cash flows are negative and bank borrowing has increased—but this is not unusual for a growth company like Cal Micro. Overall, the company's prospects look bright and the stock looks like a good buy.

But what's this? A negative article on the company appeared in this morning's newspaper:

> **DOES CAL MICRO'S BALANCE SHEET PORTEND BLOWUP?**
>
> Looking at nothing but its stock price and press releases, it would appear that California Micro Devices is on quite a roll. Not only are its earnings and sales posting impressive year-over-year increases, but the Milpitas-based company just sold 10 percent of itself to Hitachi Metals, a subsidiary of Japanese electronics giant Hitachi Ltd.
>
> As a result, its stock has doubled in the past six months, closing yesterday at 21 3/4.
>
> Yet a stroll through its balance sheet tells a very different story, especially for a company like Cal Micro, which is in the fairly low-tech business of putting such things as capacitors and resistors on semiconductor chips.
>
> Forget about its high inventories and the dilemma of negative cash flow for four out of five fiscal years. What's more troubling to some observers is the sharp rise in Cal Micro's receivables—the amount of money owed by customers. Cal Micro says its receivables rose to 126 days at the end of March from 94 days last June; according to the calculations of outside watchers, they actually grew to 156 days from 124 days.
>
> Either way, it's rarely a good sign when they stretch out for more than a quarter because it suggests a company is borrowing from future sales to maintain earnings. It's even more interesting when [Cal Micro's receivables are] more than double the receivables of one of its rivals—in this case, Vishay Intertechnology.
>
> Cal Micro blames its high receivables on favorable credit terms extended to "approximately" ten Asian customers and distributors "to avoid shipment delays."
>
> It's unclear how allowing customers to put off paying can help avoid shipment delays. What is clear, however, is that rising receivables are coming from a company that touts itself as the industry leader, and usually the only time industry leaders grant liberal payment policies is if they're desperate for the business. Several attempts to reach Cal Micro officials were unsuccessful.
>
> Source: *San Francisco Chronicle* (June 14, 1994) p. B1. Reprinted with permission of The San Francisco Chronicle.

A call to your broker confirms that Cal Micro's stock price has fallen by $2 in early trading. Should you take advantage of the price decline and buy 1,000 shares because now the company looks really cheap? Should you call your brother and tell him to sell because Cal Micro's balance sheet contains a torpedo that could potentially sink the stock? Or, should you take a closer look at company fundamentals before deciding whether to buy or sell Cal Micro shares? The receivables could indicate an increase in demand for Cal Micro's products or they could be a warning signal of problems at the company.

What do you do?

Why Financial Statements Are Important

This dilemma illustrates a fundamental point: Without adequate information, investors cannot properly judge the opportunities and risks of investment alternatives. To make informed decisions, investors rely on a variety of information, including data on the economy, various industries, companies, and products. Complete information provided by reliable sources enhances the probability that the best decisions will be made. Of course, only later will you be able to tell whether your investment decision was a good one. What we can tell you now is that ***if you want to know more about a company, its current health, and its prospects for the future, the best source of information is probably the company's own financial statements.***

The economic events and activities that affect a company and that can be translated into accounting numbers are reflected in the company's financial statements. Some financial statements provide a picture of the company at a moment in time; others describe changes that took place over a period of time. Both provide a basis for *evaluating* what happened in the past and for *projecting* what might occur in the future. For example, what is the annual rate of sales growth? Are accounts receivable increasing at an even greater rate than sales? How do sales and receivable growth rates compare to those of competitors? What rates of growth can be expected next year? These trends and relationships provide insights into a company's opportunities and risks, including growth and market acceptance, costs, productivity, profitability, and liquidity. Consequently, ***a company's financial statements can be used for various purposes: as an analytical tool, as a management report card, as an early warning signal, as a basis for prediction, and as a measure of accountability.***

As our prospective Cal Micro stockholder knows, financial statements contain information that investors need to know in order to decide whether to invest in the company. Others need financial statement information to decide whether to extend credit, negotiate contract terms, or do business with the company. Financial statements serve a crucial role in allocating capital to the most productive and deserving firms. Effective allocation of capital promotes efficient use of resources, encourages innovation, and provides a liquid market for buying and selling securities and for obtaining and granting credit.

Our stockholder has learned that published financial statements do not always contain the most up-to-date information about the company's changing economic fortunes. To ensure that important financial news reaches interested parties as soon as possible, companies send press releases or hold meetings with analysts. Press releases typically announce things like contract awards, new product introductions, capital spending plans, or anticipated acquisitions or divestitures.

Although they are not as timely as press releases, periodic financial statements do provide an economic history which is comprehensive and quantitative—and which therefore can be used to gauge company performance. ***For this reason financial statements are indispensable for developing an accurate profile of ongoing performance and prospects.*** Financial reports also help in assessing the company's viability as changes occur in input and output markets, in production technologies, among competitors, or in general economic conditions.

Our Cal Micro prospective stockholder will learn an even more important lesson: Financial statements sometimes conceal more than they reveal.

Epilogue to California Micro Devices

In August, two months after the newspaper reporter's warning about receivables, Cal Micro released its fourth quarter results and said that chips valued at \$8.3 million, or 42% of quarterly sales, were returned by customers. No reason for the returns was disclosed. The stock fell 40% that day. In October, another negative newspaper article on the company quoted former Cal Micro employees who said corporate executives were so obsessed with "making their numbers" that they resorted to desperate tactics:[2]

- They "kept the quarter open" to improve sales figures.
- They asked customers to accept additional products sooner than needed—often allowing them to delay payment for up to six months.
- They booked phony sales and shipped the products to an employee's garage where they were kept until requested by legitimate customers.
- They lowered production quality standards to meet volume goals and then shipped products of marginal quality knowing that they would be returned during the next quarter.

[2] H. Greenberg, "Cal Micro Devices: Conduct Unbecoming?" *San Francisco Chronicle* (October 17, 1994).

Figure 1.1

CALIFORNIA MICRO DEVICES
Daily Common Stock Price

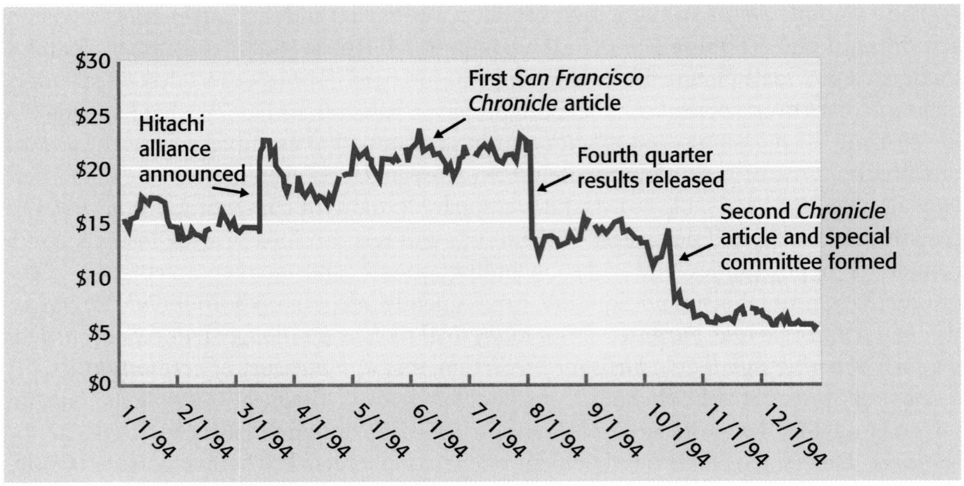

An advance copy of the article had been sent to Cal Micro's chief executive officer, but he declined comment.

The same day the news article was published, the company's Board of Directors announced the appointment of a special committee to investigate "possible revenue recognition and other accounting irregularities." The stock price dropped 46% that day. In the days and weeks that followed several things happened:

- The CEO and the chief financial officer resigned.
- The Securities and Exchange Commission (SEC) launched an investigation of the company.
- Shareholder class-action lawsuits were filed against the company and its management.
- Investors suffered a $139 million loss in company market value (see Figure 1.1).

The special committee and its audit team discovered that instead of $5.0 million profit, Cal Micro actually lost $15.2 million for the year, and sales had been overstated by 73%.

The audit uncovered fraud in financial reporting by senior corporate officers. This fraud included improper accounting for sales transactions and product returns, shipment of unwanted goods, and recording bogus sales to both legitimate and phony companies. Although the company survives today, its former CEO and CFO were both convicted of federal securities fraud charges, fined $100,000 each, required to surrender their Cal Micro shares worth roughly $2.5 million, and sentenced to jail.

Financial statement fraud is rare.[3] Most managers are honest and responsible, and their financial statements are free from the kind of intentional distortions that occurred at California Micro Devices. However, this example underscores the fact that investors and others should not simply accept the numbers in financial statements. Instead, they must analyze the numbers in sufficient detail to assess the degree to which the financial statements faithfully represent the economic events and activities affecting the company.

Company-specific data used by investors and analysts come primarily from published financial statements and from the company's willingness to provide additional financial and operating data voluntarily. Management has some latitude in deciding what financial information will be made available and when it will be released. For example, even though financial statements must conform to accepted guidelines and standards, management has considerable discretion over the particular accounting procedures used in the statements and over the details contained in supplemental footnotes and related disclosures. To further complicate matters, ***accounting is not an exact science.*** Some financial statement

[3] See *Fraudulent Financial Reporting: 1987–1997* (Washington, D.C.: Committee of Sponsoring Organizations of the Treadway Commission, 1999) and *1998 Fraud Survey* (New York: KPMG LLP., 1999).

items are measured with a high degree of precision and reliability, such as the amount of cash on deposit in a company bank account. Other items are more judgmental and uncertain because they are derived from estimates of future events, such as product warranty liabilities.

Statement readers must:

- understand that management can shape the financial information communicated to outside parties, and
- be able to distinguish between financial statement information that is highly reliable and information that is judgmental.

Both weigh heavily in determining the quality of the information in financial statements—and thus the extent to which it should be relied on for decision-making purposes. The analytical tools and perspectives in this and later chapters will enable you to understand and better interpret the information in financial statements and accompanying disclosures, as well as to appreciate fully the limitations of that information.

Economics of Accounting Information

The role of financial accounting information is to facilitate economic transactions and to foster the efficient allocation of resources among businesses and individuals.[4] Perhaps the most familiar transactions involve raising financial capital; in these cases a company seeks to attract additional financial resources by issuing common stock or debt securities. Here, financial reports provide information that can reduce investors' uncertainty about the company's opportunities and risks, thereby lowering the company's cost of capital. If you think about this, you can see demand and supply at work. Investors **demand** information regarding the company's opportunities and risks. Because companies need to raise capital at the lowest possible cost, they have an economic incentive to **supply** the information investors want. In this section we will see that the amount and type of financial accounting information provided by companies depend on demand and supply forces much like those affecting any other economic commodity.

Financial statements are demanded because of their value as a source of information about the company's performance, financial condition, and stewardship of its resources. People demand financial statements because the data reported in them improve decision making. ***The supply of financial information is guided by the costs of producing and disseminating it and the benefits it will provide to the company.*** Firms weigh the benefits they may gain from financial disclosures against the costs they incur in making those disclosures. Of course, regulatory groups such as the Securities and Exchange Commission (SEC), the Financial Accounting Standards Board (FASB), and the International Accounting Standards Committee (IASC) influence the amount and type of financial information that companies disclose as well as when it is disclosed.

Demand for Enterprise Financial Statements

A company's financial statements are demanded by several groups:

1. Shareholders and investors
2. Managers and employees
3. Lenders and suppliers
4. Customers
5. Government and regulatory agencies.

---

[4] The company may participate directly in the transaction as, for example, when it issues debt or equity securities, or when it negotiates a loan or acquires equipment on credit. However, financial statement information also facilitates transactions in secondary markets—like the New York Stock Exchange (NYSE)—where the company's debt and equity securities are subsequently traded.

Shareholders and Investors Shareholders and investors, including investment advisors, use financial information to help decide on a portfolio of securities that meets their preferences for risk, return, dividend yield, and liquidity.

Financial statements are crucial in investment decisions that use **fundamental analysis** to identify mispriced securities. Fundamental analysis uses financial statement information (including footnotes), along with industry and macroeconomic data, to forecast future stock price movements. Investors who use this approach consider past sales, earnings, cash flow, product acceptance and management performance to predict future trends in these financial drivers of a company's success or failure. Then they assess whether a particular stock or group of stocks is undervalued or overvalued at the current market price. **Technical analysis**—another school of stock market analysis—relies on price and volume movements of stocks and does not concern itself with financial statement numbers.

Investors who believe in the **efficient markets hypothesis**—and who thus presume they have no insights about company value beyond the current security price—also find financial statement data to be useful. To efficient markets investors, financial statement data provide a basis for assessing firm-specific variables (such as risk and dividend yield) that are important to portfolio selection decisions.

The **efficient markets hypothesis** says a stock's current market price reflects the knowledge and expectations of all investors. Those who adhere to this theory consider it futile to search for undervalued or overvalued stocks or to forecast stock price movements using financial statements or other public data, because any new development is quickly reflected in a firm's stock price. This perspective does not entirely preclude the use of financial statements for investment decisions, however, because financial information about a firm can still have value for predicting the stock's systematic risk (or Beta). Systematic risk remains important to the investment decision even if markets are efficient. One commercial service, BARRA, provides fundamental estimates of systematic risk to investment professionals worldwide. See T. D. Coqqin and F. J. Fabozzi, *Applied Equity Valuation* (New Hope, PA: Frank J. Fabozzi Associates, 1999).

Of course, investment analysis can be performed by shareholders and investors themselves—or by professional securities analysts who may possess specialized expertise or some comparative advantage in the acquisition, interpretation, and analysis of financial statements.

Shareholders and investors also use financial statement information when evaluating the performance of the company's top executives. When earnings and share price performance fall below acceptable levels, dissatisfied shareholders voice their complaints to management and outside directors. If this approach doesn't work, dissident shareholders may launch a campaign (**proxy contest**) to elect their own slate of directors at the next annual meeting. Activist investors often see this as a buying opportunity. By purchasing shares of the underperforming company at a bargain price, these investors hope to gain by joining forces with existing shareholders, replacing top management, and "turning the company around."

Company performance as described in recent financial statements often becomes the focal point of the proxy contest. Management defends its record of past accomplishments while perhaps acknowledging a need for improvement in some areas of the business. Dissident shareholders point to management's past failures and the need to hire a new executive team. Of course, both sides are pointing to the same financial statements. Where one side sees success, the other sees only failure—and undecided shareholders must be capable of forming their own opinion on the matter.

Managers and Employees Although managers regularly make operating and financing decisions based on information that is much more detailed and timely than the information found in financial statements, they also need—and therefore demand—financial statement data. Their demand arises from contracts (such as executive compensation agreements) that are linked to financial statement variables.

Executive compensation contracts frequently contain annual bonus and longer term pay components tied to financial statement results. Using accounting data in this manner increases the efficiency of executive compensation contracts. Rather than trying to determine whether a manager has performed capably during the year (and whether the manager deserves a bonus), the board of directors' compensation committee only needs to look at reported profitability or some other accounting measure that functions as a summary of the company's (and thus the manager's) performance.

Employees demand financial statement information for several reasons: because of the increasing popularity of employee profit sharing and employee stock ownership plans

(ESOPs, discussed in Chapter 15); to monitor the health of company-sponsored pension plans and to gauge the likelihood that promised benefits will be provided upon retirement; because union contracts may link negotiated wage increases to the company's financial performance; and more generally to help them gauge their company's current and potential future profitability and solvency.

Lenders and Suppliers Financial statements play several roles in the relationship between the company and those who supply financial capital. Commercial lenders (banks, insurance companies, and pension funds) use financial statement information to help decide the loan amount, the interest rate, and the security needed for a business loan. Loan agreements contain contractual provisions (called **covenants**) that require the borrower to maintain minimum levels of working capital, interest coverage, or other key accounting variables that provide a safety net to the lender. Violation of these loan provisions can result in technical default and allow the lender to accelerate repayment, to request additional security, or to raise interest rates. So lenders monitor financial statement data to ascertain whether the covenants are being violated.

Suppliers demand financial statements for many reasons. A steel company may sell millions of dollars of rolled steel to an appliance manufacturer on credit. Before extending credit, careful suppliers scrutinize the buyer's financial position in much the same way that a commercial bank does—and for essentially the same reason. That is, suppliers assess the financial strength of their customers in order to determine whether they will be paid for goods shipped. Suppliers continuously monitor the financial health of companies with whom they have a significant business relationship.

Customers Repeat purchases and product guarantees or warranties create continuing relationships between a company and its customers. A buyer needs to know if its supplier has the financial strength to deliver a high-quality product on an agreed-upon schedule and if the supplier will be able to provide technical support after the sale. You wouldn't buy a personal computer from a door-to-door vendor without first checking out the product and the company that stands behind it. Financial statement information can help current and potential customers monitor a supplier's financial health and thus decide on whether to purchase that supplier's goods and services.

Government and Regulatory Agencies Government and regulatory agencies demand financial statement information for various reasons.

Taxing authorities sometimes use financial statement information as a basis for establishing tax policies designed to enhance social welfare. For example, the U.S. Congress could use aggregate reported financial results as a means for justifying tax policy changes such as instituting a tax reduction during economic downturns.

> In most industrialized countries, the accounting rules that businesses use for external reporting purposes differ from the accounting rules required for taxation purposes. Only in a few countries—notably, France—are firms compelled to use financial reporting methods that conform to taxation rules. The United States allows divergence between the rules used to compute taxable income and rules used for shareholder reports. As a consequence, corporate financial reporting choices are seldom influenced by the U.S. Internal Revenue Code.

Government agencies are often customers of businesses. For example, the U.S. Army purchases weapons from suppliers whose contracts guarantee that they are reimbursed for costs and that they get an agreed-upon profit margin. So, financial statement information is essential to the resolution of contractual disputes between the Army and its suppliers, and for monitoring whether companies engaged in government business are earning profits beyond what the contracts allow.

Financial statement information is used to regulate businesses—especially public utilities, such as gas and electric companies. To achieve economies of scale in the production and distribution of natural gas and electricity, local governments have historically granted exclusive franchises to individual gas and electric companies serving a specified geographical area. In exchange for this monopoly privilege, the rates these companies are permitted to charge consumers are closely regulated. Accounting measures of profit and of asset value are essential because the accounting **rate of return**—reported profit divided by asset book value—is a key factor that regulators use in setting allowable charges.[5]

Banks, insurance companies, and savings and loan associations are also subject to regulation aimed at protecting individual customers and society from insolvency losses—for example, the inability of a bank to honor deposit withdrawal requests or the failure of an insurance company to provide compensation for covered damages as promised. Financial statements aid regulators in monitoring the health of these companies so that corrective action can be taken when needed.

Regulatory intervention (in the form of antitrust litigation, protection from foreign imports, government loan guarantees, price controls, and so on) constitutes another source of demand for financial statement information by government agencies and legislators.

Financial statement information has value either because it reduces uncertainty about a company's future profitability or economic health or because it provides evidence about the quality of its management, about its ability to fulfill its obligations under supply agreements or labor contracts, or about other facets of the company's business activities. Financial statements are demanded because they provide information that helps improve decision making or makes it possible to monitor managers' activities.

RECAP

Disclosure Incentives and the Supply of Financial Information

Investment bankers and commercial lenders sometimes possess enough bargaining power to allow them to compel companies to deliver the financial information these statement users need for analysis. For example, a cash-starved company applying for a bank loan has a strong incentive to provide all the data the lender requests. But most financial statement users are less fortunate. They must rely on mandated reporting, voluntary company disclosures that go beyond the minimum required reporting, and sources outside the company for the information needed to make decisions.

What forces induce managers to supply information? Browse through several corporate financial reports and you should notice substantial differences across companies—and perhaps over time—in the quality and quantity of the information they provide.

Some companies routinely disclose operating profits, production levels, and order backlogs by major product category so analysts can quickly spot changes in product costs and market acceptance. Other companies provide detailed descriptions of their outstanding debt and their efforts to hedge interest rate risk or foreign currency risk. Still other companies seem to disclose only the bare minimum required. What explains this diversity in the quality and quantity of financial information?

If the financial reporting environment were unregulated, disclosure would occur *voluntarily* as long as the incremental benefits to the company and its management from supplying financial information exceeded the incremental costs of providing that information. In other words, management's decisions about the scope, timing, and content of the company's financial statements and notes would be guided solely by the same cost and benefit considerations that influence the supply of any other commodity. Managers would assess the benefits created by voluntary disclosures and weigh those benefits against

[5] This regulation process is intended to enhance economic efficiency by precluding the construction of duplicate facilities that might otherwise occur in a competitive environment. Eliminating redundancies presumably lowers the ultimate service cost to consumers. Regulatory agencies specify the accounting practices and disclosure policies that must be followed by companies under their jurisdiction. As a consequence, the accounting practices that utility companies use in preparing financial statements for regulatory agencies sometimes differ from those used in their shareholder reports.

the costs of making the information available. Any differences in financial and nonfinancial disclosures across companies and over time would then be due to differences in the benefits or costs of voluntarily supplying financial information.

But, in fact, financial reporting in the United States and in many other developed countries is regulated by public agencies such as the SEC and by private agencies such as the FASB. The various public and private sector regulatory agencies establish and enforce financial reporting requirements ***designed to ensure that companies meet certain minimum levels of financial disclosure.***[6] Nevertheless, companies frequently communicate financial information that exceeds these minimum levels. They apparently believe that the benefits of the "extra" disclosures outweigh the costs. What are the perceived benefits from voluntary disclosures that exceed minimum requirements?

Disclosure Benefits Companies compete with one another in capital, labor, output, and input markets. This competition creates incentives for management to reveal "good news" financial information about the firm. The news itself may be about a successful new product introduction, increased consumer demand for an existing product, an effective quality improvement, or other matters. By voluntarily disclosing otherwise unknown good news, the company may be able to obtain capital more cheaply or get better terms from suppliers.

To see how these incentives work, consider the market for raising financial capital. Companies seek capital at the lowest possible cost. They compete with one another both in terms of the return they promise to capital suppliers and in terms of the characteristics of the financial instrument offered. The capital market has two important features:

1. Investors are uncertain about the quality of companies' debt or equity offerings because the ultimate return from the security depends on future events.
2. It is costly for the company to be mistakenly perceived as offering a low-quality stock or bond—a "lemon."[7]

This lemon cost has various forms. It could be lower proceeds received from issuing stock, a higher interest rate that will have to be paid on a commercial loan, or more stringent conditions placed on that loan.

These market factors mean that owners and managers have an economic incentive to supply the amount and type of financial information that will enable them to raise capital most cheaply. A company offering truly attractive, low-risk securities can avoid the lemon penalty by voluntarily supplying financial information that enables investors and lenders to gauge the risk and expected return of each instrument accurately. Of course, companies offering higher risk securities have incentives to mask their true condition by supplying overly optimistic financial information. However, other forces partially offset this tendency. Examples include requirements for audited financial statements and legal penalties associated with issuing false or misleading financial statements. Furthermore, managers want to maintain access to capital markets and establish a reputation for supplying credible financial information to capital market participants.

Financial statement disclosures can convey economic benefits to firms—and thus to their owners and managers. But, firms cannot obtain these benefits at zero cost.

---

[6] Corporate financial reporting in the United States has been regulated by the Securities and Exchange Commission (SEC) since its creation by an act of Congress in 1934. The SEC has historically relied on private sector organizations such as the American Institute of Certified Public Accountants (AICPA) and the FASB to formulate financial accounting and reporting standards. Another example involves the financial accounting and disclosure standards in Germany; those standards are prescribed by law in the Commercial Code (*Handelsgesetz*), the Corporation Act (*Aktiengesetz*), the Cooperatives Act (*Genossenschaftsgesetz*), and other laws related to specific types of businesses.

[7] "Lemon," a term commonly associated with automobiles, refers to an auto with hidden defects. In financial capital markets, lemon refers to an investment instrument with hidden risks. See G. Akerlof, "The Market for 'Lemons': Quality Uncertainty and the Market Mechanism," *Quarterly Journal of Economics* (August 1970), pp. 488–500.

Disclosure Costs Four costs can arise from informative financial disclosures:

1. Information collection, processing, and dissemination costs
2. Competitive disadvantage costs
3. Litigation costs
4. Political costs

The costs associated with **financial information collection, processing, and dissemination** can be large. Determining the company's obligation for postretirement employee health-care benefits provides an example.[8] This disclosure requires numerous complicated actuarial computations as well as future health-care cost projections for existing or anticipated medical treatments. Whether companies compile the data themselves or hire employee benefit consultants to do it, the cost of generating a reasonable estimate of the company's postretirement obligation can be considerable. The costs of developing and presenting financial information also include the cost incurred to audit the accounting statement item (if the information is audited). Owners ultimately pay all of these costs, just as they ultimately bear all other company costs.

Another financial disclosure cost is the possibility that competitors may use the information to harm the company providing the disclosure. Several disclosures—financial and nonfinancial—might create a **competitive disadvantage.**

- Details about the company's strategies, plans, and tactics, such as new products, pricing strategies, or new customer markets.
- Information about the company's technological and managerial innovations, such as new manufacturing and distribution systems, successful process redesign and continuous quality improvement methods, or uniquely effective marketing approaches.
- Detailed information about company operations, such as sales and cost figures for individual product lines or narrow geographical markets.[9]

Disclosing sales and profits by product line or geographical area may highlight opportunities previously unknown to competitors, thereby undermining a company's competitive advantage. For example, Uniroyal Inc. objected to disclosing its financial data by geographical area because:

> . . . this type of data would be more beneficial to our competition than to the general users of financial data. This is especially true in those countries or geographical areas where we might not be as diversified as we are in the United States. In these cases, the data disclosed could be quite specific, thereby jeopardizing our competitive situation.[10]

Labor unions or suppliers may also use the company's financial information to improve their bargaining power, which would increase the company's costs and possibly weaken its competitive advantage.

Litigation costs result when shareholders, creditors, and other financial statement users initiate court actions against the company and its management for alleged financial misrepresentations. For example, it's common for shareholders to initiate litigation when there's a sudden drop in stock price. If the price falls soon after the company has released new financial information, shareholders may sue the company and claim damages based on the disclosure. These shareholders argue they would not have committed financial capital to the company if they had known then (back when they bought the stock) what they know now (after the company's disclosure).

---

[8] See Chapter 14 for a detailed treatment of this topic.

[9] R. B. Stevenson, Jr., *Corporations and Information: Secrecy, Access, and Disclosure* (Baltimore, MD: Johns Hopkins University Press, 1980), pp. 9–11.

[10] Uniroyal Inc. correspondence as reported in G. Foster, *Financial Statement Analysis* (Upper Saddle River, NJ: Prentice Hall, 1986), p. 185.

The costs of defending against suits, even those without merit, can be substantial. Beyond legal fees and settlement costs, there is the damage to corporate and personal reputations and the distraction of executives from productive activities that would otherwise add value to the company.

There are potential **political costs** of financial reporting, especially for companies in highly visible industries like oil or pharmaceuticals. Politically vulnerable firms with high earnings are often attacked in the financial and popular press, which alleges that those earnings constitute evidence of anticompetitive business practices. Politicians sometimes respond to (or exploit) heightened public opinion. They propose solutions to the "crisis" that is causing high earnings, thereby gaining media exposure for themselves and improving their chances for reelection or reappointment. These "solutions" are usually political initiatives designed to impose taxes on unpopular companies or industries. The windfall profits tax imposed on U.S. oil companies in the late 1970s is one example. This tax was prompted, in part, by the large profit increases that oil companies reported during several years prior to the enactment of the legislation.

Antitrust litigation, environmental regulations, and the elimination of protective import quotas are other examples of the costs politicians and government bureaucrats can impose on unpopular companies and industries. Financial reports are one source of information that politicians and bureaucrats can use to identify target firms or industries. For this reason, astute managers carefully weigh political considerations when choosing what financial information to report and how best to report it. As a result, some highly profitable—but politically vulnerable—firms may make themselves appear less profitable than they really are.[11]

A company's financial reporting decisions are driven by economic considerations—and thus by cost-benefit tradeoffs. Companies that confront distinctly different competitive pressures in the marketplace and that face different financial reporting costs and benefits are likely to choose different accounting and reporting practices. A clear understanding of the economic factors that influence a company's financial reporting choices can help you to assess more keenly the quality of the provided information. That's what we'll help you do in this textbook.

RECAP

A Closer Look at Professional Analysts

Financial statements that help users make informed decisions also help allocate capital efficiently. Different types of users—investors, lenders, customers, suppliers, managers, employees, and so on—find corporate financial statements helpful in making decisions. ***Financial statement users have diverse information needs because they face different decisions or may use different approaches to making the same kind of decision.*** For example, a retail customer deciding which brand of automobile to purchase needs far less financial information about each automotive manufacturer than does a long-term equity investor who is planning to purchase stock in one of those companies. Similarly, a commercial banker engaged in asset-based lending—meaning the loan is collateralized by the borrower's inventory or receivables—needs far different financial information about the business than does a banker who lends solely on the basis of the borrower's projected future cash flows.

[11] There is another side to this "excessive profits" story. Politicians sometimes respond to public concern over record losses at highly visible companies by providing subsidies in the form of government loan guarantees (e.g., Chrysler Corporation), import tariffs (e.g., Harley Davidson), and restrictions on the activities of competitors.

It would be difficult (maybe impossible!) to frame our examination of corporate financial reporting and analysis around the diverse information needs of all potential users and the varied decisions they might possibly confront. Instead, we focus attention on professional analysts. But we define **analyst** broadly to include investors, creditors, financial advisors, and auditors—anyone who uses financial statements to make decisions as part of their job. Let's see what professional analysts do.

Analysts' Decisions

The task confronting **equity investors** like our prospective California Micro Devices stockholder is first to form an educated opinion about the value of the company and its equity securities and then to make investment decisions based on that opinion. Investors who follow a *fundamental analysis approach* estimate the value of a security by assessing the amount, timing, and uncertainty of future cash flows that will accrue to the company issuing the security. The company's financial statements and other data are used to develop projections of its future cash flows. These cash flow estimates are then discounted for risk and the time value of money. The discounted cash flow estimate is then compared, on a per-share basis, to the current price of the company's stock. This comparison allows the investor to make decisions about whether to buy, hold, or sell the stock.[12]

Other valuation approaches are used by investors. One is to estimate a company's **liquidation value**—the investor would try to determine the value the company's assets would yield if sold individually, then subtract any debt the company owes. Another is to compute the price-to-earnings (or cash flow-to-earnings) ratio for other companies in the industry and then to apply that ratio to the company's current or projected earnings. Still other approaches rely on projections of the company's quarterly earnings, changes in earnings, and changes in trends of earnings to identify possible short-term changes in the price of the company's equity securities.

Financial statement information is essential, in one way or another, to all these equity investment strategies.

Creditors' decisions require an assessment of the company's ability to meet its debt-related financial obligations through the timely payment of interest and principal, or through asset liquidation in the event interest and principal cannot be repaid. Creditors include commercial banks, insurance companies and other lenders, suppliers who sell to the company on credit, and those who invest in the company's publicly traded debt securities. Creditors form educated opinions about the company's **credit risk** by comparing required principal and interest payments to estimates of the company's current and future cash flows. Companies that are good credit risks have projected operating cash flows that are more than sufficient to meet these debt payments. Credit risk assessments are also influenced by the company's **financial flexibility**—the ability to raise additional cash by selling assets, issuing stock, or borrowing more.

Companies judged to be high credit risks are charged higher rates of interest and may have more stringent conditions—referred to as covenants—placed on their loan agreements. These loan covenants may restrict the company from paying dividends, selling nonoperating assets, buying other companies, forming joint ventures, or borrowing additional funds without prior approval by the lender. Other types of covenants, particularly those based on reported accounting figures, protect the lender from a deterioration in the borrower's credit risk. This is why creditors must monitor the company's ongoing ability to comply with lending agreement covenants.

Financial advisors include securities analysts, brokers, portfolio managers, industry consultants, and others who provide information and advice to investors and creditors. They are often able to gather, process, and evaluate financial information more economically and accurately than individual investors and creditors can, because they possess specialized skills or knowledge (e.g., industry expertise) or because they have access

[12] See Chapter 6 for additional details concerning this approach to deriving an estimate of a company's *fundamental* value and the role financial statement information plays in the valuation process.

to specialized resources provided by their organizations. As a consequence, financial advisors can play a crucial role in the decision-making process of investors and creditors. Securities analysts, in particular, are among the most important and influential users of financial statements.

Independent auditors carefully examine financial statements prepared by the company prior to conducting an audit of those statements. An understanding of management's reporting incentives coupled with an understanding of reporting rules enables auditors to recognize vulnerable areas where financial reporting abuses are likely to occur. Astute auditors choose audit procedures designed to ensure that major improprieties can be detected.

> "Consideration of Fraud in a Financial Statement Audit," *Statement of Auditing Standards No. 82* (New York: AICPA, 1997) provides examples of factors that auditors must be aware of in designing audit procedures. These examples include unduly aggressive financial targets, a significant portion of management pay tied to accounting numbers, and an excessive interest by management in maintaining or increasing the firm's stock price or earnings trend. These factors provide a motivation for managers to engage in fraudulent financial reporting.

But the Treadway Commission believes that independent auditors can (and should) do more:

> The potential of analytical review procedures for detecting fraudulent financial reporting has not been realized fully. Unusual year end transactions, deliberate manipulations of estimates or reserves, and misstatements of revenues and assets often introduce aberrations in otherwise predictable amounts, ratios, or trends that will stand out to a skeptical auditor.[13]

> **Analytical review procedures** are the tools auditors use to illuminate relationships among the data. These procedures range from simple ratio and trend analysis to complex statistical techniques—a tool kit not unlike that used by any financial analyst. The auditor's goal is to assess the general reasonableness of the reported numbers in relation to the company's activities, industry conditions, and business climate.

Current auditing standards require independent auditors to use analytical review procedures on each engagement. Why? Because they can help auditors avoid the embarrassment and economic loss of accounting "surprises," such as the one that occurred at California Micro Devices.

Independent auditors need to be well versed in the techniques of financial analysis in order to design effective audits. That's why auditors are included among those people we call analysts. Current auditing standards echo the lessons of past audit failures: ***You can't build a bulletproof audit unless you know how the game is played.*** That means understanding the incentives of managers and being a skilled financial analyst.

Analysts' Information Needs

What specific information about a company do professional analysts want? What types of information are most useful in predicting a company's earnings and cash flows when valuing its equity securities, assessing its debt repayment prospects, and evaluating audit vulnerabilities? Professional analysts say the following three types of financial information are needed:

1. Quarterly and annual financial statements along with nonfinancial operating and performance data.
2. Management's analysis of financial and nonfinancial data (including reasons for changes) along with key trends and a discussion of the past effect of those trends.
3. Information that makes it possible both to identify the future opportunities and risks confronting each of the company's businesses and to evaluate management's plans for the future.[14]

---

[13] *Report of the National Commission on Fraudulent Financial Reporting* (Washington, D.C.: 1987), p. 48. The "Treadway Commission"—officially the National Commission on Fraudulent Financial Reporting—was formed in 1985 to study the causal factors that can lead to fraudulent financial reporting and to develop recommendations for public companies and their independent auditors, for the SEC and other regulators, and for educational institutions.

[14] These findings are based on a comprehensive study of professional analysts' information needs conducted by the *Special Committee on Financial Reporting* of the AICPA. Further details can be found in *Improving Business Reporting—A Customer Focus: Meeting the Information Needs of Investors and Creditors* (New York: AICPA, 1994).

A company's financial statements provide professional investors, creditors, financial advisors, and auditors with information that heavily influences their decisions. Published financial statements of public companies also contain a **management's discussion and analysis (MD&A)** section, one that is intended to describe the company's business risks, its financial condition, and the results of its operations in considerable detail. MD&A is one of the ways management communicates the reasons for changes in financial condition and performance. Because management presumably understands the business, MD&A disclosures are an important information source for analysts. MD&A is the starting point professional analysts use in forming their own assessment of the company's profitability and health, and the reasons for changes in financial condition or performance. This is especially true when the MD&A also contains forward-looking information about changing business opportunities and risks, and about management's plans for the company.

Some of the information needed by professional analysts is contained in nonfinancial statement documents. For example, annual proxy statements furnished to shareholders contain information about the credentials of senior corporate executives and directors, about management compensation and ownership, and about the identity of major stockholders. Trade journals, industry surveys, and various other sources contain information about current and potential competitors, changing technologies and markets, threats from substitute products or services, and the bargaining power of customers and suppliers. Such information is essential to those who want to form a complete picture of a company's opportunities and risks—and its prospects for the future.

The Securities Exchange Act of 1934 requires that corporations solicit shareholders' votes, since many shareholders will not be physically present at meetings to vote on corporate matters. This solicitation is called a **proxy,** and the information that accompanies it is called the **proxy statement.** Annual meetings are required by state corporation laws. The proxy statement will—among other things—provide information about nominees for directors, the recommended auditor for the ensuing year, the compensation of the five highest paid executives, proposed changes in compensation plans, and other matters that periodically arise (such as shareholder proposals of various kinds).

Financial statement information helps investors assess the value of a firm's debt and equity securities; it helps creditors assess the company's ability both to meet its debt payments and to abide by loan terms; it helps financial advisors and securities analysts to do their job of providing information and advice to investors and creditors; and it helps auditors both to recognize potential financial reporting abuses and to choose audit procedures to detect them.

RECAP

The Rules of the Financial Reporting Game

"There's virtually no standard that the FASB has ever written that is free from judgment in its application."

—D. R. Beresford, chairman of the FASB (1987–1997)[15]

Professional analysts are forward-looking. Their goal is to predict what will happen in the future to the value of a company and its ability to repay debt. Financial statements and footnotes depict the past—an economic history of transactions and other events that affected the company. These past data provide analysts with a jumping-off point for forecasting future events, especially future earnings and cash flows.

To extrapolate into the future from financial statement data, investors, creditors, and their financial advisors must first understand the accounting measurement rules used to produce the data. Financial statements present a picture of the company at a point in time, a picture that translates many (but not all) of the economic events affecting the business into financial terms. For example, the act of providing goods and services to customers in

[15] As quoted by F. Norris, "From the Chief Accountant, a Farewell Ledger," *New York Times* (June 1, 1997).

exchange for promised future cash payments is translated by the company's accounting system into financial statement amounts known as "sales revenue" and "accounts receivable." This linkage between economic events and how those events are depicted in a financial statement can sometimes seem mysterious or confusing to the analyst. For example, some companies record sales revenue *before* goods are actually delivered to customers. Other companies record revenue at the date of delivery to customers. And still others record revenue only when payment for the goods is received from the customer, which can be long *after* delivery. We'll now look more closely at the rules that govern accounting and financial reporting practices.

Generally Accepted Accounting Principles

Over time, the accounting profession has developed a network of conventions, rules, guidelines, and procedures, collectively referred to as **generally accepted accounting principles (GAAP).** The principles and rules that govern financial reporting continue to develop and evolve in response to changing business conditions. Consider, for example, the lease of retail store space at a shopping mall. As people moved from the city to the suburbs, shopping malls emerged as convenient and accessible alternatives to traditional urban retail stores. Leasing became a popular alternative to ownership because it enabled retailing companies to gain access to store space without having to bear the burden of the large dollar outlay necessary to buy or build the store. Leasing was also attractive because it shared risks—like the competition provided by a new mall opening nearby—between the retailer and shopping mall owner. As leasing increased in popularity, the accounting profession developed guidelines—some are complex—that are followed when accounting for leases. The guidelines that evolved are now part of GAAP and are discussed in detail in Chapter 12.

The goal of GAAP is to ensure that financial statements clearly reflect the economic condition and performance of the company. To achieve this goal, financial statements should possess certain qualitative characteristics that are important to the needs of professional analysts:[16]

> This "reflect economic condition and performance" philosophy of financial reporting describes GAAP in Canada, Mexico, the United Kingdom, the United States, and many other countries. But GAAP financial reports in other countries are required to conform to tax law and/or commercial law; Chapter 18 provides details.

- **Relevance:** Financial information capable of making a difference in a decision. Relevant information helps users form more accurate predictions about the future, or it allows them to better understand how past economic events have affected the business.
- **Timeliness:** Information that is available to decision makers while it is "fresh" and capable of influencing their decisions.
- **Reliability:** Financial information that is reasonably free of error and bias, and faithfully represents what it purports to represent. Reliable financial information is factual, truthful, and unbiased. Reliability can be further described using certain characteristics:

  Verifiability: Independent measurers should get similar results when using the same accounting measurement methods. For example, the 1999 net sales of $4,725.2 million reported by Quaker Oats Company is verifiable to the extent that knowledgeable accountants and auditors would agree on this amount after examining the company's sales transactions for the year. So verifiability refers to the degree of consensus among measurers.

  Representational faithfulness: The degree to which the accounting actually represents the underlying economic event. If a company's balance sheet reports trade accounts payable of $254.3 million when the company actually owes suppliers $266.2 million, then the reported figure is not a faithful representation.

[16] A detailed discussion of these qualitative characteristics and related issues is contained in "Qualitative Characteristics of Accounting Information," *Statement of Financial Accounting Concepts No. 2* (Stamford, CT: FASB, 1980).

Neutrality: Information cannot be selected to favor one set of interested parties over another. For example, accountants cannot allow a company to reduce an estimated expense just so the company can evade a bank loan covenant.

- **Comparability:** Financial information must be measured and reported in a similar manner across companies. Comparability allows analysts to identify real economic similarities and differences among diverse companies, because those differences and similarities are not obscured by accounting methods or disclosure practices.
- **Consistency:** The same accounting methods are used to describe similar events from period to period. Consistency allows analysts to identify trends—and turning points—in the economic condition and performance of a company over time, because the trends are not obscured by changes in accounting methods or disclosure practices.

Companies can change accounting methods, but the changes are restricted to situations where it can be argued that the newly adopted accounting method is "preferable" to the old one. Companies that change accounting methods must disclose the nature and effect of the accounting change—as well as the justification for it—in the financial statements for the period in which the change is made. Common justifications include "to conform to industry practice" (i.e., improved comparability) and "to more accurately represent the company's activities" (i.e., greater representational faithfulness).

No single accounting method has all of these characteristics all of the time. In fact, GAAP frequently requires financial statement users to accept a compromise that favors some qualitative characteristics over others. For example, GAAP financial statements would show an office building investment at its historic cost (original purchase price) minus accumulated depreciation. The most *relevant* measure of the office building is often the discounted present value of its expected rental revenues. But this measure is not as *reliable* or *verifiable* as historical cost because future vacancy rates are unpredictable. GAAP's use of historical cost trades off increased reliability and verifiability for decreased relevance. Qualitative trade-offs such as this arise frequently and make it difficult to identify what are the "best" accounting methods and disclosure practices.

In evaluating whether financial reports are complete, understandable, and helpful to readers, accounting professionals use two additional conventions—**materiality** and **conservatism.** Materiality plays a critical role, first in the judgments of management in preparing the financial statements and then in the judgments of independent accountants who audit them. Suppose management unintentionally fails to record a $100,000 expense and the bookkeeping error is discovered shortly after the end of the quarter. Unless this error is corrected, quarterly earnings will be overstated by, say, 2.4% but the overstatement will reverse out next quarter. Is the misstatement material? Should the quarterly financial statements be corrected? Or, is the self-correcting misstatement immaterial and unimportant?

According to both the FASB and the SEC, the answer depends on both *quantitative* (the amount of the misstatement) and *qualitative* (the possible impact of the misstatement) considerations. Financial statements are materially misstated when they contain omissions or misstatements that would alter the judgment of a reasonable person.[17] Quantitative materiality thresholds—such as "an item is material if it exceeds 5% of pre-tax income"—are inadequate because they fail to recognize how even small misstatements can impact users' perceptions. For example, a small percentage misstatement can be material if it allows the company to avoid a loan covenant violation, reverses an earnings trend, or changes a loss to a profit.

Conservatism in accounting strives to ensure that business risks and uncertainties are adequately reflected in the financial reports. For example, it is prudent to record possible losses from product liability litigation as soon as those losses become probable and measurable. Doing so helps readers assess the potential cash flow implications of the litigation even though an exact dollar amount has not yet been determined. Unfortunately, conservatism is sometimes used to defend poor accounting judgments like overstated provisions for "big bath" restructuring costs or "cookie-jar" reserves discussed in Chapter 3.

Who Determines the Rules?

GAAP comes from two main sources:

1. Written pronouncements by designated organizations
2. Accounting practices that have evolved over time

---

[17] Material misstatements can result either from errors, which are unintentional, or fraud, which is intentional and meant to deceive financial statement users. See "Materiality," *SEC Staff Accounting Bulletin No. 99* (Washington, D.C.: SEC, August 12, 1999).

The U.S. federal government, through the SEC, has the ultimate authority to determine the rules to be followed in preparing financial statements by companies whose securities are sold to the general public. This authority was given to the Commission when it was established in 1934 by Congress in response to the severe stock market decline of 1929. The SEC requires companies to file both annual *and* quarterly financial statements as well as other types of reports. In 1990 alone, the 11,000 or so companies subject to SEC filing requirements submitted more than 280,000 documents to the Commission. By 1998, the SEC's electronic document retrieval system (EDGAR) had 650,000 connections and 25 gigabytes of downloads each day.

Although the SEC has the ultimate legal authority to set accounting principles, it has looked to private sector organizations to establish these principles. The FASB, or simply "the Board," is the organization that currently sets accounting standards in the United States. The FASB's activities are monitored by the SEC, and the SEC works closely with the FASB in formulating reporting rules. Although the FASB receives funding from various sources, it exists as an independent group with seven full-time members and a large staff. Board members are appointed to five-year terms and are required to sever all ties with the companies and institutions they served prior to joining the Board. The FASB has issued more than 140 financial accounting standards since it was created in the early 1970s. The Board has also issued seven statements of financial accounting concepts, which serve to guide the Board in setting accounting standards.

> Statements of Financial Accounting *Standards* establish new standards—such as how to value investment securities—or amend standards previously issued by the FASB and its predecessors. Statements of Financial Accounting *Concepts* establish the fundamentals—such as what qualitative characteristics accounting reports should possess. Financial accounting and reporting standards are based on the concepts.

Prior to the establishment of the FASB, the **American Institute of Certified Public Accountants (AICPA)** had the primary responsibility for setting accounting standards in the United States through its Accounting Principles Board.[18] The AICPA continues to take an active role in establishing GAAP through its participation in the FASB's deliberation process, and it is solely responsible for setting the *auditing* standards to be followed by public accounting firms.

Chapter 18 describes how financial reporting standards are determined outside the United States. In some countries it's by professional accounting organizations akin to the FASB and in other countries it's by commercial law and/or tax law requirements. The growth of global investing has spurred the development of worldwide accounting standards. These standards are written by the **International Accounting Standards Board (FASB)**, an organization established in 1973 following an agreement by professional accounting organizations in Australia, Canada, France, Germany, Japan, Mexico, the Netherlands, Ireland, the United Kingdom, and the United States. The IASC works to formulate accounting standards, promote their worldwide acceptance, and achieve greater harmonization of financial reporting regulations, standards, and procedures across countries. The IASC has issued 40 International Accounting Standards and 18 Interpretations of existing standards. Compared to U.S. GAAP, existing IASC standards allow firms much more latitude; this is a natural result of the organization's diverse constituency.

> Prior to April 2001, this group was called the International Accounting Standards Committee (IASC). We make reference to this organization both ways (IASC and IASB) at various places in the book.

Adversarial Nature of Financial Reporting

GAAP permits alternatives (LIFO versus FIFO for inventory valuation), requires estimates (the useful life of depreciable assets), and incorporates management judgments (are assets impaired?). Managers have a degree of flexibility in choosing specific accounting techniques and reporting procedures—and the resulting financial statements are sometimes open to interpretation.

Managers have reasons to exploit this flexibility. Their interests may conflict with the interests of shareholders, lenders, and others who rely on financial statement information. Some companies adopt exemplary reporting standards, while others tend to be less

[18] Before the Accounting Principles Board was formed in 1959, accounting rules were issued by a predecessor organization known as the Committee on Accounting Procedure. The evolution of U.S. GAAP is discussed in more detail in the appendix to this chapter.

forthright. Analysts who understand these conflicting incentives as well as the flexibility available under GAAP will see that a decision based on uncritical acceptance of financial statement data may turn out to be naïve—and dangerous.

The flexibility of GAAP financial reporting standards provides opportunities to use accounting tricks that make the company seem less risky than it really is. For instance, some economic liabilities like equipment leases can be transformed into off-balance sheet (and thus less visible) items. The company would then appear, from the balance sheet data, to have less debt and more borrowing capacity than is really the case. Commercial lenders who fail to spot off-balance sheet liabilities of this sort can underestimate the credit risk lurking in their loan portfolios.

> Manville Corporation's 1982 bankruptcy changed the way analysts view legal contingencies. Although some people had been asking questions about the company's exposure to asbestos-related litigation for quite some time, Manville's bankruptcy announcement on August 26, 1982 caught most analysts and investors by surprise. That's because the company's last quarterly report prior to bankruptcy estimated the total cost of settling asbestos-related claims at about $350 million, less than half of Manville's $830 million of shareholders' equity. On August 26 Manville put the potential damages at no less than $2 billion—and the company's stock plunged by 35% the next day.

As another example, companies can **smooth** reported earnings by strategically timing the recognition of revenues and expenses. This strategy projects an image of a stable company that can easily service its debt, even in a severe business downturn. The benefits of such deceptions can be large if lenders are fooled.[19] Furthermore, once the loan is granted the company has additional incentives to report its financial results in ways that circumvent default on loan covenants tied to accounting numbers.

Self-interest sometimes drives managers to manipulate the reported financial statement numbers in order to earn bonuses linked to sales or earnings targets. For example, if earnings are down late in the fiscal year, product deliveries may be accelerated to increase recognized revenues and income before year's end. Similarly, managers can delay discretionary expenses like building repairs and maintenance if earnings are expected to be too low. On the other hand, if earnings are comfortably above the bonus goal, managers may write off obsolete equipment and inventory or increase reserves for uncollectible trade receivables, whereas those same accounting adjustments may be postponed if earnings are inadequate.

Another way in which financial reporting practices can be molded to suit management's interests is to downplay the significance of contingent liabilities—like unresolved product liability lawsuits—that may affect the value of the firm. There are many reasons why management is likely to understate the true significance of a major legal contingency. In a lawsuit, candid disclosure could compromise the company's case. Similarly, public disclosure of impending financial hardships may harm the company if creditors respond by accelerating loan repayment schedules, by curtailing trade credit, or by seeking to liquidate the business.

This discussion states the case boldly and may portray the motives underlying financial reporting practices in an unflattering light. In reality, most companies strive to provide fair and reasonable disclosure of their financial affairs. Some of these companies are undoubtedly motivated as much by honor and integrity as by the knowledge that they will be rewarded for being forthright. Nevertheless, there are companies that take full advantage of the leeway available under GAAP.

The SEC and the FASB provide constraints that limit the range of financial statement discretion. Auditors and the courts further counterbalance opportunistic financial reporting practices. Nevertheless, the analyst should recognize the adversarial nature of financial reporting, maintain a healthy skepticism, and understand that financial disclosures sometimes conceal more than they reveal. The flexibility inherent in GAAP can have dire consequences for those caught unaware.

---

[19] Lenders are fooled when they mistakenly assign too little risk (thus charging too low an interest rate) to the borrowing. An interest-cost savings of one half of a percentage point on $1 billion of borrowings equates to $5 million (pre-tax) per year. If the company is in a 34% tax bracket and its stock trades at 15 times earnings, the payoff for concealing risk on financial statements is $49.5 million in share value. This value increase represents a wealth transfer to shareholders from creditors.

Aggressive Financial Reporting: A Case Study

America Online (AOL) is a leader in the expanding global market for online services and internet access. AOL offers its subscribers many services including electronic mail, conferencing, software, computing support, interactive magazines and newspapers, as well as easy access to the Internet. Since its founding in 1985, it has become the world's most popular Internet online service, with over 23 million members worldwide. AOL earned $396 million in 1999 on revenues of $4.8 billion. Its shares have yielded investors a phenomenal 112% *annual* return since the company went public in 1992. But things have not always been rosy at AOL.

In 1996, the company faced stiff competition on several fronts. Other commercial online service providers like Prodigy and CompuServ were capturing market share through aggressive pricing. The advent of the World Wide Web meant that potential subscribers who wanted just a Web ramp could now buy that service from access companies like PSINet more cheaply than at AOL. Looming on the horizon was the Microsoft Network. Despite these competitive forces, 1996 was a record year for AOL. Revenues had grown to over $1 billion from $51 million in 1993. Net income was just under $30 million, compared to $1.5 million in 1993. However, AOL's share price had suffered. From its November 1995 peak of $82 per share, the company's stock price had fallen to $29 amid concerns about subscriber growth and aggressive accounting for marketing costs. Some Wall Street analysts were uneasy about the quality of AOL's earnings, citing the company's unorthodox capitalization—rather than expensing—of certain marketing costs.

Then AOL abandoned the aggressive accounting. The announcement to do so was part of a press release that described several strategy changes at the company.

We have italicized the accounting change in the company's press release below. To put the change in perspective, the $385 million write-off represented 35% of 1996 revenues

DULLES, VA—America Online, Inc. (NYSE: AOL) announced today a series of initiatives to fully leverage its global assets in consumer networks, content, and access by more closely aligning its business structure with emerging opportunities in the interactive market, and to further distinguish its flagship online brand as the leader in value, content, and service.

Steve Case, Chairman and Chief Executive Officer of America Online, Inc., stated, "America Online has grown rapidly in recent years, and is now the global leader in interactive services. The steps we're announcing today build on that leadership by fully leveraging our assets in consumer networks, content, and access as separate business opportunities. At the same time, through new competitive 'unlimited' pricing and a superior consumer offering enhanced by new programming and design advances, we are further strengthening the position of our flagship America Online brand as the undisputed leader in value and service and the clear choice for millions of consumers worldwide." . . .

The company also announced that effective immediately it will expense all marketing costs as they are incurred. Previously, the company has deferred the cost of certain of its marketing activities, such as the costs of mailing diskettes to prospective customers, and then amortized those costs over a period of time. To reflect the changes to its evolving business model as it reduces reliance on subscriber fees by growing new revenue streams, and as a result of changing market dynamics, the company will take a charge, as of September 30, 1996, of approximately $385 million, representing the balance of deferred subscriber acquisition costs, as of that date. [Italics added for emphasis.] The company also plans to take a one-time charge in the December 1996 quarter of up to $75 million, representing costs the company expects to incur as it aligns the organization with emerging opportunities in the interactive market.

"The creation of these three new operating divisions, the rollout of new pricing and features, and this shift toward a simpler approach to financial reporting positions AOL for a business model reflecting sustained, controllable growth based on clearly establishing AOL as the best service for the widest range of consumers," Case said. "AOL is making the necessary moves to position itself as the global leader in interactive services well into the next century." . . .

Source: From *PR Newswire* (October 29, 1996). Reprinted with permission of *PR Newswire*.

and 1,283% of 1996 earnings. The write-off was more than five times as large as the total pre-tax earnings that AOL had reported for the previous five fiscal years combined.

What Was the Issue? The accounting controversy at AOL was when to expense certain "subscriber acquisition" costs such as cash outlays for subscriber starter kits, direct marketing mailers, and purchased customer lists. Under its initial accounting method, if AOL spent $24 million on advertising and free trials to lure newcomers in June of a given year, the company would not recognize an immediate expense. Instead, it would create an asset called "deferred subscriber acquisition costs." The $24 million asset would then be gradually reduced by a monthly charge to earnings, effectively spreading the cost over the average life of a subscription (about 24 months). Since AOL uses a June fiscal year end, only $1 million would be expensed the first year. The remaining $23 million would be expensed over the next 23 months. This practice [Figure 1.2(a)] was viewed by some accounting experts as unorthodox and aggressive. But it was not prohibited by GAAP! The criticism may have prompted AOL to announce in October 1996 that it would adopt the standard industry practice of recording the entire subscriber acquisition expense immediately [Figure 1.2(b)].

This accounting change had a major financial statement effect. In fiscal 1996 the company spent $363 million, a third of its revenue, on subscription promotions but it booked only $126 million of that as an expense. The company's one-time $385 million write-off to change accounting methods exceeded AOL's total revenues of $350 million for the quarter, and produced a net loss of $354 million. AOL said it would have reported quarterly earnings of $19 million under the old accounting method. The company's operating cash flows were not affected by this accounting adjustment, however, because the $385 million charge to earnings represented amounts that had already been spent.

Figure 1.2

AMERICA ONLINE'S ACCOUNTING CHANGE: (*a*) Before The Accounting Change: Capitalize and Then Expense Some Each Year; (*b*) After The Accounting Change: Expense It All When Spent

AOL has a June fiscal year end. Using its initial accounting method (part a), the $24 million spent in June would produce a $1 million expense for the year. The remaining $23 million would be charged to income over the next 23 months, or $12 million the following year and $11 million the year after.

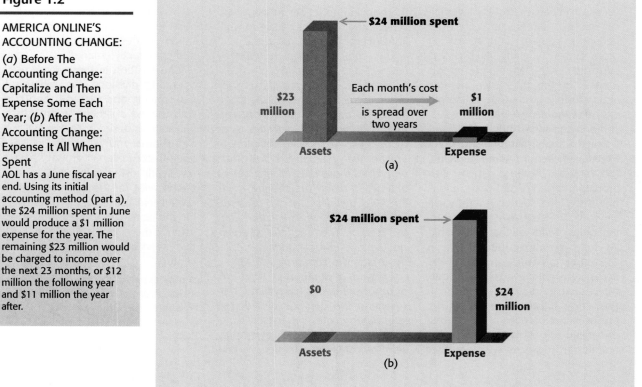

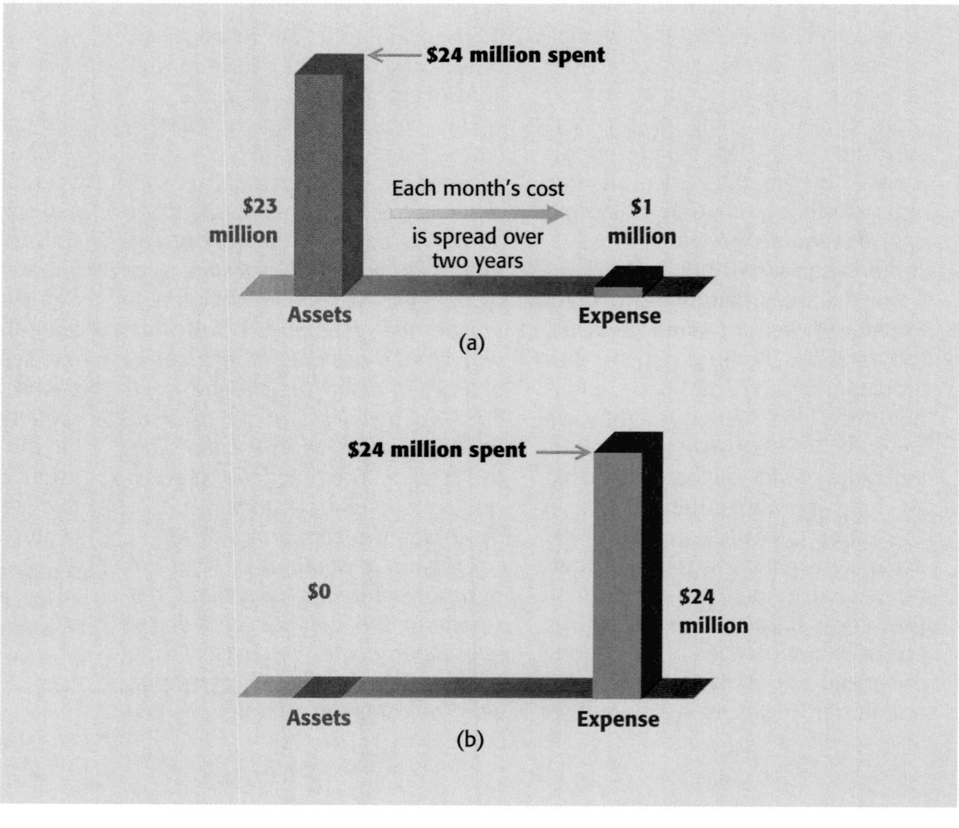

How Did Wall Street Respond? Shareholder reaction was difficult to gauge because news of the accounting change was buried in a flurry of other announcements. But the investment community clearly favored the new, more conservative accounting method. As a Merrill Lynch analyst put it, "While the earnings impact is certainly negative, we think it is more than overshadowed by the positive reaction the change in accounting should engender."[20] AOL shares closed up $1 on the day of the announcement.

Every Wall Street analyst was presumably aware that AOL was deferring its subscriber acquisition costs. But analysts who favored the stock had dismissed the accounting issue while enthusiastically trumpeting AOL's reported (now vaporized) "profits." By calling them profits, they tended to overlook or minimize that AOL was in a price war with Internet access providers and spending more cash than it was taking in. As one *Wall Street Journal* reporter observed:

> It [the accounting change] underscores just how massive the company's marketing efforts have been—and how illusory its profits may have been. The change raises the question of whether AOL will be able to report much profit at all in future quarters.[21]

Steve Case, the company's CEO, said scrapping the controversial deferred-cost method was aimed at stemming Wall Street concerns that had dogged the company for years.

> We've decided it's best not to spend all our time in this debate over accounting practices. There will be no argument over the quality of earnings.[22]

This scenario raises several intriguing questions about corporate financial reporting practices, managerial behavior, and the influence of accounting information on the decisions of investors, creditors, and others:

- How flexible is GAAP, and how much latitude is available to managers in the choice of "acceptable" accounting practices?
- What factors influence the accounting methods managers use? Why do firms change accounting methods? Does a change in accounting imply that previously reported figures (i.e., those produced by the old method) were incorrect?
- Do company disclosures make clear what accounting methods are used? Do those disclosures enable analysts to adjust reported figures when a company's accounting method either deviates from industry norms or changes through time?
- Why were analysts not surprised by AOL's decision to alter its accounting practices and by the company's $353 million loss for the quarter?
- Why didn't AOL's stock price fall when five years' worth of pre-tax profits were eliminated by the accounting change?
- How do shareholders use reported earnings and asset book values when valuing a firm's common stock?
- How does an accounting change alter creditors' opinions about a company's future cash flows and credit risk?

Perhaps the most provocative question, however, centers on the allegations raised by an SEC investigation launched shortly after AOL announced its decision to change accounting methods. Did the company violate GAAP and mislead investors by using accounting procedures that failed to provide an accurate and timely portrayal of the company's historical profit performance, current financial condition, and future prospects? Subsequent chapters of this book help you formulate answers to these and related questions about contemporary financial reporting practices in the United States and other developed countries.

In May 2000, AOL agreed to pay a $3.5 million penalty to settle SEC allegations that the company's deferred-cost accounting for subscriber acquisition costs in 1995 and 1996 violated GAAP. The SEC argued that accounting rules generally don't allow companies to book advertising costs as assets unless past performance indicates revenue from new customers will exceed the costs. At the time, AOL didn't have enough of a track record to demonstrate they could recover advertising costs, the SEC said. See M. Schroeder and N. Wingfield, "AOL Settles SEC Charges Over Its Costs," *Wall Street Journal* (May 16, 2000).

---

[20] "America Online Changes Accounting Method," *Dow Jones News Service* (October 29, 1996).

[21] J. Sandberg, "America Online Plans $385 Million Charge," *Wall Street Journal* (October 30, 1996).

[22] R. Lowenstein, "Did AOL Succeed in Spinning the Street?" *Wall Street Journal* (November 7, 1996).

An International Perspective

Because financial reporting practices vary widely in countries outside the United States, and because international business transactions are now more frequent and complex, the professional life of an analyst—in any country—has become more difficult. Multinational companies are regularly shifting resources throughout the world. These shifts cannot be accomplished efficiently without reliable financial information that permits careful analysis of investment opportunities and continuous control over how resources are deployed. Multinational companies must also resolve differences in national currencies and accounting rules when combining the financial statements of all their foreign and domestic businesses into consolidated reports.

The Coca-Cola Company, for example, generates only about 20% of its operating income from sales inside the United States. The company conducts business in 200 countries, hedges foreign currency cash flows, and uses foreign loans to finance investments outside the United States. Table 1.1 indicates the scope of Coca-Cola's worldwide operating activities from 1997 through 1999. North American (Canada and U.S.) sales were 38% of 1999 worldwide revenues but generated only 32% of worldwide operating income. By contrast, 10% of 1999 operating revenues originated in Latin America and this region produced 18% of Coca-Cola's worldwide operating income.

Understanding the economic, political, and cultural factors that contribute to regional differences in operating performance is daunting even for the most experienced financial analyst. Yet, assessing a multinational company's current performance and future prospects requires experience, knowledge, and skill with these factors.

Global competition is prevalent in most industries today, as companies facing mature domestic markets look outside their home borders for new customers and growth. Table 1.2 presents 1999 sales, net income and assets for three wireless phone manufacturers that compete on a worldwide basis. Ericsson, a Swedish firm, reports financial statement amounts in Swedish kronor; Motorola uses U.S. dollars, and Nokia, a Finnish company, uses the Euro for financial reporting purposes. Which company was the most profitable in 1999?

In the upper part of Table 1.2, the financial statement amounts reported by these three companies are not directly comparable because each firm uses a different currency. For example, Ericsson had sales of 215,403 million kronor and net income of 12,730 million kronor for 1999, but the krona/dollar exchange rate averaged 8.292 for the year. That means each U.S. dollar was worth about 8.292 kronor during 1999. Similarly, the Euro/dollar exchange rate averaged 0.945 for the year. The lower part of the table shows each company's sales, net income, and assets expressed in U.S. dollars. Here, we can see that Motorola has the largest sales ($30.931 million) but the lowest net income ($817 million) on the largest asset base ($37,327 million). Nokia has the smallest sales ($20,923 million), the largest net income ($2,727 million) and the smallest asset base ($14,377 million).

However, there is another factor that complicates our analysis. Financial statement comparisons of this sort become less meaningful when accounting standards and

Table 1.1 ■ COCA-COLA COMPANY

Operating Revenue and Income by Geographical Area

	1997		1998		1999	
	Revenue	**Income**	**Revenue**	**Income**	**Revenue**	**Income**
Africa	3%	3%	3%	4%	3%	4%
Greater Europe	29	31	26	29	23	23
Latin America	11	19	12	19	10	18
Middle and Far East	22	25	22	23	26	23
North America	35	22	37	25	38	32

Source: Coca-Cola Company 1999 Annual Report.

Table 1.2 ■ ERICSSON, MOTOROLA, AND NOKIA

Revenue, Net Income, and Assets for 1999

	Ericsson (Sweden)	Motorola (United States)	Nokia (Finland)
As reported in local currency:			
Revenue	215,403	30,931	19,772
Net income	12,730	817	2,577
Assets	202,628	37,327	14,279
U.S. dollar equivalents:			
Revenue	25,977	30,931	20,923
Net income	1,535	817	2,727
Assets	23,830	37,327	14,377
Local currency	Swedish kronor	U.S. dollars	Euros
Accounting methods	Swedish GAAP	U.S. GAAP	IAS

Source: Company reports.

Note: Sales and net income in the lower part of the table are restated into U.S. dollars using the average exchange rate for the year because the flows occurred throughout the year. *Year-end* assets are restated into U.S. dollars using the exchange rate as of the end of 1999.

measurement rules vary from one country to another. Ericsson uses Swedish GAAP, Motorola uses U.S. GAAP, and Nokia prepares its financial statements using International Accounting Standards (IAS). As a result, Motorola's lower *reported* profitability might not be attributable to economic factors if U.S. GAAP income recognition rules are more conservative than Swedish or IAS rules.

In some countries there must be conformity between the accounting methods used in shareholder financial statements and the rules used in computing taxable income. So the legislative branch of the government sets acceptable accounting principles for shareholder reporting purposes. In other countries the accounting profession, through its various committees, sets accounting principles. And these financial reporting rules differ from taxation rules.

The differing objectives of these standard-setting organizations (e.g., taxation, versus fair reporting to investors) result in diverse sets of accounting principles across countries. Analysts must be aware of this diversity and guard against the tendency to assume financial statements are readily comparable across national borders. These issues are examined in Chapter 18.

In the United States, the SEC permits foreign businesses to list their securities on a U.S. stock exchange as long as certain procedures are followed. Foreign businesses that do not use U.S. GAAP to prepare financial statements must file a Form 20-F each year with the SEC. This form transforms the foreign GAAP financial statements into U.S. GAAP. Form 20-F filings are public information, and thus they can be of considerable value to the analyst.

The financial reporting requirements for foreign companies listed on the London Stock Exchange permit greater flexibility than those that currently exist in the United States. Foreign business listed there can file financial statements that conform to any one of three accounting standards: U.K. GAAP, U.S. GAAP, or the accounting principles of the International Accounting Standards Committee (IASC). Reconciliation to a common set of accounting principles is not required. The London Stock Exchange also must allow all European Union (EU) countries to use their national GAAP—for instance, German companies can use German GAAP—under the well-established principle of mutual recognition.

Diversity is a fact of life in international accounting practice. Readers of financial statements must never lose sight of this diversity. **RECAP**

Challenges Confronting the Analyst

During the last two decades, financial statements have become increasingly complex and more accessible. Corporate financial reports are more complicated today simply because the business world has become more dynamic and complex.

Global competition and the spread of free enterprise throughout the world has prompted firms to rely increasingly on foreign countries as a market for products and services, and as a source of capital and customers. Competitive pressures have also contributed to a fundamental change in the way firms organize and finance their activities. Corporate restructurings abound. New types of financial instruments are now used by companies to raise capital and manage risk. Service firms and e-commerce companies now represent a major portion of business activity. These and other features of the changing business landscape pose difficult challenges for contemporary financial reporting practices—and for an accounting model originally developed to fit companies engaged in local manufacturing and merchandising.

There has also been explosive growth in the use of electronic means to assemble and examine financial information in the last two decades. The accessibility of computers and analytical software continues to rise as their cost falls. Quantitative methods for analyzing financial data have become increasingly popular, which in turn has meant increasing demand for and use of electronic databases containing financial information. Corporate press releases, analysts' research reports, historical financial data, and complete annual and quarterly financial reports are now readily available in electronic form through commercial vendors. Documents filed with the SEC can now be obtained from the agency's electronic data gathering and retrieval system (EDGAR, available at www. sec. gov or www. freeedgar.com).

These developments place new burdens on analysts. On the one hand, there is a wealth of financial statement data and related information available to the analyst at relatively low cost. On the other hand, firms today operate in a dynamic environment that has made the task of analyzing financial statements even more complex. The financial reporting practices of business firms are continually challenged on many fronts, and the astute analyst must remain vigilant to the possibility that financial reports sometimes do not capture underlying economic realities.

SUMMARY

Financial statements are an extremely important source of information about a company, its economic health, and its prospects. Equity investors use financial statements to form opinions about the value of a company and its stock. Creditors use statement information to assess a company's ability to repay its debt and to comply with loan covenants. Stock analysts, brokers, and portfolio managers use financial statements as the basis for their recommendations to investors and creditors. Auditors use financial statements to help design more effective audits by spotting areas of potential reporting abuses.

That's why financial statements are in demand: They provide information that helps improve decision making, and they make it possible to monitor managers' activities. But what governs the supply of financial information?

Mandatory reporting is a partial answer. Most companies in the United States and other developed countries are required to produce and send out financial statements to shareholders as well as to file a copy with a government agency—in the United States, that agency is the SEC; this requirement allows all interested parties to view the statements. That's one reason companies supply financial information.

The other reason? It's because financial information that goes beyond the minimum requirements can often benefit the company, its managers, and owners. For example, voluntary financial disclosures can help the company obtain capital more cheaply or negotiate better terms from suppliers. But benefits like these come with potential costs: information collection, processing, and dissemination costs; competitive disadvantage costs; litigation costs; and political costs. This means that two companies with different financial reporting benefits and costs are likely to choose different accounting policies and reporting strategies.

Can they do so? Yes, because financial reporting standards are often imprecise and open to interpretation. This imprecision gives managers an opportunity to shape financial statements in ways that allow them to achieve specific reporting goals. Most managers use their accounting flexibility to paint a truthful economic picture of the company; other managers mold the financial statements to mask weaknesses and to hide problems. Analysts who understand financial reporting, managers' incentives, as well as the accounting flexibility available to managers, will maintain a healthy skepticism about the numbers and recognize that financial statements sometimes conceal more than they reveal.

APPENDIX GAAP in the United States

This is a brief, historical overview of the public and private sector organizations that have influenced the development of financial accounting practices in the United States. As we shall see, some organizations have explicit statutory authority to decide what constitutes U.S. GAAP. Other organizations lack that authority but remain influential.

Early Developments

Corporate financial reporting practices in the United States prior to 1900 were primarily intended to provide accounting information for management's use. Financial statements were rarely made available to shareholders, creditors, or other interested external parties. The **New York Stock Exchange (NYSE),** established in 1792, was the primary mechanism for trading ownership in corporations. As such, it could establish specific requirements for the disclosure of financial information, and thereby dictate accounting standards for corporations whose shares it listed. Beginning in 1869, the NYSE attempted to persuade listed companies to make their financial statements public. Few companies complied. The prevailing view of corporate management was that financial information was a private concern of the company and that public disclosure would harm the company's competitive advantage.

Passage of the Sixteenth Amendment to the U.S. Constitution in 1913 and subsequent legislation allowing the federal government to tax corporate profits set the stage for expanded corporate financial disclosure. This legislation required companies to maintain accurate financial record-keeping systems; the goal of this legislation was to ensure proper tax accounting and to facilitate collection. However, corporate financial disclosures to outsiders were still limited.

The stock market crash of 1929 and the Great Depression that followed provoked widespread concern about financial disclosure. Some alleged that the collapse of the stock market was due largely to the lack of meaningful requirements for reporting corporate financial information to investors and creditors.[23] Moreover, many felt that economic conditions would not improve until investors regained confidence in the financial markets. Responding to this concern in January 1933, the NYSE began to require all companies seeking exchange listing to submit independently audited financial statements and to agree to audits of all future reports.

In an effort to bolster public confidence and restore order to the securities market, Congress enacted the Securities Act of 1933, which required companies selling capital stock or debt in interstate commerce to provide financial information pertinent to establishing the value and risk associated with those securities. One year later, the Act was amended to establish the SEC as an independent agency of the government, one whose function was to regulate both securities sold to the public and the exchanges where those securities were traded. Companies issuing stock or debt listed on organized exchanges were required to file annual audited reports with the SEC.[24] The SEC was also empowered to establish and enforce the accounting policies and practices followed by registered companies.

---

[23] See E. R. Willet, *Fundamentals of Securities Markets* (New York: Appleton-Century-Crofts, 1968), pp. 208–14.

[24] Security registration statements and other reports filed under the 1934 amendments to the Securities Act are public information and are available for inspection at the SEC and at the securities exchanges where the company's securities are listed.

These powers are given to the SEC in Section 19(a) of the Securities Act of 1933 as amended:

> . . . the Commission shall have authority, for the purposes of this title, to prescribe the form or forms in which required information shall be set forth, the items or details to be shown in the balance sheet and earning statement, and the methods to be followed in the preparation of accounts, in the appraisal or valuation of assets and liabilities, in the determination of depreciation and depletion, in the differentiation of recurring and nonrecurring income, in the differentiation of investment and operating income, and in the preparation, where the Commission deems it necessary or desirable, of consolidated balance sheets or income accounts of any person directly or indirectly controlling or controlled by the issuer, or any person under direct or indirect common control with the issuer. The rules and regulations of the Commission shall be effective upon publication in the manner which the Commission shall prescribe.

In addition to its primary pronouncement—*Regulation S-X,* which describes the principal formal financial disclosure requirements for companies—the SEC issues *Financial Reporting Releases* and other publications stating its position on accounting and auditing matters.

Accounting Series Release No. 4, issued in April 1938, first expressed the SEC's position that generally accepted accounting principles for which there is "substantial authoritative support" constitute the SEC standard for financial reporting and disclosure. The release further indicated that a company filing financial statements reflecting an accounting principle that had been formally disapproved by the SEC—or for which there was no substantial authoritative support—would be presumed to be filing misleading financial statements even though there was full disclosure of the accounting principles applied. However, the release did not provide guidance as to what the SEC meant by *substantial authoritative support.* This void was later filled.

Emergence of GAAP

The Securities Exchange Act of 1934 required the financial statements of all publicly traded firms to be audited by independent accountants. This requirement elevated the role of the independent accountants' professional organizations. These organizations were active in influencing accounting policy prior to the 1930s, but the securities acts accentuated the need for more formal accounting standards and for systematic public announcement of those standards.

During the years immediately following passage of the 1933 and 1934 securities acts, the SEC relied primarily on the American Institute of Certified Public Accountants (AICPA)—the national professional organization of certified public accountants—to develop and enforce accounting standards.[25] In response to the SEC and to the growing need to report reliable financial information, the AICPA created the Committee on Accounting Procedure in 1939 to establish, review, and evaluate accepted accounting procedures. This committee began the practice of developing U.S. financial accounting and reporting standards in the private sector.

Between 1938 and 1959, the AICPA's Committee on Accounting Procedure was responsible for narrowing the differences and inconsistencies in accounting practice. The committee issued 51 Accounting Research Bulletins (ARBs) and four Accounting Terminology Bulletins that set forth what the committee believed GAAP should be. These pronouncements were not binding on corporations or their auditors.

In 1959, the AICPA established the Accounting Principles Board (APB) to replace the Committee on Accounting Procedure. The APB's basic charge was to develop a statement

[25] The American Association of Public Accountants was established in 1887 and represented the core of the accounting profession in the United States. The name of the organization was changed to the American Institute of Accountants in 1917, and it became the AICPA in 1957.

of accounting concepts—that is, a conceptual foundation for accounting—and to issue pronouncements resolving current accounting controversies. During its existence from 1959 to 1973, the APB issued 31 Opinions and four Statements designed to improve external financial accounting and disclosure. At the outset, the force of these pronouncements, as with earlier ARBs, depended on general acceptance and persuasion. The APB sought compliance with financial reporting standards by attempting to persuade corporations and independent auditors that the standards improved the quality of financial reporting. By 1964 many accounting professionals and business leaders were convinced that persuasion alone could neither reduce the tremendous latitude available under then-existing accounting and reporting practices nor eliminate inconsistencies in the application of those practices. Critics cited instances in which identical transactions could be accounted for by any one of several different methods—and net income could be manipulated by selecting a particular accounting approach from among several considered to be "generally accepted."

A turning point in the development of corporate financial reporting standards occurred in October 1964 when the Council (or governing body) of the AICPA adopted a requirement that was incorporated into the rules of ethics for independent CPAs:

> **Rule 203—Accounting Principles:**
> A member shall not (1) express an opinion or state affirmatively that the financial statements or other financial data of any entity are presented in conformity with generally accepted accounting principles or (2) state that he or she is not aware of any material modifications that should be made to such statements or data in order for them to be in conformity with generally accepted accounting principles, if such statements or data contain any departure from an accounting principle promulgated by bodies designated by Council to establish such principles that has a material effect on the statements or data taken as a whole. If, however, the statements or data contain such a departure and the member can demonstrate that due to unusual circumstances the financial statements or data would otherwise have been misleading, the member can comply with the rule by describing the departure, its approximate effects, if practicable, and the reasons why compliance with the principle would result in a misleading statement. [As amended.][26]

This compliance requirement forced corporations and their auditors to implement the accounting standards prescribed in APB opinions and in earlier pronouncements not superseded by these opinions. This in turn caused greater attention to be focused on the activities of the APB.

Complaints about the process used to develop financial reporting and accounting standards surfaced in the 1960s and early 1970s. Corporate management, government regulators, and other interested external parties voiced concern about the lack of participation by organizations other than the AICPA, about the quality of the opinions issued, about the failure of the APB to develop a coherent conceptual foundation for external financial reporting, about the insufficient output by the APB, and about the APB's failure to act promptly to correct alleged accounting and reporting abuses.

The APB was not immune to criticism from politicians, government regulators, and the business community. One example occurred in the early 1960s when the APB attempted to resolve the question of accounting for the investment tax credit. The APB initially required the tax credit to be treated as a balance sheet item—a reduction in the asset's cost—rather than as an immediate increase to earnings. This decision met with strong resistance from business and several major accounting firms. After the SEC said it would allow both methods in filings with the Commission, the APB had no alternative but to rescind its

---

[26] The GAAP "override" provision described in the last sentence of Rule 203 is rarely seen these days in the financial statements of companies subject to SEC oversight, and most observers believe the SEC will not accept departures from GAAP.

earlier pronouncement (*Opinion No. 2*) and to permit the earnings increase (*Opinion No. 4*).[27] This change in the accounting standard enabled firms to use the accounting methods they preferred for the investment tax credit.

The 1971 Study Group on Establishment of Accounting Principles (known as the Wheat Committee) was formed to review and evaluate the private sector standard-setting process as well as to recommend improvements where possible. This committee was created because of growing concern among accounting professionals over the APB's ability to withstand pressure from the business community. The committee recommended that a new and more independent, full-time standard-setting organization be established in the private sector to replace the APB. This recommendation, which was approved by the AICPA and which became effective in July 1973, created the FASB.[28] The FASB differed from its predecessors in several important ways:

1. Board membership consisted of seven voting members, in contrast to the 18 members on the APB.
2. Autonomy and independence were enhanced by requiring members to sever all ties with their prior employers and by dictating that member salaries were paid directly by the FASB.
3. Broader representation was achieved by not requiring board members to hold a CPA license.
4. Staff and advisory support was increased substantially.

Accounting Series Release No. 150, issued by the SEC in December 1973, formally acknowledged that financial accounting pronouncements of the FASB (and its predecessor organizations) are ordinarily considered by the SEC as having "substantial authoritative support" and thus are the SEC standards for financial reporting and disclosure. Accounting practices that are contrary to FASB pronouncements are considered to not have such support. This release also reaffirmed the SEC's private sector approach to standard setting. It said,

> . . . the Commission intends to continue its policy of looking to the private sector for leadership in establishing and improving accounting principles and standards through the FASB with the expectation that the body's conclusions will promote the interests of investors.

Current Institutional Structure in the United States

The SEC still retains broad statutory powers to define accounting terms, to prescribe the methods to be followed in preparing financial reports, and to specify the details to be presented in financial statements. Under the Securities Act of 1933, companies wanting to issue securities interstate must file a prospectus with the SEC. The prospectus is a public document—prepared for each new security offering—containing information about the company, its officers, and its financial affairs. The financial section of the prospectus must be audited by an independent CPA who is registered to practice before the SEC. Once securities have been sold to the public, the company is required to file publicly accessible, audited financial statements with the SEC each year. These annual statements are known as the 10-K filing. In addition, unaudited quarterly financial reports (called 10-Q filings) are

---

[27] In fact, Congress later passed legislation permitting the investment tax credit to "flow through" to reported earnings in the year the credit was taken against the company's federal tax obligation. This situation illustrates the ultimate power of the Congress over the establishment of financial reporting and accounting standards in the United States. See "Accounting for the Investment Credit," *APB Opinion No. 2* (New York: AICPA, 1962); "Accounting for the Investment Credit," *APB Opinion No. 4* (New York: AICPA, 1964).

[28] During the transition period between the APB and FASB, the SEC seemed to take on a more active and aggressive role in policy making. During its last nine months of operation (October 1972 through June 1973), the APB issued seven opinions in an attempt to complete its agenda of in-process accounting policy considerations. The SEC issued eight releases on accounting matters during this same period and another nine during the first year of the FASB.

required. The annual 10-K disclosure requirements closely overlap the information in the company's published financial statements, but are more extensive.[29]

Although the SEC has wide statutory authority to impose financial reporting rules, it continues to rely on the accounting profession to set and enforce accounting standards and to regulate the profession. The SEC has occasionally forced the accounting profession to tackle critical problems, and it once rejected an accounting standard issued by the FASB.[30] Such situations occur rarely.

Since July 1973, the FASB has been responsible for establishing accounting standards in the United States. The FASB has issued over 140 Statements of Financial Accounting Standards, seven Statements of Financial Accounting Concepts, and numerous technical bulletins. The FASB has neither the authority nor the responsibility to enforce compliance with GAAP. That responsibility rests with company management, the accounting profession, the SEC, and the courts. Some observers believe that compliance is the weak link in the private sector standard-setting chain. These critics point to frequent litigation on financial reporting matters in the courts, the escalating cost of liability insurance premiums paid by audit firms, and criticism by the SEC's chief accountant regarding the independence of external auditors.[31]

The FASB follows a "due process" procedure in developing accounting standards. This process is designed to ensure public input in the decision process. Most accounting standards issued by the FASB go through three steps:

1. *Discussion-memorandum stage:* After the Board and its staff have considered a topic on its agenda—and perhaps consulted with experts and other interested parties—a discussion memorandum is issued. This memorandum outlines the key issues involved and the Board's preliminary views on those issues. The public is invited to comment in writing on the memorandum, and public hearings are sometimes held to permit interested individuals to express their views in person.
2. *Exposure-draft stage:* After further deliberation and modification by the Board and its staff, an exposure draft of the standard is issued. During this stage, a period of not less than 30 days, further public comment is requested and evaluated.
3. *Voting stage:* Finally, the Board votes on whether to issue the standard as contained in the exposure draft or to revise it and reissue a new exposure draft. For a proposed standard to become official and a part of generally accepted accounting principles, five of the seven Board members must approve it.

---

[29] The financial reporting and accounting requirements pertaining to SEC registrants are described in the following publications: Regulation S-X, the original and comprehensive document issued by the commission that prescribes financial reporting rules and the forms to be filed with the SEC; Accounting Series Releases, which are amendments, extensions, and additions to Regulation S-X; Special SEC Releases that relate to current issues as they arise; Accounting and Auditing Enforcement Releases (AAERs), which document the SEC response to accounting and auditing irregularities; and Financial Reporting Releases FFRs. The FFRs, together with AAERs, are the successors to Accounting Series Releases. Staff Accounting Bulletins are issued by Office of the Chief Accountant and serve as interpretations of Regulation S-X and its amendments, extensions, and additions; they do not carry the legal weight of Commission releases.

[30] "Financial Accounting and Reporting by Oil and Gas Producing Companies," *Statement of Financial Accounting Standards (SFAS) No. 19* (Stamford, CT: FASB, 1977). This statement was issued after protracted deliberation, and it identified a single method of accounting that was to be followed by all affected companies. In August 1978 the SEC ruled that a new method of accounting for oil and gas reserves needed to be developed and that in the meantime companies could use any method that had been generally accepted prior to *SFAS No. 19.* This directly contradicted the FASB and required the issuance of both a statement suspending *SFAS No. 19* and a second FASB statement finally bringing the SEC and FASB into conformity with one another. SEC involvement was, in part, due to enactment of a public law requiring an investigation into, and action on, the state of oil and gas accounting rules by December 25, 1977. Such legal deadlines in connection with the accounting standard setting process are rare. Aspects of this controversy are discussed in Chapter 10.

[31] W. P. Schuetze, "A Mountain or a Molehill?" *Accounting Horizons* (March 1994), pp. 69–75.

Influential groups and organizations use the due process of the FASB to plead for alternative solutions. The arguments often include cost-benefit considerations; claims that the proposed accounting treatment is not theoretically sound or will not be understood by users; implementation issues; and concerns that the proposed standard will be economically harmful to specific companies, industries, or the country.[32] Government agencies, preparer organizations such as the Business Roundtable, and industry trade organizations such as the Financial Executives Institute create substantial pressures on the Board. Some contend that the interests of investors, creditors, and other financial statement users are not always well represented in this political forum. Others disagree.

International Accounting Standards

When looking to register securities in U.S. markets, a major impediment foreign companies encounter is the significant differences between U.S. and foreign accounting standards. Several groups have long worked to "harmonize" worldwide accounting and reporting standards. At the center of this effort are the International Accounting Standards Committee (IASC), which sets international accounting rules, and the International Organization of Securities Commissions (IOSCO), of which the SEC is a member. As part of an agreement with IOSCO, the IASC developed a core set of International Accounting Standards (IAS), completed in 1999. IOSCO endorsed IAS for cross-border capital raising and stock exchange listing purposes in May 2000.

Formed in 1973, the IASC now has a membership that includes 153 professional accounting organizations from more than 112 countries around the world. The standard-setting function is performed by a board made up of 14 members. The IASC has issued 40 standards and 18 interpretations of existing IAS standards. Existing IASC standards typically allow firms greater latitude in their accounting and reporting practices than does U.S. GAAP.

Founded in 1974, IOSCO seeks member cooperation to improve domestic and international financial markets, to promote the development of domestic markets through information exchange, to establish standards and effective surveillance of international securities transactions, and to ensure the integrity of markets by rigorous application of standards and enforcement. In 1998, IOSCO adopted disclosure standards that enable multinational companies to prepare a single non-financial-statement disclosure document (including, for example, a description of the company's history, business, risks, and ownership) for cross-border securities offerings and stock exchange listings. In addition to greatly simplifying preparation, investors benefit from the comprehensive required disclosures and enhanced comparability of information. The SEC adopted these IOSCO disclosure standards in 1999.

The SEC continues to make it clear that U.S. financial reporting standards will not be lowered for domestic public companies. The SEC will consider international accounting standards for use by foreign companies, without reconciliation to U.S. GAAP, but only when the standards meet certain criteria:

- They include a core set of accounting pronouncements constituting a comprehensive, generally accepted basis of accounting.
- They are high quality—that is, they result in comparability and transparency, and provide for full disclosure.
- They can and will be rigorously interpreted and applied.

It remains to be seen to what extent the SEC will embrace IAS for financial statement filings.

---

[32] For example, SEC reversal of *SFAS No. 19* was justified on the grounds that implementation of the proposed accounting standard would sharply inhibit petroleum exploration and development activities.

PROBLEMS/DISCUSSION QUESTIONS

P1–1

Demand for accounting information

REQUIRED:

1. Explain why each of the following groups might want financial accounting information. What type of financial information would each group find most useful?
   a. the company's existing shareholders
   b. prospective investors
   c. financial analysts who follow the company
   d. company managers
   e. current employees
   f. commercial lenders who have loaned money to the company
   g. current suppliers
   h. debt rating agencies like Moody's or Standard and Poor's
   i. regulatory agencies like the Federal Trade Commission
2. Identify at least one other group that might want financial accounting information about the company, and describe how the information would be used.

P1–2

Incentives for voluntary disclosure

REQUIRED:

1. Describe how the following market forces influence the supply of financial accounting information:
   a. debt and equity financial markets
   b. managerial labor markets
   c. the market for corporate control (e.g., mergers, takeovers, and divestitures).
2. What other forces might cause managers to voluntarily release financial information about the company?
3. Identify five ways managers can voluntarily provide information about the company to outsiders. (You might consult a current issue of the *Wall Street Journal* for examples.) What advantages do these voluntary approaches have over the required financial disclosures contained in annual and quarterly reports to shareholders?

P1–3

Costs of disclosure

REQUIRED:

1. Define each of the following disclosure costs associated with financial accounting information, and provide an example of each cost:
   a. information collection, processing, dissemination costs
   b. competitive disadvantage costs
   c. litigation costs
   d. political costs.
2. Identify at least one other potential disclosure cost.

P1–4

Proxy statement disclosures

A company's proxy statement contains information about major shareholders, management compensation (salary, bonus, stock options, etc.), composition of the board of directors, and shares owned by top managers and members of the board of directors.

REQUIRED:

Explain why this information could be useful to a financial analyst following the firm.

P1–5

Your position on the issues

Provide a two- or three-sentence response that argues for or against (indicate which) each of these statements:

a. Accounting is an exact science.
b. Managers choose accounting procedures that produce the most accurate picture of the company's operating performance and financial condition.
c. Accounting standards in the United States are influenced more by politics than by science or economics.

(*continued*)

d. If the FASB and SEC were not around to require and enforce minimum levels of financial disclosure, most companies would provide little (if any) information to outsiders.
e. When managers possess good news about the company (i.e., information that will increase the stock price), they have an incentive to disclose the information as soon as possible.
f. When managers possess bad news about the company (i.e., information that will decrease the stock price), they have an incentive to delay disclosure as long as possible.
g. An investor who uses fundamental analysis for investment decisions has little need for financial statement information.
h. An investor who believes that capital markets are efficient has little need for financial statement information.
i. Managers who disclose only the minimum information required to meet FASB and SEC requirements may be doing a disservice to shareholders.
j. Financial statements are the only source of information analysts use when forecasting the company's future profitability and financial condition.

P1–6

How managers and professional investors rate information

A wide variety of financial and nonfinancial information is used in managing a company and in making decisions about whether or not to invest in a company. A survey of senior corporate managers and professional investors asked each group to rank the following items according to their relative importance ("1" being the most important and "14" being the least important). How do you think each item was ranked?

	Importance Ranking	
	Corporate Managers	Professional Investors
Business segment results	______	______
Capital expenditures	______	______
Cash flow	______	______
Cost control	______	______
Customer satisfaction	______	______
Earnings	______	______
Market growth	______	______
Market share	______	______
Measures of strategic achievement	______	______
New product development	______	______
Product and process quality	______	______
Research and development (R & D)	______	______
R & D productivity	______	______
Strategic goals	______	______

P1–7

Accounting quality and the audit committee

The New York Stock Exchange (NYSE), the National Association of Securities Dealers (NASD), and the American Stock Exchange (AMEX) require that listed firms have audit committees comprised of independent (i.e., outside) company directors. Audit committees review the firm's audited financial statements with management and with the outside auditor, and recommend to the full board of directors that the statements be included in the company's annual report. As a committee member, you might ask management about the following:

1. What are the key business and financial risks the company has to deal with in its financial reporting?
2. What financial reporting areas involved subjective judgments or estimates.
3. Are there significant areas where the company's accounting policies were difficult to determine?
4. How do the company's accounting practices compare with those of others in the industry?
5. How are significant accounting judgments made and estimates determined?

6. Are the financial statements and underlying accounting methods consistent with those used last year?
7. What major business transactions or events required significant accounting or disclosure judgments?
8. Are alternative accounting practices being proposed or considered that should be brought to the committee's attention?
9. Were there serious problems in preparing the financial statements?
10. Have outside parties—including the SEC, major investors, analysts, and the news media—voiced concern about the company's accounting practices?
11. Were there disagreements between management and the auditor regarding accounting practices and, if so, how were they resolved?

SOURCE: *Audit Committee Update 2000,* PriceWaterhouseCoopers LLP.

REQUIRED:

Explain for each question why the audit committee and investors might be interested in the answer.

CASES

C1–1

AST Research: Restating quarter results

AST Research Inc., a personal computer manufacturer, announced an accounting change that in many ways parallels the one made at America Online: Costs previously deferred were to be expensed immediately, and the change had no direct impact on current or future cash flows. A copy of the *Wall Street Journal* article announcing AST's accounting change follows:

AST Research said it is restating results for its fiscal 1994 fourth quarter as a result of a disagreement with the Securities and Exchange Commission over accounting rules.

The restatement will cause AST to report a loss of $8.1 million, or 25 cents a share, for the fourth quarter ended July 2, instead of the previously reported net income of $14.1 million, or 41 cents a share. The dispute arose out of an SEC review of AST's proxy statement for a $377.5 million investment in the company by Samsung Electronics Company.

The SEC staff concluded that $33.6 million of the expenses related to AST's 1993 acquisition of the computer manufacturing operations of Tandy Corporation should be charged to sales during the fourth quarter, rather than amortized over future quarters as goodwill.

AST said that the SEC didn't force it to restate the results, and that AST had agreed to the restatement to avoid delays in approval of the proxy and the Samsung investment. The redesignation of income has no material effect on AST. It's a noncash loss and will be offset by increases in net income in subsequent quarters, because of the lack of goodwill amortization.

In Nasdaq Stock Market trading yesterday, AST closed at $17,625, up 25 cents.

"They [the SEC] had a different interpretation on a piece of the accounting for the acquisition," said Bruce Edwards, AST's chief financial officer. "We decided to do the restatement to move forward on the transaction" with Samsung.

An SEC official acknowledged that the agency's corporation-finance division had been in talks with AST about its fourth-quarter earnings report but wouldn't say whether the SEC pressured AST to revise the report.

It isn't unusual for the agency to question a company's account of its own earnings, the official said. Only in rare cases does such a review spell bigger problems for the company, such as when the SEC thinks executives intentionally misstated earnings to hype a stock price. But there isn't any indication that AST did that in this case, the official added.

AST also agreed to issue additional shares to Samsung if AST incurs any uninsured losses, in excess of a certain threshold, as a result of being sued by shareholders. AST said it has now received all necessary approvals for Samsung's investment.

The company scheduled a special meeting of shareholders for June 30 to vote on the transaction.

Source: Republished with permission of the *Wall Street Journal* from "AST Research," (June 8, 1995); permission conveyed through Copyright Clearance Center, Inc.

REQUIRED:

Why was the stock market so forgiving in evaluating the accounting method change made by AST Research? How is AST Research doing today?

C1–2

Henley Manufacturing Inc. (CW): Announcing sales and earnings goals

As your first week at Henley Manufacturing Inc. draws to a close, you find a memorandum on your desk from the company's CEO. The memo outlines sales and earnings goals for next year: Sales are expected to increase 15% with net income growing by 20%.

The memo says that these goals are ambitious in light of the company's performance over the past two years—ambitious, but attainable if "everyone remains focused and committed to our business strategy."

As you finish the memo, your boss, the vice president of finance, steps into your office. She asks you what you think about the memo. You reply that it is important to have clear financial goals but that you would need to know more before making any comments on whether the goals will be easy or difficult to achieve. As she leaves your office, you ask if the CEO will be announcing these goals at next week's annual shareholders' meeting. Your boss answers, "We've never disclosed our sales and earning goals in the past." When you ask why, she says, "We aren't required to under U.S. securities regulations."

Two days later, your boss stops by again and tells you that she raised the issue of disclosing to shareholders the firm's net income and sales goals at this morning's executive committee meeting. The CEO was intrigued but requested that someone identify the costs and benefits of doing so. As she leaves your office, she asks you to prepare a briefing document for presentation at the next executive committee meeting.

REQUIRED A:

1. What are the potential costs and benefits to Henley Manufacturing of announcing its sales and earnings goals at the shareholders' meeting?
2. Would you recommend that the CEO announce both, one, or neither goal? Why?
3. If the company's sales and earnings goals covered three years rather than just next year, would your recommendation change? Why or why not?

REQUIRED B:

Suppose the memo was more detailed and described the following financial goals for next year: annual sales growth of 15%; annual earnings growth of 20%; a return on net tangible assets of 16%; a return on common equity of 20%; a minimum current ratio of 2.4; a minimum interest coverage ratio of 7.0; a minimum profit margin of 5%; a dividend payout ratio (dividends/net income) of 35% to 40%; a maximum long-term debt to common equity ratio of 40% to 45%; a minimum increase of 15% in annual capital expenditures; and a minimum inventory turnover ratio of 4.5.

Would you recommend that the CEO disclose all, some, or none of these goals at the shareholders' meeting? Which ones and why?

C1–3

Whirlpool (CW): Disclosing major customers

The following excerpt is from Whirlpool Corporation's 1999 10-K report filed with the SEC and is a required disclosure:

> The company has been the principal supplier of home laundry appliances to Sears, Roebuck and Co. ("Sears") for over 80 years. The company is also the principal supplier to Sears of residential trash compactors and microwave hood combinations and a major supplier to Sears of dishwashers, free-standing ranges, and home refrigeration equipment. The company also supplies Sears with certain other products for which the company is not currently a major supplier. Sales of such other products to Sears are not significant to the company's business. The company supplies products to Sears for sale under Sears' Kenmore and Sears brand names. Sears has also been a major outlet for the company's Whirlpool and KitchenAid brand products since 1989. In 1999 approximately 18% of the company's net sales were attributable to sales to Sears.

REQUIRED:

1. Why does the SEC require companies like Whirlpool to alert financial statement readers to the existence of major customers?
2. How might this information be of use to a financial analyst?
3. Why might Sears want to monitor the financial performance and health of Whirlpool? What specific information about Whirlpool would be of most interest to Sears?
4. Why might Whirlpool want to monitor the financial performance and health of Sears? What information about Sears would be of most interest to Whirlpool?

C1–4

The gap in GAAP (CW)

It is often alleged that the value of financial statement information is compromised by the latitude that GAAP gives to management. Companies can use different accounting methods to summarize and report the outcome of otherwise similar transactions. Inventory valuation and depreciation are examples in which GAAP allows several alternative accounting methods.

At one extreme the FASB and the SEC could limit accounting flexibility by establishing a single set of accounting methods and procedures that all companies would apply. At the other extreme, the FASB and the SEC could simply require companies to provide relevant and reliable financial information to outsiders, without placing any restrictions on the accounting methods used.

REQUIRED:

1. Why should managers be allowed some flexibility in their financial accounting and reporting choices?
2. Of the two approaches to accounting standard-setting that are mentioned above, which best describes the current financial reporting environment in the United States?
3. Describe the advantages and disadvantages of these two approaches to accounting standard-setting, and tell how these advantages and disadvantages vary across different groups of financial statement users.

C1–5

IES Industries: Voting on a merger

In early 1996 IES Industries signed a definitive merger agreement with two other neighboring utilities—Wisconsin Power and Light (WPL) and Interstate Power Company (IPC). This was the first "three way" merger in the rapidly consolidating electrical utility industry.

The merger seemed to make good economic sense. Predictions indicated that deregulation of the industry would create intense price competition. All three companies had low-cost generating capacity when compared to other utilities in the Midwest. By forming a single company, the merger partners could become even more price competitive by eliminating redundancies in energy distribution, maintenance, customer service, and corporate staffs. They could then expand their combined geographical reach to lucrative metropolitan markets in the region.

Wall Street was ambivalent about the merger. The merger announcement resulted in a 10% share price increase for IPC, but IES and WPL share prices remained flat. Part of the market's ambivalence was due to the fact that the merger required state and federal regulatory approval. Analysts predicted a lengthy approval process and voiced uncertainty about the eventual outcome.

In July 1996 MidAmerican Energy launched a hostile takeover of IES Industries. MidAmerican offered to pay $35 per share for IES stock, a $5 per-share premium over the closing price that prevailed before the takeover announcement. The board of directors at IES rejected the buyout offer and told shareholders that the company was worth more than $35 per share when combined with WPL and IPC. Shares of IES common stock closed at $33.50 following MidAmerican Energy's hostile offer, and this price was unchanged after the IES rejection.

MidAmerican's tender offer could not have been better timed. IES shareholders were scheduled to vote on the three-way merger agreement in mid-August. With MidAmerican's offer on the table, IES shareholders could vote either to approve the WPL and IPC merger or to reject the merger in favor of MidAmerican's cash bid. IES and MidAmerican launched intense advertising and public relations campaigns to sway IES shareholders. This contest for proxies (shareholder votes) cost the two companies in excess of $10 million.

REQUIRED:

1. As an employee of IES Industries and the owner of 100 shares of the company's common stock, what questions would you like answered at the August shareholders meeting just prior to submitting your vote? How might the company's financial reports help answer those questions?
2. As an institutional investor with 5% of your portfolio invested in IES shares, what questions would you like answered at the August shareholders' meeting just prior to submitting your vote? How might the company's financial reports help answer those questions?

C1–6

Trans World Airlines' (TWA) earnings announcement (CW)

Returning home from your job as a financial analyst covering the airline industry, you find a message from your father, a veteran pilot for TWA. He will be in town this evening and would like you to join him for dinner. He needs your investment advice. Having been with TWA during the company's two trips to bankruptcy court, he is ecstatic over an article in today's issue of the *Wall Street Journal.*

TWA announced net income of $623.8 million for the year, compared to a loss of $317.7 million in the prior year. At last the company seems to have recovered from its financial difficulty.

As a stockholder of TWA, your father is wondering if he should purchase more of the company's stock and if TWA might start paying dividends again now that it is profitable. He thinks the pilots' union might recover some of the wage concessions that it made during the bankruptcy process. Given the age of TWA's fleet (about 18 years), he hopes that some of the profits might be used to buy new airliners.

As you finish reading the news article, you realize that dinner is less than two hours away. What advice do you have for your father?

> ST. LOUIS—Trans World Airlines, helped by a big gain from retiring debt, posted 1993 net income of $623.8 million compared with a year-earlier loss of $317.7 million.
>
> Before the $1.08 billion gain, TWA's 1993 loss widened to $451.8 million from $317.7 million in 1992. TWA, which emerged from bankruptcy-law proceedings last November, said the gain reflected a debt-for-equity swap that was part of its reorganization plan. Creditors received a 55% stake in TWA for forgiving about $1 billion in debt.
>
> The airline's operating losses, before taxes and credits and charges, were $281.3 million in 1993 and $404.6 million in 1992. TWA's revenue fell 13% to $3.16 billion from $3.63 billion, as the company reduced its airline operations about 15% beginning in the fall of 1992.
>
> The carrier didn't break out fourth-quarter results, saying there is 'no meaningful comparison' with the year-earlier figures. Because of its emergence from Chapter 11 protection from creditors, TWA said its financial statements were prepared on both a pre- and post-reorganization basis for different parts of the fourth quarter.
>
> The company's load factor, or percentage of seats filled, slipped to 63.5% during 1993 from 64.7%. TWA's yield, or revenue per passenger mile, increased to 11.35 cents in 1993 from 10.22 cents the year before.
>
>

COLLABORATIVE LEARNING CASE

C1–7

Landfil's accounting change

You have been asked to attend a hastily called meeting of Landfil's senior executives. The meeting was called to formulate a strategy for responding to questions from shareholders, analysts, and the media about Landfil's accounting for site development costs. A major competitor, Chambers Development, announced yesterday that it would no longer capitalize site development costs but instead would expense those costs as they were incurred. Stock market reaction to the Chambers' announcement was swift and negative, with the stock down 57% at this morning's opening of the NYSE.

Landfil Inc. acquires, operates, and develops nonhazardous solid waste disposal facilities. Landfil is the third largest waste management company of its type in the United States, with 37 disposal sites. Sales have been growing at the rate of 30% annually for the last five years, and the company has established a solid record of earnings and operating cash flow performance.

Accounting Policy

Landfil capitalizes site development costs in much the same way that Chambers Development did prior to its announcement yesterday. Under the old accounting method at Chambers Development, when the firm spent $20 million on landfill site development, it would book the entire amount as a deferred asset. Then Chambers would spread the cost over 10 years by charging $2 million to earnings each year. Under the new accounting method, all $20 million is expensed in the first year.

Landfil has included the following description of its site development accounting in all annual reports issued during the last five years:

> The Company capitalizes landfill acquisition costs, including out-of-pocket incremental expenses incurred in connection with the preacquisition phase of a specific project (for example, engineering, legal, and accounting due-diligence fees); the acquisition purchase price, including future guaranteed payments to sellers; and commissions. If an acquisition is not consummated, or a development project is abandoned, all of such costs are expensed. Salaries, office expenses, and similar administrative costs are not capitalized. Landfill development and permitting costs, including the cost of property, engineering, legal, and other professional fees, and interest are capitalized and amortized over the estimated useful life of the property upon commencement of operations.

The Meeting

Discussion at the meeting became rather heated as several different points of view emerged. Some members of the executive team argued that Landfil should do nothing but reaffirm its capitalization policy, informing shareholders and others who contacted the company that this policy was consistent with GAAP and disclosed fully in the annual report. Other members of the team argued for a more proactive response involving both direct communication with shareholders and analysts as well as press releases to the media. These communications would also reaffirm the company's capitalization policy but in a more strident manner. Still other members of the executive team argued that Landfil should immediately announce that it too was discontinuing capitalization in favor of immediate expensing. No clear consensus emerged as the meeting progressed, and the group decided to take a 10-minute break before resuming discussion.

As the meeting was about to reconvene, the CEO stopped by your chair and said, "I've been handed a phone message indicating that our largest shareholder has just called. She wants to know our reaction to the events at Chambers Development. I have to call her back in 15 minutes with an answer. When the meeting starts, I'd like you to summarize the major issues we face and to state how you think we should proceed."

C1–8

AstroText Company: Questions for the stockholders' meeting

Yesterday, AstroText announced its friendly acquisition of TextTools Inc. AstroText intends to pay $20 per share for all the outstanding common stock of TextTools. At this price TextTools stockholders will be receiving a per share premium of $7 over the company's closing stock price just two days ago. There are 3 million shares outstanding, so the $7 per share premium represents $21 million in total.

AstroText and TextTools are both relatively young software development companies with similar product lines. Both companies have developed leading edge document creation software for the Internet. AstroText has focused its product line on individuals, on small businesses, and on academic markets. TextTools has targeted the corporate market, where security and encryption are extremely important. To maintain their technological edge, both companies must continue to invest heavily in software research and development. Frequent product updates are the norm for companies like AstroText and TextTools. In addition, both companies have historically spent considerable resources on product marketing and advertising.

AstroText is hosting a stockholders meeting later today to discuss details of the acquisition. So far, the company has said very little about why it's willing to pay a $7 per share premium for TextTools, about how the all-cash deal will be financed, or about why the two companies will be worth more together than they are separately.

REQUIRED:

1. Suppose you are an employee of AstroText who owns 100 shares of the company's stock. You have also received a substantial number of long-term stock options as part of your compensation package. What questions do you want answered at the stockholders meeting? What information (if any) in the company's financial reports might help answer those questions?
2. Assume you are the lead banker for AstroText. You were quite surprised to learn of the TextTools acquisition, in part because your loan to AstroText contains a provision that prohibits the company from making cash acquisitions without your approval. What questions do you want answered at the stockholders meeting? What information (if any) in the company's financial reports might help answer those questions?

2

Accrual Accounting and Income Determination

LEARNING OBJECTIVES:
After studying this chapter, you will understand:

1. The distinction between cash-basis versus accrual income, and why the latter generally is a better measure of operating performance.
2. The criteria for revenue recognition under accrual accounting, and how they are used in selected industries.
3. The matching principle, and how it is applied to recognize expenses under accrual accounting.
4. The difference between product and period costs, and why this distinction is important.
5. The format and classifications for a multiple-step income statement, and how the statement format is designed to differentiate earnings components that are more sustainable from those that are more transitory.
6. The distinction between special and unusual items, discontinued operations, extraordinary items, and the cumulative effect of accounting changes.
7. What comprises comprehensive income and alternative formats for displaying this amount in the financial statements.
8. The basic procedures for preparing financial statements and how to conduct T-account analysis.

This chapter describes the key concepts and practices that govern the measurement of annual or quarterly income (or earnings) for financial reporting purposes. Income is the difference between **revenues** and **expenses**. The cornerstone of income measurement is **accrual accounting**. Under accrual accounting ***revenues are recorded in the period when they are "earned" and become "measurable"*** —that is, when the seller has performed a service or conveyed an asset to a buyer and the value to be received for that service or asset is reasonably assured and can be measured with a high degree of reliability.[1] ***Expenses are the expired costs or assets "used up" in producing those revenues, and they are recorded in the same accounting period in which the revenues are recognized using the "matching principle."***

A natural consequence of accrual accounting is the decoupling of measured earnings from operating cash inflows and outflows. Reported revenues under accrual accounting generally do not correspond to cash receipts for the period; also, reported expenses do not always correspond to cash outlays of the period. In fact, ***accrual accounting can produce large discrepancies between the firm's reported profit performance and the amount of cash generated from operations. Frequently, however, accrual accounting earnings provide a more accurate measure of the economic value added during the period than do operating cash flows.***[2]

---

[1] In "Elements of Financial Statements," *Statement of Financial Accounting Concepts No. 6,* the Financial Accounting Standards Board (FASB) defines revenues as ". . . inflows or other enhancements of assets of an entity or settlements of its liabilities (or a combination of both) from delivering or producing goods, rendering services, or other activities that constitute the entity's ongoing major or central operations" (para. 78). Expenses are defined as ". . . outflows or other using up of assets or incurrences of liabilities (or a combination of both) from delivering or producing goods, rendering services, or carrying out other activities that constitute the entity's ongoing major or central operations" (para. 80).

[2] *Economic value added* represents the increase in the value of a product or service as a consequence of operating activities. To illustrate, the value of an assembled automobile far exceeds the value of its separate steel, glass, plastic, rubber, and electronics components. The difference between the aggregate cost of the various parts utilized in manufacturing the automobile and the price at which the car is sold to the dealer represents economic value added (or lost) by production.

This point is illustrated by the following example, which highlights the basic distinction between cash and accrual accounting measures of performance.

Example: Cash versus Accrual Income Measurement

In January 2001 Canterbury Publishing sells a three-year subscription to its quarterly publication, *Windy City Living,* to 1,000 subscribers. The subscription plan requires prepayment by the customers, so the full subscription price of \$300 (12 issues × \$25 per issue) was received by Canterbury from each of the subscribers (\$300 × 1,000 = \$300,000) at the beginning of 2001. To help finance the purchase of newsprint and other printing supplies, Canterbury takes out a \$100,000 three-year loan from a local bank on January 1, 2001. The loan calls for interest of 10% of the face amount of the loan each year (10% × \$100,000 = \$10,000), but the interest is not payable until the loan matures on December 31, 2003. The cost of publishing and distributing the magazine amounts to \$60,000 each year (\$60 per subscriber), which is paid in cash at the time of publication. The entries to record the **cash-basis** revenues and expenses for each year would be as follows:

The entries to record the initial borrowing and repayment of the loan principal are ignored since they are not revenues or expenses and do not affect the determination of cash basis income.

Throughout this book **DR** represents the debit side and **CR** represents the credit side of the accounting entry to record the transaction being discussed. See the appendix to this chapter for a review of how these transactions are recorded.

Cash-basis entries for 2001

DR Cash	\$300,000	
CR Subscriptions revenue		\$300,000

To record collection of 1,000 three-year subscriptions at \$300 each for *Windy City Living.*

DR Publishing and distribution expense	\$ 60,000	
CR Cash		\$ 60,000

To record publishing and distribution expenses paid in cash.

Cash-basis entries for 2002

DR Publishing and distribution expense	\$ 60,000	
CR Cash		\$ 60,000

To record publishing and distribution expenses paid in cash.

Cash-basis entries for 2003

DR Publishing and distribution expense	\$ 60,000	
CR Cash		\$ 60,000

To record publishing and distribution expenses paid in cash.

DR Interest expense	\$ 30,000	
CR Cash		\$ 30,000

To record interest expense paid on the three-year loan (\$100,000 × 10% × 3 years = \$30,000).

A schedule of operating cash inflows and outflows and cash-basis income would look as follows:

Cash-Basis Income Determination

(\$000 omitted)	2001	2002	2003
Cash inflows	\$300	\$ —	\$ —
Cash outflows for production and distribution	(60)	(60)	(60)
Cash outflow for interest on loan	—	—	(30)
Net income (loss)—Cash basis	\$240	(\$60)	(\$90)

Example: Cash versus Accrual Income Measurement

Publishing the magazine and servicing the subscriptions requires economic effort in each of the years 2001 through 2003, as indicated by the $60,000 of operating cash outflows each period. However, under cash-basis accounting, the entire $300,000 of cash inflow from subscription receipts would be treated as revenue in 2001, the year in which the subscriptions are sold and cash is collected, with no revenue recognized in the remaining two years of the subscription period. Likewise, the $30,000 of interest ($10,000 per year × 3 years) paid on December 31, 2003 would be recorded as an expense in year 2003 under the cash basis of accounting, with no interest expense recognized in the first two years. Consequently, on a cash basis, Canterbury Publishing would report a relatively high "profit" of $240,000 in 2001 when the subscriptions are sold and collected, and this 2001 profit would be followed by operating "losses" of $60,000 in 2002 and $90,000 in 2003 when the costs associated with publishing the remaining issues and financing the operations are paid.

Clearly, cash-basis accounting distorts our view of the operating performance of Canterbury on a year by year basis. Moreover, none of the annual cash-basis profit figures provide a reliable benchmark for predicting future operating results. This distortion is due to differences in the timing of when cash inflows and outflows occur. Recognizing cash inflows as revenue and cash outflows as expenses results in a cash-basis income number that fails to properly match effort and accomplishment.

The principles that govern revenue and expense recognition under accrual accounting are designed to alleviate the mismatching problems that exist under cash-basis accounting, making accrual earnings a more useful measure of firm performance. Accrual accounting allocates $100,000 of subscription revenue to each of the years 2001, 2002, and 2003 as the magazine is delivered to subscribers and the revenues are "earned." Likewise, accrual accounting recognizes $10,000 of interest expense in each year the bank loan is outstanding, not just in year 2003 when the interest is paid. These modifications to the cash-basis results to obtain accrual earnings are accomplished by means of the following series of "deferral" and "accrual" **adjusting entries,** which are made at the end of each year under accrual accounting (see the appendix for details).

Revenues are "earned" as a consequence of publishing magazines and servicing subscriptions—economic activities that span a three-year period. Canterbury's obligation to subscribers is fulfilled gradually over these three years as each issue is delivered, not just in 2001 when cash is collected.

Adjusting entries on December 31, 2001

DR Subscriptions revenue		$200,000	
	CR Deferred subscriptions revenue		$200,000

To adjust the subscriptions revenue account for subscriptions received but not yet earned. ($300,000 was initially credited to subscriptions revenue. Only $100,000 was earned in 2001. Therefore, subscriptions revenue must be debited for $200,000.) Deferred subscriptions revenue is a liability account reflecting Canterbury's obligation to provide subscribers with future issues of *Windy City Living.*

DR Interest expense		$ 10,000	
	CR Accrued interest payable		$ 10,000

To adjust for interest expense incurred but not yet paid, and to set up a liability for interest accrued during the period that will be paid on December 31, 2003.

Adjusting entries on December 31, 2002

DR Deferred subscriptions revenue	$100,000	
CR Subscriptions revenue		$100,000

To adjust deferred subscriptions revenue and recognize revenue for subscriptions earned during the year by providing customers with four issues of *Windy City Living.*

DR Interest expense	$ 10,000	
CR Accrued interest payable		$ 10,000

To adjust for interest expense incurred but not yet paid, and to set up a liability for interest accrued during the period that will be paid on December 31, 2003.

Adjusting entries on December 31, 2003

DR Deferred subscriptions revenue	$100,000	
CR Subscriptions revenue		$100,000

To adjust deferred subscriptions revenue and recognize revenue for subscriptions earned during the year by providing customers with four issues of *Windy City Living.*

DR Interest expense	$ 10,000	
CR Accrued interest payable		$ 10,000

To adjust for interest expense incurred during the year. After this adjusting entry, the Accrued interest payable account will have a balance of $30,000.

On December 31, 2003 the accrued interest is paid and the following entry would be made:

DR Accrued interest payable	$30,000	
CR Cash		$30,000

After these adjustments, the diagram of accrual-basis income looks like this:

Accrual-Basis Income Determination

($000 omitted)	2001	2002	2003	
Cash received	$300			
Deferred to future years	−$200			
Revenues recognized as "earned" each year	$100	$100	$100	
Expenses				
Publication and distribution (paid in cash)	(60)	(60)	(60)	
			(30)	Interest paid in cash
Interest accrued	(10)	(10)	20	Add: Amounts accrued in prior years
Net income—accrual basis	$ 30	$ 30	$ 30	

From this example, note that accrual accounting revenues for a period do not correspond to cash receipts for the same period ($100,000 of accrual-basis revenue in 2001 does not correspond to the $300,000 of cash received in that year; nor does the $100,000 of recorded accrual revenue in 2002 and 2003 correspond to $0 cash received in those years). Likewise, the reported accrual-basis expenses in a period do not correspond to cash outflows in that period ($10,000 of interest expense recorded under accrual accounting in 2001 and 2002 does not correspond to the $0 of interest paid in those periods; and the $10,000 of interest expense in 2003 does not correspond to the $30,000 of interest paid in cash in that year). As you can see, ***a consequence of accrual accounting is the decoupling of measured earnings from operating cash flows.*** Indeed, accrual accounting can result in large discrepancies between the firm's reported accrual-basis earnings and the amount of cash generated from operations (cash-basis earnings) year by year, as shown in Figure 2.1.

As this example illustrates, ***accrual accounting better matches economic benefit*** (revenues from subscriptions) ***with economic effort*** (magazine publication and

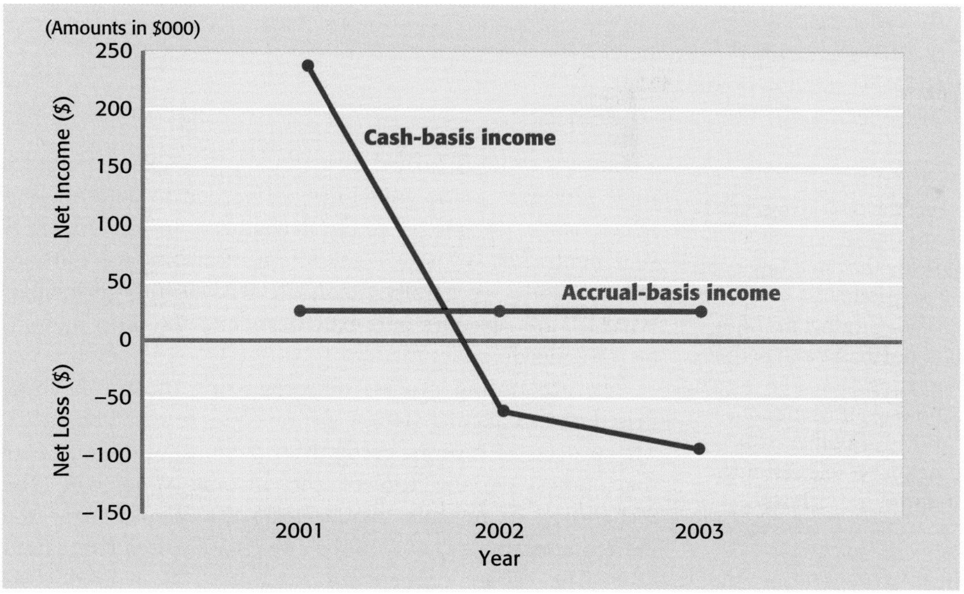

Figure 2.1

CANTERBURY PUBLISHING

Comparison of Accrual and Cash-Basis Income

distribution expenses and interest costs), ***thereby producing a measure of operating performance—accrual earnings—that provides a more realistic picture of past economic activities.*** Many believe that accrual accounting numbers also provide a better basis for predicting future performance of an enterprise.

The view that accrual earnings dominate cash flow measures of performance is asserted in *Statement of Financial Accounting Concepts No. 1*, which was issued by the Financial Accounting Standards Board (FASB) in 1978. It stated:

> "... [I]nformation about enterprise earnings and its components measured by accrual accounting generally provides a better indication of enterprise performance than does information about current cash receipts and payments."[3]

Despite the assertions of the FASB and others regarding the superiority of accrual earnings relative to net cash flows as a measure of a firm's performance, it is important to recognize that reported accrual accounting income for a given period may not always provide an accurate picture of underlying economic performance for that period. One of our objectives is to help you, as a user of accounting information, understand not only the benefits of accrual accounting numbers but also their limitations. Throughout the book we will contrast accounting measurements and their earnings impact with the underlying economic circumstances, highlighting those situations in which the two may diverge.

Measuring Profit Performance: Revenues and Expenses

We have introduced the concept of accrual accounting income and contrasted it with cash-basis earnings in a simplified setting. Now, in more realistic (and complex) settings, we will review some of the mechanics associated with measuring accrual accounting revenues and expenses.

For virtually all firms, income is not earned as a result of just one activity. A manufacturing firm, for example, earns income as a result of these separate and diverse activities:

1. Marketing the product
2. Receiving customers' orders
3. Negotiating and signing production contracts

[3] "Objectives of Financial Reporting by Business Enterprises," *Statement of Financial Accounting Concepts No. 1* (Stamford, CT: FASB, 1978), para. 44.

4. Ordering materials
5. Manufacturing the product
6. Delivering the product
7. Collecting the cash from customers.

The sequence of activities comprising the **operating cycle** of a firm that is presented here is only one of several possible sequences. The activities comprising the operating cycle can vary across firms—or even across products for a given firm. Some companies manufacture the product for inventory prior to identifying a particular purchaser and perhaps even in advance of launching a marketing campaign intended to stimulate product demand (e.g., IBM manufacturing a new model of laptop computer). In other cases the product is manufactured to customer order (e.g., Boeing manufacturing a new airplane for one of the airlines).

Since income is earned as a result of complex, multiple-stage processes, some guidelines are needed to determine at which stage income is to be recognized in the financial statements. The key issue is the *timing* of income recognition: *When,* under generally accepted accounting principles (GAAP), are revenues and expenses—and thus income—to be recognized?

The accounting process of recognizing income is comprised of two distinct steps. First, revenues must be recorded. This process of **revenue recognition** establishes the numbers that appear at the top of the income statement. The recognition of revenue then triggers the second step—the **matching** against revenue of the costs that expired (were used up) in generating the revenue. The difference between revenues and expired costs (expenses) is the **income** that is recognized for the period.

This two-step process is illustrated in the following journal entries:

	Accounting entry	Effect on income (+ or −)
(Step 1) **Revenue recognition**	**DR** Cash or accounts receivable	
	CR Sales revenues	Sales revenues (+)
(Step 2) **Matching of expense**	**DR** Cost of goods sold	Cost of goods sold (−)
	CR Inventory	
Income recognition		Net Income

Income recognition is a by-product of revenue recognition and expense matching. It is not a separate step that is independent of the other two steps. Once revenues are recognized and expenses are matched against the revenue, net income is simply the net difference that results.

The process of revenue recognition and matching expenses against revenue has an obvious effect on the income statement—the bottom-line net income number is increased by the excess of recognized revenues over expired costs. But accrual accounting affects more than income statement accounts. Due to the double-entry, self-balancing nature of accounting, important changes also occur in **net assets** (i.e., assets minus liabilities) on the balance sheet. To understand the effect that accrual accounting has on net assets, consider the following example.

ABC Company has only one asset—inventory—with a cost of $100. Its balance sheet appears as:

ABC COMPANY

Initial Balance Sheet

Assets		Liabilities + Owners' Equity	
Inventory	$100	Initial equity	$100

Assume that all of the inventory is sold for $130, which is immediately received in cash. Clearly, income should be recognized as a result of this transaction. We will focus on the balance sheet effects and analyze the transaction using the basic accounting equation:

Assets = Liabilities + Owners' equity

First we record the inflow of the asset (cash) and the source of the inflow (sales revenues):

Step 1. Revenue Recognition

Assets	=	Liabilities	+	Owners' equity
+$130 Cash				+$130 Sales revenue

Next we record the outflow of the asset (inventory) and match this expired cost against recognized revenues:

Step 2. Expense Matching

Assets	=	Liabilities	+	Owners' equity
−$100 Inventory				−$100 Cost of goods sold

After recording these transactions, the balance sheet shows:

ABC COMPANY

Subsequent Balance Sheet

Assets		Liabilities + Owners' Equity	
Cash	$130	Liabilities	$ —
Inventory	—	Initial equity	100
		+ increase in equity:	
		Income (+$130 − $100)	30
	$130		$130

Comparing the initial and subsequent balance sheets shows that equity has increased by $30, the amount of income recognized from the transaction. Equally important, net assets have also increased by $30 (i.e., $130 of cash inflow minus $100 of inventory outflow = net asset increase of $30). The point of this example is that when income is recognized in the financial statements, two things happen:

1. Owners' equity is increased by the amount of the income.
2. Net assets (i.e., gross assets minus gross liabilities) are increased by an identical amount.

Thus, there are two equivalent ways of thinking about the financial statement effects of income recognition. One perspective is that when income is recognized, the bottom-line income number (and thus, owners' equity) increases. The other is that when income is recognized, net assets are increased.

The two approaches to thinking about income recognition merely focus on different aspects of the same transaction. The approach which focuses on the net asset effect on the balance sheet provides a means for understanding the *total* financial statement effects of income recognition. This approach reminds us that income recognition simultaneously triggers an increase in the book value (carrying value) of net assets—***that is, net asset valuation and income determination are inextricably intertwined.*** When income is recognized in the financial statements, the accountant is acknowledging that the company's net assets have increased in value.[4] The real issue in income recognition is this: At what

Book value or **carrying value** refers to the amount at which an account (or set of related accounts) is reported on a company's financial statements. For example, the cost of "Property, plant, and equipment" may be reported at $1,000,000 with accumulated depreciation of $300,000. The net book value or carrying value of "Property, plant, and equipment" would be the cost minus accumulated depreciation, or $700,000.

[4] Notice that the accounting concept of income recognition is really a specific application of the economic concept of value added.

point in the cycle of operating activities is it appropriate to recognize that a firm's net assets have increased in value? The next section addresses this.

As noted, income recognition comprises two separate steps:

1. Revenue recognition
2. Expense matching.

Let's consider each step separately.

Criteria for Revenue Recognition

According to generally accepted accounting principles, revenue is recognized at the *earliest* moment in time that *both* of the following conditions are satisfied:

Condition 1. The **critical event** in the process of earning the revenue has taken place.

Condition 2. The amount of revenue that will be collected is reasonably assured and is **measurable** with a reasonable degree of reliability.

GAAP use different words to describe these two revenue recognition conditions. Condition 1, rephrased using the FASB's terminology, says revenues are not recognized until **earned.** The Board defined "earned" as:[5]

> "... [R]evenues are considered to have been earned when the entity has substantially accomplished what it must do to be entitled to the benefits represented by the revenues."

The FASB's terminology for Condition 2 says revenues must also be **realizable.** The Board defined "realizable" as (para. 83):

> "Revenues and gains are realizable when related assets received or held are readily convertible to known amounts of cash or claims to cash. Readily convertible assets have (i) interchangeable (fungible) units and (ii) quoted prices available in an active market that can rapidly absorb the quantity held by the entity without significantly affecting the price."

While the concepts embodied in "earned" and "realizable" are identical to "critical event" and "measurable," we believe that the latter terms are more easily understood and accordingly use them throughout this book.

Condition 1: The Critical Event While the earnings process is the result of many separate activities, it is generally acknowledged that there is usually one critical event or key stage considered to be absolutely essential to the ultimate increase in net asset value of the firm. The exact nature of this critical event varies from industry to industry, as we will show in subsequent examples. Unless the critical event takes place, no increase in value is added to the firm's net assets. Thus, the occurrence of the critical event is a first step that must be satisfied before revenue can be recognized. It is a "necessary," but not "sufficient," condition for revenue to be recognized.

Condition 2: Measurability It is important to understand that accountants do not immediately recognize revenue just because the critical event has taken place. There must be something else: It must be possible to measure the amount of revenue that has been earned with a reasonable degree of assurance. Condition 2 indicates that revenue cannot be recognized merely on the basis of an intuitive "feel" that certain events have added value to the firm's assets. There must be objective, verifiable evidence as to the amount of value that has been added. Unless the amount of value added can be reliably quantified, GAAP does not allow an increase in asset values to be recorded. Generally, this translates into having a readily determinable price for the goods or service, a price established in the marketplace where buyers and sellers are free to negotiate the terms of trade. So-called "list prices" assigned to the good or service by the seller often do not satisfy the measurability condition, because they can deviate from the market-clearing price paid by the buyer.

Only after Conditions 1 and 2 are *both* met can revenue be recognized under generally accepted accounting principles. To illustrate how these revenue recognition conditions are applied, let's return to the example of the three-year subscriptions sold by Canterbury Publishing in January 2001. Recall that accrual accounting would not recognize the $300,000 as revenue when the cash is received because the subscriptions revenue will be "earned" only as each magazine issue is published and delivered to the customers. If the publisher were to discontinue the magazine before all 12 issues were published, a refund would be owed to the subscribers. ***In this magazine example, the critical event in earning subscription revenue is actually providing***

---

[5] "Recognition and Measurement in Financial Statements of Business Enterprises," *Statement of Financial Accounting Concepts No. 5* (Stamford, CT: FASB, 1984), para. 83.

the product to the customers. Thus, $100,000 of revenue will be recorded in each of the three years, as the magazine is published and sent to subscribers. Stated somewhat differently, while revenue recognition Condition 2 is met in this example on initial receipt of the subscription order (i.e., the amount of ultimate revenue—$300,000—is measurable with a high degree of assurance and reliability), Condition 1 is not met at that time and, therefore, no revenue is recognized because the critical event (i.e., delivery of the magazine to the customers) has not yet occurred.

To further illustrate how the revenue recognition conditions are applied, let us consider another example. On January 2, 2001 Gigantic Motors Corporation assembles 1,000 automobiles, each with a sticker price of $18,000. Since these cars have not yet been sold to dealers, they are parked in a lot adjacent to the plant. Let's examine how revenue recognition Conditions 1 and 2 operate in this setting.

Most observers would agree that the critical event in adding value in automobile manufacturing is production itself.[6] Accordingly, the critical event occurred as the automobiles rolled off the production line. However, no revenue would be recognized at that time. Although revenue recognition Condition 1 is satisfied, Condition 2 is *not* satisfied merely on completion of production. ***This revenue recognition condition is not satisfied because the ultimate sale price of the automobiles is still unknown.*** While Gigantic Motors has established a suggested list price of $18,000 per vehicle, the ultimate amount of cash that will actually be received in the future will depend upon general economic conditions, consumer tastes and preferences, as well as the availability and asking price of competing automobile models. Thus, the specific amount of value that has been added by production is not yet measurable with a reasonable degree of assurance. Revenue will be recognized only when the cars are sold to dealers at a known price. Only then is revenue recognition Condition 2 satisfied.

The magazine subscription and automobile production examples illustrate that revenue recognition only takes place when revenue recognition Conditions 1 and 2 are *both* met. When the cash subscriptions to the magazine are received by Canterbury Publishing, Condition 2 (measurability) is satisfied but not Condition 1—no revenue is recognized until Canterbury provides the magazines to the customers and earns the revenue. When automotive production takes place at Gigantic Motors, Condition 1 (critical event) is satisfied but not Condition 2—no revenue is recognized until the sale takes place which determines with reasonable assurance the amount that Gigantic will receive from the customer.

The financial reporting rules governing revenue recognition are often misunderstood. Because revenue is usually recognized at the time of sale in most industries, some observers erroneously conclude that the sale is itself the sole criterion for recognizing revenue. But this is not correct. The financial reporting rule for recognizing revenue is more complicated and subtle. Specifically, revenue is recognized as soon as Condition 1 (critical event) *and* Condition 2 (measurability) are *both* satisfied. ***In most instances the time of sale turns out to be the earliest moment at which both Conditions 1 and 2 are satisfied, which is why revenue is most frequently recognized at the time of sale of the product or service.***

But Conditions 1 and 2 are occasionally satisfied even before a legal sale (i.e., transfer of title) occurs. The following example illustrates where revenue can be recognized prior to sale:

> Weld Shipyards has been building ocean-going oil tankers since 1951. In January 2001 Weld signs a contract to build a standard-design tanker for Humco Oil. The contract price is $60 million, and construction costs are estimated to total approximately $45 million. The tanker is expected to be completed by December 31, 2002. Weld intends to account for the project using the **percentage-of-completion** method.

---

[6] Automobile manufacturers eventually sell all units produced, although not always immediately following production or always at the sticker price.

Under the percentage-of-completion method (discussed in Chapter 3), revenues and expenses are recognized as production takes place rather than at the time of completion (the sale). For example, if the tanker is 40% complete at the end of 2001 and finished in 2002, revenues and expenses would be recognized according to the following percentage-of-completion schedule:

($ in millions)	2001	2002	Two-Year Total
Percentage	40%	60%	100%
Revenue	$24	$36	$60
Expense	(18)	(27)	(45)
Income	$ 6	$ 9	$15

This method is permitted under GAAP when certain conditions—as in the Weld Shipyard example—are met. Condition 1 (critical event) is satisfied over time as the tanker is built—just as it was in the Gigantic automotive production example. But unlike the Gigantic Motors example, *revenue recognition Condition 2* is *satisfied* for Weld Shipyards, since a firm contract with a known buyer at a set price of $60 million exists. Thus, the tanker example satisfies *both* of the two conditions necessary for revenue to be recognized. Additionally, expenses are also measurable with a reasonable degree of assurance since the tanker is of a standard design that Weld has built repeatedly in past years. This example provides an overview of why the percentage-of-completion method, when used properly, meets revenue recognition Conditions 1 and 2.

In other circumstances Conditions 1 and 2 may not both be satisfied until *after* the time of sale—for instance, until the cash is collected. In these cases it would be inappropriate to recognize income when the sale is made; instead, income recognition is deferred and is ultimately recognized in proportion to cash collections. Chapter 3 discusses the **installment sales method,** an example in which revenue and expense are recognized at the time of cash collection rather than at the time of sale.

Figure 2.2 is a time-line diagram depicting the activities comprising the revenue recognition process for some selected industries.

To justify recognizing revenue during the **production phase,** the following conditions must be met:

1. A specific customer must be identified and an exchange price agreed on. In most cases a formal contract must be signed.

Figure 2.2

THE REVENUE RECOGNITION PROCESS

Industries Recognizing Revenue at Indicated Phases

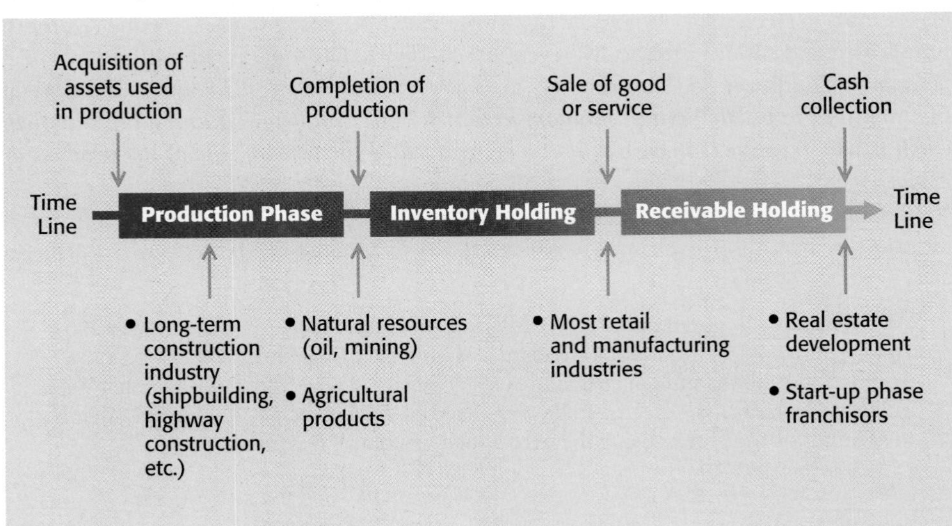

2. A significant portion of the services to be performed has been performed, and the expected costs of future services can be reliably estimated.
3. An assessment of the customer's credit standing permits a reasonably accurate estimate of the amount of cash that will be collected.

Situations where these conditions may be satisfied include long-term contracts for the construction of ships, bridges, and office buildings—as well as, for example, special-order government contracts for the production of military equipment.

As depicted in Figure 2.2, in some industries revenue may be recognized on **completion of production.** This is justified under the following conditions:

1. The product is immediately saleable at quoted market prices
2. Units are homogeneous
3. No significant uncertainty exists regarding the costs of distributing the product.

Examples where these circumstances exist include mining of natural resources and harvesting agricultural crops. These commodities are traded in active, organized markets, and thus a reliable market price can be determined at production even though the eventual buyer's identity is unknown at that time. Although GAAP permits mining and other natural resource companies to recognize revenue at completion of production, few actually do so. Instead, most delay revenue recognition until the time of sale.

Revenue recognition ***at the time of sale*** is the dominant practice in most retail and manufacturing industries. Occasionally, revenue is not recognized until ***after the time of sale.*** To justify postponing recognition of revenues, one or more of the following conditions must generally be present:

1. Extreme uncertainty exists regarding the amount of cash to be collected from customers. This uncertainty may be attributable to various factors:
   - The customer's precarious financial condition
   - Contingencies in the sales agreement that allow the buyer or seller to terminate the exchange
   - The customer having the right to return the product and this right being frequently exercised.
2. Future services to be provided are substantial, and their costs cannot be estimated with reasonable precision.

These conditions exist in circumstances like real estate sales, where collection of the sale price occurs in protracted installments, and in sales of franchises for new or unproved concepts or products.

Regardless of which basis of revenue recognition is used, the recognition of expenses must always adhere to the matching principle—all costs incurred in generating the revenue must be recorded as expenses in the same period the related revenue is recognized. Matching expenses with revenues is the second step of the income recognition process and is discussed next.

Matching Expenses With Revenues

Once gross revenues for the period are determined, the next step in determining income is to accumulate and record the costs associated with generating those revenues. Some costs are easily traced to the revenues themselves. These **traceable costs**—also called **product costs**—are described as being **matched** with revenues. Other costs are clearly also important in generating revenue, but their contribution to a specific sale or to revenues of a particular period is more difficult to quantify. Such costs are expensed in the *time periods benefited,* which is why they are called **period costs**. Let's see how the matching principle is applied to traceable or product costs—as well as to period costs.

Traceable or Product Costs This next example illustrates how product costs are matched with revenue under GAAP income measurement rules.

> Cory TV and Appliance, a retailer, sells one 24-inch color television set on the last day of February for $500 cash. The TV set was purchased from the manufacturer for $240 cash in January of that same year. Cory provides a 60-day "parts and labor" warranty to the customer. A typical 24-inch color TV requires $10 of warranty service during the first month following the sale and another $15 of service in the second month.

The expected (as well as the actually experienced) cash flows associated with this single transaction are depicted in Figure 2.3.

Figure 2.3

CASH FLOW DIAGRAM

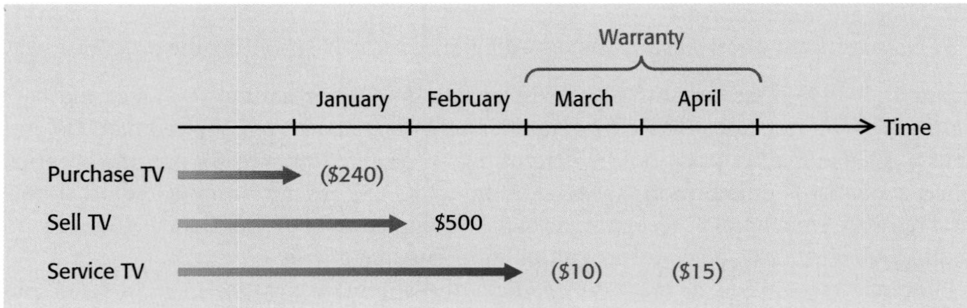

GAAP revenue recognition criteria are satisfied by the cash sale in February, so $500 of revenue is recorded in that month. The current and expected future costs of generating that revenue are $265, and these costs are recorded as expenses in the same month (February) that the revenue is recognized. Thus, accrual accounting transforms the cash flow diagram of Figure 2.3 into the revenue recognition and expense matching diagram shown in Figure 2.4.

Figure 2.4

REVENUE RECOGNITION AND EXPENSE MATCHING

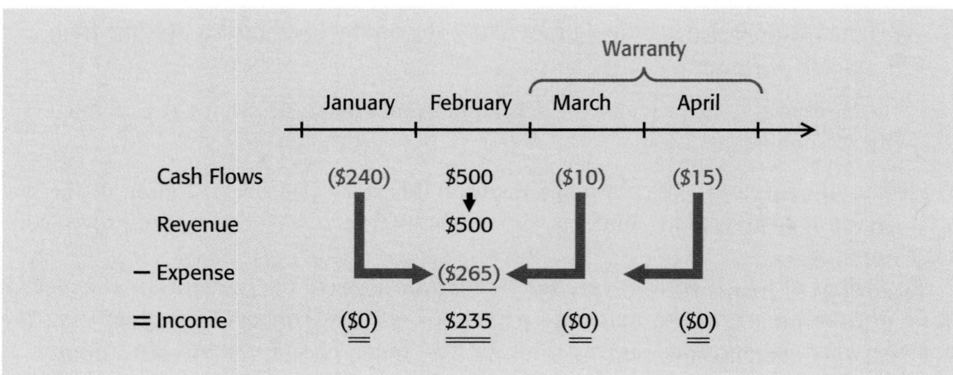

Period Costs Cory TV and Appliance incurs other types of costs that also are crucial in generating revenues. However, the linkage between these costs and individual sales is difficult to establish. One example of costs of this nature is advertising expenditures.

Assume Cory TV buys five minutes of advertising time on a local radio station each month for a monthly cost of $700. Obviously, the purpose of advertising is to generate sales. However, it is virtually impossible to associate any month's advertising expenditure with any specific sale, since consumer behavior is the result of diverse influences and repeated advertising exposure. Consequently, GAAP does not try to match advertising expenditures with specific sales. Instead, the cost of advertising is charged as an expense in the period in which the ads run. Such costs are called period costs. No effort is made to link any particular advertising campaign with particular sales, since no objective means for establishing this linkage exists.

The distinction between traceable (product) costs and period costs is discussed further in Chapter 9. At this point it is important to understand that in applying the matching concept, some costs are directly matched against revenues while others are associated with time periods.

Matching associates expired costs (expenses) with the revenues recognized in a period or with the passage of time. Costs directly matched against revenues are called product costs, while costs matched with the passage of time are called period costs.

RECAP

Income Statement Format and Classification

Virtually all decision models in modern corporate finance are based on future cash flows. Recognizing this, the FASB stated:

> "Thus, financial reporting should provide information to help investors, creditors, and others assess the amounts, timing, and uncertainty of prospective net cash inflows to the related enterprise."[7]

One way to provide users with information regarding prospective future cash flows would be to present them with cash flow forecasts prepared by management. Traditional financial reporting rejects presenting forecasted cash flow information because such numbers are considered to be too "soft"—too speculative or manipulatable.

Another way to satisfy users' needs for assessing future cash flows is to provide financial information based on past and current events in a format that gives statement users reliable and representative baseline numbers for generating *their own* forecasts of future cash flows. To accomplish this, an income statement format that segregates components of income has evolved. The intent of this format is to classify separately income components that are "transitory" and to clearly differentiate them from income components believed to be "sustainable" or likely to be repeated in future reporting periods.

VALUATION

As we survey the existing format and classification rules, we will see that the rationale behind the rules for multiple-step income statements is intended to subdivide income in a manner that facilitates forecasting. Most of the disclosure formats reviewed in this section were written into GAAP by the standard setting organization that preceded the FASB, the current private sector standard setting group.[8] Our discussion is based on the comparative income statements of Mythical Corporation for 1999–2001, presented in Exhibit 2.1 on the next page. This exhibit illustrates how existing disclosure rules are designed to help users predict future events.

The income statement isolates a key figure called **Income from continuing operations.** (See ① in Exhibit 2.1.) This component of income should include only *the normal, recurring, (presumably) more sustainable, ongoing economic activities* of the organization. As we'll discuss shortly, this intermediate income number can sometimes include gains and losses that occur infrequently—called **"Special or unusual items"** (item ② in Exhibit 2.1)—but nevertheless arise from a firm's ongoing, continuing operations. With the possible exception of some of these special or unusual items, "Income from continuing operations" summarizes the wealth effects of recurring transactions or activities that are

---

[7] "Objectives of Financial Reporting by Business Enterprises," *Statement of Financial Accounting Concepts No. 1* (Stamford, CT: FASB, 1978), para. 37.

[8] The opinions of the predecessor group—the Accounting Principles Board (APB)—continue in effect until they are either rescinded or altered by the FASB. The disclosure formats discussed in this section were developed in three separate APB opinions. These are: "Reporting the Results of Operations," *APB Opinion No. 9* (New York: AICPA, 1966); "Accounting Changes," *APB Opinion No. 20* (New York: AICPA, 1971); and "Reporting the Results of Operations—Reporting the Effects of Disposal of a Segment of a Business, and Extraordinary, Unusual and Infrequently Occurring Events and Transactions," *APB Opinion No. 30* (New York: AICPA, 1973).

Exhibit 2.1 ■ MYTHICAL CORPORATION

Income Statements
For the Years Ended December 31, 1999–2001

($ in millions)	2001	2000	1999
Net sales	$3,957	$3,478	$3,241
Costs of goods sold	(1,364)	(1,189)	(1,096)
Gross profit	2,593	2,289	2,145
Selling, general, and administrative expenses	(1,093)	(949)	(922)
2 **Special or unusual charges (Note 1)**	(251)	–	–
Income from continuing operations before income taxes	1,249	1,340	1,223
Income tax expense	(406)	(436)	(411)
1 **Income from continuing operations**	843	904	812
3 **Discontinued operations (Note 2)**			
Income from operation of discontinued business division, net of tax	203	393	528
Gain on disposal of discontinued business division, net of tax	98	–	–
Income before extraordinary item and change in accounting principle	1,144	1,297	1,340
4 **Extraordinary loss, net of tax benefit (Note 3)**	–	(170)	–
5 **Cumulative effect of change in accounting principle, net of tax effect (Note 4)**	(118)	–	–
Net income	$1,026	$1,127	$1,340
Pro forma amounts assuming the change in accounting principle had been applied retroactively			
Income from continuing operations	$ 843	$ 871	$ 774
Income from continuing operations per share	$ 9.25	$ 9.55	$ 8.49

Note 1: Special or Unusual Charges—A strike closed the Pleasant Grove manufacturing facility for five months in mid-2001. The fixed costs incurred at the idle plant totaled $251 million.

Note 2: Discontinued Operations—The Company discontinued a business segment in 2001. The 2001 operating income and gain on disposal for this segment, net of tax, were $203 million and $98 million, respectively.

Note 3: Extraordinary Loss—A fire partially destroyed the chemical plant in River City. The Company had no insurance coverage for such losses.

Note 4: Change in Accounting Principle—Effective January 1, 2001 the Company changed its method of depreciation for property, plant and equipment from the straight-line method to the sum-of-the-years' digits method. The Company believes that the sum-of-the-years' digits method is preferable since the new method corresponds to the depreciation methods used by most companies in the industry, thereby improving comparability of financial reporting. This change decreased 2001 income from continuing operations by $31 million ($0.34 per share).

expected to continue into the future. Therefore, this figure is intended to serve as the anchor or jumping-off point for forecasting future profits.

There are other components of income that are not recurring—and hence do not form a good basis for projecting future income. These other, (presumably) more transitory components of income are disclosed separately below the "Income from continuing operations" number (items ③, ④, and ⑤) and are shown net of income tax effects. These nonrecurring earnings components fall into three general categories:

- Discontinued operations
- Extraordinary items
- Cumulative effect of accounting changes.

The rules governing classification and placement of these nonrecurring items within the income statement are discussed in the following sections. These classification rules provide detailed guidance regarding what qualifies for inclusion in each statement category. As we will see, the rules standardize the format of disclosures as well as prevent certain "abuses" or distortions that might occur if firms were allowed to comingle these nonrecurring components of earnings with more sustainable, recurring revenue and expense items.

Discontinued Operations (Item ③)

Since a primary objective of financial reporting is to assist users in generating estimates of future cash flows, transactions related to operations that the firm intends to discontinue or has already discontinued must be separated from other income items.[9] The reason is straightforward since, by definition, discontinued operations will not generate *future* operating cash flows.

In Exhibit 2.1 Mythical Corporation discontinued a business segment in 2001 (item ③). Notice that the operating results of this recently discontinued segment are not included in income from continuing operations in the current period (2001) when the decision to discontinue was made; nor are they included in any of the prior years (2000 and 1999) for which comparative data are provided. Also, notice that ***income from discontinued operations is reported net of income tax effect, as are both extraordinary losses ④ and the cumulative effect of accounting changes ⑤***. This "net of tax" treatment is called **intraperiod income tax allocation.** The reason for this net of tax treatment is the belief that the income tax should be matched with the item that gave rise to it. This separation is widely thought to make the income figures more informative to users.

> Securities Exchange Commission (SEC) rules (Regulation S-X, Article 3) require that comparative income statement data for at least three years and comparative balance sheets for two years be provided in filings with the Commission. For this reason, most publicly held corporations provide these comparative income statement and balance sheet data in their annual report to shareholders as well.

Here's why: If income tax were not matched with the item giving rise to it, then total reported income tax expense would combine taxes arising both from items that were transitory as well as from other items that were more sustainable. Mixing together the tax effect of continuing activities with the tax effect of single occurrence events would make it difficult for statement readers to forecast future tax outflows arising from ongoing events. Under intraperiod income tax allocation, the income tax associated with the (presumably) sustainable income from continuing operations before income taxes is separately disclosed as $406 million in 2001. Taxes arising from the (presumably) transitory items ③, ④, and ⑤ are not included in the $406 million figure, thus facilitating forecasts of expected future flows after tax.

The revenues and expenses of the segment discontinued by Mythical Corporation in 2001 were also removed from the corresponding numbers reflecting 2000 and 1999 results (highlighted). This makes the "Income from continuing operations" number of $843 million in 2001, the year of discontinued operations, truly comparable with the "Income from continuing operations" numbers of $904 million and $812 million in 2000 and 1999, respectively. Restating the 2000 and 1999 results to make them comparable to the 2001 results means that all the numbers from the "Net sales" line through the "Income from continuing operations" line reported in the 2000 and 1999 columns of the 2001 annual report will be different from the corresponding numbers originally reported in the 2000 and 1999 statements. While initially confusing to analysts who wish to review the past sequence of earnings numbers to detect trends in a company's financial performance (often referred to as **time-series analysis**), this adjustment to the numbers is essential for valid year-to-year comparisons.

Discontinuing an operating unit of the company invariably results in other gains or losses as assets in the discontinued segment are sold or scrapped. These gains or losses are disclosed separately, again net of their income tax effect, as illustrated by the $98 million gain in Exhibit 2.1.

Consider one last point on discontinued operations. Most firms are regularly disposing of assets and altering product lines in response to changes in competitive conditions and consumer tastes and preferences. Adjustments of these sorts are a *normal, recurring* part of doing business. Consequently, the financial results of these redeployments should be included in income from continuing operations. Disclosure rules for discontinued operations were formalized because accounting standard setters were somewhat mistrustful of firms' financial reporting motives. Apparently, there was fear that managers

[9] *APB Opinion No. 30,* para. 8.

might be motivated to use abandonments or dispositions of minor segments or divisions as a way to manipulate the reported sequence or time-series of earnings from *continuing* operations. Thus, guidelines for what constituted a discontinued operation were developed to reduce this possibility.

> *APB Opinion No. 30* (New York: AICPA, 1973), para. 13 defined the concept of a discontinued operation as "a separate major line of business or class of customer" whose assets and operating activities "can be clearly distinguished, physically and operationally and for financial reporting purposes."

Gray areas exist, despite these reporting rules for discontinued operations. However, the intent of the disclosure rules is to prevent firms from manipulating the number which purports to be income from continuing operations (item ①) by treating losses (or gains) on normal asset sales and dispositions as if they had arisen from discontinued operations. To qualify for exclusion from the continuing operations number and to be reported separately as discontinued operations, entire segments of readily distinguishable assets and/or customer groupings must be discontinued.

Extraordinary Items (Item ④)

Another category of transitory items reported separately on the income statement is extraordinary items (item ④ in Exhibit 2.1). To be treated as an extraordinary item, the event or transaction must meet *both* of the following criteria:[10]

1. *Unusual nature:* The underlying event or transaction possesses a high degree of abnormality, and taking into account the environment in which the company operates, that event or transaction is unrelated to the ordinary activities of the business.
2. *Infrequent occurrence:* The underlying event or transaction is a type that would not reasonably be expected to recur in the foreseeable future, again taking into account the environment in which the business operates.

> The business environment in which an enterprise operates is a primary consideration in determining whether an underlying event or transaction is unusual in nature and infrequent in occurrence. The environment of an enterprise includes such factors as the characteristics of the industry or industries in which it operates, the geographical location of its operations, and the nature and extent of government regulation. For example, a plant explosion that results in uninsured losses would be considered an extraordinary loss by most businesses. But for a company that manufactures explosive materials (e.g., dynamite), losses from such an event may not be considered unusual in nature or infrequent in occurrence, given the environment in which the entity conducts its operations.

Like discontinued operations, extraordinary items are reported net of tax. Given the stringency of the criteria, few events qualify as extraordinary items. Examples of qualifying items include losses resulting from natural disasters (e.g., tornadoes) or losses arising from new laws or edicts (e.g., an expropriation by a foreign government).

Events that meet one—but not *both*—of the criteria do not qualify as extraordinary items. If material, these events must be disclosed as a separate line item on the income statement or in the footnotes to the financial reports. When separately reported on the income statement, they must be disclosed as a component of income from continuing operations in the section "Special or unusual items." For example, the Mythical Corporation income statement includes a "Special or unusual charge" for losses incurred in conjunction with a labor strike, which is disclosed as a separate line item and discussed in a statement note (see ②and Note 1 in Exhibit 2.1).

> As used in the authoritative accounting literature, an item is considered material if it is of sufficient magnitude or importance to make a difference in one's decision.

Other examples of special or unusual items include:[11]

1. Write-downs or write-offs of receivables, inventories, equipment leased to others, and intangibles
2. Gains or losses from the exchange or translation of foreign currencies
3. Gains or losses from the sale or abandonment of property, plant, or equipment
4. Special one-time charges resulting from corporate restructurings
5. Gains or losses from the sale of investments.

Including special or unusual items as a component of income from continuing operations complicates financial forecasting and analysis. These special items are treated as

[10] *APB Opinion No. 30,* para. 20.
[11] See *APB Opinion No. 30,* para. 23.

a part of income from continuing operations because *collectively* they represent events that arise repeatedly as a normal part of ongoing business activities.[12] However, some special items occur often while others recur sporadically. For example, firms are continuously selling or disposing of obsolete manufacturing assets as well as taking write-downs on inventory or selling investment securities. However, other special or unusual items—like strikes and reorganizations—occur less frequently. Consequently, the persistence of special or unusual items is likely to vary from period to period and from item to item. As a result, separate disclosure is provided for such special or unusual items to assist users in forecasting future results. Since these items are included as part of income from continuing operations *before* tax (sometimes referred to as being reported "above the line"), they are *not* disclosed net of tax effects.

The justification for defining extraordinary items so precisely and for requiring separate disclosure of special or nonrecurring items is to prevent statement manipulation. Without such requirements management might, in a "down" earnings year, be tempted to treat nonrecurring gains as part of income from continuing operations and nonrecurring losses as extraordinary. Precise guidelines preclude this.

RECAP

To be categorized as extraordinary and to appear below the "Income from continuing operations" line, an item must be unusual in nature *and* occur infrequently. Special or unusual items that do not meet both criteria, but are considered material, must be disclosed separately as part of pre-tax income from continuing operations.

Frequency and Magnitude of "Special" and Transitory Items

As Exhibit 2.1 illustrates, financial reporting rules for presenting operating results are designed to isolate transitory and nonsustainable components of earnings in order to assist users in predicting future earnings and cash flows. Research evidence confirms that the GAAP income statement classification framework we have discussed is useful to statement users. Specifically, subdividing earnings into three transitory components—special or unusual items, discontinued operations, and extraordinary items—and disclosing these amounts separately so that they are distinguished from the income that comes from continuing operations improves forecasts of future earnings.[13]

Figure 2.5(a) on the next page reveals that the proportion of firms reporting one or more of the kinds of transitory earnings components highlighted in the previous discussion has generally increased over time. In 1989 roughly 44% of firms listed on either the New York Stock Exchange (NYSE) or American Stock Exchange (AMEX) reported at least one of the transitory earnings components on their income statement. Ten years later, in 1998, that proportion had risen to nearly 57%. Clearly, material, separately disclosed gains and losses have become increasingly common elements of firms' earnings statements in recent years.

Figure 2.5(b) displays the proportion of NYSE and AMEX firms reporting (1) "Special or unusual items," (2) "Discontinued operations," or (3) "Extraordinary items" on their income statement from 1989–1998. The most common category of separately disclosed earnings components is for special or unusual items reported as part of income from continuing operations. Slightly more than 49% of the sample firms reported such items in 1998, compared to 34% in 1989. "Extraordinary items" are the next most common separately disclosed item, appearing on approximately 12% of the earnings statements of firms in 1998 compared to 11% in 1989. The proportion of firms disclosing gains or losses from discontinued operations didn't change much—roughly 7% to 10%—over the 1989–1998 period.

[12] Evidence that special items are likely to recur in the aggregate is provided by P. M. Fairfield, R. J. Sweeney, and T. L. Yohn, "Accounting Classification and the Predictive Content of Earnings," *The Accounting Review* (July 1996), pp. 337–55.

[13] *Ibid.*

Figure 2.5

PROPORTION OF NYSE/AMEX FIRMS REPORTING NONRECURRING ITEMS (1989–1998)

Source: *Standard & Poor's Research Insight*[SM] as data source; methodology not verified or controlled by *Standard & Poor's*.

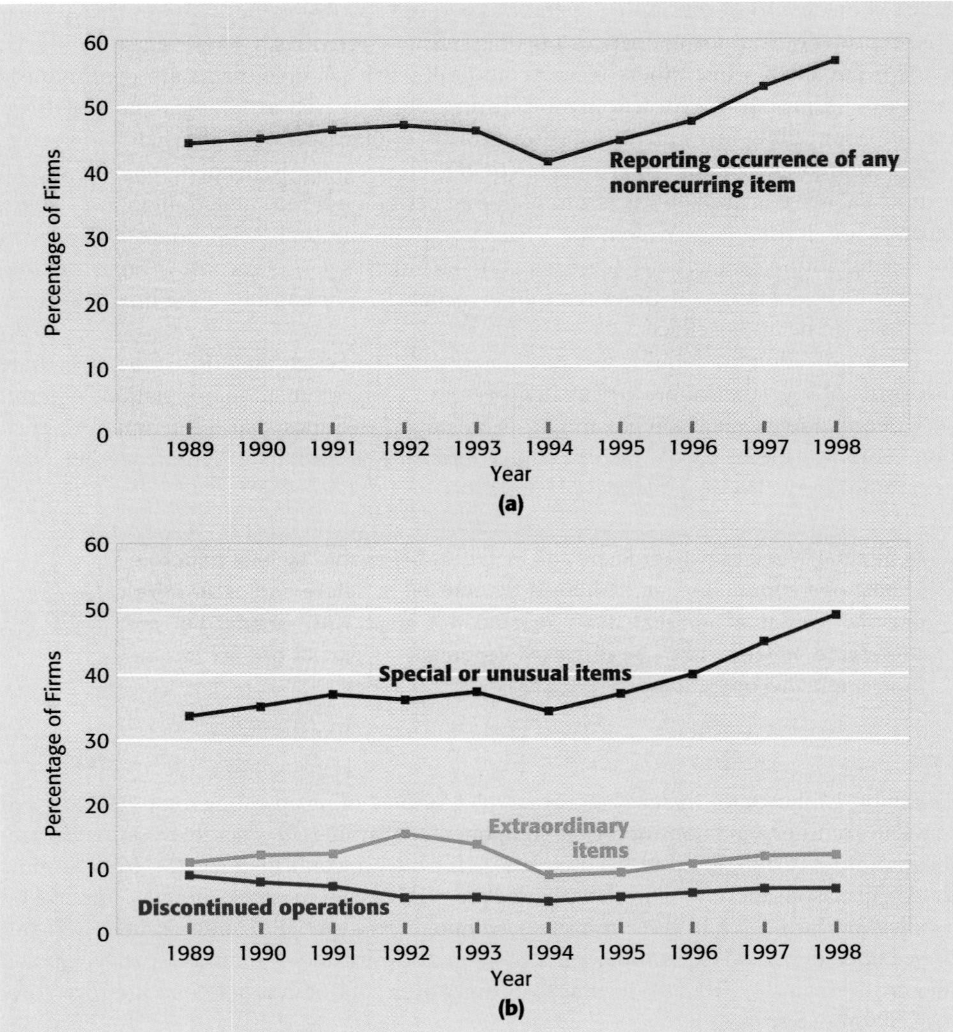

Table 2.1 shows that over the 1989–1998 period, the majority of "special or unusual" items, "discontinued operations," and extraordinary items were losses. (However for 1989–1991 most "extraordinary items" were gains.) The preponderance of special or unusual losses reflects the following two things:

1. The conservative bias of accrual accounting rules encourages early recognition of declines in asset values below cost or book value but tends to delay recognition of increases in value until the asset is sold.

Table 2.1 ■ PERCENTAGE OF NONRECURRING ITEMS RESULTING IN LOSSES (1989–1998)

	1989	1990	1991	1992	1993	1994	1995	1996	1997	1998
Special or unusual items	59.0%	64.6%	71.0%	69.2%	69.7%	66.3%	70.1%	68.9%	70.6%	73.8%
Discontinued operations	54.9	58.9	65.1	64.9	59.5	52.9	51.8	50.4	37.1	48.4
Extraordinary items	27.7	28.5	34.9	56.3	72.0	75.1	78.5	86.2	87.5	86.3
Any nonrecurring item (net)	52.6	58.2	64.7	66.3	68.6	64.9	69.3	68.7	70.3	73.6

Source: *Standard and Poor's Research Insight*[SM] as data source; methodology not verified or controlled by *Standard & Poor's*.

2. Firms have an incentive to separately disclose and clearly label losses more than gains. To merge such (presumably) nonrecurring losses undisclosed as part of the "income from continuing operations" line would cause analysts to underestimate future income. Hence, firms opt for separate line item disclosure of losses.

The higher frequency of losses in the "discontinued operations" category exists because firms tend to sell off unprofitable operating segments and/or segments that have declined in value because of shifts in consumer demand.

The bar charts in Figure 2.6 provide an indication of the relative magnitude of the gains and losses reported from 1989 to 1998 in each of the three nonrecurring item categories. Since "Special or unusual items" are reported on a pre-tax basis, we have divided these items by the absolute value of pre-tax earnings from operations. The gains and losses from "Discontinued operations" and "Extraordinary items" in the figure have been divided by the absolute value of after-tax earnings, since these latter two categories of items are reported net of tax effects. The line crossing each bar shows the median gain or loss as a percentage of the relevant earnings number. The top of each bar indicates the 75th percentile value, while the bottom of each bar shows the 25th percentile value for each category of nonrecurring items.[14]

To improve comparability, all earnings numbers have been adjusted for the non-recurring gain or loss being reported—i.e., gains have been subtracted and losses have been added to the reported earnings to arrive at an adjusted earnings number used in computing the percentages.

Three features stand out from these diagrams. First, the median value of the items disclosed in each of these categories tends to be a significant component of income, ranging approximately between 10% and 40% of the relevant earnings number. Second, for both "Special or unusual items" and "Discontinued Operations," the median value of the losses tend to be larger than the median value of the gains. Median losses reported in these two categories range between 17% and 40% of the relevant earnings number, while median

Figure 2.6

MAGNITUDES OF NONRECURRING ITEMS 1989–1998

Source: *Standard & Poor's Research Insight*SM as data source; methodology not verified or controlled by *Standard & Poor's*.

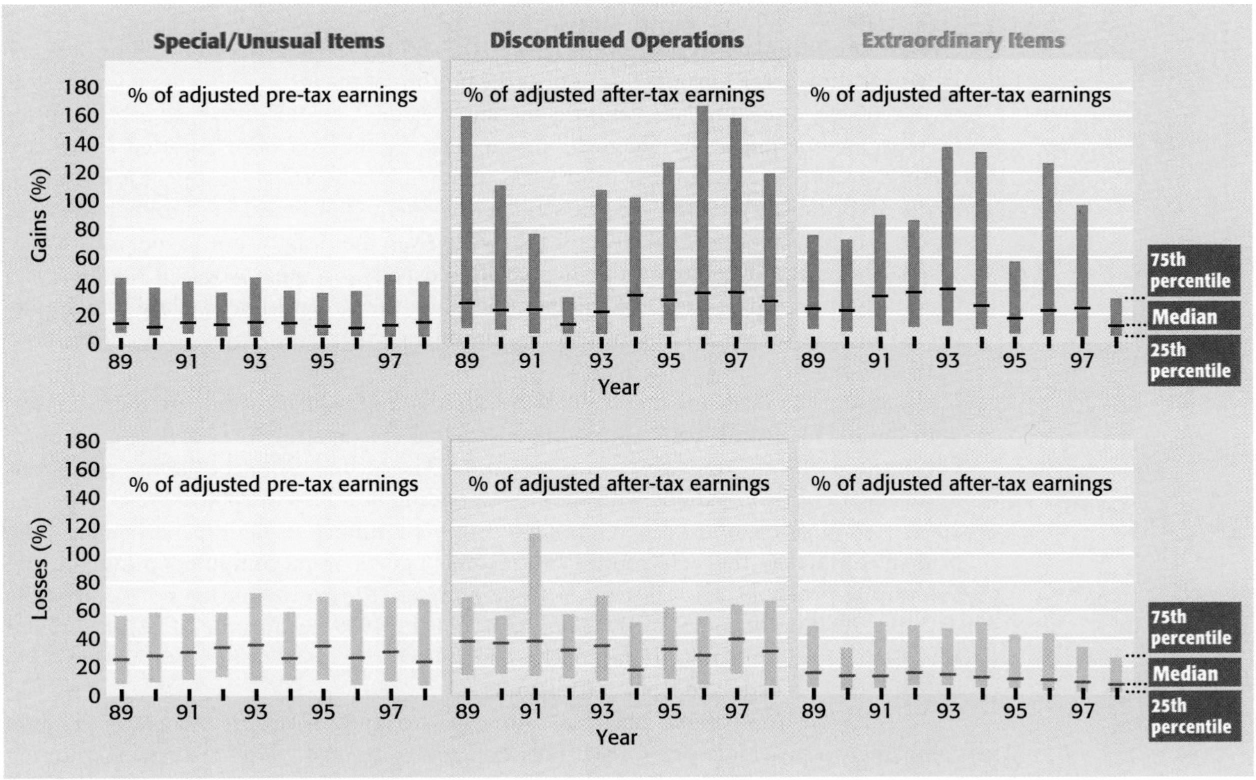

[14] The 75th percentile value means that of the firms reporting one of the three types of nonrecurring items in the indicated year, one-quarter of the firms reported items that *equaled or exceeded* the indicated percentage of income. The 25th percentile value means that one-quarter of the reported gains or losses were *equal to or below* the indicated percentage of income. The median value means that 50% were above (below) this amount.

ANALYSIS

gains range between 10% and 35% of earnings. Finally, for Discontinued operations and Extraordinary items, the upper quartile of firms reported gains in excess of 100% of adjusted after-tax earnings for a significant proportion of the sample years. The large percentage effect on earnings exists because the after-tax earnings number (before considering the effects of the gain) is close to zero. Thus, it appears that some firms try to cover up poor performance by triggering transactions that resulted in gains when their earnings were low or slightly negative.

To users of financial statements, the point of these tables and graphs is that nonrecurring and/or special gains and losses occur relatively frequently. Moreover, these items tend to have a material effect on earnings. Since they may be less sustainable than other earnings components, the weight assigned to these items when predicting future profitability and cash flows must be assessed on a case-by-case basis. (In Chapter 6 we discuss assigning weights to various earnings components for equity valuation purposes.)

Changes in Accounting Principles

Let's return to the Mythical Corporation income statement in Exhibit 2.1. The last separately disclosed item just above the bottom-line income number is the "Cumulative effect of change in accounting principle." When a firm changes from one accounting method to another, the income number for both current and past periods is usually affected. How these income effects are reported varies, depending on the nature of the principle change.

Reporting Most Accounting Changes In general, prior periods' income statements are *not* restated to reflect the income effect of changing to a new principle. Instead, the new principle is first used to compute income from continuing operations in the year of the change. For Mythical Corporation this means that depreciation expense on the 2001 income statement will be computed using the new method—that is, sum-of-the-years' digits—rather than the old straight-line method.

Next, the **cumulative effect** of the change (net of income tax effects) on all prior years' income is shown as a separate line item at the bottom of the income statement for the year of the change. The cumulative effect is measured as the after-tax difference between prior periods' income under the old method and what would have been reported if the new method had been used in those prior years. This cumulative effect treatment is illustrated in the Mythical Corporation income statement by item ⑤, where a $118 million after-tax earnings reduction appears in 2001 for the switch from the straight-line to the sum-of-the-years' digits method for computing depreciation expense. In other words, if Mythical had been using the sum-of-the-years' digits rather than the straight-line method to compute depreciation in the years *prior* to 2001, the cumulative after-tax earnings would have been $118 million lower.

Because prior years' income is not restated, it is impossible to compare the figures in both the 2001 "Income from continuing operations" line and the total 2001 "Net income" bottom-line with previous years' income figures. The income from continuing operations numbers are not comparable with the corresponding numbers in 2000 and 1999 because 2001 operating income of $843 million was determined using the new accounting principle, whereas the 2000 and 1999 income figures were computed using the old accounting principle. The 2001 net income number ($1,026 million) is not comparable with the 2000 net income of $1,127 million and the 1999 net income of $1,340 million because the full cumulative impact of the principle change on all prior years ($118 million in Exhibit 2.1) is deducted from 2001 income.

To provide comparable income numbers, existing disclosure standards require companies to provide a **pro forma** income figure computed "as if" the new accounting principle had been applied during all past periods that are presented. These pro forma income figures are shown immediately below "Net income" on the Mythical Corporation income statement in Exhibit 2.1.

In the year a change from one accounting principle to another is made, firms are compelled to highlight—as a separate line item on the income statement—the cumulative effect of the change on all prior periods' income. Retroactive restatement of prior periods' income is *not* permitted. To illustrate why, we will use the situation described in Note 4 of the Mythical Corporation statements (in Exhibit 2.1).

Mythical Corporation switched from straight-line to the sum-of-the-years' digits depreciation method, effective January 1, 2001. This change in accounting principle increased prior years' depreciation expense as follows:

Year	Gross Increase in Depreciation Expense	Net Increase After Tax Effect Is Considered
2000	$ 49	$ 33
1999	56	38
1998 and earlier	70	47
Total increase	$175	$118

In addition, the switch to the sum-of-the-years' digits depreciation method increased 2001 depreciation expense by $46 ($31 after tax effect).

In implementing the change in principle, Mythical would make the following entry:

DR Cumulative effect of change in accounting principle, net of income tax effect	$118	
DR Deferred income tax payable	57	
CR Accumulated depreciation		$175

The credit adjusts the balance sheet accumulated depreciation account to reflect the higher total amounts under the sum-of-the-years' digits method. The debit of $118 represents the decrease in after-tax net income. The difference between the credit of $175 and the income statement debit of $118 arises because of deferred income taxes which are discussed in detail in Chapter 13.

This example helps us understand why GAAP compels firms to highlight the cumulative effect of accounting principles changes in the income statement. If firms were allowed to change accounting principles and retroactively restate prior periods' income, it would be possible for them to manipulate earnings and mislead investors.

To illustrate how this might happen if retroactive restatement were permitted, let's suppose that Mythical Corporation's management had initially chosen straight-line depreciation for fixed assets even though it knew that this method overstated income in Mythical's particular economic circumstances. The motive for this overstatement might be to mislead the securities market and to allow the firm to raise capital more cheaply. Later, once it became apparent that accelerated depreciation should have been used all along, the firm would then change the accounting depreciation principle and unobtrusively adjust prior periods' income. However, ***by forcing the cumulative effect of $118 million through the income statement, all such changes must take place "in the sunshine"—and in that case the type of opportunistic accounting principle choice just discussed is made transparent.***

Figure 2.7 provides data on the frequency and magnitude of cumulative effect of accounting changes (net of tax effects) reported on the income statements of NYSE and AMEX firms from 1989 to 1998. Panel (a) shows that with the exception of 1992–1993, the percentage of firms reporting accounting change cumulative effects was generally less than 5%. During 1992–1993 the percentage of firms reporting this item on their income statements rose to 19% and 21%, respectively. The vast majority of the accounting changes reported in these two years related to the adoption of a new FASB standard (*SFAS No. 106*) on accounting for other postemployment (e.g. healthcare) benefits, which is discussed further in Chapter 14. Figure 2.7 (b) shows that the median gain from cumulative effect accounting changes ranged from roughly 9% of adjusted after-tax earnings in 1993 to nearly 33% in 1995. The median losses from cumulative effect accounting changes were generally larger and more variable, ranging from approximately 6% in 1997 to 56% in 1990.

Figure 2.7

FREQUENCY AND MAGNITUDE OF CUMULATIVE EFFECTS OF ACCOUNTING CHANGES 1989–1998

Source: *Standard & Poor's Research Insight*SM as data source; methodology not verified or controlled by *Standard & Poor's*.

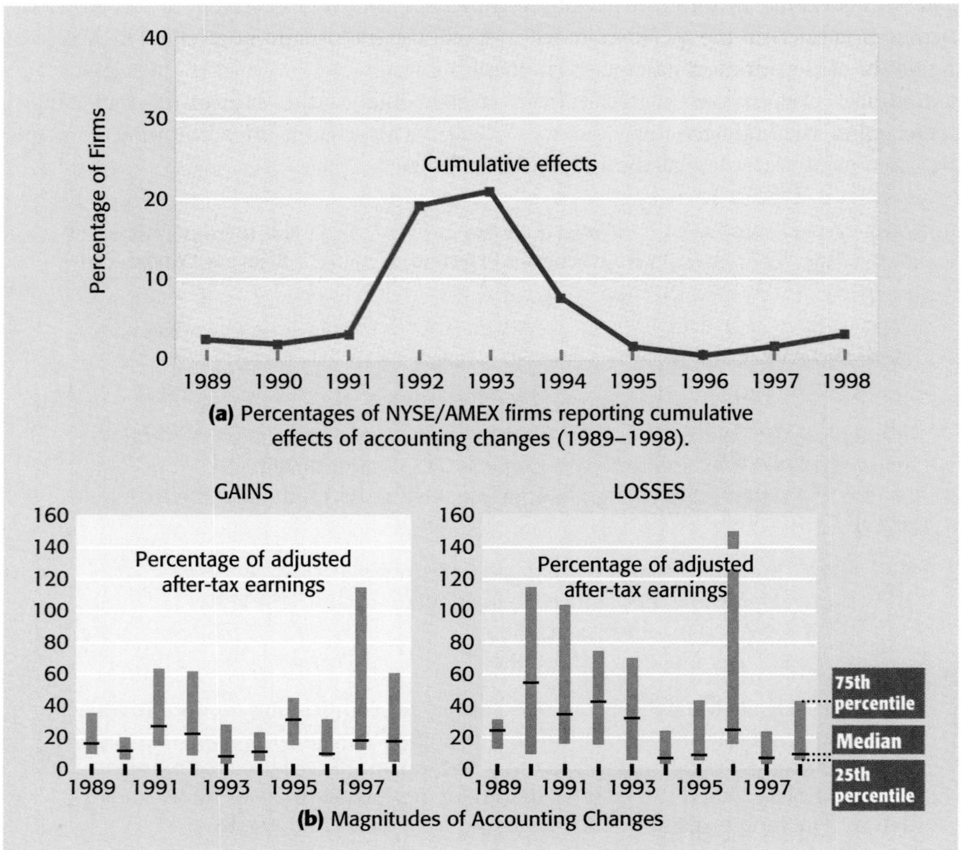

Applying Changes Retroactively There are, however, some circumstances in which GAAP requires the prior years' income effect of a newly adopted accounting principle to be applied retroactively. When this is done in the comparative income statements, there is no need for a pro forma footnote, since the retroactively adjusted income numbers will be comparable to the current period's income.

The retroactive adjustment approach has been allowed by the FASB when new accounting principles are mandated by a newly issued standard. Examples include the capitalization of leases, changes in foreign currency accounting rules, and new deferred income tax reporting requirements.[15] In circumstances such as these, the cumulative effect of the mandated change in the accounting principle is often exceedingly large relative to income from continuing operations. If, say, income from continuing operations were $400 million and if the cumulative effect of the change on prior years' income were $4.5 billion, the cumulative effect would so swamp the continuing income number that adding the two together would make the $4.9 billion net income unrepresentative of the firm's long-run sustainable earnings prospects. Under these circumstances, forcing the cumulative effect through the current period's income statement may hinder informed analysis. Furthermore, since the accounting principle change was mandated by standard setters—not made voluntarily by firms themselves—the fear of opportunistic management behavior is reduced. Accordingly, retroactive adjustment in these circumstances is allowed.

Retroactive adjustment is also required for a very small number of changes among previously existing (rather than newly mandated) accounting principles. Examples include a switch from Last-In, First-Out (LIFO) to some other inventory accounting method and a

[15] "Accounting for Leases," *Statement of Financial Accounting Standards (SFAS) No. 13* (Stamford, CT: FASB, 1976), para. 48; "Foreign Currency Translation," *SFAS No. 52* (Stamford, CT: FASB, 1981), para. 33; "Accounting for Income Taxes," *SFAS No. 109* (Norwalk, CT: FASB, 1992), para. 50.

change in accounting for long-term construction projects (e.g., from the completed-contract method to the percentage-of-completion method, or vice versa). Typically, changes of these sorts will also generate cumulative effects that swamp the income from continuing operations number. This appears to be the reason why standard setters require such changes to be adjusted retroactively.

Retroactive Effect Indeterminable The LIFO inventory accounting method requires that firms keep track of when inventory is increased as well as the cost of these new inventory layers. Therefore, LIFO entails more detailed inventory record keeping than either the FIFO or weighted average methods. A firm that switches to LIFO would have had no reason to have kept detailed inventory data on new layers of inventory costs prior to LIFO adoption. Accordingly, computing what income *would have been* for previous years on LIFO could be difficult or even impossible. For this reason the LIFO adoption disclosure is limited to reporting what income *would have been* under the old inventory method in the year of the change. The cumulative effect on prior years is deemed to be indeterminable and is therefore not disclosed. Exhibit 2.2 illustrates the disclosures arising from LIFO adoption by Ball Corporation.

Changes in Accounting Estimates

The useful life of a depreciable asset or the percentage of accounts receivable deemed uncollectible constitutes what are called **accounting estimates.** When the economic circumstances underlying an accounting estimate change, GAAP requires that the estimate also be changed. For instance, when unforeseen technological advances shorten the service life of an asset, the period over which the asset is depreciated must be similarly shortened.

When accounting estimates are changed, past income is never adjusted; instead, the income effects of the changed estimate are accounted for in the period of the change—and in future periods, if the change affects both. If the change in estimate has a material effect on current and future income, the dollar amount of the effect must be disclosed. Exhibit 2.3 shows the disclosure of the effect of a change in accounting estimate for Southwest Airlines, one that increased the useful lives of some of its aircraft.

Exhibit 2.2 ■ BALL CORPORATION

Accounting Change—Retroactive Effect Indeterminable

Inventories at December 31 consisted of the following ($ in millions):

	1995	1994
Raw materials and supplies	$ 82.8	$132.3
Work-in-process and finished goods	235.7	281.7
	$318.5	$414.0

Effective January 1, 1995, the company adopted the LIFO method of accounting for determining the cost of certain U.S. metal beverage container inventories as a preferable method for matching the cost of the products sold with the revenues generated. The impact of this change in accounting was an increase in cost of sales and a corresponding decrease in operating earnings of $17.1 million ($10.4 million after tax or 35 cents per share). The company is unable to determine the cumulative impact of this change on prior periods.

With the adoption of LIFO accounting for U.S. metal beverage container inventories, approximately 75% of total U.S. product inventories at December 31, 1995 were valued using this method. Inventories at December 31, 1995 would have been $17.1 million higher than the reported amounts if the FIFO method, which approximates replacement cost, had been used for all inventories.

Source: Ball Corporation 1995 Annual Report.

Exhibit 2.3 ■ SOUTHWEST AIRLINES

Excerpt from Footnotes to 1999 Annual Report

Effective January 1, 1999, the Company revised the estimated useful lives of its 737-300 and -500 aircraft from 20 years to 23 years. This change was the result of the Company's assessment of the remaining useful lives of the aircraft based on the manufacturer's design lives, the Company's increased average aircraft stage (trip) length, and the Company's previous experience. The effect of this change was to reduce depreciation expense approximately $25.7 million and increase net income $.03 per diluted share for the year ended December 31, 1999.

Source: Southwest Airlines, 1999 Annual Report, ftn. 2.

We'll use another example to illustrate how current and future period numbers are adjusted when a change in an accounting estimate is made. Miles Corporation purchases a production machine on January 1, 1999 for $6 million. The machine has no salvage value, an expected useful life of ten years, and it is being depreciated on a straight-line basis. On January 1, 2001 the book value of the machine is $4.8 million (i.e., $6 million of original cost minus two years of accumulated depreciation at $0.6 million per year). At that date, it becomes evident that due to changes in demand for the machine's output, its *remaining* useful life is six years, not eight years. If Miles Corporation had perfect foresight, the annual depreciation charge should have been $0.75 million ($6 million divided by eight years), amounting to $1.5 million over the first two years. Consequently, there is $0.3 million too little accumulated depreciation ($1.5 million minus $1.2 million) on January 1, 2001, and pre-tax income for the previous two years is overstated by $0.3 million. Rather than forcing Miles to retroactively adjust reported past income, the GAAP disclosure rules require the change in estimate to be reflected in higher depreciation charges over the new remaining life of the asset—in this case, from 2001 to 2006.[16] Depreciation in those years will be $0.8 million per year (i.e., the remaining book value of $4.8 million divided by the remaining useful life of six years). Over the eight-year life of the asset, depreciation will appear as follows:

1999–2000	2 years × $0.6 million per year	=	$1.2 million
2001–2006	6 years × $0.8 million per year	=	$4.8 million
Total cost of the asset			$6.0 million

From the perspective of perfect foresight, in which depreciation would have been $0.75 million per year, depreciation in the first two years is understated by $0.15 million annually, and in each of the last six years it is overstated by $0.05 million annually. Obviously, over the eight-year life of the asset, depreciation totals $6.0 million.

Why are changes in estimates "corrected" in this peculiar fashion? The reason is that accrual accounting requires many estimates; since the future is highly uncertain, a high proportion of these estimates turn out to be incorrect. If past income were corrected for each misestimate, income statements would be cluttered with numerous retroactive adjustments. The approach illustrated by this example provides an expedient way to deal with the uncertainty in financial statements without generating burdensome corrections.

Change in Reporting Entity

Another type of accounting change can arise when a company acquires another company. In such circumstances the newly combined entity presents consolidated financial statements in place of the previously separate statements of each party to the merger. Such combinations result in what is called a **change in reporting entity.**

[16] *APB Opinion No. 20,* paras. 31–3.

When a change in a reporting entity occurs, comparative financial statements for prior years must be restated for comparative purposes to reflect the new reporting entity as if it had been in existence during all the years presented. The disclosure rule states:

> . . . [A]ccounting changes which result in financial statements that are in effect the statements of a different reporting entity . . . should be reported by restating the financial statements of all prior periods presented in order to show financial information for the new reporting entity for all periods.[17]

Comparative financial statements represent an important resource for analysts, since they provide potentially valuable data for assessing trends and turning points. However, under current GAAP not all business combinations or spin-offs result in a change in the reporting entity. Consequently, analysts must understand the circumstances under which retroactive restatement takes place (and when it does not) in order to ensure that the data being used are indeed comparable. These matters are discussed in more detail in Chapter 16.

Accounting changes can dramatically affect reported earnings and distort year-to-year comparisons. For these reasons, GAAP requires special disclosures to improve interperiod comparability and to help the statement user understand what effect the accounting change has had on the current period's reported profits. The three basic types of accounting changes are: (1) change in accounting principles; (2) change in accounting estimates; and (3) change in reporting entity.

RECAP

Comprehensive Income

Generally, items included in net income are considered to be **closed transactions.** A closed transaction is one whose ultimate "payoff" results from events (1) that have already occurred and (2) whose dollar flows can be predicted fairly accurately. Recollect that income recognition automatically triggers a corresponding change in the carrying amount (book value) of net assets.

Sometimes balance sheet carrying amounts change even though the transaction is not yet closed. Let's consider a specific example, such as a bank or other financial institution that has investments in stocks or other financial instruments with readily determinable market values. Assume that these securities are held in the firm's "available-for-sale" portfolio and that their current market values exceed original purchase prices. During the early 1990s the FASB decided that the fair market value of the securities—rather than invested historical cost (the amount originally invested in them)—should appear on the balance sheet. To recognize the market value increase, the following accounting entry must be made:

DR Marketable securities	XXX	
CR Owners' equity–unrealized holding gain on investment securities		XXX

Obviously, the credit to offset the increase in the marketable securities account must be made to some sort of equity account. Notice, however, that this is not a closed transaction, since the securities have not been sold. Because such transactions are still *open*, the FASB

[17] *APB Opinion No. 20,* para. 34.

does not require the credit to run through the income statement. Instead, the owners' equity increase is reported directly as a separate component of stockholders' equity in the balance sheet.[18] Thus, selected unrealized gains (or losses) arising from incomplete (or open) transactions sometimes bypass the income statement and are reported as direct adjustments to stockholders' equity. Such items are called **other comprehensive income** components and fall into one of the three following categories:[19]

1. Unrealized gains (losses) on marketable securities held in firms' "available-for-sale" portfolios (discussed more fully in Chapter 16)
2. Unrealized gains (losses) resulting from translating foreign currency financial statements of majority-owned subsidiaries into U.S. dollar amounts for the purpose of preparing consolidated financial statements (discussed in Chapter 16)
3. In certain cases, unrealized losses resulting from recognition of minimum pension obligations under *SFAS No. 87* (discussed in Chapter 14).

Figure 2.8 provides an overview of the elements that comprise comprehensive income. *SFAS No. 130* requires firms to report comprehensive income in a statement that is displayed with the same prominence as other financial statements. Firms are permitted to display the components of other comprehensive income in one of several alternative formats:

> In "Elements of Financial Statements," *Statement of Financial Accounting Concepts Statement No. 6* (Stamford, CT: FASB, 1985), para. 70, comprehensive income is defined as "the change in equity (net assets) of a business enterprise during a period from transactions and other events and circumstances from nonowner sources. It includes all changes in equity during a period except those resulting from investments by owners and distributions to owners."

1. In a single-statement format, one in which net income and other comprehensive income are added together to disclose (total) comprehensive income
2. In a two-statement approach, one in which net income comprises one statement and a second, which presents a separate statement of comprehensive income
3. As part of the statement of changes in stockholders' equity.

Exhibit 2.4 (on the next page) from Arden Group's 1999 annual report illustrates the first approach, Exhibit 2.5 (on page 66) shows the two statement approach for Merck & Company and Exhibit 2.6 (on page 66) demonstrates the disclosure of other comprehensive income components as part of Deere & Company's 1999 Statement of Changes in Stockholders' Equity.

Figure 2.8

ELEMENTS COMPRISING COMPREHENSIVE INCOME

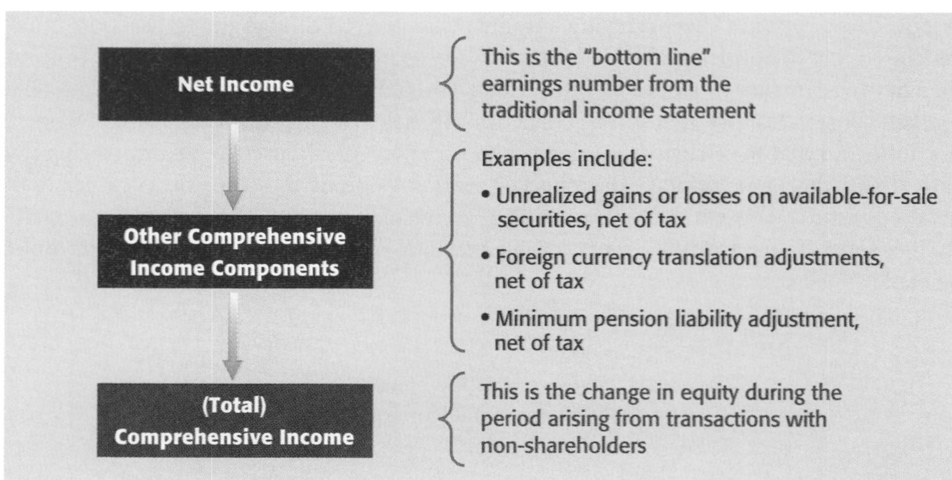

[18] "Accounting for Certain Investments in Debt and Equity Securities," *SFAS No. 115* (Norwalk, CT: FASB, 1993), para. 13.

[19] "Reporting Comprehensive Income," *SFAS No. 130* (Norwalk, CT: FASB, 1997).

Exhibit 2.4 ■ **ARDEN GROUP, INCORPORATED AND CONSOLIDATED SUBSIDIARY**

Consolidated Statements of Operations and Comprehensive Income

($ in thousands)	Years Ended December 31 1999	1998	1997
Sales	$324,168	$296,487	$274,354
Cost of sales	192,446	176,595	164,366
Gross profit	131,722	119,892	109,988
Delivery, selling, general and administrative expenses	114,892	103,882	97,127
Operating income	16,830	16,010	12,861
Interest and dividend income	1,807	1,453	1,536
Other income (expense), net	(104)	396	588
Interest expense	(694)	(764)	(702)
Income from continuing operations, before income taxes	17,839	17,095	14,283
Income tax provision	6,122	7,014	5,586
Income from continuing operations, net of income taxes	11,717	10,081	8,697
Loss from discontinued operations, net of income tax benefits of $1,602 in 1997	–	–	(2,738)
Net income	$ 11,717	$ 10,081	$ 5,959
Other comprehensive income (loss), net of tax:			
Unrealized gain (loss) from available-for-sale securities:			
Unrealized holding gains (losses) arising during the period	(951)	(89)	496
Reclassification adjustment for gains (losses) included in net income	112	66	(80)
Net unrealized gain (loss), net of income tax expense (benefits) of $(572) for 1999, $(9) for 1998, and $275 for 1997	(839)	(23)	416
Comprehensive income	$ 10,878	$ 10,058	$ 6,375

RECAP

Comprehensive income measures the change in equity (net assets) of a company that results from all nonowner transactions and events. It is comprised of both bottom-line accrual income that is reported on the income statement and other comprehensive income components. Other comprehensive income is comprised of selected unrealized gains and losses on incomplete (or open) transactions that bypass the income statement and that are reported as direct credits or debits to stockholders' equity. Firms are required to report comprehensive income in a statement that is displayed with the same prominence as other financial statements. But firms are free to choose the format of presentation—either as a separate statement or as part of a statement that is combined with the income statement or a statement of changes in stockholders' equity.

Exhibit 2.5 ■ MERCK & COMPANY, INCORPORATED AND SUBSIDIARIES

Consolidated Statements of Income

($ in millions)	Years Ended December 31 1999	1998	1997
Sales	$32,714.0	$26,898.2	$23,636.9
Costs, Expenses, and Other			
Materials and production	17,534.2	13,925.4	11,790.3
Marketing and administrative	5,199.9	4,511.4	4,299.2
Research and development	2,068.3	1,821.1	1,683.7
Acquired research	51.1	1,039.5	—
Equity income from affiliates	(762.0)	(884.3)	(727.9)
Gains on sales of businesses	—	(2,147.7)	(213.4)
Other (income) expenses, net	3.0	499.7	342.7
	24,094.5	18,765.1	17,174.6
Income before taxes	8,619.5	8,133.1	6,462.3
Taxes on Income	2,729.0	2,884.9	1,848.2
Net Income	$ 5,890.5	$ 5,248.2	$ 4,614.1

MERCK & COMPANY, INCORPORATED AND SUBSIDIARIES

Consolidated Statement of Comprehensive Income

($ in millions)	Years Ended December 31 1999	1998	1997
Net Income	$ 5,890.5	$ 5,248.2	$ 4,614.1
Other Comprehensive Income (Loss)			
Net unrealized gain (loss) on investments, net of tax and net income realization	25.6	(5.6)	(17.6)
Minimum pension liability, net of tax	3.8	(24.7)	(12.4)
	29.4	(30.3)	(30.0)
Comprehensive Income	$ 5,919.9	$ 5,217.9	$ 4,584.1

Exhibit 2.6 ■ DEERE & COMPANY

Statement of Changes in Consolidated Stockholders' Equity

Year Ended October 31, 1999 (in millions of dollars)	Total Equity	Common Stock	Treasury Stock	Unamortized Restricted Stock*	Retained Earnings	Other Comprehensive Income (Loss)
Balance October 31, 1998	$4,079.8	$1,789.8	($1,467.6)	($7.2)	$3,839.5	($74.7)
Comprehensive income (loss)						
Net income	239.2				239.2	
Other comprehensive income						
Minimum pension liability adjustment	(.2)					(.2)
Cumulative translation adjustment	(26.9)					(26.9)
Unrealized loss on marketable securities	(18.9)					(18.9)
Total comprehensive income	193.2					
Repurchases of common stock	(49.0)		(49.0)			
Treasury shares reissued	47.2		47.2			
Dividends declared	(204.2)				(204.2)	
Other stockholder transactions	27.3	60.6		(14.1)	(19.2)	
Balance October 31, 1999	$4,094.3	$1,850.4	($1,469.4)	($21.3)	$3,855.3	($120.7)

*Unamortized restricted stock includes restricted stock issued at market price net of amortization to compensation expense.

SUMMARY

This chapter highlights the key differences between cash and accrual income measurement. In most instances accrual-basis revenues do not equal cash receipts, and accrual expenses do not equal cash disbursements. The principles that govern revenue and expense recognition under accrual accounting are designed to alleviate the mismatching of effort and accomplishment that occurs under cash basis accounting.

Revenue is recognized when *both* the "critical event" and "measurability" conditions are satisfied. The critical event establishes when the entity has done something to "earn" the asset being received, and measurability is established when the revenue can be measured with a reasonable degree of assurance. These two conditions may be satisfied before or after the point of sale. The matching principle determines how and when the assets that are "used up" in generating the revenue—or that expire with the passage of time—are expensed. Relative to current operating cash flows, accrual earnings generally provide a more useful measure of firm performance, and serve as a more useful benchmark for predicting future cash flows.

Predicting future cash flows and earnings is critical to assessing the value of a firm's shares and its creditworthiness. Multiple-step income statements are designed to facilitate this forecasting process by isolating the more recurring or sustainable components of earnings from the nonrecurring or transitory earnings components. GAAP disclosure requirements for various types of accounting changes also facilitate the analysis of company performance over time.

Occasionally, changes in assets and liabilities resulting from incomplete or "open" transactions bypass the income statement and are reported as direct adjustments to stockholders' equity. Comprehensive income provides a measure of all changes in equity of an enterprise that result from transactions with nonowners. When used with related disclosures in the financial statements, comprehensive income and its components can provide valuable information to investors and creditors for assessing the magnitude and timing of an entity's future cash flows.

APPENDIX Review of Accounting Procedures and T-Account Analysis

The basic accounting equation is the foundation of financial reporting:

$$A = L + OE$$

The basic accounting equation says that at all times, the dollar sum of a firm's assets (A) must be equal to the dollar sum of the firm's liabilities (L) plus its owners' equity (OE). To understand why this equality must always hold, keep two things in mind:

1. Assets don't materialize out of thin air—they have to be financed from somewhere.
2. There are only two parties that can provide financing for a firm's assets:
   a. Creditors of the company—for example, when a supplier ships inventory to a firm on credit (an asset—inventory—is received).
   b. Owners of the company—for example, when owners buy newly issued shares directly from the firm (an asset—cash—is received).

Putting these two things together explains why the two sides of the basic accounting equation must be equal. The equation says the total resources a firm owns or controls (its assets) must, by definition, be equal to the total of the financial claims against those assets held by either creditors or owners.

We'll now use the basic accounting equation to show how various transactions affect its components. Notice, each transaction maintains the basic equality; for example, any increase in an asset must be offset by (1) a corresponding increase in a liability or owners' equity account or (2) a decrease in some other asset.

Assume that Chicago Corporation sells office furniture and provides office design consulting services. It is incorporated on January 1, 2001 and issues $1,000,000 of stock to investors for cash. Here's how the basic accounting equation will be affected by this and subsequent transactions:

For simplicity, we ignore nuances of the par value of the stock, etc., and simply treat the entire amount as "common stock." The details of stock transactions are explored further in Chapter 15.

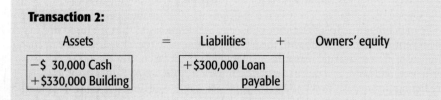

Transaction 1:

Assets	=	Liabilities	+	Owners' equity
+$1,000,000 Cash				+$1,000,000 Common stock

On the next day, Chicago Corporation buys a combination office building and warehouse for $330,000, paying $30,000 in cash and taking out a $300,000 loan at 8% interest per year.

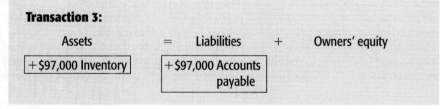

Transaction 2:

Assets	=	Liabilities	+	Owners' equity
−$ 30,000 Cash +$330,000 Building		+$300,000 Loan payable		

Suppliers ship a wide assortment of inventory costing $97,000 to the firm on credit on January 11.

Transaction 3:

Assets	=	Liabilities	+	Owners' equity
+$97,000 Inventory		+$97,000 Accounts payable		

On January 15, Chicago corporation sells a portion of its inventory costing $50,000 to several customers for $76,000.

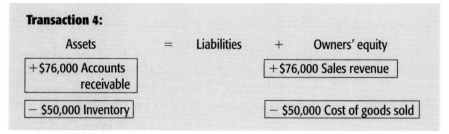

Transaction 4:

Assets	=	Liabilities	+	Owners' equity
+$76,000 Accounts receivable				+$76,000 Sales revenue
− $50,000 Inventory				− $50,000 Cost of goods sold

A sale causes assets to flow into the company. Who benefits from this inflow of assets? The owners do. That's why owners' equity is increased by $76,000 in Transition 4. The source of this increase is labeled—in this case, the source of the increase is sales revenue. But in making a sale, the firm must relinquish an asset, inventory. Whose claims are reduced as a result of this outflow of assets? The owners'. That's why owners' equity is decreased by $50,000 in the second part of Transaction 4. Again, the reason for the decrease in owners' equity is labeled—in this case, the need to deliver inventory to the customer reduces owners' equity claims on the firm's assets by $50,000—the cost of goods sold.

In addition to the balance sheet (which follows the "balancing" format of the basic accounting equation), there is another financial statement called the income statement. Recollect that "Sales revenue" is the top line of the income statement and that "Cost of goods sold" is deducted from revenues. So Transaction 4, which was illustrated in a basic accounting equation (i.e., balance sheet) format, really includes income statement accounts. ***Another way of saying the same thing is that the revenue and expense accounts that appear on the income statement are really owners' equity accounts. Revenues are owners' equity increases; expenses are owners' equity decreases.*** (Later in this appendix, we'll show how these accounts are "closed" into retained earnings—a component of owners' equity—as part of the adjusting and closing process.)

Understanding Debits and Credits

Keeping track of transactions using the basic accounting equation—as we did in Transactions 1 through 4—is cumbersome. For this reason, a streamlined approach is used for recording how transactions either increase or decrease financial statement accounts. Increases and decreases in accounts are based on the convention of "debits" and "credits." Debit (abbreviated DR) means "left-side" of accounts and credit (abbreviated CR) means "right-side" of accounts.

We now depict the basic accounting equation in T-account form and show the rules for how debits and credits operate to reflect increases or decreases to various accounts.

Asset Accounts		=	**Liability Accounts**		+	**Owners' Equity Accounts**	
Debits (DR)	Credits (CR)		Debits (DR)	Credits (CR)		Debits (DR)	Credits (CR)
increase the account balance	**decrease** the account balance		**decrease** the account balance	**increase** the account balance		**decrease** the account balance	**increase** the account balance

Since Transaction 4 showed us that revenue accounts increase owners' equity and expense accounts decrease it, the DR and CR rules treat revenue and expense accounts just like any other owners' equity accounts. The rules can be summarized as follows:

Revenues (i.e., OE increases)		**Expenses (i.e., OE decreases)**	
Debits (DR)	Credits (CR)	Debits (DR)	Credits (CR)
decrease the account balance	**increase** the account balance	**increase** the account balance	**decrease** the account balance

Let's elaborate on the debit/credit rules for expense accounts. Expense accounts are increased by debits. An increase in an expense *decreases* owners' equity. Owners' equity is decreased by debits. That's why increases in an expense account (which decrease owners' equity) are debits.

The basic accounting equation must always be "in balance"—the total of the assets must always equal the total of the liabilities plus owners' equity. ***Similarly, for each transaction, the dollar total of the debits must equal the dollar total of the credits.*** Adherence to the debit and credit rules for each transaction automatically keeps the basic accounting equation "in balance." To help you visualize how this happens, we will redo Transactions 1–4 in debit/credit format and show (in brackets to the right of the account) what happens to the basic accounting equation:

Transaction 1: Stock issued for cash

DR Cash [+A]	$1,000,000	
CR Common stock [+OE]		$1,000,000

Transaction 2: Purchase of building

DR Building [+A]	$330,000	
CR Cash [−A]		$ 30,000
CR Loan payable [+L]		300,000

Transaction 3: Purchase of inventory on credit

DR Inventory [+A]	$97,000	
CR Accounts payable [+L]		$97,000

Transaction 4: Sale of inventory on account

DR Accounts receivable [+A]	$76,000	
DR Cost of goods sold [−OE]	50,000	
CR Sales revenue [+OE]		$76,000
CR Inventory [−A]		50,000

As the pluses and minuses to the right of the debits and credits show, adherence to the DR/CR rules automatically maintains the balance of the basic accounting equation.

We next introduce four additional transactions for Chicago Corporation. Assume that Chicago purchases a one-year fire and theft insurance policy on the building and its contents on January 15, 2001 for $6,000. They make the following journal entry upon purchasing the policy:

Transaction 5: Purchase of prepaid insurance

DR Prepaid insurance [+A]	$6,000	
CR Cash [−A]		$6,000

Prepaid insurance is an asset account because the policy provides a valuable benefit to the company—insurance coverage for the ensuing 12 months.

Next, assume the company receives a $10,000 fee, in advance, from a law firm to help the firm design their new office space. The fee is received on January 17, and the consulting/design services are to be provided over the next month. The following journal entry is made by Chicago Corporation:

Transaction 6: Receipt of consulting fees in advance

DR Cash [+A]	$10,000	
CR Fee received in advance [+L]		$10,000

The credit is to a liability account "Fee received in advance" because the firm has an obligation to provide the consulting services (or return the fee).

Further assume, Chicago Corporation pays certain suppliers $37,000 for inventory recorded in Transaction 3. Other suppliers will be paid in ensuing periods.

Transaction 7: Payment on account

DR Accounts payable [−L]	$37,000	
CR Cash [−A]		$37,000

Finally, $30,000 is received from one of the customers to whom inventory was sold in Transaction 4.

Transaction 8: Collections on account

DR Cash [+A]	$30,000	
CR Accounts receivable [−A]		$30,000

Adjusting Entries

Before financial statements are prepared (either monthly, quarterly, or annually), a firm's financial accounts must be reviewed to determine whether all economic events that have occurred are reflected in the accounts. It is usually the case that certain readily identifiable types of events will *not* be reflected in the accounts. To include these events in the accounts, **adjusting entries** must be made. These adjusting entries fall into four categories:

1. Adjustments for prepayments
2. Adjustments for unearned revenues
3. Adjustments for accrued expenses
4. Adjustments for accrued revenues.

We now assume that Chicago Corporation is preparing financial statements for the month ended January 31, 2001. Adjusting entries in each of the four categories are necessary and discussed next.

Adjustments for Prepayments The insurance policy acquired for $6,000 on January 15 in Transaction 5 has partially expired. One-half of one-month's coverage has now elapsed; consequently, 1/24 of the original *annual* premium payment is no longer an asset. The passage of time means that *past* insurance coverage has no future value. So the following adjusting entry is made:

Adjusting Entry A1:

DR Insurance expense [−OE]	$250	
CR Prepaid insurance [−A]		$250
($6,000 ÷ 12= $500 × 1/2 mo.)		

After this entry is made, the balance in the Prepaid insurance account will be $5,750; this is the original $6,000 balance minus the $250 credit in Adjusting entry A1. The $5,750 represents the remaining asset—insurance coverage for the ensuing 11 1/2 months. The adjusting entry has *simultaneously* accomplished two things:

1. The DR recognizes that portion of the premium that has "expired"—i.e., the portion that is an expense of January. This is the matching principle in action, since the expense is matched against revenues of January.
2. The CR reduces the carrying amount in the asset account by $250. As a result of this reduction, the prepaid insurance account is shown at $5,750; this is the portion of the original $6,000 insurance premium that has not yet expired.

We will discuss the various methods for estimating depreciation in Chapter 10.

The building acquired in Transaction 2 also represents a prepayment. Chicago Corporation paid for the building in early January 2001 but this building is expected to be used in operations over a series of *future* years. As the building is used, a portion of its future service potential declines. This decline in service potential value is an expense of the period called **depreciation.** Assume Chicago Corporation estimates building depreciation for January totaled $1,250. The following adjusting entry will then be made:

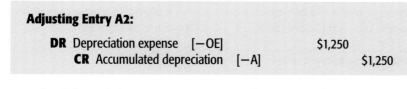

Adjusting Entry A2:

DR Depreciation expense [−OE]	$1,250	
CR Accumulated depreciation [−A]		$1,250

(The accumulated depreciation account represents a "contra-asset" account that is deducted from the cost of the building, as we shall see later.)

A **contra** account is an account that is *subtracted* from another account to which it relates. Contra-asset accounts carry credit balances because they are subtracted from asset accounts that carry debit balances.

Adjustments for Unearned Revenues By the end of January, let's assume 60% of the design work for the law firm has been completed. Consequently, the following adjusting entry is made:

Adjusting Entry A3:

DR Fee received in advance [−L]	$6,000	
CR Consulting fees revenue [+OE]		$6,000

Notice this entry also accomplishes two things. One, the debit lowers the balance in the liability account "Fee received in advance" to $4,000 (i.e., the original $10,000 minus the $6,000 liability reduction arising from the debit). Two, the credit properly recognizes that 60% of the $10,000 advance has been earned in January and thereby increases owners' equity.

Adjustments for Accrued Expenses Salaries and wages for the month of January totaled $16,000. The paychecks will not be issued to employees until Monday, February 3. Because the expense arose in January and a liability exists for money owed to the employees, the following entry must be made:

Adjusting Entry A4:

DR Salary and wages expense [−OE]	$16,000	
CR Salary and wages payable [+L]		$16,000

Adjusting entries like this one must be made for a wide range of expenses that *accrue* over the reporting period. ***Accrual accounting recognizes expenses as the underlying real economic event occurs, not necessarily when the cash flows out.*** Consequently, adjusting entries for accrued expenses must be made not only for accrued wages payable, but also for items like heat, light and power that was used during the month and interest that has accumulated during the period but has not yet been paid. Assume the utility bill arrives on January 31 but will not be paid until February 9, the due date of the bill. If the utility bill for January totaled $9,000, the following additional adjusting entry is necessary:

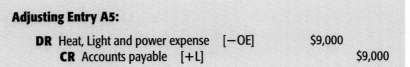

Adjusting Entry A5:

DR Heat, Light and power expense [−OE]	$9,000	
CR Accounts payable [+L]		$9,000

Furthermore, interest of $2,000 has accrued on the loan principal that was used to buy the building. (The accrued interest is determined as follows: $300,000 × 8% = $24,000 × 1/12 of year = $2,000.) The following entry is made:

Adjusting Entry A6:

DR Interest expense [−OE]	$2,000	
CR Accrued interest payable [+L]		$2,000

Adjustments for Accrued Revenues During the last week in January, Chicago Corporation provides design consulting services to a physician who is remodeling her office. The physician is billed for the $2,100 due. The adjusting entry is:

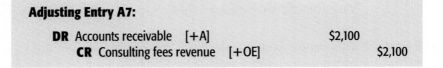

Adjusting Entry A7:

DR Accounts receivable [+A]	$2,100	
CR Consulting fees revenue [+OE]		$2,100

Again, the adjusting entry simultaneously accomplishes two things:

1. The DR reflects the asset that the firm expects to collect as a result of consulting services rendered in January.
2. The CR shows the corresponding increase in owners' equity that arises when the asset write-up is recognized.

Posting Journal Entries to Accounts and Preparing Financial Statements

Throughout this book, we will use journal entries as a streamlined mechanism for showing you how economic events affect financial statement accounts. In this section of the appendix we provide a terse overview of how professional accountants use journal entries as the building blocks for preparing financial statements. We will use T-accounts to demonstrate this. We will also show how analysis of T-accounts can be used to infer what transactions (and dollar amounts) a firm entered into between two balance sheet dates.

The DRs and CRs in each journal entry that is made are posted to T-accounts. **Posting** means the DR or CR is entered in the appropriate left (or right) side of the affected T-account. A separate T-account is maintained for each asset, liability, and owners' equity account. (Remember: revenue and expense accounts are effectively owners' equity accounts, too. The balances accumulated in these accounts for a particular reporting period will be "closed out" or transferred to owners' equity at the end of the period.) Exhibit 2.7 shows all the T-accounts that arise from the transactions of Chicago Corporation during

Exhibit 2.7 ■ POSTING TO T-ACCOUNTS

ASSETS = LIABILITIES + OWNERS' EQUITY

ASSETS

Cash

(1)	$1,000,000	(2)	$30,000
(6)	10,000	(5)	6,000
(8)	30,000	(7)	37,000
Bal.	$ 967,000		

Accounts Receivable

(4)	$76,000	(8)	$30,000
(A7)	2,100		
Bal.	$48,100		

Inventory

(3)	$97,000	(4)	$50,000
Bal.	$47,000		

Prepaid Insurance

(5)	$6,000	(A1)	$250
Bal.	$5,750		

Building

(2)	$330,000		
Bal.	$330,000		

Accumulated Depreciation

		(A2)	$1,250
		Bal.	$1,250

LIABILITIES

Accounts Payable

(7)	$37,000	(3)	$97,000
		(A5)	9,000
		Bal.	$69,000

Salary and Wages Payable

		(A4)	$16,000
		Bal.	$16,000

Accrued Interest Payable

		(A6)	$2,000
		Bal.	$2,000

Loan Payable

		(2)	$300,000
		Bal.	$300,000

Fee Received in Advance

(A3)	$6,000	(6)	$10,000
		Bal.	$ 4,000

OWNERS' EQUITY

Common Stock

		(1)	$1,000,000
		Bal.	$1,000,000

Retained Earnings

(Revenue and expense account balances will be closed out to this account at end of the accounting period.)

Consulting Fees Revenue

		(A3)	$6,000
		(A7)	2,100
		Bal.	$8,100

Sales Revenue

		(4)	$76,000
		Bal.	$76,000

Cost of Goods Sold

(4)	$50,000		
Bal.	$50,000		

Insurance Expense

(A1)	$250		
Bal.	$250		

Depreciation Expense

(A2)	$1,250		
Bal.	$1,250		

Salary and Wages Expense

(A4)	$16,000		
Bal.	$16,000		

Heat, Light and Power Expense

(A5)	$9,000		
Bal.	$9,000		

Interest Expense

(A6)	$2,000		
Bal.	$2,000		

January 2001. The journal entry DR or CR that gave rise to the amount posted in the T-account is indicated by a number to the left of each item. For example, in the cash T-account, the (1) to the left of the DR of $1,000,000 indicates that this item arose from the $1,000,000 DR in transaction 1. The (1) to the left of the $1,000,000 credit to common stock indicates that this item resulted from the balancing CR in Transaction 1. Posting *both* the DR and CR to the T-accounts reflected in the original entry maintains the equality of the basic accounting equation.

The adjusting entries are also posted to the T-accounts shown in those entries. For example, in Exhibit 2.7, the (A1) to the left of the $250 DR to the "Insurance expense" T-account tells us that this item arose from adjusting entry A1. (Notice the CR from that entry was posted as a credit to the "Prepaid insurance" account, with the A1 designation to the left of the posting.)

The accountant preparing the financial statements would use the balances in the revenue and expense accounts (entered in maroon in Exhibit 2.7) to prepare the January 2001 income statement. As shown in Exhibit 2.8, income for January (ignoring taxes) is $5,600. This amount represents the **net** increase in owners' equity for the month arising from operations. Consequently, the $5,600 appears again *in the balance sheet* as an owners' equity increase labeled "retained earnings" (shown by the arrows). The asset, liability, and common stock T-accounts (entered in black) comprise the other balance sheet accounts. (Notice, the credit balance in accumulated depreciation is deducted from the building account. That's why this is a "contra-asset" account.)

> This is true because revenues increase owners' equity and expenses decrease owners' equity (review transaction 4). So, the excess of revenues over expenses represents the ***net*** increase in owners' equity.

Exhibit 2.8 ■ CHICAGO CORPORATION

Income Statement
For the Month Ended January 31, 2001

Revenues:		
Sales revenue		$76,000
Consulting fees revenue		8,100
Total revenue		84,100
Expenses:		
Cost of goods sold	$50,000	
Salary and wages expense	16,000	
Heat, light and power expense	9,000	
Depreciation expense	1,250	
Insurance expense	250	
Interest expense	2,000	
Total expense		78,500
Pretax income		$ 5,600

Statement of Financial Position
January 31, 2001

Assets:			**Liabilities and Equity:**	
Cash		$ 967,000	Liabilities:	
Accounts receivable		48,100	Accounts Payable	$ 69,000
Inventory		47,000	Fees received in advance	4,000
Prepaid insurance		5,750	Salary and wages payable	16,000
Building	$330,000		Accrued interest payable	2,000
Less: Accumulated depreciation	(1,250)	328,750	Loan payable	300,000
Total Assets		$1,396,600	Equity:	
			Common stock	1,000,000
			Retained earnings	5,600
			Total Liabilities and Equity	$1,396,600

Closing Entries

After the income statement for the month of January 2001 is prepared, the revenue and expense accounts have served their purpose. So balances in these accounts are "zeroed out" (or closed) to get them ready to reflect February transactions. To get the revenue and expense account balances to zero, a **closing journal entry** is made. All revenue account balances (which are credits) are *debited* (to get them to zero); all expense account balances (which are debits) are *credited* (to get them to zero). The difference between the closing entry debits and credits—in this case a credit of $5,600—is made to retained earnings. Here's the entry:

DR Sales revenue	$76,000	
DR Consulting fees revenue	8,100	
CR Cost of goods sold		$50,000
CR Salary and wages expense		16,000
CR Heat, light and power expense		9,000
CR Depreciation expense		1,250
CR Insurance expense		250
CR Interest expense		2,000
CR Retained earnings		5,600

After this entry is posted to the accounts, all of the revenue and expense accounts will have zero balances. The accounts are now clear to receive February income statement transactions.

T-accounts Analysis as an Analytical Technique

Understanding the various events or transactions that affect individual account balances is critical to analyzing financial statements. Users of financial statements can't "see" the individual transactions that underlie various account balances and changes in account balances in comparative balance sheets. Nevertheless, it's often possible to deduce the aggregate amount of certain common events or transactions that have taken place during the reporting period. Armed with the following knowledge, one can reconstruct transactions that have occurred during a given reporting period.

- Start with beginning and ending balances in various balance sheet T-accounts (which are always available from comparative balance sheets)
- Know the major types of transactions or events that cause increases or decreases in individual T-accounts
- Know how various accounts and financial statement items articulate with one another.

A comparative balance sheet reflects the asset, liability and owners' equity account balances as of the end of the current reporting period (typically a quarter or year) and for one or more previous reporting periods. Firms are required to show ending account balances for at least two years in annual reports issued to shareholders.

T-account analysis also can be used to gain insights into why accrual basis earnings and cash basis earnings (i.e., cash flows from operations) differ.

Let's use a new example, Trevian Corporation, to illustrate how T-account analysis can be used to infer or deduce unknown or unobservable transactions. Consider the following analysis of Accounts receivable (net of the Allowance for doubtful accounts):

Accounts Receivable—Net

Beginning Balance	$1,000,000		
		Collections on account	(B)
Sales on account	(A)		
Ending Balance	$1,200,000		

Note that the major transaction that increases accounts receivable (debit to this account) is sales on account, while the major transaction causing a decrease in accounts receivable (credits to this account) is the collections on account. Assuming these are the only events that affected Accounts receivable during the period, we can infer from the $200,000 increase in Trevian's Accounts receivable that sales on account exceeded collections on account during the period by $200,000. But can we go a step further and deduce the aggregate amounts of the debits (A) and credits (B) to this account? Yes, we can. However, to do so we need to understand how parts of the income statement and balance sheet articulate with one another.

Other transactions that can affect the Accounts receivable account include write-offs of specific accounts determined to be uncollectible, sales returns and allowances, and customers that take advantage of sales discounts by paying off their account balance within the discount period. Typically, these events have a minimal effect on the Accounts receivable balance for the period.

Recall that the first line of the income statements of most companies is sales revenue. Typically, when one business sells a product or service to another company the sale is a credit sale, meaning that the sale is "on account" and will be collected within 30, 60, or 90 days depending upon industry credit terms. Suppose sales revenue for Trevian was $3,500,000 and all sales were credit sales. We can recreate the following entry that summarizes the credit sales for the period and shows directly how income statement and balance sheet accounts reflect opposite sides of the same transaction and, thus, articulate with one another.

DR Accounts receivable	$3,500,000	
CR Sales revenue		$3,500,000

Knowing that all sales on account are reflected in an offsetting debit to Accounts receivable allows us to deduce the amount (A) = $3,500,000 in the Accounts receivable T-account presented above. Next, we can combine this information with the fact that the net increase in Accounts receivable was $200,000 to deduce that the collections on account during the period—unknown amount (B)—must have been $3,300,000 In other words,

Beginning accounts receivable balance	$1,000,000	
+ Sales on account	3,500,000	
− Collections on account	(3,300,000)	← (Plug to balance = B)
= Ending accounts receivable balance	$1,200,000	

Analysis of the Accounts receivable T-account also provides information for understanding differences between accrual basis income and cash from operations. The important insight from the analysis of the Accounts receivable T-account is that sales on account (reflected as revenue in accrual basis income) is recorded on the debit side of this account, while collections on account (reflected as revenue in cash basis income measurement—i.e., cash flow from operations) is recorded on the credit side of this account. Knowing that Trevian's Accounts receivable has increased by $200,000 tells us that accrual basis revenue exceeded cash basis revenue for the period by $200,000. Therefore, we would need to *subtract* this increase in Accounts receivable from the accrual basis income number to convert accrual earnings to cash flow from operations. Conversely, if collections on account had exceeded sales on account by $200,000, this *decrease* in Accounts receivable would have to be *added* to accrual basis net income to arrive at cash flow from operations.

Analogous reasoning can be used to gain insights into transactions that affect Accounts payable and the differences between accrual basis expenses and cash basis expenses. The following T-account summarizes the key events that cause changes in Trevian's Accounts payable for a period:

Accounts Payable

Debit		Credit	
		Beginning balance	$2,000,000
Payments on account	(B)		
		Purchases of inventory on account	(A)
		Ending balance	$1,500,000

Here we can see that payments on account exceeded purchases of inventory on account by $500,000, resulting in a decrease in the Accounts payable T-account for the period. We can deduce the amount of purchases on account by again referring to the income statement and recalling the components that comprise the cost of goods sold computation for a merchandising firm. For purposes of this illustration, assume Trevian's cost of goods sold is $2,100,000, and the beginning and ending inventory from its comparative balance sheets are $1,500,000 and $1,800,000, respectively. Purchases of inventory for the period can be deduced as follows:

Beginning inventory	$1,500,000	
+ Purchases of inventory	2,400,000	← (Plug to balance = A)
− Ending inventory	(1,800,000)	
Cost of goods sold	$2,100,000	

Assuming that all purchases of merchandise inventory was purchased on credit (generally the case for most businesses), we can determine through T-account analysis that payments on account must have been $2,900,000 determined as follows:

Beginning accounts payable balance	$2,000,000	
+ Purchases on account (see above)	2,400,000	
− Payments on account	(2,900,000)	← (Plug to balance = B)
= Ending accounts payable balance	$1,500,000	

Changes in the Accounts payable and Inventory T-accounts help us understand the differences between accrual accounting's cost of goods sold expense and the cash-basis expense for inventory purchases. We'll use the schedules above for Trevian's cost of goods sold and Accounts payable to demonstrate this point:

Accrual accounting cost-of-goods-sold deduction included in determining income	$2,100,000
Add: Inventory increase	300,000
Equals: Total inventory purchases in 2001	2,400,000
Add: Accounts payable decrease	500,000
Equals: Cash basis expense for inventory purchases	$2,900,000

As shown, two adjustments are required to convert accrual-basis cost of goods sold ($2,100,000) to cash-basis expense for inventory purchases ($2,900,000). The first adjustment for the inventory increase is because beginning inventory is a ***non-cash addition*** to cost of goods sold, while ending inventory is a ***non-cash deduction*** in arriving at cost of goods sold (see cost of goods sold schedule above). Therefore, to remove the net non-cash effects of beginning and ending inventory from cost of goods sold, we must add the increase in inventory. (If inventory had declined, we would subtract the decrease.) Making this adjustment to cost of goods sold gives us the total inventory purchased in 2001. (We've assumed that all inventory purchases are on account. Consequently, all inventory purchases during the year would be credited to Accounts payable.)

The second adjustment—for the decrease in Accounts payable—is because Trevian's cash *payments* for inventory purchased on account exceeded new inventory *purchases* on account in the current period (see Accounts payable schedule above). Thus, Trevian's cash payments for inventory actually exceeded the credit purchases of inventory that's included in the accrual-basis cost of goods sold number. Accordingly, to convert the accrual-basis cost-of-goods-sold expense to a cash-basis expense, the decrease in accounts payable must be added. (If Accounts payable had increased, this change would have been subtracted.)

Note that in the previous discussion the adjustments made are to convert accrual basis *expense* to cash-basis *expense*. To adjust accrual-basis *income* to obtain cash-basis *income* (cash flow from operations), the adjustment for the changes in Inventory and Accounts Payable would be in the opposite direction. That is, the increase in inventory and the decrease in Accounts payable would be *subtracted* from accrual income to obtain cash flow from operations. This is because adjustments to expense have the opposite effect on income.

In general, analyses similar to that used for Accounts receivable and Accounts payable can be carried out for Accrued revenue, Accrued expense, Deferred (unearned) revenue, and Deferred (prepaid) expense accounts to deduce other differences between accrual basis income and cash basis income. Understanding that differences between accrual basis and cash basis income can be gleamed from most working capital accounts (i.e., current asset and current liability accounts reported on the balance sheet) is one of the key lessons in financial statement analysis that we will return to repeatedly throughout later chapters in this book.

EXERCISES

E2–1

Determining accrual- and cash-basis revenue

AICPA adapted

In November and December 2001 Gee Company, a newly organized magazine publisher, received $36,000 for 1,000 three-year subscriptions at $12 per year, starting with the January 2002 issue of the magazine.

REQUIRED:

How much should Gee report in its 2001 income statement for subscriptions revenue on an accrual basis? How much revenue would be reported in 2001 on a cash basis?

E2–2

Determining unearned subscription revenue

AICPA adapted

Aneen's Video Mart sells one- and two-year mail-order subscriptions for its video-of-the-month business. Subscriptions are collected in advance and credited to sales. An analysis of the recorded sales activity revealed the following:

	2000	2001
Sales	$420,000	$500,000
Less cancellations	(20,000)	(30,000)
Net sales	$400,000	$470,000
Subscription expirations		
2000	$120,000	
2001	155,000	$130,000
2002	125,000	200,000
2003		140,000
	$400,000	$470,000

REQUIRED:

What amount of unearned subscription revenue should Aneen report on its December 31, 2001 balance sheet?

E2–3

Converting from accrual to cash-basis revenue

AICPA adapted

In its accrual-basis income statement for the year ended December 31, 2001, Dart Company reported revenue of $1,750,000. Additional information was as follows:

Accounts receivable 12/31/00	$375,000
Uncollectible accounts written off during 2001	20,000
Accounts receivable 12/31/01	505,000

REQUIRED:

Under the cash basis of income determination, how much should Dart report as revenue for 2001?

Tara Company reported accrual-basis revenue of $1,980,000 in its income statement for the year ended December 31, 2001. Additional information was as follows:

E2–4

Converting from accrual- to cash-basis revenue

AICPA adapted

	2000	2001
Accounts receivable	$415,000	$550,000
Allowance for doubtful accounts	25,000	40,000

No uncollectible accounts were written off during 2001.

REQUIRED:

Had the cash basis of accounting been used instead, how much revenue would Tara Company have recognized for 2001?

John Tracey, M.D., keeps his accounting records on the cash basis. During 2001 Dr. Tracey collected $150,000 in fees from his patients. At December 31, 2000 Dr. Tracey had accounts receivable of $20,000. At December 31, 2001 Dr. Tracey had accounts receivable of $35,000 and unearned fees of $5,000.

E2–5

Converting from cash- to accrual-basis revenue

AICPA adapted

REQUIRED:

On the accrual basis, what was Dr. Tracey's patient service revenue for 2001?

Marr Corporation reported rental revenue of $2,210,000 in its cash-basis income statement for the year ended November 30, 2001. Additional information is as follows:

E2–6

Converting from cash- to accrual-basis revenue

AICPA adapted

Rents receivable – November 30, 2001	$1,060,000
Rents receivable – November 30, 2000	800,000
Uncollectible rents written off during the fiscal year	30,000

REQUIRED:

On the accrual basis, how much gross rental revenue should Marr report in 2001?

Under Hart Company's accounting system, all insurance premiums paid are debited to prepaid insurance. For interim financial reports, Hart makes monthly estimated charges to insurance expense with credits to prepaid insurance. Additional information for the year ended December 31, 2001 is as follows:

E2–7

Converting from accrual- to cash-basis expense

AICPA adapted

Prepaid insurance at December 31, 2000	$210,000
Charges to insurance expense during 2001, including a year-end adjustment of $35,000	875,000
Unexpired insurance premiums at December 31, 2001	245,000

REQUIRED:

What was the total amount of insurance premiums paid by Hart during 2001?

Dix company operates a retail store and must determine the proper December 31, 2001 year-end accrual for the following expenses:

E2–8

Determining accrued liabilities

AICPA adapted

- The store lease calls for fixed rent payments of $1,200 per month, payable at the beginning of the month, and additional rent equal to 6% of net sales over $250,000 per calendar year, payable on January 31 of the following year. Net sales for 2001 are $450,000.
- An electric bill of $850 covering the period December 16, 2001 through January 15, 2002 was received January 22, 2002.
- A $400 telephone bill was received January 7, 2002 covering:

Service in advance for January 2002	$150
Local and toll calls for December 2001	250

REQUIRED:

What amount should Dix Company report as accrued liabilities on its December 31, 2001 balance sheet?

E2–9

Determining gain (loss) from discontinued operations

Munn Corporation's income statements for the years ended December 31, 2002 and 2001 included the following information before adjustments:

	2002	2001
Operating income	$ 800,000	$600,000
Gain on sale of division	450,000	–
	1,250,000	600,000
Provision for income taxes	375,000	180,000
Net income	$ 875,000	$420,000

On January 1, 2002 Munn Corporation agreed to sell the assets and product line of one of its operating divisions for $1,600,000. The sale was consummated on December 31, 2002, and it resulted in a gain on disposition of $450,000. This division's net losses were $320,000 in 2002 and $250,000 in 2001. The income tax rate for both years was 30%.

REQUIRED:

In preparing revised comparative income statements, Munn should report a gain (loss) from discontinued operations of how much?

E2–10

Determining cumulative effect of accounting change

AICPA adapted

Effective January 1, 2001 Younger Company adopted the accounting principle of expensing incurred advertising and promotion costs. Previously, advertising and promotion costs applicable to future periods were recorded in prepaid expenses. Younger can justify the change, which was made for both financial statement and income tax purposes. Younger's prepaid advertising and promotion costs totaled $500,000 at December 31, 2000. Assume that the income tax rate is 40% for 2000 and 2001.

REQUIRED:

The adjustment for the effect of this change in accounting principle should result in a net charge against income in the 2001 income statement of how much?

E2–11

Determining cumulative effect of accounting change

AICPA adapted

On January 1, 2001 Roem Corporation changed its inventory method to FIFO from LIFO for both financial and income tax reporting purposes. The change resulted in a $500,000 increase in the January 1, 2001 inventory. Assume that the income tax rate for all years is 30%.

REQUIRED:

Determine the cumulative effect of the accounting change that Roem should report in its 2001 income statement.

E2–12

Determining period versus product costs

REQUIRED:

Classify the following costs as period or product costs. If a product cost, indicate which will be matched with sales as part of cost of goods sold, and which will be shown as a direct deduction from sales.

Depreciation on office building	Depreciation on factory
Insurance expense for factory building	Bonus to factory workers
Product liability insurance premium	Salary to marketing staff
Transportation charges for raw materials	Administrative expenses
Factory repairs and maintenance	Bad debt expense
Rent for inventory warehouse	Advertising expenses
Cost of raw materials	Research and development
Factory wages	Warranty expense
Salary to chief executive officer	Electricity for plant

E2–13

Converting from cash to accrual basis

The following information is provided for Kelly Plumbing Supply.

Cash received from customers during December 2001	$387,000
Cash paid to suppliers for inventory during December 2001	$131,000

Cash received from customers includes November accounts receivables of $139,000. Sales totaling $141,000 were made on account during December and are expected to be collected in January 2002. Cash paid to suppliers in December included payments of $19,000 for inventory purchased and used in November. All inventory purchased in December and $39,000 of inventory purchased in November was used in December.

REQUIRED:

What is gross profit for the month of December under accrual accounting?

E2–14

Accrual basis revenue recognition

Runway Care, Inc. provides contract-mowing services for private airfields with grass runways. Some clients prepay for their mowing services early in the spring and their payment is credited to unearned revenue. The following information was taken from Runway's 2001 financial statements.

	Balance at	
	June 30	July 31
Accounts receivable	$30,000	$29,000
Unearned revenue	5,000	3,000

Runway received $73,000 of payments on account during June.

REQUIRED:

How much revenue should Runway report for the month of June?

E2–15

Determining effect of omitting year-end adjusting entries

Hentzel Landscaping commenced its business on January 1, 2001.

1. During the first year of its operations, Hentzel purchased supplies in the amount of $12,000 (debited to "Supplies inventory"), and of this amount, $3,000 were unused as of December 31, 2001.
2. On March 1, 2001 Hentzel Landscaping received $18,000 for landscaping services to be rendered for 18 months (beginning July 1, 2001). This amount was credited to "Unearned landscaping revenue."
3. The company's gasoline bill for $2,500 for the month of December 2001 was not received until January 15, 2002.
4. The company had borrowed $50,000 from HomeTown Financing on April 1, 2001 at an interest rate of 12% per annum. The principal, along with all the interest, is due on April 1, 2002.
5. On January 1, 2001 the company purchased 10 lawnmowers at $3,000 per unit. The lawnmowers are expected to last for three years with no salvage value.

On December 31, 2001 Hentzel Landscaping did not record any adjusting entries with respect to these transactions.

REQUIRED:

Using the table format below, show the effect of the *omission* of each year-end adjusting entry on the following: (Indicate both the amount and the direction of the effect.) Use "OS" for overstated, "US" for understated, and "NE" for no effect.

Item Number		Assets	Liabilities	Net Income
	Direction of effect			
	Dollar amount of effect			

PROBLEMS/DISCUSSION QUESTIONS

P2–1

Journal entries and statement preparation

- On January 1, 2001 Frances Corporation started doing business and the owners contributed $200,000 capital in cash.
- The company paid $24,000 to cover the rent for the office space for the 24-month period from January 1, 2001 to December 31, 2002.
- On March 1, 2001 MSK Inc. entered into a consulting contract under which Frances Corporation promised to provide consulting to MSK Inc. for the ten-

month period from March 1, 2001 to December 31, 2001. In return MSK promised to pay a monthly consulting fee of $15,000, which was to be paid in January 2002. Frances Corporation fulfilled its contractual obligation during 2001.

- On July 1, 2001 Frances Corporation purchased office equipment for $100,000 cash. The equipment has an estimated useful life of five years and no salvage value. The equipment was immediately placed into use. Frances Corporation uses the straight-line method of depreciation. Frances Corporation records depreciation expense in proportion to the number of months' usage.
- Through November 30, 2001, the company had paid $66,000 to its employees for 11 months of salaries. Accrued salaries on December 31, 2001 were $6,000. On December 31, 2001, Norbert Corporation advanced $20,000 to Frances Corporation for consulting services to be provided during 2002.

REQUIRED:

1. Provide journal entries for each of these transactions.
2. Provide adjusting entries at the end of the year.
3. Prepare an income statement for the year ended December 31, 2001.
4. Prepare a balance sheet as of December 31, 2001.

P2–2

Converting accounting records from cash basis to accrual basis

AICPA adapted

The following information pertains to Baron Flowers, a calendar-year sole proprietorship, which maintained its books on the cash basis during the year.

BARON FLOWERS

Trial Balance December 31, 2001

	DR	CR
Cash	$ 25,600	
Accounts receivable 12/31/00	16,200	
Inventory 12/31/00	62,000	
Furniture and fixtures	118,200	
Land improvements	45,000	
Accumulated depreciation 12/31/00		$ 32,400
Accounts payable 12/31/00		17,000
Baron, drawings		–0–
Baron, capital 12/31/00		124,600
Sales		653,000
Purchases	305,100	
Salaries	174,000	
Payroll taxes	12,400	
Insurance	8,700	
Rent	34,200	
Utilities	12,600	
Living expenses	13,000	
	$827,000	$827,000

The "Baron, drawings" account is used to record any distributions to Mr. Baron. The "Baron, capital" account is used to record any capital contributions that Mr. Baron makes to the business and any profits or losses retained in the business.

Baron has developed plans to expand into the wholesale flower market and is in the process of negotiating a bank loan to finance the expansion. The bank is requesting 2001 financial statements prepared on the accrual basis of accounting from Baron. During the course of a review engagement, Mr. Muir, Baron's accountant, obtained the following additional information:

1. Amounts due from customers totaled $32,000 at December 31, 2001.
2. An analysis of the receivables revealed that an allowance for uncollectible accounts of $3,800 should be provided.
3. Unpaid invoices for flower purchases totaled $30,500 and $17,000 at December 31, 2001 and December 31, 2000, respectively.
4. A physical count of the goods at December 31, 2001 determined that the inventory totaled $72,800. The inventory was priced at cost, which approximates market value.
5. On May 1, 2001 Baron paid $8,700 to renew its comprehensive insurance coverage for one year. The premium on the previous policy, which expired on April 30, 2001, was $7,800.
6. On January 2, 2001 Baron entered into a 25-year operating lease for the vacant lot adjacent to Baron's retail store, which was to be used as a parking lot. As agreed to in the lease, Baron paved and fenced in the lot at a cost of $45,000. The improvements were completed on April 1, 2001, and they have an estimated useful life of 15 years. No provision for depreciation or amortization has been recorded. Depreciation on furniture and fixtures was $12,000 for 2001.
7. Accrued expenses at December 31, 2000 and 2001 were as follows:

	2000	2001
Utilities	$ 900	$1,500
Payroll taxes	1,100	1,600
	$2,000	$3,100

8. Baron was notified late in the year of a lawsuit filed against his business for an injury to a customer. Baron's attorney believes that the unfavorable outcome is probable and that a reasonable estimate of the settlement exclusive of amounts covered by insurance is $50,000.
9. The salaries account includes $4,000 per month paid to the proprietor. Baron also receives $250 per week for living expenses. These amounts should have been charged to Baron's drawing account.

REQUIRED:

1. Determine the adjustments that are required to convert the trial balance of Baron Flowers to the accrual basis of accounting for the year ended December 31, 2001. Prepare formal journal entries to support your adjustments.
2. Write a brief memo to Baron explaining why the bank would require financial statements prepared on the accrual basis instead of the cash basis.

P2–3 The following is the preclosing trial balance of Antonia Retailers, Inc.:

Adjusting entries and statement preparation

ANTONIA RETAILERS, INC.

Preclosing Trial Balance as of December 31, 2001

	DR	CR
Cash	$ 42,000	
Accounts receivable	67,500	
Prepaid rent	15,000	
Inventory	100,000	
Equipment	60,000	
Building	90,000	
Allowance for doubtful accounts		$ 5,000
Accumulated depreciation–equipment		30,000
Accumulated depreciation–building		9,000
Advance from customers		25,000
Accounts payable		18,000
Salaries payable		4,000
Capital stock		70,000
Retained earnings 1/1/01		187,500
Sales revenue		350,000
Cost of goods sold	185,000	
Salaries expense	50,000	
Bad debt expense	10,500	
Rent expense	30,000	
Insurance expense	18,000	
Depreciation expense–building	5,000	
Depreciation expense–equipment	2,000	
Dividends	23,500	
Totals	$698,500	$698,500

The following additional information is provided to you:

1. The company paid a salary advance of $10,000 to one of its employees, a total which was debited to the salaries expense account. This was an advance against the employee's salary for the year 2002.
2. On January 1, 2001 the company paid an insurance premium of $18,000, which was debited to the insurance expense account. The premium provided insurance coverage for 18 months beginning on January 1, 2001.
3. The company decided to revise its estimate of bad debts expense by calculating it at 10% of its sales revenue.
4. On January 1, 2002 the board of directors of the company declared an additional dividend of $10,000 for the year 2001.

REQUIRED:

1. Prepare the necessary adjusting entries for the year ended December 31, 2001.
2. Prepare an income statement for the year ended December 31, 2001.
3. Prepare a balance sheet as of December 31, 2001.

P2–4 At the top of the next page is selected information from the balance sheet for Flaps Inc. Solve for the missing amounts for each of the five years.

Understanding the accounting equation

	2000	2001	Year 2002	2003	2004
Total liabilities and stockholders' equity	$13,765	**F**	**K**	**P**	**U**
Current liabilities	**A**	3,420	3,467	3,517	**V**
Common stock	138	139	**L**	142	144
Contributed capital	2,340	**G**	2,387	2,422	**W**
Non-current assets	8,667	8,721	**M**	8,968	**X**
Retained earnings	2,795	2,813	2,851	**Q**	**Y**
Total assets	**B**	**H**	14,040	**R**	14,351
Non-current liabilities	5,231	**I**	5,335	**S**	5,454
Additional paid-in capital	**C**	2,216	2,247	**T**	2,296
Current assets	**D**	**J**	5,200	5,275	5,315
Total liabilities	8,630	8,683	**N**	8,929	**Z**
Total stockholders' equity	**E**	5,168	**O**	5,314	5,354

P2–5

Understanding the accounting equation

Below is selected information from, Flightscape Adventures' financial statements. Solve for the missing amounts for each of the five years. You may have to use some numbers from the year before or the year after to solve from certain current year numbers. (NA = not available.)

	2000	2001	Year 2002	2003	2004
Current assets (CA)	**A**	$2,285	**L**	$2,150	**X**
Non-current assets	3,665	**F**	3,604	**R**	3,732
Total assets	5,821	**G**	**M**	5,805	**Y**
Current liabilities (CL)	1,437	**H**	**N**	**S**	1,463
Non-current liabilities	**B**	2,345	**O**	2,206	2,252
Contributed capital	990	**I**	**P**	1,049	**Z**
Retained earnings (ending)	1,182	**J**	1,087	**T**	1,204
Total stockholders' equity	**C**	2,302	2,136	**U**	**AA**
Total liabilities and stockholders' equity	**D**	**K**	5,724	5,805	**BB**
Working capital (CA − CL)	**E**	762	707	**V**	732
Net income (loss)	NA	85	**Q**	40	99
Dividends	NA	14	9	**W**	12

P2–6

Converting from cash to accrual

During August 2001, Packer Manufacturing had the following cash receipts and disbursements:

Cash received from customers	$319,000
Cash received from selling equipment	11,200
Cash paid for salaries	47,000
Cash paid to suppliers for inventory purchases	130,000

In addition, the following balance sheet account balances were shown on Packer's books:

	July 31	August 31
Accounts receivable	$128,000	$135,000
Inventory	33,000	25,000
Accounts payable	21,000	25,000
Salaries payable	8,000	5,000

Assume all sales and purchases are on account.

REQUIRED:

1. Determine sales for August 2001.
2. Determine salary expense for August 2001.
3. Determine cost of goods sold for August 2001.

P2–7

Converting from cash to accrual basis

During the month of October 2001, HAWK-I Rentals had the following cash receipts and payments:

Rental receipts (cash) received	$43,000
Cash paid for insurance	5,000
Cash paid for taxes	6,000
Cash received from sale of used equipment	11,000

Of the rental receipts collected, $2,000 was reported as rent receivable at September 30, and $3,500 was a prepayment of November's rent. An insurance premium of $1,000 was owed at the end of October. Taxes of $1,000 and $700 were owed at October 1 and October 31, respectively. Equipment sold in October had a book value (cost minus accumulated depreciation) of $12,200 at the time of sale.

REQUIRED:

1. Determine rental income for October 2001.
2. Determine insurance expense for October 2001.
3. Determine tax expense for October 2001.
4. Assuming the accumulated depreciation on the equipment sold was $1,300, what is the appropriate journal entry to record the sale of the used equipment?

P2–8

Journal entries and statement preparation

Bob's Chocolate Chips and More, a bakery specializing in gourmet pizza and chocolate chip cookies, started business October 1, 2001. The following transactions occurred during the month.

a. Common stock of $90,000 was sold to start the business.
b. Equipment consisting of mixers and ovens were acquired October 1 for $30,000 cash. The equipment is expected to last five years and can be sold, at that time, for $5,000. Management uses the straight-line method to calculate depreciation expense.
c. Ingredients costing $15,000 were purchased on account during the month and all but $5,000 was paid for by the end of the month.
d. Rent is $500 a month. October, November and December's rent were paid October 5.
e. A payment of $800 for utilities was made during the month.
f. Sixty percent of the ingredients purchased in (c) were prepared and sold for $35,000 on account; $26,000 was collected on account receivable during the month.
g. Wages of $5,200 were paid during the month. Moreover, wages for the last three days of the month amounted to $400 and will be paid during the first week of November.
h. $12,000 was borrowed from the bank for additional working capital requirements, and $3,000 was repaid by month-end. Interest on the unpaid loan balance amounted to $450 at the end of October and was paid on November 5.

REQUIRED

Prepare the required journal entries and adjustments as well as an income statement and balance sheet, in good form, for Bob's Chocolate Chips and More as of October 31, 2001. (*Hint*: You may want to consider using T-accounts to classify and accumulate the above transactions prior to preparing the statements.)

P2–9

Journal entries and statement preparation

The following is the pre-adjusted trial balance of JetCo Fuel Services as of December 31, 2001.

JETCO FUEL SERVICES

Pre-Adjusted Trial Balance
December 31, 2001

	Debits	Credits
Cash	$ 39,800	
Accounts receivable, net	70,700	
Fuel inventory	42,600	
Equipment	30,000	
Fuel tanker	75,000	
Accumulated depreciation		$ 3,000
Accounts payable		35,100
Accrued expenses		12,500
Customer deposits		2,400
Notes payable		75,000
JetCo capital stock		75,000
Retained earnings		15,300
Fuel sales		840,000
Fuel expense	641,200	
Salary expense	75,000	
Insurance expense	72,000	
Rent expense	12,000	
	$1,058,300	$1,058,300

ADDITIONAL INFORMATION:

a. A fuel tanker was purchased July 1, 2001 by issuing a three-year 10% interest-bearing note payable for $75,000. The tanker is expected to last ten years and then be scrapped. JetCo uses the straight-line depreciation method.
b. After taking a physical inventory it was discovered that fuel inventories were overstated by $6,100.
c. Equipment on the balance sheet was acquired January 1, 2000 and has a ten-year life.
d. A search of unrecorded liabilities reveals unrecorded fuel expenses of $4,800.
e. A 36-month insurance policy was acquired for $72,000 on August 31, 2001 and charged to insurance expense.
f. On June 1, 2001 one-year's rent ($12,000) was paid and charged to rent expense.
g. The balance in the Customers' deposit account was earned in 2001.
h. During 2001, JetCo paid a dividend of $75,000, which was subtracted from retained earnings.

REQUIRED:

1. Prepare any required adjustments as of December 31, 2001.
2. Prepare JetCo's income statement for the year ending 2001 and its balance sheet.

P2–10

IVAX Corporation Determining missing amounts on income statement

STRETCH

The information on the following page was taken from a recent income statement of IVAX Corporation. IVAX is a holding company with subsidiaries providing research, development, manufacturing and marketing of brand name pharmaceutical products.

(continued)

	($ in 000)
Amortization of intangible assets	$?
Cost of goods sold	?
Cumulative effect of change in accounting principle, net of taxes (debit)	(3,048)
Extraordinary gain on extinguishment of debt, net of taxes	1,121
General and administrative expenses	88,434
Gross profit	241,171
Income before cumulative effect of change in accounting principle	74,642
Income before extraordinary item and cumulative effect of change in accounting principle	?
Income from continuing operations	?
Income from continuing operations before income taxes	34,664
Income from discontinued operations, net of taxes	48,904
Interest expense	?
Interest income	11,972
Net income	?
Net revenues	?
Operating income	?
Other income, net	20,830
Provision for income taxes	(10,047)
Research and development	48,615
Restructuring costs and asset write-downs	12,222
Selling expenses	79,508
Gross profit as percent of sales	37.81%
Total operating expenses	$232,452

REQUIRED:

1. Recast IVAX's income statement and present it in good form. Fill in the missing data.
2. Consider the item "Restructuring costs and asset write-downs." What impact did this charge have on IVAX's cash flows?
3. IVAX's income statements over the last three years report Research and development expenses averaging $51.3 million per year. These expenses are incurred by IVAX to enhance current products and to develop new products in the hope of generating higher future sales. Generally accepted accounting principles require that all such costs be expensed in the year incurred. Consider the following statement:

   Research and development expenditures are really assets because they will benefit the future operations of the firm (i.e., lead to higher sales).

   If you agree, suggest an alternative way to account for research and development expenditures rather than expensing them in the year incurred. If you disagree, what are your reasons?
4. Assume that you are a financial analyst for IVAX Corporation. Your boss has asked you to project next year's net earnings. What earnings number from the information provided above would you use as the basis for your projection? Why?

P2–11

Determining income from continuing operations and gain (loss) from discontinued operations

AICPA adapted

The following condensed statement of income of Helen Corporation, a diversified company, is presented for the two years ended December 31, 2002 and 2001:

	2002	2001
Net sales	$10,000,000	$9,600,000
Cost of sales	(6,200,000)	(6,000,000)
Gross profit	3,800,000	3,600,000
Operating expenses	(2,200,000)	(2,400,000)
Operating income	1,600,000	1,200,000
Gain on sale of division	900,000	–
Net income before taxes	2,500,000	1,200,000
Provision for income taxes	(1,250,000)	(600,000)
Net income	$ 1,250,000	$ 600,000

On January 1, 2002 Helen entered into an agreement to sell for $3,200,000 the assets and product line of one of its separate operating divisions. The sale was consummated on December 31, 2002, and resulted in a gain on disposition of $900,000. This division's contribution to Helen's reported income before taxes for each year was as follows:

2002	$640,000 loss
2001	$500,000 loss

Assume an income tax rate of 50%.

REQUIRED:

1. In the preparation of a revised comparative statement of income, Helen should report income from continuing operations after income taxes for 2002 and 2001, respectively, amounting to how much?
2. In the preparation of a revised comparative statement of income, Helen should report "Discontinued operations" for 2002 and 2001, respectively, of what amounts? (Indicate income or loss.)

P2–12

Determining sustainable earnings

STRETCH

This problem is based on the financial statements of Ingersoll Rand. The operating income before taxes (all numbers in thousands) for the years ended Year 2 and Year 1 are $161,136 and $160,945, respectively. These income numbers were arrived at without considering the following items (all numbers provided in this problem are on a pre-tax basis):

a. A loss associated with a restructuring of operations during Year 1 totaled $23,000. The management felt that this significant charge merited a separate line item disclosure in that portion of the income statement permitted by GAAP.
b. During Year 1 the company sold certain unused property for a gain of $33,694. The company had not reported similar events in the past several years.
c. During Year 1 the company wrote off investments of $17,305 in some depressed energy-related businesses. The management felt that this item should be treated as a nonrecurring charge.
d. During Year 1 the company incurred a before-tax loss of $11,100 for the early extinguishment of long-term debt. This is treated as an extraordinary item.
e. Effective January 1, Year 2 the company changed its method of accounting to include in inventory certain manufacturing overhead costs that were previously charged to operating expense. The cumulative effect of this change for the years prior to January 1, Year 2 amounted to a net benefit of $16,260. Assume the new method of accounting had been applied retroactively for Year 1 and Year 0. In this case the before-tax income would have been lower by $890 and $2,468, respectively. Note this change is considered to be a change in accounting principle by GAAP.

REQUIRED:

1. Assume a tax rate of 40% for all items. After incorporating the preceding items, prepare comparative income statements for Year 2 and Year 1 as required by GAAP.
2. Assume you are an analyst following the stock of the company. Compute the growth rate in "sustainable earnings" from Year 1 to Year 2. Sustainable earnings can be considered as that portion of a given period's earnings which can be used to form an expectation about the next period's earnings. If the company maintains the same growth rate in Year 3, provide a forecast for the sustainable earnings for Year 3.

P2–13

Preparing a multiple-step income statement

The following balances in the revenue and expense T-accounts of Murphy Oil are extracted from its trial balance as of December 31, Year 1:

($ in 000)	DR	CR
Sales		$1,646,053
Other operating revenues		45,189
Nonoperating revenue (interest income, etc.)		19,971
Income tax benefit		15,415
Crude oil, products, and related expenses	$1,274,780	
Exploration expenses	65,755	
Selling and general expenses	67,461	
Depreciation, depletion, and amortization	225,924	
Impairment of long-lived assets	198,988	
Provision for reduction in work force	6,610	
Interest expense	5,722	

The component "Impairment of long-lived assets" represents a write-down of property, plant, and equipment. The asset impairment resulted from management's expectation of a continuation into the foreseeable future of the low-price environment for crude oil, natural gas, and petroleum products that confronted the oil and gas industry throughout most of Year 1. Although asset impairment is not unusual in the oil industry, it is not expected to occur frequently.

REQUIRED:

1. Prepare the income statement of Murphy Oil Corporation for the year ended December 31, Year 1 in good form.
2. On December 31, Year 2 Murphy completed a tax-free spin-off to its stockholders of all the common stock of its wholly owned farm, timber, and real estate subsidiary, Deltic Farm & Timber Company, Inc. (reincorporated as "Deltic Timber Corporation"). The following balances in the revenue and expense T-accounts of Deltic Farm & Timber Company, Inc. are taken from its trial balance as of December 31, Year 1:

($ in 000)	DR	CR
Sales		$74,124
Other operating revenues		4,618
Nonoperating revenue (interest income, etc.)		691
Product and other expenses	$56,697	
Selling and general expenses	3,673	
Depreciation and amortization	4,053	
Interest expense	309	
Provision for income taxes (income tax expense)	5,394	

As a result of the spin-off transaction, activities of the farm, timber, and real estate segment have to be accounted for as discontinued operations by Murphy Oil, with the Year 1 income statement restated to conform to the Year 2 presentation. On the basis of the additional information, reconstruct Murphy Oil's Year 1 income statement after considering the spin-off as a discontinued operation.

C2–1

Fuentes Corporation: Preparation of a multiple-step income statement

Fuentes Corporation reported the following in its 2001 annual report:

FUENTES CORPORATION

Income Statements
For the Years Ended December 31, 2000–2001

($ in millions)	2001	2000
Net sales	$7,475	$6,952
Costs and expenses		
Cost of goods sold	(5,803)	(5,284)
Selling, general, and administrative	(793)	(820)
Income from continuing operations before income taxes	879	848
Income tax expense	(317)	(305)
Income from continuing operations	$ 562	$ 543

One year later in its 2002 annual report Fuentes disclosed a number of significant financial events:

1. A loss associated with a corporate headquarters restructuring during 2002 totaled $60 million (net of tax benefit of $31 million). A previous managerial restructuring occurred in 1999. Fuentes' management felt that this significant change merited separate line item disclosure in that portion of the income statement permitted by GAAP.
2. In October 2002, Fuentes discontinued its Geegaw product line entirely, choosing to concentrate its efforts on its remaining two products, Chatchkies and Baubles. All Geegaws were manufactured at the Kishinev, MD, plant, which was closed in November. The 2002 income from the Geegaw operation, net of tax, was $143 million. The loss on disposal of this segment (net of a tax benefit of $25 million) was $53 million. The 2001 and 2000 results of the discontinued operations are shown below:

($ in millions)	2001	2000
Net sales	$3,125	$3,063
Costs and expenses		
Cost of goods sold	(2,515)	(2,419)
Selling, general, and administrative	(465)	(478)
Income before tax	145	166
Income tax expense	(52)	(60)
Income after tax	$ 93	$ 106

3. Effective January 1, 2002 Fuentes changed from the sum-of-the-years' digits method for depreciating production equipment to the straight-line method in the Chatchkies and Baubles divisions. (The depreciation method used in the Kishinev plant where Geegaws were manufactured was not changed.) The cumulative effect of this change in accounting principle on all prior years' income as of January 1, 2002 was to increase income by $56 million, net of an income tax effect of $29 million. If the new accounting principle had been in use in those years, the 2001 and 2000 results would have been as shown on the next page:

($ in millions)	2001	Adjusted Amounts Change	2000	Change
Net sales	$7,475	$ 0	$6,952	$ 0
Costs and expenses				
Cost of goods sold	(5,793)	−10	(5,270)	−14
Selling, general, and administrative	(791)	−2	(817)	−3
Income from continuing operations before income taxes	891	+12	865	+17
Income tax expense	(321)	+(4)	(311)	+(6)
Income from continuing operations	$ 570	$+8	$ 554	$+11

4. A "partial" income statement for 2002 follows:

($ in millions)	2002
Net sales	$5,002
Costs and expenses	
Cost of goods sold	(3,927)
Selling, general, and administrative	(350)
Income before tax	725
Income tax expense	(261)
Income after tax	$ 464

This statement is partial because it *excludes entirely* the events described in parts 1 and 2 of this question—that is, the discontinued operation has already been removed from these figures; also excluded is the restructuring cost (and its tax effect). The partial income statement does, however, compute depreciation expense using the new straight-line depreciation method described in part 3.

REQUIRED:

Prepare comparative income statements for the years 2002 and 2001, as they would be reflected under GAAP.

C2–2

The Quaker Oats Company: Classification of gains versus losses

In 1991 and again in 1995 Quaker Oats Company disposed of business segments. The 1991 transaction was a spin-off of Fisher-Price (a toy manufacturing operation) to the company's shareholders. The 1995 transaction was principally composed of the sale of both the North American and European pet food businesses.

Exhibit 1 contains the consolidated statements of income from the 1991 Annual Report as well as the financial statement footnote on discontinued operations, which also appeared in that report. Exhibit 2 reflects the consolidated statements of income from the 1995 Annual Report; in addition Exhibit 2 also contains excerpts from two 1995 financial statement footnotes.

Notice that Quaker treated the 1991 transaction as a discontinued operation "below the line," while the 1995 transaction was treated differently.

Exhibit 1 ■ THE QUAKER OATS COMPANY AND SUBSIDIARIES

Consolidated Statements of Income

($ in millions, except per-share data)	Year ended June 30 1991	1990	1989
Net sales	$5,491.2	$5,030.6	$4,879.4
Cost of goods sold	2,839.7	2,685.9	2,655.3
Gross profit	2,651.5	2,344.7	2,224.1
Selling, general, and administrative expenses	2,121.2	1,844.1	1,779.0
Interest expense—net of $9.0, $11.0, and $12.4 interest income	86.2	101.8	56.4
Other expense—net	32.6	16.4	149.6
Income from continuing operations before income taxes	411.5	382.4	239.1
Provision for income taxes	175.7	153.5	90.2
Income from continuing operations	235.8	228.9	148.9
Income (loss) from discontinued operations—net of tax	(30.0)	(59.9)	54.1
Net income	205.8	169.0	203.0
Preferred dividends—net of tax	4.3	4.5	—
Net income available for common	$ 201.5	$ 164.5	$ 203.0
Per common share			
Income from continuing operations	$ 3.05	$ 2.93	$ 1.88
Income (loss) from discontinued operations	(.40)	(.78)	.68
Net income	$ 2.65	$ 2.15	$ 2.56
Dividends declared	$ 1.56	$ 1.40	$ 1.20
Average number of common shares outstanding (in thousands)	75,904	76,537	79,307

Note 2: Discontinued Operations—In April 1990 the Company's Board of Directors approved in principle the distribution of Fisher-Price to the Company's shareholders. Accordingly, Fisher-Price has been reflected as a discontinued operation in the accompanying financial statements for all periods presented. The tax-free distribution was completed on June 28, 1991 and Fisher-Price, Inc., an independent free-standing company, was created. The distribution reduced reinvested earnings by $200 million. The $29.6 million payable to Fisher-Price at June 30, 1991 represents an estimate of the final cash settlement pursuant to the Distribution Agreement. Each holder of Quaker common stock on July 8, 1991 received one share of Fisher-Price, Inc. common stock for every five shares of Quaker common stock held as of such date. Fisher-Price, Inc. common stock is publicly traded.

The loss from discontinued operations for fiscal 1990 was $59.9 million, or 78 cents per share, including $25.5 million, or 33 cents per share, for the loss from the first nine months of fiscal 1990 and an after-tax provision of

$34.4 million, or 45 cents per share, recorded in the fourth quarter. The third-quarter results included charges of $10.7 million, or 8 cents per share, for the East Aurora, New York manufacturing facility closing and $17 million, or 23 cents per share, for anticipated transaction expenses of the planned spin-off and projected operating losses (including allocated interest expense) through the expected completion date of the spinoff. The fourth-quarter provision included charges of $8.6 million, or 7 cents per share, for the pending closing of Fisher-Price's Holland, New York manufacturing facility and $4.8 million, or 4 cents per share, for costs relating to staff reductions. The fourth-quarter provision also included $25.4 million, or 21 cents per share, for inventory write-downs and the cost of maintaining related trade programs and $18.1 million, or 13 cents per share, for higher projected operating losses through the spin-off date due to lower than previously anticipated sales volumes.

During fiscal 1991, the Company recorded an additional $50 million pretax charge ($30 million after tax), or 40 cents per share to discontinued operations. The charge related primarily to receivables credit risk exposure, product recall reserves, and severance costs.

The following summarizes the results of operations for discontinued operations ($ in millions):

	1991	1990	1989
Sales	$601.0	$702.6	$844.8
Pretax earnings (loss)	(50.0)	(96.2)	89.6
Income tax benefit (expense)	20.0	36.3	(35.5)
Income (loss) from discontinued operations	($ 30.0)	($ 59.9)	$ 54.1

Fisher-Price operating loss for fiscal 1991 was approximately $35 million. Fisher-Price operating losses for the fourth quarter of fiscal 1990, including the Holland, New York plant closing and severance charges, were $40 million, including allocated interest expense of $1.2 million. Interest expense of $6.7 million, $7.4 million, and $7.1 million was allocated to discontinued operations in fiscal 1991, 1990, and 1989, respectively.

Exhibit 2 ■ THE QUAKER OATS COMPANY AND SUBSIDIARIES

Consolidated Statements of Income

($ in millions, except per-share data)	1995	Year ended June 30 1994	1993
Net sales	$6,365.2	$5,955.0	$5,730.6
Cost of goods sold	3,381.5	2,926.2	2,870.0
Gross profit	2,983.7	3,028.8	2,860.6
Selling, general, and administrative expenses	2,603.2	2,425.6	2,302.3
Gains on divestitures and restructuring charges—net	(1,094.3)	108.6	20.5
Interest expense—net of $6.3, $8.9, and $10.5 interest income, respectively	110.7	89.7	55.1
Foreign exchange loss—net	4.2	26.2	15.1
Income before income taxes and cumulative effect of accounting changes	1,359.9	378.7	467.6
Provisions for income taxes	553.8	147.2	180.8
Income before cumulative effect of accounting changes	806.1	231.5	286.8
Cumulative effect of accounting changes—net of tax	(4.1)	—	(115.5)
Net income	802.0	231.5	171.3
Preferred dividends—net of tax	4.0	4.0	4.2
Net income available for common	$ 798.0	$ 227.5	$ 167.1
Per common share amounts			
Income before cumulative effect of accounting changes	$ 6.00	$ 1.68	$ 1.96
Cumulative effect of accounting changes	(0.03)	—	(0.79)
Net income	$ 5.97	$ 1.68	$ 1.17
Dividends declared	$ 1.14	$ 1.06	$ 0.96
Average number of common shares outstanding (in thousands)	133,763	135,236	143,948

Acquisitions and Divestitures Footnote Excerpt—On March 14, 1995 the Company completed the sale of its North American pet food business to H. J. Heinz Company for $725.0 million and realized a gain of $513.0 million. On April 24, 1995 the Company completed the sale of its European pet food business to Dalgety PLC for $700.0 million and realized a gain of $487.2 million. Other divestitures in fiscal 1995 included the Dutch honey business in February 1995, the Mexican chocolate business in May 1995, and the U.S. bean and chili businesses in June 1995. The Company realized gains on these divestitures of $4.9 million, $74.5 million, and $91.2 million, respectively.

The following table presents sales and operating income from the businesses divested in fiscal 1995 through the sale dates. Operating income includes certain allocations of overhead expenses and excludes gains on divestitures and restructuring charges in all fiscal years.

(*continued*)

($ in millions)	1995	1994	1993
Sales			
U.S. and Canadian grocery products	$ 554.6	$ 757.3	$ 720.8
International grocery products	760.4	876.0	969.8
Sales from divested business	$1,315.0	$1,633.3	$1,690.6
Operating income			
U.S. and Canadian grocery products	$ 39.3	$ 54.2	$ 55.6
International grocery products	34.1	50.6	63.7
Operating income from divested business	$ 73.4	$ 104.8	$ 119.3

Restructuring Charges—In fiscal 1995 the Company recorded a restructuring charge of $76.5 million for cost-reduction and realignment activities in order to address the changes in its business portfolio and to allow it to quickly and effectively respond to the needs of trade customers and consumers. These changes result in the elimination of approximately 850 positions and primarily include the realignment of the corporate, shared services and business unit structures, the European cereals business, and the U.S. distribution center network. Savings from these activities are expected to be about $50 million annually beginning in calendar 1996. Approximately 90% of the annual savings will be in cash.

REQUIRED:

1. Why do you think the 1991 and 1995 divestiture transactions were treated so differently?
2. Do you agree with each year's financial statement placement?
3. What factors do you think were used to justify the fact that each treatment was in conformity to GAAP?

C2–3

Baldwin Piano and Organ I (KR): Identifying critical events for revenue recognition

The following information is based on the 1993 annual report and 10-K statement of Baldwin Piano and Organ Company.

The company is the largest domestic manufacturer of keyboard musical instruments, and it manufactures or distributes all major product classes of pianos and electronic organs. The company believes that the breadth and quality of its line of keyboard musical instruments, its large and well-established dealer distribution networks, and its efficient and low-cost manufacturing capabilities have enabled it to maintain its strong market share in the keyboard musical instrument market.

Over the company's 131-year history, its principal products have been pianos and organs. The company significantly expanded its principal business lines through its 1988 acquisition of the keyboard operations of The Wurlitzer Company, which now operates as a wholly owned subsidiary of the company. Over the years, the company has also expanded and diversified its product line in order to utilize excess capacity and its woodworking, electronics, and technical expertise. The company manufactures printed circuit boards, electronic assemblies, grandfather and other quality clocks, and wooden cabinets.

The company ships keyboard instruments and clocks to its dealer network on a consignment basis. Accordingly, revenue is recognized at the time the dealer sells the instrument to a third party. The company charges a monthly display fee on all consigned inventory held by dealers longer than 90 days. This display fee, on an annual basis, ranges from 12% to 16% of the selling price of such inventory to the dealer. Display fee income is included under the component "Other operating income, net."

The company distributes its Baldwin keyboard musical instruments in the United States through approximately 500 independent dealers (600 outlets) and 11 company-owned stores operating in six major metropolitan areas. Most of the independent dealers carry Baldwin products as their principal line—and often their exclusive one.

The company has been engaged in financing the retail purchase of its products for over 80 years. In 1993 approximately 35% of the company's domestic sales were financed by the company in retail installment programs offered through the company's dealers. Installment contract receivables are recorded at the principal amount of the contracts. Interest on the contracts is recorded as income over the life of the contracts. The company has entered into agreements with an independent financial institution to sell substantially all its installment receivable contracts. The company continues to service (collect cash and perform other administrative services) all installment receivables sold. Over the lives of the contracts, the difference between the original interest earned on the contracts and the interest paid to the independent financial institution is recognized as the component labeled "Income on the sale of installment receivables." The installment contracts are written generally at fixed rates ranging from 12% to 16% with terms extending over three to five years. The interest paid to the independent financial institution is around 5%. Under the agreement with the independent financial institution, the company is required to repurchase either installment receivables that become more than 120 days past due or accounts that are deemed uncollectible.

Wurlitzer and the electronic contract business transfer title and recognize revenue at the time of shipment to their dealers and customers, respectively.

The company distributes its Wurlitzer products through approximately 400 independent dealers. The company's networks of Baldwin dealers and Wurlitzer dealers are separate and distinct, with no significant overlap. Certain Wurlitzer dealers finance their inventory from an independent bank. Dealers can borrow money from the bank based upon the value of the inventory purchased from Wurlitzer, with the musical instruments pledged as collateral. The dealers are required to pay the bank monthly interest payments and pay the principal balance after inventory is sold or if it is held longer than twelve months. The bank may request Wurlitzer to repurchase notes due from delinquent dealers. The company believes that its financial statements contain adequate provisions for any loss that may be incurred as a result of this commitment.

The electronic contract business consists of manufacturing printed circuit boards and electro-mechanical assemblies for manufacturers outside the music industry. These products were a natural extension of the company's production and those research and development capabilities developed in connection with its electronic keyboard musical instrument business. The company currently produces printed circuit boards and other electronic assemblies for a diverse group of original equipment manufacturers, which sell to the medical electronics, telecommunications, computer peripheral, specialty consumer, data communications, and industrial control markets.

Required:

1. Baldwin uses different critical events to recognize revenue from the sale of inventory for its different business segments. Identify the critical events and rank them from the most to the least conservative policy based on your judgment of the circumstances. For each source of revenue, does the chosen revenue recognition method satisfy both the critical event and the measurability criteria? If you don't have enough information, discuss what additional information is needed to form a judgment on this issue.
2. In addition to income from the sale of inventory, Baldwin also earns income from financing the sale of some of its inventories. Identify the critical event used by Baldwin to record the financing income. Discuss whether the revenue recognition method for the financing income satisfies the critical event and measurability criteria. Total financing income includes gain or loss on sale of installment receivables and interest income.

C2–4

Baldwin Piano and Organ II (KR): Analysis and interpretation of income statement

In addition to the information provided in Baldwin Piano I, consider the following information we've provided along with information from the 1993 annual report and 10-K statement of Baldwin Piano and Organ company.

BALDWIN PIANO AND ORGAN COMPANY

Income Statements for the Year Ended December 31

	1993	1992	1991
Net sales	$120,657,455	$110,076,904	$103,230,431
Cost of goods sold	(89,970,702)	(79,637,060)	(74,038,724)
Gross profit	30,686,753	30,439,844	29,191,707
Income on the sale of installment receivables	5,746,125	5,256,583	4,023,525
Interest income on installment receivables	443,431	308,220	350,058
Other operating income, net	3,530,761	3,803,228	3,768,760
	40,407,070	39,807,875	37,334,050
Operating expenses			
Selling, general, and administrative expense	(26,187,629)	(25,118,465)	(23,970,568)
Provision for doubtful accounts	(1,702,234)	(2,053,189)	(2,131,644)
Operating profit	12,517,207	12,636,221	11,231,838
Interest expense	(2,232,258)	(2,610,521)	(3,932,830)
Income before income taxes	10,284,949	10,025,700	7,299,008
Income taxes	(4,120,000)	(4,090,000)	(2,884,000)
Income before cumulative effects of change in accounting principles	6,164,949	5,935,700	4,415,008
Cumulative effect of changes in postretirement and postemployment benefits	(1,604,000)	–	–
Net income	$ 4,560,949	$ 5,935,700	$ 4,415,008

Interest income on installment receivables represents interest on receivables not sold to the independent financial institution.

The following summary table was prepared on the basis of the business segment data reported by Baldwin:

Business	Segment Revenue as a Percentage of Total Revenue 1993	1992	Segment Profit as a Percentage of Segment Revenue 1993	1992
Musical products	72.70%	81.50%	5.00%	7.60%
Electronic	22.20	13.30	14.80	13.90
Financing services	5.20	5.10	52.80	49.20

The cash flow statement indicates that the company has repaid long-term debt of about $8.6 million, $5.6 million, and $8.3 million during the years 1991, 1992, and 1993, respectively. The balance sheet indicates that the book value of the company's finished goods inventory decreased by about 8% from 1992 to 1993.

In March 1993 the contents of one of the company's finished goods warehouses were damaged by exposure to smoke from a fire adjacent to the warehouse. The company has received insurance proceeds equal to the wholesale value of the destroyed inventory. Accordingly, a gain of approximately $1,412,000 on the insurance settlement is included in the 1993 Consolidated Statements of Earnings in the component labeled "Other operating income, net."

On January 27, 1993 the company entered into an agreement in principle whereby Peridot Associates, Inc. (Peridot) would acquire all outstanding shares of the company's common stock at a per-share price of $18.25, subject to certain contingencies. The agreement expired on May 16, 1993. Under the agreement, the company was obligated to reimburse Peridot $800,000 for certain expenses incurred by Peridot. Additionally, the company incurred other expenses of approximately $305,000 related to the proposed acquisition. These combined expenses are included in the 1993 Consolidated Statements of Earnings as the component labeled "Other operating income, net."

REQUIRED:

Identify and explain the sources of the change in Baldwin's profitability from 1992 to 1993 with a view to evaluating its current earnings quality and future prospects. To what extent can this change be attributed to changes in the management's estimates?

Hint: Preparing a common-size income statement and/or year-to-year percentage change analysis of income statement items will help you formulate your response. Additional information regarding Baldwin Piano can be found in case C2–3.

3

Additional Topics in Income Determination

LEARNING OBJECTIVES:

After studying this chapter, you will understand:

1. The conditions under which it is appropriate to recognize revenues and profits either before or after the point of sale.
2. The procedures for recognizing revenue and adjusting associated asset values in three specific settings—long-term construction contracts, agricultural commodities and installment sales.
3. How the flexibility in GAAP for income determination invites earnings management.
4. The various techniques used by firms to manage earnings.
5. SEC guidance on revenue recognition designed to curb earnings management.

This chapter covers special topics in income determination. The first part of the chapter outlines the conditions and describes the accounting procedures for recognizing revenue and profit either before or after a sale occurs. The second part looks at earnings management and how firms can sometimes exploit the flexibility in GAAP to manage annual earnings up or down.

Because revenue is usually recognized at the time of sale in most industries, some people erroneously conclude that the sale is itself the *sole* criterion in recognizing revenue. This is not correct! The correct rule for recognizing revenue is more complicated and subtle. As noted in Chapter 2, revenue is recognized at the earliest moment in time that Condition 1 (the "critical event") *and* Condition 2 ("measurability") are *both* satisfied. ***The earliest moment at which Conditions 1 and 2 are both satisfied is usually the time of sale.*** That is why revenue is usually recognized when the sale is made.

But there are cases in which Conditions 1 and 2 are satisfied *before* the sale—for example, as production takes place. When this happens and when expenses are *also* measurable with a reasonable degree of assurance, GAAP allows income to be recognized before the sale.

In other circumstances Conditions 1 and 2 may not both be satisfied until *after* the time of sale—for instance, not until the cash is collected. In these cases GAAP disallows revenue recognition when the sale occurs; instead, revenue recognition is deferred until cash is received.

Revenue Recognition Prior to Sale

Percentage-of-Completion Method

Long-term construction projects—such as roads and bridges, military hardware, and costly items such as oil tankers—frequently satisfy both revenue recognition conditions prior to the time of sale.

These types of projects are usually begun only after a formal contract with a purchaser has been signed. Since a buyer for the completed project is assured, the critical event in the earning of revenue is the actual construction—that is, revenue recognition Condition 1 is satisfied as construction progresses. Furthermore, since the contract price is specified, the amount of the revenue that has been earned is measurable with a reasonable degree of assurance, thus satisfying revenue recognition Condition 2.

In many construction projects it is also possible to estimate with reasonable accuracy the cost of the project and to measure its stage of completion. Furthermore, construction contracts usually require purchasers to make progress payments to the contractor as construction progresses. These interim payment requirements help ensure that the contractor will receive payment for the work performed.

When long-term construction contracts possess all these attributes, revenue recognition Conditions 1 and 2 are both satisfied as construction progresses, and expenses can be matched against revenues to determine income. This is called the **percentage-of-completion method.** Here's how it works.

Solid Construction Corporation signs a contract with the City of Springfield on January 1, 2001 to build a highway bridge over Stony Creek. The contract price is \$1,000,000; construction costs are estimated to be \$800,000; and the project is scheduled to be completed by December 31, 2003. Periodic cash payments are to be made by the City of Springfield as construction progresses.

	Actual experience on the project as of December 31		
	2001	**2002**	**2003**
Costs incurred to date	\$240,000	\$544,000	\$ 850,000
Estimated future costs	560,000	306,000	—
Billings to date	280,000	650,000	1,000,000
Cash collections to date	210,000	600,000	1,000,000

Under the percentage-of-completion method, the profit to be recognized in any year is based on the ratio of incurred contract costs divided by estimated total contract costs. Using the data in the example, we compute the profit for 2001 using the following steps:

Step 1 **Compute the percentage-of-completion ratio by dividing costs incurred to date by estimated total costs.**

This is done to estimate the percentage of completion at any given point during the project. At the end of 2001 estimated total costs on the project are \$800,000—that is, \$240,000 of costs incurred in 2001 plus \$560,000 of estimated future costs. The cost ratio is:

$$\frac{\$240{,}000}{\$800{,}000} = 0.30 \text{ or } 30\%$$

Step 2 **Determine the estimated total profit on the contract by comparing the contract price with the estimated total costs.**

At the end of 2001 the estimated profit on the contract is still \$200,000—that is, the difference between the contract price of \$1,000,000 and estimated total costs of \$800,000.

Step 3 **Compute the estimated profit earned to date.**

The estimated profit earned to date is the cost ratio (or percentage-of-completion) computed in Step 1 multiplied by the estimated profit computed in Step 2—that is, $.30 \times \$200{,}000 = \$60{,}000$.

Notice that 30% of the total estimated costs of $800,000 have been incurred by the end of 2001, so 30% of the total estimated profit of $200,000 can be recognized in that same year—that is, profit is recognized in proportion to costs incurred. Since no profit has been recognized prior to 2001, all the $60,000 is recognizable in 2001.

Because cost estimates and completion stages change, these computations must be repeated in each subsequent year. Furthermore, the profit computation for each subsequent contract year must incorporate an additional step. The computation for 2002 illustrates this.

Step 1 **Compute the completion ratio that is determined by dividing incurred costs by estimated total costs.**

At the end of 2002 estimated total costs on this contract have risen to $850,000—$544,000 of costs incurred through 2002 plus $306,000 of estimated future costs. The cost ratio (or percentage of completion) is:

$$\frac{\$544{,}000}{\$850{,}000} = 0.64 \text{ or } 64\%$$

Step 2 **Determine the estimated profit on the contract.**

The estimated profit on the contract has now dropped to $150,000—the difference between the contract price of $1,000,000 and the newly estimated total costs of $850,000 as of the end of 2002.

Step 3 **Compute the estimated profit earned to date.**

Since 64% of the total estimated costs have already been incurred (Step 1), 64% of the revised estimated profit of $150,000 (Step 2), or $96,000, has been earned through December 31, 2002.

Notice that a portion of the profit on this contract—$60,000—has already been recognized in 2001. Therefore, only the *incremental profit* earned in 2002 should be recognized. This requires an additional computation.

Step 4 **Compute the incremental profit earned in the current year.**

The estimated total profit earned through December 31, 2002 is $96,000 (Step 3). Since $60,000 of the estimated profit was recognized on this contract in 2001, only $36,000 ($96,000 − $60,000) of additional profit can be recognized in 2002.

These four steps can be expressed succinctly using the following profit computation formula:

$$\underbrace{\left[\frac{\text{Costs incurred to date}}{\text{Estimated total costs}} \times \begin{matrix}\text{Estimated}\\ \text{total profit}\end{matrix}\right]}_{\text{Profit earned to date}} - \underbrace{\begin{matrix}\text{Profit recognized}\\ \text{in previous years}\end{matrix}}_{\text{Previously recognized profit}} = \begin{matrix}\text{Profit recognized}\\ \text{in current year}\end{matrix} \quad \textbf{(3.1)}$$

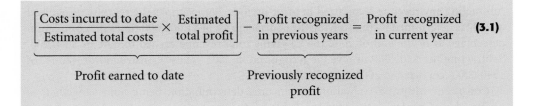

The previously recognized profit is the sum of all profits (or losses) recognized on the contract in prior years—that is, the sum of all profits (or losses) that were determined by multiplying the cost-completion ratio by the total profit estimated at those earlier dates. Again, the reason for subtracting this amount from the profit-earned-to-date figure is to avoid double-counting profits recognized in prior years.

Repeating the computations for 2001 and 2002 using the formula in equation (3.1) gives the following results:

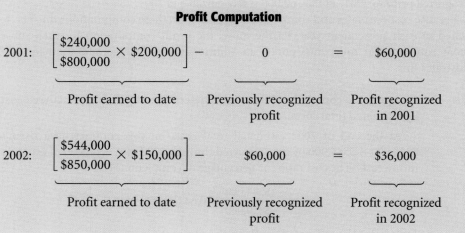

Profit Computation

$$2001: \quad \underbrace{\left[\frac{\$240{,}000}{\$800{,}000} \times \$200{,}000\right]}_{\text{Profit earned to date}} - \underbrace{0}_{\text{Previously recognized profit}} = \underbrace{\$60{,}000}_{\text{Profit recognized in 2001}}$$

$$2002: \quad \underbrace{\left[\frac{\$544{,}000}{\$850{,}000} \times \$150{,}000\right]}_{\text{Profit earned to date}} - \underbrace{\$60{,}000}_{\text{Previously recognized profit}} = \underbrace{\$36{,}000}_{\text{Profit recognized in 2002}}$$

Of course, these results are identical to those derived using the multiple-step approach illustrated previously. The computation for 2003 would be:

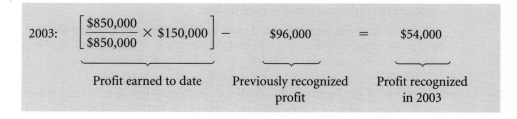

$$2003: \quad \underbrace{\left[\frac{\$850{,}000}{\$850{,}000} \times \$150{,}000\right]}_{\text{Profit earned to date}} - \underbrace{\$96{,}000}_{\text{Previously recognized profit}} = \underbrace{\$54{,}000}_{\text{Profit recognized in 2003}}$$

Using percentage-of-completion, the cumulative profit recognized over the three years totals \$150,000 (\$60,000 + \$36,000 + \$54,000). This total equals the difference between the contract price of \$1,000,000 and the actual costs of \$850,000.

The journal entries shown in Exhibit 3.1 would be used to record these events on the books of Solid Construction Corporation.

Entries (2) and (3) of Exhibit 3.1 require elaboration. Income is recognized in entry (2) using the income recognition formula of equation (3.1). An alternative to entry (2) which provides more detailed information is to separately record the construction expense as shown in Exhibit 3.1. The amount debited to "Construction expense" each period is the actual construction costs incurred in that period. The credit to "Construction revenue" is determined by multiplying the total contract price by the completion percentage and then subtracting any revenue recognized in prior periods. For example, the revenue recognized in 2002 is determined by multiplying the contract price of \$1,000,000 times the completion percentage as of the end of 2002 (64%) giving total revenue earned to date of \$640,000. Subtracting the \$300,000 of revenue recognized in 2001 yields "Construction revenue" of \$340,000 recognized in 2002.

Consistent with asset valuation and income determination being linked together, as discussed in Chapter 2, the carrying value of net assets is also increased as income is recognized. This is why the entry (2) debit increases the "Construction in progress" account, which is a part of inventory. Thus, entry (2) reflects the dual financial statement impact of income recognition: ***both net assets and income increase.***

In entry (3) the account labeled "Billings on construction in progress" is a contra-account (reduction) to the inventory subcomponent labeled "Construction in progress." The net of these two accounts is shown as a current asset (if there is a debit balance) or as a

Exhibit 3.1 ■ SOLID CONSTRUCTION CORPORATION

Journal Entries
Percentage-of-Completion Method

	2001		2002		2003	
(1) To record costs incurred						
DR Inventory: Construction in progress	$240,000		$304,000		$ 306,000	
CR Accounts payable, cash, etc.		$240,000		$304,000		$ 306,000
(2) To record income recognized						
DR Inventory: Construction in progress	$ 60,000		$ 36,000		$ 54,000	
CR Income on long-term construction contract		$ 60,000		$ 36,000		$ 54,000
Alternative entry						
DR Inventory: Construction in progress	$ 60,000[1]		$ 36,000[1]		$ 54,000[1]	
DR Construction expense	240,000[2]		304,000[2]		306,000[2]	
CR Construction revenue		$300,000[3]		$340,000[3]		$ 360,000[3]
[1]Gross profit earned in current period	30% × ($1,000,000 − $800,000)		64% × ($1,000,000 − $850,000) − $60,000		($1,000,000 − $850,000) − $96,000	
[2]Actual construction costs incurred in current period	$ 240,000		$544,000 − $240,000		$850,000 − $544,000	
[3]Revenues earned in current period	30% × $1,000,000		(64% × $1,000,000) − $ 300,000		$1,000,000 − $300,000 − $340,000	
(3) To record customer billings						
DR Accounts receivable	$280,000		$370,000		$ 350,000	
CR Billings on construction in progress		$280,000		$370,000		$ 350,000
(4) To record cash received						
DR Cash	$210,000		$390,000		$ 400,000	
CR Accounts receivable		$210,000		$390,000		$ 400,000
(5) To record completion and acceptance of the project						
DR Billings on construction in progress					$1,000,000	
CR Construction in progress						$1,000,000

current liability (if there is a credit balance). In our example, the balance sheet presentation for Solid Construction Corporation would be as follows for 2001 and 2002:

2001		
Current Assets		
Accounts receivable		$70,000
Inventory: Construction in progress	$300,000	
Less: Billings on construction in progress	(280,000)	
		$20,000

2002		
Current Assets		
Accounts receivable		$50,000
Current Liabilities		
Inventory: Construction in progress	($640,000)	
Less: Billings on construction in progress	650,000	
		$10,000

The component "Billings on construction in progress" must be treated as a contra-inventory account to avoid balance sheet double-counting. Typically, a sale results in a receivable being recognized and a simultaneous decrease in inventory. However, inventory is not reduced in long-term construction accounting since the sale is not made until completion. The contra-account treatment avoids including certain costs and profits twice—once in inventory ("Inventory: Construction in progress") and a second time in the receivables account.

Finally, although profits are recognized proportionately as construction progresses, ***estimated losses on a contract are recognized in their entirety as soon as it becomes known that a contract loss will ensue.***

In our example, income is recognized by using the ratio of incurred costs divided by estimated total costs. This cost ratio is widely used since it provides a simple index of progress toward completion—i.e., work done to date. However, there are situations in which this cost ratio may not accurately reflect construction progress. For example, consider a case in which raw materials to be used in construction are stockpiled in advance of use. In such situations costs are being incurred as the raw materials are received and recorded on the books. Yet these costs do not increase the stage of completion until the raw materials are actually *used.* In projects in which this stockpiling is significant, some other means for measuring progress toward completion would be preferable. Possibilities include labor hours worked or various output measures (such as miles of roadway completed).

Completed-Contract Method

There are cases in which it is not possible to determine expected costs with a high degree of reliability under long-term construction contracts, making the use of the percentage-of-completion method inappropriate. In these situations, the **completed-contract method** is used instead.

The completed-contract method defers recognition of income until the project is completed. Journal entries under the completed-contract method are identical to those illustrated previously for the percentage-of-completion method except that entry (2) in Exhibit 3.1, which records income as construction progresses, is omitted. Instead, all the income on the contract is recognized when the contract is completed. The entry for recognizing income under the completed-contract method in 2003 is shown at the top of the facing page.

DR Billings on construction in progress	$1,000,000	
CR Construction in progress		$850,000
CR Income on long-term construction contract		150,000

Although income is recognized only on completion, losses are recognized in their entirety as soon as their probable existence is known.

Table 3.1 illustrates that total income for the three years is the same under both the completed-contract method and the percentage-of-completion method ($150,000). However, the timing of income recognition differs considerably.

Table 3.1 ■ YEARLY INCOME COMPARISON OF TWO LONG-TERM CONTRACT ACCOUNTING METHODS

Year	Completed-Contract Method	Percentage-of-Completion Method
2001	−0−	$ 60,000
2002	−0−	36,000
2003	$150,000	54,000
Total income	$150,000	$150,000

The net asset balance at intermediate construction stages will also differ between the two methods. As shown in column (g) of Table 3.2, ***the amount of this net asset balance difference in any year is precisely equal to the difference in cumulative profit recognized on each basis.*** This difference in net asset balances exists because the recognition of income has a corresponding effect on net asset balances.

Revenue Recognition on Commodities

The timing of revenue recognition for producers of agricultural and mining commodities raises some interesting issues. There is general agreement that in both mining and farming, the critical event in adding value usually comes *before* the actual sale. The critical event in mining is extracting the resource from the ground. In agriculture the critical event is harvest. (The critical event is harvest, since prior to harvest the crop may still be lost because of drought, hail, insects, or disease. Only after the crop is safely out of the field have these income threatening possibilities been avoided.) Thus, revenue recognition Condition 1 is satisfied prior to the sale itself.

Table 3.2 ■ COMPARATIVE ACCOUNT BALANCES

Percentage-of-Completion Versus Completed-Contract Method

December 31, Year-End Account Balances

	Completed-Contract Method			Percentage-of-Completion Method			
	(a) Construction in Progress	(b) Billings	(c) Net Asset Balance Col. (a) − Col. (b)	(d) Construction in Progress	(e) Billings	(f) Net Asset Balance Col. (d) − Col. (e)	(g) Difference in Net Asset Balances Between Methods Col. (f) − Col. (c)
2001	$240,000	$280,000	$− 40,000	$300,000	$280,000	$+20,000	$+60,000[1]
2002	544,000	650,000	−106,000	640,000	650,000	−10,000	+96,000[2]
2003	−0−	−0−	−0−	−0−	−0−	−0−	−0−

[1]Also equals difference between cumulative profit on percentage-of-completion method ($60,000) and the completed-contract method ($0) from Table 3.1.
[2]Also equals difference between cumulative profit on percentage-of-completion method ($60,000 + $36,000 = $96,000) and the completed-contract method ($0 + $0) from Table 3.1.

However, the precise time at which revenue recognition Condition 2 ("measurability") is satisfied for commodities producers is open to some dispute. The following example explores the issues.

A farmer harvests 110,000 bushels of corn on September 30, 2001. On this date the posted market price per bushel was $3.50. The total cost of growing the crop was $220,000, or $2.00 per bushel. The farmer decides to sell 100,000 bushels for cash on September 30 at the posted price of $3.50 and stores the remaining 10,000 bushels. On January 2, 2002 the market price drops to $3.00. Fearing further price declines, the farmer immediately sells the bushels in storage at a price of $3.00 per bushel.

Completed-Transaction (Sales) Method The timing of revenue recognition on the 100,000 bushels of corn that were sold on September 30 is straightforward. Revenue recognition Conditions 1 and 2 are both satisfied at September 30, and income would be recognized at the time of sale. The income statement would show:

2001 Income Statement	
Revenues (sale of 100,000 bushels at a market price of $3.50 per bushel)	$ 350,000
Expenses (costs of $2.00 per bushel for 100,000 bushels sold)	(200,000)
Income from sale	$ 150,000

Under the traditional view, which we call the **completed-transaction (sales) method,** no income would be recognized at September 30 on the 10,000 bushels that were harvested but not sold. For these 10,000 bushels, revenue recognition Condition 2 is considered not to have been met since the eventual selling price is still unknown—that is, the sale transaction is not yet completed. The bushels in storage would be reflected on the farmer's balance sheet at their *cost* of $20,000 ($2.00 per bushel × 10,000 bushels).

When the bushels in storage are sold in 2002, the income statement would reflect a profit on the sale of the 10,000 bushels:

As costs are incurred during the year, the direct costs of crop production—things like seed, fertilizer, fuel and depreciation on machinery—are charged to a "Production in process" or "Crop inventory" account with offsetting credits to Cash, Accounts payable or Accumulated depreciation.

2002 Income Statement	
Revenues (sale of 10,000 bushels at a market price of $3.00 per bushel)	$ 30,000
Expenses (costs of $2.00 per bushel for 10,000 bushels sold)	(20,000)
Income from sale	$ 10,000

Note the traditional approach avoids recognizing any income on the 10,000 unsold bushels until the sales transaction is completed in 2002.

Market Price (Production) Method There is another way for measuring income in the previous example. This alternative recognizes that well-organized markets exist for most agricultural and many mining commodities. In addition, the quantities offered for sale by any individual producer are usually very small in relation to the total size of the market. Producers face an established price for as many units as they choose to sell. These factors mean that a readily determinable market price at which output *could be sold* is continuously available. In this view, revenue recognition Condition 2 ("measurability") is satisfied prior to the actual sale of actively traded commodities.

Since revenue recognition Condition 1 ("critical event") occurs at harvest, both conditions necessary to recognize revenue are satisfied as soon as the crop is safely out of the field (i.e., at the point of production). Thus, farming income on all 110,000 bushels is recognized under this approach on September 30:

Revenues (100,000 bushels sold at a market price of $3.50)	$ 350,000
Expenses (costs of $2.00 per bushel for 100,000 bushels sold)	(200,000)
Market gain on unsold inventory (10,000 bushels times the difference between the $3.50 market price at the date of harvest and the $2.00 cost per bushel)	15,000
Total income from farming activities	$ 165,000

This **market price (or production) method** recognizes farming income on the 10,000 unsold bushels as well as on the 100,000 bushels sold. This view emphasizes the fact that the farmer *could have sold* these 10,000 bushels at the time of harvest for a readily determinable price of $3.50 per bushel. Since the critical event in farming is harvest and since the potential sales price at the time of harvest is known, both revenue recognition conditions relating to farming are deemed to be satisfied on September 30. Therefore, farming income of $165,000 is immediately determinable.

Under the market price method, the bushels in storage are reflected on the farmer's balance sheet at $35,000 ($3.50 market price at harvest times 10,000 bushels). If the corn was initially carried at its *cost* of $20,000 ($2.00 per bushel times 10,000 bushels), the entry necessary to reflect the value added by farming is:

DR Crop inventory	$15,000	
CR Market gain on unsold inventory		$15,000

The credit would appear as shown on the income statement for 2001.

After the corn is harvested, the activity called farming has ended. However, this farmer is actually engaged in another business in addition to farming. By withholding 10,000 bushels from the market, the farmer is also pursuing a separate (nonfarming) activity called **speculation.** This speculation is undertaken in the hope that prices will rise above their September 30 level of $3.50 per bushel. Subsequent changes in the market price of corn will thus give rise to speculative gains or losses—also called **inventory holding gains and losses.**

To illustrate, recollect that at the start of 2002, the market price of corn drops from $3.50 to $3.00 per bushel. This decline in price gives rise to a speculative (holding) loss in 2002 of $5,000 (a decline of $0.50 per bushel times 10,000 bushels). The inventory is marked-to-market, and the journal entry to reflect the loss is:

DR Inventory (holding) loss on speculation	$5,000	
CR Crop inventory		$5,000

After this entry is posted, the carrying value of the inventory is now reduced to $30,000 (10,000 bushels times $3.00 per bushel).

Fearing further price declines, the farmer immediately sells the remaining 10,000 bushels at $3.00 on January 2. The entry is:

DR Cost of goods sold	$30,000	
CR Crop inventory		$30,000
DR Cash	$30,000	
CR Crop Revenue		$30,000

Comparison: Completed-Transaction (Sales) and Market Price (Production) Methods Although total income over the two periods is the same under each approach, the income recognized in each period is not the same, and the activities to which the income is attributed also differ:

Completed-Transaction (Sales) Method			Market Price (Production) Method	
Income from sales	$150,000	**2001**	Income from farming activities	$165,000
Income from sales	10,000	**2002**	Holding loss on speculation	(5,000)
Total income	$160,000		Total income	$160,000

The completed-transaction (sales) method avoids recognizing any income on the 10,000 unsold bushels until the transaction is completed (when the grain is sold). However, in emphasizing completed transactions, this traditional approach—the completed-transaction method—merges the results of the farmer's speculative and farming activities and does not reflect the separate results of either.

This example illustrates why income recognition can be controversial. In practice the completed-transaction method is far more prevalent. However, the market price method is deemed to be in conformity with generally accepted accounting principles when readily determinable market values are continuously available. The market price method has the dual advantages of (1) explicitly recognizing the separate results arising from the farming and speculative activities that the farmer is engaged in, and (2) conforming more closely to the income recognition conditions introduced in Chapter 2.

For long-term construction contracts and commodities (natural resources and agricultural products), the two conditions for revenue recognition—"critical event" and "measurability"—are frequently satisfied prior to sale. The percentage-of-completion method recognizes revenue and profits (losses) on long-term construction contracts as work progresses. The market price (production) method recognizes the difference between the cost of the natural resource or agricultural commodity and its prevailing market price as income at the time of production or harvest. In both cases an inventory account—"Construction in progress" for long-term construction contracts and "Crop inventory" for commodities—is debited to reflect the increase in value that is recognized on the income statement, thereby maintaining the linkage between income determination and asset valuation.

RECAP

Revenue Recognition Subsequent to Sale

Installment Sales Method

Sometimes revenue is not recognized even though a valid sale has taken place. This accounting treatment is acceptable only under highly unusual circumstances. One instance in which revenue recognition might be delayed beyond the point of sale is when sales are made under very extended cash collection terms. Examples include installment sales of consumer durables and retail land sales of vacation or retirement property. A lengthy collection period considerably increases the risk of nonpayment. ***Where the risk of noncollection is unusually high and where there is no reasonable basis for estimating the proportion of installment accounts likely to prove uncollectible, then revenue recognition may be deferred.***

When these extreme risk situations exist, neither of the two revenue recognition conditions are satisfied. Specifically, when it's highly uncertain that customers will make the cash payments called for in the contract, then the sale itself is not the critical event in creating value. In such circumstances the actual cash collection is the critical event, and revenue recognition Condition 1 is satisfied only as the amounts due from customers are received. Similarly, revenue recognition Condition 2 is not satisfied either since the amount ultimately collectible from customers is not measurable with a reasonable degree of certainty at the time of sale.

Since Conditions 1 and 2 are both satisfied only over time as cash collections take place, a revenue recognition method tied to cash collections has been devised to deal with such situations. This revenue recognition approach is called the **installment sales method.**

Installment Sales Method Illustrated The installment sales method recognizes revenue and income proportionately as cash is collected. The amount recognized in any period is based on two factors:

1. The installment-sales gross-profit percentage (gross profit/sales).
2. The amount of cash collected on installment accounts receivable.

Here's an example of revenue and income recognition under the installment sales method:

	2001	2002
Installment sales	$1,200,000	$1,300,000
Cost of installment goods sold	840,000	884,000
Gross profit	$ 360,000	$ 416,000
Gross profit percentage	30%	32%
Cash collections		
On 2001 installment sales	$ 300,000	$ 600,000
On 2002 installment sales		340,000

During 2001 installment sales of $1,200,000 were made. The potential gross profit on these sales was $360,000. The installment contracts call for cash payments over each of the next four years. Because of the extreme uncertainties regarding ultimate collectibility, this gross profit will be recognized only as customers pay on their accounts. Since $300,000 of cash was collected in 2001, the gross profit recognized in 2001 will be $90,000—that is, $300,000 multiplied by 30%, the gross profit percentage (gross profit/sales) on 2001 installment sales. This $90,000 is shown on the 2001 income statement as 2001 income from installment sales. The difference between the total potential gross profit of $360,000 and the $90,000 of recognized income—or $270,000—is deferred gross profit (see entries [4] and [5] in Exhibit 3.2 on the following page).

Income recognized in 2002 from installment sales comprises two components:

1. A component relating to 2002 cash collections on 2001 installment sales.
2. A component relating to 2002 cash collections on 2002 installment sales.

The computation for installment sales income recognized in 2002 is:

Total 2002 Installment Sales Income	Gross Profit Recognized
Component relating to 2001 sales	
Cash collections in year 2002 from 2001 sales	$600,000
Multiplied by year 2001 gross profit percentage	30%
	$180,000
Component relating to year 2002 sales	
Cash collections in year 2002 from 2002 sales	$340,000
Multiplied by year 2002 gross profit percentage	32%
	$108,800
Total installment sales income recognized in year 2002	$288,800

Journal entries to record these facts for years 2001 and 2002 are shown in Exhibit 3.2.

Exhibit 3.2 ■ INSTALLMENT SALES METHOD

Journal Entries

	2001		2002	
(1) To record installment sales				
DR Accounts receivable—2001 installment sales	$1,200,000			
DR Accounts receivable—2002 installment sales			$1,300,000	
CR Installment sales revenue		$1,200,000		$1,300,000
(2) To record cost of goods sold				
DR Cost of installment goods sold	$ 840,000		$ 884,000	
CR Inventory		$ 840,000		$ 884,000
(3) To record cash collections				
DR Cash	$ 300,000		$ 940,000	
CR Accounts receivable—2001 installment sales		$ 300,000		$ 600,000
CR Accounts receivable—2002 installment sales				340,000
(4) To defer gross profit on portion of current-period sales that are not yet collected				
DR Deferred gross profit (income statement)	$ 270,000		$ 307,200	
CR Deferred gross profit—Adjustment to accounts receivable		$ 270,000		$ 307,200
(5) To recognize realized gross profit on installment sales of prior periods				
DR Deferred gross profit—Adjustment to accounts receivable			$ 180,000	
CR Recognized gross profit on installment sales—prior year				$ 180,000

The income statement would appear as follows:

	2001	2002
Installment sales	$1,200,000	$1,300,000
Cost of installment goods sold	(840,000)	(884,000)
Gross profit	360,000	416,000
Less: Deferred gross profit on installment sales of current year	(270,000)	(307,200)
Gross profit recognized on current year's sales	90,000	108,800
Plus: Gross profit recognized on installment sales of prior years	–	180,000
Total gross profit recognized this year	$ 90,000	$ 288,800

Some additional internal record keeping is necessary when applying the installment sales method. Installment sales and the related cost of goods sold must be tracked by individual year in order to compute the gross profit percentage that applies to each year. In addition, the accounting system must match cash collections with the specific sales year to which the cash collections relate. This matching is needed in order to apply the correct gross profit percentage to cash receipts.

On the balance sheet, the "Accounts receivable—installment sales" components are classified as current assets if they are due within 12 months of the balance sheet date. Amounts not expected to be collected within the next year may also be classified as current assets if installment sales are a normal part of the company's operations, since the company's operating cycle would include the installment collection period. Existing practice typically classifies the deferred gross profit account as a contra-asset, which is shown as a reduction to accounts receivable.

Selling, general, and administrative expenses relating to installment sales are treated as period costs—that is, as costs that are expensed in the period in which they are incurred—because they provide no future benefits. This treatment is consistent with the manner in which period costs are handled for normal (non-installment) sales.

Interest on Installment Contracts The essence of an installment sales contract is that the cash payments arising from the sale are spread over multiple periods. Because of this delay in receiving the sales proceeds, sellers charge interest on installment sales contracts. Consequently, the required monthly or quarterly installment payments include both interest and principal. This complication was omitted from the example we just illustrated. GAAP requires that the interest component of the periodic cash proceeds must be recorded separately. This means that interest payments are not considered when computing the recognized gross profit on installment sales. Chapter 8 outlines the procedures for differentiating between principal and interest payments on customer receivables.

The installment sales method of revenue recognition is used when the risk of non-collection is high or when it is impractical to estimate the amount of uncollectibles. Under the installment sales method, the gross profit on sales is deferred and recognized in income in subsequent periods—that is, when the installment receivables are collected in cash. The linkage between income determination and asset valuation is maintained by showing deferred gross profit as a contra-account (reduction) to installment accounts receivable.

RECAP

Earnings Management

"Executives rarely have to violate the law to put a gloss on dreary earnings. Accepted accounting principles leave ample room for those who want to fudge the numbers."[1]

The criteria for revenue and expense recognition outlined in Chapter 2 provide general guidelines for accrual accounting income determination. But applying these rules in specific settings still leaves room for considerable latitude and judgment. For example, determining when revenue has been earned (critical event) and is realizable (measurability)—the two conditions for revenue recognition—are often judgment calls. Managers can sometimes exploit the flexibility in GAAP to manipulate reported earnings in ways that mask the underlying performance of the company. Some managers have even resorted to outright financial fraud to inflate reported earnings, but this is relatively rare.

The growing propensity of managers to bolster earnings by exploiting the flexibility in GAAP or by resorting to financial fraud recently led former SEC Chairman Arthur Levitt to warn:

> "Increasingly, I have become concerned that the motivation to meet Wall Street earnings expectations may be overriding common sense business practices. Too many corporate managers, auditors, and analysts are participating in a game of nods and winks. In the zeal to satisfy consensus earnings estimates and project a smooth earnings path, wishful thinking may be winning the day over faithful representation. As a result, I fear that we are witnessing an erosion in the quality of earnings, and therefore, the quality of financial reporting. Managing may be giving way to manipulation; integrity may be losing to illusion."[2]

[1] F. S. Worthy, "Manipulating Profits: How It's Done," *Fortune,* June 25, 1984, pp. 50–54.

[2] Statements made by Arthur Levitt, Chairman of the Securities and Exchange Commission, in a speech entitled, "The Numbers Game," delivered at the New York University Center for Law and Business, September 28, 1998.

Earnings management is not new. But the perception is that it has become increasingly common in today's marketplace because of pressure to meet analysts' earnings forecasts. Companies that miss analysts' earnings per share estimates by even a few pennies frequently experience significant stock price declines. Several highly publicized examples of alleged accounting "irregularities"[3] and recent research studies[4] lend support to Chairman Levitt's concerns about earnings management.

One way to avoid a market penalty for reporting a loss is to make sure to report a profit—real or artificial. Results from a recent research study suggest that artificially inflating earnings is a common occurrence, especially for firms that would otherwise report small losses.[5] Figure 3.1(a) shows a frequency distribution of annual reported earnings for a large number of firms over a 20-year period. The horizontal axis represents groupings of reported earnings divided by beginning-of-year market value of equity. The interval width of each grouping is 0.005. Thus, the grouping labeled −1 includes scaled earnings from −.005 to just less than .000, grouping 0 contains values from .000 to just less than +.005, while grouping +1 contains values from +.005 to just less than +.010. The vertical axis measures the number of firms whose reported earnings fall into the various categories.

> Let's use a number example for clarity. Assume Hong Company reports 2001 earnings of $500,000 and the market value of its equity on January 1, 2001 was $62,500,000. Thus, $500,000 ÷ $62,500,000 = .008. Since .008 is within the interval of .005 to .010, Hong Company would appear in interval +1.

The striking feature of this graph is the discontinuity in the number of firms reporting slightly negative earnings versus slightly positive earnings. Substantially fewer firms fall just

Figure 3.1(a)

DISTRIBUTION OF ANNUAL NET INCOME

Source: P. Dechow, S. Richardson and A. Tuna (see footnote 4).

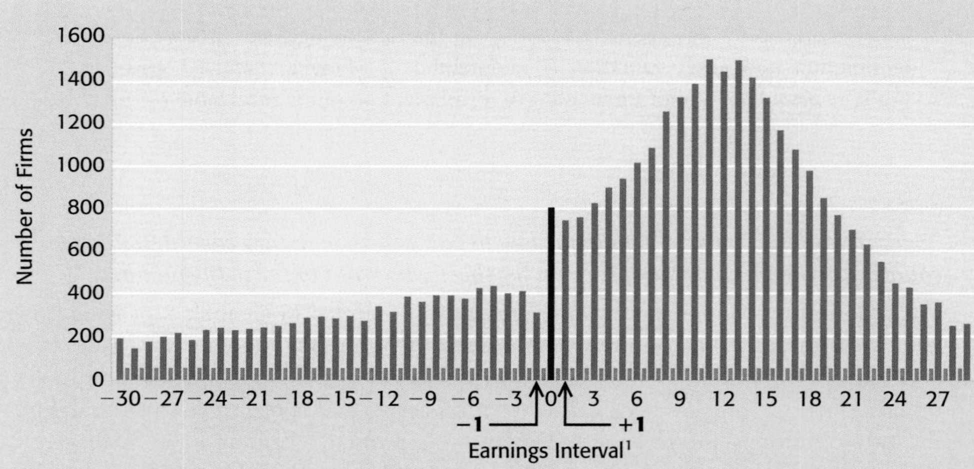

[1]Earnings intervals are based on annual net income divided by beginning-of-year market value of equity. The interval width is .005, e.g., interval −1 includes values from −.005 to just less than .000, while interval +1 includes values from +.005 to just less than +.010.

(a)

[3] D. Bank, "Informix Says Accounting Problems Were More Serious Than First Disclosed," the *Wall Street Journal,* September 23, 1997; T. O'Brien, "KnowledgeWare Accounting Practices Are Questioned," the *Wall Street Journal,* September 7, 1994; M. Maremont, "Anatomy of a Fraud: How Kurzweil's Straight-Arrow CEO Went Awry," *Business Week,* September 16, 1996, pp. 90–93; S. Lipin, "How Telxon Corp. Came to Restate Earnings," the *Wall Street Journal,* December 23, 1998; J. Laing, "Dangerous Games: Did 'Chainsaw Al' Dunlap Manufacture Sunbeam's Earnings Last Year?" *Barron's Online,* June 8, 1998, pp. 1–8; E. Nelson and J. Lublin, "Whistle-Blowers Set Off Cendant Probe," the *Wall Street Journal,* August 13, 1998, p. A1.

[4] D. Burgstahler and I. Dichev, "Earnings Management to Avoid Earnings Decreases and Losses," *Journal of Accounting and Economics* (December 1997), pp. 99–126; F. Degeorge, J. Patel, R. Zeckhauser, "Earnings Management to Exceed Thresholds," *Journal of Business* (January, 1999), pp. 1–33; P. Dechow, S. Richardson, and A. Tuna, "Are Benchmark Beaters Doing Anything Wrong?" Working Paper, University of Michigan Business School, April 2000.

[5] Dechow et al., op. cit.

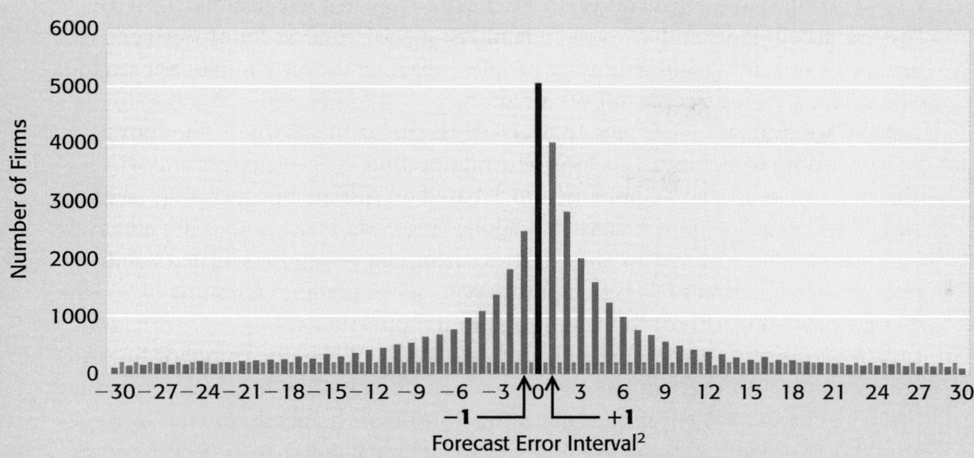

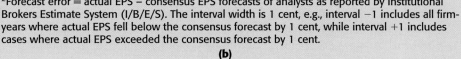

[2]Forecast error = actual EPS − consensus EPS forecasts of analysts as reported by Institutional Brokers Estimate System (I/B/E/S). The interval width is 1 cent, e.g., interval −1 includes all firm-years where actual EPS fell below the consensus forecast by 1 cent, while interval +1 includes cases where actual EPS exceeded the consensus forecast by 1 cent.

(b)

Figure 3.1(b)

DISTRIBUTION OF ANNUAL FORECAST ERRORS (IN CENTS) AS REPORTED BY I/B/E/S

Source: P. Dechow, S. Richardson and A. Tuna (see footnote 4).

below zero (grouping −1) compared to those reporting earnings at or just above zero (groupings 0 and +1). This suggests that managers try to avoid reporting losses. One way of doing so even in troubled times is to exploit the flexibility in GAAP to push earnings into the positive range.

As noted above, investors often penalize companies that fail to meet analysts' earnings expectations. Figure 3.1(b) reflects the strong incentive managers have to meet or beat analysts' earnings estimates. This graph shows the distribution of analysts' annual earnings per share (EPS) forecast errors—that is, actual EPS minus analysts' consensus EPS estimate. The interval width of each bar is one cent. Thus, forecast error bar −1 (+1) reflects the number of firm-years where actual earnings per share falls below (above) the analysts' consensus forecasts by 1 cent. Note the large number of observations clustered in the zero forecast error interval where actual EPS equals the consensus estimate. Also, note the much smaller number of forecast errors that fall in the bar just below zero (−1) compared to the number that fall just above zero (+1). One explanation of this result is that some companies are managing earnings upward to "meet or beat" analysts' earnings projections.

The analysts' consensus EPS estimates come from I/B/E/S. This acronym stands for Institutional Brokers Estimate System and provides institutional analyst earnings per share forecasts (both annual and quarterly) for over 18,000 companies in over 50 countries.

Popular Earnings Management Devices

What are some of the more popular techniques firms use to manage earnings? Former Chairman Levitt singles out five areas that the SEC finds particularly troublesome and pervasive.[6]

- *"Big Bath" restructuring charges:* The 1990s was the decade of **restructuring** in corporate America. To remain competitive and become more efficient, hundreds of companies closed plants, consolidated operations, reduced their labor force and sold off non-core business units. Once a decision to restructure is made, GAAP requires companies to estimate the future costs they expect to incur to carry out the restructuring—for such things as employee severance payments and plant closings. These estimated restructuring costs are then charged to an expense account with an off-setting credit to a liability account ("Restructuring reserve") in the current period. In an effort to "clean up" company balance sheets, managers have often taken excessive restructuring write-offs and overstated estimated charges for future expenditures. Examples of questionable items that the SEC has found in

[6] Levitt, op. cit.

restructuring charges include services to be provided in some future period by lawyers, accountants and investment bankers; special bonuses for officers; and expenses for retraining and relocating people. Amazingly, some companies even took charges for training people not yet hired!

Why are companies tempted to overstate restructuring charges? The conventional wisdom is that investors look beyond one-time special charges and write-offs and, instead, value a company's stock based on sustainable operating earnings (see Chapter 6). So, many believe that taking "big bath" charges does not adversely affect stock price.[7] Moreover, these restructuring charges and associated liability reserves are sometimes reversed in future years when earnings fall short of targets, thereby providing a boost to the bottom line at opportune times.

- *Creative acquisition accounting and purchased R&D:* When one company buys another company and uses the **purchase method** of accounting for the combination (see Chapter 16), the buyer must allocate a portion of the purchase price to the acquired firm's identifiable net assets, including intangibles like in-process (incomplete) research and development (R&D) activities. *Statement of Financial Standards (SFAS) No. 2* states that "while future benefits from a particular research and development project may be foreseen, they generally cannot be measured with a reasonable degree of certainty."[8] Accordingly, values assigned to R&D projects that have no alternative future use are immediately expensed (i.e., in the period in which the acquisition occurs). This treatment results in an economic asset (potential benefits from in-process R&D) that never appears on the balance sheet. If and when revenues from these R&D investments materialize, there are no offsetting charges to expense because the cost of the purchased R&D was written off in the period acquired. This is a classic example of mismatching revenues and expenses that gives the appearance of excessive profitability in later years.

  The fair value of in-process R&D is difficult to measure and, therefore, difficult to verify. This creates considerable opportunity to manage post-acquisition earnings by allocating a disproportionate share of the initial purchase price to in-process R&D. This problem has been particularly acute for acquisitions of technology and software development companies where a major portion of the purchase price has been allocated to in-process R&D activities that are then immediately written off.
- *Miscellaneous "cookie jar reserves":* Accrual accounting allows companies to estimate and accrue for obligations that will be paid in *future periods* as a result of transactions or events in the *current period.* Similar reserves are allowed for estimated declines in asset values. Examples include provisions for bad debts and loan losses, warranty costs, sales returns and reserves for various future expenditures related to corporate restructuring. Some companies use unrealistic assumptions to arrive at these estimated charges. They over-reserve in good times and cut back on estimated charges, or even reverse previous charges, in bad times. As a result, these "cookie jar reserves" become a convenient income smoothing device.
- *Intentional errors deemed to be "immaterial" and intentional bias in estimates:* Materiality thresholds are another way of using financial reporting flexibility to inflate earnings. Sometimes, companies intentionally misapply GAAP—e.g., capitalizing an expenditure that should be expensed. If this incorrect treatment is subsequently caught by the auditor, management might justify the error by arguing that the earnings effect is "immaterial" and, therefore, not worth correcting. The problem, of course, is that a series of these "immaterial" errors spread across several accounts can, in the aggregate, have a material affect on bottom line earnings.

---

[7] J. Elliott and D. Hanna, "Repeated Accounting Write-Offs and the Information Content of Earnings," *Journal of Accounting Research, Supplement,* 1996, pp. 135–155.

[8] "Accounting for Research and Development Costs," *Statement of Financial Accounting Standards (SFAS) No. 2* (Stamford, CT: Financial Accounting Standards Board [FASB], 1974), para. 45.

Intentional misstatement of estimates is another area of abuse. Estimates abound in accrual accounting. Examples include estimated useful lives and salvage values for fixed assets, estimates of bad debts, and the amount of write-down for obsolete inventory. Management can often shade these estimates in one direction or the other to achieve a desired earnings target. As long as these estimates fall within "acceptable" ranges, the biased estimate is unlikely to draw attention from the external auditor.

- *Premature or aggressive revenue recognition:* Another common abuse is to recognize revenues before they have been "earned" (the critical event criterion) or become "realized" (the measurability criterion). This important earnings management device is discussed in the next section.

Revenue Recognition Abuses The SEC says that revenue is earned (critical event) and is realized or realizable (measurability)–and, therefore, can be recognized–when all of the following criteria are met:

1. Persuasive evidence of an exchange arrangement exists,
2. Delivery has occurred or services have been rendered,
3. The seller's price to the buyer is fixed or determinable, and
4. Collectibility is reasonably assured.

"Arrangement" means there is a final understanding between the parties as to the specific nature and terms of the agreed-upon transaction.

The following scenarios taken from a recent SEC Staff Accounting Bulletin (SAB) illustrate some troublesome areas of revenue recognition as well as the SEC's interpretive response as to the appropriate treatment.[9]

- ***Scenario 1—Goods shipped on consignment:*** A software manufacturer (seller) ships 100,000 copies of a new video game to distributors, charging $50 per copy. Under terms of the signed agreement, distributors have the right (a) to return unsold copies of the video game, and (b) not to pay the seller until they resell the product to final customers through their retail outlets. The software manufacturer wants to recognize $5,000,000 of revenue upon delivery of the video games to the distributors. Can the company do this?

  SEC interpretive response: No revenue can be recognized on delivery. The reason is the seller retains the risks and rewards of ownership of the product. Title does not pass to the distributor when the goods are shipped. Also, under criterion 4 above, there is considerable uncertainty as to ultimate collectibility of the sales price on the goods shipped.
- ***Scenario 2—Sales with delayed delivery:*** Prior to the close of its September 30 fiscal quarter, a manufacturer (seller) completes production of 50,000 specialized gas valves. The valves sell for $60 each and were ordered by customers that assemble and sell gas fireplaces. The customers are unable to take delivery by September 30 for reasons that include: (1) lack of available storage space, (2) having ample inventory on hand to cover production for the next month, and (3) delayed production schedules. The seller segregates the valves awaiting shipment from other unsold products in its own warehouse and wishes to recognize $3,000,000 of revenue in the current quarter from these goods produced, but not shipped.

  SEC interpretive response: Without further conditions being spelled out in the sales agreement (criterion 1), the seller cannot recognize revenue until delivery has taken place (criterion 2). Generally, delivery is *not* considered to have occurred unless the customer (a) takes title, and (b) assumes the risks and rewards of ownership of the products. Typically, this occurs when a product is received at the

[9] "Revenue Recognition in Financial Statements," *Staff Accounting Bulletin No. 101* (Washington, D.C., Securities and Exchange Commission, December 3, 1999).

customer's place of business or when the product is shipped to the customer. If the buyer requests in the sales agreement that the transaction be on a "bill and hold" basis, and has a substantial business purpose for doing so, then the seller may recognize revenue when the production of the goods is complete.

- ***Scenario 3—Goods sold on layaway:*** Company R, a retailer, offers layaway sales to its customers. Company R collects an initial cash deposit from the customer but retains the merchandise and sets it aside in its inventory. Although a date may be specified within which the customer must finalize the purchase, Company R does not require the customer to sign a fixed payment agreement. The merchandise is not released to the customer until full payment is received. Company R wants to recognize revenue equal to a pro-rata portion of the merchandise sales price as cash is collected.

  SEC interpretive response: Company R should postpone recognizing revenue until merchandise is delivered to the customer (criterion 2). Until then, the cash received to date should be recognized as a liability such as "Deposits from layaway customers." Because Company R retains the risks of ownership, receives only deposits, and does not have an enforceable right to the remainder of the purchase price, it is not entitled to recognize revenue until the sales price is received in full.

- ***Scenario 4—Nonrefundable up-front fees:*** Increasingly, service providers negotiate agreements with customers that require the customer to pay a nonrefundable up-front "initiation" or service "activation" fee. For example, companies that provide telecommunications services typically charge each new customer a nonrefundable activation fee. Once enrolled for service, customers then pay monthly usage fees that just cover the company's operating costs. The costs to activate the telecommunications service are minimal. Thus, the up-front fee more than covers these costs. The key question here is when should revenue from nonrefundable up-front activation fees be recognized?

  SEC interpretive response: Unless the up-front fee is in exchange for products delivered or services performed that represent the culmination of a separate earnings process, deferral of revenue is appropriate because service has not been rendered (criterion 2). In such circumstances the up-front fees, even if nonrefundable, are deemed to be earned as the services are delivered over the full term of the service agreement. This means that the up-front fees should be deferred and recognized pro-rata over the periods when services are provided because that's when the fees are earned.

- ***Scenario 5—Gross versus net basis for Internet resellers:*** Another troublesome area is the method used to record sales by certain Internet companies that simply act as an agent or broker in a transaction. For example, assume Dot.com Company operates an Internet site from which it sells airline tickets. Customers place orders by selecting a specific flight from Dot.com's Web site and providing a credit card number for payment. Dot.com receives the order and credit card authorization and passes this information along to the airline. The airline sends the tickets directly to the customer. Dot.com does not take title to the tickets and, therefore, has no ownership risk or other responsibility for the tickets. The airline is fully responsible for all returned tickets and disputed credit card charges. (So, Dot.com is just an agent or broker that facilitates the transaction between the customer and the airline.) The average ticket price is $500 of which Dot.com receives a $25 commission. In the event a credit card sale is rejected, Dot.com loses its $25 margin on sale. Because the management of Dot.com believes that revenue growth is what drives its share price, it seeks to report the revenue from this transaction on a "gross" basis at $500, along with cost of sales of $475.

  SEC interpretive response: Dot.com should report the revenue from this transaction on a "net" basis—$25 as commission revenue and $0 for cost of sales. In determining whether revenue should be reported gross (with separate display of cost of sales) or on a net basis, the SEC stipulates that the following factors be considered:

1. Is Dot.com acting as a principal or as an agent/broker in the transaction?
2. Does Dot.com take title to the ticket?
3. Does Dot.com assume the risks of ownership such as possible losses from bad debts or returns?

If Dot.com acts as a principal in the transaction, takes title to the tickets or assumes the ownership risks, then the gross method is deemed appropriate. Otherwise, the net method must be used.

It is important to note that SAB 101 was not meant to change GAAP. Instead, it is intended to close some loopholes and eliminate gray areas in how GAAP is being applied in practice. A recent survey of annual reports indicates that the SEC guidelines have diminished abuses.[10] However, aggressive revenue recognition still occurs. So analysts must be vigilant for firms that overstate true earnings performance by bending revenue recognition rules.

The criteria for revenue and expense recognition are intended to provide general guidance for accrual accounting income determination. However, these general criteria leave ample room for judgment and interpretation that creates flexibility in GAAP. Analysts and investors must be alert for management's attempts to exploit this flexibility in ways that push the boundaries of acceptable revenue and expense recognition.

RECAP

SUMMARY

The "critical event" and "measurability" conditions for revenue recognition are typically satisfied at point of sale. However, there are circumstances—long-term construction contracts, production of natural resources, and agricultural commodities—where it is appropriate to recognize revenue prior to sale. Revenue recognition may also be delayed until after the sale—specifically, when cash is collected. This approach is used when there is considerable uncertainty about the collectibility of the sales price or where there are significant costs that will be incurred after the sale that are difficult to predict. This chapter outlines the special accounting procedures used when revenue recognition doesn't occur at the point of sale.

The broad criteria for revenue and expense recognition leave room for considerable latitude and judgment. This flexibility in GAAP can sometimes be exploited by management to hide or misrepresent the underlying economic performance of a company. This chapter outlines some of the more common ways of managing earnings that have come under SEC scrutiny. Later chapters provide further examples of how earnings can be manipulated. Auditors and financial statement users must be aware of management's incentives to manage earnings, and the ways in which this is accomplished. Armed with this knowledge, you will be in a much better position to spot "accounting irregularities" and to avoid their unpleasant consequences.

---

[10] P. McConnell, J. Pegg and D. Zion, "Revenue Recognition 101," *Accounting Issues,* Bear, Stearns & Co. Inc., New York, March 10, 2000.

EXERCISES

E3-1

Long-term construction contract accounting

AICPA adapted

The following data pertain to Pell Company's construction jobs, which commenced during 2001:

	Project 1	Project 2
Contract price	$420,000	$300,000
Costs incurred during 2001	240,000	280,000
Estimated cost to complete	120,000	40,000
Billed to customers during 2001	150,000	270,000
Received from customers during 2001	90,000	250,000

REQUIRED:

1. If Pell used the completed-contract method, what amount of gross profit (loss) would be reported in its 2001 income statement?
2. If Pell used the percentage-of-completion method, what amount of gross profit (loss) would be reported in the 2001 income statement?

E3-2

Determining gross profit under percentage-of-completion

AICPA adapted

Haft Construction Company has consistently applied the percentage-of-completion method. On January 10, 2001, Haft began work on a $3,000,000 construction contract. At the inception date, the estimated cost of construction was $2,250,000. The following data relate to the progress of the contract:

Income recognized at 12/31/01	$ 300,000
Costs incurred 1/10/01 through 12/31/02	1,800,000
Estimated cost to complete at 12/31/02	600,000

REQUIRED:

In its income statement for the year ended December 31, 2002, what amount of gross profit should Haft report?

E3-3

Determining gross profit using installment sales

AICPA adapted

Lang Company uses the installment method of revenue recognition. The following data pertain to Lang's installment sales for the years ended December 31, 2001 and 2002:

	2001	2002
Installment receivables at year-end on 2001 sales	$60,000	$30,000
Installment receivables at year-end on 2002 sales	–	69,000
Installment sales	80,000	90,000
Cost of sales	40,000	60,000

REQUIRED:

What amount should Lang report as deferred gross profit in its December 31, 2001 and 2002 balance sheets?

E3-4

Determining gross profit using the installment sales method

AICPA adapted

Since there is no reasonable basis for estimating the degree of collectibility, Astor Company uses the installment method of revenue recognition for the following sales:

	2001	2000
Sales	$900,000	$600,000
Collections from:		
2000 sales	100,000	200,000
2001 sales	300,000	–
Accounts written off:		
2000 sales	150,000	50,000
2001 sales	50,000	–
Gross profit percentage	40%	30%

REQUIRED:

What amount should Astor report as deferred gross profit in its December 31, 2001 balance sheet for the 2000 and 2001 sales?

On January 2, 2001, Yardley Company sold a plant to Ivory Inc. for $1,500,000. On that date, the plant's carrying cost was $1,000,000. Ivory gave Yardley $300,000 cash and a $1,200,000 note, payable in four annual installments of $300,000 cash plus 12% interest. Ivory made the first principal and interest payment of $444,000 on December 31, 2001. Yardley uses the installment method of revenue recognition.

E3–5

Determining gross profit using the installment method

AICPA adapted

REQUIRED:

In its 2001 income statement, what amount of realized gross profit should Yardley report?

Taft Corporation, which began business on January 1, 2001, appropriately uses the installment sales method of accounting. The following data are available for December 31, 2001 and 2002:

E3–6

Determining installment accounts receivable

AICPA adapted

	2001	2002
Balance of deferred gross profit on sales on account for:		
2001	$300,000	$120,000
2002		440,000
Gross profit on sales	30%	40%

REQUIRED:

The installment accounts receivable balances at December 31, 2001 and 2002 would be how much?

Kul Company, which began operations on January 1, 2001, appropriately uses the installment sales method of accounting. The following information is available for 2001:

E3–7

Determining realized gross profit on installment sales

AICPA adapted

Installment accounts receivable, December 31, 2001	$400,000
Deferred gross profit, December 31, 2001 (before recognition of realized gross profit for 2001)	280,000
Gross profit on sales	40%

REQUIRED:

For the year ended December 31, 2001, cash collections and realized gross profit on installment sales should be how much?

On December 31, 2001, Rice, Inc. authorized Graf to operate as a franchise for an initial franchise fee of $150,000. Of this amount, $60,000 was received upon signing the agreement and the balance, represented by a note, is due in three annual payments of $30,000 each, beginning December 31, 2002. The present value on December 31, 2001 of the three annual payments appropriately discounted is $72,000. According to the agreement, the nonrefundable down payment represents a fair measure of the services already performed by Rice; however, substantial future services are required of Rice. Collectibility of the note is reasonably certain.

E3–8

Determining deferred franchise fee revenue

AICPA adapted

REQUIRED:

In Rice's December 31, 2001 balance sheet, unearned franchise fees from Graf's franchise should be reported as how much?

For $50 a month, Rawl Company visits its customers' premises and performs insect control services. If customers experience problems between regularly scheduled visits, Rawl makes service calls at no additional charge. Instead of paying monthly, customers may pay an annual fee of $540 in advance.

E3–9

Determining revenue recognized with advanced fees

AICPA adapted

REQUIRED:

For a customer who pays the annual fee in advance, Rawl should recognize the related revenue in what amounts and when?

E3–10

Determining deferred service contract revenue

AICPA adapted

Dunne Company sells equipment service contracts that cover a two-year period. The sales price of each contract is $600. Dunne's past experience is that, of the total dollars spent for repairs on service contracts, 40% is incurred evenly during the first contract year and 60% evenly during the second contract year. Dunne sold 1,000 contracts evenly throughout 2001.

REQUIRED:

In its December 31, 2001 balance sheet, what amount should Dunne report as deferred service contract revenue?

E3–11

Determining account balances under installment sales method

AICPA adapted

Bear Company, which began operations on January 2, 2001, appropriately uses the installment sales method of accounting. The following information is available for 2001:

Installment sales	$1,400,000
Realized gross profit on installment sales	240,000
Gross profit percentage on sales	40%

REQUIRED:

For the year ended December 31, 2001, what amounts should Bear report as accounts receivable and deferred gross profit?

E3–12

Determining gross profit and deferred gross profit under the installment method

AICPA adapted

Baker Company is a real estate developer that began operations on January 2, 2001. Baker appropriately uses the installment method of revenue recognition. Baker's sales are made on the basis of a 10% down payment, with the balance payable over 30 years. Baker's gross profit percentage is 40%. Relevant information for Baker's first two years of operations is as follows:

	2002	2001
Sales	$16,000,000	$14,000,000
Cash collections	2,020,000	1,400,000

REQUIRED:

1. At December 31, 2001, Baker's deferred gross profit was how much?
2. Baker's realized gross profit for 2002 was how much?

PROBLEMS/DISCUSSION QUESTIONS

P3–1

Income measurement under alternative revenue recognition rules

Ms. Fuji started a business on January 1, 2001. Key operating statistics for 2001 were as follows:

Beginning inventory	0
Number of units produced	20,000
Number of units sold (delivery basis)	16,000
Number of units sold for which cash has been received by December 31, 2001	14,000

Direct production costs were $12 per unit. There were no fixed costs or selling/delivery expenses. The selling price per unit was $16.00.

On January 1, 2002, Ms. Fuji decided to liquidate the business. She sold the remaining inventory at $13.00 per unit for cash. By January 15, 2002, she collected the amount due from customers for sales made during 2001.

REQUIRED:

Based on the above information, compute the net income of Ms. Fuji for the years 2001 and 2002 under:

1. Production basis
2. Sales (or delivery) basis
3. Cash collection basis.

P3–2

Income determination under alternative bases of revenue recognition

Agri Pro, a farm corporation, produced 15,000 bushels of wheat in its first year of operations. During the year, Agri Pro sold 10,000 bushels of the grain produced for $2.40 per bushel and collected three-fourths of the selling price on the grain sold; the balance is to be collected in equal amounts during each of the two following years. The local grain elevator is quoting a year-end market price of $3.00 per bushel. Additional data for the first year are as follows:

Depreciation on equipment	$ 3,000
Other production costs (cash)—per bushel	0.50
Miscellaneous administrative costs (cash)	4,000
Selling and delivery costs (incurred and paid at time of sale), per bushel	0.10
Dividends paid to stockholders during year 1	10,000
Interest on borrowed money (1/2 paid in cash)	5,000

Agri Pro is enthusiastic about the accountant's concept of matching product costs with revenues.

REQUIRED:

Compute net income under each of the methods indicated below and determine the carrying (book) value of inventory and accounts receivable at the end of the first year of operation for each of these methods.

1. Recognize revenue when production is complete.
2. Recognize revenue at point of sale.
3. Recognize revenue on an installment (cash collection) basis.

P3–3

Determining pre-tax income and accounts receivable using the installment method

Lowery, Inc., an Arizona land speculator, started business on May 1, 2001. Lowery sold 700 acres of desert sand to a local developer for $960 an acre. Lowery is paid 60% of the selling price at the time the contract is signed, with the balance due in 24 months; however, collection is not assured. Lowery's property acquisition costs were $350 per acre and property taxes of $75,000 were paid during the year.

REQUIRED:

Compute Lowery's 2001 pre-tax income and determine its accounts receivable balance at December 31, 2001 using the installment sales method.

P3–4

Determining pre-tax income, inventory carrying value, and accounts receivable under sales and production basis

Howe, Inc., a Texas crude oil producer, started business on May 1, 2001. Howe sells all its production, f.o.b. shipping point, to a single customer at the current spot price for West Texas crude. The customer pays Howe 60% of the selling price at the time of delivery with the remaining to be paid in 10 months. Throughout 2001 the spot market price for the oil was $28.00 per barrel; however, on December 31, 2001 the market price jumped to $31.00 per barrel, where it is expected to remain. Howe's direct production costs are $12.00 per barrel, drilling equipment depreciation expense totaled $180,000 for the eight-month period ending December 31 and property taxes of $75,000 were paid during the year. Howe produced 30,000 barrels of oil of which 6,000 barrels were included in January 1, 2002 opening inventory.

REQUIRED:

Compute Howe's 2001 pre-tax income and determine its inventory carrying value and accounts receivable balance at December 31, 2001 under the following:

1. Production basis
2. Sales (completed transaction) basis
3. Installment (cash collection) basis.

P3–5

Percentage of completion accounting

AICPA adapted

In 2001, Long Construction began work under a three-year contract. The contract price is $800,000. Long uses the percentage-of-completion method for financial accounting purposes. The income to be recognized each year is based on the proportion of cost incurred to total estimated costs for completing the contract. The financial-statement presentations relating to this contract at December 31, 2001 follow:

Balance Sheet	
Accounts receivable—construction contract billings	$15,000
Construction in progress	$50,000
Less contract billings	(47,000)
Construction in progress less billings	$ 3,000
Income Statement	
Income (before tax) on the contract recognized in 2001	$10,000

REQUIRED:

1. How much cash was collected in 2001 on this contract?
2. What was the initial estimated total cost on this project?
3. What is the estimated total income (before tax) on this contract?

P3–6

Long-term construction contract accounting

MSK Construction Company contracted to construct a factory building for $525,000. Construction started during 2001 and was completed in 2002. Information relating to the contract is provided below:

	2001	2002
Costs incurred during the year	$290,000	$150,000
Estimated additional cost to complete	145,000	–
Billings during the year	260,000	265,000
Cash collections during the year	240,000	285,000

REQUIRED:

Record the above transactions in the books of MSK Construction Company under the completed-contract and the percentage-of-completion methods. Determine amounts that will be reported on the balance sheet at the end of 2001.

P3–7

Determining income under installment sales method

AICPA adapted

The Maple Corporation sells farm machinery on the installment plan. On July 1, 2001, Maple entered into an installment sale contract with Agriculture, Inc., for an eight-year period. Equal annual payments under the installment sale are $100,000 and are due on July 1. The first payment was made on July 1, 2001. Additional information is as follows:

- The amount that would be realized on an outright sale of similar farm machinery is $556,000.
- The cost of the farm machinery sold to Agriculture is $417,000.
- The finance charges relating to the installment period are $244,000 based on a stated interest rate of 12%, which is appropriate.
- Circumstances are such that the collection of the installments due under the contract is reasonably assured.

REQUIRED:

What income or loss before income taxes should Maple record for the year ended December 31, 2001 as a result of the above transaction? Show supporting computations in good form.

P3–8

Revenue recognition for goods on consignment

Englewood Marine is a builder of 30-foot fiberglass fishing boats. The boats are marketed through a network of third-party dealers on a consignment basis. The consignment agreement stipulates that Englewood retains title to the boats until final sale to the customer. Dealers can return unsold boats to Englewood by paying shipping expenses and a financing fee for the time held. Each boat's cost to dealers is fixed at $28,000. Englewood's gross profit margin per boat is 30%.

Englewood shipped 41 boats to dealers during the six months ending October 31. Shipments were:

Monthly Boat Shipments to Dealers	
May–3	August–9
June–6	September–8
July–8	October–7

Dealers had three Englewood boats on hand for the quarter ended July 31 and two boats on hand at October 31.

REQUIRED:

1. Prepare a schedule showing Englewood Marine's revenues, cost of goods sold and gross profit for the quarters ending July 31 and October 31.
2. Indicate how Englewood Marine would report the unsold boats and for how much at July 31 and October 31.

P3–9

Revenue recognition based on delivery performance

STRETCH

Composite, Inc. is a manufacturer of modular homes. Due to lack of storage space for raw material inventories, Composite implemented a just-in-time inventory process in early 1999. Composite contracts with qualified vendors to be sole suppliers for a given raw material. In return, the vendors guarantee performance in accordance with Composite's purchase order.

On Friday, November 2, 2001, Composite placed a purchase order with Mogul Chemical Company for plastic resins. Composite's purchase order specifically states that all material is shipped so that Composite takes title to the goods when they are received. Delivery is to be made at 6:00 AM on the designated delivery date. Designated delivery date, pounds, and selling price per pound are:

Delivery Date	Pounds	Selling Price per Pound
Friday, November 30, 2001	75,000	$1.00
Friday, December 7, 2001	80,000	1.00
Friday, December 14, 2001	60,000	1.10
Friday, December 21, 2001	50,000	1.20
Friday, January 4, 2002	50,000	1.20

In December, Mogul Chemical was experiencing a slowdown in sales and decided to produce Composite's January 2002 order over the Christmas holidays. After completing the production on December 29, the material was promptly loaded on a staged trailer, which was immediately locked and sealed. An invoice and a bill of lading were prepared. The invoice was then sent to Composite on a "bill and hold" basis.

Upon receiving the invoice, Composite contacted Mogul and was told that the material was invoiced because Mogul wanted to include the sale in the quarter ended December 31, 2001. However, actual delivery would take place according to the purchase order terms. Composite accepted the explanation.

REQUIRED:

1. Determine the sales revenue that Mogul should recognize on transactions with Composite for the quarter ended December 31, 2001.
2. What would Mogul's justification be for including the production on December 29 in its December sales?
3. Should Mogul include the December 29 production in its December sales? Why or why not?

P3–10

Revenue recognition on layaways

STRETCH

DW Hooks is a customer-oriented retailer of high-definition televisions and other similar electronic and computer equipment. Hooks will accept layaway sales provided the customer makes a minimum down payment of 20% of the retail price and pays the balance off within 90 days. After the customer makes the initial deposit, Hooks transfers the merchandise from a "Retail Inventory" account to a "Layaway—Merchandise Inventory" account. Inventory is valued at approximately 80% of the retail-selling price. When the layaway sale is paid in full, Hooks will deliver the merchandise to the customer.

At January 31, 2001 Hooks had $72,000 of merchandise on layaway, for which customers have made cash deposits totaling $55,000. For the quarter ending April 30, 2001 Hooks had the following layaway transactions:

Month	Amounts Added to Layaway Inventory	Deposits Made During Month	Deliveries	
			Cost	Retail
February	$49,000	$45,000	$24,000	$30,000
March	50,000	67,000	56,000	70,000
April	40,000	51,000	48,000	60,000

REQUIRED:

1. Prepare the journal entries required to record these transactions.
2. Prepare a schedule showing sales revenue earned for the period, and reconcile the balances in layaway and customer deposits at January 31, 2001 to April 30, 2001.
3. How should Hook report the customer deposits in its financial statements?

CASES

C3–1

Smith's Farm: Alternative bases of income determination

Thomas Smith owns and operates a farm in Kansas. During 2001, he produced and harvested 40,000 bushels of wheat. Smith had no inventory of wheat at the start of the year. Immediately after harvesting the wheat in the late summer of 2001, Smith sold 30,000 bushels to a local grain elevator operator. As of December 31, 2001, Smith had received payment for 20,000 bushels. Additional information relating to the farm follows:

Price:	
Market price per bushel at the time of harvest and sale to the grain elevator operator	$ 3.60
Market price per bushel at December 31, 2001	3.60
Costs:	
Variable production costs per bushel	0.50
Delivery costs per bushel	0.20
Annual fixed cost of operating the farm that are unrelated to the volume of production	$25,000

REQUIRED:

1. Prepare a 2001 income statement for Smith's Farm under each of the following assumptions regarding what constitutes the "critical event" in the process of recognizing income:

   a. Assuming that production is the critical event
   b. Assuming that the sale is the critical event
   c. Assuming that cash collection is the critical event.

   (For simplicity, treat the fixed operating costs as period—rather than product—costs.)

2. Determine the December 31, 2001 balances for wheat inventory and accounts receivable under each of the three income recognition methods in requirement (1).
3. Assume that the farm is left idle during 2002. Since there is no harvest, Smith's only transaction consists of an October 2002 sale of the 10,000 bushels in inventory at a price of $2.80 per bushel. Further assume that no fixed costs are incurred while the farm is idle.

   Compute 2002 income on both the sale and production basis. Discuss the causes for any profit or loss reported under each income determination alternative.

C3–2

London, Inc.: Determining gross profit under the percentage-of-completion method

AICPA adapted

London, Inc. began operation of its construction division on October 1, 2001 and entered into contracts for two separate projects. The Beta project contract price was $600,000 and provided for penalties of $10,000 per week for late completion. Although during 2002 the Beta project had been on schedule for timely completion, it was completed four weeks late in August 2003. The Gamma project's original contract price was $800,000. Change orders during 2003 added $40,000 to the original contract price. The following data pertains to the separate long-term construction projects in progress:

	Beta	Gamma
As of September 30, 2002:		
Costs incurred to date	$360,000	$410,000
Estimated costs to complete	40,000	410,000
Billings	315,000	440,000
Cash collections	275,000	365,000
As of September 30, 2003:		
Cost incurred to date	450,000	720,000
Estimated costs to complete	—	180,000
Billings	560,000	710,000
Cash collections	560,000	625,000
Additional Information:		

London accounts for its long-term construction contracts using the percentage-of-completion method for financial reporting purposes and the completed-contract method for income tax purposes.

REQUIRED:

1. Prepare a schedule showing London's gross profit (loss) recognized for the years ended September 30, 2002 and 2003 under the percentage-of-completion method.
2. Prepare a schedule showing London's balances in the following accounts at September 30, 2002 under the percentage-of-completion method:
   Accounts receivable
   Costs and estimated earnings in excess of billings
   (Billings in excess of costs and estimated earnings)
3. Determine how much income would be recognized for tax purposes under the completed-contract method for the 2002 and 2003 fiscal years.

C3-3

Stewart & Stevenson Services, Inc. (KR): Understanding accounts used for long-term construction contract accounting

STRETCH

Stewart & Stevenson Services, Inc. manufactures motors and generators. Following is extracted from the Year 2 financial statements of Stewart & Stevenson Services, Inc.

STEWART AND STEVENSON SERVICES, INC.

	Year 2	Year 1
Balance Sheet Items		
Accounts receivable	$143,166	$121,030
Costs incurred on uncompleted contracts	190,670	70,766
Accrued profits	13,117	9,857
Cost incurred + accrued profits	203,787	80,623
Less: Customer progress payments	(164,078)	(55,258)
Cost in excess of billings (net)	$ 39,709	$ 25,365
Income Statement Items		
Sales revenue	$812,526	$686,363
Cost of sales	685,879	569,695
Gross margin	$126,647	$116,668
Gross margin rate	15.6%	17.0%

Assumption: All sales revenue are from long-term construction contracts.

REQUIRED:

1. Using the information provided above, reconstruct the following T-accounts, showing how the accounts changed from their beginning to ending balances in Year 2.

STEWART AND STEVENSON SERVICES, INC.

CONSTRUCTION IN PROCESS INVENTORY

Beginning balance	$ 80,623		
Ending balance	203,787		

BILLINGS ON CONTRACT (PROGRESS PAYMENTS)

		$ 55,258	Beginning balance
		164,078	Ending balance

ACCOUNTS RECEIVABLE

Beginning balance	$121,030		
Ending balance	143,166		

2. Compute sales revenue, cost of goods sold, and gross margin assuming the company was using the completed-contract method during Year 2.
3. Assuming a tax effect rate of 40% and further assuming that the company switched from the percentage-of-completion method to the completed-contract method at the end of Year 2, provide the effect of this change of accounting principle on the accounting equation at the end of Year 2.
4. Assuming the information on accrued profits is not available, estimate the gross margin assuming the company was using the completed-contract method during Year 2.
5. Explain the difference in the gross margins obtained from (2) and (4).
6. Assuming the information on accrued profits is not available, estimate the gross margin if revenue were recognized on a cash collected basis.

C3–4

Revenue recognition—membership fees

Uncle Mike's is a discount club retailer that generates revenues through membership fees and from selling products at discounted prices to its club members. To shop at its stores, the customer must purchase a $40 annual membership, which expires on December 31. The cost of the membership is pro-rated over the remaining months of the year; for example, the cost of a membership purchased in July would be $20 ($40 × 6 months/12 months). However, the customer has the right to cancel the membership at any time during the year and receive a full refund, at the end of the respective calendar quarter, of the membership fee originally paid.

Based on historical data and industry averages, Uncle Mike's estimates that 30% of its members will request a refund before the end of their membership period. Uncle Mike's data for the past ten years indicates that significant variations between actual and estimated cancellations have not occurred. Furthermore, Uncle Mike's does not expect significant variations to occur in the foreseeable future.

During the calendar year ended December 31, 2001, Uncle Mike's quarterly membership refunds were as follows: March $54,900; June $18,715; September $8,803; and December $4,667. Memberships issued during the year were:

Month	Number	Month	Number
January	2,000	July	500
February	2,000	August	500
March	1,500	September	1,000
April	1,000	October	800
May	900	November	900
June	500	December	800

REQUIRED:

1. Prepare a schedule showing quarterly and annual membership fees earned by Uncle Mike's during 2001.
2. How would you initially classify the membership fees in Uncle Mike's financial statements?
3. How would your answer change (in Requirement 1) if Uncle Mike's could not accurately predict membership refunds?

4

Structure of the Balance Sheet and Statement of Cash Flows

LEARNING OBJECTIVES:

After studying this chapter, you will understand:

1. How the various asset, liability, and stockholders' equity accounts found on a typical corporate balance sheet are measured and classified.
2. How to use balance sheet information to understand key differences in the nature of firms' operations and how those operations are financed.
3. Differences in balance sheet terminology and presentation format in countries outside the United States.
4. How successive balance sheets and the income statement can be used to determine cash inflows and outflows for a period.
5. How information provided in the cash flow statement can be used to explain changes in noncash accounts on the balance sheet.
6. The distinction between operating, investing, and financing sources and uses of cash.
7. How changes in current asset and liability accounts can be used to adjust accrual earnings to obtain cash flows from operations.

The **balance sheet** contains a summation of the assets owned by the firm, the liabilities incurred to finance these assets, and the shareholders' equity representing the amount of financing provided by owners at a specific date.

The Financial Accounting Standards Board (FASB) defines the three basic elements of the balance sheet:[1]

1. **Assets:** Probable future economic benefits obtained or controlled by an entity as a result of past transactions or events.
2. **Liabilities:** Probable future sacrifices of economic benefits arising from an entity's *present* obligations to transfer assets or provide services to other entities in the *future* as a result of *past* transactions or events.
3. **Equity:** The residual interest in the assets of an entity that remains after deducting its liabilities. For a corporate form of organization, this interest is referred to as shareholders' or stockholders' equity.

The balance sheet tells us how management has invested its money and where the money came from. It provides information for assessing rates of return, capital structure, liquidity, solvency, and financial flexibility of an enterprise.

Two **rate of return** measures for evaluating operating efficiency and profitability of an enterprise are return on assets (ROA) and return on common equity (ROCE). (The precise calculation of these two performance

[1] "Elements of Financial Statements of Business Enterprises," *Statement of Financial Accounting Concepts No. 6,* (Stamford, CT: FASB, 1985), paras. 25, 35, 49.

measures is detailed in Chapter 5.) By comparing ROA to ROCE, statement users can see whether debt financing is being used to enhance the return earned by shareholders.

The balance sheet provides critical information for understanding an entity's **capital structure.** Capital structure refers to how much of an entity's assets are financed from debt versus equity sources. An important decision in corporate finance is determining the proper mix of debt and equity financing. Management must weigh the benefits of using debt financing (with tax-deductible interest) against the dangers of becoming over-leveraged and the possibility of defaulting on required interest and principal payments.

In addition to assessing the mix of debt versus equity financing, the balance sheet and related footnotes provide information for evaluating the **maturity structure** of the various obligations within the liability section. This information is critical to assessing the **liquidity** of an entity. Liquidity measures how readily assets can be converted to cash relative to how soon liabilities will have to be paid in cash. The balance sheet is the source of information for a variety of liquidity measures (detailed in Chapter 5) used by analysts and commercial lending officers to assess the credit worthiness of an entity.

Maturity structure refers to how far into the future the obligations will come due.

In addition to the liquidity measures that focus on short-term cash inflows and cash needs, balance sheets provide information for assessing long-term **solvency**—the ability of a company to generate sufficient cash flows to maintain its productive capacity and still meet interest and principal payments on long-term debt. A company that cannot make debt payments when due is technically insolvent and may be forced to reorganize or liquidate.

Operating and financial flexibility refers to an entity's ability to adjust to unexpected downturns in the economic environment in which it operates or to take advantage of profitable investment opportunities as they arise. Balance sheets provide information for making these assessments. A firm with most of its assets invested in specialized manufacturing facilities (e.g., a foundry) has limited ability to adjust to economic downturns and, thus, has limited operating flexibility. Similarly, a firm with minimal cash reserves and large amounts of high interest debt on its balance sheet will have limited ability to take advantage of profitable investment opportunities that may arise.

Now that we have outlined the information contained in balance sheets and how it is used, we next turn our attention to how various balance sheet accounts are measured and classified.

Classification Criteria and Measurement Conventions for Balance Sheet Accounts

We will use the financial statements of Motorola to illustrate the classification criteria and measurement methods used in a typical balance sheet. While many people characterize generally accepted accounting principles (GAAP) balance sheet carrying amounts as **historical costs,** what they really represent is more complicated. In fact, carrying amounts in a GAAP balance sheet are a mixture of historical costs, **current costs** (also called **fair value**), **net realizable value,** and **discounted present values.**

Exhibit 4.1 shows Motorola's balance sheet, which uses a typical U.S. disclosure format. In the "Assets" section, cash and any other assets expected to be converted into cash within the next 12 months (or within the **operating cycle,** if the operating cycle is longer than 12 months) are classified as "Current assets." Assets not expected to be converted into cash within this period are categorized separately. Within the "Current assets" category, items are disclosed in descending order of liquidity—how quickly the items will be converted into cash through the normal course of business. In the "Liabilities" section of the balance sheet, items expected to be settled from current assets within the next 12 months (or within the operating cycle, if longer) are categorized as "Current liabilities." All other liabilities appear in a separate section as noncurrent or long-term obligations. Equity claims also appear in their own separate section of the balance sheet, which is often referred to as the "Stockholders' equity" section.

A firm's **operating cycle** is the elapsed time beginning with the initiation of production and ending with the cash collection of the receivables from the sale of the product.

Exhibit 4.1 ■ MOTOROLA INC. AND CONSOLIDATED SUBSIDIARIES

Balance Sheet

($ in millions)	December 31 1999	1998
Assets		
Current assets		
Cash and cash equivalents	$ 3,345	$ 1,453
Short-term investments	699	171
Accounts receivable, net	5,125	5,057
Inventories	3,422	3,745
Deferred income taxes	3,162	2,362
Other current assets	750	743
Total current assets	16,503	13,531
Property, plant, and equipment, net	9,246	10,049
Other assets	11,578	5,148
Total assets	$37,327	$28,728
Liabilities and Stockholders' Equity		
Current liabilities		
Notes payable and current portion of long-term debt	$ 2,504	$ 2,909
Accounts payable	3,015	2,305
Accrued liabilities	6,897	6,226
Total current liabilities	12,416	11,440
Long-term debt	3,089	2,633
Deferred income taxes	3,481	1,188
Other liabilities	1,513	1,245
Total liabilities	20,499	16,506
Company-obligated mandatorily redeemable preferred securities of subsidiary trust holding solely company-guaranteed debentures	484	–
Stockholders' equity		
Preferred stock, $100 par value issuable in series Authorized shares: 0.5 (none issued)	–	–
Common stock, $3 par value Authorized shares: 1999 and 1998, 1,400 Issued and outstanding: 1999, 612.8; 1998, 601.1	1,838	1,804
Additional paid-in capital	2,572	1,894
Retained earnings	8,780	8,254
Non-owner changes to equity	3,154	270
Total stockholders' equity	16,344	12,222
Total liabilities and stockholders' equity	$37,327	$28,728

To convey a feeling for the diversity of the measurement bases used in a typical balance sheet, we will discuss selected accounts from Motorola's 1999 comparative balance sheet (see Exhibit 4.1). Many of the measurement issues introduced in this section are explored in greater depth in subsequent chapters.

Cash The balance sheet carrying amount for cash reflects the amount of money or currency the firm has on hand or in bank accounts. If cash consists exclusively of U.S. dollar amounts, the balance sheet cash account reflects the *historical* amount of net dollar units arising from past transactions. But due to the unique liquidity of cash, this historical amount of net dollar units is identical to the current market value of the cash.

If some of the cash amounts are denominated in foreign currency units (likely for Motorola, a multinational firm), then those amounts in foreign currency units must be

> **Monetary assets** are fixed in dollar amounts irrespective of price changes. A $300,000 cash deposit remains fixed at $300,000 even if the general level of prices goes up and the purchasing power of that $300,000 declines. **Nonmonetary assets** like inventory and buildings are *not* fixed in dollar amounts—that is, inventory purchased for $300,000 can conceivably increase in value if prices go up. While not assured, this potential for changing value is the distinguishing characteristic of nonmonetary items—their value is *not* expressed in a fixed number of monetary units.

translated into U.S. dollar equivalents. For **monetary assets** like cash, accounts receivable, and notes receivable, the current rate of exchange in effect at the balance sheet date is used to translate foreign currency units into dollars. As a consequence of using the current rate of exchange (rather than the historical rate of exchange that was in effect at the time of the foreign currency cash inflow), this portion of the cash account is carried at its **current market price**—*not* at its historical transaction amount. For these foreign currency deposits, current market exchange values are used irrespective of whether they are higher or lower than the historical rate. Consequently, the GAAP measurement convention for cash is, in reality, current market price rather than historical cost.

> A U.S. company with 1 million pesos in the bank account of its Mexican manufacturing subsidiary would value the cash at $105,374 U.S. dollars on December 31, 1999 when the exchange rate was 9.49 pesos to the dollar. This same bank account (with 1 million pesos) would have been valued at $101,112 U.S. dollars on December 31, 1998 when the exchange rate was 9.89 pesos to the dollar.

Short-term Investments This category of assets comprises items like U.S. Treasury bills, notes, equity securities, or other financial assets that companies use to earn a return on funds not currently needed in operations. The FASB has recently changed the measurement rules for certain investments in debt and equity securities. Under the new rules, a distinction is made between debt securities, which the reporting company intends to hold to maturity, and all other securities (both debt and equity), which are intended to be held only for short periods of time.[2] The new rules are as follows:

1. Debt securities the company intends to hold to maturity are carried at amortized cost. (When debt securities are sold at a premium or discount, the premium or discount is amortized over time—hence the term **amortized cost.**)
2. Debt and equity securities held for short-range investment purposes are carried at market (i.e., the price at which these securities can be bought and sold), irrespective of whether market is above or below cost.

> When the balance sheet carrying amount of the securities investment is written up or down to current market value, the offsetting gain or loss appears on the income statement if the securities are **trading securities** where the intent is to generate profits on short-term differences in price. When less actively traded securities (termed **available-for-sale securities**) are marked-to-market, the offsetting gain or loss goes directly to stockholders' equity rather than through the income statement. (These accounting rules are discussed further in Chapter 16.)

How long the company intends to hold the debt securities determines how they are measured in the balance sheet. Some will be carried at amortized cost and others at current market prices. Short-term equity securities are always measured at current market prices.

Net Accounts Receivable The balance sheet carrying amount for gross accounts receivable is equal to the face amount arising from the past transaction. Thus, if a company sold goods with a sales price of $100,000 on November 15, 2001, the following entry would be made:

DR Accounts receivable	$100,000	
CR Sales revenue		$100,000

If the receivable is still outstanding at December 31, 2001, it would be shown on the balance sheet at $100,000. However, accrual accounting requires that any future costs be matched

[2] "Accounting for Certain Investments in Debt and Equity Securities," *Statement of Financial Accounting Standards (SFAS) No. 115* (Norwalk, CT: FASB 1993). Under the old rules that *SFAS No. 115* replaced, short-term investments were carried at lower of cost or market.

against the revenues recognized in that period. When sales are made for credit (on account), some sales may unknowingly be made to customers who will prove incapable of making the required payment. The expense associated with these uncollectible accounts must be recognized—on an estimated basis—in the period in which the sales arise. This compels companies to prepare an estimate of the proportion of existing accounts receivable balances that they reasonably believe will ultimately not be collected. In Motorola's case the 1999 accounts receivable disclosure shows net accounts receivable of $5,125 million, after adjustment for the allowance account. Notice that as a consequence of this "netting" of accounts, the total for net accounts receivable is carried at expected **net realizable value** as of the balance sheet date, not at original historical cost.

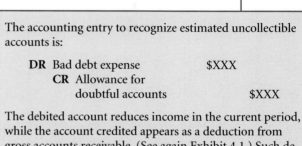

> The accounting entry to recognize estimated uncollectible accounts is:
>
> | | | |
> |---|---|---|
> | **DR** Bad debt expense | $XXX | |
> | **CR** Allowance for doubtful accounts | | $XXX |
>
> The debited account reduces income in the current period, while the account credited appears as a deduction from gross accounts receivable. (See again Exhibit 4.1.) Such deductions from asset accounts are called **contra-asset** accounts. (Estimating and recognizing bad debt expense is discussed in Chapter 8.)

Inventories In the notes to its financial statements, Motorola discloses that inventories are carried at **lower of cost or market,** where cost is computed using the weighted average method. Therefore, the measurement basis for inventories depends on the relationship between historical cost and current market price. When costs are lower than market price, the carrying amounts for inventory conform to the historical cost convention. When cost exceeds market, inventories on the balance sheet are carried at current market price, where that market price is the cost to replace the item (subject to special GAAP rules—see Chapter 9).

Property, Plant, and Equipment—Net This item appears on the balance sheet at its net amount—historical cost minus accumulated depreciation. Motorola, like most companies, provides information about the components of this figure in the financial statement notes.

	December 31 1999	1998
Land	$ 251	$ 284
Buildings	5,989	6,288
Machinery	15,608	16,316
	21,848	22,888
Less: Accumulated depreciation	(12,602)	(12,839)
Property, plant, and equipment–net	$ 9,246	$ 10,049

When a long-lived asset becomes impaired—that is, when its carrying amount may no longer be recoverable—the fixed asset account is reduced to its lower **fair value.**[3] If available, quoted current market prices are the best measure of fair value. However, market prices for long-lived assets are not always readily available. So, fair value may need to be estimated by discounting expected future net operating cash flows. (This topic is covered in Chapter 10.)

> *SFAS No. 121, (para. 7),* defines *fair value* of an asset as "... the amount at which the asset could be bought or sold in a current transaction between willing parties, that is, other than a forced or liquidation sale."

Accounts Payable and Accrued Liabilities These items are reflected on the balance sheet at the amount of the original liability—that is, at the amount arising at the inception of the transaction. Consequently, the numbers are shown at historical cost.

[3] "Accounting for the Impairment of Long-Lived Assets and for Long-Lived Assets to Be Disposed of," *SFAS No. 121* (Norwalk, CT: FASB, 1995).

Long-term Debt When long-term debt (typically, notes or bonds) is issued, the initial balance sheet carrying amount is determined by computing the **discounted present value** of the sum of (1) the future principal repayment *plus* (2) the periodic interest payments. The rate used for discounting these amounts is the effective yield on the notes or bonds at the date they were issued. Here, we'll simply provide a brief overview of the general measurement rules for long-term debt. More on bonds and other long-term debt instruments is presented in Chapter 11.

When bonds are sold at par, the amount received is equal to the recorded face amount of the debt. For example, if Motorola sells $100,000,000 of 15-year, 10% coupon bonds for $100,000,000, the accounting entry is:

DR Cash	$100,000,000	
CR Bonds payable		$100,000,000

The $100,000,000 carrying amount is equal to the present value of the principal *and* interest payments over the life of the bond discounted at 10%, the effective yield at the time of issue. The effective yield is 10% since the effective yield on bonds sold at par is equal to the coupon rate. (We'll show why in Chapter 11.) When bonds are sold at a premium or at a discount, the initial carrying amount is again equal to the present value of the future payments, where the discount rate is the effective yield on the bonds. In general, at balance sheet dates after the bonds' issuance date, the subsequent carrying amount of *all* bonds outstanding is equal to the present value of the future principal and interest flows discounted at the *original effective yield rate.* This carrying amount will differ from the current market price of the bonds whenever interest rates have changed subsequent to issuance. Consequently, long-term debt is also carried at historical cost, where the carrying amount is determined by calculating the discounted present value of the future principal and interest cash flows using the original effective yield on the bonds as the discount rate.

Deferred Income Taxes This liability account represents taxes on income recognized in Motorola's income statement in current and prior periods that will not be paid to the government until future periods. So this is a **deferred income tax liability.** In the United States, the rules used to determine income for financial reporting purposes (called **book income**) frequently do not conform to the rules used to determine income for taxation purposes (called **taxable income**). Book income also diverges from taxable income in many other industrialized countries. Income determination rules for financial reporting differ from rules for determining income for taxation purposes because of the very different objectives of the two computations. The objective in measuring book income is to reflect a firm's underlying economic success: Was the firm profitable during the period? The objective in measuring taxable income is to conform to laws designed to provide a basis for funding government operations. Since the rules that govern income determination for tax purposes result from a national political process, these rules do not necessarily measure changes in firms' underlying economic condition. Most companies maintain two sets of accounting records (or books) to facilitate both accurate financial reporting and compliance with tax laws.

The amount reported as book income is the basis for the deduction reported on the income statement for tax expense. However, the amount actually owed and paid to the government—that is, the sum of the credits to cash and to income taxes payable on the balance sheet—is determined by firms' taxable income. As a consequence, the debit to the income statement account (tax expense) and the credit to the balance sheet accounts (cash or taxes payable) ***will usually be for different amounts.*** To balance the entry, deferred income taxes—reflecting the difference in the *timing* of revenue and expense in computing book income versus taxable income—must be debited or credited. (The measurement and reporting rules for deferred taxes are covered in Chapter 13.)

In Motorola's case, the deferred income tax liability account has a credit balance of $3,481 million due to the **timing differences** that caused book income to exceed taxable income in past years.[4] Book income can exceed taxable income for at least two possible reasons:

> Note that Motorola also reports "Deferred income taxes" totaling $3,162 million in the asset section of its balance sheet. This amount arises because certain timing differences caused taxable income to be *greater* than book income in prior years.

1. Internal Revenue Service (IRS) rules allow Motorola to claim deductions for tax purposes before these items are reflected as GAAP expenses on the books.
2. GAAP allows Motorola to reflect revenues on the income statement before they are deemed to be taxable by the IRS.

Since these timing differences are expected to reverse in subsequent years, *future* taxable income will exceed book income. So, credit balances in deferred income taxes reflect the expected future liability associated with these timing difference reversals. Even though these reversals may be expected to take place in, say, three years in the future, GAAP reflects these amounts at their *undiscounted amount.* In other words, existing GAAP treats expected reversals in the years 2002 and 2012 identically—that is, the time-value of money is ignored.

> There are other reasons why book income may differ from taxable income—called permanent differences—but they do not give rise to deferred taxes. For example, U.S. income tax law does not tax municipal bond interest. Consequently, if a firm owns municipal bonds and receives interest on these bonds, the interest is tax free. Book income will include the interest income, but taxable income will not.

The accounting treatment for deferred income taxes is inconsistent with the measurement rules used to reflect long-term debt. The future outflows associated with long-term debt are shown at their discounted present value; *but the future outflows associated with book–tax timing differences are reflected at their full undiscounted amounts.* We note this inconsistency to reemphasize the fact that the measurement rules used to value different balance sheet accounts differ from item-to-item. *Balance sheet items are not all measured at historical costs—some are, some aren't.* And among those balance sheet amounts that are measured at historical cost, some—like long-term debt—are measured using a discounting approach, while other accounts—like deferred taxes—are reflected at their full, undiscounted historical amounts.

Mandatorily Redeemable Preferred Stock Motorola, like several other companies, has issued a type of preferred stock called trust preferred securities (TPS) to provide financing for their operations.[5] (We'll just provide an overview here—further details on the complicated transactions that give rise to these securities are discussed in Chapter 15.) The shares pay monthly or quarterly dividends and are redeemable at Motorola's option. Because of the mandatory redemption feature and the required periodic dividend payments, these hybrid securities incorporate elements of both debt and equity. So where to classify them within the balance sheet is controversial. Notice that Motorola finessed the issue by disclosing them in a section between debt and equity—often called the "mezzanine" section. The FASB is currently developing standards for reporting these securities that will hopefully help resolve the classification issue.

Common Stock This account represents the **par value** of shares issued and outstanding. The par value is determined by the company's articles of incorporation. Par values were originally established to ensure that a corporation would maintain a minimum level of investment by shareholders in order to protect the interests of creditors. Some states preclude companies from paying dividends to shareholders that would result in a reduction of stockholders' equity below the par value of shares issued and outstanding. As a practical matter, debt covenant provisions in lending agreements generally place restrictions on firms' distributions to shareholders that are more stringent than the statutory par-value

[4] *Credits* to deferred income tax arise because the debit to tax expense exceeds the credit to taxes payable. Since tax expense is based on book income and taxes payable is based on taxable income, this means that in past years book income for Motorola exceeded taxable income.

[5] For a further discussion of the key features of trust preferred securities, see P. J. Frischmann, P. D. Kimmel, and T. D. Warfield, "Innovation in Preferred Stock: Current Developments and Implications for Financial Reporting," *Accounting Horizons* (September 1999), pp. 201–18.

restrictions. Therefore, the par value of shares has limited economic significance, as discussed in Chapter 15. The common stock account is carried at the historical par value of the shares.

Additional Paid-in Capital This account reflects the amounts in excess of par or stated value that were received by the corporation when the shares were originally issued. For example, if Motorola issued 100,000 shares of \$3 par-value stock for \$15 per share, the "Additional paid-in capital" component would be credited for

$$(\$15 - \$3) \times 100{,}000 = \$1{,}200{,}000$$

Thus, paid-in capital is also shown at historical cost.

Retained Earnings This account measures the net of cumulative earnings less cumulative dividend distributions of the company since inception. Therefore, it represents the cumulative earnings that have been reinvested in the business. The "Retained earnings" account is increased (decreased) by the net income (net loss) for the period and is decreased for dividends that are declared in the period. For many firms, like Motorola, retained earnings represents the major portion of stockholders' equity. Thus, the book value of equity is largely determined by the past earnings that have been retained and reinvested in the business. As we will see in Chapters 5 and 6, book value of equity is a key element of many performance measures—like return on common equity (ROCE)—and it plays an important role in equity valuation.

Different measurement bases pervade the balance sheet. Because these items ultimately appear on the income statement, income is a mixture of historical costs, current values, and present values. This means that retained earnings is also a mixture of many different measurement bases.

Non-owner Changes to Equity This account measures the cumulative unrealized gains and losses from *other comprehensive income components* recognized in current and prior years. This component of stockholders' equity is also called "Accumulated other comprehensive income." As noted in Chapter 2, the most common components of other comprehensive income are (1) fair value adjustments made to securities classified as "available for sale," (2) foreign currency translation adjustments, and (3) unrealized losses resulting from recognition of the minimum liability provision under SFAS No. 87. This account is credited for unrealized gains and debited for unrealized losses. All amounts are shown net of tax effects. For Motorola, we see this account balance increased from a \$270 million credit balance at the end of 1998 to a whopping \$3,154 million credit balance at the end of 1999, an increase of \$2,884 million. Motorola's consolidated statement of stockholders' equity (not shown) explains the components of this change:

1. Unrealized gains on available for sale securities	\$2,990
2. Unrealized losses on foreign currency translation adjustments	(33)
3. Adjustment related to minimum pension liability provision	(73)
Total 1999 increase	\$2,884

Analytical Insights: Understanding the Nature of a Firm's Business

ANALYSIS

One tool for gaining insights into the nature of a company's operations and for analyzing its asset and financial structure is to prepare a **common-size balance sheet.** In a common-size balance sheet, each balance sheet account is expressed as a percentage of total assets or, equivalently, as a percentage of total liabilities plus shareholders' equity. Exhibit 4.2 presents common-size balance sheets for four companies operating in four distinctly different industries—E-Trade Group, an Internet company specializing in online investing services;

Exhibit 4.2 ■ COMMON-SIZE BALANCE SHEET COMPARISON

1999 Fiscal Year

($ in millions)	Company A Amounts	Company A %	Company B Amounts	Company B %	Company C Amounts	Company C %	Company D Amounts	Company D %
Assets								
Current assets								
Cash and marketable securities	$ 611.0	3.5	$ 344.0	2.3	$1,655.4	20.9	$ 301.9	4.3
Current receivables	10,297.8	58.6	—	—	5,067.1	64.1	295.0	4.3
Inventories	1,294.3	7.4	7,101.0	47.0	—	—	192.0	2.8
Other current assets	1,654.7	9.4	715.0	4.7	—	—	35.9	0.5
Total current assets	13,857.8	78.9	8,160.0	54.0	6,722.5	85.0	824.8	11.9
Noncurrent assets								
Property, plant, and equipment, net	1,782.3	10.1	6,410.0	42.5	178.8	2.3	4,524.4	65.5
Goodwill and intangibles, net	295.1	1.7	—	—	17.2	0.2	—	—
Other assets, net	1,643.0	9.3	534.0	3.5	989.7	12.5	1,561.4	22.6
Total assets	$17,578.2	100.0	$15,104.0	100.0	$7,908.2	100.0	$6,910.6	100.0
Liabilities and Stockholders' Equity								
Total current liabilities	$ 7,136.7	40.6	$ 4,076.0	27.0	$6,458.3	81.6	$ 783.5	11.3
Long-term liabilities	6,347.2	36.1	3,738.0	24.7	—	—	3,991.8	57.8
Total liabilities	13,483.9	76.7	7,814.0	51.7	6,458.3	81.6	4,775.3	69.1
Redeemable preferred stock and other preferred stock	—	—	986.0	6.5	30.6	0.4	225.0	3.3
Stockholders' equity								
Contributed capital and other equity items	239.0	1.4	2,036.0	13.5	1,427.7	18.1	1,129.2	16.3
Retained earnings (deficit)	3,855.3	21.9	4,268.0	28.3	(8.4)	(0.1)	781.1	11.3
Total liabilities and stockholders' equity	$17,578.2	100.0	$15,104.0	100.0	$7,908.2	100.0	$6,910.6	100.0

Deere & Company, a manufacturer of agricultural and heavy construction equipment with a large finance subsidiary; K-Mart, a well-known discount retailer; and Potomac Electric Power Company, an electrical utility providing service to Washington D.C. and the surrounding area. Can you match up the common-size statements with each of these companies? Think about the industry in which each firm operates and about the economic activities the firms might engage in. Then try to figure out how these activities might impact a typical balance sheet.

Note that Company C has a very large proportion of its assets in cash, marketable securities and accounts receivable with no inventory and a relatively small amount of property, plant, and equipment (PP&E). Most of Company C's debt financing comes from short-term liabilities, as the company carries no long-term debt. Finally, note that retained earnings is negative (a deficit), indicating that the company has suffered cumulative losses since it was formed. The lack of inventory rules out Deere and K-Mart as the source of Company C's data since both would hold significant inventories. Also, the relatively low amount of property, plant, and equipment further rules out these two firms as well as Potomac Power since all three need significant amounts of fixed assets to conduct business. This leaves E-Trade Group as the obvious match. A corroborating piece of evidence is the deficit in retained earnings. Because of heavy start-up costs, many of the relatively young Internet companies like E-Trade have yet to turn a profit.

Both Company A and Company B have relatively high amounts of current assets, but the mix of current assets is quite different. For Company A, current receivables represent nearly 60% of total assets, while Company B has no current receivables but 47% of its assets are in inventory. Since many of Deere's agricultural and heavy construction equipment products sell for well in excess of $100,000, dealers and customers often need to finance their purchases. Deere offers this financing through John Deere Credit, its wholly-owned finance subsidiary, whose operations are included in the consolidated numbers. Thus, the large receivables balance for Company A coupled with significant amounts invested in inventories and PP&E provide strong clues that Deere is Company A.

Like most national discount retailers, K-Mart would be expected to have large amounts of inventory. Because most sales are for cash or paid through bank credit cards (e.g., Visa or Master Card), K-Mart would likely have little or no current receivables on its balance sheet. Moreover, with a large number of stores either purchased or leased under capital lease arrangements, we would expect to see relatively large investments in PP&E. This profile seems to match up well with Company B's data.

This leaves Potomac Power as Company D. Note the relatively low amount of current assets and the large investment in PP&E to generate electricity. The large amount of long-term debt financing is also quite common for utilities. Regulated utilities are allowed to build a "reasonable and fair return" to stockholders into the energy rates charged customers. Therefore, they have a relatively steady and predictable earnings and cash flow stream. This allows utilities like Potomac Power to use proportionately more long-term debt to finance their operations relative to companies with more volatile earnings patterns.

The preceding exercise demonstrates how statement readers can extract useful information from common-size balance sheets to learn about the underlying economics of an industry and the nature of the firm's operations. Chapter 5 will introduce additional analytical tools for conducting in-depth analyses of companies.

International Differences in Balance Sheet Presentation

The account titles and format of balance sheets prepared in other countries can sometimes differ rather dramatically from those prepared under U.S. GAAP.[6] In contrast to the United States, where assets are presented in decreasing order of liquidity, in the United Kingdom,

[6] In addition, the measurement bases used for various accounts can sometimes be quite different from country to country. Throughout the book, we will alert you to some of these important differences as we discuss the recognition, measurement, and disclosure rules that govern financial reporting.

Germany, Netherlands, and some other European countries, fixed assets are presented first followed by the current assets displayed in increasing order of liquidity. This format is illustrated in Exhibit 4.3, which presents the 1999 balance sheet of Cadbury Schweppes PLC, a British confectionery and beverage company.

Exhibit 4.3 ■ CADBURY SCHWEPPES PLC

Balance Sheets at 2 January 2000

	Group		Company	
(in millions of sterling pounds)	**1999 £m**	1998 £m	**1999 £m**	1998 £m
Fixed Assets				
Intangible assets and goodwill	**1,725**	1,607	**–**	–
Tangible assets	**1,091**	1,126	**19**	19
Investments in associates	**296**	170	**11**	11
Investments	**89**	1	**3,838**	3,612
	3,201	2,904	**3,868**	3,642
Current Assets				
Stocks	**404**	409	**–**	–
Debtors				
– Due within one year	**769**	741	**75**	54
– Due after one year	**29**	19	**5**	6
Investments	**410**	416	**–**	–
Cash at bank and in hand	**151**	104	**–**	–
	1,763	1,689	**80**	60
Current Liabilities				
Creditors: amounts falling due within one year				
–Borrowings	**(432)**	(527)	**(1,435)**	(927)
– Other	**(1,283)**	(1,217)	**(304)**	(286)
Net Current Assets/(Liabilities)	**48**	(55)	**(1,659)**	(1,153)
Total Assets Less Current Liabilities	**3,249**	2,849	**2,209**	2,489
Non-Current Liabilities				
Creditors: amounts falling due after more than one year				
–Borrowings	**(311)**	(499)	**(736)**	(850)
– Other	**(51)**	(52)	**–**	–
Provisions for liabilities and charges	**(263)**	(158)	**(1)**	(1)
	(625)	(709)	**(737)**	(851)
Net Assets	**2,624**	2,140	**1,472**	1,638
Capital and Reserves				
Called up share capital	**253**	254	**253**	254
Share premium account	**942**	916	**942**	916
Capital redemption reserve	**90**	87	**90**	87
Revaluation reserve	**61**	63	**1**	1
Profit and loss account	**894**	523	**186**	380
Shareholders' Funds	**2,240**	1,843	**1,472**	1,638
Minority Interests				
Equity minority interests	**139**	61	**–**	–
Non-equity minority interests	**245**	236	**–**	–
	384	297	**–**	–
Total Capital Employed	**2,624**	2,140	**1,472**	1,638

Source: *Cadbury Schweppes 1999 Annual Report and Form 20-F.*

Note that within the fixed assets category, intangible assets are presented first followed by tangible assets (i.e., property, plant, and equipment) and finally financial assets or investments. The British balance sheet format is presented in a way that emphasizes the firm's liquidity and solvency. Notice, instead of reporting a figure for total assets, Cadbury Schweppes reports a subtotal for current assets less current liabilities, which highlights their working capital or liquidity position. Also notice the presentation of a subtotal for total assets less current liabilities. This figure can readily be compared with the long-term debt obligations appearing next to assess Cadbury's solvency position.

The Cadbury Schweppes balance sheet also introduces some account titles unique to British accounting that can be confusing to the unwary. For example, two accounts in the current assets section that can be particularly confusing are the "Stocks" and "Debtors" accounts. In the United Kingdom, Stocks is the common term for inventory. The Debtors account is analogous to the Accounts receivable account in the United States. The Capital and Reserves section, which is analogous to the Stockholders' equity section in U.S. balance sheets, contains several account titles unique to British accounting. Table 4.1 shows the accounts under U.S. GAAP that correspond to these British accounts. Two of the British equity accounts require brief elaboration since they have no U.S. counterpart:

- **Capital redemption reserve:** In the United Kingdom, when a company repurchases its own shares, these shares are cancelled. Where the repurchase is paid for from profits, an amount equivalent to the par or stated value of the shares repurchased is transferred from the Called up share capital account to a Capital redemption reserve account, which is not available for dividend distribution.
- **Revaluation reserve:** U.K. GAAP allows companies to periodically revalue both tangible and intangible fixed assets. Any surplus arising from a revaluation is credited to a revaluation reserve in the equity section of the balance sheet.

Finally, note that Cadbury Schweppes reports two sets of numbers on its balance sheet—one for the "Group" and another for the "Company." The Group numbers reflect the financial position of Cadbury Schweppes and all of its subsidiaries. This is equivalent to the "consolidated" financial statement numbers of a parent and its subsidiaries under U.S. GAAP. The company numbers reflect the financial position of the Cadbury Schweppes holding company.

This example provides a brief glimpse of how balance sheet format and terminology used in other countries differ from those used under U.S. GAAP. Examples of differences in accounting standards across countries appear throughout the book and are discussed extensively in Chapter 18.

Table 4.1 ■ COMPARISON OF U.K. AND U.S. ACCOUNT TITLES

U.K. Equity Accounts	Equivalent U.S. Accounts
Called up share capital	Common stock–par
Share premium account	Capital in excess of par
Capital redemption reserve	No equivalent in U.S. GAAP
Revaluation reserve	No equivalent in U.S. GAAP
Profit and loss account	Retained earnings

The balance sheet provides a snapshot of the financial position of a company at a given point in time. It shows the various types of assets held at the balance sheet date and the claims against those assets (i.e., how those assets have been financed).

Balance sheet accounts reflect a variety of measurement bases, including historical cost, current costs (also called fair value), net realizable value, and discounted present value. Therefore, users of balance sheet information must be careful to recognize the effects that these different measurement bases can have both when aggregating numbers across accounts as well as when computing ratios that are used in making inter-company comparisons.

With the tremendous growth in international business and the increased frequency of cross-border financing, it is likely that you will encounter statements prepared under non–U.S. GAAP sometime during your career. When you do, you must be aware of differences in recognition and measurement criteria, statement format, and terminology in order to properly interpret and analyze those statements.

RECAP

Statement of Cash Flows

The balance sheet shows a firm's investments (assets) and financial structure (liabilities and stockholders' equity) at a given *point in time.* By contrast, the **statement of cash flows** shows the user why a firm's investments and financial structure have *changed* between two balance sheet dates. The connection between successive balance sheet positions and the statement of cash flows can be demonstrated through simple manipulation of the basic accounting equation:

$$\text{Assets} = \text{Liabilities} + \text{Stockholders' equity} \tag{4.1}$$

Partitioning the assets into cash and all other assets yields:

$$\text{Cash} + \text{Noncash assets} = \text{Liabilities} + \text{Stockholders' equity} \tag{4.2}$$

Rearranging yields:

$$\text{Cash} = \text{Liabilities} - \text{Noncash assets} + \text{Stockholders' equity} \tag{4.3}$$

From basic algebra we know that an equality like this must also hold for the algebraic sum of the changes on both sides of the equation. Representing equation (4.3) in the form of the change (Δ) in each term results in

$$\Delta\text{Cash} = \Delta\text{Liabilities} - \Delta\text{Noncash assets} + \Delta\text{Stockholders' equity} \tag{4.4}$$

Thus, the cash flow statement—which provides an explanation of why a firm's cash position has changed between successive balance sheet dates—simultaneously explains the changes that have taken place in the firm's noncash asset, liability, and stockholders' equity accounts over the same time period.

The change in a firm's cash position between successive balance sheet dates will *not* equal the reported earnings for that period. There are three reasons for this:

1. Reported net income usually will not equal cash flow from **operating activities** because (a) noncash revenues and expenses are often recognized as part of accrual earnings, and (b) certain operating cash inflows and outflows are not recorded as revenues or expenses under accrual accounting in the same period the cash flows occur.
2. Changes in cash are also caused by nonoperating **investing activities** like the purchase or sale of fixed assets.
3. Additional changes in cash are caused by **financing activities** like the issuance of stock or bonds, the repayment of a bank loan, or dividends paid to stockholders.

Cash flows are critical to assessing a company's liquidity and creditworthiness. Firms with cash flows that are smaller than currently maturing obligations can be forced into liquidation or bankruptcy. Because cash flows and accrual earnings can differ dramatically, current reporting standards mandate that firms prepare a statement of cash flows as well as an income statement and balance sheet. The cash flow statement is designed to explain the causes for year-to-year changes in the balance of cash and cash equivalents.[7] We provide a brief introduction to the statement of cash flows here, focusing on the format of the statement and on the nature of some of the basic adjustments that are needed to convert accrual earnings to cash flow from operations. Later, after you have reviewed the accrual and cash flow effects of the transactions that affect various balance sheet and income statement accounts in the intervening chapters, you will find a more detailed explanation of the cash flow statement in Chapter 17.

The cash flow statement summarizes the cash inflows and outflows of a company broken down into its three principal activities:

- **Operating activities:** Cash flows from operating activities result from the cash effects of transactions and events that affect operating income—both production and delivery of goods and services.
- **Investing activities:** Cash flows from investing activities include making and collecting loans; investing in and disposing of debt or equity securities of other companies; and purchasing and disposing of assets, like equipment, that are used by a company in the production of goods or services.
- **Financing activities:** Cash flows from financing activities include obtaining cash from new issues of stock or bonds, paying dividends or buying back a company's own shares (treasury stock), borrowing money, and repaying amounts borrowed.

Companies that are able to satisfy most of their cash needs from operating cash flows are generally considered to be in stronger financial health and better credit risks.

Cash Flows Versus Accrual Earnings

The following example illustrates the major differences between cash flows and accrual earnings and why a cash flow statement is needed to fully understand the distinction between the two.

HRB Advertising Company opened for business on April 1, 2001. The corporation's activities and transactions for the remainder of 2001 are summarized as follows:

1. Herb Wilson, Robin Hansen, and Barbara Reynolds each contributed $3,500 cash on April 1 for shares of the company's common stock.
2. HRB rented office space beginning April 1, and paid the full year's rental of $2,000 per month—or $24,000—in advance.
3. The company borrowed $10,000 from a bank on April 1. The principal plus accrued interest is payable January 1, 2002 with interest at the rate of 12% per year.
4. HRB purchased office equipment with a five-year life for $15,000 cash on April 1. Salvage value is zero and the equipment is being depreciated straight-line.
5. HRB sold and billed customers for $65,000 of advertising services rendered between April 1 and December 31. Of this amount, $20,000 was still uncollected by year-end.
6. By year-end, the company incurred and paid the following operating costs: (a) utilities, $650; (b) salaries, $36,250; and (c) supplies, $800.
7. The company had accrued (unpaid) expenses at year-end as follows: (a) utilities, $75; (b) salaries, $2,400; and (c) interest, $900.
8. Supplies purchased on account and unpaid at year-end amounted to $50.

---

[7] The format for preparing the cash flow statement is specified in "Statement of Cash Flows," *SFAS No. 95* (Stamford, CT: FASB, 1987). As defined in *SFAS No. 95*, **cash equivalents** are short-term, highly liquid investments that are readily convertible to cash.

9. Supplies inventory on hand at year-end amounted to $100.
10. Annual depreciation on office equipment is $15,000 ÷ 5 years = $3,000. Since the equipment was acquired on April 1, the depreciation expense for 2001 is $3,000 × 9/12 = $2,250.

Herb, Robin, and Barbara were delighted to discover that the company earned a profit (before taxes) of $3,725 in 2001. However, they were shocked to learn that the company's checking account was overdrawn by $11,200 at year-end. This overdraft was particularly disconcerting since the bank loan was now due.

Is HRB Advertising Company profitable? Or is it about to go bankrupt? What are its prospects for the future? Exhibit 4.4 helps us examine these issues.

While HRB Advertising generated *positive* accrual accounting earnings of $3,725 during 2001, its operating cash flow was a *negative* $16,700. Columns (b) and (c) show the causes for the divergence between the components of accrual income (column [a]) and operating cash flows (column [d]). Because of a net infusion of cash from financing activities (column [d]), the net change in cash (a negative $11,200) was much smaller than the negative cash flow of $16,700 from operating activities.

We now discuss the rationale behind the adjustments in columns (b) and (c). We examine each adjustment in terms of how it affects "bottom-line" *accrual basis net income*—not how the adjustment affects revenues or expenses that comprise net income. Because expenses are treated as negative amounts in computing net income, an adjustment that reduces (increases) an expense is treated as a plus (negative) amount in columns (b) and (c). This way of designating positive and negative amounts will facilitate our discussion of the adjustments to accrual basis income needed to arrive at operating cash flows.

Exhibit 4.4 ■ **HRB ADVERTISING COMPANY**

Analysis of Accrual Income Versus Change in Cash for Year Ended December 31, 2001

ITEM	(a) Accrual Income	(b) Noncash Accruals: Revenue Earned (or Expenses Incurred)	(c) Prepayments and Supplies Buildup	(d) a + b + c Cash Received (or Paid) During 2001
Operating Activities				
Advertising revenues	$65,000	−$20,000(5)		$45,000
Salaries	−38,650	+2,400(7b)		−36,250
Rent	−18,000		−$6,000(2)	−24,000
Utilities	−725	+75(7a)		−650
Supplies	−750	+50(8)	−100(9)	−800
Interest	−900	+900(7c)		−0−
Depreciation	−2,250	+2,250(10)		−0−
Operating cash flow				−$16,700
Net income	$ 3,725			
Investing Activities				
Equipment purchase				−$15,000(4)
Financing Activities				
Stock issuance				$10,500(1)
Bank borrowing				10,000(3)
				$20,500
Change in cash				−$11,200

Note: Numbers in parentheses refer to numbered transactions on pages 144–145.

- Advertising revenues recognized under accrual accounting totaled \$65,000. However, \$20,000 of this remains as uncollected accounts receivable at year-end. Thus, the ending balance in the "Accounts receivable" account must be *subtracted* from the accrual-basis revenues to derive the cash received during the year for advertising services.
- The salaries expense of \$38,650 for the year includes the \$36,250 of salaries incurred and paid in cash plus the \$2,400 of salary expense accrued at year-end. Therefore, the accrued (unpaid) salaries, which is the ending balance in the "Accrued salaries payable" (liability) account, must be *added back* to total salaries expense to derive the salaries paid in cash.
- HRB recognized rent expense of \$2,000 × 9 months = \$18,000 in 2001. The difference between the amount paid out in cash and the amount recognized as expense under accrual accounting (\$24,000 minus \$18,000 or \$6,000) would be the ending balance in the "Prepaid rent" (asset) account. This amount is shown as a negative adjustment (*subtraction*) in column (c), since the cash outflow for rent was greater than the amount of rent expense recognized.
- The utilities expense of \$725 for the year includes the \$650 of utilities paid in cash plus \$75 of utilities expense accrued at year-end. The utilities expense incurred but not yet paid, which is the ending balance in the "Accrued utilities payable" (liability) account, must be *added back* to the total utilities expense to obtain the cash payments for utilities in 2001.
- Total supplies purchased during the year included \$800 paid in cash and \$50 purchased on account ("Accounts payable"). Of the amount purchased, \$100 of supplies remains on hand in the "Supplies inventory" account at the end of the year. So, supplies expense under accrual accounting is \$800 + \$50 − \$100 = \$750. To adjust the accrual basis expense to derive the cash outflow for supplies requires that we *add back* the ending balance in accounts payable (which was a noncash increase to the supplies expense) and *subtract* the \$100 ending balance in supplies inventory (which was a noncash decrease to the supplies expense).
- Accrued interest expense for the year is \$10,000 × 12% × 9/12 = \$900. Since none of this has been paid in cash, the ending balance in the "Accrued interest payable" (liability) account must be *added back* to the "Interest expense" account to obtain the cash paid out for interest in 2001.
- Depreciation is a noncash expense under accrual accounting. So, this amount, which is reflected in the increase in the "Accumulated depreciation" (contra-asset) account, must be *added back* to depreciation expense.

> Remember, for a start-up company, beginning account balances are zero.

Except for depreciation, each of the adjustments outlined above uses the ending balance (which is also the *change* in the account balance in the first year of a company's life) of a current asset account (e.g., "Accounts receivable," "Supplies inventory," or "Prepaid rent") or a current liability account (e.g., "Accounts payable," "Salaries payable," "Utilities payable," or "Interest payable") to adjust accrual basis revenues or expenses in order to derive cash flows from operations. The adjustments to accrual basis income (revenues minus expenses) for changes in current asset and current liability accounts that represent accrued revenues, deferred (unearned) revenues, accrued expenses, or deferred (prepaid) expenses are summarized in Figure 4.1.

> Only adjustments for changes in working capital accounts are summarized in Figure 4.1. Other adjustments (such as depreciation and gains/losses on asset sales) will be discussed in Chapter 17.

Exhibit 4.5 illustrates how the adjustments to accrual earnings due to *changes* in various current asset and liability accounts would be reflected in a GAAP statement of cash flows. The item numbers appearing next to each element in the cash flow statement correspond to the numbers in columns (b), (c), and (d) of Exhibit 4.4. The presentation format illustrated is called the **indirect approach,** since it does not show the individual operating cash inflows and outflows *directly.* (The **direct approach** is shown in column [d] of Exhibit 4.4). In Exhibit 4.5, net cash flows from operations is arrived at indirectly by adjusting earnings for the differences between accrual basis revenues and expenses and cash inflows and outflows during the period.

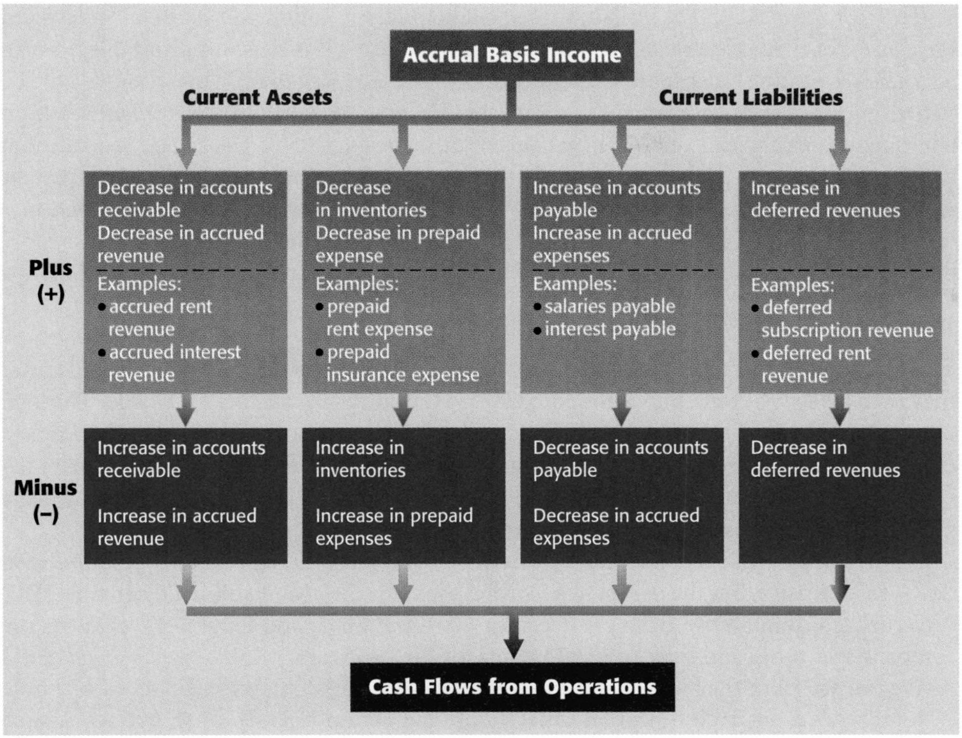

Figure 4.1

ADJUSTMENTS TO ACCRUAL EARNINGS FOR CHANGES IN WORKING CAPITAL ACCOUNTS TO OBTAIN CASH FLOWS FROM OPERATIONS.

Exhibit 4.5 ■ HRB ADVERTISING COMPANY

Statement of Cash Flows for Year Ended December 31, 2001

Operating Cash Flows		
Net income		$ 3,725
Plus:		
Depreciation[10]	$ 2,250	
Increase in salaries payable[7b]	2,400	
Increase in accounts payable[8]	50	
Increase in utilities payable[7a]	75	
Increase in interest payable[7c]	900	5,675
Minus:		
Increase in receivables[5]	(20,000)	
Increase in prepaid rent[2]	(6,000)	
Increase in supplies inventory[9]	(100)	(26,100)
Cash flows from operations		($16,700)
Investing Cash Flows		
Equipment purchase[4]		($15,000)
Financing Cash Flows		
Stock issuance[1]		$10,500
Bank borrowing[3]		10,000
		$20,500
Change in cash		($11,200)

The cash flow statement in Exhibit 4.5 will help Herb, Robin, and Barbara understand the causes for their overdrawn checking account. While the business was profitable from an accrual accounting standpoint, total cash flows were negative. This should not be surprising since start-up companies often spend a large portion of their available cash on equipment purchases, inventory build-up, and the production of goods and services that are frequently sold on account—and, therefore, that generate no cash immediately. Although the company is profitable, it may be forced into bankruptcy unless quick action is taken to resolve the cash flow deficit. To remain in business, the owners must infuse more equity capital, arrange for an extension of their bank loan, or speed up cash collections.

Deriving Cash Flow Information

The three owners were able to convince their banker to refinance the loan but only after they each agreed to contribute another $2,000 to the company—a total of $6,000. The loan was replaced by a three-year note, but the interest rate was increased to 13.50% to reflect the additional risk associated with the refinanced borrowing. Herb, Robin, and Barbara felt confident that with careful attention to both earnings and cash flow, they could successfully grow the business and repay the note before its maturity.

During 2002—the second year of business—revenues increased and operating cash flows were positive, but the company recorded a loss for the year. Exhibit 4.6 contains HRB Advertising's comparative balance sheets for 2001 and 2002, and Exhibit 4.7 presents the company's earnings and cash flow statements for the two years.

We can see from the balance sheet that the $10,000 bank loan was refinanced as a note ("Note payable" in Exhibit 4.6) and that additional common stock of $6,000 was issued during 2002. Also notice that the company's cash account ended the year with a positive balance of $500.

Highlights from the income statement (Exhibit 4.7[a]) include substantial growth in advertising revenues from $65,000 to $92,000, a 41.5% increase. At the same time, the company was able to speed up its collection of credit sales and reduce its "Accounts

Exhibit 4.6 ■ HRB ADVERTISING COMPANY

Comparative Balance Sheets
December 31, 2001 and 2002

	2001	2002
Assets		
Cash	($11,200)	$ 500
Accounts receivable	20,000	15,775
Supplies inventory	100	225
Prepaid rent	6,000	6,000
Office equipment	15,000	16,500
Less: Accumulated depreciation	(2,250)	(5,500)
Total assets	$27,650	$33,500
Liabilities and Equities		
Utilities payable	$ 75	$ 50
Interest payable	900	675
Accounts payable (supplies)	50	75
Salaries payable	2,400	4,200
Bank loan	10,000	—
Note payable	—	10,000
Total liabilities	$13,425	$15,000
Common stock	10,500	16,500
Retained earnings	3,725	2,000
Total liabilities and stockholders' equity	$27,650	$33,500

Exhibit 4.7 ■ HRB ADVERTISING COMPANY

Comparative Income and Cash Flow Statements for Years Ended December 31, 2001 and 2002

	2001	2002
Income Statement		
Revenue from advertising services	$65,000	$92,000
Less:		
Salaries expense	(38,650)	(62,875)
Supplies expense	(750)	(1,200)
Rent expense	(18,000)	(24,000)
Utilities expense	(725)	(1,050)
Interest expense	(900)	(1,350)
Depreciation	(2,250)	(3,250)
Net income	$ 3,725	($ 1,725)

(a)

	2001	2002
Cash Flow Statement		
Net income	$ 3,725	($ 1,725)
Depreciation	2,250	3,250
	5,975	1,525
Working capital adjustments:		
Accounts receivable decrease (increase)	(20,000)	4,225
Supplies inventory (increase)	(100)	(125)
Prepaid rent decrease (increase)	(6,000)	—
Utilities payable increase (decrease)	75	(25)
Accounts payable (supplies) increase	50	25
Interest payable increase (decrease)	900	(225)
Salaries payable increase	2,400	1,800
Cash flow from operations	($16,700)	$ 7,200
Equipment purchases	($15,000)	($ 1,500)
Cash flow from investing activities	($15,000)	($ 1,500)
Bank loan (repayment)	$10,000	($10,000)
Note payable issued	—	10,000
Common stock issued	10,500	6,000
Cash flow from financing activities	$20,500	$ 6,000
Change in cash balance	($11,200)	$11,700

(b)

receivable" balance, as shown in Exhibit 4.6. Unfortunately, salary expense increased nearly 63%, from $38,650 to $62,875, which seems to be the major factor contributing to the company's $1,725 loss for the year. From the cash flow statement (see Exhibit 4.7[b]), we see that 2002 cash flows from operations totaled a positive $7,200 even though the business sustained a loss for the year. The company's overall cash balance increased by $11,700 during the year, with $6,000 of that amount representing cash contributed by the owners in exchange for additional common stock.

Although U.S. companies must now include a cash flow statement similar to Exhibit 4.7(b) in their annual report to shareholders, this was not always the case. Moreover, quarterly cash flow statements are not required, although some companies voluntarily make them available to shareholders. Companies that don't provide quarterly cash flow statements challenge the analyst. How can cash flow information be derived from a company's balance sheet and income statement when the cash flow statement itself is not available?

The answer is not very complicated, as we will see. Deriving information about a company's cash receipts and disbursements from balance sheet and income statement information involves little more than a careful and systematic analysis of the changes in individual balance sheet accounts and their corresponding income statement effects. From this analysis you can deduce individual cash flows and construct a summary schedule of cash receipts (inflows) and disbursements (outflows) that closely resembles the cash flow statement presented in Exhibit 4.7(b).

The starting point for this analysis is the cash account itself. Notice from the balance sheet (Exhibit 4.6) that the company's cash position increased by $11,700 during 2002, from the $11,200 deficit at the beginning of the year to a $500 positive balance at year-end. Consequently, we know that total cash receipts for the year must have been $11,700 greater than total cash payments. Now let's uncover some individual cash flow items.

Exhibit 4.8 illustrates the general T-account analysis that can be used to derive cash flow information from selected balance sheet accounts of HRB Advertising for 2002. From the comparative balance sheet in Exhibit 4.6, the beginning and ending balances can be obtained for each *balance sheet* account that is affected when a revenue or expense item is recorded. The accrual basis revenue or expense that results in a debit or credit to the related balance sheet account can then be entered (see circled items in Exhibit 4.8). The cash received or cash paid, which results in an offsetting entry to each of these accounts, is the

Exhibit 4.8 ■ HRB ADVERTISING COMPANY

Analysis of Income Statement and Balance Sheet Accounts for Year Ended December 31, 2002

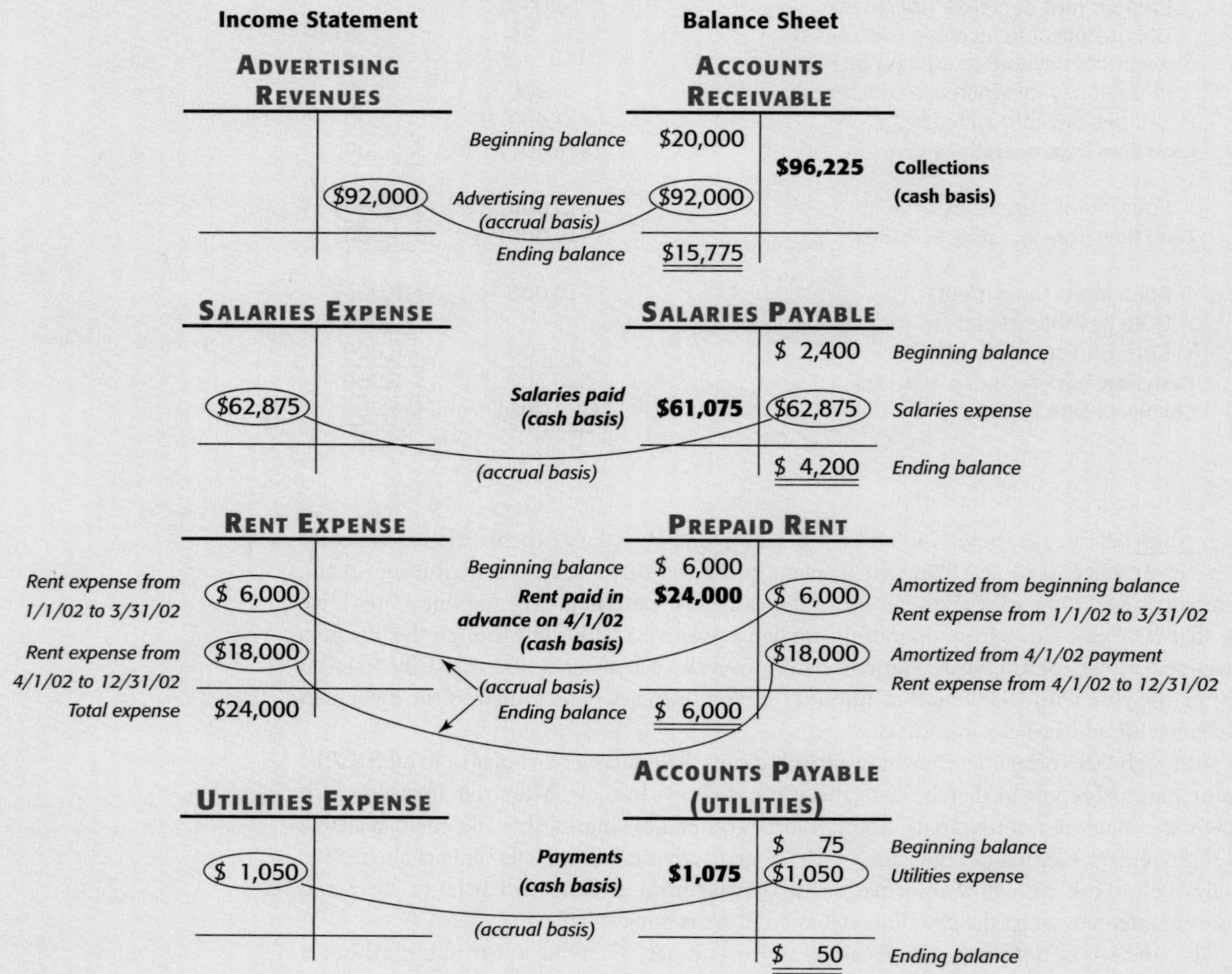

Exhibit 4.8 (cont.) ■ HRB ADVERTISING COMPANY

Analysis of Income Statement and Balance Sheet Accounts for Year Ended December 31, 2002

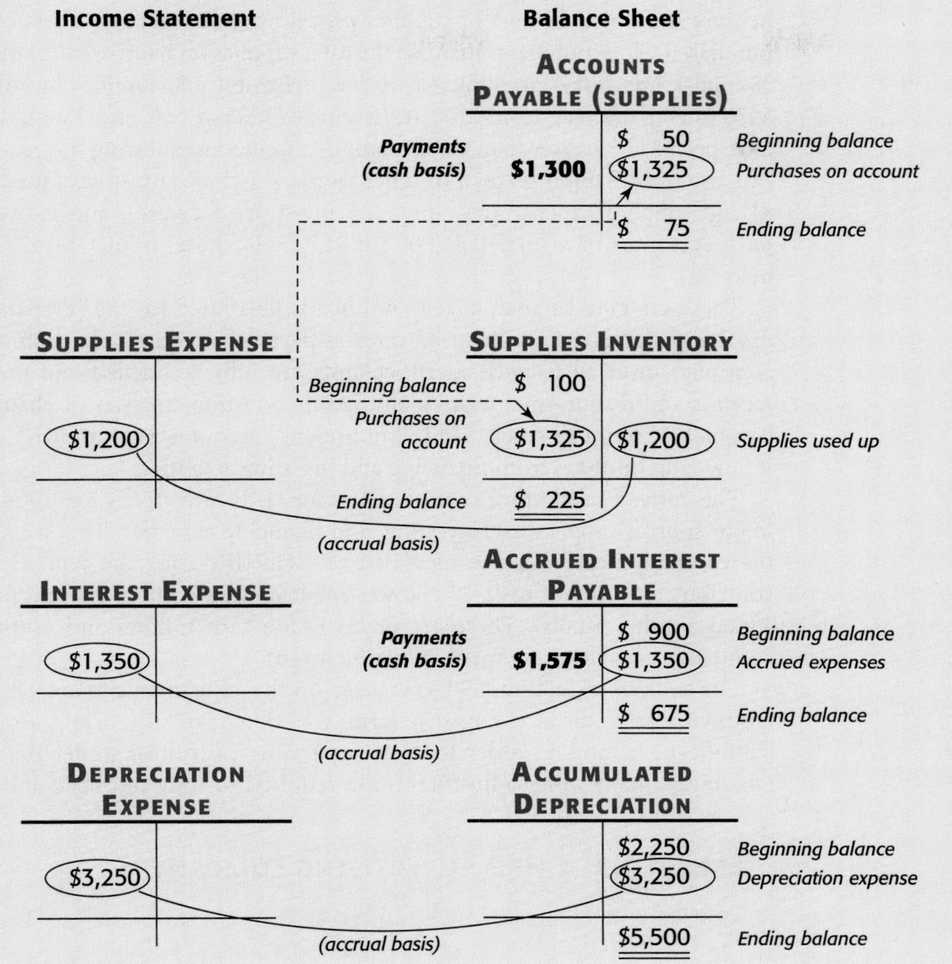

"plug" figure (in bold) that is needed to arrive at the ending balance that is given. We now illustrate this analysis for selected accounts in Exhibit 4.8.

The company's only source of operating cash inflows is customer receipts, so we begin with an analysis of the "Accounts receivable" account. As shown in Exhibit 4.8, the balance in the "Accounts receivable" account declined by $4,225 during 2002, from a beginning balance of $20,000 to a year-end balance of $15,775. Since billings for advertising services performed during 2002 totaled $92,000 (i.e., advertising revenues in the earnings statement of Exhibit 4.7[a]), HRB must have collected $96,225 from its customers. To see this, note that collections must have been $4,225 greater than new billings, because the "Accounts receivable" balance decreased by this amount during the year. Another way to think about this calculation is to assume that all customers pay on a timely basis. In this case, HRB would have collected $20,000 cash from customers billed in 2001 and another $76,225 from customers billed in 2002 (or $92,000 billings minus the $15,775 that was uncollected at year-end).

Salary payments represent the company's largest operating cash outflow. Exhibit 4.8 shows that salaries payable increased by $1,800 during the year, from a beginning balance of $2,400 to $4,200 at year-end. Consequently, salary payments must have been $61,075 for the year, or $1,800 less than the total salaries expense of $62,875 that shows up in the income statement in Exhibit 4.7(a).

Some cash inflows and outflows involve more than one balance sheet account. Exhibit 4.8 shows this for supplies. As shown there, "Accounts payable (supplies)" increased $25 during the year, from a beginning balance of $50 to $75 at year-end. This means that payments for supplies must have been $25 less than purchases. But, where can we find information about purchases? Certainly not from the income statement (Exhibit 4.7[a]), because it reports the cost of supplies *used* during the year regardless of when they were purchased. Since purchases increase the total supplies on hand, we turn our attention to the "Supplies inventory" account. As we see in Exhibit 4.8, supplies inventory increased by $125 during the year, from $100 at the start to $225 at year-end. Purchases must therefore have been $125 greater than the amount of supplies used during the year (i.e., the supplies expense from Exhibit 4.7[a]). In other words, purchases must have totaled $1,325 (or the $1,200 supplies expense plus the $125 inventory increase), and consequently, supplier payments must have totaled $1,300 (or $1,325 purchases minus the $25 accounts payable increase).

The same kind of analysis just outlined is illustrated for the "Prepaid rent," "Accounts payable (utilities)," and "Accrued interest payable" accounts in Exhibit 4.8. The process continues until all balance sheet accounts are fully reconciled and the company's cash receipts and disbursements are identified. In addition, analysis of changes in the "Notes payable," "Common stock," and "Equipment" accounts (not shown) can identify cash inflows and outflows from financing and investing activities.

The derived cash inflows and outflows for HRB Advertising are listed in Exhibit 4.9 by major sources—operating, investing, and financing activities. This schedule explains why the company's cash balance increased by $11,700 during the year. Operating activities contributed $7,200 of cash, $1,500 was spent on new equipment, and financing activities added another $6,000. These are precisely the cash inflows and outflows listed in the company's cash flow statement in Exhibit 4.7(b).

The analysis in Exhibit 4.9 has focused on the adjustments to accrual earnings that are required as a result of changes in various working capital (current assets minus current liabilities) accounts in order to derive operating cash flows under the indirect method. Obviously, many other adjustments are required to fully reconcile accrual earnings and

Exhibit 4.9 ■ HRB ADVERTISING COMPANY

Schedule of Cash Receipts and Disbursements for the Years Ended December 31, 2001 and 2002

	2001	2002	
Operating Activities			
Advertising services	$45,000	$96,225	← *from Accounts Receivable*
Salaries	(36,250)	(61,075)	← *from Salaries Payable*
Rent	(24,000)	(24,000)	← *from Prepaid Rent*
Utilities	(650)	(1,075)	← *from Utilities Payable*
Supplies	(800)	(1,300)	← *from Supplies Payable*
Interest	—	(1,575)	← *from Interest Payable*
Operating cash flow	($16,700)	$ 7,200	
Investing Activities			
Equipment purchase	($15,000)	($ 1,500)	← *from Office Equipment*
Financing Activities			
Bank borrowing	$10,000	($10,000)	← *from Notes Payable*
Note issuance	—	10,000	← *from Notes Payable*
Stock issuance	10,500	6,000	← *from Common Stock*
	20,500	6,000	
Change in cash	($11,200)	$11,700	← *from Cash*

cash flows from operations. These will be discussed in Chapter 17 after you have had a chance to review in some detail the accrual accounting entries related to noncurrent asset and liability accounts.

Accrual earnings and cash flows capture different aspects of a firm's performance and often differ by a wide margin from year to year. Cash flows are critical to assessing a company's liquidity and creditworthiness. The cash flow statement provides a detailed summary of the cash inflows and outflows that are derived from a company's three primary activities—operations, investing, and financing. This section has outlined the basic techniques for deriving operating cash flows from an analysis of comparative balance sheets and income statement information. To do this, you must analyze changes in current asset and current liability accounts (as well as other non-cash revenues and expenses like depreciation) that capture differences between the cash flow effects and accrual earnings effects of revenue and expense transactions.

RECAP

SUMMARY

The balance sheet and statement of cash flows are two of the primary financial statements required under GAAP. The balance sheet shows the assets owned by a company at a given point in time and how those assets are financed (debt versus equity). A variety of measurement bases are used to report the various asset, liability, and stockholders' equity accounts. When making intercompany comparisons, financial statement users must be careful to recognize how the different measurement bases affect key financial ratios and how account titles and statement formats vary across countries.

The statement of cash flows shows the change in cash for a given period, broken down into operating, investing, and financing activities. Successive balance sheets and the statement of cash flows articulate with one another, because changes in noncash balance sheet accounts can be used to explain changes in cash for a period. Analysis of changes in selected balance sheet accounts also can be used to explain why operating cash flows differ from accrual income. Conversely, the statement of cash flows provides information that enables users to understand changes in balance sheet accounts that have occurred over the reporting period. Understanding the interrelationships between successive balance sheets and the statement of cash flows, and being able to exploit these interrelationships to derive unknown account balances are important skills for analysts and lending officers.

EXERCISES

E4–1

Determining collections on account

AICPA adapted

During 2001 Kew Company, a service organization, had $200,000 in cash sales and $3,000,000 in credit sales. The accounts receivable balances were $400,000 and $485,000 at December 31, 2000 and 2001, respectively.

REQUIRED:

What was Kew Company's cash receipts from sales in 2001?

E4–2

Determining cash from operations

AICPA adapted

The following information is available from Sand Corporation's accounting records for the year ended December 31, 2001:

Cash received from customers	$870,000
Rent received	10,000
Cash paid to suppliers and employees	510,000
Taxes paid	110,000
Cash dividends paid	30,000

REQUIRED:

Compute cash flow provided by operations for 2001.

E4–3

Determining cash collections on account

AICPA adapted

Fresh Company is preparing its cash budget for the month of May. The following information is available concerning its accounts receivable:

Estimated credit sales for May	$200,000
Actual credit sales for April	$150,000
Estimated collection in May for credit sales in May	20%
Estimated collection in May for credit sales in April	70%
Estimated collection in May for credit sales prior to April	$ 12,000
Estimated write-offs in May for uncollectible credit sales	$ 8,000
Estimated bad debts expense in May for credit sales in May	$ 7,000

REQUIRED:

What are the estimated cash receipts from accounts receivable collections in May?

E4–4

Determining ending accounts receivable

AICPA adapted

The following information is available for Alex Corporation's first year of operation:

Payment for merchandise purchases	$200,000
Ending merchandise inventory	60,000
Accounts payable (balance at end of year)	40,000
Collections from customers	170,000

All merchandise items were marked to sell at 30% above cost.

REQUIRED:

What should be the ending balance in accounts receivable, assuming all accounts are deemed collectible?

E4–5

Determining cash disbursements

AICPA adapted

Serven Corporation has estimated its accrual-basis revenue and expenses for June 2001 and would like your help in estimating cash disbursements. Selected data from these estimated amounts are as follows:

- Sales — $700,000
- Gross profit (based on sales) — 30%
- Increase in trade accounts receivable for the month — $ 20,000
- Change in accounts payable during month — 0
- Increase in inventory during month — $ 10,000
- Variable selling, general, and administrative expenses include a charge for uncollectible accounts of 1% of sales.
- Total selling, general, and administrative expenses are $71,000 per month plus 15% of sales.
- Depreciation expense of $40,000 per month is included in fixed selling, general, and administrative expense.

REQUIRED:

On the basis of the preceding data, what are the estimated cash disbursements from operations for June?

E4–6

Determining cash collections on account

AICPA adapted

The following information was taken from the 2001 financial statement of Planet Corporation:

Accounts receivable, January 1, 2001	$ 21,600
Accounts receivable, December 31, 2001	30,400
Sales on accounts and cash sales	438,000
Uncollectible accounts (bad debts)	1,000

No accounts receivable were written off or recovered during the year.

REQUIRED:

Determine the cash collected from customers by Planet Corporation in 2001.

E4–7

Determining cash received from customers

AICPA adapted

Lance Corporation's statement of cash flows for the year ended September 30, 2001 was prepared using the indirect method, and it included the following items:

Net income	$60,000
Noncash adjustments	
Depreciation expense	9,000
Increase in accounts receivable	(5,000)
Decrease in inventory	40,000
Decrease in accounts payable	(12,000)
Net cash flows from operating activities	$92,000

Lance reported revenues from customers of $75,000 in its 2001 income statement.

REQUIRED:

What amount of cash did Lance receive from customers during the year ended September 30, 2001?

E4–8

Determining cash from operations and reconciling with accrual net income

The following information was taken from the 2001 financial statements of Eiger Corporation, a maker of equipment for mountain and rock climbers:

Net income	$100,000
Depreciation	30,000
Increase (decrease) in	
Accounts receivable	110,000
Inventories	(50,000)
Prepaid expenses	15,000
Accounts payable	(150,000)
Salaries payable	15,000
Other current liabilities	(70,000)

REQUIRED:

1. Calculate Eiger's cash flow from operating activities for 2001.
2. Explain the reasons for the difference between the firm's net income and its cash flow from operating activities in 2001.

E4–9

Determining cash from operations and reconciling with accrual net income

The following information was taken from the 2001 financial statements of Zurich Corporation, a maker of fine Swiss watches:

Net income	($200,000)
Depreciation	50,000
Increase (decrease) in	
Accounts receivable	(140,000)
Inventories	25,000
Other current assets	10,000
Accounts payable	120,000
Accrued payables	(25,000)
Interest payable	50,000

REQUIRED:

1. Calculate Zurich's cash flow from operating activities for 2001.
2. Explain the reasons for the difference between the firm's net income and its cash flow from operating activities in 2001.

E4–10 Determining amounts shown on statements of cash flows

The following information was taken from Abbott Laboratory's financial statements. Abbott makes a variety of health-care products and uses the indirect method to determine cash flows from operations:

Cost of goods sold	$ 6,563,978
Acquisitions of property, plant, and equipment	1,007,247
Decrease in inventories	109,087
Repayments of obligations under long-term leases	112,876
Decrease in salaries payable	534,281
Gain on sale of land	271,986
Increase in receivables	181,085
Purchases of long-term investment securities	178,727
Repayments of long-term borrowings	234,848
Increase in accrued payables	154,873
Proceeds from short-term borrowings	196,487
Decrease in accounts payable	121,741
Proceeds from sales of property, plant, and equipment	23,878
Proceeds from the sale of long-term borrowings	381,848
Proceeds from sales of long-term investment securities	496,120
Decrease in other current assets	114,009
Purchases of common stock for treasury	607,598
Increase in prepaid expenses	34,875
Dividends paid	488,413
Sales	10,978,387
Depreciation and amortization	427,782
Repayments of short-term borrowings	213,833
Increase in current assets	3,978,911
Proceeds from the exercise of executive stock options	74,027

REQUIRED:

Determine which of the preceding items would appear as a separate line-item on Abbott Laboratory's statement of cash flows. In each case, indicate whether the item is related to cash flows from operations, from investing activities, or from financing activities.

PROBLEMS/DISCUSSION QUESTIONS

P4–1 Preparing the income statement and statement of cash flows

Consider the following transactions pertaining to Retail Traders Company. Amounts in parentheses indicate a decrease in the account.

	Assets		= Liabilities +	Owners' Equity	
Explanation	**Cash**	**Inventory**	**Accounts Payable**	**Common Stock**	**Retained Earnings**
Beginning balance		$ 10,000	$ 5,000	$3,000	$ 2,000
Credit purchases		100,000	100,000		
Cash sales	$115,000				115,000
Cost of goods sold		(90,000)			(90,000)
Cash paid to suppliers	(85,000)		(85,000)		
Ending balance	$ 30,000	$ 20,000	$ 20,000	$3,000	$ 27,000

REQUIRED:

1. Based on this information, prepare an income statement and statement of cash flows.
2. Provide an intuitive explanation of how the adjustments made to net income in the cash flow statement converts the accrual numbers to cash flow numbers.

P4–2

Explaining the differences between cash flow from operations and accrual net income

CFA adapted

In reviewing the financial statements of Graceland Rock Company, you note that net income increased but cash flow from operations decreased from 2001 to 2002.

REQUIRED:

1. Explain how net income could increase for Graceland Rock Company while cash flow from operations decreased. Your answer must include three illustrative examples.
2. Explain why cash flow from operations may be a good indicator of a firm's "quality of earnings" when analyzed in conjunction with accrual-basis earnings.

P4–3

Common-size financial statements

Below are the common-size balance sheets from four companies: Amazon.com, an Internet book retailer; Alcoa, a major producer of aluminum products; Wendy's, a fast-food services organization; and Delta Air Lines, a major supplier of air transportation.

REQUIRED:

Based on your general business knowledge, the economic activities of these four firms, and information derived from the balance sheet analysis below, match the company with its respective balance sheet. Explain your reasoning for the choices that you make.

COMMON-SIZE BALANCE SHEET COMPARISONS

	Company A	Company B	Company C	Company D
Assets				
Current assets				
Cash and marketable securities	1.84%	6.91%	28.57%	11.19%
Current receivables	13.85	3.64	–	4.22
Inventories	9.48	–	8.93	2.14
Other current assets	2.95	5.60	3.45	1.02
Total current assets	28.12	16.15	40.95	18.57
Noncurrent assets				
Property, plant, and equipment, net	53.52	69.32	12.85	73.76
Goodwill and intangibles, net	7.78	9.56	29.55	2.56
Other assets, net	10.58	4.97	16.65	5.11
Total assets	100.00%	100.00%	100.00%	100.00%
Liabilities and Stockholders' Equity				
Current liabilities				
Total current liabilities	17.60%	32.20%	29.90%	15.09%
Long-term liabilities	36.84	39.73	59.33	17.73
Total liabilities	54.44	71.93	89.23	32.82
Minority interest	8.53	–	–	–
Redeemable preferred stock	–	–	–	10.62
Stockholders' equity				
Contributed capital and other equity items	1.51	11.41	46.46	(0.18)
Retained earnings (deficit)	35.52	16.66	(35.69)	56.74
Total liabilities and stockholders' equity	100.00%	100.00%	100.00%	100.00%

P4–4

Common-size financial statements

On the next page are the common-size balance sheets from four companies: Merck & Co., a global research-driven pharmaceutical manufacturing company; Target, a national discount retailer; Gannett, a newspaper publisher and broadcasting company; and Wisconsin Electric Power Company, a regional electric utility.

REQUIRED:

Based on your general business knowledge, the environment in which the above firms operate, and information derived from the balance sheet analysis, match the company with its respective balance sheet. Explain your reasoning for the choices that you make.

COMMON-SIZE BALANCE SHEET COMPARISONS

	Company A	Company B	Company C	Company D
Assets				
Current assets				
Cash and marketable securities	1.28%	8.99%	0.40%	0.51%
Current receivables	10.72	11.47	5.91	9.80
Inventories	22.16	7.99	3.16	1.05
Other current assets	3.66	3.15	1.61	0.58
Total current assets	37.82	31.60	11.08	11.94
Noncurrent assets				
Property, plant, and equipment, net	57.74	27.15	62.75	24.69
Goodwill and intangibles, net	—	21.28	—	59.94
Other assets, net	4.44	19.97	26.17	3.43
Total assets	100.00%	100.00%	100.00%	100.00%
Liabilities and Stockholders' Equity				
Current liabilities				
Total current liabilities	34.13%	24.58%	13.41%	9.81%
Long-term liabilities	31.68	28.55	50.04	38.79
Total liabilities	65.81	53.13	63.45	48.60
Redeemable preferred stock	—	—	3.23	—
Stockholders' equity				
Contributed capital and other equity items*	4.70	(18.93)	14.37	(9.72)
Retained earnings (deficit)	29.49	65.80	18.95	61.12
Total liabilities and stockholders' equity	100.00%	100.00%	100.00%	100.00%

*Net of cost of shares repurchased for treasury.

P4–5

Determining cash flows from operating and investing activities

AICPA adapted

Karr, Inc. reported net income of $300,000 for 2001. Changes occurred in several balance sheet accounts as follows:

Equipment	$25,000 increase	Inventories	$20,000 decrease
Accumulated depreciation	40,000 increase	Accounts receivable	15,000 increase
Note payable	30,000 increase	Accounts payable	5,000 decrease

ADDITIONAL INFORMATION:

- During 2001 Karr sold equipment costing $25,000, with accumulated depreciation of $12,000, for a gain of $5,000.
- In December 2001 Karr purchased equipment costing $50,000, with $20,000 cash and a 12% note payable of $30,000.
- Depreciation expense for the year was $52,000.

REQUIRED:

1. In Karr's 2001 statement of cash flows, calculate net cash provided by operating activities.
2. In Karr's 2001 statement of cash flows, calculate net cash used in investing activities.

P4–6

Determining operating cash flow components

AICPA adapted

The following data have been extracted from the financial statements of Prentiss, Inc., a calendar-year merchandising corporation:

Balance sheet data	December 31 2001	December 31 2002
Trade accounts receivable–net	$ 84,000	$ 78,000
Inventory	150,000	140,000
Accounts payable–merchandise (credit)	(95,000)	(98,000)

- Total sales for 2002 were $1,200,000 and for 2001 were $1,100,000. Cash sales were 20% of total sales each year.
- Cost of goods sold was $840,000 for 2002.
- Variable general and administrative (G&A) expenses for 2002 were $120,000. These expenses have varied in proportion to sales and have been paid at the rate of 50% in the year incurred and 50% the following year. Unpaid G&A expenses are ***not*** included in accounts payable.
- Fixed general and administrative expenses—including $35,000 depreciation and $5,000 bad debt expense—totaled $100,000 each year. The amount of such expenses involving cash payments was paid at the rate of 80% in the year incurred and 20% the following year. In each year there was a $5,000 bad debt estimate and a $5,000 write-off. Unpaid G&A expenses are ***not*** included in accounts payable.

REQUIRED:

Compute the following:

1. The amount of cash collected during 2002 that resulted from total sales in 2001 and 2002.
2. The amount of cash disbursed during 2002 for purchases of merchandise.
3. The amount of cash disbursed during 2002 for variable and fixed general and administrative expenses.

P4–7

Understanding the relation between the income statement, cash flow statement, and changes in balance sheet accounts

The following cash flow information pertains to the 2001 operations of Matterhorn, Inc., a maker of ski equipment:

Cash collections from customers	$16,670
Cash payments to suppliers	19,428
Cash payments for various operating expenses	7,148
Cash payments for current income taxes	200
Cash provided (used) by operating activities	(10,106)

The following additional information comes from Matterhorn's 2001 income statement:

Net income	$ 609
Depreciation of equipment	2,256
Amortization of patents	399
Loss on sale of equipment	169

The following additional information comes from Matterhorn's 2000 and 2001 comparative balance sheets (decreases are in parentheses):

Change in accounts receivable	$ 3,630
Change in inventory	3,250
Change in accounts payable	(3,998)
Change in accrued operating expenses	(2,788)
Change in deferred taxes payable	127

REQUIRED:

1. Use the preceding information to derive Matterhorn's 2001 income statement.
2. Use the same information to compute Matterhorn's 2001 cash flow from operating activities under the indirect method (i.e., derive cash flow from operating activities by making the necessary adjustments to net income).
3. Provide a brief explanation for the difference observed between net income and cash provided by operating activities.

P4–8

Understanding the relation between the income statement, cash flow statement, and changes in balance sheet accounts

The following cash flow information pertains to the 2001 operations of Divemaster, Inc., a maker of scuba diving equipment:

Cash collections from customers	$72,481
Cash payments to suppliers	51,768
Cash payments for selling and administrative expenses	9,409
Cash payments for interest	1,344
Cash payments for current income taxes	671
Cash provided by operating activities	9,289

The following additional information comes from Divemaster's 2001 income statement:

Net income	$1,085
Depreciation of equipment	7,380
Gain on sale of equipment	327

The following additional information comes from Divemaster's 2000 and 2001 comparative balance sheets (decreases are in parentheses):

Change in accounts receivable	($4,603)
Change in inventory	7,400
Change in accounts payable	3,146
Change in accrued selling and administrative expenses	772
Change in deferred taxes payable	(87)
Change in accrued interest payable	117

REQUIRED:

1. Use the preceding information to derive Divemaster's 2001 income statement.
2. Use the same information to compute Divemaster's 2001 cash flow from operating activities under the indirect method (i.e., derive cash flow from operating activities by making the necessary adjustments to net income).
3. Provide a brief explanation for the difference observed between net income and cash provided by operating activities.

P4–9

Understanding the relation between operating cash flows and accrual earnings

The following information is taken from the operating section of the statement of cash flows (direct method) of Battery Builders, Inc.:

Collections from customers	$ 28,000
Payments to suppliers for purchases	(13,000)
Payments for operating expenses	(9,000)
Payments for current period income taxes	(4,000)
Cash provided by operating activities	2,000

The following information is obtained from the income statement of Battery Builders:

Net income	$4,000
Depreciation expense	4,000
Gain on sale of equipment	2,000
Write-off of goodwill	1,000

In addition, the following information is obtained from the comparative balance sheets of Battery Builders (+/− refers to increase/decrease):

Change in accounts receivable	$+3,000
Change in inventory	+3,000
Change in accounts payable	+2,000
Change in accrued payable (related to operating expense)	−2,000
Change in deferred income taxes payable	+1,000

REQUIRED:

1. Prepare a complete accrual-basis income statement for the current year.
2. Compute the cash flows from operations using the indirect approach (i.e., start with accrual-basis net income and adjust for various items to obtain cash flows from operations).

The following information was taken from Microsoft Corporation's Year 2 balance sheet; Microsoft is one of the largest independent computer software makers in the United States.

P4–10

Microsoft (Finding missing values on a classified balance sheet and analyzing balance sheet changes)

	($ in millions)
Total current liabilities	$5,730
Other current assets	?
Equity investments	?
Property, plant, and equipment, net	1,505
Common stock and paid-in capital	?
Other assets	260
Cash and short-term investments	13,927
Total stockholders' equity	?
Accounts payable	759
Retained earnings	7,622
Unearned revenue	?
Accrued compensation	359
Accounts receivable, net	1,460
Total assets	?
Other current liabilities	809
Preferred stock	980
Total current assets	15,889
Income taxes payable	915
Total liabilities and stockholders' equity	22,357

The following is Microsoft's Year 1 balance sheet.

MICROSOFT CORPORATION

Consolidated Balance Sheets

($ in millions)	June 30, Year 1
Assets	
Current assets	
Cash and short-term investments	$ 8,966
Accounts receivable, net	980
Other	427
Total current assets	10,373
Property, plant, and equipment	1,465
Equity investments	2,346
Other assets	203
Total assets	$14,387
Liabilities and Stockholders' Equity	
Current liabilities	
Accounts payable	$ 721
Accrued compensation	336
Income taxes payable	466
Unearned revenue	1,418
Other	669
Total current liabilities	3,610
Stockholders' equity	
Convertible preferred stock: shares authorized 100; issued and outstanding 13	980
Common stock and paid-in capital: shares authorized 8,000; issued and outstanding 2,408	4,509
Retained earnings	5,288
Total stockholders' equity	10,777
Total liabilities and stockholders' equity	$14,387

REQUIRED:

1. Solve for the missing values and present Microsoft's Year 2 balance sheet in good form.
2. Microsoft has recently become a customer of your firm. In fact, their accounts receivable is one of your firm's largest current assets. The amount is so large that the chief executive officer (CEO) of your firm is concerned because if Microsoft doesn't pay in a timely fashion your firm would experience severe cash flow problems. Use Microsoft's balance sheet to assess Microsoft's ability to make timely payment of its current liabilities.
3. Using your Year 2 balance sheet and the Year 1 balance sheet provided, compare and contrast the financial position of the firm at the end of these two years. For example, were there any major changes in Microsoft's financial position from the end of Year 1 to the end of Year 2? In what ways did the firm's financial position improve or deteriorate over this time period?
4. Assume that you are a financial analyst. Based on the financial position of Microsoft as portrayed in the Year 1 and Year 2 balance sheets, would you advise your clients to invest in the common stock of the firm? Why or why not?
5. Before advising your clients about whether or not to purchase the common stock of Microsoft, what information beyond the Year 1 and Year 2 balance sheets would you seek?

P4–11

Finding missing values on a classified balance sheet and analyzing balance sheet accounts

The following information was taken from one of Hewlett-Packard Company's recent balance sheets. Hewlett-Packard is a major designer and manufacturer of electronic measurement and computing equipment, including workstations, PCs, and laser printers.

	($ in millions)
Total liabilities and shareholders' equity	?
Inventories: Finished goods	$1,100
Other current assets	347
Employee compensation and benefits payable	837
Total current assets	6,716
Land	?
Total shareholders' equity	7,269
Long-term debt	?
Machinery and equipment	2,792
Taxes payable	381
Long-term receivables and other assets	1,912
Other long-term liabilities	210
Cash and cash equivalents	625
Total assets	11,973
Notes payable and short-term borrowings	?
Deferred revenues (current)	375
Short-term investments	495
Buildings and leasehold improvements	2,779
Total current liabilities	4,063
Inventories: Purchased parts and fabricated assemblies	1,173
Deferred taxes payable	243
Common stock and capital in excess of $1 par value	1,010
Accumulated depreciation	2,616
Other accrued liabilities	583
Retained earnings	?
Accounts and notes receivable	?
Accounts payable	686

REQUIRED:

1. Use the information in the problem to determine the missing amounts and present Hewlett-Packard's balance sheet in good form.
2. Does Hewlett-Packard obtain financing primarily from stockholders or from creditors? Explain.
3. What is Hewlett-Packard's largest current asset?
4. What is Hewlett-Packard's largest current liability?
5. Calculate the ratio of Hewlett-Packard's current assets to current liabilities and comment on Hewlett-Packard's short-term liquidity position.
6. Hewlett-Packard's balance sheet lists an item called "Other current assets." What assets might be included under this heading?

P4–12

Analyzing the difference between operating cash flows and accrual earnings

The following are Food Tiger's 2000 and 2001 balance sheets and 2001 income statement.

FOOD TIGER, INC.

Comparative Balance Sheets

	December 31 2001	December 31 2000
Assets		
Current assets		
Cash and cash equivalents	$ 6,804	$ 428
Receivables	97,106	76,961
Inventories	844,539	673,606
Prepaid expenses	9,401	16,684
Total current assets	957,850	767,679
Property, at cost	1,446,896	1,094,804
Less: Accumulated depreciation	(407,641)	(303,027)
Total assets	$1,997,105	$1,559,456
Liabilities and Shareholders' Equity		
Current liabilities		
Accounts payable – trade	$ 343,163	$ 290,064
Accrued expenses	184,017	138,921
Accrued interest payable	1,067	3,394
Income taxes payable	37,390	42,958
Total current liabilities	565,637	475,337
Long-term debt	504,913	415,561
Total liabilities	$1,070,550	$ 890,898
Shareholders' equity		
Common stock	$ 263,155	$ 162,298
Retained earnings	663,400	506,260
Total shareholders' equity	$ 926,555	$ 668,558
Total liabilities and shareholders' equity	$1,997,105	$1,559,456

FOOD TIGER, INC.

Income Statement
For Year Ended December 31, 2001

Net sales	$6,438,507
Cost of goods sold	(5,102,977)
Gross profit	1,335,530
Selling and administrative expenses	(855,809)
Interest expense	(34,436)
Depreciation	(104,614)
Income before income taxes	340,671
Provision for income taxes	(135,500)
Net income	$ 205,171

ADDITIONAL INFORMATION:

1. The "Accounts payable, trade" account is used only for purchases of merchandise inventory.
2. The balance in the "Prepaid expenses" account represents prepaid selling and administrative expenses for the following year.
3. Except for the prepaid selling and administrative expenses noted in (2), the company records all selling and administrative expenses in the accrued expenses account prior to making payment.
4. The company records all interest expense in the "Accrued interest payable" account prior to making payment.
5. The company records all income tax expense in the "Income taxes payable" account prior to making payment.
6. Cash dividends declared and paid during 2001 were $48,031.
7. No long-term assets were disposed of in 2001.

REQUIRED:

1. Prepare an analysis of Food Tiger's 2001 operating cash flows and accrual based net income by completing the following table. The table follows the format of Exhibit 4.4 in this chapter.
2. Prepare Food Tiger's "Statement of cash flows" for 2001. Follow the format of Exhibit 4.5 in this chapter.

Table 1 ■ FOOD TIGER, INC.

Analysis of Change in Cash Versus Income for 2001

Item	(a) Accrual Income	(b) Noncash Accruals: Revenue Earned or Expenses Incurred	(c) Prepayments/ Buildups/Other Adjustments	(d) (a+b+c) Cash Received (+) or Paid (−)
Operating Activities				
.				
.				
.				
Operating cash flow				
Net Income				
Investing Activities				
.				
.				
.				
Financing Activities				
.				
.				
.				
Change in cash				

P4–13

Preparing the balance sheet and income statement

AICPA adapted

Vanguard Corporation is a distributor of food products. The corporation has approximately 1,000 stockholders; and its stock, which is traded "over-the-counter," is sold throughout 2001 at about $7 a share with little fluctuation. The corporation's balance sheet at December 31, 2000 appears below.

VANGUARD CORPORATION

Balance Sheet
December 31, 2000

Assets		
Current assets		
Cash		$ 4,386,040
Accounts receivable	$3,150,000	
Less allowance for doubtful accounts	(94,500)	3,055,500
Inventories—at the lower of cost (FIFO) or market		2,800,000
Total current assets		10,241,540
Fixed assets—at cost	$3,300,000	
Less accumulated depreciation	(1,300,000)	2,000,000
Total assets		$12,241,540
Liabilities and Stockholders' Equity		
Current liabilities		
Notes payable due within one year		$ 1,000,000
Accounts payable and accrued liabilities		2,091,500
Federal income taxes payable		300,000
Total current liabilities		3,391,500
Notes payable due after one year		4,000,000
Stockholders' equity		
Capital stock—authorized 2,000,000 shares of $1 par value; issued and outstanding 1,000,000 shares	$1,000,000	
Additional paid-in capital	1,500,000	
Retained earnings	2,350,040	
Total stockholders' equity		4,850,040
Total liabilities and stockholders' equity		$12,241,540

Information concerning the corporation and its activities during 2001 follows:

1. Sales for the year were $15,650,000. The gross profit percentage for the year was 30% of sales. Merchandise purchases and freight-in totaled $10,905,000. Depreciation and other expenses do not enter into cost of goods sold.
2. Administrative, selling, and general expenses (including provision for state taxes) other than interest, depreciation, and provision for doubtful accounts amounted to $2,403,250.
3. The December 31, 2001 accounts receivable amounted to $3,350,000, and the corporation maintains an allowance for doubtful accounts equal to 3% of the accounts receivable outstanding. During the year $50,000 of 2000 receivables were deemed uncollectible and charged off to the allowance account.
4. The rate of depreciation of fixed assets is 13% per annum, and the corporation consistently follows the policy of taking one-half year's depreciation in the year of acquisition. The depreciation expense for 2001 was $474,500.
5. The notes are payable in 20 equal quarterly installments—commencing March 31, 2001—with interest at 5% per annum also payable quarterly.
6. Accounts payable and accrued liabilities at December 31, 2001 were $2,221,000.
7. The balance of the 2000 federal income tax paid in 2001 was in exact agreement with the amount accrued on the December 31, 2000 balance sheet.

8. The 2001 estimated tax payments made in 2001 totaled $400,000. Income tax expense for 2001 on an accrual accounting basis was $530,000.
9. During the second month of each quarter of 2001, dividends of $0.10 a share were declared and paid. In addition, in July 2001 a 5% stock dividend was declared and paid.

REQUIRED:

Prepare the following statements in good form and support them by well-organized and developed computations for the year ending December 31, 2001:

a. Balance sheet
b. Income statement

CASES

C4-1

Debbie Dress Shops, Inc.: Determining cash flow amounts from comparative balance sheets and income statement

AICPA adapted

STRETCH

The balance sheet and income statement for Debbie Dress Shops are presented along with some additional information about the accounts. You are to answer the questions that follow concerning cash flows for the period.

DEBBIE DRESS SHOPS, INC.

Balance Sheet

	December 31 2001	2000
Assets		
Current assets		
Cash	$ 300,000	$ 200,000
Accounts receivable—net	840,000	580,000
Merchandise inventory	660,000	420,000
Prepaid expenses	100,000	50,000
Total current assets	1,900,000	1,250,000
Long-term investments	80,000	—
Land, building, and fixtures	1,130,000	600,000
Less: Accumulated depreciation	(110,000)	(50,000)
	1,020,000	550,000
Total assets	$3,000,000	$1,800,000
Liabilities and Stockholders' Equity		
Current liabilities		
Accounts payable	$ 530,000	$ 440,000
Accrued expenses	140,000	130,000
Dividends payable	70,000	—
Total current liabilities	740,000	570,000
Note payable—due year 2003	500,000	—
Stockholders' equity		
Common stock	1,200,000	900,000
Retained earnings	560,000	330,000
Total stockholders' equity	1,760,000	1,230,000
Total liabilities and stockholders' equity	$3,000,000	$1,800,000

DEBBIE DRESS SHOPS, INC.

Income Statements

	Year ended December 31 2001	2000
Net credit sales	$6,400,000	$4,000,000
Cost of goods sold	5,000,000	3,200,000
Gross profit	1,400,000	800,000
Expenses (including income taxes)	1,000,000	520,000
Net income	$ 400,000	$ 280,000

1. All accounts receivable and accounts payable are related to trade merchandise. Accounts payable are recorded net and always are paid to take all the discounts allowed. The allowance for doubtful accounts at the end of 2001 was the same as at the end of 2000; no receivables were charged against the allowance during 2001.
2. The proceeds from the note payable were used to finance a new store building. Capital stock was sold to provide additional working capital.

REQUIRED:

1. Calculate cash collected during 2001 from accounts receivable.
2. Calculate cash payments during 2001 on accounts payable to suppliers.
3. Calculate cash provided from operations for 2001.
4. Calculate cash inflows during 2001 from financing activities.
5. Calculate cash outflows from investing activities during 2001.

C4–2

Snap-On-Tools Corporation (CW): Determine missing amounts on the cash flow statement

The purpose of this case is to familiarize you with the statement of cash flows of a publicly held company. Its primary objective is to test your understanding of the relationships underlying the cash flow statement. It also serves as a natural way to expand your understanding of accounting terminology. This is an important feature because the financial statements of publicly held companies often use terms that are different from those appearing in financial accounting textbooks.

The information on the next page was taken from Snap-On-Tools Corporation's Year 2 statement of cash flows. Snap-On-Tools Corporation makes and sells hand tools for mechanics, tool storage units, and related items. Most of the company's sales come from dealers who visit customer locations with their walk-in vans.

	($ in thousands)
Cash and cash equivalents at beginning of year	$ 10,930
Increase in notes payable	52,503
Decrease in deferred income taxes	6,005
Decrease in accounts payable	8,202
Net cash provided by operating activities	?
Capital expenditures	21,081
Depreciation	25,484
Acquisition of Sun Electric, net of cash acquired	110,719
Increase in receivables	5,458
Net cash used in investing activities	?
Payment of long-term debt	8,332
Increase in other noncurrent assets	3,609
Decrease in inventories	5,928
Proceeds from stock option plans	4,940
Net earnings	65,975
Increase in accruals, deposits, and other liabilities	23,330
Cash dividends paid	45,718
Increase in long-term debt	78,650
Net cash provided by (used in) financing activities	?
Effect of exchange rate changes	1,916
Increase in cash and cash equivalents	?
Disposal of property and equipment	3,379
Cash and cash equivalents at end of year	?
Amortization	3,973
Increase in prepaid expenses	4,829
Gain on sale of assets	250

REQUIRED:

Use the following information to solve for the missing values, and recast Snap-On-Tools's Year 2 statement of cash flows in proper form. (*Note*: The item "Effect of exchange rate changes" captures gains or losses that arise when a firm converts its foreign subsidiaries' financial statements from the respective currencies [e.g., French francs] into U.S. dollars.) In Snap-On's case, these translations were not favorable in Year 2. While the amount of this item reflects events and transactions affecting various items in the statement of cash flows, it is not separately identified with any individual section of the statement. Rather, it is treated as an adjustment to aggregate net cash flows to arrive at the change in cash. This adjustment usually appears near the bottom of the statement of cash flows.

C4–3 **Drop Zone Corporation (CW): Understanding the relation between successive balance sheets and the cash flow statement**

STRETCH

Following is Drop Zone Corporation's balance sheet at the end of 2000 and its cash flow statement for 2001. Drop Zone manufactures equipment for sky divers.

DROP ZONE CORPORATION

Balance Sheet
December 31, 2000

Assets	
Current assets	
Cash	$ 7,410
Accounts receivable—net	6,270
Inventory	13,395
Prepaid assets	1,995
Total current assets	29,070
Land	27,930
Buildings and equipment	194,655
Less: Accumulated depreciation, buildings and equipment	(40,185)
Total assets	$211,470

DROP ZONE CORPORATION (*continued*)

Balance Sheet
December 31, 2000

Liabilities and Stockholders' Equity	
Current liabilities	
Accounts payable	$ 11,400
Accrued payables	3,135
Total current liabilities	14,535
Long-term debt	19,950
Stockholders' equity	
Common stock, $10.00 par value	18,525
Paid-in capital	31,920
Retained earnings	144,780
Less: Treasury stock	(18,240)
Total liabilities and stockholders' equity	$211,470

DROP ZONE CORPORATION

Statement of Cash Flows
For Year Ended December 31, 2001

Operating Activities	
Net income	$11,400
Plus (minus) noncash items	
+ Depreciation expense	5,415
Plus (minus) changes in current asset and liability accounts	
+ Decrease in inventory	1,425
+ Decrease in prepaid assets	855
+ Increase in accrued payables	1,140
– Increase in accounts receivable	(3,990)
– Decrease in accounts payable	(2,850)
Cash provided by operating activities	$13,395
Investing Activities	
Purchase of equipment	($39,615)
Proceeds from the sale of land	8,550
Cash used by investing activities	($31,065)
Financing Activities	
Issuance of long-term debt	$16,245
Issuance of common stock	12,825
Cash dividends paid	(6,270)
Purchase of treasury stock	(2,565)
Cash provided by financing activities	$20,235
Net cash flow	$ 2,565

ADDITIONAL INFORMATION:

1. During 2001, 500 shares of common stock were sold to the public.
2. Land was sold during 2001 at an amount that equaled its original cost.

REQUIRED:

Use the preceding information to derive Drop Zone Corporation's balance sheet at the end of 2001.

C4–4

Long Distance Runner Corporation (CW): Understanding the relation between successive balance sheets and the cash flow statement

Long Distance Runner Corporation manufactures footwear and clothing for runners and hikers. Its balance sheet at the end of 2001 and its cash flow statement for 2001 follow.

LONG DISTANCE RUNNER CORPORATION

Balance Sheet
December 31, 2001

Assets	
Current assets	
Cash	$ 39,825
Accounts receivable—net	147,825
Inventory	27,000
Prepaid expenses	6,750
Total current assets	221,400
Land	202,500
Buildings	202,500
Equipment	40,500
Less: Accumulated depreciation, buildings and equipment	(27,000)
Patents, net	40,500
Total assets	$680,400
Liabilities and Stockholders' Equity	
Current liabilities	
Accounts payable	$ 62,100
Accrued salaries payable	20,250
Accrued interest payable	20,250
Total current liabilities	102,600
Notes payable—long term	148,500
Long-term debt	158,625
Stockholders' equity	
Common stock $1.00 par value	23,500
Paid-in capital	233,000
Retained earnings	14,175
Less: Treasury stock	–0–
Total liabilities and stockholders' equity	$680,400

LONG DISTANCE RUNNER CORPORATION

Statement of Cash Flows
for the Year Ended December 31, 2001

Operating Activities	
Net income	$ 20,925
Plus (minus) noncash items	
+ Depreciation expense	16,875
+ Amortization of patent	13,500
+ Loss on sale of equipment	675
	$ 51,975
Plus (minus) changes in current asset and liability accounts	
+ Decrease in prepaid assets	6,750
+ Increase in accrued salaries payable	13,500
– Increase in accounts receivable	(73,575)
– Increase in inventory	(6,750)
– Decrease in accounts payable	(22,275)
– Decrease in accrued interest	(10,125)
Cash used by operating activities	($ 40,500)
Investing Activities	
Purchase of land	($ 67,500)
Purchase of building	(202,500)
Proceeds from the sale of equipment	9,450
Cash used by investing activities	($260,550)
Financing Activities	
Issuance of long-term debt	$158,625
Issuance of common stock	175,500
Cash dividends paid	(47,250)
Sale of treasury stock	6,750
Principal repayment on note payable	(6,750)
Cash provided by financing activities	$286,875
Net cash flow	($ 14,175)

ADDITIONAL INFORMATION:

1. During 2001, 7,500 shares of common stock were sold to the public.
2. Equipment with an original cost of $13,500 and with accumulated depreciation of $3,375 was sold for $9,450 in 2001.

REQUIRED:

Use the preceding information to derive Long Distance Runner Corporation's balance sheet at the end of 2000 (i.e., at the beginning of 2001).

Collaborative Learning Case

C4–5

Kellogg Company (CW): Determine missing amounts on the cash flow statement and explain the causes for change in cash

The following information was taken from Kellogg Company's Year 2 statement of cash flows. Kellogg is the world's largest maker of ready-to-eat cereals. Its cereal products account for about 38% of the U.S. market and 52% of the non-U.S. market. Some of its more famous brand name products include Frosted Flakes, Rice Krispies, Fruit Loops, and Apple Jacks.

	($ in millions)
Increase (decrease) in cash and temporary investments	$77.5
Issuance of common stock	17.7
Other noncash expenses	16.8
Decrease in accounts receivable	10.2
Additions to properties	?
Purchase of treasury stock	83.6
Depreciation	222.8
Increase in prepaid expenses	22.9
Cash and temporary investments at end of year	?
Decrease in deferred income taxes	5.4
Borrowings on notes payable	182.1
Cash used by investing activities	319.9
Issuance of long-term debt	4.3
Cash dividends	?
Property disposals	25.2
Cash provided by operations	934.4
Increase in accounts payable	42.7
Other financing activities	1.1
Reduction of long-term debt	126.0
Increase in inventories	41.4
Cash used by financing activities	?
Effect of exchange rate changes on cash	0.7
Net earnings	?
Cash and temporary investments at beginning of year	100.5
Increase in accrued liabilities	105.6
Other acquisitions	11.6
Reduction of notes payable	274.0

Required:

1. Determine the missing values and recast Kellogg's Year 2 statement of cash flows, showing in good form cash flows from operations, investing, and financing activities. (*Note*: The item "Effect of exchange rate changes on cash" captures the gains or losses that arise when a firm converts its foreign subsidiaries' financial statements from the respective currencies (e.g., French francs) into U.S. dollars. In Kellogg's case, these translations were favorable in Year 2. This item should be treated as an adjustment to aggregate net cash flows to arrive at the change in cash. This adjustment usually appears near the bottom of the statement of cash flows.)
2. How did Kellogg fund its investing activities during Year 2?
3. How much cash did depreciation provide during Year 2?
4. Cash provided by operations was $934.4 million in Year 2, yet Kellogg's cash account balance only increased by $77.5 million during the year. How can this be?

5

Essentials of Financial Statement Analysis

"Investors would be well advised to shut out all the yammering about earnings expectations, consensus forecasts, and whisper numbers and focus instead on the financial information reported by companies themselves."[1]

LEARNING OBJECTIVES:
After studying this chapter, you will understand:

1. How competitive forces and a company's business strategy influence its operating profitability and the composition of its balance sheet.
2. Why analysts worry about the quality of financial statement information and how quality is determined.
3. How return on assets (ROA) can be used to analyze a company's profitability, and what insights are gained from separating ROA into its profit margin and asset turnover components.
4. How return on common equity (ROCE) can be used to assess the impact of financial leverage on a company's profitability.
5. How short-term liquidity risk differs from long-term solvency risk, and what financial ratios are used to assess these two dimensions of credit risk.
6. How to interpret the results of an analysis of profitability and risk.
7. Why EBITDA (earnings before interest, taxes, depreciation, and amortization) can be a misleading indicator of profitability and cash flow.

A firm's financial statements are like an optical lens. If you know how to look through them, you can more clearly see what is going on at the firm. Has profitability improved? Are customers paying their bills more promptly? How was the new manufacturing plant financed? Financial statements hold the answers to these and other questions. They can tell us how the company got to where it is today, and they can help us forecast where the company might be tomorrow.

This chapter provides an overview of three financial analysis tools—**common size statements, trend statements,** and **financial ratios.** We show how each tool is used, and we explain how to interpret the results from each. But the important message in this chapter is that all financial analysis tools are built around reported accounting data, and these tools can be no better than the data from which they are constructed. ***What financial data a company chooses to report and how the data are reported affect not only the financial statements themselves but also the ratios and other numbers used to analyze those statements.***

Introducing financial analysis tools at this early point prepares you for later chapters where we describe various financial reporting alternatives and their impact on ratios, trends, and other comparisons.

Basic Approaches

Analysts use financial statements and financial data in many ways and for many different purposes. Two purposes you should know are time-series analysis and cross-sectional analysis.

[1] G. Morgenson, "Flying Blind in a Fog of Data," *New York Times* (June 18, 2000).

Time-series analysis helps identify financial trends over time for a *single* company or business unit. The analyst might be interested in determining the rate of growth in sales for Intel Corporation, or the degree to which Intel's earnings have fluctuated historically with inflation, business cycles, foreign currency exchange rates, or changes in economic growth in domestic or foreign markets.

Cross-sectional analysis helps identify similarities and differences *across* companies or business units at a single moment in time. The analyst might compare the 2001 profitability of one company in an industry to a competitor's profitability. A related analytic tool—**benchmark comparison**—measures a company's performance or health against some predetermined standard. For example, commercial lending agreements often require the borrowing company to maintain minimum dollar levels of working capital or tangible net worth. Once the loan has been granted, the lender—a bank or insurance company—monitors compliance by comparing the borrower's reported financial amounts and ratios to those specified in the loan agreement.

Tangible net worth is usually defined as total *tangible* assets minus total liabilities, where tangible assets exclude things like goodwill, patents, trademarks, and other *intangible* items.

Analysts use a mixture of time-series and cross-sectional tools when evaluating a particular company or business unit. Both can reveal meaningful details about current profitability and financial condition, and they can also reveal details about recent changes that might affect future profitability or financial condition. However, these comparisons make use of financial statement data, and hence they are influenced by distortions of that data—if they are indeed distorted.

Evaluating the "Quality" of Accounting Numbers

Analysts use financial statement information to "get behind the numbers"—that is, to see more accurately the economic activities and condition of the company and its prospects, as depicted in Figure 5.1. However, financial statements do not always provide a complete and faithful picture of a company's activities and condition. The raw data needed for a complete and faithful picture do not always reach the financial reports because the information is filtered by generally accepted accounting principles (GAAP) and by management's accounting discretion. Both factors can distort the quality of the reported information and the analyst's view of the company.

Let's see how the financial reporting "filter" phenomenon works with equipment leases. GAAP requires each lease to be classified as either a **capital lease** or an **operating lease,** and it requires only capital leases to be reported as balance sheet assets and liabilities. Operating leases are "off-balance sheet" items—meaning they are not included in the reported asset and liability numbers but are instead disclosed in supplemental footnotes that accompany the financial statements. (We'll see how and why this is so in Chapter 12.) So GAAP lets

Figure 5.1

THE FINANCIAL REPORTING FILTER AND THE ANALYST'S TASK

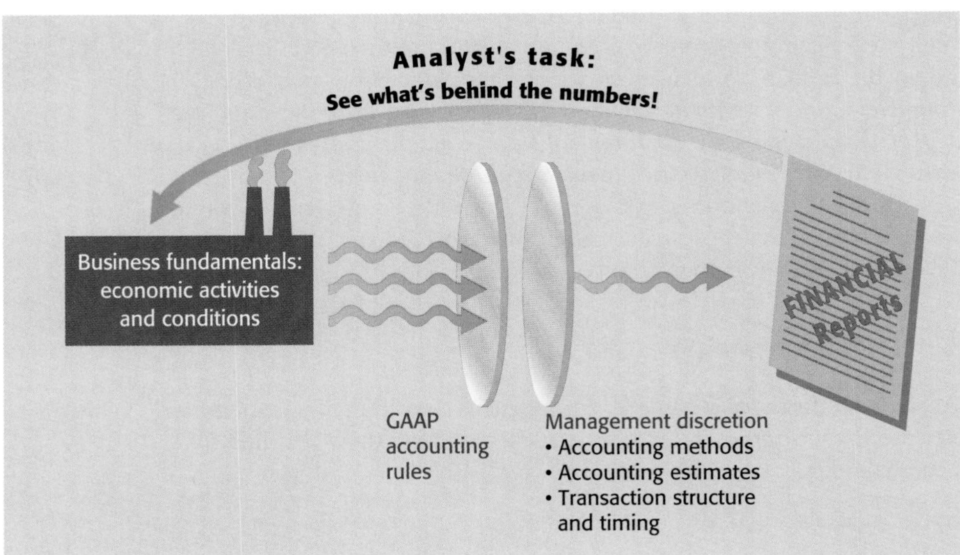

capital leases pass to the balance sheet, but it filters out operating leases, sending them to the statement footnotes. Analysts can—and do—use these footnotes to recast the balance sheet so that all equipment leases are treated the same way. The GAAP filter is then overcome.

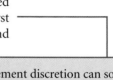

Management discretion can cloud financial analysis in several ways. For example, managers who understand GAAP can use it to structure business transactions so that financial reporting goals are achieved. Do you, as a manager, want to keep equipment leases off the balance sheet? Then just make certain your company's lease contracts meet the GAAP rules for an operating lease. Doing so keeps your leases off the balance sheet and lowers your reported debt.

Management discretion can also complicate the analyst's task in areas like inventory accounting, where GAAP allows managers to freely choose among several alternative reporting methods. Because each inventory method leads to a different set of reported earnings and asset numbers, financial comparisons can be affected. Here, too, the analyst can sometimes use footnote information to recast the reported financial results and thereby eliminate management discretion as an information filter.

> GAAP and management discretion can sometimes make the analyst's task easier by illuminating aspects of the company's activities and condition. For example, GAAP requires companies to disclose sales and operating income by business segment—information that some companies would not otherwise make available. Similarly, management sometimes goes far beyond GAAP's minimum reporting requirements by disclosing financial and nonfinancial operating details that are useful to analysts.

Management also has discretion over accounting estimates and the timing of business transactions. Consider estimated "bad debt expense," management's forecast of the amount of current sales that will never be collected from credit customers. A reduction in estimated bad debt expense could mean customer credit quality has improved (i.e., more credit customers are now expected to pay their bills). Or, it could mean bad debt expense was temporarily reduced to meet a quarterly earnings goal. Similar questions arise over the timing of discretionary expenditures for advertising, research and development (R&D), or information technology. Did advertising expense decline because the current ad program was such a resounding success, or because management curtailed spending this quarter just to meet an earnings goal? In other words, have business fundamentals improved or is it simply "earnings management"?

RECAP

Analysts need to understand what accounting data do and do not reveal about a company's economic activities and condition. They must also know how to adjust the reported numbers, when necessary, to overcome distortions caused by GAAP or by management's accounting and disclosure choices. The first step to informed financial statement analysis is a careful evaluation of the quality of the reported accounting numbers. No tool of financial statement analysis is completely immune to distortions caused by GAAP or by management's reporting choices.

Quaker Oats Company—an Illustration

> We have a unique combination of powerhouse food brands plus a growth engine like no other—Gatorade. In 1999, our business grew in all the right ways: volumes, revenues, margins, and ultimately profits. We are disciplined stewards of capital, using our resources effectively, reducing operating costs, and driving greater efficiencies in our businesses around the world. [Quaker Oats Company 1999 Annual Report]

With annual sales of $5 billion and a market capitalization of over $7 billion, the Quaker Oats Company is one of the 10 largest food processors in the United States. The company was formed in 1901 as the successor to American Cereal, an Ohio company that was organized in 1891. Quaker Oats manufactures and sells grocery products in the United States, Canada, Europe, Latin America, and the Pacific. The company operates 46 manufacturing plants in 13 states and 14 foreign countries, and it has distribution centers and sales offices in 22 states and 20 foreign countries.

Quaker's portfolio of grocery products includes ready-to-eat and hot cereals, grain-based snacks, syrups, frozen breakfast products, thirst-quenching beverages, rice and pasta products, as well as institutional and food-service products. Included in the company's product line are such well-known brand names as Quaker Oatmeal, Cap'n Crunch cereal, Rice-A-Roni flavored rice dishes, and Gatorade. Ninety-three percent of Quaker's 1999 sales came from brands holding the number one or number two position in their product category, and nearly 40% of sales and profits came from Gatorade.

The U.S. food processing industry is now quite mature. The amount of food consumed per person remains essentially unchanged from one year to the next. With the U.S. population growing at only about 1% annually, companies like Quaker have focused their attention on demographic shifts, on the growing ethnic diversity of the U.S. population, and on expanding their presence in foreign markets.

Labor is the largest component of food production costs; it represents about one-third of total manufacturing costs. Grains, sweeteners, and other food commodities that are the raw materials for Quaker's products account for another 20%. Other manufacturing costs include packaging, transportation, and energy. The business requires substantial investments in manufacturing and distribution facilities, but the pace of technological change in the industry is slow.

Competition centers around reinforcing established brands, developing new value-added products, and reducing manufacturing and logistics costs to achieve lower selling prices. Established brands are reinforced through marketing, advertising, and promotion programs that build brand awareness and increase repeat product purchases. The emphasis on cost reduction by food processing companies reflects intense competition both in the mature markets of North America and Europe and among price-conscious consumers worldwide.

Now that you have an understanding of the business and the industry, let's take a look at the company's financial statements.

Quaker's Financial Statements

Comparative income statements for the Quaker Oats Company are shown in Exhibit 5.1(a). Sales decreased from roughly $6 billion in 1995 to $5 billion in 1997, and then they fell to $4.7 billion in 1999. The company's pre-tax income was also erratic during these years: It declined from $1,220.5 million in 1995 to only $415.6 million the next year, and then declined again to a $1,064.3 million loss in 1997. By 1999, pre-tax income had rebounded to $618.3 million.

Exhibit 5.1(a) ■ QUAKER OATS COMPANY

Comparative Income Statements

($ in millions)	1999	1998	1997	1996	1995
Sales	$4,725.2	$4,842.5	$5,015.7	$5,199.0	$5,954.0
Cost of goods sold	2,136.8	2,374.4	2,564.9	2,807.5	3,294.4
Gross profit	2,588.4	2,468.1	2,450.8	2,391.5	2,659.6
Selling, general and administrative expenses	1,904.1	1,872.5	1,938.9	1,981.0	2,358.8
(Gains) losses on divestitures and restructurings	(2.3)	128.5	1,486.3	(113.4)	(1,053.5)
Interest expense	61.9	69.6	85.8	106.8	131.6
Other (revenues) expenses	6.4	0.9	4.1	1.5	2.2
Pre-tax income	618.3	396.6	(1,064.3)	415.6	1,220.5
Income taxes	163.3	112.1	(133.4)	167.7	496.5
Net income (loss)	455.0	284.5	(930.9)	247.9	724.0
Preferred dividends	4.4	4.5	3.5	3.7	2.0
Net income (loss) available for common	$ 450.6	$ 280.0	($ 934.4)	$ 244.2	$ 722.0

Why were sales and pre-tax earnings so volatile? After all, Quaker Oats is a mature company operating in a stable industry, one in which gyrations in sales and earnings are virtually nonexistent. What's been happening?

A closer look at the income statements gives us part of the answer. Pre-tax earnings in 1995 benefited from a $1,053.5 million net-of-tax divestiture gain—the result of selling some product lines. Divestiture gains of $113.4 million and $2.3 million helped boost pre-tax earnings for 1996 and 1999, respectively. Pre-tax earnings in 1997 and 1998 suffered from divestiture and restructuring charges of $1,486.3 million and $128.5 million, respectively. Information elsewhere in the annual report tells us that the 1995 gain came from selling off several U.S. and international businesses—pet foods, bean and chili products, Mexican chocolate, and Dutch honey. Divestitures in 1996 included some of the company's frozen foods and Italian products business. The 1997 divestiture charge was for Snapple, a beverage business Quaker Oats bought in 1994 for $1.7 billion and sold in 1997 for $300 million.

Removing these divestiture and restructuring items from pre-tax income helps clarify matters—that is, sales have been declining but *adjusted* pre-tax income has increased each year! Let's find the source of that improvement.

Adjustments to Remove Divestiture/Restructuring Gains and Losses

	1999	1998	1997	1996	1995
Pre-tax income	$618.3	$396.6	($1,064.3)	$415.6	$1,220.5
− Divestiture/restructuring (gains) losses	(2.3)	128.5	1,486.3	(113.4)	(1,053.5)
= Adjusted pre-tax income	$616.0	$525.1	$ 422.0	$302.2	$ 167.0

Financial analysts use *common size* and *trend* statements to help spot changes in a company's cost structure and profit performance. **Common size income statements,** shown in Exhibit 5.1(b) on the next page recast each statement item as a percentage of sales. For example, Quaker's expense for cost of goods sold for 1999 is shown as 45.2% of 1999 sales (45.2% = $2,136.8 cost of goods sold$_{99}$/$4,725.2 sales$_{99}$) instead of $2,136.8 million. The **trend statements** shown in Exhibit 5.1(b) also recast each statement item in percentage terms, but they do so using a base year number rather than sales. For instance, a trend statement of income shows Quaker's 1999 expense for cost of goods sold as 64.9% of base year (1995) cost of goods sold (64.9% = $2,136.8 cost of goods sold$_{99}$/$3,294.4 cost of goods sold$_{95}$).

Several aspects of the company's profit performance are revealed by these statements:

- Sales in 1999 are only 79.4% of what they were in 1995, having fallen steadily since 1995 [trend statements].
- Cost of goods sold in 1999 is 64.9% of its 1995 level [trend statements].
- Quaker enjoys a hefty gross profit—54.8% in 1999—up from 44.7% in 1995 [common size statements].
- Selling, general, and administrative expenses have increased to 40.3% of each sales dollar in 1999 from a low in 1996 of 38.1% [common size statements].
- After divestiture/restructuring charges and gains are eliminated, pre-tax income in 1999 represents 13.0% of sales compared to only 2.8% in 1995 [common size statements].

The past several years have been difficult for the company and its employees. Quaker Oats sold several food businesses in 1995 and used the cash to pay for the Snapple acquisition, only to sell Snapple two years later. These divestitures explain why sales dropped more than 20% from 1995 to 1999. But there is some good news. By selling off its under-performing brands and by increasing operating efficiencies at its manufacturing plants, Quaker Oats was able to reduce cost of goods sold from 55.3% of sales in 1995 to

Exhibit 5.1(b) ■ QUAKER OATS COMPANY

Common Size and Trend Analysis of Income

Common size statements (% of sales)	**1999**	**1998**	**1997**	**1996**	**1995**
Sales	100.0	100.0	100.0	100.0	100.0
Cost of goods sold	45.2	49.0	51.1	54.0	55.3
Gross profit	54.8	51.0	48.9	46.0	44.7
Selling, general and administrative expenses	40.3	38.7	38.7	38.1	39.6
(Gains) losses on divestitures, restructurings and asset impairment	0.0	2.7	29.6	−2.2	−17.6
Interest expense	1.3	1.4	1.7	2.1	2.2
Other (revenues) expenses	0.1	0.0	0.1	0.0	0.0
Pre-tax income	13.1	8.2	−21.2	8.0	20.5
Income taxes	3.5	2.3	−2.6	3.2	8.3
Net income (loss)	9.6	5.9	−18.6	4.8	12.2
Preferred dividends	0.1	0.1	0.1	0.1	0.0
Net income (loss) available for common	9.5	5.8	−18.5	4.7	12.2
Adjusted pre-tax income	13.0	10.8	8.4	5.8	2.8

Trend statements (1995 = 100%)	**1999**	**1998**	**1997**	**1996**	**1995**
Sales	79.4	81.3	84.2	87.3	100.0
Cost of goods sold	64.9	72.1	77.9	85.2	100.0
Gross profit	97.3	92.8	92.1	89.9	100.0
Selling, general and administrative expenses	80.7	79.4	82.2	84.0	100.0
(Gains) losses on divestitures, restructurings and asset impairment	0.2	−12.2	−141.1	10.8	100.0
Interest expense	47.0	52.9	65.2	81.2	100.0
Other (revenues) expenses	290.9	40.9	186.4	68.2	100.0
Pre-tax income	50.7	32.5	−87.2	34.1	100.0
Income taxes	32.9	22.6	−26.9	33.8	100.0
Net income (loss)	62.8	39.3	−128.6	34.2	100.0
Preferred dividends	220.0	225.0	175.0	185.0	100.0
Net income (loss) available for common	62.4	38.8	−129.4	33.8	100.0

only 45.2% of sales in 1999. This improvement explains why adjusted pre-tax income grew from 2.8% of sales to 13.0% of sales during the same period. While sales have fallen, more of each sales dollar has hit the bottom line!

Now let's see what we can learn from the balance sheet.

Exhibit 5.2(a) shows Quaker's comparative balance sheets using reported dollar amounts. The company's assets are concentrated in cash, trade accounts receivable, finished goods (under "Inventories"), manufacturing and distribution facilities (called "Property, plant, and equipment"), and (before 1997) intangibles. To finance these assets, Quaker has relied on a combination of short-term and long-term debt, vendor payables, preferred and common stock, along with internally generated resources (represented by "Retained earnings").

Several important changes in the company's asset mix and financial structure have occurred since 1995. These changes can be easily seen from the common size and trend statements in Exhibits 5.2(b) ("Assets") and 5.2(c) ("Liabilities and Owners' Equity").

Consider the composition of Quaker's assets in 1999. The company's common size statements in Exhibit 5.2(b) show that trade accounts receivable made up 10.6% of total assets that year, up from 8.6% in 1995. Inventories represent another 11.1% of total 1999 assets, also up somewhat from 1995 levels. Quaker's gross (before depreciation) investment in property, plant, and equipment (PP&E) is 77.3% of total 1999 assets, but the net (after subtracting accumulated depreciation) book value of PP&E is only 46.2% of total assets. This asset mix of roughly 11% trade accounts receivable, 11% inventories, and 46% net PP&E is typical for an established manufacturing company operating in a mature industry

Exhibit 5.2(a) ■ QUAKER OATS COMPANY

Comparative Balance Sheets

($ in millions)	1999	1998	1997	1996	1995
Assets					
Cash and cash equivalents	$ 282.9	$ 326.6	$ 84.2	$ 110.5	$ 93.2
Marketable securities	0.3	27.5	–	–	–
Trade accounts receivable—net of allowances	254.3	283.4	305.7	294.9	398.3
Inventories:					
Finished goods	186.6	189.1	172.6	181.8	203.6
Grains and raw materials	50.0	48.4	59.0	62.1	69.7
Packaging materials and supplies	29.6	23.9	24.5	31.0	33.4
Total inventories	266.2	261.4	256.1	274.9	306.7
Other current assets	193.0	216.1	487.0	209.4	281.9
Total current assets	996.7	1,115.0	1,133.0	889.7	1,080.1
Other assets	55.9	79.4	48.8	66.8	63.3
Property, plant and equipment at cost	1,851.9	1,818.8	1,913.1	1,943.3	1,946.0
Less accumulated depreciation	(745.2)	(748.6)	(748.4)	(742.6)	(778.2)
	1,106.7	1,070.2	1,164.7	1,200.7	1,167.8
Intangible assets—net of amortization	236.9	245.7	350.5	2,237.2	2,309.2
Total assets	$2,396.2	$2,510.3	$2,697.0	$4,394.4	$4,620.4
Liabilities and Owners' Equity					
Short-term debt	$ 73.3	$ 41.3	$ 61.0	$ 517.0	$ 643.4
Current portion of long-term debt	81.2	95.2	108.4	51.1	68.6
Trade accounts payable	213.6	168.4	191.3	210.2	298.4
Various accrued payables	570.2	704.2	585.0	576.4	691.3
Total current liabilities	938.3	1,009.1	945.7	1,354.7	1,701.7
Long-term debt	715.0	795.1	887.6	993.5	1,051.8
Other liabilities	523.1	533.4	615.2	797.3	769.9
Preferred stock	61.0	70.1	77.7	19.0	17.7
Common stock	840.0	840.0	840.0	840.0	840.0
Treasury stock	(1,457.4)	(1,176.0)	(898.6)	(959.8)	(998.4)
Retained earnings	776.2	438.6	229.4	1,349.7	1,237.7
Total common shareholders' equity	158.8	102.6	170.8	1,229.9	1,079.3
Total liabilities and equity	$2,396.2	$2,510.3	$2,697.0	$4,394.4	$4,620.4

where credit sales—and thus trade receivables—are an important component of the distribution channel. Quaker's other assets—cash, other assets, miscellaneous current assets, and intangibles—make up the remaining 32% of the company's total assets for 1999. The company's cash balance, 11.8% of 1999 total assets, is high for a manufacturing firm where 2% to 3% is the norm.

Quaker Oats had a substantial investment in intangible assets: $2.3 billion (Exhibit 5.2[a]) in 1995, or 50% of total assets (Exhibit 5.2[b]). This investment is a natural result of the company's growth strategy. Faced with mature markets for its existing products, Quaker Oats and other large food processors have sought to increase market share by acquiring smaller companies with established and successful regional products. Quaker then uses its own manufacturing, distribution, and marketing expertise to penetrate national or international markets. The company's investment in intangible assets includes amounts paid to acquire trademarks and patented processes from smaller firms. It also includes **goodwill**—the amount in the acquisition price that represents a premium paid for the target company over and above the value of its identifiable assets. (Chapter 16 has more on goodwill.) In fact, most of the company's $2.3 billion of intangible assets in 1995

Exhibit 5.2(b) ■ QUAKER OATS COMPANY

Common Size and Trend Analysis of Assets

Common Size Statements (% of total assets)	**1999**	**1998**	**1997**	**1996**	**1995**
Assets					
Cash and cash equivalents	11.8	14.1	3.1	2.5	2.0
Trade accounts receivable—net of allowances	10.6	11.3	11.3	6.7	8.6
Inventories:					
Finished goods	7.8	7.5	6.4	4.2	4.4
Grains and raw materials	2.1	1.9	2.2	1.4	1.5
Packaging materials and supplies	1.2	1.0	0.9	0.7	0.7
Total inventories	11.1	10.4	9.5	6.3	6.6
Other current assets	8.1	8.6	18.1	4.8	6.1
Total current assets	41.6	44.4	42.0	20.3	23.3
Other assets	2.3	3.2	1.8	1.5	1.4
Property, plant and equipment at cost	77.3	72.4	70.9	44.2	42.1
Less accumulated depreciation	−31.1	−29.8	−27.7	−16.9	−16.8
	46.2	42.6	43.2	27.3	25.3
Intangible assets—net of amortization	9.9	9.8	13.0	50.9	50.0
Total assets	100.0	100.0	100.0	100.0	100.0

Trend Statements (1995 = 100%)	**1999**	**1998**	**1997**	**1996**	**1995**
Assets					
Cash and cash equivalents	303.9	379.9	90.3	118.6	100.0
Trade accounts receivable—net of allowances	63.8	71.2	76.8	74.0	100.0
Inventories:					
Finished goods	91.7	92.9	84.8	89.3	100.0
Grains and raw materials	71.7	69.4	84.6	89.1	100.0
Packaging materials and supplies	88.6	71.6	73.4	92.8	100.0
Total inventories	86.8	85.2	83.5	89.6	100.0
Other current assets	68.5	76.7	172.8	74.3	100.0
Total current assets	92.3	103.2	104.9	82.4	100.0
Other assets	88.3	125.4	77.1	105.5	100.0
Property, plant and equipment at cost	95.2	93.5	98.3	99.9	100.0
Less accumulated depreciation	95.8	96.2	96.2	95.4	100.0
	94.8	91.6	99.7	102.8	100.0
Intangible assets—net of amortization	10.3	10.6	15.2	96.9	100.0
Total assets	51.9	54.3	58.4	95.1	100.0

can be traced to a single acquisition—the 1994 purchase of Snapple beverages for $1.7 billion. This one transaction added $1.4 billion to goodwill.

What happened in 1997 when Quaker's intangibles fell to $350 million (Exhibit 5.2[a]) or only 13% of total assets (Exhibit 5.2[b])? If you guessed the company sold a product line, you are correct. Quaker sold the Snapple beverage business for about $300 million—that's $1.4 billion less than it had paid for Snapple three years earlier. As a result, the company's intangible assets decreased 81.7% in that year alone (1996 intangible assets of 96.9% minus 1997 intangibles of 15.2% from the trend statements in Exhibit 5.2[b]).

Because of the company's huge investment in Snapple intangibles, trade receivables made up only 8.6% of 1995 total assets (Exhibit 5.2[b]). Inventories added 6.6%, with another 25.3% coming from net PP&E. But does this mean that Quaker Oats increased its investment in all of these assets after selling Snapple? Not necessarily! The trend statements show that trade receivables in 1999 were 63.8% and inventories were 86.8% of their 1995 levels—but PP&E changed very little (both gross and net book values in 1999 were about

95% of their 1995 levels). ***Trend statements provide a clearer indication of growth and decline than do common size statements.***

What changes in the company's financial structure have occurred since 1995? Has the mix of debt and equity capital remained constant over the past five years? And what about the proportion of short-term versus long-term borrowing? The common size and trend statements in Exhibit 5.2(c) provide the answers. We can see the following from the common size statements:

- Current liabilities are 39.2% in 1999, up slightly from 36.8% in 1995, but short-term debt has fallen to 3.1% from 13.9% in 1995.
- Long-term debt has grown to 29.8% in 1999, up from 22.8% in 1995, while the balance in the "Other liabilities" component increased to 21.8% from 16.7%.
- Preferred stock increased but common shareholders' equity decreased over these five years, especially in 1997 when "Retained earnings" fell because of the Snapple divestiture loss.

Exhibit 5.2(c) ■ QUAKER OATS COMPANY

Common Size and Trend Analysis of Liabilities and Equity

Common Size Statements (% of total assets)	**1999**	**1998**	**1997**	**1996**	**1995**
Liabilities and Owners' Equity					
Short-term debt	3.1	1.6	2.3	11.8	13.9
Current portion of long-term debt	3.4	3.8	4.0	1.2	1.5
Trade accounts payable	8.9	6.7	7.1	4.8	6.4
Various accrued payables	23.8	28.1	21.7	13.1	15.0
Total current liabilities	39.2	40.2	35.1	30.9	36.8
Long-term debt	29.8	31.7	32.9	22.6	22.8
Other liabilities	21.8	21.2	22.8	18.1	16.6
Preferred stock	2.6	2.8	2.9	0.4	0.4
Common stock	35.0	33.4	31.1	19.1	18.2
Treasury stock	−60.8	−46.8	−33.3	−21.8	−21.6
Retained earnings	32.4	17.5	8.5	30.7	26.8
Total common shareholders' equity	6.6	4.1	6.3	28.0	23.4
Total liabilities and equity	100.0	100.0	100.0	100.0	100.0

Trend Statements (1995 = 100%)	**1999**	**1998**	**1997**	**1996**	**1995**
Liabilities and Owners' Equity					
Short-term debt	11.4	6.4	9.5	80.4	100.0
Current portion of long-term debt	118.4	138.8	158.0	74.5	100.0
Trade accounts payable	71.6	56.4	64.1	70.4	100.0
Various accrued payables	82.5	101.9	84.6	83.4	100.0
Total current liabilities	55.1	59.3	55.6	79.6	100.0
Long-term debt	68.0	75.6	84.4	94.5	100.0
Other liabilities	67.9	69.3	79.9	103.6	100.0
Preferred stock	344.6	396.0	439.0	107.3	100.0
Common stock	100.0	100.0	100.0	100.0	100.0
Treasury stock	146.0	117.8	90.0	96.1	100.0
Retained earnings	62.7	35.4	18.5	109.0	100.0
Total common shareholders' equity	14.7	9.5	15.8	114.0	100.0
Total liabilities and equity	51.9	54.3	58.4	95.1	100.0

So, the common size statements show a relatively stable financial structure, with some decrease in short-term debt offset by an increase in the percentage of long-term debt. The trend statements show the following:

- Short-term debt in 1999 fell to only 11.4% of its 1995 level.
- Long-term debt fell to 68% of its 1995 level by 1999.
- Common stock was unchanged, but preferred stock grew 344.6%.

An unusual feature of Quaker's financial structure is its stock repurchase program, as indicated by the size and growth in treasury stock on the balance sheet. This statement item represents the amount paid by Quaker Oats to buy back its own previously issued common and preferred stock. We can learn more about Quaker's stock repurchase program by examining the company's cash flow statements.

Exhibit 5.3(a) presents comparative cash flow statements, with some statement items reported as combined figures to simplify the presentation. Common size and trends for selected cash flow items are shown in Exhibit 5.3(b). The common size statements are constructed by dividing each cash flow item by sales for that year. For example, Quaker's operating activities generated $631.1 million cash (Exhibit 5.3[a]) in 1999, or 13.4% of sales of $4,725.2 million (Exhibit 5.1[a]). In other words, cash from operations in 1999 was 13.4 cents for each sales dollar, up from 6.8 cents in 1995 (Exhibit 5.3[b]).

How does Quaker use these operating cash flows? Like most manufacturing companies, Quaker must devote resources to plant modernization and improvement. In addition, as mentioned earlier, much of the company's growth comes from buying established product lines from others. Therefore, a major cash use is capital expenditures and acquisitions; this use consumed $194.3 million in 1999 (Exhibit 5.3[a]), or 4.1 cents per sales dollar (4.1% in Exhibit 5.3[b]). The company's cash dividends, $156.2 million in 1999, or 3.3 cents per sales dollar, are comparable to those of many other mature companies with substantial operating cash flows. Debt payments consumed another $60.4 million of cash in 1999, or 1.3 cents per sales dollar. This leaves 4.7 cents (13.4 − 4.1 − 3.3 − 1.3) of operating cash flow per sales dollar to cover the company's stock repurchases, other financing and investing activities, exchange rate effects, and the net increase in cash.

Now that we understand where the cash came from and how it was used, let's take a closer look at Quaker's stock repurchasing activities. The firm spent $382.3 million (Exhibit 5.3[a]) buying back common and preferred stock in 1999, and another $384.9 million in 1998. These cash payments to stockholders represented 8.1 cents (Exhibit

Exhibit 5.3(a) ■ QUAKER OATS COMPANY

Comparative Cash Flow Statements

($ in millions)	1999	1998	1997	1996	1995
Net income	$455.0	$284.5	($930.9)	$247.9	$724.0
Adjustments	176.1	229.0	1,420.9	162.5	(316.9)
Cash from operations	631.1	513.5	490.0	410.4	407.1
Capital expenditures and acquisitions—net	(194.3)	68.9	84.3	(68.3)	920.2
Other investments	33.9	217.6	—	0.2	4.2
Cash used in investing activities	(160.4)	286.5	84.3	(68.1)	924.4
Cash dividends	(156.2)	(159.7)	(159.4)	(157.0)	(154.8)
Reduction of debt—net	(60.4)	(124.0)	(499.0)	(199.8)	(1,090.9)
Repurchase of common and preferred stock	(382.3)	(384.9)	(56.2)	(5.5)	(5.7)
Other financing activities	82.6	112.0	121.2	31.0	(91.6)
Cash used in financing activities	(516.3)	(556.6)	(593.4)	(331.3)	(1,343.0)
Effect of exchange rate changes on cash	1.9	(1.0)	(7.2)	6.3	1.7
Net increase (decrease) in cash	($ 43.7)	$242.4	($ 26.3)	$ 17.3	($ 9.8)

5.3[b]) per sales dollar in 1999 and 7.9 cents in 1998, compared to 13.4 cents and 10.6 cents, respectively, in operating cash flows. That means the company spent more than half of its operating cash flows in those two years on stock repurchases. Buybacks also occurred in 1995 through 1997, but the dollar amounts involved were substantially smaller.

Why did Quaker Oats accelerate its stock repurchases in 1998? ***Buybacks often increase when companies no longer need to use operating cash flows for other purposes like business acquisitions and debt repayment.*** That's exactly what happened at Quaker Oats.

The cash flow statements in Exhibit 5.3(a) show that Quaker Oats generated about $920 million in 1995 by selling off some product lines. These funds, when combined with nearly $407 million in cash from operations, were more than enough to cover the company's $1,091 million debt repayment that year. Debt repayments of $200 million in 1996 and $499 million in 1997 were made primarily from operating cash flows. By 1998, Quaker's cash from operations ($514 million) far exceeded its cash needs for debt repayment ($124 million) and acquisitions (+$69 million because the company sold more businesses that year). The problem: what should be done with the extra cash?

Cash dividends to common and preferred shareholders provide part of the answer. Quaker Oats paid out nearly $160 million in dividends in 1998, about the same amount that was paid out in 1997 and 1996. But that left an operating cash flow surplus of $299 million ($514 − $124 + $69 − $160). Rather than put the money in a bank account, Quaker used it and some other cash to buy back $385 million of common stock from its

Exhibit 5.3(b) ■ QUAKER OATS COMPANY

Common Size and Trend Analysis of Selected Cash Flow Items

Common Size Statements (% of sales)	**1999**	**1998**	**1997**	**1996**	**1995**
Selected Items					
Cash from operations	13.4	10.6	9.8	7.9	6.8
Capital expenditures and acquisitions—net	−4.1	1.4	1.7	−1.3	15.5
Other investments	0.7	4.5	0.0	0.0	0.1
Cash used in investing activities	−3.4	5.9	1.7	−1.3	15.6
Cash dividends	−3.3	−3.3	−3.2	−3.0	−2.6
Reduction of debt—net	−1.3	−2.6	−10.0	−3.9	−18.3
Repurchase of common and preferred stock	−8.1	−7.9	−1.1	−0.1	−0.1
Other financing activities	1.8	2.3	2.4	0.6	−1.6
Cash used in financing activities	−10.9	−11.5	−11.9	−6.4	−22.6
Effect of exchange rate changes on cash	0.0	0.0	−0.1	0.1	0.0
Net increase (decrease) in cash	−0.9	5.0	−0.5	0.3	−0.2

Trend Statements (1995 = 100%)	**1999**	**1998**	**1997**	**1996**	**1995**
Selected Items					
Cash from operations	155.0	126.1	120.4	100.8	100.0
Capital expenditures and acquisitions—net	−21.1	7.5	9.2	−7.4	100.0
Other investments	807.1	5181.0	0.0	4.8	100.0
Cash used in investing activities	−17.4	31.0	9.1	−7.4	100.0
Cash dividends	100.9	103.2	103.0	101.4	100.0
Reduction of debt—net	5.5	11.4	45.7	18.3	100.0
Repurchase of common and preferred stock	6707.0	6752.6	986.0	96.5	100.0
Other financing activities	−90.2	−122.3	−132.3	−33.8	100.0
Cash used in financing activities	38.4	41.4	44.2	24.7	100.0
Effect of exchange rate changes on cash	111.8	−58.8	−423.5	370.6	100.0
Net increase (decrease) in cash	445.9	−2473.5	268.4	−176.5	100.0

shareholders. The company repurchased another $382 million of its common shares in 1999. Returning excess cash to shareholders makes good business sense when there are no attractive investment opportunities available to the company.

RECAP

From our analysis of the Quaker Oats Company and its financial statements, we can come to three conclusions:

- **Informed financial statement analysis begins with knowledge of the company and its industry.**
- **Common size and trend statements provide a convenient way to organize financial statement information so that major financial components and changes are easily recognized.**
- **Financial statements help the analyst gain a sharper understanding of the company's economic condition and its prospects for the future.**

Profitability, Competition, and Business Strategy

The mechanics of running a business are not really very complicated when you get down to essentials. You have to make some stuff and sell it to somebody for more than it cost you. That's about all there is, except for a few million details.

–John L. McCaffey

Financial ratios are another powerful tool analysts use in evaluating profit performance and assessing credit risk. Most evaluations of profit performance begin with the **return on assets (ROA)** ratio,

$$\text{ROA} = \frac{\text{NOPAT}}{\text{Average assets}}$$

where *NOPAT* refers to the company's **net operating profit after taxes** for a particular period (such as a year), and *average assets* is the average book value of total assets over that same time period. Before computing ROA, analysts adjust the company's reported earnings and asset figures. These adjustments fall into three broad categories:

1. Adjustments aimed at ***isolating a company's sustainable operating profits*** by removing nonoperating or nonrecurring items from reported income.
2. An adjustment that ***eliminates after-tax interest expense*** from the profit calculation so that *operating* profitability comparisons over time or across companies are not clouded by differences in financial structure.[2]

[2] To illustrate how financial structure can affect profitability comparisons, consider two companies that have (a) identical after-tax operating profits of $500 before interest expense is considered, and (b) the same total asset base of $5,000. One company has no interest-bearing debt, the other has $2,000 of 12% debt outstanding. Annual interest expense on this debt is $240 = $2,000 × 0.12, but the deductibility of interest expense for tax purposes saves the company $84 = $240 × 0.35 each year when the corporate income tax rate is 35%. Consequently, the company with debt would report net income of $344 or $500 − $240 × (1 − 0.35). If financing costs are ignored, the all-equity company would have an ROA of 10% ($500/$5,000), while the company with debt would have an ROA of 6.88% ($344/$5,000). The analyst might mistakenly conclude that one company's profit performance is superior to the other when, in fact, the only difference between these two companies is their choice of financing. The "adjusted" ROA for the company with debt would confirm that identical levels of *operating* profit performance had been achieved:

$$\text{ROA} = \frac{\text{After-tax operating profits} + \text{Interest expense} \times (1 - \text{Tax rate})}{\text{Average assets}}$$

$$= \frac{\$344 + \$240 \times (1 - 0.35)}{\$5{,}000} = .10 \textit{ or } 10\%$$

3. Adjustments for ***distortions related to accounting quality concerns,*** which involve potential adjustments to both income and assets for items such as nonoperating income from short-term investments or the off-balance sheet operating leases mentioned earlier.

Exhibit 5.4 summarizes the ROA calculations for Quaker Oats using the company's earnings and balance sheet information from Exhibits 5.1(a) and 5.2(a). The adjustments made to reported earnings each year eliminate the restructuring charges, gains and interest, on an after-tax basis. ROA for 1999 thus becomes:

$$ROA_{96} = \frac{\text{Net income} + \text{Charges and gains} \times (1 - \text{Tax rate}) + \text{Interest} \times (1 - \text{Tax rate})}{\text{Average assets}}$$

$$= \frac{\$455.0 - \$2.3 \times (1 - 0.35) + \$61.9 \times (1 - 0.35)}{(\$2{,}510.3 + \$2{,}396.2)/2} = .201 \textit{ or } 20.1\%$$

After all adjustments, Quaker's ROA increased from 5.4% in 1996 to 20.1% in 1999. Here's why.

There are just two ways a company can increase its operating profits per asset dollar. One is to increase the profit yield on each sales dollar. The other is to expand the amount of sales generated from each asset dollar. In other words, a company that wants to ***increase its rate of return on assets*** can strive to do so in two different ways:

1. By increasing the operating profit margin
2. By increasing the intensity of asset utilization.

Both approaches are embedded in the ROA calculation:

$$ROA = \frac{\text{NOPAT}}{\text{Average assets}} = \left(\frac{\text{NOPAT}}{\text{Sales}}\right) \times \left(\frac{\text{Sales}}{\text{Average assets}}\right)$$

$$= \text{Operating profit margin} \times \text{Asset turnover}$$

Changes in the profit yield per sales dollar show up as changes in the ***operating profit margin,*** and changes in the amount of sales generated from each asset dollar are reflected as ***asset turnover*** changes.

Consider a company that earns \$9 million of NOPAT on sales of \$100 million and that has an average asset base of \$50 million. The ROA for this company is:

$$ROA = \left(\frac{\text{NOPAT}}{\text{Sales}}\right) \times \left(\frac{\text{Sales}}{\text{Average assets}}\right)$$

$$= \left(\frac{\$9}{\$100}\right) \times \left(\frac{\$100}{\$50}\right) = .09 \times 2 = .18 \text{ or } 18\%$$

Exhibit 5.4 ■ QUAKER OATS COMPANY

Return on Assets

	1999	1998	1997	1996
Net income as reported	\$ 455.0	\$ 284.5	(\$ 930.9)	\$ 247.9
Restructuring/divestitures after-taxes	(1.5)	83.5	1,246.3	(73.7)
Interest expense after-taxes	40.2	45.2	55.8	69.4
Net operating profit after-tax (NOPAT)	\$ 493.7	\$ 413.3	\$ 371.2	\$ 243.6
Assets at year-end	\$2,396.2	\$2,510.3	\$2,697.0	\$4,394.4
Assets at beginning of year	2,510.3	2,697.0	4,394.4	4,620.4
Average assets	\$2,453.3	\$2,603.7	\$3,545.7	\$4,507.4
Return on assets (NOPAT/Average assets)	20.1%	15.9%	10.5%	5.4%

Note: Following common practice, an approximate tax rate (35% in this case) is used to compute after-tax restructuring charges (gains) and interest expense. For the 1997 restructuring loss, the income tax effect of \$240 million (or 16%) was taken directly from a footnote in the Quaker Oats annual report.

Now suppose that some efficiencies in inventory and accounts receivable management are possible so that average assets can be reduced to \$45 million without sacrificing sales. Assets turnover will increase to 2.22 and ROA will rise to 20%:

$$\text{ROA} = \left(\frac{\text{NOPAT}}{\text{Sales}}\right) \times \left(\frac{\text{Sales}}{\text{Average assets}}\right)$$
$$= \left(\frac{\$9}{\$100}\right) \times \left(\frac{\$100}{\$45}\right) = .09 \times 2.22 = .20 \text{ or } 20\%$$

However, there is another way to boost ROA from 18% to 20%—that is, increase the operating profit margin to 10% through aggressive cost reductions. Sales are unchanged and asset turnover stays at 2, but ROA is now:

$$\text{ROA} = \left(\frac{\text{NOPAT}}{\text{Sales}}\right) \times \left(\frac{\text{Sales}}{\text{Average assets}}\right)$$
$$= \left(\frac{\$10}{\$100}\right) \times \left(\frac{\$100}{\$50}\right) = .10 \times 2 = .20 \text{ or } 20\%$$

Exhibit 5.5 extends the ROA analysis of Quaker Oats by presenting margin and asset turnover figures for each of the four years. Here we learn that Quaker's improved profitability stems from a combination of better operating margins and increased turnover. For example, in 1996 the company was generating \$1.15 of sales from each asset dollar, and each sales dollar produced 4.7 cents of NOPAT for an ROA of 5.4%. By contrast, Quaker generated \$1.93 of sales per asset dollar in 1999, and each sales dollar produced 10.4 cents of NOPAT, so ROA that year was 20.1%.

The explanation for Quaker's profitability improvement lies in the numbers—and in the business decisions that lurk behind the numbers. By shedding Snapple and other under-performing food brands, sales were reduced (Exhibit 5.1[a]) but the operating profit margin more than doubled. Manufacturing efficiency gains may have also played a role in the company's margin increase. But there is another part to the story. Fewer food brands means fewer resources tied up in receivables, inventories, and facilities (property, plant and equipment). Quaker's asset base was considerably more productive in 1999 (\$1.93 of sales per dollar of assets) than it was in 1995 (\$1.15 of sales per asset dollar).

Can Quaker Oats sustain its current level of profitability? It is hard to say. Increased manufacturing costs, brand erosion, and competitive price pressures could reduce the company's ROA. For example, an increase in the cost of cereal grains could easily cause the operating margin to decline to 10.0% from its 1999 level of 10.4%. This small change when amplified by the asset turnover ratio would result in ROA declining from 20.1% to 19.3% (= 10.0% × 1.93). To sustain ROA at 20.1%, Quaker would then need to generate an additional \$0.08 of sales per asset dollar (20.1% = 10.0% × 2.01). Growing sales is always difficult in a mature industry, however.

Exhibit 5.5 ■ QUAKER OATS COMPANY

ROA Decomposition

	1999	1998	1997	1996
Sales	\$4,725.2	\$4,842.5	\$5,015.7	\$5,199.0
NOPAT	493.7	413.3	371.2	243.6
Average assets	2,453.3	2,603.7	3,545.7	4,507.4
Operating profit margin (*NOPAT/Sales*)	10.4%	8.5%	7.4%	4.7%
Asset turnover (*Sales/Average assets*)	1.93	1.86	1.41	1.15
ROA = Margin × Asset turnover	20.1%	15.9%	10.5%	5.4%

Some analysts find it helpful to further decompose ROA by isolating individual factors that contribute to a company's operating profit margin and asset turnover. For example, the operating profit margin for Quaker Oats can be expressed as:

$$\begin{aligned}\text{Operating profit margin} &= \frac{\text{NOPAT}}{\text{Sales}} = \frac{(\text{Sales} - \text{CGS} - \text{SG\&A} - \text{Other} - \text{Taxes})}{\text{Sales}} \\ &= \left(\frac{\text{Sales}}{\text{Sales}}\right) - \left(\frac{\text{CGS}}{\text{Sales}}\right) - \left(\frac{\text{SG\&A}}{\text{Sales}}\right) - \left(\frac{\text{Other}}{\text{Sales}}\right) - \left(\frac{\text{Taxes}}{\text{Sales}}\right) \\ &= 100\% - \left(\frac{\text{CGS}}{\text{Sales}}\right) - \left(\frac{\text{SG\&A}}{\text{Sales}}\right) - \left(\frac{\text{Other}}{\text{Sales}}\right) - \left(\frac{\text{Taxes}}{\text{Sales}}\right)\end{aligned}$$

where, from Exhibit 5.1(a), *CGS* is the company's cost-of-goods-sold expense; *SG&A* is Quaker's selling, general, and administrative expense; *Other* is other expenses and revenues, and *Taxes* is adjusted income tax expense. These margin components (which happen to correspond to the common size earnings statement items we've already described) can help the analyst identify areas where cost reductions have been achieved or where cost improvements are needed.

The asset turnover component of ROA can be decomposed as:

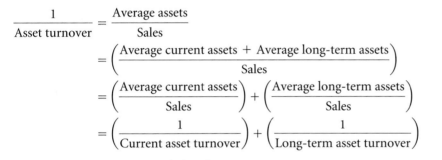

$$\begin{aligned}\frac{1}{\text{Asset turnover}} &= \frac{\text{Average assets}}{\text{Sales}} \\ &= \left(\frac{\text{Average current assets} + \text{Average long-term assets}}{\text{Sales}}\right) \\ &= \left(\frac{\text{Average current assets}}{\text{Sales}}\right) + \left(\frac{\text{Average long-term assets}}{\text{Sales}}\right) \\ &= \left(\frac{1}{\text{Current asset turnover}}\right) + \left(\frac{1}{\text{Long-term asset turnover}}\right)\end{aligned}$$

The **current asset turnover** ratio helps the analyst to spot efficiency gains from improved accounts receivable and inventory management, while the **long-term asset turnover** ratio captures information about property, plant, and equipment utilization.

> Using the information in Quaker's 1999 income statement to illustrate the tax expense adjustment, we find that adjusted taxes would equal \$184.2 instead of the reported income tax expense of \$163.3 shown in the statement. The various adjustments made in arriving at NOPAT also cause the tax component of ROA to differ from the reported figure. The correct figure for *Taxes* is computed by solving:
>
> $$\text{NOPAT} = \text{Sales} - \text{CGS} - \text{SG\&A} - \text{Other} - \text{Taxes}$$
>
> Substitution for NOPAT and the other statement items yields:
>
> $$\$493.7 = \$4{,}725.2 - \$2{,}136.8 - \$1{,}904.1 - 6.4 - \text{Taxes}$$
>
> meaning that *Taxes* = \$184.2 that year.

ROA and Competitive Advantage

Our analysis of Quaker's profit performance has thus far revealed that the company's ROA for 1999 was 20.1%, up from 5.4% in 1996. This profitability increase was traced to a combination of higher operating margins and increased asset utilization. Now we want to know how Quaker's profit performance compares with other companies in the industry.

Exhibit 5.6 presents a decomposition of 1999 ROA for Quaker and one of its competitors, Kellogg Company, a manufacturer of ready-to-eat cereals and convenience

Exhibit 5.6 ■ QUAKER OATS AND THE COMPETITION

1999 ROA Decomposition

	Quaker	Kellogg	Grain Mill Products Industry
Operating profit margin (NOPAT/Sales)	10.4%	9.8%	4.1%
Assets turnover (Sales/Average assets)	1.93	1.42	1.38
Return on assets (ROA)	**20.1%**	**13.9%**	**5.7%**

foods. Also shown are average ROA and component values for the industry—grain mill products—to which Quaker and Kellogg belong. Industry data like these are available from a variety of sources, including Standard & Poor's *Industry Survey,* Robert Morris and Associates' *Annual Statement Studies,* and many on-line financial information services.

Quaker Oats was more profitable than Kellogg in 1999, earning an ROA of 20.1% compared to Kellogg's 13.9%. Moreover, both companies beat the industry average ROA of 5.7%. How did Quaker achieve superior profit performance? The ROA decomposition reveals that Quaker's NOPAT margin was 10.4 cents per sales dollar—slightly better than Kellogg's 9.8% margin but considerably above the industry-wide margin of 4.1 cents. So, a strong operating margin was key to the success of both companies. And the reason Quaker Oats outperformed Kellogg? Better asset turnover. Quaker generated $1.93 in sales per asset dollar compared to only $1.42 in sales per asset dollar at Kellogg and just $1.38 for the industry.

The key to Quaker's success in 1999 is found in both its profit margin and its asset turnover. Quaker outperformed the competition by earning a higher operating profit margin on each dollar of sales and by generating more sales per asset dollar.

Can Quaker maintain this level of ROA performance? The answer can be found only by identifying Quaker's competitive advantage—that is, the source of its superior operating profit margin and turnover rate—and by determining whether that competitive advantage is sustainable over time. There are several factors that can explain why companies operating in the same industry—and that therefore are confronting similar economic conditions—can earn markedly different rates of return on their assets. Some companies gain a competitive advantage over rivals by developing unique products or services. Others do so by providing consistent quality or exceptional customer service and convenience. Still others get ahead because of their innovative production technologies, distribution channels, or sales and marketing efforts. The sustainability of these advantages, however, varies.

Competition in an industry continually works to drive down the rate of return on assets toward the competitive floor—that is, the rate of return that would be earned in the economist's "perfectly competitive" industry. This competitive floor is approximated by the yield on long-term government securities (i.e., the **risk-free rate of return**), adjusted upward for the risk of business failure and capital loss in the industry. Companies that consistently earn rates of return above the floor are said to have a **competitive advantage.** However, rates of return that are higher than the industry floor stimulate more competition as existing companies innovate and expand their market reach or as new companies enter the industry. These developments lead to an erosion of profitability and advantage.

To see how these forces work, consider the simplified representation of the ready-to-eat cereals industry comprising four firms in Figure 5.2.

Firm A and Firm B earn exactly the same competitive floor rate of return, which we assume to be 12%, but they do so in different ways. Firm A earns a 12% ROA by combining a high margin (say 8%) with low turnover (say 1.5). Firm B has a low margin (say 2%) and a high turnover (6 times). Despite their differences, both companies achieve the same level of economic success: ROA $= 12\% = 8\% \times 1.5 = 2\% \times 6$.

Company C enjoys a competitive advantage that allows it to earn a return greater than 12%; Company D is disadvantaged and earns a return less than 12%.

Company C's superior profitability stems from the wide acceptance of its successful new breakfast cereal (Vita-Flakes) among health-conscious consumers. C's current edge is that Vita-Flakes are unique in the marketplace.

The particular competitive advantage C now enjoys may not persist. Other cereal companies can and will develop products that rival Vita-Flakes in taste and nutritional benefits. As rival products become available, they will compete directly with Vita-Flakes for each consumer dollar, and C's sales volume will thus decline. This will prompt a reduction in C's asset turnover, and it will shift C leftward (dotted arrow) in Figure 5.2 toward the competitive ROA of 12%. Of course, C's management is unlikely to ignore the introduction of rival breakfast products. Faced with the threatened loss of its competitive advantage, C

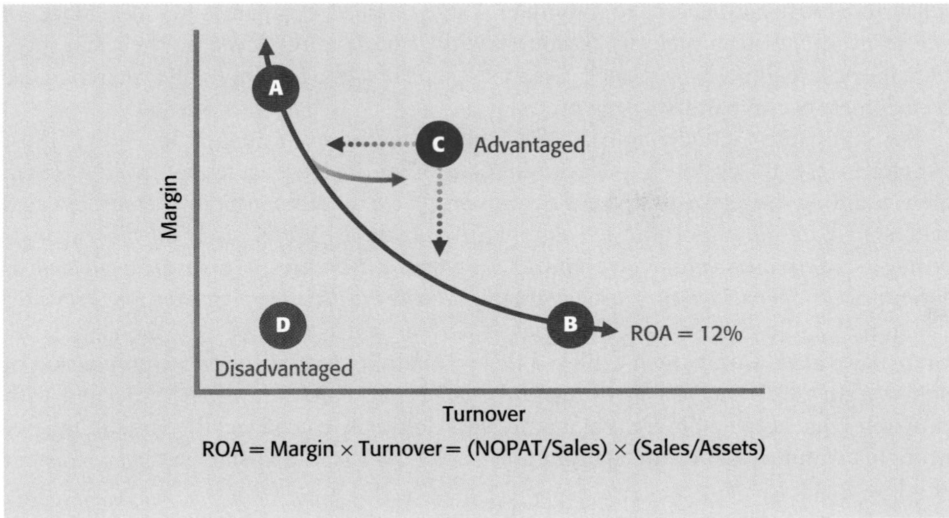

Figure 5.2

ILLUSTRATION OF HOW MARGIN AND TURNOVER AFFECT RETURN ON ASSETS (ROA)

could respond by reducing product prices or by increasing advertising expenditures. Both responses could stimulate additional consumer sales and increase turnover, causing a shift back to the right (as depicted by the curved arrow in Figure 5.2). However, price reductions and increased advertising costs also lower the company's NOPAT margin, and thus they produce a downward shift (dotted arrow) toward the competitive ROA floor.

While the challenge to C is sustaining its Vita-Flakes advantage in the face of escalating competition, Company D is facing different challenges. D's current level of profitability is below the industry floor of 12%. Investors and creditors will be reluctant to commit additional financial resources to D unless its profit picture improves. Why? Because D is not currently earning a rate of return large enough to compensate investors for business and financial risk. If D is unable to rectify the situation quickly, its cost of capital will increase, its profit margin will become even lower, and its long-term financial viability may be threatened. What turnaround strategies can D pursue?

According to most observers, there are only two strategies for achieving superior performance in any business. One strategy is product and service **differentiation,** the other is **low-cost leadership.**[3] A differentiation strategy focuses customer attention on "unique" product or service attributes to gain brand loyalty and attractive profit margins. The idea is quite simple: People are willing to pay premium prices for things they value and can't get elsewhere.

Differentiation can take several forms. Examples include advanced technology and performance capabilities, consistent quality, availability in multiple colors or sizes, prompt delivery, technical support services, customer financing, distribution channels, or some other factor of real or perceived importance to customers. Our hypothetical cereal companies, for instance, are likely to focus customer attention on superior taste and nutritional benefits when introducing products intended to compete with Vita-Flakes. Retailers like Bloomingdales, Neiman Marcus, and Nordstrom achieve differentiation by emphasizing customer service, merchandise quality, and a "unique" shopping experience.

A low-cost leadership strategy focuses customer attention on product pricing, often using slogans like "everyday low prices" or "the lowest price in town." The goal is to become the lowest cost producer in the marketplace so that you can underprice the competition, achieve the highest sales volumes, and still make a profit on each sale. Companies can attain a low-cost position in various ways. Examples include quantity discount purchases, a lean administrative structure, and production efficiencies from

[3] See W. K. Hall, "Survival Strategies in a Hostile Environment," *Harvard Business Review* (September–October 1980), pp. 78–85; M. E. Porter, *Competitive Strategy* (New York: Free Press, 1980). Porter also describes a "niche" or "focused" strategy whereby companies achieve uniqueness within a narrowly defined market segment.

outsourcing or vigorous cost containment. Large retailing companies like Wal-Mart are able to negotiate steep quantity discounts with manufacturers because their size gives them more bargaining power; such discounts then allow the retailer to offer merchandise to customers at comparatively low prices.

Few companies actually pursue one strategy to the exclusion of the other. Most companies try to do both—developing customer loyalty while controlling costs. Understanding the relative emphasis a company places on differentiation versus low-cost leadership can be important for competitive analysis. ***Differences in the business strategies companies adopt give rise to economic differences, which are reflected as differences in operating margins, earnings, and asset utilization.*** For example, consider in Figure 5.2 the two cereal companies A and B, which earn exactly the same 12% competitive ROA. Company A achieved this profitability level through a combination of high margin (8%) and low asset turnover (1.5), a combination often associated with companies that adopt a differentiation strategy. Company B achieved the same ROA level through a combination of low margin (2%) and high turnover (6), a pattern consistent with low-cost leadership.

The choice confronting D company's management should now be clear. There are three ways D can return to a competitive profit level: (1) improve the operating margin, (2) increase asset turnover (more sales volume or fewer assets), or (3) both. Margin improvements will shift D upward in Figure 5.2, whereas better turnover will shift it horizontally to the right. In both cases, D moves closer to the industry ROA of 12%. So, D's management must choose one path or the other—or a combination of the two. That's all they need to do—and attend to a few million details to do it.

RECAP

Not every company in an industry earns the same rate of return on its assets. Some earn more than the industry average ROA while others earn less. Companies that fall below the industry average ROA strive to grow sales, improve operating efficiency, and better manage assets so that they can become competitive again. Those who are fortunate enough to earn more than the industry average ROA struggle to maintain their competitive advantage—through differentiation or low-cost leadership—and to stay on top. This ebb and flow of competition shows up as differences in ROA and in its profit margin and asset turnover components.

Credit Risk and Capital Structure

Credit risk refers to the ability and willingness of a borrower (an individual or organization) to pay its debt. Ability and willingness influence the likelihood that the lender (typically a bank or insurance company) will receive promised principal and interest payments when due. In the corporate arena, two factors must be kept in mind:

- A company's *ability to repay debt* is determined by its capacity to generate cash from operations, asset sales, or external financial markets in excess of its cash needs.
- A company's *willingness to pay* depends on which of the competing cash needs is viewed by management as most pressing at the moment. Those needs include working capital and plant capacity requirements to sustain current operating activities, capital expenditures for new product and service development or market expansion, and shareholder dividends or debt service requirements.

There are numerous and interrelated risks that influence a company's ability to generate cash. Multinational companies, for example, must cope with possible changes in host government regulations, potential political unrest, and fluctuating currency exchange rates. Domestic companies are exposed to the kind of risk associated with political or demographic changes, recession, inflation, and interest rate fluctuations. Companies within a particular industry confront risks related to technological change, shifting competition, regulation, and availability of raw materials and labor. Management competency, litigation, and the company's strategic direction are additional sources of risk. Each of these risks ultimately affects a company's operating performance, net income, and cash flows. In fact, the statement of cash flows—which reports the net amount of cash generated or used by operating, investing, and financing activities—is an important source of information for analyzing a company's credit risk.

For instance, the comparative cash flow statements for Quaker Oats in Exhibit 5.3(a) reveal strong, and growing, operating cash flows. The company's $631 million of operating cash flows in 1999 were more than sufficient to cover its net investing needs ($160 million), leaving a cash surplus of $471 million ($631 − $160) available for other purposes. How did the company use this cash surplus? Quaker spent $156 million that year on cash dividend payments and $382 million on stock repurchases while also paying down its short-term and long-term debt by over $60 million. Some of the money for these payments came from other financing activities ($83 million) and Quaker's existing cash reserves ($44 million). Based on this cursory analysis, it appears that Quaker is a low credit risk company because it generates operating cash flows substantially in excess of what is required to sustain its business activities.

Although cash flow statements contain information enabling a user to assess a company's credit risk, financial ratios are also useful for this purpose. ***Credit risk analysis using financial ratios typically involves an assessment of liquidity and solvency.*** **Liquidity** refers to the company's *short-term* ability to generate cash for working capital needs and immediate debt repayment needs. **Solvency** refers to the *long-term* ability to generate cash internally or from external sources in order to satisfy plant capacity needs, fuel growth, and repay debt when due. Our discussion of financial ratios as an analytical tool for assessing credit risk is based on the distinction between concerns for short-term liquidity and for long-term solvency.

Short-Term Liquidity Short-term liquidity problems arise because operating cash inflows don't match outflows. To illustrate the mismatching problem, let's consider the *operating cycle* of a retailer like Wal-Mart. It acquires merchandise from suppliers on credit, promising to pay within 30 or 60 days. The merchandise is first shipped to Wal-Mart warehouses. Later it is sent on to Wal-Mart stores where it is displayed for purchase and promoted through in-store and regular advertising. Wal-Mart pays for some transportation, labor, and advertising costs immediately and delays payment of other costs. Eventually, Wal-Mart sells the merchandise to customers, who pay by cash or charge card; receivables (if any) are collected some time later; and the company then pays the remaining amounts owed to suppliers and others. Liquidity problems arise when cash inflows from customers lag behind the cash outflows to employees, suppliers, and others.

The operating cycle must not only generate sufficient cash to supply working capital needs, it must also provide cash to service debt as payments become due. For some companies, interest expense is their largest single cost. Such companies may discover that operating cash flows are sufficient to cover periodic interest payments but that the need to repay loan principal causes a liquidity problem. Companies that are not liquid—and are therefore not able to pay obligations as they come due—may be forced into bankruptcy.

One index of a company's short-term liquidity is its **current ratio:**

$$\text{Current ratio} = \frac{\text{Current assets}}{\text{Current liabilities}}$$

Current assets include cash and "near cash" items. For example, receivables become cash as they are collected, so they are only one step removed from cash. Inventories are converted into cash in two steps:

1. They must be sold, usually on credit.
2. The resulting receivable must later be collected.

By including receivables and inventory in current assets, the current ratio reflects existing cash as well as amounts soon to be converted to cash in the normal operating cycle.

A more short-run reflection of liquidity is the **quick ratio:**

$$\text{Quick ratio} = \frac{\text{Cash} + \text{Marketable securities} + \text{Receivables}}{\text{Current liabilities}}$$

Few businesses can instantaneously convert their inventories into cash. So, the quick ratio does not include inventory in the numerator and thus provides a measure of *very* immediate liquidity.

Activity ratios tell us how efficiently the company is using its assets. Activity ratios can highlight causes for operating cash flow mismatches. For example, the **accounts receivable turnover** ratio is an activity ratio that can help analysts determine whether receivables are excessive when compared to existing levels of credit sales:

$$\text{Accounts receivable turnover} = \frac{\text{Net credit sales}}{\text{Average accounts receivable}}$$

To illustrate how to interpret this ratio, suppose annual credit sales totaled \$10 million and that customer accounts receivable were \$2 million at the beginning of the year and \$3 million at year-end. The accounts receivable turnover ratio value is then:

$$\frac{\$10}{(\$2 + \$3)/2} = 4 \text{ times per year}$$

The average annual balance of receivables (\$2.5 million) represents one-fourth of yearly credit sales ($\$2.5/\$10 = 1/4$), so receivables must turn over four times per year.

The accounts receivable turnover ratio can also be used by the analyst to spot changing customer payment patterns. For example, if we divide the accounts receivable turnover ratio into 365 days, the result tells us the number of days that the average customer receivable is "on the books" before it is collected—that is:

$$\text{Days accounts receivable outstanding} = \frac{365 \text{ days}}{\text{Accounts receivable turnover}}$$

$$= \frac{365 \text{ days}}{4} = 91.25 \text{ days}$$

In our example the average accounts receivable is collected about 91 days after the credit sale occurs. This is the same as saying accounts receivable "turn over" four times per year.

> Most companies just report a single "Sales" number that is the sum of cash plus credit sales. Using total "Sales" instead of "Credit sales" in the accounts receivable turnover calculation can sometimes produce misleading results. Companies for which cash sales comprise a large proportion of total "Sales" will have relatively low accounts receivable balances and correspondingly large receivable turnover ratios. Fortunately, cash sales are rare in a surprisingly large number of businesses today. In certain industries like discount retailing, however, cash sales are the rule rather than the exception.

Another activity ratio is the **inventory turnover ratio,** which tells us how effectively inventories are managed:

$$\text{Inventory turnover} = \frac{\text{Cost of goods sold}}{\text{Average inventory}}$$

Assume that beginning inventory was \$8 million, that year-end inventory was \$9 million, and that cost of goods sold was \$43.35 million. Therefore inventory turnover is:

$$\frac{\$43.35}{(\$8 + \$9)/2} = 5.1 \text{ times per year}$$

Amazon.com and other e-commerce retailing companies exhibit large inventory turnover ratios as a consequence of adopting business models that emphasize high sales volume and avoid the need to stock inventory in brick-and-mortar stores. As a result, Amazon's inventory turnover ratio (24.4 in 1998) has a large numerator (\$476 million, reflecting high volume) and a small denominator (\$19.5 million, reflecting low inventory levels).

The inventory turnover ratio can also be used to determine the average **days inventory held** as follows:

$$\text{Days inventory held} = \frac{365 \text{ days}}{\text{Inventory turnover}} = \frac{365 \text{ days}}{5.1} = 71.57 \text{ days}$$

In our example, it takes about 72 days for inventory to move from the company to its customers. In other words, average inventory is sufficient to cover almost 72 days of customer sales. This is just another way of saying that inventory turns over 5.1 times (i.e., 365 days/71.57 days) each year.

The calculation of inventory turnover and days inventory held for a manufacturing firm is more complicated than for the merchandising firm illustrated here. That's because inventory in a manufacturing firm must pass through three stages of the operating cycle:

1. As *raw material*, from purchase to the start of production.
2. As *work-in-process*, over the length of the production cycle.
3. As *finished goods*, from completion of production until it is sold.

Inventory in a merchandising firm passes only through Stage 3.

To calculate how long inventory is held at each stage, analysts use the following:

$$\text{Raw materials: } 365 \text{ days} \times \frac{\text{Average raw materials inventory}}{\text{Raw materials used}}$$

$$\text{Work-in-process: } 365 \text{ days} \times \frac{\text{Average work-in-process inventory}}{\text{Cost of goods manufactured}}$$

$$\text{Finished goods: } 365 \text{ days} \times \frac{\text{Average finished goods inventory}}{\text{Cost of goods sold}}$$

Cost of goods sold and the breakdown of inventory into raw materials, work-in-process, and finished goods is reported in the financial statements. Cost of goods manufactured can be calculated as "cost of goods sold" *plus* ending "finished goods inventory" *minus* beginning "finished goods inventory." However, the amount of raw materials used in production is rarely disclosed in financial statements. It may be available in the company's fact book or obtained by contacting the company's investor relations group.

The **accounts payable turnover** ratio—and its **days payable outstanding** counterpart—helps the analyst understand the company's pattern of payments to suppliers:

$$\text{Accounts payable turnover} = \frac{\text{Inventory purchases}}{\text{Average accounts payable}}$$

$$\text{Days accounts payable outstanding} = \frac{365 \text{ days}}{\text{Accounts payable turnover}}$$

Suppose trade accounts payable averaged $7.4 million and inventory purchases totaled $44.350 million during the year. The accounts payable turnover ratio would then equal almost 6 (i.e., turnover occurs six times per year), and the days accounts payable outstanding would be about 60 days. (You should verify both calculations!) ***More timely payment of accounts payable would lead to a lower average payable balance, a higher turnover ratio, and fewer days outstanding.***

For retail companies like Amazon.com and Wal-Mart, inventory purchases equal cost-of-goods-sold expense plus the year's inventory increase—that is, $44.350 = $43.350 + ($9 − $8) in our example.

Let's piece these activity ratios together to get a picture that will help us analyze the financial condition of our company.

- Inventory remains on hand for about 72 days
- Inventory is sold and another 91 days elapse before cash is collected from the customer
- Suppliers are paid about 60 days after inventory is purchased.

Cash outflows and inflows seem dangerously mismatched by 103 days (72 + 91 − 60). The company's **operating cycle** spans 163 days—that is how long it takes to sell inventory (72 days) and collect cash from the customers (91 days). But the company pays for inventory purchases in just 60 days, so its **cash cycle** is 103 days—suppliers are paid 103 days before the company has received cash from product sales. This hypothetical company may face a short-term liquidity problem because cash outflows and inflows are mismatched by 103 days. It must rely on other cash sources—like bank loans—to sustain its operating working capital requirements over the 103-day gap.

Exhibit 5.7 on the next page reports the operating cycle and cash cycle for three retailers: Amazon.com, Wal-Mart and Nordstrom. Each company has adopted a different business model, and differences in these business models show up as differences in working capital activity ratios, operating cycles, and cash cycles. Amazon.com is an e-commerce retailer that doesn't have to stock inventory on store shelves. Consequently, inventory levels at Amazon.com are quite low—just 15.0 days. Amazon's customers pay by bank credit card so Amazon gets cash (from the customer's credit card company) almost instantaneously when

Exhibit 5.7 ■ AMAZON.COM, WAL-MART, AND NORDSTROM

Comparison of 1998 Operating and Cash Cycles

	Amazon.com	Wal-Mart	Nordstrom
Working capital activity ratios:			
1. Days inventory held	15.0	72.1	120.9
2. Days accounts receivable outstanding	0.0	4.0	42.6
3. Days accounts payable outstanding	154.7	33.4	34.3
Operating cycle (1 + 2)	15.0	76.1	163.5
Cash cycle (1 + 2 − 3)	(139.7)	42.7	129.2

it makes a sale. The operating cycle at Amazon.com is 15.0 days but the cash cycle is *minus* 139.7 days. That's because Amazon waits 154.7 days after buying inventory to pay its suppliers.

Wal-Mart and Nordstrom are traditional brick-and-mortar retailers that target different market segments. Wal-Mart carries a broad line of merchandise, emphasizes low prices, and most customers pay cash or use a credit card. Nordstrom is known for its fashion apparel and shoes. The company emphasizes product quality and customer service, including its in-store credit card. Wal-Mart has a 76.1 day operating cycle compared to 163.5 days at Nordstrom. It takes Nordstrom longer to sell inventory (120.9 days compared to 72.1 days at Wal-Mart), and longer to collect cash from customers once the sale has been made (42.6 days, compared to 4.0 days at Wal-Mart). However, both companies pay suppliers in about 34 days. So, the difference in cash cycle at the two companies—42.7 days at Wal-Mart compared to 129.2 days at Nordstrom—can be traced back to Nordstrom's emphasis on fashion apparel (slower to sell) and its in-store credit card (slower to collect cash). Both companies must carefully manage their short-term liquidity because cash outflows and inflows are mismatched.

Let's return to our analysis of the Quaker Oats Company. Exhibit 5.8 reports data on the company's short-term liquidity ratios. Quaker's current ratio is 1.06 in 1999, down from 1.20 two years earlier. The quick ratio is 0.57 in 1999, suggesting some improvement since 1997. The quick ratio means cash and receivables at Quaker are sufficient to cover 57% of the company's 1999 current liabilities. Adding inventories further improves the picture—a current ratio of 1.06 means that total current assets cover 106% of Quaker's current liabilities.

Exhibit 5.8 ■ QUAKER OATS COMPANY

Credit Risk Analysis: Short-Term Liquidity

	1999	1998	1997
Current ratio	1.06	1.10	1.20
Quick ratio	0.57	0.63	0.41
Working capital activity ratios			
1. Days inventory held	45.1	39.8	37.8
2. Days accounts receivable outstanding	20.8	22.2	21.9
3. Days accounts payable outstanding	33.1	27.9	28.4
Operating cycle (1 + 2)	65.9	62.0	59.7
Cash cycle (1 + 2 − 3)	32.8	34.1	31.3

Quaker's credit customers are paying more promptly in 1999 than they did in 1997, with days receivable outstanding at 20.8 compared to 21.9 two years earlier. However, Quaker is paying its bills less promptly—days payable outstanding has risen from 28.4 in 1997 to 33.1 in 1999. Inventory turnover has also deteriorated, and inventory levels are up from 37.8 days in 1997 to 45.1 days in 1999.

There is some misalignment of operating cash flows, since payments to suppliers occur about 33 days after purchase; in contrast, it takes 66 days (20.8 + 45.1) to generate a sale and collect cash from customers. In view of the company's overall level of positive operating cash flows, this misalignment is unlikely to cause concern.

Long-Term Solvency Solvency refers to the ability of a company to generate a stream of cash inflows sufficient to maintain its productive capacity and still meet the interest and principal payments on its long-term debt. A company that cannot make timely payments in the amount required becomes insolvent and may be compelled to reorganize or liquidate.

Debt ratios provide information about the amount of long-term debt in a company's financial structure. The more a company relies on long-term borrowing to finance its business activities, the higher its debt ratio and the greater the long-term solvency risk. There are several variations in debt ratios. Two commonly used ratios are:

$$\text{Long-term debt to assets} = \frac{\text{Long-term debt}}{\text{Total assets}}$$

$$\text{Long-term debt to tangible assets} = \frac{\text{Long-term debt}}{\text{Total tangible assets}}$$

Suppose a company has $20 million of outstanding long-term debt and $100 million of total assets, of which $35 million are intangibles like goodwill or purchased patents, trademarks, or copyrights. The two debt ratios would be:

$$\text{Long-term debt to assets} = \frac{\$20}{\$100} = 0.200$$

$$\text{Long-term debt to tangible assets} = \frac{\$20}{\$100 - \$35} = 0.307$$

These results tell us that only 20 cents of each asset dollar was financed using long-term debt. The remaining 80 cents came from other sources—internally generated resources, short-term borrowing, or equity capital in the form of common and preferred stock. This level of debt—only 20 cents of each asset dollar—would be surprisingly high for a discount retailer like Wal-Mart but surprisingly low for an electric utility company. Retailers use short-term debt and trade credit to finance their inventory purchases, and they usually lease (but don't own) their retail stores. Electric utilities, on the other hand, rely on long-term debt to support their sizable investment in power generating facilities and transmission lines. Electric utilities also have relatively predictable operating cash flows because energy demand is reasonably stable and competition is limited by regulators. Companies whose sales fluctuate widely due to changing economic conditions generally prefer to avoid debt, since the fixed interest charges are difficult to meet during bad times. These cyclical companies tend to have smaller debt-to-asset ratios.

Analysts devote considerable attention to refining both the numerator and denominator of debt ratios. For example, analysts include in the numerator hybrid securities having the cash flow characteristics of debt even though these hybrids are not classified as long-term debt on the balance sheet. Operating leases and other off-balance sheet obligations are routinely included as debt equivalents. The exclusion of intangible assets from the ratio denominator is also common. This adjustment is intended to remove "soft" assets—those difficult to value reliably—from the analysis.

Comparative debt ratios for Quaker Oats are shown in Exhibit 5.9. The company's debt to total asset ratio was 0.33 in 1999, a slight decrease from the 0.37 level in 1997. The long-term debt to tangible assets ratio stands at 0.37, also down from 0.42 in 1997. The two debt ratios moved in the same direction and are consistent with a manufacturing company that requires significant long-term financing to support its business and yet is financially sound.

Exhibit 5.9 ■ QUAKER OATS COMPANY

Credit Risk Analysis: Long-Term Solvency

	1999	1998	1997
Long-term debt to assets ratio	0.33	0.36	0.37
Long-term debt to tangible assets ratio	0.37	0.39	0.42
Interest coverage ratio	11.05	8.56	5.97
Operating cash flow to total liabilities	0.29	0.22	0.20

Although debt ratios are useful for understanding the financial structure of a company, they provide no information about its ability to generate a stream of inflows sufficient to make principal and interest payments. One financial ratio commonly used for this purpose is the **interest coverage ratio:**

$$\text{Interest coverage} = \frac{\text{Operating income before taxes and interest}}{\text{Interest expense}}$$

This ratio indicates how many times interest expense is covered by operating profits before taxes and interest are factored in. It reflects the cushion between operating profit inflows and required interest payments. If the company must also make periodic principal payments, then the analyst could include those amounts in the calculation.

> Many analysts use an *adjusted* operating income figure that removes nonoperating and nonrecurring items from reported income and that corrects for accounting quality distortions.

Suppose a company has \$200 million of operating income before taxes and interest, and \$50 million of interest expense. The company's interest coverage ratio is:

$$\frac{\$200}{\$50} = 4$$

This shows that operating profit is four times larger than interest expense—a substantial cushion for the lender. But now suppose our company is also required to make a \$100 million debt principal payment. The revised interest coverage ratio is:

$$\frac{\$200}{\$50 + \$100} = 1.33$$

When required debt payments are factored in, the lender's cushion now looks thin.

A criticism of the traditional interest coverage ratio is that it uses earnings rather than operating cash flows in the numerator. Some analysts prefer to compute a **cash flow coverage ratio** in which the numerator represents operating cash flows before interest and tax payments are factored in. When operating profits and cash flows move in tandem, both versions of the ratio will yield similar results. However, when the two measures do diverge—as during a period of rapid growth—income may be a poor substitute for cash flow, and in that case the cash flow coverage ratio is preferable.

Another useful measure of long-term solvency compares **operating cash flow** to the company's **total liabilities** (excluding deferred taxes):

$$\begin{array}{c}\text{Operating cash flow}\\ \text{to total liabilities}\end{array} = \frac{\text{Cash flow from continuing operations}}{\text{Average current liabilities plus long-term debt}}$$

This ratio shows the ability of a company to generate cash from operations in order to service both short-term and long-term borrowings.

Referring to Exhibit 5.9, we see an interest coverage ratio of 11.05 in 1999—a significant improvement from the 5.97 in 1997. Two factors help explain this. Net income is up in 1999 compared to 1997, and interest expense is down because Quaker repaid some of the long-term borrowing used to finance its Snapple purchase. As a result, interest coverage in 1999 benefits from a larger income flow and a lower level of interest expense.

Quaker's operating cash flow to total liabilities ratio clearly demonstrates why the company is regarded by most analysts as financially solvent and a low credit risk. Operating cash flow in 1999 is sufficient to repay 29% of the company's total debt, up somewhat from the 1997 level. It is remarkable that a company of Quaker's size can generate enough cash from operations to repay all borrowings in three and one-half years (1 year/0.29% repayment per year = 3.45 years).

When lenders want to know about a company's ability to pay debts on time, they assess its credit risk. A cash flow statement is often the starting point for credit risk assessment because it shows the company's operating cash flows along with its financing and investment needs. A low-credit-risk company generates operating cash flows substantially in excess of what are required to sustain its business activities. Liquidity and solvency ratios are additional tools the lender can use to assess credit risk.

RECAP

Return on Equity and Financial Leverage

Profitability and credit risk both influence the return that common shareholders earn on their investment in the company. To see how, let's look at what happens when a successful company borrows money to fund its growth.

ParsTech develops and distributes home financial planning software nationwide. Assume the company has $1 million in assets and no debt—ParsTech is an "all equity" firm. Earnings in 2001 are $150,000 and the entire amount is paid to shareholders as a dividend. These events are summarized in the first row of Exhibit 5.10.

ParsTech's ROA for 2001 is 15% ($150,000 in earnings/$1 million in assets). Since the company has no debt, all the earnings belong to shareholders, so **return on common equity** (ROCE) is also 15% ($150,000 in earnings/$1 million in common equity).

Early in 2002 the company borrows $1 million to expand its manufacturing, distribution, and customer support facilities. Lenders charge only 10% interest on the loan because the company has steady cash flows and a track record of successful new product introductions.

Exhibit 5.10 ■ PARSTECH

Financial Leverage

	Earnings Before Interest[1]	Assets	Common Shareholders' Equity	Return on Assets (ROA)	Interest Charges	Net Income Available to Common Stockholders	Return on Common Equity (ROCE)
2001	$150,000	$1 million	$1 million	15%	—	$150,000	15%
2002	300,000	2 million	1 million	15	$100,000	200,000	20
2003	450,000	3 million	1 million	15	300,000	150,000	15

[1]Earnings are before interest but after taxes, and they are distributed to lenders (as interest) and shareholders (as dividends) each year.

Strong consumer demand plus expanded plant capacity produce a banner year for the company. Earnings before interest total $300,000 in 2002, and ParsTech's ROA is again 15% (shown in the second row of Exhibit 5.10). Who gets the $300,000? Lenders must receive their share—$100,000 in interest on the loan—but the rest belongs to common shareholders. Shareholders receive $200,000 and ROCE is 20%.

Why did ROCE increase while ROA was unchanged? The answer is **financial leverage.** ParsTech borrowed $1 million at 10% (or $100,000 annual interest) but earned 15% (or $150,000) on the money. After the company paid interest charges, common shareholders gained $50,000 without investing more of their own money in the company. Financial leverage benefits shareholders whenever the cost of debt (10% in our example) is less than what the company earns on the borrowed funds (15% in our example).

There's a downside here, however, because financial leverage can sometimes be costly to shareholders. For instance, suppose that ParsTech borrowed another $1 million in 2003 to further expand its facilities. But this time, lenders assign a higher credit risk to the company and charge 20% interest. Earnings before interest but after taxes are $450,000 in 2000 and ParsTech's ROA is again 15%. What is ROCE?

> More precisely, it's the *after-tax* cost of debt that must be less than what the company earns on borrowed funds. If the corporate income tax rate is 35%, ParsTech has an after-tax cost of debt of 6.5% [10% × (1 − 0.35)] even though lenders are charging 10% interest. Financial leverage benefits ParsTech shareholders as long as the company earns more than 6.5% on its debt-financed investment.

Now lenders receive $300,000 in interest—$100,000 for the first loan plus $200,000 for the second—leaving only $150,000 of earnings for common shareholders. ROCE in 2000 is 15% ($150,000/$1 million in common equity), down from the previous year. Stockholders are no better off now than they were two years earlier when the company was smaller and earnings were lower. What happened?

The second loan cost more (20% or $200,000 in annual interest) than ParsTech was able to earn ($150,000) on the borrowed funds, and shareholders had to make up the difference. ***Financial leverage is beneficial—but only when the company earns more than the incremental after-tax cost of debt.*** If the cost of debt becomes too high, increased leverage can actually harm shareholders.

If you want to gauge a company's profit performance from its shareholders' viewpoint, use ROCE.

$$\text{ROCE} = \frac{\text{Net income available to common shareholders}}{\text{Average common shareholders' equity}}$$

ROCE measures a company's performance in using capital provided by common shareholders to generate earnings.[4] It explicitly considers how the company's assets are financed. Interest charged on loans and dividends on preferred stock are both subtracted in arriving at "Net income available to common shareholders." The capital provided by common shareholders during the period can be computed by averaging the aggregate par value of common stock, capital contributed in excess of par, and retained earnings (minus common treasury shares) at the beginning and end of the period. For example, using the data in Exhibits 5.1(a) and 5.2(a), the ROCE for Quaker Oats in 1999 is:

$$\text{ROCE} = \frac{\text{Net income} - \text{Restructuring and gains} - \text{Preferred dividends}}{\text{Average common stockholders' equity}}$$

$$= \frac{\$455.0 - \$1.5 - \$4.4}{(\$158.8 + \$102.6)/2} = \frac{\$449.1}{\$130.7} = 3.436 \text{ or } 343.6\%$$

where $455.0 is reported net income, $1.5 is the after-tax restructuring charges and gains (i.e., $2.3 × 65%), and $4.4 is preferred dividends. A 35% tax rate has been assumed. The restructuring charges and gains are eliminated from reported net income so that ROCE

[4] If the analysts' goal is to isolate *sustainable* ROCE, "Net income available to common shareholders" should be purged of nonoperating and nonrecurring items and corrected for accounting quality distortions. These are discussed in later chapters.

reflects only continuing operations. Quaker's ROCE is uncommonly high in 1999 compared to the industry average of 12.0% or the company's 14.8% ROCE in 1996. The reason? Common shareholders' equity was reduced by about $1.3 billion when Quaker sold Snapple back in 1997. Average common shareholders' equity was $131 million in 1999, compared to $1,155 million in 1996. This smaller equity base, when combined with strong earnings, produces an exceptionally high ROCE.

Components of ROCE We can break down ROCE into several components to aid in our interpretation, much as we did earlier with ROA. The components of ROCE are ROA, common earnings leverage, and financial leverage:

$$\text{ROCE} = \text{ROA} \times \text{Common earnings leverage} \times \text{Financial structure leverage}$$

$$= \left(\frac{\text{NOPAT}}{\text{Average assets}}\right) \times \left(\frac{\text{Net income available to common shareholders}}{\text{NOPAT}}\right)$$

$$\times \left(\frac{\text{Average assets}}{\text{Average common shareholders' equity}}\right)$$

$$= \frac{\text{Net income available to common shareholders}}{\text{Average common shareholders' equity}}$$

ROA measures the profitability of operations before considering how the company's assets are financed. The **common earnings leverage ratio** shows the proportion of NOPAT (net operating profits before interest but after taxes) that belongs to common shareholders. The **financial structure leverage ratio** measures the degree to which the company uses common shareholders' capital to finance assets.

The ROCE breakdown for Quaker Oats in 1999 is:

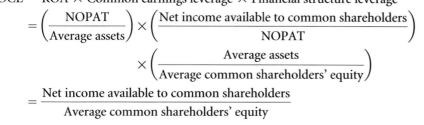

$$\text{ROCE} = \text{ROA} \times \text{Common earnings leverage} \times \text{Financial structure leverage}$$

$$= \left(\frac{\$493.7}{(\$2{,}510.3 + \$2{,}396.2)/2}\right) \times \left(\frac{\$449.1}{\$493.7}\right) \times \left(\frac{(\$2{,}510.3 + \$2{,}396.2)/2}{(\$158.8 + \$102.6)/2)}\right)$$

$$= 0.2012 \times 0.910 \times 18.770$$

$$= 3.436 \text{ or } 343.6\%$$

Quaker's higher ROCE (343.6%) compared to ROA (20.1%) occurs because the company has a lot of debt in its financial structure, resulting in a high financial structure leverage ratio (18.77). (Recall from Exhibit 5.2(c) that common shareholders' equity represents only 6.6% of total assets in 1999.) Interest on this debt contributes to a moderate common earnings leverage ratio (0.910). The two factors in combination produce a return on common equity that is 17.1 times (0.910 × 18.770) greater than what the company earns on all assets (20.1% ROA).

To see how the components of ROCE work together, consider two companies—NoDebt and HiDebt—both having $2 million in assets. NoDebt raised all its capital from common shareholders; HiDebt borrowed $1 million at 10% interest. Both companies pay income taxes at a combined federal and state rate of 40%.

Exhibit 5.11 on the next page shows how the two companies compare in different earnings years. Let's start with a good earnings year, one in which both companies earn $240,000 before interest but after taxes. This represents an ROA of 12% for both companies, and 12% is also NoDebt's ROCE. HiDebt's ROCE is 18%, since $180,000 of earnings ($240,000 − $60,000) is available to common shareholders. Leverage increased the return to HiDebt's shareholders because the capital contributed by lenders earned 12% but required an after-tax interest payment of only 6%—that is, (1 − 40%) × 10%. The extra 6% earned on each borrowed dollar of assets increased the return to common shareholders.

But what happens when earnings are low? That situation is illustrated by the bad earnings year in Exhibit 5.11. Both companies earn $60,000 before interest but after taxes, for a 3% ROA. All of these earnings are available to NoDebt shareholders, so ROCE at the

Exhibit 5.11 ■ NODEBT AND HIDEBT

Profitability and Financial Leverage

	Total Assets	Shareholders' Equity	Earnings Before Interest[1]	After-Tax Interest	Available to Common Shareholders	ROA	ROCE
Good Earnings Year							
HiDebt	$2 million	$1 million	$240,000	$60,000	$180,000	12.0%	18.0%
NoDebt	2 million	2 million	240,000	—	240,000	12.0	12.0
Neutral Earnings Year							
HiDebt	2 million	1 million	120,000	60,000	60,000	6.0	6.0
NoDebt	2 million	2 million	120,000	—	120,000	6.0	6.0
Bad Earnings Year							
HiDebt	2 million	1 million	60,000	60,000	—	3.0	0.0
NoDebt	2 million	2 million	60,000	—	60,000	3.0	3.0

[1]Earnings are before interest but after taxes. HiDebt has after-tax interest charges of $60,000—that is $1 million × 10% × (1 – 40%)—each year.

company is also 3%. At HiDebt, after-tax interest charges wipe out earnings and ROCE becomes 0% because there's nothing left for shareholders. HiDebt earns 3% on each asset dollar but must pay 6% to lenders for each dollar borrowed. Here leverage decreases the return to common equity.

In the neutral year, leverage neither helps nor hurts shareholders. That's because the 6% return earned on each asset dollar just equals the 6% after-tax cost of borrowing. Figure 5.3 illustrates the key results from this example.

RECAP

Financial leverage works two ways. It can make good years better by increasing the shareholders' return, but it can also make bad years worse by decreasing the shareholders' return. It all depends on whether the company earns more on each borrowed dollar than it pays out in interest.

Earnings, Cash Earnings, or EBITDA?

It's the quarterly earnings season, that three-week period each quarter when analysts and investors nervously watch the financial wire services as companies report their quarterly results. One company whose stock you own, Millbrae Technologies, is expected to report

Figure 5.3

FINANCIAL LEVERAGE AND ROCE

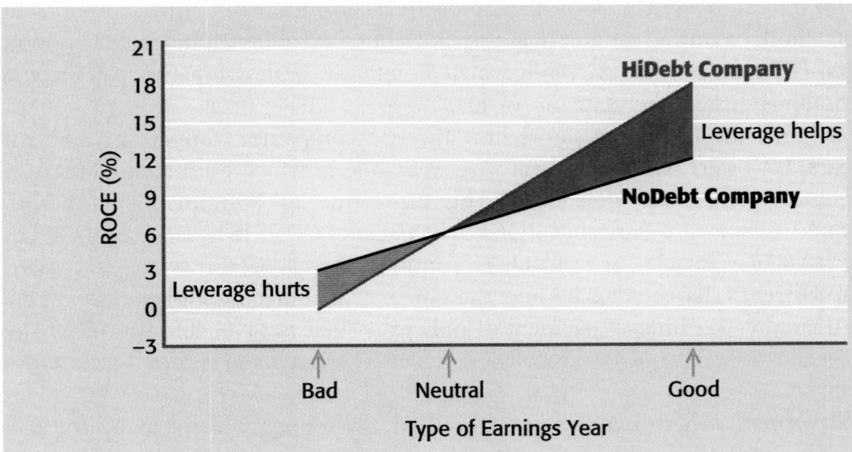

record per share earnings of $1.50 this quarter. That's what analysts covering the company are saying. You, however, are confident that Millbrae will beat the $1.50 consensus "Wall Street" estimate. You scan your e-mail for the company's press release, and sure enough the headline reads: "Millbrae has a blockbuster quarter—earns $2.10 per share." Great news! But wait—the stock is trading down as if investors are punishing the company for reporting an earnings disappointment. What's going on?

A closer look at Millbrae's press release reveals the problem. The company's GAAP earnings for the quarter were only $1.20 per share, considerably below what analysts were expecting. No wonder the stock is trading down on the earnings disappointment. And the "$2.10 per share" the company said it earned? It turns out that wasn't GAAP earnings at all but instead something called **EBITDA** (earnings before interest, taxes, depreciation, and amortization).

Many companies today are highlighting a non-GAAP earnings figure in press releases, in analyst conference calls, and in quarterly and annual reports. Sometimes the earnings figure is called EBITDA, sometimes "cash earnings," and sometimes "pro forma earnings." But these distinctions are often vague, so you have to look closely to find out what's really going on. For example, here is what Amazon.com said in its annual report about its 1999 earnings:

Pro forma information regarding our results, which excludes amortization of goodwill and other intangibles, stockbased compensation, equity in losses of equity-method investees, and merger, acquisition and investment-related costs, is as follows:

YEAR ENDED DECEMBER 31, 1999 ($ in thousands except per share amounts)	
Pro forma loss from operations	$(352,371)
Pro forma net loss	$(389,815)
Pro forma basic and diluted loss per share	$ (1.19)

Using the methodology described above to derive pro forma loss from operations, our U.S. book business was profitable in the fourth quarter of 1999 and we expect this business to be profitable in 2000. The pro forma results are presented for informational purposes only and are not prepared in accordance with generally accepted accounting principles.

Amazon reported a "pro forma" loss of about $390 million or $1.19 per share for 1999. More important, the company said its U.S. book business became profitable—on a "pro forma" basis—in the fourth quarter of 1999 and is expected to be profitable in 2000. Of course, the profit measure Amazon highlights in its annual report is one that the company itself has constructed. Pro forma profits at Amazon.com exclude a variety of costs that are routinely included in GAAP earnings. Once these costs are included, the company's 1999 loss increases to $720 million or $2.20 per share. Was Amazon's U.S. book business profitable in the fourth quarter of 1999? The answer depends on which profit benchmark is used—the company's own "pro forma" calculation or GAAP earnings. The more cost items Amazon excludes from its profit computation, the more "profitable" the company's book business will appear. But appearances don't necesssarily mirror reality!

Let's take a closer look at the computation and origin of these non-GAAP profit measures. Exhibit 5.12 on the next page presents a GAAP income statement for Marconi Communications, an emerging telecommunications company. Marconi has a GAAP loss of $51 million for 2001. This loss includes a charge for depreciation, goodwill amortization, restructuring and merger costs, interest and taxes. By selectively including or excluding these items, Mar-

Exhibit 5.12 ■ MARCONI COMMUNICATIONS

GAAP Earnings, "Pro forma" Earnings, EBITDA, and "Cash" Earnings

GAAP Earnings ($ in millions)	**2001**
Sales	$500
Cost of goods sold (excluding depreciation)	(200)
Depreciation expense	(100)
Selling, general and administrative expenses	(75)
Goodwill amortization	(100)
Restructuring and merger expenses	(50)
Interest expense	(60)
Taxes	34
Net income (loss)	($ 51)

"Pro forma" earnings

Net income (loss)	($ 51)
Excluded costs:	
Goodwill amortization	100
Restructuring and merger expenses	50
Pro forma earnings	$ 99

EBITDA earnings

Net income (loss)	($ 51)
Excluded costs:	
Interest expense	60
Tax expense	(34)
Depreciation expense	100
Goodwill amortization	100
EBITDA	$175

"Cash" earnings

Net income (loss)	($ 51)
Excluded costs:	
Goodwill amortization	100
Cash earnings	$ 49

coni can highlight any of several different profit numbers. For example, Marconi adds back goodwill amortization along with its restructuring and merger costs to arrive at "pro forma" earnings of $99 million. The company's $175 million of EBITDA excludes interest, taxes, depreciation and goodwill amortization. "Cash" earnings of $49 million, on the other hand, incorporate a single adjustment for goodwill amortization. Be forewarned, however, that standard definitions for these non-GAAP profit benchmarks do not presently exist. Companies today can and do exercise considerable discretion over which cost items are included or excluded in the profit numbers they choose to highlight. Of course, the financial statements themselves must still report GAAP earnings (e.g., Marconi's $51 million loss) but some firms try to overshadow these GAAP numbers with other, more creative, profit benchmarks.

The origins of EBITDA date back to before 1980 when EBIT (earnings before interest and taxes) or *operating earnings* was often used as a key indicator of a company's ability to service its debt.[5] One important advantage of EBIT is that it "leveled the playing field" for differences in capital structure and taxation by removing interest and taxes from the profit benchmark, thus making comparisons across companies more transparent. (Recall our earlier discussion of interest coverage.) However, EBIT is not a cash flow measure—we will see why in a moment—and it may overstate or understate the degree to which operating cash is available to service debt.

EBITDA displaced EBIT in the 1980s as a financial benchmark for measuring a company's cash flow and thus its ability to service debt. EBITDA removes from the profit calculation two non-cash items—depreciation and amortization—that are major expense items for many companies today, especially technology and telecommunications companies. Proponents claim EBITDA really is an accurate measure of cash flow—

[5] P. Stumpp, T. Marshella, M. Rowan, R. McCreary, and M. Coppola, "Putting EBITDA in Perspective: Ten Critical Failings of EBITDA as the Principal Determinant of Cash Flow," *Global Credit Research Report,* Moody's Investors Service (June 2000).

assuming the company does not have to spend money on equipment or pay taxes and interest on debt. Critics respond that EBITDA isn't the same as cash flow. Quite simply, cash flow is what's left in the till after you account for all the cash coming in and all the cash going out during a given period. EBITDA ignores the cash required for working capital growth and for reinvestment (i.e., money spent replacing worn out equipment). EBITDA also says nothing about the quality of earnings because it takes operating revenues and expenses at face value without considering whether those revenues and expenses affect cash directly. As a result, EBITDA can easily be manipulated through aggressive accounting policies relating to revenues and expenses.

"Pro forma" earnings emerged in the late 1990s as a label for adjusted GAAP earnings where everything but the kitchen sink may be excluded from the profit figure. At firms like Amazon.com, the adjustments include the elimination of goodwill amortization, merger costs, stock-based employee pay, and losses at affiliates. Some companies also exclude interest, taxes, and depreciation to produce an "adjusted pro forma" EBITDA. These and other "pro forma" adjustments to GAAP earnings are rationalized by analysts and company management because they involve non-cash charges, or they are non-recurring, or because they somehow mask the company's true profitability. Skeptics argue that "pro forma" profits are nothing more than EEBS—earnings excluding bad stuff![6]

"Cash" earnings also emerged in the late 1990s as a term used to describe GAAP earnings without goodwill amortization, although it is sometimes mistakenly used as a synonym for EBITDA. Goodwill is now a significant balance sheet asset for many U.S. companies, often representing more than 50% of total assets. The growing importance of goodwill on balance sheets reflects a shift in the economy away from companies built around physical capital ("bricks and mortar") and toward companies built around intellectual capital (knowledge and information). As more companies grow through purchase acquisitions of other firms, and more goodwill accumulates on the balance sheet, GAAP earnings falls because of escalating goodwill amortization. "Cash" earnings ignores the goodwill charge to income and thus provides, proponents argue, a clearer picture of profitability for acquisitive growth companies. In fact, as we go to press, the Financial Accounting Standards Board (FASB) is proposing to eliminate the requirement for amortizing goodwill.[7]

> Accounting goodwill arises when one company purchases another, and the price paid exceeds the fair market value of the seller's brick-and-mortar net assets (see Chapter 16). Suppose Bidder.com bought Target.com for $40 million cash. Target's net brick-and-mortar assets—cash, receivables, inventories, buildings, and equipment *minus* current liabilities and debt—total only $5 million. Why is Bidder willing to pay $35 million more than Target's net assets are worth? Because Bidder will get access to a valuable technology, subscriber base, or market opportunity that is not currently reflected on Target's balance sheet. The *excess* purchase price ($35 million) will show up on Bidder's books as goodwill to be amortized (charged) against future earnings.

Why are companies resorting to EBITDA and "pro forma" earnings instead of just highlighting their GAAP earnings performance? The answer is simple—impression management! It's a whole lot easier to transform a GAAP loss into a "profit" by changing how profits are measured rather than changing the economics of the business itself. Just cross out a few expense items here and there, and suddenly the business looks profitable again. Sometimes the adjustments are well-intentioned attempts to describe the company's sustainable operating profits and cash flows. But not always. In either case, you will be well served to remember:

- There are no standard definitions for non-GAAP earnings numbers. EBITDA at one company may be "pro forma" earnings at another and "cash" earnings at still another. Worse, a company may change its EBITDA or "pro forma" earnings definition each quarter.
- Some real costs of the business are ignored, resulting in an incomplete picture of company profitability. For example, buildings and equipment wear out over time. GAAP accounting recognizes this economic reality as depreciation expense and requires that it be included in the profit calculation. Ignoring it understates the true costs of the business.

[6] J. Fox, "Forget Earnings—Try Fully Diluted EEBS!" *Fortune* (May 11, 1998).

[7] "*Business Combinations and Intangible Assets—Accounting for Goodwill*," Exposure Draft (Stamford, CT: FASB, February 14, 2001).

- Using these non-GAAP earnings as a measure of cash flow can be misleading. They ignore cash required for working capital growth and replacement capital expenditures. They also overlook the non-cash elements of revenues and expenses and can easily be manipulated using aggressive accounting policies.

Despite the growing acceptance of these non-GAAP profit measures on Wall Street, in corporate boardrooms, and among credit analysts, informed financial statement readers must be wary and look behind the numbers to understand what's really going on in the business. For the credit analyst, the message is simple: You can't buy a cup of coffee with EBITDA, "pro forma" earnings, or "cash" earnings. It takes real cash!

RECAP

SUMMARY

Financial ratios, along with common size and trend statements, provide analysts with powerful tools for tracking a company's performance over time, for making comparisons among different companies, and for assessing compliance with contractual benchmarks.

Some companies account for inventory using the First-In First-Out (FIFO) method; others use Last-In First-Out (LIFO). These alternative methods can produce very different balance sheet and income statement figures, and as a result, numerous financial ratios can be affected. Analysts must be alert to this possibility and know how to recognize when differences in the GAAP accounting methods that a company uses, rather than economic fundamentals, are affecting the analysis.

Another problem arises because under GAAP, fixed assets are measured using the historical cost convention. Two companies with identical assets that were purchased at different times will show those assets at different amounts. The company with the older (presumably lower cost) assets would likely report a higher ROA as well as a higher asset turnover ratio. Here, too, the analyst must guard against accounting distortions that mask economic fundamentals.

These and other accounting influences complicate financial analysis and the interpretation of ratio differences. That's why we examine the effects of accounting method choices, inflation, and other potential distortions of reported financial statement numbers in subsequent chapters.

EXERCISES

E5–1
Inventory turnover
AICPA adapted

Motley Company's merchandise inventory and other related accounts for 2001 follow:

Sales	$3,000,000
Cost of goods sold	2,200,000
Merchandise inventory	
Beginning of year	500,000
End of year	600,000

REQUIRED:

Assuming that the merchandise-inventory buildup was relatively constant during the year, how many times did the merchandise inventory turn over during 2001?

E5–2
Receivable and inventory turnover
AICPA adapted

Selected data of the Islander Company follow:

	As of December 31	
Balance Sheet Data	**2001**	**2000**
Accounts receivable	$500,000	$470,000
Allowance for doubtful accounts	(25,000)	(20,000)
Net accounts receivable	$475,000	$450,000
Inventories—lower of cost or market	$600,000	$550,000

Income Statement Data	Year Ended December 31 2001	2000
Net credit sales	$2,500,000	$2,200,000
Net cash sales	500,000	400,000
Net sales	$3,000,000	$2,600,000
Cost of goods sold	$2,000,000	$1,800,000
Selling, general, and administrative expenses	300,000	270,000
Other	50,000	30,000
Total operating expenses	$2,350,000	$2,100,000

REQUIRED:

1. What is the accounts receivable turnover for 2001?
2. What is the inventory turnover for 2001?

E5–3

Inventory turnover

AICPA adapted

On January 1, 2001 River Company's beginning inventory was $400,000. During 2001 the company purchased $1,900,000 of additional inventory, and on December 31, 2001 River's ending inventory was $500,000.

REQUIRED:

What is the inventory turnover for 2001?

E5–4

Receivable turnover

AICPA adapted

Utica Company's net accounts receivable was $250,000 at December 31, 2001 and $300,000 at December 31, 2002. Net cash sales for 2002 were $100,000. The accounts receivable turnover for 2002 was 5.0, and this turnover figure was computed from net credit sales for the year.

REQUIRED:

What were Utica's total net sales for 2002?

E5–5

Current and quick ratios

AICPA adapted

Todd Corporation wrote off $100,000 of obsolete inventory at December 31, 2001.

REQUIRED:

What effect did this write-off have on the company's 2001 current and quick ratios?

E5–6

Current ratio

AICPA adapted

Gil Corporation has current assets of $90,000 and current liabilities of $180,000.

REQUIRED:

Compute the effect of each of the following transactions on Gil's current ratio:

1. Refinancing a $30,000 long-term mortgage with a short-term note
2. Purchasing $50,000 of merchandise inventory with short-term accounts payable
3. Paying $20,000 of short-term accounts payable
4. Collecting $10,000 of short-term accounts receivable.

E5–7

Interest coverage

AICPA adapted

The following data were taken from the financial records of Glum Corporation for 2001:

Sales	$3,600,000
Bond interest expense	120,000
Income taxes	600,000
Net income	800,000

REQUIRED:

How many times was bond interest earned in 2001?

E5–8

Why inventory turnover increased

AICPA adapted

In a comparison of 2001 to 2000 performance, Neir Company's inventory turnover increased substantially, although sales and inventory amounts were essentially unchanged.

REQUIRED:

Which of the following statements best explains the increased inventory turnover ratio?

1. Cost of goods sold decreased
2. Accounts receivable turnover increased
3. Total asset turnover increased
4. Gross profit percentage decreased

E5–9

Days sales outstanding

AICPA adapted

Selected information taken from the accounting records of Vigor Company follows:

Net accounts receivable at December 31, 2000	$ 900,000
Net accounts receivable at December 31, 2001	$1,000,000
Accounts receivable turnover	5 to 1
Inventories at December 31, 2000	$1,100,000
Inventories at December 31, 2001	$1,200,000
Inventory turnover	4 to 1

REQUIRED:

1. What was Vigor's gross margin for 2001?
2. Suppose there are 360 business days in the year. What was the number of days' sales outstanding in average receivables and the number of days' sales outstanding in average inventories for 2001, respectively?

PROBLEMS/DISCUSSION QUESTIONS

P5–1

Ratio analysis

CFA adapted

Margaret O'Flaherty, a portfolio manager for MCF Investments, is considering an investment in Alpine Chemical 7% bonds, which mature in 10 years. She asks you to analyze the company to determine the riskiness of the bonds.

ALPINE CHEMICAL COMPANY FINANCIAL STATEMENTS

	Year Ended December 31					
($ in millions)	1996	1997	1998	1999	2000	2001
Assets						
Cash	$ 190	$ 55	$ -0-	$ 157	$ 249	$ -0-
Accounts receivable	1,637	2,087	1,394	2,143	3,493	3,451
Inventory	2,021	945	1,258	1,293	1,322	1,643
Other current assets	17	27	55	393	33	171
Current assets	3,865	3,114	2,707	3,986	5,097	5,265
Gross fixed assets	4,650	5,038	5,619	5,757	6,181	7,187
Less: accumulated depreciation	2,177	2,543	2,841	3,138	3,465	3,893
Net fixed assets	2,473	2,495	2,778	2,619	2,716	3,294
Total assets	$ 6,338	$ 5,609	$ 5,485	$ 6,605	$ 7,813	$ 8,559

(continued)

($ in millions)	1996	1997	1998	1999	2000	2001
			Year Ended December 31			
Liabilities and net worth						
Notes payable	$ 525	$ 750	$ -0-	$ 1,300	$ 1,750	$ 1,900
Accounts payable	673	638	681	338	743	978
Accrued liabilities	303	172	359	359	483	761
Current liabilities	1,501	1,560	1,040	1,997	2,976	3,639
Long term debt	1,985	1,044	1,401	1,457	1,542	1,491
Deferred tax credits	352	347	363	336	345	354
Total liabilities	3,838	2,951	2,804	3,790	4,863	5,484
Common stock	50	50	100	100	100	100
Capital surplus	100	100	-0-	-0-	-0-	-0-
Retained earnings	2,350	2,508	2,581	2,715	2,850	2,975
Net worth	2,500	2,658	2,681	2,815	2,950	3,075
Total liabilities and net worth	$ 6,338	$ 5,609	$ 5,485	$ 6,605	$ 7,813	$ 8,559

Income statement	1996	1997	1998	1999	2000	2001
Net sales	$14,100	$15,508	$13,875	$14,750	$19,133	$19,460
Cost of goods sold	10,200	11,220	9,366	10,059	13,400	13,117
Gross profit	3,900	4,288	4,509	4,691	5,733	6,343
Operating expense	2,065	2,203	2,665	2,685	3,472	3,885
Operating profit	1,835	2,085	1,844	2,006	2,261	2,458
Interest expense	275	465	275	319	376	318
Depreciation expense	475	477	479	478	495	511
Profit before tax	1,085	1,143	1,090	1,209	1,390	1,629
Income taxes	193	115	265	145	192	150
Net income	$ 892	$ 1,028	$ 825	$ 1,064	$ 1,198	$ 1,479

REQUIRED:

1. Using the data provided in the accompanying financial statement, calculate the following ratios for Alpine Chemical for 2001:
   a. EBIT/interest expense
   b. Long-term debt/total capitalization
   c. Funds from operations/total debt
   d. Operating income/sales

   Use the following conventions: EBIT is earnings before interest and taxes; total capitalization is interest-bearing long-term debt plus net worth; funds from operations means net income plus depreciation expense; and total debt includes interest-bearing short-term and long-term debt.
2. Briefly explain the significance of each ratio calculated in part (1) to the assessment of Alpine Chemical's creditworthiness.
3. Insert your answers to part (1) into Table 1 that follows. Then from Table 2 on the next page, select an appropriate credit rating for Alpine Chemical.

Table 1 ■ ALPINE CHEMICAL COMPANY

	1996	1997	1998	1999	2000	2001
EBIT / interest expense	4.95x	3.46x	4.96x	4.79x	4.70x	?
Long-term debt / total capitalization	44%	28%	34%	34%	34%	?
Funds from operations / total debt	54%	84%	93%	56%	51%	?
Operating income / sales	13%	13%	13%	14%	12%	?

Table 2 ■ INDUSTRY DATA

Three-Year Medians (1999–2001) by Credit Rating Category

	AAA	AA	A	BBB	BB	B
EBIT / interest expense	11.0	9.5	4.5	3.0	2.0	1.0
Long-term debt / total capitalization	13.0	16.5	29.5	39.0	45.5	63.5
Funds from operations / total debt	83.0	74.0	45.5	31.5	18.5	8.0
Operating income / sales	21.5	16.0	15.0	12.0	11.0	9.0

P5–2

Financial statement analysis

AICPA adapted

STRETCH

Here is a cash flow statement and partial balance sheet for Woods Company, along with supplemental information. The omitted items are numbered from (1) through (16) and can be calculated from the other information given.

WOODS COMPANY

2001 Statement of Cash Flows

Operations	
Net loss for 2001	($ 2,885)
Adjustments:	
Bond premium amortization	(500)
Deferred income taxes	(200)
Depreciation expense	3,000
Goodwill amortization	2,000
Increase in (noncash) working capital	(700)
Total from operations	715
Proceeds from equipment sold	10,000
Proceeds from reissue of treasury stock	11,400
Par value of common stock issued to reacquire preferred stock	7,500
Purchase of land	(14,715)
Payment on long-term bond debt	(7,200)
Par value of preferred stock reacquired by issuing common stock	(7,500)
Increase in cash	$ 200

Woods Company: Supplemental Information—Selected 2001 Income Statement Items

Bond interest expense (net of amortization)	$3,500
Loss before tax adjustment	(3,900)
Less: Income tax adjustment for refund due	815
Deferred income taxes	200
Net loss after tax adjustment	($2,885)

Selected Ratios	January 1, 2001[1]	December 31, 2001
Current ratio	?	3:1
Total stockholders' equity divided by total liabilities	4:3	?

Woods Company had neglected to amortize $2,000 of goodwill in 2000. The correction of this material error has been appropriately made in 2001. The book value and selling price of the equipment sold was two-thirds of the cost of the equipment.

[1]The above ratios were computed prior to the error correction.

WOODS COMPANY

Balance Sheets

	January 1, 2001[1]	December 31, 2001
Current assets	$22,000	$ (5)
Building and equipment	92,000	(6)
Accumulated depreciation	(25,000)	(7)
Land	(1)	(8)
Goodwill	12,000	(9)
Total assets	$ (?)	$ (?)
Current liabilities	$ (2)	(10)
Bonds payable (8%)	(3)	(11)
Bond premium	(?)	(12)
Deferred income taxes	(4)	1,700
Common stock	66,000	(13)
Paid-in capital	13,000	(14)
Preferred stock	16,000	(15)
Retained earnings (deficit)	(6,000)	(16)
Treasury stock (at cost)	(9,000)	-0-
Total liabilities and stockholders' equity	$ (?)	$ (?)

[1]The January 1, 2001 items are shown prior to restatement.

REQUIRED:

Number your answer sheet from (1) through (16). Place the correct balance for each balance sheet item next to the corresponding number on your answer sheet. Question mark (?) amounts may be needed to calculate the numbered balances. Do not restate the January 1 balance sheet for the error. Working capital was $16,500 at January 1, 2001.

P5–3

Explaining changes in financial ratios

AICPA adapted

Items 1 through 6 describe what an auditor discovered about changes in a client's financial statement ratios or amounts from the prior year's figures. For each item, select the most likely explanation from the list provided. The items are independent of each other.

1. Inventory turnover increased substantially from the prior year. (Select three explanations.)
2. Accounts receivable turnover decreased substantially from the prior year. (Select three explanations.)
3. Allowance for doubtful accounts increased in dollars from the prior year, but it decreased from the prior year as a percentage of accounts receivable. (Select three explanations.)
4. Long-term debt increased from the prior year, but interest expense increased more than the percentage increase in long-term debt. (Select one explanation.)
5. Operating income increased from the prior year, although the company was less profitable than in the prior year. (Select two explanations.)
6. Gross margin percentage was unchanged from the prior year, although gross margin increased from the prior year. (Select one explanation.)

EXPLANATIONS LIST:

a. Items shipped on consignment during the last month of the year were recorded as sales.
b. A significant number of credit memos for returned merchandise issued during the last month of the year were not recorded.
c. Year-end inventory purchases were overstated because items received in the first month of the subsequent year were incorrectly included.

(continued on next page)

d. Year-end inventory purchases were understated because items received before year-end were incorrectly excluded.
e. A larger percentage of sales occurred during the last month of the year, compared to the prior year.
f. A smaller percentage of sales occurred during the last month of the year, compared to the prior year.
g. The same percentage of sales occurred during the last month of the year, compared to the prior year.
h. Sales increased at the same percentage as cost of goods sold, compared to the prior year.
i. Sales increased at a lower percentage than cost of goods sold increased, compared to the prior year.
j. Sales increased at a higher percentage than cost of goods sold increased, compared to the prior year.
k. Interest expense decreased, compared to the prior year.
l. The effective income tax rate increased, compared to the prior year.
m. The effective income tax rate decreased, compared to the prior year.
n. Short-term borrowing was refinanced on a long-term basis at the same interest rate.
o. Short-term borrowing was refinanced on a long-term basis at lower interest rates.
p. Short-term borrowing was refinanced on a long-term basis at higher interest rates.

P5–4 The following information was taken from Alpha Corporation's 2001 annual report:

Current asset ratios
AICPA adapted

ALPHA CORPORATION

Selected Balance Sheet Data

	As of December 31	
	2001	**2000**
Cash	$ 10,000	$ 80,000
Accounts receivable (net)	50,000	150,000
Merchandise inventory	90,000	150,000
Short-term marketable securities	30,000	10,000
Land and buildings (net)	340,000	360,000
Mortgage payable (no current portion)	270,000	280,000
Accounts payable (trade)	70,000	110,000
Short-term notes payable	20,000	40,000

ALPHA CORPORATION

Selected Income Statement Data

	Year Ended December 31	
	2001	**2000**
Cash sales	$1,800,000	$1,600,000
Credit sales	500,000	800,000
Cost of goods sold	1,000,000	1,400,000

REQUIRED:

Determine the following:

1. Alpha's quick ratio as of December 31, 2001
2. Alpha's receivable turnover for 2001
3. Alpha's merchandise inventory turnover for 2001
4. Alpha's current ratio at December 31, 2001.

P5–5

Financial ratios and the balance sheet

STRETCH

REQUIRED:

Use the following information along with your knowledge of financial ratios and balance sheet relationships to fill in the missing items on the balance sheet of Clapton Corporation. Round all amounts to the nearest dollar.

ADDITIONAL INFORMATION:

1. Days accounts payable outstanding was 45.6 days in 2001, compared to 66.3 days in 2000.
2. The current ratio at the end of 2001 was 2.5, compared to 2.0 at the end of 2000.
3. The firm's gross profit rate was 25% in 2001 and 28% in 2000.
4. Net income for 2001 was $1,250,000, compared to $1,000,000 in 2000.
5. No common or preferred stock was issued during 2001.
6. Return on average assets was 5% for 2001, compared to 8% in 2000.
7. Cash dividends declared and paid in 2001 were $250,000; in 2000 they were $200,000.
8. Days accounts receivable outstanding was 36.5 days in 2001 and 50.5 days in 2000.
9. The long-term debt to total asset ratio at the end of 2001 was 0.40, compared to 0.30 at the end of 2000.
10. The quick ratio at the end of 2001 was 1.6875, compared to 1.5 at the end of 2000.
11. Days inventory held was 60.8 days in 2001 and 75.7 days in 2000.
12. Net sales in 2001 were $20,000,000, compared to $18,000,000 in 2000.
13. Net operating profit after taxes—but before interest—for 2001 was $1,750,000, compared to $1,400,000 in 2000.

CLAPTON CORPORATION

Consolidated Balance Sheets

	As of December 31 2001	2000
Assets		
Current assets		
Cash	$ (a)	$ 500,000
Marketable securities	3,200,000	(b)
Accounts receivable	(c)	1,800,000
Inventories	(d)	(e)
Prepaid expenses	550,000	450,000
Total current assets	10,000,000	(f)
Property, plant, and equipment (net)	(g)	18,000,000
Noncurrent assets		
Long-term receivables	2,500,000	2,000,000
Investments	1,500,000	1,000,000
Other	1,000,000	(h)
Total assets	$ (i)	$ (j)

(continued)

	As of December 31 2001	2000
Liabilities and Stockholders' Equity		
Current liabilities		
Accounts payable	$ (k)	$ (l)
Wages and employee benefits payable	775,000	(m)
Income taxes	300,000	750,000
Advances and deposits	100,000	200,000
Other current liabilities	200,000	400,000
Total current liabilities	(n)	(o)
Long-term liabilities		
Long-term debt	(p)	9,000,000
Deferred income taxes	3,000,000	2,000,000
Other	(q)	500,000
Total liabilities	(r)	15,000,000
Stockholders' equity		
Preferred stock	1,000,000	(s)
Common stock	(t)	2,000,000
Paid-in capital	(u)	9,000,000
Retained earnings	(v)	(w)
Total stockholders' equity	(x)	(y)
Total liabilities and stockholders' equity	$ (z)	$ (zz)

HELPFUL HINTS:

- Start by calculating the missing values for common and preferred stock. Then compute total assets for 2000.
- Total assets for 2001 can be found using 2000 total assets along with the information in (6) and (13).
- Accounts receivable for 2001 can be found using 2000 accounts receivable along with the information in (8) and (12).

P5–6

Why financial ratios change

AICPA adapted

Daley, Inc. is consistently profitable. Daley's normal financial statement relationships are as follows:

Current ratio	3 to 1
Inventory turnover	4 times
Total debt/total assets ratio	0.5 to 1

REQUIRED:

Determine whether each transaction or event that follows increased, decreased, or had no effect on each ratio.

1. Daley declared, but did not pay, a cash dividend.
2. Customers returned invoiced goods for which they had not paid.
3. Accounts payable were paid at year-end.
4. Daley recorded both a receivable from an insurance company and a loss from fire damage to a factory building.
5. Early in the year, Daley increased the selling price of one of its products because customer demand far exceeded production capacity. The number of units sold this year was the same as last year.

P5–7

Working backward to the statements

AICPA adapted

The December 31, 2001 balance sheet of Ratio, Inc. is presented next. These are the *only* accounts in Ratio's balance sheet. Amounts indicated by a question mark (?) can be calculated from the additional information given.

Assets	
Cash	$ 25,000
Accounts receivable (net)	?
Inventory	?
Property, plant, and equipment (net)	294,000
	$432,000

Liabilities and Stockholders' Equity	
Accounts payable (trade)	?
Income taxes payable (current)	25,000
Long-term debt	?
Common stock	300,000
Retained earnings	?
	$432,000

ADDITIONAL INFORMATION:

Current ratio at year-end	1.5 to 1
Total liabilities divided by total stockholders' equity	0.8
Inventory turnover based on sales and ending inventory	15 times
Inventory turnover based on cost of goods sold and ending inventory	10.5 times
Gross margin for 2001	$315,000

REQUIRED:

Compute the December 31, 2001 balance for each missing item.

Hint: $\frac{\text{Gross margin}}{\text{Inventory}} = \frac{\text{Sales} - \text{CGS}}{\text{Inventory}} = \left(\frac{\text{Sales}}{\text{Inventory}}\right) - \left(\frac{\text{CGS}}{\text{Inventory}}\right)$

P5–8

EBITDA and revenue recognition

Giddings & Lewis, Inc. (G&L) supplies industrial automation equipment and machine tools to the automotive industry. G&L uses the "percentage of completion" method for recognizing revenue on its long-term contracts. Customer orders have long lead times because they involve multi-year capital investment programs. Sometimes orders are cancelled. Selected items from the company's financial statements are shown below.

($ in millions)	1993	1994	1995
Sales	$571.5	$619.5	$730.6
Accounts receivable—billed	141.6	94.5	147.9
Accounts receivable—unbilled	104.5	249.4	202.7
Total accounts receivable	246.1	343.9	350.6
Inventory	57.4	74.8	102.3
Earnings before interest and taxes (EBIT)	74.8	75.8	38.1
Depreciation and amortization	14.8	15.4	19.3
Plant writedown	-0-	-0-	30.3

REQUIRED:

1. Compute EBITDA and "adjusted EBITDA"—after excluding the plant writedown—for each year shown in the schedule.
2. Are profits at G&L keeping pace with sales?
3. Compute "days receivables outstanding"—use year-end receivables—for each year shown in the schedule.
4. Why might analysts be concerned about earnings quality at G&L?

P5–9

Maytag Corporation: Profitability analysis

Maytag Corporation manufactures and distributes a broad line of home appliances including gas and electric ranges, dishwashers, refrigerators, freezers, laundry equipment, and vacuum cleaning products. The home appliance segment contributes about 87% of Maytag's total sales. The company's other two segments are commercial appliances and international appliances, both of which have grown over the last three years. Roughly 89% of Maytag's sales come from North American markets.

Refer to Maytag's 1999 financial statements. As shown, consolidated sales increased 19.4% from 1997 to 1998 and 6.3% from 1998 to 1999. Earnings varied considerably over these years with net income (before extraordinary items) increasing from $183.49 million in 1997 to $286.51 million in 1998 and to $328.53 million in 1999.

REQUIRED:

Prepare an analysis of Maytag's profitability for 1999, 1998, and 1997 following the steps outlined below. For all ratios requiring balance sheet values, use the average of beginning and ending balances. Ratios using earnings numbers should be based on net income before extraordinary items. Assume a 35% tax rate.

Step 1. Calculate average total assets, liabilities and stockholders' equity for 1999.

	1999	1998	1997
Average total assets	?	$ 2,550,909	$ 2,422,047
Average total liabilities and minority interest	?	1,989,222	1,827,148
Average total shareholders' equity	?	561,687	594,900

Step 2. Calculate Maytag's return on assets (ROA) for each year. Use margin and turnover analysis together with common size income statements to explain the year-to-year change in ROA.

Step 3. What is the after-tax interest rate that Maytag has been paying for its debt? Analyze the portion of average total assets that Maytag has been financing with debt over the last three years and comment on any apparent strategy.

Step 4. Calculate Maytag's return on common equity (ROCE) for each year. Has leverage benefited Maytag shareholders? How can you tell?

MAYTAG CORPORATION

Consolidated Statements of Income

($ in thousands)	1999	1998	1997
Net sales	$4,323,673	$4,069,290	$3,407,911
Cost of sales	3,072,253	2,887,663	2,471,623
Gross profit	1,251,420	1,181,627	936,288
Selling, general, and administrative expense	675,927	658,889	578,015
Operating income	575,493	522,738	358,273
Interest expense	(59,259)	(62,765)	(58,995)
Other, net	14,617	10,912	1,277
Income before taxes, minority interest and extraordinary item	530,851	470,885	300,555
Income taxes	195,100	176,100	109,800
Income before minority interest and extraordinary item	335,751	294,785	190,755
Minority interest	(7,223)	(8,275)	(7,265)
Income before extraordinary item	328,528	286,510	183,490
Extraordinary item—loss on early retirement of debt	–	(5,900)	(3,200)
Net income	$ 328,528	$ 280,610	$ 180,290

MAYTAG CORPORATION

Consolidated Balance Sheets

($ in thousands)	1999	1998
Assets		
Current assets		
Cash and cash equivalents	$ 28,815	$ 28,642
Accounts receivable	494,747	472,979
Inventory	404,120	383,753
Deferred income taxes	35,484	39,014
Other current assets	58,350	44,474
Total current assets	1,021,516	968,862
Noncurrent assets		
Deferred income taxes	106,600	120,273
Prepaid pension costs	1,487	1,399
Intangible pension asset	48,668	62,811
Other intangible assets	427,212	424,312
Other noncurrent assets	54,896	44,412
Total noncurrent assets	638,863	653,207
Property, plant, and equipment		
Land	19,660	19,317
Buildings and improvements	349,369	333,032
Machinery and equipment	1,622,764	1,499,872
Construction in progress	74,057	102,042
	2,065,850	1,954,263
Less allowance for depreciation	1,089,742	988,669
Total property, plant, and equipment	976,108	965,594
Total assets	$2,636,487	$2,587,663
Liabilities and Shareholders' Equity		
Current liabilities		
Notes payable	$ 133,041	$ 112,898
Accounts payable	277,780	279,086
Accrued liabilities	271,729	258,537
Current portion of long-term debt	170,473	140,176
Total current liabilities	853,023	790,697
Noncurrent liabilities		
Deferred income taxes	22,842	21,191
Long-term debt	337,764	446,505
Postretirement benefit obligations	467,386	460,599
Accrued pension cost	56,528	69,660
Other noncurrent liabilities	101,776	117,392
Total noncurrent liabilities	986,296	1,115,347
Mandatorily redeemable preferred securities	200,000	-0-
Minority interest	169,788	174,055
Shareholders' equity		
Common stock	146,438	146,438
Additional paid-in capital	503,346	467,192
Retained earnings	1,026,288	760,115
Treasury stock	(1,190,894)	(805,802)
Employee stock plans	(38,836)	(45,331)
Accumulated comprehensive income	(18,962)	(15,048)
Total shareholders' equity	427,380	507,564
Total liabilities and equity	$2,636,487	$2,587,663

P5–10

Nike and Reebok: Comparative analysis of footware manufacturers

Nike designs, develops, and markets quality footwear, apparel, athletic equipment, and accessories worldwide. The company sells its products to approximately 20,000 retail accounts in the United States and through a mix of independent distributors, licensees, and subsidiaries in approximately 110 countries around the world.

Reebok International Ltd. designs and markets sports, fitness, and "casual use" footwear and apparel. The company has four major brands: Reebok, Greg Norman, Rockport (shoes), and the Ralph Lauren Footwear Company, which manufactures footwear sold under the Ralph Lauren and Polo Shirt brands. Financial statements for Nike and Reebok appear below.

ADDITIONAL INFORMATION:

1. Reebok's cash flow from operations was $281,625 in 1999, $151,777 in 1998, and $126,925 in 1997. Nike's cash flow from operations was $961,000, $517,500, and $323,100, respectively.
2. If a tax rate is needed, use a rate of 35%.

REQUIRED:

1. Using the information in the financial statements, calculate the following financial ratios for fiscal 1999 for each company. Financial ratio values for 1998 have already been computed.

	1999		1998	
	Nike	Reebok	Nike	Reebok
Current ratio	?	?	2.07	2.22
Quick ratio	?	?	1.25	1.35
Accounts receivable turnover	?	?	5.57	5.97
Days receivable outstanding	?	?	65.5	61.1
Inventory turnover	?	?	4.44	3.71
Days inventory held	?	?	82.2	98.4
Accounts payable turnover	?	?	9.63	10.16
Days accounts payable outstanding	?	?	37.9	35.9
Return on assets	?	?	9.7%	4.9%
Long-term debt to total assets	?	?	7.0%	31.9%
Long-term debt to total tangible assets	?	?	7.6%	33.2%
Interest coverage	?	?	11.9	1.6
Operating cash flow to total liabilities	?	?	23.9%	13.2%
Operating profit margin	?	?	5.5%	2.7%
Asset turnover	?	?	1.78	1.84

2. Use the results of the ratio analysis to identify similarities and differences in the profitability, liquidity, and long-term solvency of the two firms.
3. As a financial analyst following the two firms, what other information (beyond what's in the financial statements) would you seek to supplement the ratio analysis?

REEBOK INTERNATIONAL LTD.

Consolidated Statements of Income

($ in thousands)	1999	1998	1997
Net sales	$2,899,872	$3,224,592	$3,643,599
Other income (expenses)	(8,635)	(19,167)	(6,158)
	2,891,237	3,205,425	3,637,441
Cost and expenses			
Cost of sales	1,783,914	2,037,465	2,294,049
Selling, general and administrative expenses	971,945	1,043,199	1,069,433
Special charges	61,625	35,000	58,161
Amortization of intangibles	5,183	3,432	4,157
Minority interest	6,900	1,178	10,476
Interest expense	49,691	60,671	64,366
Interest income	(9,159)	(11,372)	(10,810)
	2,870,099	3,169,573	3,489,832
Income before income taxes	21,138	35,852	147,609
Income taxes	10,093	11,925	12,490
Net income	$ 11,045	$ 23,927	$ 135,119

NIKE, INC.

Consolidated Statements of Income

($ in thousands)	1999	1998	1997
Revenues	$8,776,900	$9,553,100	$9,186,500
Cost and expenses			
Cost of sales	5,493,500	6,065,500	5,503,000
Selling and administrative expenses	2,426,600	2,623,800	2,303,700
Interest expense	44,100	60,000	52,300
Other (income) expense (net)	21,500	20,900	32,300
Restructuring charges	45,100	129,900	–0–
	8,030,800	8,900,100	7,891,300
Income before income taxes	746,100	653,000	1,295,200
Income taxes	294,700	253,400	499,400
Net income	$ 451,400	$ 399,600	$ 795,800

REEBOK INTERNATIONAL LTD.

Consolidated Balance Sheets

($ in thousands)	1999	1998
Assets		
Current assets		
Cash and cash equivalents	$ 281,744	$ 180,070
Accounts receivable (net)	417,404	517,830
Inventories	414,616	535,168
Deferred income taxes	88,127	78,419
Prepaid expenses	41,227	50,309
Total current assets	1,243,118	1,361,796
Property and equipment (net)	178,111	172,585
Intangibles (net)	68,892	68,648
Deferred income taxes	43,868	99,212
Other	30,139	37,383
Total assets	$1,564,128	$1,739,624
Liabilities and Stockholders' Equity		
Current liabilities		
Notes payable to bank	$ 27,614	$ 48,070
Current portion of long-term debt	185,167	86,640
Accounts payable	153,998	203,144
Accrued expenses	248,822	191,833
Income taxes payable	8,302	82,597
Total current liabilities	623,903	612,284
Long-term debt (net)	370,302	554,432
Minority interest	41,107	31,972
Outstanding redemption value of equity put options	–0–	16,559
Shareholders' equity		
Common stock	930	933
Retained earnings	1,170,885	1,156,739
Treasury stock	(617,620)	(617,620)
Unearned compensation	–0–	(26)
Accumulated comprehensive income	(25,379)	(15,649)
Total shareholders' equity	528,816	524,377
Total liabilities and shareholders' equity	$1,564,128	$1,739,624

NIKE, INC.

Consolidated Balance Sheets

($ in thousands)	1999	1998
Assets		
Current assets		
Cash and cash equivalents	$ 198,100	$ 108,600
Accounts receivable (net)	1,540,100	1,674,400
Inventories	1,199,300	1,396,600
Deferred income taxes	120,600	156,800
Income tax receivable	15,900	-0-
Prepaid expenses	190,900	196,200
Total current assets	3,264,900	3,532,600
Property and equipment (net)	1,265,800	1,153,100
Identifiable intangible assets and goodwill	426,600	435,800
Deferred income taxes	290,400	275,900
Total assets	$5,247,700	$5,397,400
Liabilities and Stockholders' Equity		
Current liabilities		
Current portion of long-term debt	$ 1,000	$ 1,600
Notes payable	419,100	480,200
Accounts payable	373,200	584,600
Accrued liabilities	653,600	608,500
Income taxes payable	-0-	28,900
Total current liabilities	1,446,900	1,703,800
Long-term debt (net)	386,100	379,400
Deferred income taxes and other liabilities	79,800	52,300
Redeemable preferred stock	300	300
Shareholders' equity		
Common stock, Class A convertible	200	200
Common stock, Class B	2,700	2,700
Capital in excess of stated value	334,100	262,500
Foreign currency translation adjustment	(68,900)	(47,200)
Retained earnings	3,066,500	3,043,400
Total shareholders' equity	3,334,600	3,261,600
Total liabilities and shareholders' equity	$5,247,700	$5,397,400

P5–11

Toy's "R" Us , Inc: Common-size statements of cash flow

Shown below is the comparative statements of cash flows for Toys "R" Us, Inc. for 2000, 1999, and 1998. The company reported sales (in millions) of $11,862, $11,170, and $11,038, respectively, in these years.

TOYS "R" US, INC. AND SUBSIDIARIES

Consolidated Statements of Cash Flows

($ in millions)	2000	1999	1998
Cash Flows from Operating Activities			
Net (loss) earnings	$ 279	$ (132)	$ 490
Adjustments:			
Depreciation, amortization, and asset write-offs	278	255	253
Deferred income taxes	156	(90)	18
Restructuring and other charges	–0–	546	–0–
Changes in operating assets and liabilities:			
Accounts and other receivables	35	(43)	(40)
Merchandise inventories	(192)	233	(265)
Prepaid expenses and other operating assets	(69)	(27)	(9)
Accounts payable, accrued expenses, and other liabilities	497	229	22
Income taxes payable	(119)	(7)	40
Net cash provided by operating activities	865	964	509
Cash Flows from Investing Activities			
Capital expenditures (net)	(533)	(373)	(494)
Other assets	(28)	(49)	(22)
Purchase of Imaginarium, net of cash acquired	(43)	–0–	–0–
Net cash used in investing activities	(604)	(422)	(516)
Cash Flows from Financing Activities			
Short-term borrowings (net)	95	4	(142)
Long-term borrowings	593	771	11
Long-term debt repayments	(604)	(412)	(176)
Exercise of stock options	14	16	62
Share repurchase program	(200)	(723)	(253)
Net cash used in financing activities	(102)	(344)	(498)
Effect of exchange rate changes	15	(2)	(42)
Cash and Cash Equivalents			
Increase (decrease) during year	174	196	(547)
Beginning of year	410	214	761
End of year	$ 584	$ 410	$ 214

REQUIRED:

1. What is the purpose of preparing common-size statements of cash flows? For example, what can a financial analyst learn about a firm by preparing a set of common-size statements of cash flows?
2. Prepare common-size statements of cash flows (expressed as a percentage of sales) for the fiscal years ending 2000, 1999, and 1998 for Toys "R" Us, Inc.
3. Interpret your common-size statements of cash flows. For example, what interesting features of the company's operating, financing, and investing activities do they reveal?

CASES

C5–1

J.C. Penney (A) (CW): Common size and trend income statements

The comparative statements of income for J.C. Penney Company, Inc. covering the years 1997–1999 are reproduced below.

REQUIRED:

1. Prepare common-size income statements for each year.
2. What do the common size statements reveal about the company's operating results?
3. Using 1997 as the base year, prepare a trend analysis of J.C. Penney's income statement through 1999.
4. What does the trend analysis reveal about the company's operating results?
5. Which approach—common size or trend analysis—was most revealing? Why?

J.C. PENNEY COMPANY, INC. AND SUBSIDIARIES

Consolidated Statements of Income

($ in millions)	1999	1998	1997
Revenue			
Retail sales (net)	$31,391	$29,439	$29,482
Direct marketing revenue	1,119	1,022	928
Total revenue	32,510	30,461	30,410
Costs and expenses			
Cost of goods sold	23,374	21,642	21,294
Selling, general, and administrative expenses	7,164	6,623	6,566
Costs and expenses of direct marketing	872	785	711
Real estate and other	(28)	(26)	(39)
Net interest expense and credit operations	299	391	457
Amortization of intangible assets	129	113	117
Other charges (net)	169	(22)	379
Total costs and expenses	31,979	29,506	29,485
Income before income taxes	531	955	925
Income taxes	195	361	359
Net income	$ 336	$ 594	$ 566

C5–2

J.C. Penney (B) (CW): Earnings forecast

This case builds on the earlier J.C. Penney (A) case (C5–1) and illustrates how common-size statements and trend analysis can be used to forecast a company's earnings. Such projections are often referred to as *pro forma* ("as if") financial statements. The following assumptions (listed in no particular order) should be used:

1. J.C. Penney's combined federal and state income tax rate was about 38% during 1997–1999.
2. Interest expense fell from 1997 to 1999 because the company retired some long-term debt. It does not intend to retire any debt (or issue new debt) during 2000.
3. Retail sales for the industry are expected to grow in 2000 at the average annual growth rate of the last two years. J.C. Penney's direct marketing revenue is expected to grow 10% in 2000.
4. No nonrecurring charges, accounting method changes, or "other" charges are anticipated in 2000.
5. Because of heavy competition from discount retailers (e.g., Wal-Mart) and full-service retail firms (e.g., Sears), J.C. Penney will need to increase its advertising expenditures in 2000 to achieve the projected sales growth. Selling, general, and administrative expenses as a percentage of total revenue will increase by three percentage points from the 1999 level. Costs and expenses of direct marketing are expected to remain at their three-year average percentage of direct marketing revenue.
6. Amortization expense is expected to remain constant (unchanged) in 2000.
7. "Real estate and other" costs for 2000 are expected to be the average of the 1997–1999 period.

8. J.C. Penney expects to improve its inventory management procedures in 2000. This improvement should yield a two-percentage point increase in the 2000 gross margin when compared to 1999.
9. Direct marketing revenue should grow in 2000 at the average annual growth rate of the last two years.

REQUIRED:

1. Prepare a projected 2000 income statement for J.C. Penney. (*Hint*: Start by forecasting sales for the year.)
2. Based on your forecast, will J.C. Penney have a better year in 2000 than it did in 1999? Why or why not?
3. How did the company do in 2000?

C5–3

Iomega Corporation (CW): Attending an analysts meeting

Iomega Corporation designs, manufactures, and markets removable data storage devices for use with personal computers and workstations. These storage devices include magnetic disk drives, tape backup drives, and ZIP removable cartridge drives.

You were recently hired by Wean Ditter, a firm providing investment advisory services to individual investors, as their head analyst for the computer industry. Next week you are scheduled to attend an analysts meeting at Iomega where the company's chief executive officer and chief financial officer will be available to field your questions.

REQUIRED:

Prepare a list of the questions that you want answered by Iomega's chief executive officer and chief financial officer. These questions should clarify your understanding of the company's past performance, current financial condition, and future prospects.

IOMEGA CORPORATION AND SUBSIDIARIES

Consolidated Statements of Operations

($ in thousands)	1999	1998	1997
Sales	$1,525,129	$1,694,385	$1,739,972
Cost of sales	1,155,556	1,271,451	1,192,310
Gross profit	369,573	422,934	547,662
Operating expenses			
Selling, general and administrative expenses	292,061	386,304	291,930
Research and development	76,481	101,496	78,026
Restructuring charges	65,773	–0–	–0–
Purchased in-process technology	–0–	11,100	–0–
Total operating expenses	434,315	498,900	369,956
Operating income (loss)	(64,742)	(75,966)	177,706
Interest income	6,414	4,239	6,931
Interest expense	(7,161)	(10,163)	(6,443)
Other expenses	(5,768)	(1,535)	(879)
Income (loss) before income taxes	(71,257)	(83,425)	177,315
Benefit (provision) for income taxes	(32,232)	29,203	(61,963)
Net income (loss)	$ (103,489)	$ (54,222)	$ 115,352

IOMEGA CORPORATION AND SUBSIDIARIES

Consolidated Balance Sheets

($ in thousands)	1999	1998
Assets		
Current assets		
Cash and cash equivalents	$172,706	$ 90,273
Temporary investments	38,209	-0-
Accounts receivable	188,482	238,810
Inventories	94,626	165,132
Income taxes receivable	19,910	24,974
Deferred income taxes	-0-	49,827
Other current assets	21,585	20,246
Total current assets	535,518	589,262
Property, plant, and equipment, at cost	365,036	373,227
Less accumulated depreciation and amortization	(227,336)	(165,112)
	137,700	208,115
Intangibles, net	31,743	33,580
Other assets	2,848	4,350
Total assets	$707,809	$835,307
Liabilities and Stockholders' Equity		
Current liabilities		
Related party notes payable	$ 1,569	$ 101
Current portion of notes payable	-0-	40,000
Accounts payable	135,615	166,125
Accrued payroll, vacation, and bonus	13,189	21,048
Deferred revenue	29,832	33,114
Accrued advertising	36,971	30,226
Accrued warranty	17,211	7,435
Accrued restructuring charges	17,843	-0-
Other accrued liabilities	83,947	61,020
Current portion of capital lease obligations	3,973	4,307
Total current liabilities	340,150	363,376
Capital lease obligations—net of current portion	1,366	4,119
Notes payable—net of current portion	-0-	488
Deferred income taxes	-0-	4,903
Convertible subordinated notes	45,505	45,655
Stockholders' equity		
Preferred stock	-0-	-0-
Common stock	9,027	8,937
Additional paid-in capital	293,627	286,206
Retained earnings	24,222	127,711
Less: common stock treasury shares at cost	(6,088)	(6,088)
Total stockholders' equity	320,788	416,766
Total liabilities and stockholders' equity	$707,809	$835,307

IOMEGA CORPORATION AND SUBSIDIARIES

Consolidated Statements of Cash Flows

($ in thousands)	1999	1998	1997
Cash Flows from Operating Activities			
Net income (loss)	$(103,489)	$ (54,222)	$ 115,352
Non-cash revenue and expense adjustments			
Depreciation and amortization expense	97,286	68,280	39,272
Purchased in-process technology	–0–	11,100	–0–
Deferred income tax provision (benefit)	44,924	(7,262)	397
Bad debt provision	5,846	(1,204)	2,274
Restructuring charges	34,796	–0–	–0–
Tax benefit from disposition of employee stock	2,145	7,435	5,767
Other	4,269	8,772	703
Changes in operating assets and liabilities			
Trade receivables (net)	44,557	55,433	(71,723)
Inventories	62,313	84,335	(74,463)
Other current assets	3,254	(6,594)	15,662
Accounts payable	(30,585)	(108,324)	111,437
Other current liabilities	46,150	(13,723)	58,747
Income taxes	5,064	(47,414)	19,830
Net cash provided by (used in) operating activities	216,530	(3,388)	223,255
Cash Flows from Investing Activities			
Purchase of property, plant and equipment—net of lease proceeds	(46,814)	(94,775)	(85,871)
Purchase of Nomai S.A.—net of cash acquired	–0–	(41,902)	–0–
Purchase of temporary investments	(38,209)	–0–	(59,918)
Sale of temporary investments	–0–	36,319	23,599
Purchase of SyQuest assets	(12,093)	–0–	–0–
Net decrease (increase) in other assets	(90)	(2,943)	246
Net cash used in investing activities	(97,206)	(103,301)	(121,944)
Cash Flows from Financing Activities			
Proceeds from sales of common stock	5,216	5,283	3,991
Proceeds from issuance of related notes payable	–0–	40,000	–0–
Proceeds from issuance of notes payable and capital leases	3,532	80,000	87,295
Payments on notes payable and capital leases obligations	(45,639)	(87,778)	(139,251)
Purchase of common stock	–0–	(465)	(1,736)
Net cash (used in) provided by financing activities	(36,891)	37,040	(49,701)
Cash and Cash Equivalents			
Net change in cash and cash equivalents	82,433	(69,649)	51,610
Cash and cash equivalents at beginning of year	90,273	159,922	108,312
Cash and cash equivalents at end of year	$ 172,706	$ 90,273	$ 159,922

C5–4

Nike, Inc. and Reebok International Ltd. (CW): Management's discussion and analysis

This case builds on Problem P5–10. The Management's Discussion and Analysis (MD&A) section of a company's annual report to shareholders contains an interpretive review of operating results, liquidity, and capital resources. One can think of the MD&A section as a narrative discussion of the company's financial past, one which can help investors chart the future. Management is encouraged to disclose prospective or forward-looking data. These data might include specific earnings or sales forecasts, or a discussion of recent trends and events and how they may affect future operations and cash flows.

REQUIRED:

1. Obtain the MD&A section of the annual reports of Nike (year-end May 31, 1999) and Reebok (year-end December 31, 1999) from www.prenhall.com/revsine.

2. What are the key themes of each company's MD&A? For example, what positives and negatives about past performance or about the future outlook for the firm are mentioned?
3. Does the MD&A reinforce your financial ratio analysis in Problem P5–10? What contradictions surface, if any?
4. As an analyst, is there anything not discussed in the MD&A that you feel should have been mentioned?
5. Access the EDGAR system at the SEC (www.sec.gov or www.freeedgar.com) and obtain the MD&A section of the most recent annual reports of Nike and Reebok. What new insights do these MD&A discussions provide?

C5–5

Sun Microsystems and Micron Electronics (CW): Comparative financial statement analysis

Micron Electronics develops, markets, manufactures, sells, and supports personal computer (PC) systems for consumer, government, and business use. The company provides end-users with memory intensive PC systems that include the latest hardware and software features commercially at competitive prices.

Sun Microsystems is a leading supplier of network computing products including workstations, servers, software, microprocessors, and a full range of services and support. Sun's products command a significant share of a rapidly growing segment of the computer industry—networked workstations and servers. The company's products are used for many demanding commercial and technical applications. Sun has differentiated itself from its competitors by its commitment to the network computing model and the UNIX operating system, its rapid innovation, and its open systems architecture.

The accompanying exhibits contain the comparative income statements and balance sheets of Micron Electronics and Sun Microsystems for 1997 through 1999. The statements are presented on a common-size basis and on a trend basis (with 1997 data omitted for trend statement brevity).

SUN MICROSYSTEMS, INC. AND MICRON ELECTRONICS, INC.

Comparative Common Size and Trend Analysis of Earnings

	Sun Microsystems			Micron Electronics		
Common Size Statements (% of sales)	**1999**	**1998**	**1997**	**1999**	**1998**	**1997**
Net sales	100.0	100.0	100.0	100.0	100.0	100.0
Cost of sales	48.2	47.9	50.3	81.2	87.2	82.7
Gross profit	51.8	52.1	49.7	18.8	12.8	17.3
R&D expenditures	11.8	12.2	9.9	0.3	0.6	0.5
Selling, general and administrative expenses	27.0	28.4	27.9	15.2	16.4	10.1
Other operating expenses (income)	–0–	–0–	–0–	0.3	0.6	(0.3)
Operating income (loss)	13.0	11.5	11.9	3.0	(4.8)	7.0
Non-operating (income) expense	(0.7)	(0.5)	(1.2)	(1.1)	(9.8)	(0.4)
Interest expense	–0–	–0–	0.1	–0–	–0–	–0–
Income before tax	13.7	12.0	13.0	4.1	5.0	7.4
Provision for income taxes	4.9	4.2	4.2	1.6	2.2	2.9
Net income	8.8	7.8	8.8	2.5	2.8	4.5
Trend Statements (1997 = 100%)	**1999**	**1998**		**1999**	**1998**	
Net sales	136.4	113.9		73.5	88.6	
Cost of sales	130.7	108.6		72.2	93.4	
Gross profit	142.1	119.2		80.0	65.8	
R&D expenditures	162.9	140.2		47.0	105.4	
Selling, general, and administrative expenses	132.1	115.6		110.5	143.4	
Other operating expenses (income)	–0–	–0–		(0.5)	(1.8)	
Operating income (loss)	148.2	110.1		31.7	(61.5)	
Non-operating (income) expense	82.8	46.7		201.3	2,153.0	
Interest expense	–0–	–0–		–0–	–0–	
Income before tax	143.2	104.9		41.0	59.6	
Provision for income taxes	160.1	115.2		39.6	66.8	
Net income	135.3	100.1		41.9	55.0	

SUN MICROSYSTEMS, INC. AND MICRON ELECTRONICS, INC.

Comparative Common Size Analysis of Balance Sheets

	Sun Microsystems			Micron Electronics		
Common Size Statements (% of assets)	**1999**	**1998**	**1997**	**1999**	**1998**	**1997**
Cash and cash equivalents	12.9	14.4	14.1	27.5	47.4	24.3
Marketable securities	18.7	8.3	9.6	18.7	4.2	1.3
Receivables	27.2	32.3	35.5	20.8	18.5	29.5
Inventories	3.7	6.1	9.3	2.4	4.5	15.2
Deferred income taxes	5.8	6.5	6.1	2.0	2.8	3.5
Other current assets	4.3	5.0	4.8	2.8	0.4	0.5
Total current assets	72.6	72.6	79.4	74.2	77.8	74.3
Net property, plant, and equipment	19.1	22.8	17.0	21.8	21.3	25.2
Other assets	8.3	4.6	3.6	4.0	0.9	0.5
Total assets	100.0	100.0	100.0	100.0	100.0	100.0
Notes payable	0.0	0.9	2.1	1.0	2.4	2.5
Accounts payable	9.0	8.7	10.0	30.0	31.0	40.1
Accrued payroll	6.2	5.5	7.2	–0–	–0–	–0–
Deferred revenue	5.0	4.6	4.2	–0–	–0–	–0–
Accrued liabilities and other	18.2	17.5	15.8	2.8	2.7	4.8
Total current liabilities	38.4	37.2	39.3	33.8	36.1	47.4
Long-term debt and other obligations	4.5	1.3	2.3	3.8	3.7	4.4
Total liabilities	42.9	38.5	41.6	37.6	39.8	51.8
Common stock (net)	0.0	0.0	0.0	0.1	0.1	0.1
Capital surplus	20.7	23.6	26.2	17.4	17.7	15.8
Retained earnings	49.0	55.2	51.3	44.9	42.3	32.3
Treasury stock	(12.3)	(17.7)	(19.5)	–0–	–0–	–0–
Other comprehensive income (loss)	(0.1)	0.4	0.4	–0–	0.1	–0–
Stockholders' equity	57.1	61.5	58.4	62.4	60.2	48.2
Total liabilities and net worth	100.0	100.0	100.0	100.0	100.0	100.0

SUN MICROSYSTEMS, INC. AND MICRON ELECTRONICS, INC.

Comparative Trend Analysis of Balance Sheets

	Sun Microsystems		Micron Electronics	
Trend Statements (1997 = 100%)	**1999**	**1998**	**1999**	**1998**
Cash and cash equivalents	165.0	124.6	109.3	178.6
Marketable securities	348.2	105.2	1,366.0	290.1
Receivables	137.2	110.8	68.3	57.4
Inventories	70.3	79.1	15.2	26.7
Deferred income taxes	169.9	129.7	56.5	73.1
Other current assets	164.6	127.0	524.2	61.9
Total current assets	164.0	111.2	96.6	95.6
Net property, plant, and equipment	201.1	162.6	83.5	77.2
Other assets	411.5	155.6	808.5	165.7
Total assets	179.3	121.6	96.7	91.3
Notes payable	1.6	46.7	37.6	90.2
Accounts payable	160.8	105.7	72.3	70.6
Accrued payroll	154.1	93.6	–0–	–0–
Deferred revenue	213.6	134.1	–0–	–0–
Accrued liabilities and other	205.5	134.3	56.1	51.6
Total current liabilities	174.5	114.8	68.8	69.7
Long-term debt and other obligations	359.0	70.1	82.7	75.3
Total liabilities	184.5	112.4	70.0	70.2
Common stock (net)	201.7	100.0	100.7	100.3
Capital surplus	141.7	109.4	106.5	102.3
Retained earnings	171.2	130.8	134.4	119.5
Treasury stock	114.3	109.6	–0–	–0–
Other comprehensive income (loss)	(57.9)	115.3	–0–	(5.9)
Stockholders' equity	175.5	128.1	125.4	114.0
Total liabilities and net worth	179.3	121.6	96.7	91.3

REQUIRED:

1. What similarities and differences about the companies do the common-size and trend statements reveal? Which company has the stronger profit performance?
2. As an equity research analyst working for one of Micron Electronics' institutional investors, what questions would you ask of Micron management?

C5–6

Sun Microsystems and Micron Electronics, Inc. (CW): Management discussion and analysis

This builds on the preceding case (C5–5). The MD&A section of a company's annual report to shareholders contains an interpretive review of operating results, liquidity, and capital resources. One can think of the MD&A section as a narrative discussion of the firm's financial past, one that can help investors chart the future. Management is encouraged to disclose prospective or forward-looking data. These data might include specific earnings or sales forecasts, or a discussion of recent trends and events and how they may affect future operations and cash flows.

REQUIRED:

1. Access the EDGAR system at the SEC (www.sec.gov or www.freeedgar.com) and obtain the MD&A sections of the annual reports of Sun Microsystems (year-ended June 30, 1999) and Micron Electronics (year-ended September 2, 1999).
2. What key themes are stressed in each company's MD&A? For example, what positives and negatives about past performance or about the future outlook of each company are mentioned?
3. Does the MD&A complement or reinforce your financial ratio analysis in C5–5? What contradictions surface, if any?

(continued)

4. As an analyst, is there anything not discussed in the MD&A that you feel should have been mentioned?

C5–7

Argenti Corporation: Evaluating credit risk

It's late Tuesday evening, and you've just received a phone call from Dennis Whiting, your boss at GE Capital. Dennis wants to know your reaction to the Argenti loan request before tomorrow's loan committee meeting.

> We've provided seasonal loans to Argenti for the past 20 years, and they've always been a first-rate customer, but I'm troubled by several recent events. For instance, the company just reported a $141 million loss for the first quarter of 2001. This comes on top of a $237 million loss in 2000 and a $9 million loss in 1999. What's worse, Argenti changed inventory accounting methods last year, and this change reduced the 2000 loss by $22 million. I can't tell if the company's using other accounting tricks to prop up earnings, but I doubt it.
>
> I believe Argenti's problem lies in its core business—customers just aren't buying its merchandise these days. Management's aggressive price discount program in the fourth quarter of 2000 helped move inventory, but Argenti doesn't have the cost structure needed to be competitive as a discounter. Take a look at the financials I'm sending over, and let me know what you think.

Argenti Corporation operates a national chain of retail stores ("Argenti's") which sells appliances and electronics, home furnishings, automotive parts, apparel, and jewelry. The company's first store opened in New York City in 1904. Today, the company owns or leases more than 900 stores located in downtown areas of larger cities and in suburban shopping malls. Customer purchases are financed in-house using ArgentiCredit cards. The company employs more than 58,000 people.

The Seasonal Credit Agreement with GE Capital—dated October 4, 2000—provides a revolving loan facility in the principal amount of $165 million. The purpose of this facility is to provide backup liquidity as Argenti reduces its inventory levels. Under the credit agreement, Argenti may select among several interest rate options, which are based on market rates. Unless GE Capital agrees, loans may be made under the seasonal credit facility only after the commitments under the company's other debt agreements are fully used.

ARGENTI CORPORATION

Balance Sheets and Selected Other Data

($ in millions)	2000	1999	1998	1997	1996
Assets					
Cash and securities	$ 35	$ 38	$ 36	$ 117	$ 92
Receivables	213	166	112	62	47
Inventories	1,545	1,770	1,625	1,242	1,038
Other current assets	13	22	6	4	312
	1,806	1,996	1,779	1,425	1,489
Property, plant, and equipment—net	1,308	1,366	1,396	1,263	1,222
Investments	317	345	314	296	277
Other assets	1,448	1,177	1,048	851	445
	$4,879	$4,884	$4,537	$3,835	$3,433

(continued)

($ in millions)	2000	1999	1998	1997	1996
Liabilities and shareholders' equities					
Notes payable	$1,028	$ 160	$ 144	$ 0	$ 0
Accounts payable	1,812	2,040	1,955	1,595	1,399
Accrued expenses	1,232	1,201	1,248	1,204	1,148
	4,072	3,401	3,347	2,799	2,547
Long-term debt	87	423	228	213	125
Other liabilities	112	185	203	216	208
Preferred stock	175	175	75	–0–	–0–
Common stock	54	46	23	19	16
Retained earnings	518	768	750	661	583
Less: Treasury stock	(139)	(114)	(89)	(73)	(46)
	$4,879	$4,884	$4,537	$3,835	$3,433
Selected earnings and cash flow data					
Sales	$6,620	$7,085	$7,029	$6,023	$5,806
Cost of goods sold	4,869	5,211	5,107	4,258	4,047
Gross margin	1,751	1,874	1,922	1,765	1,759
Net income	(237)	(9)	137	101	60
Operating cash flow	(356)	(182)	153	132	157
Dividends	9	4	24	23	19

Argenti management has asked GE Capital for a $1.5 billion refinancing package that would be used to pay off all or a substantial portion of its outstanding debt. Excerpts from the company's financial statements follow.

MANAGEMENT DISCUSSION AND ANALYSIS
(2000 ANNUAL REPORT)

The company has obtained waivers under the Long-Term Credit Agreement and the Short-Term Credit Agreement with respect to compliance for the fiscal quarter ending March 29, 2001 — with covenants requiring maintenance of minimum consolidated shareholders' equity, a minimum ratio of debt to capitalization, and minimum earnings before interest, taxes, depreciation, amortization, and rent (EBITDAR). These waivers and amendments reduce the maximum amount of debt permitted to be incurred, and the maturity of the Long-Term Agreement was changed from February 28, 2002 to August 29, 2001.

The company is currently in discussions with financing sources with a view toward both a longer term solution to its liquidity problems and obtaining refinancing for all or a substantial portion of its outstanding indebtedness, including a total of $1,008 million which will mature on or about August 29, 2001. This would include repayment of the current bank borrowings and amounts outstanding under the Note Purchase Agreements. The company's management is highly confident that the indebtedness can be refinanced. Its largest shareholder, GE Capital, also expects the company to be able to refinance such indebtedness. However, there can be no assurance that such refinancing can be obtained or that amendments or waivers required to maintain compliance with the previous agreements can be obtained.

FOOTNOTE TO FINANCIAL STATEMENTS (2000 ANNUAL REPORT)

The company intends to improve its financial condition and reduce its dependence on borrowing by slowing expansion, controlling expenses, closing certain unprofitable stores and continuing to implement its inventory reduction program. Management is in the process of reevaluating the company's merchandising, marketing, store operations, and real estate strategies. The company is also consider-

(continued)

ing the sale of certain operating units as a means of generating cash. Future cash is also expected to continue to be provided by ongoing operations, sale of receivables under the Accounts Receivable Purchase Agreement with GE capital, borrowings under revolving loan facilities, and vendor financing programs.

Quarterly Income

		Fiscal 2000			
	Mar. 01	**Dec. 00**	**Sep. 00**	**Jun. 00**	**Mar. 00**
Sales	$1,329	$2,084	$1,567	$1,534	$1,435
Cost of goods sold	997	1,525	1,096	1,210	1,038
Gross profit	$ 332	$ 559	$ 471	$ 324	$ 397
Net income	($ 141)	($ 165)	($ 35)	$ 11	($ 48)
Gross profit (% sales)	25.0%	26.8%	30.1%	21.1%	27.7%
Net income (% sales)	−10.6%	−7.9%	−2.2%	0.7%	−3.3%

REQUIRED:

1. Why did Argenti need to increase its notes payable borrowing to over $1 billion in 2000?
2. What recommendation would you make regarding the company's request for a $1.5 billion refinancing package?

C5–8

Amazon.com: Analysis of an Internet retailer

Amazon.com, Inc. is the world's leading online retailer with over 17 million customer accounts in over 150 countries. The company sells books, music, DVDs, videos, toys, electronics software, video games, and home improvement products. Through its marketplace services—Amazon.com Auctions, zShops and sothebys.amazon.com—the company has created Web-based marketplaces where buyers and sellers enter into transactions involving a wide range of products. As the company states in its 1999 10-K:

> We offer our customers a superior shopping experience by providing high value through selection, convenience, ease of use, low prices, product information and an intense focus on customer service. We are a proven technology leader, having developed electronic commerce innovations such as 1-Click technology, personalized shopping services, easy-to-use search and browse features, secure payment protections, and wireless access to our stores.

The company's quarterly income statement and balance sheet appear on the next page.

REQUIRED:

1. Comment on the company's "year over year" sales growth for the March and December quarters. Why do you suppose December 1999 sales outpaced March 2000 sales?
2. Compute the gross profit margin for each quarter and comment on any trend.
3. How well has the company been managing its "Selling, general, and administrative expense"?
4. Why doesn't Amazon.com have any "Receivables" on its balance sheet?
5. Compute inventory turnover for each quarter (using the quarter-end inventory amount) and comment on any trend.
6. Analysts who cover Internet stocks use the "cash burn rate" as an index of company health. The cash burn rate (in months) is:

$$\text{Cash burn rate} = \frac{\text{Cash on hand}}{\text{Operating cash flow needs (per month)}}$$

Suppose an Internet company is generating *negative* operating cash flows of −$300 each quarter, or −$100 per month. If it has $1,000 of cash on hand, its cash burn rate is 10 months. Unless operations turn cash flow positive, the company will run out of money in 10 months. Based on Amazon's historical growth and operating cash flows, what is its cash burn rate as of March 2000?

7. Why are analysts interested in Amazon's cash burn rate?

AMAZON.COM, INC.

Quarterly Income Statements

($ in millions)	Mar. 00	Dec. 99	Sep. 99	Jun. 99	Mar. 99	Dec. 98
Sales	$573.9	$676.0	$355.8	$314.4	$293.6	$252.9
Cost of goods sold	427.6	670.5	417.7	246.8	223.6	199.5
Gross profit	146.3	5.5	(61.9)	67.6	70.0	53.4
Selling, general, and administrative expenses	342.2	277.2	161.5	139.5	121.6	95.4
Operating profit	(195.9)	(271.7)	(223.4)	(71.9)	(51.6)	(42.0)
Interest income (net)	27.6	18.2	21.5	28.3	16.6	8.6
Non-operating expense	(140.2)	(69.7)	4.8	(94.4)	(26.7)	(13.0)
Pre-tax income	(308.4)	(323.2)	(197.1)	(138.0)	(61.7)	(46.4)
Total income taxes	–0–	–0–	–0–	–0–	–0–	–0–
Net income	($308.4)	($323.2)	($197.1)	($138.0)	($ 61.7)	($ 46.4)
Cash flows from operations	($320.5)	$ 31.5	($ 75.6)	($ 29.6)	($ 17.2)	$ 38.9

AMAZON.COM, INC.

Quarterly Balance Sheets

($ in millions)	Mar. 00	Dec. 99	Sep. 99	Jun. 99	Mar. 99	Dec. 98
Cash and equivalents	$1,008.8	$ 706.3	$ 905.7	$1,144.3	$1,443.0	$373.4
Net receivables	–0–	–0–	–0–	–0–	–0–	–0–
Inventories	172.3	220.6	118.8	59.4	45.2	29.5
Other current assets	89.8	85.3	55.6	53.3	37.1	21.4
Total current assets	1,270.9	1,012.2	1,080.1	1,257.0	1,525.3	424.3
Net property, plant, and equipment	334.4	317.6	221.2	156.3	60.6	29.8
Other assets	1,124.4	1,141.8	938.5	884.9	227.1	194.4
Total assets	$2,729.7	$2,471.6	$2,239.8	$2,298.2	$1,813.0	$648.5
Current portion of long-term debt	$ 16.0	$ 14.3	$ 12.8	$ 9.9	$ 7.2	$ 0.7
Accounts payable	255.8	463.0	236.7	166.0	133.0	113.4
Other current liabilities	295.4	261.6	108.2	102.0	61.4	47.6
Total current liabilities	567.2	738.9	357.7	277.9	201.6	161.7
Long-term debt	2,137.0	1,466.3	1,462.2	1,449.2	1,533.9	348.1
Common stock	3.5	3.5	3.4	1.7	1.6	0.5
Capital surplus	1,258.9	1,146.6	994.3	940.5	304.0	298.5
Retained earnings	(1,236.8)	(883.7)	(577.8)	(371.1)	(228.1)	(160.3)
Total common equity	25.6	266.4	419.9	571.1	77.5	138.7
Total liabilities and equity	$2,729.7	$2,471.6	$2,239.8	$2,298.2	$1,813.0	$648.5

6

The Role of Financial Information in Valuation, Cash Flow Analysis, and Credit Risk Assessment

LEARNING OBJECTIVES:

After studying this chapter, you will understand:

1. The basic steps in corporate valuation.
2. What free cash flows are and how they are used to value a company.
3. How accounting earnings are used in valuation and why *current* earnings are considered more useful than *current* cash flows for assessing *future* cash flows.
4. What an earnings multiple is and what factors contribute to variation in price-earnings multiples.
5. How the permanent, transitory, and valuation-irrelevant components of earnings each affects price-earnings multiples.
6. The notion of earnings quality and what factors influence the quality of earnings.
7. The abnormal earnings approach to valuation and how it is applied in practice.
8. The notion of "earnings surprises" and how stock returns relate to "good news" and "bad news" earnings surprises.
9. The importance of cash flow analysis and credit risk assessment in lending decisions.

We introduced the key financial ratios used to assess a company's operating performance, liquidity, and solvency in the previous chapter. In this chapter we examine the role that financial accounting information plays in valuation, cash flow analysis, and credit risk assessment. Along the way, we will also build a framework for understanding what academic and professional research has to say about how useful accounting numbers are to investors and creditors.

Corporate valuation involves estimating the worth—or intrinsic value—of a company, one of its operating units, or its ownership shares. Although there are several approaches to valuation, equity investors and analysts often use **fundamental analysis** to estimate the value of a company. This valuation approach uses basic accounting measures, or "fundamentals," to assess the amount, timing, and uncertainty of a firm's future operating cash flows or earnings. The data in a firm's financial statements, along with industry and economy-wide data, are used to develop projections of future earnings or cash flows. These projections are then discounted at a risk-adjusted cost of capital to arrive at an initial valuation estimate. This initial estimate is further refined by adding the current value of nonoperating assets (such as a corporate art collection) and subtracting off-balance sheet obligations. This refined valuation becomes the basis for buy, hold, or sell decisions.

Cash flow assessment plays a central role in analyzing the **credit risk** of a company. Lenders use the firm's financial statements and other information to estimate its future cash flows. These cash flow projections are then compared to the firm's future debt-service requirements. Companies with projected operating cash flows that comfortably exceed debt principal and interest payments are deemed good credit risks. Less favorable operating cash flow prospects may suggest the firm is a high credit risk and, therefore, should be charged higher rates of interest, have more stringent conditions placed on its loans, or be refused credit.

Corporate Valuation

Valuing an entire company, an operating division of that company or its ownership shares involves three basic steps:

1. **Forecasting** future values of some financial attribute—what we call the **value-relevant attribute**—that drives a firm's value. Common value-relevant attributes include:
   - Distributable or free cash flows (defined and discussed later)
   - Accounting earnings
   - Balance sheet book values
2. Determining the **risk** or **uncertainty** associated with the attribute's forecasted future values.
3. Determining the **discounted present value** of the expected future values of the value-relevant attribute, where the discount rate reflects the risk or uncertainty from step 2.

Dividends are another value-relevant attribute discussed in finance texts. However, the "dividend discount" valuation approach is of limited practical use despite its intuitive appeal. This is because dividends represent the *distribution* of wealth. The accounting measures considered here focus on wealth *creation,* the prosperity and growth of the business.

The Discounted Free Cash Flow Approach

The **distributable—or free—cash flow valuation model** combines the elements in these three steps to express current stock price as the discounted present value of expected future distributable cash flows. **Free cash flow**—a term popular among analysts—is sometimes defined as the company's operating cash flows (before interest) minus cash outlays for the replacement of existing operating capacity like buildings, equipment, and furnishings. It's the amount available to finance planned expansion of operating capacity, to reduce debt, to pay dividends, or to repurchase stock. This is the best way to measure free cash flows if you are interested in valuing the company as a whole and without regard to its capital structure.

But what if you want to value just the company's common stock? Then we need to refine our free cash flow measure by also subtracting cash interest payments, debt repayments, and preferred dividends. What's left is the free cash flow (denoted *CF*) that's available to common stockholders.[1] Of course, *CF* can be used to pay common dividends, buy back common stock, or expand operating capacity. The free cash flow equity valuation model can be written as:[2]

Expected free cash flow each period ⟶ ∞

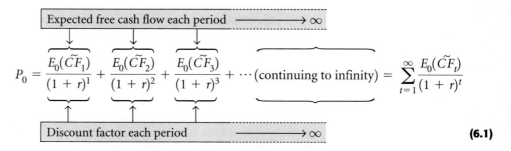

$$P_0 = \frac{E_0(\tilde{CF}_1)}{(1+r)^1} + \frac{E_0(\tilde{CF}_2)}{(1+r)^2} + \frac{E_0(\tilde{CF}_3)}{(1+r)^3} + \cdots \text{(continuing to infinity)} = \sum_{t=1}^{\infty} \frac{E_0(\tilde{CF}_t)}{(1+r)^t} \qquad \textbf{(6.1)}$$

Discount factor each period ⟶ ∞

[1] One of the earliest accounting treatments of this concept appeared in L. Revsine, *Replacement Cost Accounting* (Upper Saddle River, NJ: Prentice Hall, 1973), pp. 33–5 and 95–100.) There, free cash flow was defined as "the portion of net operating flows that can be distributed as a dividend without reducing the level of future physical operations" (p. 34).

[2] See E. F. Fama and M. H. Miller, *The Theory of Finance* (New York: Holt, Rinehart & Winston, 1972), Ch. 2; R. Brealey and S. Myers, *Principles of Corporate Finance* (New York: McGraw-Hill, 1988), Ch. 4; S. A. Ross, R. W. Westerfield, and J. F. Jaffee, *Corporate Finance* (Homewood, IL: Richard D. Irwin, 1993), Ch. 5.

The price, P_0, that the market sets today (at time $t = 0$) for a company's stock equals the sum (Σ) of the stream of *expected future free cash flows* [the $E_0(\tilde{CF})$ terms in the numerators] per share of stock *discounted back to the present* [the $(1 + r)^t$ terms in the denominators].[3] The E_0 signifies that the cash flows are *expected.* The subscript 0 on E indicates that today's stock price (P_0) is based on investors' *current assessment* (at time $t = 0$) of the company's expected future cash flows.

The cash flow stream begins one period from now at $t = 1$, and it continues over an infinite horizon to $t = \infty$, but each future free cash flow is currently unknown and therefore uncertain.[4]

The discount rate, r, commonly referred to as the **equity cost of capital,** is adjusted to reflect the uncertainty or riskiness of the cash flow stream.[5] Streams that are more uncertain or risky will be discounted at a higher rate.

Simply put, the discounted free cash flow valuation model in equation (6.1) says that today's market price of each common share depends on investors' current *expectations* about the future economic prospects of the firm as measured by free cash flows. These future cash flows are discounted by a factor that reflects the risk (or uncertainty) and timing of the anticipated flows.

To apply this valuation model as represented, we would have to estimate free cash flows for each and every future period, starting one year hence and going forward forever. Obviously, this would be a daunting task. In practice some simplifying assumptions are made to facilitate the valuation process.[6]

One simplification for a mature firm with a stable cash flow pattern is to assume that the *current level* of cash flows (CF_0) will continue in perpetuity—a zero-growth perpetuity. This means the *expected* free cash flows in each future period can be replaced with the *known* current period cash flow so that equation (6.1) becomes:

Expected free cash flow in each year set equal to the free cash flow realized in year 0 $\longrightarrow \infty$

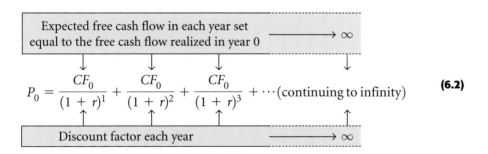

$$P_0 = \frac{CF_0}{(1 + r)^1} + \frac{CF_0}{(1 + r)^2} + \frac{CF_0}{(1 + r)^3} + \cdots \text{(continuing to infinity)} \qquad \textbf{(6.2)}$$

Discount factor each year $\longrightarrow \infty$

---

3 We depict uncertain future amounts with a tilde (~). Thus, $E_0(\tilde{CF}_3)$ indicates the currently expected uncertain free cash flow for period 3 in the future. By contrast, the already known past cash flow in period 0 would be shown without the tilde (i.e., CF_0).

4 An alternative representation of the discounted cash flow valuation model presumes that the future cash flow stream continues only through some finite terminal period, T, at which point the company is liquidated and a liquidating or terminal distribution, $\tilde{CF}_T$, is paid to stockholders:

$$P_0 = \sum_{t=1}^{T-1} \frac{E_0(\tilde{CF}_t)}{(1 + r)^t} + \frac{E_0(\tilde{CF}_T)}{(1 + r)^T}$$

5 There is no clear consensus in the finance literature on how to best estimate the cost of equity capital. However, one popular approach is to use the **capital asset pricing model** (CAPM), which expresses the equity cost of capital as the sum of the return on a riskless asset (r_f) plus an equity risk premium $[E(r_M) - r_f]$ multiplied by the company's systematic (beta) risk-that is,

$$r_e = r_f + [E(r_M) - r_f]\beta.$$

See J. Pettit, "Corporate Capital Costs: A Practitioners' Guide," *Journal of Applied Corporate Finance* (Spring 1999), pp. 115–20.

6 These simplifying assumptions and other detailed aspects of the valuation process are described in B. Cornell, *Corporate Valuation* (Homewood, IL: R. D. Irwin, 1993); T. Copeland, T. Koller, and J. Murin, *Valuation* (New York: Wiley, 2000); A. Damadoran, *Investment Valuation* (New York: Wiley, 1996); and S. Penman, *Financial Statement Analysis and Security Valuation* (New York: McGraw Hill/Irwin, 2001).

The present value of the same dollar cash flow over an infinite horizon—called a **constant perpetuity**—simplifies to:[7]

$$P_0 = \frac{CF_0}{r} \tag{6.3}$$

Thus, if a company is currently generating a free cash flow of \$5 per share, which is expected to continue indefinitely, and if the discount rate is 10%, the estimated share price would be \$5/.10 = \$50.

The Role of Earnings in Valuation

We have just described a free cash flow valuation model linking investors' expectations about a company's future cash flow prospects to today's stock price. *But what role does earnings play in valuation?* If investors are truly interested in knowing the company's future cash flows, why would they care about current earnings? The answer hinges on the belief that *current* accrual accounting earnings are more useful than *current* cash flows in predicting *future* cash flows. The Financial Accounting Standards Board (FASB), for example, makes this assertion. It states:

> "Information about enterprise earnings and its components measured by accrual accounting generally provides a better indication of enterprise performance than information about current cash receipts and payments."[8]

The Board stresses that the primary objective of financial reporting is to provide information useful to investors and creditors in assessing the *amount, timing,* and *uncertainty* of prospective enterprise net cash flows.[9] The FASB contends that users pay attention to a firm's accounting earnings because these measures of periodic firm performance improve their ability to forecast companies' future cash flows.

The FASB's belief that *current* earnings outperform *current* cash flows in predicting *future* cash flows stems from the *forward-looking* nature of accrual accounting. To illustrate, consider this example. Under generally accepted accounting principles (GAAP), a \$100,000 cash expenditure for production equipment would not be expensed in its entirety when pur-

The following quote from the "Intrinsic Value" column of the *Wall Street Journal* underscores the importance of accrual earnings as an indicator of future free cash flows:

> "As per usual, this column values stocks by their expected future free cash flow, discounted back to the present. Earnings are a proxy—imperfect but the best we have—for free cash flow, which is the spare change that the underlying business throws off to their owners after paying for salaries, interest, capital maintenance, taxes and Danish for their chief executives, in addition to their eight-figure bonuses." (R. Lowenstein, "S&P 500: Cheap, Fair, Going, Gone . . . ," *Wall Street Journal,* June 19, 1997).

---

[7] A constant perpetuity is a stream of constant cash flows without end. To see why the present value of a cash flow perpetuity

$$PV = \frac{CF}{(1+r)^1} + \frac{CF}{(1+r)^2} + \frac{CF}{(1+r)^3} + \cdots + \frac{CF}{(1+r)^\infty}$$

reduces to

$$PV = \frac{CF}{r}$$

consider this example. Assume that the market price (i.e., present value) of an investment is \$1,000 and that this investment will yield a return of 9%, or \$90, in perpetuity. Since the amount of this perpetual cash flow is $PV \times r$, we can express the amount of the perpetuity as:

$$PV \times r = CF$$

Dividing both sides of the equation by r immediately yields the formula for the present value of a perpetuity:

$$PV = \frac{CF}{r}$$

In our example,

$$\$1{,}000 = \frac{\$90}{.09}$$

[8] "Objectives of Financial Reporting by Business Enterprises," *Statement of Financial Accounting Concepts No. 1* (Stamford, CT: FASB, 1978), para. 43.

[9] Ibid., para. 37. The term **net cash flows** refers to the difference between cash receipts (inflows) and cash payments (outflows).

chased. Instead, that expenditure is charged to an asset account and the asset is depreciated over future years as it is used to produce the products that are sold to customers. Both the depreciable life and depreciation method are chosen to reflect the *expected future benefit pattern* that arises from the use of the asset. Accrual accounting automatically incorporates this long-horizon, multiple-period view for such capital expenditure transactions.

Consider another example. Under accrual accounting an up-front cash advance from a customer is recognized as income not when the cash is received but rather over a series of future periods as the advance is earned (recall the Canterbury Publishing example from Chapter 2). Cash flows are "lumpy"—but as these examples illustrate—accrual accounting earnings measurement takes a long-horizon perspective that smoothes out the "lumpiness" in year-to-year cash flows. This explains why the FASB contends that current earnings provide a much better measure of long-run expected operating performance than do current cash flows.

The FASB's contention is supported by empirical research that shows two results:

- Current earnings are a better forecast of future cash flows than are current cash flows.[10]
- Stock returns correlate better with accrual earnings than with realized operating cash flows.[11]

These results imply that investors are better able to predict a company's future free cash flows using the company's accrual earnings than by using realized cash flows.

Figure 6.1 illustrates the linkage between a company's current earnings, future free cash flows, and current stock price, as suggested by the FASB and by the empirical evidence.[12]

The analyst combines information about the company's current earnings, its business strategy, and the industry's competitive dynamics to forecast sustainable future free cash flows. ***Through the use of accruals and deferrals, accrual accounting produces an earnings number that smoothes out the unevenness or "lumpiness" in year-to-year cash flows, and it provides an estimate of sustainable "annualized" long-run future free cash flows.***

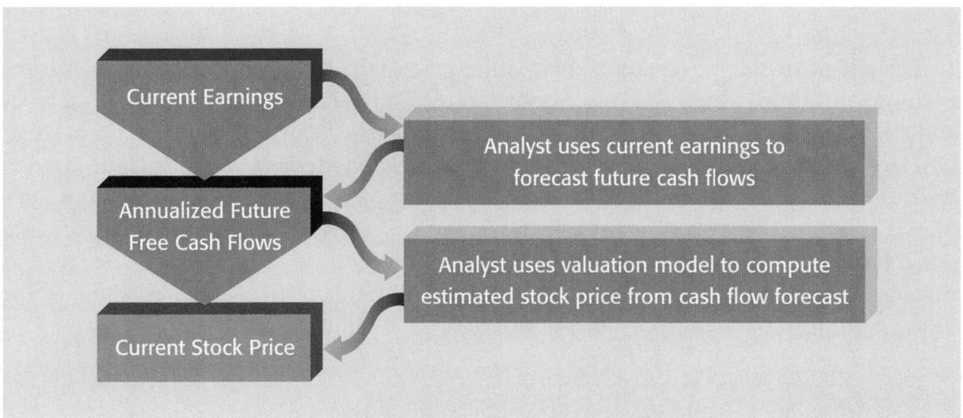

Figure 6.1

LINKAGE BETWEEN STOCK PRICE AND ACCRUAL EARNINGS

[10] See M. Barth, D. Cram, and K. Nelson, "Accruals and the Prediction of Future Cash Flows," *The Accounting Review* (January 2001), pp. 27–58; and P. Dechow, S. P. Kothari, and R. Watts, "The Relation Between Earnings and Cash Flow," *Journal of Accounting and Economics* (May 1998), pp. 133–68. Additional evidence on the usefulness of *current earnings* in predicting *future cash flows* is provided by R. Greenberg, G. Johnson, and K. Ramesh, "Earnings Versus Cash Flow as a Predictor of Future Cash Flow," *Journal of Accounting, Auditing and Finance* (Fall 1986), pp. 266–77; and C. Finger, "The Ability of Earnings to Predict Future Earnings and Cash Flow," *Journal of Accounting Research* (Autumn 1994), pp. 210–23.

[11] P. Dechow, "Accounting Earnings and Cash Flows as Measures of Firm Performance: The Role of Accounting Accruals," *Journal of Accounting and Economics* (July 1994), pp. 3–42.

[12] For a slightly different discussion of these linkages, see W. H. Beaver, *Financial Reporting: An Accounting Revolution* (Upper Saddle River, NJ: Prentice Hall, 1981), Ch. 4.

The final step in this process involves using the annualized free cash flow estimate together with the risk-adjusted discount rate to arrive at an estimated value for the firm's stock.

To appreciate the implications of these linkages, let's revisit the simplified zero-growth perpetuity setting and our free cash flow valuation model in equation (6.2). Assuming zero growth means that one way to estimate a firm's equity value (or stock price) is to use its free cash flow in the current period (CF_0) as our forecast of free cash flow in each future period. But according to the FASB's assertion, the current period accrual income is a better proxy for sustainable future cash flows than is the current period free cash flow. This means replacing the current period cash flow, CF_0 in equation (6.2), with the current period's earnings (denoted X_0). In this case the free cash flow valuation model simplifies to:

Free cash flow discount model from equation (6.1)

Expected future free cash flow set equal to current accrual earnings in year 0 ⟶ ∞

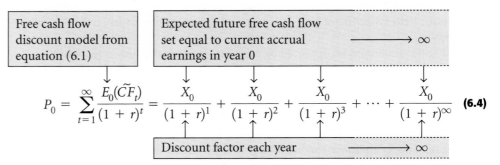

$$P_0 = \sum_{t=1}^{\infty} \frac{E_0(\tilde{CF}_t)}{(1+r)^t} = \frac{X_0}{(1+r)^1} + \frac{X_0}{(1+r)^2} + \frac{X_0}{(1+r)^3} + \cdots + \frac{X_0}{(1+r)^{\infty}} \tag{6.4}$$

Discount factor each year ⟶ ∞

As in equation (6.2), the right-hand side of equation (6.4) is a perpetuity with a discounted present value of X_0/r. Thus, given our simplifying assumptions, the current stock price estimate can be expressed as a capitalized rate $(1/r)$ times a perpetuity equal to the current earnings:

$$P_0 = \frac{1}{r}(X_0) = \frac{X_0}{r} \tag{6.5}$$

or alternatively:

$$\frac{P_0}{X_0} = \frac{1}{r} \tag{6.6}$$

The left-hand side of equation (6.6) is the **price/earnings (P/E) ratio,** also called the **earnings multiple,** which is a measure of the relation between a firm's current earnings and its share price. Under the assumption of zero growth, the price/earnings ratio in equation (6.6) is the reciprocal of the risk-adjusted interest rate (equity cost of capital) used to discount future earnings. If the current risk-adjusted interest rate is 8%, the earnings multiple is $1/.08 = 12.5$, which is the rate at which \$1 of current earnings is capitalized into price. If the company reports current earnings of \$5 per share and if investors believe this earnings level will persist in perpetuity at \$5 per share, then the capitalized value of the future earnings stream implies a share price of $\$5 \times 12.5 = \$62.50$.

In theory, equity valuation involves discounting the expected value of some measure of wealth creation—like free cash flow or earnings—over an infinite horizon using a risk-adjusted discount rate (equity cost of capital). In practice, simplifying assumptions are made to facilitate the valuation process. One simplification is to assume that future periods' free cash flows will be a perpetuity equal to the current period's accrual earnings. Accrual accounting produces an earnings number that smoothes out the unevenness in the year-to-year cash flows, thereby providing a measure of firm performance that is generally a better indicator of the long-run sustainable free cash flows of an enterprise. Using this valuation approach, stock price is stated as a multiple of current period earnings, where the multiple (in the no-growth case) is the reciprocal of the firm's equity cost of capital.

RECAP

Research on Earnings and Equity Valuation

Research on Earnings and Equity Valuation

Over the past 30 years, researchers have investigated the **value-relevance** of financial accounting information.[13] Many of these studies seek to further our understanding of the relation between stock prices and earnings.

To illustrate, let's consider equation (6.5). That equation suggests that current earnings (X_0) can "explain" current stock price (P_0) in the sense that perpetual earnings of \$5 per share give rise to a \$62.50 share price. It immediately follows that *differences* in current earnings across firms should help explain *differences* in stock prices across firms at a particular point in time. ***That is, if accounting earnings are viewed by investors as an important piece of information for assessing firm value, then earnings differences across firms should help explain differences in these firms' stock prices.*** This is just another way of saying that earnings are value-relevant.

One way to test whether reported earnings are value-relevant is to examine the statistical association between stock prices and earnings across many firms at a given point in time. Studies of this type are called **cross-sectional tests.** Researchers explored this statistical association using the following simple earnings valuation equation:

$$P_i = \alpha + \beta X_i + e_i \qquad \textbf{(6.7)}$$

where:

- P_i is the end-of-period closing stock price for firm *i*, and X_i is the firm's reported accounting earnings for that period.
- The intercept (α) and slope (β) terms in the equation represent coefficients to be estimated using standard regression analysis or similar techniques.
- e_i denotes a random error which reflects the variation in stock prices that cannot be explained by earnings.

If accounting earnings are relevant for determining stock prices, then the estimated slope coefficient β, which measures the covariance between earnings and prices, should be positive. A statistically positive β means that differences in earnings across firms explain a significant portion of the variation in share prices across firms. Moreover, if current earnings were a perfect forecast of future free cash flows, and if all companies had the same cost of equity capital and conformed to the zero-growth assumption, current earnings would explain 100% of the cross-sectional variation in share prices.

Figure 6.2 on the next page plots 1999 year-end stock prices (measured on the vertical axis) against annual earnings per share (EPS, measured on the horizontal axis) for 39 retail grocery companies. The upward-sloping line represents the estimated price-earnings relation for the regression equation (6.7) for this group of companies at the end of 1999. The regression line has a vertical axis intercept (α) estimate of \$9.80 per share and a slope (β) coefficient estimate of 9.55—that is:

$$P_i = \underset{\substack{\uparrow \\ \text{Stock} \\ \text{price at} \\ \text{\$0 EPS}}}{\overset{\substack{\text{Intercept} \\ \downarrow}}{9.80}} + \underset{\substack{\uparrow \\ \text{Earnings} \\ \text{multiple}}}{\overset{\substack{\text{Slope} \\ \downarrow}}{9.55}} \times \underset{\substack{\uparrow \\ \text{EPS}}}{(\$X_i)} \qquad \textbf{(6.8)}$$

---

[13] For an overview of this research, see B. Lev and J. Ohlson, "Market-Based Empirical Research in Accounting: A Review, Interpretation, and Extension," *Journal of Accounting Research* (*Supplement,* 1982), pp. 249–322; B. Lev, "On the Usefulness of Earnings and Earnings Research: Lessons and Directions from Two Decades of Empirical Research," *Journal of Accounting Research* (*Supplement,* 1989), pp. 153–92, and S. P. Kothari, "Capital Markets Research in Accounting," *Journal of Accounting and Economics* (forthcoming 2001).

Figure 6.2

1999 P/E RELATION FOR RETAIL GROCERY STORES

Regression Result:
$P_i = \$9.80 + 9.55\ X_i$
$R^2 = 34.2\%$

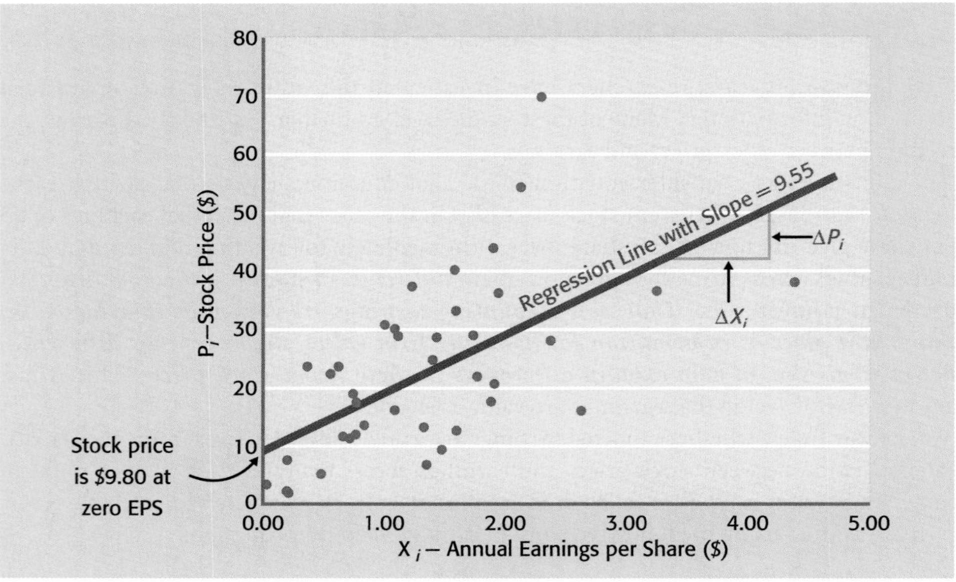

A grocery company that reported earnings per share of $X_i = \$1$ in 1999 would be predicted to have a stock price of $\$19.35 = \$9.80 + 9.55 \times \$1$. The estimated slope coefficient ($\beta = 9.55$) is positive and statistically significant, indicating that reported earnings explains some of the cross-sectional variation in stock prices of grocery companies. However, the proportion of variation in share prices explained by earnings (the R^2 for the regression) is only 34.2%. Some points lie well above the average price-earnings relation in Figure 6.2, while others fall far below the regression line.[14] The next section discusses reasons why current earnings do not explain 100% of the variation in current prices and why some firms' P/E ratios are well above (below) average.

Sources of Variation in P/E Multiples

Risk Differences Two firms with the same level of current and future earnings can sell for different prices because of differences in the risk or uncertainty associated with those earnings. Riskier firms have a higher risk-adjusted cost of capital, which means the discount rate in capitalizing earnings will be *higher,* resulting in a *lower* price.

To illustrate, suppose Firm A and Firm B both report current earnings of $10 per share and it is expected, on average, that these earnings will persist into the future. However, Firm A's earnings exhibit greater volatility over time—therefore, greater risk—thus, resulting in a 15% cost of equity capital. Firm B's earnings exhibit lower volatility—thus, lower risk—and a 10% cost of equity capital is appropriate. The estimated price for these two firms' shares would be:

Firm A	Firm B
$\frac{\$10}{.15} = \$66.67$	$\frac{\$10}{.10} = \$100$

Thus, despite having equal earnings, Firm A's stock price will be one-third less than Firm B's ($66.67 versus $100) because Firm A is riskier and its cost of capital (15%) is higher than Firm B's (10%).

[14] The error term (e_i) in equation (6.7) does not show up in equation (6.8) because the latter equation is the expression for the *fitted regression line.* The vertical deviations between the fitted regression line and the data points that plot the combination of earnings and price for individual firms are the e_i error terms in equation (6.7).

Growth Opportunities Most firms' P/E ratios run between 10 and 30. However, it is not uncommon to find start-up companies like Ebay and high-tech companies like Qualcomm trading at prices that are 100 times (or more) current earnings. What explains these exceptionally high P/E ratios?

In addition to valuing earnings generated from existing assets, the market values **growth opportunities**—that is, the firm's *potential earnings* from reinvesting current earnings in new projects that will earn a rate of return in excess of the cost of equity capital. The net present value of growth opportunities (NPVGO) from the reinvestment of current earnings adds a positive increment to the firm's stock price, resulting in above-average P/E multiples. For a firm with positive growth opportunities, the pricing equation (6.5) can be rewritten as:

$$P_0 = \underbrace{\frac{X_0}{r}}_{\text{Present value of earnings from assets in place}} + \underbrace{\text{NPVGO}}_{\text{Net present value of future growth opportunities}} \qquad \textbf{(6.9)}$$

The first term is the current operations value of a firm that has no growth opportunities and distributes all its earnings to stockholders in the form of dividends. The second term is the future growth value of a firm—the *additional* value if the firm retains its earnings to fund new investment projects that have positive net present values.

To illustrate the incremental value derived from growth opportunities, suppose Firm A has 100,000 shares outstanding and can generate earnings of $1 million per year in perpetuity if it undertakes no new investment projects. Thus, its earnings per share is $10 ($1 million/100,000 shares). If Firm A's cost of equity capital is 10%, the price per share is:

$$P_0 = \frac{X_0}{r} = \frac{\$10}{.10} = \$100$$

Now assume that Firm A can reinvest all earnings from period 0 in a project that is expected to increase earnings in period 1 and *in every subsequent period* by $150,000, or $1.50 per share. This represents a 15% return on the reinvested earnings ($150,000/ $1 million). If Firm A's cost of capital remains at 10%, the net present value of this investment as of the start of period 1 is:

$$\underbrace{-\$1{,}000{,}000}_{\text{Earnings invested at beginning of period 1}} + \underbrace{\frac{\$150{,}000}{.10}}_{\text{Present value at beginning of period 1 of incremental return from reinvested earnings}} = \$500{,}000$$

Since $500,000 is the net present value as of the beginning of period 1, the value at time 0 can be determined by discounting back one period:

$$\frac{\$500{,}000}{(1 + .10)^1} = \$454{,}545$$

Thus, NPVGO per share $\frac{\$454{,}545}{100{,}000}$ + $4.55. The price per share of Firm A with growth opportunities is:

$$\begin{aligned} P_0 &= \frac{X_0}{r} + \text{NPVGO} \\ &= \frac{\$10}{.10} + 4.55 = \$104.55 \end{aligned}$$

Note the stock is more valuable now than it was with no-growth ($100). That's because the firm is able to reinvest earnings in a project expected to earn a 15% rate of return (forever) when the firm's cost of capital or discount rate is only 10%. In this simplified example, the retention rate on earnings was 100%—meaning that none of the earnings were paid as dividends to shareholders. But this need not be the case for a firm to have growing earnings.

In general, the growth rate in earnings will depend on

- the portion of earnings reinvested each period, called the **retention rate** (k)[15]
- the rate of return earned on new investment (r^*).

As long as the retention rate is positive and as long as the return earned on new investment is greater than the firm's cost of equity capital $(r^* > r)$, NPVGO will be positive and will contribute to the P/E multiple. Return on equity (ROE), one of the key accounting performance measures introduced in Chapter 5, can be used to assess whether a firm is likely to earn a return on reinvested earnings that exceeds its cost of equity capital.

Permanent, Transitory, and Valuation-Irrelevant Components of Earnings If investors view firms' current earnings levels as likely to persist in perpetuity, then the slope coefficient (β) in equation (6.7) should equal the average earnings multiple for the particular companies and time period being examined. This prediction follows directly from the equity valuation model in equation (6.5), where current earnings are translated into share price using an earnings multiple based on the risk-adjusted cost of equity capital. For example, if the average risk-adjusted cost of capital is 8%, then β should be 1/.08 or 12.5. However, for many firms, the earnings multiple falls well below this theoretical value.[16] Why?

One explanation is that reported earnings numbers often contain three distinctly different components, each subject to a different earnings capitalization rate:[17]

1. A **permanent earnings** component (X_i^P) which is valuation-relevant and expected to persist into the future. In theory, the multiple for this component should approach $1/r$.
2. A **transitory earnings** component (X_i^T) which is valuation-relevant but is not expected to persist into the future. Since transitory earnings result from one-time events or transactions, the multiple for this component should approach 1.0.
3. A **value-irrelevant earnings** or **noise** component (X_i^0) which is unrelated to future free cash flows or future earnings and, therefore, is *not* pertinent to assessing current share price. Such earnings components should carry a multiple of zero.

These three earnings components correspond roughly to the three broad classifications in the multiple-step income statements as described in Chapter 2. For example:

- ***Income from continuing operations (with the possible exception of special items)*** is generally regarded as a recurring, sustainable component of a company's profit performance, and thus it would fall into the permanent earnings category.
- ***Income (loss) from discontinued operations and extraordinary gains and losses,*** on the other hand, are nonrecurring. These items are more likely to be viewed as transitory com-

> Some items that comprise income from continuing operations may correctly be viewed by investors as highly transitory and/or value-irrelevant, and would be capitalized accordingly. Examples include inventory holding gains and losses embedded in First-In First-Out (FIFO) earnings and Last-In, First-Out (LIFO) liquidation profits that result when old LIFO inventory layers are sold. Later chapters discuss the value-relevance of these and other earnings and balance sheet items in considerable detail.

[15] The earnings retention rate (k) is [(earnings − dividends)/earnings]. One minus the retention ratio $(1 - k)$ is the **dividend payout ratio.**

[16] Notice that the slope coefficient of 9.55 for retail grocery stores in Figure 6.2 suggests an earnings capitalization rate of 10.47% because 1/.1047 = 9.55.

[17] For a more formal discussion of these three earnings components and their valuation implication, see R. Ramakrishnan and J. Thomas, "Valuation of Permanent, Transitory, and Price-Irrelevant Components of Reported Earnings," *Journal of Accounting, Auditing and Finance* (1998), pp. 301–36.

ponents of earnings and, therefore, to be valued at a much lower multiple than those items associated with permanent earnings components.

- A ***change in accounting principles***, which gives rise to a ***cumulative effect adjustment*** to income that has no future cash flow consequences to shareholders, may be viewed as "noise" that is valuation-irrelevant.

The idea that reported earnings may sometimes contain permanent, transitory and value-irrelevant components suggests that X_i (total earnings) in the simple price-earnings regression model of equation (6.7) should be rewritten as the sum of permanent, transitory, and valuation-irrelevant components—that is

$$X_i = X_i^P + X_i^T + X_i^0$$

This modification allows for a different multiple or capitalization rate for each earnings component:[18]

Permanent component of earnings ↓ | Transitory component of earnings ↓ | Value-irrelevant component of earnings ↓

$$P_i = \alpha + \beta_P X_i^P + \beta_T X_i^T + \beta_0 X_i^0 + e_i \qquad \textbf{(6.10)}$$

↑ Earnings multiple on permanent (β_P), transitory (β_T), and value-irrelevant (β_0) components of earnings

Equation (6.10) expresses share price as a function of the permanent, transitory, and valuation-irrelevant components of earnings. Each earnings component has a different earnings multiple—β_P, β_T, and β_0, respectively.

In theory, permanent (sustainable) earnings should have a higher earnings multiple than transitory earnings because we expect the former to persist longer into the future—that is, β_P should be greater than β_T.[19] Likewise, the multiple for transitory earnings should exceed the multiple for value-irrelevant earnings since the latter have no bearing on future cash flows and, therefore, have no bearing on price—that is, β_0 should be 0 while β_T should be approximately 1.0. Figure 6.3 on the next page illustrates these predictions about earnings multiples for different earnings components. The slope of each line corresponds to the earnings multiple for that particular earnings component, where *r* equals 20%.

To illustrate the importance of distinguishing between permanent, transitory, and value-irrelevant earnings components, let's suppose two companies report identical bottom-line earnings of $10 per share, as in Table 6.1 on the following page. Does this mean they would necessarily sell for the same price? Perhaps not, as we will see.

A careful analysis of the financial statements and related footnotes of Firm A reveals that total earnings can be decomposed into three categories: (1) 60% that is judged to be value-relevant and permanent, (2) 30% that is value-relevant but transitory, and (3) 10% that is considered value-irrelevant. Analysis of Firm B's financial report indicates its earnings composition is 50% permanent, 20% transitory, and 30% value-irrelevant. This decomposition of each firm's reported EPS is shown in Table 6.1.

---

[18] You may wonder about the distinction between the value-irrelevant component (X_i^0) and the error term (e_i) in equation (6.10). X_i^0 is a component of earnings that is not relevant to assessing price, while e_i represents "other information" that is *not* a component of current earnings but *is* relevant to assessing price. For example, e_i may represent news about a new scientific breakthrough or discovery the firm has just made. Such news would have a positive effect on price, but it would not yet be reflected in current earnings.

[19] Lipe presents evidence consistent with this conjecture. He finds a greater stock price reaction to earnings components that exhibit greater permanence than to those components that are more transitory in nature. See R. Lipe, "The Information Contained in the Components of Earnings," *Journal of Accounting Research* (Supplement 1986), pp. 33–64.

Figure 6.3

PRICE/EARNINGS MULTIPLES FOR PERMANENT, TRANSITORY, AND VALUE-IRRELEVANT EARNINGS COMPONENTS WITH $r = 20\%$

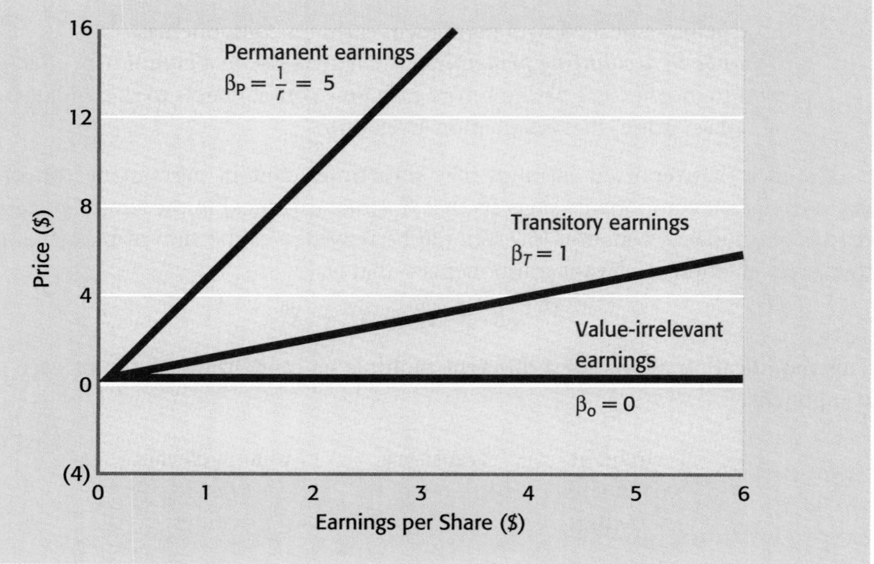

Using a 20% cost of capital to capitalize the permanent component of earnings, we find that the valuation model in equation (6.10) implies a stock price of $33 for Firm A and $27 for Firm B. Firm A's stock price is approximately 20% greater than Firm B's price, even though both companies report the same earnings per share. In the vernacular of the analyst community, Firm A's stock sells for a higher earnings multiple because investors perceive its **earnings quality** to be superior to that of Firm B.

Table 6.1 ■ APPLYING P/E MULTIPLES TO EARNINGS COMPONENTS

	Firm A	Firm B
EPS as reported	$10	$10
Analyst's EPS decomposition		
Permanent component	60% of $10 = $6	50% of $10 = $5
Transitory component	30% of $10 = $3	20% of $10 = $2
Value-irrelevant component	10% of $10 = $1	30% of $10 = $3
Earnings multiple applied to each earnings component at cost of capital of r = 20%		
Permanent component ($\beta_P = 5 = 1/20$)	5 × $6 = 30	5 × $5 = 25
Transitory component ($\beta_T = 1$)	1 × $3 = 3	1 × $2 = 2
Value-irrelevant component ($\beta_0 = 0$)	0 × $1 = 0	0 × $3 = 0
Implied share price	**$33**	**$27**
Implied total earnings multiple (Share price/EPS as reported)	3.3	2.7

The Concept of Earnings Quality ◗ A *Wall Street Journal* article described earnings quality and its implications for stock prices:

> Quality of earnings measures how much the profits companies publicly report diverge from their true operating earnings. Low quality means the bottom line is padded with

paper gains—such as the profit-fattening effect of inflation on a company's reported inventory values, or gains produced by "underdepreciation," when a company doesn't write off plant and equipment as fast as their real value is falling.

Because a decline in quality means companies' reported earnings are weaker and less sustainable than they appear, it indicates likely trouble for future earnings—whether or not a recession arrives. If history is any guide, those lower quality earnings also will come home to roost in lower stock prices. . . .[20]

The notion of earnings quality is multifaceted, and there is no consensus on how to measure it.[21] Basically, earnings are considered to be high quality when they are *sustainable*—for example, those that are generated from repeat customers or from a high quality product that enjoys steady customer demand based on clear brand name identity. Examples of *un*sustainable earnings items include gains or losses from debt retirement; asset write-offs from corporate restructuring and plant closings; or temporary reductions in discretionary expenditures for advertising, research and development, or employee training.

Accrual accounting treats these discretionary expenditures as expenses. One way a firm can boost earnings temporarily is by cutting back on the amount spent for these activities. However, earnings increases of this sort are not sustainable because the expenditures are critical to creating future demand for the firm's products, and to creating new products or developing competent management—all important determinants of long-run sustainable earnings.

Earnings quality is also affected by the accounting methods chosen by management to describe the routine, ongoing activities of a company (e.g., LIFO rather than FIFO inventory accounting), and by the subjectivity—it's unavoidable!—of accounting estimates (e.g., allowance for future uncollectibles).

Does earnings quality matter? One study finds that when reported earnings are adjusted for quality differences—for example, subtracting (adding back) transitory gains (losses) or adjusting for differences in inventory methods (FIFO versus LIFO)—the "quality-adjusted" earnings numbers better explain why firms' stocks sell for different prices.[22] These results suggest that differences in earnings quality are associated with differences in the overall earnings capitalization rate (earnings multiple) that investors assign to reported earnings when determining share prices. It should be easy enough to see that as transitory (X_i^T) or value-irrelevant (X_i^0) components become a larger part of a firm's reported earnings:

- the quality of those reported earnings is eroded,
- reported earnings become a less reliable indicator of the company's long-run sustainable cash flows,
- hence earnings are a less reliable indicator of fundamental value.

This is illustrated in Table 6.1, where we see that Firm B (with a higher proportion of transitory or value-irrelevant components of earnings) has an overall earnings multiple of 2.7 compared to 3.3 for Firm A. Suppose all the reported earnings were considered permanent. Then the stock would sell for $10/.20 = $50, and the earnings multiple would be 5. Low-quality earnings will be assigned a lower overall earnings multiple and capitalized at a lower rate.

The research to date suggests that the capital market is rather sophisticated—it does not react naively to reported earnings, but instead, it appears to distinguish among permanent, transitory, and value-irrelevant earnings components. Investors recognize differences in the quality of reported earnings numbers and take these differences into account when assessing the implications of earnings reports for share prices. From time to time throughout this book, we will come back to this idea as we discuss alternative accounting treat-

---

[20] B. Donnelly, "Profits' 'Quality' Erodes, Making Them Less Reliable," *Wall Street Journal* (October 18, 1990).

[21] See L. Bernstein and J. Siegel, "The Concept of Earnings Quality," *Financial Analysts Journal* (July–August 1979), pp. 72–5; J. Siegel, "The 'Quality of Earnings' Concept—A Survey," *Financial Analysts Journal* (March–April 1982), pp. 60–8.

[22] See B. Lev and R. Thiagarajan, "Fundamental Information Analysis," *Journal of Accounting Research* (Autumn 1993), pp. 190–215. To arrive at "quality-adjusted" earnings, the researchers started with reported earnings and then eliminated revenue or expense items thought to be transitory or value-irrelevant.

ments, both for ongoing events and for specialized transactions, and as we review the academic and professional research literature on the valuation relevance of alternative accounting methods and footnote disclosures.

RECAP

Firms' shares often sell at prices that differ from multiplying current reported earnings by the average earnings multiple for their industry. A variety of factors contribute to variation in price/earnings (P/E) multiples. These factors include differences in risk; in growth opportunities; and in what proportions of current earnings are considered persistent, transitory, and value-irrelevant. The persistence of earnings is related to earnings quality—higher quality earnings are more persistent and sustainable. Assessing earnings quality involves using information from a multiple-step income statement, a balance sheet, a cash flow statement, financial footnotes, and management's discussion and analysis to identify components of current earnings that are likely to be sustainable in contrast to those that are transitory or price-irrelevant.

The Abnormal Earnings Approach to Equity Valuation

In the previous section, we found that the role of accounting earnings information is *indirect*—earnings are only useful because they help generate forecasts of future free cash flows. Recently, another valuation approach has emerged in practice that uses earnings and equity book value numbers themselves as *direct* inputs to the valuation process. Under many circumstances this approach leads to valuation estimates that are equivalent to the discounted free cash flow approach. But this new approach helps us better understand the economic forces that influence share prices over time and across firms.

This new approach is based on the notion that the value of a company (and its share price) is driven not by the level of earnings themselves but by the level of earnings *relative to a fundamental economic benchmark.* That benchmark is the cost of capital, expressed in dollars, and it reflects the level of earnings investors demand from the company as compensation for the risks of investment. Investors willingly pay a premium only for those firms that earn more than the cost of capital—meaning firms that produce **positive abnormal earnings.** For firms whose earnings are "ordinary" or "normal"—that is, where the earnings rate is equal to the cost of capital—investors are only willing to pay an amount equal to the underlying book value of assets. Firms that earn less than the cost of capital—that produce **negative abnormal earnings**—have a share price *below* book value and thus sell at a discount. This relationship between share prices, book value, and abnormal earnings performance is expressed mathematically as:[23]

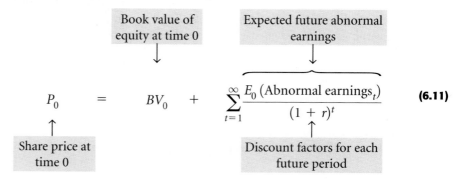

Book value of equity at time 0 → BV_0; Expected future abnormal earnings → numerator of the sum

$$P_0 = BV_0 + \sum_{t=1}^{\infty} \frac{E_0(\text{Abnormal earnings}_t)}{(1+r)^t} \qquad \textbf{(6.11)}$$

Share price at time 0 → P_0; Discount factors for each future period → $(1+r)^t$

[23] Several variations of the abnormal earnings valuation model have appeared in the literature. Recent examples include J. Ohlson, "Earnings, Book Values, and Dividends in Equity Valuation," *Contemporary Accounting Research* (Spring 1995), pp. 661–87; T. Copeland, T. Koller, and J. Murrin, *Valuation: Measuring and Managing the Value of Companies* (New York: Wiley, 1994); B. Madden, *CFROI Valuation* (Boston, MA: Butterworth-Heinemann, 1999); S. Penman, *Financial Statement Analysis and Security Valuation* (New York: McGraw-Hill/Irwin, 2001); and G. B. Stewart, III, *The Quest for Value* (New York: Harper Business, 1991).

where:

- BV denotes the equity book value (assets minus liabilities) per share that shareholders have invested in the firm,
- E_0 denotes the expectation about future abnormal earnings per share formed at time 0,
- r is the cost of equity capital.

The cost of equity capital, r, also corresponds to the risk-adjusted return stockholders *require* from their investment. So the earnings level the company must generate in period t to satisfy stockholders is $r \times BV_{t-1}$, or stockholders' required rate of return multiplied by the beginning of period (i.e., $t - 1$) invested capital. Any difference between actual earnings for period t (X_t) and stockholder's required dollar return on invested capital for the period ($r \times BV_{t-1}$) represents **abnormal earnings.**

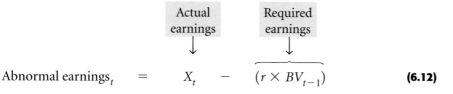

$$\text{Abnormal earnings}_t = \underbrace{X_t}_{\text{Actual earnings}} - \underbrace{(r \times BV_{t-1})}_{\text{Required earnings}} \quad \textbf{(6.12)}$$

To illustrate, suppose a company's equity book value (BV) at the beginning of the year is \$100 per share, and the cost of equity (r) is 15%. Stockholders therefore require earnings of at least \$100 × 15% or \$15 per share. If investors expect the company to report earnings equal to the benchmark earnings but it does even better and earns \$20 per share—thus exceeding the benchmark—the stock price will increase to reflect the company's superior performance. If actual earnings are only \$10—thus falling short of the benchmark expected earnings—the stock price will fall. The amount of the stock price increase (or decline) depends on the degree to which stockholders believe that abnormal (above *or* below normal) earnings are permanent rather than transitory.

Financial statements and related footnotes provide a wealth of information for assessing the relationships expressed by equations (6.11) and (6.12). The balance sheet provides detailed information on the book value of equity (assets minus liabilities). The income statement provides detailed information for assessing a firm's earnings. Chapter 5 described how asset and equity book values and earnings numbers can be combined into two key ratios—return on assets (ROA) and return on equity (ROE)—for assessing firm performance.

If ROE exceeds ROA, then the firm has the ability to earn a return on its investments that exceeds its cost of debt financing. This is because ROA measures the company's earnings return on *all* invested capital (since total assets must equal debt plus equity), whereas ROE is the return on *equity* capital. Recall from the previous chapter that interest paid on debt financing (net of taxes) is added back to net income to form the numerator of the ROA calculation. Thus, this adjusted earnings number measures the return on all invested capital—both debt and equity—which equals total assets.

A firm's ROE can be compared to its required rate of return on equity (cost of equity capital) or to the ROEs of other companies in the industry to evaluate its prospects for generating "abnormal earnings." Companies with ROEs that consistently exceed the industry average generally will have shares that sell for a higher premium relative to book value (i.e., a higher market-to-book ratio).

In making comparisons across firms, the analyst must be careful to gauge the quality and comparability of the accounting policies or methods used. For example, does the company being analyzed tend to select liberal accounting methods (i.e., those that may increase earnings and net asset values) or more conservative methods (i.e., those that may decrease earnings and net asset values). The degree of conservatism associated with a firm's accounting choices will have a direct bearing on the relationship among share price, earnings, and equity book value components of equation (6.11). To see this, let us consider a company that has a $10 share price and an $8 per share equity book value. Analysts who understand the accounting complexities described later in this book know there are two reasons why this company's stock may be valued at a $2 premium to equity book value. One reason is that shareholders believe the company will produce abnormal earnings in the future and those future earnings are worth—according to equation (6.11)—$2 today. A second possibility, however, is that stockholders only expect the company to produce "normal" earnings in the future (i.e., zero abnormal earnings), but they recognize that the company's conservative accounting methods understate equity book value by $2 per share.[24]

Much of the information needed for assessing the quality and value-relevance of a company's reported accounting numbers appears in footnotes that accompany the financial statements. These footnotes describe accounting policies for such matters as depreciation (straight-line versus accelerated), inventory valuation (LIFO versus FIFO), and methods of accounting for business combinations (purchase versus pooling of interests). Later chapters will clarify the important differences in these and other accounting methods and their impact on earnings and balance sheet book values. In certain instances, we show how you can adjust reported numbers to put firms that use different methods on a more equal footing before using those numbers for valuation purposes.

The combined book value–abnormal earnings approach to valuation says a company's future earnings are determined by (1) the resources (net assets) available to management; and (2) the rate of return or profitability earned on those net assets. If a firm can earn a return on net assets (equity book value) that exceeds (falls below) its cost of equity capital, then it will generate positive (negative) abnormal earnings. Its stock will then sell at a premium (discount) relative to book value. A key feature of this valuation model is that it explicitly takes into account a cost for the capital (net assets) provided by the owners of the business. Value is added only if the earnings generated from those net assets exceed the equity cost of capital benchmark. Appendix A to this chapter illustrates how to use this valuation model for a real company.

RECAP

Earnings Surprises

Both the earnings capitalization model (equation [6.4]) and the abnormal earnings model (equation [6.11]) share a common characteristic: Each requires estimates of future earnings. But estimates can (and usually do) prove to be incorrect. When this happens, an "earnings surprise" results.

If securities markets are rational and efficient in the sense of fully and correctly impounding available information into prices, then stock prices will reflect investors' *unbiased* expectations about the company's future earnings and cash flows. These expectations incorporate a vast array of information, including knowledge of the company's earnings and cash flow history, product market conditions, competitor actions, and other factors. For example, the stock prices of General Motors and Ford incorporate information about unit sales figures published weekly in the financial press, as well as expectations about changes in interest rates, because interest rates influence consumers' car-buying behavior. Stock prices move up or down as investors receive new information and then revise their expectations about the future earnings and cash flow prospects of the company. Financial reports are an important source of information that investors use in updating their expectations.

Unbiased means that, on average, the market's earnings expectations will be correct—not systematically high or systematically low.

Stock price changes can also occur because of unanticipated changes in interest (discount) rates over time.

[24] For a further discussion of these points and the implications of the abnormal earnings valuation model, see G. Feltham and J. Ohlson, "Valuation and Clean Surplus Accounting for Operating and Financial Assets," *Contemporary Accounting Research* (Spring 1995), pp. 689–731; V. Bernard, "The Feltham-Ohlson Framework: Implications for Empiricists," *Contemporary Accounting Research* (Spring 1995), pp. 733–47; Penman, ibid. and Stewart, ibid.

Consider a typical General Motors' quarterly earnings announcement that is released through major financial wire services. If reported quarterly earnings correspond exactly to the earnings investors expected before the announcement, they have no reason to alter their expectations about GM's future earnings or cash flows. The reported quarterly earnings would simply *confirm* market expectations. The earnings release may resolve market uncertainty about current earnings—but it does not provide new information to investors. On the other hand, if reported quarterly earnings deviate from investors' expectations, this **earnings surprise** represents new information that investors will use to revise their expectations about the company's future earnings and cash flow prospects. Of course, this change in investor expectations will cause the company's stock price to change following the earnings announcement.

The way stock prices change in response to new information about earnings can be expressed mathematically as follows:

Price change from period $t-1$ to t		Current earnings surprise		Change (Δ) in expectations about future earnings
↓		↓		↓

$$P_t - P_{t-1} = \overbrace{X_t - E_{t-1}(\tilde{X}_t)} + \sum_{k=1}^{\infty} \frac{\Delta E_t(\tilde{X}_{t+k})}{(1+r)^k} \tag{6.13}$$

where

- $P_t - P_{t-1}$ is the stock price change from just before to just after the earnings announcement;
- $X_t - E_{t-1}(\tilde{X}_t)$ is the earnings "surprise" or deviation of reported earnings from the market's expectation just *before* the earnings announcement;
- $\sum_{k=1}^{\infty} \frac{\Delta E_t(\tilde{X}_{t+k})}{(1+r)^k}$, the summation term, represents the valuation impact of revised expectations about all future earnings.

The change in stock price from one point in time to another can also be influenced by dividends. Consequently, some versions of equation (6.13) incorporate a dividend term so that the price change is defined as: $P_t + D_t - P_{t-1}$. A similar (but more complicated) expression for earnings announcement induced stock price changes can be derived from the abnormal earnings valuation model in equation (6.10). Until recently, however, most "earnings surprise" research has used variations of equation (6.13).

Figure 6.4 illustrates the typical behavior of stock returns leading up to, and following quarterly earnings announcements for three different scenarios described on page 250:

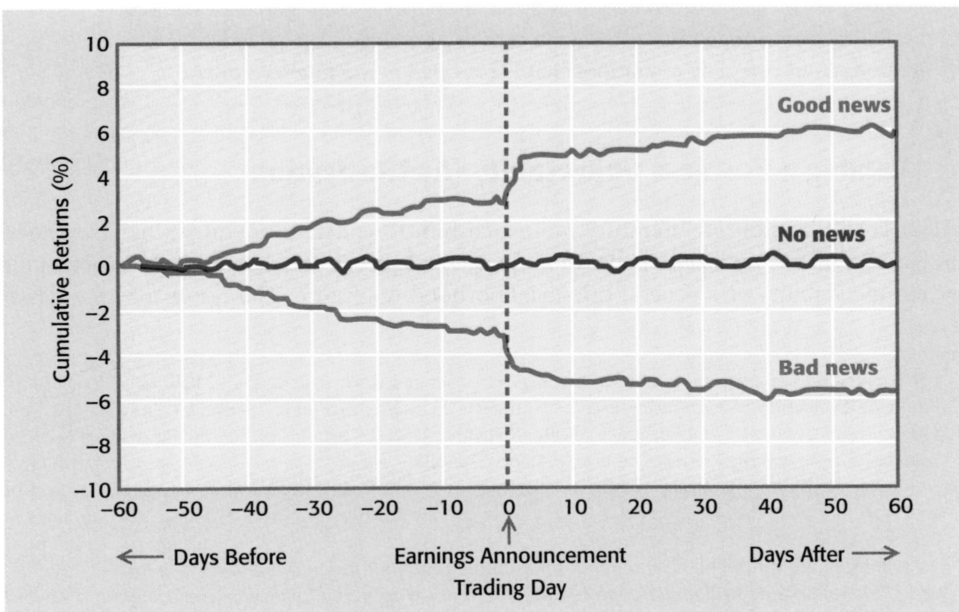

Figure 6.4

STOCK RETURNS AND QUARTERLY EARNINGS "SURPRISES"

1. Reported earnings are viewed as a "*good news*" earnings surprise because they exceed market expectations.
2. Reported earnings contain "*no news*" because they correspond exactly to market expectations.
3. Reported earnings are viewed as a "*bad news*" earnings surprise because they fall below market expectations.[25]

Companies that report good news earnings (a positive earnings surprise) tend to have an upward drift in stock returns before the actual earnings announcement date (day 0 in Figure 6.4), followed by another stock return increase on announcement. The stock returns of companies reporting "bad news" earnings surprises exhibit a negative drift before the announcement, followed by another decrease in stock returns at the announcement date. Modest post-announcement drifts in stock returns are also not uncommon, especially when the earnings surprise is quite large.[26] Quarterly earnings announcements that contain "no news" lead to stock returns that hover around zero before and after announcement.

It's easy to explain why stock prices sometimes exhibit a positive or negative drift *before* the actual earnings announcement date. Take the case of General Motors. Investors learn about the company's automobile sales on a weekly basis and therefore can anticipate fairly well the actual quarterly earnings number prior to its formal announcement by GM. The fact that GM's stock price changes at the announcement date indicates that not all the information contained in the earnings release is fully anticipated by investors. Small companies—and those followed by just a few securities analysts—tend to exhibit less pre-announcement stock return drift because investors usually have very limited information about the company and its earnings prospects for the quarter. Large companies, whose performance is tracked by many analysts, are more likely to exhibit the stock return behavior illustrated in Figure 6.4.

Stock price at any given point in time reflects investors' aggregate expectations about the company's future earnings. Information that changes investors' expectations about future earnings will cause prices to rise or fall depending on whether the information represents "good news" or "bad news." Research evidence demonstrates that quarterly and annual earnings announcements are important information events. Stock prices tend to increase (positive returns) or decrease (negative returns) when the reported earnings turn out to be greater (less) than expected. The amount of surprise conveyed by earnings announcements depends on the amount of pre-earnings announcement information about company operations that is provided in the financial press.

RECAP

Valuing a Business Opportunity (An Illustration)

Allen Ford's passion for literature motivated him to consider opening a neighborhood bookstore. Allen convinced a colleague who was an expert in market research to look at the economic viability of a general title neighborhood bookstore. The results of his analysis

---

[25] For research on the association between earnings surprises and stock returns, see R. Ball and P. Brown, "An Empirical Evaluation of Accounting Income Numbers," *Journal of Accounting Research* (Autumn 1968), pp. 159–178; and G. Foster, C. Olsen, and T. Shevlin, "Earnings Releases, Anomalies, and the Behavior of Security Returns," *The Accounting Review* (October 1984), pp. 574–603.

[26] A number of studies investigate whether post-earnings announcement drift provides opportunities to earn abnormal returns in the stock market. For a review of this literature, see V. Bernard, "Stock Price Reactions to Earnings Announcements: A Summary of Recent Anomalous Evidence and Possible Explanations," in R. Thaler (ed.), *Advances in Behavioral Finance* (New York: Russell Sage Foundation, 1992); and V. Bernard, J. Thomas, and J. Abarbanell, "How Sophisticated Is the Market in Interpreting Earnings News," *Journal of Applied Corporate Finance* (Summer 1993), pp. 54–63.

fueled Allen's enthusiasm: The market demographics were favorable, and there was little competition. Annual sales were projected to ultimately reach $350,000.

Allen rejected the notion of opening his own independent bookstore, and instead focused on several franchise opportunities. By affiliating with a national or regional company, Allen would enjoy brand name recognition, economies of scale in purchasing and advertising, and employee training and support programs. After investigating several possibilities, Allen settled on "The BookWorm," an expanding regional chain of franchised bookstores that emphasized convenience, price, selection, and neighborhood friendliness. Each store had a coffee bar surrounded by soft seating, with abundant natural light encouraging patrons to browse leisurely. This concept had a proven record of success in similar communities, and it appealed to Allen's tastes.

A BookWorm franchise could be established with a franchise investment of about $100,000, including the initial franchise fee of $21,000, fixtures of $20,000 to $25,000, and an inventory cost of $55,000 to $60,000. The inventory and fixtures would be purchased from the corporate parent, BookWorm, Inc. Corporate staff would conduct a site location study, assist in negotiating lease terms for retail space, help with store layout and renovation, train employees on operating policies and procedures, and provide all grand opening advertising and promotional materials. Once a new BookWorm franchise opens, the corporate parent receives royalties (typically as a percentage of sales) determined in accordance with a 15-year renewable franchise contract.

The prospectus that Allen obtained from the parent company contained the selected financial highlights for a typical BookWorm franchise store shown in Table 6.2. The notes accompanying the table indicated that store fixtures are depreciated over 10 years using the straight-line method; that the initial franchise fee is amortized over 15 years; that operating expenses include a competitive salary for a store manager; and that income taxes have been ignored because they are owner-specific, thus making them highly variable across locations.

With these financial projections and his understanding of the marketplace, Allen Ford must decide whether to invest $100,000 in a BookWorm franchise. Influencing the decision may be several nonfinancial considerations, such as the degree of confidence Allen has in BookWorm's corporate staff or the proposed interior design and ambiance of the shop. However, viewed through the stark lens of economics, Allen's decision problem simplifies to the standard net present value rule—invest if the estimated value of the franchise (adjusted for the risk of investment) exceeds its $100,000 cost. From trade sources, Allen learned that 16% was a reasonable estimate of the cost of equity capital for franchised neighborhood bookstores. Allen used two different approaches to estimate the value of the bookstore, relying on predictions contained in the **pro forma** (i.e., forecasted) financial statements whenever possible.

Table 6.2 ■ BOOKWORM FRANCHISE

Projected Sales, Earnings, Free Cash Flows, and Owner's Investment

	Year 1	Year 2	Year 3	Year 4	Year 5
Sales	$200,000	$250,000	$300,000	$325,000	$350,000
Franchise royalty (5%)	10,000	12,500	15,000	16,250	17,500
Pre-tax earnings	(6,832)	3,600	13,750	22,000	26,000
Free cash flows[1]	(3,000)	5,500	15,000	16,000	24,500
Assets at year-end	100,000	100,000	100,000	100,000	100,000
Owner's investment:					
Beginning of year	100,000	100,000	100,000	100,000	100,000
+ Pre-tax earnings	(6,832)	3,600	13,750	22,000	26,000
− Distribution to owner	6,832	(3,600)	(13,750)	(22,000)	(26,000)
= End of year	$100,000	$100,000	$100,000	$100,000	$100,000

[1] Free cash flows are cash from operations minus required capital expenditures.

The first approach, based on expected future *free cash flows,* is summarized in Table 6.3. Sales and free cash flow projections for Years 1 through 5 are taken directly from the pro forma financial statement data in Table 6.2. Allen believes that sales will remain flat after Year 5 and that free cash flows will average about $24,500 per year. These assumptions produce a Year 5 **terminal value** estimate of $153,125—that is, the present value (at the end of Year 5) of the perpetual $24,500 free cash flow per year, discounted at a 16% cost of equity capital.

When the terminal value at the end of Year 5 is discounted back to the present (beginning of Year 1) and added to the sum of the present value of expected free cash flows for Year 1 through Year 5, the result is a free cash flow value estimate for the bookstore of $104,517, as shown in Table 6.3. This amount is *greater* than Allen's required capital investment of $100,000—this means Allen will be earning a return in excess of 16% per year on his investment *if* he opens the bookstore and the financial projections underlying the valuation estimate prove correct.

A second approach for estimating the value of Allen's business opportunity relies on expected future *abnormal earnings*—the amount by which operating earnings each year exceed the dollar cost of capital for the bookstore. This valuation, also based on projections contained in the pro forma financial statements, is summarized in Table 6.4.

Part (a) of Table 6.4 summarizes the pro forma earnings forecasts for the bookstore. As before, Allen believes sales and pre-tax earnings will be flat beyond Year 5.

Part (b) describes the calculation of yearly abnormal earnings. First, the 16% "Cost of equity capital" is multiplied by the beginning book value of equity to produce a figure called **"Normal earnings"** in each year. The component "Normal earnings" is the profit level that investors (including Allen) demand from the business in order to earn their 16% per year required rate of return. Then "Normal earnings" is subtracted from "Projected pre-tax earnings" to produce an estimate of expected "Abnormal earnings" for each year.

In part (c), the Year 5 "Terminal value" estimate of $56,250 represents the present value (at the end of Year 5) of the perpetual $9,000 per year abnormal earnings flow from Year 6 to infinity, discounted at a 16% cost of equity capital. The present value (as of the beginning of Year 1) of all abnormal earnings sums to $4,517. This amount, when added to the $100,000 of capital required to start the business, yields a valuation estimate for the bookstore of $104,517. Once again, the analysis supports opening the bookstore.

> Before investing, Allen should perform a **sensitivity analysis** of the free cash flow and abnormal earnings valuation estimates. Sensitivity analysis involves constructing "best case" and "worst case" scenarios for the business that incorporate alternative assumptions about sales, costs, and competitor behavior. Each scenario produces financial forecasts that become the basis for revised free cash flow and abnormal earnings valuation estimates. In this way Allen could learn how alternative economic conditions might affect the bookstore's value and his return on investment.

Table 6.3 ■ BOOKWORM FRANCHISE

Valuation of Expected Future Cash Flows

	Year 1	Year 2	Year 3	Year 4	Year 5	Beyond Year 5
(a) Financial Projections						
Sales	$200,000	$250,000	$300,000	$325,000	$350,000	$350,000
Free cash flows	($3,000)	$ 5,500	$ 15,000	$ 16,000	$ 24,500	$ 24,500
As a percentage of sales	*−1.5%*	*2.2%*	*5.0%*	*4.9%*	*7.0%*	*7.0%*
					Estimated terminal value =	$24,500/0.16
(b) Valuation Estimate at 16%						
Expected future cash flow	($3,000)	$ 5,500	$ 15,000	$ 16,000	$ 24,500	$153,125
× Discount factor at 16%	0.86207	0.74316	0.64066	0.55229	0.47611	0.47611
= Present value of each flow	($2,586)	$ 4,087	$ 9,610	$ 8,837	$ 11,665	$ 72,904*
(c) Estimated Value (sum of all present values above)	$104,517					

* Rounded

Table 6.4 ■ BOOKWORM FRANCHISE

Valuation of Expected Abnormal Earnings

	Year 1	Year 2	Year 3	Year 4	Year 5	Beyond Year 5
(a) Financial Projections						
Sales	$200,000	$250,000	$300,000	$325,000	$350,000	$350,000
Pre-tax earnings (loss)	($ 6,832)	$ 3,600	$ 13,750	$ 22,000	$ 26,000	$ 25,000
As a Percentage of Sales	*−3.4%*	*1.4%*	*4.6%*	*6.8%*	*7.4%*	*7.1%*
(b) Computation of Abnormal Earnings						
Equity book value (beginning of year)	$100,000	$100,000	$100,000	$100,000	$100,000	$100,000
× Cost of equity capital = 16%	0.16	0.16	0.16	0.16	0.16	0.16
= Normal earnings	$ 16,000	$ 16,000	$ 16,000	$ 16,000	$ 16,000	$ 16,000
Projected pre-tax earnings (loss)	($ 6,832)	$ 3,600	$ 13,750	$ 22,000	$ 26,000	$ 25,000
× Normal earnings	(16,000)	(16,000)	(16,000)	(16,000)	(16,000)	(16,000)
= Abnormal earnings (loss)	($ 22,832)	($ 12,400)	($ 2,250)	$ 6,000	$ 10,000	$ 9,000
(c) Valuation Estimate at 16%				*Estimated terminal value* = $9,000/0.16		
Expected abnormal earnings (loss)	($ 22,832)	($ 12,400)	($ 2,250)	$ 6,000	$ 10,000	$ 56,250
× Discount factor at 16%	0.86207	0.74316	0.64066	0.55229	0.47611	0.47611
= Present value of each abnormal earnings flow	($ 19,683)	($ 9,215)	($ 1,441)	$ 3,314	$ 4,761	$ 26,781
(d) Sum of All Present Values	**$ 4,517**					
+ Capital to start the business	100,000					
= Estimated value	$104,517					

Cash Flow Analysis and Credit Risk

Equity investors analyze financial statements to determine the value of a firm's shares. Creditors, on the other hand, are primarily concerned with assessing a firm's ability to meet its debt obligations through timely payment of principal and interest. Commercial banks, insurance companies, pension funds, and other lenders form opinions about a company's **credit risk** by comparing current and future debt-service requirements to estimates of the company's current and expected future cash flows.

Financing the BookWorm Franchise After reviewing the investment opportunity, Allen Ford decided to purchase a BookWorm franchise. The evaluation process was lengthy; it included interviews with 10 current franchise owners. These interviews enabled Allen to gain a deeper understanding of the business and its key risks and success factors. He was able to identify several proven marketing and promotional strategies for launching the franchise. With this information and an assessment of local market conditions, Allen refined the financial projections supplied by the corporate parent, performed a valuation analysis, and concluded that the franchise was likely to earn an acceptable risk-adjusted rate of return over time. There was still one hurdle—financing a portion of the $100,000 franchise purchase price.

Allen needed a bank loan for two reasons. First, the total market value of Allen's personal investment portfolio was $50,000. Second, Allen's interviews with other franchise owners revealed that a $100,000 initial investment might not provide an adequate cash cushion for the first year of operations.

After describing to a local banker the business opportunity and his cash needs in the $50,000 to $100,000 range, Allen learned that ample funds were currently available at attractive interest rates. Allen was asked to complete a detailed loan application, including a personal credit history and business plan, and to prepare monthly earnings and cash flow projections for the first two years of franchise operations. Filled with optimism, Allen began assembling the financial and other information required and thinking about the kind of loan he would seek from the bank.

Traditional Lending Products

Commercial bank loans are a common source of cash for most companies today. These loans can be structured either as short-term or long-term, fixed or floating rate, payable on demand or with fixed maturity, and secured or unsecured.

Short-term Loans Loans with maturities of one year or less, called short-term loans, comprise more than half of all commercial bank loans. **Seasonal lines of credit** and special purpose loans are the most common short-term borrowing. Short-term loans are used primarily to finance working capital needs when inventory or receivables increase temporarily. They may be **secured** by the inventories or receivables themselves, or they may be **unsecured.** Loan repayment usually comes from the routine conversion of these current assets into cash.

> Seasonal lines of credit are commonly used by companies with sales cycles that are also seasonal (e.g., lawn and garden equipment retailers). These loans provide the cash to support increases in current assets during the peak selling period. The borrower draws on the seasonal credit line as funds are required and repays as seasonal sales produce net cash inflows. **Special purpose business loans** are often used to finance, on a temporary basis, increases in current assets resulting from unusual or unexpected circumstances.

Long-term Loans Called **term lending agreements,** long-term loans have a maturity of more than one year, with maturities ranging from two to five years being the most common. The principal and interest repayment schedule, along with other conditions of the loan, are detailed in a signed contractual agreement between the borrower and the bank. Term loans are often used to finance the purchase of fixed assets, the acquisition of another company, the refinancing of existing long-term debt, or permanent working capital needs. They are frequently secured by pledging the assets acquired with the loan proceeds, although lenders rarely look to asset liquidation as the primary source of funds for loan repayment. Scheduled principal and interest payments are generally presumed to come from the borrower's future operating cash flows.

Revolving Loans Revolving loans are a variation on the seasonal credit line. They have a commitment period extending beyond one year, and allow borrowing up to a maximum level at any time over the life of the loan. Revolving loans are often used to finance cash imbalances that arise in day-to-day operations, seasonal needs, or permanent working capital needs when normal trade credit is inadequate to support a company's sales volume. Borrowers have the right to *prepay* the revolving loan and later re-borrow those funds, but they must comply with the terms and conditions specified in the loan agreement. The interest rate on the revolving line of credit is usually the bank's prime lending rate plus an additional percentage, and the rate will usually change (or "float") as the prime rate rises or falls over the life of the credit line. In addition to interest, the borrower pays a "commitment fee" that is based on the total amount of the credit extended.

Commercial banks are not the only source of debt financing for businesses. Another source of financing is **commercial paper**—short-term notes sold directly to investors by large and highly rated companies. These notes usually mature in 270 days or less and carry a fixed interest rate. Because commercial paper is issued directly to investors and is usually secured by a bank credit line, the interest rate the company pays is often significantly below the rate a bank would charge for a direct loan.

> The word **bond** is commonly used to refer to all kinds of secured and unsecured debt although, strictly speaking, a bond is a secured debt. A **debenture** is an unsecured bond, one in which no specific pledge of property is made, although the debenture holder does have a claim on property not otherwise pledged as collateral or security. The term **note** is generally used for unsecured debt instruments issued with an original maturity of 10 years or less.

Long-term forms of public debt financing include bonds, debentures, or notes. Long-term debt securities are promises made by the issuing company to pay principal when due and to make timely interest payments on the unpaid balance. Bonds can have numerous special features. For example, **secured bonds** specify collateral that protects the bondholder if and when the borrower defaults. Other bonds contain **seniority** features that specify which bondholders will be paid first in the event of bankruptcy. Some may contain **sinking fund provisions** that require the borrowing company to make annual payments to the trustee, who then uses the funds to retire a portion of the debt prior to its maturity. Still others may contain **call provisions,** which allow the company to repurchase or "call" part or all of the debt issue at stated prices over a specific period.

Regardless of the special features attached, virtually all bonds or notes contain numerous **protective covenants** designed to protect the interests of the creditor. These covenants place restrictions on the borrower's activity and are described in the **indenture,** a written agreement between the borrowing company and its creditors. The role that accounting numbers play in these debt covenants is discussed in Chapter 7.

Credit Analysis

To lend funds to a company, a commercial loan officer of a bank must first evaluate the prospective borrower's ability to repay the proposed loan at maturity. This evaluation typically involves financial analysis and includes the preparation of forecasted financial statements, "due diligence" (a qualitative assessment of the business, its customers and suppliers, and management's character and capability), and analysis of credit risk.

Financial analysis of a potential borrower begins with an understanding of the firm, its business, its key risks and success factors, and the competitive dynamics of the industry. Next, an evaluation of the quality of its accounting earnings and financial reporting choices is made to determine whether traditional ratios and statistics derived from the financial statements can be relied on to measure accurately the company's economic performance and financial condition. Lenders and credit analysts frequently adjust reported financial statement numbers. For example, nonrecurring gains and losses and other transitory components of earnings are removed from the reported bottom-line earnings number to arrive at a measure of operating performance that is more representative of a firm's long-run sustainable profitability. Off-balance sheet obligations (e.g., operating lease commitments) are frequently added to a firm's reported debt. Finally, other adjustments are made to improve the comparability of the financial data across potential loan candidates.

The next step is evaluating the company's profit performance and balance sheet strength. Financial, operating, and leverage ratios (discussed in Chapter 5) as well as trends in revenues and expenses are examined and compared to industry averages. This phase of the analysis identifies positive and negative changes in the prospective borrower's profitability, financial health, and industry position. However, the historical performance and condition of the borrower is only a partial indication of creditworthiness. Loan approval is largely determined by the borrower's ability to repay the proposed loan from *future* operating cash flows. ***Consequently, an estimate of the company's future financial condition is indispensable to most lending decisions.***

Pro forma (i.e., "as if") financial statements are prepared by the credit analyst to assess the borrower's ability to generate sufficient cash flows to make interest and principal payments when due.[27] These projections incorporate the analyst's understanding of the company's plans and business strategy, the potential responses of rival companies, and factors that shape the prospective borrower's economic environment. The pro forma financial statements and their underlying assumptions are then tested to establish the borrower's vulnerability to changing economic circumstances. This testing involves examining plausible "worst-case" scenarios that indicate just how poorly the company can perform before it defaults. This enables the analyst to gauge the company's **financial flexibility**—that is, the

[27] Techniques for constructing financial statement forecasts are described in T. Copeland, et al., op. cit.; K. Palepu, V. Bernard, and P. Healy, *Business Analysis and Valuation* (Cincinnati, OH: South-Western Publishing, 2000); and C. Stickney and P. Brown, *Financial Statement Analysis: A Strategic Perspective* (Fort Worth, TX: Dryden Press, 1999).

degree to which the company can satisfy its cash needs during periods of fiscal stress by drawing on existing credit lines, accessing capital markets, curtailing discretionary cash expenditures, or selling assets.

Due diligence evaluation is like "kicking the tires" of the prospective borrower by conducting plant tours, trade checks, and interviews with competitors, suppliers, customers, and employees. Comprehensive due diligence may also include asset appraisals, reviews of the company's other debt obligations, internal controls, planned capital expenditures, potential environmental liabilities, and other matters that bear on the company's future success and ability to repay debt at maturity.

The final step of credit analysis is a **comprehensive risk assessment** that involves evaluating and summarizing the various individual risks associated with the loan. Some risks will be unique to the specific borrower; others will be associated with potential changes in the economy or industry, new regulations, or unanticipated events. The credit analyst evaluates the severity of each risk in terms of (1) its probability of occurrence, (2) how it could affect the borrower's ability or willingness to repay, and (3) the bank's estimated costs if the borrower defaults.

Credit evaluations performed by rating agencies such as Standard & Poor's or Moody's involve procedural steps similar to those described here for commercial bank loans. Ratings are assigned to long-term debt, medium-term notes, and commercial paper based on analysts' evaluations of (1) the likelihood of default, (2) the nature and provisions of the debt, and (3) the protection afforded debtholders in the event of bankruptcy. See *Corporate Finance Criteria* (New York: Standard & Poor's, 1994).

If the prospective borrower is judged to be creditworthy, the final terms and conditions of the loan are negotiated with the borrower. Obviously, lenders are compensated for anticipated credit risks through the interest rate charged on the loan. The yield on a loan must be sufficient to cover the lender's (1) cost of borrowing funds; (2) costs of administering, monitoring, and servicing the loan; (3) normal (competitive) return on the equity capital needed to support the bank's lending operations; and (4) premium for exposure to default risk. Collateralized loans or loans with personal guarantees lower credit risk and enable lenders to lower the borrower's cost of debt.

Interpretation of Cash Flow Components

Cash flow analyses and forecasts are central to all credit evaluations and lending decisions. A company's obligation to make interest and principal payments cannot be satisfied out of earnings, because earnings includes many noncash accruals and deferrals. Rather, payment has to be made with cash! Consider the situation confronting your client, G. T. Wilson Company.

Wilson Company has been a client of your bank for over 40 years. The company owns and operates nearly 850 retail furniture stores throughout the United States and has over 38,000 employees. Sales and earnings growth have exceeded the industry average until recently, and the company has paid dividends consistently for almost 100 years. Prior to 1992 Wilson built its reputation on sales of moderately priced upholstered furniture, case goods (wooden tables, chairs, and bookcases), and decorative accessories. The company's stores were located in large, urban centers where occupancy costs were quite low. Increased competition and changing consumer tastes caused Wilson to alter its strategy beginning in 1992. One aspect of this strategic shift involved expanding the company's product line to include higher quality furniture, consumer electronics, and home entertainment systems. To complement this expanded product line, Wilson also introduced a credit card system so that customers could more easily pay for their purchases. Wilson used commercial paper, bank loans, and trade credit to finance the growth of receivables and inventories. The company's strategy also focused on closing unprofitable downtown stores; at the same time it chose to expand by opening new stores in suburban shopping centers.

Your bank has extended two loans to Wilson, a \$50 million secured construction loan that matures in 2004, and a \$200 million revolving credit line that is currently up for renewal. Wilson has always complied with the terms of the revolving line-of-credit, but the company's borrowing has been at or near the maximum amount allowed for the past two years. Exhibit 6.1 presents comparative cash flow statements for the company and Exhibit 6.2 on page 258 reports selected financial statistics. What do these cash flow statements and summary statistics tell us about the company's credit risk?

Exhibit 6.1 ■ G. T. WILSON COMPANY

Comparative Statements of Cash Flow

($ in thousands)	1992	1993	1994	1995	1996	1997	1998	1999	2000
				Year Ended January 31					
Operating									
Net income	$ 31,600	$ 33,000	$ 38,200	$ 41,900	$ 36,400	$ 31,600	$ 34,950	$ 10,900	($145,400)
Depreciation	7,500	8,200	8,400	9,000	9,600	10,600	12,000	13,600	14,600
Other adjustments to income	70	(850)	(1,100)	(1,600)	(2,500)	(1,800)	(1,700)	(1,350)	(17,000)
(Increase) Decrease in receivables	(57,700)	(42,000)	(40,300)	(55,500)	(12,000)	(49,900)	(60,300)	(72,200)	9,600
(Increase) in inventories	(23,300)	(9,100)	(24,900)	(13,500)	(38,400)	(38,200)	(100,850)	(51,100)	(4,350)
(Increase) Decrease in prepayments	(450)	100	(400)	(650)	(200)	(150)	(1,250)	(650)	700
Increase (Decrease) in accounts payable	17,600	3,800	22,400	2,050	13,900	6,900	(12,100)	(8,000)	42,400
Increase (Decrease) in other current liabilities	8,100	11,900	8,500	15,400	(21,900)	13,900	14,950	15,650	(1,500)
Cash flow from operations	**($16,580)**	**$ 5,050**	**$ 10,800**	**($ 2,900)**	**($15,100)**	**($27,050)**	**($114,300)**	**($93,150)**	**($100,950)**
Investing									
Acquisition of property, plant, and equipment	(15,250)	(7,800)	(10,600)	(14,400)	(16,100)	(25,900)	(26,250)	(23,150)	(15,500)
Acquisition of investments	(250)	(400)	–	–	(450)	(6,000)	(2,200)	(5,700)	(5,300)
Cash flow from investing	**($15,500)**	**($ 8,200)**	**($10,600)**	**($14,400)**	**($16,550)**	**($31,900)**	**($ 28,450)**	**($28,850)**	**($ 20,800)**
Financing									
Increase (Decrease) in short-term borrowing	60,300	1,600	18,900	64,000	64,300	(8,650)	152,300	63,050	147,600
Increase (Decrease) in long-term borrowing	–	(1,500)	(1,500)	(1,650)	(1,500)	98,450	(1,600)	93,900	(4,000)
Increase (Decrease) in capital stock	2,700	4,000	850	(17,900)	(8,900)	7,400	(8,200)	1,800	850
Dividends	(14,100)	(14,400)	(17,700)	(19,700)	(20,800)	(21,100)	(21,150)	(21,100)	(4,500)
Cash flow from financing	**$ 48,900**	**($10,300)**	**$ 550**	**$ 24,750**	**$ 33,100**	**$ 76,100**	**$ 121,350**	**$137,650**	**$ 139,950**
Other	(450)	(400)	(100)	–	(400)	(1,350)	2,450	(650)	(700)
Change in cash	**$ 16,370**	**($13,850)**	**$ 650**	**$ 7,450**	**$ 1,050**	**$ 15,800**	**$ (18,950)**	**$ 15,000**	**$ 17,500**

Cash Flow From Operations A company's "cash flow from operations" is the amount of cash it was able to generate from ongoing core business activities. Generating cash from operations is essential to the long-term economic viability of the business. However, not every company can be expected to produce positive operating cash flows every year. Even financially healthy companies must sometimes spend more cash on their operating activities than they receive from customers.

The comparative cash flow statements in Exhibit 6.1 show that Wilson produced positive operating cash flows in 1993 and 1994. Since then, its operating cash flows have been consistently negative and declining, with the average level for the last three years approximately equal to *minus* $100 million. This sharply contrasts with the company's sales and earnings performance as shown in Exhibit 6.2 on the next page. Sales have grown steadily from $920 million in 1992 to $1.85 billion in 1999, with a small decline in 2000. Net income (shown in Exhibit 6.1) increased from $31.6 million in 1992 to a peak of $41.9 million in 1995, followed by three years of relative stability where earnings averaged about $33 million each year. Net income declined in 1999 to $10.9 million, and the company reported a $145.4 million loss in 2000.

Exhibit 6.2 ■ G. T. WILSON COMPANY

Selected Financial Statistics

	Year Ended January 31								
	1992	1993	1994	1995	1996	1997	1998	1999	2000
Operations									
Sales ($ millions)	$920	$980	$1,095	$1,210	$1,250	$1,375	$1,665	$1,850	$1,762
Number of new stores (net of closures)	4	6	13	21	52	40	37	41	21
Gross profit/sales	31.8%	32.1%	32.8%	33.0%	36.5%	35.8%	35.3%	35.1%	30.1%
Selling, general, and administrative/sales	24.8%	25.1%	25.2%	25.2%	29.9%	30.7%	30.6%	30.4%	41.3%
Net income/sales	3.4%	3.4%	3.5%	3.5%	2.9%	2.3%	2.1%	0.6%	−8.3%
Dividends/net income	44.6%	43.6%	46.3%	47.0%	57.1%	66.8%	60.5%	193.6%	−3.1%
Short-term Liquidity									
Current assets/current liabilities	3.7	3.6	3.3	3.4	3.7	4.6	4.5	5.0	6.2
Operating cash flows as a % of sales	−1.8%	0.5%	1.0%	−0.2%	−1.2%	−2.0%	−6.9%	−5.0%	−5.7%
Days receivable	91.3	95.3	104.1	115.1	126.2	131.1	130.5	140.0	142.5
Allowance for uncollectibles (%)	3.8%	4.1%	3.8%	4.0%	3.6%	3.2%	2.8%	3.0%	3.3%
Days inventory	100.9	100.2	102.7	104.3	112.8	117.1	129.6	131.2	130.5
Days payable	42.4	42.5	48.6	45.7	48.9	47.1	33.6	30.7	42.6
Long-term Solvency									
Total debt as a % of assets	32.7%	29.3%	25.9%	30.8%	37.3%	41.8%	49.8%	56.4%	75.7%
Interest coverage	8.8	8.1	8.7	6.4	4.7	4.5	3.9	1.2	(2.4)
Short-term debt as a % of total debt	33.3%	46.5%	59.4%	70.8%	81.6%	64.0%	75.8%	70.0%	78.3%

What aspects of Wilson's operations consumed cash during the company's profitable years? Exhibit 6.1 shows that the primary factors contributing to the company's negative operating cash flows are increases in accounts receivable and increases in inventories. Some growth in receivables and inventories is to be expected because of the company's decision to expand its product line and to introduce a customer credit card. However, increases in receivables or inventories can sometimes signal unfavorable business conditions. For example, the average collection period for customer accounts (days receivables in Exhibit 6.2) increased from 91.3 days in 1992 to 142.5 days in 2000. This trend could reflect expanded credit card use, more lenient credit policies toward customers, or a deterioration in customers' ability to pay. Similarly, the increase in days inventory (Exhibit 6.2) from 100.9 in 1992 to 130.5 in 2000 could be due to product line extensions, escalating merchandise costs, or slack consumer demand. The credit analyst must evaluate each possible explanation to discover what economic forces are responsible for the company's negative operating cash flows and whether positive cash flows from operating activities are likely to be generated in the future.

> It is interesting to note that Wilson's allowance for uncollectibles actually declined in percentage terms after 1995 (Exhibit 6.2) even though the average collection period increased. Why do you suppose this happens?

A business that spends more cash on its operating activities than it generates must find ways to finance the operating cash shortfall. Typically, this means using up cash reserves, borrowing additional cash, issuing additional equity, or liquidating investments like real estate and other fixed assets. None of these options can be sustained for prolonged periods of time. For example, Wilson could finance the company's continued operating cash flow deficit by selling some retail stores. Doing this might jeopardize the company's ability to generate positive operating cash flows in the future. Similarly, creditors are unlikely to keep lending to a business that continuously does not generate an acceptable level of cash flow from its operations. In this regard, Wilson's inability to generate positive operating cash flows in recent years is troublesome.

Investing Activities In this section of the cash flow statement, companies disclose capital expenditures, acquisitions of other firms, and investments in marketable securities. Of course, disinvestment generates cash (examples include the sale of equipment or investment securities).

The cash flow statements of Wilson Company (Exhibit 6.1) show sustained investment in property, plant, and equipment that is consistent with the company's expansion into new stores (Exhibit 6.2). Analysts should carefully investigate the capital expenditures of the company and any fixed asset retirements during the year. Capital expenditures and asset sales should be consistent with the company's business strategy and growth opportunities. For example, consider the following scenarios.

- *Emerging companies* require substantial investments in property, plant, and equipment at a stage when operating cash flows are typically negative.
- *Established growth companies* also require substantial fixed asset investments to further expand their market presence. Operating cash flows for established growth companies can be positive or negative depending on the pace of expansion, the degree to which expansion also requires working capital investment, and the ability of the company to generate a positive operating cash flow from established markets.
- *Mature companies'* capital expenditures, on the other hand, are limited to the amount needed to sustain current levels of operation. Mature companies usually rely on internal sources (operating cash flows and fixed asset sales) to finance their capital expenditure needs.

Changes in a company's capital expenditures or fixed asset sales over time must be carefully analyzed. For example, a sharp reduction in capital expenditures for an emerging growth company may indicate that the company is suffering from a temporary cash shortage. Decreased capital expenditures may also signal a more fundamental change in management's expectations about the company's growth opportunities and competitive environment. Similarly, an unexplained increase in fixed asset sales could mean that management needs to raise cash quickly or that it is eliminating excess production capacity. The analyst needs to evaluate each of these possibilities because they have very different implications for the company's future operating cash flows.

Financing Activities The most significant source of external financing for most companies is debt. There is a large research literature in finance which explores the "optimal" amount of debt financing that companies should include in their capital structure. Determining this optimal debt level involves a tradeoff between two competing economic forces—taxes and bankruptcy costs.[28] The advantage of debt financing is that interest on debt is tax deductible. The disadvantage is that highly leveraged firms have a greater risk of bankruptcy. The precise point at which these two forces counterbalance one another varies from company to company and over time. One way analysts can assess the optimal level of debt is to evaluate the company's historical and estimated future ability to meet scheduled debt payments. In this regard the situation at G. T. Wilson Company would appear bleak.

The financing section of Wilson's cash flow statements (Exhibit 6.1) reveals a heavy reliance on short-term debt to finance the company's capital expenditures and operating cash flow deficits. The company issued $98.45 million of long-term debt in 1997 and $93.9 million in 1999. But the vast majority of Wilson's external financing has been in the form of short-term debt. Total debt as a percentage of assets (Exhibit 6.2) has grown from 32.7% in 1992 to 75.7% in 2000; short-term debt as a percentage of total debt has increased from 33.3% in 1992 to 78.3% in 2000; and the company's interest coverage ratio has deteriorated from 8.8 times to *minus* 2.4 times.

---

[28] See Ross, Westerfield, and Jaffe, op. cit., Ch. 16. These and other authors identify a third economic force that influences firms' capital structure decisions—that is, agency costs. These costs are considered in more detail in Chapter 7.

Wilson's cash flow needs and growing debt burden raise questions about the wisdom of its dividend policy. Recall that Wilson has paid cash dividends to shareholders for almost 100 years, and it continued to do so during 2000 when the company reported a $145.4 million loss. Cash dividend payments totaled $14.1 million in 1992, grew to $20.8 million in 1996, and then held steady at that level until falling to $4.5 million in 2000. These cash flows could instead have been used to finance the company's operating deficits and capital expenditures—or to pay down debt.

Why was management so reluctant to curtail dividends? The payment of a cash dividend is viewed as an important signal by many financial analysts and investors. Management presumably "signals" its expectations about the future through its dividend policy. A cash dividend increase is viewed as an indication that management expects future operating cash flows to be favorable—to the extent it can sustain the higher dividend. A reduction in cash dividends is interpreted as an indication that management expects future operating cash flows to decrease and remain at this decreased level. Research tends to corroborate dividend signaling. Increases and decreases in cash dividend payments are (on average) associated with subsequent earnings and operating cash flow changes in the same direction. Of course, the degree of association between dividend changes and future earnings or operating cash flow performance is less than perfect. So, financial analysts and investors must evaluate carefully the specific circumstances confronting each company.

This illustration is based loosely on the financial statements of a real company, W. T. Grant for the years 1967 through 1975. At the time that it filed for bankruptcy in late 1975, Grant was the seventeenth largest retailer in the United States. The company's collapse has been traced to a failed business strategy that involved rapid store expansion, product line extensions, and customer credit terms that contributed to delayed payment and increased customer default risk.[29]

RECOMMENDATION Wilson's use of short-term debt financing, coupled with its inability to generate positive cash flows from operations, places the company in a precarious position. Unless other external sources of financing are identified or unless operating activities start to generate positive cash flows, the company will be forced to declare bankruptcy if (and when) short-term creditors demand payment on existing loans. Wilson Company is a serious credit risk to the bank, and renewal of the $200 million revolving credit line is probably not justified. In fact, the bank may consider taking immediate steps to improve the likelihood of loan repayment and to protect its creditor position in the event of bankruptcy.

Timing differences between cash inflows and cash outflows create the need to borrow money. Cash flow analysis helps lenders identify why cash flow imbalances occur and whether the imbalance is temporary. Commercial banks, insurance companies, pension funds, and other lenders will lend the needed cash only if there is a high probability that the borrower's future cash inflows will be sufficient to repay the loan. Credit analysts rely on their understanding of the company, its business strategy and the competitive environment, and the adequacy of its past cash flows as a basis for forecasting future cash flows and assessing the company's financial flexibility under stress.

RECAP

SUMMARY

In *Concepts Statement No. 1,* the FASB sets forth the primary objectives of financial reporting. One of those objectives states:

> Financial reporting should provide information to help present and potential investors and creditors and others in assessing the amounts, timing and uncertainty of prospective cash receipts from dividends or interest and the proceeds from the sale, redemption, or maturity of securities or loans. Since investors' and creditors' cash flows are related to enterprise cash flows, financial reporting should provide informa-

[29] See J. Largay and C. Stickney, "Cash Flows, Ratio Analysis and the W. T. Grant Company Bankruptcy," *Financial Analysts Journal* (July–August, 1980), pp. 51–84.

tion to help investors, creditors, and others assess the amounts, timing, and uncertainty of prospective net cash inflows to the related enterprise.[30]

This chapter provides a framework for understanding how financial reporting meets this important objective. Specifically, we show how accounting numbers are used in valuation, cash flow analysis, and credit risk assessment. Alternative valuation models and approaches to credit risk assessment are presented to illustrate what it means to "assess the amounts, timing, and uncertainty of prospective net cash inflows" of a business.

A critical part of understanding the **decision-usefulness** of accounting information—a major focus of this book—is understanding *which* accounting numbers are used, *why* they are used, and *how* they are used in investment and credit decisions. Knowing how earnings, book values, and cash flows are used in investment and credit decisions will help you to evaluate the alternative accounting measures discussed in subsequent chapters of this book—not only those recognized in the financial statements but also those disclosed outside the financial statements in footnotes.

Knowing what, why, and how accounting numbers are used in investment and credit decisions also helps us understand the incentives that management has for structuring transactions in certain ways or for choosing among alternative GAAP treatments for a particular transaction. We will come back to this point repeatedly as we explore the underlying economics of business transactions and the alternative accounting methods used to describe those transactions.

APPENDIX A Abnormal Earnings Valuation

This Appendix illustrates how the abnormal earnings valuation model can be combined with security analysts' published earnings forecasts to produce an **intrinsic stock price estimate** for a company. To make this illustration real, we focus on Reebok International Ltd. and those analysts' earnings forecasts that were available in March 2000 when the company's common stock was trading at $9.25 per share. Then we show how this valuation model can also be used to understand the market's expectations for an Internet company, Amazon.com.

Reebok (named after the *reebok*, a swift and agile African gazelle) entered the U.S. market in 1979 following several decades of success as a designer and manufacturer of high-performance running shoes sold in the United Kingdom. By merging high-performance technology with style and fashion, the company successfully rode the sports and fitness wave in the United States in the mid-1980s. In 1989 Reebok introduced "The Pump" technology into its basketball shoes. Today, the company continues to emphasize both high performance and fashion in its products.

SHARE PRICE VALUATION There are five steps to deriving a share price estimate using analysts' earnings forecasts and the abnormal earnings valuation model:

1. Obtain analysts' earnings-per-share (EPS) forecasts for some finite horizon, say the next five years.
2. Combine the EPS forecasts with projected dividends to forecast common equity book value over the horizon.
3. Compute yearly *abnormal* earnings by subtracting *normal* earnings (i.e., beginning equity book value multiplied by the equity cost of capital) from analysts' EPS forecasts.
4. Forecast the perpetual (terminal year) *abnormal* earnings flow that will occur beyond the explicit forecast horizon.
5. Add the current book value and the present value of the two abnormal earnings components—the first five years and for years beyond the terminal period—to obtain an intrinsic value estimate of the company's share price.

Each of these steps is illustrated in the Reebok valuation in Table 6.5.

[30] "Objectives of Financial Reporting by Business Enterprises," *Statement of Financial Accounting Concepts No. 1* (Stamford, CT: FASB, 1978), p. viii.

Table 6.5 ■ REEBOK INTERNATIONAL LTD.

Abnormal Earnings Valuation as of March 1, 2000

	Historical Results		Forecasted Results					
	1998	1999	2000	2001	2002	2003	2004	Beyond 2004
(a) Earnings Forecasts								
Reported earnings per share[1]	$1.04	$1.30						
Last year's earnings per share			$ 1.30	$ 1.19	$ 1.39	$ 1.53	$ 1.69	
× (1 + Forecasted earnings growth)			0.9154	1.1681	1.1020	1.1020	1.1020	
= Forecasted earnings per share			$ 1.19	$ 1.39	$ 1.53	$ 1.69	$ 1.86	
(b) Equity Book Value Forecasts								
Equity book value at beginning of year	$8.99	$9.56	$ 9.40	$10.59	$11.98	$13.51	$15.20	
+ Earnings per share from (a)	1.04	1.30	1.19	1.39	1.53	1.69	1.86	
+ Stock issued (repurchased)	0.03	(0.24)	0.00	0.00	0.00	0.00	0.00	
+ Other comprehensive income per share	(0.50)	(1.22)	0.00	0.00	0.00	0.00	0.00	
− Dividends per share	0.00	0.00	0.00	0.00	0.00	0.00	0.00	
= Equity book value at year-end	$9.56	$9.40	$10.59	$11.98	$13.51	$15.20	$17.06	
ROE = EPS/Equity book value at beginning of year	11.6%	13.6%	12.7%	13.1%	12.8%	12.5%	12.2%	
(c) Abnormal Earnings								
Equity book value at beginning of year	$8.99	$9.56	$ 9.40	$10.59	$11.98	$13.51	$15.20	
× Equity cost of capital	13.0%	13.0%	13.0%	13.0%	13.0%	13.0%	13.0%	
= Normal earnings	$1.17	$1.24	$ 1.22	$ 1.38	$ 1.56	$ 1.76	$ 1.98	
Actual or forecasted earnings	$1.04	$1.30	$ 1.19	$ 1.39	$ 1.53	$ 1.69	$ 1.86	
− Normal earnings	1.17	1.24	1.22	1.38	1.56	1.76	1.98	
= Abnormal earnings	($0.13)	$0.06	($ 0.03)	$ 0.01	($ 0.03)	($ 0.07)	($ 0.12)	
(d) Valuation								
Future abnormal earnings in forecast horizon			($ 0.03)	$ 0.01	($ 0.03)	($ 0.07)	($ 0.12)	
× Discount factor at 13%			0.88496	0.78315	0.69305	0.61332	0.54276	
= Abnormal earnings discounted to present			($ 0.03)	$ 0.01	($ 0.02)	($ 0.04)	($ 0.06)	
Abnormal earnings in year 2005[2]								($ 0.12)
Assumed long-term growth rate								3.0%
Perpetuity factor for year 2004								10.0
Discount factor at 13%								0.54276
Present value of terminal year abnormal earnings[3]								($ 0.67)
(e) Estimated Share Price								
Sum of discounted abnormal earnings over horizon			($ 0.14)					
+ Present value of terminal year abnormal earnings			(0.67)					
= Present value of all abnormal earnings			(0.81)					
+ Current equity book value			9.40					
= Estimated current share price at March 1, 2000			$ 8.59					
Actual share price at March 1, 2000			$ 9.25					

[1] Adjusted for nonrecurring gains and losses.
[2] This is forecasted abnormal earnings for 2004, multiplied by one plus the long-term growth rate: ($0.12) × (1 + .03) = ($0.1236), or ($0.12) rounded.
[3] This is just ($0.1236) × 10.0 × 0.54276 = ($0.6709), or ($0.67) rounded.

Our forecast horizon—and the one used by analysts covering the company—is the five-year period from 2000 through 2004. There are at least three reasons why analysts focus on the short- to intermediate-term forecast horizon in valuing a company. First, competitive pressures make it difficult for the company to sustain growth in sales, profits, and cash flows in the long run. Thus, it is unrealistic to forecast that a growing company can maintain high short-term growth rates for an indefinite period. Second, long-range projections are more uncertain and, therefore, subject to greater error. Simply put, projected earnings or dividend payouts to shareholders become less and less reliable the farther removed they are from the current forecast date. And third, because of the time value of money, the discounted present values of future abnormal earnings (or free cash) flows become smaller as the forecast horizon increases. In other words, longer range forecasts simply do not matter very much in terms of determining current share price. For example, the present value of a dollar received 25 years from now discounted at 15%—a very realistic estimate for the cost of equity capital—is equal to $\$1 \div (1 + .15)^{25} = \$0.03$.

In late March 2000 securities analysts who covered Reebok were forecasting EPS of $1.19 for 2000 and $1.39 for 2001. These same analysts were forecasting annual EPS growth of 10.2% for 2002 through 2004. Based on the company's projected EPS of $1.39 for 2001, this means that analysts were forecasting 2002 EPS of $1.53 (or $1.39 × 1.1020). These same analysts were forecasting 2003 EPS of $1.69 (or $1.53 × 1.1020), and so on. These EPS forecasts are presented in part (a) of Table 6.5.

Next, we need to compute the book value of common equity for each year of the five-year forecast horizon. From the historical information contained in part (b) of the table, we learn that Reebok has not been paying dividends for the last two years or buying back much of its common stock. We assume that no dividend distributions or additional stock repurchases will occur over the next five years. These assumptions are combined with the EPS forecasts from part (a) to produce the equity book value forecasts of $10.59 per share at the end of 2000 and $17.06 per share at the end of 2004.

The abnormal earnings calculation for each of the five years in our forecast horizon are shown in part (c) of Table 6.5. Here, "normal" earnings are subtracted from the annual EPS forecasts. Normal earnings are just Reebok's common equity book value at the *beginning* of each year—as computed in part (b)—multiplied by the company's cost of equity capital, which is 13%.[31] For example, the −$0.03 per share of abnormal earnings for 2000 is simply analysts' $1.19 EPS forecast minus the $1.22 normal earnings (13% × $9.40 beginning equity book value) for the year.

These abnormal earnings forecasts from part (c) become the basic inputs to the valuation calculation in part (d), where abnormal earnings are discounted at the company's 13% equity cost of capital. A *terminal value* calculation intended to represent the value of the company's abnormal earnings flow beyond our five-year forecast horizon is also shown in part (d). To arrive at this terminal value estimate, we assume that Reebok's abnormal earnings of −$0.12 in 2004 will continue to grow by 3% each year for the foreseeable future.[32] The present value of this growing perpetual flow at the beginning of 2005 is −$1.236, which is the 2004 earnings multiplied by one plus the long-term growth rate (1 + 0.03), and then multiplied again by the perpetuity factor 10.0.[33] This quantity is then discounted using the present value factor for five periods discounted at 13% (0.54276), which translates the present value of abnormal earnings at the beginning of 2005 into a current day present value of −$0.67. Part (e) shows that the sum of all discounted abnormal earnings flows (−$0.81) plus the company's current equity book value ($9.40) produces an estimated share price of $8.59; this contrasts with Reebok's actual $9.25 share price.

What does this tell us? For one thing, Reebok's $9.25 per share stock price on March 1, 2000 was somewhat higher than that implied by securities analysts' five-year EPS and dividend payout forecasts coupled with our own predictions about earnings growth beyond the forecast horizon (year 2004). In this regard, Reebok's stock may appear to be somewhat overpriced in the marketplace. However, the market may have been anticipating abnormal earnings to stop declining beyond year 2004 and instead return to breakeven ($0.00) or

---

[31] This figure was derived from the capital asset pricing model (CAPM) using the then-current risk-free rate of 6.33% for 30-year treasury bonds, Reebok's equity beta of 1.10 as reported by *Zacks Investment Research,* and a long-term market risk premium of 6%. The CAPM formula applied to Reebok is:

$$6.33\% + (1.10 \times 6\%) = 12.93\% \text{ or about } 13\%.$$

[32] Because of competitive pressures, the assumed growth rate of abnormal earnings beyond year 2004 is less than the growth rate in abnormal earnings from 2000 to 2004, which averages 7.8%.

[33] This discount factor is equal to one divided by the difference between the equity cost of capital (13%) and the abnormal earnings growth rate (3%), or $1/(.13 - .03)$.

become slightly positive. The rub, of course, is that we cannot know at the time which of the forecasts will prove correct in the future.

The abnormal earnings valuation model in Table 6.5 can be used to value almost any publicly traded company. It's easy to implement because it requires just a handful of data items—earnings forecasts from analysts, a beginning book value of equity, forecasts of dividends and stock repurchases, an equity cost of capital (discount rate), and a long-term growth rate for abnormal earnings beyond the terminal year. But how well does it work?

There are several ways to answer this question. One approach compares the accuracy of stock price estimates from several different valuation models—for example, the abnormal earnings model versus the free cash flow valuation model. A recent study did just that using a sample of nearly 3,000 firm-year observations over 1989 through 1993.[34] Earnings, dividends and cash flow forecasts were gathered from *Value Line* for each sample firm and year. These forecasts were then used as inputs to an abnormal earnings valuation model (like the one in Table 6.5) and as inputs to a separate free cash flow valuation model. The two value estimates—one based on abnormal earnings and the other based on free cash flows—were then compared to actual stock prices. Which valuation model was best? Abnormal earnings value estimates were more accurate and explained more of the variation in actual stock prices than did free cash flow value estimates.

> In theory, both valuation models should produce the same stock price estimate. But in practice, the two valuation models often do not produce the same stock price estimate.

A related study asked if money can be made from the abnormal earnings valuation model in Table 6.5.[35] Using a sample of nearly 18,000 firm-year observations covering 1979 to 1991, the researchers computed valuation estimates for each firm and year. These estimates were then used to construct a *value index*—it's the estimated value divided by the actual share price—for each company and year. (The value index for Reebok would be \$8.59/\$9.25 = 0.929.) The simulated trading strategy involved "buying" the most undervalued companies (high value index) and "selling short" the most overvalued companies (low value index). This strategy produced a three-year portfolio return of 35%, which implies investors can profit from using the abnormal earnings valuation model.

Valuing a Dot-Com

"Trying to get your arms around the value of an Internet stock is like trying to hug the air."[36]

Determining a company's worth is difficult enough for firms like Reebok or Wal-Mart that have an established business model, a solid customer base, and a proven record of profits and cash flows. But how do you value an Internet company like Amazon.com—a company with no profits to date? Is Amazon.com really worth the \$40 billion the stock market gave it in December 1999 when the company's shares were selling for \$113 each? The \$6.7 billion the stock market gave it in January 2001 (\$19 per share)? Or, is it worth something else?

Internet stocks and other emerging growth companies are difficult to value using the free cash flow or abnormal earnings models described in this chapter. The problem is that these valuation methods require forecasts of future revenue growth, profit margins, cash investment needs, and other important inputs. But how do you forecast the future when it's a company with little history and an unproven business plan? Even thoughtful forecasts are still guesses, and a bad one will throw a valuation off-kilter—making the stock seem either too cheap or too expensive. To overcome this problem, some analysts have turned to so-called "new economy" valuation metrics (e.g., eyeballs, Internet time, and page views) intended to minimize the guesswork.[37]

---

[34] J. Francis, P. Olsson, and D. R. Oswald, "Comparing the Accuracy and Explainability of Dividends, Free Cash Flow, and Abnormal Earnings Equity Value Estimates," *Journal of Accounting Research* (Spring 2000), pp. 45–70.

[35] R. Frankel and C. Lee, "Accounting Valuation, Market Expectation, and Cross-Sectional Stock Returns," *Journal of Accounting and Economics* (June 1998), pp. 283–320.

[36] R. D. Hof, E. Neuborne and H. Green, "Internet Stocks: What's Their Real Worth," *Business Week* (December 14, 1998).

[37] N. Byrnes, "Eyeballs, Bah! Figuring Dot-Coms' Real Worth," *Business Week* (October 30, 2000).

Here's how one "new economy" valuation metric is used. Let's suppose 25.2 million people visited the Internet portal Yahoo! at least once in January. If you divide the number of Yahoo! visitors into the company's market capitalization of $18.4 billion—that's just January's $33 stock price multiplied by 558.4 million Yahoo! shares outstanding—you get a market value of $731 per visitor. In other words, the stock market says each Yahoo! visitor is worth $731. Compare that to one of Yahoo's rivals, Lycos Inc., where the numbers work out to be about $135 per visitor. According to analysts who use the new metrics, this disparity in visitor value means Yahoo! shares are expensive while Lycos shares are cheap—even though neither company is currently making a profit on its visitors!

A different approach to valuation turns the whole process on its head.[38] Instead of forecasting all the inputs to come up with a number for what the stock should be worth, this method starts with the stock price and works backward to answer the question: What kind of profitability and growth does this company have to deliver to justify the price? This method does not avoid making some assumptions, but it's a way to perform a reality check on the stock market.

To see how this approach works, let's take a closer look at Amazon.com. For the 12 months ended September 30, 2000, the company had a net loss of $1.2 billion on sales of $2.5 billion. (That's a loss of $0.48 on each sales dollar.) Amazon's stock price fell from a record $113 in December 1999 to $19 by January 2001. But even at the price of $19, the stock market had lofty expectations for the company—a one-year leap to profitability followed by revenue and earnings growth of 39% a year for the next 10 years, as we show you next.

To arrive at that conclusion, we derived the market-implied growth rate from the current stock price. Here's how. From our discussion earlier in this chapter, a company's market value has two components. One relates to assets in place and the other to future growth opportunities (see equation 6.9). In the context of the abnormal earnings valuation model, these two components are called *current operations value* (COV), a measure of the worth of the company as it now operates, and *future growth value* (FGV), a measure of the company's expected growth.

$$\text{Market value (MV)} = \text{Current operations value (COV)} + \text{Future growth value (FGV)}$$

Once you determine the COV—and that's the easier of the two—you can figure out the market-implied future growth value. And once you know the FGV, you can determine the implied revenue and earnings growth rate. Then you can make a judgment about whether that growth rate is achievable.

Sounds easy enough, although some aspects of the analysis can be troublesome. The details behind our Amazon.com calculations are in Table 6.6. To keep things simple, let's focus only on the highlights. First, we determine the company's *total* market value—the value of common stock, preferred stock, and debt. At the price of $19, Amazon's common stock is worth $6,762 million ($19 per share times the 355.9 million shares outstanding). The company has no preferred stock and $2,100 million in debt. So, the company's *total* market value is $8,862 million.

Next to be determined is the company's COV—what Amazon would be worth if there were no further growth. But hold on—it's not making money now. Sure, but that's because of large startup costs—dollars spent on information technology, e-commerce software, and on acquiring customers. Once those costs are out of the way, assume that the company will earn an operating margin of 10%. So, to determine COV, we will assume the company is now earning its average long-term margin and is thus profitable.

To get COV from the abnormal earnings valuation model, we start with expected sales for the next 12 months of $3,600 million (obtained from management or from analysts who follow the company—we used an analyst's forecast). Then we multiply the sales forecast by the long-term operating margin of 10% to arrive at expected operating profits

[38] G. Milano, "EVA and the 'New' Economy," *Journal of Applied Corporate Finance* (Summer 2000), pp. 118–28.

Table 6.6 ■ AMAZON.COM

Valuing an Internet Company

A. Determining the Market-Implied Growth Rate ($ in millions, except per share amounts)

(a) Market Value of the Company		
Stock price per share—January 2001	$19.00	
× Common shares outstanding (in millions)	355.9	
= Market value of common stock		$6,762
+ Value of preferred stock		—
+ Value of interest-bearing debt		2,100
= Market value of the company		$8,862
(b) Operating Assumptions and Capital		
Sales for the next 12 months	$3,600	
× Long-term average operating margin	10%	
= Long-term average NOPAT		$ 360
Book value of interest-bearing debt	$2,100	
+ Book value of stockholders' equity	(229)	
= Capital invested in the company	$1,871	
Cost of capital	15%	
Required NOPAT (rounded)		281
Abnormal NOPAT		$ 79
(c) Current Operations Value (COV)		
Abnormal NOPAT from current operations	$ 79	
÷ Cost of capital (discount rate)	15%	
= Value of abnormal NOPAT from current operations (rounded)	$ 529	
+ Current capital in the company	1,871	
= Current operations value of the company		$2,400
(d) Future Growth Value (FGV)		
Market value of the company		$8,862
Current operations value of the company		(2,400)
Future growth value of the company		$6,462
Implied annual growth rate		39.0%

B. Getting Behind the Numbers

The abnormal earnings valuation model is used as our benchmark for evaluating Amazon.com's $19 stock price. But two modifications are made to adapt the abnormal earnings valuation equation (6.11) for our purposes here. The first modification involves isolating the COV and FGV components of the model:

$$\begin{aligned} P_0 &= BV_0 + \sum_{t=1}^{\infty} \frac{E_0\,(\text{Abnormal earnings}_t)}{(1+r)^t} \\ &= BV_0 + \frac{E_0\,(\text{Current abnormal earnings})}{r} + FGV \\ &= COV + FGV \end{aligned} \tag{6.11}$$

The second modification is made because Amazon.com has a deficit balance in stockholders' equity. To overcome problems associated with a negative value for BV_0 and its impact on the abnormal earnings calculation, we redefine all components of the valuation model to reflect *total* capital (debt plus equity). A weighted-average cost of capital for debt and equity is used, with the cost of equity capital calculated as described in footnote 31.

The implied annual growth rate is found by solving a complex expression that equates FGV with the present value of abnormal earnings growth over a 10-year horizon.

(required NOPAT) of $360 million per year. Next, we need to find out how much capital—stockholders' equity and debt—is invested currently in the company. Amazon's most recent balance sheet showed $2,100 million of debt and a deficit of $229 million in stockholders' equity, so total capital is $1,871 million. What level of profits must the company generate to satisfy its debt and equity investors? To get that number, we need a cost of capital estimate so that we can compute *normal* earnings. Because the stock is volatile, we assume a high cost of capital—15% (footnote 31 describes our approach). The company thus needs to generate $281 million in earnings (or $1,871 million multiplied by 15%) to satisfy its investors. That's less than the $360 million of expected operating profits, so abnormal earnings are $79 million more than investors require ($360 million minus $281 million).

To get the COV, we divide expected abnormal earnings by 15%—which yields $529 million—and then add current investor capital of $1,871 million. This gives Amazon a current operations value of $2,400 million. With no future growth, that's what the company would be worth.

Now it's easy to determine Amazon's future growth value (FGV). We simply subtract $2,400 million from the total market value ($8,862 million), which gives an FGV of $6,462 million. How fast do revenues and operating profits have to grow over the next 10 years to give you a future growth value of $6,462 million? The answer is 39% a year, assuming margins of 10% and a 15% cost of capital.

Can Amazon achieve a 39% average annual revenue (and profit) growth rate over 10 years? That's where investors and analysts must turn to industry fundamentals and common sense. For instance, Amazon's sales would need to reach $96 billion, and its operating profits $9.6 billion, in 10 years. Is that realistic? Not if the company sells only books. The total of all U.S. retail book sales in 1999 was about $12 billion. Even if book sales expanded by 3% a year, total retail sales would be only around $16 billion ten years out. If Amazon captured the entire U.S. retail book market, it would still fall $86 billion short of the projected sales target.

Clearly, Amazon must sell more than just books if it is to achieve the market-implied growth rate. And it does sell more—including CDs, consumer electronics, and a variety of other items on a global basis. So, let's turn to Wal-Mart, a "bricks and mortar" retailer, for a different perspective on Amazon's growth prospects. Wal-Mart had sales of $165 billion and operating profits of $622 million in 1999. Can Amazon become more than half as large as Wal-Mart in 10 years? Some analysts clearly think so because the consensus five-year earnings growth rate forecast for Amazon was 41% in January 2001. On the other hand, as e-commerce draws more competitors—including Wal-Mart—it may be unrealistic to assume that Amazon can achieve the levels of growth and profitability needed to sustain its $19 stock price. Of the 29 Wall Street analysts who covered the company in January 2001, 18 rated Amazon a "buy" or "strong buy" and 11 said investors should continue to "hold" the stock. Stay tuned.

APPENDIX B Measuring Cash Flow at Standard & Poor's

Discussions about cash flow often suffer from lack of uniform definition of terms. Table 6.7 illustrates the terminology used at the credit-rating agency Standard & Poor's. At the top is the item from the funds flow statement usually labeled **"funds from operations" (FFO)** or **"working capital from operations."** This quantity is net income adjusted for depreciation and other noncash debits and credits factored into it. Back out the changes in working capital investment to arrive at **"operating cash flow."**

Next, capital expenditures and cash dividends are subtracted out to arrive at **"free operating cash flow"** and **"discretionary cash flow,"** respectively. Finally, the purchase cost of acquisitions is subtracted from the running total, proceeds from asset disposals added, and other miscellaneous sources and uses of cash netted together. **"Prefinancing cash flow"** is the end result of these computations, which represents the extent to which company cash flow from all internal sources has been sufficient to cover all internal needs.

Table 6.7 ■ XYZ CORPORATION

Cash Flow Summary

($ in millions)	Year One	Year Two
Funds from operations (FFO)	$18.58	$22.34
Decrease (increase) in noncash current assets	(33.12)	1.05
Increase (decrease) in noncash current liabilities	15.07	(12.61)
Operating cash flow	$ 0.53	$10.78
Capital expenditures	(11.06)	(9.74)
Free operating cash flow	($10.53)	$ 1.04
Cash dividends	(4.45)	(5.14)
Discretionary cash flow	($14.98)	($ 4.10)
Acquisitions	(21.00)	–
Asset disposals	0.73	0.24
Net other sources (uses) of cash	(0.44)	(0.09)
Prefinancing cash flow	($35.69)	($ 3.95)
Increase (decrease) in short-term debt	$23.00	–
Increase (decrease) in long-term debt	6.12	13.02
Net sale (repurchase) of equity	0.32	(7.07)
Decrease (increase) in cash and securities	6.25	(2.00)
	$35.69	$ 3.95

Source: Standard & Poor's *Corporate Finance Criteria* (New York: Standard & Poor's, 1994), p. 25.

The bottom part of the table reconciles prefinancing cash flow to various categories of external financing and changes in the company's own cash balances. In the example, XYZ Corporation experienced a $35.7 million cash shortfall in year one, which had to be met with a combination of additional borrowings and a drawdown of its own cash.

PROBLEMS/DISCUSSION QUESTIONS

P6–1

Quality of earning essay

1. Define the term *quality of earnings.*
2. List the techniques that management can use to improve earning performance in the short run.
3. Give examples of low quality earnings components.

P6–2

Discussion questions on the role of accounting numbers in valuation

1. Describe the role of accounting numbers in corporate valuation.
2. Describe the role of accounting numbers in cash flow assessment.
3. What is meant by sustainable earnings? What types of earnings are not sustainable?
4. Briefly describe what the process of valuation involves.
5. What are free cash flows? Describe the key features of the free cash flow approach to valuation.
6. What is abnormal earnings? Describe the key features of the abnormal earnings approach to valuation.
7. What is an earnings surprise? How does an earnings surprise impact the value of a firm's equity?

P6–3

Explaining differences in P/E ratios

The price/earnings (P/E) ratios in July 1999 for two groups of companies were:

Company	P/E Ratio
Group A	
General Motors	6.3
Merck & Company	26.3
Microsoft	38.6
Group B	
Compaq Computer	40.0
Dell Computer	64.6
Gateway	35.4

REQUIRED:

1. What factors might explain the difference in the P/E ratios of the firms in Group A?
2. What factors might explain the difference in the P/E ratios of the firms in Group B?

P6–4

Abnormal earnings—some examples

As discussed in the chapter, abnormal earnings (AE) are:

$$AE_t = \text{Actual earnings}_t - \text{Required earnings}_t$$

which may be expressed as

$$AE_t = \text{NOPAT}_t - (r \times BV_{t-1})$$

where NOPAT is the firm's net operating profit after taxes, r is the cost of equity capital and BV_{t-1} is the (beginning) book value of equity at $t - 1$.

REQUIRED:

Solve the following problems:

1. If NOPAT is \$5,000, $r = 15\%$, and BV_{t-1} is \$50,000, what is AE?
2. If NOPAT is \$25,000, $r = 18\%$, and BV_{t-1} is \$125,000, what is AE?
3. Assume that the firm in (2) can increase NOPAT to \$30,000 by instituting some cost-cutting measures. What is the new AE?
4. Assume that the firm in (2) can divest \$25,000 of unproductive capital, with NOPAT falling by only \$2,000. What is the new AE?
5. Assume that the firm in (2) can add a new division at a cost of \$40,000, which will increase NOPAT by \$7,600 per year. Would adding the new division increase AE?
6. Assume that the firm in (1) can add a new division at a cost of \$25,000, which will increase NOPAT by \$3,500 per year. Would adding the new division increase AE?

P6–5

Value creation by two companies

As discussed in the chapter, abnormal earnings (AE) are:

$$AE_t = \text{Actual earnings}_t - \text{Required earnings}_t$$

which may be expressed as

$$AE_t = \text{NOPAT}_t - (r \times BV_{t-1})$$

where NOPAT is the firm's net operating profit after taxes, r is the cost of equity capital, and BV_{t-1} is the (beginning) book value of equity at $t - 1$.

Appearing below is the NOPAT, BV_{t-1}, and cost of equity capital of two firms.

Company A	1997	1998	1999	2000	2001
NOPAT	\$ 66,920	\$ 79,632	\$ 83,314	\$ 89,920	\$ 92,690
BV_{t-1}	\$478,000	\$504,000	\$541,000	\$562,000	\$598,000
Cost of equity capital	0.152	0.167	0.159	0.172	0.166

Company B	1997	1998	1999	2000	2001
NOPAT	\$192,940	\$ 176,341	\$227,700	\$ 198,900	\$ 282,964
BV_{t-1}	\$877,000	\$943,000	\$989,999	\$1,020,000	\$1,199,000
Cost of equity capital	0.188	0.179	0.183	0.175	0.186

(continued)

REQUIRED:

1. Calculate each firm's AE each year from 1997 to 2001.
2. Which firm was a better investment for its shareholders over the 1997–2001 period? Why?

P6–6

Determinants of P/E ratios

A firm's P/E ratio can be written using equation 6.9 as:

$$\text{P/E} = \frac{\text{Market price per share}}{\text{Earnings per share}} = \frac{1}{\text{r}} + \frac{\text{Present value of growth opportunities per share}}{\text{Earnings per share}}$$

where *r* is the cost of equity capital (discount rate).

REQUIRED:

Briefly discuss how a firm's P/E ratio is related to (a) the present value of the firm's growth opportunities, (b) the firm's risk, and (c) the firm's choice of accounting methods.

P6–7

Valuing growth opportunities

As shown in equation 6.9, the price equation for a firm with positive growth opportunities is

$$P_0 = \frac{X_0}{r} + \text{NPVGO}$$

where P_0 is the current stock price, X_0 is current reported earnings per share, *r* is the cost of equity capital, and NPVGO is the net present value of future growth opportunities. The values of P_0, X_0, and *r* for several companies are:

	P_0	X_0	r
Dell Computer	$38.44	$ 0.68	0.176
eToys	8.84	−1.78	0.183
Ford Motor	53.31	5.29	0.124
Home Depot	56.63	1.08	0.125
United Airlines	77.56	12.55	0.137
Wal-Mart	54.75	1.30	0.135

REQUIRED:

1. Why does eToys have a higher cost of equity capital (*r*) than does Wal-Mart?
2. Compute NPVGO for each company.
3. Why is the NPVGO of United Airlines negative?
4. Why do Ford Motor and Wal-Mart have such different NPVGO amounts?

P6–8

Interpreting stock price changes

Assume that General Motors (GM) announces on September 30, 2000 that it expects its earnings per share (EPS) to be $4.50 for the year 2000. At the time of the announcement financial analysts' were forecasting GM's annual EPS to be $5.00.

REQUIRED:

1. Would you expect to observe a change in GM's stock price on September 30? Explain why or why not.
2. Consider the following two scenarios:
   a. The $0.50 deviation of GM's management forecast from analysts' forecast is completely attributable to a month-long labor strike at one of GM's parts plants, a strike which disrupted production at most of the firm's car manufacturing facilities.
   b. The $0.50 deviation of GM's management forecast from analysts' forecast is attributable to GM's (previously undisclosed) decision to discontinue production of its line of sports utility vehicles and small trucks.

   Do you expect the magnitude of the stock price change to be greater in case (a) or case (b)? Why?

P6–9

Components of earnings

The chapter discusses the following three components of earnings: permanent, transitory, and valuation-irrelevant.

REQUIRED:

1. Provide a one-sentence explanation for each component.
2. Provide some examples of each component. (You might examine the income statements of two or three publicly traded companies to aid your answer.)

P6–10

Stock price assimilation of earnings information

Figure 6.4 in this chapter illustrates the behavior of stock returns over the period before a quarterly earnings announcement (i.e., trading days −60 to −1), at the time of an earnings announcement (i.e., day 0), and over the period following an earnings announcement (i.e., trading days +1 to +60) for three groups of firms. (*Note:* A 60 trading day period is almost equal to the 90 calendar days that make up a fiscal quarter.) The three groups are "good news" firms (earnings are greater than what the market expected), "no news" firms (earnings are what the market expected), and "bad news" firms (earnings are less than what the market expected).

REQUIRED:

1. Why do the stock returns of "good news" firms drift upward before the earnings announcement date (i.e., over the −60 to −1 trading day period).
2. Why do the stock returns of "bad news" firms drift downward before the earnings announcement date (i.e., over the −60 to −1 trading day period).
3. Why don't the stock returns of "no news" firms drift upward or downward during the −60 to −1 trading day period?
4. For each group, explain the behavior of the stock returns at the time of the earnings announcement (i.e., on trading day 0).
5. While not immediately obvious from Figure 6.4, there is a tendency for the stock returns of "good news" firms to continue to drift upward after the earnings announcement (i.e., trading days +1 to +60), and for the stock returns of "bad news" firms to continue to drift downward after the earnings announcement. Explain why these post-announcement drifts occur.
6. Suppose a separate Figure 6.4 was produced for a sample of large publicly traded firms and for a sample of small publicly traded firms. Would you expect the two figures to look the same? Explain why or why not.

P6–11

Applying P/E multiples to earnings components

Consider the following information:

	ABC Corporation	XYZ Corporation
Reported EPS	$5.00	$5.00
EPS decomposition		
Permanent	75%	55%
Transitory	20%	25%
Value-irrelevant	5%	20%

REQUIRED:

1. Use a risk-adjusted cost of capital of 15% to calculate the implied share price and earnings multiples for each firm. Why are the implict share prices and earnings multiples for the two firms different?
2. Repeat (1) using a risk-adjusted cost of capital of 8%.

P6–12

Abnormal earnings valuation–Compaq Computer

STRETCH

Compaq Computer Corporation (Compaq) was founded in 1982. Compaq manufactures and markets a wide range of computing products, including desktop computers, portable computers, workstations, communications products, and tower personal computer (PC) servers and peripheral products that store and manage data in network environments. Compaq markets its products primarily to business, home, government, and education customers.

Compaq's industry is intensely competitive with many U.S., Japanese, and other international companies vying for market share. The market continues to be characterized by rapid technological advances in both hardware and software-development that have substantially increased the capabilities and applications of information management products and have resulted in the frequent introduction of new products. The principal elements of competition are price, product performance, product quality and reliability, service and support, marketing and distribution capability, and corporate reputation.

1. Appearing in the accompanying table are Compaq's earnings per share and equity book value per share for the 1997–1999 period.
2. Assume that Compaq will pay a $0.10 dividend on its common stock in the future.
3. In the past three years Compaq has issued some common stock through stock option plans. Assume that this practice will continue in the future and will add $1.50 of book value per share each year.
4. In April 2000, the financial analysts following Compaq were projecting annual earnings per share (EPS) of $1.07 for 2000, $1.47 for 2001, and an annual EPS growth rate of 20% for the next three years (2002–2004).
5. After an initial five-year horizon, assume that Compaq's abnormal earnings will grow by 7.5% per year.
6. Compaq's beta is 1.30, and the risk-free rate of return is 6.33%. Use this information, along with a market risk premium of 6.0% to estimate Compaq's cost of equity capital. (See footnote 31 in this chapter for a description of how to calculate the equity cost of capital.)
7. Compaq's actual stock price was $29.19 at the end of April 2000.

COMPAQ COMPUTER

		December 31	
	1997	1998	1999
As reported earnings per share	$1.23	($1.71)*	$0.35
Equity book value beginning of year	$4.49	$6.21	$6.73
+ Earnings per share	1.23	(1.71)	0.35
+ Stock issued (repurchased)	0.50	2.29	1.75
− Dividends per share	0.01	0.06	0.09
= Equity book value, end of year	$6.21	$6.73	$8.74

* $0.41 before a special $2.12 restructuring charge in 1998.

REQUIRED:

1. Use the abnormal earnings valuation model from Appendix A of this chapter to derive an estimate of Compaq's stock price as of April 2000. How does the price you derive compare to the company's actual stock price?
2. Some analysts were forecasting the company's EPS to be $1.50 in 2000, $2.00 in 2001, and to grow at 30% each year from 2002 to 2004. Repeat (1) using these analyst forecasts in your calculation.
3. Which valuation—(1) or (2)—do you think is more reasonable? Why?

P6–13

Abnormal earnings valuation—Dell Computer

STRETCH

Dell Computer Corporation (Dell) designs, manufactures, and markets a wide range of computer systems, including desktops, notebooks, and network servers; it also markets software, peripherals, and service and support programs. The company is the world's leading direct-computer systems company and one of the top five computer vendors in the world.

The company was founded on the principle that delivering computers custom-built to specific customer orders is the best business model for providing solutions that are truly relevant to end-user needs. This build-to-order, flexible manufacturing process enables the company to achieve faster inventory turnover and reduced inventory levels, and it allows the company to rapidly incorporate new technologies and components into its product offerings. The company also offers a broad range of service and support programs through its own technical personnel and its direct management of specialized service suppliers. These services range from telephone support to on-site customer-dedicated systems engineers.

1. Appearing in the accompanying table are Dell's earnings per share and equity book value per share for the 1997–1999 fiscal years (Dell's fiscal year ends on January 31).
2. Dell has not been paying any dividends on its common stock. Assume that this will continue in the future.
3. Dell has issued common stock and also repurchased some common stock in the open market. Assume that no stock will be issued or repurchased in the future.

4. In April 2000, the financial analysts following Dell were forecasting annual earnings per share (EPS) of $0.92 in 2000, $1.21 in 2001, and an annual EPS growth rate of 33% for 2002–2004.
5. After an initial five-year horizon, assume that Dell's abnormal earnings will grow by 7.5% per year.
6. Dell's beta is 1.62 and the risk-free rate of return is 6.33%. Use this information, along with a market risk premium of 6.0% to estimate Dell's cost of equity capital. (See footnote 31 in this chapter for a description of how to calculate the equity cost of capital.)
7. Dell's actual stock price was $50.13 at the end of April 2000.

DELL COMPUTER	1997	1998	1999
As reported earnings per share	$0.36	$0.57	$0.66
Equity book value beginning of year	$0.39	$0.50	$0.91
+ Earnings per share	0.36	0.57	0.66
+ Stock issued (repurchased)	(0.25)	(0.16)	0.49
− Dividends per share	0	0	0
= Equity book value, end of year	$0.50	$0.91	$2.06

REQUIRED:

1. Use the abnormal earnings valuation model from Appendix A of this chapter to derive an estimate of Dell's stock price as of April 2000. How does the price you derive compare to the company's actual stock price?
2. Some analysts were forecasting the company's EPS to be $1.20 in 2000, $1.50 in 2001, and to grow at 45% each year from 2002 to 2004. Repeat (1) using these analyst forecasts in your calculation.
3. Why might Dell's actual stock price differ from the share price estimates derived in (1) and (2)?

P6–14

Calculating sustainable earnings

Colonel Electric Company is one of the largest and most diversified industrial corporations in the world. From the time of its incorporation in 1892 the company has engaged in developing, manufacturing, and marketing a wide variety of products for the generation, transmission, distribution, control and utilization of electricity. The company's products include lamps and other lighting products; major appliances for the home; industrial automation products and components; motors; electrical distribution and control equipment; locomotives; power generation and delivery products; nuclear reactors, nuclear power support services, and fuel assemblies; commercial and military aircraft jet engines; materials, including plastics, silicones, and superabrasives; and a wide variety of high-technology products, including products used in medical diagnostic applications.

Appearing in the accompanying table are the 1998–2000 income statements of Colonel Electric Company.

COLONEL ELECTRIC COMPANY

Comparative Income Statements
For Years Ended December 31

($ in millions)	2000	1999	1998
Revenues			
Sales of goods	$54,196	$53,177	$52,767
Sales of services	11,923	10,836	8,863
Royalties and fees	1,629	753	783
Total revenues	67,748	64,766	62,413

(continued)

COLONEL ELECTRIC COMPANY (*continued*)

Comparative Income Statements
For Years Ended December 31

($ in millions)	2000	1999	1998
Costs and Expenses			
Cost of goods sold	(24,594)	(24,308)	(22,775)
Cost of services sold	(8,425)	(6,785)	(6,274)
Restructuring (charges) reversals	1,000	–	(2,500)
Interest charges	(595)	(649)	(410)
Other costs and expenses	(6,274)	(5,743)	(5,211)
Litigation charges (income)	550	–	(250)
(Losses) gains on sales of investments	(75)	–	25
(Losses) gains on asset sales	25	55	(35)
Inventory write-offs	–	(18)	–
Asset impairment write-offs	–	–	(24)
Special item charges	(34)	–	(8)
Loss from labor strike	–	(20)	–
Total costs and expenses	(38,422)	(37,468)	(37,462)
Earnings from continuing operations before income taxes	29,326	27,298	24,951
Provision for income taxes (34%)	(9,971)	(9,281)	(8,483)
Earnings from continuing operations	$19,355	$18,017	$16,468
Income (loss) from discontinued operations (net of tax)	–	(250)	1,100
Gain (loss) on sale of discontinued operations (net of tax)	750	–	–
Extraordinary gain (loss) on early debt retirement (net of tax)	(50)	–	10
Cumulative gain (loss) from change in accounting methods (net of tax)	(110)	–	55
Net earnings	$19,945	$ 17,767	$ 17,633

In 2000 the company earned "Royalties and fees" revenue of $1 billion from a one-time six month contract with the U.S. government. The company does not expect to do any further business with the U.S. government in the future.

REQUIRED:

1. Calculate Colonel Electric's sustainable earnings for each year.
2. How does Colonel Electric's sustainable earnings compare to its reported net earnings in each year?

P6–15

Net accruals and discretionary accruals

Companies that want to "manage" their reported earnings can do so through operating cash flows or net income accruals (the noncash revenue and expense components of GAAP earnings).

The 1999–2000 balance sheets and 2000 income statement of Runner's World Inc. follow. The company's operating cash flow for 2000 was –$38,460, a net outflow.

RUNNER'S WORLD INC.

Income Statement
for the Year Ended December 31, 2000

Sales	$120,000
Cost of goods sold	(60,000)
Selling, general, and administrative expenses	(22,000)
Depreciation expense	(14,000)
Operating income	24,000
Interest expense	(6,000)
Interest income	1,000
Income before taxes	19,000
Income taxes (34%)	(6,460)
Net income	$12,540

RUNNER'S WORLD INC.

Balance Sheet

	December 31	
	2000	**1999**
Assets		
Cash	$ 100,000	$ 80,000
Accounts receivable	95,000	75,000
Inventories	120,000	90,000
Prepaid expenses	15,000	20,000
Plant, property, and equipment (net)	924,000	850,000
Long-term investments	175,000	232,000
Total assets	$1,429,000	$1,347,000
Liabilities and stockholders' equity		
Liabilities		
Accounts payable	$ 220,000	$ 155,000
Accrued payables	195,000	275,000
Interest payable	22,000	10,000
Income tax payable	45,000	62,000
Long-term debt	350,000	270,000
Total liabilities	832,000	772,000
Stockholders' equity		
Common stock	175,000	145,000
Retained earnings	422,000	430,000
Total stockholders' equity	597,000	575,000
Total liabilities and stockholders' equity	$1,429,000	$1,347,000

REQUIRED:

1. Calculate the net accruals (i.e., the difference between accrual earnings and operating cash flows) recorded by Runner's World in 2000.
2. Identify the individual components of net accruals in (1).
3. Which accruals identified in (2) are subject to the greatest degree of management discretion?
4. Why might managers manipulate the firm's discretionary accruals?

P6–16

Earnings-based equity valuations

In each of the following situations assume a zero-growth rate for earnings and dividends (NPVGO is zero), that all earnings are paid out as dividends, and that the earnings-based valuation model in equation 6.9 is being used.

(continued)

1. Dennison Corporation's earnings are expected to be $7.00 per share and its stock price is $28.00. What is the required rate of return on the firm's equity?
2. Sampson Corporation's earnings are expected to be $5.00 per share and its required rate of return on equity is 22%. What is the current price of the stock?
3. Johnson Corporation's current stock price is $40.00 and its required rate of return on equity is 15%. What is the firm's expected earnings?

P6–17

Growth, expansion, and equity valuation

Allison Manufacturing and BSJ Manufacturing both produce after-market accessories for sports utility vehicles. Both companies are about to launch strategic initiatives that will increase sales and net income for the foreseeable future. Allison Manufacturing has decided to launch an expensive advertising compaign that will increase sales from $20 million to $30 million a year, and net income from $2 million to $2.5 million a year. BSJ Manufacturing has decided to issue an additional $10 million of common stock and then use the proceeds to buy a smaller accessories manufacturer. The acquisition is expected to increase BSJ's sales by $10 million a year and net income by $1 million. Key financial statement figures for both companies are shown below. The "Before" amounts describe each company's current operations while the "After" amounts incorporate the expected results from the strategic initiatives.

	Before	After
Allison Manufacturing:		
Annual sales	$20 million	$30 million
Annual net income	$2 million	$2.5 million
Equity book value	$10 million	$10 million
Number of shares outstanding	100,000	100,000
BSJ Manufacturing:		
Annual sales	$20 million	$30 million
Annual net income	$2 million	$3 million
Equity book value	$10 million	$20 million
Number of shares outstanding	100,000	200,000

Both companies pay all net income out as dividends each year and have a 10% cost of equity capital. Use the abnormal earnings valuation model from Equation 6.11 to answer the required questions.

REQUIRED:

1. Calculate the per share value of each company *before* they undertake their strategic initiatives assuming that the current level of annual net income can be sustained forever.
2. Calculate the percentage growth rate in sales and net income that each company will experience as a result of their strategic initiatives. What is the return on equity (ROE) for each company before and after the strategic initiative?
3. Calculate the per share value of each company after they implement their strategic initiatives assuming that the expected level of annual net income can be sustained forever.
4. Explain why the per share value of one company increases while the per share value of the other company declines.

P6–18

The usefulness of management earnings forecasts to financial analysts and investors

The excerpt below is from an article appearing in the *Wall Street Journal.*

REQUIRED:

1. Briefly discuss why management forecasts of earnings may be useful to financial analysts and investors.
2. Why might managers steer analysts toward conservative earnings estimates by issuing earnings forecasts that they know are below the earnings they expect to report?
3. As an analyst, what action(s) would you take with firms that consistently issue conservative earnings forecasts?
4. Are there any disadvantages to firms (or their managers) that issue conservative earnings forecasts?

(continued)

5. The article claims that firms can consistently "low-ball" analysts by issuing conservative earnings forecasts and then expect to see their stock prices increase when reported earnings are higher "than expected." Do you agree or disagree with this claim? Why?

"LOW-BALLING: HOW SOME COMPANIES SEND STOCKS ALOFT"—What makes a stock a high flyer? Consistently beating the analysts' estimates helps a lot. And many companies seem to have figured out a way to try to help ensure that happens.

Each quarter, after securities analysts estimate what the companies they follow will earn, the game begins. Chief financial officers or investor relations representatives traditionally "give guidance" to analysts, hinting whether the analysts should raise or lower their earnings projections so the analysts won't be embarrassed later.

And these days, many companies are encouraging analysts to deflate earnings projections to artificially low levels, analysts and money managers say. If the game is played right, a company's stock will rise sharply on the day it announces its earnings—and beats the analysts' too-conservative estimates.

Take U.S. Healthcare Inc. Late last year, some analysts say, executives of the health-care services company led them to figure it would post fourth-quarter earnings of about 45 cents a share. On Jan. 28, U.S. Healthcare announced a "preliminary" earnings estimate of 55 cents a share. Then, only two weeks later, U.S. Healthcare shocked Wall Street by posting a whopping 68 cents a share for the quarter. The company's stock surged 10% that day, closing at $40.625.

Several analysts think that they were misled. "U.S. Healthcare may have beat its own internal estimates, but it also wanted to guide analysts to numbers they knew they could beat," says Kenneth Abramowitz, a health-care analyst who follows the company for Sanford Bernstein and Co.

Costas Nicolaides, the company's chief financial officer, says U.S. Healthcare simply did better than it expected. "I don't guide analysts," he says. "But if someone were to come up with a ridiculous figure, I might raise my eyebrow, or my body language would be such that they'd know."

Money managers and analysts say an increasing number of companies are leading analysts to underestimate their earnings. "More companies," especially those in such growth areas as health-care and technology, "are starting to coerce us to a high degree about what our estimates should be," says Michael Stark, a research analyst with Robertson Stephens & Co. in San Francisco. "They're always low-balling."

Analysts and portfolio managers say that some companies consistently report earnings that are just a little bit better than what they lead analysts to believe. They mention T2 Medical Inc. and Cirrus Logic Inc.; both "understate by pennies," says Robert Czepial, who runs the Robertson Stephens & Co. Growth Fund. "Of course they're managing the information," he says.

A spokesman for T2 declines to comment. Cirrus's chief financial officer, Sam Srinivasan, says that "Cirrus doesn't play the game of being conservative with the numbers for the analysts."

One corporate chief financial officer, speaking on the condition of anonymity, says that analysts, not the company he works for, are to blame for the company's low-balling its projected earnings. "If the Street's looking for 10 cents and you do nine, you're a moron," he says. "If they're looking for 10 and you do 11, you're a hero."

But low-balling may not work forever. That's the conclusion that some analysts draw from the case of AST Research Inc. For more than five quarters, several analysts and money managers say, the Irvine, Calif., computer maker consistently led them to believe it would earn at least five cents a share less than the actual results.

But for this year's first quarter, analysts lifted their projections, running far ahead of the company's "guidance."

Last month, when AST announced its earnings for the quarter, its stock fell $1.875 to $28.125—even though AST's results were in line with numbers it had given analysts.

P6–19 The following excerpts were taken from an article about apparel retailers that appeared in the *Wall Street Journal.*

Information disclosures by retail firms

DEPARTMENT AND APPAREL STORES SAW WEAK MARCH SALES; CHILLY WEATHER DELAYED MANY SPRING PURCHASES; DISCOUNT CHAINS GAINED—Blaming unseasonably cool weather, many of the nation's largest apparel retailers posted weak sales gains in March. But the discount-store sector fared far better, aided by brisk sales of Easter-related gifts.

Department stores and specialty apparel chains in particular reported flat or lower sales. Federated Department Stores Inc. saw sales at stores open at least a year drop 0.2% from a year earlier. May Department Stores Co. said same-store sales were flat compared with a year earlier. And Limited Inc. reported a same-store decline of 6%.

Analysts added that while a March Easter helped sales, store closings on the holiday reduced results by as much as several percentage points. (Last year, Easter fell in April.) Also, many retailers delayed until April some promotions that usually occur in March so they didn't coincide with Easter demand. "March was less promotional than a year ago," said Jeffrey Edelman, an analyst at Deutsche Morgan Grenfell. . . .

Overall, March same-store sales rose about 4.4%, according to Salomon's index. Another index, compiled by Goldman, Sachs & Co. and using a larger number of retailers, showed a same-store rise of about 4% from a year earlier. . . .

Chilly weather in some areas encouraged many consumers to put off buying spring clothing, contributing to weak results at apparel stores. The Limited chain's results were hurt mostly by its women's units, where same-store sales declined 14%. Limited's Express unit in particular has been saddled with poor-selling merchandise, analysts said. The Intimate Brands lingerie operation, of which Limited owns an 83% stake, performed better, posting a same-store gain of 4%. . . .

A few department-store chains, though, posted far better gains. Carson Pirie Scott & Co. said same-store sales rose 7% from a year earlier. And luxury chain Neiman Marcus Group Inc. reported a gain of 8.7%.

	Latest Month Total Sales 1997 ($ in millions)	Comparable Stores Change from Year Earlier[1]
Wal-Mart	$10,287.0	+7.2%
Kmart	2,840.0	+13.0
Dayton Hudson	2,312.0	+1.9
Federated	1,289.8	−0.2
May	1,010.0	+0.0
Dillard	641.1	+1.0
Neiman Marcus	201.1	+8.7
Carson Pirie Scott	103.9	+7.0
Limited	719.1	−6.0
Gap	524.0	−3.0
Talbots	111.6	+1.0
Charming Shoppes	100.8	+14.0
AnnTaylor	78.6	+7.4
Costco	1,960.0	+11.0

[1] U.S. sales of stores open at least one year.

REQUIRED:

1. As a financial analyst following this industry, how might you use the disclosures to generate forecasts of the firms' earnings for the next fiscal quarter or year?
2. Why do you think that the article reports a comparison of the current month's sales with the same month of the previous year?
3. What information beyond monthly sales would you like to see these firms report to help forecast future earnings? Why?
4. What reasons might the firms have for not wanting to disclose the data you suggest in (3)?
5. Recently, some of the companies mentioned in the article have sought to end the practice of disclosing monthly sales data to the *Wall Street Journal.* As a financial analyst following this industry, would you object or support ending this practice? Why?

P6–20

Restructuring charges (and reversals) and the quality of earnings

The following excerpt is from an article that appeared in the *Wall Street Journal.*

ABREAST OF THE MARKET: WRITE-OFFS MAY BECOME "WRITE-ONS"; REVERSAL OF CHARGES COULD PROVE CUSHION IN THE NEXT DOWNTURN—With the Dow Jones Industrial Average hitting another record last week, investors wonder if earnings next year can support today's stock prices. But they may be pleasantly surprised by reserves buried in some corporate balance sheets.

Companies ranging from General Motors to USAir Group took huge write-offs in the early 1990s to account for previously unrecognized liabilities, especially for retired employees' health care. Now, analysts at Goldman, Sachs & Co. say many write-offs, which wiped billions in book value from balance sheets and crushed earnings, appear overly conservative. Many companies could reduce or reverse charges in the next year or two. Such "write-ons" as Goldman calls them, could provide a cushion to profits in the next cyclical downturn, the firm says.

As a result of the write-offs, the earnings and book values investors see today are "the cleanest" in many years, writes Gabrielle Napolitano, an analyst at Goldman, in a study. And she says "many of the write-offs taken in earlier years may actually be reversed in full or in part."

Ms. Napolitano says it's difficult to forecast when and how write-ons may occur, but adds, "They could be substantial." Ms. Napolitano says she believes companies may use write-ons to smooth their earnings over the next year or two if growth in the economy and profits slows.

The problem for investors trying to predict write-ons is that the nature and size of the original write-offs were unprecedented, so it's difficult to predict how, or whether, companies will take write-ons. A reversal might show up as an unusual gain, leaving operating earnings untouched. Companies offer few details on how they might adjust write-offs. Write-off reversals or reductions would vary depending on the industry.

Goldman says conservative accounting now in place has produced the highest-quality earnings and book values in years. David Shulman, chief stock strategist at Salomon Brothers, says earlier charges "may very well have been overstated." But he's concerned that if companies bury write-ons in such things as labor costs without identifying the source of the cost reduction, investors could think earnings are stronger than conditions warrant.

REQUIRED:

1. The *Wall Street Journal* article contains the following two statements: (a) "As a result of the write-offs, the earnings and book values investors see today are the cleanest in many years" and (b) "Conservative accounting now in place has produced the highest-quality earnings and book values in years." What is meant by these statements? Do you agree with them? Why or why not?
2. How do restructuring charges and subsequent reversals affect the quality of reported earnings?

3. Why might management tend to over-estimate future restructuring costs?
4. Why might analysts be concerned about the potential for firms to make "write-ons" in future years?
5. What is the biggest difficulty that you foresee in dealing with write-ons?

CASES

C6–1

Illinois Tool Works (JB): Abnormal earnings valuation

The abnormal earnings model for estimating common share value is:

$$P_0 = BV_0 + \sum_{t=1}^{\infty} \frac{E_0(X_t - rBV_{t-1})}{(1 + r)^t}$$

where P is the total value of all outstanding shares, BV is the (beginning) book value of stockholders' equity, r is the cost of equity capital, E is the expectations operator, and X is net income. In words, the model says that share value equals the book value of stockholders' equity plus the present value of future expected abnormal earnings (where abnormal earnings is net income minus the cost of equity capital multiplied by the beginning-of-period book value of stockholders' equity).

The model is amazingly simple. Two "rubs" are that the model is silent on just how one comes up with expected net income for future years (and therefore future expected abnormal earnings) and just how many future years should be used. Owing to the way present value is calculated, abnormal earnings amounts expected for years in the distant future have a small present value and are essentially irrelevant to valuation. In addition, competitive market forces tend eventually to drive abnormal earnings to zero. Thus, it isn't important to make the forecasting horizon terribly long. Professional analysts rarely use more than 15 years, often fewer than 10.

Comparative income statements and balance sheets for Illinois Tool Works (ITW) for 1997–1999 are presented on the following pages.

REQUIRED:

1. Assume a ten-year forecasting horizon. Also assume that ITW's 1999 return on beginning stockholders' equity (net income divided by beginning 1999 stockholders' equity) of 25% is expected to persist throughout the forecasting horizon (i.e., expected net income is always equal to .25 multiplied by beginning-of-the-year stockholders' equity). Also assume no additional stock issuances or repurchases, and that dividends equal 20% of net income in each year (ITW's approximate historical dividend payout ratio). Given these assumptions, the book value of stockholders' equity at the *end* of 2000 (beginning of 2001) equals book value at the *beginning* of 2000 plus (1 − .20) times 2000 net income. Finally assume that the cost of equity capital is 12.5% (ITW's approximate cost of equity capital). With these relatively simple assumptions, use the abnormal earnings model to estimate the total value of Illinois Tool Work's common shares as of the end of 1999. Ignore terminal values at the end of the ten-year forecast horizon in your calculations.
2. As of the end of 1999, 300 million common shares were outstanding. Convert your estimate in (1) to a per-share estimate. For purposes of comparison, the actual market value of ITW's common shares ranged from $67 to $73 during the fourth quarter of 1999.
3. Now assume that ITW will maintain just a 20% return on beginning stockholders equity over the 10-year forecast horizon. What would the company's shares then be worth?

ILLINOIS TOOL WORKS

Consolidated Statement of Income

($ in millions)	1999	1998	1997
Sales	$9,333	$5,648	$5,220
Cost of goods sold	5,773	3,459	3,230
Gross profit	3,560	2,189	1,990
Selling and administrative expenses	1,730	898	878
Depreciation and amortization	343	212	185
Operating profit	1,487	1,079	927
Interest expense	68	14	19
Non-operating income/expense	(15)	5	(17)
Special Items	81	0	0
Pre-tax Income	1,353	1,060	925
Total income taxes	512	387	337
Net income	$ 841	$ 673	$ 588

ILLINOIS TOOL WORKS

Consolidated Statement of Shareholders' Equity

($ in millions)	1999	1998	1997
Balance at beginning of year	$3,338	$2,806	$2,396
Net income (loss)	841	673	587
Stock issued (repurchased)	830	(6)	(64)
Common stock dividends	(194)	(135)	(113)
Balance at end of year	$4,815	$3,338	$2,806

C6–2

General Motors Corporation (CW): Income statement discussion

Because you are president of your investment club and have a strong background in corporate financial reporting, the other club members typically rely on you to lead the discussion of the group's investment decisions. A special meeting has been called for Monday night (two days from now) to discuss the club's investment in the common stock and unsecured bonds of General Motors (GM). This previously unscheduled meeting was prompted by yesterday's announcement by GM that it had both a net loss of $651.8 million for the fourth quarter of fiscal 1992 and a net loss of $23.5 billion for the entire year (see the following *Wall Street Journal* article).

GM'S DEFICIT IN QUARTER HIT $651.8 MILLION; HUGE ONE-TIME CHARGES CAUSED THE LOSS WHILE OPERATIONS REBOUNDED

DETROIT—General Motors Corp., weighed down by huge one-time charges, reported a fourth-quarter loss of $651.8 million and a world record-breaking $23.5 billion deficit for the year. But excluding the charges, GM was in the black.

Analysts called the $3.5 billion improvement in GM's annual operating performance a positive surprise, as it was accomplished despite more conservative accounting. Investors boosted the company's shares to $40.50, up $1.25, in heavy New York Stock Exchange composite trading. "It's a turnaround we can be proud of," GM's Chief Financial Officer, G. Richard Wagoner, said during a news conference. "But we've got a way to go."

Indeed, GM's unfunded pension liabilities soared to $14 billion from $8.4 billion a year earlier, representing a claim on future cash flow. And Mr. Wagoner reaffirmed GM's "aggressive but achievable target" of reversing $3.5 billion in North American Operations losses this year, even though sales aren't expected to improve strongly.

The No. 1 auto maker said it earned $273.3 million, or 10 cents a share, in the fourth quarter before two big charges and a smaller gain. That marked a rebound from a year-earlier loss of $519.8 million, or $1.09 a share, before a restructuring charge. Including charges, GM had a loss of $2.47 billion, or $4.25 a share, a year earlier. In the latest quarter, GM's net loss was $1.25 a share. Revenue rose 6.4% to $35.76 billion in the latest fourth quarter.

When GM "can earn 10 cents a share with conservative accounting, that's a major surprise," said Morgan Stanley analyst Scott Merlis. If the economy rebounds, GM "could show the same type of earnings surprises as Chrysler," he added.

(continued)

More importantly, GM added $1.98 billion in cash to its coffers during the fourth quarter as cash flow from operations rebounded strongly. GM ended the year with $7.2 billion in cash, up from $3.98 billion a year earlier.

The rebound in cash flow is critical, because GM's cash outflow during the past two years had undermined its efforts to develop new products and fix its badly dented balance sheet.

For the first time, GM disclosed the magnitude of the losses that drove the auto maker's outside directors last year to oust former President Lloyd E. Reuss and then Chairman Robert C. Stempel. GM had a loss of $3.5 billion on its core North American auto business in all of 1992, on top of 1991's $6.89 billion deficit. In the fourth quarter, GM narrowed its North American loss "before interest and taxes" to $966 million from $1.27 billion a year earlier. But the North American loss in the 1992 quarter was deepened by a one-time $333 million expense for a larger-than-expected early retirement program, and an unspecified addition to warranty-claims reserves taken as part of a broad move to make GM's accounting more conservative.

GM's overseas automotive operations earned $218.4 million in the fourth quarter, down 24% from a year earlier before a $165.1 million gain from GM's sale of its stake in South Korea's Daewoo Motor Corp. The drop reflects weakness in key European markets, and Mr. Wagoner said business will be "tougher" for GM's European operations this year.

GM's three big nonautomotive units contributed a total of $703.1 million in the latest quarter. For all of 1992, GM earned $92 million before a $22.2 billion charge to recognize liabilities for retiree medical benefits and $1.5 billion in other restructuring charges. That compares with a 1991 loss of $3.45 billion before one-time write-offs. GM's revenue for all of 1992 climbed 7.6% to $132.43 billion.

Mr. Wagoner said GM is still confident it can make good on President John F. Smith Jr.'s promise to produce break-even results in North American operations, before interest, taxes and a continuing charge for retiree medical benefits.

But he conceded that GM "has work to do" to shore up its balance sheet. The $20.8 billion charge for retiree medical benefits reduced GM's net worth to just $6.23 billion from $27.34 billion. That won't affect GM's ability to pay dividends or secure financing, Mr. Wagoner said. But it does dramatize the huge claim health care will put on GM's future cash flow, particularly as the ratio of U.S. automotive retirees to U.S. active workers rises above the current 1-to-1.

"We have at GM a very rich benefits program," Mr. Wagoner said. "We need to work with our unions" to lower medical costs that GM estimates are escalating now at about 10% annually.

That process began yesterday, as Mr. Smith met with United Auto Workers union local leaders in Detroit for an unprecedented session to discuss the state of GM's business and the impact of the retiree-benefits issue.

As for the huge unfunded pension liability, GM took steps to tighten up its pension accounting and begin contributing more to its retirement funds. "We're going to start funding more than we're expensing," a GM spokesman said. GM lowered to 10% from 11% the assumed rate of earnings on its pension assets. That move will raise the company's continuing pension expenses about $428 million a year, the spokesman said.

Although the club has investments in the common stock and bonds of 15 to 20 different companies, its investment in GM common stock and bonds represents about 15% of the total value of the club's portfolio. Several club members are concerned about GM's net losses and by other information in the earnings announcement. They wonder if it is time to sell some or all the club's GM common stock and bonds. Some of the concerns raised by club members (which are sure to come up for discussion at the meeting) include:

1. "With such a large loss, will the company still have enough cash to continue to pay dividends?"
2. "Where will the company get the cash to pay for these one-time charges?"
3. "I heard that GM could have written off the $22.2 billion charge for retiree medical benefits over 20 years rather than all in one year. Why did they write it all off in one year?"
4. "In a couple of places the article mentions 'conservative accounting.' What does that mean?"
5. "In the article, GM's chief financial officer states, 'It's a turnaround we can be proud of, . . . but we've got a way to go.' How in the world can a $23.5 billion loss for the year be a turnaround to be proud of?"

6. "Given the size of the $23.5 billion net loss for the year, I don't understand why the share price rose by $1.25 on the day of the announcement."
7. "Since its net worth (i.e., assets minus liabilities or just stockholders' equity) fell from $27.34 billion to $6.23 billion for the year, isn't GM now more highly leveraged than before, and hence more risky? Won't the leverage increase mean that bond rating agencies like Moody's and Standard & Poor's will reduce GM's credit rating, thereby reducing the value of our bonds?"
8. "I'm confused by all of the 'earnings' numbers referred to in the article. Which one is the best indicator of GM's future profitability?"
9. "The article states that during 1992, GM added $3.98 billion to its cash. How can this be? They lost $23.5 billion!"
10. "The article states that the reduction in GM's net worth from $27.34 billion to $6.23 billion won't affect its ability to pay dividends or secure financing. How can this be?"

REQUIRED:

1. To focus discussion at the meeting, you decide that you should identify the key positives and negatives about GM that are contained in the *Wall Street Journal* article. What positives and negatives would you put forth for the group to consider?
2. What specific comments would you make in response to the issues raised by your fellow club members?
3. Based on your analysis of GM's earnings-related disclosures, how much (if any) of the club's GM common stock and bonds would you vote to sell?
4. If you had more time before the meeting, what other information would you gather and why?

C6–3 Financial variables/ratios and prediction of bankruptcy and loan default (CW)

BACKGROUND:

On graduating from business school, you took a job as the senior loan officer at a bank in your hometown. Virtually all the bank's lending activities involve five to seven year loans to publicly held companies that are traded on regional or national stock exchanges. The bank president called you into his office this morning and said that he wants you to develop a statistical model for predicting which of the bank's corporate customers will go bankrupt or otherwise default on their loans within one year.

REQUIRED:

1. Prepare a list of the financial variables and ratios that you think should be included in the model.
2. In one or two sentences, provide the economic intuition for why each of the variables and ratios in (1) is a useful predictor of bankruptcy or default.
3. Briefly discuss how you might go about developing and testing your model.

C6–4 Intel and Xerox: Free Cash Flow

Standard & Poor's, the credit rating agency, has assigned its top rating (A+) to Intel Corporation and a lower rating (A–) to Xerox. Selected cash flow information for the two companies follows.

INTEL ($ in millions)	**1999**	**1998**	**1997**	**1996**	**1995**
Operating cash flow	$11,335	$9,191	$10,008	$8,743	$4,026
Capital expenditures	3,403	3,557	4,501	3,024	3,550
Free cash flow	7,932	5,634	5,507	5,719	476
Cash dividends	366	217	180	148	116
Common stock sold (repurchased)	(4,069)	(4,658)	(3,015)	(1,041)	(842)
Debt issued (repaid)	187	86	(305)	360	(183)

(continued)

XEROX ($ in millions)	1999	1998	1997	1996	1995
Operating cash flow	$1,252	$ (987)	$1,264	$ 200	$513
Capital expenditures	594	566	520	510	438
Free cash flow	658	(1,553)	744	(310)	75
Cash dividends	586	531	475	438	389
Common stock sold (repurchased)	144	(46)	24	(221)	70
Debt issued (repaid)	(97)	2,468	642	990	766

REQUIRED:

1. Explain why Intel received a higher credit rating than did Xerox.
2. What other factors beyond cash flows are likely to influence Standard & Poor's decision to give a lower credit rating to Xerox?

C6–5

Microsoft Corporation (CW): Unearned revenues and earnings management

Microsoft develops, manufactures, licenses, sells, and supports a wide range of software products, including operating systems for personal computers (PCs) and servers; server applications for client/server environments; business and consumer productivity applications; software development tools; and Internet and intranet software and technologies. The company has expanded its interactive content efforts, including MSN (the Microsoft Network on-line service), various Internet-based services, and entertainment and information software programs. Microsoft also sells PC books and input devices, and it researches and develops advanced technologies for future software products.

The following excerpt is from an article that appeared in the *Wall Street Journal.*

MICROSOFT'S EARNINGS GROWTH SLOWED IN THE LATEST QUARTER—Microsoft Corp.'s growth juggernaut slowed in its fiscal fourth quarter, but the numbers masked a surprisingly potent performance by the software giant.

The Redmond, Wash., company's earnings barely topped Wall Street's consensus, breaking a pattern of dramatic upside surprises for the company. But the company's profit would have been considerably higher had it not salted away revenue in a special reserve account for use in future quarters. That account, dubbed "unearned revenues," continued to swell and underscore the returns Microsoft is reaping as a near-monopoly supplier of personal computer operating-software and key application programs. The account represents revenues Microsoft has collected but hadn't yet reported. It was established because the company faces future costs to deliver upgrades and customer support for products that already have been paid for. The policy helps smooth out sharp swings in the company's quarterly results.

Microsoft reported net income of $1.06 billion, or 80 cents a share, for the quarter ended June 30, an increase of 89% from $559 million, or 43 cents a share, a year earlier. Analysts had expected per-share earnings of about 79 cents, according to First Call Corp. Quarterly revenue was $3.18 billion, up 41% from $2.26 billion a year earlier.

OTHER INFORMATION:

1. Appearing in the accompanying tables are the comparative income statements for the fourth quarters of fiscal 1996 and 1997 and for the fiscal years 1996 and 1997. Also shown are comparative balance sheets for fiscal 1996 and 1997.
2. The balance in the unearned revenues account on March 31, 1997 (the end of the third fiscal quarter of 1997) was $1,285 (in millions).
3. The following description of Microsoft's unearned revenues account is taken from the company's SEC filings:

The portion of the Company's revenues that are earned later than billed is reflected in the unearned revenues account. Of the March 31, 1997 balance of $1,285 million, approximately $765 million represented the unearned portion of Windows desktop operating systems revenues and $150 million represented the unearned portion of Office 97 revenues. Unearned revenues associated with upgrade rights for Microsoft Office 97 were $190 million and the balance of unearned revenues was primarily attributable to maintenance and other subscription contracts.

MICROSOFT CORPORATION

Income Statements

($ in millions, except earnings per share)	Three Months Ended June 30, 1996	Three Months Ended June 30, 1997	Year Ended June 30, 1996	Year Ended June 30, 1997
Net revenues	$2,255	$3,175	$8,671	$11,358
Cost of revenues	241	242	1,188	1,085
Research and development	453	516	1,432	1,925
Sales and marketing	661	744	2,657	2,856
General and administrative	90	94	316	362
Total operating expenses	1,445	1,596	5,593	6,228
Operating income	810	1,579	3,078	5,130
Interest income	92	127	320	443
Other expenses	(42)	(80)	(19)	(259)
Income before income taxes	860	1,626	3,379	5,314
Provision for income taxes	301	569	1,184	1,860
Net income	$ 559	$1,057	$2,195	$ 3,454
Preferred stock dividends	-0-	7	-0-	15
Net income available for common shareholders	$ 559	$1,050	$2,195	$ 3,439
Earnings per share	$ 0.43	$ 0.80	$ 1.71	$ 2.63
Average shares outstanding	1,290	1,327	1,281	1,312

REQUIRED:

1. Calculate Microsoft's net profit margin for the fourth quarter of 1996 and 1997 and for the fiscal years 1996 and 1997. Comment on the results.
2. Calculate Microsoft's working capital and current ratio. Comment on the results.
3. Did Microsoft fall short of, meet, or exceed analysts' expectations for fourth-quarter EPS?

MICROSOFT CORPORATION

Balance Sheets

($ in millions)	June 30, 1996	June 30, 1997
Assets		
Current assets		
Cash and short-term investments	$ 6,940	$ 8,966
Accounts receivable	639	980
Other	260	427
Total current assets	7,839	10,373
Property, plant, and equipment	1,326	1,465
Equity investments	675	2,346
Other assets	253	203
Total assets	$10,093	$14,387
Liabilities and Stockholders' Equity		
Current liabilities		
Accounts payable	$ 808	$ 721
Accrued compensation	202	336
Income taxes payable	484	466
Unearned revenues	560	1,418
Other	371	669
Total current liabilities	2,425	3,610

(continued)

MICROSOFT CORPORATION (*continued*)

Balance Sheets

($ in millions)	June 30, 1996	June 30, 1997
Liabilities and Stockholders' Equity		
Minority interest	125	—
Put warrants	635	—
Stockholders' equity		
Convertible preferred stock	—	980
Common stock and paid-in capital	2,924	4,509
Retained earnings	3,984	5,288
Total stockholders' equity	6,908	10,777
Total liabilities and stockholders' equity	$10,093	$14,387

4. If no reductions were made from the "Unearned revenues" account during the fourth quarter of fiscal 1997, how much did Microsoft add to the account during that quarter?
5. Continuing (4), how much higher or lower would Microsoft's fourth-quarter income before tax have been (on a per-share basis) if this accrual adjustment had not been made?
6. Assume that Microsoft reduced its "Unearned revenues" account by $188.0 million during the first three quarters of fiscal 1997. How much did Microsoft add to the account during the fiscal year?
7. Continuing (6), how much higher or lower would Microsoft's annual income before tax have been (on a per-share basis) if this accrual adjustment had not been made?
8. How much income before tax (on a per-share basis) does Microsoft have "stored" in the "Unearned revenues" account at the end of 1997?
9. How can the "Unearned revenues" account be used to manage EPS?
10. How can analysts monitor the extent to which the "Unearned revenues" account is being used to manage EPS?
11. Does the existence of the "Unearned revenues" account necessarily mean that Microsoft intends to manage its reported earnings? Explain.

C6–6

M&W Retailing (CW): Cash flow assessments and credit analysis

Founded in 1872 and incorporated in Illinois in 1968, M&W Retailing Corporation (not its real name) is one of the nation's oldest and largest retail merchandising organizations with over $6.6 billion in annual revenues. The company operates 408 retail stores in 43 states with approximately 29 million square feet of selling space. The major product offerings by the company are: appliances and consumer electronics; furniture and home furnishings; apparel; jewelry; and automotive parts and repairs. In 1988 the company was taken private by its management in a $3.8 billion leveraged buyout.

The company has been a client of your bank for 35 years. It is early January 2001, and management has approached your bank to ask for an increase in the firm's line of credit from $1.0 to $2.0 billion.

As part of the loan application process, your bank asked M&W to provide some financial information about its operations over the last five years. Because the company's fiscal year ends on December 31, 2000, the results for 2000 are not yet available, so the company has provided information covering the 1995–1999 period.

Although the firm's 2000 financial statements have not yet been finalized, management has provided the following information that it expects to report for the fiscal year ended December 31, 2000 ($ in millions):

Total revenues of $6,620 versus $7,085 in 1999
Net loss of ($237) versus net income of $11 in 1999
Cash flows from operating activities of –$356 versus –$182 in 1999
Cash flows from investing activities of –$148 versus –$109 in 1999

Cash flows from financing activities of $499 versus $295 in 1999
(Proceeds from the issuance of short-term debt of $588 were the primary source of the financing cash flows in 2000)
Overall a net cash flow of −$5 for 2000

The income statements and balance sheets that follow are prepared on both a trend basis and on a common size basis. In the trend statements, 1995 serves as the base year with all subsequent years' amounts expressed as a percent of the 1995 amount. For example, in the trend income statements, sales for 1995, 1996, and 1997 are reported at $5,655,000, 102.21, and 106.14, respectively. This means sales for 1996 were 102.21% of 1995 sales, while 1997 sales were 106.14% of 1995 sales. The trend balance sheets are constructed in a similar fashion. In the common size income statements all items are expressed as a percent of sales for that year. In the common size balance sheets all items are expressed as a percent of total assets for that year.

Note: In responding to these questions you should provide a detailed discussion and analysis of the financial statements given in the case including appropriate trend and ratio analysis.

REQUIRED:

1. Should the increase in the firm's line of credit be granted? Why or why not?
2. What other information would you like to have before finalizing your decision?

M&W RETAILING CORPORATION

Partial Trend Income Statement

	1995 ($ in millions)	1996 (%)	1997 (%)	1998 (%)	1999 (%)
Sales	$5,655	102.21	106.14	124.46	125.29
Cost of goods sold	(4,103)	102.53	107.90	123.86	125.74
Gross profit	1,552	101.35	101.48	126.03	124.10
Selling, general, and administrative expense	(1,243)	103.14	102.49	129.53	137.25
Operating income					
Before depreciation	309	94.17	97.41	111.97	71.20
Depreciation	(95)	102.11	103.16	114.74	125.26
Operating profit	214	90.65	94.86	110.75	47.20
Interest expense	(75)	68.00	58.67	80.00	125.33
Nonoperating income	19	36.84	5.26	10.53	15.79
Special items	17	0.00	0.00	0.00	0.00
Pre-tax income	175	85.71	91.43	102.29	5.71
Income taxes	(40)	125.00	147.50	155.00	(2.50)
Income from continuing operations	$ 135	74.07	74.81	86.67	8.15

M&W RETAILING CORPORATION

Partial Common Size Income Statement

	1995	1996	1997	1998	1999
Sales	100.00%	100.00%	100.00%	100.00%	100.00%
Cost of goods sold	(72.56)	(72.79)	(73.76)	(72.21)	(72.82)
Gross profit	27.44	27.21	26.24	27.79	27.18
Selling, general, and administrative expense	(21.98)	(22.18)	(21.23)	(22.88)	(24.08)
Operating income before depreciation	5.46	5.03	5.01	4.91	3.10
Depreciation	(1.68)	(1.68)	(1.63)	(1.55)	(1.68)
Operating profit	3.78	3.35	3.38	3.36	1.42

M&W RETAILING CORPORATION (*continued*)

Partial Common Size Income Statement

	1995	1996	1997	1998	1999
Interest expense	(1.33)	(0.88)	(0.73)	(0.85)	(1.33)
Nonoperating income	0.34	0.12	0.02	0.03	0.04
Special items	0.30	0.00	0.00	0.00	0.00
Pre-tax income	3.09	2.59	2.67	2.54	0.13
Income taxes	(0.71)	(0.87)	(0.98)	(0.88)	0.01
Income from continuing operations	2.38%	1.72%	1.69%	1.66%	0.14%

M&W RETAILING CORPORATION

Partial Trend Balance Sheet

	1995 ($ in millions)	1996 (%)	1997 (%)	1998 (%)	1999 (%)
Cash and equivalents	$ 623	18.94	25.04	10.75	11.24
Net receivables	73	93.15	90.41	161.64	257.53
Inventories	1,000	103.80	124.20	162.50	177.00
Accounts payable	1,227	98.61	110.68	140.10	147.03

M&W RETAILING CORPORATION

Partial Common Size Balance Sheet

	1995	1996	1997	1998	1999
Assets					
Cash and equivalents	16.08%	3.44%	4.07%	1.48%	1.43%
Net receivables	1.88	1.98	1.72	2.60	3.85
Inventories	25.81	30.24	32.39	35.79	36.24
Total assets	100.00%	100.00%	100.00%	100.00%	100.00%
Liabilities and Equity					
Accounts payable	31.66%	35.25%	35.41%	37.86%	36.94%
Long-term debt	13.94	5.97	7.35	6.48	9.17
Total liabilities	84.26	83.89	84.17	83.22	82.08
Total equity	15.74	16.11	15.83	16.78	17.92
Total liabilities and equity	100.00%	100.00%	100.00%	100.00%	100.00%

M&W RETAILING CORPORATION

Annual Statement of Cash Flows

($ in millions)	1995	1996	1997	1998	1999
Operating Activities					
Income before extraordinary items	$135	$100	$101	$117	$ 11
Noncash adjustments					
Depreciation and amortization	95	97	98	109	119
Deferred taxes	(16)	32	25	29	(7)
Gain on sale of property, plant, and equipment	0	0	0	0	(11)
Other	0	0	0	0	(12)

M&W RETAILING CORPORATION (*continued*)

Annual Statement of Cash Flows

($ in millions)	1995	1996	1997	1998	1999
Changes in operating assets and liabilities					
Receivables	21	8	5	(40)	(70)
Inventory	(73)	(38)	(204)	(243)	(145)
Deferred taxes	(8)	(34)	(1)	5	(9)
Other assets and liabilities	70	(10)	105	179	(58)
Operating activities—net cash flow	224	155	129	156	(182)
Investing Activities					
Increase in investments	(751)	(707)	(688)	(691)	(803)
Sale of investments	729	698	669	671	775
Net change in short-term investments	55	146	(8)	16	2
Capital expenditures	(128)	(146)	(142)	(184)	(122)
Sale of property, plant, and equipment	3	7	3	4	39
Acquisitions	0	0	0	(120)	0
Investing activities—other	2	2	3	0	0
Investing activities—net cash flow	(90)	0	(163)	(304)	(109)
Financing Activities					
Sale of common and preferred stock	0	1	1	78	193
Purchase of common and preferred stock	(7)	(97)	(11)	(9)	(98)
Cash dividends	(13)	(19)	(23)	(24)	(4)
Long-term debt—issuance	0	0	100	168	205
Long-term debt—reduction	(137)	(403)	(18)	(275)	(17)
Current debt—changes	0	0	0	144	16
Financing activities—other	3	2	2	1	0
Financing activities—net cash flow	(154)	(516)	51	83	295
Cash and equivalents—change	($ 20)	($361)	$ 17	($ 65)	$ 4

M&W RETAILING CORPORATION

Selected Ratios

	1995	1996	1997	1998	1999
Liquidity and Activity					
Cash flow per share	4.98	4.31	4.46	5.10	(2.94)
Inventory turnover	4.26	4.13	3.88	3.55	3.04
Receivables turnover	67.72	81.99	89.58	76.50	46.31
Total asset turnover	1.47	1.58	1.65	1.68	1.50
Collection period (days)	5	4	4	5	8
Days to sell inventory	85	87	93	102	118
Operating cycle (days)	90	92	97	106	126
Profitability					
Pre-tax profit margin (%)	3.09	2.60	2.67	2.54	0.14
Net profit margin (%)	2.39	1.73	1.68	1.66	0.16
Return on assets (%)	3.48	2.91	2.63	2.58	0.23
Return on equity (%)	25.96	18.08	16.64	17.03	1.57
Leverage					
Interest coverage	3.33	3.94	4.64	3.98	1.11
Total debt/total assets (%)	16.13	6.41	7.87	9.98	13.29
Total assets/common equity	7.45	6.21	6.32	6.61	6.98
Long-term debt/capital	46.98	27.04	31.72	27.84	33.86
Long-term debt/common equity	103.85	37.07	46.46	42.79	64.00

C6–7

Monsanto Corporation (CW): Economic value Added (EVA™)

Economic Value Added (EVA™) is a performance measure developed by Stern Stewart & Company.[39] It is designed to measure the economic value added or lost by a firm's operations. In its simplist form, EVA is just operating profits minus a capital charge for the use of the firm's assets. It can be expressed as:

$$\text{EVA} = (r - k) \times \text{Capital}$$

where r is the firm's rate of return, k is the firm's cost of capital, and Capital is the value of the net assets invested in the business.

EVA can also be expressed as:

$$\text{EVA} = \text{NOPAT} - (k \times \text{Capital}) = \text{NOPAT} - \text{Capital charge}$$

NOPAT (net operating profit after taxes), as measured by Stern Stewart, is not exactly the same as the NOPAT we used in Chapter 5. Stern Stewart makes numerous adjustments to the reported accounting numbers in arriving at its own measures of NOPAT and Capital (e.g., capitalization of operating leases, capitalization of research and development expenditures, elimination of goodwill amortization). They also have their own approach to measuring the firm's cost of capital.

To illustrate the basic features of the EVA performance metric, this case uses some simplifying assumptions with regard to how NOPAT and Capital are measured. These assumptions are discussed in the "Other Information" section that follows.

ADOPTION OF EVA BY MONSANTO:

Monsanto Company and its subsidiaries manufacture and sell a diversified line of agricultural products, chemical products, pharmaceuticals, and food ingredients (e.g., NutraSweet brand sweetener) worldwide.

MONSANTO CORPORATION

Statement of Consolidated Income

($ in millions)	1995	1994	1993
Net sales	$8,962	$8,272	$7,902
Cost of goods sold	5,109	4,774	4,564
Gross profit	3,853	3,498	3,338
Marketing expenses	1,282	1,191	1,199
Administrative expenses	598	589	548
Technological expenses	713	674	695
Amortization of intangible assets	119	81	81
Restructuring expenses—net	156	40	5
Operating income	985	923	810
Interest expense	(190)	(131)	(129)
Interest income	59	81	40
Gain on sale of styrenics plastics business	189	—	—
Other income (expense)—net	44	22	8
Income before income taxes	1,087	895	729
Income taxes	348	273	235
Net income	$ 739	$ 622	$ 494

Balance sheet data	1995	1994	1993
Total debt and total stockholders' equity (beginning of the year)	$8,891	$8,640	$9,085

[39] For a detailed discussion of the EVA™ model, see G. B. Stewart, III, The *Quest for Value* (New York: Harper Business, 1991). EVA is a trademark of Stern Stewart & Company.

The following information is from Monsanto's 1995 annual report to shareholders:

> The company has had a decade-long goal of sustaining a 20 percent ROE. When it was implemented in 1986, it was a major stretch goal for a company delivering ROE in the low teens. It subsequently led to the portfolio of businesses that has contributed to our recent success. Management now feels that most of the value has been extracted from an ROE-based target. Therefore, we wanted to find a financial metric that would create new levels of shareowner value and would be more directly correlated with the stock price. It had to be a measure that was economic-based and tied to cash flow, rather than one that is accounting based.
>
> In 1996, we will be putting in place a new system of financial metrics that features Economic Value Added (EVA™). For Monsanto, its appealing features are that it's easy to understand, it can be used by all employees, and it can be tied to incentive compensation.
>
> There are four types of value drivers in this new measurement system. The first is a focus on operational excellence. Substantial and ongoing cost reductions, redesign efforts and productivity improvements are the bread-and-butter of an EVA™ system. The second is a zero tolerance for underperforming capital. Third, growth has to add value. Alliances, joint ventures and acquisitions only are acceptable if the risk-adjusted return is greater than the cost of capital. Fourth, we can enhance EVA™ by lowering or optimizing the company's weighted cost of capital. This means using the appropriate amount of debt in our capital structure.
>
> This year, we'll be determining the targets for increasing shareowner value during our planning process. By the start of 1997, we'll begin measuring our performance against the EVA™ targets.

Other Information:

- Assume that Monsanto's cost of capital is 16%.
- Measure Capital as total debt plus total stockholders' equity.
- Measure NOPAT as net (sustainable) operating profits after taxes, excluding interest expense. Refer to Chapter 5 for details.
- Assume an income tax rate of 34% when necessary.

Required:

1. Using the 1993–1995 comparative income statement and the information above, calculate Monsanto's EVA for 1993–1995. Comment on the results.
2. How might top executive compensation be tied to EVA so that executives are motivated to improve shareholder value?

Collaborative Learning Case

C6–8

IBM Corporation (CW): Firm-specific information releases and large stock price changes

Consider the following three cases:

Required:

A. IBM (A)

1. What aspects of the following *Wall Street Journal* article are likely to have caused IBM's stock price to change?
2. As an analyst, would you recommend that your clients sell their IBM shares, buy more shares, or maintain existing holdings? Why?
3. What other information might you gather before making the recommendation in (2)?
4. Suppose one of your clients called and expressed concern that the market may have overreacted to the information in the announcement. How would you respond?

(continued)

A. IBM SHARES FALL 11% AS FIRM SAYS IT WILL CUT 25,000 JOBS AND MAY TRIM DIVIDEND; PRETAX CHARGE OF $6 BILLION EXPECTED IN 4TH PERIOD; MAINFRAME WOES MOUNT – IBM Corp. plunged deeper into the worst crisis in its history, declaring that it expects to make its first layoffs in half a century and warning that its once-sacrosanct dividend is in danger.

In a news conference a day after a special Monday board meeting, Chairman John F. Akers said IBM will take a $6 billion pretax charge for the fourth quarter to pay for cutting its work force by 25,000 more employees and shedding assets in its fading mainframe computer business.

Mr. Akers also stunned the computer industry by disclosing that IBM's business continues to deteriorate much faster than expected, with no end in sight. He said IBM will break even on an operating basis in the fourth quarter and said there's no sign of improvement in early 1993.

IBM stock, already at 10-year lows, plummeted $6.75, or almost 11%, to $56.125 in New York Stock Exchange composite trading. It was the most actively traded issue, with 12.2 million shares changing hands. Securities analysts said the stock, now trading well below IBM's Sept. 30 book value of $62, could go even lower, possibly into the 40s.

Mr. Akers said IBM will make a major shift away from its core business, the mainframe computers used by the world's big companies and governments, and into the newer software and services market. He said IBM's mainframe revenue will drop 10% this year and keep dropping next year.

Frank Metz, IBM's chief financial officer, also said the company is reevaluating its long-standing goal to show an 18% return on equity by the mid-1990s. "Clearly the path to get to that goal is longer than it was; 1994 or so is not in the cards," said Mr. Metz.

As recently as September, IBM assured Wall Street that its annual dividend of $4.84 a share was secure. But yesterday Mr. Akers said IBM's weakness over the past few months, particularly in the crucial markets of Japan and Germany, caught the company off guard. "The decline has been precipitous and it has happened at a much faster rate than we expected," he said.

In further signs of its more modest ambitions for the future, IBM said it will slash development spending next year by $1 billion and said it expects to cut its administrative overhead by another $1 billion. It also said it will keep cutting its capital spending, which fell by about $1 billion in 1992. In 1991, IBM reported that it spent more than $5 billion on plant and other property. Research and development and engineering spending consumed $6.64 billion in 1991.

IBM got a further slap from Moody's Investors Service Inc., which said it is considering downgrading the ratings of $18 billion in the debt of Big Blue and its subsidiaries. Last week, the other major rating agency, Standard & Poor's Corp., placed its triple-A rating of IBM under review. Moody's has already downgraded IBM's debt once from its top rating; most IBM issues are now rated double-A-2.

B. IBM (B)

1. What aspects of the April 30, 1997 *Wall Street Journal* article are likely to have caused IBM's stock price to change?
2. Suppose that one of your clients called and expressed concern that IBM's stock is now overvalued and that he should sell his shares. How would you respond?

B. IBM BOOSTS PAYOUT 14%, PLANS BUYBACK—IBM, underscoring its confidence in its future, boosted its dividend 14%, the second such rise in a year, and announced a $3.5 billion stock-repurchase plan.

IBM's moves sent the company's stock soaring 8% (a 5.3% increase). IBM Chairman Louis V. Gerstner told shareholders that computer networking, especially the Internet, was driving much of IBM's profit. But in a cautionary note, he acknowledged IBM's sluggish revenue growth, declaring that it was "imperative" for the company to rev up sales.

IBM's directors raised the quarterly payout to 40 cents a share from 35 cents. The dividend increase wasn't completely unexpected, but the move added to recent optimism about IBM since it reported better-than-expected earnings last week for the first quarter, and a top executive expressed confidence about the rest of 1997.

Mr. Gerstner expressed optimism about the Armonk, N.Y., company's prospects, telling the approximately 900 shareholders that IBM is benefiting from the growth in computer services and in networking, including the Internet boom. Such networking plays to the company's skills in integrating complex technology and its strength in building and selling the big 'server' computers that pump information to clients and personal-computer users. "If the shift to network computing seems suspiciously convenient to IBM, well, we got lucky," Mr. Gerstner said in his matter-of-fact way. "It's not often that a company gets a second shot at leadership."

But, he continued. "That's all it is—a shot, an opportunity. We still have to compete. We still have to execute our strategy." He added that boosting IBM's revenue—a concern of many analysts—"remains an imperative for us."

IBM last increased its quarterly dividend in April 1996, when it went to 35 cents from 25 cents a share. That increase came after a series of cutbacks from its once-rich $1.21 a share, as IBM slipped into trouble in the early 1990s.

The increased amount of money IBM's board authorized for share buybacks comes on top of more than $13.2 billion of stock IBM has repurchased since Jan. 31, 1995. Share buybacks boost per-share earnings simply by reducing the number of shares outstanding, which pleases many analysts but doesn't improve a company's underlying profitability.

Source: Republished with permission of the *Wall Street Journal*, from the *Wall Street Journal* (April 30, 1997); permission conveyed through Copyright Clearance Center, Inc.

C. Nike

1. What aspects of the following *Wall Street Journal* article are likely to have caused Nike's stock price to change?
2. Assume that you are a financial analyst. Would the information in the article cause you to alter your forecast of Nike's earnings for next year (1998)? Why? Would the article alter your earnings forecasts for each of the next five years? Why?
3. Do you think that the stock prices of Nike's competitors (e.g., Reebok, Converse, L.A. Gear, and Adidas) would change on the day that Nike made the preceding announcement? If so, how and why? If not, why not?

C. NIKE'S STOCK DROPS 13% AS FIRM SEES QUARTERLY NET FALLING SHORT OF FORECASTS—Nike Inc. warned that shifts in order patterns and other factors would drag fiscal fourth-quarter earnings below Wall Street forecasts. The news hammered the Beaverton, Ore., athletic-footwear maker's highflying shares. In New York Stock Exchange composite trading yesterday, Nike dropped $8.625, or 13%, to $55.375.

The issues crimping profits for the period ending tomorrow are relatively minor and short term, analysts said. But Wall Street and investor expectations about Nike have been high because of the company's turbocharged growth over the past several quarters. Moreover, the stock has surged in recent days on unconfirmed rumors that investor Warren Buffett has been buying Nike shares. The developments do represent the first stumble in a long time for Nike, which has had profit increases as high as 80% in recent quarters.

Nike said that it expects earnings of between 51 and 56 cents a share for the fourth quarter, including a one-time pretax charge of $18 million for the planned shutdown of a manufacturing facility. Wall Street had been expecting earnings of 69 cents a share. In the year-earlier fourth quarter, Nike earned $156.4 million, or 53 cents a share, on revenue of $1.92 billion.

Nike said several factors damped fourth-quarter profits. One was a shift in order patterns, particularly in Europe. Nike said more retailers bought more items in advance. Typically, Nike retailers buy shoes in advance, and if they sell out, make emergency "at once" orders that are delivered quickly. But Nike said retailers are making fewer "at once" orders in the current quarter. That implies that retailers' sales are lower than they expected. Some analysts said that, because of Nike's torrid growth in recent quarters, Nike retailers ordered aggressively, betting that sales would continue to surge. "Some got stuck because sales may not have gone up as rapidly as they have," said Jennifer Black Groves, an analyst with Black & Co.

Nike also said it had a "slight" increase in order cancellations in the U.S. Nike's international business has been booming, but U.S. sales still make up more than 60% of total revenue. In an analysts call, the company said it had about $30 million of canceled orders in the quarter, slightly more than it has typically had in recent quarters.

Analysts said the domestic market for Nike is mature, and suggested Nike may have priced shoes at a point where competitors can cut into Nike sales. Reebok, Converse, and Adidas all have recently introduced shoes that sell in the $80 to $110 a pair range; many Nike models cost more. "They've been walking up the price ladder and they may have gone up as far as they can go," said Alice Ruth, an analyst at Montgomery Securities.

Even with pinched fourth-quarter profit, Nike said it expects a record year, with revenue and profit increasing 40% from year-earlier levels. It also said it expects revenue growth in 1998 to surpass the company's stated goal of 15%. Last fiscal year, Nike earned $553.2 million, or $3.77 a share, on sales of $6.5 billion.

Nonetheless, the fourth-quarter projection prompted many analysts to adjust their fiscal 1997 and 1998 projections. Shelly Hale Young, analyst at Hambrecht & Quist, lowered her 1997 projection to $2.68 a share from $2.83, and dropped her 1998 forecast to $3.24 from $3.40.

Source: Republished with permission of the *Wall Street Journal*, from the *Wall Street Journal* (May 30, 1997); permission conveyed through Copyright Clearance Center, Inc.

D. General Questions

1. In situations like A (IBM) and C (Nike), firms often release important news after the market has closed for the day. Why might they do this (i.e., what are the costs and benefits of such a strategy)?
2. Beyond these news releases, what other types of firm-specific information would cause large price changes at the time of announcement?

7

The Role of Financial Information in Contracting

"A verbal contract isn't worth the paper it's written on."

—Sam Goldwyn, film producer

LEARNING OBJECTIVES:

After studying this chapter, you will understand:

1. What conflicts of interest arise between managers and shareholders, lenders, or regulators.
2. How and why accounting numbers are used in debt agreements, in compensation contracts, and for regulatory purposes.
3. How managerial incentives are influenced by accounting-based contracts and regulations.
4. What role contracts and regulations play in shaping managers' accounting choices.
5. What accounting "gimmicks" are sometimes used to hide a company's true performance, and how to spot them.

Business contracts include formal written agreements, such as Allen Ford's franchise contract with BookWorm, Inc.[1] Financial accounting numbers are often used to define contract terms and to monitor compliance with those terms.

Commercial lending agreements, for example, may require the borrower to maintain a current ratio or interest coverage ratio above a certain level. This requirement protects the lender from a deterioration of the borrower's credit risk. The lender then uses earnings, cash flow, and balance sheet data to monitor the borrower's compliance with the loan covenants. Financial data are also used in executive compensation contracts and in formal agreements with government agencies, joint-venture partners, suppliers, distributors, and customers. Figure 7.1 identifies the parties in each of these kinds of contracts.

The benefit of financial statement data for contracting purposes depends on the accounting methods used by the company and its freedom to change them. For example, an interest coverage provision is *unlikely* to protect the lender if the borrowing company can achieve the required coverage level by changing its accounting methods or through other artificial means. Contracting parties understand that financial reporting flexibility affects how contracts are written and enforced. This chapter describes these influences and addresses these questions:

- What role do accounting numbers play in contracts?
- What incentives do accounting-based contracts create for the parties involved?

[1] Chapter 6 explains why Allen Ford decided to purchase a BookWorm franchise. In this chapter, Allen must obtain a bank loan to finance the purchase.

Figure 7.1

SIGNIFICANT CONTRACTING RELATIONSHIPS IN CORPORATE ORGANIZATIONS

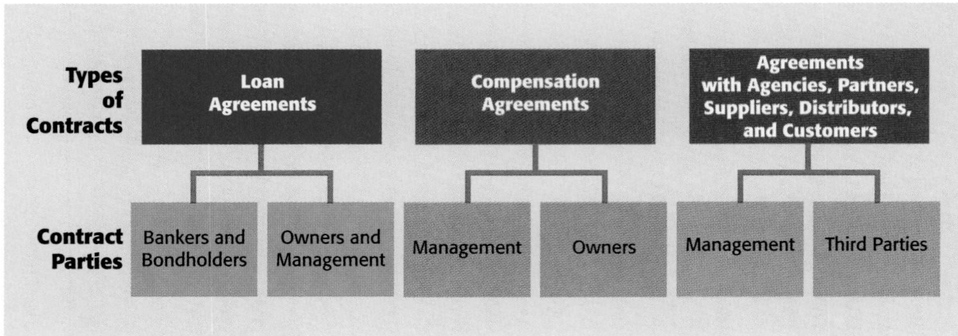

- How do these incentives help us understand why managers choose certain accounting methods and avoid others?
- How do these incentives influence when transactions are recorded?

Finalizing the BookWorm Loan

Allen Ford assembled the monthly cash flow projections and other materials requested by the loan officer. This was not easy, but it produced an unintended benefit: Allen was forced again to evaluate the economic viability of the bookstore and the financial challenges ahead. His detailed cash flow projections revealed the need for a revolving credit line, one that was slightly larger than he anticipated originally. Otherwise, the prospects for the business seemed bright, and Allen was eager to finalize the two loans.

Several days after Allen completed the loan application, the bank phoned him to indicate preliminary approval of both the term loan and the revolving credit line. Allen was elated with the approval but surprised by the interest rate. It seemed higher than other local banks were charging for similar business loans. Allen and the loan officer agreed to meet to discuss the final terms and conditions of both loans. The loan officer advised Allen to consider accepting more stringent loan covenant restrictions in exchange for a lower rate of interest. Allen was not quite sure what the loan officer had in mind, but it seemed worth exploring. Allen knew that some loan covenants were tied directly to the borrower's financial statements, and he wanted to be certain that the accounting-based covenants proposed by the bank agreed with his financial projections for the bookstore. In preparation for this negotiation, Allen reviewed the types of covenants commonly used in commercial bank loans.

Conflicts of Interest in Business Relationships

Delegating decision-making authority is an essential feature of the modern corporation and most business relationships. Capital providers (stockholders and lenders) delegate authority to professional managers. In turn, managers delegate authority over aspects of a company's business affairs to others—inside and even outside the company—who have expertise or timely access to information that is critical for decision making. (Wal-Mart and Costco, for example, allow some suppliers to monitor product sales electronically at the checkout stand and to replenish shelf inventory without first seeking company approval.) But delegation of authority can cause **conflicts of interest.** The conflicts arise when one party to the business relationship can take actions that benefit him or her but harm the other party.

Suppose that rather than operating the store himself, Allen Ford hired a bookstore manager. Would the bookstore manager always make decisions that are in Allen's (the owner's) best interest? Probably not, because some business decisions that benefit the owner may not always benefit the manager. Conversely, there will be other business decisions that directly benefit the manager at Allen's expense. Consider this example: A long-time friend of the manager arrives in town unexpectedly and suggests a leisurely lunch at the country club. The manager is tempted to agree even though it would mean closing the bookstore for two hours. Allen would prefer to keep the bookstore open because he absorbs the profit lost from closing the store and receives no benefit from the manager's luncheon reunion.

Potential conflicts of interest permeate many business relationships. Allen's franchise loans provide an illustration. The interest rate on each loan compensates the bank for credit risk and the other costs associated with providing financial capital to the BookWorm business. Once the loans are granted, however, Allen might be tempted to divert the cash toward other, more risky investment opportunities—like buying tickets in the state lottery. The chance of winning $40 million is quite remote and if the loan proceeds are diverted, the lender's risk of nonpayment jumps.

Contract terms can be designed to eliminate or reduce conflicting incentives that arise in business relationships. Allen's loan agreements will describe the business purpose for each loan and require that the borrowed funds be used only for those purposes. By agreeing to such conditions, Allen is providing the bank with a written assurance that borrowed funds will not be diverted to other (unspecified) uses—such as buying lottery tickets. Business contracts specify the mutual expectations—the rights and responsibilities—of each participant in the relationship, and thus they provide a low-cost mechanism for addressing any conflicts of interest that may arise.

Lending Agreements and Debt Covenants

Most companies have debt in the form of either commercial bank loans or bonds. In addition, managers frequently own shares of the companies they manage. As we will see, the interests of creditors and stockholders often diverge, particularly after the lender has handed over the cash. This divergence creates incentives for managers to take actions that transfer part of the company's value from creditors to the managers themselves as well as to other stockholders. ***These incentives arise because business decisions affect not only the value of the firm but also the relative share of that value which belongs to owners rather than to creditors.*** So lending agreements contain restrictions—called **covenants**—that protect lenders from these actions. Before we discuss covenants, let's more fully explore the types of creditor/owner conflicts that raise the need for covenants. Two sources of conflict can arise between creditors and owners:

- **Asset substitution:** If a company borrows to engage in low-risk investment projects and the interest rate charged reflects that low risk, the value of the business to owners is increased—and the value to creditors is reduced—by substituting higher-risk projects.
- **Repayment:** If a company borrows money for a new project and the interest rate charged presumes the company's current dividend policy will be maintained, the value of the creditor's stake is reduced when the borrowed funds are used instead to pay larger dividends. At the extreme, if the company sells all its assets and pays owners a liquidating dividend, creditors are left with a worthless business.[2]

> Investment outcomes cannot be known in advance with certainty. So it is convenient to represent outcome possibilities using a **probability distribution** like the one in Figure 7.2, which shows the likelihood that each investment project will yield a particular dollar outcome. For example, one project may have a 10% chance of earning $5,000 or less, a 40% chance of earning from $5,000 to $20,000, a 40% chance of earning between $20,000 and $35,000, and a 10% chance of earning more than $35,000.

We begin by looking at **asset substitution** and the conflicting incentives of creditors and owners. Figure 7.2 shows the probability distribution of dollar returns associated with two investment projects.[3] Each curve spans the entire range of possible dollar

[2] Descriptions of these—and other—creditor–stockholder conflicts of interest are contained in A. Barnea, R. Haugen, and L. Senbet, *Agency Problems and Financial Contracting* (Upper Saddle River, NJ: Prentice Hall, 1985); P. Milgrom and J. Roberts, *Economics, Organization and Management* (Upper Saddle River, NJ: Prentice Hall, 1992); C. Smith and J. Warner, "On Financial Contracting: An Analysis of Bond Covenants," *Journal of Financial Economics* (1979), pp. 117–61; and R. Watts and J. Zimmerman, *Positive Accounting Theory* (Upper Saddle River, NJ: Prentice Hall, 1986).

[3] This illustration of asset substitution is adapted from R. Watts and J. Zimmerman, *Positive Accounting Theory* (Upper Saddle River, NJ: Prentice Hall, 1986), p. 187.

Figure 7.2

PROBABILITY DISTRIBUTIONS OF DOLLAR RETURNS FOR TWO INVESTMENT PROJECTS

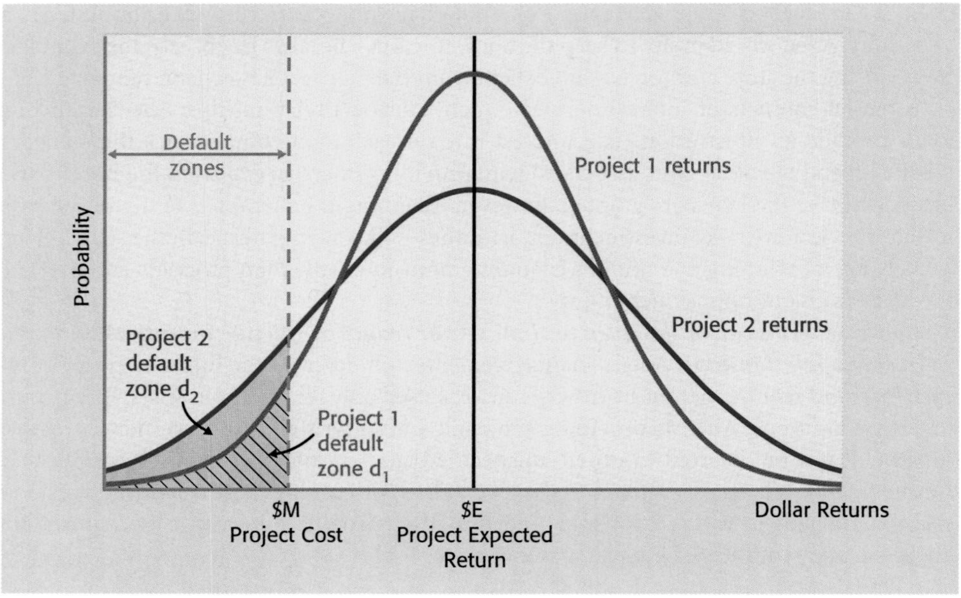

returns for the project, with the height of the curve at any given point indicating the probability of receiving that particular dollar return. Both investment projects have the same cost ($M), the same expected dollar return ($E), the same investment horizon (one year), and the same market risk.[4] But, as shown, the potential returns from Project 2 have greater dispersion (higher variance) than do those from Project 1. In other words, the extreme dollar returns—those at the far left and right in the figure—have a greater probability of occurrence for Project 2 than for Project 1.

If both projects require the same dollar investment, which one would the owner-manager select? With no debt outstanding, stockholders—including the owner-manager—would be indifferent between the two projects. That's because the value of the company is the same no matter which project is chosen, since both projects have the same cost ($M), the same expected dollar return ($E), and the same market risk.

But what if the company has debt with principal and interest payments that also total $M one year from now? Would shareholders still be indifferent between the two projects? What about creditors who supplied debt financing to the company? Would they too be indifferent?

When companies have debt outstanding, the *dispersion* of dollar returns for each investment project—the likelihood of extreme outcomes—has a bearing on the **relative value** of the project to creditors and stockholders. So even though the two projects in Figure 7.2 have the same expected value ($E), one will now be worth more to some faction than the other because they don't have the same dispersion.

To see this, consider the viewpoint of creditors who expect to be paid from the dollars earned by the chosen project. Notice that the *probability* of Project 1 generating dollar returns less than the required $M loan payment is given by the crosshatched area d_1 under the Project 1 curve. We refer to this region as the "default zone" because if Project 1 produces returns to the left of $M, the company will default on part or all of its required loan payment. Since the probability of all possible dollar returns from a given project must sum to one, the probability that creditors will receive full payment is $(1 - d_1)$; this is shown by the *unshaded area* under the Project 1 curve to the right of $M.

The default zone for Project 2 is the grey area d_2 (which includes the crosshatched area d_1). The probability that creditors will receive full payment from Project 2 is $(1 - d_2)$, and

[4] These project attributes greatly simplify the discussion. **Market risk** is the covariance of project returns with market returns in the sense commonly used when discussing capital asset pricing models. See, for example, S. A. Ross, R. W. Westerfield, and J. F. Jaffe, *Corporate Finance* (Homewood, IL: Irwin, 1993), p. 295.

because d_2 is larger than d_1, the probability of debt repayment for Project 1 is greater than the probability of debt repayment for Project 2.

Compare the default regions of the two investments. Creditors prefer Project 1 over Project 2 because Project 1 has a lower default probability than does Project 2—and thus, it has a correspondingly higher probability that creditors will be paid in full. Obviously, the value of the business to creditors will be greater if Project 1 is chosen because it has less default risk.

But what do stockholders prefer? Project 2 has a higher probability of very large dollar returns to stockholders. But, what about the project's higher risk of a large loss? Stockholders are not obligated to pay a company's debts when corporate cash flows are inadequate to cover what is owed. This limits stockholders' "downside" exposure: When project returns fall below \$M, stockholders don't have to make up the shortfall so that creditors can be paid. Creditors, on the other hand, have limited "upside potential" because their **fixed claim** (the \$M loan payment in our example) to corporate cash flows does not get larger when project returns exceed \$M. ***All other things being equal, stockholders of companies with debt financing prefer investment projects with high dispersion (like Project 2), because they receive all payoffs greater than \$M while creditors absorb the loss associated with payoffs less than \$M.***

If the company borrows \$M for low-risk Project 1 but then invests the funds in high-risk Project 2, stockholder value is increased but creditor value falls. Substituting the high-risk Project 2 for the low-risk Project 1 leaves shareholders with more upside potential—but creditors have more "downside risk" of default. Asset substitution transfers wealth from creditors to shareholders but leaves the total value of the business unchanged. This result is illustrated in Figure 7.3(a).

The situation we've just described involved projects with the same cost, expected return, and market risk—and thus, the same total value. We've also seen that asset substitution changes how the company's total value is shared between owners and creditors—but that it does not change the value of the company.

Another kind of asset substitution—illustrated in Figure 7.3(b)—occurs when the high-risk Project 2 has a lower expected value (or greater market risk) than Project 1. Here

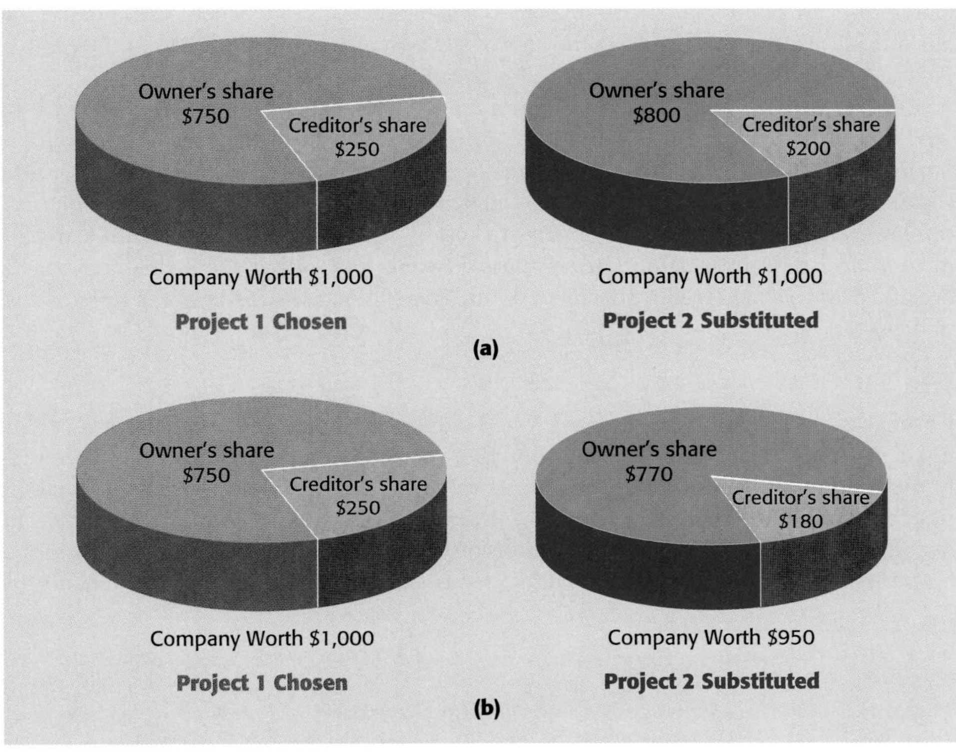

Figure 7.3

THE CONSEQUENCES OF ASSET SUBSTITUTION FOR OWNERS AND CREDITORS

(a) Investment projects with the same expected dollar returns (and market risk) but different dispersions.
(b) Investment projects with different expected dollar returns (and market risk) and different dispersions.

the creditors' loss is even greater because the company itself becomes less valuable. Skipping the details, we see that the end result is that borrowing for Project 1 but then putting the money into Project 2 instead makes:

- the company worth less because Project 2 has a smaller total value than Project 1 ($950 versus $1,000), and
- the owners' share of the company worth more ($770 versus $750) and the creditors' share worth less because Project 2 has more dispersion than Project 1.

Stockholders are willing to substitute projects that *reduce* the total value of the company when the wealth transfer from creditors more than compensates them for the overall value loss. The company is worth less ($950 versus $1,000), but substitution results in more value for shareholders ($770 versus $750) and less for creditors ($180 versus $250).

The **repayment problem** involves how to use the cash generated by the company's operating activities. Management has one of three choices:

1. Reinvest the cash back into the business
2. Repay amounts owed to lenders
3. Pay dividends to or buy back shares from stockholders.

When companies are financed partially with debt, owner-managers have incentives to distribute cash to stockholders (including themselves).[5] This could be done in several ways. Management could forego investments in positive net present value projects and instead pay dividends to shareholders or repurchase outstanding shares; or management could sell existing business assets and distribute the proceeds to shareholders (again by means of dividends or share repurchases). Both actions leave creditors with a company of greatly reduced value or worse—an "empty corporate shell." The value of the business to creditors is reduced because there are fewer total corporate resources available for debt repayment, making loan default more likely.

Creditors know that their interests will sometimes conflict with the interests of shareholders and owner-managers. Without protections in lending agreements, creditors will demand a higher return (interest rate) on business loans as compensation for the added risk of asset substitution and repayment. This higher interest rate is the way creditors get paid for the possibility that owner-managers will take actions that benefit shareholders but harm creditors. But this increases the cost of debt financing and shifts $M to the right in Figure 7.2—thus causing shareholder value to fall!

Another way to reduce conflicts of interest between creditors and shareholders is by writing contracts that restrict—explicitly or implicitly—the owner-manager's ability to harm creditors.[6] To do this, loan provisions are specifically designed to address asset substitution and repayment. These covenants effectively lower the default risk of creditors, and this lower risk, in turn, lowers the borrower's cost of debt financing and shifts $M loan payment to the left. ***Debt covenants benefit both creditors and shareholders.*** Creditors benefit because debt covenants reduce default risk, and shareholders benefit from the lowered cost of debt.

The Structure of Debt Covenants

Covenants are intensively negotiated. They require the borrower to maintain a certain financial status for the loan's duration, and they set minimum standards for the borrower's future conduct and performance. Covenants vary with the borrower's business characteristics, financial condition, and the length of the loan. If credit risk is high, covenants may be tied directly to detailed financial projections provided by the borrower; where credit risk is low, a few general financial benchmarks may be sufficient. In either case covenants are

---

5 S. C. Myers, "Determinants of Corporate Borrowing," *Journal of Financial Economics* (November 1977), pp. 147–75.

6 See M. C. Jensen and W. H. Meckling, "Theory of the Firm: Managerial Behavior, Agency Costs and Ownership Structure," *Journal of Financial Economics* (October 1976), pp. 305–60 or Smith and Warner, op. cit.

designed to protect the creditor and to give an early warning of deterioration in the financial condition of the borrower.

Affirmative covenants stipulate actions the borrower *must* take. Generally, these include:

1. Using the loan for the agreed-upon purpose
2. Financial covenants and reporting requirements
3. Compliance with laws
4. Rights of inspection
5. Maintenance of insurance, properties, and records.

Financial covenants establish minimum financial tests with which a borrower must comply. These tests can specify dollar amounts (such as required minimum levels of net worth and working capital) or ratios (such as minimum debt-to-equity and interest coverage ratios). Financial covenants are intended to signal financial difficulty and to trigger intervention by the creditor—we explain how later—long before bankruptcy or liquidation become necessary. To keep the lender informed about the company's financial and operating performance, the borrower is required to provide financial reports to the lender in a timely manner. Here is an example from TCBY Enterprises—"The Country's Best Yogurt":

> [The company] will furnish . . . not later than one hundred twenty days (120) after the close of each fiscal year . . . consolidated balance sheets, income statements and statements of cash flow . . . and such other comments and financial details as are usually included in similar reports. (para. 5.1 of TCBY term loan agreement)

Financial covenants often do not stipulate the accounting methods to be used when preparing the statements, except that they must comply with generally accepted accounting principles (GAAP):

> Such reports shall be prepared in accordance with GAAP and shall be audited by independent certified public accountants of recognized standing . . . and shall contain unqualified opinions . . . (para. 5.1 of TCBY term loan agreement).

Loan agreements guard against asset substitution by placing restrictions on how the money can be used:

> Borrower will use the proceeds of the term loans for the loan purposes set forth . . . in Section 1.1 of this agreement. (para. 5.5 of TCBY term loan agreement).

The financial covenants establish specific levels of performance as well as conditions that must be met, and they give precise meaning to the financial terms and ratios mentioned in the contract:

> Borrower will at all times maintain a ratio of Current Assets to Current Liabilities . . . that is greater than 2.0 to 1.0 . . . a Profitability Ratio greater than 1.5 to 1.0 . . . [defined as] the ratio of Net Income for the immediately preceding period of twelve calendar months to Current Maturities of Long Term Debt . . . a Fixed Charge Coverage Ratio greater than 1.0 to 1.0 . . . [defined as] the ratio of Net Income of the Borrower and Subsidiaries for the immediately preceding period of twelve calendar months plus Noncash Charges of the Borrower and Subsidiaries for the same period to Current Maturities of Long Term Debt of the Borrower and Subsidiaries plus cash dividends paid by TCBY to the shareholders of TCBY for the preceding period of twelve calendar months plus Replacement CapEx of the Borrower and Subsidiaries for the preceding twelve calendar months . . . (paras. 5.7, 5.8, and 5.9 of TCBY term loan agreement).

Notice that TCBY is required to maintain a **fixed charge coverage** ratio greater than 1.0, and the ratio is defined as:

$$\text{Fixed charge coverage} = \frac{\text{Net income} + \text{Noncash charges}}{\text{Current maturities} + \text{Dividends} + \text{Replacement CapEx}}$$

all measured over the most recent 12 months. Noncash charges—like depreciation and goodwill amortization—are added back to net income because they don't reduce the cash available for debt repayment. Replacement CapEx—capital expenditures required to maintain (but not expand) the business—is viewed by TCBY's lender as a necessary cash outflow, like debt repayment.

Also notice how the fixed charge coverage requirement indirectly limits the company's ability to pay dividends. Suppose TCBY had net income of \$50, noncash charges of \$35, current loan maturities of \$40, and replacement capital expenditures of \$30. How large a dividend could TCBY pay to shareholders? A simple calculation shows the answer to be \$15.

$$\text{Fixed charge coverage} = \frac{\$50 + \$35}{\$40 + \text{Dividend} + \$30} = 1.0$$
$$= \frac{\$50 + \$35}{\$40 + \$15 + \$30} = 1.0$$

Dividends in excess of \$15 would put TCBY in violation of its fixed-charge coverage requirement.

Negative covenants tend to be more significant and even more intensively negotiated than affirmative covenants, because they place direct *restrictions* on managerial decisions. These restrictions prevent actions that might impair the lender's claims against the company's cash flows, earnings, and assets. Negative covenants include limits on total indebtedness, investment of funds, capital expenditures, leases, and corporate loans, as well as restrictions on the payment of cash dividends, share repurchases, mergers, asset sales, voluntary prepayment of other indebtedness, and on new business ventures. This example is from the TCBY loan agreement:

> [Borrower agrees that it will not] sell, lease, transfer, or otherwise dispose of any assets . . . except the sale of inventory in the ordinary course of business and disposition of obsolete or worn-out equipment upon the replacement thereof . . . [or to] repurchase the stock of TCBY using, directly or indirectly, the proceeds of any loan. (paras. 6.6 and 6.12 of TCBY term loan agreement).

The prohibition on stock repurchases addresses the repayment problem described earlier in the chapter.

Restrictions on total indebtedness limit the amount of additional debt the company may incur over the term of the loan. These restrictions are stated as a dollar amount or in the form of a ratio (e.g., total debt to assets, or working capital, or tangible net worth):

> [Borrower agrees that it will not take on any new loans if] the aggregate amount of all such loans, advances and extensions of credit . . . would exceed twenty-five percent (25%) of the consolidated Tangible Net Worth of the Borrower . . . (para. 6.3 of TCBY term loan agreement).

Covenants restricting the use of funds for dividend payments, share repurchases, capital expenditures, and other business purposes are included so the creditor has greater assurance that cash will be available to make interest and principal payments when due. In limiting the borrower's ability to sell, merge, or transfer operating assets, the creditor is ensuring the survival of the borrower's repayment potential.

It is also common for a borrower to agree not to use any of its existing property as collateral on future loans without first obtaining consent from the current lender:

> [Borrower agrees that it will not] [c]reate, incur, assume or suffer to exist any Lien, encumbrance, or charge of any kind (including any lease required to be capitalized under GAAP) upon any of its properties and/or assets other than Permitted Liens. (para. 6.1 of TCBY term loan agreement).

An unusual feature of this **negative pledge**—a promise to not take a particular action—is that TCBY agrees to limit its property leasing activities, but it does so only for leases required to be capitalized under GAAP. The agreement does not restrict TCBY from utilizing more operating leases.

The **events of default** section of a loan agreement describes circumstances in which the creditor has the right to terminate the lending relationship. Situations leading to default include the failure to pay interest or principal when due, inaccuracy in representations, failure to abide by a covenant, failure to pay other debts when due (known as "cross default"), impairment of collateral, change in management or ownership, and bankruptcy.

Most lending agreements require the borrower to provide a **Certificate of Compliance,** which affirms that management has reviewed the financial statements and found no violation of any covenant provision. If a covenant has been violated, the nature and status of the violation must be specified.[7] Remedies for breach of covenant restrictions include renegotiation of the debt contract terms (e.g., an increase in the interest rate), seizure of collateral, acceleration of the maturity of the debt, or initiation of legal bankruptcy proceedings.

The common remedy creditors exercise in the event of default is renegotiation of the loan agreement. All aspects of the loan—payment schedule, interest rate, collateral, affirmative and negative covenants—may be renegotiated. In cases where the circumstances of default are considered relatively insignificant, the creditor may waive the violation or give the borrower a period of time—a "grace period"—to correct its covenant breach. In cases where the default is severe, the creditor may accelerate loan repayment (with interest) and terminate its relationship with the borrower. Although creditors rarely exercise the right to accelerate repayment, having this right substantially strengthens a lender's negotiating position with the borrower if problems arise.

RECAP

When it comes to a company's business decisions, what's best for managers and shareholders isn't always best for creditors. Debt covenants—including those based on accounting numbers—help reduce this conflict of interest. Creditors benefit because debt covenants reduce default risk, and shareholders benefit from the lowered cost of debt financing.

Managers' Responses to Potential Debt Covenant Violations

Violating a covenant is costly. So managers have strong incentives to make accounting choices that reduce the likelihood of technical default. Accounting choices include not only the selection of alternative accounting techniques (e.g., LIFO versus FIFO inventory methods) but also accrual adjustments (e.g., changing the amount of bad debt provisions), and decisions about when to initiate transactions that result in accounting gains or losses (e.g., asset sales or corporate restructuring). Readers of financial statements must be able to recognize and understand these incentives and their effect on managers' accounting choices.

A **technical default** occurs when the borrower violates one or more loan covenants but has made all interest and principal payments. A **payment default** occurs when the borrower is unable to make the scheduled interest or principal payment.

A number of studies have examined how incentives arising out of debt contracts affect managers' accounting choices. One study looked at voluntary accounting changes made by 130 companies reporting covenant violations from 1980 to 1989. This study found that net worth and working capital restrictions are the most frequently violated accounting-based covenants and that companies approaching default often made accounting changes that increased reported earnings.[8] The most common techniques

---

[7] Any covenant breach that existed at the date of the most recent balance sheet and that subsequently has not been cured (i.e., remedied or corrected) should be disclosed in the notes to the financial statements (Rule 4–08[c] of Securities and Exchange Commission [SEC] Regulation S-X). When covenants are violated, the related debt must be reclassified as current if it is probable that the borrower will not be able to cure the default within the next 12 months. See "Classification of Obligations that are Callable by the Creditor," *Statement of Financial Accounting Standards [SFAS] No. 78* (Stamford, CT: Financial Accounting Standards Board [FASB] 1983) and "Classification of Obligations When a Violation Is Waived by the Creditor," *Emerging Issues Task Force 86–30* (Stamford, CT: FASB, 1986).

[8] A. P. Sweeney, "Debt-Covenant Violations and Managers' Accounting Responses," *Journal of Accounting and Economics* (May 1994), pp. 281–308.

used to increase earnings are changes in pension cost assumptions (to be discussed later in Chapter 14), the liquidation of LIFO layers, and the adoption of the FIFO inventory method (Chapter 9).

Another study examined what are called **discretionary accounting accruals**—noncash financial statement adjustments which "accrue" revenue (e.g., debits to accounts receivable and credits to sales) or accrue expenses (e.g., debits to warranty expense and credits to accrued warranties payable).[9] This study, which looked at discretionary accruals by 94 companies reporting covenant violations from 1985 to 1988, found that "abnormal" accruals in the year prior to violation significantly increased reported earnings by accelerating revenue and postponing expenses. (Normal accruals were determined by examining each company's past accruals and by benchmarking against average accruals reported by other firms in the same industry that year.) Moreover, these accrual adjustments were also more likely to increase working capital in the year of covenant violation.

These and other studies suggest that ***management tends to make accounting changes and/or to manipulate discretionary accruals to avoid violating debt covenants.*** Earnings increases that arise from management's efforts to avoid violating covenant provisions are unlikely to reflect the true underlying economic condition of the company and, therefore, are not likely to be sustainable. Unsustainable earnings increases are unlikely to translate into permanent cash flow increases (Chapter 2). These "tenuous" earnings components should be interpreted with caution.

Throughout the remainder of the book, we highlight how alternative accounting methods and accrual adjustments affect earnings and key financial ratios. We'll alert you to accounting choices that can have substantial implications for debt covenants—implications you should keep in mind as you go about interpreting and using accounting numbers for making economic decisions.

Management Compensation

Most modern corporations are not run by descendants of those who founded the organization but instead are controlled by professional managers—that is, "hired hands" who may lack the passion for corporate excellence that comes with substantial share ownership. This separation of ownership and control creates potential conflicts of interest between shareholders and managers.

Consider a top executive whose job requires extensive travel and who, for reasons of "comfort and convenience," prefers the corporate jet to a commercial airline. Who receives the benefits of the comfort and convenience? And who pays the cost? If the comfort and convenience that comes from using the corporate jet leads to increased managerial productivity, both parties stand to gain. Shareholders lose, however, when the benefits of comfort and convenience accrue only to the executive and there are no productivity improvements. That's because shareholders alone bear the added cost of travel by corporate jet.

> The corporate jet example illustrates one type of conflict between shareholders and managers—the tendency of managers to "overconsume" corporate resources. But there are others. For example, managers who are close to retirement age may have little incentive to adopt a long-term focus by investing in R&D.

Obviously, managers have incentives to use corporate assets for their personal benefit at the expense of owners. Potential conflicts of interest can be overcome if managers are given incentives which cause them to behave like owners. One way is a compensation package that links managerial pay to improvements in firm value.[10] If the manager's compensation goes up as the organization's value increases, managers have an incentive to take actions that lead to increased firm value—that is, managers and owners benefit simultaneously.

---

[9] M. L. DeFond and J. Jiambalvo, "Debt Covenant Violation and Manipulation of Accruals," *Journal of Accounting and Economics* (January 1994), pp. 145–76.

[10] A more complete discussion of compensation incentives and owner–manager conflicts of interest is contained in Jensen and Meckling, op. cit., Milgrom and Roberts, op. cit., and Watts and Zimmerman, op. cit.

Two ways of aligning managers' incentives with owners' interests are to link compensation to stock returns and/or financial performance measures such as accounting earnings. Both are widely used. Neither is perfect.

Consider stock returns. Managerial strategies and decisions clearly affect share prices in the long run. But in the short run, share prices could rise or fall due to factors like interest rate changes that are beyond management's control.

Changes in interest rates affect stock prices for two reasons. To see why, consider the effect of a *decrease* in marketwide interest rates. First notice that a decrease in marketwide interest rates will reduce the company's cost of equity capital. As you know from Chapter 6, this will increase share price. Second, as interest rates decrease, the yields on fixed-rate bond investments fall, making them less attractive to investors. Both factors contribute to an increase in the demand for stocks and to an increase in stock prices.

Similar problems cloud the linkage between compensation and financial performance measures like earnings. On the positive side, earnings are probably less susceptible to the influence of temporary and external economic forces, and unlike stock returns, accounting-based financial performance measures can be tied to a manager's specific responsibilities, such as the profitability of a single product line or geographical region. On the other hand, using accounting earnings as a measure is frequently criticized for its reliance on accruals, deferrals, allocations, and valuations that involve varying degrees of subjectivity and judgment.

A good compensation plan must overcome the incentive alignment problems we have discussed and motivate managers to act like owners.[11]

How Executives Are Paid

Most compensation packages involve a base salary, an annual (or short-term) incentive, and a long-term incentive:

- **Base salary** is typically dictated by industry norms and the executive's specialized skills.
- **Short-term incentives** set annual financial performance goals that must be achieved if the executive is to earn various bonus awards. For example, a plan may stipulate that a bonus of 10% of salary is earned only if the after-tax return on assets for the company exceeds 12%. But a 20% bonus can be earned if the return on assets is 15% or more. Such plans link pay to performance; since compensation is "at risk," managers have an incentive to achieve plan goals.
- **Long-term incentives** motivate and reward executives for the company's long-term growth and prosperity (typically three to seven years). Long-term incentives are designed to counterbalance the inherently short-term orientation of other incentives.

Figure 7.4 illustrates the size and mix of compensation for chief executive officers (CEOs) based on a recent survey of pay practices at 500 industrial companies. At medium-sized companies, base salary represents only 37% of the median total CEO pay. Variable compensation, in the form of short-term (i.e., annual) and long-term incentives, makes up the largest portion of top executive pay at both medium and large companies. Notice also that the amount of CEO pay "at risk"—the combined percentage of short-term and long-term incentive compensation—is substantially greater for large companies (51% + 21% = 72%) than for small companies (21% + 11% = 32%).

Within a given organization, the proportion of pay "at risk" falls off steeply for executives on lower rungs of the corporate ladder. One compensation survey found that corporate executives in large industrial companies had 71% of their 1997 pay at risk, mid-level managers had 20% of their pay at risk, and nonmanagerial professionals had only 8% of their pay at risk.[12]

[11] Certain features of executive compensation packages are also designed to reduce the combined tax liability of the company and its managers. Tax considerations undoubtedly contribute to the popularity of certain pay practices and help explain their use by some companies and not others. See C. W. Smith and R. L. Watts, "Incentive and Tax Effects of Executive Compensation Plans," in R. Ball and C. W. Smith (eds.), *The Economics of Accounting Policy Choice* (McGraw-Hill: New York, 1992).

[12] *1998 Hay Compensation Report,* Hay Group, Inc., 1998.

Figure 7.4

CEO TOTAL EXECUTIVE COMPENSATION

A typical "small" company has revenues of about $500 million, a "medium" company has revenues of about $2 billion, and a "large" company has revenues of about $10 billion.

Source: J. D. England, "Executive Pay, Incentives, and Performance," in D. E. Logue (ed.), *Handbook of Modern Finance* (Boston: Warren, Gorham & Lamont, 1996), p. E9-3.

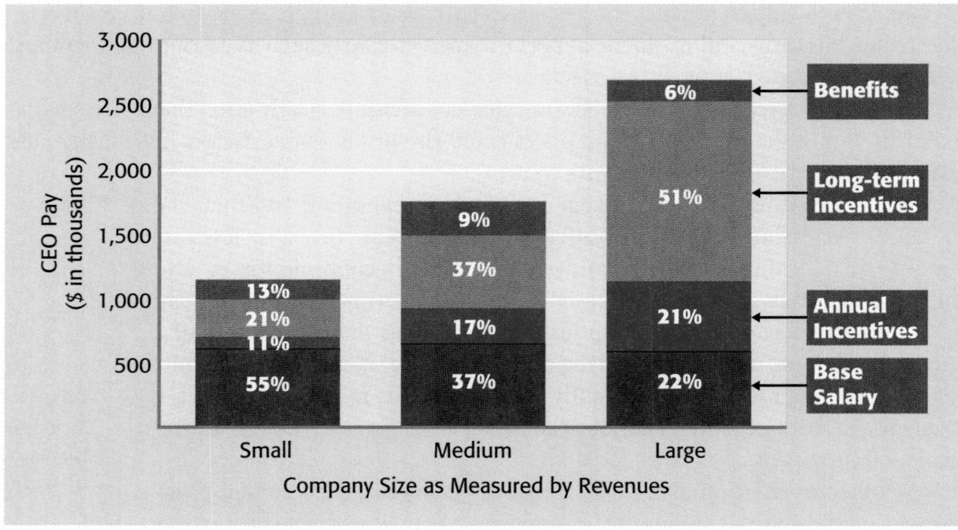

Long-term incentives comprise a large portion of total compensation for most CEOs, although many long-term plans are not tied directly to accounting numbers. Figure 7.5 shows the prevalence of long-term incentives by type.

Stock options are the most common long-term incentive device. Because the option has value only if the market price of the underlying stock rises, the executive has an incentive to increase shareholder value as measured by stock price. So-called **incentive stock options** qualify for favorable tax treatment—that is, the executive is taxed at the capital gains rate, which is usually lower than the ordinary income tax rate. So-called **nonqualified stock options** do not have this personal tax advantage.

Stock appreciation rights (SARs) are a stock option variation developed to ease the cash flow burden faced by executives when stock options are exercised. The executive does not have to pay anything to receive the cash value of an appreciated SAR. When granted in tandem with traditional stock options, SARs can provide all of the cash needed to exercise the options, including any associated tax liability.

Restricted stock is typically an award of stock that is nontransferable or subject to forfeiture for a period of years. Restricted stock grants provide a set of "golden handcuffs" for retaining executives with desirable skills, at least during the restriction period. **Phantom stock** has all the characteristics of restricted stock, except that the executive receives the cash value of shares "earned out," not the shares themselves.

Performance plans award shares or cash units earned according to the degree of achievement of predetermined performance goals. From a financial reporting perspective, these plans are important because performance goals are often tied to financial targets (e.g., earnings-per-share growth or return-on-equity hurdles). Occasionally, the performance goals are strategic—increasing market share, reducing costs, or raising product quality. Performance goals are established at the beginning of the award period, which usually ranges from four to seven years, and may be stated in absolute terms or relative to the performance levels achieved by peer companies over the award period.

Performance unit (or cash) plans allocate to each executive a given number of "units" of fixed dollar value at the start of the award period. At the end of the award period, the executive receives cash equal to the number of units "earned out" times the fixed dollar value, with the proportion of units earned determined by the degree to which performance goals have been achieved.

Performance shares are similar to unit plans in that each executive is allocated a fixed number of common shares, with the proportion earned out again contingent upon the extent

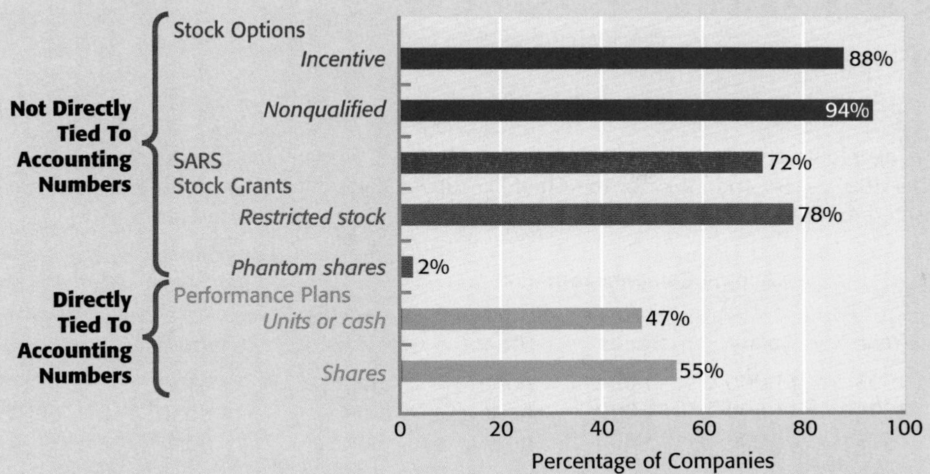

Stock options come in various forms, the choice of which is largely dependent on the tax treatment for the executive and the company. Stock options give the executive the right to buy shares at a stated (exercise) price, typically the fair market price on the grant date, for a period of years. If the stock price rises, the executive may trade in (or "exercise") each option plus pay the stated exercise price in exchange for a share of company stock. *Nonqualified stock options* require the executive to pay ordinary income tax at the exercise date on the difference between the stated exercise price and the stock's current fair market value. Under certain Internal Revenue Code provisions, *incentive stock options* may be awarded that offer capital gains tax treatment; however, the corporate tax deductibility of the options is also limited by Code provisions.

Stock appreciation rights (SARs) do not require the manager to exercise the option and pay the stated exercise price in order to capture the gain. Instead, with SARs an executive receives an amount equal to the difference between the current stock price and the exercise price. This "appreciation" can be paid in stock, cash, or both. SARs enable companies and their executives to reduce the transaction costs associated with exercising options.

Stock grants give the executive outright ownership of company shares. With *restricted stock,* only after all restrictions lapse are the shares "earned out" and unconditionally owned by the executive. The most prevalent restriction is one of continued employment, although performance-related conditions are sometimes applied. Dividends can be paid to the executive even when the stock is restricted, and many restricted stock awards carry immediate voting rights. With *phantom* (hypothetical) *shares,* the executive "owns" the share value but not the stock itself.

Performance plans require the manager to achieve certain multiyear financial performance goals such as a three-year average return on equity above 20%. The payout could be either cash or company shares.

Figure 7.5

PREVALENCE OF LONG-TERM INCENTIVES

Source: England, op cit.

to which financial and strategic goals are met. Since performance plans comprise an important element of long-term incentive compensation, analysts and other statement readers must be aware that financial reporting choices have a potential impact on managers' long-term compensation.

Information about a company's executive compensation practices can be found in the annual proxy statement, a notification of the annual shareholders meeting, filed with the SEC. Among other disclosures, this document describes both the compensation payments and awards made to the five highest paid executives of the company and any new executive compensation plans submitted for shareholder approval. Exhibit 7.1 presents excerpts from the 1996 proxy statement of Reebok International Ltd.

Why did Reebok require its top executives to use part of their 1995 cash bonus to buy restricted shares of the company's common stock? (See highlighted section of Exhibit 7.1.) Bonuses do not provide a very strong incentive for managers to act like owners since earnings can be "managed." Stock ownership can strengthen managers'

Although performance plans have been a key element of long-term incentive compensation in many companies for a number of years, passage of the Tax Reform Act of 1993 provided further impetus for pay plans linked to specific performance goals. See the discussion in Reebok's proxy statement (Exhibit 7.1).

Exhibit 7.1 ■ REEBOK INTERNATIONAL LTD.

Notice of Annual Meeting of Shareholders
(May 7, 1996)

Executive Compensation

The following table sets forth the aggregate compensation paid or accrued by the Company for services rendered during the years ended December 1993, 1994 and 1995 for the Chief Executive Officer and each of the Company's four other most highly compensated executive officers. [Authors' note: Three executives are omitted for brevity.]

		Annual Compensation ($k)			Long-Term Compensation		
Name and Position	**Year**	**Salary**	**Bonus**	**Other**	**Restricted Stock ($k)**	**Options**	**Other ($k)**
Paul B. Fireman	1995	$1,000	none	none	none	87,300	$ 97
Chairman, President and	1994	1,000	$1,000	none	none	none	69
Chief Executive Officer	1993	1,000	650	none	none	none	231
Paul R. Duncan	1995	600	120	none	none	40,000	52
Executive Vice President	1994	583	525	none	none	none	16
	1993	500	357	none	none	25,000	77

Certain of the Company's executive officers are required to defer twenty-five percent (25%) of their 1995 bonus award and to invest it into restricted shares of Reebok Common Stock. Fifty percent (50%) of such shares vest on each of January 1, 1997 and January 1, 1998. Any unvested portion of such shares will be forfeited if the executive officer leaves the Company prior to such vesting dates.

Approval of Executive Performance Incentive Plan

On February 15, 1996 the Compensation Committee of the Board of Directors unanimously approved, subject to approval by shareholders at the 1996 Annual Meeting, the Reebok International Ltd. Executive Performance Incentive Plan (the "Incentive Plan") which provides for the awarding of bonuses to certain executive officers or other key employees of the Company and its subsidiaries subject to attainment of certain performance criteria.

In 1993, the Internal Revenue Code was amended by adding Section 162(m) which limits to $1 million the federal income tax deduction which public corporations may claim for compensation paid to any of its top five executives except in certain limited circumstances. One such exception is for compensation based solely on the attainment of one or more performance criteria which are established by an independent compensation committee and approved by shareholders. The Incentive Plan is intended to comply with this exclusion for performance-based compensation and is being submitted to shareholders for approval in order to preserve the deductibility of compensation paid under the Incentive Plan.

The following is a brief description of certain material features of the Incentive Plan.

Term. Subject to approval by shareholders, the Incentive Plan will be effective as of January 1, 1996 and will continue until December 31, 2000 unless reapproved by the Company's shareholders or unless amended or terminated.

Participants. Participants in the Incentive Plan will be those corporate officers and other key employees of the Company and its subsidiaries who are selected annually to participate in the Plan by the Compensation Committee. It is anticipated that the participants selected by the Compensation Committee will be those officers and other key employees whose compensation may be subject to the deductibility limits of Section 162(m) of the Code and will include annually less than twenty individuals . . .

incentives and reduce potential owner-manager conflicts of interest. The restriction on the stock—some or all of the bonus investment is lost if the executive leaves within two years—exists to make certain that the executives don't just "take the money and run." The two-year vesting provision encourages managers to worry about the company's longer-term financial success.

Exhibit 7.1 ■ **REEBOK INTERNATIONAL LTD. (*continued*)**

Notice of Annual Meeting of Shareholders (May 7, 1996)

Performance Criteria. Within 90 days after the beginning of each fiscal year of the Company, the Compensation Committee will establish for each participant an objective performance goal or goals based on one or more of the following performance criteria: net income (before or after taxes); operating income; revenue; advance orders or bookings; expenses; return on sales; gross or net margin; cash flow; earnings per share; return on assets; return on equity; total shareholder return; market share; inventory turnover; and stock price. In establishing such performance goals, the Compensation Committee may apply the performance criteria as a measure of the Company or a subsidiary, or any product category or categories. The Compensation Committee will also determine the amounts of the target awards that will be paid if the performance goal or goals are met and the method by which such amounts will be calculated. In addition, at the Committee's option, it may determine that all or any part of the award will be paid in shares of Reebok Common Stock having an equivalent value to the amount of the award, which shares will be subject to such restrictions as the Compensation Committee may determine. In any case, the maximum award that may be paid to any participant under the Incentive Plan for any year is the lesser of 300% of such participant's base salary in effect such year or $3 million.

Determination of Award. . . . In order to reflect additional considerations relating to performance, the Compensation Committee may, in its discretion, reduce or eliminate any calculated award to be paid to a participant, but may not increase such award.

An affirmative vote of a majority of the shares present, in person or by proxy, and entitled to vote at the Annual Meeting is required to approve the Incentive Plan.

The Board of Directors unanimously recommends that shareholders vote FOR [the proposal].

A second feature of Reebok's executive compensation is that both financial (e.g., earnings per share, cash flow, return on assets) and nonfinancial (e.g., bookings, market share) performance measures were used.[13] Financial metrics like last year's earnings per share tell us about the past. However, nonfinancial metrics like sales orders booked are lead indicators of future economic performance. Also, some of the financial metrics used at Reebok were accounting-based (e.g., gross margin, operating income, revenue) while others were market-based (e.g., total shareholder return, stock price). The end result is a mixture of internal and external financial metrics combined with some nonfinancial metrics to produce a "balanced scorecard" for evaluating managerial performance.[14]

At Reebok and most other companies today, it's the **compensation committee** that is responsible for implementing the executive pay plan. This committee is comprised of the company's outside (nonmanagement) directors. It selects the performance metrics to be used and sets the annual or multiyear performance goals for each executive. The committee can also override the bonus formula when circumstances warrant. Reebok's compensation committee is allowed to reduce or eliminate any calculated award but it may not increase the award. As we will see in a moment, compensation committees play an important role in reducing managers' incentives to meet the performance target using accounting "gimmickry."

Incentives Tied to Accounting Numbers

Figure 7.5 showed that 47% to 55% of all companies use performance plans, which are usually tied to accounting numbers, as *long-term* compensation incentives. For *annual* bonus plans, accounting numbers become overwhelmingly important. Let's take a closer look at

---

13 To learn more about the use of nonfinancial performance measures in bonus plans, see C. D. Ittner, D. F. Larcker and M. U. Rajan. "The Choice of Performance Measures in Annual Bonus Contracts," *The Accounting Review* (April 1997), pp. 231–55.

14 See R .S . Kaplan and D. P. Norton, *The Balanced Scorecard* (Boston, MA: Harvard Business School Press, 1996).

how these "at risk" compensation components—annual bonus plans and long-term compensation—are tied to accounting numbers.

The common performance measures used in *annual* incentive plans for senior corporate executives are shown in Figure 7.6. Virtually every company included in the survey from which Figure 7.6 is taken has an annual performance-based incentive compensation plan for executives. Most plans link bonus awards to one or more accounting-based performance measure, such as earnings per share, or return on equity. Operating cash flows are the performance measure in 15% of the bonus plans. Total return to shareholders—dividends plus share price appreciation—is the performance measure in 8% of the bonus plans.

Figure 7.7 paints a similar picture of the performance measures used in *long-term* incentive plans. Although some companies (14%) tie long-term incentive awards to total return to shareholders, most use earnings performance to determine long-term compensation awards. Together, Figures 7.6 and 7.7 show how extensively accounting numbers serve as the basis for annual bonus and long-term performance awards.

This wide use of accounting-based incentives is controversial for at least four reasons.

First, earnings growth does not automatically translate into increased shareholder value. Management can "grow" earnings by expanding the size of the business through acquisitions or new investment. This strategy can produce substantial dollar increases in sales volume, operating earnings, and EPS. But these added profits don't always increase shareholder value. For shareholder value to increase, the company must earn more on new investments than its incremental cost of capital. Alas, not all acquisitions and investments clear the cost of capital "hurdle" even though they may show an accounting profit. So earnings-based incentive compensation plans can reward managers for launching new investments that increase earnings but not shareholder value.

> ROA for 2002 is equal to the $100 of net income, divided by net assets of $950 (after subtracting $50 of accumulated depreciation) or 10.5%. The 11.1% ROA calculation for 2003 is $100 of net income, divided by net assets of $900 (after subtracting $100 of accumulated depreciation).

Second, the accrual accounting process itself can sometimes distort traditional measures of company performance. Take return on assets (ROA), for example. Companies that show improving ROA often do so because of real profitability gains—greater revenues or lower expenses. However, some ROA improvements are due to nothing more than depreciation accounting. To see this, consider a business that generates $100 of net income each year and pays that same amount out as a dividend. The business opens on January 1, 2001 with total assets of $1,000 and no debt. Half of those assets ($500) are invested in new equipment. The annual depreciation charge for the equipment is $50. The company's ROA for 2001 is 10% ($100 of net income, divided by $1,000 of beginning assets). But next year ROA will grow to about 10.5%. And the year after that, ROA will be 11.1%. Why? Not because profits at the company have increased but instead because depre-

Figure 7.6

PERFORMANCE MEASURES IN ANNUAL BONUS PLANS

The individual percentages sum to more than 100% because some companies use multiple measures of performance.

Source: Hay Group, Inc., 1993.

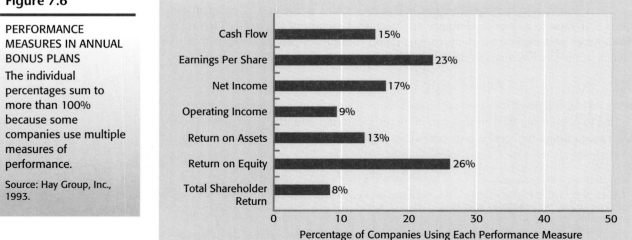

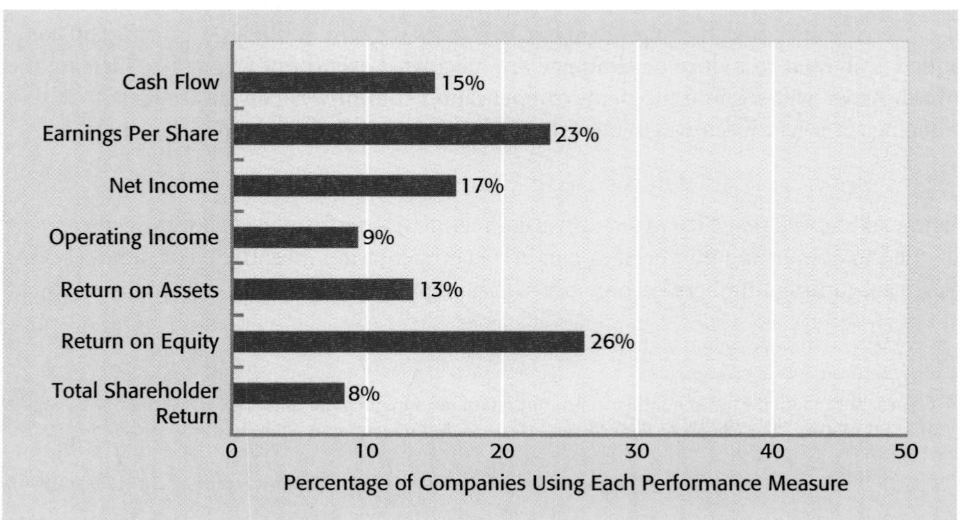

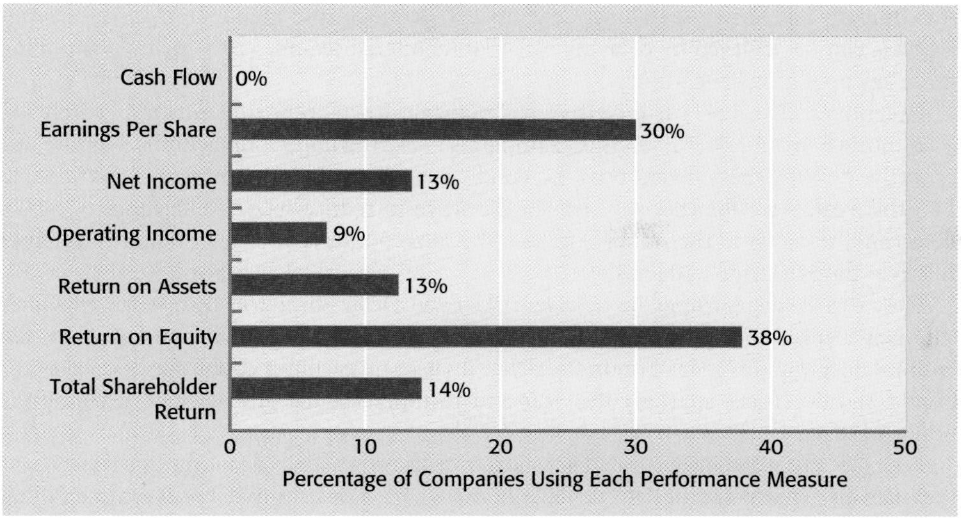

Figure 7.7

PERFORMANCE MEASURES IN LONG-TERM INCENTIVE PLANS

The individual percentages sum to more than 100% because some companies use multiple measures of performance.

Source: Hay Group, Inc., 1993.

ciation accounting has reduced the book value of total assets. (Inflation exacerbates this problem, as discussed in Chapter 10.)

As a stockholder in the company, you probably don't want to pay an ROA bonus for depreciation accounting. It's better instead to reward management for real profitability improvement and to ignore the profit growth illusion created by depreciation accounting. That's why some companies prefer ROGI (Return on Gross Investment, or net income divided by total *gross* assets) as a performance metric in their bonus plans.

Third, accounting-based incentive plans can encourage managers to adopt a short-term business focus. Consider the typical bonus plan in Figure 7.8. The executive receives a bonus equal to 100% of base salary if annual EPS reaches the $3.50 target. The bonus award declines to 50% of base salary for EPS performance at the $3.00 level, and it escalates to 150% for EPS at the $4.00 level. If EPS falls below $3.00, no bonus is awarded; at EPS above $4.00, the bonus remains 150% of base salary.

To see how accounting-based incentives might contribute to a short-term focus, consider an executive who believes current business conditions will only allow the company to earn $2.80 EPS for the year. Despite these unfavorable (no bonus) conditions, the executive can still achieve the $3.00 EPS minimum required for a bonus by curtailing needed expenditures—simply cut back on critical research and development. Research expenses go down, reported earnings go up, and bonuses are paid! This short-term strategy can prove costly in the long term if a competitor introduces a new product based on the technology

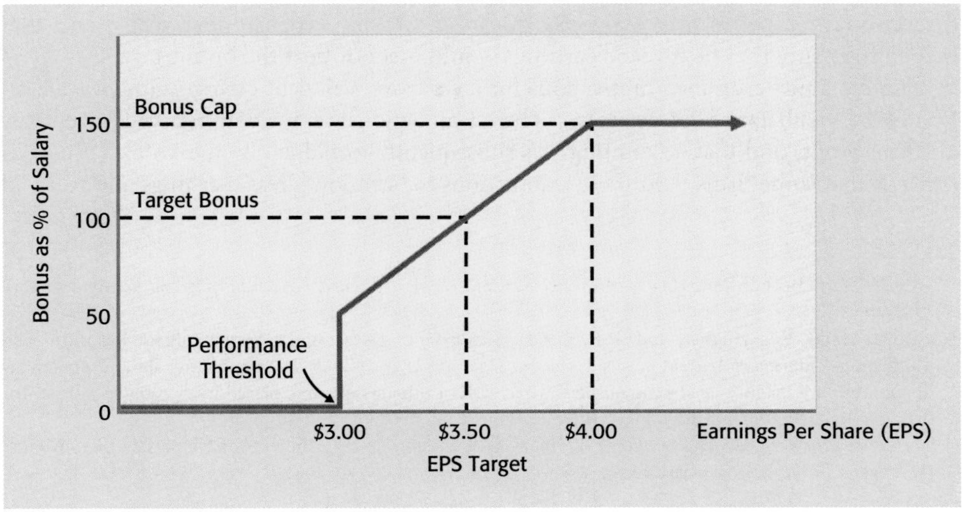

Figure 7.8

STRUCTURE OF ANNUAL PERFORMANCE BONUS

the company had been researching. Of course, the same unsustainable short-term earnings increase can be achieved by delaying essential maintenance and repairs or by postponing other key operating expenditures.

Executives also have an incentive to "manage down" reported earnings when the accounting benchmark (EPS in this example) is *above* the upper bonus limit. Suppose our executive believes that current business conditions will enable the company to earn $4.20 EPS this year. Here the executive has an incentive to reduce reported earnings to $4.00, deferring the excess to the future. After all, the same bonus is awarded no matter whether EPS is at the $4.00 or $4.20 level!

How can excess earnings be deferred? It's easy! Delay some fourth-quarter customer shipments until the beginning of next year. Current year's sales decline and earnings fall without affecting this year's bonus; the delayed sales and earnings count toward next year's bonus. You don't lose anything this year and you increase the probability of earning the bonus next year.

Fourth, executives have some discretion over the company's accounting policies, and they can use that discretion to achieve bonus goals. For example, an executive falling short of the $3.00 EPS minimum might deliberately reduce fourth-quarter inventories, report a "LIFO liquidation" gain, and boost earnings to a level above the bonus threshold. (LIFO liquidations are discussed in Chapter 9.) On the other hand, if earnings performance is so low that reaching the bonus threshold is impossible, the manager has an incentive to further reduce earnings. The objective of these deliberate earnings reductions—called "big baths"—is simple. Today's write-offs lower future expenses, thereby increasing future earnings—and future bonuses! Examples of "big bath" write-offs include higher bad debt allowances, large restructuring charges, and goodwill reductions. Accounting discretion also allows managers who believe earnings will exceed the $4.00 ceiling to play bonus "games"—reduce reported earnings down to the bonus maximum and defer the excess.

Research Evidence Do managers use accounting flexibility to achieve bonus goals? One study, which looked at annual bonus plans like the one in Figure 7.8, revealed two things:[15]

1. When annual earnings already exceeded the $4.00 bonus ceiling, managers used discretionary accounting options to *reduce* earnings.
2. When it was clearly evident that earnings would be below the bonus threshold ($3.00 in Figure 7.8), managers used their financial reporting flexibility to reduce earnings still further.

These reductions in earnings had no impact on that year's bonus but improved managers' chances of receiving bonuses the following year. That's because taking a larger discretionary expense this year often meant a smaller expense next year—and that helped to ensure that next year's earnings would meet or beat the bonus target.

Another study examined motivations for a controversial, debt extinguishment transaction called **insubstance defeasances.**[16] These transactions were widely believed to generate artificial profits and that accounting was subsequently forbidden by the FASB.[17] The evidence is that some firms used these transactions to "window-dress" earnings and to avoid

---

[15] P. Healy, "The Effect of Bonus Schemes on Accounting Decisions," *Journal of Accounting and Economics* (April 1985), pp. 85–108.

[16] J. R. M. Hand, P. J. Hughes, and S. E. Sefcik, "Insubstance Defeasances: Security Price Reactions and Motivations," *Journal of Accounting and Economics* (May 1990), pp. 47–89. The transaction allowed a company to account for a liability "as if extinguished" when cash or other assets were placed irrevocably in a trust that then made all remaining principal and interest payments on the debt.

[17] "Accounting for Transfers and Servicing of Financial Assets and Extinguishments of Liabilities," *SFAS No. 125* (Norwalk, CT: FASB, 1996), para.16.

restrictions in bond covenants. Again, the research findings show that managers sometimes use accounting flexibility to evade contract constraints and to gain bonus benefits.

Yet another research study found evidence that R&D expenditures tend to decline during the years immediately prior to a CEO's retirement.[18] Existing GAAP requires R&D expenditures to be expensed as incurred, thereby reducing income and bonuses.[19] By reducing R&D expenditures before retirement, these CEOs were able to increase the payout from their bonus contracts.

Compensation plans should align managers' incentives with the objectives of shareholders. Many compensation plans link incentive pay to accounting numbers; this linkage is an effective management incentive since improved financial performance generally translates into greater shareholder wealth. Unfortunately, accounting numbers can be manipulated. Consequently, compensation plans tied to financial goals sometimes backfire because of the short-term, self-interest focus of executives.

RECAP

Protection Against Short-Term Focus These abuses explain why compensation plans must also be designed to include long-term incentive components (primarily stock options) that are specifically intended to mitigate the short-term focus of executives. Stock options give managers a strong incentive to avoid shortsighted business decisions and instead operate the company in ways that create shareholder value.

Another factor that can reduce short-term focus is the fact that incentive compensation plans are administered by a compensation committee comprised of the company's outside (nonmanagement) directors. It can intervene when circumstances warrant modification of the scheduled incentive award. For example, intervention might arise when a change in an accounting principle occurs since the full cumulative effect of the change on all prior years usually appears in the current year's income statement (see Chapter 2). In general, the compensation committee can adjust the incentive award whenever it believes that current earnings have been unduly influenced by special items or other possible accounting distortions.

For example, language of the following sort is typical in many compensation agreements:

> "At any time prior to the payment of performance awards, the compensation committee may adjust previously established performance targets and other terms and conditions . . . to reflect major unforeseen events such as changes in laws, regulations, or accounting practices, mergers, acquisitions, divestitures, or extraordinary, unusual, or nonrecurring items or events."[20]

Compensation committees *can* adjust incentive awards for unusual or nonrecurring items and events—but do they? One study looked at the pay practices of 376 large public companies from 1970 through 1996 and found that nonrecurring gains tend to flow through to compensation but losses do not.[21] Compensation committees apparently do shield top managers from bonus reductions when net income is decreased by nonrecurring losses. But when net income is increased by nonrecurring gains, top managers reap the benefits in the form of higher bonus awards.

[18] P. M. Dechow and R. G. Sloan, "Executive Incentives and The Horizon Problem: An Empirical Investigation," *Journal of Accounting and Economics* (March 1991), pp. 51–89.

[19] "Accounting for Research and Development Costs," *SFAS No. 2* (Stamford, CT: FASB, 1974).

[20] J. D. England, "Executive Pay, Incentives and Performance," in D. E. Logue (ed.), *Handbook of Modern Finance* (Boston: Warren, Gorham & Lamont, 1996), p. E9-18.

[21] J. J. Garver and K. M. Garver, "The Relation Between Nonrecurring Accounting Transactions and CEO Cash Compensation," *The Accounting Review* (April 1998), pp. 235–54.

Regulatory Agencies

Financial statements used by creditors and shareholders are prepared using GAAP. But companies like J. P. Morgan, Chase, Allstate Insurance, New England Power, and many others must also provide financial statements to the government agencies that regulate them. Those statements may be prepared on another basis—RAP—to satisfy specific regulatory objectives.

RAP stands for **regulatory accounting principles,** the methods and procedures that must be followed when putting together financial statements for regulatory agencies. RAP tells a company how to account for its business transactions—from when to record revenue and in what amount, to how depreciation expense must be calculated and what account title to use.

Regulators use RAP financial reports to set the prices customers are charged, as a basis for supervisory action, as a source of statistical information, and as an early warning signal for monitoring a company's financial health. To achieve these goals, regulators sometimes require the use of accounting principles that deviate from GAAP. Here's an example of such a deviation from the telecommunications industry:

> Under regulatory accounting, the company capitalizes both interest and equity costs during periods of construction. (*SBC Communications,* 1994 annual report)

GAAP allows interest to be treated as just another cost of the company's construction project, but "equity costs" are not capitalized under GAAP (see Chapter 10). So, SBC Communications is telling annual report readers that its treatment of equity costs complies with RAP but deviates from GAAP. As a result, the company's completed construction projects—its telephone lines and related facilities—are shown at higher book values than would be the case if GAAP were used.

Why do shareholders, creditors, and other statement readers care about RAP if companies only use it when preparing financial reports for regulatory agencies? The answer is that ***RAP sometimes shows up in the company's GAAP financial statements too.*** Why? Because *SFAS No. 71* allows rate-regulated companies like SBC Communications to account for and report assets and liabilities consistent with the way in which regulators establish rates as long as:

- the rates are designed to recover the costs of providing the regulated service, and
- the competitive environment makes it reasonable to assume that such rates can be charged and collected.[22]

So, SBC Communications not only capitalized equity costs in its financial reports to industry regulators, but also did so in its published financial statements for shareholders and creditors.

> The published balance sheets of rate-regulated companies will also contain **regulatory assets and liabilities** that reflect anticipated future rate adjustments, deferred costs, and delayed obligations specific to the regulatory process.

Knowing how a company accounts for its business transactions—whether it uses GAAP or RAP—is essential to gaining a clear understanding of its financial performance and condition.

There's another reason why shareholders and creditors need to understand RAP as well as GAAP. Regulated companies can suffer because financial reports affect the regulatory process—for example, a rate increase may be denied based on the reported numbers. This possibility can influence both 1) management's GAAP accounting choices and 2) when transactions are recorded.

To see how, let's take a look at banks, savings institutions, and credit unions.

Capital Requirements in the Banking Industry

Banks and other financial institutions are required by federal and state regulatory agencies to meet **minimum capital requirements.** The purpose of these requirements is to

[22] "Accounting for the Effects of Certain Types of Regulation," *SFAS No. 71* (Stamford, CT: FASB, 1982).

ensure that the bank (or institution) remains financially sound and can meet its obligations to depositors.

The test for capital adequacy is a simple one: Does the amount of investor capital (think of "adjusted" stockholders' equity) or the ratio of investor capital to gross assets—both defined by RAP—exceed the minimum level allowed by the regulator? If it does, the bank is in compliance and considered to have adequate capital. If bank capital falls below the minimum allowed, regulatory intervention can be triggered.

Suppose Hometown Bank & Trust has gross assets of $900 million and investor capital of $135 million, and suppose the bank's regulators set a 10% minimum capital ratio. Hometown is in compliance with the capital requirement because it has a capital adequacy ratio of 15%, calculated as:

$$\text{Capital adequacy ratio} = \frac{\text{Invested capital (as defined by RAP)}}{\text{Gross assets (as defined by RAP)}}$$
$$= \frac{\$135 \text{ million}}{\$900 \text{ million}} = 15\%,$$

which is above the 10% minimum allowed.

Regulators have a powerful weapon to encourage compliance with minimum capital guidelines. They can impose costs on banks and financial institutions found to be in noncompliance. For example, a noncomplying bank:

- is required to submit a comprehensive plan describing how and when its capital will be increased
- can be examined more frequently by the regulator
- can be denied a request to merge, open new branches, or expand its services
- can be subject to dividend payment restrictions if it has inadequate or "potentially inadequate" capital (e.g., Hometown Bank & Trust might be prohibited from paying any dividends if its capital adequacy ratio falls to the minimum level allowed—10%).

Because regulators can restrict bank operations, a bank with "inadequate" capital incurs greater regulatory costs than does a bank with adequate capital.

There are several ways bank managers can avoid costly penalties as a result of failing to meet minimum capital requirements. The best approach is to operate profitably and invest wisely so that the bank remains financially sound. Another way is to choose accounting policies that increase RAP invested capital or decrease RAP gross assets so that the bank can pass its capital adequacy test. Let's examine this "artificial" approach to regulatory compliance.

The cash that banks receive from depositors is used to make loans. These loans show up as balance sheet receivables; they typically represent the bank's single largest asset. Uncollected loans are a significant cost in the banking industry. But bank managers have some discretion over the timing and amount of recorded uncollectibles. This discretion can be used to improve the bank's capital adequacy ratio. How?

It's easy: Understate the true loan loss provision and loan charge-offs for the year. This improves the bank's capital adequacy ratio, and simultaneously increases the net income figure reported to shareholders. But these improvements are just an illusion. In reality the bank expects more uncollectibles than are shown on the financial reports. Understating loan loss provisions and charge-offs may help avoid noncompliance with bank capital requirements, but this strategy hides the bank's true performance and condition from both regulators and shareholders. So evading RAP guidelines can impede accurate financial analysis.

A bank's **loan loss provision** is just the estimated bad debt expense associated with its loan receivables. **Loan charge-offs** are loans the bank no longer expects to collect. The debit that arises when a loan loss provision is established decreases net income while loan charge-offs decrease bank capital.

Rate Regulation in the Electric Utilities Industry

Electric utility companies like New England Power have their prices set by state and federal agencies—that is, by public utility commissions. The rate formulas of most commissions use accounting-determined costs and asset values. A typical rate formula for an electric utility looks like this:

$$\text{Allowed revenue} = \text{Operating costs} + \text{Depreciation} + \text{Taxes} + (\text{ROA} \times \text{Asset base})$$

where ROA is the return on assets allowed by the regulator. The rate formula sets total allowed revenues equal to an amount that covers the company's operating costs (fuel, labor, and administrative expenses plus depreciation and taxes) and provides a "fair" return on the capital invested in operating assets (things like generating stations, transmission lines, fuel inventory, and so on).

Suppose Midwest Power & Light has annual operating costs, depreciation, and taxes of $300 million. Suppose also that $500 million of capital is invested in operating assets. Finally, suppose that the state public service commission sets ROA at 10%. The annual revenue allowed would be:

$$\begin{aligned}\text{Allowed revenue} &= \$300 \text{ million} + (10\% \times \$500 \text{ million})\\ &= \$300 \text{ million} + \$50 \text{ million} = \$350 \text{ million}\end{aligned}$$

To arrive at a rate per kilowatt-hour of electricity, the $350 million of revenue allowed is divided by the company's *estimate* of total kilowatt-hours to be sold during the year.

Industry RAP governs which items can be included in a regulated utility's operating costs and asset base—and which cannot be included. The difference is important because included items are charged to customers but disallowed items are charged to shareholders. Consider this example: Suppose Midwest Power & Light spends $10 million on customer safety advertising and $50 million on corporate "image" advertising. Customer safety advertising is an allowed operating cost, so it is included in the rate formula. Customers ultimately pay for the $10 million spent on safety advertising through higher electricity rates.

Corporate image advertising is not an allowed cost in most states, so the $50 million that Midwest Power & Light spent promoting itself cannot be passed on to customers in the form of higher electricity rates. Who pays the bill? Shareholders do, because there's $50 million less cash in the company. Regulators apparently see image advertising as unnecessary. Consequently, they do not require customers to pay for it through higher electricity rates.

The example illustrates how RAP can influence rate regulation and the revenues ultimately received by utility companies. But there's another important point to the example. Industry RAP treats customer safety advertising and corporate image advertising differently. GAAP does not—both kinds of advertising would be included in operating costs on the company's income statement. Other differences between public utility RAP and GAAP are:

- **deferring costs** that would otherwise be charged to expense by nonregulated companies—utilities can postpone expensing storm damage costs, for example, as long as it is probable that those specific deferred costs are subject to recovery in future revenues,
- **capitalization of equity costs** on construction projects when interest alone can be capitalized by nonregulated companies.

Because of *SFAS No. 71,* RAP gets included in the financial statements that utility companies prepare for shareholders and creditors.

Rate regulation also creates incentives for public utility managers to artificially increase the asset base. Suppose Midwest Power & Light signs a $700,000 one-year rental agreement for service vehicles. If the rental payment is an allowed operating cost for rate-making purposes, customers would pay $700,000 in higher electricity rates. On the other hand, if the rental could be included in the company's regulatory asset base, customers would pay $770,000, or 10% more—$700,000 for depreciation (the full cost of the one-year asset) plus another $70,000 so that shareholders receive the allowed 10% return on the $700,000 asset.

Given the choice, shareholders would prefer to have the rental payment treated as an asset for rate-making purposes. The company could then charge customers an extra $70,000 and use the cash to cover "disallowed" costs—like image advertising—or to pay stockholder dividends. One way to make this happen is to design the rental contract so that it qualifies for RAP treatment as an asset. (We show you how in Chapter 12.) Another approach is to lobby regulators to relax the rules governing when a rental contract qualifies for asset treatment. ***Change the contract or change the accounting rules***—the result is the same. Adding more dollars to the asset base increases the allowed revenue stream for a rate-regulated company.

Taxation

All companies are "regulated" by state and federal tax agencies. When it comes to income taxes and the U.S. government, the regulators are Congress and the Internal Revenue Service (IRS). Congress writes the rules, but the IRS interprets and administers them, and it collects the income tax.

IRS regulations govern the computation of net income for tax purposes. These IRS accounting rules are just another type of RAP. Many IRS accounting rules are the same as GAAP rules. Consider this example: Revenue is generally recognized for tax and GAAP purposes at the time of sale, not later when cash is collected from customers. However, there are situations in which IRS accounting rules differ from GAAP.

A case in point is "goodwill"—the excess price paid to acquire a business over and above its net asset value. GAAP allows companies to expense goodwill gradually over a period of time—up to 40 years for most companies currently, although this may soon change.[23] IRS rules do not permit companies to expense goodwill (and thereby reduce taxable income) except in very rare circumstances. For many companies, this means that taxable net income (computed without goodwill expense) is higher than the GAAP net income figure (computed after subtracting goodwill expense) reported to shareholders. This may explain why some managers avoid recorded goodwill—it lowers GAAP net income but it doesn't lower the company's IRS tax payments.

> To see how **goodwill** arises, suppose a business with assets worth $80 million and debt of $40 million is purchased by Raider Corporation for $55 million. Raider will record the purchase as
>
> | | | |
> |---|---|---|
> | **DR** Assets purchased (at fair value) | $80 million | |
> | **DR** Goodwill (excess purchase price) | $15 million | |
> | **CR** Cash paid out | | $55 million |
> | **CR** Liabilities assumed by Raider | | $40 million |
>
> Notice that the goodwill increase of $15 million is required to make the journal entry balance. (Goodwill is discussed in Chapter 16.)

When inventory costs are rising, companies like to use LIFO for tax purposes because it lowers their taxable income. But the IRS rules on LIFO inventory accounting contain an unusual requirement—companies that elect to use LIFO for tax purposes must also use LIFO in their shareholder reports. So the tax benefits of LIFO can only be obtained when LIFO is also used in GAAP financial statements—but doing so lowers GAAP net income when prices are rising. Since the

> LIFO means **"Last-In, First-Out,"** and here's how it works. Suppose a start-up bicycle retailer begins the year with no inventory. Ten bicycles are purchased for $150 each during the first week of operations and another five bicycles are purchased mid-month for $180 each—same brand and model, just a higher price from the manufacturer. Eight bicycles are sold during the month, leaving seven still in inventory. Using LIFO, the retailer would calculate the cost of goods sold to be $1,350 (or five bicycles at $180 each plus three more at $150 each). Notice that this calculation presumes the ***last*** bicycles to come into the shop (those bought for $180 each) are the ***first sold.*** Notice also that with rising inventory costs, LIFO produces a larger cost of goods sold expense ($1,350 in our example) than does FIFO or **"First-In, First-Out"** (eight bicycles at $150 each, or $1,200). A larger cost-of-goods-sold expense means a lower taxable income. Chapter 9 tells you more.

[23] The FASB proposes that goodwill should not be amortized but should instead be written down if impaired. See "Business Combinations and Intangible Assets—Accounting for Goodwill," *Exposure Draft* (Norwalk, CT: FASB, February 14, 2001).

LIFO method is widely used, many corporate managers must believe that the tax benefits of LIFO outweigh its negative impact on GAAP net income.

Taxation and GAAP accounting are related in another way. Companies reporting large GAAP earnings sometimes attract the attention of politicians who threaten to impose "windfall profits" taxes. This has been true for big U.S. oil companies during periods of rapidly increasing oil prices and/or oil "shortages" caused by governmental policies.

For example, during the 1970s the price of gasoline was controlled by the federal government in an effort to reduce consumption and to dampen the inflationary impact of escalating oil prices. In 1979 the price of gasoline at the pump was decontrolled one week before big oil companies announced record third-quarter profits that were labeled by politicians as "obscene." After the earnings announcements, a "windfall profits" tax on oil company earnings was proposed, and politicians voted to reimpose gasoline price controls. These actions occurred even though part of the reported profit increase was due to an accounting change required by the FASB; most of the rest of the increase was due to overseas operations and inventory holding gains.

Sometimes it just doesn't pay to be seen as a highly profitable company. When that's the case, managers have incentives to use accounting methods that make the company look less profitable than it really is. That way they can avoid attracting the attention of politicians and regulators who might impose a "windfall profits" tax or other cost on the company.

RECAP

Government regulatory agencies and taxing authorities can write their own accounting rules, and many do. The result is that some financial statements for shareholders and creditors contain special regulatory items or use regulatory accounting methods which deviate from normal GAAP. Accounting-based regulations—including IRS rules—also influence the choice of GAAP accounting methods for shareholder reports and when transactions are recorded.

ANALYSIS

Analytical Insights: Identifying "Managed" Earnings

It is essential for financial statement users to identify companies that achieve incremental increases in earnings resulting from strength in business fundamentals rather than earnings management techniques or accounting 'gimmickry.'[24]

We said in Chapter 6 that the key measure of corporate value is **permanent** ("sustainable") **earnings** from core businesses—the "above the line" income from continuing operations discussed in Chapter 2. Most analysts, investors and lenders agree. Compared to bottom-line net income, core earnings provide a truer picture of a company's ability to generate profits from its major business activities. Core earnings are also more predictive of the company's sustainable economic performance, its long-term growth trends, and its financial viability.

But uncovering a company's core earnings and assessing its overall performance is not easy. The challenge comes from several sources. As an analyst, you must do the following:

- Wrestle with differences in accounting methods and reporting practices across companies—even in the same industry.
- Identify areas where accounting choices can hide potential earnings surprises—so-called "accounting torpedoes"—such as a major write-off of bad debts or intangibles.

---

[24] G. Napolitano, *Earnings Management Revisited: Minimizing the Torpedoes in Financial Reports* (New York: Goldman Sachs, November 1998), p. 3.

- Assess the degree to which the firm has "managed" earnings and used accounting gimmickry.
- Adjust the reported financial statement amounts to eliminate the impact of these potential accounting "abuses."

This book is devoted to helping you meet the challenge.

The message from this chapter and from Chapter 3 is that managers sometimes have powerful incentives to "manage" the reported profitability and financial condition of their companies. These incentives are motivated by loan covenants, compensation contracts, regulatory agency oversight, tax avoidance efforts, a desire to "meet or beat" analysts' quarterly earnings forecasts and to increase the company's stock price. Financial statement gimmicks are likely to be most prevalent when these accounting incentives are especially strong. For example, when the company is in danger of violating its debt covenants; or when a large portion of top management pay comes from bonuses tied to earnings per share or sales growth; or when management has a lengthy record of beating "the Street's" earnings forecast by a penny. What's the penalty for failing to "make" the numbers? Loan default, lost bonuses, and an abrupt stock price decline.

> Accounting gimmicks sometimes backfire. In 1997, top officers and directors at Leslie Fay agreed to pay back $34.7 million to shareholders of the company. The payment settled shareholder lawsuits filed because of alleged accounting gimmicks used in 1991 and 1992. Among other things, the suits charged that earnings gimmicks artificially increased officers' bonuses in those years. See L. Vickery, "Leslie Fay's Ex-Financial Chief, Polishan, is Found Guilty of Fraud," *Wall Street Journal* (July 7, 2000).

So now you know *when* to look for potential accounting distortions, but what exactly do you look *for* and *where* do you look? How do companies "manage" earnings? What accounting gimmicks are used?

The remaining chapters of this book explore these topics in detail. For now, we'll simply give you a "broad-brush" overview to sensitize you to the danger areas.

Look to areas where subjective judgments or estimates have a significant impact on the financial statements. For some companies, the areas to scrutinize might be revenue recognition, deferred marketing and customer acquisition costs, or reserves for bad debts and inventory obsolescence. For other companies, the critical areas may involve intangible asset valuation, asset impairment, warranty and product liability reserves, restructuring charges, or litigation and environmental contingencies. Also take a close look at areas where it is difficult to evaluate the company's accounting practices because no authoritative standards exist or because established practices are controversial. And watch out for large business transactions, especially those that are unusually complex in structure or in their financial statement effects. And take a magnifying glass to the financial statement footnotes and other financial disclosures. They should be complete and transparent—allowing you to look behind the numbers to see what's really going on in the company. If not, there may be an accounting torpedo headed in your direction.[26]

> A recent professional pronouncement requires independent auditors to adopt this incentives-driven financial analytic perspective when conducting audits.[25]

Exhibit 7.2 contains a partial list of tell-tale signs for identifying "aggressive" accounting choices. Keep this list handy as you read the rest of the book. We have a lot more to say about the "red flags" in Exhibit 7.2 and why they are helpful. Each chapter discusses other warning signals that you may want to add to this list.

---

[25] "Consideration of Fraud in a Financial Statement Audit," *Statement on Auditing Standards No. 82* (New York: American Institute of Certified Public Accountants, 1997), paras. 16–17.

[26] Recent examples of accounting torpedoes can be found in N. Byrnes and J. M Laderman, "Help for Investors: How to Spot Trouble," *Business Week* (October 5, 1998); N. Byrnes, R. A. Melcher, and D. Sparks, "Earnings Hocus-Pocus," *Business Week* (October 5, 1998); C. Loomis, "Lies, Damned Lies, and Managed Earnings," *Fortune* (August 2, 1999); M. Maremount, "Anatomy of a Fraud," *Business Week* (September 16, 1996); S. Pulliam, "Earnings Management Spurs Selloffs Now," *Wall Street Journal* (October 29, 1999); and S. Tully, "The Earnings Illusion," *Fortune* (April 20, 1999).

Exhibit 7.2 ■ TELL-TALE SIGNS OF POTENTIAL ACCOUNTING DISTORTIONS

- Unexplained changes in accounting methods like a switch from LIFO to FIFO inventory methods.
- LIFO "dipping" or excessive year-end inventory purchases for LIFO companies when prices are rising.
- Changes in estimates for asset useful life, lease residual value, and pension or post-retirement health care benefit assumptions.
- Receivables or inventory growth that outpaces sales growth.
- Bad debt reserves that are low relative to receivables, past credit losses, or peer companies.
- Sudden "off-loading" of receivables by sale or securitization.
- Unusually long depreciation lives and amortization periods.
- Increasing gap between earnings and operating cash flows.
- Increasing gap between earnings and taxable income.
- Unexplained large increases or decreases in deferred income tax balances.
- Off-balance-sheet financing arrangements including significant use of joint ventures, "take-or-pay" contracts, or operating leases.
- Unexpected write-offs of receivables and loans, inventories, buildings and equipment, or intangibles.
- Large changes in discretionary expenses such as advertising and R&D.
- Unusual business transactions that boost earnings.
- Audit qualifications or changes in the outside auditor.

Note: These (and other) accounting "red flags" are described more fully in later chapters.

SUMMARY

Conflicts of interest among managers, shareholders, lenders, or regulators are a natural feature of business. Contracts and regulations help address these conflicts of interest in ways that are mutually beneficial to the parties involved. Accounting numbers often play an important role in contracts and regulations because they provide useful information about the company's performance and financial condition, as well as about the management team's accomplishments.

Accounting-based lending agreements, compensation contracts, and regulations shape managers' incentives—after all, that's why accounting numbers are included in contracts and regulations. They also help explain the accounting choices managers make. Understanding why and how managers exercise their discretion in implementing GAAP can be extremely helpful to those who are analyzing and interpreting a company's financial statements.

And what happened to Allen Ford? The bank provided the loans Allen needed to open his first BookWorm, and the concept proved so successful he now owns three stores. Allen is currently developing a business plan for a used-book store to be called Second Time Around.

EXERCISES

E7–1

Conflicts of interest and agency costs

Suppose you and two friends each invested $100,000 in an oil and gas partnership. The general partner—Huge Gamble, Inc.—invests no cash but makes all operating decisions for the partnership, including where and how deep to drill for oil. Drilling costs plus a management fee are charged against the $300,000 of cash you and your friends invested. If oil is found, you each get 15% of partnership net income, with the remaining 55% going to Huge Gamble. But if the wells are dry, you get nothing except any cash that remains.

REQUIRED:

What is an agency relationship and what are agency costs? How do these concepts apply to your investment in the oil and gas partnership?

REQUIRED:

What is a debt covenant? Why do lenders include them in loan agreements? Why do borrowers agree to include covenants in loan agreements?

E7–2

Understanding debt covenants

REQUIRED:

What are affirmative debt covenants? What are negative covenants? Provide two examples of each.

E7–3

Affirmative and negative debt covenants

The debt covenants in TCBY's loan agreement do not explicitly mention the accounting methods that must be used when TCBY prepares financial statements for submission to the lender.

REQUIRED:

Why don't lenders require the use of specific accounting methods rather than letting management pick from among GAAP alternatives?

E7–4

Debt covenants and accounting methods

REQUIRED:

What are the advantages of loan agreements that contain covenants tied to accounting numbers? Are there any disadvantages? Explain.

E7–5

Contracts and accounting numbers

REQUIRED:

What are regulatory costs and why are they important for understanding a company's financial reporting choices?

E7–6

Regulatory costs

Some public service commissions let utilities include "Construction in progress"—construction dollars spent for projects not yet completed—in the rate-making asset base. Other states only allow completed projects to be included.

REQUIRED:

Which approach favors shareholders? Why?

E7–7

Regulatory accounting principles

Illinois Power & Heat just spent $5 million repairing one of its electrical generating stations that was damaged by a tornado. The loss was uninsured. Management has asked the public service commission for approval to treat the $5 million as an asset for rate-making purposes rather than as an allowed expense.

REQUIRED:

What difference will this make to customers and shareholders?

E7–8

Equipment repairs and rate regulation

REQUIRED:

Why are banks and insurance companies required by regulators to maintain minimum levels of investor capital? What impact does this type of regulatory requirement have on the financial statements that banks and insurance companies prepare for shareholders?

E7–9

Capital adequacy

The top five executives at Marvel Manufacturing are paid annual bonuses based on predetermined earnings goals. These bonuses can be as much as 500% of salary. As a member of the company's compensation committee, you've been asked to comment on the following proposed changes to the annual bonus plan:

- Use after-tax income from continuing operations as the earnings performance measure instead of bottom-line net income.
- Set performance goals based on return on assets (ROA) rather than on earnings.
- Set performance goals—net income or ROA—based on beating the industry average rather than using an absolute performance target.

E7–10

Incentive design

REQUIRED:

What are the advantages and disadvantages of each suggested change?

E7–11

Medical malprofits

REQUIRED:

Explain the potential conflict of interest that arises when doctors own the hospitals in which they work. The following news article may help.

The executive who became the most visible symbol of profit-driven medical care stepped down yesterday as the top officer of the Columbia/HCA Healthcare Corporation amid a criminal investigation of whether the company's pursuit of profits has stretched beyond the legal limits . . . [He] will be replaced by Thomas F. Frist, Jr., a surgeon by training, who has made his career in the hospital business . . . Dr. Frist said he was ending Columbia's practice of selling ownership stakes in its hospitals to its doctors. That has been a critical piece of the strategy that helped propel Columbia's growth but led to great legal and ethical criticism that the company was compromising the medical independence of its doctors.

Source: *New York Times* (July 26, 1997).

E7–12

Bonus tied to EPS performance

Mr. John Brincat is the president and chief executive of Mercury Finance, an auto lender that specializes in high credit-risk customers.

Mr. Brincat is eligible for an annual incentive bonus equal to 1% of Net After-tax Earnings of the Company and is eligible for an additional bonus based upon annual increases in Net After-tax Earnings per share only after earnings exceed 20% over the prior year. The additional bonus is determined as follows:

- Earnings per share increases of 0% to 19.99%, no additional bonus is paid.
- Earnings per share increases of 20% to 29.99%, additional bonus will be equal to 2.5% of the amount of increase from the prior year.
- Earnings per share increases of 30% to 39.99%, additional bonus will be equal to 3.0% of the amount of increase from the prior year.
- Earnings per share increases of 40% or more, additional bonus will be equal to 3.5% of the amount of increase from the prior year.

In addition, at the time the employment contract was entered into, Mr. Brincat was issued a stock option grant . . . of 2,500,000 shares at a price of $17.375 per share, the fair market value on the date of the grant. The options vest equally during the next five years of the contract and are exercisable in increments of 500,000 shares annually only if earnings per share each year exceeds the prior year's earnings per share by 20%. If earnings per share do not increase by 20%, Mr. Brincat forfeits that year's options and has no further right or claim to that year's options.

Source: Mercury Finance 1995 proxy.

REQUIRED:

As a shareholder, how comfortable would you be if your company's managers had contracts with these types of bonus and stock option incentives? Why?

PROBLEMS/DISCUSSION QUESTIONS

P7–1

Managerial incentives and stock ownership

REQUIRED:

1. Suppose Mr. Johnson received a base salary (before personal income taxes) of $800,000 in 1993. His personal tax rate was 35% that year, and the year-end value of his Campbell stock was $1.6 million. How much of his after-tax salary for 1993 would go toward buying more stock in the company?

2. What are the advantages and disadvantages of Campbell's stock ownership plan?
3. Do you think that institutional investors (e.g., pension portfolio managers and mutual fund managers) would favor or oppose Campbell's plan? Why?

Campbell's Soup Executives Must Own Firm's Stock

Campbell Soup Co. said Tuesday it is introducing a stock ownership plan for its chief executive and about 70 other senior executives. Under the plan, David Johnson, president and chief executive officer, is required to hold three times his 1992 base salary of $757,500 in shares by the end of 1994. He must maintain the three times-earnings stake every year until he leaves the company. Executive or senior vice presidents are expected to buy and hold at least two times their annual base salary by 1994. Corporate vice presidents who have been with the company for three or more years will buy and hold the equivalent of one year's base salary. Senior executives will buy shares equal to at least one-half their annual salary. All corporate officers must hold at least 1,000 shares of Campbell stock by the end of this year.

Source: *Bloomberg Business News* (May 1993).

P7–2

Managerial incentives and pay

Required:

1. Mr. Hudgens has five minutes to speak on his proposal at the ConAgra shareholders' meeting. What key points do you think Mr. Hudgens will make?
2. ConAgra's vice president for human resources will also have five minutes to defend the current incentive plan and to oppose the Hudgens proposal. What arguments will the vice president make?
3. Will ConAgra's institutional investors (e.g., pension portfolio managers and mutual fund managers) favor or oppose the Hudgens plan? Why?
4. How did the shareholder vote turn out? How does the company pay its top executives today?

ConAgra Holder is Seeking Changes in Incentive Plan

Donald Hudgens thinks ConAgra Inc.'s chairman and chief executive officer, Philip B. Fletcher, has it too easy. "Maybe I'm naive," says Mr. Hudgens, a retired railroad chemist. "I've never had a high-powered job." Still, he contends that ConAgra's CEO should be working harder for his millions.

As a consequence, ConAgra shareholders will vote later this month on Mr. Hudgens's proposal that the company revise a special long-term incentive plan directors approved for Mr. Fletcher last year. Under that plan, the chairman would receive 50,000 ConAgra common shares for every percentage point over 10% that the company's per-share earnings rise during the next four fiscal years.

For example, if earnings grow at a compound annual rate of 14%, as they did last year, Mr. Fletcher would get 200,000 shares of stock—that is, four percentage points times 50,000 shares. The payout would occur in July 1998. At ConAgra's current price, every 50,000 shares would be valued at $1.6 million.

"They'll do it [exceed 10%] in spite of any incentive award," Mr. Hudgens says. He has some statistical support. Prudential Securities food analyst John McMillin calculates that over the past five years ConAgra's per-share earnings have grown at a 15.4% compounded annual rate; ConAgra's longtime internal goal is for per-share earnings growth to exceed 14% a year, on average.

Thus, Mr. Hudgens wants ConAgra to compare its performance with that of other food companies, and he has drawn up a list of 13—Archer-Daniels-Midland Co., Borden, Inc., CPC International, Inc., Campbell Soup Co., General Mills, Inc., H.J. Heinz Co., Kellogg Co., PepsiCo, Inc., Philip Morris Co., Quaker Oats Co., Ralston Purina Co., Sara Lee Corp. and Tyson Foods, Inc. Moreover, per-share growth must come from continuing operations, the 54-year-old shareholder says.

"I have no problem with management making a lot of money," Mr. Hudgens says. "More power to 'em. But I want them to work their tails off for us."

Source: Republished with permission of the *Wall Street Journal*, from the *Wall Street Journal* (September 6, 1994); permission conveyed through Copyright Clearance Center, Inc.

P7–3

Corporate governance

In June 1997, the Calpers pension fund announced that it wanted to strengthen the power and independence of corporate boards by urging companies to do the following:

1. Adopt a tougher definition of independent director. To count as independent, for example, a board member couldn't serve more than 10 years, hold a personal-services contract with a senior executive, or be affiliated with a nonprofit group that gets "significant contributions" from the company.
2. Appoint these independent directors to a majority of board seats. Only those directors meeting 10 strict measures of independence could serve on key board committees, such as the audit or compensation panel.
3. Pick an independent "lead" director, who would help the chairman run the board. About 36% of the biggest industrial companies had lead directors last year (1996), up from 21% in 1995, according to a survey of 1,058 directors by recruiters Korn/Ferry International in New York.
4. Publish guidelines in the annual proxy statement describing how the board handles competing time commitments when directors serve on multiple boards.
5. Decide what proportion of board members may exceed a certain age.

CALPERS TO BACK CORPORATE GOVERNANCE STANDARDS

The nation's biggest public pension fund soon will demand that the nation's biggest businesses bolster their boards' power and independence through much stronger corporate-governance practices.

Directors of the California Public Employees' Retirement System [Calpers] today are expected to endorse corporate-governance standards for the first time. The standards, which define board independence more rigidly than ever before, mark the latest burst of activism by a giant fund that played an influential role in the departure of chief executives from General Motors Corp., Eastman Kodak Co., International Business Machines Corp. and other companies.

Calpers will grade the 300 largest U.S. companies in its $113 billion stock portfolio on whether they meet its new minimum standards, dubbed "fundamental principles." Fund officials say they plan to withhold votes for the re-election of directors at concerns scoring the worst grades. Though other activist investors praised the standards, some executives said full compliance could be difficult.

. . . A majority of the 300 companies that Calpers will grade probably don't meet every fundamental principle, suggested Kayla Gillan, the fund's general counsel. But many will revamp their corporate-governance practices "simply because they don't want to get a bad grade."

. . . Some boards undoubtedly will resist Calpers's sweeping corporate-governance push. The stricter definition of director independence "doesn't make sense at all," said Terence J. Gallagher, corporate governance vice president at Pfizer Inc. For instance, he noted, about four of Pfizer's 13 nonemployee directors have served more than a decade and they're all highly valued.

. . . The Calpers board today probably also will approve a set of tougher "ideal" principles, which Ms. Gillan said she may use to grade the 300 companies again in the future. These standards include: a) appointment of an independent director as chairman; b) board term limits; c) removal of directors who don't achieve certain performance criteria; d) limiting employees' board seats to just the chief executive officer; and e) a 10% limit on the number of directors more than 70 years old.

REQUIRED:

1. Why do companies have boards of directors?
2. Outside board members at some companies are long-time personal friends of the CEO and own no company stock. Some serve on 10 or more boards and earn substantial fees from doing so. Company funded retirement plans for board members are also common. How might each of these factors weaken corporate governance?
3. How will each of Calpers's proposals improve corporate governance?
4. Will these corporate governance changes help companies achieve better financial performance?

P7–4

Compensation of outside directors

REQUIRED:

1. What are the advantages of paying outside directors in stock and stock options? Are there any disadvantages?
2. Stock prices are sometimes influenced by factors that are beyond management's control—like interest rates, the health of the economy and industry, changing consumer tastes, and so on. Should directors' pay be influenced by these factors?
3. As a director of Times Mirror, would you vote in favor of a management proposal to eliminate all dividends on the company's common stock? Why?

TIMES MIRROR JOINS COMPANIES THAT PAY OUTSIDE DIRECTORS BY STOCK PERFORMANCE

Times Mirror Co., joining a small group of publicly traded companies, ended fixed pay for outside directors in favor of a more risk-prone, entirely stock-based compensation plan. The new program, which gives directors a substantial raise this year, reflects the market-minded views of Chairman and Chief Executive Officer Mark Willes.

Under the media company's revised pay plan, directors who aren't company employees receive as an annual retainer 500 shares of Times Mirror common stock and a cash payment equal to the value of 500 shares, effective January 1, 1997, the company said. Although the proxy information didn't set a value, the package adds up to $50,375 for each director, based on the $50.375 per-share price of Times Mirror shares on January 2, the first trading day of the year. That's a 68% raise from the $30,000 fixed retainer paid half in cash and half in stock during 1996.

The new plan eliminates fees of $1,000 for each board and committee meeting, along with pensions, for nonemployee directors. Instead, nonemployee board members will each be granted options for 5,000 shares of common stock annually, this year at an option price of $46.6875 a share. Times Mirror shares closed down $1.625 Thursday at $57.25 in New York Stock Exchange composite trading.

Switching to such risk-based pay for directors puts Times Mirror in a small group of major companies that have taken similar steps, including Sunbeam Corp. and Scott Paper Co. Advocates of shareholders' rights have long urged widespread use of stock-linked compensation for directors.

Half the compensation is in cash in order to cover taxes, Mr. Willes said, adding that the company wanted to set up a system under which "it didn't cost you money to be a director." While the package for directors may appear richer than those used by some other firms, Mr. Willes said that's largely because "it accounts for the risk involved."

P7–5

Earnings quality and pay

Following your retirement as senior vice president of finance for a large company, you joined the board of Cayman Grand Cruises, Inc. You serve on the compensation committee and help set the bonuses paid to the company's top five executives. According to the annual bonus plan, each executive can earn a bonus of 1% of annual net income.

No bonuses were paid in 2000 because the company reported a net loss of $6,588,000.

Shortly after the end of the year, the compensation committee received a letter signed by all five executives, indicating that they felt the company had performed well in 2000. The letter identified the following items from the 2000 income statement which the executives felt painted a less favorable view of their performance than was actually the case:

Proposed Adjustments to 2000 Earnings

($ in thousands)	
Restructuring and other nonrecurring charges	$63,000
Loss from discontinued operations	22,851
Extraordinary charge, early retirement of debt	6,824
Cumulative effect of required changes in accounting principles for postretirement benefits other than pensions	88,847
Cumulative effect of management-initiated changes in accounting principles for:	
Depreciation	14,180
Warehouse and catalog costs	2,110

The letter asked the compensation committee to add these items back to the reported net loss and to then recalculate the bonus awards for 2000. The fiscal year 2000 income statement follows. Assume the tax rate is 34%.

REQUIRED:

1. As a member of the compensation committee, how would you respond to each suggested adjustment? Why?
2. What 2000 net income figure do you suggest be used to determine bonuses for the year?

CAYMAN GRAND CRUISES, INC.

Consolidated Statement of Income

($ in thousands)	June 30, 2000
Net revenues	$1,024,467
Cost of sales	535,178
Gross margin	489,289
Selling, general, and administrative	299,101
Research, development, and engineering	94,172
Gain on sale of joint venture	(33,000)
Restructuring and other nonrecurring charges	63,000
Operating income	66,016
Gain on sale of investment	40,800
Interest expense	(7,145)
Interest income	2,382
Other income (expense)—net	(2,121)
Income before income taxes	99,932
Provision for income taxes	(29,980)
Income from continuing operations	69,952
Income (loss) from discontinued operations (net of tax effect)	(22,851)
Gain on disposal of discontinued operations (net of tax effect)	38,343
Extraordinary charge, early retirement of debt (net of tax effect)	(6,824)
Income before cumulative effect of changes in accounting principles	78,620
Cumulative effect on prior years of changes in accounting principles for:	
Postretirement benefits other than pensions (net of tax effect)	(88,847)
Income taxes (net of tax effect)	19,929
Depreciation (net of tax effect)	(14,180)
Warehouse and catalog costs (net of tax effect)	(2,110)
Net income (loss)	$ (6,588)

P7–6

Avoiding debt covenant violations

Food Lion, Inc. operates a chain of retail supermarkets principally in the southeastern United States. The company's stores sell groceries, produce, meats, dairy products, seafood, frozen food, deli/bakery, and nonfood items (such as tobacco, health and beauty aids, and other household and personal products). The supermarket business is highly competitive, and it is characterized by low profit margins. Food Lion competes with national, regional, and local supermarket chains; discount food stores; single unit stores; convenience stores; and warehouse clubs.

On June 4, 1993, Food Lion entered into a credit agreement with a group of banks. Excerpts taken from the loan agreement follow.

Section 5.19. Limitation on Incurrence of Funded Debt

The Borrower will not create, assume or incur or in any manner be or become liable in respect of any Funded Debt . . . after January 1, 1994 [unless] the ratio of Income Available for Fixed Charges for the immediately preceding four Fiscal Quarters to Pro Forma Fixed Charges for such four Fiscal Quarters shall have been at least 2.00 to 1.00.

Section 5.20. Fixed Charges Coverage

At the end of each Fiscal Quarter . . . the ratio of Income Available for Fixed Charges for the immediately preceding four Fiscal Quarters then ended to Consolidated Fixed Charges for the immediately preceding four Fiscal Quarters then ended, shall not be less than . . . 1.75 to 1.0.

Section 5.21. Minimum Consolidated Tangible Net Worth

Consolidated Tangible Net Worth will at no time be less than (i) $706,575,475 plus (ii) 30.0% of the cumulative Consolidated Net Income of the Borrower during any period after January 2, 1993, calculated quarterly but excluding from such calculations of Consolidated Net Income for purposes of this clause (ii), any quarter in which the Consolidated Net Income of the Borrower and its Consolidated Subsidiaries is negative.

Source: Food Lion, Inc. loan agreement.

REQUIRED:

1. In two more weeks, the company's books will be closed for the quarter and the *fixed charges coverage* might fall below the level required by the loan agreement. How can management avoid violating this covenant?
2. The company's *tangible net worth* may also fall below the amount specified in the loan agreement. How can management avoid violating this covenant?
3. Elsewhere in the loan agreement it says that the company's *ratio of consolidated debt to total capitalization* must be at least 0.75 to 1.0. How can management avoid violating this covenant?
4. Suppose you were one of Food Lion's bankers, and you were thinking about making changes to the loan covenants. What management activities would you most want to limit? Why?

P7–7

How debt covenants are structured

Delhaize America operates retail food supermarkets in the Southeastern and Mid-Atlantic regions of the United States. The Company's stores—"Food Lion," "Kash 'n' Karry," and "Save 'n' Pack"—sell a wide variety of groceries, produce, meats, dairy products, seafood, frozen food, deli/bakery and nonfood items such as health and beauty care, prescriptions, and other household and personal products.

In November, 1999 the company entered into a credit agreement with a group of banks. Excerpts taken from the loan agreement follow:

SECTION 6.07. Fixed Charges Coverage

At the end of each Fiscal Quarter set forth below, the ratio of (i) Consolidated EBITDAR for the period of four Fiscal Quarters then ended to (ii) Consolidated Fixed Charges for such period, shall not have been less than the ratio set forth below opposite such Fiscal Quarter:

(*continued*)

Fiscal Quarter	Ratio
First Fiscal Quarter ended on or immediately after the Effective Date—Third Fiscal Quarter 2001	2.25:1
Fourth Fiscal Quarter 2001—Third Fiscal Quarter 2002	2.50:1
Fourth Fiscal Quarter 2002—Third Fiscal Quarter 2003	2.75:1
Fourth Fiscal Quarter 2003 and thereafter	3.00:1

SECTION 6.08. Ratio of Consolidated Adjusted Debt to Consolidated EBITDAR

At no date will the ratio of (i) Consolidated Adjusted Debt at such date to (ii) Consolidated EBITDAR for the period of four consecutive Fiscal Quarters ended on or most recently prior to such date exceed the ratio set forth below opposite the period in which such date falls:

Period	Ratio
Effective Date—day immediately preceding last day of Fourth Fiscal Quarter 2001	4.50:1
Last day of Fourth Fiscal Quarter 2001—day immediately preceding last day of Fourth Fiscal Quarter 2002	4.00:1
Last day of Fourth Fiscal Quarter 2002—day immediately preceding last day of Fourth Fiscal Quarter 2003	3.75:1
Last day of Fourth Fiscal Quarter 2003 and thereafter	3.50:1

Source: Delhaize America loan agreement.

"EBITDAR" is Earning Before Interest, Taxes, Depreciation, Amortization, and Rent and "Consolidated Fixed Charges" means debt payments and interest expenses plus rent payments.

REQUIRED:

1. Why does the loan agreement include rent as a "fixed charge" in the EBITDAR coverage ratio described in Section 6.07?
2. The minimum acceptable EBITDAR coverage ratio (Section 6.07) increases from 2.25 at inception of the loan to 3.00 in the fourth quarter of 2003. How does the company benefit from this requirement? How does the lender benefit?
3. The debt-to-EBITDAR ratio described in Section 6.08 serves what purpose?
4. The maximum acceptable debt-to-EBITDAR ratio (Section 6.08) decreases from 4.50 at inception of the loan to 3.50 in the fourth quarter of 2003. How does the company benefit from this requirement? How does the lender benefit?

P7–8

Investment projects and stockholder–bondholder conflict

ABC Corp. must choose between two projects, both of which require an investment of $250,000. Project A has a 0.5 probability of generating a net payoff of $250,000 and a 0.5 probability of generating a net payoff of $500,000. Project B has a 0.5 probability of generating a net payoff of $100,000 and a 0.5 probability of generating a net payoff of $650,000.

REQUIRED:

1. What is the expected value of each project? Which project do shareholders prefer? Why?
2. ABC Corp. will issue $250,000 in bonds to finance the chosen project. The bonds will be repaid from project cash flows. Which project do bondholders prefer? Why?
3. Suppose bondholders plan to loan the company $250,000 for Project A, and they know nothing about Project B. Management knows about both projects, and will invest the borrowed funds in the project that's most valuable for shareholders. What problem does Project B create for bondholders? What should bondholders do to guard against this Project B possibility before giving money to the company?

A recent *Wall Street Journal* article described how Microsoft records revenue from software sales.

P7–9

Microsoft's "unearned revenue" account

STRETCH

SOME SAVVY FANS COOL TO MICROSOFT

Some savvy investors, detecting fissures in Microsoft's armor, are pulling back from the world's most highly valued company.

The concern: the first-ever drop in an arcane but closely watched indicator of Microsoft's future results.

The balance in Microsoft's "unearned revenue" accounting, which declined to $4.13 billion on Sept. 30 from $4.24 billion in June, has become a lightning rod for more general concerns about the price of the company's shares. . . . Managers of several large funds . . . are shedding part of their Microsoft holdings. The immediate trigger was the first quarter-to-quarter decline in Microsoft's unearned revenue account. . . .

In the software industry, Microsoft pioneered the practice of recording a portion of the revenue from some products as "unearned," starting with the release of Windows 95. The practice is common in some other fields: Many magazine publishers, for instance, record subscription revenues only when issues are shipped.

Similarly, Microsoft now holds back a portion of revenues from Windows 98, Windows NT and Office until it "earns" the revenue by delivering interim upgrades, bug fixes and other customer support. The account also includes the value of coupons that customers receive, which entitle them to free upgrades when they buy a Microsoft product before the next version is ready.

A delay in the shipment of Office 2000 earlier this year caused the company to add $400 million to the unearned revenue account in the March quarter to cover the coupons issued to buyers of Office 97. As copies of Office 2000 were shipped, half of that amount flowed into the June quarterly results; another $150 million was transferred in the fiscal quarter ended in September.

The effect was to bolster earned revenues in those quarters and lower unearned revenues. . .

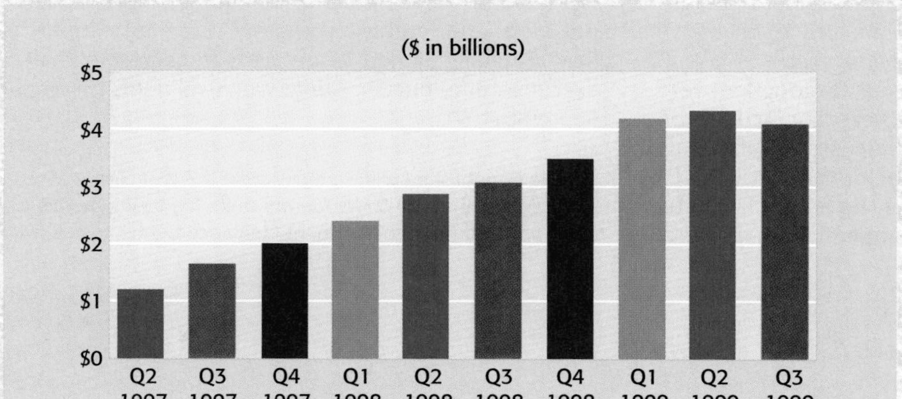

Future or Fallout?
Microsoft's unearned revenue account consists of revenues set aside from the sales of Windows 98, Windows NT and Office to pay for future improvements. It also includes the value of coupons that entitle users to upgrade to newer versions of Microsoft software.

Source: Republished with permission of the *Wall Street Journal*, from the *Wall Street Journal* (October 28, 1999); permission conveyed through Copyright Clearance Center, Inc.

REQUIRED:

1. Based on the revenue recognition principles discussed in Chapters 2 and 3, explain why a company like Microsoft would set aside some software sales revenues as "unearned"?
2. How would you determine how much sales revenue to set aside each quarter? Is this number easy to calculate?

(continued)

3. Suppose the "unearned revenue" account is reduced by $100 million. Where do these dollars go? (The "unearned revenue" account is reduced by a debit. What account receives the offsetting credit?)
4. Describe how contracting and regulatory incentives might influence how much revenue is set aside as "unearned." How might these incentives influence when the "unearned revenue" account is reduced and by how much?
5. Why do analysts and investors pay such close attention to changes in Microsoft's unearned revenue account?

P7–10

Executive pay when the CEO nears retirement

REQUIRED:

1. Why might it make sense to change a CEO's incentive pay plan as the CEO nears retirement? What conflicts of interest arise as a CEO gets close to retirement age?
2. In early 1997, Ralston Purina Company changed the way its CEO was paid. As a shareholder, what are the advantages and disadvantages of the compensation committee's new strategy for paying Mr. Stiritz?
3. Suppose you are an independent compensation consultant hired by a group of Ralston Purina shareholders. What changes would you suggest be made to the compensation committee's plan?
4. According to the committee, Mr. Stiritz's compensation was changed to "facilitate greater focus on succession planning" and to locate the right successor "so the company will do well after his retirement." In May 1997 Ralston Purina named two of its officers as co-chief executives. As a shareholder, would you be surprised by this outcome? Why or why not?

CEOs HAVE LESS SAY IN DESIGNATING SUCCESSORS

Not long ago, chief executive officers called all the shots in the crucial corporate game of "Pass the Baton."

Today, it's a whole new game. Assertive boards and influential investors are playing bigger parts in the timing of a CEO's exit and choice of successor. Their increased involvement weakens business titans' authority over abdication and can turn transfers of leadership into messy succession struggles.

Bowing to shareholder demands for tougher oversight, more boards now link a chief's pay increase or yearly performance review to succession-planning progress. Ralston Purina Co. directors gave William P. Stiritz options on 600,000 shares last fall to "facilitate greater focus on succession planning." To make sure the 62-year-old chief executive tapped a replacement soon, Ralston froze his salary and ended certain bonuses and stock grants until he retires.

The package rewards Mr. Stiritz, ensconced in the top post since 1981, for locating the right successor "so the company will do well after his retirement," says W. H. Danforth, an outside director of the St. Louis pet-food and battery company. Late last month, Ralston finally named two officers to share the chief-executive title, but Mr. Stiritz won't relinquish it until September 30.

Source: Republished with permission of the *Wall Street Journal*, from the *Wall Street Journal* (June 24, 1997); permission conveyed through Copyright Clearance Center, Inc.

RALSTON PURINA COMPANY:
COMPENSATION FOR THE CHAIRMAN AND CHIEF EXECUTIVE OFFICER

The Compensation Committee recognized, as it evaluated Mr. Stiritz's overall compensation at the end of fiscal 1996, that he is likely to retire in the next few years from the position of Chief Executive Officer. Taking that into consideration, the Committee determined it to be in the best interest of the Company to change its approach to compensating Mr. Stiritz. The Committee wishes to facilitate a greater focus by Mr. Stiritz on succession planning and believes that sequential grants of long-term awards which are intended to retain key employees are not appropriate with respect to the Chief Executive Officer when there are relatively few years until retirement. To that end, the Committee decided to award Mr. Stiritz a special performance stock option grant of 600,000 shares (see the table below), in exchange for which it would (i) freeze Mr. Stiritz's base pay until retirement at the level it was during fiscal year 1996; (ii) exclude him from future annual stock award grants; and (iii) exclude him from any further intermediate or long-term cash bonus plans.

The size of the performance stock option grant was determined based on a calculation of the anticipated decrease in the value of Mr. Stiritz's total compensation package, caused not only by the direct effect of freezing his salary, but also by the indirect effect such a freeze will have on the calculation of benefits which are based on a percentage of base pay: e.g., his future annual cash bonuses; Company match on deferrals of salary or bonus into savings or deferred compensation plans; anticipated value of a second long-term incentive plan, to be implemented in fiscal year 1997, from which he was excluded; and value of annual stock option grants it was anticipated would have been awarded to him.

The purpose of the grant which, in the Committee's opinion, has an approximate value equal to the benefits described above which he will forgo, is to tie the majority of Mr. Stiritz's compensation to the Company's Common Stock price performance during the last years of his employment.

The following table sets forth the CEO's compensation over the last three years:

		Annual Compensation			Long-Term Compensation Awards	
Name & Principal Position	Year	Salary	Bonus	Other Annual Compensation	Securities Underlying Options (#)	All Other Compensation
W. P. Stiritz	1996	$1,000,000	$1,071,000	$79,527	600,000	$621,289
Chairman of the	1995	900,000	1,071,000	14,135	195,000	601,862
Board/CEO	1994	825,000	500,000	38,060	0	345,355

The following table sets forth the CEO's 600,000 share option grant in 1996:

Name	Number of Securities Underlying Options Granted	% of Total Options Granted to Employees in Fiscal Year	Exercise or Base Price(1) ($/share)	Expiration Date	Grant Date Value
W. P. Stiritz	200,000(2)	10.37%	$67.25	9/25/06	$5,528,000
	200,000(2)	10.37	$67.25	9/25/06	5,528,000
	200,000(2)	10.37	$67.25	9/25/06	5,528,000

(1)Market price on date of grant.

(2)Reflects one of three tranches each equal to 33⅓% of stock price performance options granted to the executive on a single date. The options are exercisable in such tranches on 9-26-98, 9-26-01, and 9-26-04, provided that, with respect to each tranche, a target market price (reflecting a 5% per year increase in the market price of the Common Stock) is met on the respective date. If the target market price is not met on the relevant date, shares of that tranche will not become exercisable until and unless the target market price for a subsequent fiscal quarter end or award anniversary date is met. All shares become exercisable, in any event, on the ninth anniversary of the date of grant. The target market prices for the dates on which each tranche of such shares would first become exercisable are $74.14, $85.83, and $99.36, respectively.

Source: Ralston Purina Company 1996 proxy.

REQUIRED:

1. The proxy statement excerpt on the next page describes how Walt Disney Company pays its CEO, Mr. Eisner. What is the purpose of the annual bonus plan? Are the performance goals reasonable?
2. Why does Disney also award stock options to Mr. Eisner?
3. Some of Mr. Eisner's options have an exercise price above the stock's market price on the grant date. Why?
4. How does stock return performance of Disney compare to the peer group and the market (S&P 500). How does Mr. Eisner's compensation compare to the performance of Disney's stock?
5. Disney's management selects the companies in its peer group. What problems does this create for an analyst or investor trying to evaluate Mr. Eisner's pay and performance relative to Disney's competitors?

P7–11

CEO compensation at Walt Disney Company

EXCERPTS FROM WALT DISNEY COMPANY PROXY STATEMENT FOR 1997

Pursuant with an employment agreement dated January 11, 1989, Mr. Eisner's base salary is $750,000 per year through the entire term of the agreement. The agreement provides for a nondiscretionary annual bonus equal to 2% of the amount by which the Company's net income for the fiscal year exceeded the amount representing a return on stockholder's equity of 11% (9% for 1989 and 1990).

The agreement provides for a single stock option grant (made on January 11, 1989) of 8,000,000 shares of common stock. Of the options granted, 25% were granted at an exercise price $10 above the then current fair market value of the common stock, with the remaining 75% granted at a price equal to fair market value.

Appearing below are tables setting forth the total compensation earned or paid to Mr. Eisner during each of the last three fiscal years and a comparison of the cumulative return of the company, a peer group, and the market (the S&P 500 index).

	Annual Compensation		Long-Term Compensation	
Fiscal Year	Salary	Bonus	Restricted Stock Awards	Other
1996	$750,000	$7,900,000	0	$3,520
1995	750,000	8,024,707	$5,996,522	6,877
1994	750,000	7,268,807	2,638,394	9,730

Comparison of Five-Year Cumulative Total Return among the Company, S&P 500 Index, and Peer Group Index

Measurement Period	Walt Disney Company	S&P 500	Peer Group Index
1991	100	100	100
1992	128	111	119
1993	134	125	174
1994	138	130	163
1995	206	169	206
1996	229	203	226

The peer group includes Capital Cities/ABC, Club Med, Hasbro, Hilton Hotels, King World Productions, Mattel, Paramount Communications, Time Warner, Turner Broadcasting System, and Viacom Inc. All dividends are reinvested.

Source: Walt Disney Company 1997 proxy.

P7–12

A new employment agreement at Disney

REQUIRED:

1. How does Mr. Eisner's new bonus plan (described below) differ from the old plan described in Problem 7–11?
2. Are the performance goals in the new bonus plan reasonable?
3. As a shareholder, would you vote for or against the new employment contract? Why?

EXCERPTS FROM WALT DISNEY COMPANY PROXY STATEMENT FOR 1997

On September 30, 1996, a new employment agreement with Mr. Eisner was approved by the Compensation Committee and the Board of Directors. The new agreement provides for Mr. Eisner's employment through September 30, 2006 at his current base salary of $750,000 per year.

If this plan is approved by stockholders, commencing with fiscal 1999, Mr. Eisner's bonus will be tied to the growth of the Company's earnings per share (EPS). The "threshold EPS" for each fiscal year reflects a 7.5% growth over the threshold EPS of the prior year (or the "base EPS," in the case of fiscal 1999). Thus, on a hypothetical basis, if there were a constant growth rate of 7.5% (starting from the base EPS) in each year of the agreement beginning with fiscal 1999, no bonuses would be payable to Mr. Eisner. If actual EPS for fiscal 1999 reflected a 20% growth rate from the base EPS, but EPS grew by 0% in fiscal 2000 over fiscal 1999, a bonus would be payable for both years, since the EPS for fiscal 2000 would still represent compound growth in excess of the minimum required for the payment of a bonus under the formula.

The Committee also granted to Mr. Eisner stock options on 8,000,000 shares of common stock. Of this total, options on 5,000,000 shares bear an exercise price of $63.31 (fair market value at the grant date). Three additional options, each with respect to 1,000,000 shares, bear exercise prices $79.13 (125% of fair market value) vesting on September 30, 2004; $94.96 (150% of fair market value) vesting on September 30, 2005; and $126.62 (200% of fair market value) vesting on September 30, 2006.

The following table sets forth the option grants and their potential value:

Number of Options Granted	Exercise Price ($/share)	Expiration Date	Hypothetical Value at Grant Date
5,000,000	$ 63.31	9/30/08	$134,096,924
1,000,000	79.14	9/30/11	25,390,861
1,000,000	94.97	9/30/11	21,194,406
1,000,000	126.62	9/30/11	14,901,090

Source: Walt Disney Company 1997 proxy.

P7–13

Understanding rate regulation and accounting choices

Alliant Energy just received regulatory approval for its 2001 electricity rate. The company has been authorized to charge customers $0.10 per kilowatt-hour (kwh), a rate lower than what other utilities in the state charge. Details of the rate calculation are as follows:

ALLIANT ENERGY
2001 Rate Authorization

Allowed operating costs			$ 1,120 million
Assets in service	$3,200 million		
× Allowed rate of return	8.75%	=	$ 280 million
Revenue requirement			$ 1,400 million
÷ Estimated energy demand			14,000 million kwh
Rate allowed per kwh			$ 0.10

Shortly after the 2001 rate was set, the company's financial reporting staff circulated an internal memo recommending the following accounting changes:

1. Extend plant depreciation life by five years to reflect current utilization forecasts. This would add $175 million to the asset base and reduce annual depreciation (an operating cost) by $5 million.
2. Increase estimated bad debt expense from 1% to 1.5% of sales to reflect current forecasts of customer defaults. This would add $7 million to operating costs and reduce total assets by the same amount.
3. Amortize 2000 hostile takeover defense costs of $4.5 million over three years rather than take the entire expense in 2000 (last year). This would increase 2001 operating costs by $1.5 million and add $3 million to the asset base.
4. Write up fuel and materials inventories to their current replacement value. This would add $60 million to the asset base, but it would have no impact on 2001 operating costs.

REQUIRED:

1. Assess the impact of each proposed change on the company's 2001 revenue requirement and rate per kilowatt-hour, assuming that regulators will approve the accounting changes and adjust the allowed rate accordingly.
2. As a member of the state utility commission, comment on the merits of each proposed accounting change.

C7–1

Genesco, Inc., Worthington Industries, Inc., and Symantec Corporation (CW): A tale of three dividend constraints

Loan agreements often contain provisions that limit the borrower's ability to pay cash dividends or buy back stock to an amount called the **"inventory of payable funds"** or IPF. The IPF is increased by earnings and the proceeds from stock sales, and it is reduced by losses and cash payments to shareholders (dividends or buybacks).

Here's an example: A loan agreement signed in January 2001 says: "cash dividends and stock redemptions (buybacks) are limited to the sum of $5 million plus (i) 25% of net income after December 31, 2000 and (ii) 60% of the proceeds received from issuing common or preferred stock after February 1, 2001."

Suppose the company reports 2001 net income of $12 million and issues $10 million of stock during the year. According to the loan agreement, dividends and stock buybacks cannot exceed $15 million—the $5 million base amount plus 25% of the $12 million net income and 60% of the $10 million stock proceeds. If cash dividends of $3 million were paid out during the year and there were no stock buybacks, the IPF would total $12 million at year-end. This is the most that can be paid to shareholders without more earnings or stock sales.

Several factors in addition to earnings, stock issues, and shareholder payouts determine the level of a company's IPF. First, there's the base IPF amount described in the covenant ($5 million in our example). Next, there's the earnings cumulation date (beginning December 31, 2000) and the percentage allowed (25%). Finally, there's the stock sale cumulation date (February 1, 2001) and the percentage allowed (60%). These details are negotiated as part of the loan approval and acceptance process.

Reproduced next are dividend constraint descriptions for three companies. Genesco, Inc. manufactures and sells branded men's and women's shoes and boots, including Johnston & Murphy, Dockers, and Nautica shoes as well as Laredo, Code West, and Larry Mahan boots.

> The February 1, 1993 indenture, under which the Company's 10⅜% senior notes due 2003 were issued, limits the payment of dividends and redemptions of capital stock to the sum of $10 million plus (i) 50% of Consolidated Net Income (as defined) after April 30, 1993 and (ii) the aggregate Net Proceeds (as defined) received from the issuance or sale of capital stock after February 1, 1993.
>
> At February 1, 1997, the Company was in a deficit position of $91.3 million in its ability to pay dividends. Due to the above restrictions, the Company suspended dividends in the fourth quarter of Fiscal 1994 and now has cumulative dividend arrearage in the amount of $277,494 for Series 1, $300,553 for Series 3, $253,360 for Series 4, and $146,333 for $1.50 Subordinated Cumulative Preferred Stock.

Worthington Industries, Inc. is the largest independent flat rolled steel processor in the United States with over 1,700 industrial customers.

> Various debt agreements place restrictions on financial conditions and require maintenance of certain ratios. One of these restrictions limits cash dividends and certain other payments to $3,000,000 plus 75% of net earnings, as defined, subsequent to May 31, 1976. Retained earnings of $347,333,000 were unrestricted at May 31,1996.

Symantec Corporation develops, markets, and supports a diversified line of application and system software products designed to enhance individual and workgroup productivity as well as manage networked computing environments.

> On April 2, 1993, the Company issued convertible subordinated debentures totaling $25.0 million. The debentures limit the payment of cash dividends and the repurchase of capital stock to a total of $10.0 million plus 25% of cumulative net income subsequent to April 2, 1993.

The information at the top of the facing page was taken from the Symantec Corporation's March 31, 1996 annual report to shareholders.

SYMANTEC CORPORATION Selected Financial Statement Items			
($ in thousands)	1994	1995	1996
Net income (loss)	($44,421)	$33,409	($39,783)
Proceeds from sale of common stock	47,969	21,395	20,770
Cash dividends paid	-0-	-0-	-0-
Stock repurchases	-0-	-0-	-0-

REQUIRED:

1. Calculate Symantec's inventory of payable funds (IPF) at the end of fiscal 1996.
2. What percentage of net income (loss) is added to (subtracted from) the IPF of each company? Why does the percentage vary across companies?
3. Why do lenders treat both cash dividends and stock buybacks as a reduction to the IPF?
4. Why do lenders treat proceeds from new stock sales as an IPF increase?
5. How might Genesco's management eliminate the company's IPF deficit?
6. Why does Worthington Industries maintain such a large IPF balance?

C7–2

Huffy Corporation, Caesars World, and Lands' End (CW): Accounting-based incentive bonus plans

Huffy Corporation manufactures and sells recreation and leisure products through its subsidiaries—Huffy Bicycle, Huffy Sports, and True Temper Hardware. The company's profit sharing bonus plan was described in a recent proxy statement:

> PROFIT SHARING BONUS PLAN
>
> Bonus opportunity is extended to virtually all managerial employees of the Company, including its Executive Officers. Individual and corporate performance objectives are established at the beginning of each year. The corporate performance measure for bonus payments is based on return on average net assets ("RONA"), and for 1992 the Committee determined that the target level bonus would be achieved when RONA was 10 percent, with threshold level bonus and maximum level bonus being achieved when RONA was 8.5 percent and 14.2 percent, respectively.

The company reported 1992 net income of $4,215,000 and earnings before the cumulative effect of accounting changes of $11,843,000. An accounting change made that year explains the difference between these two numbers. In addition, the company's net assets at the end of 1991 and 1992 were $124,997,000 and $117,687,000 respectively.

Caesars World, Inc. and its subsidiaries provide domestic and international customers with a broad range of entertainment, gaming, and resort experiences at its three hotel/resort properties. The company's incentive compensation plans were described in a recent proxy statement:

> INCENTIVE COMPENSATION PLANS
>
> The Company has adopted Incentive Compensation Plans for fiscal 1993 with respect to certain officers of the Company. Basically, the Plans provide for incentive compensation for each officer designated to participate based on a designated percentage of corporate pre-tax income (before extraordinary and certain unusual items) in excess of 12% of shareholders' equity as of July 31, 1992 (subject to adjustment if certain stock sales or repurchases occur).

The company's financial statements show:

CAESARS WORLD
Selected Financial Statement Items

($ in thousands)	Year-End Amounts 1992	1993	1994
Income before taxes and extraordinary loss	$117,360	$133,976	$128,555
Extraordinary loss	6,073	-0-	-0-
Net income	66,005	83,215	78,361
Total stockholders' equity	384,648	472,890	556,867
Proceeds from stock issued	2,454	1,369	2,111
Stock repurchases	1,986	1,338	2,337

Lands' End, Inc. is a leading direct marketer of traditionally styled apparel, soft luggage, and other products offered through its regular and specialty catalogs. The company's incentive bonus plan was described in a recent proxy statement:

Incentive Bonuses

The Plan provides participants with bonuses in the form of Company Common Stock, cash or a combination thereof in the event the Company earns pre-tax income in excess of 6% of net sales for the fiscal year of participation. The amount of each incentive bonus is a function of two factors: (i) the participant's level of eligibility ("Bonus Eligibility Amount") as determined by the Committee, and (ii) the extent to which the Company's pre-tax income exceeds 6% of net sales. Each participant's bonus will be calculated as that employee's Bonus Eligibility amount (as determined by the Committee) multiplied by the earned participation level for such year in accordance with the following table:

Pre-tax Income to Net Sales (%)	Participation Level (% of Incentive Bonus Earned)
6%	0%
7	15
8	35
9	70
10	100
11	150

The company's financial statements show:

LANDS' END
Selected Financial Statement Items

($ in thousands)	1995	1994	1993	1992	1991
Net sales	$992,106	$869,975	$733,623	$683,427	$601,991
Pre-tax income	59,663	69,870	54,033	47,492	29,943

REQUIRED:

1. Why do Huffy, Caesars World, and Lands' End use bonus plans?
2. Did Huffy's managers achieve a RONA greater than 8.5% in 1992?
3. Did Caesars World's managers earn their required minimum rate of return on beginning equity in 1993? How about 1994?
4. Did executives at Lands' End meet their minimum rate of return on sales over the 1991–1995 period?

5. Why don't all companies use the same financial performance measure in their bonus plans?
6. As a member of the board's compensation committee at each company, what financial reporting decisions would you want to carefully monitor? Why?
7. Are the performance targets in these plans reasonable? What information would help you answer this question?

C7–3

Sunny Day Stores, Inc. (CW): Debt covenants and financial distress

Sunny Day Stores operates convenience stores throughout much of the United States. The industry is highly competitive, with low profit margins. The company's competition includes national, regional, and local supermarkets; oil companies; and convenience store operators.

A footnote to the 2001 financial statements described the company's long-term debt:

> Note payable to the Prudential Insurance Company of America ("Prudential") with annual principal payments of $900,000, interest at 8.93%. Amount outstanding: $5,700,000 in 2001 and $6,600,000 in 2000.
>
> Term note payable to First Florida Bank ("First Florida") maturing in September 2006, with quarterly principal payments of $125,000 through June 30, 2002 and $250,000 thereafter, with interest at 1% in excess of prime (7.5% at December 26, 2001). Amount outstanding: $3,563,956 in 2001 and $3,000,000 in 2000.
>
> Revolving note payable to First Florida Bank with interest at 1% in excess of prime (7.5% at December 26, 2001). Amount outstanding: $7,400,000 in 2001 and 2000.
>
> Certain of the Company's loan agreements pertaining to the borrowings from the Prudential Insurance Company of America ("Prudential") and First Florida Bank ("First Florida") require the Company to maintain minimum interest coverage ratio, working capital, and net worth levels, impose restrictions on additional borrowings, and prohibit the payment of dividends. Specifically, at the end of fiscal 2001 Sunny Day must have a net worth of $22,850,000, working capital (on a FIFO inventory basis) must be at least $1,300,000, and the interest coverage ratio must be at least 1.6.

The company's 2001 financial statements that follow show that Sunny Day Stores was not in compliance with these loan covenants at year-end.

SUNNY DAY STORES, INC.

Comparative Balance Sheets

	2001	2000
Cash and cash equivalents	$ 1,451,688	$ 2,971,457
Accounts receivable less allowances for doubtful accounts of $82,000 and $63,000 in 2001 and 2000, respectively	985,987	705,923
Refundable income taxes	400,000	135,831
Inventories—FIFO basis	10,640,125	8,690,734
Less LIFO reserve	(3,057,715)	(2,845,703)
Total inventories	7,582,410	5,845,031
Prepaid expenses and other assets	764,627	547,705
Refundable deposits	700,000	380,522
Total current assets	$ 11,884,712	$ 10,586,469

	2001	2000
Accounts payable		
Trade	$ 9,237,416	$ 6,208,733
Money orders	1,637,255	1,442,811
Fuel taxes	1,106,713	635,556
Accrued liabilities		
Salaries and wages	774,519	846,131
Self-insurance reserves	1,186,613	966,770
State and local taxes	1,136,241	569,160
Current portion of long-term debt	1,956,369	1,082,429
Total current liabilities	$ 17,035,126	$ 11,751,590

(continued)

SUNNY DAY STORES, INC. (*continued*)

Comparative Balance Sheets

	2001	2000		2001	2000
Property and equipment			Deferred income taxes	400,000	1,477,323
Land	11,016,168	13,603,304	Unearned revenue	111,426	179,224
Buildings	19,673,636	19,801,221			
Fixtures and equipment	32,232,643	32,749,133	Long-term debt, less		
Leaseholds and			current portion	13,969,745	16,693,772
improvements	5,084,679	4,929,748			
	$ 68,007,126	$71,083,406			
Less allowances for					
depreciation and					
amortization	(31,008,778)	(28,988,173)	Stockholders' equity		
	$36,998,348	$42,095,233	Common stock	170,165	170,165
Other assets			Additional paid-in capital	5,124,245	5,124,245
Land held for sale	2,641,735		Retained earnings	15,171,001	17,735,240
Other	456,913	449,857		$20,465,411	$23,029,650
			Total liabilities and		
Total assets	**$51,981,708**	**$53,131,559**	**stockholders' equity**	**$51,981,708**	**$53,131,559**

SUNNY DAY STORES, INC.

Statement of Cash Flows

	2001	2000	1999
Cash Flows from Operating Activities			
Net income (loss)	($2,564,239)	($1,042,297)	$ 613,423
Adjustments			
Depreciation and amortization	3,980,186	4,460,529	3,793,119
Deferred income taxes	(1,077,323)	(512,995)	577,235
Gain on sale of property	(532,570)	(174,657)	(100,322)
Decrease in unearned revenue	(67,798)	(83,804)	(84,235)
Changes in assets and liabilities			
(Increase) in accounts receivable	(280,064)	53,121	(358,982)
(Increase) in refundable income taxes	(264,169)	244,085	(113,675)
(Increase) in inventories	(1,737,379)	2,908,024	412,647
(Increase) in other assets	(263,981)	(141,910)	(241,347)
Increase in refundable deposits	(319,478)	(15,107)	(145,866)
Increase in accounts payable and other liabilities	4,409,596	(4,304,076)	3,807,200
Total adjustments	3,847,020	2,433,210	7,545,774
Net cash flow from operations	$1,282,781	$1,390,913	$8,159,197
Cash Flows from Investing Activities			
Purchase of property and equipment, net	(2,390,832)	(2,871,399)	(9,593,270)
Sale of property and equipment	1,428,051	668,656	821,641
Collections of notes and loans receivables	10,318	(103,610)	7,775
Net cash used in investing activities	$ (952,463)	($2,306,353)	($8,763,854)
Cash Flows from Financing Activities			
Issuance of long-term debt	82,515	2,633,454	4,528,915
Dividends	–0–	–0–	(204,198)
Payment of long-term debt	(1,932,602)	(3,108,251)	(1,588,391)
Net cash provided by financing activities	($1,850,087)	$ (474,797)	$2,736,326
Net increase (Decrease) in Cash	($1,519,769)	($1,390,237)	$2,131,669

SUNNY DAY STORES, INC.

Statement of Operations

	2001	2000	1999
Net revenue	$217,710,782	$202,393,136	$191,243,016
Cost and expenses			
Costs of goods sold	176,102,027	158,643,287	146,652,853
Selling, general, and administrative	44,631,749	43,687,704	41,805,330
Interest expense—net	1,551,138	1,728,650	1,658,732
Net gain from sale of property	(532,570)	(174,657)	(100,322)
	221,752,344	203,884,984	190,016,593
Income (loss) before taxes	(4,041,562)	(1,491,848)	1,226,423
Provision (benefit) for income taxes			
Current	(400,000)	63,444	50,000
Deferred	(1,077,323)	(512,995)	563,000
	(1,477,323)	(449,551)	613,000
Net income (loss)	$ (2,564,239)	$ (1,042,297)	$ 613,423
Earnings per common share	($1.51)	($0.61)	$0.36

Required:

It's late January 2002 and you've been hired by Prudential and First Florida to act on their behalf in negotiations with Sunny Day Stores, Inc. Both lenders want to restructure their loans to address the company's current financial problems, and the restructured loans may require covenant changes.

Prudential and First Florida seek your advice on the type and amount of collateral to be required, revised interest rates, and possible changes to the payment schedules. In addition, the lenders have asked you to suggest new minimum net worth, working capital, and interest coverage ratios for 2002 and 2003. Specifically:

1. What type and amount of collateral do you suggest be required?
2. Should a higher interest rate be charged? Why or why not?
3. What changes would you suggest be made to the payment schedule?
4. What new minimum net worth, working capital, and interest coverage limits would you suggest the lenders set?
5. Suppose the company asked permission to resume payment of its $0.12 per-share common stock dividend, which was suspended in 2000. What advice would you give Prudential and First Florida?

C7–4

Maxcor Manufacturing: Compensation and earnings quality

Margaret Magee has served both as an outside director to Maxcor Manufacturing since 1990 and as a member of the company's compensation committee since 1997. Margaret has been reviewing Maxcor's 2000 preliminary earnings statement (reproduced on the next page) in preparation for the February 2001 board and compensation committee meetings. She is uneasy about the company's definition and computation of "Operating profits" for 2000, particularly since management bonuses at Maxcor are based on achieving specific operating profit goals. *(continued)*

MAXCOR MANUFACTURING

Consolidated Results of Operations

($ in millions)	Year Ended December 31 2000	1999
Sales	$98.4	$111.2
Operating costs		
Cost of goods sold	(81.5)	(92.2)
Selling, general, and administrative expenses	(12.5)	(12.9)
Operating profit	4.4	6.1
Research and development expenses (see note)	(5.7)	(2.4)
Provision for plant closings (see note)	(2.6)	-0-
Interest expense	(2.9)	(2.6)
Other income	0.7	1.2
Profit (loss) before taxes	(6.1)	2.3
Provision (credit) for income taxes	2.1	(0.8)
Profit (loss) of consolidated companies	(4.0)	1.5
Equity in profit of affiliated companies	0.2	0.3
Profit (loss)	$ (3.8)	$ 1.8

The preliminary financial statements also contained the following footnotes:

Research and Engineering Expenses. Research and engineering expenses include both "Research and development expenses" for new product development and charges to "Cost of goods sold" for ongoing efforts to improve existing products. The amounts (in millions) for 2000 and 1999 were:

	2000	1999
Research and development expenses	$5.7	$2.4
Cost of goods sold	2.9	6.3
Research and engineering expense	$8.6	$8.7

Plant Closing Costs. In 2000, the Company recorded provisions for plant closing and staff consolidation costs totaling $2.62 million. Included in this total are charges related to the probable closing of the Company's York, Pennsylvania facility ($1.75 million), the consolidation of the North American operations of the Building Construction Products Division ($0.63 million), and charges to reflect lower estimates of the market value of previously closed U.S. facilities ($0.24 million). These costs include the estimated costs of employee severance benefits, the estimated net losses on disposal of land, buildings, machinery and equipment, and other costs incidental to the closing and planned consolidation.

Maxcor Manufacturing is an established, privately held manufacturer that operates in two principal business segments: *Building Construction Products,* which involves the design, manufacturing, and marketing of construction and materials-handling machinery; and *Engines* for various off-highway applications. Before 2000 the company had experienced 15 years of steadily increasing sales and operating profits.

The company was founded in 1938 by Hugh Maxwell, a former Ford Motor Company engineer. Neither Mr. Maxwell nor any members of his family are currently officers of the company. Maxcor's common stock is held by the Maxwell Family Trust (35%), the Maxwell Employee Stock Ownership Plan (ESOP) Trust (50%), a venture capital firm (13%), and current management (2%). Margaret Magee also serves as an outside trustee for the Maxwell ESOP Trust.

Maxcor's senior management participates in an incentive bonus plan that was first adopted in 1996. The bonus formula for 2000 was approved by the compensation committee at its February 1999 meeting. According to the plan, each senior manager's 2000 bonus is to be determined as follows:

Bonus as Percentage of 2000 Salary	2000 Operating Profits ($ in millions)
0%	Below $4.0
100	At least $4.0
200	At least $6.0
300	At least $8.0

The compensation committee can award a lesser amount than that indicated by the plan formula if circumstances warrant such action. No bonus reductions have occurred since the plan was adopted in 1996.

REQUIRED:

Why might Ms. Magee feel uneasy about Maxcor's computation of 2000 operating profits? Should Ms. Magee approve the 100% bonus payment for 2000 as specified by the plan formula? What changes (if any) would you recommend be made to the bonus formula for next year?

C7–5

Relative performance and stock options

Here's how Level 3 Communication's stock option plan works. Suppose options are granted on January 1, 2000 when the company's stock is selling for $50 a share. The options cannot be exercised until January 1, 2003 and the exercise price on that date is $50 plus a factor reflecting the change in the S&P Index between the grant date and the exercise date. If the Index increases 50%, so does the exercise price (to $75). If the Index falls by 10% between the grant date and the exercise date, the exercise price also falls (to $45).

REQUIRED:

1. On January 1, 2003, the company's stock is trading at $90 a share. The S&P Index has increased 60 percent from its level at the grant date. What is the exercise price of Level 3's options? Have employees benefited from the company's stock option plan?
2. What if the January 1, 2003 stock price was only $70? Calculate the option exercise price and determine if employees have benefited from the stock option plan. How well have Level 3 stockholders done since the grant date?
3. Stock prices and the S&P Index tend to increase when Mr. Alan Greenspan, Chairman of the Federal Reserve Bank, lowers interest rates. What is the rationale for raising the exercise price when interest rates decline? What other macroeconomic risks can influence the value of employee stock options at Level 3?
4. Why hasn't the Level 3 plan been adopted by other companies?

THE MOVING-TARGET OPTION

Nineteen ninety-eight was a good year for Harvey Golub, the chief executive of American Express. His stock options zoomed from $45 million to $60 million in value. But it was a bad year for Golub's shareholders. They underperformed the S&P 500 by 13 percentage points.

The disappointed Amex holders have a lot of company. It's common these days for executives to get rich off options even as they deliver subpar results to their investors. It's the simple arithmetic of a bull market: Options can be worth a lot of money on a stock that rises, even if it badly lags the averages . . .

How do we stop this madness? One bold telecom executive, James Crowe, shows how. When he founded fiber-optics network Level 3 Communications three years ago, he vowed to align his interests with investors'. His option plan, which covers all employees, ties exercise prices to the S&P 500 Index. If Level 3 just keeps up with the average, the options are worthless. If it outperforms, the options are worth a decent amount to rank and file employees and big money to top managers.

Level 3 investors aren't hurting and neither is Chief Executive Crowe. Since the stock was first offered to the public just under two years ago,

(continued)

it has tripled in price. Crowe has a $300 million paper profit so far on his options.

Crowe thinks every company should adopt an option plan like this one. "All kinds of companies have hurt their investors, yet managements are getting enormous payoffs," he scolds.

Crowe is a lonely crusader. We don't know of a single other public company that ties option prices to the S&P.

Former Securities & Exchange Commissioner Joseph Grundfest, now a Stanford Law School professor, presented Level 3's plan at his annual directors' conference last year. Directors of companies like American International Group, Bank America, Lucent and Time Warner attended. Grundfest reports their reaction: "Many thought it was a great idea—for other companies." He adds: "A Level 3-style plan would eliminate the Lake Wobegon effect, where all CEOs are above average. Which is why it's frightening to many." . . .

Source: Reprinted by permission of Forbes Magazine © 2000 Forbes. From an article by T. Mack (March 20, 2000).

8

Receivables

LEARNING OBJECTIVES:
After studying this chapter, you will understand:

1. The methods used to estimate uncollectible accounts in order to determine the expected net realizable value of accounts receivable.
2. How firms estimate and record sales returns and allowances.
3. How to evaluate whether or not reported receivables arose from real sales and how to spot danger signals.
4. How to impute and record interest when notes receivable yield either no explicit interest or an unrealistically low interest rate.
5. How companies transfer or dispose of receivables in order to accelerate cash collection and how to distinguish between transactions that represent sales of receivables from those that are borrowings.
6. Why receivables are sometimes restructured when a customer experiences financial difficulty and how to account for the troubled-debt restructuring.

Receivables are amounts owed to a business firm by outsiders. In U.K. financial reports, receivables are called "debtors" — a term clearly connoting the legal obligation of outsiders to make payments to a firm. Most receivables arise from credit sales and are called **trade receivables** or **accounts receivable.** Receivables that result from other types of transactions and events (e.g., insurance claims from casualty losses) are separately disclosed, if significant, on the balance sheet to facilitate informed financial analysis.

Assessing the Net Realizable Value of Accounts Receivable

Generally accepted accounting principles (GAAP) requires that accounts receivable be reflected in the balance sheet at their **net realizable value.**[1] Two things must be estimated to determine the net realizable value of receivables:

1. The amount that will not be collected because customers are unable to pay—called **uncollectibles.**
2. The amount that will not be collected because customers return the merchandise for credit or are allowed a reduction in the amount owed—called **returns** and **allowances.**

The next sections discuss financial reporting issues relating to uncollectibles, returns, and allowances.

---

[1] "Net realizable value" means the selling price of an item minus reasonable further costs both to make the item ready to sell and to sell it. When applied to trade receivables, net realizable value means the amount of money the business can reasonably expect to collect from its credit customers.

Estimating Uncollectibles

Some credit sales never get collected. These losses are an unavoidable cost of doing business. Companies could adopt such stringent credit standards that "bad debt" losses would be virtually zero. But if they only sold to customers with impeccable credit records, they would forego many otherwise profitable sales opportunities.

Most companies establish credit policies by weighing the expected cost of credit sales—customer billing and collection costs plus potential bad debt losses—against the benefit of increased sales. Companies choose what they believe is a profit maximizing balance. This trade-off between increased costs and additional profits from credit sales illustrates that bad debts are often unavoidable. Consequently, the accrual accounting matching principle requires that some *estimate* of uncollectible accounts be offset against current period sales—that is, ***estimated losses from customers who are ultimately unable to pay are treated as an expense of the period in which the sale is made.*** Obviously, companies can't know at the time of sale which customers will ultimately be unable to pay. So proper matching of revenues and expenses is achieved by estimating the proportion of current period credit sales that will not be collected in the future, and then by charging this amount as an expense.

Suppose Bristol Corporation estimates that, based on current industry trends and the company's experience, bad debt losses arising from first quarter 2001 sales are expected to be $30,000. The entry Bristol would make under GAAP is:

DR Bad debt expense	$30,000	
CR Allowance for uncollectibles		$30,000

The allowance for uncollectibles is a contra-asset account that is subtracted from gross accounts receivable. If Bristol's gross accounts receivable and allowance for uncollectibles balances *before* recording this bad debt entry were $1,500,000 and $15,000, respectively, then after recording bad debts, its balance sheet would show:

Accounts receivable (gross)	$1,500,000	
Less: Allowance for uncollectibles	(45,000)	(15,000) Initial balance (30,000) Addition
Accounts receivable (net)	$1,455,000	

There are two approaches companies use to estimate uncollectible accounts. One multiplies a specific loss percentage by sales revenues; the other multiplies a (usually different) loss percentage by gross accounts receivable. Each approach is illustrated as follows.

1. *The sales revenue approach.* Assume that Bristol Corporation prepares quarterly financial statements and must estimate bad debt expense at the end of each quarter. Analyzing customer payment patterns, Bristol determined that bad debt losses average about 1% of sales. If first quarter sales in 2001 total $3,000,000, then bad debt losses from those sales are expected to total $30,000. The entry previously illustrated would then be made to record the company's estimate of bad debt expenses arising from current quarter sales.

Sales Revenue Approach Estimate the current period bad debt expense as a percentage of current period sales. For Bristol Corporation, the estimate is:

$$.01 \times \$3{,}000{,}000 \text{ Sales for the quarter} = \$30{,}000 \text{ Bad debt expense}$$

So the entry is:

DR Bad debt expense	$30,000	
CR Allowance for uncollectibles		$30,000

2. *The gross accounts receivable approach.* Suppose that instead of estimating bad debts as a percentage of sales, Bristol determined that at any given time approximately 3% of gross accounts receivable eventually prove uncollectible. Gross receivables at March 31, 2001 total $1,500,000, which means that on that date the required allowance for uncollectibles is 3% of this amount, or $45,000. Because the allowance-account balance is only $15,000, $30,000 must be added to the uncollectibles account at the end of the quarter. Doing this would bring the allowance for uncollectibles balance up to $45,000.

Gross Receivables Approach Estimate the required allowance account balance as a percentage of gross receivables, then adjust the allowance to this figure. For Bristol Corporation, the required allowance account balance is:

.03 × $1,500,000 Outstanding receivables = $45,000 Allowance

The allowance account currently has a $15,000 balance, so $30,000 is added:

DR Bad debt expense	$30,000	
CR Allowance for uncollectibles		$30,000

Writing Off Bad Debts When a specific account receivable is known to be definitely uncollectible, the entire account must be removed from the books. For example, if Bristol determines that a $750 receivable from Ralph Company cannot be collected, the following entry is made:

DR Allowance for uncollectibles	$750	
CR Account receivable–Ralph Company		$750

Notice that this entry has no effect on income. A specific account receivable (Ralph Company) is eliminated from the books and the allowance contra-account is reduced, ***but no bad debt expense is recorded.*** This is consistent with the accrual accounting philosophy of recording estimated bad debt expense when the sale was made rather than at some later date when the nonpaying customer is identified. Of course, Bristol Corporation does not know at the time of each sale which particular customers will be unable to pay. That's why the offsetting credit for bad debt expense was originally made to the contra-asset account "Allowance for uncollectibles." ***Only when the seller knows which specific receivable is uncollectible can the individual account (Ralph Company) be written off.*** This is what the preceding entry accomplishes.

Assessing the Adequacy of the Allowance for Uncollectibles Account Balance

No matter which method—percentage of sales or percentage of gross receivables—is used to estimate bad debts, management must periodically assess the reasonableness of the allowance for uncollectibles balance. Given existing economic conditions and customer circumstances, is the balance in the allowance-for-uncollectibles account adequate, excessive, or insufficient?

To make this judgment, management performs an **aging of accounts receivable.** As the name implies, an aging of receivables is simply a determination of how long each receivable has been on the books. Receivables that are long past due often arise because customers are experiencing financial difficulties and may ultimately be unable to pay. An aging is performed by subdividing total accounts receivable into several age categories, as shown in Exhibit 8.1.

Obviously, considerable judgment goes into evaluating the adequacy of the allowance-for-uncollectibles balance. Most companies make careful appraisals in this area, since audit guidelines are well-developed and auditors' scrutiny is intense.

Exhibit 8.2 on page 346 contains selected financial statement figures taken from the 1996 annual report of Heilig-Meyers Company, the largest furniture retailer in the United

Exhibit 8.1 ■ BRISTOL CORPORATION

Allowance for Uncollectibles Based on Aging of Receivables

On December 31, 2001 Bristol Corporation's gross accounts receivable are $1,600,000, and the allowance-for-uncollectibles balance is $39,000. Bristol's normal sales terms require payment within 30 days after the sale is made and the goods are received by the buyer. Bristol determines that the receivables have the following age distribution:

	Current	31–90 days old	91–180 days old	Over 180 days old	Total
Amount	$1,450,000	$125,000	$15,000	$10,000	$1,600,000

Once the receivables have been grouped by age category, a separate estimate of uncollectibles by category is developed. Based on past experience, Bristol determines the following estimate of expected bad debt losses by category:

	Current	31–90 days old	91–180 days old	Over 180 days old
Estimated % of bad debt losses	2.5%	6%	20%	40%

The required balance in the allowance-for-uncollectibles account would then be as follows:

	Current	31–90 days old	91–180 days old	Over 180 days old	Total
Amount	$1,450,000	$125,000	$15,000	$10,000	$1,600,000
Estimated % of bad debt losses	2.5%	6%	20%	40%	
Allowance for uncollectibles	$ 36,250	$ 7,500	$ 3,000	$ 4,000	$ 50,750

Because the allowance-for-uncollectibles balance is only $39,000, the account must be increased by $11,750. To bring the balance up to the $50,750 figure indicated by the aging, Bristol would make the following adjusting entry:

DR Bad debt expense	$11,750	
CR Allowance for uncollectibles		$11,750

States. Over 80% of all Heilig-Meyers customers buy on credit using the company's in-house installment financing plan. Store managers are authorized to make customer credit decisions within corporate guidelines.

1996 was a difficult year for Heilig-Meyers. Sales increased 19% (from $956.0 million to $1,138.5 million), but pre-tax earnings fell 39% (from $105.9 million to $64.5 million). Earnings declined because aggressive price competition caused margins to narrow throughout the industry, and the company's growth strategy resulted in high costs for new-store openings. Bad debt expense for the year ($65.4 million) roughly equaled the company's pre-tax earnings ($64.5 million). Despite a poor profit performance, both bad

Exhibit 8.2 ■ HEILIG-MEYERS COMPANY

Analysis of Uncollectible Accounts Receivable

	1996	1995
A. Reported Amounts ($ in millions)		
Sales of merchandise	$1,138.5	$956.0
Pre-tax earnings	64.5	105.9
Customer receivables (gross)	$ 573.7	$584.9
Allowance for uncollectibles	54.7	46.7
Bad debt expense	65.4	45.4
B. Analysis		
Bad debt expense as % of sales	5.7%	4.8%
Allowance as % of customer receivables	9.5%	8.0%

Source: Heilig-Meyers 1996 Annual Report to Shareholders.

debt expense (as a percentage of sales) and the allowance for uncollectibles (as a percentage of gross customer receivables) increased in 1996. This suggests that Heilig-Meyers was taking a more conservative view of receivable collections than it had in the past, perhaps because the customer credit quality had recently deteriorated.

What impact did this conservative view have on the company's 1996 pre-tax earnings? The data in Exhibit 8.2 provide the answer.

Suppose Heilig-Meyers had maintained 1996 bad debt expense at 4.8% of sales (the same rate used in 1995). Bad debt expense would then have been $54.6 million (4.8% of $1,138.5 million sales)—or $10.8 million lower. This would have meant a corresponding $10.8 million (or 16.7%) increase in pre-tax earnings for the year.

Now suppose Heilig-Meyers had kept the allowance for uncollectibles at 8% of gross receivables (the rate used in 1995). In this case, the allowance account balance for 1996 would have been $45.9 million (8% of $573.7 million gross customer receivables)—or $8.8 million lower than what the company actually reported. Of course, this would have meant an $8.8 million reduction in bad debt expense for the year, and an $8.8 million (or almost 14%) increase in pre-tax earnings.

This analysis shows that the decision to be more conservative about receivable collections penalized reported earnings in what was already a poor profit year.

For companies like Heilig-Meyers, where most customer purchases are financed with in-house credit, a small change in the percentage rate used to estimate bad debt expense or the allowance for uncollectibles can have a big impact on reported earnings.

Determining whether the allowance for uncollectibles is adequate requires judgment. Consequently, the temptation to "manage" earnings by using bad debt accruals can be strong. As the Heilig-Meyers example illustrates, not all companies succumb to this temptation. However, research evidence does show that companies tend to reduce bad debt expense when earnings are otherwise low—and then to increase the expense when earnings are high.[2]

Estimating Sales Returns and Allowances

Sometimes the wrong goods are shipped to customers or the correct goods arrive damaged. In either case the customer will return the item or request a price reduction. When goods are returned or price allowances granted, the customer's account receivable must be reduced and an income statement charge made. Assume that Bristol Corporation agrees to reduce by $8,000 the price of goods that arrived damaged at Bath Company. Bristol would record this price adjustment as:

DR Sales returns and allowances	$8,000	
CR Accounts receivable–Bath Company		$8,000

Bath now owes $8,000 less than the amount it was previously billed, as reflected by the reduction to accounts receivable. The account that is debited here is an offset to sales revenues—termed a contra-revenue account. Sales revenues are not reduced directly; the contra-revenue account allows Bristol Corporation to keep a running record of the frequency and amount of returns and price reductions, since these events represent potential breakdowns in customer relations.

[2] See M. McNichols and G. P. Wilson, "Evidence of Earnings Management From the Provision for Bad Debts," *Journal of Accounting Research* (Supplement 1988), pp. 1–31; S. Moyer, "Capital Adequacy Ratio Regulations and Accounting Choices in Commercial Banks," *Journal of Accounting and Economics* (July 1990), pp. 123–54; M. Scholes, P. Wilson, and M. Wolfson, "Tax Planning, Regulatory Capital Planning and Financial Reporting Strategy for Commercial Banks," *Review of Financial Studies* (Vol. 3, No. 4, 1990), pp. 625–50; J. Collins, D. Shackelford, and J. Wahlen, "Bank Differences in the Coordination of Regulatory Capital, Earnings, and Taxes," *Journal of Accounting Research* (Autumn 1995), pp. 263–91; A. Beatty, S. Chamberlain, and J. Magliolo, "Managing Financial Reports of Commercial Banks: The Influence of Taxes, Regulatory Capital, and Earnings," *Journal of Accounting Research* (Autumn 1995), pp. 231–61. As the titles of these studies suggest, regulatory capital requirements in commercial banks and financial services companies also influence bad debt accruals.

At the end of the reporting period, companies estimate the expected amount of future returns and allowances arising from receivables currently on the books. If the estimated number is large in relation to the accounts receivable balance or to earnings, then the adjusting entry is:

DR Sales returns and allowances	$$$$	
CR Allowance for sales returns and allowances		$$$$

The debit is again to a contra-revenue account that reduces net sales by the estimated amount. Since it is not yet known which *specific* customer accounts will involve future returns and allowances, the credit entry must be made to a contra-asset account that offsets gross accounts receivable. In practice, estimated sales returns and allowances are seldom material in relation to receivables. Consequently, no end-of-period accrual is typically made for these items.

Ignoring *estimated* future returns and allowances has a trivial effect on income when the amount of *actual* returns and allowances does not vary greatly from year to year.

Ordinary returns and allowances are seldom a major issue in financial reporting. On the other hand, companies occasionally adopt "aggressive" revenue recognition practices—meaning that revenue is recognized either prematurely or inappropriately. This revenue recognition aggressiveness generates significant returns in later periods. Aggressive revenue recognition overstates both accounts receivable and income. Consequently, analysts must understand that a sudden spurt in accounts receivable may be a danger signal, as we see next.

Analytical Insight: Do Existing Receivables Represent Real Sales?

ANALYSIS

When a company's sales terms, customer credit standing, and accounting methods do not change from period to period, the growth rates in sales and in accounts receivable will be roughly equal. If sales grow by 10%, accounts receivable should also grow by about 10%. Understanding this fact, astute statement readers carefully monitor the relationship between sales growth and receivables growth. When receivables grow faster than sales, this represents a potential "red flag." Receivables could grow at a higher rate than sales for several reasons. For example, the disparity in growth rates might reflect something positive like a deliberate change in sales terms designed to attract new customers. Suppose that instead of requiring payment within 30 days of shipment, the company allows customers to pay in four months. Changes like this broaden the potential market for the company's products and services by allowing slightly less creditworthy customers to buy the firm's products. In this case, receivables growth will far outpace sales growth. (Assume that before introducing more lenient credit terms, the company had annual sales of $12 million and customers, on average, paid within 30 days. Outstanding accounts receivable, therefore, represent one month's sales, or $1 million. Under the new credit program, customer receivables would represent four months' sales, or $4 million; this represents a 300% increase in receivables even if total sales remain unchanged.)

Alternatively, when receivables growth exceeds sales growth, this could be an early warning signal of emerging problems. It might be caused by deteriorating creditworthiness among existing customers. If customers are unable to pay, receivables will not be collected when due and accounts receivable will grow at a faster rate than sales. However, this problem should be uncovered in careful audits by the company's independent auditor. Accordingly, when the cause for the unusual growth in receivables is due to an inability of customers to pay on time, GAAP financial statements would ordinarily show a large increase in estimated uncollectibles.

Collectibility of receivables requires forecasts of future conditions. Forecasts are often inaccurate. However, existing auditing procedures for accounts receivable are very detailed and stringent, requiring auditors to send confirmations to customers verifying the legitimacy of the recorded receivables. Aging schedules to uncover payment problems are also required. Furthermore, auditors undertake credit-checks on the company's largest customers to ascertain the probability of eventual collection. As a consequence of these procedures, while collectibility requires forecasts that could be wrong, extreme overstatement of net (collectible) receivables is rare.

Another reason why receivables growth might exceed sales growth is that the firm has changed its financial reporting procedures, which determine *when* sales are recognized. Consider Table 8.1, which presents selected financial statement data for Bausch & Lomb Inc. for the years 1990 through 1993.

Table 8.1 shows that net trade accounts receivable grew dramatically in both 1992 and 1993. This growth shows up in absolute dollar amounts (an increase of $72,076 in 1992 and $107,635 in 1993) as well as in relation to total balance sheet assets (11.8% in 1991 versus 14.8% in 1992 and 15.3% in 1993). But what makes this growth seem "unusual" is the disparity in growth rates between sales and receivables. While sales grew at 12.43% in 1992 and 9.54% in 1993, receivables jumped by 35.11% and 38.81% in those same years, respectively (highlighted areas in Table 8.1). Clearly, something unusual was happening in both years. A partial explanation was provided one year later in the company's 1994 annual report, which stated:

> In the fourth quarter of 1993, the Company adopted a business strategy to shift responsibility for the sale and distribution of a portion of the U.S. traditional contact lens business to optical distributors. A 1993 fourth quarter marketing program to implement this strategy was developed, contributing one-time net income of approximately $10 million. Subsequently, this strategy proved unsuccessful.

Prior to this change in Bausch & Lomb's business strategy, revenues and associated receivables were recognized when sales were made to retailers or ultimate consumers. In the fourth quarter of 1993, however, shipments to distributors appear to have been treated as sales. This change in revenue recognition was in keeping with the shift in sales strategy, but the worry is that if distributors are unable to sell their inventory they will return it to Bausch & Lomb for credit. This is exactly what happened, as described in the company's 1994 annual report:

> *In October 1994, the Company announced it had implemented a new pricing policy for traditional contact lenses and agreed on a one-time basis to accept returns from these distributors.* As a result, the Company recorded sales reserves and pricing adjustments which reduced operating earnings by approximately $20 million in the third quarter. The new pricing policy sought to enhance the Company's competitive position in a market segment where industry prices had declined since the business strategy was implemented. *The returns program allowed U.S. distributors to send back the excess portion of unsold traditional lenses and balance their overall contact lens inventories.* [Emphasis added.]

Table 8.1 ■ BAUSCH & LOMB, INC.

Selected Financial Statement Data, 1990–93

($000 omitted)	1990	1991	1992	1993
Net Sales	$1,368,580	$1,520,104	$1,709,086	$1,872,184
Net trade accounts receivable	$ 202,967	$ 205,262	$ 277,338	$ 384,973
Days sales outstanding[1]	54 days[1]	49 days	59 days	75 days
Receivables as a % of total assets	12.1%	11.8%	14.8%	15.3%
Year-to-year growth in				
Net sales		$151,524	$188,982	$163,098
Net trade accounts receivable		$ 2,295	$ 72,076	$107,635
Net sales		11.07%	12.43%	9.54%
Net trade accounts receivable		1.13%	35.11%	38.81%

[1]"Days sales outstanding" is "Net trade accounts receivables" divided by "Net sales" per day. For example, the calculation for 1990 "Days sales outstanding" is

$202,967 net trade receivables/($1,368,580 net sales/365 days) = 54 days.

Source: Bausch & Lomb Inc. Annual Reports.

This statement suggests that the changes in sales strategy and revenue recognition only began in 1993. Yet the data in Table 8.1 reveal that a large disparity in sales and receivables growth rates occurred earlier. What explains this pre-1993 disparity?

A *Business Week* article published six months after Bausch & Lomb released its 1994 annual report suggests several possible explanations.[3] The article asserts that top-down pressure to achieve sales and profit goals caused Bausch & Lomb managers to loosen revenue recognition standards in the early 1990s, an assertion that was vehemently denied by top Bausch & Lomb executives. Specifically, Bausch & Lomb sales representatives allegedly "gave customers extraordinarily long payment terms, knowingly fed gray markets, and threatened to cut off distributors unless they took on huge quantities of unwanted products. Some also shipped goods before customers ordered them and booked the shipments as sales. . . ."[4] The article further contends that this type of deal making "became frantic" from the last quarter of 1992 through early 1994 and that the U.S. contact lens division "had a habit of constantly rolling over unpaid bills so that customers wouldn't return unwanted goods for credit."[5] If *Business Week*'s interpretations are correct, these practices would explain the unusual pre-1993 receivables growth.

Figure 8.1 depicts the company's days sales outstanding (DSO) for receivables by quarter for March 1989 through the end of 1995. DSO receivables is just the dollar amount of outstanding receivables divided by average daily sales. From March 1989 to March 1992, DSO receivables at Bausch & Lomb averaged about 50 days and fluctuated little from quarter to quarter. By the end of 1992, however, outstanding receivables had grown to 59 days, and by the fourth quarter of 1993 they stood at 72 days. This unusual pattern of growth in DSO receivables at Bausch & Lomb undoubtedly caused some financial statement readers to become skeptical about the company's revenue recognition practices.

One last point regarding Bausch & Lomb. The *Business Week* article contends that the reported December 31, 1993 accounts receivable number of $385 million (see Table 8.1) *understates* the real growth of outstanding customer credit. The understatement occurs, according to the article, because Bausch & Lomb sold some receivables to a third-party financing company for cash. Receivable sales of this sort are called **factoring.** If the receivables had not been factored, then the reported disparity in sales and receivables growth rates for 1992 and 1993 would have been even larger!

Scrutiny of changes in accounts receivable balances is essential. Large increases in accounts receivable relative to sales frequently represent a danger signal. The two most likely causes are (1) collection difficulties, and (2) sales contingencies or disputes that may lead to potential returns.

Figure 8.1

BAUSCH & LOMB INC.
DSO Receivables by Quarter

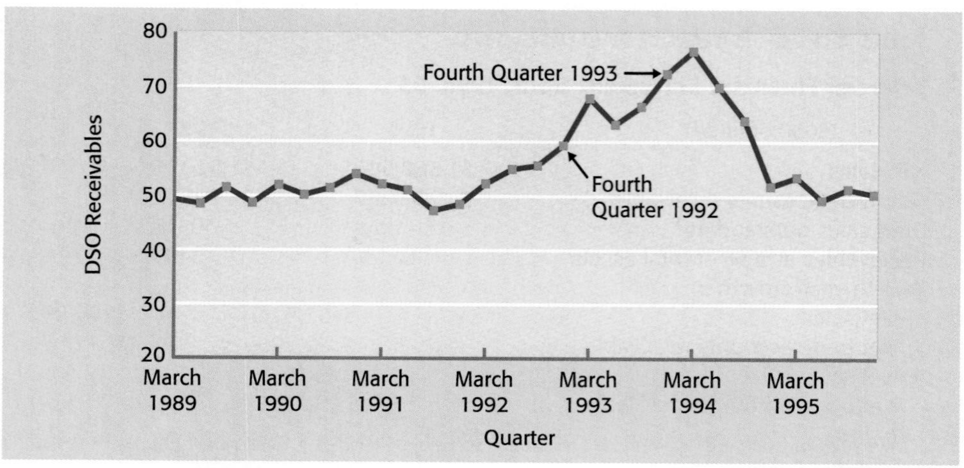

[3] M. Maremont, "Blind Ambition," *Business Week* (October 23, 1995), pp. 78–92.
[4] Ibid., pp. 79–80.
[5] Ibid., p. 86.

Many revenue recognition "irregularities" can be discovered by tracking the relationship between changes in sales and receivables. Another example is provided by the 1997 Sunbeam Corporation annual report.

Albert J. Dunlap joined Sunbeam Corporation as Chairman and Chief Executive Officer in July 1996. He had earned a reputation as a "turnaround" specialist because of his aggressiveness in restructuring and downsizing companies he previously ran, such as Scott Paper. By cutting costs and eliminating waste, Dunlap restored the companies to profitability. Sunbeam had mediocre performance in the years prior to Dunlap's arrival. But reported 1997 quarterly and annual financial results seemed to indicate considerable improvement.

At the start of his letter to shareholders in the 1997 annual report, Dunlap stated:

> We had an amazing year in 1997! During the past 12 months we set new records in almost every facet of the Company's operations. We experienced significant sales growth and concurrently increased margins and earnings.

The letter concluded:

> Stay tuned, the best is yet to come!

Soon after the 1997 Sunbeam annual report appeared, some analysts raised questions about the quality of the reported earnings and the economic validity of the results.[6] Sales for 1997 and 1996 and year-end receivables were as follows:

($000 omitted)	1997	1996
Net sales	$1,168,182	$984,236
Gross trade accounts receivable	305,219	227,043

Sales grew by 18.69% ([$1,168,182 − $984,236] ÷ $984,236) while receivables grew by 34.43% ([$305,219 − $227,043] ÷ $227,043). The disparity in growth rates is a clue that there may be a problem. Investigation is warranted since the following notes to the 1997 annual report disclose "bill and hold sales" and disposal of receivables—events that affect both sales and receivables.

Revenue Recognition

The Company recognizes revenues from product sales principally at the time of shipment to customers. In limited circumstances, at the customer's request the Company may sell seasonal product on a bill and hold basis provided that the goods are completed, packaged and ready for shipment, such goods are segregated and the risks of ownership and legal title have passed to the customer. *The amount of such bill and hold sales at December 29, 1997 was approximately 3% of consolidated revenues.* [Emphasis and highlighting added.]

Credit Facilities

In December 1997, the Company entered into a revolving trade accounts receivable securitization program to sell without recourse, through a wholly-owned subsidiary, certain trade accounts receivable. The maximum amount of receivables that can be sold through this program is $70 million. *At December 28, 1997, the Company had received approximately $59 million from the sale of trade accounts receivable.* [Emphasis and highlighting added.]

Source: Sunbeam Corporation 1997 Annual Report.

Let's look at **bill and hold** sales. One issue is whether these are real sales. The note states that these terms were at the customer's request and legal title had passed. So it's reasonable to conclude that the sales were legitimate even though the inventory hadn't been shipped. But the other issue is whether these are really sales of 1997 or instead 1998 sales that have

> In a bill and hold sale, the company recognizes revenue and the associated account receivable, but does not ship the product to the customer until later.

[6] See Jonathan R. Laing, "Dangerous Games," *Barron's* (June 8, 1998).

been pulled into 1997 by the bill and hold terms. The amount in question isn't trivial—3% of sales ($1,168,182,000) is $35,045,000. This represents 19.05% of the reported $183,946,000 growth in sales between 1996 and 1997.

Furthermore, the true growth in receivables is understated by the amount of receivables sold at the end of 1997. The $59 million cash received is the book value of the receivables minus the financing charge. So $59 million roughly approximates the amount of receivables removed from the books.

Let's summarize the clues that were available to the careful analyst:

1. Receivables growth greatly exceeded sales growth.
2. Bill and hold sales raise the possibility that some of this disparity is because sales were booked too early, thus generating receivables that won't be collected quickly. Worse yet, collection may never occur if delivery of "sold" items is ultimately refused.
3. Had Sunbeam not sold approximately $59 million of receivables, the "real" growth rate of receivables would have exceeded the reported rate of 34.43%, further increasing the disparity between sales and receivables growth rates. This even larger disparity increases the likelihood that some "channel stuffing"—that is, overly aggressive revenue recognition on items "sold" to dealers—was occurring.

These, as well as other issues unrelated to receivables, prompted a reaudit of Sunbeam's financial statements from the fourth quarter of 1996 through the first quarter of 1998. The reaudit disclosed that 1997 sales were overstated by $95,092,000 and profits were $38,301,000 rather than $109,415,000, as reported.[7]

Albert J. Dunlap was fired by Sunbeam's Board of Directors on June 15, 1998.

And it was careful scrutiny by informed analysts that led to inquiries which resulted in these corrections!

RECAP

Evaluating the net realizable value of accounts receivable requires an analysis of the adequacy of estimated uncollectibles and provisions for returns and price adjustments. When receivables growth exceeds sales growth, this could be an indication of aggressive revenue recognition policies. Statement readers who carefully examine receivables trends and levels can discern potential problems as they evolve.

Imputed Interest on Trade Notes Receivable

In certain industries the seller sometimes extends long-term credit to the buyer, who then signs a note. If the note bears an interest rate approximating prevailing borrowing and lending rates, the accounting is straightforward. Assume that Michele Corporation manufactures and sells a machine to Texas Products Company. The cash selling price of the machine is $50,000. Michele accepts a three-year $50,000 note signed by Texas Products, with interest of 10% per annum to be paid in quarterly installments each year. Assume that 10% approximates prevailing borrowing rates for companies as creditworthy as Texas Products. Upon making the sale, Michele would record:

DR Note receivable–Texas Products Company	$50,000	
CR Sales revenues		$50,000

Interest income would accrue each quarter, and when the cash payment is received, the accrued interest receivable would be reduced. These are the entries:

[7] See Dana Canedy, "Sunbeam Restates Results, and 'Fix' Shows Significant Warts," *New York Times* (October 21, 1998).

DR Accrued interest receivable	$1,250	
CR Interest income		$1,250
(To accrue three months' interest = [$50,000 × .10] ÷ 4)		
DR Cash	$1,250	
CR Accrued interest receivable		$1,250
(To record receipt of the interest payment)		

A complication arises for a note that does not state an interest rate or when the stated rate is lower than prevailing rates for loans of similar risk. Suppose Monson Corporation sells equipment it manufactured to Davenport Products in exchange for a $50,000 note due in three years. The note bears no explicit interest. It just says that the entire $50,000 is to be paid at the end of three years. Monson's published cash selling price for the equipment is $37,566, and the current borrowing rate for companies like Davenport is 10%.

The present value factor for a payment three years away at a 10% rate is .75132 (see Appendix 1 Table 1). Therefore, the present value of the note is $50,000 times .75132, or $37,566—which is exactly equal to the cash selling price of the equipment. Although the $50,000 note itself does not contain any mention of interest, Monson will earn a return of 10% per year for financing Davenport's long-term credit purchase. This is easily demonstrated:

Present value of $50,000 payment in 3 years (cash sales price)	$37,566.00
Plus: Year 1 interest: 10% × $37,566.00	3,756.60
Equals: Present value of $50,000 payment due in 2 years	41,322.60
Plus: Year 2 interest: 10% × $41,322.60	4,132.26
Equals: Present value of $50,000 payment due in 1 year	45,454.86
Plus: Year 3 interest: 10% × $45,454.86	4,545.14[1]
Equals: Payment by Davenport at the end of year 3	$50,000.00

[1]Rounded.

At the end of year 3, Monson receives a payment of $50,000, which consists of the cash sales price ($37,566) plus interest ($12,434 = $3,756.60 + $4,132.26 + $4,545.14).

Monson Corporation would record the sale to Davenport Products as:

DR Note receivable–Davenport	$37,566.00	
CR Sales revenue		$37,566.00

Over the next three years, the note receivable is increased and interest income recognized. For example, at the end of year 1, the entry would be:[8]

DR Note receivable–Davenport	$3,756.60	
CR Interest income		$3,756.60

Notice that after Monson records interest income of $4,132.26 in year 2 and $4,545.14 in year 3, the carrying amount of the note receivable will be exactly $50,000. When Davenport makes the required payment at maturity of the note, Monson Corporation would record:

[8] For simplicity, we ignore the periodic recording of interest on a monthly or quarterly basis during the year. In reality, if quarterly statements were prepared, the first year interest income of $3,756.60 would be apportioned to each quarter.

DR Cash	$50,000.00	
CR Note receivable–Davenport		$50,000.00

An additional complication arises when the note receivable contains a stated interest rate ***but the stated rate is lower than prevailing borrowing rates at the time of the transaction.*** When this happens, interest must again be imputed. Assume that Quinones Corporation sells a machine to Linda Manufacturing in exchange for a $40,000, three year, 2.5% note from Linda. At the time of the sale, the interest rate normally charged to companies with Linda's credit rating is 10%. Since the note's stated interest rate is far below Linda's normal borrowing rate, Quinones must determine the machine's implied sales price by computing the note's present value at the 10% rate:

Nominal Interest-Bearing Note

Calculation of Present Value at 10% Effective Interest Rate

Present value of $40,000 principal repayment in three years at 10%:					
	$40,000	×	.75132	=	$30,052.80
Present value of three interest payments of $1,000 (i.e., $40,000 × .025), each at 10%:					
Year 1:	$ 1,000	×	.90909	=	909.09
Year 2:	$ 1,000	×	.82645	=	826.45
Year 3:	$ 1,000	×	.75132	=	751.32
TOTAL					$32,539.66

(Note: All present value factors are from Appendix 1 Table 1, 10% column.)

This computation shows that the implied cash selling price of the machine is $32,539.66, because this amount equals the discounted present value of the note Quinones received in exchange for the machine. Quinones makes the following entry:

DR Note receivable–Linda Mfg.	$32,539.66	
CR Sales revenue		$32,539.66

Since payment was deferred, Quinones will earn 10% over the duration of the note on the amount of the credit sale ($32,539.66). The interest earned consists of three $1,000 payments over each of the ensuing years and another imputed interest payment of $7,460.34 ($40,000 minus the $32,539.66 implied cash selling price) at maturity. The composition of yearly interest income is shown in Table 8.2, and Figure 8.2 shows the note receivable from the time of sale to maturity.

As shown in Table 8.2 and Figure 8.2, the present value of the note, and thus its carrying value, increases each year (see column (d) of Table 8.2). The increase equals the difference between the annual 10% interest income earned—column (a)—and the cash received—column (b). For example, in year 1 Quinones would record:

DR Note receivable–Linda Mfg.	$ 2,253.97	
DR Cash	1,000.00	
CR Interest income		$ 3,253.97

Table 8.2 ■ QUINONES CORPORATION

Computation of Interest on Note Receivable

	(a) Interest Income—10% of Column (d) Balance for Prior Year	(b) Cash Interest Received	(c) Increase in Present Value of Note (a) Minus (b)	(d) End of Year Present Value of Note
Inception	—	—	—	$32,539.66
Year 1	$3,253.97	$1,000.00	$2,253.97	34,793.63
Year 2	3,479.36	1,000.00	2,479.36	37,272.99
Year 3	3,727.01[1]	1,000.00	2,727.01	40,000.00
Total	$10,460.34			

[1]Rounded.

Similar entries would be made in years 2 and 3 using the amounts shown in Table 8.2. At the end of year 3, the carrying amount of the note will be $40,000. When Linda pays the note on maturity, Quinones will record the payment as:

DR Cash	$40,000.00	
CR Note receivable—Linda Mfg.		$40,000.00

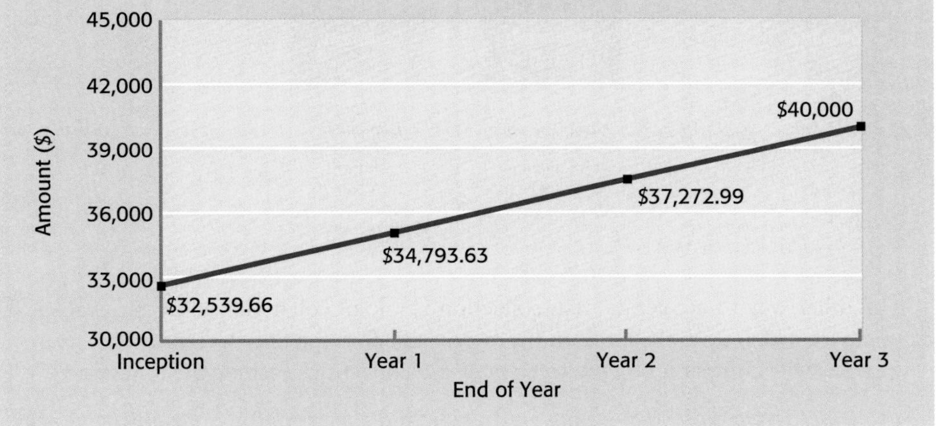

Figure 8.2

QUINONES CORPORATION

Carrying Value of Note Receivable

RECAP

For long-term credit sales transactions utilizing notes receivable:

- **Sales revenue is recorded at the known cash price (Monson Corporation) or at the implied cash price (Quinones Corporation) of the item sold. The implied cash price is determined by computing the note receivable's present value using the prevailing borrowing rate (i.e., the effective market rate of interest).**
- **Interest income is recorded each period over the note's term to maturity using the prevailing borrowing rate.**

This approach achieves a clear separation between the two income sources—credit sales and interest earned. Income from the credit sale is recorded when the sale is made. Interest income from financing the customer's purchase, on the other hand, is recorded over time as it is earned. This separation of income sources makes it possible to assess the degree to which a company's overall earnings are due to profitable credit sales versus profitable customer financing—a potentially important distinction.

Accelerating Cash Collection: Selling Receivables and Collateralized Borrowings

Companies collect cash from their credit customers according to the payment schedule called for in the note or trade receivable. Sometimes companies prefer not to wait until customer payments arrive in the normal course of business. Instead, they accelerate cash collection with the help of a bank or financing company.

There are two ways to accelerate cash collections, as depicted in Figure 8.3. One is **factoring,** where the company sells its receivables outright to the bank in exchange for cash. Customer payments flow directly to the bank in most cases. Factoring can be **without recourse** (also called **nonrecourse**), meaning that the bank cannot turn to the company for payment in the event that some customer receivables prove uncollectible. Factoring can also be **with recourse,** meaning that the company is willing to buy back any bad receivables from the bank.

Figure 8.3

SELLING RECEIVABLES AND COLLATERALIZED BORROWINGS

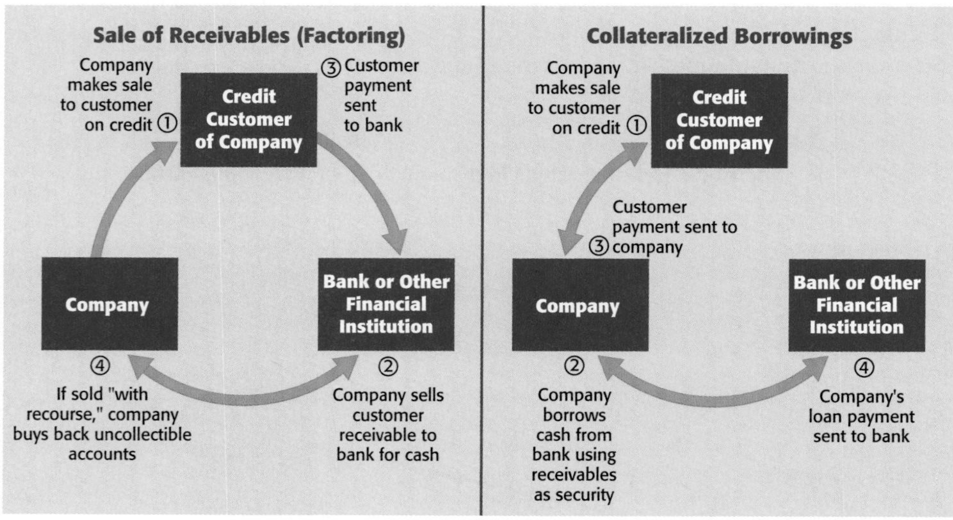

The other way to accelerate cash collection is a loan collateralized by receivables. The company gets cash from the bank and is responsible for repaying the loan.

Reasons why companies might accelerate cash collections include the following:

1. ***Competitive conditions require credit sales but the company is unwilling to bear the cost of processing and collecting receivables.*** Restaurants are an example of this. Customers of upscale restaurants expect to be able to charge meals rather than pay cash. Yet, most restaurants are reluctant to incur the costs of servicing receivables. Consequently, restaurants rely on third parties like VISA, American Express, and Diners' Club, companies which, in effect, "buy" the customer receivable from the restaurant.

Credit card companies "buy" the receivables at a discount—they pay the restaurant, say, 97 cents for every dollar of receivables. The three cent "discount" is the fee charged for accelerating cash receipts.

2. ***There may be an imbalance between the credit terms of the company's suppliers and the time required to collect customer receivables.*** Suppliers might extend credit on six-month terms to a company while inventory turnover plus receivables turnover total 210 days. To pay suppliers within the due date, early cash collection is necessary.
3. ***The company may have an immediate need for cash but be short of it.*** Selling receivables to a financial institution allows the company to raise cash quickly. Using receivables as collateral for a bank loan also represents a way to obtain quick cash (and perhaps low-cost financing).

Let's look at the accounting issues that arise when receivables are sold or used in a collateralized loan.

Sale of Receivables (Factoring)

To illustrate a factoring transaction *without* recourse, suppose Hervey Corporation sells $80,000 of its customer receivables to Leslie Financing. The purchaser (Leslie Financing) is called the **factor.** Leslie charges a 5% fee (5% × $80,000 = $4,000) for this service and pays Hervey $76,000. The entry to record the nonrecourse sale of the receivables on Hervey Corporation's books is:

DR Cash	$76,000	
DR Interest expense	4,000	
CR Accounts receivable		$80,000

The $4,000 is charged to interest expense because this amount represents the financing charge Hervey incurred to accelerate cash collection. In a sale without recourse, if some of Hervey's customers fail to pay the amount owed, Leslie Financing has no recourse against Hervey (hence the term)—and thus, Leslie bears the loss.

Usually, the bank or financing company refuses to bear the costs of sales returns, discounts, or allowances. Consequently, a holdback to cover these items may be included in the transaction. For example, if the holdback is $3,000 and if all other facts regarding the nonrecourse sale are unchanged, the entry on Hervey's books is:

DR Cash	$73,000	
DR Interest expense	4,000	
DR Due from Leslie Financing	3,000	
CR Accounts receivable		$80,000

Any returns, discounts, or allowances reduce the amount paid to Hervey by Leslie. If these items totaled $1,800 on the sold receivables, Leslie would ultimately pay an additional $1,200 to Hervey and Hervey would make the following entry:

DR Cash	$ 1,200	
DR Sales returns, discounts, and allowances	1,800	
CR Due from Leslie Financing		$ 3,000

Next we illustrate the sale of accounts receivable *with* recourse. Again, assume Hervey Corporation sells $80,000 of trade receivables to Leslie Financing. If any of the receivables are not paid, Hervey bears the loss. Leslie's fee is reduced to 4% with a recourse transaction rather than 5% because the risk to Leslie is lower. Assume Leslie withholds $5,000 to cover possible noncollections. The entry on Hervey Corporation's books is:

DR Cash	$71,800	
DR Interest expense	3,200	
DR Due from Leslie Financing	5,000	
CR Accounts receivable		$80,000

The $5,000 holdback account "Due from Leslie Financing" represents a cushion to absorb credit losses that must ultimately be borne by Hervey in a sale with recourse.

Assume all but $3,750 of receivables are collected. Once collections are known, the financing company remits the final settlement amount. The entry on Hervey's books is:

DR Cash	$ 1,250	
DR Allowance for uncollectibles	3,750	
CR Due from Leslie Financing		$5,000

The $3,750 debit to allowance for uncollectibles is appropriate if normal allowances had been accrued on the receivables that were sold. Allowance accounts are usually maintained when the sale is with recourse. If no allowance was maintained, then the debit of $3,750 would be made to an account entitled "loss on sale of receivables" or some other similarly titled income statement loss account.

Borrowing Using Receivables As Collateral

If the transaction between Hervey Corporation and Leslie Financing had been a **collateralized loan** rather than a sale of receivables, then the accounts receivable would not be removed from Hervey's books. Instead, a liability account would be created to reflect the loan. Suppose that $80,000 of receivables were pledged as collateral for a loan; interest is 4% of $80,000. Then the entry is:

DR Cash	$76,800	
DR Prepaid interest	3,200	
CR Loan payable—Leslie Financing		$80,000

The fact that the receivables have been pledged as collateral for this loan must be disclosed in the notes to the financial statements, if material.[9] Once the loan is due, Hervey would make these entries:

DR Loan payable—Leslie Financing	$80,000	
CR Cash		$80,000
DR Interest expense	$ 3,200	
CR Prepaid interest		$ 3,200

Notes receivable can also be assigned or sold. Accelerating cash collection on notes in this way is called **discounting,** because the financial institution advances cash to the company based on the *discounted present value* of the notes. For example, suppose Abbott Manufacturing received a $9,000 six-month, 8% per year interest-bearing note from Weaver Company, a customer. That same day, Abbott discounted the note at Second State Bank. If the bank discounts the note at 12%, Abbott would receive only $8,798.40. The cash proceeds to Abbott are:

Face amount of the note	$9,000.00
Interest on note ($9,000 × .08 × ½*)	360.00
Maturity amount of the note	9,360.00
Interest charged by bank:	
($9,360 × .12 × ½*)	561.60
Cash proceeds	$8,798.40

*Multiplication by ½ represents 6 months' interest

At maturity, the bank will present the note to Weaver Company for payment. Abbott would make the following entry when the note is discounted:

DR Cash	$8,798.40	
DR Interest expense	201.60	
CR Note receivable		$9,000

Accelerating cash collection generates interest expense of $201.60, the difference between the book value of the note and the cash proceeds.

Notes can be discounted either with or without recourse. If discounted *with* recourse, then Second State Bank would collect $9,360 ($9,000 principal plus $360 interest) from Abbott if Weaver failed to pay the note at maturity. When notes are discounted with recourse and the note is removed from the books of the seller, a contingent liability must be disclosed in the footnotes.[10]

Ambiguities Abound: Is It a Sale or a Borrowing?

Usually, the nature of the transaction is clear when receivables are sold or assigned. But in some situations, it is not obvious whether the receivables have been sold or are instead

[9] "Accounting for Contingencies" *Statement of Financial Accounting Standards (SFAS) No. 5* (Stamford, CT: Financial Accounting Standards Board [FASB], 1975), para. 12.

[10] Ibid., para. 12.

being used as collateral for a loan. The ambiguity arises whenever certain obligations, duties, or rights regarding the transferred receivables are retained by the firm undertaking the transfer (which is called the **transferor**).

The FASB has provided guidelines in *SFAS No. 140* for distinguishing between sales and collateralized borrowings involving receivables.[11] The guidelines hinge on the issue of whether the transferor ***surrenders control over the receivables.*** If control is surrendered, then the transaction is treated as a sale, and any gain or loss is recognized in earnings. However, if the criteria for a sale are not met because control has not been surrendered, then the transaction is accounted for as a collateralized borrowing.

> *SFAS No. 140* states that the transferor surrenders control over the receivables when *all* of the following conditions are met:
>
> 1. The transferred assets are beyond the reach of the transferor and its creditors.
> 2. The transferee has the right to dispose of the assets.
> 3. There is no agreement obligating the transferor to repurchase or redeem the transferred assets in the future nor can the transferor unilaterally force the holder to return the assets.
>
> (See para. 9 and para. 27–28.)

The issues addressed in *SFAS No. 140* have assumed great importance with the growth of **financial asset securitization.** ***Securitization occurs when receivables (like mortgages or automobile loans) are bundled together and sold or transferred to another organization which issues securities that are collateralized by the transferred receivables.*** For example, the financing subsidiary of General Motors (General Motors Acceptance Corporation) sells Certificates of Automobile Receivables to investors. The collateral supporting these certificates are bundled automobile loans. By bundling large numbers of receivables, the seller creates value because the risk of loss is reduced by the portfolio effect of the bundling itself.

Home mortgages, car loans, credit card debt, and health club membership fees are just a few of the receivables that have been securitized and sold to investors. An estimated $2.5 trillion of securitized instruments were outstanding at the end of 1998.[12] As more of these transactions were undertaken, the FASB felt compelled to provide guidelines for when securitizations should be treated as sales and for when they must be treated as borrowings.

Ambiguities arise, for example, when a bank transfers a group of mortgages (which, to the bank, are receivables) to some other organization but retains the responsibility for servicing the mortgages. The bank often continues to collect the mortgage payments or to handle customer inquiries, or it even promises to buy back the mortgages at some future date if certain conditions occur. How these transactions are treated has important financial reporting implications. For example:

ANALYSIS

1. If the transaction is really a borrowing but is erroneously treated as a sale, then both assets and liabilities are understated (i.e., the loan does not appear on the company's balance sheet and neither do the receivables). Ratios like debt-to-equity and rate of return on assets are consequently distorted.
2. If the transaction is really a sale, then a gain or loss on the transaction should be recognized. To erroneously treat such transactions as borrowings misrepresents the company's net assets.

A Closer Look at Securitizations

Securitizations are popular for two reasons. First, investors have a strong appetite for acquiring securitized assets. Second, firms with large amounts of receivables have powerful incentives to engage in securitizations. It's a "win-win" situation for investors and firms; both parties benefit.

Investors benefit because they are able to obtain highly liquid financial instruments that diversify their risk. A simple example shows this. Suppose the prevailing rate of return on debt instruments with "moderate" risk is 9% per year. The 9% yield is determined by the credit standing of large corporate and government issuers of bonds and other instruments. By contrast, people who take out home mortgages with banks do not have the same high

[11] "Accounting for Transfers and Servicing of Financial Assets and Extinguishments of Liabilities," *SFAS No. 140* (Norwalk, CT: FASB, 2000).

[12] Fitch IBCA, "Securitization and Its Impact on Bank Ratings," *Financial Services Special Report* (New York, March 9, 1999).

credit-standing as these bond issuers. Understandably, the rates people pay on their mortgages are higher—let's say 10% per year.

Assume that a bank forms a bundled portfolio of these home mortgages and is prepared to sell them at a price that yields the investor a return of 9%. The risk associated with the individual mortgages ranges from "low" to "moderately high" *but the risk of the bundled portfolio in the aggregate is "moderate."* So the investors have an investment option that also provides a 9% per year yield at the same "moderate" risk level but responds differently than other debt instruments to changes in interest rates and other economic events. This diversifies risk. That's attractive. Furthermore, the investors could not form a "moderate" risk, 9% return mortgage portfolio themselves since the costs of identifying potential mortgagees and doing a credit analysis are high and would lower their return below 9%. And even if they could construct their own portfolio, if investors later wanted to liquidate the investment, they'd have difficulty finding buyers for individual mortgages. So investors benefit from securitizations by gaining liquid portfolio diversification opportunities that they could not achieve on their own.

If you don't understand this now, it's too early to panic. We'll explain why there's a gain in Chapter 11. You'll be able to follow the discussion in this section without a detailed understanding of the specifics underlying the gain.

But the bank also wins! If the bank sells the 10% mortgages at a price that yields the purchasers a return of 9%, this means that the selling price is higher than the carrying value of the mortgages on the bank's books. So the bank records a gain on the sale of the receivables. ***This gain exists because the bank has created value.*** As we just saw, the individual investors would never consider lending directly to, say, two or three home purchasers. (It's too risky. Who knows how many will default?) But the large portfolio is much less risky. So investors who are unable to duplicate the bank's return on their own without assuming high risks (and costs) are very willing to accept the 9% return.

It's even better for the investors! To make the securities more attractive, the bank will provide investors with a return that slightly exceeds 9%.

Banks and other firms that engage in securitization transactions do not transact directly with the investors. The format of securitizations is somewhat convoluted, for reasons we'll soon explain. Figure 8.4 shows how a typical securitization is structured.

The firm doing the securitization (the transferor) forms what is called a **special purpose entity** or **SPE.** The SPE is usually a trust or corporation that is legally distinct from the

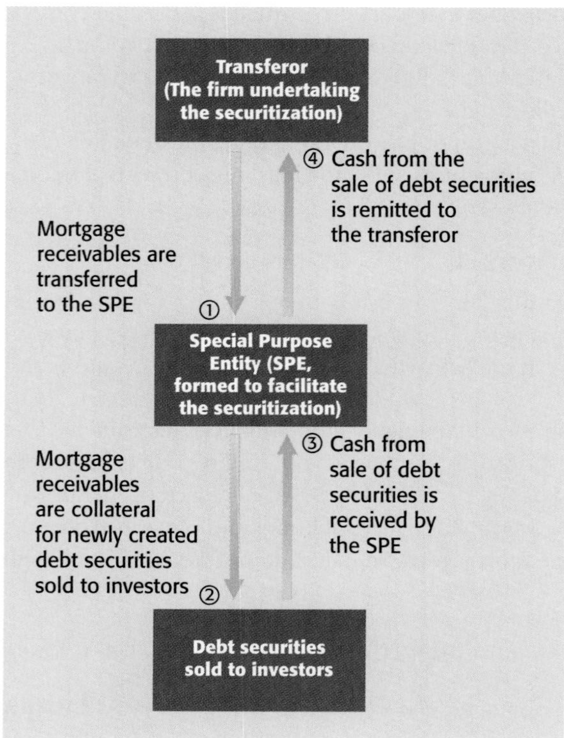

Figure 8.4

THE STRUCTURE OF A SECURITIZATION

transferor and is created solely for the purpose of undertaking the securitization transaction. The transferor then sells the receivables (mortgages in our example) to the SPE. The SPE creates and issues debt securities (with the mortgages as collateral) that are sold to outside investors. The cash received from the investors by the SPE is then remitted to the transferor. In many situations the transferor continues to service the assets (that is, handle cash collections, record-keeping, etc.) usually for a fee that is paid by the SPE.

The cash flows from the mortgages themselves (i.e., principal repayment and interest) are later used to make the periodic interest and principal repayments to the investors who bought the debt securities.

The SPE is created for two reasons. One is to protect the investors who bought the debt securities. Because the receivables were sold to the SPE, they are beyond the reach of the transferor and its creditors. ***So even if the transferor were to declare bankruptcy, the collateral underlying the notes is safe from seizure.*** The other reason for creating the SPE is because its existence allows the transferor to receive favorable financial reporting treatment for the transaction. Here's why. If there were no SPE, the transferor would issue the notes directly to investors. This would constitute a collateralized borrowing; the receivables would appear on the transferor's books and so would the notes (as a liability). But by creating the legally distinct entity, the receivables are removed from the transferor's books. Furthermore, the notes are the SPE's debt, not the transferor's. Since the SPE is not consolidated, the debt securities never appear on the transferor's balance sheet. ***So both the receivables and the debt are "off balance sheet."***

> Securitizations are carefully designed to enable the transferor to avoid consolidating the SPE. To accomplish this, the SPE must meet four conditions stated in *SFAS No. 140*, para. 35:
>
> 1. *It is demonstrably distinct from the transferor.* This condition is met if the transferor cannot unilaterally dissolve the SPE and either of two other highly technical circumstances apply.
> 2. *Its activities are narrowly limited.* These are restricted to holding title to the transferred assets, issuing the collateralized debt securities, collecting cash flows from the transferred assets, and making interest and principal payments to holders of the debt securities.
> 3. *It holds only rigidly defined types of assets.* The assets must not require decision-making by the SPE.
> 4. *Its ability to dispose of assets is limited to narrowly defined circumstances.* This means that the SPE must be an unthinking robot that cannot exercise discretion.
>
> Why does the FASB allow favorable off-balance sheet treatment for these contorted transactions? One reason is because they are economically beneficial. That is, the transferor creates value through the portfolio effect of bundling the assets, and the investors diversify their risk and earn slightly higher returns.

Some Cautions for Statement Readers

Factoring, assignment, and securitization of receivables raise some issues for those who analyze financial statements. The main issue is the level of disclosure in statement footnotes when receivables have been transferred during the reporting period. When the transfer is with recourse (the "selling" company is still responsible for uncollected receivables), *SFAS No. 5* requires footnote disclosure of the contingent liability.[13] ***But there is no similar unequivocal disclosure requirement when receivables are sold without recourse.*** Some observers contend that receivables sold without recourse are a financing transaction that must be separately disclosed in the cash flow statement.[14] But even if this interpretation is correct, GAAP only requires that disclosures be made when they are **material.** The FASB has defined materiality as:

ANALYSIS

> A decision not to disclose certain information may be made, say, . . . because the amounts involved are too small to make a difference (they are not material). . . . The Board's present position is that no general standards of materiality can be formulated to take into account all the considerations that enter into an experienced human judgment.[15]

[13] *SFAS No. 5*, para. 12.

[14] This position is based on an interpretation of "Statement of Cash Flows," *SFAS No. 95* (Stamford, CT: FASB, 1987), para. 16.

[15] "Qualitative Characteristics of Accounting Information," *Statement of Financial Accounting Concepts No. 2* (Stamford, CT: FASB, 1980), para. 125 and 131.

Materiality is defined loosely as information that, if disclosed, would change the decision-maker's judgment. But since the guidelines are unclear, some companies might purposely not disclose sales of receivables and, if asked about the omission, declare the information "immaterial."

Here's what this means for statement readers. Earlier in the chapter we saw that one way to assess whether reported receivables arose from legitimate sales was to compare the growth rate of sales and the growth rate of receivables. This comparison in Table 8.1 for Bausch & Lomb showed that receivables growth far outstripped sales growth between 1991 and 1993. Our conclusion—based on disclosures from the 1994 Bausch & Lomb annual report—was that the leap in receivables growth arose from "forcing" inventory on distributors and treating these shipments as sales. The way to recognize these potential trouble areas is to monitor receivables growth. ***But when firms sell receivables, the receivables number reported in the balance sheet will understate the true growth in receivables over the period.***

The Securities and Exchange Commission has issued a Staff Accounting Bulletin (SAB) on materiality to establish clearer guidelines.* (SABs inform registrants about the criteria the SEC staff will use in resolving reporting issues.) SAB No. 99 rejects arbitrary, across-the-board percentages like 5% as the materiality threshold. Instead, through a series of examples, the SEC reaffirms that materiality is contextual. So consider a firm where the consensus analysts' quarterly EPS forecasts are $1.00 per share. The firm knows that actual earnings will fall short at 99¢ per share. If the firm evades GAAP rules to raise earnings by one cent per share, *in that specific context,* the inappropriate earnings boost is material because it is designed to change investors' perceptions of whether the firm is performing up to expectations.

* *SEC Staff Accounting Bulletin: No. 99,—Materiality,* August 12, 1999.

This is precisely what *Business Week* says happened at Bausch & Lomb, whose "internal financial documents," they claim, show year-end 1993 receivables to be $506 million rather than the $385 million reported on the company's balance sheet (see again Table 8.1). According to *Business Week,* Bausch & Lomb felt the factored receivables didn't need to be disclosed under GAAP.[16]

Irrespective of whose interpretation of disclosure requirements is correct here, the opportunity to transfer receivables provides a way for companies to disguise the *real* extent of receivables growth. Suppose a company is "aggressively" booking sales to artificially raise current earnings. To avoid discovery, the company could factor or securitize some of its "good" receivables—those that don't arise from the questionable sales—and thus understate the true disparity in the growth of receivables and sales. So the receivables remaining on the books are the "bad" ones and the factoring has disguised the deterioration in the *quality* of reported receivables. Consequently, statement readers must scrutinize footnotes and the financing activities section of the cash flow statement for evidence of dispositions of receivables that may be masking overly aggressive revenue recognition policies or bad receivables management.

The transferred receivables "disappear" from the balance sheet. Because receivables are lower, certain ratios like return on assets and receivables turnover improve when compared to previous periods. But is the ratio improvement sustainable? Should the analyst "undo" the transfer and recompute the ratios with the receivables included? At a minimum, the analyst must be aware of the extent of the disruption in the year-to-year ratio pattern and its impact on financial forecasts. Other adjustments depend on the circumstances. Also, did the transferor "cherry-pick" the best receivables in order to make the transaction attractive to the purchasers? If it did, the analyst must scrutinize the quality of the remaining receivables as well as the adequacy of the allowance for uncollectibles.

The Sunbeam sale of trade accounts receivable on page 351 was a securitization. Sunbeam fully disclosed the transaction. But if the securitization had not taken place, the year-to-year growth in Sunbeam's receivables would have approximated 60%, not the 34.43% reported on the comparative financial statements themselves.

Troubled Debt Restructuring

What happens to a lender when a customer is financially unable to make the interest and principal payments required by an installment loan or other receivable? Rather than force the customer into bankruptcy, lenders frequently agree to **restructure** the loan receivable,

[16] M. Maremont, op. cit., p. 90.

thus allowing the customer to remain in business. The restructured loan can differ from the original loan in several ways:

- Scheduled interest and principal payments may be reduced or eliminated.
- The repayment schedule may be extended over a longer time period.
- The customer and lender can settle the loan for cash, other assets, or equity interests.

Lenders are willing to restructure a customer's loan to help the customer resolve present financial difficulties and stay in business. And lenders often receive more through restructuring than through foreclosure or bankruptcy.

Consider the debt restructuring described in Exhibit 8.3. On December 31, 1999, Hudson Hotels Corporation owned and/or managed 47 hotel properties located primarily in the northeastern and southeastern United States. These investments were financed using long-term debt—a Convertible Subordinated Debenture. During 1999, the company suffered operating losses and cash flow difficulties. The Convertible Subordinated Debenture originally carried an interest rate of 7.5% per year and a maturity date of July 1, 2001. The conversion price on December 31, 1998 was $4.50 per common share. Because the Company could not make the required loan payments, the lender (a mutual fund) canceled $4.5 million of the debt in exchange for the following:

Exhibit 8.3 ■ HUDSON HOTELS CORPORATION

Debt Restructuring

In July 1999, the Company replaced its outstanding $7.5 million Convertible Subordinated Debenture to Oppenheimer Convertible Securities Fund with a new Convertible Subordinated Debenture bearing the following terms: principal balance of $3.0 million; interest rate of 18.75%; maturity date of April 15, 2000; and a conversion price of $1.80 per share. As a result, the Company reported an extraordinary gain from the debt restructuring, net of expenses, of approximately $4 million or $0.64 per common share—basic.

Source: Hudson Hotels Corporation 1999 10-K Report.

- An acceleration of the maturity date by 8 1/2 months.
- An increase in the annual interest rate from 7.5% to 18.75%.
- A decrease in the conversion price of $2.70 per share.

Obviously, the lender would have preferred that Hudson Hotels pay the original debt and interest on time. Faced with the company's inability to do so, it chose to restructure the debt rather than force the company into bankruptcy.

This example illustrates a key feature of **troubled debt restructurings** not present in ordinary debt refinancings. *SFAS No. 15* gives this definition:

> A restructuring of debt constitutes a troubled debt restructuring . . . if the creditor for economic or legal reasons related to the debtor's financial difficulties grants a **concession** to the debtor that it would not otherwise consider. [Emphasis added.][17]

In other words, for the restructuring to be "troubled," the borrower (Hudson Hotels Corporation) must be unable to pay off the original debt and the lender (the mutual fund) must grant a concession to the

To help you understand this financial instrument, we'll define each of the three words, in reverse order. **Debentures** are bonds that have no underlying collateral that could be seized if Hudson Hotels defaulted on the debt. It is an unsecured borrowing. **Subordinated** means that Hudson has other debt issues that "ranked-ahead" of this debt in the event of liquidation—that is, investors in the other debt would be paid before investors in the Convertible Subordinated Debenture. **Convertible** bonds allow the investor—at the investor's option—to convert the bond into equity shares of Hudson. A conversion price of $4.50 on December 31, 1998 means that each $1,000 bond could be converted into 222.222 shares ($1,000 ÷ $4.50 = 222.222). This is an attractive feature for bond investors because it provides a potentially valuable "upside" option if the issuer prospers.

[17] "Accounting by Debtors and Creditors for Troubled Debt Restructuring," *SFAS No. 15* (Stamford, CT: FASB, 1977), para. 2.

borrower. What the FASB means by "concession" is quite specific: In exchange for canceling the original debt, the lender must accept ***new debt or assets with an economic value less than the book value of the original debt plus any accrued interest.***

Our Hudson Hotels example meets these guidelines. The company was unable to make its interest and principal payments. The lender then agreed to restructure the debt, and in so doing, it granted the company a substantial economic concession—the $4.5 million of debt cancellation.

Troubled debt restructurings can be accomplished in two different ways:

- **Settlement,** where the original loan is canceled by a transfer of cash, other assets, or equity interests (borrower's stock) to the lender.
- **Continuation with modification** of debt terms, where the original loan is canceled and a new loan agreement is signed.

Some troubled debt restructurings contain elements of both settlement and modification.

The accounting issues related to troubled debt restructuring encompass both the measurement of the new (modified) loan and a report of any gain or loss. The following examples illustrate these issues.[18]

Suppose that Harper Companies purchased $75,000 of corn milling equipment from Farmers State Cooperative on January 1, 1998. Harper paid $25,000 cash and signed a five-year 10% installment note for the remaining $50,000 of the purchase price. The note calls for annual payments of $10,000 plus interest on December 31 of each year. Harper made the first two installment payments on time but was unable to make the third annual payment on December 31, 2000. After much negotiation, Farmers State agreed to restructure the note receivable. At that time, Harper owed $30,000 in unpaid principal plus $3,000 in accrued interest. We will assume that the restructuring was agreed to on January 1, 2001 and that both companies have already recorded interest up to that date.

Settlement

Suppose Farmers State agrees to cancel the loan if Harper pays $5,000 cash and turns over the company car. The car was purchased 18 months ago for $21,000 cash, has a current fair market value of $18,000, and is carried on Harper's books at $16,000 ($21,000 original cost minus $5,000 accumulated depreciation). Notice that the combined economic value of the cash ($5,000) and automobile ($18,000) is $23,000—or $10,000 less than the $33,000 Harper owes Farmers State.

The January 1, 2001 entries made to record settlement of the troubled debt are:

Harper Companies (Borrower)

(a) To increase the net carrying amount of the automobile ($16,000) to its fair market value ($18,000):

DR Automobile	$ 2,000	
CR Gain on disposal of asset		$ 2,000

(b) To record the settlement:

DR Note payable	$30,000	
DR Interest payable	3,000	
DR Accumulated depreciation	5,000	
CR Cash		$ 5,000
CR Automobile		23,000
CR Extraordinary gain on debt restructuring		10,000

---

[18] Troubled debt restructurings often involve complexities that are beyond the scope of our discussion here. See *SFAS No. 15,* ibid.; "Accounting by Creditors for Impairment of a Loan," *SFAS No. 114* (Norwalk, CT: FASB, 1993); and "Accounting by Creditors for Impairment of a Loan—Income Recognition and Disclosures," *SFAS No. 118* (Norwalk, CT: FASB, 1994).

Farmers State Cooperative (Lender)

(a) To record the settlement:

DR Cash	$ 5,000	
DR Automobile	18,000	
DR Loss on receivable restructuring	10,000	
CR Note receivable		$30,000
CR Interest receivable		3,000

What do these entries accomplish? The settlement creates two earnings gains for Harper: (1) a gain on asset disposal of $2,000—the difference between the car's fair market value ($18,000) and its book value ($16,000); and (2) an extraordinary debt restructuring gain of $10,000—the difference between the note's book value plus accrued interest ($30,000 plus $3,000) and the fair market value of assets transferred ($5,000 cash plus $18,000 automobile). Farmers State has a debt restructuring loss for the same $10,000 figure. Both companies record all interest up to the restructuring date and then cancel the note and related interest receivable and payable.

Farmers State Cooperative's settlement loss would not be extraordinary but would instead be included in the computation of income from continuing operations. Because it's a lender, restructurings are a normal part of its business and are likely to recur. So these transactions meet *neither* criterion for extraordinary items.

Continuation with Modification of Debt Terms

Instead of reaching a negotiated settlement of the note receivable, Harper and Farmers State could have resolved the troubled debt by modifying the terms of the original loan. The possibilities are endless. For accounting purposes, what matters is whether the ***undiscounted sum of future cash flows under the restructured note is above or below the note's book value (including accrued interest) at the restructuring date.***

Suppose Farmers State agrees to postpone all principal and interest payments on the note receivable to maturity. Harper's final (and only) payment on December 31, 2002 would total $39,000 (the $30,000 principal plus $9,000 representing three years interest at 10%). Harper and Farmers State have already recorded $3,000 in accrued interest as of January 1, 2001. So the book value of the note plus accrued interest is $33,000 at the restructuring date.

Because the sum of future cash flows on the restructured note ($39,000) is *greater* than the carrying value of the original payable ($33,000), Harper will not show a restructuring gain. Instead, Harper will compute a new (and lower) effective interest rate for the restructured note and accrue interest at that new rate until the loan is fully paid. The new effective interest rate is that rate which equates the present value of the restructured cash flows to the carrying value of the debt at the date of restructure. The new effective interest rate for Harper Companies is 8.7% per year.

To see this, notice that the restructured note calls for Harper to make a single payment of $39,000 on December 31, 2002—two years from the January 1, 2001 restructuring date. We need to find a discount rate that equates the present value of this $39,000 payment with the $33,000 carrying value of the note receivable. This means finding the rate *r* that solves the following equation:

$$\underbrace{\text{Carrying value}}\quad = \quad \underbrace{\text{Present value of future cash flows}}$$

$$\$33{,}000 = \frac{\$39{,}000}{(1 + r)^2}$$

The value of *r* is .087. The present value factor for a single payment due in two periods at 8.7% is 0.84615, and $39,000 multiplied by this factor equals $33,000 (rounded).

Farmers State will continue using the 10% interest rate on the original note.[19] To do so, it must value the restructured note payments using a 10% effective interest rate. Farmers State will then show a loss for the difference between the present value of the restructured note, which is $32,232, and the carrying value of the original note ($33,000). The entries made by both companies are:

The present value factor for a single payment due in two years at 10% is .82645. The value of the note is $39,000 × .82645, or $32,232 (rounded).

[19] *SFAS No. 114*, para. 14.

Harper Companies (Borrower)

(a) To record the modified note (when sum of restructured cash flows is greater than note book value plus accrued interest):

DR Note payable	$30,000	
DR Interest payable	3,000	
CR Restructured note payable		$33,000

Farmers State Cooperative (Lender)

(a) To record the modified note (when sum of restructured cash flows is greater than note book value plus accrued interest):

DR Restructured note receivable	$32,232	
DR Loss on receivable restructuring	768	
CR Note receivable		$30,000
CR Interest receivable		3,000

Both companies accrue interest beginning on the debt restructuring date (January 1, 2001) and ending on the maturity date of the restructured note (December 31, 2002). But they will *not* use the same interest rate. The borrower, Harper, will record annual interest at 8.7% of the note's carrying value at the beginning of each year, whereas Farmers State will use a 10% annual rate. The entries for the next two years are:

Harper Companies (Borrower)

(a) To record interest on December 31, 2001:

DR Interest expense	$2,871	
CR Restructured note payable		$2,871

($2,871 = $33,000 × 8.7%)

(b) To record interest on December 31, 2002:

DR Interest expense	$3,121	
CR Restructured note payable		$3,121

($3,121 = [$33,000 + $2,871] × 8.7%)

Farmers State Cooperative (Lender)

(a) To record interest on December 31, 2001:

DR Restructured note receivable	$3,223	
CR Interest income		$3,223

($3,223 = $32,232 × 10%)

(b) To record interest on December 31, 2002:

DR Restructured note receivable	$3,546	
CR Interest income		$3,546

($3,546 = [$32,232 + $3,223] × 10%)

Over time, Harper Companies' note payable and Farmers State Cooperative's note receivable grow to the final balance of $39,000, the required payment at maturity, as shown on the next page.

This example illustrates a restructured loan in which the total restructured cash flows are *greater* than the carrying value of the troubled debt. Next let's examine a situation in which the sum of the future cash flows is *less* than the carrying value of the troubled debt.

Suppose Farmers State waives all interest payments and defers all principal payments until December 31, 2002. The restructured cash payments ($30,000) are *less* than the carrying value of the original receivable ($33,000). Harper will show an extraordinary gain on the debt restructuring, and all subsequent payments will be treated as a reduction of the restructured principal. No interest expense is recorded by Harper. But Farmers State follows the procedures

	Harper Companies	Farmers State Cooperative
Restructured note, initial carrying amount	$33,000	$32,232
Accrued interest expense, Harper		
2001	2,871	
2002	3,121	
Accrued interest revenue, Farmers State		
2001		3,223
2002		3,546
Note carrying amount, December 31, 2002	$39,000*	$39,000*

*Rounded.

outlined in the previous example. The restructured note is valued at $24,794 (using the 10% effective interest rate from the original note), a debt restructuring loss is recorded, and interest income is accrued to maturity. The entries made at the restructuring date are:

The $24,794 is just the present value of $30,000 received in two years at 10%, or $24,794 = $30,000 × 0.82645.

Harper Companies (Borrower)

(a) To record the modified note (restructured cash flows less than note book value):

DR Note payable	$30,000	
DR Interest payable	3,000	
CR Restructured note payable		$30,000
CR Extraordinary gain on debt restructuring		3,000

Farmers State Cooperative (Lender)

(a) To record the modified note (restructured cash flows less than note book value):

DR Restructured note receivable	$24,794	
DR Loss on receivable restructuring	8,206	
CR Note receivable		$30,000
CR Interest receivable		3,000

Harper would not record any interest over the life of the restructured note. The $30,000 cash payment on December 31, 2002 would reduce the outstanding balance of Harper's restructured note payable. Farmers State still records interest income over the life of the note. These entries would be:

Harper Companies (Borrower)

(No entries are made until the cash payment at maturity.)

Farmers State Cooperative (Lender)

(a) To record interest on December 31, 2001:

DR Restructured note receivable	$2,479	
CR Interest income		$2,479

($2,479 = $24,794 × 10%)

(b) To record interest on December 31, 2002:

DR Restructured note receivable	$2,727	
CR Interest income		$2,727

($2,727 = [$24,794 + $2,479] × 10%)

The note receivable balance at Farmers State will grow to $30,000 at maturity.

International Accounting Standards for debt restructurings from the lender's perspective are virtually identical to U.S. GAAP. (See "Financial Instruments: Recognition and Measurement," International Accounting Standard (IAS) 39 [London, 1998], para. 113.) There are no explicit international standards governing troubled-debt restructuring from the borrower's perspective.

Evaluating Troubled Debt Restructuring Rules

The GAAP rules for troubled debt restructurings are subject to several criticisms. First there is an obvious (and uncomfortable) lack of symmetry in the financial reporting of the borrower and lender. Different measurement rules are used to value the borrower's restructured note payable and the lender's restructured receivable. Consequently, the initial book value GAAP assigns to the payable is not the same as that assigned to the receivable. This also results in a difference between the borrower's restructuring gain and the lender's restructuring loss.

Second, the GAAP restructuring gains and losses do not always correspond to real economic gains and losses for the companies involved. For one thing, GAAP often assigns the gain or loss to the wrong time period. Take the case of Farmers State Cooperative. Although the accounting loss was shown in 2001, most of the economic loss occurred earlier when Harper became unable to make the loan payments.

Third, one could also question GAAP's use of the original loan's effective interest rate to value the restructured receivable and the lender's restructuring loss. Turning again to Farmers State, the original 10% loan to Harper used an interest rate that reflected the borrower's credit risk at the time. Over the ensuing three years, Harper's credit risk undoubtedly increased to the point where lenders would charge a higher rate of interest (say 15%) on new loans to the company. After all, Harper failed to meet its financial obligations in 2000. A higher effective interest rate on the restructured receivable will produce a lower initial book value and a larger restructuring loss for the lender. The GAAP approach is a practical solution because it avoids the sometimes difficult task of estimating the borrower's real effective interest rate at the restructuring date. However, this approach also fails to fully reflect the economic realities of troubled debt restructurings.

Table 8.3 summarizes, in general terms, the accounting illustrated in each of the Harper–Farmers State troubled debt restructurings. **RECAP**

Table 8.3 ■ SUMMARY OF ACCOUNTING PROCEDURES FOR TROUBLED DEBT RESTRUCTURINGS

		Restructured Loan Cash Flows Are:	
	Settlement Gain or Loss	**Lower Than Current Book Value of Loan[1]**	**Higher Than Current Book Value of Loan[1]**
Borrower			
New loan payable	—	Total of restructured cash flows	Current book value
Gain on debt restructuring	Extraordinary	Extraordinary	None
Gain (loss) on transfer of assets	Ordinary	—	—
Future interest expense	—	None, all payments applied to principal	Based on rate which equates current book value and restructured cash flows
Lender			
New loan receivable	—	Present value of new cash flows at original effective interest rate	Present value of new cash flows at original effective interest rate
Loss on debt restructuring	Ordinary	Ordinary	Ordinary
Future interest income	—	Based on original loan rate	Based on original loan rate

[1]Includes unpaid accrued interest.

SUMMARY

GAAP requires that accounts receivable be shown at their net realizable value. This means gross accounts receivable must be reduced by the amount of estimated uncollectibles and returns/allowances. Companies use one of two methods to estimate uncollectible accounts: (1) the sales revenue approach, or (2) the gross accounts receivable approach. Under either approach, firms must periodically assess the reasonableness of the uncollectibles balance by performing an aging of accounts receivable. Analysts should scrutinize the allowance for uncollectibles balance over time. Increases in the allowance as a percent of accounts receivable may indicate collection problems or other customer difficulties. Decreases in the allowance percentage might be a sign of earnings management.

Receivables growth can exceed sales growth for several reasons, including a change in customer mix or credit terms. But a disparity in the growth rate of receivables and sales could also indicate that aggressive revenue recognition practices are being used. For this reason, careful analysis of period-to-period trends is necessary to determine whether the reported receivables arise from real sales.

In certain long-term credit sales transactions, interest must be imputed by determining the note receivable's present value. This is necessary to distinguish between income from the sale and interest income, which might be recognized in different periods.

Firms sometimes transfer or dispose of receivables before their due date in order to accelerate cash collection. Sales of receivables—also called factoring—can be with or without recourse. Receivables are also occasionally used as collateral for a loan. In analyzing these transactions, it is sometimes not obvious whether the transaction to accelerate cash collection represents a sale or a borrowing; however, the FASB has provided guidelines in *SFAS No. 140* for distinguishing between sales (where the transferor surrenders control over the receivables) and borrowings (where control is not surrendered). Receivables that are transferred get removed from the balance sheet. Analysts should examine receivables transfer transactions. Is it a sale or a borrowing? Any divergence between the accounting treatment and the economics of the transaction misstates assets and liabilities. Furthermore, sale of receivables changes ratios like receivables turnover as well as potentially masking the underlying real growth in receivables. Keep these factors in mind when using these ratios in valuations or other forecasts.

Banks and other holders of receivables will frequently restructure the terms of the receivable when a customer is unable to make required payments. These troubled debt restructurings can take one of two forms: (1) settlement, or (2) continuation with modification of debt terms. When terms are modified, the precise accounting treatment depends on whether the sum of future cash flows under the restructured note is above or below the note's book value at the restructuring date. Remember that the interest rate used in troubled debt restructurings may not reflect the real economic loss suffered by the lender.

Self-Study Problem: Roomkin & Juris Department Stores Securitization

Roomkin & Juris is a department store chain in the western United States. In September 2001 it created a legally separate trust (R & J Trust) to serve as the special purpose entity for securitizing $1,000,000 of customer receivables. Customers are charged an interest rate of 12% per year on unpaid receivable balances. The receivables were sold to the trust which in turn issued $1,000,000 of two-year 9% per annum notes collateralized by the receivables. Interest on the notes is paid quarterly. Roomkin & Juris services the accounts and remits a portion of the cash collected to the trust. The R & J Trust uses this cash to make all required payments to the investors. Because the receivables are constantly turning over, this is what is called a **revolving securitization.** The amount of collateral must be maintained at the original amount (here $1,000,000) less any credit losses (which, assume, are borne by the investors). Three transactions in 2001 were related to the securitization:

- *September 30:* Roomkin & Juris sells receivables with a book value of $980,000 (i.e., gross receivables of $1,000,000 and an allowance for uncollectibles of $20,000) to the trust for $995,000.

- *October 1–December 29:* Roomkin & Juris collects $692,500 from customers on the receivables sold to the trust. This amount represents payment of both the principal portion of the receivables and interest.
- *December 30:* Roomkin & Juris transfers $692,500 of new receivables and cash to the trust to replenish the collateral base and to allow it to make required interest payments.

1. Record the sale of the receivables on Roomkin & Juris' books.

The journal entry is:

DR Cash	$995,000	
DR Allowance for uncollectibles	20,000	
CR Accounts receivable		$1,000,000
CR Gain on sale of receivables		15,000

Because the investors bear all credit losses, the allowance that relates to the sold receivables is removed from the books. The journal entry presumes that Roomkin & Juris do not charge a fee for servicing the accounts. The $15,000 gain is the value created by securitization—it's what investors are willing to pay over and above the book value of the receivables.

2. Record Roomkin & Juris' cash collections on the sold receivables.

The journal entry is:

DR Cash	$692,500	
CR Due to R & J Trust		$692,500

The collateral must be maintained at $1,000,000 less any credit losses. (Remember, investors bear all credit losses in this securitization.) So Roomkin & Juris must replace the receivables principal that has been repaid by the customers, plus $22,500 cash to cover the fourth quarter 2001 interest payment on the notes ($\$1{,}000{,}000 \times 9\% \times {}^{1}/_{4} = \$22{,}500$). This total is $692,500.

3. Record the asset transfer to the R & J Trust.

The journal entry is:

DR Due to R & J Trust	$692,500	
CR Accounts receivable		$670,000
CR Cash		22,500

Since some of the original accounts receivable have been collected, the collateral is now replenished by a transfer of $670,000 of *new* receivables to the R & J Trust. The $22,500 cash enables the trust to make the quarterly interest payment on the notes.

4. What happens in September 2003 when the R & J Trust repays the principal amount of the notes?

Over the two years, the collateral has been maintained at $1,000,000 minus any credit losses. Let's assume that the receivables collateral balance is $984,000 on September 30, 2003 when the notes are due; that is, credit losses were $16,000 ($1,000,000 − $984,000). The amount of principal repayment that the investors will receive is $984,000. Roomkin & Juris will remit that amount in cash to the R & J Trust. Since the securitization has terminated, collateral is no longer needed and the receivables are transferred back from the R & J Trust to the department store. The entry on Roomkin & Juris' books is:

DR Accounts receivable	$984,000	
CR Cash		$984,000

Exercises

E8–1

Account analysis

AICPA adapted

For the month of December 2001 the records of Ranger Corporation show the following information:

Cash received on accounts receivable	$35,000
Cash sales	30,000
Accounts receivable, December 1, 2001	80,000
Accounts receivable, December 31, 2001	74,000
Accounts receivable written off as uncollectible	1,000

Required:

Determine the gross sales for the month of December 2001.

E8–2

Account analysis

AICPA adapted

At the close of its first year of operations, on December 31, 2001, the Walker Company had accounts receivable of $250,000, which were *net* of the related allowance for doubtful accounts. During 2001, the company had charges to bad debt expense of $40,000 and wrote off, as uncollectible, accounts receivable of $10,000.

Required:

What should the company report on its balance sheet at December 31, 2001, as accounts receivable *before* the allowance for doubtful accounts?

E8–3

Ratio effects of write-offs

AICPA adapted

Delta Corporation wrote off a $100 uncollectible account receivable against the $1,200 balance in its allowance account.

Required:

For the following amounts or ratios, determine the relationship between the amount or ratio before the write-off (x) with the amount or ratio after the write-off (y):

Amount or Ratio	Possibilities
1. Current ratio	a. x greater than y
2. Net accounts receivable balance	b. x equals y
3. Gross accounts receivable balance	c. x less than y
	d. Cannot be determined

E8–4

Bad debt expense

AICPA adapted

The following information is available for the Parker Company:

Credit sales during 2001	$100,000
Allowance for doubtful accounts at December 31, 2000	1,200
Accounts receivable deemed worthless and written off during 2001	1,600

During 2001 Parker estimated that its bad debt expense should be 1% of all credit sales.

As a result of a review and aging of accounts receivable in early January 2002, it has been determined that an allowance for doubtful accounts of $1,100 is needed at December 31, 2001.

Required:

What is the total amount that Parker should record as "bad debt expense" for the year ended December 31, 2001?

E8–5

Amortization table

AICPA adapted

The Lake Company sold some machinery to the View Company on January 1, 2001, for which the cash selling price was $758,200. View entered into an installment sales contract with Lake at an interest rate of 10%. The contract required payments of $200,000 a year over five years, with the first payment due on December 31, 2001.

Required:

Prepare an amortization schedule that shows what portion of each $200,000 payment will be shown as interest income over the period 2001–2005.

E8–6 **Discounted note** AICPA adapted

Weaver, Inc. received a $60,000, six month, 12% interest-bearing note from a customer. The note was discounted the same day at Third National Bank at 15%.

REQUIRED:

Compute the amount of cash received by Weaver from the bank.

E8–7 **Note receivable carrying amount** AICPA adapted

On January 1, 2001, Carpet Company loaned $100,000 to its supplier, Loom Corporation, which was evidenced by a note, payable in five years. Interest at 5% is payable annually, with the first payment due on December 31, 2001. The going rate of interest for this type of loan is 10%. The parties agreed that Carpet's inventory needs for the loan period will be met by Loom at favorable prices. Assume that the present value (at the going rate of interest) of the $100,000 note is $81,000 at January 1, 2001.

REQUIRED:

1. Show the journal entry that Carpet would make to record interest and the receipt of cash at December 31, 2001.
2. What is the nature of the account that arises as a consequence of the difference between the 5% cash interest and the effective yield of 10%?

E8–8 **Aging analysis** AICPA adapted

On December 31, 2001, Vale Company had an unadjusted credit balance of $1,000 in its allowance for uncollectible accounts. An analysis of Vale's trade accounts receivable at that date revealed the following:

Age	Amount	Estimated Uncollectible
0 – 30 days	$60,000	5%
31 – 60 days	4,000	10
Over 60 days	2,000	70

REQUIRED:

What amount should Vale report as allowance for uncollectible accounts in its December 31, 2001 balance sheet?

E8–9 **Account analysis** AICPA adapted

The following information relates to Jay Company's accounts receivable for 2001:

Accounts receivable, 1/1/01	$ 650,000
Credit sales for 2001	2,700,000
Sales returns for 2001	75,000
Accounts written off during 2001	40,000
Collections from customers during 2001	2,150,000
Estimated future sales returns at 12/31/01	50,000
Estimated uncollectible accounts at 12/31/01	110,000

REQUIRED:

What amount should Jay report for accounts receivable, before allowances for sales returns and uncollectible accounts, at December 31, 2001?

E8–10 **Consignments** AICPA adapted

Mare Company's December 31, 2001 balance sheet reported the following current assets:

Cash	$ 70,000
Accounts receivable	120,000
Inventories	60,000
Total	$250,000

An analysis of the accounts disclosed that accounts receivable consisted of the following:

Trade accounts	$ 96,000
Allowance for uncollectible accounts	(2,000)
Selling price of Mare's unsold goods out on consignment, at 130% of cost, *not* included in Mare's ending inventory	26,000
Total	$120,000

REQUIRED:

What are the correct totals for cash, accounts receivable, and inventories at December 31, 2001?

PROBLEMS/DISCUSSION QUESTIONS

P8–1

Balance sheet presentation and journal entries for various receivables transactions

Baer Enterprises's balance sheet at October 31, 2001 (fiscal year end) includes the following:

Accounts receivable	$379,000
Less: Allowance for uncollectible accounts	(33,000)
Accounts receivable (net)	$346,000

Transactions for fiscal 2002 include the following:

1. Due to a product defect, previously sold merchandise totaling $10,500 was returned.
2. Customer accounts totaling $29,750 were written off during the year.
3. On November 1, 2001, Baer sold teleconferencing equipment and received a $75,000 non-interest-bearing note receivable due in three years. The normal cash-selling price for the equipment is $56,349. Assume the appropriate interest rate for these transactions is 10%.
4. Credit sales during the year were $395,000, while collections totaled $355,000.
5. Baer sold Hartman, Inc. $45,000 of accounts receivable without recourse. Hartman's fee for factoring receivables is 9%.
6. Utilizing the gross receivables approach, Baer determined that the 2002 fiscal year-end allowance for uncollectible accounts should be $35,000.

REQUIRED:

1. Prepare journal entries for each of these events. Also prepare the entry to accrue interest income on the note.
2. Show Baer's balance sheet presentation for accounts and notes receivable at October 31, 2002.

P8–2

Allowance for uncollectibles

Avillion Corporation had a $45,000 debit balance in accounts receivable and a $3,500 credit balance in allowance for uncollectibles on December 31, 2001. The company prepared the following aging schedule to record the adjusting entry for bad debts:

Age of Receivables	Amount	Expected Bad Debts
0 – 30 days old	$30,000	5%
31 – 90 days old	10,000	11
Over 90 days old	5,000	30

a. On January 1, 2002 the company was informed that one of its customers (Smith Corporation), which owed $2,000, has filed for bankruptcy and may be unable to pay the amount due.
b. On March 1, 2002 Smith Corporation's bankruptcy was finalized and the bankruptcy court notified all its creditors (including Avillion Corporation) that Smith Corporation will pay 60 cents on the dollar for the amount owed to its creditors.
c. On May 7, 2002 Avillion Corporation received a check from Smith Corporation for the amount indicated by the court.

REQUIRED:

1. Provide journal entries to record the preceding transactions in the books of Avillion Corporation. In addition, using the table format provided below, show the effects of each of the transactions on the following financial statement items. Clearly indicate the amount and the direction of the effects (use "+" for increase, "−" for decrease, and "NE" for no effect).

	Assets	Liabilities	Net Income	Cash Flow from Operations
Direction of effect				
Dollar amount of effect				

2. Assume that Avillion Corporation had instead prepared the following aging schedule on December 31, 2001:

Age of Receivables	Amount	Expected Bad Debts
0–30 days old	$30,000	3%
31–90 days old	10,000	8
Over 90 days old	5,000	22

Redo requirement (1) using the revised aging schedule.

P8–3

Journal entries, aging analysis and balance sheet presentation

At December 31, 2001, Oettinger Corporation, a premium kitchen cabinetmaker for the home remodeling industry, reported the following accounts receivable information on its year-end balance sheet:

Gross accounts receivable	$850,000
Less: Allowance for uncollectibles	(25,000)
Accounts receivable (net)	$825,000

During 2002, the company had credit sales of $8,200,000 of which $7,975,000 was collected. Oettinger employs the sales revenue approach to estimate bad debt expense and continues to use the same 1% used in previous years.

Although 2002 started off well, the industry experienced a slowdown in the last four months of the year and cash collections consequently dropped off substantially. Moreover, a major customer, who owed Oettinger $85,000, unexpectedly filed for bankruptcy and went out of business during November. Oettinger's controller is concerned that other customers are experiencing similar cash flow problems and that the company's allowance for uncollectible accounts is too low. As a result she prepared the following schedule:

% of Accounts Receivable Balance	Number of Days Past Due	Estimated % Collectible
20.0%	0–30	98.0%
40.0	31–60	95.0
35.0	61–90	85.0
3.0	91–120	75.0
2.0	120 or more	50.0

REQUIRED:

1. Determine Oettinger's accounts receivable balance at December 31, 2002. Prepare a journal entry for each of the transactions affecting the accounts receivable balance for 2002.
2. Prepare an aging analysis to compute the required balance in the allowance for uncollectible accounts at December 31, 2002.

3. Prepare all required journal entries affecting the allowance for uncollectible accounts for the year ended December 31, 2002.
4. Show Oettinger's balance sheet presentation of accounts receivable at December 31, 2002.

P8–4

Account analysis

AICPA adapted

The following information is available for the Hokum Company ($ in thousands):

	2001	2002	2003
Charge sales	$ 900	$1,100	$1,000
Cash sales	600	800	700
Total	$1,500	$1,900	$1,700
Accounts receivable (end of year)	$170	$230	$220
Allowance for doubtful accounts (end of year)	47	30	56
Accounts written off as uncollectible (during the year)	2	50	4

REQUIRED:

Assuming that there was *no* change in the method used for estimating doubtful accounts during 2001–2003, determine the balance in the allowance for doubtful accounts at the beginning of 2001.

P8–5

Comprehensive receivables and allowance analysis

On January 1, 2001 Hussain Corporation reports the following information pertaining to its accounts receivable:

Accounts receivable (gross)	$20,000
Less: Allowance for uncollectibles	(2,000)
Accounts receivable (net)	$18,000

For the year ended December 31, 2001, Hussain Corporation had credit sales of $100,000. Collections for the year amounted to $92,000, of which $16,000 was from 2000 sales and $76,000 was from current year's sales. Bad debts written off during the year totaled $9,000; $4,000 of this total pertained to receivables outstanding as of January 1, 2001, and $5,000 was from this year's sales. On December 31, 2001, the company prepared the following aging schedule to determine the ending balance in the allowance for uncollectibles:

Aging Information	Book Value	Expected Bad Debts
Over 90 days old	$2,000	30%
31–90 days old	7,000	20
Current (0–30 days)	(To be computed by you)	10

REQUIRED:

1. Provide journal entries to record the preceding transactions as well as year-end bad debt expense. Compute the ending accounts receivable and allowance balances.
2. Show how the accounts receivable balance you computed will be disclosed in the balance sheet as of December 31, 2001.
3. Show how much of the bad debt expense for 2001 relates to actual and expected future write-offs from 2001 sales versus prior years' sales.

P8–6

Interest schedule

On December 31, 1995, Sea Containers Ltd., a company located in Hamilton, Bermuda, reported notes receivable of $63,930,000. This amount represents the present value of future cash flows (both principal and interest) discounted at a rate of 11.12% per annum. The schedule of collections of the receivables is provided next ($ in thousands):

Year Ending December	Collections
1996	$20,724
1997	15,896
1998	11,559
1999	7,179
2000	8,559
2001	13
	$63,930

Assume that the interest due is paid along with the face value of the receivables at the end of each year.

REQUIRED:

Provide journal entries to record the interest received as well as the collection of the notes receivable.

P8–7

Account analysis

The following information is adapted from the financial statements of Buck Hill Falls Company. The company provides recreational facilities, water and sewage services, miscellaneous maintenance services, etc., to residents of Buck Hill Falls, Monroe County, Pennsylvania.

BUCK HILL FALLS COMPANY
Fiscal Years Ended October 31

	1996	1995	1994
From Income Statements			
Revenues	$2,175,475	$2,218,139	$2,203,529
Provision for doubtful accounts	20,585	150,631	95,241
From Balance Sheets			
Gross accounts receivable	$ 353,723	$ 325,229	$ 210,758
(−) Allowance for doubtful accounts	(100,445)	(79,860)	(35,000)
Net accounts receivable	$ 253,278	$ 245,369	$ 175,758

Note: Bad debt expense is frequently referred to as "provision for doubtful accounts."

REQUIRED:

1. Reconstruct all the journal entries pertaining to "Gross accounts receivable" and "Allowance for doubtful accounts" (i.e., "Allowance for uncollectibles") for the fiscal years ended October 31, 1995 and October 31, 1996. You may assume that all revenues are from credit sales.
2. Try to identify scenarios consistent with the allowance and write-off activity reported over the 1994–1996 period.

P8–8

Cash discounts and returns

STRETCH

On January 1, 2001 Hillock Brewing Company sold 50,000 bottles of beer to various customers for $45,000 using credit terms of 3/10, n/30. These credit terms mean that customers will get a cash discount of 3% of invoice price for payments made within 10 days of the sale (this is what the 3/10 signifies). If payment is not made within 10 days, then the entire invoice price is due no later than the 30th day (this is what the n/30 signifies). At the time of sale, Hillock expects sales returns of 5%. On January 9, 2001 customers made payment on one half of the total receivables. They returned goods with a selling price of $2,000 on January 15, 2001. The balance due was paid on January 28, 2001.

REQUIRED:

1. Provide journal entries to record the preceding transactions in the books of Hillock Company; assume that Hillock records *expected* sales returns at the time of sales.
2. Redo requirement (1) assuming that customers returned goods with a selling price of $3,000 on January 15, 2001.

3. Provide journal entries to record the preceding transactions in the books of Hillock Company; assume that Hillock records sales returns when customers *actually* return the goods.
4. Since the net sales revenue is the same under both methods—requirements (1) and (3)—what is the advantage of recording anticipated sales returns rather than waiting to record them when the customers actually return the goods?
5. Assuming that the incremental annualized borrowing rate for a customer is 18%, are customers better off paying within 10 days to get the discount or should they wait to pay until the 30th day?

P8–9

Collateralized borrowing

Mik-Gen Corporation has a $100,000 bond sinking fund payment due in early August. In order to meet its obligation, on August 1 Mik-Gen decided to accelerate collection of accounts receivable by assigning $130,000 of specified accounts to a commercial lender as collateral for a loan. Under the agreement, Mik-Gen guarantees the accounts and will notify its customers to make their payments directly to the lender; in return the lender will advance Mik-Gen 85% of the accounts assigned. The remaining 15% will be paid to Mik-Gen once the commercial lender has recovered its fees and related cash advances. The lender receives a fee of 5% of the total accounts assigned, which is immediately deducted from the initial cash advance. The lender also assesses a monthly finance charge of 1/2 of 1% on any uncollected balances. Finance charges are to be deducted from the first payment due Mik-Gen after the lender has recovered its cash advances.

On August 31, Mik-Gen received a statement from the lender saying it had collected $80,000. On September 30, Mik-Gen receives a check from the lender together with a second statement saying an additional $40,000 has been collected.

REQUIRED:

1. Prepare all necessary journal entries.
2. Show the balance sheet presentation of the assigned accounts receivable and any related liabilities at August 31.

P8–10

Factoring receivables

Atherton Manufacturing Company sold $200,000 of accounts receivable (with a corresponding balance of $4,000 in the allowance for uncollectibles) without recourse to a factor with notification (i.e., the customers were instructed to mail their checks directly to the factor). While the factor was liable for all bad debts, Atherton was responsible for sales returns. The factor charged 12% per annum interest on the gross receivables for a period of one month (which is the expected weighted average time to maturity of the receivables) plus a factoring fee of 6%, both of which were deducted by the factor from the value of receivables. A 5% holdback was retained by the factor for expected sales returns. The customers returned inventory with a selling price of $3,000. All remaining accounts were settled and the factor paid the balance due. The factor incurred actual bad debts of $7,500. Assume that Atherton records sales returns only when goods are returned (i.e., it does not record an allowance for sales returns).

REQUIRED:

1. Provide journal entries to record the preceding transactions.

In answering parts (2) and (3), make the following modified assumptions:

- Atherton Manufacturing Company transfers $200,000 of accounts receivable (with a corresponding balance of $4,000 in the allowance for uncollectibles) *with full recourse* to a factor *without notification* (i.e., the customers continue to mail the checks to Atherton). Using the cash collected from the customers, Atherton repays the factor.
- The factor charged a factoring fee of 2.5%.
- A 7% holdback was retained by the factor; 5% of this holdback pertained to expected sales returns and the additional 2% to bad debts.
- The actual bad debts were $5,500.

2. In answering this part, assume that the transfer of receivables was considered a "sale" under the provisions of *SFAS No. 140.* Provide journal entries to record the preceding transactions.
3. In answering this part, assume that the transfer of receivables was considered a "borrowing" under the provisions of *SFAS No. 140.* Provide journal entries to record the preceding transactions.

P8–11 **Reconstructing T-accounts**

The following information is taken from the financial statements of Ramsay Health Care Inc.:

	Excerpts from Balance Sheets as of end of	
	Year 3	Year 2
Gross accounts receivable	$26,944,000	$31,651,000
Allowance for doubtful accounts	(3,925,000)	(4,955,000)
Net accounts receivable	$23,019,000	$26,696,000

	Excerpts from Income Statements for the Years Ended		
	Year 3	Year 2	Year 1
Revenue	$137,002,000	$136,354,000	$136,946,000
Provision for doubtful accounts	5,846,000	8,148,000	8,628,000
Operating income before taxes	6,900,000	(1,048,000)	9,321,000

Note: Bad debt expense is frequently referred to as "provision for doubtful accounts."

REQUIRED:

1. Reconstruct all the journal entries relating to "Gross accounts receivable" and "Allowance for doubtful accounts" (i.e., "Allowance for uncollectibles") for the year ended December 31, Year 3. You may assume that all revenues are from credit sales.
2. Assume that the company computes its bad debt expense by multiplying sales revenues by some percentage. (This is called the sales revenue approach.) Recalculate the bad debt expense (i.e., "Provision for doubtful accounts") for Year 3; assume that Ramsay estimated the Year 3 bad debts at the same percentage of revenue as it did in Year 2. Based on the revised figure, show how "Gross accounts receivable" and "Allowance for doubtful accounts" would be presented as of the end of Year 3. Also calculate a revised operating income before taxes using the revised figure for bad debt expense.
3. In answering this part, assume that the company is using the gross accounts receivable approach to estimate its bad debt expense (i.e., assume that "Allowance for doubtful accounts" is fixed as a percentage of gross receivables). Recalculate the bad debts expense for Year 3 *and* the ending balance in "Allowance for doubtful accounts" at the end of Year 3; assume that Ramsay estimated the expected bad debts at the same percentage of receivables as it did in Year 2. Also, calculate the revised operating income before taxes using the revised figure for bad debt expense.
4. Based on your answers to requirements (2) and (3), what inferences can be drawn about Ramsay's accounts receivables management and the adequacy of the allowance for doubtful accounts?

P8–12 **Restructured note receivable**

Fish Spotters, Inc. purchased a single-engine aircraft from National Aviation on January 1, 2001. Fish Spotters paid $55,000 cash and signed a three-year 8% note for the remaining $45,000. Terms of the note require Fish Spotters to pay accrued interest annually on December 31, with the remaining $45,000 balance due with the last interest payment on December 31, 2003. Fish Spotters made the first two interest payments but was unable to make the principal and interest payment due December 31, 2003. On January 1, 2004 National Aviation agreed to restructure the note receivable.

REQUIRED:

Provide the journal entries that National Aviation would record under each of the following independent scenarios.

1. National Aviation agrees to take the aircraft back in return for the outstanding note. Assume that the aircraft has a market value of $40,000.
2. National agrees to accept a $5,000 cash payment and a new $35,000 note receivable due in five years. The note stipulates that annual interest of $4,200 will be

paid each December 31. Prepare the note receivable amortization table through December 31, 2008 and all entries through December 31, 2006.

P8–13

Restructured note receivable

Warren Companies purchased equipment for $72,000 from General Equipment Manufacturers on January 1, 1999. Warren Companies paid $12,000 in cash and signed a five-year, 5% installment note for the remaining $60,000 of the purchase price. The note calls for annual payments of $12,000 plus interest on December 31 of each year. Warren Companies made the first installment on time, but it was not able to make the next installment (due on December 31, 2000). On January 1, 2001 General Equipment Manufacturers agreed to restructure the note receivable.

REQUIRED:

Provide journal entries in the books of both Warren Companies and General Equipment Manufacturers for the period 2001–2003 under the following *independent* scenarios:

1. General Equipment Manufacturers accepted $20,000 in cash and old equipment fully depreciated in the books of Warren Companies (with a market value of $14,000) in exchange for the outstanding note.
2. General Equipment Manufacturers agreed to receive a total of $57,600 ($48,000 plus $9,600, representing four years interest at 5%) on December 31, 2003 in exchange for the outstanding note. (Interpolate for Warren's new effective interest rate.)
3. General Equipment decides to waive all interest and defers all principal payments until December 31, 2003.

P8–14

Accounting for transfer of receivables

The following footnotes are excerpted from the financial statements of three companies:

RICOH COMPANY LTD., MARCH 31, 1994

NOTE NO. 7—SHORT-TERM BORROWINGS AND TRADE NOTES RECEIVABLE DISCOUNTED WITH BANKS

The Company and certain of its domestic subsidiaries regularly discount trade notes receivable on a full recourse basis with banks. These trade notes receivable discounted are contingent liabilities. The weighted average interest rates on these trade notes receivable discounted were 4.2% and 3.2% as of March 31, 1993 and 1994, respectively.

CROWN CRAFTS INC., MARCH 31, 1994

NOTE NO. 4—FINANCING ARRANGEMENTS

Factoring Agreement

The Company assigns substantially all of its trade accounts receivable to a commercial factor. Under the terms of the factoring agreement, the factor remits invoiced amounts to the Company on the approximate due dates of the factored invoices. The Company does not borrow funds from its factor or take advances against its factored receivables balances. Accounts are factored without recourse as to credit losses but with recourse as to returns, allowances, disputes and discounts. Factoring fees included in marketing and administrative expenses in the consolidated statements of earnings were: $1,501,000 (1994), $1,223,000 (1993) and $1,077,000 (1992).

FOXMEYER CORPORATION, MARCH 31, 1994

NOTE C—ACCOUNTS RECEIVABLE FINANCING

On October 29, 1993, the Corporation entered into a one-year agreement to sell a percentage ownership interest in a defined pool of the Corporation's trade accounts receivable with limited recourse. Proceeds of $125.0 million from the sale were used to reduce amounts outstanding under the Corporation's revolving credit facilities. Generally, an undivided interest in new accounts receivable will be sold daily as existing accounts receivable are collected to maintain the participation interest at $125.0 million. Such accounts receivable sold are not included in the accompanying consolidated balance sheet at March 31, 1994. An allowance for doubtful accounts has been retained on the participation interest sold based on estimates of the Corporation's risk of credit loss from its obligation under the recourse provisions. The cost of the accounts receivable financing program is based on a 30-day commercial paper rate plus certain fees. The total cost of the program in 1994 was $2.2 million and was charged against "Other income" in the accompanying consolidated statements of income. Under the agreement, the Corporation also acts as agent for the purchaser by performing recordkeeping and collection functions on the participation interest sold. The agreement contains certain covenants regarding the quality of the accounts receivable portfolio, as well as other covenants which are substantially identical to those contained in the Corporation's credit facilities.

REQUIRED:

How do the three companies record the transfer of their receivables—that is, as a sale or borrowing? Is their accounting treatment consistent with the economics of the transactions? Explain.

P8–15

Do existing receivables represent real sales?

Moto-Lite Company is an original equipment manufacturer of high-quality aircraft engines that have traditionally been sold directly to aero clubs building their own aircraft. The engine's selling price is dependent on its size and horsepower; Moto-Lite's average gross profit per engine is 35%.

In an effort to expand its sales, Moto-Lite entered into an agreement with Macco Corporation, a British manufacturer of light aircraft, to be the sole supplier of its 80 horsepower, 2 stroke engines. Under the terms of the agreement, Moto-Lite will stock a minimum of 10 engines at Macco's production facility in order to service aircraft production requirements. Each engine has a firm selling price of $6,000. Title to the engines does not pass until the engine is used in Macco's production process.

During its quarter ending October 31, Moto-Lite shipped and billed 19 engines (DR accounts receivable, CR sales) to Macco Corporation. As of that date, Macco had used nine engines in its production process. All but three of the engines used had been paid for prior to October 31. The remaining ten engines will be used in November.

REQUIRED:

1. What type of agreement does this appear to be? Was Moto-Lite correct to record all 19 motors shipped as sales in the quarter ending October 31?
2. How should the transaction be accounted for and by how much, if at all, were Moto-Lite's sales, receivables, and gross profit overstated at October 31?

P8–16

Do existing receivables represent real sales?

Aurora Aluminum, a vendor to Bostian Enterprises, receives Bostian's purchase order for computer drill sheet. Bostian, a maker of electronic circuit boards, implemented a production process that is designed to take advantage of just-in-time inventory management techniques. Accordingly, their purchase order specifically states that delivery is to be made to Bostian's assembly plant at 1 P.M. on January 16, 2002 and that payment will be 30 days after delivery.

Aurora had a lull in production activity and decided to produce Bostian's order over the Christmas holidays. After producing the material on December 27, it was promptly loaded on a staged trailer, which was immediately locked and sealed. An invoice and a bill of lading were prepared. The invoice was immediately sent to Bostian on a "bill and hold" basis.

Upon receiving the invoice, Bostian contacted Aurora and was told that the material was invoiced because Aurora wanted to include the sale in its just closed calendar year-end; however, actual delivery would take place in accordance with the purchase order terms and that payment would be expected 30 days after delivery. Moreover, risk of ownership would remain with Aurora until delivery. Bostian accepted the explanation, and reminded Aurora that it could not accept the material prior to its scheduled delivery date due to space constraints.

REQUIRED:

Was Aurora correct to include the Bostian transaction as a sale and account receivable in calendar year 2001? Explain.

CASES

C8–1

Ralston Purina Company (CW): Comprehensive receivables

Appearing next is information pertaining to the "Allowance for doubtful accounts" account of Ralston Purina Company. Examine this information and answer the following questions ($ in millions).

	Year Ended September 30		
	1999	**1998**	**1997**
Allowance for Doubtful Accounts			
Balance, beginning of year	?	?	$26.7
Provision charged to expense	?	3.9	3.1
Write-offs, less recoveries	8.3	4.2	?
Balance, end of year	24.5	?	24.8

REQUIRED:

1. Solve for the unknowns in the schedule above.
2. Make all entries related to the "Allowance for doubtful accounts" account for fiscal years 1997–1999.
3. Make all entries for bad debts for fiscal years 1997–1999 assuming Ralston did not accrue for estimated bad debt losses but instead recorded bad debt expense once receivables were determined to be uncollectible. (This is called the direct write-off method.)
4. Why does GAAP require the allowance method over the direct write-off method?
5. Calculate the cumulative difference in reported pre-tax income under the allowance and direct write-off methods over the 1997–1999 period.
6. Assume that it is the end of fiscal year 2000 and Ralston's managers are trying to decide on the amount of the bad debt expense for 2000. Based on an aging of accounts receivable, the accounting department feels that a provision of $9.0 million is appropriate. However, the company just found out that a customer with an outstanding accounts receivable of $6.0 million may have to file for bankruptcy. The decision facing Ralston managers is whether to increase the initial provision of $9.0 million by $6.0 million, by some lesser amount, or by nothing at all. What is your recommendation?
7. Consider the following information. Assume that you are a manager of Ralston Purina and have a cash bonus plan that is a function of reported earnings before income taxes. Specifically, assume that you receive an annual cash bonus of zero if earnings before income taxes is below $100 million and 1.0% of the amount by which earnings before income taxes exceeds $100 million and up to a maximum bonus of $1 million (i.e., when net income reaches $200 million, no further bonus is earned). What adjustment to the initial $9.0 bad debt provision might you decide on in each of the following scenarios?

    a. Earnings before income taxes (including the initial $9.0 provision for bad debts) is $65.0 million.
    b. Earnings before income taxes (including the initial $9.0 provision for bad debts) is $106.0 million.
    c. Earnings before income taxes (including the initial $9.0 provision for bad debts) is $225.0 million.
    d. Earnings before income taxes (including the initial $9.0 provision for bad debts) is $203.0 million.

8. What other scenarios can you identify in which managers may use the provision for bad debts to accomplish some contract-related strategy?
9. Identify other items in the financial statements (besides the bad debt provision) that managers have the ability to "manage."

C8–2

Great Southwest Corporation (KR): Valuing notes and recording interest

Great Southwest Corporation, Inc. (GSC) was a real estate development company headquartered in the southwestern United States. GSC was also engaged in constructing, developing, and operating amusement parks. On January 1, 1969 GSC sold its amusement park "Six Flags over Texas," which had been carried on the books of GSC at a value of $22 million. GSC received a down payment of $2 million immediately and received a 35-year, 6.5% note for $35 million from the buyer. In addition, GSC immediately received another $3,412,500, representing prepayments of stated interest for the first three years. Beginning in 1972 payments of $2,137,500 (which include interest payment of $1,137,500 and principal payment of $1,000,000) per year were to be made for the next 35 years. Since the average book value of the note is $17.5 million (one half of $35 million), the annual stated interest payments were calculated at 6.5% of $17.5 million.

Assume that the company can justify recording the sale of the amusement park on January 1, 1969 when the contract was signed. Also, assume that all cash transactions took place on the first day of each year.

GSC recorded the following journal entries to reflect the sale:

DR Cash	$ 2,000,000	
DR Notes receivable	35,000,000	
CR Amusement park in Dallas		$22,000,000
CR Gain on sale		15,000,000
DR Cash	3,412,500	
CR Unearned interest revenue		3,412,500

REQUIRED:

1. Are these journal entries consistent with GAAP? If not, explain how GSC should have recorded the sale and the receipt of initial cash payments. Show all relevant calculations.
2. Assuming that the prevailing effective interest rate for comparable transactions is 10%, redo requirement (1). In addition, provide the necessary journal entries for the first four years of the note's life (i.e., 1969 to 1972) to record the interest revenue and the receipt of the periodic payments.

C8–3

Spiegel, Inc. (KR): Analyzing receivables growth

You have recently been hired as an equity analyst at a large mutual fund. During your first week, you receive the following memo:

Welcome to Vitality Mutual Funds. I am sure you are excited to join our firm as a financial analyst. I am currently looking at the financial statements of Spiegel, Inc., which is a multi-channel specialty company that owns Spiegel, Eddie Bauer, and Newport News. The company also owns First Consumers National Bank ("FCNB"). FCNB is a special purpose bank limited to the issuance of credit cards, primarily FCNB Preferred Charge cards for use by Spiegel, Eddie Bauer and Newport News customers. I need your assistance in analyzing the company's accounts receivable. I did some cursory analysis and identified some very interesting trends. During 1994 and 1995, the growth in sales has outpaced the growth in receivables. In fact, during 1995, while the company's net sales grew at around 7%, its receivables decreased by more than 30%! I am quite pleased with the improvement in receivables management. In fact, the receivable collection period has dropped from around 140 days to less than 120 days. This is quite impressive given that the company relies very heavily on installment sales to generate a substantial majority of its revenue. However, I am not sure how Spiegel is accounting for the sale of receivables or how the factoring of receivables impacts my calculations. One additional thing that I can't understand is why Spiegel is showing a portion of the allowance for sales returns under accrued liabilities. I am under the impression that such allowance accounts are contra-asset accounts. What I need from you is a succinct report (with supporting analysis) addressing the issues that I have raised in this memo. To help you in your analysis, I have included below some information that I have on the company. Good luck.

Sincerely,
Maria S. Kang
Senior Analyst
Vitality Mutual Funds

The following table provides an adapted breakdown of the net receivables balance reported in comparative balance sheets:

	As of December 31 1995	1994	1993
Receivables generated from operations	$2,001,081	$1,683,444	$1,403,618
Receivables sold	(1,180,000)	(480,000)	(330,000)
Receivables owned	821,081	1,203,444	1,073,618
Less: Allowance for returns	(37,769)	(27,762)	(28,238)
Less: Allowance for doubtful accounts	(40,832)	(49,954)	(46,855)
Receivables—net (from balance sheet)	$ 742,480	$1,125,728	$ 998,525

During 1995, 1994, and 1993, the company transferred portions of its customer receivables to trusts which, in turn, sold certificates representing undivided interests in the trusts to investors. These transactions are similar to the factoring of receivables, except that a group of investors, as opposed to a single factor, is investing in the receivables of Spiegel. That is, this was a securitization of the receivables. Certificates sold were $700,000 in 1995 (under two separate transactions of $350,000 each) and $150,000 and $330,000 (in 1994 and 1993, respectively). As a result of these transactions, other revenue increased by $18,637 and $10,658 in 1995 and 1994, respectively, representing the gain on the sold receivables that existed at the date of the transaction. The receivables were *sold without recourse,* and the bad debt reserve related to the net receivables sold has been reduced accordingly. Note that Spiegel is still responsible for sales returns, although the investors in the securitized receivables bear the bad debt risk. As cash is collected from the customers, Spiegel pays only the required interest portion to the investors and reinvests the remaining cash flows in new accounts receivables that are generated (i.e., the investors are continually refinancing the receivables of Spiegel over the duration of the securitization agreement). The company owns the remaining undivided interest in the trusts not represented by the certificates (i.e., Spiegel is retaining ownership of a portion of the securitized receivables which is included under "Receivables Owned"). In addition, the company *will service all receivables for the trusts* (i.e., Spiegel is performing the administrative aspects of collecting and distributing the cash flows from the receivables).

The company reported the following sales figures over the three-year period:

	For the Years Ended December 31 1995	1994	1993
Net sales	$2,886,225	$2,706,791	$2,337,235

In addition, the following table provides information on the company's allowance for doubtful accounts over the same period:

	Allowance for Doubtful Accounts 1995	1994	1993
Beginning balance	**$49,954**	**$46,855**	**$37,231**
Charged to earnings	91,612	79,183	69,160
Reduction for receivables sold	(33,600)	(6,300)	(1,609)
Other	-0-	-0-	695
Accounts written off	(67,134)	(69,784)	(58,622)
Ending balance	**$40,832**	**$49,954**	**$46,855**

"Other" represents the beginning balance of Newport News, which was acquired in 1993.

The company's accrued liabilities at the end of 1995 include "Allowance for returns" of $31,927. This breakdown is not available for the prior two years.

The following footnote describes the company's revenue recognition policy:

> REVENUE RECOGNITION
> Sales made under installment accounts represent a substantial portion of net sales. The Company provides for returns at the time of sale based upon projected merchandise returns.

REQUIRED:

Provide the analysis requested by Ms. Kang including journal entries which show how Spiegel accounts for the sale of receivables.

C8–4

Thompson Traders (KR): Bad-debt analysis

Thompson Traders started its business on January 1, 1997. The following information pertains to the company's accounts receivable during the first five years of its operations:

Year	Revenue	Bad Debts Written Off	Bad Debts Pertaining to Sales Made During 1997	1998	1999	2000	2001
1997	$30,000	$ 600	$600				
1998	40,000	1,000	300	$700			
1999	60,000	1,500	–0–	500	$1,000		
2000	80,000	2,400	–0–	–0–	800	$1,600	
2001	90,000	3,000	–0–	–0–	–0–	800	$2,200

The company typically sells on credit to its customers. All sales made in a given calendar year are fully settled by the following year, by which time all uncollected receivables are written off. Since inception, Thompson has recorded bad debts expense at 2.75% of its revenue. After five years of operation, the company is now considering a reevaluation of its bad debts formula before finalizing its financial statements for the year 2001. The following are excerpts taken from a recent meeting of Thompson's managers discussing this issue:

> Our experience suggests that the bad debts written off have ballooned from 2% of revenues to almost 3.5%. So, while we were being very conservative in the earlier years, currently our provisions are much below our actuals. Conservatively, I recommend a formula of 3.5% of revenues.
>
> (Tony Barclay, Corporate Accounting)

> While I agree with Tony's computations, my experience suggests that the quality of our receivables has pretty much remained the same and I don't expect them to change in the near future. Therefore, I recommend that we retain our current formula.
>
> (Ian Spencer, Manager, Accounts Receivable)

> If you believe that you have under- or over-provided for bad debts over the last four years, you have to revise the formula to reflect your past experience and current expectations. While revising the formula will lead to correct expensing in the future, you also have to adjust the allowance account for past estimation errors. More importantly, since this will be considered as a change in accounting methods, you have to restate the past financial statements.
>
> (Brian Joshi, Outside Consultant)

REQUIRED:

You have been hired as a summer intern in the corporate controller's office to examine the bad debt accounting at Thompson. Based on the information provided, write a report to the top management providing an assessment of the company's bad debt formula and provide specific recommendations to improve its accounting, if needed. In completing the report, please address all the issues raised during the recent company meeting.

C8–5

Software Toolworks, Inc. (KR): Account reconciliation and analysis

The following information is adapted from the financial statements of Software Toolworks, Inc:

	For the Years Ended March 31	
	1993	1992
Revenues (net of provision for returns)	$119,598,000	$102,646,000
Provision for returns	10,942,000	8,863,000
Provision for doubtful accounts	946,000	3,673,000

	Balances as of March 31	
	1993	1992
Accounts receivable	$ 38,895,000	$34,754,000
Allowance for returns	(5,264,000)	(6,363,000)
Accounts receivable minus returns	33,631,000	28,391,000
Allowance for doubtful accounts	(3,570,000)	(4,151,000)
Net accounts receivable	$ 30,061,000	$24,240,000

Note: Bad debt expense is frequently referred to as "provision for doubtful accounts." Similarly, expected sales returns are sometimes labeled as "provision for returns."

The fiscal 1992 provision for doubtful accounts of $3,673,000 included both a $2,167,000 allowance for estimated uncollectible amounts from a major customer which filed for Chapter 11 bankruptcy protection and a $583,000 allowance related to Original Equipment Manufacturer receivables of $2,333,000 which were in arbitration. No such provisions were necessary during fiscal 1993.

Assume all sales are credit sales.

REQUIRED:

1. Reconcile beginning and ending account balances for gross receivables, allowance for returns, and allowance for doubtful accounts for the year ended March 31, 1993.
2. Analyze the growth and level of Software Toolworks' receivables as well as both the allowance for returns and allowance for doubtful accounts.

9

Inventories

A wholesaler or retailer buys assets like suits or shoes that are immediately saleable in their current form. Assets held for sale are called **inventories.** A typical wholesaler or retailer will have only one inventory account, called *merchandise inventory,* on its balance sheet.

A manufacturing firm makes a final product like dishwashers using inputs from many different suppliers. Manufacturers' balance sheet inventory classifications typically include three categories:

1. **Raw materials inventory,** which consists of components like steel that will eventually be used in the completed product.
2. **Work-in-process inventory,** which contains the aggregate cost of units that have been started but not completed at the balance sheet date. Work-in-process inventory includes the cost of the raw materials, direct labor, and overhead that has been incurred in the manufacture of the partially completed units.[1]
3. **Finished goods inventory,** which represents the total costs incorporated in completed but unsold units.

Inventories are usually a significant asset, both in absolute size and in proportion to all other assets. Furthermore, selling inventories for a price greater than their cost represents the main source of a firm's sustainable income. For these reasons, inventory accounting is exceedingly important.

LEARNING OBJECTIVES:
After studying this chapter, you will understand:

1. The two methods used to determine inventory quantities—the perpetual inventory system and the periodic inventory system.
2. What specific items and kinds of costs are included in inventory.
3. What absorption costing is and how it complicates financial analysis.
4. The difference between various cost flow assumptions—weighted average, FIFO, and LIFO.
5. How to use the LIFO reserve disclosure to estimate inventory holding gains and to transform LIFO firms to a FIFO basis.
6. How LIFO liquidations distort gross profit and how to adjust for these distortions to improve forecasts.
7. What research tells us about the economic incentives guiding the choice of inventory accounting methods.
8. How to eliminate realized holding gains from FIFO income.
9. How to apply the lower of cost or market method and on what assumptions the method rests.
10. How and why the dollar-value LIFO method is applied.

[1] Manufacturing overhead includes items such as depreciation of production equipment and buildings, power, indirect labor, and so on.

An Overview of Inventory Accounting Issues

We will use an example of a retailer who sells refrigerators to illustrate the basic issues in inventory accounting. Assume the retailer started the year with a beginning inventory of one refrigerator, which costs $300. During the year the cost of identical refrigerators increases to $340, and the retailer purchases another refrigerator at this $340 cost. At the end of the year the retailer sells one of the refrigerators for $500. Further assume that it is not possible to ascertain which of the two refrigerators was actually sold.

It is easy to determine the total cost of the goods that were available for sale. This total cost is determined by adding the cost of the beginning inventory and the cost of any purchases during the period—that is,

The total cost of the goods available for sale during the period was $640, a total that represents the aggregate *historical cost* of the two refrigerators.

The cost of the refrigerator that has been sold must be removed from the inventory account and charged to cost of goods sold, while the cost of the other refrigerator remains in inventory. In other words, the total cost of the goods available for sale ($640) must be allocated between ending inventory and cost of goods sold. This allocation process can be represented as follows:

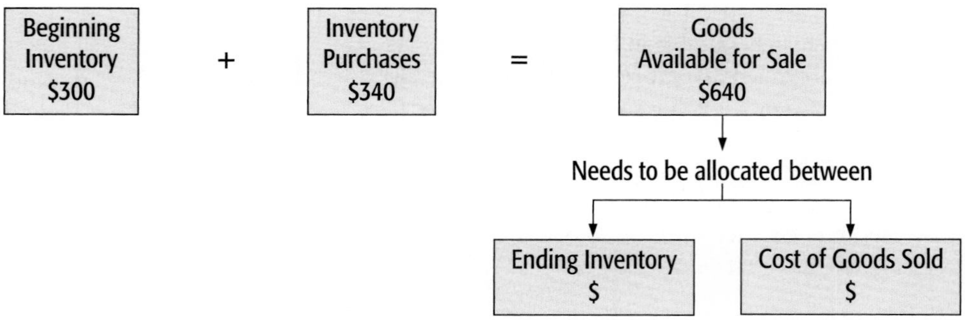

The choice of the method for making this allocation between ending inventory and cost of goods sold represents the major issue in inventory accounting.

Even in this simple case, there are at least three ways the total for the goods available for sale ($640) can be allocated between ending inventory and cost of goods sold:

1. One is to assume the refrigerator that was sold should reflect the average of the cost of the two refrigerators (i.e., $640/2 = $320), which would make the allocation:

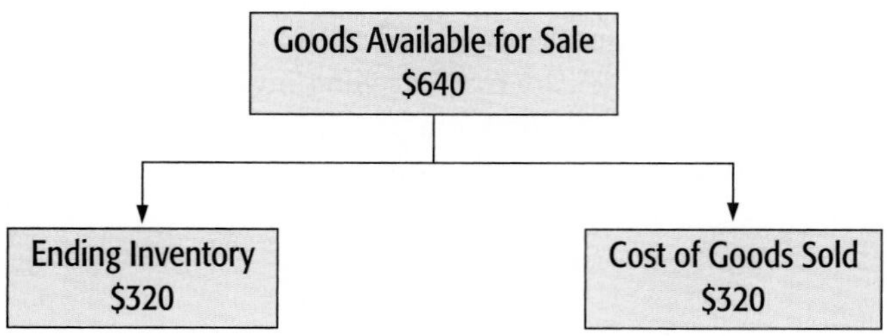

This is called the **weighted average** inventory costing method.

2. Another possibility is to assume that the refrigerator that was sold was the oldest refrigerator in stock—the $300 unit from the beginning inventory. This would mean the cost assigned to the refrigerator still on hand at the end of the year would be the $340 cost of the most recently purchased unit. Here, the allocation is:

Goods Available for Sale
$640

Ending Inventory	Cost of Goods Sold
$340	$300

This method assumes the first unit purchased is the first unit sold. Accountants call this **first-in, first-out (FIFO).**

3. Yet another alternative is to assume the refrigerator that was sold was the most recently purchased refrigerator—the one costing $340. This would mean the cost assigned to the refrigerator still on hand at the end of the year would be the $300 cost of the oldest available unit that was in inventory at the start of the year, making the allocation:

Goods Available for Sale
$640

Ending Inventory	Cost of Goods Sold
$300	$340

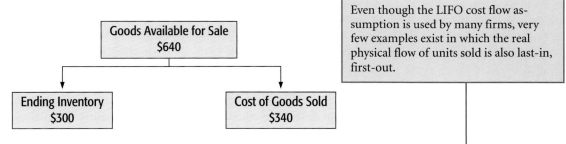

This method assumes the last unit purchased is the first unit sold. This is called **last-in, first-out (LIFO).**

> Even though the LIFO cost flow assumption is used by many firms, very few examples exist in which the real physical flow of units sold is also last-in, first-out.

Each of these cost allocations assumes a different flow of inventory costs—average cost, FIFO, or LIFO—from goods available for sale to the ending inventory account and to the cost of goods sold expense account; this is why these methods are called *cost flow assumptions.* GAAP does not require the *cost flow* assumption to correspond to the *physical flow* of inventory. ***If the cost of inventory never changed, all three cost flow assumptions would yield the same financial statement result.*** Also, under historical cost accounting, no matter what cost flow assumption is used, the total dollar amount allocated between cost of goods sold and ending inventory is always equal to the historical dollar cost of the goods available for sale ($640 in this case). This important point is shown in the following schedule:

> We don't discuss the weighted average method in the cost flow assumptions section later in the chapter because it generates numbers that are between the LIFO and FIFO approaches, and it introduces no additional issues. However, we do illustrate weighted average in more detail in the self-study problem at the end of the chapter.

Cost Flow Assumption	Total Historical Cost of Goods Available for Sale	=	Amount Allocated to Ending Inventory	+	Amount Allocated to Cost of Goods Sold
Weighted average	$640	=	$320	+	$320
First-in, first-out (FIFO)	$640	=	$340	+	$300
Last-in, first-out (LIFO)	$640	=	$300	+	$340

Once an inventory cost flow assumption is selected, the cost of goods sold can be determined using the following formula:

Beginning Inventory	+	Inventory Purchases	=	Goods Available for Sale
Goods Available for Sale	−	Ending Inventory	=	Cost of Goods Sold

For example, assume that the FIFO cost flow assumption is selected, so ending inventory is $340. Then, cost of goods sold is calculated as:

Beginning inventory	$300
Inventory purchases	+340
Goods available for sale	640
Ending FIFO inventory	−340
Cost of goods sold	$300

This simple example should refresh your memory about basic inventory accounting points. Actual business situations are more complex and encompass issues such as:

- How should physical quantities in inventory be determined?
- What items should be included in ending inventory?
- What costs should be included in inventory purchases (and eventually in ending inventory)?
- What cost flow assumption should be used for allocating goods available for sale between cost of goods sold and ending inventory?

Determining Inventory Quantities

There are two different methods for determining inventory quantities: (1) perpetual and (2) periodic. A **perpetual inventory system** keeps a running (or "perpetual") record of the amount in inventory. Purchases are debited to the inventory account itself, and the cost of units sold is removed from the inventory account as sales are made. Usually, these inventory records are maintained in both physical units and dollars. The physical amount of inventory on hand at any point in time should correspond to the unit balance in the inventory account.

The inventory T-account under a perpetual inventory system contains the following information at any point in time:

INVENTORY

Beginning inventory (units and $s) Plus: Cost of units purchased (units and $s)	Minus: Cost of units transferred to cost of goods sold (units and $s)
Equals: Ending inventory on hand (units and $s)	

A **periodic inventory system** does not keep a running record of the amount of inventory on hand. Purchases are accumulated in a separate "inventory purchases" account and no entry is made at the time of sale to reflect cost of goods sold. The records for a periodic inventory system look like this:

INVENTORY PURCHASES

Cost of units purchased ($s only)	

INVENTORY

Beginning inventory ($s only)	

In a periodic inventory system, ending inventory and cost of goods must be determined by physically counting the goods on hand at the end of the period. The computation is:

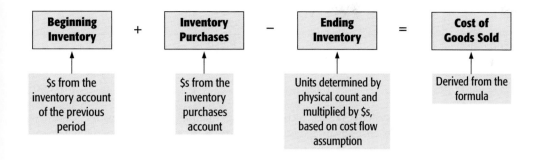

Beginning Inventory	+	**Inventory Purchases**	−	**Ending Inventory**	=	**Cost of Goods Sold**
↑		↑		↑		↑
$s from the inventory account of the previous period		$s from the inventory purchases account		Units determined by physical count and multiplied by $s, based on cost flow assumption		Derived from the formula

To illustrate the accounting entries under each system, assume the following data:

Sales	$10,000
Beginning inventory	1,400
Inventory purchases	9,100
Ending inventory	3,500

The entries under the perpetual and periodic inventory systems are compared below.

Comparison of Entries—Perpetual Versus Periodic Inventory System

Perpetual Inventory System			**Periodic Inventory System**		
			Entry (1) **To Record Purchases:**		
DR Inventory	$ 9,100		**DR** Inventory purchases	$ 9,100	
CR Accounts payable (or cash)		$ 9,100	**CR** Accounts payable (or cash)		$ 9,100
			Entry (2) **To Record Sales:**		
DR Cash or Accounts receivable	$10,000		**DR** Cash or Accounts receivable	$10,000	
CR Sales revenues		$10,000	**CR** Sales revenues		$10,000
DR Cost of goods sold	$ 7,000*				
CR Inventory		$ 7,000	(NO ENTRY)		

*(Computed as Beginning inventory [$1,400] + Purchases [$9,100]−Ending inventory [$3,500] = Cost of goods sold [$7,000])

			Entry (3) **To Close the Accounts:**		
(NO ENTRY)			**DR** Inventory (ending)	$ 3,500	
			DR Cost of goods sold	7,000	
			CR Inventory (beginning)		$ 1,400
			CR Inventory purchases		9,100

The inventory-related accounts would appear as follows under each method (entry numbers are indicated):

Perpetual Inventory System

INVENTORY

Beg. bal.	$1,400		
(1)	9,100	(2)	$7,000
End. bal.	$3,500		

COST OF GOODS SOLD

(2)	$7,000		

SALES

		(2)	$10,000

Periodic Inventory System

INVENTORY

Beg. bal.	$1,400		
(3)	3,500	(3)	$1,400
End. bal.	$3,500		

INVENTORY PURCHASES

(1)	$9,100	(3)	$ 9,100
End. Bal.	–0–		

COST OF GOODS SOLD

(3)	$7,000		

SALES

		(2)	$10,000

Periodic inventory systems reduce record keeping, making these systems less costly to maintain. However, this cost advantage is achieved at the expense of far less management control over inventory. For those who use a periodic inventory system, there is no running inventory record, and quantities on hand must be determined by physical count. Furthermore, the cost-of-goods-sold number under the periodic system is a "plug" figure—that is, the computation assumes that goods not on hand when the physical count is taken were sold. But some of the goods not on hand may have been stolen or wasted. Under the periodic system, there is no way to determine the extent of these potential losses.

A perpetual inventory system is more complicated and usually more expensive. It does not eliminate the need to take a physical inventory, since the book inventory figures must be verified for accuracy at least annually. But a perpetual system gives management greater control over inventories. For example, the running balance in inventory allows careful monitoring of stock levels. This is useful in avoiding stockouts, particularly in manufacturing where "just-in-time" inventory purchasing is practiced. Furthermore, the comparisons that must be made between book inventories and physical count figures reveal discrepancies that may be attributable to theft, employee carelessness, or natural shrinkage.

When the physical count reveals inventory shortages, the accounting records must be adjusted to conform to the actual amount on hand. If a shortage of $310 was indicated, the adjustment is:

DR Loss from inventory shortage (or Cost of goods sold)	$310	
CR Inventory		$310

Choosing between the two systems depends on weighing their costs and benefits. Perpetual inventory systems are typically used where:

- *a small number of inventory units with high unit value exists.* An example is the inventory of vehicles in an automobile dealership.
- *continuous monitoring of inventory levels is essential.* An example is a production line where raw materials shortages would shut the operation down.

Periodic systems are used in situations of high volume and low per-unit cost. However, the widespread use of computerized optical scanning equipment has led to the adoption of perpetual systems in supermarkets and other high volume settings where such systems were previously not cost-effective. Wal-Mart and Costco were among the first companies to utilize optical scanning and perpetual inventory systems. These firms share the information captured by their electronic inventory management systems with suppliers who are authorized to automatically ship new merchandise directly to their stores when inventory levels fall below prescribed minimum levels. This approach shortens inventory restocking cycles at Wal-Mart and Costco and reduces the need for warehouse inventories.

One morning, a Costco store in Los Angeles began running a little low on size-one and size-two Huggies. Crisis loomed.

So what did Costco managers do? Nothing. They didn't have to, thanks to a special arrangement with Kimberly-Clark Corp., the company that makes the diapers.

Under this deal, responsibility for replenishing stock falls on the manufacturer, not Costco. In return, the big retailer shares detailed information about individual stores' sales. So, long before babies in Los Angeles would ever notice it, diaper dearth was averted by a Kimberly-Clark data analyst working at a computer hundreds of miles away in Neenah, Wis. . . . A Kimberly-Clark spokeswoman says the benefits of the program "more than offset" additional labor costs. Last year, Kimberly-Clark posted a 51% rise in net income to $1.67 billion on $13 billion in sales, capping three years of improving results.

For Costco, the benefits of such close cooperation with a major supplier are equally clear: Costco saves money not only on staffing in its inventory department, but also on storage.

Source: Republished with permission of the *Wall Street Journal* from "Kimberly-Clark Keeps Costco in Diapers, Absorbing Costs Itself" by E. Nelson and A. Zimmerman (September 7, 2000). Permission conveyed through Copyright Clearance Center, Inc.

Items Included in Inventory

All inventory items to which the firm has legal title should be included in the inventory account. However, in day-to-day operations, most firms do not attempt to use the passage of legal title as the criterion for including items in the inventory records, since this would be a time-consuming process. Instead, firms adopt the expedient of recording inventory only when it is physically received.

The use of this physical-receipt expedient creates no difficulties except when it comes time to prepare financial statements. At that time, the firm must determine whether all goods that were in fact legally owned have been included in the inventory account. Goods in transit are the primary concern, since legal title to such goods may transfer to the purchaser before they are physically received by the purchaser. The purchaser determines the legal status of goods in transit by examining invoices pertaining to goods received during the first few days of the next accounting period, and then uses this information to determine precisely when title passed.

Sometimes goods may be physically in the possession of a firm but not legally owned by the firm. One example is goods shipped on **consignment.** Here, the firm that holds the goods (the consignee) acts as an agent for the owner (the consignor) in selling the goods. The consignee receives a sales commission and forwards the net sales price (after deducting the commission and any selling expenses) to the consignor. Consignment goods should not be included in the inventory of the consignee; instead, they must appear as part of the inventory of the consignor, the legal owner.

> Consignment goods also raise potential revenue recognition issues for the consignor that analysts must consider. For example, manufacturers may ship products to their dealers on consignment and nevertheless try to treat such shipments as sales, thereby recognizing income prematurely. Consequently, if "sales" terms provide the "purchaser" with the right to return unsold goods or if the cash payment terms on the "sale" are unusually long, it is possible that the manufacturer has treated consignment shipments as sales, thereby overstating both sales revenues and income and understating inventory (see Chapter 3).

ANALYSIS

Costs Included in Inventory

The carrying cost of inventory should include all costs required to obtain physical possession and to put the merchandise in saleable condition. This includes the purchase cost, sales taxes and transportation costs paid by the purchaser, insurance costs, and storage costs. For a manufacturing firm, inventory costs also include those production costs—such as labor and overhead—that are incurred in making a finished saleable product.[2]

In principle, inventory costs should also include the costs of the purchasing department and other general administrative costs associated with the acquisition and distribution of inventory. As a practical matter, however, such costs are extremely difficult to associate with individual purchases and would have to be allocated on some arbitrary basis. From a cost-benefit perspective, the effort that would be expended in trying to assign these indirect inventory costs to unit purchases generally exceeds the benefits. That's why inventory cost shown in the accounting records is usually limited to *direct* acquisition and processing costs that can be objectively associated with specific goods. Costs that do not meet this criterion—such as purchasing department costs—are generally treated as period costs and expensed in the period in which they arise. Cash purchase discounts that are lost because of late payment represent interest expense rather than a cost of acquiring inventory. These costs are excluded from inventory and expensed.

Manufacturing Costs

The inventory costs of a manufacturer include raw material, labor, and certain overhead items. Costs of this type are called **product costs.** Product costs are assigned to inventory

[2] In certain cases interest incurred during the time that inventory is being developed for sale can be capitalized, as described in Chapter 10. Examples include discrete projects such as shipbuilding or real estate development—that is, cases in which money is borrowed to finance construction over several reporting periods. See *Statement of Financial Accounting Standards (SFAS) No. 34,* "Capitalization of Interest Cost" (Stamford, CT: Financial Accounting Standards Board [FASB], October 1979).

and treated as assets until the inventory is sold. When sold, the inventory carrying value is charged to cost of goods sold, and at that point all inventoried costs become an expense.

A manufacturer also incurs costs not considered to be closely associated with production. Examples include general administrative costs (such as the president's salary) and selling costs. These costs are not inventoried. Instead, they are treated as expenses of the period in which they are incurred and are called **period costs.**

The flow of product costs through the inventory accounts and, eventually, to the cost-of-goods-sold account is illustrated in Exhibit 9.1.

Exhibit 9.1 ■ FLOW OF PRODUCT COSTS FOR MANUFACTURING BUSINESSES

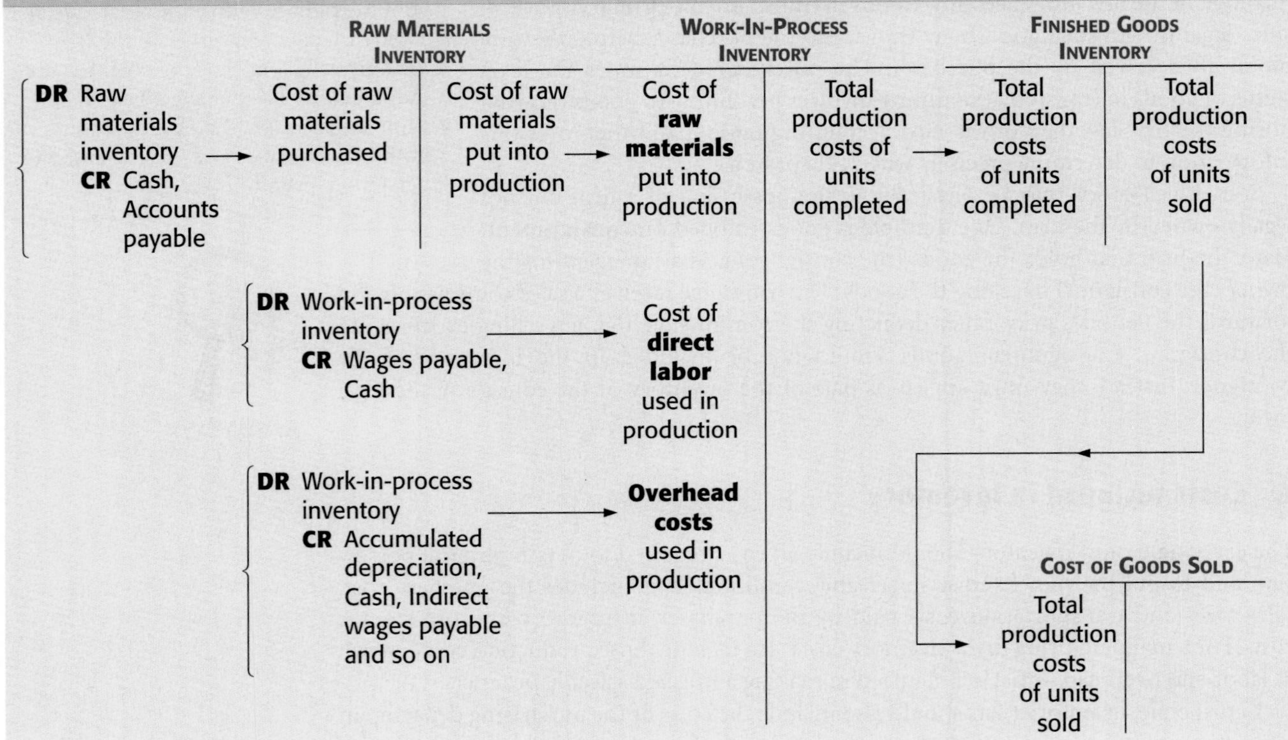

Absorption Costing Versus Variable Costing

As indicated in Exhibit 9.1, manufacturing overhead costs comprise one element of product costs and are accordingly included in inventory. However, there are two views regarding the appropriate treatment of ***fixed*** manufacturing overhead costs. One view is called **variable costing** (or direct costing), while the other view is called **absorption costing** (or full costing).

Variable costing includes in inventory only the variable costs of production. **Variable costs** are those that change in proportion to the level of production. Examples include raw materials cost, direct labor, and certain overhead items such as electricity used in running production equipment. **Fixed costs** of production are costs that do not change as production levels change. Examples include rental of production facilities, depreciation of production equipment, and property taxes. ***When variable costing is used, these fixed overhead costs are not included as part of inventory cost.*** Instead, fixed production overhead costs are treated as period costs and are expensed in the period in which they are incurred.

The logic underlying variable costing is that incurred costs are considered to be includable in inventory only if they provide future benefits to the firm. Proponents of variable costing argue that fixed production overhead costs are *not* assets since they expire in the period in which they are incurred and thus do not provide future benefit to the firm. For example, factory insurance carried in June provides no benefit after June 30; for insurance protection in July, another month's premium must be paid. But future benefits *do* derive from variable costs such as materials used in production; once materials have been purchased and used in making an inventory unit, that cost can be "stored" and will provide a future benefit when the inventory is eventually sold. These kinds of costs are considered to be includable in inventory under variable costing.

Under absorption costing, all production costs are inventoried. Fixed production overhead costs are not written-off to expense as incurred. Instead they are treated as product costs and carried as assets in the appropriate inventory accounts. The rationale is that *both* variable and fixed production costs are assets since *both* are needed to produce a saleable product.

Both absorption costing and variable costing treat all selling, general, and administrative (SG&A) costs as period costs. These SG&A costs are *never* inventoried under *any* circumstances under either method. Table 9.1 shows the treatment of costs by category under each inventory costing approach. The only cost category treated differently is fixed production overhead, which is highlighted in the table.

VALUATION

The variable and absorption costing alternatives provide statement readers with potentially very different pictures of year-to-year changes in performance—that is, the trend of earnings over a series of years can differ markedly under the two approaches, as we will illustrate. These different earnings trends could influence analysts' forecasts. Analysts must understand the financial statement effects of *both* methods even though ***generally accepted accounting principles do not allow variable costing to be used in external financial statements.*** Accounting rules require inventory cost to include both fixed and variable production costs; therefore, ***only absorption costing is permitted under GAAP.***

International Accounting Standards (IAS) also require the use of absorption costing. See IAS 2 (revised 1993), "Inventories" (London: International Accounting Standards Committee, 1993, para. 10.) GAAP in most non-U.S. settings also requires absorption costing. Mexican GAAP permits variable costing, but it is not widely used.

Unfortunately, absorption costing makes it difficult to interpret year-to-year changes in reported income. These problems arise when inventory levels change between one year and the next. This is illustrated in the example whose basic assumptions are shown in Exhibit 9.2 on the following page.

Over the two years in the example, there was a constant selling price, constant variable production costs per unit (e.g., material, labor, and variable overhead) and constant total fixed production costs. Units produced increased in 2002 (125,000 versus 100,000 in 2001), but units sold in 2002 dropped (90,000 versus 110,000 units in 2001).

Exhibit 9.3 shows that reported GAAP gross margin under FIFO absorption costing increases from $110,000 in 2001 to $130,000 in 2002—an 18.2% increase. Income *increases* despite the fact that variable production cost and selling price per unit were constant, fixed cost did not change in total, and unit sales decreased.

Table 9.1 ■ SUMMARY OF COST TREATMENT BY CATEGORY UNDER VARIABLE AND ABSORPTION COSTING

Cost Category	Inventoried under Variable Costing?	Inventoried under Absorption Costing?
Production materials	Yes	Yes
Production labor	Yes	Yes
Variable production overhead	Yes	Yes
Fixed production overhead	No	Yes
Selling, general and administrative	No	No

Exhibit 9.2 ■ ABSORPTION VERSUS VARIABLE COSTING ILLUSTRATION

Selling price and cost data:
Selling price = $8 per unit in both 2001 and 2002
Variable production costs = $3 per unit in both 2001 and 2002
Fixed production costs = $400,000 per year in both 2001 and 2002
Beginning inventory (FIFO basis), January 1, 2001 = 50,000 units @ $7

Production and sales volume data:	2001	2002
Units produced	100,000	125,000
Units sold	110,000	90,000
Ending inventory (in units)*	40,000	75,000

*Computations—2001: 50,000 + 100,000 − 110,000 = 40,000 units
2002: 40,000 + 125,000 − 90,000 = 75,000 units

Exhibit 9.3 ■ ABSORPTION VERSUS VARIABLE COSTING STATEMENTS: CONTRASTING THE OUTCOMES

Absorption Cost Income Statements (GAAP)

2001			2002		
Sales revenues (110,000 @ $8)		$880,000	Sales revenues (90,000 @ $8)		$720,000
Cost of goods sold:			Cost of goods sold:		
From beginning inventory (50,000 @ $7)	$350,000		From beginning inventory (40,000 @ $7)	$280,000	
From 2001 production (60,000 @ $7*)	420,000		From 2002 production (50,000 @ $6.20**)	310,000	
		(770,000)			(590,000)
GAAP Gross margin		$110,000	GAAP Gross margin		$130,000
Gross margin %		12.50%	Gross margin %		18.06%
Ending inventory: 40,000 units @ $7*			Ending inventory: 75,000 units @ $6.20**		
*This cost is determined as follows:			**This cost is determined as follows:		
Variable production costs (given)	$3.00/unit		Variable production costs (given)	$3.00/unit	
Fixed production costs, unitized $400,000/100,000 =	4.00/unit		Fixed production costs, unitized $400,000/125,000 =	3.20/unit	
Total production cost for 2001	$7.00/unit		Total production cost for 2002	$6.20/unit	

Variable Cost Income Statements (Not GAAP)

2001			2002		
Sales revenues (110,000 @ $8)		$880,000	Sales revenues (90,000 @ $8)		$720,000
Variable cost of goods sold:			Variable cost of goods sold:		
From beginning inventory (50,000 @ $3)	$150,000		From beginning inventory (40,000 @ $3)	$120,000	
From 2001 production (60,000 @ $3)	180,000		From 2002 production (50,000 @ $3)	150,000	
		(330,000)			(270,000)
Variable contribution margin		550,000	Variable contribution margin		450,000
Less: Fixed production costs treated as a period expense		(400,000)	Less: Fixed production costs treated as a period expense		(400,000)
Variable cost gross margin		$150,000	Variable cost gross margin		$ 50,000
Gross margin %		17.05%	Gross margin %		6.94%
Ending inventory: 40,000 units @ $3			Ending inventory: 75,000 units @ $3		

Why do we get this strange result? The answer reveals a major deficiency of absorption cost financial statements. Production increased in 2002 to 125,000 units and exceeded sales, which totaled 90,000 units. Inventory therefore increased by 35,000 units (125,000 minus 90,000) to a year-end total of 75,000 units. When inventory increases under absorption costing, as in this illustration, the amount of fixed cost assigned to inventory increases. ***As inventory absorbs more fixed cost, less fixed cost gets charged to the income statement and income goes up.*** Very large inventory increases produce a favorable income effect that can offset an unfavorable income effect caused, say, by a sales decrease. This is what happened in Exhibit 9.3, and it is this effect that explains the jump in 2002 income.

> In Exhibit 9.3, the fixed costs in inventory at January 1, 2002, totaled $160,000 (i.e., 40,000 units times $4 of fixed cost per ***unit***). At December 31, 2002, fixed cost included in inventory had risen to $240,000 (i.e., 75,000 units times $3.20 of fixed cost per unit).

By contrast, variable cost income in Exhibit 9.3 falls from $150,000 in 2001 to $50,000 in 2002. Critics of absorption costing contend that in situations similar to this example, variable costing better reflects underlying economics. Nonetheless, external financial statements must conform to absorption costing, as required by GAAP.

Generalizing from this example, the mechanics of absorption costing can lead to year-to-year income changes that may delude the unwary. This can happen whenever production and sales are not in balance—that is, whenever physical inventory levels (in units) are either increasing or decreasing. When the number of units in inventory is increasing, absorption cost gross margins tend to rise. This effect may be so large that it could obscure offsetting unfavorable effects (for example, sales decreases or deteriorating efficiency) that are taking place simultaneously. When physical inventory levels are decreasing, absorption cost income tends to fall, since fixed overhead that was previously in inventory gets charged against income as part of the cost of goods sold.

> Companies rarely disclose absorption costing effects on income. But Vacu-Dry Company did in its 1996 Annual Report:
>
> > In fiscal 1995, the increase in the cost of sales percentage was predominantly due to the lower production volume as a result of the decreased sales volume and the resultant *decrease in overhead absorption.* [Emphasis added.]

RECAP

To analyze comparative income statements, you must understand the mechanics of absorption costing and bear in mind that any imbalance between units produced and units sold may have a pronounced effect on reported income. Furthermore, the absorption cost income effect can obscure underlying economic changes of interest to statement readers. For example, a sudden, unexpected sales jump—clearly a good news event—may cause an inventory depletion. With GAAP absorption costing, the inventory reduction forces an additional dose of fixed overhead through the income statement, thereby masking part of the income benefit arising from the sales jump.

Cost Flow Assumptions: The Concepts

For most publicly-held firms, inventory is continuously purchased in large quantities. It is difficult to determine the purchase lot from which units have been sold, especially in firms where manufacturing alters the form of the raw materials acquired. Consider an automobile manufacturer. It's not easy to know what specific steel purchase batch was used in the hood of a specific car.

In a few industries, it is possible to identify which particular units have been sold. In retail businesses like jewelry stores and automobile dealerships, which sell a small number of high value items, cost of goods sold can be measured by reference to the known cost of the actual units sold. This inventory accounting method is called **specific identification.** But this method suffers from a serious deficiency, since specific identification makes it relatively easy to manipulate income. Consider a large jewelry dealer with three identical watches in inventory that were acquired at three different purchase costs. Under the specific identification method, the reported profit on sale can be raised (or lowered) by simply delivering the lowest (or highest) cost watch. An inventory method allowing latitude like this is open to criticism.

Specific identification is usually not feasible for most businesses. Even when it is feasible, it has some serious drawbacks, as just illustrated. For these reasons, a **cost flow assumption** is usually required to allocate goods available for sale between ending inventory and cost of goods sold—that is:

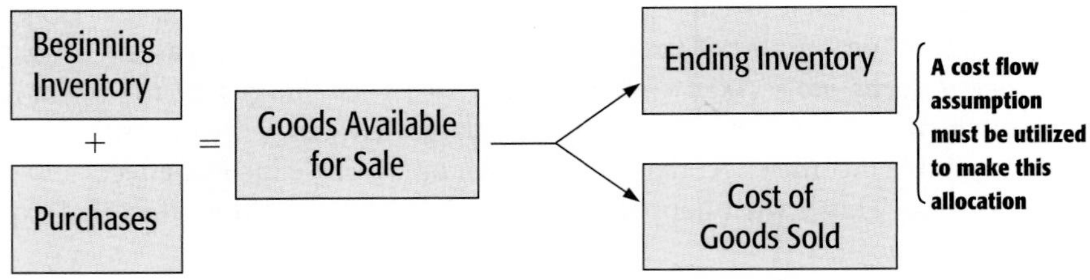

It is important to understand that GAAP does not require the cost flow assumption to conform to the actual physical flow of the goods.

International Accounting Standards designate FIFO and weighted average cost as the "benchmark" treatments. LIFO is an "allowed alternative" treatment. (See *IAS 2*, paras. 21–23.)

Six hundred companies were surveyed by the American Institute of Certified Public Accountants, and the inventory cost flow assumptions that they used, as shown in Table 9.2, indicate two things. First, the most popular inventory costing method is FIFO, followed closely by LIFO; weighted average cost is the next most popular method. Second, the total frequencies of all methods exceed the total number of firms surveyed (600), which means most firms use a combination of inventory costing methods. For example, of the 301 firms using LIFO in 1999, only 8% (24 firms) exclusively used LIFO for all inventories, largely because LIFO is prohibited in most countries outside the United States. Thus, U.S.-domiciled multinational companies that use LIFO for domestic inventories would usually be required to use some other cost flow assumption for their foreign subsidiary inventories.

Table 9.2 ■ FREQUENCY OF INVENTORY COST FLOW ASSUMPTIONS (1996–1999)

	Number of Companies			
	1999	**1998**	**1997**	**1996**
Methods				
First-in, first-out (FIFO)	404	409	415	417
Last-in, first-out (LIFO)	301	319	326	332
Weighted average cost	176	176	188	181
Other	34	40	32	37
Use of LIFO				
For all inventories	24	30	17	15
50% or more of inventories	159	152	170	178
Less than 50% of inventories	83	95	99	92
Not determinable	35	42	40	47
Companies Using LIFO	**301**	**319**	**326**	**332**

Source: A. Mrakovcic (ed.) *Accounting Trends and Techniques,* 2000. Copyright by the American Institute of Certified Public Accountants, Inc. Reprinted with permission.

Let's revisit the refrigerator dealer to explore the underlying cost flow concepts. This simple example highlights key issues without cluttering the analysis with details that hinder comprehension. Recall the facts of the example.

> The retailer started the year with a beginning inventory of one refrigerator, which had an invoice cost of $300. During the year, the dealer-cost of identical refrigerators increased to $340. Assume that the retailer purchases another refrigerator at this $340 cost. At the end of the year, one of the two refrigerators is sold for $500.

First-In, First-Out (FIFO) Cost Flow

The first-in, first-out (FIFO) method assumes the oldest units available in inventory are the first units that are sold. This means that ending inventory on the FIFO basis will always consist of the cost of the most recently acquired units. In the refrigerator example, the computations are:

Income statement:		
Sales revenues	$500	
Cost of goods sold (FIFO)	300	(Cost of oldest unit)
Net income	$200	
Balance sheet:		
Ending inventory (FIFO)	$340	(Cost of newest unit)

FIFO cost flow for a more realistic case, one in which numerous purchases and sales are made throughout the year, is shown in Figure 9.1.The FIFO cost flow in this diagram illustrates that sales are presumed to have been made from the oldest available goods (in this case, from beginning inventory and the goods purchased in January through September) and that ending inventory consists of the most recently acquired goods (October through December).

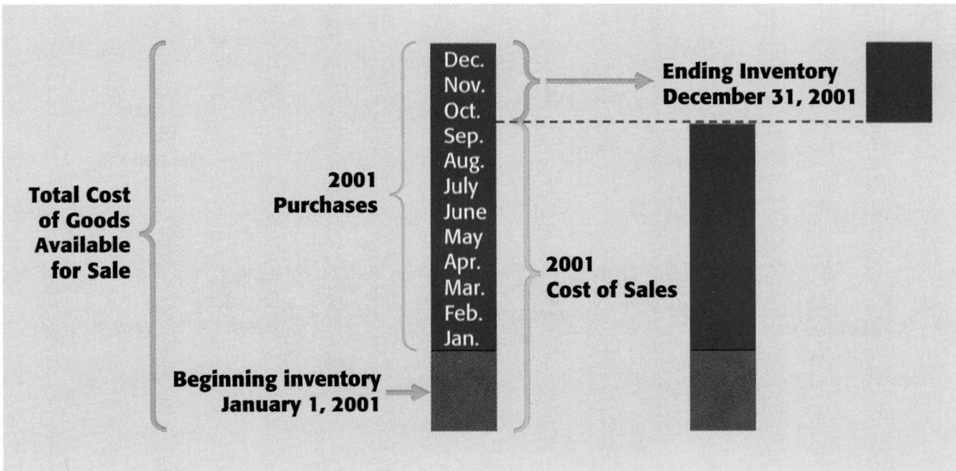

Figure 9.1

FIFO COST FLOW

FIFO charges the oldest costs against revenues on the income statement. This characteristic is often viewed as a deficiency of the FIFO method, since the current cost of replacing the units sold is not being matched with current revenues. However, on the balance sheet, FIFO inventory represents the most recent purchases and—if inventory turnover is reasonably rapid—-will usually approximate current replacement cost.

Last-In, First-Out (LIFO) Cost Flow

The last-in, first-out (LIFO) method presumes sales were made from the most recently acquired units. In the refrigerator example, the computations are:

Income statement:		
Sales revenues	$500	
Cost of goods sold (LIFO)	340	(Cost of newest unit)
Net income	$160	
Balance sheet:		
Ending inventory (LIFO)	$300	(Cost of oldest unit)

This method will seldom correspond to the actual physical flow of goods, but remember, GAAP does not require conformity between the assumed cost flow and the physical flow of units.

LIFO matches the most recently incurred costs against revenues. When purchases and sales occur continuously, the most recently incurred costs will be virtually identical to current replacement cost. So LIFO provides a good match between current costs and current revenues. But on the balance sheet, LIFO inventory consists of the oldest costs ($300 in the refrigerator example), which usually will not approximate the current replacement cost of inventory.

For firms that have used the LIFO method for many years, the LIFO inventory amount may reflect only a small fraction of what it would cost to replace this inventory at today's prices. A diagram of LIFO cost flow in Figure 9.2 shows how old **layers** can accumulate in ending inventory.

Figure 9.2

LIFO COST FLOW

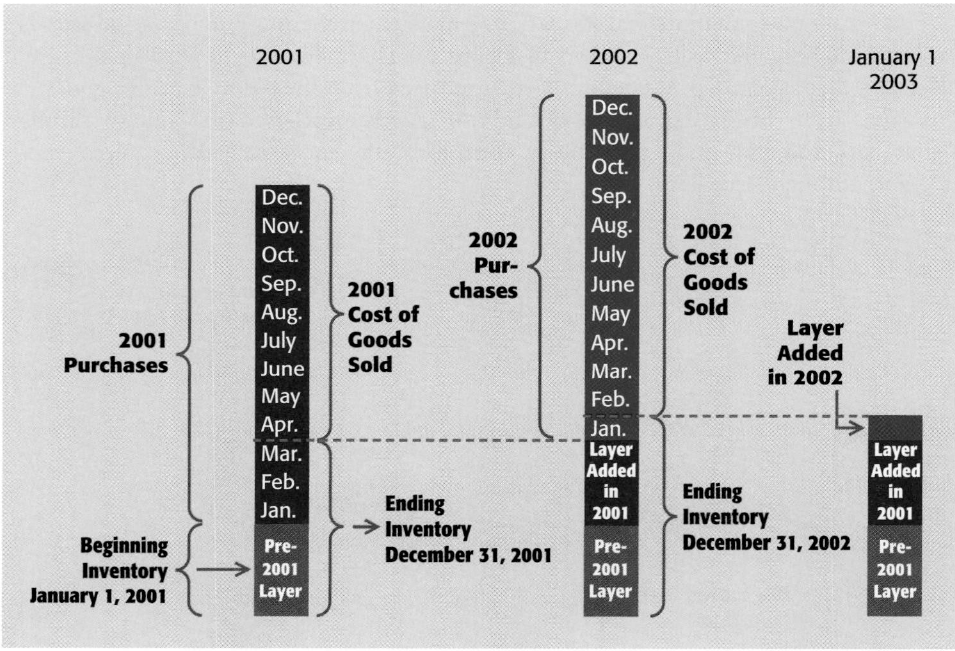

As Figure 9.2 shows, when purchases exceed sales in any year, a new LIFO layer is formed. New inventory layers are valued using the *oldest* costs incurred during that year. For example, the LIFO layer added in 2001 is comprised of the inventory purchase costs expended from January through March 2001. Since sales under LIFO are always presumed to have been made from the most recent purchases, the 2001 LIFO layer will remain on the books at the end of 2002 as long as units sold in 2002 do not exceed units purchased in 2002. As Figure 9.2 shows, not only did the 2001 LIFO layer remain, but a small additional LIFO layer was added in 2002, because unit purchases exceeded unit sales. A firm that has been on LIFO since, say, 1954 could still be carrying a portion of its inventory at 1954 costs, a portion at 1955 costs, and so on.

FIFO, LIFO, and Inventory Holding Gains

FIFO and LIFO give different financial statement results because each method treats inventory holding gains and losses in a different way. To understand the differences, we first need to understand inventory holding gains and losses.

Inventory holding gains and losses are the input cost changes that occur following the purchase of inventory. Let's go back to the refrigerator example. Assume the replacement cost of each refrigerator at the end of the year was $340. However, both FIFO and LIFO are historical cost methods, and therefore goods available for sale will reflect only the *historical cost* that was paid to acquire the two units on hand:

Beginning inventory (1 unit @ $300)	$300
Purchases (1 unit @ $340)	+ 340
Historical cost of goods available for sale	$640

Notice that historical cost accounting ignores the $40 holding gain that arose on the unit of beginning inventory as its replacement cost increased from $300 to $340. Thus, goods available for sale are shown at their historical cost of $640 rather than at their current replacement cost of $680 (i.e., to replace the two units would cost $340 each).

There is an accounting method called **current cost accounting** that records holding gains on financial statements as they arise. ***Because it is a departure from historical cost, this method is not permitted in the basic financial statements.*** However, the FASB does allow voluntary supplementary disclosure of current cost data in the annual report.[3]

> The holding gain takes place as the replacement cost of the inventory increases. But since the gain has not yet been included in income, it is an **unrealized holding gain.** Once the gain gets included in income (as described in this section), it is a **realized holding gain.**

In a current cost (non-GAAP) accounting system, the following entry would be made at the time that inventory replacement cost increases:

DR Inventory	$40	
CR Unrealized holding gain		$40

The "Unrealized holding gain" account represents an owners' equity increase. Whether these holding gains should be treated as a component of net income or instead included in other comprehensive income is a controversial issue that we discuss in Chapter 18. In this chapter we ignore the controversy and treat holding gains as an element of other comprehensive income.

Once the holding gains entry has been made, the *current* cost of goods available for sale is:

Beginning inventory (1 unit @ $300)	$300
Increase in the replacement cost of beginning inventory	+40
Purchases (1 unit @ $340)	+340
Current cost of goods available for sale (2 units @ $340)	$680

When the unit is sold for $500, the partial financial statements under current cost are:

Income statement:	
Sales revenues	$500
Replacement cost of goods sold (1 unit @ $340)	340
Current cost operating profit	$160
Balance sheet:	
Ending inventory	$340

The current cost operating profit figure is the margin that results from matching current replacement cost against current revenues. It reflects the expected ongoing profitability of current operations at current levels of costs and selling prices.

Figure 9.3 on the following page contrasts the treatment of goods available for sale under (a) historical cost accounting and (b) current cost accounting. Notice that the total amount to be allocated between inventory and cost of goods sold is $40 higher under current costing ($680 versus $640). This difference is attributable to the holding gain that

[3] "Financial Reporting and Changing Prices," *Statement of Financial Accounting Standards No. 89* (Stamford, CT: FASB, 1986).

Figure 9.3

ALLOCATION OF GOODS AVAILABLE FOR SALE: HISTORICAL COSTING VERSUS CURRENT COSTING:
(a) Historical Cost of Goods Available for Sale = $640; and
(b) Current Cost of Goods Available for Sale = $680

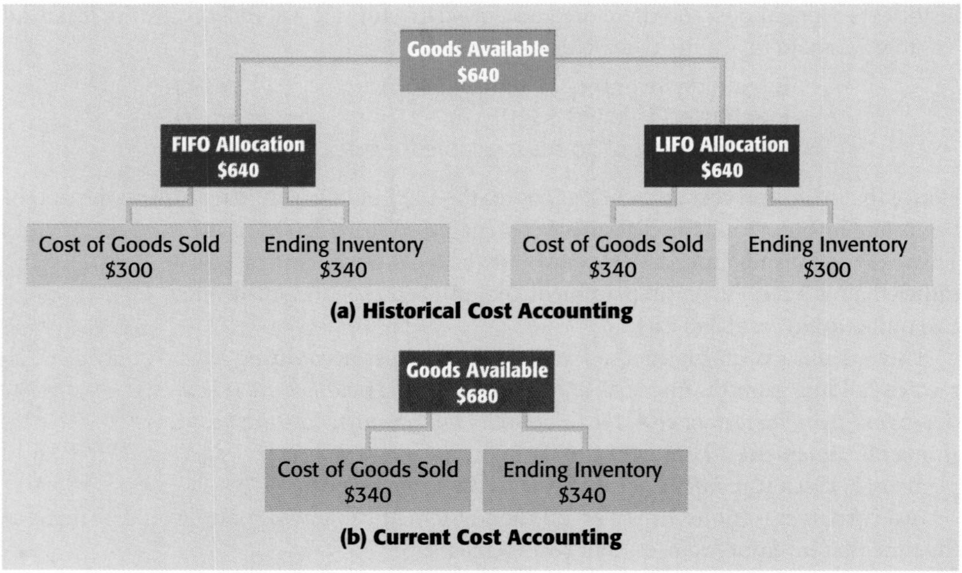

was added to goods available for sale under current costing. With current costing, the total to be allocated is carried at current cost (two units at $340 each, for a total of $680). ***This means that the balance sheet inventory number and the cost of goods sold number are both shown at current cost.***

By contrast, the historical cost figures for goods available for sale under both FIFO and LIFO ($640) are $40 less than the total current cost of the two units available ($680). This means that under either LIFO or FIFO it is impossible to simultaneously reflect both inventory *and* cost of goods sold at current cost: One can be shown at current cost, but the other must then be shown at historical cost. ***The primary difference between FIFO and LIFO is that each method makes a different choice regarding which element is shown at the out-of-date cost.*** FIFO shows inventory at approximately[4] current cost but is then forced to reflect cost of goods sold at historical cost. LIFO shows cost of goods sold at approximately current cost but is then forced to reflect inventory on the balance sheet at historical cost.

Inventory quantity decreases—reductions in physical units in inventory—can produce a distortion known as a LIFO liquidation, discussed later in the chapter.

When input costs are rising, LIFO income will be lower than FIFO income as long as inventory quantities remain constant or increase. In the refrigerator example, LIFO income is $160, whereas FIFO income is $200. Income is *lower under LIFO because LIFO charges the new, higher cost units to cost of goods sold.*

The income number under LIFO will *usually* (but not always) closely approximate the income number under current costing:

LIFO Income		**Current Cost Income**	
Sales revenues	$500	Sales revenues	$500
Cost of goods sold	340	Replacement cost of goods sold	340
LIFO operating profit	$160	Current cost operating profit	$160

When purchases occur continuously, this near equivalence exists because LIFO charges the most recently acquired goods to cost of goods sold.

Now let's reexamine the FIFO income number. ***By charging the oldest costs to the income statement, FIFO automatically includes in income the holding gain on the unit that was***

[4] In our example, FIFO inventory is shown at *exactly* current cost. In more complicated situations that occur in real organizations, FIFO inventory amounts will *approximate* current costs. The faster the inventory turnover (cost of goods sold divided by average inventory), the closer will be the correspondence between inventory at FIFO cost and inventory at replacement cost.

sold. This result is seen by comparing the total income figures under FIFO and current costing:

FIFO Income		**Current Cost Income**	
Sales revenues	$500	Sales revenues	$500
Cost of goods sold	300	Replacement cost of goods sold	340
FIFO operating profit	$200	Current cost operating profit	$160

A comparison of the two income numbers shows that FIFO income is $40 higher. This $40 difference is, of course, the holding gain on the oldest refrigerator, which is the one that the FIFO assumption considers to have been sold. Another way to visualize this income difference is to decompose FIFO income into its component parts.

Components of FIFO Income	
Current cost operating profit	$160
Holding gain on unit considered sold	40
FIFO operating profit	$200

This reformulation tells us that FIFO income comprises two components:

- Current cost operating profit of $160
- A realized holding gain of $40 on the unit that was sold.

Remember, the notion of "current cost operating profit" represents a matching against sales revenue of the then-current replacement cost of the inventory at the time of sale.

While these components are easy to extract in the refrigerator example, in actual financial statements the components of FIFO profit are not disclosed and only the total figure is reported.

Some analysts argue that by merging current cost operating profits and realized holding gains, FIFO gives misleading signals about the sustainable operating profits of the company. For example, operating profit is generally considered to be potentially sustainable if existing conditions continue. By contrast, holding gains are dependent on external price increases, which may or may not be sustainable. But FIFO gives the impression that operating profit is $200, thus suggesting that $200—not $160—is sustainable. Because the higher FIFO income number includes potentially unsustainable gains, that $40 portion of FIFO income is considered to represent low quality earnings.[5]

ANALYSIS

But remember, LIFO is also an historical cost accounting method with its own deficiencies. There is only $640 (rather than $680) to allocate between cost of goods sold and inventory in our refrigerator example. Because LIFO allocates the most recent cost of $340 to the income statement, that leaves only $300—the old historical cost—for allocation to the balance sheet. Therefore, the LIFO balance sheet inventory number will not reflect current replacement cost. This leads to another set of issues that further cloud financial reporting. Let's examine them.

The LIFO Reserve Disclosure

Because LIFO inventory costs on the balance sheet frequently include old inventory layers, they are carried at amounts that are much lower than FIFO inventory amounts. This can make it very difficult to compare LIFO versus FIFO firms meaningfully. To remedy this difficulty, the Securities and Exchange Commission adopted a disclosure policy in 1974 that requires LIFO firms to disclose the dollar magnitude of the difference between LIFO and FIFO inventory costs. This disclosure is called the **LIFO reserve** and must be reported at each balance sheet date. Exhibit 9.4, from the

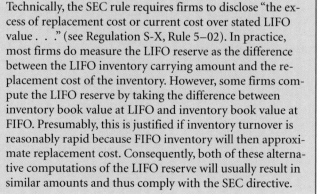

Technically, the SEC rule requires firms to disclose "the excess of replacement cost or current cost over stated LIFO value . . ." (see Regulation S-X, Rule 5–02). In practice, most firms do measure the LIFO reserve as the difference between the LIFO inventory carrying amount and the replacement cost of the inventory. However, some firms compute the LIFO reserve by taking the difference between inventory book value at LIFO and inventory book value at FIFO. Presumably, this is justified if inventory turnover is reasonably rapid because FIFO inventory will then approximate replacement cost. Consequently, both of these alternative computations of the LIFO reserve will usually result in similar amounts and thus comply with the SEC directive.

[5] See, for example, J. G. Siegel, "The 'Quality of Earnings' Concept—A Survey," *Financial Analysts Journal* (March–April 1982), pp. 60–68.

Exhibit 9.4 ■ VACU-DRY COMPANY

Inventories footnote disclosure

	June 30 1996	June 30 1995
Inventories [at LIFO]		
Finished goods	$ 2,757,000	$4,926,000
Work-in-process	233,000	239,000
Raw materials and containers	440,000	249,000
Total	$3,430,000	$5,414,000

Disclosure on the face of the balance sheet

	June 30 1996	June 30 1995
Inventories, less LIFO reserves of $2,114,000 and $1,334,000 in 1996 and 1995, respectively	$3,430,000	$5,414,000

Source: Vacu-Dry Company 1996 Annual Report

Vacu-Dry Company 1996 annual report, illustrates a typical disclosure of this divergence between LIFO and FIFO inventory amounts. (Vacu-Dry is a California firm that produces and markets fruit products.)

The disclosure in Exhibit 9.4 provides statement readers with an important tool. By adding the reported LIFO reserve amount at June 30, 1996 to the June 30, 1996 balance sheet LIFO inventory number, one can estimate June 30, 1996 FIFO inventory. Specifically, the sum of the ending LIFO inventory ($3,430,000) and the fiscal year end LIFO reserve ($2,114,000) totals $5,544,000. This sum represents an estimate of June 30, 1996 FIFO ending inventory of Vacu-Dry. Notice that this result immediately follows from the definition of the LIFO reserve, which is the difference between FIFO inventory amounts and LIFO inventory amounts—that is:

$$\text{Inventory}_{\text{FIFO}} \quad - \quad \text{Inventory}_{\text{LIFO}} \quad = \quad \text{LIFO Reserve}$$
$$\$5{,}544{,}000 \quad - \quad \$3{,}430{,}000 \quad = \quad \$2{,}114{,}000$$

Therefore, rearranging the equation yields the following:

$$\text{Inventory}_{\text{FIFO}} \quad = \quad \text{Inventory}_{\text{LIFO}} \quad + \quad \text{LIFO Reserve}$$
$$\$5{,}544{,}000 \quad = \quad \$3{,}430{,}000 \quad + \quad \$2{,}114{,}000$$

Thus, one can think of the FIFO inventory cost as being comprised of LIFO inventory cost plus a LIFO reserve adjustment which measures the difference between the current cost of inventory units and the historical cost of all LIFO layers. The LIFO reserve disclosure allows the analyst to convert reported LIFO inventory amounts to FIFO amounts. This adjustment can be performed for all dates for which LIFO reserve amounts are disclosed. To illustrate this point specifically, a similar adjustment using the beginning LIFO reserve disclosure in Exhibit 9.4 can also be made to estimate Vacu-Dry's June 30, 1995 FIFO inventory:

> Remember, this conversion to FIFO is an approximation. As long as inventory turns fairly rapidly, the approximation is close.

$$\text{Inventory}_{\text{FIFO}} \quad = \quad \text{Inventory}_{\text{LIFO}} \quad + \quad \text{LIFO Reserve}$$
$$\$6{,}748{,}000 \quad = \quad \$5{,}414{,}000 \quad + \quad \$1{,}334{,}000$$

FIFO inventory at June 30, 1995 equals $6,748,000. This number is also, of course, the FIFO beginning inventory for July 1, 1995.

Using the LIFO reserve disclosure in this way also makes it possible for analysts to convert LIFO cost of goods sold to a FIFO basis. This is most easily understood by looking at the basic cost-of-goods-sold formula in column (1) of Exhibit 9.5. Notice that both the beginning and ending inventory *and* the cost-of-goods-sold amounts in column (1) are

Exhibit 9.5 ■ ADJUSTING COST OF GOODS SOLD FROM LIFO TO FIFO

(1)		(2)		(3)
Beginning Inventory$_{LIFO}$	+	**Beginning LIFO Reserve**	=	**Beginning Inventory$_{FIFO}$**
Plus: Purchases				Plus: Purchases
Equals: Goods Available$_{LIFO}$				Equals: Goods Available$_{FIFO}$
Minus: **Ending Inventory$_{LIFO}$**	+	**Ending LIFO Reserve**	=	Minus: **Ending Inventory$_{FIFO}$**
Equals:				Equals:
Cost of Goods Sold$_{LIFO}$	− / +	**Increase in LIFO Reserve** or **Decrease in LIFO Reserve**	=	**Costs of Goods Sold$_{FIFO}$**

measured at LIFO. (Inventory purchases represent the actual events of the period and do not require a cost flow assumption.) Column (2) shows the addition of the respective LIFO reserves to beginning and ending LIFO inventory. As we just saw, the sum that results from this addition yields FIFO inventory amounts, which are shown in column (3). Using the basic cost-of-goods-sold formula on the column (3) FIFO numbers plus actual purchases yields FIFO cost of goods sold. Thus, the LIFO reserve disclosures make it possible to convert LIFO cost of goods sold to a FIFO basis.

We apply this adjustment process to convert Vacu-Dry's reported LIFO cost-of-goods-sold number to a FIFO basis in Exhibit 9.6. FIFO cost of goods sold is $23,362,000. To make valid comparisons across firms that use different inventory accounting methods, you must make adjustments like those in Exhibit 9.6.

A shortcut procedure can be used to convert cost of goods sold from LIFO to FIFO. The shortcut focuses on the *change* in the LIFO reserve between the beginning and end of the year, as reflected at the bottom of column (2) in Exhibit 9.5. (This shortcut avoids the need to successively add the respective LIFO reserve amounts to beginning and ending inventory.) Applying this shortcut adjustment to the Vacu-Dry data given in Exhibit 9.6, we see that the change in the LIFO reserve was an *increase* of $780,000 (i.e., $1,334,000 at the start of the fiscal year versus $2,114,000 at the end of the year) and that LIFO cost of goods

Exhibit 9.6 ■ VACU-DRY COMPANY

Adjusting From LIFO to FIFO Cost of Goods Sold

($ in thousands)	As Reported in Financial Statements (LIFO)		LIFO Reserve		Adjusted to FIFO Basis
Beginning inventory, July 1, 1995	$ 5,414	+	$1,334	=	$ 6,748
Purchases	22,158				22,158
Goods available	27,572				28,906
Ending inventory, June 30, 1996	3,430	+	2,114	=	5,544
Cost of goods sold	$24,142	−	$ 780 increase	=	$23,362

sold exceeds FIFO cost of goods sold by $780,000. So, when the LIFO reserve amount *increases,* the shortcut conversion procedure is:

$$\text{Cost of goods sold}_{\text{LIFO}} - \text{Increase in LIFO reserve} = \text{Cost of goods sold}_{\text{FIFO}}$$

When the LIFO reserve amount *decreases,* the conversion is:

$$\text{Cost of goods sold}_{\text{LIFO}} + \text{Decrease in LIFO reserve} = \text{Cost of goods sold}_{\text{FIFO}}$$

The adjustment process can provide insights about inventory price movements. For example, since LIFO cost of goods sold is higher than FIFO cost of goods sold, we know inventory purchase costs incurred by Vacu-Dry were rising during 1996.

Vacu-Dry uses LIFO for all of its inventory. But as we saw in Table 9.2, most companies use a combination of inventory cost flow assumptions. This is illustrated in the following disclosure from the 2000 Winn-Dixie Stores, Inc., annual report:

> Inventories are stated at the lower of cost or market. The "dollar value" last-in, first-out (LIFO) method is used to determine the cost of approximately 84% of inventories consisting primarily of merchandise in stores and distribution warehouses. Manufacturing, pharmacy and produce inventories are valued at the lower of first-in, first-out (FIFO) cost or market. . . . At June 28, 2000, inventories valued by the LIFO method would have been $232,368 higher ($217,274 higher at June 30, 1999) if they were stated at the lower of FIFO cost or market.

The LIFO-to-FIFO adjustment for a company like Winn-Dixie, which uses LIFO for only a portion of its inventory, is identical to the method used in Exhibit 9.6 for Vacu-Dry. The beginning and ending LIFO reserves are added, respectively, to beginning and ending reported inventory amounts. It doesn't matter that LIFO was used for only 84% of the inventory. By adding the LIFO reserve to the reported inventory, *the LIFO portion is adjusted* and what results is inventory on a 100% FIFO basis.

Under both FIFO and LIFO, the allocation of costs between ending inventory and cost of goods sold is limited to the *historical* costs incurred. As costs change, LIFO puts the "oldest" costs on the balance sheet, while FIFO runs the "oldest" costs through the income statement. The LIFO reserve disclosure permits analysts to transform LIFO financial statements to a FIFO basis, thus making comparisons between firms more meaningful when one firm is using LIFO and the other FIFO.

RECAP

Inflation, LIFO Reserves, and the LIFO Effect on Income

Figure 9.4 provides descriptive statistics on the magnitude of LIFO reserves and the LIFO income effect for a broad cross-section of firms that used LIFO for all or part of their inventories from 1976 to 1998.[6] Figure 9.4(a) shows the median LIFO reserve amount stated as a percentage of stockholders' equity along with the 25th and 75th percentile values.[7] Figure 9.4(c) shows the median, 25th, and 75th percentile values of the *change* in LIFO reserve each year stated as a percentage of the absolute value of pre-tax income for that year. The change in LIFO reserve shows how much higher (lower) the cost of goods sold is under LIFO as compared to FIFO and, hence, how much lower (higher) pre-tax LIFO income is as compared to FIFO income. Finally, Figure 9.4(b) relates the annual inflation rates (as

[6] The 1976 to 1991 data for these graphs are adapted from R. Jennings, P. J. Simko, and R. B. Thompson, II, "Does LIFO Inventory Accounting Improve the Income Statement at the Expense of the Balance Sheet?" *Journal of Accounting Research* (Spring 1996), pp. 85–109. The data from 1992–1998 came from Standard & Poor's Research Insight.®

[7] The 75th percentile value is the value that is equal to or greater than the observation for 75% of the firms in the sample. Therefore, 25% of the firms will have an observed value that is *greater* than the 75th percentile.

measured by the percentage change in the Consumer Price Index) to the amounts reported in the (a) and (c) graphs over the 1976 to 1998 time frame.

The median LIFO reserve in Figure 9.4(a) ranged from a high of 13.3% of stockholders' equity in 1980 to low of 2.9% in 1998. Since stockholders' equity equals the book value of net assets (i.e., assets minus liabilities), the results in Figure 9.4(a) also reveal how much *higher* the reported net assets of firms would have been had they valued their LIFO inventories under the FIFO method. Clearly, the decision to use the LIFO inventory method reduces the net asset values below what they would have reported under the FIFO inventory method.

The LIFO pre-tax income in Figure 9.4(c) was substantially *lower* than what firms would have reported under the FIFO inventory method throughout the 1976–1998 time period. The median pre-tax LIFO "earnings effect" ranged from a reduction of 13.6% in 1979 to a reduction of 1.7% in 1997. In Figure 9.4(b) the higher LIFO reserves and larger LIFO earnings "drag" during 1976–1982 correspond to the relatively higher inflation rates

You may ask why the LIFO reserve amounts as a percentage of stockholders' equity show a general downward trend through the 1980s and early 1990s despite annual inflation rates from 4–6% in most years. With constant inventory levels (in units) and positive price increases from year to year, you would expect to see LIFO reserves that increase through time. The general downward trend in the LIFO reserve as a percentage of owners' equity from 1981 to 1998 can be explained by a combination of (1) the growing owners' equity through time; and (2) the increasing tendency of firms to reduce inventory *levels* throughout the 1980s and 1990s as they downsized and restructured their operations, and as they adopted just-in-time inventory management.

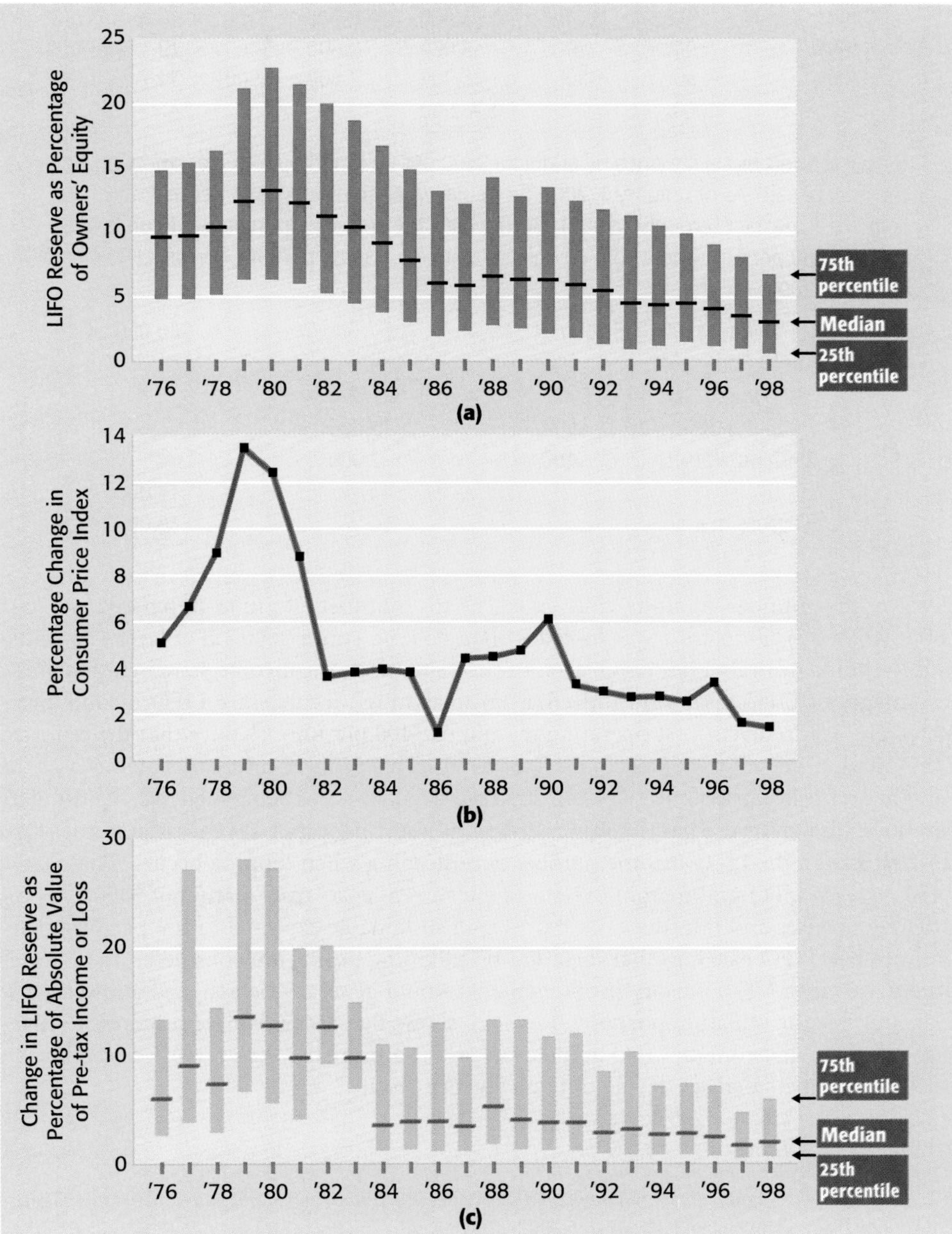

Figure 9.4

MAGNITUDE OF LIFO RESERVES AND LIFO EARNINGS EFFECT.

(a) Distribution of LIFO Reserve Amounts as a Percentage of Owners' Equity; (b) Percentage Change in CPI for Benchmark; and (c) LIFO Effect as Percentage of Pre-tax Income. (1976–1998).

Source: (a): R. Jennings, P. J. Simko, and R. B. Thompson, II, op. cit., 1976 to 1991; Standard & Poor's Research Insight,® 1992 to 1998; (c) Standard and Poor's Research Insight.®

in these years as compared to 1983–1998. This makes sense because you would expect the greatest differences between LIFO and FIFO inventory values and cost-of-goods-sold amounts to occur during periods of significant price changes.

LIFO Liquidation

When a LIFO firm liquidates old LIFO layers, the net income number under LIFO can be seriously distorted. This is because the older (and usually lower) costs in the LIFO layers that are liquidated are "matched" against sales dollars that are stated at higher current prices. This results in an inflated or illusory profit margin. The following example illustrates the point.

The Bernazard Company had the following layers in its LIFO inventory at January 1, 2001, at which time the replacement cost of the inventory was $600 per unit.

Year LIFO Layer Added	Units	Unit Cost	Total	LIFO Reserve as of 1/1/01
1998	10	$300	$ 3,000	($600 − $300) × 10 = $ 3,000
1999	20	400	8,000	($600 − $400) × 20 = 4,000
2000	30	500	15,000	($600 − $500) × 30 = 3,000
	60		$26,000	$10,000

Bernazard sets its selling price by adding a $400 per unit markup to replacement cost at the time of sale. As of January 1, 2001, the replacement cost was $600 per unit; this cost remained constant throughout 2001. During 2001 the company purchased 45 units at a cost of $600 per unit, and it sold 80 units at a price of $1,000 per unit. Pre-tax LIFO income for 2001 would be:

Sales revenues, 80 @ $1,000		$80,000
Cost of goods sold:		
2001 purchases, 45 @ $600	$27,000	
2000 purchases, 30 @ $500	15,000	
1999 purchases, 5 @ $400	2,000	
		44,000
LIFO gross margin		$36,000

Because the number of units sold exceeded the number of units purchased in 2001 $(80 - 45 = 35)$, Bernazard was forced to liquidate its entire 2000 LIFO layer (30 units) and five units from its 1999 LIFO layer. In such situations the income statement matching advantages of LIFO disappear. Indeed, a "mismatching" occurs since LIFO income overstates the "real" current cost operating margin of $400 per unit. (Notice that the reported LIFO margin per unit is $36,000 ÷ 80, or $450.) This $50 per unit overstatement of the margin occurs because some 1999 and 2000 purchase costs are being matched against 2001 revenues. If analysts use past margin numbers as a starting point in generating future cash flow estimates, the LIFO income number is misleading when dipping occurs. That is, the $450 *reported* LIFO unit margin overstates the current cost "*real*" margin of $400 used for pricing purposes and thus does not represent a sustainable expected future per-unit margin number. LIFO earnings that include LIFO dipping profits are considered to be lower quality earnings.[8] The illusory profit elements would generally be assigned a lower earnings multiple for valuation purposes. Research shows that security price reactions to earnings numbers that contain LIFO liquidation profits are smaller than the price reactions to earnings numbers that are devoid of these illusory profits.[9]

VALUATION

---

[8] For example, see Siegel, op. cit., pp. 60–68.

[9] T. Carroll, D. W. Collins, and W. B. Johnson, "The LIFO–FIFO Choice and the Quality of Earnings Signals" (Working Paper, University of Iowa, August 1997).

To understand better what happens when LIFO dipping occurs, let's examine the reported current cost operating margin for 2001:

Sales revenues (80 × $1,000)	$80,000
Replacement cost of goods sold (80 × $600)	48,000
Current cost operating margin (80 × $400)	$32,000

The 2001 LIFO income of $36,000 exceeds the 2001 current cost margin of $32,000. ***This "extra" LIFO income of $4,000 is the result of mismatching.*** In more technical terms, as LIFO layers are liquidated, some of the inventory holding gains of 2000 and 1999 that were ignored under historical cost LIFO in the years they occurred suddenly get recognized as income as the old, lower cost inventory layers are matched against current selling prices. This can be seen by examining the December 31, 2001 LIFO inventory computation:

Year LIFO Layer Added	Remaining Units	Unit Cost	Ending Inventory 12/31/01 Total	LIFO Reserve as of 12/31/01
1998	10	$300	$3,000	($600 − $300) × 10 = $3,000
1999	15	$400	6,000	($600 − $400) × 15 = 3,000
	25		$9,000	$6,000

The LIFO reserve was $10,000 at January 1, 2001 (see p. 408). Notice that the LIFO dipping has reduced the LIFO reserve to $6,000 at December 31, 2001. This $4,000 reduction in the LIFO reserve represents another way of visualizing how LIFO dipping creates a mismatching on the income statement. Previously ignored unrealized holding gains get included in income as old LIFO layers are liquidated. The earnings "boost" of $4,000 is equal to the difference between the current cost to replace the liquidated layer of LIFO inventory (at date of sale) and the original cost of those units. This is demonstrated in Exhibit 9.7. When old LIFO layers are invaded, LIFO income jumps, but the increase is not sustainable.

Exhibit 9.7 ■ CALCULATION OF LIFO LIQUIDATION PROFITS

LIFO Layer Liquidated								
Year Added	Units Liquidated		Current Cost		Historical Cost		LIFO Liquidation Effect on Earnings
2000	30	×	($600	−	$500)	=	$3,000
1999	5	×	($600	−	$400)	=	1,000
Total increase in pre-tax earnings due to LIFO liquidation							$4,000

When the income effect of a LIFO liquidation is material, the SEC requires that the 10-K report disclose the dollar impact of LIFO dipping on income. Most companies that provide the 10-K disclosure also disclose the dollar impact of dipping in the annual report. The statement user should be alert to the fact that the earnings effect of LIFO dipping can be reported on either a *before-tax* or *after-tax* basis. Exhibit 9.8 shows this disclosure (on both a before- and after-tax basis) from Vacu-Dry Company's 1996 annual report.

Exhibit 9.8 ■ VACU-DRY COMPANY

1996 Annual Report Disclosure of LIFO Dipping

During 1996, the Company liquidated certain LIFO inventories that were carried at lower costs prevailing in prior years. The effect of this liquidation was to increase earnings before income taxes by $642,000 ($384,000 increase in net earnings, or an increase of $.23 per share).

The LIFO dipping disclosure in Exhibit 9.8 indicates that 1996 earnings before income taxes were increased by $642,000 as a consequence of matching old LIFO layer costs against 1996 revenues. This number represents the *pre-tax* effect of LIFO liquidation, indicating that the reported LIFO gross margin in 1996 overstated sustainable earnings by $642,000. Equivalently, the LIFO cost-of-goods-sold number was lower than current cost of goods sold by $642,000.

We are now able to explain more precisely the LIFO–FIFO cost-of-goods-sold (COGS) difference computed for Vacu-Dry in Exhibit 9.6. As we see in that exhibit, LIFO cost of goods sold exceeds FIFO cost of goods sold by $780,000—the dollar increase in the LIFO reserve. The LIFO reserve increases when input costs increase. But LIFO dipping reduces the LIFO reserve because old, lower cost LIFO layers are reduced. To explain the LIFO-FIFO cost-of-goods-sold difference, we need to explain the change in the LIFO reserve. This is done in Exhibit 9.9.

Exhibit 9.9 ■ VACU-DRY COMPANY

Change in the LIFO Reserve

Beginning LIFO reserve, July 1, 1995	$1,334,000
Decrease in LIFO reserve due to LIFO dipping (Exhibit 9.8)	(642,000)
Increase in LIFO reserve due to increases in input costs during the year (Plug)	1,422,000
Ending LIFO reserve, June 30, 1996	$2,114,000

We know the beginning and ending balance of the reserve as well as the decrease caused by LIFO dipping. To reconcile to the June 30, 1996 amount, the reserve had to increase by $1,422,000 (the Plug figure in Exhibit 9.9). This increase is attributable to rising input costs. So the $780,000 difference between the LIFO and FIFO cost-of-goods-sold numbers can be explained as:

1. Rising input costs *increased* LIFO cost of goods sold by:	$1,422,000
2. LIFO dipping undercharged expense and thus *reduced* cost of goods sold by:	(642,000)
3. Result: LIFO cost of goods sold exceeds FIFO cost of goods sold by:	$ 780,000

ANALYSIS

Reconciling the LIFO reserve as in Exhibit 9.9 provides the analyst with information about the direction of input costs. When linked to other data, this cost information can be valuable. For example, if the analyst knows that input costs are rising but competition limits output price increases, the analyst can deduce that future margins will suffer.

The LIFO to FIFO adjustment is also used in trend analysis, as illustrated in Exhibit 9.10, where comparative gross profit data for Vacu-Dry are shown for 1994–1996.

The Exhibit 9.10 data show that the gross profit percentage dropped sharply in 1995 and slightly in 1996. But we have also seen in Exhibit 9.8 that there was LIFO dipping in 1996, which increased the reported gross profit in 1996 over what it would have been without the

Exhibit 9.10 ■ VACU-DRY COMPANY

Comparative Gross Profit Data as Reported

	Year Ended June 30		
($ in thousands)	1996	1995	1994
Net sales	$26,533	$21,438	$ 27,773
Cost of goods sold	24,142	19,270	23,521
Gross profit	$ 2,391	$ 2,168	$ 4,252
Gross profit as a percentage of sales	9.0%	10.1%	15.3%

liquidation. You might ask what the profit trend looks like after adjusting for LIFO dipping. We can extend the previous analysis to address this question, as shown in Exhibit 9.11.

Exhibit 9.11 ■ VACU-DRY COMPANY

Gross Profit Data Adjusted for LIFO Dipping

	Year Ended June 30		
($ in thousands)	1996	1995	1994
Gross profit as reported	$ 2,391	$ 2,168	$ 4,252
Pre-tax effect of LIFO dipping on gross profit	642	—	—
Gross profit after eliminating LIFO dipping effect	$ 1,749	$ 2,168	$ 4,252
Net sales (as reported)	$26,533	$21,438	$ 27,773
Adjusted gross profit percentage	6.6%	10.1%	15.3%
Exhibit 9.10 gross profit percentage	9.0%	10.1%	15.3%
Difference	−2.4	N/A	N/A

The computations reveal that after removing the illusory income effect arising from LIFO dipping, the gross profit percentage for Vacu-Dry shows a dramatic downward trend over the 1994–1996 period. The adjusted gross profit percentage (highlighted in Exhibit 9.11) fell from 15.3% in 1994 to 6.6% in 1996. This continuing deterioration is not immediately evident in the reported gross margin figures. Analysis of trend data provides potentially important information regarding management's performance in adapting to new market conditions. Neglecting to adjust the year-to-year data for nonsustainable factors (such as the artificial margin improvement that results from LIFO dipping) could easily lead to erroneous conclusions.

VALUATION

Consider one final point regarding Exhibit 9.11. Many analysts believe that the most recent margin percentage provides the least-biased estimate of the next year's margin percentage. (This belief is correct when margins follow a random-walk pattern. When they do, the best estimate of the next period's value is generated by simply extrapolating the most recently observed past value.) ***After eliminating the effects of LIFO dipping, the adjusted gross margin percentage provides a clearer picture of the underlying real sustainable gross margin in each year.*** Analysts trying to estimate Vacu-Dry's future performance must understand that it is the 6.6% adjusted margin percentage—not the 9.0% unadjusted figure—that represents the starting point for estimating the sustainable margin in subsequent periods.

Vacu-Dry disclosed both the pre-tax *and* after-tax income effect of LIFO dipping. Some companies only disclose the increase in net (after-tax) earnings. In these instances analysts can still easily convert the LIFO dipping effect to a pre-tax basis and evaluate year-to-year changes in gross margin.

Here's how. Assume that a company discloses that LIFO dipping increased its (after tax) net income by $3,055,000. Further assume that the income tax rate is 35%. Then:

$$\text{After-tax effect} = \text{Pre-tax effect} \times (1 - \text{marginal tax rate})$$

or

$$\$3{,}055{,}000 = \text{Pre-tax effect} \times (1 - .35)$$

or

$$\frac{\$3{,}055{,}000}{.65} = \text{Pre-tax effect of } \$4{,}700{,}000$$

The $4,700,000 pre-tax impact of LIFO dipping would then be used to undertake an analysis like Exhibit 9.11.

The Frequency of LIFO Liquidations

Figure 9.5 on the following page provides information regarding the frequency of LIFO liquidations from 1985 to 1998 for manufacturing and merchandising firms using LIFO. The vertical axis represents the percentage of firms that reported a LIFO liquidation in any given year. In most years, between 10% and 20% of firms using LIFO experience a LIFO liquidation; clearly, liquidations are not uncommon. Inventory costs tended to increase over this period. When LIFO dipping occurred, roughly 60% to 80% of the time the older costs that were matched against current revenues were below current replacement costs, as shown in Figure 9.6. This causes a transitory boost to earnings.

Figure 9.7 shows the earnings impact for those firms in the sample that reported LIFO liquidations with positive earnings effects. From 1985 to 1998, the median effect of LIFO dipping on pre-tax earnings ranged from a high of 10.4% in 1991 to a low of 3.1% in 1995.

Figure 9.5

PERCENTAGE OF MANUFACTURING AND MERCHANDISING FIRMS USING LIFO AND EXPERIENCING A LIFO LIQUIDATION

Source: 1985–1993 data, *National Automated Accounting Research System* (NAARS). The NAARS service is offered jointly by Lexis-Nexis, a division of Reed Elsevier, Inc., and the American Institute of Certified Public Accountants; 1994–1998 data, 10-K Wizard.®

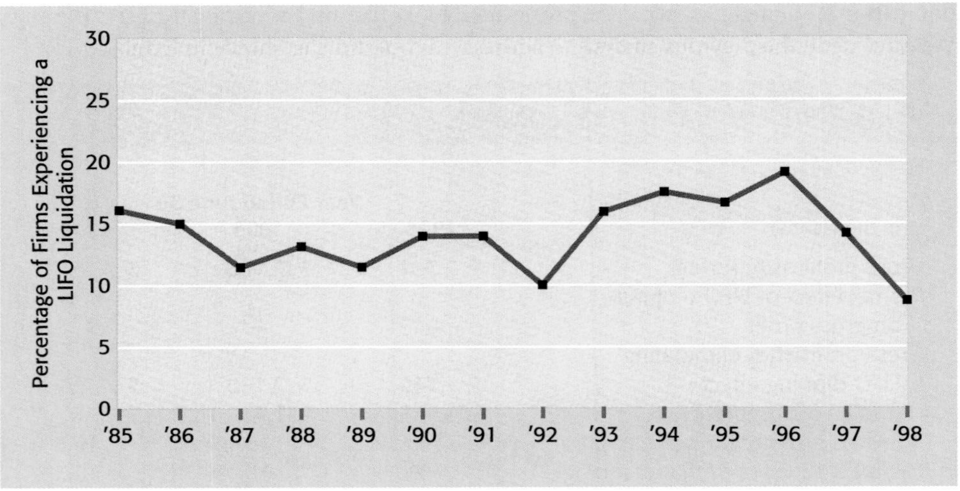

Figure 9.6

PERCENTAGE OF FIRMS WITH LIFO LIQUIDATIONS EXPERIENCING A POSITIVE, NEGATIVE, OR IMMATERIAL EFFECT ON PRE-TAX EARNINGS

Source: 1985–1993 data, *National Automated Accounting Research System* (NAARS); 1994–1998 data, 10-K Wizard.®

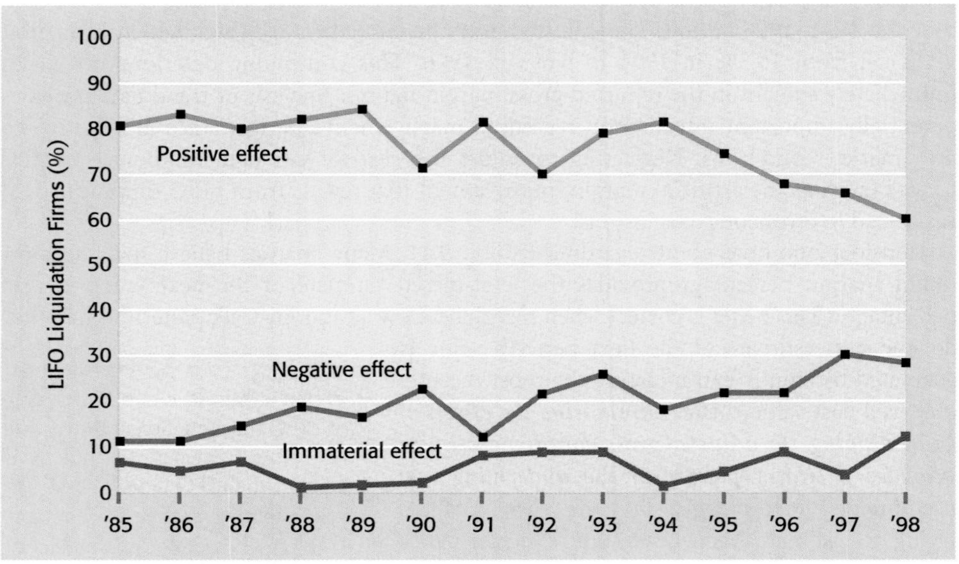

Figure 9.7

PRE-TAX EARNINGS EFFECT OF LIFO LIQUIDATIONS WITH POSITIVE EFFECTS ON EARNINGS

Source: 1985–1993 data, *National Automated Accounting Research System* (NAARS); 1994–1998 data, 10-K Wizard.®

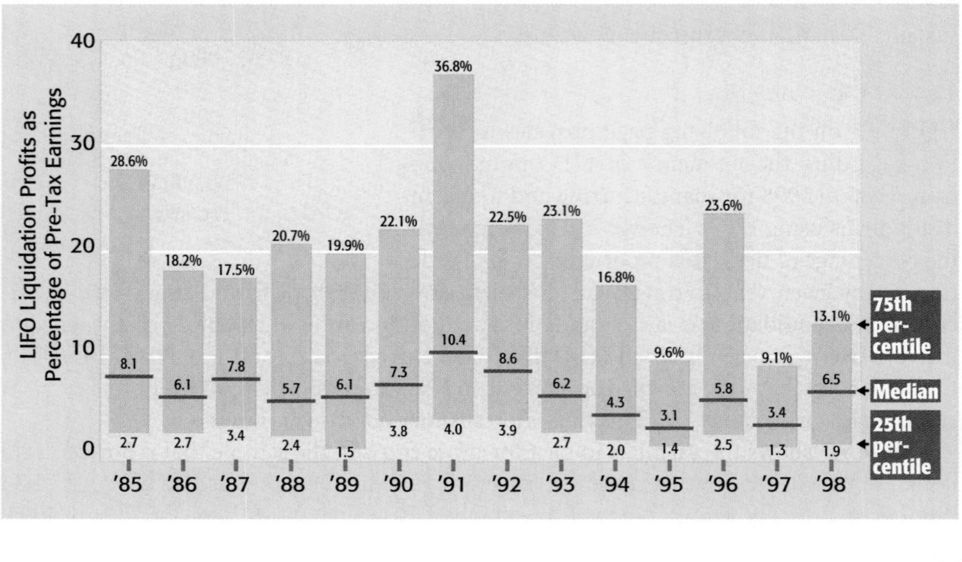

The numbers above the bars represent the 75th percentile of the distribution. So, for example, 25% of the firms with 1991 LIFO liquidations boosted pre-tax earnings by 36.8% or more. Clearly, LIFO liquidations occur frequently, and their impact on earnings is large enough to warrant close attention. To avoid being mislead by transitory LIFO liquidation profits, statement users should carefully scrutinize the LIFO inventory footnote. The objective is to determine if a LIFO liquidation occurred during the period and, if so, what impact this had on reported profits for the period.

LIFO liquidations occur frequently and often have a large impact on reported earnings. The earnings effect arises from a mismatching, since LIFO layers carried at "old" costs are matched against current period revenues. Reported margins are distorted and so is the income trend.

RECAP

Eliminating LIFO Ratio Distortions

ANALYSIS

LIFO inventory costing can lead to ratio distortions that can be corrected easily. For example, on its June 30, 1996 balance sheet, Vacu-Dry Company reported total current assets of \$6,669,000 and total current liabilities of \$2,533,000. Utilizing these numbers, the current ratio at June 30, 1996 is:

$$\frac{\text{Current assets}}{\text{Current liabilities}} = \frac{\$6{,}669{,}000}{\$2{,}533{,}000} = 2.63$$

However, Exhibit 9.4 disclosed that the LIFO inventory carrying amount understated FIFO (and replacement cost) inventory by \$2,114,000. This is the LIFO reserve that we must add to the numerator to reflect the current ratio in truly *current* terms. The adjusted current ratio is (\$000 omitted):

$$\frac{\$6{,}669 + \$2{,}114}{\$2{,}533} = 3.47$$

The current ratio improves after making the LIFO adjustment. Most other ratios deteriorate once the adjustments for LIFO effects are included. To illustrate the general deterioration, consider the inventory turnover ratio:

$$\frac{\text{Cost of goods sold}}{\text{Average inventory}} = \text{Inventory turnover}$$

The inventory turnover ratio is designed to reflect the physical turnover of product—that is, how long the typical unit remains in inventory. Most firms have many inventory categories. This diversity renders unit measures of inventory turnover meaningless since unit turnover is difficult to interpret in a diversified firm. That's why dollar—rather than unit—inventory measures are used to compute the turnover ratio. For Vacu-Dry, using the inventory amounts from Exhibit 9.4 and cost of goods sold from Exhibit 9.10, inventory turnover for 1996 is (\$000 omitted):

$$\frac{\$24{,}142}{(\$3{,}430 + \$5{,}414)/2} = 5.5 \text{ times per year}$$

The typical unit turns over 5.5 times per year. Another way to understand what this means is to divide 5.5 into 365, the number of days in a year. The result $365/5.5 = 66.4$ shows that the typical unit remains in inventory for 66.4 days.

The inventory turnover ratio is structured to approximate *physical* unit flow. The numerator is the cumulative dollar cost of units that have been sold; the denominator is the average cost of units on hand during the year. Under "normal" circumstances, the quotient should reflect the physical unit turnover. Unfortunately, LIFO frequently distorts the representation of physical unit flow. To see why, consider the denominator of the Vacu-Dry ratio; it does *not* reflect the then-current cost of the inventory at the beginning or end of fiscal year 1996, since the LIFO reserve at these times was, respectively, $1,334,000 and $2,114,000. For a firm using LIFO:

- the numerator of the ratio—cost of goods sold—is predominantly current period, here, 1996 costs;
- the denominator—average inventory—consists of old LIFO costs.

The quotient will not capture physical unit turnover unless an adjustment is made to the denominator. Furthermore, an adjustment to the numerator is also required because the pre-tax impact of the LIFO dipping ($642,000) causes the cost-of-goods-sold numerator to understate *current* cost of goods sold by this amount. To correctly gauge physical turnover, the analyst must *always* adjust the denominator of LIFO firms' turnover by adding the LIFO reserve amounts to beginning and ending inventory. In addition, the numerator must also be adjusted for LIFO liquidation profits whenever LIFO dipping occurs. The Vacu-Dry 1996 inventory turnover ratio adjusting both the numerator and the denominator is ($000 omitted):

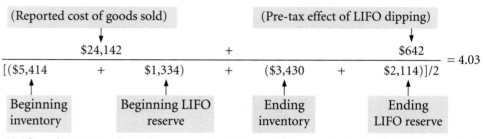

(Reported cost of goods sold) → $24,142; (Pre-tax effect of LIFO dipping) → $642

$$\frac{\$24{,}142 + \$642}{[(\$5{,}414 + \$1{,}334) + (\$3{,}430 + \$2{,}114)]/2} = 4.03$$

Beginning inventory → $5,414; Beginning LIFO reserve → $1,334; Ending inventory → $3,430; Ending LIFO reserve → $2,114

Dividing this LIFO adjusted turnover (4.03) into 365 days reveals that the typical unit, in fact, remains in inventory for 90.6 days—considerably longer than the 66.4 days suggested by the unadjusted analysis.

Tax Implications of LIFO

In the United States, the accounting principles that a firm uses in preparing its external financial statements need not be the same as the principles used in computing income taxes. The only exception to this statement occurs under LIFO. U.S. tax rules specify that if LIFO is used for tax purposes, the external financial statements must also use LIFO. This is called the **LIFO conformity rule.**

> Footnote disclosure of the LIFO reserve, as required by GAAP, is allowed by the IRS.

The LIFO conformity rule partially explains the widespread use of LIFO for financial reporting purposes. To gain the tax advantage of LIFO, firms must also use this method in their external financial statements.

LIFO's tax advantage is that it provides a lower income number than FIFO during periods of rising prices and nondecreasing inventory quantities, thus lowering the immediate tax liability. However, this effect can be reversed if LIFO layers are liquidated or if future purchase costs fall.

The dollar amount of the tax saving provided by LIFO can easily be computed by reference to the LIFO reserve number. For example, in Exhibit 9.4 we saw that Vacu-Dry's LIFO reserve at June 30, 1996 was $2,114,000. This number is equal to the cumulative excess of LIFO cost of goods sold over what the cost of goods sold would have been if FIFO had been used. The $2,114,000 also represents the cumulative unrealized holding gain on the old LIFO layers. Under FIFO, the old, lower cost inventory would have been charged to cost of goods sold, thereby raising cumulative pre-tax income by this amount. Assuming an average tax rate over the past years of 40%, Vacu-Dry has *postponed* approximately $845,600 in taxes (that is, $2,114,000 × 40%) since it began using LIFO.

> The marginal federal corporate tax rate immediately prior to 1986 was 46% and from 1986 to 1992 the rate was 34%. Since 1992 the rate has been 35%. With state and local taxes the overall marginal tax rates obviously would be even higher. We use a flat 40% rate to simplify the calculations.

The amount of taxes that companies can postpone by using LIFO can be substantial, as shown in Table 9.3. This table lists the twelve firms with the largest LIFO reserves as of year-end 1999 together with their estimated tax savings (based on using a 40% marginal tax rate). As shown, the LIFO tax benefit ranges from $1.069 billion for Exxon Mobil

Table 9.3 ■ ESTIMATED TAX SAVINGS FOR FIRMS WITH THE LARGEST LIFO RESERVES

($ in millions)	1998 LIFO Reserve	Estimated Cumulative Tax Benefit[1]
Exxon Mobil Corporation	$2,673.00	$1,069.20
General Motors Corporation	2,268.00	907.20
Caterpillar, Inc.	2,067.00	826.80
Ford Motor Company	1,397.00	558.80
General Electric Company	1,098.00	439.20
Chevron Corporation	1,089.00	435.60
Deere & Company	1,012.00	404.80
Philip Morris Companies, Inc.	1,000.00	400.00
Alcoa, Inc.	769.80	307.92
Sears, Roebuck & Company	713.00	285.20
Royal Dutch/Shell Group	628.00[2]	251.20
Du Pont (E I) de Nemours	363.86	145.54

[1] Based on an average marginal tax rate of 40%
[2] Converted from British pounds to U.S. dollars based on the exchange rate on December 31, 1998.

Source: Standard & Poor's Research Insight[SM] as data source; methodology not verified or controlled by Standard & Poor's.

Corporation to $146 million for Du Pont. The average amount of taxes postponed by these twelve firms was $502.6 million. Clearly, these companies have received a substantial cumulative cash flow benefit from using LIFO relative to FIFO.

Although clear cash flow benefits result from using LIFO, critics argue that LIFO may induce undesirable managerial behavior. This may happen if a firm has depleted its inventory quantities toward the end of a year. If inventories are allowed to remain at the depleted level, the tax liability could increase considerably because of the liquidation of old, low-cost LIFO layers. However, a manager can avoid this increase in taxes by simply purchasing a large amount of inventory at the end of the year in order to bring the inventory back up to beginning-of-year levels. Doing this to avoid tax increases may cause unwise purchasing behavior—excessive stocks may be carried, or year-end purchases may be made despite the fact that future purchase costs are expected to fall.[10]

Eliminating Realized Holding Gains for FIFO Firms

ANALYSIS

LIFO puts realized holding gains into income when old LIFO layers are eliminated. In contrast, reported income for FIFO firms *always* includes some realized holding gains during periods of rising inventory costs since FIFO charges the *oldest* inventory to cost of goods sold. Another way of saying the same thing is that FIFO cost of goods sold is understated because of the inventory holding gains that have occurred during the period. Since holding gains are potentially unsustainable, astute analysts try to remove them from reported FIFO income (or, equivalently, add them to FIFO costs of goods sold).

The size of the divergence between FIFO cost of goods sold and replacement cost of goods sold depends on two factors:

1. *The severity of input cost changes.* All other factors being equal, the greater the amount of cost change, the larger the divergence between FIFO and replacement cost of goods sold.
2. *The rapidity of physical inventory turnover.* The slower inventory turnover, the larger the divergence.

[10] Results consistent with the potential for tax-driven inventory management inefficiencies are reported in M. Frankel and R. Trezevant, "The Year-End LIFO Inventory Purchasing Decision: An Empirical Test," *The Accounting Review* (April 1994), pp. 382–398.

We illustrate a simple procedure to convert cost of goods sold from FIFO to replacement cost—and thereby eliminate realized holding gains from FIFO income.[11] The procedure requires an estimate of inventory cost change and assumes rapid inventory turnover. Consider the following example.

Ray Department Store experienced the following inventory transactions during 2001:

Beginning inventory (FIFO basis)	$1,000,000
Merchandise purchases	+8,000,000
Goods available for sale	9,000,000
Ending inventory (FIFO basis)	−1,100,000
Cost of goods sold (FIFO basis)	$7,900,000

Assume, on average, Ray's input costs for inventory increased by 10% during 2001. The adjustment procedure comprises three steps:

1. Determine FIFO cost of goods sold. In the example, this is $7,900,000. This amount is *not* adjusted.
2. Adjust the *beginning* inventory for one full year of specific price change. In the example, this is $1,000,000 times 10% or $100,000.
3. Determine the replacement cost of goods sold, which is the sum of the amount in step 1 ($7,900,000) and the amount in step 2 ($100,000)—that is, $8,000,000.

The difference between the computed replacement cost of goods sold ($8,000,000) and FIFO cost of goods sold ($7,900,000) equals the amount of realized holding gains included in the FIFO income figure ($100,000). This simple procedure gives results that accurately approximate tedious calculation approaches.

(In Appendix A to this chapter, we provide an intuitive explanation for why this procedure for isolating realized holding gains for FIFO firms "works." We also discuss how analysts can use either price indices or competitors' data to estimate the rate of inventory cost change—10% in the example.)

Inventory Errors

Errors in computing inventory are rare and almost always accidental. For example, a computer programming mistake might assign the wrong costs to inventory items. But there are also occasional instances where companies deliberately (and fraudulently) misstate inventories to manipulate reported earnings. You must first understand how inventory errors affect reported results in order to understand why some managers use this misrepresentation technique.

To visualize the effect of inventory errors, let's assume that due to a miscount in the 2001 year-end physical inventory, Jones Corporation's ending inventory is *overstated* by $1 million. Further assume there are no other inventory errors. Using the cost-of-goods-sold formula, we see that this error *understates* 2001 cost of goods sold by $1 million:

	Effect of 2001 Error on:
Beginning inventory	No error
Plus: Purchases	No error
Equals: Goods available	No error
Minus: Ending inventory	Overstated by $1 million
Equals: Cost of goods sold	Understated by $1 million

[11] See A. Falkenstein and R. L. Weil, "Replacement Cost Accounting: What Will Income Statements Based on the SEC Disclosures Show?—Part II," *Financial Analysts Journal* (March–April 1977), pp. 48–57. We have altered the Falkenstein and Weil procedural description slightly to simplify the exposition.

Because ending inventory is subtracted in the cost-of-goods-sold computation, an overstatement of ending inventory leads to an understatement of cost of goods sold. By understating cost of goods sold by $1 million, pre-tax income is overstated by $1 million. Furthermore, if the error is not detected and corrected in 2001, the error will also cause 2002 pre-tax income to be misstated. The reason that the error carries over into 2002 is because the December 31, 2001 ending inventory becomes the January 1, 2002 beginning inventory. So the carryforward effect (assuming no other 2002 inventory errors) is:

	Effect of 2001 Error on the 2002 COGS Computation
Beginning inventory	Overstated by $1 million
Plus: Purchases	No error
Equals: Goods available	Overstated by $1 million
Minus: Ending inventory	No error
Equals: Cost of goods sold	Overstated by $1 million

The overstatement of 2002 cost of goods sold (COGS) results in a $1 million understatement of 2002 pre-tax income. The carryforward effect in 2002 is equal in amount but in the opposite direction from the 2001 effect. Because the first year's income is overstated by $1 million and the second year's income is understated by the same amount, by December 31, 2002—the end of the two-year cycle—the retained earnings account (which is cumulative, of course) will be correct.

If we assume that Jones Corporation's inventory error was discovered in January 2002 and that the income tax rate is 35%, the entry to correct the error is:

DR Retained earnings	$650,000	
DR Income tax payable	350,000	
CR Inventory		$1,000,000

If an inventory error is discovered during the reporting year, it is corrected immediately. However, if an error is not discovered until a subsequent year (say 2002 in our example), then the retained earnings balance as of the beginning of the discovery year (2002) is corrected. If the error has a material effect on the company's financial statements, it must be separately disclosed.

ANALYSIS

In recent years, the media have coined the phrase "accounting irregularities." Some of these irregularities simply relate to exuberant use of the flexibility within GAAP; others involve fraud. Accounting fraud is relatively rare, but it does happen. And some of the more spectacular frauds involve inventory misstatement. Leslie Fay Companies, Inc., is an example. The company manufactures women's apparel. 1992 was expected to be a difficult year for the firm because of pricing and style issues. To offset the emerging profit shortfall, quarter-end inventory was overstated. As we just saw, overstating ending inventory decreases cost of goods sold, increases income, and masks the adverse real conditions facing the company. Subsequent shareholder litigation alleged that this behavior was partly motivated by a bonus plan tied to reported profits.[12] But as our numerical example illustrates, the phony earnings boost in the overstatement year reverses in the following year. So if the economic adversity that motivated the deliberate initial inventory overstatement continues, the inventory overstatements have to continue as well.

This is exactly what happened at Comptronix Corporation, an electronics manufacturer who lost an important customer in 1989.[13] After succumbing to the temptation of overstating profits by overstating inventory, the practice could not be abandoned without causing a reversal. So the overstatement continued until late 1992.[14] The fraud was eventually discovered at both companies. Can analysts do the same? For outsiders, fraud is

---

[12] L. Vickery, "Leslie Fay's Ex-Financial Chief, Polishan, Is Found Guilty of Fraud," *Wall Street Journal* (July 7, 2000).

[13] See C. Mulford and E. Comiskey, *Financial Warnings* (New York: John Wiley & Sons, Inc., 1996), pp. 228–233.

[14] For a comprehensive discussion of the accounting issues at Comptronix, see J. L. Boockholdt, "Comptronix, Inc.: An Audit Case Involving Fraud," *Issues in Accounting Education* (February 2000), pp. 105–128.

difficult to detect. But, there are sometimes clues.[15] For example, the reduction in cost of goods sold arising from inventory overstatement increases gross margins. So an unexplained increase in gross margins during troubled economic times warrants investigation.

Analytical Insights: LIFO Dangers

CONTRACTING

LIFO makes it possible to manage earnings. To see how, consider a firm that has an executive bonus plan linked to earnings per share, as depicted in Figure 7.8 on p. 311. Assume it is December 15, 2001, the firm reports on a calendar year basis, and the managers expect EPS for 2001 to be $4.40. (Since year-end is only two weeks away, this estimate is likely to be very accurate.) As described in Chapter 7, the bonus "tops-out" at $4.00 per share. From the managers' perspective 40¢ of expected earnings is "wasted" in the sense that it doesn't increase bonus payouts. So the executives have an incentive to "manage down" reported earnings back toward $4.00. LIFO makes this easy to do when input costs are rising. Here's why.

LIFO is applied using the periodic inventory method. Firms wait until the end of the year to compute cost of goods sold. So inventory purchased on December 31, 2001 is the "last-in" and is considered to be the "first out" when LIFO cost of goods sold is computed. Similarly, inventory purchased on December 30 is considered to have been sold next, and so on. Since input costs are rising, if the managers buy extra, unneeded higher cost inventory during the last two weeks of 2001, this will raise cost of goods sold, lower income, and drive EPS down toward $4.00. Lowering earnings in this way doesn't decrease their bonus so long as they don't let EPS fall below $4.00. But this unneeded inventory *does* increase inventory carrying costs as well as the risk of loss from obsolescence and spoilage. So managers don't suffer from the inventory build-up but shareholders do.

> Using the perpetual method defeats the purpose of LIFO. Here's why. Suppose a calendar year firm makes a sale on January 4 and uses the perpetual method; under LIFO, the units sold are presumed to come from the most recent purchase, say January 3. But if the firm instead uses the periodic method and computes cost of goods sold on December 31, those early-in-the-year January purchases will be the *oldest* purchases and less likely to be considered sold. So perpetual LIFO is seldom used.

But the story isn't over. In 2002 the firm now has too much inventory—remember, the purchases at the end of 2001 were unneeded. So in 2002, managers reduce inventory down to proper levels—a LIFO liquidation occurs. If input costs and output prices move together (that's the norm), then 2002 selling prices are higher than those in 2001. The LIFO dipping in 2002 results in old, low cost, early 2001 purchases being matched against higher 2002 selling prices. This artificially raises 2002 income. So it's a win-win situation for the managers! Playing this 2001 year-end LIFO game costs the managers no 2001 bonus and promises to increase 2002 income. At the end of 2001 they can't accurately forecast 2002 income. It might be below $3.00 per share, out of the bonus range. But the LIFO dipping income might be enough to raise 2002 income above $3.00 per share—back into the bonus range. The effect of the income shift from 2001 into 2002 improves the likelihood that the managers will earn a bonus in 2002.

> Remember, under LIFO, 2001 cost of goods sold assumed December purchases were sold first, then November, and so on working backward through the year. The new LIFO inventory layers added during the last two weeks of 2001 are costed out at cost levels in effect early in 2001, say, costs incurred in January and February.

To see the full range of earnings management "opportunities" using LIFO, let's go to a totally new scenario. It's November 15, 2001. Again there's a bonus plan like the one in Figure 7.8 and input costs and output prices have been rising. But here, assume that forecasted EPS is only $2.60. At this earnings level, the managers won't qualify for a bonus. But if the managers deliberately stop normal purchases for the last six weeks of the year, LIFO layers will be depleted. Again a mismatching occurs as December sales revenues are matched against pre-November 15 costs. When this is done aggressively, EPS can be driven into the bonus area above $3.00 per share. But do managers engage in this type of deliberate LIFO dipping? Unfortunately, research evidence here is sparse. However, if bonus contracts do not subtract-out LIFO dipping "profits," there is an incentive to dip deliberately.

---

[15] For a discussion of these clues, see Mulford and Comiskey, op. cit.

LIFO provides significant tax benefits when costs are rising. To obtain these tax benefits, Congress specified that companies must use LIFO not just for tax purposes but for financial reporting as well. Despite this constraint, only about 50 percent of companies in an AICPA survey use LIFO, as shown in Table 9.2. Since costs have tended to rise consistently over most of the past 60 years, you can ask why the other 50% of companies do *not* use LIFO. Are they squandering available tax benefits? Why many companies do not use LIFO has intrigued accounting researchers for years. Conjectures about why some companies do not use LIFO include the following:[16]

1. The estimated tax savings from using LIFO are too small to justify the added complexity of the LIFO approach. There are two possible reasons for small tax savings:
   a. Inventory holding gains are trivial for non-LIFO firms.
   b. These non-LIFO firms have large tax loss carryforwards and are not currently paying taxes.
2. Firms in cyclical industries that are subject to extreme fluctuations in physical inventory levels would find LIFO unattractive because of the high probability of LIFO liquidations and consequent adverse tax effects.
3. Inventory obsolescence poses difficult issues under LIFO; consequently, firms subject to a high rate of inventory obsolescence may be reluctant to adopt LIFO.
4. During periods of generally rising prices, LIFO leads to lower profits. Managers may be reluctant to adopt LIFO under these conditions for either one—or both—of the following reasons:
   a. They believe that lower LIFO earnings will lead to lower stock price.
   b. They believe that the lower LIFO earnings will lead to lower compensation, since management bonuses are often linked to reported earnings.
5. In a period of rising prices, LIFO causes certain ratios used in loan agreements to deteriorate—for example, the leverage ratio. Firms might be reluctant to adopt LIFO because adoption could result in loan covenant violations.
6. Smaller firms might not adopt LIFO because of the higher costs associated with maintaining the more complicated LIFO accounting records.

Research evidence is consistent with many (but not all) of these conjectures about why some firms don't use LIFO. Several studies have found that the potential inventory holding gains are much higher for LIFO firms than for non-LIFO firms.[17] Accordingly, the tax saving for LIFO adopters is much higher than the potential savings for firms not using LIFO. Furthermore, non-LIFO firms generally have significantly larger tax loss carryforwards than LIFO firms, thereby obviating the need to adopt LIFO.[18] Research evidence is also generally consistent with the fact that LIFO adopters have lower levels of inventory fluctuations[19] and lower leverage in comparison with non-LIFO adopters.[20] In the aggregate, these studies suggest rational economic explanations for the behavior of firms who do not adopt LIFO.

Another aspect of inventory accounting that has intrigued researchers is whether the stock market differentiates between LIFO earnings and FIFO earnings. In inflationary

---

[16] See B. E. Cushing and M. J. LeClere, "Evidence on the Determinants of Inventory Accounting Policy Choice," *The Accounting Review* (April 1992), pp. 355–366.

[17] Two examples of such studies are Cushing and LeClere, ibid., and N. Dopuch and M. Pincus, "Evidence on the Choice of Inventory Accounting Methods: LIFO vs. FIFO," *Journal of Accounting Research* (Spring 1988), pp. 28–59.

[18] Cushing and LeClere, ibid., and F. W. Lindahl, "Dynamic Analysis of Inventory Accounting Choice," *Journal of Accounting Research* (Autumn 1989), pp. 201–226.

[19] Examples include Dopuch and Pincus, op. cit., and C. J. Lee and D. A. Hsieh, "Choice of Inventory Accounting Methods: Comparative Analysis of Alternative Hypotheses," *Journal of Accounting Research* (Autumn 1985), pp. 468–485.

[20] Examples include Lindahl, op. cit., and Cushing and LeClere, op. cit.

periods LIFO firms would—on average—report lower profits than FIFO firms but would have higher after-tax cash flows. From an economic perspective the LIFO firms are better off, despite the lower reported earnings. Furthermore, the quality of reported LIFO earnings is presumably higher than FIFO earnings, since LIFO earnings usually exclude inventory holding gains from net income; accordingly, LIFO earnings are presumably more sustainable than FIFO earnings during inflationary periods. Thus, the research question is whether investors differentiate between the quality of LIFO versus FIFO earnings or, instead, simply penalize LIFO firms for their lower reported earnings.

VALUATION

Many of the early studies of market reaction to LIFO versus FIFO examined instances in which firms switched from FIFO to LIFO as inflation accelerated. The research question frequently posed was:

> If the market simply reacts to bottom-line earnings, then stock prices of firms shifting to LIFO should, on average, fall. On the other hand, if the market considers earnings *quality,* then the relatively higher reported (and expected future) after-tax cash flows of new LIFO adopters should lead—on average—to stock price increases as the switch is announced.

Researchers studied the stock price reaction to announcements by firms that they had switched to LIFO as well as to the announcements of the new LIFO earnings numbers. These studies generated conflicting results, probably because of the failure to control for other factors influencing stock price behavior during the year of the inventory switch.

A more recent study that included such controls found consistent evidence that the market perceives LIFO earnings to be of higher quality than FIFO earnings.[21] This study produced the following findings:

1. When reported earnings include highly-transitory inventory holding gains (either under FIFO or when LIFO liquidation occurs), the market perceives these earnings to be lower quality earnings, and thus the share price response is small relative to high quality (sustainable) earnings.
2. The market response to earnings news is greater after LIFO adoption. This suggests that the market believes that LIFO produces a higher quality earnings signal.
3. Across all firms, there is a higher market response to a given amount of earnings-surprise under LIFO in comparison to FIFO. Again, this result is consistent with LIFO being perceived as the higher quality earnings number.

SUMMARY

This chapter is designed to allow readers to understand existing GAAP inventory methods and disclosures; it can also help readers conduct informed comparisons and analysis of profitability and net asset positions across firms with varying inventory methods. Here are the important messages from this chapter.

Absorption costing can lead to potentially misleading period-to-period income changes whenever inventories increase or decrease sharply. Furthermore, financial reporting rules allow firms latitude in selecting a cost flow assumption for determining the cost of goods sold reported on the income statement and the inventory values reported on the balance sheet. Some firms use FIFO, some use LIFO, and some use weighted average; others use a combination of these methods. This diversity in practice can severely hinder interfirm comparisons when inventory purchase costs are changing over time, which is the usual case. Before undertaking inter-firm comparisons, numbers for the LIFO firms should be transformed to the FIFO basis.

Reported FIFO income merges together sustainable operating profits and potentially unsustainable realized holding gains. Analysts must disentangle these elements when preparing cash flow forecasts. Similarly, LIFO dipping distorts reported margins because it matches "old" costs with current selling prices. Old, out-of date LIFO inventory carrying amounts can distort

[21] Carroll, Collins, and Johnson, op. cit. Additional evidence on how the market values LIFO versus FIFO earnings can be found in Jennings, Simko and Thompson, op. cit.

various ratios like inventory turnover. Analysts should use the LIFO reserve to adjust inventories before computing ratio values. Users of financial statements must understand these differences and know how to adjust for them using various footnote disclosures. Only by doing so can valid comparisons be made across firms that utilize different inventory cost flow assumptions.

Self-Study Problem: Mitsuru Corporation

Mitsuru Corporation began business operations on January 1, 2001 as a wholesaler of macadamia nuts. Its purchase and sales transactions for 2001 are listed in Exhibit 9.12. Mitsuru uses a periodic inventory system.

Exhibit 9.12 ■ MITSURU CORPORATION

Inventory Purchases and Sales

	Purchases			Sales
Date	**Pounds**	**Dollars/Pound**	**Total Dollars**	**Pounds**
January 1	1,000	$10.00	$ 10,000	
February 3	4,000	10.20	40,800	
February 9				3,600
April 1	4,000	10.30	41,200	
May 29				3,500
June 28	5,000	10.40	52,000	
July 20				4,100
September 14	5,000	10.50	52,500	
September 17				4,200
December 18	4,000	10.60	42,400	
December 22				3,600
	23,000		$238,900	19,000

1. Compute 2001 ending inventory and cost of goods sold for Mitsuru Corporation using the weighted average cost flow assumption.

Ending inventory totals 4,000 pounds—that is, purchases of 23,000 pounds minus sales of 19,000 pounds. The average cost per pound (rounded) is:

$$\frac{\text{Total cost of goods available for sale} \rightarrow \$238{,}900}{\text{Total pounds available for sale} \rightarrow 23{,}000} = \$10.39/\text{pound}$$

Ending inventory is 4,000 pounds times $10.39 or $41,560. Cost of goods sold is then determined as follows:

Total cost of goods available for sale	$238,900
Less: Ending inventory computed above	41,560
Cost of goods sold (weighted average method)	$197,340

2. Compute 2001 ending inventory and cost of goods sold for Mitsuru Corporation using the FIFO cost flow assumption.

Under the first-in, first-out cost flow assumption, the ending inventory consists of the 4,000 most-recently-purchased pounds of macadamia nuts. This ending inventory amount consists entirely of the December 18 purchase of 4,000 pounds for $42,400. Accordingly, FIFO cost of goods sold is:

Total cost of goods available for sale	$238,900
Less: Ending FIFO inventory	42,400
FIFO cost of goods sold	$196,500

3. Compute 2001 ending inventory and cost of goods sold for Mitsuru Corporation using the LIFO cost flow assumption.

Under LIFO, the ending inventory is comprised of the 4,000 pounds of oldest macadamia nut purchases. This 4,000 pounds would consist of two layers:

January 1	1,000 pounds	@	$10.00	=	$10,000
February 3	3,000 pounds	@	$10.20	=	30,600
	4,000 pounds				$40,600

Then, LIFO cost of goods sold is:

Total cost of goods available for sale	$238,900
Less: Ending LIFO inventory	40,600
LIFO cost of goods sold	$198,300

4. Assume that the December 31, 2001 macadamia nut replacement cost is $10.60 per pound. Compute Mitsuru's LIFO reserve and use the beginning and ending LIFO reserve amounts to reconcile between LIFO and FIFO cost of goods sold.

The LIFO reserve at a given point in time is the difference between the LIFO inventory book value and its then-current replacement cost. At January 1, 2001, Mitsuru Corporation's LIFO reserve was $0 since the LIFO book value and replacement cost both equaled $10,000. At December 31, 2001, the LIFO reserve was $1,800, computed as follows:

December 31, 2001 inventory replacement cost: 4,000 pounds @ $10.60	$42,400
December 31, 2001 LIFO inventory	40,600
December 31, 2001 LIFO reserve	$ 1,800

Using the formula for converting cost of goods sold from a LIFO to FIFO basis in conjunction with the answers to parts 2 and 3 of this self-study problem yields:

$$\text{COGS}_{\text{LIFO}} + \text{Beginning LIFO reserve} - \text{Ending LIFO reserve} = \text{COGS}_{\text{FIFO}}$$
$$\$198{,}300 + 0 - \$1{,}800 = \$196{,}500$$

Notice that $196,500 equals the FIFO cost-of-goods-sold number computed in part 2.

As discussed in the text, the reconciliation procedure is an approximation. Adding the LIFO reserve to the LIFO inventory equals replacement cost. If the inventory turns quickly, then inventory replacement cost *approximates* FIFO inventory. In this self-study problem, ending FIFO inventory at $10.60 per pound exactly equals replacement cost. Hence, the adjustment is precise.

APPENDIX A Eliminating Realized Holding Gains From FIFO Income

In the chapter we show a simple way to estimate the amount of realized holding gains included in the FIFO income figure. In this appendix we provide a simple example to illustrate why this method works.

Consider a firm buying and selling inventory *in equal amounts daily* as you contemplate Figure 9.8. The *quantity* of inventory purchased during the year is the area denoted "P." Beginning inventory *quantity* is the area denoted "B," and ending inventory *quantity* is the area denoted "E." Let's assume that B equals E—that is, inventory quantity did not change over the year. Under these conditions the *units* comprising FIFO cost of goods sold would consist of the area B + (P − E). In other words, under the FIFO cost flow assumption, cost of goods sold consists of the first—or oldest—units available, which is beginning inventory plus the earliest purchases. Under LIFO, cost of goods sold would comprise the

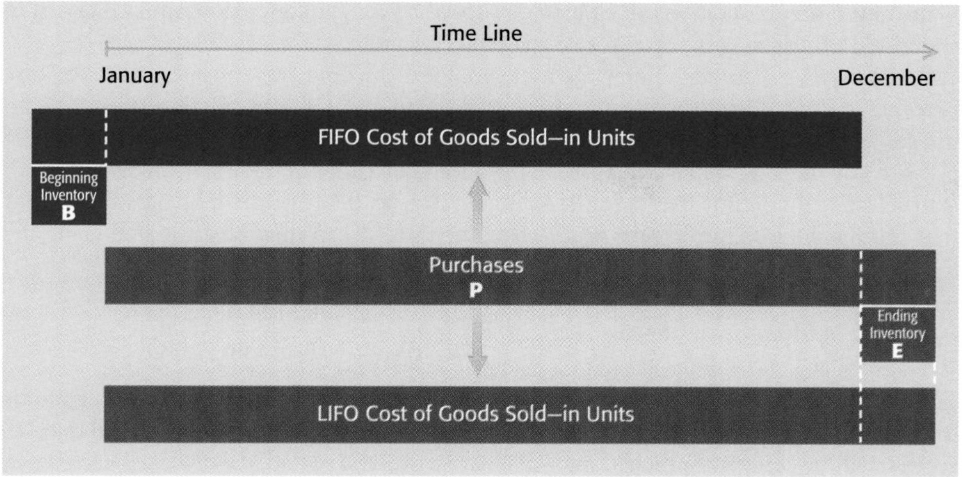

Figure 9.8

FIFO TO LIFO COST OF GOODS SOLD APPROXIMATION TECHNIQUE

area P—that is, the most *recently* purchased units. The difference between the units comprising the two cost-of-goods-sold measures is the area E minus B. Expressed in units:

$$CGS_{LIFO} = CGS_{FIFO} + E - B \tag{9.1}$$

Expressed in dollars:

$$\$CGS_{LIFO} = \$CGS_{FIFO} + \$E - \$B \tag{9.2}$$

Notice that if inventory costs do not change over the year, $\$E = \$B$ and $\$CGS_{LIFO} = \$CGS_{FIFO}$. In general it's reasonable to expect inventory costs to change from the beginning to the end of the year. If we assume that inventory purchase costs changed over the year at the rate "r," then \$E will not equal \$B, even though E units equals B units. Specifically, the dollar amount of ending inventory will equal $(1 + r)$ times the dollar amount of beginning inventory—that is,

$$\$E = \$B \times (1 + r) \tag{9.3}$$

Substituting the equation (9.3) value of \$E into equation (9.2) yields:

$$\$CGS_{LIFO} = \$CGS_{FIFO} + \$B \times (1 + r) - \$B \tag{9.4}$$

or

$$\$CGS_{LIFO} = \$CGS_{FIFO} + \$B \times r \tag{9.5}$$

In this example, daily unit purchases and sales are equal. Under these conditions LIFO cost of goods sold will equal current cost of goods sold. So equation (9.5) can be rewritten:

$$\$CGS_{CC} = \$CGS_{FIFO} + \$B \times r \tag{9.6}$$

where $\$CGS_{CC}$ is current cost of goods sold. As we saw on page 403, the difference between FIFO pre-tax income and current cost income (or, equivalently, FIFO cost of goods sold and current cost of goods sold) is the inventory holding gain or loss. Thus, the product $\$B \times r$ provides an estimate of the inventory holding gain (loss) that is embedded in the FIFO earnings number.[22]

Notice that equation (9.6) is equivalent to the simple holding gain estimation procedure used in the chapter. This approximation "works" as long as inventory unit quantities do not change very much over the year and as long as inventory purchases and sales take place

[22] Analysts generally perceive such inventory holding gains as low quality earnings items because they cannot be sustained in the future unless inventory costs continue to increase; see Siegel, op. cit., situation 7, p. 68. Consistent with this view, Carroll, Collins, and Johnson, op. cit., find that the market price adjustments associated with earnings surprises of firms whose earnings contain relatively large inventory holding gains are substantially smaller than those of firms with relatively smaller FIFO inventory holding gains.

frequently. If these conditions aren't met for a specific firm, the conversion from FIFO cost of goods sold to current cost of goods sold will not be accurate.

To eliminate realized holding gains from FIFO income, we must estimate "r," the percentage change in inventory purchase costs. One means for estimating this rate is to use some input cost price index, such as one of the various producer price indices (PPI) prepared by the U.S. Department of Labor, Bureau of Labor Statistics. Another approach is to select a competitor that is in the same industry as the FIFO firm being adjusted but that utilizes the LIFO inventory procedure. The rate "r" can then be estimated using the following ratio computed from the LIFO competitor's disclosures:

$$\text{Rate of inventory input cost change ("r")} = \frac{\text{Change in LIFO reserve}}{BI_{LIFO} + \text{Beginning LIFO reserve}}$$

The denominator of the ratio is the initial current cost of the inventory, and the numerator is the change in current cost over the period. The quotient is an estimate of the desired rate, "r." However, if the competitor dipped into LIFO layers over the period, the disclosed decrease in cost of goods sold because of the dipping must be added back to the numerator. The reason is that LIFO dipping reduces the LIFO reserve. Adding back the dipping effect generates a more accurate measure of "r." But, if the competitor's year-to-year inventory levels changed substantially, the derived rate will differ from the true rate of inventory cost increase.

APPENDIX B Lower of Cost or Market Method

This appendix covers a widely used method in inventory accounting called the lower of cost or market method.

An asset represents a cost that has been incurred which possesses future service potential value to a firm. If subsequent events cause the future service potential value of an asset to drop below its cost, then its carrying value must be reduced. In inventory accounting this is called the **lower of cost or market method.**

It is more complicated than its name implies, although the reasoning underlying lower of cost or market is simple. Whenever the replacement cost of inventory declines below its original cost, the presumption is that the service potential value of the inventory has been impaired and a write-down is warranted. If a unit of inventory originally cost $10 but if its replacement cost falls to $8, a decrease in carrying value of $2 would be required. ***What's implied here is that inventory replacement cost and eventual selling price move together.*** The decline in replacement cost is presumed to signal that the price at which the inventory can be sold—its future service potential value—has fallen. Thus, a loss has occurred which must be recognized in the accounts.

In practice the relationship between cost decreases and selling price decreases is unlikely to be perfect. For this reason the market value used in applying lower of cost or market is subject to two constraints:

1. **Ceiling.** "Market" should not exceed the inventory's **net realizable value**—that is, the estimated selling price in the ordinary course of business less reasonably predictable costs of completion and disposal.
2. **Floor.** "Market" should not be less than the inventory's net realizable value reduced by an allowance for an approximately normal profit margin.[23]

The constraint that market should not exceed net realizable value represents a ceiling designed to avoid overstating obsolete goods. For example, a motor originally cost $80 but is now obsolete and has a net realizable value of only $50. Even if its replacement cost is $65, the inventory should be valued at its net realizable value of $50. To value it at its replacement cost of $65 would fail to recognize the full extent of the expected loss that has occurred.

---

[23] "Restatement and Revision of Accounting Research Bulletins," *Accounting Research Bulletin No. 43* (New York: AICPA, 1953), Chapter 4, para. 8.

The floor constraint covers situations in which declines in input replacement cost do not move perfectly with declines in selling price. To illustrate, assume the following:

	Original Cost	Replacement Cost	Net Realizable Value	Net Realizable Value Less Normal Profit of $11
Inventory item	$60	$46	$70	$59

This scenario assumes that the normal per unit profit margin is $11. An inventory write-down to $46 would lead to an abnormally high unit profit margin of $24 (i.e., net realizable value of $70 less $46) when the inventory is sold in a later period. This $24 profit exceeds the $11 normal profit margin. A write-down to $59 would still afford the company a normal profit margin; any larger write-down would result in excess profits in future periods. The floor provides a lower bound for write-downs in situations where input replacement cost and selling price do not move together.

Together, these two constraints mean that the market value used in applying the lower of cost or market rule is the *middle value* of (1) replacement cost, (2) net realizable value, and (3) net realizable value less a normal profit margin. This is depicted in Figure 9.9.

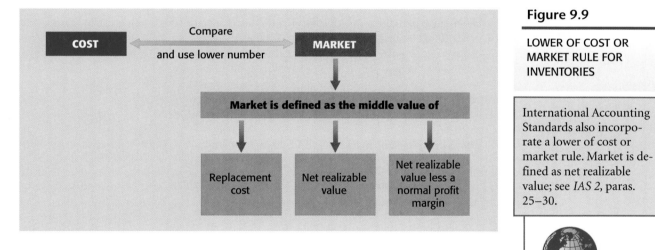

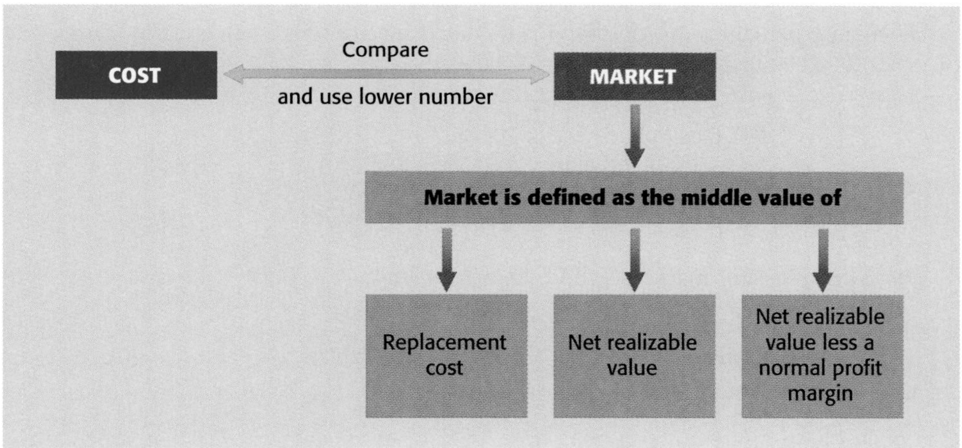

Figure 9.9

LOWER OF COST OR MARKET RULE FOR INVENTORIES

International Accounting Standards also incorporate a lower of cost or market rule. Market is defined as net realizable value; see *IAS 2*, paras. 25–30.

Applying the lower of cost or market rule is illustrated in Exhibit 9.13 using four scenarios.

Exhibit 9.13 ■ APPLICATION OF LOWER OF COST OR MARKET RULE

		Market				
Scenario	Original Cost	Replacement Cost	Net Realizable Value	Net Realizable Value Less a Normal Profit Margin	Middle of the Three Market Values	Inventory Value Used
1	$20	$23	$27	$21	$23	$20
2	20	19	24	18	19	19
3	20	19	18	12	18	18
4	20	15	25	19	19	19

Scenario 1. Inventory is valued at cost ($20) since cost is lower than the middle of the three market values ($23). This illustrates the traditional rule for inventory carrying values in historical cost accounting: Inventories are carried at original cost unless the future service potential value of the item has been impaired.

Scenario 2. Inventory is carried at replacement cost ($19). Market is defined as the middle value of the three definitions in Figure 9.9. The values are 18, 19, and 24; since 19 is between 18 and 24, it is market. Since market is less than original cost, it is presumed that a portion of the original service potential value of the inventory has been impaired. Therefore, the inventory is written down.

Scenario 3. Inventory is valued at net realizable value ($18) since net realizable value is the middle "market" value (i.e., 18 is between 12 and 19) and is below cost. Here we see the operation of the ceiling. This rule is intended to avoid carrying obsolete goods at a cost in excess of the net value that will be realized upon sale. If the rule were not invoked, inventory would be carried at $19 (its replacement cost), which is more than the $18 that it is expected to yield.

Scenario 4. Inventory is valued at net realizable value less a normal profit margin ($19) because this number is lower than original cost and is the middle value of the market price constraints. Scenario 4 illustrates the floor. If the rule were not invoked, inventory would be carried at $15 (its replacement cost). This would be an excessive write-down, because a $15 carrying cost would result in an above-normal margin when the goods are sold.

When a perpetual inventory system is used and inventory is written down from a cost of, say, $1,000,000 to a market value of $970,000, the entry is:

> If a periodic inventory system is used, this entry would not be made. Instead, the ending *market* value of inventory ($970,000) would be used as ending inventory in the cost-of-goods-sold computation. This treatment essentially "buries" the $30,000 loss as an undisclosed element of cost of goods sold.

DR Loss from decline in market value of inventory	$30,000	
CR Inventory		$30,000

The lower of cost or market method can be applied to

- individual inventory items
- classes of inventory—say, fertilizers versus weed-killers
- the inventory as a whole.

Companies have discretion regarding how inventories are aggregated when applying the lower of cost or market rule, as illustrated in Exhibit 9.14. Depending on whether the aggregation is by item of inventory, inventory class, or total inventory, the lower of cost or market value could be $27,000, $31,000, or $32,000.

Income tax regulations do not permit the use of the lower-of-cost-or-market rule in conjunction with LIFO. The reason for this prohibition is that LIFO provides tax

Exhibit 9.14 ■ AGGREGATION ALTERNATIVES IN APPLYING THE LOWER OF COST OR MARKET RULE

			Lower of Cost or Market Aggregated by:		
Inventory Item	**Cost**	**Market**	**Item**	**Class**	**Total**
Class 1:					
Item 1	$10,000	$ 6,000	$ 6,000		
Item 2	3,000	8,000	3,000		
	$13,000	$14,000		$13,000	
Class 2:					
Item 3	20,000	18,000	18,000	$18,000	
	$33,000	$32,000	$27,000	$31,000	$32,000

advantages when prices are rising; if LIFO firms were permitted to use lower of cost or market, then such firms would also gain tax advantages when prices are falling. Congress is unwilling to provide LIFO firms with tax savings that would arise irrespective of the direction of input cost movements.

The Contracting Origins of the Lower of Cost or Market Method

CONTRACTING

The lower of cost or market method for inventories was widely practiced in the United States before the 1920s. Presumably, it evolved in the formative years of modern financial reporting to satisfy the information needs of what was then the most important external user group—commercial lenders. Banking in that era consisted mainly of securitized lending. Loans required collateral from the borrower, primarily in the form of inventory, accounts receivable, or fixed assets. Clearly, lenders wanted to avoid basing their decisions on overstated asset values, since overstated asset values resulted in inadequate amounts of collateral. The conservatism inherent in lower of cost or market represented a mechanism for protecting the then-dominant user group from unpleasant surprises—lower than expected collateral values.[24] Thus, the lower-of-cost-or-market rule evolved because of the dominant form of lending contracts in use years ago.

Evaluation of the Lower of Cost or Market Rule

Individual and institutional equity investors are now important users of financial statements. The conservative bias built into the lower of cost or market rule protects lenders but it may sometimes harm these other users. Consider a prospective seller of an equity security of a company whose inventory is written down to market. If the write-down was unwarranted (e.g., because the decline in replacement cost did not presage a decline in eventual selling price), the prospective seller's position is worsened by lower of cost or market accounting, since the share price obtainable may be lower than the price that would exist with less conservative accounting. Clearly, conservative rules designed to systematically understate asset amounts favor lenders and equity purchasers over borrowers and equity sellers. This absence of neutrality that pervades lower of cost or market has troubled numerous financial reporting experts and has led to repeated criticisms of the approach.

In addition to its bias against those seeking loans and those selling equity securities, the lower of cost or market rule has another deficiency. It assumes that input costs and output prices generally move together. Therefore, a decline in input cost triggers a loss recognition because it is presumed that the cost decrease presages a selling price decrease. But there is

---

[24] Evidence about the role that lenders played in the evolution of modern financial reporting and the lower-of-cost-or-market rule is contained in a proposal from the Federal Reserve Board that was designed to standardize financial reporting (*Federal Reserve Bulletin*, April 1, 1917, p. 270):

> *Because this matter was clearly of importance to banks and bankers, and especially to the Federal Reserve Banks* which might be asked to rediscount commercial paper based on borrowers' statements, the Federal Reserve Board has taken an active interest in the consideration of the suggestions which have developed as a result of the Trade Commission's investigation, and now submits in the form of a tentative statement certain proposals in regard to suggested standard forms of statements for merchants and manufacturers. [Emphasis added]
>
> The problem naturally subdivides itself into two parts. (1) The improvement in standardization of the forms of statements; (2) the adoption of methods which will insure greater care in compiling the statements and the proper verification thereof.

The proposal (which was subsequently adopted) contained a specific reference to the importance of the lower-of-cost-or-market rule for inventories (p. 275):

> . . . The auditor should satisfy himself that inventories are stated at cost or market prices, whichever are the lower at the date of the balance sheet. No inventory must be passed which has been marked up to market prices and a profit assumed that is not and may never be realized. . . . It may be found that inventories are valued at the average prices of raw materials and supplies on hand at the end of the period. *In such cases the averages should be compared with the latest invoices in order to verify the fact that they are not in excess of the latest prices.* . . . [Emphasis added]

little empirical evidence to corroborate this assumption. It is possible that input costs and selling prices will move together. It is also possible that they may not. When input costs and selling prices do not move together, a loss may be recognized when, in fact, no loss has occurred. Consider, for example, the following illustration:

	Original Cost	Replacement Cost	Net Realizable Value	Net Realizable Value Less Normal Profit Margin
Cost relationships on January 1, 2001	$100	$100	$115	$90
Cost relationships on December 31, 2001	100	95	115	90

Strict application of the lower of cost or market rule at year end would require a write-down of the inventory to $95 from its original cost of $100. However, the selling price of the inventory has not changed, since its net realizable value is still $115. Therefore, no loss exists but GAAP would require a $5 write-down!

> Worse yet, after a write-down, International Accounting Standards permit inventory to be *written back up* to a number not exceeding original cost if selling prices recover (see IAS2 [revised 1993], para. 30). So companies might conceivably recognize losses in "good" earnings years that can comfortably absorb the "hit," then write the inventory back up in "bad" earnings years (recognizing gains) to mask the real extent of earnings deterioration.

In summary, the lower of cost or market rule reflects conservatism. As financial statement users have become more diverse, the rule has been subjected to mounting criticism. First, conservatism is itself an elusive concept; while inventory write-downs may initially be conservative, the resulting higher margin in the period following the write-down provides opportunities for earnings management. Second, as the use of published financial statements has broadened over the years, conservatism strikes many observers as a violation of the neutrality posture that financial reporting rules are designed to achieve. For example, if downward changes in replacement cost are considered to be reliable evidence of a loss, logic suggests that upward changes in replacement cost should similarly be considered reliable evidence of a gain. Finally, the lower of cost or market rule relies on an implicit relationship between input costs and output prices that may not prevail. When the input/output relationship does not exist, inventory losses may be recognized even though no real loss has occurred. As a consequence of these limitations, the lower of cost or market approach constitutes GAAP but it does not hold a secure place in accounting theory.

APPENDIX C Dollar Value LIFO

The LIFO inventory method requires data on each separate product or inventory item, and it therefore has two drawbacks. First, item-by-item inventory records are *costly* to maintain; and second, when LIFO records are kept by individual item, the likelihood of *liquidating* a LIFO layer is greatly increased.

- *Cost.* Traditional LIFO systems kept by individual item necessitate considerable clerical work. Detailed records for each separate product or item in beginning inventory must be kept both in terms of physical units and unit cost. Similar detail must be accumulated for all purchases during the period. Finally, ending inventory must also be costed individually by item. These data requirements quickly become unwieldy for firms with numerous inventory categories.
- *Liquidation.* One of the motivations for adopting LIFO is that this method tends to keep inventory holding gains out of income and thereby lowers taxes. However, when old LIFO layers are liquidated, this objective is subverted and both income and income taxes rise. The possibility of liquidating a LIFO layer is very high when item-by-item LIFO is used. Consider the case of a computer store that sells print-

ers. As laser printers were introduced, such stores reduced their inventories of dot-matrix printers. If LIFO always had to be kept on a per-item basis, this decrease in the obsolete models would cause a liquidation of old LIFO layers and negate the benefits of LIFO.

To overcome both the cost and liquidation problems, a method has been developed in which LIFO cost can be estimated for broad categories of inventory from simple inventory records that are kept in terms of end-of-period costs. This method is called **dollar value LIFO.**

Overview of Dollar Value LIFO

Dollar value LIFO avoids much of the detailed record keeping required under standard LIFO. Ending inventory is determined in terms of year-end prices, just as it is under FIFO. The ending inventory at end-of-year prices is then adjusted by a price index to estimate LIFO inventory.[25] To illustrate the procedure in simplified form, let's assume that a firm first adopts LIFO on January 1, 2001 and elects to use dollar value LIFO. The time of initial LIFO adoption is termed the **base period.** The facts of the example are:

Beginning inventory, LIFO, at base period (1/1/01) costs	\$100,000
Ending inventory at 12/31/01 costs	\$140,000
Inventory price index at base period (1/1/01)	1.00
Inventory price index at 12/31/01	1.12

Under LIFO, a new LIFO layer is added only when the unit (or physical) quantity of inventory increases. In this example we cannot compare the ending inventory dollars (\$140,000) with the beginning inventory dollars (\$100,000) to determine whether physical quantities increased. Why? Because the December 31 inventory is stated at end-of-year costs while the beginning inventory is stated at base-period costs.

However, we can use the inventory price index to restate ending inventory (expressed in end-of-year costs) to base-period costs by dividing \$140,000 by 1.12. The result, \$125,000, is the December 31, 2001 inventory expressed in base-period (January 1, 2001) costs.

---

[25] A price index is simply a ratio that compares prices during the current period with prices during some base period. Separate indices are computed for each period. If a price index for a given year is 1.12, this means that prices in that year are 12% higher than they were in the base period.

In applying dollar value LIFO, the index used must reflect price changes for the specific inventory. General price indices are not permitted except in unusual situations. One method for computing the index is to determine the following ratio by reference to detailed purchase records:

$$\frac{\text{Cost of ending inventory at end-of-period prices}}{\text{Cost of ending inventory at base period prices}} = \text{Index for year}$$

However, this computation can be burdensome when the inventory consists of many different types of items. In such situations an index can be computed based upon a sample of representative purchases. One such approach is:

	Ending Inventory Units (1)	Base-Period Cost Per Unit (2)	Current-Period Cost Per Unit (3)	Total Base-Period Cost (1) × (2)	End-of-Period Cost (1) × (3)
Item A	20,000	\$3	\$ 4	\$ 60,000	\$ 80,000
Item B	5,000	7	8	35,000	40,000
Item C	11,000	9	10	99,000	110,000
				\$194,000	\$230,000

The resulting index is:

$$\frac{\$230{,}000}{\$194{,}000} = 1.186$$

Once ending inventory is restated, it is possible to determine whether the physical quantity of inventory has increased during 2001:

Ending inventory expressed in base-period costs ($140,000/1.12)	$125,000
Beginning inventory expressed in base-period costs	100,000
Inventory increase expressed in base-period costs	$ 25,000

Clearly, a new LIFO layer was added in 2001. However, the new LIFO layer must be recorded at the cost level that was in effect when the layer was added. Since the inventory increase expressed in terms of base period costs was $25,000—and since costs went up 12 percent during 2001—then the new LIFO layer would be costed at $25,000 × 1.12, or $28,000. Therefore, the December 31, 2001 ending inventory computed under the dollar value LIFO method would be comprised of two layers:

	Base-Period Costs	Adjustment Factor	Dollar Value LIFO Carrying Amount
Beginning inventory (1/1/01)	$100,000	1.00	$100,000
2001 layer	25,000	1.12	28,000
Ending inventory, dollar value LIFO			$128,000

To continue the example, let's assume that the December 31, 2002 inventory price index is 1.20 and that ending inventory at December 31, 2002 is $146,400 (expressed in year-end 2002 costs).

As before, it is necessary to determine whether a new LIFO layer was added in 2002. To do this, we must restate the December 31, 2002 inventory in terms of base-period costs and compare it to the January 1, 2002 inventory (expressed in base-period costs):

Ending inventory expressed in base-period costs ($146,400/1.20)		$122,000
Beginning inventory expressed in base-period costs:		
Base-period layer	$100,000	
2001 layer ($28,000/1.12)	25,000	
		125,000
Inventory decrease expressed in base-period costs		$ (3,000)

Expressed in base-period costs, inventory decreased in 2002. Since the cost flow is LIFO, this decrease is assumed to have come from the 2001 layer. At base-period costs, the 2001 layer would be reduced to $22,000—that is, $25,000 minus the $3,000 inventory decrease. The December 31, 2002 dollar value LIFO inventory would again be comprised of two layers:

	Base-Period Costs	Adjustment Factor	Dollar Value LIFO Carrying Amount
Beginning inventory	$100,000	1.00	$100,000
2001 layer	22,000	1.12	24,640
Ending inventory, dollar value LIFO			$124,640

Finally, assume that inventory at December 31, 2003 totals $170,100 at year-end costs and that the inventory price index at that date is 1.26. In order to determine whether a new LIFO layer was added in 2003, we must restate the December 31, 2003 inventory in terms of base-period costs:

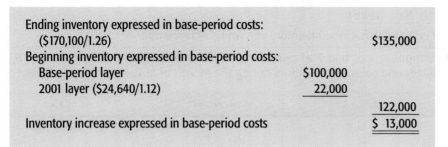

Ending inventory expressed in base-period costs:		
($170,100/1.26)		$135,000
Beginning inventory expressed in base-period costs:		
Base-period layer	$100,000	
2001 layer ($24,640/1.12)	22,000	
		122,000
Inventory increase expressed in base-period costs		$ 13,000

The new 2003 LIFO layer must be added to LIFO inventory using the cost level in effect in 2003. To do this, we must multiply the inventory increase expressed in base-period costs ($13,000) by the December 31, 2003 price index, which is 1.26. Thus, the December 31, 2003 dollar value LIFO inventory would consist of three layers:

	Base-Period Costs	Adjustment Factor	Dollar Value LIFO Carrying Amount
Beginning inventory	$100,000	1.00	$100,000
2001 layer	22,000	1.12	24,640
2003 layer	13,000	1.26	16,380
Ending inventory, dollar value LIFO			$141,020

The steps required to compute dollar value LIFO are summarized as follows:

1. Ending inventory is initially computed in terms of year-end costs. This simplifies record keeping.
2. To determine whether a new LIFO layer had been added (or whether an existing layer has been liquidated), the ending inventory must be restated to base-period cost and compared to the beginning inventory at base-period cost. This eliminates the effect of input cost changes. After restatement, any difference between beginning and ending inventory is the inventory change expressed in base-period cost. It indicates whether inventory *quantities* have changed.
3. Any inventory change determined from step 2 must be costed as follows:
   a. New LIFO layers are valued using costs of the year in which the layer was added.
   b. Decreases in old LIFO layers are removed using costs that were in effect when the layer was originally formed.

The procedures for costing new dollar value LIFO layers are technically inconsistent with a strict LIFO flow assumption. For example, notice that the 2003 layer added in the example is costed at 1.26, a figure which represents 2003 *year-end* costs. Under traditional LIFO, new layers are added using beginning-of-year costs, not end-of-year costs. Since dollar value LIFO is a computational convenience, this inconsistency in costing new layers is usually ignored in order to simplify the computations.

EXERCISES

E9–1

Account analysis

AICPA adapted

On January 1, 2001 the merchandise inventory of Manuel Company was $300,000. During 2001 Manuel purchased $1,900,000 of merchandise and recorded sales of $2,000,000. The gross profit (gross margin) on these sales was 20%.

REQUIRED:

What is the merchandise inventory of Manuel at December 31, 2001?

E9–2

Cost flow computations

AICPA adapted

City Stationers, Inc., had 200 calculators on hand at January 1, 2001 costing $18 each. Purchases and sales of calculators during the month of January were as follows:

Date	Purchases	Sales
January 12		150 @ $28
14	100 @ $20	
29	100 @ $22	
30		100 @ $32

City does not maintain perpetual inventory records. According to a physical count, 150 calculators were on hand at January 31, 2001.

REQUIRED:

1. What is the cost of the inventory at January 31, 2001 under the FIFO method?
2. What is the cost of the inventory at January 31, 2001 under the LIFO method?

E9–3

Account analysis

AICPA adapted

The following information is available for Day Company for 2001:

Cash disbursements for purchases of merchandise	$290,000
Increase in trade accounts payable	25,000
Decrease in merchandise inventory	10,000

REQUIRED:

What is the cost of goods sold for 2001?

E9–4

Account analysis

AICPA adapted

For the year 2001, the gross profit of Dumas Company was $96,000; the cost of goods manufactured was $340,000; the beginning inventories of goods in process and finished goods were $28,000 and $45,000, respectively; and the ending inventories of goods in process and finished goods were $38,000 and $52,000, respectively.

REQUIRED:

What is the dollar amount of Dumas Company sales for 2001?

E9–5

Account analysis

AICPA adapted

Hestor Company's records indicate the following information:

Merchandise inventory, January 1, 2001	$ 550,000
Purchases, January 1 through December 31, 2001	2,250,000
Sales, January 1 through December 31, 2001	3,000,000

On December 31, 2001 a physical inventory determined that ending inventory of $600,000 was in the warehouse. Hestor's gross profit on sales has remained constant at 30%. Hestor suspects some of the inventory may have been taken by some new employees.

REQUIRED:

At December 31, 2001, what is the estimated cost of missing inventory?

E9–6

Account analysis

AICPA adapted

On June 30, 2001 a flash-flood damaged the warehouse and factory of Padway Corporation, completely destroying the work-in-process inventory. There was no damage to either the raw materials or finished goods inventories. A physical inventory taken after the flood revealed the following valuations:

Raw materials	$ 62,000
Work-in-process	–0–
Finished goods	119,000

The inventory of January 1, 2001 consisted of the following:

Raw materials	$ 30,000
Work-in-process	100,000
Finished goods	140,000
	$270,000

A review of the books and records disclosed that the gross profit margin historically approximated 25% of sales. The sales for the first six months of 2001 were $340,000. Raw material purchases were $115,000. Direct labor costs for this period were $80,000, and manufacturing overhead has historically been applied at 50% of direct labor.

REQUIRED:

Compute the value of the work-in-process inventory lost at June 30, 2001. Show supporting computations.

E9–7

Cost flow computations

AICPA adapted

The Frate Company was formed on January 1, 2001. The following information is available from Frate's inventory records for Product Ply:

	Units	Unit Cost
January 1, 2001		
(Beginning inventory)	800	$ 9.00
Purchases:		
January 5, 2001	1,500	10.00
May 25, 2001	1,200	10.50
July 16, 2001	600	11.00
November 26, 2001	900	11.50

A physical inventory on December 31, 2001 shows 1,600 units on hand.

REQUIRED:

Prepare schedules to compute the ending inventory at December 31, 2001 under each of the following inventory methods:

1. FIFO
2. LIFO
3. Weighted average

Show supporting computations in good form.

E9–8

Absorption versus variable costing

AICPA adapted

Information from Peterson Company's records for the year ended December 31, 2001 is available as follows:

Net sales	$1,400,000
Cost of goods manufactured:	
Variable	$ 630,000
Fixed	$ 315,000
Operating Expenses:	
Variable	$ 98,000
Fixed	$ 140,000
Units manufactured	70,000
Units sold	60,000
Finished goods inventory, 1/1/01	None

There were no work-in-process inventories at the beginning and end of 2001.

REQUIRED:

1. What would be Peterson's finished goods inventory cost at December 31, 2001 under the variable (direct) costing method?
2. Under the absorption costing method, what would Peterson's operating income be?

E9–9

Absorption versus variable costing

AICPA adapted

Selected information concerning the operation of Kern Company for the year ended December 31, 2001 is available as follows:

Units produced	10,000
Units sold	9,000
Direct materials used	$40,000
Direct labor incurred	$20,000
Fixed factory overhead	$25,000
Variable factory overhead	$12,000
Fixed selling and administrative expenses	$30,000
Variable selling and administrative expenses	$ 4,500
Finished goods inventory, January 1, 2001	None

There were no work-in-process inventories at the beginning and end of 2001.

REQUIRED:

1. What would be Kern's finished goods inventory cost at December 31, 2001 under the variable (direct) costing method?
2. Which costing method—absorption or variable costing—would show a higher operating income for 2001, and by what amount?

E9–10

Change to LIFO method

AICPA adapted

The Hastings Company began operations on January 1, 2001 and uses the FIFO method in costing its raw material inventory. Management is contemplating a change to the LIFO method in 2002 and is interested in determining what effect such a change will have on net income. Accordingly, the following information has been developed:

	2001	2002
Final inventory		
FIFO	$240,000	$270,000
LIFO	200,000	210,000
Net income		
(Computed under the FIFO method)	$120,000	$170,000

REQUIRED:

Based on the above information, what would 2002 net income be after the change to the LIFO method?

E9–11

Inventory errors

CMA adapted

The following inventory valuation errors have been discovered for Knox Corporation:

- The 1999 year-end inventory was overstated by $23,000.
- The 2000 year-end inventory was understated by $61,000.
- The 2001 year-end inventory was understated by $17,000.

The reported income before taxes for Knox was:

Year	Income Before Taxes
1999	$138,000
2000	254,000
2001	168,000

REQUIRED:

Compute what income before taxes for 1999, 2000, and 2001 should have been after correcting for the errors.

E9–12

Lower of cost or market

AICPA adapted

Moore Corporation has two products in its ending inventory; each is accounted for at the lower of cost or market. A profit margin of 30 percent on selling price is considered normal for each product. Specific data with respect to each product follows at the top of the next page:

	Product 1	Product 2
Historical cost	$17.00	$ 45.00
Replacement cost	15.00	46.00
Estimated cost to dispose	5.00	26.00
Estimated selling price	30.00	100.00

REQUIRED:

In pricing its ending inventory using the lower of cost or market rule, what unit values should Moore use for products 1 and 2, respectively?

E9–13

Dollar-value LIFO

AICPA adapted

The Acute Company manufactures a single product. On December 31, 1998, Acute adopted the dollar-value LIFO inventory method. The inventory on that date using the dollar-value LIFO inventory method was determined to be $300,000. Inventory data for succeeding years are as follows:

Year Ended December 31	Inventory at Respective Year-End Prices	Relevant Price Index (Base Year 1998)
1999	$363,000	1.10
2000	420,000	1.20
2001	430,000	1.25

REQUIRED:

Compute the inventory amounts at December 31, 1999, 2000, and 2001, using the dollar-value LIFO inventory method for each year.

E9–14

Dollar-value LIFO

AICPA adapted

On December 31, 2000 Fern Company adopted the dollar-value LIFO inventory method. All of Fern's inventories constitute a single pool. The inventory on December 31, 2000 using the dollar-value LIFO inventory method was $600,000. Inventory data for 2001 are as follows:

December 31, 2001 inventory at year-end prices	$780,000
Relevant price index at year-end (base year 2000)	1.20

REQUIRED:

Under the dollar-value LIFO inventory method, what would Fern's inventory be at December 31, 2001?

E9–15

Inventory costing concepts

AICPA adapted

Cost for inventory purposes should be determined by the inventory cost flow method most clearly reflecting periodic income.

REQUIRED:

1. Describe the fundamental cost flow assumptions for the average cost, FIFO, and LIFO inventory cost flow methods.
2. Discuss the reasons for using LIFO in an inflationary economy.
3. Where there is evidence that the utility of goods, in their disposal in the ordinary course of business, will be less than cost, what is the proper accounting treatment and under what concept is that treatment justified?

PROBLEMS/DISCUSSION QUESTIONS

P9–1

Account analysis

The following information pertains to Yuji Corporation:

	January 1, 2001	December 31, 2001
Raw materials inventory	$ 34,000	$ 38,000
Work-in-process inventory	126,000	145,000
Finished goods inventory	76,000	68,000
Costs incurred during the year 2001 were as follows:		
Raw material purchased		$116,000
Wages to factory workers		55,000
Salary to factory supervisors		25,000
Salary to selling and administrative staff		40,000
Depreciation on factory building and equipment		10,000
Depreciation on office building		12,000
Utilities for factory building		5,000
Utilities for office building		7,500

REQUIRED:

Sales revenue during 2001 was $300,000. The income tax rate is 40%. Compute the following:

1. Cost of raw materials used
2. Cost of goods manufactured/completed
3. Cost of goods sold
4. Gross margin
5. Net income

P9–2

Inventory accounting—comprehensive

Alex Wholesalers Inc. began its business on January 1, 2001. Information on its inventory purchases and sales during 2001 are provided below:

	Inventory Purchases		
	Units	**Cost per Unit**	**Total**
January 1	10,000	$4.00	$ 40,000
March 10	8,000	4.10	32,800
April 12	12,000	4.30	51,600
September 15	7,500	4.45	33,375
November 11	6,000	4.75	28,500
December 29	6,500	5.00	32,500
Units available for sale	**50,000**		**$218,775**

	Inventory Sales		
	Units	**Price per Unit**	**Total**
March 1	7,000	$8.00	$ 56,000
September 1	20,000	8.50	170,000
December 1	11,000	9.00	99,000
Units sold	**38,000**		**$325,000**

Assume a tax rate of 40 percent.

REQUIRED:

1. Compute the cost of ending inventory and cost of goods sold under each of the following methods: (1) FIFO, (2) Weighted average cost, and (3) LIFO. Assume that Alex uses the periodic inventory procedure.
2. Assume that Alex uses the periodic LIFO method.
   a. Calculate the replacement cost of the ending inventory and the LIFO reserve as of the end of the year. You may assume that year-end purchase cost was still $5.00 per unit.
   b. Provide an estimate of Alex's cost of goods sold under the periodic FIFO method based only on the information that will be publicly available to the investors of Alex. Explain why your answer differs from FIFO cost of goods sold computed in part 1.
   c. The purchasing manager of Alex was planning to acquire 10,000 units of inventory on January 5, 2002, at $5.00 per unit. The accountant for Alex suggests that the company will be better off if Alex acquires the inventory instead on December 31, 2001. What are the pros and cons of the accountant's suggestion? Wherever possible, show supporting calculations.
3. Calculate cost of goods sold assuming that Alex uses the perpetual FIFO method.

P9–3

LIFO liquidation

The inventory footnote to the 2001 annual report of the Ruedy Company reads in part as follows:

> Because of a prolonged strike in one of our supplier's plants, inventories were unavoidably reduced during 2001. Under the LIFO system of accounting, this "eating into LIFO layers" resulted in an increase in *after-tax* net income of $36,000 over what it would have been had inventories been maintained at their physical levels which existed at the start of the year.

The price of Ruedy Company's merchandise purchases was $22 per unit for 20,000 units during 2001. Prior to 2001, inventory prices had risen steadily for many years. Ruedy Company uses the periodic inventory method. The company's inventory positions at the beginning and end of the year are summarized below. Ruedy's income tax rate is 40%.

Date	Physical Count of Inventory	LIFO Cost of Inventory
January 1, 2001	30,000 units	$?
December 31, 2001	20,000 units	260,000

REQUIRED:

1. Was 2001 cost of goods sold higher or lower as a result of the LIFO liquidation? By how much?
2. Were 2001 income taxes higher or lower as a result of "eating into LIFO layers"? By how much?
3. What was the average cost per unit of the 10,000 units removed from the January 1, 2001 LIFO inventory?
4. What was the January 1, 2001 LIFO cost of inventory?
5. What was the reported 2001 cost of goods sold for Ruedy Company?

P9–4

Criteria for choosing a cost flow assumption

The president of Jeanette Corporation is in a dilemma regarding which inventory method (LIFO or FIFO) to use. The controller of Jeanette Corporation provides the following list of factors that should be considered before making a choice.

1. Jeanette Corporation has borrowed money during the current month and has entered into a debt contract. The covenants of this contract require Jeanette Corporation to achieve a certain amount of net income and maintain a certain amount of working capital.
2. The Board of Directors of Jeanette is contemplating a proposal to reward the top management of Jeanette Corporation with an incentive bonus that is based on accounting net income.

3. The vice president of finance suggests using the LIFO method for tax purposes and the FIFO method for financial reporting purposes. With lower taxable income, Jeanette Corporation can save on the current tax it pays, and at the same time, it can show higher income in the financial reports and "look good."
4. The controller cautions that while the LIFO method may reduce the current period tax liability, "it could hit us hard when things are not going so well." This potential problem with the LIFO method could be "avoided if we use FIFO in the first place."
5. However, the president would like to adopt the method that provides both a better application of the matching principle and a more current measure of inventory on the balance sheet.
6. The controller suggests that Jeanette should adopt the FIFO method since higher accounting income means a higher stock price.

REQUIRED:

The president of Jeanette has asked you to write a report evaluating the pros and cons of each of the issues raised above. Given her busy schedule, the president would like the report to be brief. In answering this question, assume that Jeanette Corporation expects an upward trend in inventory prices.

P9–5

Inventory alternatives

Princess Retail Stores started doing business on January 1, 2001. The following data reflect its inventory purchases and sales during the year:

	Inventory Purchases		
	Units	**Cost per Unit**	**Total**
January 1	20,000	$ 7.00	$140,000
March 1	16,000	9.00	144,000
June 1	14,000	11.00	154,000
September 1	10,000	13.00	130,000
December 1	12,000	15.00	180,000
	72,000		**$748,000**

	Sales		
	Units	**Price per Unit**	**Total**
March 2	24,000	$14.00	$336,000
September 2	18,000	16.00	288,000
December 2	20,000	18.00	360,000
	62,000		**$984,000**

REQUIRED:

1. Compute gross margin and cost of ending inventory using the periodic FIFO cost flow assumption.
2. Compute gross margin and cost of ending inventory using the periodic LIFO cost flow assumption. Compute the dollar amount of the LIFO reserve. Using this additional disclosure, how might an analyst estimate the cost of goods sold of Princess under the FIFO method based only on publicly available information? Show supporting calculations.
3. Under historical cost accounting, gross margin is calculated as current output price minus historical input price. For analytical convenience, we can break the gross margin into two components:

   a. "True" operating margin = current output price − current input price, and
   b. Inventory profits = current input price − historical input price.

   Provide an estimate of the "true" operating margin for Princess Retail Stores.
4. The following are excerpts from a recent top management meeting at Princess Retail Stores. Your assignment is to clearly provide guidelines to the top manage-

ment team on each of the issues raised in the meeting. Show calculations where necessary.

a. "I am most concerned about appropriately matching revenues and expenses. I suggest that we look for an inventory accounting method that achieves this objective both during inflationary and deflationary times." (Frances Iyer, Chairman)
b. "Frances, I think the choice is obvious. What other method can achieve better matching of revenues and expenses than the specific identification method? By choosing this method, we would send a clear signal to the stock market that we are not playing any earnings management games." (Sandra Kang, VP Investor Relations)
c. "I would like to maximize our current profits. What inventory method might help us achieve this most important goal and why?" (Antonia Iyer, CEO)
d. "Antonia, I know you can't stop thinking about your earnings-based bonus. My primary objective is to minimize the present value of future income tax outflows." (Juanita Kang, CFO)
e. "I would like to have our cake and eat it too. Why don't we follow Juanita's suggestion for income tax accounting and follow Antonia's idea for external financial reporting?" (B. T. Kang, VP Operations)

P9–6

Inventory turnover

STRETCH

The following is excerpted from the financial statements of Baldwin Piano and Organ Company:

CONSOLIDATED STATEMENTS OF EARNINGS

	Years Ended December 31 Year 3	Year 2	Year 1
Net sales	$120,657,455	$110,076,904	$103,230,431
Cost of goods sold	89,970,702	79,637,060	74,038,724
Gross profit	$ 30,686,753	$ 30,439,844	$ 29,191,707

Inventories consist of the following:

	Year 3	Year 2
FIFO cost:		
Raw materials	$ 9,930,923	$ 9,500,765
Work in process	7,081,883	5,943,672
Finished goods	36,149,809	39,328,177
	53,162,615	54,772,614
Excess of FIFO cost over LIFO inventory value	(8,085,250)	(6,828,615)
	$45,077,365	$47,943,999

At December 31, Year 3, approximately 77% of the company's inventories were valued on the LIFO method.

During the past three years, certain inventories were reduced. This reduction resulted in the liquidation of LIFO inventory layers carried at the lower costs prevailing in prior years as compared with the current cost of inventories. The effect of these inventory liquidations was to increase net earnings for Year 3, Year 2, and Year 1 by approximately $694,000 ($.20 per share), $519,000 ($.15 per share) and $265,000 ($.08 per share), respectively.

REQUIRED:

1. Estimate Baldwin's cost of goods sold and the cost of goods manufactured for Year 3; assume the company had used FIFO instead of LIFO.
2. On the basis of these FIFO numbers, compute Baldwin's finished goods and work-in-process inventory turnovers (expressed in days) for Year 3. What do these turnovers tell you about Baldwin's operating cycle?

P9–7

Gross margins and cash flow sustainability

Parque Corporation applied to Fairview Bank early in 2001 for a $400,000 five-year loan to finance plant modernization. The company proposes that the loan be unsecured and repaid from future operating cash flows. In support of the loan application, Parque submitted an income statement for 2000. Prepared using the FIFO inventory cost flow approach, this income statement reflected annual profit that was approximately 50% of the principal amount of the loan. This was offered as evidence that the loan could easily be repaid within the five-year term.

Parque is in the business of recycling yelpin, an industrial lubricant. The company buys used yelpin from large salvage companies and, after cleaning and reconditioning it, sells it to manufacturing companies. The recycling business is very competitive and has typically generated small gross margins. The salvage companies set yelpin prices on the first day of each quarter, and Parque purchases yelpin at the established price for the entire quarter. Yelpin prices fluctuate with business conditions. Prices paid to salvage companies by Parque have risen in recent years but tend to fall during economic downturns.

Parque sells the recycled yelpin at $1 per pound above the currently prevailing price that it pays to acquire the used yelpin from salvage companies. December 31, 1999 inventory was 300,000 pounds at a cost of $7.00 per pound. Purchases and sales in 2000 were:

	Purchases	Sales
First quarter 2000	600,000 lbs. @ $7.20/lb.	700,000 lbs. @ $8.20/lb.
Second quarter 2000	700,000 lbs. @ $7.40/lb.	600,000 lbs. @ $8.40/lb.
Third quarter 2000	800,000 lbs. @ $7.80/lb.	700,000 lbs. @ $8.80/lb.
Fourth quarter 2000	600,000 lbs. @ $8.10/lb.	650,000 lbs. @ $9.10/lb.

Cash operating costs during 2000 totaled $2,800,000.

REQUIRED:

1. Compute 2000 income for Parque Corporation using the FIFO inventory flow assumption. Ignore income taxes.
2. Did Parque Corporation really earn a profit from its *operating* activities in 2000?
3. Given the circumstances described, what risks exist that could threaten ultimate repayment of the loan?

P9–8

Evaluating inventory cost-flow changes

1. The following is an excerpt from the financial statements of Trinity Industries:

> Effective September 30, 1987, the Company changed its method of accounting for inventories from the LIFO method principally to the Specific Identification method, because, in the opinion of management, there is a better matching of revenues and expenses, better correlation of accounting and financial information with the method by which the Company is managed, and better presentation of inventories at values that more fairly present the inventories' cost.

REQUIRED:

Evaluate each of the justifications provided by Trinity for changing its inventory cost flow assumption.

2. During 1990, SPS Technologies changed its inventory cost flow assumption from LIFO to the average cost method. The following is an excerpt from the financial statements of SPS Technologies.

> The change to the average cost method will conform all inventories of the Company to the same method of valuation. The Company believes that the average cost method of inventory valuation provides a more meaningful presentation of the financial position of the Company since it reflects more recent costs in the balance sheet. Under the current economic environment of low inflation and an expected reduction in inventories and low production costs, the Company be-

lieves that the average cost method also results in a better matching of current costs with current revenues.

REQUIRED:

Evaluate each of the justifications provided by SPS Technologies for changing its inventory cost flow assumption.

P9–9

Interfirm comparisons

Fraser Corporation uses the LIFO method of inventory valuation and is in the process of preparing its financial statements for the year 2001. The controller of Fraser Corporation provided the following income statement for the year ended December 31, 2001 to top management for review:

Sales Revenue		$1,000,000
Less: Cost of goods sold		
Beginning Inventory	150,000	
Add: Purchases	650,000	
Less: Ending Inventory	(200,000)	
		(600,000)
Gross Profit		400,000
Less: Selling and administrative expenses		(150,000)
Net Income before Taxes		250,000
Less: Income taxes		(75,000)
Net Income		$ 175,000

The CEO of Fraser had mixed emotions after examining the income statement. He wanted to know how Fraser compares with its closest rival, KAS Corporation, and he instructed the controller to "compute some ratios for both companies." KAS uses the FIFO method of inventory valuation. The following are excerpts from the controller's report:

	Fraser	KAS
Gross margin rate (Gross margin/sales)	?	49%
Return on sales (Net income/sales)	?	21%
Inventory turnover (COGS/average inventory)	?	1.8

REQUIRED:

1. Complete the controller's report by computing the ratios for Fraser based on the information given in the income statement above. For each ratio, how does Fraser compare with KAS? Explain how the choice of inventory methods biases the comparisons in favor of either Fraser or KAS.
2. After reviewing the controller's report, the CEO was concerned about Fraser's performance relative to KAS on two out of the three ratios. However, the controller pointed out to the CEO that the "perceived underperformance" of Fraser is primarily driven by differences in accounting methods. In addition, the controller added that if one takes into account "our current period LIFO tax savings, Fraser has outperformed KAS." The CEO asked the controller, "Why don't you show me how an analyst might adjust our income statement to make it comparable to that of KAS?" Your task is to help the controller by preparing a pro forma income statement for Fraser, one that is comparable to that of KAS. Assume that if Fraser had used the FIFO method, the beginning and ending inventories would have been higher by $50,000 and $150,000, respectively. On the basis of the "adjusted" income statement, recompute the three ratios given in the controller's report, and explain how and why the CEO's earlier conclusions are altered by the revised figures.

P9–10

LIFO and ratio effects

STRETCH

The original Bacardi® rum business was founded in Cuba in 1862 by Don Facundo Bacardy Maso. The following information is excerpted from the annual report of Bacardi Corporation for the year ended December 31, Year 2. The effective tax rate of Bacardi was 17% in Year 2.

> The company follows the last-in, first-out (LIFO) method of determining inventory cost. The LIFO method is considered by management to be preferable because it more closely matches current costs with current revenues in periods of price level changes. Under this method, current costs are charged to costs of sales for the year.
>
> In Year 2, LIFO liquidation was caused primarily by a substantial reduction during the year in [the inventory of] molasses (the major raw material). This LIFO liquidation, which resulted in cost of products sold being charged with higher inventory costs from prior years, caused a decrease in Year 2 net income of approximately $1,400,000 or $0.14 per share.
>
> LIFO inventories at December 31, Year 2 and Year 1 were $51,892,000 and $53,812,000 respectively, which is approximately $700,000 and $20,800,000 less than replacement cost at those dates.
>
> In accordance with generally recognized trade practices, inventories of distilled spirits in bonded aging warehouses have been included in current assets, although the normal aging period is usually from one to three years.

[Ending] inventories consist of the following:

($ in thousands)	Year 2	Year 1
Finished goods	$ 2,684	$ 2,420
Aging rum in bond	40,285	39,921
Raw materials and supplies	8,923	11,471
	$51,892	$53,812

Cost of goods sold and net income (after tax) during Year 2 were $65,374,000 and $45,568,000 respectively.

REQUIRED:

1. Compute the cost of goods manufactured (i.e., rum fully aged) during Year 2. Without using the LIFO reserve information, compute the finished goods inventory turnover (i.e., number of days from when inventory is completed until it is sold) and the work-in-process inventory turnover (i.e., number of days the inventory is in the production cycle). Is the difference between the two inventory turnover ratios consistent with the nature of Bacardi's business? Explain.
2. On the basis of available information, provide an estimate of Bacardi's net income if the company had used FIFO during Year 2. By comparing the reported LIFO income with your estimate of FIFO income, what do you learn about the business conditions faced by Bacardi during Year 2?
3. Using all available information, compute a total inventory turnover measure (expressed in number of days). Does your estimate of inventory turnover capture the "true" physical turnover of Bacardi (based on what you know about the business)? Explain. If it does not capture the "true" physical turnover, provide possible reasons. Be specific.

P9–11

LIFO Inventory—Comprehensive

The comparative income statements and edited inventory footnote for Oxford Industries, Inc. for 2000 follow. Located in Atlanta, Oxford designs, manufactures, markets and sells consumer apparel products for both men and women. Its ticker symbol is OXM. Using the information provided, answer the questions at the end of this problem.

OXFORD INDUSTRIES, INC. AND SUBSIDIARIES

Consolidated Statements of Earnings

($ in thousands, except per share amounts)	June 2, 2000	Year Ended May 28, 1999	May 29, 1998
Net sales	$839,533	$862,435	$774,518
Costs and expenses:			
Cost of goods sold	685,841	698,170	619,690
Selling, general and administrative	112,056	116,284	111,041
Interest, net	3,827	4,713	3,421
	801,724	819,167	734,152
Earnings before income taxes	37,809	43,268	40,366
Income taxes	14,368	16,875	15,743
Net earnings	$ 23,441	$ 26,393	$ 24,623
Basic earnings per common share	$3.04	$3.15	$2.79
Diluted earnings per common share	$3.02	$3.11	$2.75

OXFORD INDUSTRIES, INC. AND SUBSIDIARIES

Edited Inventory Footnote*

The components of inventories are summarized as follows:

($ in thousands)	June 2, 2000	May 28, 1999
Finished goods	$ 90,961	$ 92,195
Work in process	25,903	24,579
Fabric	28,255	23,280
Trim and supplies	8,118	6,874
	$153,237	$146,928

The excess of replacement cost over the value of inventories based upon the LIFO method was $37,154,000 at June 2, 2000, $37,367,000 at May 28, 1999, and $39,205,000 at May 29, 1998. Changes in the LIFO reserve increased earnings $0.02 per share basic in 2000, $0.13 per share basic in 1999, and decreased earnings $0.06 per share basic in 1998.

During fiscal 2000, inventory quantities were reduced, which resulted in a liquidation of LIFO inventory layers carried at lower costs which prevailed in prior years. The effect of the liquidation was to decrease cost of goods sold by approximately $147,000 and to increase net earnings by $91,000 or $0.01 per share basic. During fiscal 1999, the effect of [the 1999] liquidation was to decrease cost of goods sold by approximately $1,174,000 and to increase net earnings by $716,000 or $0.09 per share basic. During fiscal 1998, the effect of [the 1998] liquidation was to decrease cost of goods sold by approximately $591,000 and to increase net earnings by $361,000 or $0.04 per share basic.

*The footnote was edited to include selected 1998 data. Items in the footnote *text* have no zeroes omitted.

Assume that the effective tax rate is 35%.

REQUIRED:

1. Based on the available information, provide an estimate of Oxford Industries' "Earnings before income taxes" for the years 2000 and 1999 if the company had used FIFO accounting.

(*continued*)

2. Using the available data, provide estimates of the amount of realized holding gains (inventory profits) that were included in 2000, 1999 and 1998 "Earnings before income taxes" under the LIFO method.
3. Explain why the estimated FIFO income numbers (see requirement [1]) are higher or lower than those under the LIFO method. (*Hint*: To do this, prepare a reconciliation of changes in the LIFO reserve for 2000 and 1999 as illustrated on page 410 of the text.)
4. As of the end of the fiscal years 2000 and 1999, compute the total amount of income tax saved by Oxford from the time of its initial adoption of LIFO. Ignore present value effects in your calculations. For the fiscal year 2000 alone, did Oxford pay higher or lower income tax under LIFO compared to what it would have paid under FIFO? How much?
5. Compute Oxford's inventory turnover ratio (without making any adjustments) for the year 2000 under the LIFO cost flow assumption. (Express it in number of days.) Does this number provide a good estimate of the days' inventory held by Oxford Industries? If not, propose (and defend) an alternative approach to calculating the inventory turnover. Show supporting calculations.

P9–12

LIFO reporting–comprehensive

Maple Company has used the LIFO method of inventory accounting since its inception in 1960. At December 31, 1999, the ending inventory was:

Base layer	5,000 units @ $1.00	= $5,000
1968 layer	2,000 units @ $1.30	= 2,600
		$7,600

The company uses the periodic inventory system in which sales are assumed to have been made from the last inventory units acquired during the year. Purchase prices for Maple Company's inventory are adjusted twice a year by its supplier—on January 1 and July 1.

Purchase and sales transactions for 2000 and 2001 were:

	Units Purchased	Units Sold
2000		
January–June	40,000 units @ $2.50	30,000 units @ $3.80
July–December	40,000 units @ $2.70	50,000 units @ $3.90
2001		
January–June	40,000 units @ $2.75	43,000 units @ $4.00
July–December	40,000 units @ $3.00	43,000 units @ $4.30

Other expenses totaled $60,000 in 2000 and $66,000 in 2001. Inventory purchase prices in effect during the last half of 1999 were $2.40 per unit.

REQUIRED:

1. Compute operating income for the Maple Company on the LIFO historical cost basis for 2000 and 2001.
2. Compute current cost income from continuing operations for the Maple Company for 2000 and 2001.
3. Determine the total increases in current cost amounts (i.e., unrealized cost savings or holding gains) occurring in 2000 and 2001.
4. What portion of the reported 2000 and 2001 LIFO income consisted of realized holding gains (i.e., "inventory profits")?
5. What was the dollar amount of Maple Company's LIFO reserve at December 31, 1999? Compute the increases and decreases to the LIFO reserve in 2000 and 2001. Identify the cause for each increase and decrease.
6. LIFO, a method which supposedly is designed to keep inventory profits out of income, does not accomplish this result for the Maple Company in either 2000 or 2001. Why?

P9–13

LIFO–comprehensive

Sirotka Retail Company began business in 1999. The following information pertains to Sirotka for the first three years of its operation:

		Purchases		Sales	
Year	**Operating Expenses**	**Units**	**Unit Cost**	**Units**	**Unit Price**
1999	$60,000	15,000	$20.00	12,000	$35.00
2000	90,000	20,000	25.00	18,000	40.00
2001	65,000	5,000	30.00	10,000	40.00

Assume the following:

- The income tax rate is 40%.
- Purchase and sale prices change only at the beginning of the year.
- Sirotka uses the LIFO cost flow assumption.
- Operating expenses are primarily selling and administrative expenses.

REQUIRED:

1. Compute cost of goods sold and the cost of ending inventory for each of the three years. (Identify the number of units and the cost per unit for each LIFO layer in the ending inventory.)
2. Prepare income statements for each of the three years.
3. Compute the LIFO reserve at the end of 1999, 2000, and 2001.
4. Compute the effect of LIFO liquidation on the net income of the company for the years 2000 and 2001.
5. Compute the inventory turnover ratio for the years 2000 and 2001. Do not make adjustments for any potential biases in LIFO accounting. Comment on the direction of the bias (i.e., understated/overstated) in the inventory turnover ratio under LIFO. Is the ratio in one year more biased than in the other? Explain.
6. How best can the physical turnover of inventory (i.e., "true" inventory turnover) be approximated using *all* the information available in a LIFO financial statement? Illustrate your approach by recomputing Sirotka's inventory turnover ratios for 2000 and 2001.
7. Compute the gross margin rates for the years 2000 and 2001. Explain whether the difference in the gross margin rates between 2000 and 2001 reflect the change in Sirotka's economic condition from 2000 to 2001.
8. Provide an *estimate* of the FIFO cost of goods sold for the years 1999, 2000, and 2001 using the information available in the financial statements.
9. Based on your answers to subparts (1) and (8), estimate Sirotka's tax savings for 1999, 2000, and 2001.
10. Assuming a discount rate of 10%, compute the present value as of December 31, 1998 of the tax savings over the period 1999–2001 (i.e., discount the 1999 tax savings one period, and so on).

P9–14

Identifying FIFO holding gains

Caldwell Corporation operates an ice-cream processing plant and uses the FIFO inventory cost flow assumption. A partial income statement for the year ended December 31, 2001 appears below:

CALDWELL CORPORATION

Statement of Income
For the Year Ended December 31, 2001

Sales revenues	$680,000,000
Cost of goods sold	360,000,000
Gross margin	320,000,000
SG&A expenses	200,000,000
Income before taxes	$120,000,000

Caldwell's physical inventory levels were virtually constant throughout 2001. The FIFO dollar amount of inventory at January 1, 2001 was $60,000,000. During 2001, the Consumer Price Index (an index of overall average purchasing power for typical urban-dwelling consumers) increased by 4%.

Caldwell Corporation's largest competitor, Cohen Confections, uses LIFO for inventory accounting. Excerpts from its December 31, 2001 inventory footnote were:

INVENTORY FOOTNOTE (COHEN CONFECTIONS):
Inventories are computed using the LIFO cost flow assumption. Comparative amounts were:

	December 31	
	2001	**2000**
Raw materials	$ 8,100,000	$ 8,000,000
Finished goods	76,000,000	80,000,000
	$84,100,000	$88,000,000

The difference between the LIFO inventory amounts and the replacement cost of the inventory at December 31, 2001 and 2000, respectively, was $18,000,000 and $12,000,000. A LIFO liquidation occurred in 2001 which increased the reported gross margin by $1,000,000.

REQUIRED:

Using the above information, what is the *best* estimate of the amount of realized holding gains (or inventory profits) included in Caldwell Corporation's "income before taxes."

CASES

C9–1

Barbara Trading Company (KR): Understanding LIFO distortions

Barbara Trading Company has used the LIFO method of inventory accounting since its inception in 1970. At December 31, 1999 the ending inventory was:

Base layer	10,000 units @ $ 7.00	$ 70,000
1980 layer	5,000 units @ $12.00	$ 60,000
		$130,000

The company uses the periodic inventory method, in which sales are assumed to have been made from the last inventory units acquired during the year (periodic LIFO). The purchase and sales prices change only once a year (i.e., on January 1). Operating expenses are $600,000 per year and the income tax rate is 40%.

Year	Units Purchased	Units Sold
2000	100,000 units @ $25.00	100,000 units @ $35.00
2001	90,000 units @ $30.00	100,000 units @ $40.00

During 2001, Barbara Trading Company implemented a new inventory management program to reduce the level of inventory carried.

REQUIRED:

1. Prepare Barbara's income statements for the years 2000 and 2001.
2. The CEO of Barbara Trading Company, Ms. I. M. Greedy, examined the effect of the new inventory management program on the company's inventory turnover. After doing some quick calculations, Ms. Greedy was overjoyed. "When our competitors are turning their inventory over 12 to 15 times a year, our inventory turnover for 2001 has exceeded 30!" How did the CEO estimate the inventory turnover ratio for 2001? Based on all available information, provide an estimate of the "true" inven-

tory turnover of Barbara Trading Company during 2001. Assume the competitors' turnovers were based on data from their financial statements. What might be the potential limitations of comparing Barbara's inventory turnover with its competitors'? Show supporting figures where necessary.

3. The CEO was also quite ecstatic about the company's overall performance during the year 2001. "I am extremely pleased with the growth in our bottom line. Although some of the growth is probably due to the increase in selling price, most of it appears to be the result of our new inventory management program." Prepare a memo to the CEO explaining the "true" reasons behind the change in net income from 2000 to 2001. Show supporting figures where necessary. Also critically evaluate the rationale provided by the CEO for the growth in earnings.
4. The CFO of Barbara Trading Company, Mr. I. M. Taxed, was rather concerned about the tax implications of reducing inventory levels. He was lamenting, "I told you all about the LIFO Boomerang. We could have avoided paying a lot of taxes that resulted from our inventory liquidations had we adopted FIFO in the first place." Evaluate the CFO's analysis of the tax effects.

C9–2

General Electric: Interpreting a LIFO footnote

http://www

The following inventory footnote appears in the 1999 General Electric annual report.

GENERAL ELECTRIC COMPANY

Edited Inventory Footnote

($ in millions)	December 31 1999	1998
GE		
Raw materials and work in process	$3,438	$3,154
Finished goods	3,054	2,967
Unbilled shipments	233	195
	6,725	6,316
Less revaluation to LIFO	(927)	(1,011)
	5,798	5,305
GE Capital Services		
Finished goods*	1,209	744
	$7,007	$6,049

LIFO revaluations decreased $84 million in 1999, compared with decreases of $87 million in 1998 and $119 million in 1997. Included in these changes were decreases of $4 million, $29 million and $59 million in 1999, 1998 and 1997, respectively, that resulted from lower LIFO inventory levels. There were net cost decreases in each of the last three years.

*Including $773 million of Wards' retail inventory at year-end 1999. [*Authors' note:* GE Capital Services acquired control of the formerly bankrupt retailer on August 2, 1999.]

GE's earnings before income taxes were $15.577 billion in 1999. Assume a 35% marginal tax rate.

REQUIRED:

1. What are the total cumulative tax savings as of December 31, 1999 that GE has realized as a result of using the LIFO inventory method?
2. What would GE's pre-tax earnings have been in 1999 if it had been using FIFO?
3. What December 31, 1999 balance sheet figures would be different—and by how much—if GE had been using FIFO to account for its inventories?
4. What were the LIFO liquidation profits reported in 1999 both pre-tax and after tax?
5. Explain what factors cause the difference between the LIFO pre-tax income number and the FIFO pre-tax income number you estimated in requirement 2. (*Hint*: Reconcile the change in the LIFO reserve for 1999.)
6. Repeat requirements 1–3 using GE's 2000 financial statements.

C9–3

Harsco Corporation: Interpreting a LIFO footnote

The following inventory footnote is taken from Harsco Corporation's 1999 annual report. You are to use this information in answering the questions that follow. Inventories are summarized as follows:

HARSCO CORPORATION

Edited 1999 Inventory Footnote

Inventories consist of:

($ in thousands)	1999	1998
Finished goods	$ 37,715	$ 45,259
Work-in-process	37,198	36,060
Raw materials and purchased parts	76,911	71,576
Stores and supplies	20,374	22,909
	$172,198	$175,804
Valued at lower of cost or market:		
LIFO basis	$132,366	$129,708
FIFO basis	16,483	28,473
Average cost basis	23,349	17,623
	$172,198	$175,804

Inventories valued on the LIFO basis at December 31, 1999 and 1998 were approximately $28.4 million and $32.5 million, respectively, less than the amounts of such inventories valued at current costs.

As a result of reducing certain inventory quantities valued on the LIFO basis, net income increased . . . by $1.1 million, $0.2 million and $0.1 million in 1999, 1998 and 1997, respectively.

REQUIRED:

1. By how much would net income after taxes have differed for 1999 if Harsco had used FIFO to value those inventory items valued under LIFO? Assume a 35% marginal tax rate. Be sure to indicate whether FIFO income would be higher or lower than LIFO income.
2. What would the "LIFO Reserve" have been on December 31, 1999 if no LIFO liquidation had occurred in 1999?
3. What was the net difference in 1999 income taxes that Harsco experienced as a result of using LIFO rather than FIFO? Assume a 35% tax rate and indicate whether FIFO or LIFO would yield the higher tax and by how much.
4. What was the approximate rate of change in input costs in 1999 for Harsco's inventory?

C9–4

Baines Corporation: Absorption versus variable costing

Baines Corporation is a manufacturer of fireplace tools and accessories. The company has been prosperous since its incorporation in 1960, largely due to a small, exceptionally skilled, and highly motivated managerial staff. Baines has been able to attract and retain its excellent management team because of a very attractive managerial incentive plan. The plan allocates 23% of total pre-tax FIFO-absorption cost profits into a pool that is distributed to managers as a year-end bonus. The bonus pool is allocated to individual managers using a point system based upon each manager's performance relative to a budgeted goal.

Data relating to 2000 operations were as follows:

Beginning inventory	1,500,000 units @ $2.95
Ending inventory	1,500,000 units @ $2.95
Production	4,000,000 units
Sales	4,000,000 units @ $3.50
Variable production costs	$1.45/unit
Fixed production costs	$6,000,000/year

Reported pre-tax profit for 2000 was:

Sales revenues	(4,000,000 @ $3.50)		$14,000,000
Costs of goods sold:			
Variable production costs	(4,000,000 @ $1.45)	$5,800,000	
Fixed production costs	(4,000,000 @ $1.50)	6,000,000	
			11,800,000
Operating profit			2,200,000
Interest expense			200,000
Pre-tax profit			$ 2,000,000

Early in 2001, interest rates increased and the president of Baines Corporation, Mr. Eldred, was concerned about the rising cost of financing the inventory. After a careful study of the situation, Mr. Eldred became convinced that inventory levels could be reduced considerably without adversely affecting sales or delivery performance, provided certain changes in purchasing, production, and sales procedures were adopted. Accordingly, Mr. Eldred called a meeting of the management group in February 2001 and outlined his multifaceted plan for reducing inventories.

His basic strategy met with immediate acceptance, and various additional efficiencies and other inventory management improvements were suggested by several of the participants. The meeting adjourned with each manager resolving to do all that was possible to decrease inventory levels and thereby reduce interest expenses.

As the year progressed, Mr. Eldred's proposals and the refinements suggested by the other managers were put into practice; as a result, inventory levels were significantly reduced by December 31, 2001. The managers were quite pleased with their successful implementation of the new strategy, and morale was quite high.

Basic facts concerning 2001 performance were as follows:

Beginning inventory	1,500,000 units @ $2.95
Ending inventory	700,000 units @ $3.325
Production	3,200,000 units
Sales	4,000,000 units @ $3.50
Variable production costs	$1.45/unit
Fixed production costs	$6,000,000/year
Interest expense	$100,000/year

Shortly after the final 2001 profit figures were reported early in 2002, a general management meeting was held. As he walked into the room, Mr. Eldred was somewhat surprised to see a rather sullen and dispirited group of managers confronting him. One was heard to mumble, "Well, I wonder what this year's double cross will be!"

REQUIRED:

1. What do you think caused the abrupt change in the mood of the management team at Baines Corporation? Cite figures to support your explanation.
2. How might this problem have been prevented? Cite figures to support your explanation.

C9–5

Handy & Harman: Comprehensive LIFO analysis

Founded shortly after the U.S. Civil War, Handy & Harman is a New York based manufacturer dealing in both precious and nonprecious metal products. In 1980 precious metals segments comprised 76% of total revenues and 83% of pre-tax profit contribution before allocation of general corporate expenses.

Handy & Harman's business activities span a range of industries and applications. For example, in the precious metals sector, the company makes gold and silver alloys for jewelry and silverware in many gauges, finishes, and colors. In addition, the company operates a refining service in which gold, silver, and platinum metals are recovered from manufacturing scrap. Precious metals alloys supplied by Handy & Harman are used, for example, as electrical contacts, fuse links, switches and relays in electronic components; they are also used to join metals in airplane hydraulic systems.

Their silver-cadmium-indium control rods govern the rate of chain reactions in nuclear power plants, and other precious metal products are used as circuitry materials in television sets, home computers, and electronic games. Nonprecious metal products include tubing, piping, and cable. These products are supplied to firms in energy, transportation, electronic, and leisure product sectors.

LIFO inventory accounting was originally permitted by the Revenue Act of 1938 and extended to a wide range of U.S. industries by the Revenue Act of 1939. The 1939 Act included a "conformity" rule which prohibited companies that used LIFO for tax purposes from reporting to shareholders using non-LIFO methods. Many believe that this conformity rule led to the widespread adoption of LIFO for external reporting purposes.

Handy & Harman has used LIFO for precious metals inventory accounting since the early 1940s. However, a change in the Canadian income tax law, which prohibited LIFO accounting for income tax purposes, caused the company to liquidate the Canadian subsidiary's LIFO layers in 1979. As explained in Exhibit 2, the pre-tax "inventory profits," which were recognized as a consequence of this liquidation totaled $10,157,000. Exhibit 1 contains both the comparative "Consolidated Statement of Income" from the 1980 Annual Report and the comparative edited "Consolidated Balance Sheet" as well as the balance sheet inventory footnote. Exhibit 2 contains excerpts from "Management Discussion and Analysis" from the 1980 report. Exhibit 3 contains New York monthly average market prices for gold and silver during the 1979 and 1980 period in addition to average yearly price data over the 1975–1980 period. Exhibit 3 reflects the substantial increases in precious metals prices that occurred between 1977 and 1980. These increases, in turn, led to significant differences between the LIFO carrying cost of the precious metals inventory and their then current market replacement cost. These differences (the "LIFO reserve") are separately reported in the inventories footnote included in Exhibit 1.

Exhibit 1 ■ HANDY & HARMAN AND SUBSIDIARIES

Consolidated Balance Sheet

	December 31 1980	December 31 1979
Assets		
Current assets:		
Cash	$ 5,166,000	$ 5,243,000
Receivables	205,349,000	429,722,000
Refundable federal income taxes	—	4,320,000
Inventories	102,897,000	90,432,000
Deferred income tax benefit	1,607,000	1,173,000
Prepaid expenses and deposits	2,157,000	2,385,000
Total current assets	317,176,000	533,275,000
Property, plant, and equipment	125,578,000	103,121,000
Less accumulated depreciation and amortization	44,256,000	38,350,000
	81,322,000	64,771,000
Intangibles, net of amortization	4,708,000	3,204,000
Deferred charges	328,000	365,000
Other assets	893,000	1,633,000
Total assets	$404,427,000	$603,248,000

Exhibit 1 (*continued*) ■ HANDY & HARMAN AND SUBSIDIARIES

Liabilities and shareholders' equity		
Current liabilities:		
Notes payable	$119,500,000	$339,302,000
Current maturities of long-term liabilities	5,607,000	5,703,000
Accounts payable	62,302,000	89,292,000
Accrued liabilities:		
Smelters' charges and other expenses	20,622,000	20,189,000
United States and foreign taxes on income	21,822,000	2,069,000
Other taxes	4,513,000	1,758,000
Total current liabilities	234,366,000	458,313,000
Long-term liabilities, less current maturities	54,763,000	53,129,000
	289,129,000	511,442,000
Deferred income taxes	3,888,000	3,277,000
Total Liabilities	293,017,000	514,719,000
Shareholders' equity:		
Common stock—par value $1; 16,000,000 shares authorized; issued: 1980—14,611,432; 1979—14,611,432 shares	14,611,000	14,611,000
Capital surplus	7,011,000	6,621,000
Retained earnings	94,122,000	71,796,000
	115,744,000	93,028,000
Deduct treasury stock: 1980—964,128 shares; 1979—1,009,728 shares—at cost	4,334,000	4,499,000
Total shareholders' equity	111,410,000	88,529,000
Total liabilities and shareholders' equity	$404,427,000	$603,248,000

Consolidated Statements of Income

	Year Ended December 31		
	1980	1979	1978
Sales and service revenues	$760,957,000	$630,924,000	$467,955,000
Cost of sales and service	639,481,000	541,582,000	405,333,000
Gross profit	121,476,000	89,342,000	62,622,000
Selling, general, and administrative expenses	46,776,000	38,886,000	27,702,000
	74,700,000	50,456,000	34,920,000
Other deductions (income):			
Interest expense	17,820,000	26,754,000	9,063,000
Other (net)	1,970,000	1,196,000	(256,000)
	19,790,000	27,950,000	8,807,000
Income before income taxes	54,910,000	22,506,000	26,113,000
Provision for taxes on income	27,162,000	8,725,000	13,192,000
Net income	$ 27,748,000	$ 13,781,000	$ 12,921,000
Net income per share of common stock	$2.04	$1.02	$0.95

Exhibit 1 (*continued*) ■ HANDY & HARMAN AND SUBSIDIARIES

Supplemental Information:
Inventories footnote

	1980	1979	1978
Precious metals:			
Fine and fabricated metals in various stages of completion	$ 54,961,000	$ 39,098,000	$ 41,698,000
Non-precious metals:			
Base metals, factory supplies, and raw materials	23,122,000	29,521,000	18,997,000
Work in process	10,283,000	14,797,000	9,289,000
Finished goods	14,531,000	7,016,000	8,269,000
	$ 102,897,000	$ 90,432,000	$ 78,253,000
Precious metals stated at LIFO cost	$ 54,072,000	$ 38,775,000	$ 41,589,000
LIFO inventory—excess of year-end market value over cost	$431,554,000	$646,795,000	$151,892,000
12/31 market value per ounce:			
Silver	$ 15.65	$ 28.00	$ 6.07
Gold	$586.00	$512.00	$226.00
Market value of precious metals held for customers and returnable in commercial bar or fabricated form	$ 82,962,000	$ 91,842,000	$ 31,996,000

Exhibit 2 ■ EXCERPTS FROM MANAGEMENT DISCUSSION AND ANALYSIS, HANDY & HARMAN

1980 Annual Report

LIQUIDITY

The nature of the Company's business, which is primarily that of fabricating and refining precious metals, in many respects makes it unique insofar as liquidity is concerned. Its inventories, consisting principally of gold and silver, may be considered as an equivalent to cash. Furthermore, these precious metals inventories which are stated in the balance sheet at LIFO cost have a market value substantially in excess of such cost. . . .

OPERATIONS

Comparison of 1980 versus 1979

Sales for the precious metals segment increased $132,974,000 (30%) resulting from higher average prices for gold and silver, partially offset by lower unit sales volume. The average price for gold was $612.51 per ounce and the average price for silver was $20.63 per ounce, representing increases of 99% and 86% respectively over the previous year.

Profit contribution (pre-tax income before deducting interest and corporate expenses) increased $28,671,000 (88%) for the segment. The higher precious metals prices caused a surge in the refining end of the precious metals business, as explained in the Letter to Shareholders. The 1979 profit contribution included a pre-tax LIFO gain of $10,157,000, resulting from the liquidation of the Canadian subsidiary's gold and silver inventory. The 1979 figures were adversely affected by a strike of almost six months duration at two principal plants in the precious metal segment. . . .

Exhibit 3 ■ MONTHLY AVERAGE AND ANNUAL PRICE DATA

Gold

Annual average $ per troy oz.		Monthly average $ per troy oz.	1979	1980
1975	161.165	January	227.384	675.377
1976	124.939	February	246.147	665.513
1977	147.978	March	242.207	553.629
1978	193.436	April	238.853	516.771
1979	307.615	May	257.441	513.912
1980	612.509	June	279.162	600.717
		July	295.331	643.273
		August	301.993	627.510
		September	356.968	675.774
		October	392.734	660.343
		November	392.160	622.476
		December	461.006	594.814

Silver

Annual average cents per troy oz.		Monthly average cents per troy oz.	1979	1980
1975	441.852	January	625.455	3,825.682
1976	435.346	February	741.716	3,508.500
1977	462.302	March	744.518	2,413.333
1978	540.089	April	749.250	1,450.000
1979	1,109.418	May	837.345	1,253.286
1980	2,063.157	June	853.833	1,574.762
		July	913.505	1,605.932
		August	933.387	1,589.714
		September	1,395.916	2,014.381
		October	1,678.073	2,018.136
		November	1,660.265	1,864.824
		December	2,179.278	1,639.333

REQUIRED:

1. Using the data contained in the exhibits, estimate what Handy & Harman's income before taxes would have been for 1979 and 1980 had the FIFO inventory flow assumption been used.
2. Discuss the two potential causes for the difference between income as reported in 1979 and 1980 and income that would have been reported under FIFO. Which of these alternatives appears to be the more likely cause for the income divergence computed in your response to question 1?
3. Estimate the total tax savings that Handy & Harman gained as of December 31, 1979 and as of December 31, 1980 because of its use of LIFO in prior years. Assume a tax rate of 46%. What factor explains the tax savings changes between year-end 1979 and year-end 1980?

COLLABORATIVE LEARNING CASE

C9–6 **Weldotron Corporation (KR): Strategic choice of accounting methods**

The following excerpts are taken from Weldotron's financial statements.

WELDOTRON CORPORATION AND SUBSIDIARIES

Condensed Consolidated Balance Sheets
February 28, 1994, and February 28, 1993

($ in thousands)	1994	1993
Assets		
Total current assets	$15,449	$16,162
Net property, plant, and equipment	3,417	3,725
Other assets	220	170
Total assets	$19,086	$20,057
Liabilities and stockholders' equity		
Total current liabilities	$ 7,144	$ 7,021
Long-term debt less current portion	1,527	1,585
Other long-term liabilities	683	637
Total liabilities	9,354	9,243
Minority interest	722	700
Stockholders' equity:		
Common stock, par value $0.05 per share; issued 2,352,720 in 1994 and 1,882,720 in 1993	118	94
Additional paid in capital	9,798	8,715
(Deficit) Retained earnings	(783)	1,428
	9,133	10,237
Less: Common stock in treasury	(123)	(123)
Total stockholders' equity	9,010	10,114
Total liabilities & stockholders' equity	$19,086	$20,057

WELDOTRON CORPORATION AND SUBSIDIARIES

Condensed Consolidated Statements of Operations
For the Years Ended February 28, 1994, February 28, 1993, and February 29, 1992

($ in thousands)	1994	1993	1992
Net sales	$30,440	$26,400	$29,061
Costs and expenses:			
Cost of sales	22,375	19,322	21,372
Selling, general, and administrative	9,258	9,471	8,902
Depreciation and amortization	558	612	678
Restructuring charges	625	–0–	–0–
	32,816	29,405	30,952
Loss from operations	(2,376)	(3,005)	(1,891)
Other income (expenses)	128	(33)	606
Income tax (benefit) provision	(59)	26	–0–
Minority interest share of (income) loss	(22)	(57)	123
Loss from continuing operations	(2,211)	(3,121)	(1,162)
Discontinued operations:	–0–	–0–	(1,059)
Net Loss	$ (2,211)	$ (3,121)	$ (2,221)

Excerpts from Footnotes: ($ in thousands)

1. Summary of Significant Account Policies

Inventories: Substantially all inventories are valued at the lower of cost, determined by the use of the first in, first out method (FIFO) or market (see Note 2).

Income Taxes: Weldotron Corporation and its subsidiaries file a consolidated federal income tax return. Accumulated undistributed earnings of the Company's foreign subsidiary were approximately $352 at February 28, 1994. No provision has been made for U.S. income taxes on these earnings as the Company has reinvested or plans to reinvest overseas.

2. Change In Accounting Principle for Inventories

Effective February 28, 1994, the Company changed its basis of valuing inventories from the last in, first out (LIFO) method to the first in, first out (FIFO) method.

In previous years, the Company experienced significant operating losses and has addressed these problems by discontinuing certain products and related parts. The results of inventory reductions in previous years resulted in the liquidation of LIFO layers which resulted in a mismatching of older costs with current revenues, which defeats the primary objective of LIFO. Further reductions of inventory levels are expected from the discontinuance of products and parts as well as better manufacturing methods which will reduce production lead times. Under these circumstances, the FIFO method of inventory valuation is the preferable method due to the improved matching of revenues and expenses and the current industry practice.

The change has been applied retroactively by restating prior years' financial statements. The effects of the reversal of the previous LIFO reserve were partially offset by the appropriate application of FIFO costing requirements. The effects of this change in the method of valuing inventory were to increase the net loss previously reported in 1993 by $128 and to decrease the net loss previously reported in 1992 by $97. The effects on 1994 were not material. The effects of this restatement were also to increase retained earnings as of March 1, 1991 by $2,356 (i.e., the retroactive effect).

7. Long Term Debt and Short Term Borrowings

On June 25, 1991, the Company entered into a credit facility (the "Credit Facility") with Congress Financial Corporation ("Congress"), a CoreStates Company, to provide a revolving line of credit and term loan for working capital purposes not to exceed $5,000, which replaced the Company's existing credit facility. The interest rate is 3.75% over the CoreStates floating base rate, which was 6% at February 28, 1994. The Credit Facility further requires that the Company pay fees on the unused line of credit, for administration and upon early termination of the Credit Facility. On April 13, 1994, the Credit Facility was extended for one year. It expires and is due and payable on or before June 25, 1995.

The Credit Facility is collateralized by substantially all of the assets of the Company and its domestic subsidiaries. Borrowings under the Credit Facility are limited to certain percentages of eligible inventory and accounts receivable including stipulations as to the ratio of advances collateralized by receivables compared to advances collateralized by inventory.

The Credit Facility's covenants stipulate that tangible domestic net worth of greater than $8,200 and consolidated working capital greater than $9,500 be maintained. In addition, the Credit Facility restricts the payment of dividends, limits the amount of the advances to and guarantees for the Company's foreign subsidiary and limits annual capital expenditures to $500. At February 28, 1994 the Company was in compliance with the covenants of the Credit Facility.

Borrowings under the Credit Facility aggregated $3,215, including a $1,500 long-term loan at February 28, 1994. The remaining borrowing under the Credit Facility is included in current liabilities.

Tax Note:

At February 28, 1994, $8,400 of Federal tax loss carryforwards are available for regular income tax purposes.

Note 2 states that Weldotron changed its inventory method from LIFO to FIFO effective February 28, 1994. In the same note, the Company has provided justifications for the change in the inventory cost flow assumption. Note 7 discloses details of the Company's credit facility and covenants. This note states that the Company was in compliance with the covenants on February 28, 1994.

REQUIRED:

Financial reporting choices can sometimes allow companies to achieve strategic objectives and benefit shareholders. Using this perspective, evaluate the effect of Weldotron's inventory accounting change on its debt covenants, specifically on the tangible domestic net worth constraint of $8,200 and the consolidated working capital constraint of $9,500. (Note: In answering this question you should keep in mind that when applying the working capital constraint, lenders often ignore current liabilities related to the borrowing itself.)

10

Long-Lived Assets and Depreciation

LEARNING OBJECTIVES:

After studying this chapter, you will understand:

1. What measurement base is used in accounting for long-lived assets and why this base is used.
2. What specific costs can be capitalized and how joint costs are allocated among assets.
3. How generally accepted accounting principles (GAAP) measurement rules complicate both trend analysis and cross-company analysis and how to avoid misinterpretations.
4. Why balance sheet carrying amounts for internally developed intangibles usually differ from their real value.
5. When long-lived asset impairment exists and how it is recorded.
6. How different depreciation methods are computed.
7. How analysts can adjust for different depreciation assumptions and improve interfirm comparisons.
8. How long-lived asset accounting and depreciation practices differ internationally.

An asset is something that generates future economic benefits and is under the exclusive control of a single entity. Assets can be tangible items like inventories and buildings or intangible items like patents and trademarks.

The previous two chapters—receivables and inventories—examined current assets. Current assets represent a large part of total assets for many companies. Recall that a current asset is expected to be converted into cash within one year or within the operating cycle, whichever is longer.

> The *operating cycle* begins with the receipt of raw materials inventory and ends when the cash is received for the completed product that has been sold. If inventory turns over every 90 days and if the average receivables collection period is 50 days, then the operating cycle is 140 days (i.e., 90 + 50).

This chapter concentrates on operating assets expected to yield their economic benefits (or service potential) over a period longer than one year. Such assets are called **long-lived assets.**

Long-lived assets represent a significant percentage of total assets in industries like oil exploration and refining, automobile manufacturing, and steel. Exhibit 10.1 shows a condensed version of the asset portion of Phillips Petroleum Company's balance sheet in both dollar and common-sized terms at December 31, 1999. Notice that long-lived assets (properties, plants and equipment) comprises 72.9% of total assets. Firms have latitude in how much detail they provide about separate long-lived asset components. Phillips chose to provide a footnote breakdown of the total properties by industry segment, as shown in Exhibit 10.2. Notice that the highlighted net properties total from Exhibit 10.1 ($11,086) appears again in Exhibit 10.2. Statement readers can then see the breakdown of gross and net property, plants and equipment across industry segments.

Exhibit 10.1 ■ PHILLIPS PETROLEUM COMPANY

Condensed Partial Consolidated Statement of Financial Position

($ in millions)	December 31, 1999	Percentage
Assets:		
Cash and cash equivalents	$ 138	
Accounts and notes receivable (less allowances: 1999—$19; 1998—$13)	1,808	
Inventories	515	
Deferred income taxes	143	
Prepaid expenses and other current assets	169	
Total current assets	2,773	18.2%
Investments and long-term receivables	1,103	7.3
Properties, plants and equipment (net)	11,086	72.9
Deferred income taxes	83	0.6
Deferred charges	156	1.0
TOTAL	$15,201	100.0%

Source: Phillips Petroleum Company 1999 Annual Report.

Clearly, there's a high proportion of long-lived assets in some industries. However, the GAAP rules used to measure the carrying amounts of long-lived assets are frequently criticized, and we'll see why next.

Exhibit 10.2 ■ PHILLIPS PETROLEUM COMPANY

Condensed Footnote Breakdown of Property, Plants and Equipment

The Company's investment in properties, plants and equipment (PP&E), with accumulated depreciation, depletion and amortization (DD&A), at December 31 was:

	1999		
($ in millions)	Gross PP&E	DD&A	Net PP&E
Exploration and production	$12,326	$ 6,744	$ 5,582
Gas gathering, processing and marketing	2,316	1,275	1,041
Refining, marketing and transportation	4,611	2,131	2,480
Chemical	2,963	1,210	1,753
Corporate and other	512	282	230
	$22,728	$11,642	$11,086

Source: Phillips Petroleum Company 1999 Annual Report.

Measuring the Carrying Amount of Long-Lived Assets

There are two ways that long-lived assets could potentially be measured:

1. Assets could be measured at their estimated value in an ***output*** market. An output market refers to a market where assets are ***sold.*** We will call measures that use output market numbers **expected benefit approaches.**
2. Assets could be measured at their estimated cost in an ***input*** market. An input market refers to a market where assets are ***purchased.*** Measures that use input costs will be called **economic sacrifice approaches.**

Expected benefit approaches recognize that assets are valuable because of the ***future cash inflows*** they are expected to generate. Consequently, these approaches measure various definitions of future cash inflows generated by the asset. One example of an expected benefit approach is **discounted present value.** Here, the value of an item of manufacturing equipment would be measured by estimating the discounted present value of the stream of future net operating cash inflows it's expected to generate over its operating life. Another example of an expected benefit approach is the cash inflow that the asset would bring if it were sold instead of being used in operations. Under this variant of the expected benefit approach, long-lived assets would be reported at their **net realizable value**—the amount that would be received if the asset were sold in the used asset market.

Economic sacrifice approaches to asset measurement focus on the amount of resource expenditure necessary to acquire it. One example of an economic sacrifice approach is **historical cost** (the dominant GAAP measurement method)—that is, the historical amount spent to buy the asset constitutes the *past* sacrifice incurred to bring the asset into the firm. Another example of an economic sacrifice approach involves measuring the current (or replacement) cost of the asset. Under a **replacement cost** approach, assets would be carried at their current purchase cost—the expenditure (sacrifice) needed *today* to buy the asset.

The Approach Used by GAAP

Table 10.1 shows a hypothetical range of long-lived asset carrying amounts as measured under each approach. Assume the fixed asset is a truck used by a freight hauler to transport heavy industrial equipment. Let's say the truck originally cost $100,000, is two years old, has a remaining useful life of eight years, is being depreciated straight-line, and is expected to have no salvage value (market value) at the end of its useful life.

GAAP uses historical cost—an economic sacrifice approach—for measuring long-lived assets in almost all circumstances. The choice of historical cost is not an accident. It results from several pragmatic aspects of the existing financial reporting environment.

CONTRACTING

As discussed in Chapter 1, financial reports play a critical role in resource allocation decisions such as equity investing and lending. Furthermore, accounting numbers are widely used in contracts such as loan agreements, incentive compensation plans, and union contracts. Because of these uses, ***parties whose transactions are explicitly or implicitly tied to accounting numbers expect them to be reliable numbers.*** By **reliable,** we mean the

Table 10.1 ■ HYPOTHETICAL LONG-LIVED ASSET CARRYING AMOUNTS

Expected Benefit Approaches

1. Discounted present value:

   Expected net operating cash inflows = $18,000 per year (assumed) for eight remaining years, discounted at a 10% (assumed) rate

   $$5.33493^{1} \times \$18,000 = \$96,029$$

2. Net realizable value:

   Current resale price from an over-the-road equipment listing (Purple Book) for the specific vehicle model

   $85,000 (Assumed)

Economic Sacrifice Approaches

3. Historical cost less accumulated depreciation:

   $$\$100,000 - \left(\frac{\$100,000}{10 \text{ years}} \times 2 \text{ years}\right) = \$80,000$$

4. Replacement cost:

   Replacement cost of a two-year-old vehicle in equivalent condition

   $90,000 (Assumed)

[1] Discount factor for an ordinary annuity for eight years at 10%.

numbers must not be prone to manipulation. If the numbers were not reliable (e.g., if they could be easily manipulated by one party to the contract), then cautious decision makers would be reluctant to enter into contracts using such "soft" numbers. The reason is that manipulation by one party could circumvent the contract terms.

Auditors also prefer that financial statement numbers have certain characteristics. One is that the numbers be verifiable. **Verifiability** means the numbers should arise from readily observable, corroborable facts, rather than from subjective beliefs. Verifiable numbers are important to auditors because of the many legal suits arising from audited financial statements. Auditors believe that verifiable data help provide a defense in court, reducing potential litigation losses.

As modern financial reporting evolved, reliability and verifiability were used as qualitative criteria, or guidelines, for selecting acceptable long-lived asset measurement rules. Expected benefit approaches, such as discounted present value reporting, were discarded because the resulting numbers were deemed to be neither reliable nor verifiable. That's because present value computations require inherently subjective forecasts of future net cash flows as well as an assumed discount rate. This is illustrated in Table 10.1 where alternative 1—the discounted present value/expected benefit approach—requires an estimate of expected net operating cash inflows ($18,000) and a choice of discount rate (10%). Most decision makers won't tie contracts to such numbers since the other party to the contract could easily evade certain contract terms by simply altering the cash flow forecast amounts or the discount rate.

Another expected benefit approach—the net realizable value from selling the asset—has also been rejected as a measurement base because of its frequent lack of verifiability. Our example in Table 10.1 assumed that the long-lived asset had a readily determinable market price, as some do. However, many long-lived assets are immobile (e.g., buildings), and others are highly specialized and therefore traded in thin markets; consequently, selling prices are often not readily determinable. The current selling price of these long-lived assets would need to be estimated using past transaction prices or transactions involving similar (but not necessarily identical) assets. Numbers obtained from such procedures often fail the verifiability test.

> Depreciation is an allocation of historical cost to time periods. Except by coincidence, the net book value number at a point in time—original cost less accumulated depreciation—does not reflect the economic worth of the asset at that time.

The economic sacrifice approach that uses replacement cost (i.e., the estimated current cost of *replacing* the asset), has also been disqualified on the basis of similar assertions that the numbers lack verifiability.

The only long-lived asset measurement method that survives the dual screens of reliability and verifiability is the economic sacrifice approach called historical cost. Consequently, long-lived assets are generally reflected in U.S. financial statements at the original historical cost of acquiring the asset (minus accumulated depreciation). Long-lived assets typically last for many years, and their replacement cost tends to increase. But GAAP prohibits adjustment for upward revisions in the replacement cost of the asset. However, when asset values are impaired, GAAP mandates write-downs.

> **RECAP**
>
> **Since long-lived assets are predominantly carried at depreciated historical cost, statement users should not expect balance sheet numbers for such assets to necessarily approximate their real economic worth. This is a serious deficiency (with important implications for statement users) that we explore later in this chapter.**

Long-Lived Asset Measurement Rules Illustrated

The initial carrying amount of a long-lived asset is governed by two rules:

1. All costs necessary to acquire the asset and make it ready for use are included in the asset account. Costs included in the asset account are called **capitalized costs.** (Expenditures excluded from asset categories are "charged-off" to income—i.e., expensed.)

2. **Joint costs** incurred in acquiring more than one asset are apportioned among the acquired assets.

Both rules are illustrated in the Canyon Corporation example that follows in Exhibit 10.3.

Exhibit 10.3 ■ CANYON CORPORATION

Joint Cost Allocation, Fixed Asset Purchase

Canyon Corporation acquired a tract of land on June 1, 2001 by paying $6,000,000 and by assuming an existing mortgage of $1,000,000 on the land. Canyon demolished an empty structure on the property at a cost of $650,000. Bricks and other materials from the demolished building were sold for $10,000. Regrading and clearing the land cost $35,000. Canyon then began constructing a new factory on the site. Architectural fees were $800,000, and the payments to contractors for building the factory totaled $12,000,000. Canyon negotiated a bank loan to help ease the cash flow crunch during construction. Interest payments over the construction period totaled $715,000. Legal fees incurred in the transaction totaled $57,000, of which $17,000 was attributable to both examination of title covering the land purchase and legal issues linked to the assumption of the existing mortgage. The remaining $40,000 of legal fees related to contracts with the architect and the construction companies. The construction project was completed on December 31, 2001.

The amounts allocated to the land and building accounts, respectively, are:

Land		
Cash payment		$ 6,000,000
Mortgage assumed		1,000,000
Demolition of existing structure	$650,000	
Less: Salvage value of material	(10,000)	
		640,000
Regrading and clearing land		35,000
Legal fees allocated		17,000
Capitalized land costs		$ 7,692,000
Building		
Architectural fees		$ 800,000
Building costs		12,000,000
Interest capitalized		715,000
Legal fees allocated		40,000
Capitalized building costs		$13,555,000

Capitalized land costs include many items in addition to the $6,000,000 cash payment. For example, the cost of demolishing the existing structure (net of salvaged materials) is added to the land account, since the land had to be cleared before the new building could be erected. This illustrates initial carrying amount Rule 1—all costs necessary to prepare the asset for its intended use are capitalized—here as land costs. The legal fees illustrate Rule 2—joint costs are apportioned among assets, both the land and building in this case.

The costs allocated to the building include the interest arising from the loan Canyon negotiated to finance construction. GAAP requires capitalizing what are called **avoidable interest** payments. *Statement of Financial Accounting Standards (SFAS) No. 34* (para. 12) defines this as interest that "could have been avoided . . . if expenditures for the as-

Apportionment is also necessary when more than one asset is acquired for a lump-sum price. Assume two tracts of land are acquired for $1,000,000. For property tax purposes, the land tracts are assessed as follows:

		Percentage
Tract 1	$240,000	40%
Tract 2	360,000	60%
Total	$600,000	100%

The $1,000,000 purchase price would be apportioned between the tracts in proportion to their assessed value—40% to Tract 1 and 60% to Tract 2.

International Accounting Standards (IAS) allow more latitude than FASB standards for interest capitalization. The "benchmark" (or standard) treatment is to expense all borrowing costs in the period incurred. However, the "allowed alternative treatment" permits capitalization. The guidelines for allowable capitalization are similar to those in *SFAS No. 34;* see "Borrowing Costs," *IAS 23* (revised 1993)(London: International Accounting Standards Committee [IASC] 1993, paras. 7, 13, 17).

sets had not been made."[1] To qualify as avoidable interest, the interest doesn't have to arise from borrowing that is directly linked to a construction loan. So long as some debt was outstanding during the construction period, a portion of the interest was avoidable and qualifies for capitalization. Here's why. Building the asset required spending cash. ***If the asset had not been built, that cash could have been used to retire debt, thereby lowering interest costs.*** This is why the interest is *avoidable,* and this is why the capitalized interest doesn't have to arise from a dedicated construction loan. Capitalizing interest is another application of Rule 1—interest paid to lenders during the construction period is considered to be a cost necessary to prepare the asset for its intended use.

Interest can also be capitalized for borrowings that are outstanding during construction of assets intended for sale or lease. To qualify for interest capitalization, the inventory being constructed must be an identifiable, discrete project (e.g., a three-year military contract to construct two aircraft carriers).

Avoidable interest is the product of the interest rate times cumulative weighted average expenditures. For example, assume the following timing of expenditures in Exhibit 10.3 on Canyon's construction project completed on December 31:

Date and Amount		Portion of Year		Cumulative Weighted Average Expenditures
June 1	$10,000,000	58.630%[1]	=	$5,863,000
August 22	3,555,000	36.203%	=	1,287,000
				$7,150,000

[1]June 1 through December 31 = 214 days, and 214 ÷ 365 = 58.630% of a year. The 36.203% is computed similarly.

Assuming a 10% interest rate on the outstanding debt, avoidable interest is $715,000 (10% × $7,150,000). GAAP limits the amount of interest that can be capitalized to the *lower* of (1) interest actually incurred or (2) avoidable interest. If Canyon's interest actually incurred had been $800,000, the capitalized amount would be limited to avoidable interest, $715,000. If interest actually incurred was only $600,000, then just $600,000 would be capitalized.

As discussed in Chapter 15, GAAP utilizes what is called the proprietary view of the firm. The proprietary view deems the firm and its owners to be indistinguishable. Consequently, funds contributed by owners do not come from "outsiders." ***The firm can't charge itself interest on contributed ownership capital.***

However, ***capitalization is restricted to interest arising from actual borrowings from outsiders.*** To see the financial statement effect of this restriction, let's assume that Canyon had not borrowed from a bank but had instead issued more common stock and used the proceeds to finance construction. Further assume that Canyon had absolutely no interest-bearing debt outstanding. Equity funds are not "free"—stockholders expect to earn a return, and they get angry when it doesn't materialize! Despite this, GAAP does not allow Canyon to calculate an artificial interest charge on the equity financing and capitalize this "imputed interest" as a part of the cost of the building. ***So the way the construction is financed can alter the cost capitalized under GAAP when a company initially has no outstanding debt.***

Treating equity that is issued to finance construction as "free" (when there is no interest-bearing debt outstanding) is consistent with the traditional accounting model, which ignores the cost of capital provided by owners when periodic income is computed—that is, GAAP allows no expense recognition for the cost associated with capital provided by stockholders. These funds are treated as if they are costless. In summary, the cost of equity capital is ignored in both income determination and asset costing.

Interest capitalization can complicate analysis of firms' performance over time. Because of interest capitalization, an increase in capital expenditures can temporarily decrease the amount of interest *expense* shown on the income statement and—all other factors being

[1] "Capitalization of Interest Cost," *Statement of Financial Accounting Standards (SFAS) No. 34* (Stamford, CT: Financial Accounting Standards Board [FASB], 1979).

equal—increase income. But this income increase does not result from increased sales, lower costs, or other operating efficiencies. Consequently, the year-to-year profit improvement is unrelated to operating activities and may not be sustainable. Of course, a decrease in year-to-year construction activity has just the opposite effect—the dollar amount of capitalized interest falls, thereby reducing income growth. To see this, consider the following example, taken from USX Corporation's 1999 10-K.

($ in millions)	Year ended December 31 1999	1998	Year-to-year Change
Income from continuing operations before income taxes	$1,054	$989	+ 6.6%
Minus: Capitalized interest	26	46	−43.5%
Income from continuing operations before income taxes and *without* interest capitalization	$1,028	$943	+ 9.0%

ANALYSIS

Notice, capitalized interest fell by $20 million, or 43.5%. With capitalization, USX income from continuing operations before income tax increased by 6.6% between 1998 and 1999. Without interest capitalization, the growth would have been 9.0%. The *decline* in capitalized interest reduced the rate of year-to-year income growth. By capitalizing interest, GAAP makes year-to-year income changes a function of *both* changes in operating performance *and* changes in construction levels. This complicates the analysis of earnings sustainability.

Tax Versus Financial Reporting Incentives The way incurred costs are allocated between land and building has an impact on the amount of income that will be reported in future periods. Land is a permanent asset—that's why it's not depreciated. A factory building has a finite life and is depreciated over future years. For *financial reporting purposes,* the manner in which costs are allocated—between, say, land and building—is guided by which one (land or building) generated the cost.

For *tax purposes* the incentives for allocating costs between land and building asset categories are completely different, because the objective of most firms is to minimize tax payments, not to "correctly" allocate costs. The larger are the costs allocated to land for tax purposes, the *higher* the future taxable income becomes since land cannot be depreciated. Aggressive taxpayers seek to minimize the amount of joint expenditures allocated to nondepreciable assets like land. Similarly, taxpayers would prefer not to capitalize interest payments for tax purposes since the benefits of the deduction would be spread over the depreciable life of the asset rather than being deductible immediately. However, U.S. income tax rules generally parallel financial reporting rules and *require* interest capitalization for qualifying assets.

Capitalization Criteria—An Extension Winger Enterprises, another example to help further clarify which costs are included in the determination of asset carrying amounts and which are not, follows in Exhibit 10.4 on the next page.

In Exhibit 10.4, total expenditures that are capitalized—that is, those that are included in the carrying amount of the machine—include *all* of the costs ($88,500) associated with getting the machine ready for production use, not just the invoice cost of $80,000.

To further illustrate the capitalization criteria, suppose that in January 2004 Winger spent an additional $8,000 on the machine. The total expenditure consisted of:

- $2,000 for ordinary repairs and maintenance, required every several years
- $6,000 for the installation of a new component that allowed the machine to consume less raw material and operate more efficiently.

In this example, the $2,000 would be treated as a period expense, while the $6,000 would be capitalized in 2004 and added to the carrying amount of the machine.

Exhibit 10.4 ■ WINGER ENTERPRISES

Determination of Capitalized Costs

On January 1, 2001 Winger Enterprises purchased a machine that will be used in operations. The cash purchase price of the machine was $80,000. The freight cost to transport the machine to Winger's factory was $1,200. During the month of January 2001 Winger's employees spent considerable time calibrating the machine and making adjustments and test-runs to get it ready for use. Costs incurred in doing this were:

Allocated portion of production manager's salary for coordinating machine adjustments	$2,200
Hourly wages of production workers engaged in test-runs of the machine	3,600
Cost of raw materials that were used in test-runs (the output was not saleable)	1,500

Given these facts, the capitalized amount of the machine would be the total of all of the costs ($80,000 + $1,200 + $2,200 + $3,600 + $1,500 = $88,500).

GAAP capitalizes an expenditure on a long-lived asset when the expenditure causes any of the following conditions:

- The useful life of the asset is extended;
- The capacity of the asset is increased (i.e., when there is an increase in attainable units of output);
- The efficiency of the asset is increased (i.e., when fewer labor hours or raw material inputs are required);
- There is any other type of increase in the economic benefits (or future service potential value) of the asset that results as a consequence of the expenditure.

Financial Analysis and Fixed Asset Reporting

ANALYSIS

Using depreciated historical cost as the measure of fixed asset values introduces many potential pitfalls for unwary statement readers. Here's a simple example.

Chen Corporation purchases long-lived assets and begins operations on January 1, 1999. The assets cost $1,000,000, have a 10-year expected life, no salvage value, and will be depreciated using the straight-line method. Assume that net operating cash flows (i.e., revenues minus variable operating expenses) for 1999 are $220,000. Chen's reported pre-tax return on beginning assets for 1999 is 12%, computed as:

Pre-tax net operating cash flow	$220,000
Depreciation ($1,000,000/10 years)	100,000
Pre-tax profit	$120,000

The pre-tax return on beginning net assets is calculated as:

$$\frac{\text{Pre-tax profit}}{\text{Beginning net assets}} = \frac{\$120{,}000}{\$1{,}000{,}000} = 12\%$$

Let's assume Chen makes no additional capital expenditures over the ensuing four years. Consequently, the average age of its operating assets increases over this period. Further assume that, on average, prices in the economy are increasing at 3% per year and that Chen is able to keep pace by increasing its net operating cash flow by 3%. Our example incorporates two features—aging assets and inflation—which complicate statement analysis. Table 10.2 shows why.

Table 10.2 ■ CHEN CORPORATION

Time-Series Distortions from Aging Assets and Inflation

	January 1, 1999	December 31, 1999	December 31, 2000	December 31, 2001	December 31, 2002	December 31, 2003
Asset book value	$1,000,000	$900,000	$800,000	$700,000	$600,000	$500,000
Net operating cash flow (increasing by 3% per year):		$220,000	$226,600	$233,398	$240,400	$247,612
Depreciation		100,000	100,000	100,000	100,000	100,000
Pre-tax profit		$120,000	$126,600	$133,398	$140,400	$147,612
Return on beginning assets		12%	14.1%	16.7%	20.1%	24.6%
Average age of assets		1 year	2 years	3 years	4 years	5 years

Notice that the return on beginning assets rises from 12% to 24.6% over the five years, highlighted in Table 10.2. As we are about to explain, this increase is caused by two factors:

1. An aging asset base
2. Increasing costs and prices.

While our example is contrived, it does help us understand how historical cost reporting for fixed assets may make trend analyses misleading. Specifically, how should the increasing return be interpreted? Is Chen's year-to-year performance really improving? Is the 2003 rate of return sustainable?

"Is year-to-year performance improving?" Probably not. The upward drift in reported return on assets is caused by operating cash flows that just keep pace with inflation, while depreciation and the asset's original cost do not change under historical cost reporting. To know whether the rate of return increase is "real," we need each year's numbers expressed in terms of current year prices. That is, to determine whether the return increase from 12% to 14.1% (in 2000) represents real improvement, we would need to know the replacement cost of the assets and we would need to recompute the rate of return using replacement cost depreciation and asset value. Only then could we assess whether some portion of the year-to-year "improvement" is real—as opposed to being an artifact of the historical cost basis of accounting for fixed assets.

"Is the 2003 return sustainable?" No, it's not. If the rate of return for 2003 were recomputed on a replacement cost basis, it would not be 24.6%. Statement readers seldom have enough information to adjust for year-to-year distortions like those in Table 10.2. However, they must understand that ***when asset reinvestment is not continuous, the increasing age of the asset base in conjunction with rising prices introduces distortions*** like those in Table 10.2—and thus, projections must be made with caution.

Historical cost accounting for long-lived assets also creates problems for statement readers who try to make comparisons between companies like Chen Corporation and its competitors. To see why, suppose Chen's biggest competitor is Rizzo Corporation. As of January 1, 1999 Rizzo had assets with a net book value of $1,000,000. Recall that Chen also had an asset net book value of $1,000,000 on that same date. While Chen's assets were new, let's assume Rizzo's were, on average, five years old and had a ten-year expected life. Rizzo also uses straight-line depreciation with no salvage value. Given these assumptions, Rizzo's asset net book value consisted of:

Long-lived assets at original cost	$2,000,000
Less: Accumulated depreciation	1,000,000
Net asset book value	$1,000,000

Rizzo's policy is to replace 10% of its assets each year at the end of their useful lives. Assume that Rizzo's pre-tax net operating cash flow for 1999 is $320,000 and that its pre-tax return on beginning net assets is 12%, as shown here:

Pre-tax net operating cash flow	$320,000
Depreciation ($2,000,000/10 years)	200,000
Pre-tax profit	$120,000

The pre-tax return on beginning net assets is calculated as:

$$\frac{\text{Pre-tax profit}}{\text{Beginning net assets}} = \frac{\$120{,}000}{(\$2{,}000{,}000 - \$1{,}000{,}000)} = 12\%$$

Rizzo's 1999 pre-tax return on assets is 12%, the same as Chen's. Rizzo is also able to keep pace with inflation by increasing its net operating cash flow by 3% each year. We will assume that its annual capital expenditures to replace 10% of its January 1, 1999 asset base ($2,000,000 × 10% = $200,000) also increases at the inflation rate of 3% and that the new assets are purchased on the last day of the year. These assumptions yield the performance data for 1999–2003 in Table 10.3.

Here's what our Chen (Table 10.2) versus Rizzo Corporation (Table 10.3) comparison illustrates. Both firms start in identical financial reporting positions on January 1, 1999. Each has assets with a *net* book value of $1,000,000. The *only* difference is that Chen's assets are new and Rizzo's are five years old, on average. Rizzo constantly replaces a portion of its

Table 10.3 ■ RIZZO CORPORATION

Time-Series Without Distortion from Aging Assets

		Year Ended				
	January 1, 1999	**December 31, 1999**	**December 31, 2000**	**December 31, 2001**	**December 31, 2002**	**December 31, 2003**
Asset net book value	$1,000,000	$1,006,000*	$1,017,580	$1,034,307	$1,055,736	$1,081,408
Capital expenditures (increasing by 3% per year)		206,000	212,180	218,545	225,102	231,855
Net operating cash flow (increasing by 3% per year):		$ 320,000	$ 329,600	$ 339,488	$ 349,673	$ 360,163
Depreciation (see details below)		200,000	200,600	201,818	203,673	206,183
Pre-tax profit		$ 120,000	$ 129,000	$ 137,670	$ 146,000	$ 153,980
Return on beginning assets		12%	12.8%	13.5%	14.1%	14.6%
Average age of assets		5 years	5 years	5 years	5 years	5 years

Depreciation details explained:	**1999**	**2000**	**2001**	**2002**	**2003**
1. Beginning-of-year **gross** original cost of assets	$2,000,000	→ $2,006,000	→ $2,018,180	→ $2,036,725	→ $2,061,827
2. Gross cost of assets retired at year-end	(200,000)	(200,000)	(200,000)	(200,000)	(200,000)
3. Capital expenditure on new assets (increases by 3%)	206,000	212,180	218,545	225,102	231,855
4. End-of-year **gross** original cost of assets	$2,006,000 →	$2,018,180 →	$2,036,725 →	$2,061,827 →	$2,093,682
Depreciation for year: Item 1 × 10%	$ 200,000	$ 200,600	$ 201,818	$ 203,673	$ 206,183

* Computed as: Beginning net book value ($1,000,000) + Capital expenditure ($206,000) − Depreciation ($200,000) = $1,006,000. All other years are computed similarly.

assets and maintains an average asset age of five years as highlighted in Table 10.3, while the average age of Chen Corporation's assets is increasing, as highlighted in Table 10.2. Rizzo's reported return on beginning assets at the end of 2003 is 14.6%; Chen's is 24.6%. Both firms experienced identical economic conditions and were able to respond identically. The only difference is that over this period Rizzo constantly maintained a long-lived asset age of five years, while the average age of Chen's assets increased from one year to five years. An analyst who is unaware of the asset age differential might erroneously conclude that Chen is more profitable than Rizzo in 2003 (a 24.6% versus a 14.6% return on assets) and that Chen's more dramatic upward trend implies a rosier future. As we have just seen, such inferences are unwarranted since the difference across firms is driven by the way that historical-cost, fixed-asset accounting rules affect firms with aging assets.

Table 10.2 is intended to convey the problems analysts face in doing a trend analysis for a single firm. These problems exist because of the GAAP rules used in long-lived asset financial reporting. Table 10.3 extends this critique of GAAP rules by showing how firms whose assets are continually being replaced cannot easily be compared to firms with aging assets.

While the issues raised in Tables 10.2 and 10.3 are real, the problems confronting analysts in practice are not usually as extreme. To understand why, let's focus on year-to-year (time-series) analyses, like those in Table 10.2. Unlike Chen, most firms replace some assets each year. Established firms with continuous capital expenditures do not experience the increasing average asset age shown in Table 10.2. Instead, with regular replacement, the average age of long-lived assets remains fairly constant from year-to-year. For these firms, the year-to-year pattern of returns more closely resembles that of Rizzo Corporation (highlighted in Table 10.3). That is why we introduced an example of a firm whose average asset age remained constant, like Rizzo's. As long as the rate of asset price increases is low (like 3% in our example), the distortions caused by GAAP are small. If the *average age* of assets is relatively constant and if prices change at a constant rate, reported rate of return ultimately stabilizes. Of course, in those rare instances in which capital expenditures are "lumpy," statement readers must recognize the possibility that an aging asset base can lead to distorted returns on assets, like those of Table 10.2.

Continuing the assumptions of Table 10.3 to December 31, 2009 shows that the rate of return on assets ultimately stabilizes at approximately 15.4%. Thus, with constant (and small) rates of price change, the distortion caused by historical cost accounting for long-lived assets is small.

GAAP for long-lived assets does significantly impede rate-of-return comparisons across companies in certain situations. Within the same industry, differences like those between Chen and Rizzo would be unusual, since competition often leads firms to pursue similar investment and operating strategies. Firms that don't modernize or innovate are ultimately left behind. Consequently, market forces lead to commonalities that usually make comparisons across firms *within the same industry* meaningful.

The historical cost basis used for long-lived assets does create potentially significant problems for those comparing firms in *different industries.* Operating conditions, capital expenditure policies, and the rate of input cost change can vary significantly across industries. For example, if there is little technological change in one industry, there is little incentive for firms to replace old—but still functional—assets. In stagnated industries, the average age of assets can increase, and this tendency contrasts with industries in which technological advancements have proliferated. This average age differential can lead to misleading comparisons, like those illustrated in Table 10.2 (where Chen experienced an increase in asset age) as compared to Table 10.3 (where Rizzo's asset age remained stable).

GAAP rules for fixed-asset accounting complicate financial analysis. Statement readers need to understand what factors might cause trend and across-firm distortions and adjust for them. Often, information to make the adjustment is unavailable. In these circumstances, knowing the approximate direction of any biases may help the statement reader avoid unwarranted inferences.

RECAP

Intangible Assets

Intangible assets, like patents, trademarks, and copyrights, convey future benefits to their owners. When one firm purchases an intangible asset from another—for example, a valuable trademark—few new accounting or reporting issues arise. The acquired intangible asset is recorded at the arm's-length transaction price and is amortized over its expected useful life, as described later in the chapter. (Another category of acquired intangible assets, called goodwill, arises as a consequence of certain types of corporate takeovers. This category of intangible is discussed in Chapter 16).

Difficult financial reporting issues exist when the intangible asset is developed internally instead of being purchased from another company. These difficulties arise because of the accounting treatment of the expenditures that ultimately create the valuable intangible (such as a patent or trademark). A patent, for example, is the result of successful research and development expenditures; a valuable trademark is the result of successful advertising, a great product, clever packaging, or brand loyalty.

The recoverability of research and development expenditures is highly uncertain at the start of a project. Consequently, the FASB requires that virtually all R&D expenditures be expensed as incurred.[2] This mandated financial reporting uniformity was viewed as a practical way of dealing with the risk of nonrecoverability of R&D expenditures. Similarly, prevailing accounting principles have long required companies to treat advertising and creative product development expenditures as period costs, again because of the highly uncertain, difficult-to-predict, future benefits.

The major categories of cash outflows most likely to result in intangibles-creation are immediately expensed (e.g., R&D, advertising, etc.). ***When past outflows successfully create intangible assets, the outflows have already been expensed and there are usually few remaining future outflows to capitalize!*** Consequently, the balance sheet carrying amount for intangible assets is often far below the value of the property right. For example, the 1991 Annual Report of Polaroid Corporation indicates that "Patents and trademarks" are valued at $1. However, a footnote in that same annual report discloses that Polaroid was awarded a court judgment arising from a suit which alleged that Eastman Kodak Company's instant cameras and film infringed on Polaroid patents. The judgment was ultimately settled for $924.5 million. The size of the judgment and settlement indicates that the Polaroid patents are extremely valuable. Nevertheless, the real economic value of these internally developed intangible assets does not appear on Polaroid's balance sheet, since the costs incurred in developing the valuable patents were expensed as incurred. This situation is not unusual.

> *SFAS No. 86* states that technological feasibility has been established "when the enterprise has completed all planning, designing, coding and testing activities that are necessary to establish that the product can be produced to meet its design specifications including functions, features, and technical performance requirements" (para. 4).

As software development companies proliferated in the 1980s, the FASB ultimately provided guidance in accounting for software development costs.[3] *SFAS No. 86* applies the previously described R&D rules to the particular circumstances faced by companies developing computer software products. Specifically, *prior to* establishing the **technological feasibility** of a computer software product, a company expenses *all* R&D costs incurred to develop it. After technological feasibility is established, additional costs incurred to get the product ready for general release to customers can be capitalized. Capitalization of additional costs ceases when the final product is available for sale. The costs incurred before technological feasibility is established can be considerable; because feasibility may not be assured until late in the expenditure cycle, there may be few costs left to capitalize. Accordingly, the recorded intangible software asset may be far less than its value to the software development firm, just as in other (nonsoftware) R&D settings.

---

[2] "Accounting for Research and Development Costs," *SFAS No. 2* (Stamford, CT: FASB, 1974). The only exception to immediate expensing is when the R&D expenditures will be reimbursed by some outside group.

[3] "Accounting for the Costs of Computer Software to Be Sold, Leased, or Otherwise Marketed," *SFAS No. 86* (Stamford, CT: FASB, 1985).

The GAAP bias that leads to an understatement of internally developed intangible assets has hindered financial analysis for many years, and the problem has worsened as modern economic activity shifted in the 1980s. In high technology industries like software development and biotechnology, research has contributed to large increases in the value of intellectual property rights such as patents and trademarks. Yet accounting rules for internally developed intangibles have not kept pace.

The FASB justified expensing all R&D for three reasons:

1. The future benefits accruing from these expenditures are highly uncertain.
2. A causal relationship between current R&D and future revenue has not been demonstrated.
3. Whatever benefits may arise cannot be objectively measured.[4]

But recent research indicates that these assertions are probably incorrect. One study examined the relationship between R&D expenditures and both future earnings and share values.[5] The study found that a one-dollar increase in R&D expenditures results in a cumulative two-dollar profit increase over a seven-year period. Furthermore, a one-dollar increase in R&D expenditures leads to a five-dollar increase in market value, on average. So R&D expenditures *are* related to future benefits and logic suggests that a causal relationship exists. Another study developed statistically reliable estimates of unrecorded R&D asset costs.[6] These asset cost estimates were then used to adjust reported earnings and book values to reflect capitalization of R&D. The adjusted numbers that reflected R&D capitalization (and subsequent amortization) were strongly associated with stock prices and returns and, thus, value-relevant to investors. So investors' behavior suggests that the adjusted numbers are measuring R&D benefits. Together, the results of these two studies contradict the three reasons the FASB used to justify expensing R&D.

VALUATION

Some portion (often small) of total software development costs does get capitalized once technological feasibility is established. But the proportion of total software development costs that gets capitalized is subjectively determined and varies across firms, as shown in Figure 10.1. More than 50% of the firms included in the Figure 10.1 sample capitalized between 0 to 20% of software development costs while about 5% capitalized

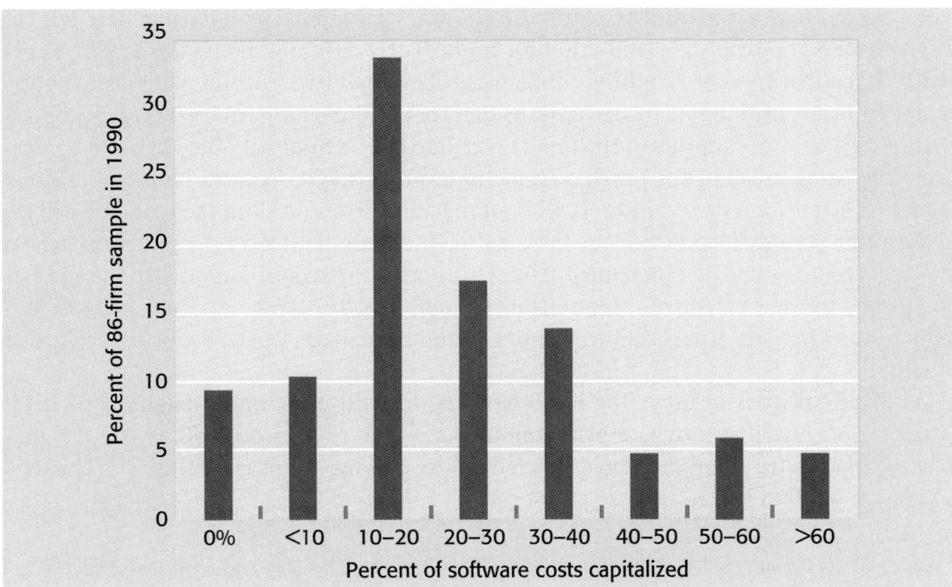

Figure 10.1

SOFTWARE CAPITALIZATION RATES

Source: Elizabeth A. Eccher, "Managerial Discretion in Financial Reporting," Working Paper, Massachusetts Institute of Technology, August 1988. Reprinted with permission.

---

4 *SFAS No. 2,* paras. 39–46.

5 T. Sougiannis, "The Accounting Based Valuation of Corporate R&D," *The Accounting Review* (January 1994), pp. 44–68.

6 B. Lev and T. Sougiannis, "The Capitalization, Amortization, and Value-Relevance of R&D," *Journal of Accounting and Economics* (February 1996), pp. 107–138.

more than 60%. So one question that arises is whether a GAAP standard that conveys such latitude also provides information that is relevant to investors. One study found that it does since the capitalization-related variables (annual amount capitalized, amount of the software asset, and annual amortization) were significantly associated with stock prices, returns and future earnings.[7] But the next question is whether value relevance would *increase* if GAAP permitted even larger amounts of software development costs to be capitalized. Another study explored this.[8] The author found that capitalizing 100% of software development costs and amortizing them over three years produced accounting numbers that are more consistent with observed market prices than are *SFAS No. 86* partial capitalization numbers. ***Relaxing the expense charge-off criteria improved value relevance.***

VALUATION ANALYSIS

To summarize, research findings almost uniformly indicate that existing GAAP for both R&D and software development is too conservative. The expenditures create assets that do not appear on balance sheets, and income for current as well as future years is misstated. Fortunately, analysts can adjust for these problems using required GAAP disclosures. For example, firms are required to disclose separately total expensed R&D.[9] Similarly, *SFAS No. 86* requires disclosure of unamortized software assets, amortization and write-downs of the assets in each period, and all costs that are expensed prior to technological feasibility.[10] ***Analysts can use these disclosures to reconstruct what asset and amortization amounts would be if GAAP allowed full capitalization.*** (Analysts can create their own estimation procedures or use the models in the articles cited in footnotes 6 and 8.) Unhappily, disclosures of marketing and advertising expenditures are too cryptic to permit a similar adjustment approach for trademarks or brands. So it's harder to undo the deficiencies of GAAP for these intangible assets.

Intangibles and Mergers The merger boom of the late 1990s increased the understatement of R&D assets. Here's why. When one firm acquires another and uses the **purchase method** to account for the acquisition (discussed in Chapter 16), the total purchase price must be apportioned to the individual assets acquired. The firms that were taken-over often had ongoing R&D projects. Managers of the acquiring firm have strong incentives to allocate a large portion of the acquisition cost to this **purchased in-process R&D.** Why? Well, GAAP requires R&D to be written-off as incurred. Allocating a large portion of the purchase price to in-process R&D provides a justification for immediately charging the *acquired* R&D to expense. Some managers of acquiring companies believe that large income statement charges arising from acquisitions are treated as transitory (or even valuation irrelevant) events by analysts. So their impact on firm valuation is presumed to be minimal. They feel that aggressively allocating much of the purchase price to in-process R&D reduces both consolidated assets and acquisition period income, without reducing firm value. But the write-off will *increase* future periods' income because there are fewer dollars of asset cost to amortize later. So managers get to write-off a (potentially large) portion of the acquisition price to the acquisition period income statement—presumably without penalty—and, by reducing assets, also reduce future periods' amortization expenses. From the managers' perspective, it's a win-win situation!

As this book goes to press, the FASB is trying to reduce the understatement of R&D assets. GAAP says that purchase price amounts assigned to in-process R&D projects that *have no alternative future use* must be charged to expense upon acquisition.[11] This is a reiteration of SFAS No. 2.

---

[7] D. Aboody and B. Lev, "The Value Relevance of Intangibles: The Case of Software Capitalization," *Journal of Accounting Research* (Supplement 1998), pp. 161–191.

[8] K. Den Adel, "The Value-Relevance of Alternative Accounting Treatments of Software Development Costs" (Unpublished manuscript, Purdue University, May 2000).

[9] *SFAS No. 2,* para. 13.

[10] *SFAS No. 86,* paras. 11–12.

[11] "Applicability of FASB Statement No. 2 to Business Combinations Accounted for by the Purchase Method," *FASB Interpretation No. 4* (Norwalk, CT: FASB, 1975).

A current exposure draft addresses the acquisition "abuses" of the late 1990s. The draft states:

> An enterprise shall recognize any intangible assets acquired from other enterprises . . . or as part of a business combination and shall initially measure those assets based on their fair value.[12]

Since the acquired intangible assets must be recorded at their fair value, this compels the acquiring firm (and their auditors) to determine whether the acquired R&D has "no alternative future use." If there *is* a future use, the acquired in-process R&D cannot be written-off. Will this portion of the exposure draft survive? Will it reduce the unwarranted write-offs of real R&D assets? Stay tuned.

Intangibles Accounting in the United Kingdom: Similarities and Differences

The financial reporting rules for research and development in the United Kingdom are generally similar to those in the United States. Marketing and advertising costs are treated as period costs in the United Kingdom, just as they are in the United States. As a result, U.K. balance sheet numbers for patents, trademarks, and similar intangibles are subject to the same type of understatement as those in the United States.

However, there is a difference between the application of the historical cost accounting principle in the United Kingdom and the United States. United Kingdom accounting rules allow companies to write long-lived assets up to new higher carrying values when market value exceeds cost—making adherence to the cost principle more flexible in the United Kingdom. The understatement of intangibles on U.K. firms' books prompted a few U.K. companies to abandon the historical cost treatment of trademarks (called "brands" in British English) and to write these intangible assets up to their estimated fair value. One author summarizes the U.K. treatment of brands as follows:

> A case can be made that the brand value should be placed on the balance sheet or at least reported to shareholders as part of a firm's financial report. In fact, several British firms have added brand equity to the balance sheet. For example, in 1988 Ranks Hovis McDougall decided to put a balance sheet value of $1.2 billion on its 60 brands. First, such an intangible asset can easily exceed in value that of tangible assets which are scrupulously reported and affect shareholders' valuation of firms. Second, reported brand equity can focus attention upon intangible assets and thus make it easier to justify brand building activities that are likely to pay off in the long term. Without such information, shareholders must rely upon short-term financials.
>
> The major difficulty involves a question of whether any valuation of brand equity can be both objective and verifiable. Unless brand valuation can be defended, it will not be helpful and can result in legal liability. It is no coincidence that in England, where brand value has been placed upon the balance sheet, there is a less litigious environment.[13]

While only a few U.K. firms have actually written brands up to fair value, the fact that some have chosen to do so indicates the perceived limitations of existing accounting for intangibles.

However, the latitude for recognizing internally developed intangibles in the U.K. has recently been restricted. The U.K. standard setting group, the Accounting Standards Board, stated:

> "An internally developed intangible asset may be capitalised only if it has a readily ascertainable market value." ["Goodwill and Intangible Assets," *Financial Reporting Standard* (FRS) 10 (London: Accounting Standards Board, 1997), para. 14].

Balance sheet carrying amounts for internally developed intangible assets like patents or trademarks are not dependable indicators of their value to the firm. Because the assets are understated, so too is income statement amortization in later years.

RECAP

[12] "Business Combinations and Intangible Assets," *FASB Exposure Draft* (Norwalk, CT: FASB, September 7, 1999), para. 35.

[13] D. A. Aaker, *Managing Brand Equity* (New York: Free Press, 1991), p. 28.

A Case Study of Ambiguities in Capitalization Criteria: Oil and Gas Exploration Costs

Earlier, we described two characteristics that tend to make the book values of long-lived assets unreliable indicators of their value to the firm. First, for pragmatic reasons historical cost is used as the primary basis for measuring long-lived assets. So past economic sacrifice—rather than current expected benefit—determines balance sheet carrying amounts. Second, the ultimate benefit from research and product development expenditures cannot be forecast at the start of a project; this uncertainty causes these items to be written off as period costs even if they eventually lead to the creation of an asset. That's why many development expenditures designed to create intangible assets never get capitalized.

Now we explain a third cause for the discrepancy between long-lived asset numbers and economic reality—***ambiguities in capitalization criteria.*** Ambiguities in capitalization criteria arise in several settings, including the treatment of oil and gas exploration costs. Consider the following example.

> Calaboga Oil paid $50 million for a large oil field in Alaska. During 2001 Calaboga explored for oil throughout the field. Twenty wells were drilled at a total cost of $200 million, or $10 million per well. Nineteen of the wells proved to be unproductive dry holes, while one was found to contain a considerable amount of oil. The financial reporting question is this: What is the appropriate carrying amount of the producing well?

Over time, two different approaches to determining the cost of the producing well emerged. The two approaches differ in their treatment of the $190 million that was spent in drilling the 19 dry holes.

One alternative, called the **full-cost approach,** considers the $190 million to be a necessary cost of finding the one producing oil well. That well would be carried on the books at $250 million using the full-cost approach; this is the $50 million land purchase price plus the $200 million of total drilling costs.

Another alternative, the **successful-efforts approach,** would reflect the producing well at only $60 million. This is the sum of the $50 million land purchase price plus the $10 million cost of drilling the specific well that became a producer. The $190 million of drilling costs incurred on the unproductive wells would be written off to the 2001 income statement as a period expense.

The two approaches in this example can be summarized as shown on the following page.

From year-to-year, reported profits would be more volatile using the successful-efforts approach, especially for small firms that do not have a large portfolio of drilling projects. Furthermore, small growth firms that engage in extensive exploration activities would tend to report lower near-term profits under successful efforts. To avoid this volatility and potentially lower average earnings, most smaller oil companies use the full-cost approach. Notice that under the full-cost option, unsuccessful drilling outcomes do not penalize current periods' earnings.

We focus on accounting options for oil and gas exploration because this topic contains many of the issues that typify financial reporting controversies. Specifically,

- The debate regarding the alternative accounting treatments is endless—there is no "right" or "wrong" answer.
- The reporting options have the potential to influence managerial behavior.
- The securities market appears to recognize that the differing managerial incentives have implications for valuing firms.

We now address these issues.

Full Cost	
Balance Sheet:	
Petroleum production property	
Land cost	$ 50,000,000
Drilling costs on dry holes	190,000,000
Drilling costs on producer	10,000,000
Capitalized Amount	$250,000,000
Income Statement:	
2001 Charge =	-0-
Successful Efforts	
Balance Sheet:	
Petroleum production property	
Land cost	$ 50,000,000
Drilling costs on producer	10,000,000
Capitalized Amount	$ 60,000,000
Income Statement	
2001 Charge =	$190,000,000

Debate Is Endless As world energy prices increased during the 1970s, public scrutiny of oil companies' profits also increased. The diversity in financial reporting within the oil industry was deemed undesirable by the U.S. Congress because it made comparisons across firms difficult and hindered effective regulation. Congress passed the Energy Policy and Conservation Act in 1975, which directed the SEC to standardize oil and gas reporting.[14] The SEC initially delegated this task to the FASB.

In 1977 the FASB issued *SFAS No. 19*,[15] which eliminated the choice allowed between the full-cost and successful-efforts options. *SFAS No. 19* mandated that all companies had to use successful-efforts accounting. This elicited an outcry from smaller oil companies that, remember, were predominantly using full costing. These companies lobbied Congress by arguing that the profit volatility from successful-efforts accounting would hinder their ability to raise capital, inhibit their domestic energy exploration, and ultimately increase U.S. dependence on foreign oil, thereby negating the intent of the 1975 energy act.

These lobbying efforts were successful. The SEC was pressured to reexamine the FASB's approach. The SEC subsequently concluded that neither full-cost nor successful-efforts accounting reflected oil and gas producers' true performance. To see why, let's return to the Calaboga Oil illustration, above.

The SEC argued that if the value of the oil that had been discovered was estimated to be worth, say, $3 billion, it is pointless to debate whether this significant discovery should be reflected at $60 million or $250 million, since both totals fail to capture the economic substance. Instead, the SEC announced that statements filed with the Commission could be prepared under either full-cost or successful-efforts reporting methods. The SEC further expressed an intention to develop a new method—called **reserve recognition accounting**—which would be designed to measure the estimated worth of the discoveries. The SEC never succeeded in gaining acceptance for reserve recognition accounting, primarily because of the assumptions and forecasts it entailed.

---

[14] Public Law 94–163, Energy Policy and Conservation Act [42 U.S. Code, Sec. 6383].

[15] "Financial Accounting and Reporting by Oil and Gas Producing Companies," *SFAS No. 19* (Stamford, CT: FASB, 1977).

After the SEC refused to require that *SFAS No. 19* be used in filings with the Commission, the FASB was compelled to suspend it.[16] Today, oil and gas companies continue to have the option of using either the full-cost or the successful-efforts approach. In other words, after years of endless heated debate, neither approach was considered "wrong." In addition, a footnote disclosure similar to reserve recognition accounting has been required since 1983.[17] This footnote is intended to provide approximate data regarding the estimated worth of proven oil and gas reserves.

CONTRACTING

Reporting Options Influence Managerial Behavior The protest resulting from the FASB's attempt to eliminate full-cost accounting is revealing. The arguments raised by managers of full-cost companies were designed to evoke sentiments about U.S. energy self-sufficiency, national security, economic growth, and other emotional topics. While these issues may have been important, many observers concluded that the real reasons that firms objected to the successful-efforts accounting method were due to other factors—factors that managers were reluctant to raise openly! For example, because the successful-efforts method results in more volatile earnings numbers for small producers, managers' bonuses tied to reported earnings would be lost in certain years. Another reason (indeed, this one was raised openly by some firms) is that the lower near-term profits under the successful-efforts method could lead to violation of loan covenants tied to debt-to-equity ratios.

If one basis for the objection to *SFAS No. 19* was managers' fears of losing bonuses, then it is likely that managers would adapt their behavior if successful-efforts accounting were mandated. For example, managers of small companies might decide to forego riskier drilling projects to avoid the chance of lower successful-efforts earnings if the riskier projects failed. By limiting their drilling efforts to "surer things," the managers would increase the probability of achieving bonus targets.

What we have just explained underscores the issues raised in Chapters 1 and 7 regarding how reporting rules exert a potentially powerful impact on the behavior of managers. Since bonus contracts are often tied to accounting numbers like net income, managers' operating decisions can be influenced by financial reporting rules.

VALUATION

Securities Market Implications If securities markets are reasonably efficient, investors would be aware of the effect of these incentives on managers' behavior. Indeed, the anticipated cutback in drilling levels would be expected to lower the discounted value of affected firms' future cash flows. Why? Because the riskier drilling projects that would be eliminated would still in the aggregate have had positive expected payoffs. Following this logic, we would expect to observe an adverse price reaction for those firms whose accounting would have been altered by *SFAS No. 19*.

Several accounting researchers tested aspects of this hypothesis.[18] These studies found that as it became evident that *SFAS No. 19* would be issued, the security prices of full-cost firms fell relative to those of successful-efforts firms. This result is consistent with the market anticipating that full-cost managers will change their behavior in a way that lowers future operating cash flows. Other studies provided further evidence that the adverse share price effects for full-cost companies were related to factors like bonus effects and bond covenant violations.[19]

---

[16] "Suspension of Certain Accounting Requirements for Oil and Gas Producing Companies," *SFAS No. 25* (Stamford, CT: FASB, 1979).

[17] "Disclosures About Oil and Gas Producing Activities," *SFAS No. 69* (Stamford, CT: FASB, 1982).

[18] See, for example, D. W. Collins and W. T. Dent, "The Proposed Elimination of Full Cost Accounting in the Extractive Petroleum Industry: An Empirical Assessment of the Market Consequences," *Journal of Accounting and Economics* (March 1979), pp. 3–44; and B. Lev, "The Impact of Accounting Regulation on the Stock Market: The Case of Oil and Gas Companies," *The Accounting Review* (July 1979), pp. 485–503.

[19] See, for example, D. W. Collins, M. S. Rozeff, and D. S. Dhaliwal, "The Economic Determinants of the Market Reaction to Proposed Mandatory Changes in the Oil and Gas Industry: A Cross-Sectional Analysis," *Journal of Accounting and Economics* (March 1981), pp. 37–71; T. Lys, "Mandated Accounting Changes and Debt Covenants: The Case of Oil and Gas Accounting," *Journal of Accounting and Economics* (April 1984), pp. 39–65; and D. F. Larcker and L. Revsine, "The Oil and Gas Accounting Controversy: An Analysis of Economic Consequences," *The Accounting Review* (October 1983), pp. 706–32.

GAAP capitalization criteria for long-lived assets are sometimes ambiguous. Managers have an incentive to exploit this ambiguity in order to derive benefits for themselves and the firm in various contractual arrangements.

RECAP

Asset Impairment

Here, we review guidelines for determining when and how assets that have already been capitalized should be treated once their value subsequently becomes impaired.

The notion of **asset impairment** is straightforward. A firm acquires an asset because the future benefits expected to be generated by that asset exceeds its cost. Subsequently, if the asset's remaining expected future benefits fall below its net book value, that asset is considered to have become impaired.

Measuring impairment encompasses two stages. First, some threshold loss level must be established to determine when a write-down must be made. Second, once the threshold is triggered, the amount of the write-down must be determined and recorded.

The standards for determining when an asset is impaired and the guidelines for reporting it are contained in *SFAS No. 121* and summarized in Figure 10.2.[20]

We now explain the impairment guidelines step-by-step using the lettered stages in Figure 10.2.

Stage A. *SFAS No. 121* states that an impairment review should be made whenever external events raise the possibility that an asset has become

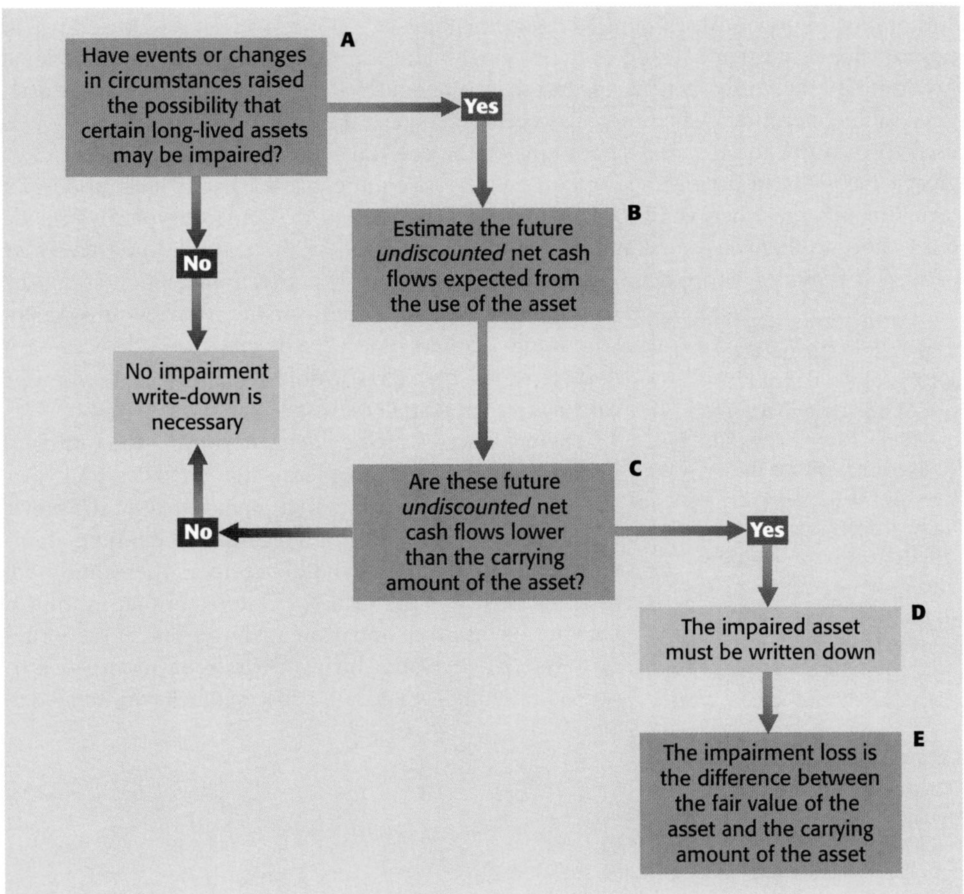

Figure 10.2

LONG-LIVED ASSET IMPAIRMENT GUIDELINES

[20] "Accounting for the Impairment of Long-Lived Assets and for Long-Lived Assets to Be Disposed Of," *SFAS No. 121* (Norwalk, CT: FASB, 1995).

impaired. Examples of such external events include a significant decrease in the asset's market value or deterioration in the business climate.

Stage B. ***This stage defines the threshold loss level that triggers the write-down.***

Stage C. The threshold is triggered whenever the expected future *net* cash inflow—undiscounted total future inflows minus future outflows—is *lower* than the current carrying amount of the asset.

Stage D. When an impairment loss is recognized, the long-lived asset is written down. The income statement charge is included "above the line"—that is, as a component of income from continuing operations before income taxes.

Stage E. ***This stage defines the amount of the write-down that must be recognized.*** The write-down loss is measured as the difference between the fair value of the asset and the current carrying amount of the asset.

The FASB defines the fair value of an asset as ". . . the amount at which the asset could be bought or sold in a current transaction between willing parties. . . ."[21] When market prices are not available, fair value must be estimated using techniques such as discounted present values, the price of similar assets, and other information.[22]

CONTRACTING

Impairment write-downs present managers with another set of potential earnings management opportunities. For example, in a very good earnings year, managers might be tempted to take an impairment write-down and then write the asset back up (through earnings) in some subsequent year when earnings are down. *SFAS No. 121* eliminates this opportunity for earnings management across years. The FASB prohibits firms from "restoration of previously recognized impairment losses."[23] Once an asset is written down, it cannot later be written back up to the original higher carrying amount. But International Accounting Standards permit reversals of previously recognized impairment losses. Reversals are permitted when there has been a change in the estimates that were previously used to measure the loss.[24] The amount of the reversal increases income.[25] The IASC's greater flexibility in permitting impairment reversals represents a specific illustration of a recurring difference between IAS standards and U.S. GAAP: IAS standards typically provide more latitude than do U.S. standards. Some observers view the extra latitude favorably because it provides an opportunity for managers to convey private information about the firm's expected future performance to the investment community. Others object to the extra latitude because it also provides managers with opportunities to manage earnings and potentially mislead analysts.

> The degree of latitude that ought to exist in financial reporting has been debated for years. It's called the **uniformity** versus **flexibility** controversy. At one extreme, some believe that all firms should report using a single (i.e., uniform) approach; immediate capitalization of R&D under *SFAS No. 2* is an example of uniformity. At the opposite extreme, others believe that potentially different underlying economic circumstances justify different allowable reporting methods; LIFO versus FIFO inventory accounting illustrates flexibility. This issue is analyzed in R. A. Dye and R. E. Verrecchia, "Discretion vs. Uniformity: Choices Among GAAP," *The Accounting Review* (July 1995), pp. 389–415.

There is also research evidence regarding the timing of impairment write-offs, evidence that predates *SFAS No. 121*. This research indicates that managers used the previous absence of clear guidelines regarding the timing of impairment recognition to influence users' perceptions of how the firm was performing. One study that examined recognition of asset impairment found that these write-offs were often made during periods of sustained economic difficulty—that is, the observed behavior tended to

[21] Ibid., para. 7.
[22] Ibid.
[23] Ibid., para. 11.
[24] "Impairment of Assets," *IAS 36* (London: IASC, 1998).
[25] This assumes that the originally impaired asset was carried at historical cost. But as you will see later in the chapter, IAS rules allow firms to revalue assets to an amount *above* their historical cost. When the impairment reversal applies to an asset that was originally revalued and subsequently deemed to be impaired, the reversal "gain" is credited directly to owners' equity. (Ibid., para. 104.)

conform to "big bath" bunching of expenses and losses.[26] But does impairment really occur only in bad times? This bunching of write-offs reinforces the need for the clear guidelines in this area that are contained in *SFAS No. 121.*

Obligations Arising from Retiring Long-Lived Assets

When an electric utility builds a nuclear plant, or an oil company constructs an offshore drilling rig, regulatory authorities require public welfare and safety expenditures at the end of the asset's life. Nuclear plants must be decontaminated and drilling rigs must be disassembled. This costs money. And by law, these expenditures must take place. ***So when certain kinds of assets are built, a liability simultaneously arises.*** Until recently, GAAP often ignored these required outflows at the end of an asset's life and no liability appeared on firms' books. But this is changing. The FASB has issued an exposure draft that would require firms to record a liability when such assets are placed into service.[27]

> Sometimes the liability arises *after* the asset is placed into service. For example, suppose a new law is passed requiring removal of gasoline storage tanks at the end of their useful lives. For firms utilizing these tanks, the liability arises when the law is passed, not when the tank was first placed into service. Also, liabilities may arise over time, as the asset is used. If a coal strip mine must be reclaimed, the liability arises proportionately as the mining occurs.

Here's how the FASB proposal works. Firms would be required to estimate the expected present value of the outflows that will occur when assets are eventually retired. These outflows would be discounted using what the Board terms a **credit-adjusted risk-free rate.** The discounted present value of the liability would be recorded along with an increase in the carrying amount of the related long-lived asset. Consider the following example:

> This is the risk-free rate of interest on zero-coupon U.S. Treasury instruments plus an adjustment for the credit standing of the firm. So, if the risk-free rate is 5% and the firm's credit standing allows it to borrow at 3% over the risk-free rate, the credit adjusted risk-free rate is 8%.

> Kalai Oil Corporation constructs an oil drilling rig off the Texas coast which is placed into service on January 1, 2002. The rig cost $300 million to build. Texas law requires that the rig be removed at the end of its estimated useful life of five years. Kalai estimates that the cost of dismantling the rig will be $12 million and its credit adjusted risk-free rate is 8%. The discounted present value of the liability is $8,167,000. Assume that Kalai has already capitalized the $300 million cost of the rig in an account called "Drilling rig."

> The present value factor for a payment five years away at 8% is 0.68058. So rounded to the nearest thousand, the present value is $12 million × 0.68058 = $8,167,000.

When the asset is placed into service, Kalai records the asset retirement obligation (ARO) as:

DR Drilling rig (asset retirement cost)	$8,167,000	
CR ARO liability		$8,167,000

The $8,167,000 debit to the asset account is allocated to expense using some systematic method. Assuming straight-line depreciation over the expected useful life of five years, the entry is:

DR Depreciation expense	$1,633,400	
CR Accumulated depreciation–drilling rig		$1,633,400

The liability is initially recorded at its present value but grows over time as retirement nears. The present value of the liability will be increased by 8% per year, as the schedule on the next page shows.

[26] J. A. Elliott and W. H. Shaw, "Write-Offs as Accounting Procedures to Manage Perceptions," *Journal of Accounting Research* (Supplement 1988), pp. 91–119.

[27] "Accounting for Obligations Associated with the Retirement of Long-Lived Assets," *Exposure Draft* (revised) (Norwalk, CT: FASB, February 17, 2000).

	(a) Present Value of the Liability at Start of Year	(b) Interest Expense [8% × Column (a) Amount]	(c) Present Value of the Liability at End of Year [Column (a) + Column (b)]
2002	$ 8,167,000	$653,360	$ 8,820,360
2003	8,820,360	705,629	9,525,989
2004	9,525,989	762,079	10,288,068
2005	10,288,068	823,045	11,111,113
2006	11,111,113	888,887*	12,000,000

*Rounded.

The entry to record the increase in the liability in 2002 is:

DR Interest expense	$653,360	
CR ARO liability		$653,360

Assume that an outside contractor dismantles the rig early in January 2007 at a cost of $11,750,000. The journal entry is:

DR ARO liability	$12,000,000	
CR Cash		$11,750,000
CR Gain on settlement of ARO liability		250,000

As this book goes to press, the FASB has not issued a final document regarding asset retirement obligations. It may tweak the existing exposure draft before issuing final rules, which are expected in mid-2001.

DEPRECIATION

Productive assets like buildings, equipment, and machinery eventually wear out. So do assets like patents, which have a finite economic life. Consequently, the cost of these assets must be apportioned to the periods in which they provide benefits. This is the application of the matching principle (Chapter 2) to long-lived assets. This matching process is called **depreciation**. For intangible assets, the allocation of costs to periods is referred to as **amortization.** For mineral deposits and other wasting assets, the assignment of expired costs to periods is called **depletion.** For simplicity, we will refer collectively to any of these allocations of costs to periods as the **depreciation process.**

In financial reporting, the cost to be allocated to periods through the depreciation process is the asset's original historical cost minus its expected salvage value. The objective is to spread the original cost over the period of asset use; ***depreciation is not intended to track the asset's declining market value.*** Realistically, the asset's end-of-period book value (its original cost minus cumulative depreciation) would approximate its market value only by sheer coincidence. We stress this *absence of correspondence* between accounting measures of depreciation and value decrement because accounting depreciation, computed following GAAP, is a process of cost allocation, *not* asset valuation.

When applied to long-lived assets, the matching process requires the reporting entity to estimate three things:

1. The expected useful life of the asset
2. The depreciation pattern which will reflect the asset's declining service potential
3. The expected salvage value that will exist at the time the asset is retired.

Each requires estimates of future events, especially the pace of technological change and shifts in consumer tastes and preferences. Assets whose economic benefits expire evenly over time are depreciated on a straight-line basis, while those that provide more valuable services in the early years are depreciated on an accelerated basis. The following example in Exhibit 10.5 illustrates the procedures.

The **straight-line** (SL) depreciation method simply allocates cost minus salvage value evenly over the asset's expected useful life.

The depreciation rate for the **double-declining balance** method (DDB) is double the straight-line rate (in Exhibit 10.5, 20% per year for SL, 40% per year for DDB). Applying a constant DDB depreciation percentage to a declining balance will never depreciate book value down to salvage value. To depreciate down to an asset's expected salvage value using DDB, two steps must be employed. First, in years 1 and 2, the 40% rate is applied to the

Exhibit 10.5 ■ DEPRECIATION EXAMPLE

Facts

Cost of the asset	\$10,500
Expected salvage value	\$ 500
Expected useful life	5 years

Straight-line Depreciation (SL)

$$(\text{Constant rate} \times \text{Constant base}) = \frac{\text{Cost} - \text{Salvage value}}{\text{Estimated life}}$$

$$\left(\frac{1}{5}\right) \times (\$10{,}500 - \$500) = \$2{,}000 \text{ per year for all 5 years}$$

Double-declining Balance Depreciation (DDB)

(Constant rate × Changing base) = Double the straight-line rate × Book value at beginning of each period

Straight-line rate = 20% (i.e., 5 year life)

Double straight-line rate = 20% × 2 = 40%

Year	Beginning of Year Book Value	Depreciation (40% of Beginning of Year Book Value)	End of Year Book Value
1	\$10,500.00	\$4,200.00	\$6,300.00
2	6,300.00	2,520.00	3,780.00
3	3,780.00	1,093.33†	2,686.67
4	2,686.67	1,093.33	1,593.34
5	1,593.34	1,093.34	500.00

†Year 3: Switch to straight-line method (as explained in the text).
\$3,780 − \$500 = \$3,280; \$3,280 ÷ 3 = \$1,093.33

Sum-of-the-years' Digits Depreciation (SYD)

$$\left(\begin{matrix}\text{Changing} \\ \text{rate}\end{matrix} \times \begin{matrix}\text{Constant} \\ \text{base}\end{matrix}\right) = \frac{\text{Years remaining in life}}{\text{Sum-of-the years' digits*}} \times (\text{Cost} - \text{Salvage})$$

Sum-of-the-years' digits = 5 + 4 + 3 + 2 + 1 = 15

Year	Depreciable Basis (\$10,500 − \$500)	Applicable Fraction	Depreciation
1	\$10,000	5/15	\$ 3,333.33
2	10,000	4/15	2,666.67
3	10,000	3/15	2,000.00
4	10,000	2/15	1,333.33
5	10,000	1/15	666.67
Total		15/15	\$10,000.00

*The formula for determining the sum-of-the-years' digits is: $n(n + 1) \div 2$ where n equals the estimated life of the asset. In our example: $5(5 + 1) \div 2 = 15$. This, of course, is the answer we get by tediously summing the years' digits—that is 5 + 4 + 3 + 2 + 1 = 15.

book value of the assets, without subtracting the salvage value. Second, once the DDB depreciation amount falls below what it would be with straight-line depreciation, a switch to the straight-line method is made. This happens in year 3, when DDB depreciation would have been \$3,780 × 40%, or \$1,512, which is less than the straight-line depreciation of \$2,000. Therefore, straight-line depreciation is used beginning in year 3. The SL amount of \$1,093.33 is determined by taking the end of year 2 remaining book value of \$3,780, subtracting the salvage value of \$500, and dividing the result, \$3,280, by 3.

Sum-of-the-years' digits (SYD) is another accelerated depreciation method. SYD will depreciate an asset to precisely its salvage value, so a switch to SL is unnecessary.

Figure 10.3(a) shows the annual depreciation charges under the alternative depreciation methods; Figure 10.3(b) shows the resulting net book value at each year-end.

In preparing external financial reports, companies are free to select the depreciation method they believe best reflects both the pattern of an asset's use and the services it provides. Within the same industry, different companies may use different methods. Even within the same company, different types of assets may be depreciated using different methods. For example, buildings might be depreciated using the straight-line method, while trucks might be depreciated using the sum-of-the-years' digits method. Table 10.4 illustrates an annual survey of book depreciation choices used by 600 companies.

This annual AICPA survey shows that straight-line depreciation predominates for financial reporting purposes. However, accelerated depreciation is almost universally used

Figure 10.3

ALTERNATIVE DEPRECIATION METHODS

(a) Annual Depreciation Charges; and (b) Net Book Value

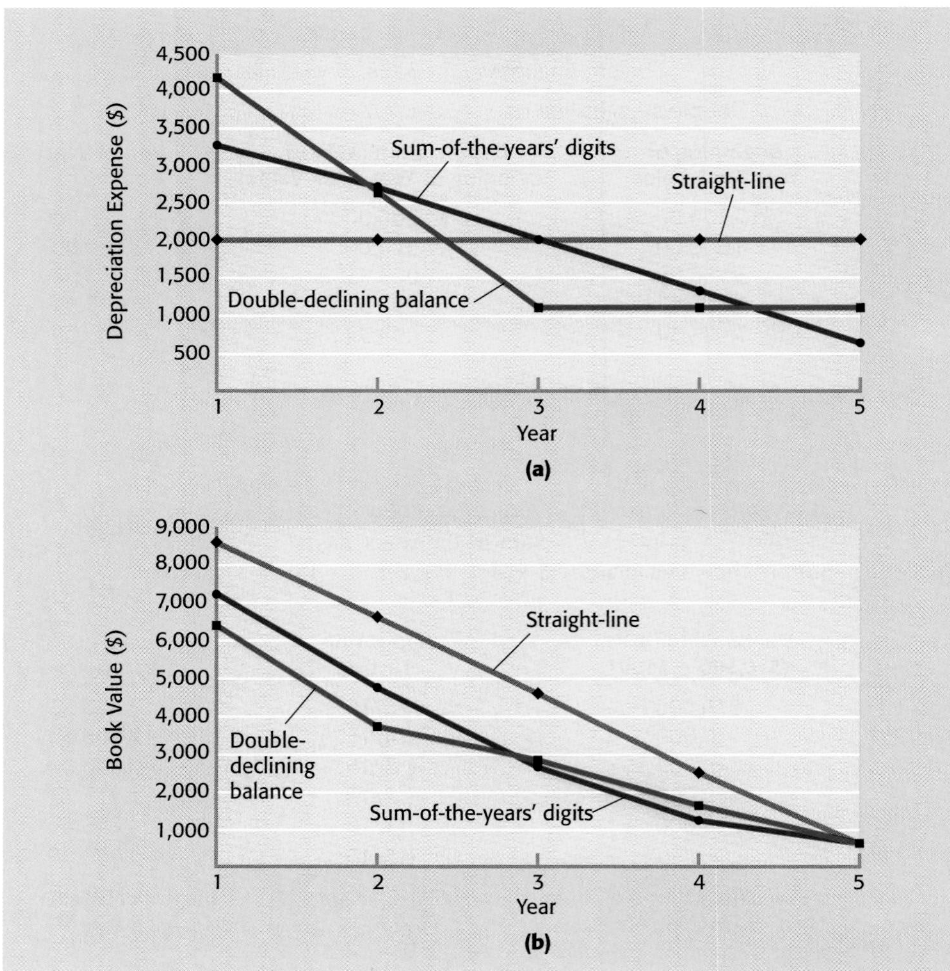

Table 10.4 ■ DEPRECIATION CHOICES

	Number of Companies			
	1999	1998	1997	1996
Straight-line	577	577	578	575
Declining-balance	27	25	26	28
Sum-of-the-years' digits	7	9	10	12
Accelerated method—not specified	53	43	50	48
Units-of-production	31	36	39	42
Other	6	9	10	12

Source: Reprinted with permission from A. Mrakovcic (ed.), *Accounting Trends and Techniques,* 2000, page 391. Copyright © 2000 by American Institute of Certified Public Accountants, Inc. The numbers for each year do not total 600 since companies use more than one depreciation method (e.g., straight-line for buildings and accelerated for automobiles).

for tax purposes. While there is some evidence that the market adjusts for differences in depreciation methods when establishing securities prices,[28] the diversity of depreciation methods across firms complicates security analysis.

> Firms that are not currently paying taxes because of losses or operating loss carryforwards have an incentive not to use accelerated depreciation. But even here, tax rules require certain depreciation methods. Consequently, companies are constrained in efforts to abandon accelerated tax depreciation methods when losses materialize.

Disposition of Long-Lived Assets

When long-lived assets are disposed of before their useful lives are completed, any difference between the net book value of the asset and the disposition proceeds is treated as a gain or loss. Assume that the asset in the previous example is being depreciated using the double-declining balance method and is sold at the end of year 2 for $5,000 when its book value is $3,780. The following entry is made:

DR Cash	$5,000	
DR Accumulated depreciation	6,720	
CR Long-lived asset		$10,500
CR Gain on sale of asset		1,220

Dispositions of assets take place frequently as firms respond to changing production and consumer-demand conditions. For this reason, gains and losses from asset sales do not satisfy the criteria for the extraordinary item treatment described in Chapter 2. Accordingly, such items are included in the income statement "above the line" as an element of pre-tax income from continuing operations.

Financial Analysis and Depreciation Differences

ANALYSIS

Most U.S. firms use straight-line depreciation for financial reporting purposes. Nevertheless, making valid comparisons across firms is often hindered by other depreciation assumptions, especially differences in useful lives. Two firms in the same industry often depreciate their otherwise similar assets over different estimated lives. When this happens, potentially significant income differences arise.

We now illustrate this problem and discuss ways to adjust depreciation to achieve greater comparability across firms. Exhibit 10.6(a) on the following page shows information extracted from the 1999 annual report of UAL Corporation (parent of United Air Lines, Inc.); Exhibit 10.6(b) on page 483 contains similar data from the 1999 annual report of Southwest Airlines Co., one of United's competitors. Both companies depreciate all their long-lived assets using the straight-line method. However, UAL depreciates aircraft over useful lives of 4 to 30 years; for Southwest useful lives range from 20 to 25 years. A difference in useful life assumptions also exists for ground equipment; UAL's estimated lives

[28] W. H. Beaver and R. E. Dukes, "Interperiod Tax Allocation and δ-Depreciation Methods: Some Empirical Results," *The Accounting Review* (July 1973), pp. 549–59.

Exhibit 10.6(a) ■ UAL CORPORATION BALANCE SHEET FIXED ASSETS

($ in millions)	December 31 1999	1998
Operating property and equipment		
Owned–		
Flight equipment	$13,518	$12,006
Advances on flight equipment	809	985
Other property and equipment	3,368	3,134
	17,695	16,125
Less–Accumulated depreciation and amortization	5,207	5,174
	12,488	10,951
Capital leases–		
Flight equipment	2,929	2,605
Other property and equipment	93	97
	3,022	2,702
Less–Accumulated amortization	645	599
	2,377	2,103
	$14,865	$13,054

Partial Footnote on Operating Property and Equipment

Depreciation and amortization of owned depreciable assets is based on the straight-line method over their estimated service lives. Leasehold improvements are amortized over the remaining period of the lease or the estimated service life of the related asset, whichever is less. Aircraft are depreciated to estimated salvage values, generally over lives of 4 to 30 years; buildings are depreciated over lives of 25 to 45 years; and other property and equipment are depreciated over lives of 3 to 15 years.

Properties under capital leases are amortized on the straight-line method over the life of the lease, or in the case of certain aircraft, over their estimated service lives. Lease terms are 10 to 30 years for aircraft and flight simulators and 25 years for buildings. Amortization of capital leases is included in depreciation and amortization expense.

Selected Income Statement Information

($ in millions)	Year Ended December 31 1999	1998
Depreciation and amortization	$ 867	$793
Earnings before taxes, distributions on preferred securities and extraordinary item	$1,243	$827

Source: UAL Corporation 1999 Annual Report

range from 3 to 45 years, while Southwest's are from 3 to 30 years. (See highlighted sections in Exhibit 10.6[a] and [b]).

Clear differences exist but the level of disclosure is too cryptic to allow analysts to compute precise adjustments. Despite this drawback, by making reasonable assumptions, we can estimate the effect on income arising from the differences in asset lives for UAL and Southwest. Let's see how.

Because both companies use straight-line depreciation, the ratio of average *gross* property, plant, and equipment divided by depreciation expense gives us a rough approximation of the estimated useful (depreciable) life of the average asset. Here's why. Straight-line depreciation expense (SL) is computed as:

(10.1) $$\text{SL} = \frac{\text{Gross property, plant, and equipment (minus salvage value)}}{\text{Average useful life}}$$

Rearranging terms:

(10.2) $$\text{SL} \times (\text{Average useful life}) = \text{Gross property, plant, and equipment (minus salvage value)}$$

**Exhibit 10.6(b) ■ SOUTHWEST AIRLINES CO.
BALANCE SHEET FIXED ASSETS**

($ in thousands)	December 31 1999	1998
Property and equipment, at cost		
Flight equipment	$5,768,506	$4,709,059
Ground property and equipment	742,230	720,604
Deposits on flight equipment purchase contracts	338,229	309,356
	6,848,965	5,739,019
Less—Allowance for depreciation	1,840,799	1,601,409
	$5,008,166	$4,137,610

Footnote on Property and Equipment Accounting Policy

PROPERTY AND EQUIPMENT Depreciation is provided by the straight-line method to estimated residual values over periods ranging from 20 to 25 years for flight equipment and 3 to 30 years for ground property and equipment. Property under capital leases and related obligations are recorded at an amount equal to the present value of future minimum lease payments computed on the basis of the Company's incremental borrowing rate or, when known, the interest rate implicit in the lease. Amortization of property under capital leases is on a straight-line basis over the lease term and is included in depreciation expense.

Selected Income Statement Information

($ in thousands)	Year Ended December 31 1999	1998
Depreciation	$248,660	$225,212
Income before income taxes	$773,611	$705,112

Source: Southwest Airlines 1999 Annual Report

Further rearranging yields:

$$\text{Average useful life} = \frac{\text{Gross property, plant, and equipment (minus salvage value)}}{\text{SL}} \qquad \textbf{(10.3)}$$

The ratio in equation (10.3) is only a rough approximation for many reasons. One is that we cannot estimate the salvage values assumed by UAL and Southwest. Other factors that make the computation approximate are discussed next. The computation of average useful lives using the equation (10.3) approximation is shown in Exhibit 10.7 on the following page. End-of-year and start-of-year gross property are added together in Exhibit 10.7 and then divided by 2 in order to estimate average gross property for 1999. Applying the equation (10.3) approach suggests that, *on average,* UAL is using shorter estimated lives (21.8 years) than Southwest (24.0 years).[29]

[29] To understand why the Exhibit 10.7 answer is in years (i.e., 21.8 years and 24.0 years), let's express average gross property divided by depreciation expense in terms of the underlying measurement dimensions:

$$\frac{\text{Average gross property, plant, and equipment}}{\text{Depreciation expense}} \quad \begin{matrix}\leftarrow \text{The underlying measurement dimension is \$s} \\ \leftarrow \text{The underlying measurement dimension is \$s per year}\end{matrix}$$

Expressing the computation in underlying measurement dimensions, the division in Exhibit 10.7 becomes:

$$\frac{\$s}{\$s/\text{Year}}$$

Following algebraic rules for division by fractions, we invert the denominator and multiply it by the numerator:

$$\$s \times \frac{\text{Year}}{\$s}$$

The $s cancel and the answer is expressed dimensionally in years (e.g., 21.8 years and 24.0 years).

Exhibit 10.7 ■ COMPUTING APPROXIMATE AVERAGE USEFUL LIVES

($ in millions)	UAL	Southwest
Average gross property, plant, and equipment[1] / Depreciation expense	$\dfrac{\frac{\$19{,}908 + \$17{,}842}{2}}{\$867}$	$\dfrac{\frac{\$6{,}510.7 + \$5{,}429.7}{2}}{\$248.7}$
	$\dfrac{\$18{,}875}{\$867} = 21.8$ years	$\dfrac{\$5{,}970.2}{\$248.7} = 24.0$ years

[1]Excludes deposits and advances on flight equipment. For example, year-end 1999 numbers were computed as follows using Exhibit 10.6(a) and 10.6(b) data: UAL: $13,518 + $3,368 + $2,929 + $93 = $19,908; Southwest: $5,768.5 + $742.2 = $6,510.7

To improve comparisons of profitability between UAL and Southwest, the analyst would like to undo these differences in depreciation lives. One way to undo these differences is to divide UAL's average gross property number by Southwest's estimated depreciable life—that is,

$$\frac{\$18{,}875}{24.0 \text{ years}} = \$786.5$$

The quotient, $786.5 million, is the approximate annual UAL depreciation expense number that would result from using Southwest's longer estimated useful life assumption. If these rough approximations are correct, UAL's 1999 depreciation would fall by $80.5 million (i.e., $867 million − $786.5 million) and earnings before taxes, extraordinary items, and the cumulative effect of accounting change would rise by the same amount. This represents a pre-tax earnings increase of 6.5%.

> It is possible that the useful life differences reflect real economic differences rather than accounting choices. For example, Southwest's aircraft might be newer and, on average, have longer useful lives. If the useful lives differences are "real," then analysts' attempts to "undo" the differences may impede, rather than improve, profit comparisons.

This adjustment process is crude and relies on assumptions. The adjustment assumes that the useful life differences are artificial. It assumes that the salvage value proportions are roughly equivalent for both firms. It further assumes that the dollar breakdown within asset categories is similar for both UAL and Southwest—that is, the computation assumes that UAL and Southwest Airlines both have roughly the same proportionate dollar amount of trucks, gate equipment, aircraft, and so on. If these assumptions are incorrect, then the average age computation for one airline cannot legitimately be applied to the other's asset base to estimate "adjusted" depreciation. However, if these assumptions hold, the adjusted numbers should make a comparison of UAL and Southwest more accurate.

In Chapter 13 we illustrate another adjustment approach for depreciation differences that uses data from the deferred income tax footnote.

International Perspective

In the United States, the purpose of financial reporting rules is to capture the underlying economic activities of a firm. In the auditor's opinion, this is indicated by the phrase "these statements *present fairly*. . . ." A similar philosophy governs the preparation of financial statements in the United Kingdom, where the auditor opines that "these statements give a *true and fair view*. . . ." The underlying economic position of the reporting entity also dominates the accounting principles in other countries, such as The Netherlands, Canada, Australia, and New Zealand.

This reporting perspective is not universal. In many countries, publicly disseminated financial reports have other, overriding objectives. In France all companies' financial reports must conform to a specified format using tax accounting measurement rules. Constraining companies to use a specific set of accounts and narrow measurement rules is thought to provide comparable data to government decision makers, thus enabling them to better regulate the economy. A similar philosophy governs financial reporting in other European countries, such as Italy and Belgium.

To illustrate how some countries' financial reporting departs from the Anglo-American tradition, consider the following example from the 1993 annual report of Lufthansa, a German airline. A note in the financial statement says:

> [German income tax law] makes it possible to claim depreciation up to 30 percent of the acquisition costs on new aircraft *in addition to normal depreciation.* [emphasis added] [Another facet of the German income tax law] allows higher depreciation for measures which benefit environment protection.

This excerpt illustrates how tax or other government policy considerations could obscure economic performance in German (as well as in other countries') financial statements. German tax law allows companies to take special depreciation deductions ***in excess of the estimated historical costs incurred.*** To get these "extra" tax deductions, German companies must also deduct the same amount on the income statement in the annual report. The accounting entry is:

As discussed in Chapter 18, these tax-driven effects on financial statements are weakening. Some countries now allow firms to deviate from the tax rules in their consolidated (group) financial statements and require them to adhere to the tax rules only in the holding company (parent) financial statements.

DR Other operating expenses (an income statement charge for the "extra" expense recognized)	XXXX	
CR Special reserve items subject to future taxation (a balance sheet liability account appearing just above shareholders' equity)		XXXX

These "other operating expenses" do not represent a permanent tax deduction since they must be reversed (i.e., taken into income) in subsequent years. Specifically, Lufthansa disclosed in its 1993 annual report that

> [T]he tax on income resulting from the release of special items . . . will be spread over the course of up to a twelve-year release period [in the consolidated statements].

Since these "extra" income statement deductions result in higher income—and higher income taxes—in future years, the credit in the preceding journal entry ("Special reserve items subject to future taxation") represents a liability.

Our point is simple. Both U.S. and German financial reporting rules use the historical cost principle. Nevertheless, German financial statements may not be comparable to U.S. statements for certain companies because German accounting allows income statement charges in excess of historical cost amounts.

The United Kingdom has reporting rules similar to those in the United States. Nevertheless, there are differences in long-lived asset measurement procedures between the two countries. United Kingdom companies are permitted to periodically revalue land and buildings. When this is done, the accumulated depreciation account is removed and the revalued amount becomes the new book value. The amount of the write-up is credited to an owners' equity account called **revaluation reserve.** Assume a building that originally cost £20,000,000 and has an accumulated depreciation balance of £10,000,000 is appraised at £35,000,000 and accordingly written up, as permitted by U.K. standards. The accounting entry is:

DR Building	£15,000,000	
DR Accumulated depreciation	10,000,000	
CR Revaluation reserve		£25,000,000

The new net book value becomes £35,000,000 after this entry is made, as follows on the next page:

	Net Book Value Prior to Revaluation	Revaluation	Net Book Value After Revaluation
Building	£20,000,000	**DR** £15,000,000	£35,000,000
Less: Accumulated depreciation	(10,000,000)	**DR** 10,000,000	–
Net book value	£10,000,000		£35,000,000

The revaluation reserve account that is credited in the previous entry is an owners' equity account. Under GAAP in the United Kingdom, this amount would be disclosed as a separate line item in the owners' equity section of the balance sheet.

Depreciation in subsequent periods is based on the revaluation net book value (£35,000,000). If the building has an expected remaining useful life of 20 years at the time of the revaluation, annual depreciation on the income statement will be £1,750,000 (i.e., £35,000,000 ÷ 20).

> The amount in the owners' equity revaluation reserve account would be transferred year-by-year to retained earnings as the revalued asset is depreciated. For example, if we assume that the asset is not subsequently revalued over the ensuing 20 years, £1,250,000 (i.e., £25,000,000 ÷ 20) would be reclassified each year. The entry is:
>
> | | | |
> |---|---|---|
> | **DR** Revaluation reserve | £1,250,000 | |
> | **CR** Retained earnings | | £1,250,000 |
>
> This reclassification entry is made in order to reduce the revaluation reserve as the asset ages. If no entry were made, there would still be a revaluation reserve amount on the books even after the asset is removed from service. The year-by-year transfer ultimately reduces the reserve to zero.

Revaluations are not uncommon among U.K. companies. A recent report indicated that approximately 25% of surveyed U.K. companies revalued at least some of their long-lived assets in 1993 and 1994.[30] While U.K. reporting rules encourage companies to update revaluations periodically, they do not require it. Consequently, even when balance sheets show revaluation reserves, readers cannot assume that a *recent* revaluation occurred or that the reported net book values approximate current cost. In addition to the updating problem, many U.K. firms never revalue fixed assets at all. This complicates comparisons across companies in the United Kingdom.

The International Accounting Standards Committee also allows fixed asset revaluations. The revaluation procedure in *IAS 16* roughly parallels the U.K. approach.[31] However, *IAS 16* requires that revaluations be updated periodically—that is, whenever the revalued carrying amount differs materially from fair value.[32]

This example illustrates that despite the general similarities among U.S., U.K., and IAS reporting rules, important differences do exist. Writing up fixed assets to reflect reappraisal increases is forbidden in the U.S. Differences of this sort make financial analyses of foreign companies—even companies in "similar" reporting environments—a perilous activity.

SUMMARY

GAAP for long-lived assets is far from perfect. The need for reliable and verifiable numbers causes these assets to be measured in terms of the economic sacrifice incurred to obtain them—their historical cost—rather than in terms of their current expected benefit—or worth—to the firm. Since it is uncertain whether future benefits result from research and brand development costs, these costs are generally expensed in the period incurred. Consequently, balance-sheet carrying amounts for intangible assets often differ from their real value to the firm. Analysts must scrutinize disclosures of R&D expenses to undo the overly conservative accounting. Managers may deliberately allocate an excessive portion of the total purchase price in a takeover to in-process R&D in order to increase post-takeover earnings.

Changes in the amount of capitalized interest from one period to the next can distort earnings trends. A thorough understanding of how the GAAP measurement rules are applied

---

[30] L. C. L. Skerratt and D. J. Tonkin (eds.), *Financial Reporting 1993–1994: A Survey of U.K. Reporting Practice* (London: The Institute of Chartered Accountants in England and Wales, 1994), p. 195.

[31] "Property, Plant and Equipment," *IAS 16* (London: IASC, 1993).

[32] Ibid., para. 34.

allows statement readers to avoid pitfalls in trend analysis when investment in new assets is sporadic. When comparing return on assets (ROA) ratios across firms, one must remember that—all other factors being equal—there is an upward drift in reported ROA as assets age. So analysts must determine whether the average age of the long-lived assets for firms being analyzed is stable or rising. Inflation also injects an upward bias into reported ROA. Similarly, an understanding of differences in depreciation choices across firms permits better inter-firm comparisons. When making inter-firm comparisons, analysts should use footnote disclosures to overcome differences in the long-lived asset useful lives chosen by each firm and where possible, in their depreciation patterns. Finally, international practices for long-lived assets and book depreciation charges are sometimes very different from those in the United States. Asset impairment write-downs depend on subjective forecasts and could be used to manage earnings, especially under IAS rules. Statement users who make cross-country comparisons must exercise caution.

EXERCISES

E10–1

Determining asset cost and depreciation expense
AICPA adapted

In January 2001 Action Corporation entered into a contract to acquire a new machine for its factory. The machine, which had a cash price of $150,000, was paid for as follows:

Down payment	$ 15,000
Note payable due June 1, 2001	120,000
500 Shares of Action common stock with a value of $50 per share	25,000
Total	$160,000

Prior to the machine's use, installation costs of $4,000 were incurred. The machine has an estimated useful life of 10 years and an estimated salvage value of $5,000.

REQUIRED:

What should Action record as depreciation expense for 2001 under the straight-line method?

E10–2

Determining depreciation expense
AICPA adapted

Turtle Company purchased equipment on January 2, 2001 for $50,000. The equipment had an estimated five-year service life. Turtle's policy for five-year assets is to use double-declining balance depreciation for the first two years of the asset's life and then to switch to the straight-line depreciation method.

REQUIRED:

In its December 31, 2003 balance sheet, what amount should Turtle report as accumulated depreciation for equipment?

E10–3

Depreciation base
AICPA adapted

The Apex Company purchased a tooling machine on January 3, 1991 for $30,000. The machine was being depreciated on the straight-line method over an estimated useful life of 20 years, with no salvage value.

At the beginning of 2001, when the machine had been in use for 10 years, the company paid $5,000 to overhaul the machine. As a result of this improvement, the company estimated that the remaining useful life of the machine was now 15 years.

REQUIRED:

What should be the depreciation expense recorded for this machine in 2001?

E10–4

Analysis of various costs
AICPA adapted

On June 18, 2001 Dell Printing Company incurred the following costs for one of its printing presses:

Purchase of collating and stapling attachment	$84,000
Installation of attachment	36,000
Replacement parts for overhaul of press	26,000
Labor and overhead in connection with overhaul	14,000

The overhaul resulted in a significant increase in production capability. Neither the attachment nor the overhaul increased the estimated useful life of the press.

REQUIRED:

What is the total amount of the preceding costs that should be capitalized?

E10–5

Deferred payment contract

On January 1, 2001 Hardy, Inc. purchased certain plant assets under a deferred payment contract. The agreement called for making annual payments of $10,000 per year for five years. The first payment is due on January 1, 2001, and the remaining payments are due on January 1 of each of the next four years. Assume an imputed interest rate of 10%.

REQUIRED:

What entry should be made to record the purchase of these plant assets on January 1, 2001?

E10–6

Analysis of various costs

AICPA adapted

Samson Manufacturing Company, a calendar-year company, purchased a machine for $65,000 on January 1, 1999. At the date of purchase, Samson incurred the following additional costs:

Loss on sale of old machinery	$1,000
Freight-in	500
Installation cost	2,000
Testing costs prior to regular operation	300

The estimated salvage value of the machine was $5,000, and Samson estimated the machine would have a useful life of 20 years, with depreciation being computed on the straight-line method. In January 2001 accessories costing $3,600 were added to the machine in order to reduce its operating costs. These accessories neither prolonged the machine's life nor provided any additional salvage value.

REQUIRED:

What should Samson record as depreciation expense for 2001?

E10–7

Classification of costs

AICPA adapted

On February 1, 2001 Reflection Corporation purchased a parcel of land as a factory site for $50,000. An old building on the property was demolished, and construction began on a new building, completed on November 1, 2001. Costs incurred were:

Demolition of old building	$ 4,000
Architect's fees	10,000
Legal fees for title investigation and purchase contract	2,000
Construction costs	500,000

Salvaged materials resulting from demolition were sold for $1,000.

REQUIRED:

What cost should be recorded for the land and new building, respectively?

E10–8

Classification of costs

AICPA adapted

On July 1, 2001 Town Company purchased for $540,000 a warehouse building and the land on which it is located. The following data were available concerning the property:

	Current Appraised Value	Seller's Original Cost
Land	$200,000	$140,000
Warehouse building	300,000	280,000
	$500,000	$420,000

REQUIRED:

At what amount should Town record the land?

E10–9

Capitalized interest

AICPA adapted

Clay Company started construction on a new office building on January 1, 2000, and it moved into the finished building on July 1, 2001. Of the building's $2,500,000 total cost, $2,000,000 was incurred in 2000 evenly throughout the year. Clay's incremental borrowing rate was 12% throughout 2000, and the total amount of interest incurred by Clay during 2000 was $102,000.

REQUIRED:

What amount should Clay report as capitalized interest at December 31, 2000?

E10–10

Capitalized interest

AICPA adapted

Cole Company began constructing a building for its own use in January 2001. During 2001 Cole incurred interest of $50,000 on specific construction debt and $20,000 on other borrowings. Interest computed on the weighted-average amount of accumulated expenditures for the building during 2001 was $40,000.

REQUIRED:

What amount of interest cost should Cole capitalize? Prepare the journal entry to record payment of the interest.

E10–11

Account analysis

AICPA adapted

Weir Company uses straight-line depreciation for its property, plant, and equipment, which, stated at cost, consisted of the following:

	December 31	
	2001	**2000**
Land	$ 25,000	$ 25,000
Buildings	195,000	195,000
Machinery and equipment	695,000	650,000
	915,000	870,000
Less accumulated depreciation	(400,000)	(370,000)
	$515,000	$500,000

Weir's depreciation expense for 2001 and 2000 was $55,000 and $50,000, respectively.

REQUIRED:

What amount was debited to accumulated depreciation during 2001 because of property, plant, and equipment retirements?

E10–12

Depreciation expense patterns

AICPA adapted

The following graph depicts three depreciation expense patterns over time.

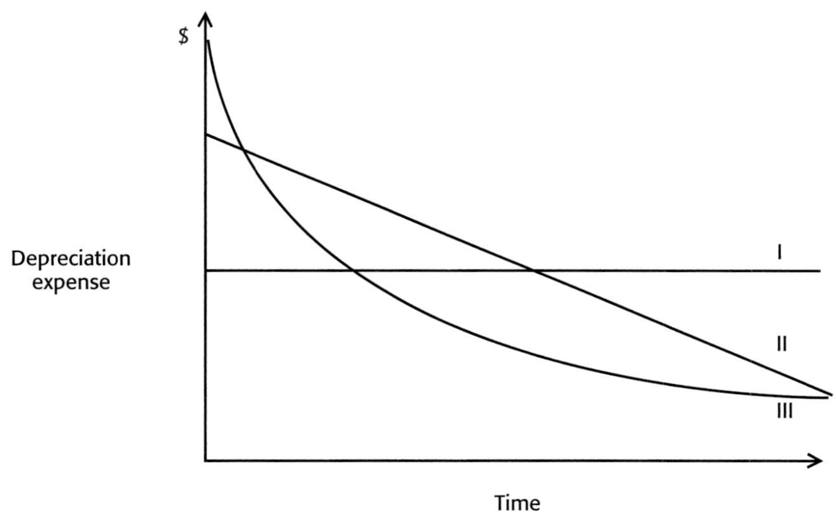

REQUIRED:

Pattern I, of course, is straight-line depreciation. Which depreciation expense pattern corresponds to the sum-of-the-years' digits method and which corresponds to the double-declining balance method? Explain why the shape of the Pattern II and Pattern III lines differs.

E10–13

Intangibles amortization

AICPA adapted

On January 1, 1997 Vick Company purchased a trademark for $400,000, which had an estimated useful life of 16 years. In January 2001 Vick paid $60,000 for legal fees in a successful defense of the trademark.

REQUIRED:

How much should Vick record as trademark amortization expense for 2001?

E10–14 **Intangibles** AICPA adapted

On January 2, 1998 Lava, Inc. purchased a patent for a new consumer product for $90,000. At the time of purchase, the patent was valid for 15 years; however, the patent's useful life was estimated to be only 10 years due to the competitive nature of the product. On December 31, 2001 the product was permanently withdrawn from sale under governmental order because of a potential health hazard in the product.

REQUIRED:

What should the total charge against income be in 2001 on this patent?

E10–15 **R&D cost treatment** AICPA adapted

During 2001 Orr Company incurred the following costs:

Research and development services performed by Key Corporation for Orr	$150,000
Design, construction, and testing of preproduction prototypes and models	200,000
Testing in search for new products or process alternatives	175,000

REQUIRED:

How much research and development expense should Orr report in 2001?

E10–16 **R&D cost treatment** AICPA adapted

In 2001 Ball Labs incurred the following costs:

Direct costs of doing contract research and development work for the government to be reimbursed by a governmental unit	$400,000

Research and development costs not included above were:

Depreciation	$300,000
Salaries	700,000
Indirect costs appropriately allocated	200,000
Materials	180,000

REQUIRED:

What was Ball's total research and development expense in 2001?

E10–17 **Depletion** AICPA adapted

In January 2001 Vorst Company purchased a mineral mine for $2,640,000, with removable ore estimated at 1,200,000 tons. After it has extracted all the ore, Vorst will be required by law to restore the land to its original condition at an estimated cost of $180,000. Vorst believes it will be able to sell the property for $300,000. During 2001 Vorst incurred $360,000 of development costs to prepare the mine for production, and it removed and sold 60,000 tons of ore.

REQUIRED:

In its 2001 income statement, what amount should Vorst report as depletion expense?

PROBLEMS/DISCUSSION QUESTIONS

P10–1 **Depreciation expense computations** AICPA adapted

On January 2, 2000 Half, Inc. purchased a manufacturing machine for $864,000. The machine has an eight-year estimated life and a $144,000 estimated salvage value. Half expects to manufacture 1,800,000 units over the life of the machine. During 2001 Half manufactured 300,000 units.

REQUIRED:

For each item, calculate depreciation expense for 2001 (the second year of ownership) for the machine just described under the method listed:

1. Straight-line
2. Double-declining balance
3. Sum-of-the-years' digits
4. Units of production

(*Hint*: The units of production method was not discussed in the text but is easy to understand. Depreciation is based on a ratio; the ratio numerator is production during the period and the denominator is estimated total production over the life of the machine. This ratio is then multiplied by the machine's cost minus salvage value to determine depreciation expense.)

P10–2

Lump-sum purchases

On June 30, 2001 Macrosoft Company acquired a 10-acre tract of land. On the tract was a warehouse that Macrosoft intended to use as a distribution center. At the time of purchase, the land had an assessed tax value of $6,300,000 and the building had an assessed tax value of $11,200,000. Macrosoft paid $15,000,000 for the land and building. After the purchase the company paid $1,000,000 to have various modifications made to the building.

REQUIRED:

1. At what amount should Macrosoft record the land and building?
2. For financial reporting purposes, why might the managers of Macrosoft prefer to assign a larger portion of the $15,000,000 to the land rather than to the building?

P10–3

Asset cost under a deferred payment plan

Cayman Diving Inc. needs to acquire a new dive boat. The seller will accept a noninterest bearing note for $400,000 due in four years or $250,000 in cash. The company's incremental cost of borrowing is 10%.

REQUIRED:

Which option should Cayman Diving select? Would your answer change if Cayman's incremental borrowing rate was 13%? Why?

P10–4

Allocation of acquisition costs among asset accounts

On April 23, 2001 Starlight Department Stores Inc. acquired a 75-acre tract of land by paying $25,000,000 in cash and by issuing a six-month note payable for $5,000,000 and 1,000,000 shares of its common stock. On April 23, 2001 Starlight's common stock was selling for $80.00 a share and had a par value of $2.50. The land had two existing buildings, one that Starlight intended to renovate and use as a warehouse, and another that Starlight intended to demolish to make way for the construction of a new department store. At the time of the purchase, the assessed values for property tax purposes of the land and the building to be renovated were $105,000,000 and $20,000,000, respectively. To complete the purchase, Starlight incurred legal fees of $25,000. The cost of demolishing the unneeded building was $50,000. Starlight paid $250,000 to have the land graded so that the new store could be built. Starlight paid a total of $100,000,000 to have the new department store built and another $25,000,000 to renovate the old building. To fund the work on the renovation and the new store, Starlight obtained a loan from Gotham City bank. Starlight made total interest payments of $10,000,000 during the period the buildings were being completed. (Assume that all of the interest payments qualify for capitalization.) Since parking would be needed for both the new department store and the warehouse, Starlight had a portion of the land covered with asphalt at a cost of $450,000. Starlight also paid $200,000 to install lighting for the parking lots and $75,000 to install decorative fencing and a parking access gate. During 2001 Starlight paid property taxes of $150,000 on the new property. All work was completed by December 31, 2001, and the new store and warehouse were placed in service on January 1, 2002.

REQUIRED:

Determine what costs should be assigned to the (1) land, (2) building, and (3) land improvements asset accounts. (*Hint*: The allocation of the original purchase price between the land and building should be made in proportion to the relative assessed values of the land and building at the time of the purchase.)

P10–5

Capitalize or expense various costs

Formidable Express provides overnight delivery of letters and small parcels to numerous locations throughout the United States. As part of its operations, the company maintains a sizable fleet of delivery trucks. Assume that Formidable Express made the following expenditures related to the fleet during 2001:

1. The company has the engines in its trucks serviced (i.e., "tuned-up") once every two years. The cost of the servicing in 2001 was $11.0 million.
2. Due to the high mileage put on the delivery vehicles, the company normally replaces 20% of its fleet's engines every year. In 2001 the cost incurred to replace engines amounted to $7.8 million.

(*continued*)

3. The tires on each vehicle are replaced once every three years. The cost of the new tires installed in 2001 amounted to $1.0 million.
4. In 2001 the company paid $3.5 million to have the trucks in the fleet rustproofed. Management expects that the trucks will now last an extra three years.
5. Because each truck was out of service for about a week due to the rust-proofing in (4), the company estimates that it lost $12.0 million in revenue during the course of the year.

REQUIRED:

Which expenditures should Formidable capitalize and which should be expensed?

P10–6

Capitalize or expense various costs

Fly-by-Night is an international airline company. Its fleet includes Boeing 757s, 747s, 727s, Lockheed L-1011s, and McDonnell Douglas MD-83s, MD-80s, and DC-9s. Assume that Fly-by-Night made the following expenditures related to these aircraft in 2001:

1. New jet engines were installed on some of the MD-80s and MD-83s at a cost of $25.0 million.
2. The company paid $2.0 million to paint one-eighth of the fleet with the firm's new colors in order to create a new public image. The company intends to paint the remainder of the fleet over the next seven years.
3. Routine maintenance and repairs on various aircraft cost $8.0 million.
4. Noise abatement equipment (i.e., "hush kits") was installed on the fleet of DC-9s to meet FAA maximum allowable noise levels upon takeoff. Equipment and installation cost $7.5 million.
5. The avionics systems were replaced on the Lockheed L-1011s. This will allow the aircraft to be used four more years than originally expected.
6. The existing seats on all 747s were replaced with new, more comfortable seats at a cost of $0.5 million.
7. The jet engines on 50% of the Boeing 727s received a major overhaul at a cost of $5.0 million. As a result, the aircraft should be more fuel efficient.

REQUIRED:

1. Which of these expenditures should Fly-by-Night capitalize? Why?
2. How might Fly-by-Night use expenditures like these to manage its earnings?

P10–7

Determining an asset's cost

On July 23, 2001 Consolidated Parcel Service (CPS) acquired a new "de-icing" machine for use at its facility at Chicago's O'Hare airport. The machine is used to de-ice the wings of the firm's aircraft in winter months. The invoice price of the machine was $15,000,000. The seller offered CPS a 2% cash discount on the gross invoice price if CPS paid for the machine by August 1, 2001. The cost to ship the machine from the seller's warehouse was $15,000 and was paid by CPS. Insurance during transport amounted to $5,000, also paid by CPS. Many CPS employees were involved with the assembly and testing of the machine. Their wages totaled $20,000. As part of testing the machine, $35,000 worth of "de-icing" fluid was used to ensure that the machine operated properly. During testing, one of CPS's cargo planes was inadvertently damaged. The cost to repair the aircraft (not covered by insurance) amounted to $250,000. As a result of the damaged aircraft being out of service while it was being repaired, CPS lost $750,000 in revenue. Finally, because the machine was larger than the previous one, CPS had to erect a new storage facility. The cost of doing so was $75,000 for materials, $25,000 for labor, and $5,000 for salaries of the supervisory personnel who directed the construction.

REQUIRED:

Assuming that CPS paid for the machine on July 29, 2001, determine the capitalizable cost of the machine to CPS.

P10–8

Asset impairment

Four years ago Omega Technology Inc. acquired a machine for use in its computer chip manufacturing operations at a cost of $35,000,000. The firm expected the machine to have a seven-year useful life and a zero salvage value. The company has been using straight-line depreciation for the asset. Due to the rapid rate of technological change in the industry, at the end of year four, Omega estimates that the machine is capable of generating (undiscounted) future cash flows of $11,000,000. Based on the quoted market prices of similar assets, Omega estimates the machine to have a fair market value of $9,500,000.

REQUIRED:

1. What is the book value of the machine at the end of year four?
2. Should Omega recognize an impairment of this asset? Why or why not? If yes, what is the amount of the impairment loss that should be recognized?
3. At the end of year four, at what amount should the machine appear in Omega's balance sheet?

P10–9

Accounting for computer software costs

In its 1995 balance sheet, IBM reported the following account:

($ in millions)	1995	1994
Software, less accumulated amortization (1995: $11,276; 1994: $10,793)	$ 2,419	$ 2,963

In the footnotes to its financial statements, IBM reported that it spent $2,997 on computer software-related activities. Assume that these expenditures were related to projects in which technological feasibility has been proved.

REQUIRED:

1. How is IBM required to account for computer software-related expenditures?
2. As of the end of 1995, how much has IBM spent on existing computer software-related activities in past years?
3. As of the end of 1995, how much of its computer software-related expenditures has IBM capitalized?
4. Based on the information given, estimate IBM's amortization of computer software costs in 1995.
5. Assume that IBM amortizes its capitalized software costs using the straight-line method. Estimate the average useful life of the software products developed as of the end of 1995.
6. How might firms use the accounting for computer software costs to manage their earnings?

P10–10

Asset impairment

National Sweetener Company owns the patent to the artificial sweetener known as Supersweet. Assume that National Sweetener acquired the patent on January 1, 1995 at a cost of $300 million dollars, expected the patent to have an economic useful life of 12 years, and has been amortizing the patent on a straight-line basis. Assume that at the time the patent was acquired, National Sweetener expected that the process would generate future net cash flows of $30 million the first year of its useful life and that the cash flows would grow at a rate of 10% each year over the remainder of its useful life. By the year 2007 (i.e., after 12 years), National Sweetener expected that there would be several other artificial sweeteners on the market and therefore that it would sell the Supersweet patent at that time for about $60.0 million.

Year	Expected Future Cash Flows ($ in millions)	Year	Expected Future Cash Flows ($ in millions)
1995	$30.0	2002	$ 58.7
1996	33.0	2003	64.3
1997	36.3	2004	70.7
1998	39.9	2005	77.8
1999	43.9	2006	85.6
2000	48.3	Total	$641.6
2001	53.1		

On December 31, 2001 when the patent's book value was $160.0 million ($300.0 – $140.0), National Sweetener learned that one of its competitors had come up with a revolutionary new sweetener that could be produced much more cheaply than Supersweet. National Sweetener expects that the introduction of this product on January 1, 2002 will substantially reduce the cash flows from its Supersweet patent process.

Consider the following two independent scenarios:

- ***Scenario I:*** National Sweetener expects that the cash flows from Supersweet over the 2002–2006 period will be only 50% of those originally projected and that the sale of the Supersweet patent will bring only $25 million when sold as originally planned. When discounted at a rate of 15% (which National Sweetener feels is appropriate), these amounts yield a present value of $129.0 million. National Sweetener estimates that the market value of the Supersweet patent on December 31 2001, is $160.0 million.
- ***Scenario II:*** National Sweetener expects that the cash flows from Supersweet over the 2002–2006 period will be only 25% of those originally projected and that the sale of the Supersweet patent will bring only $25 million when sold as originally planned. When discounted at a rate of 15%, these amounts yield a present value of $70.7 million. National Sweetener estimates that the market value of the Supersweet patent on December 31, 2001 is $68.0 million.

REQUIRED:

1. Should National Sweetener recognize an impairment of its Supersweet patent in Scenario I? If so, what is the amount of the loss and at what amount should the patent be reported in National Sweetener's 2001 ending balance sheet?
2. Repeat requirement (1) for the second scenario.

P10–11

Interest capitalization

To meet the increasing demand for its microprocessors, on January 1, 2001 Intelligent Micro Devices began construction of a new manufacturing facility. Construction costs were incurred uniformly throughout 2001 and were recorded in the firm's "Construction-in-progress" account. The average balance in the "Construction-in-progress" account during 2001 was $150,000,000.

To facilitate the construction of the facility, the firm arranged for an $80,000,000 construction loan on January 1 at a rate of 13%. The firm also issued $40,000,000 of common stock to help finance the project. Management estimates that the firm's cost of equity capital is 16%. On January 1, 2001 the firm also issued bonds in the amount of $200,000,000, carrying a weighted-average interest rate of 11.5%.

REQUIRED:

1. What is the total amount of interest incurred by the firm in 2001?
2. Assume that the firm bases the amount of capitalized interest on the average balance in the "Construction-in-progress" account. How much of the interest in (1) should be capitalized?
3. How much of the amount in (2) will be related to the firm's common stock issue? Why?
4. Where will the amount in (2) appear in the firm's 2001 financial statements?
5. What amount of interest expense will appear in the firm's 2001 income statement?
6. Assume that the facility is completed on December 31, 2001 and that it is placed in service on January 1, 2002. How, if at all, will the amount in (2) affect the future income of the firm?
7. Calculate the firm's interest coverage ratio (income before interest and taxes divided by interest expense) with and without the interest capitalization. Which coverage ratio would be more useful to a creditor in the evaluation of the firm's risk of insolvency?

P10–12

Accounting for internally developed patents versus purchased patents

Consider the following two scenarios:

- ***Scenario I:*** Over the 1998–2001 period, Micro Systems, Inc. spends $10,000,000 a year to develop patents on new computer hardware manufacturing technology. While some of its projects failed, the firm did develop several new patents each year during the period.
- ***Scenario II:*** Over the 1998–2001 period, Macro Systems, Inc., a competitor of Micro Systems, Inc., paid $10,000,000 each year to acquire patent rights from other firms. The firm assigned a five-year useful life to all of the patents.

1. Each firm had sales of $200,000,000, $242,000,000, $290,000,000, and $350,000,000, respectively, over the 1998–2001 period.
2. Each firm's operating expenses (excluding the preceding patent-related information) were $140,000,000, $170,000,000, $205,000,000, and $245,000,000, respectively over the 1998–2001 period.
3. Assume that a 34% income tax rate applies to both firms.

REQUIRED:

1. How would the two firms account for their patent-related expenditures?
2. Calculate the net income and net income as a percent of sales (i.e., profit margin) of each firm for the 1998–2001 period. Contrast the reported profitability of the two firms.
3. Assume that the firms continue to spend $10,000,000 per year in the fashion just described. How would the comparability of their income statements be affected?

P10–13

Earnings effects of changes in useful lives and salvage values

Assume that Major Motors Corporation, a large automobile manufacturer, reported in a recent annual report to shareholders that buildings had an original cost of $4,694,000,000.

1. Major Motors uses the straight-line depreciation method to depreciate the buildings over a useful life of 34 years.
2. Assume that the ratio of end-of-year accumulated depreciation on the buildings to their depreciable cost is 35.3%. This implies that the buildings, on average, are about 12 years old. Assume that Major Motors depreciates them to a salvage value of 5% of their original cost.
3. Assume that Major Motors' management is considering both extending the original useful lives of the buildings to 40 years from 34 years and increasing the salvage value to 10% of the buildings' original cost.
4. Assume a tax rate of 34%.

REQUIRED:

1. What is the book value of the buildings at the end of the current year (i.e., before adjusting for any change in useful lives or salvage values)?
2. What would be the dollar amount and direction of the effect on Major Motors' net income if the proposed changes to the useful lives and salvage values were implemented at the start of the next fiscal year?

P10–14

Straight-line versus accelerated depreciation ratio effects

STRETCH

The 2000 income statement and other information for Mallard Corporation, which is about to purchase a new machine at a cost of $500 and a new computer system at a cost of $300, appears next.

Sales	$1,000
Cost of goods sold	600
Gross profit	400
Operating expenses	150
Income before tax	250
Income taxes	85
Net income	$ 165

ADDITIONAL INFORMATION:

- The two new assets are expected to generate a 25% annual rate of growth in the firm's sales.
- The firm will include the depreciation expense on the machine as part of cost of goods sold and the depreciation expense on the computer system as part of operating expenses.
- *Excluding* the depreciation on the new machine, the firm's cost of goods sold is expected to increase at an annual rate of 7.5%.
- *Excluding* the depreciation on the new computer system, the firm's operating expenses are expected to increase at an annual rate of 4.0%.

(*continued*)

- The firm's gross total assets (net of asset retirements) are expected to grow at a rate of 20% per year. Average gross total assets in 2000 were $1,000. Assume that asset retirements generate no gains or losses.
- Both the machine and the computer system have a three-year useful life and a zero salvage value.
- Assume an income tax rate of 34%.

REQUIRED:

1. Assume that the assets are purchased on January 1, 2001. Prepare pro forma income statements for 2001 through 2003. Assume the firm elects to use the straight-line depreciation method for depreciating the new assets.
2. Repeat (1), assuming instead that the firm elects to use the sum-of-the-years' digits method for depreciating the new assets.
3. For both (1) and (2), calculate the firm's gross profit rate (gross profit divided by sales), NOPAT margin (net operating profit after tax divided by sales), and return on assets (NOPAT divided by average total assets). How does the use of the different depreciation methods affect the behavior of the ratios over the 2001–2003 period?

P10–15

Approaches to long-lived asset valuation

1. Contrast the economic sacrifice and expected benefit approaches to long-lived asset valuation.
2. GAAP requires firms to use historical cost (in most cases) to report the value of long-lived assets. As a statement reader, do you think that firms should be encouraged to voluntarily report their asset values under alternative valuation approaches? Why or why not?
3. As the manager of a publicly held company, what costs and benefits do you see associated with the voluntary disclosure of asset values using approaches other than historical cost?

CASES

C10–1

Microsoft (CW): Capitalization versus expensing of R&D

Microsoft develops, manufactures, licenses, sells, and supports a wide range of software products, including operating systems for personal computers (PCs) and servers; server applications for client/server environments; business and consumer productivity applications; interactive media programs; and Internet platform and development tools. Microsoft also offers on-line services, sells PC books and input devices, and researches and develops advanced technology software products. Microsoft products are available for most PCs, including Intel microprocessor-based computers and Apple computers. Microsoft's business strategy emphasizes the development of a broad line of PC software products for business and personal use.

Income statement and balance sheet information from Microsoft's recent annual reports to shareholders follows. Assume an income tax rate of 35%.

Microsoft: Selected Financial Information ($ in millions)	1996	1997	1998	1999	2000
Sales	$ 8,671	$11,358	$15,262	$19,747	$22,956
Net income (NOPAT)	2,195	3,454	4,490	7,785	9,421
Total assets	10,093	14,387	22,357	38,625	52,150
Total shareholders' equity	6,908	10,777	16,627	28,438	41,368
Research and development	$ 1,432	$ 1,925	$ 2,897	$ 2,970	$ 3,775

REQUIRED:

1. How does current GAAP require firms to account for their research and development expenditures?
2. Use the reported information to calculate Microsoft's NOPAT margin (net operating profit after taxes divided by sales), asset turnover (sales divided by average total assets), return on assets (NOPAT divided by average total assets), and return on

shareholders' equity (NOPAT divided by average shareholders' equity) for 1998, 1999, and 2000.

3. Assume that Microsoft expects its research and development expenditures to benefit the current accounting period as well as the next two accounting periods. Briefly describe how Microsoft's 1998 income statement and balance sheet would have been different if it had capitalized rather than expensed its research and development expenditures.
4. Repeat (2) after capitalizing research and development expenditures and amortizing them as described in (3). As a statement reader, would you find the differences in the ratios in (2) and (4) to be significant? Why?

C10–2

Southwest Airlines (CW): Financial statement effects of capitalized interest

The following information was taken from Southwest Airlines Co.'s annual report to shareholders.

SOUTHWEST AIRLINES COMPANY

Consolidated Statement of Income

($ in thousands)	1999	Years Ended December 31 1998	1997
Interest expense	$ 54,145	$ 56,276	$ 63,454
Capitalized interest	(31,262)	(25,588)	(19,779)
Income before income taxes	773,611	705,112	516,956
Net income	$474,378	$433,431	$317,772

Consolidated Statement of Cash Flows

	1999	1998	1997
Cash payments for interest, net of amount capitalized	$ 26,604	$ 33,384	$ 42,372

REQUIRED:

Assume a 35% income tax rate.

1. What is the underlying rationale for the capitalization of interest?
2. Assume that none of the assets to which the 1999 capitalized interest applies have been completed and placed into service. Calculate the firm's 1999 income before income taxes, assuming that no interest had been capitalized in 1999. What is the percentage change from the reported amount?
3. Starting with net income of $474,378 as reported in 1999, assume the same facts as in (2), and recalculate Southwest's *net* income.
4. Briefly discuss the impact of capitalized interest on a firm's future reported earnings.

C10–3

Delta Air Lines (CW): Financial statement effects of depreciation policy changes

The following information is taken from Delta Air Lines Inc.'s 1995 annual report to shareholders.

DEPRECIATION AND AMORTIZATION:

Prior to April 1, 1993, the Company depreciated substantially all of its flight equipment on a straight-line basis over a 15-year period from the dates placed in service. As a result of a fleet plan review, effective April 1, 1993, the Company increased the estimated useful lives of substantially all of its flight equipment. Flight equipment that was not already fully depreciated is being depreciated on a straight-line basis over a 20-year period from the dates placed in service. The effect of this change was a $34 million decrease in depreciation expense in 1993.

REQUIRED:

Assume a 34% income tax rate.

1. Calculate the impact of the depreciation policy change on Delta's 1993 net income.
2. How will the change affect Delta's reported earnings over the next few years?

(*continued*)

3. How might a financial analyst determine if the change made by Delta is reasonable in light of industry conditions?
4. How might firms use depreciation policy changes to manage their earnings? Is there anything to prevent rampant use of depreciation policy changes as a tool to manage reported earnings?
5. In light of the contracting issues discussed in Chapter 7, speculate as to the possible reasons Delta might have made the change in its depreciation policy.

C10–4

Target Corporation and Kmart (CW): Depreciation differences and financial statement analysis

Target Corporation is a general merchandise retailer. Its divisions include Target, an upscale discount chain; Mervyn's, a middle-market promotional department store; and upscale department stores in the Midwest (Dayton's, Hudson's, and Marshall Field's).

Kmart Corporation is one of the world's largest mass merchandise retailers. The dominant portion of the firm's operations is general merchandise retailing through the operation of a chain of 2,170 Kmart discount stores with locations in each of the 50 states, Puerto Rico, the U.S. Virgin Islands, and Guam.

Information taken from both firms' 2000 annual reports to shareholders follows.

TARGET CORPORATION

($ in millions)	January 29 2000	January 30 1999
Property and Equipment		
Land	$2,069	$1,868
Buildings and improvements	7,807	7,217
Fixtures and equipment	3,422	3,274
Construction in progress	526	378
Accumulated depreciation	(3,925)	(3,768)
Property and equipment—net	$9,899	$8,969

Property and long-lived assets are recorded at cost less accumulated depreciation or amortization. Depreciation and amortization are computed using the straight-line method over estimated useful lives. Accelerated depreciation methods are generally used for income tax purposes.

Estimated useful lives by major asset category are as follows:

Asset	Life (in Years)
Buildings and improvements	8–50
Fixtures and equipment	5–8
Computer hardware and software	4
Intangible assets and goodwill	3–20

On an ongoing basis, we evaluate our long-lived assets for impairment using undiscounted cash flow analysis.

($ in millions)	January 29 2000	January 30 1999
Depreciation and amortization	$ 854	$ 780
Earnings before income taxes and extraordinary charge	1,936	1,556
Net earnings	$1,144	$ 935

KMART CORPORATION

($ in millions)	January 26 2000	January 27 1999
Property:		
Land	$ 374	$ 334
Buildings	1,008	944
Leasehold improvements	2,502	2,156
Furniture and fixtures	5,509	5,142
Construction in progress	123	62
Property under capital leases	2,038	2,140
	$11,554	$10,778
Less–accumulated depreciation and amortization:		
Property owned	(3,977)	(3,674)
Property under capital leases	(1,167)	(1,190)
Total	$ 6,410	$ 5,914

Depreciation and amortization, including amortization of property held under capital leases, are computed based on the estimated useful lives of the respective assets using the straight-line method for financial statement purposes and accelerated methods for tax purposes. The general range of lives are 25 to 50 years for buildings, 5 to 25 years for leasehold improvements, 3 to 5 years for computer systems and equipment and 3 to 17 years for furniture and fixtures.

Selected income statement information follows.

($ in millions)	January 26 2000	January 27 1999
Depreciation and amortization	$ 770	$671
Income before income taxes, dividends on convertible preferred securities, and discontinued operations	1,020	798
Net income	$ 403	$518

REQUIRED:

Assume a 35% tax rate.

1. Estimate the average useful life of each firm's long-lived assets.
2. Calculate a revised estimate of Kmart's 2000 depreciation expense using the estimated average useful life of Target's assets. Use this amount to recalculate Kmart's 2000 income before taxes and net income.
3. Calculate a revised estimate of Target's 2000 depreciation expense using the estimated average useful life of Kmart's assets. Use this amount to recalculate Target's 2000 income before taxes and net income.
4. Why might a financial analyst want to make the adjustments in (2) or (3)?
5. What factors will affect the reliability and accuracy of the adjustments performed in (2) and (3)?

C10–5

Dallas versus Houston (CW): Financial analysis and fixed asset reporting

Dallas Inc. began operations on January 1, 2001 when it purchased some long-lived assets at a cost of $120,000. The assets have a 12-year useful life and no salvage value; Dallas Inc. intends to use the straight-line depreciation method. Assume that the firm will generate net operating cash flows of $33,000 in 2001 and that its net operating cash flows will grow at an annual rate of 10%. Assume that Dallas does not intend to make any capital expenditures over the next five years.

Houston Inc. is a competitor of Dallas Inc. On January 1, 2001 the book value of Houston's assets is $120,000 (original cost of $240,000). Houston's assets, like those of Dallas Inc., have a 12-year useful life, no salvage value, and are depreciated on a straight-line basis. However, they are six years old and are halfway through their useful life of 12 years. Houston has a policy of replacing one-twelfth of its assets each year at the end of the assets' useful lives. Assume that Houston Inc. will generate net operating cash flows of $43,000 in 2001 and that the firm's net operating cash flows will grow at an annual rate of 10%. To keep pace with inflation, the management of Houston Inc. will increase the capital expenditures of the firm by 10% per year.

REQUIRED:

1. Prepare a schedule of Dallas Inc.'s net book value of assets, net operating cash flow, depreciation expense, income before tax, income taxes, net income, average asset age, and return on net assets (net income divided by beginning book value of net assets) for the 2001–2005 period. Assume an income tax rate of 34%.
2. Repeat requirement (1) for Houston Inc.
3. Compare the return on net assets of the firms over the 2001–2005 period.
4. Which firm's 2005 income is more sustainable? Why?

C10–6

ShopKo (CW): Long-lived assets reporting

ShopKo Stores, Inc. (ShopKo) is a leading regional discount store chain operating 109 discount retail stores in 13 states. ShopKo stores carry a wide selection of branded and private label nondurable "hardline" goods such as housewares, music videos, health and beauty aids, toys, and sporting goods; and "softline" goods such as home textiles, apparel (men's, women's, and children's), shoes, jewelry, cosmetics and accessories. In addition, 106 of the company's stores include pharmacy departments and 99 include optical departments.

Information taken from a recent copy of ShopKo's annual report to shareholders and the firm's 10-K reports that were filed with the SEC appears next.

Property and Equipment

Property and equipment are carried at cost. The cost of buildings and equipment is depreciated over the estimated useful lives of the assets. Buildings and certain equipment (principally computer and retail store equipment) are depreciated using the straight-line method. Remaining properties are depreciated on an accelerated basis. Useful lives generally assigned are: buildings—25 to 40 years; retail store equipment—8 years; warehouse, transportation, and other equipment—3 to 10 years. Costs of leasehold improvements are amortized over the period of the lease or the estimated useful life of the asset, whichever is shorter, using the straight-line method. Property under capital leases is amortized over the related lease term using the straight-line method. Interest on property under construction of $1.1, $1.1, and $1.0 million was capitalized in fiscal years 3, 2, and 1, respectively.

The components of property and equipment are as follows:

($ in thousands)	February 27 Year 3	February 29 Year 2
Property and equipment at cost:		
Land	$102,394	$ 89,196
Buildings	352,426	309,382
Property under construction	8,664	18,648
Leasehold improvements	40,914	40,903
Equipment	221,454	191,907
Property under capital leases	14,216	14,975
	740,068	665,011
Less accumulated depreciation and amortization:		
Property and equipment	(239,344)	(212,242)
Property under capital leases	(7,656)	(7,546)
Net property and equipment	$493,068	$445,223

SHOPKO STORES, INC. AND SUBSIDIARIES

Property and Equipment

($ in thousands)	Balance at Beginning of Year 3	Additions at Cost	Retirements and Transfers	Balance at End of Year 3
Land	$ 89,196	$13,328	$ 130	$102,394
Buildings:				
Owned	309,382	35,687	(7,357)	352,426
Leased	14,975		759	14,216
Property under construction	18,648		9,984	8,664
Leasehold improvements	40,903	1,603	1,592	40,914
Equipment	191,907	40,442	10,895	221,454
	$665,011	$91,060	$16,003	$740,068

SHOPKO STORES, INC. AND SUBSIDIARIES

Reserve for Depreciation and Amortization Property and Equipment

($ in thousands)	Balance at Beginning of Year 3	Additions at Cost	Retirements and Transfers	Balance at End of Year 3
Buildings:				
Owned	$ 80,286	$15,663	$ 2,509	$ 93,440
Leased	7,546	869	759	7,656
Leasehold improvements	11,654	2,625	1,592	12,687
Equipment	120,302	23,889	10,974	133,217
	$219,788	$43,046	$15,834	$247,000

SHOPKO STORES, INC. AND SUBSIDIARIES

Consolidated Statement of Cash Flows

	Fiscal Years Ended		
($ in thousands)	February 27 Year 3 (52 weeks)	February 29 Year 2 (53 weeks)	February 23 Year 1 (52 weeks)
Cash Flows from Operating Activities			
Net earnings	$ 50,059	$ 49,589	$45,080
Adjustments to reconcile net earnings to net cash provided by operating activities:			
Depreciation and amortization	43,275	40,372	39,134
Provision for losses on receivables	143	139	215
Gain on the sale of property and equipment	(240)	(120)	(783)
Deferred income taxes	(68)	(3,899)	829
Change in assets and liabilities:			
Receivables	(3,926)	(430)	(2,461)
Merchandise inventories	(30,122)	2,016	(19,600)
Other current assets	(1,213)	(1,031)	(1,894)
Other assets	(558)		
Accounts payable	9,258	(13,859)	13,530
Accrued liabilities	8,649	3,675	5,581
Net cash provided by operating activities	75,257	76,452	79,631

(continued on next page)

SHOPKO STORES, INC. AND SUBSIDIARIES (*continued*)

Consolidated Statement of Cash Flows

	Fiscal Years Ended		
($ in thousands)	February 27 Year 3 (52 weeks)	February 29 Year 2 (53 weeks)	February 23 Year 1 (52 weeks)
Cash Flows from Investing Activities			
Payments for property and equipment	($ 91,060)	($ 53,391)	($59,100)
Proceeds from the sale of property and equipment	408	1,327	1,341
Net cash (used in) investing activities	(90,652)	(52,064)	(57,759)
Cash Flows from Financing Activities			
Payments to related party	(181,167)	(22,867)	(19,417)
Net proceeds from long-term debt	197,112		
Proceeds from short-term debt	15,025		
Net proceeds from sale of common stock		240,830	
Dividends paid	(14,080)	(240,830)	
Reduction in capital lease obligations	(784)	(1,446)	(2,263)
Net cash provided by (used in) financing activities	16,106	(24,313)	(21,680)
Net increase in cash	711	75	192
Cash at beginning of year	2,081	2,006	1,814
Cash at end of year	$ 2,792	$ 2,081	$ 2,006
Supplemental Cash Flow Information			
Noncash investing and financial activities			
Capital lease obligations incurred	$ -0-	$ 1,871	$ 333
Cash paid during the period for:			
Interest	$ 15,642	$ 18,339	$22,331
Income taxes	31,879	42,430	27,237

REQUIRED:

1. How much cash was expended on new property and equipment during fiscal Year 3? Make the journal entry.
2. How much depreciation and amortization did ShopKo record on its property and equipment in fiscal Year 3? Make the journal entry.
3. Assume that retirements of property and equipment consist exclusively of sales for cash. What was the original cost of the property and equipment sold in fiscal Year 3? What was the book value of the property and equipment sold in fiscal Year 3? What was the gain or loss recognized on the sale of the property and equipment sold in fiscal Year 3? Make the journal entry to record the sale of property and equipment during fiscal Year 3.

C10–7

Intel Corporation (CW): Long-lived asset reporting

Appearing on the following pages is information pertaining to the "Plant, Property, and Equipment" accounts of Intel Corporation. This information was taken from Intel's Year 2 10-K report. A 10-K is an annual report firms must file with the SEC within 90 days of the end of their fiscal year. (All figures are in thousands.)

ADDITIONAL INFORMATION:

All amounts under the heading "Retirements and Sales" are retirements.

REQUIRED:

1. Solve for the unknowns in Intel's "Property, Plant, and Equipment" and "Accumulated Depreciation" schedules for Year 2.
2. What was the total amount expended on the acquisition of new property, plant, and equipment in Year 2? Where would this amount appear in the financial statements?

3. What was the net gain (or net loss) reported in Year 2 on the retirement of property, plant, and equipment? Where would this amount appear in the financial statements?
4. Make all the journal entries related to the "Property, plant, and equipment" and "Accumulated Depreciation" accounts for Year 2.
5. Prepare a schedule of the depreciation expense to be taken for financial reporting purposes on the new machinery and equipment acquired in Year 2. Prepare separate schedules assuming straight-line, sum-of-the-years' digits, and double-declining balance. Assume a zero salvage value for all assets and a three-year useful life; also assume that Intel takes a full year of depreciation in the year an asset is purchased.
6. Assume that one of Intel's long-term debt contracts requires that Intel maintain a minimum interest coverage ratio of 5.0. If Intel's interest coverage ratio falls below 5.0, the lenders have the option of requiring immediate payment of their debt or renegotiating the interest rate. Assume that Intel's interest coverage ratio at the end of Year 1 was 4.9. Briefly describe how the restriction on the firm's interest coverage ratio could affect management's choice of depreciation policy for all or some of the new long-term assets acquired in Year 2.
7. What other settings can you identify in which management may be tempted to use depreciation policy strategically to influence the numbers reported in the financial statements?
8. Identify other items in the financial statements (besides depreciation expense) that management is capable of "managing." Are some easier for outside parties to observe?
9. Several years ago, the SEC decided to stop requiring firms to report the detailed information about the underlying changes in the long-term asset and accumulated depreciation accounts that appear in the following two schedules. As a financial analyst, do you approve or disapprove? Explain why.

INTEL CORPORATION

Property, Plant, and Equipment

($ in thousands)	Balance at Beginning of Year 2	Additions at Cost	Retirements and Sales	Transfers, Reclassifications and Other In (Out)	Balance at End of Year 2
Land and buildings	$ (a)	$ 24,612	$12,455	$124,001	$1,097,526
Machinery and equipment	1,764,623	596,068	(b)	30,322	2,288,200
Construction in progress	87,614	(c)	2,470	(d)	258,430

INTEL CORPORATION

Accumulated Depreciation, Property, Plant, and Equipment

($ in thousands)	Balance at Beginning of Year 2	Additions at Cost	Retirements and Sales	Transfers, Reclassifications and Other In (Out)	Balance at End of Year 2
Buildings and improvements	$226,533	$ (a)	$ 1,812	$(116)	$ 283,954
Machinery and equipment	(b)	358,903	91,044	116	1,197,479

C10–8

Tuesday Morning Corporation (CW): Long-lived assets reporting

Tuesday Morning Corporation operates a chain of 246 deep discount retail stores in 32 states. As a deep discount retailer, the company purchases close-out merchandise at prices generally ranging from 10% to 50% of normal wholesale prices and sells the merchandise at prices that are 50% to 80% lower than retail prices generally charged by department and specialty stores. Merchandise offered by Tuesday Morning stores primarily consists of dinnerware, silver serving pieces, gourmet housewares, bathroom, bedroom, and kitchen accessories, linens and domestics, Christmas trim, luggage, toys, stationery, and silk plants.

Appearing next is information taken from Tuesday Morning's annual report to shareholders for a recent year.

TUESDAY MORNING CORPORATION AND SUBSIDIARIES

Consolidated Balance Sheets

($ in thousands, except share amount)	December 31 1994	1993
Assets		
Current assets:		
Cash and cash equivalents	$ 4,535	$ 1,728
Income taxes receivable	–	2,133
Inventories	46,815	53,551
Prepaid expenses	1,674	991
Other current assets	649	1,246
Total current assets	53,673	59,649
Property, plant, and equipment:		
Land	8,356	8,356
Buildings	12,852	12,748
Furniture and fixtures	15,017	15,120
Equipment	12,578	5,287
Leasehold improvements	1,713	1,491
	50,516	43,002
Less accumulated depreciation and amortization	(17,563)	(14,411)
Net property, plant, and equipment	32,953	28,591
Due from officer	1,799	–
Other assets	978	727
Total assets	$89,403	$88,967
Liabilities and Shareholders' Equity		
Current liabilities:		
Current installments on mortgages	$ 2,747	$ 1,402
Current installments on capital lease obligation	607	–
Accounts payable	12,916	15,859
Accrued expenses:		
Sales tax	1,574	1,760
Other	1,945	3,118
Deferred income taxes	303	146
Due to officer	–	599
Income taxes payable	988	–
Total current liabilities	21,080	22,884
Mortgages on property, plant, and equipment, excluding current installments	4,952	7,595
Capital lease obligations, excluding current installments	1,821	–
Deferred income taxes	2,920	2,764
	9,693	10,359
Shareholders' equity:		
Preferred stock of $1 par value per share Authorized 2,000,000 shares, none issued	–	–
Common stock of $0.01 par value per share Authorized 20,000,000 shares; issued 8,099,586 shares in 1994 and 8,059,586 in 1993	81	81
Additional paid-in capital	18,171	18,091
Retained earnings	42,545	39,894
Less: Treasury stock (299,500 shares in 1994 and 329,500 shares in 1993)	(2,167)	(2,342)
Total shareholders' equity	58,630	55,724
Total liabilities and shareholders' equity	$89,403	$88,967

Note 9: Supplemental cash flow information	1994	1993	1992
Net earnings (loss)	$ 2,651	$(1,052)	$ 8,171
Adjustments to reconcile net earnings to cash provided by operations:			
Depreciation and amortization	3,862	2,805	2,071
Deferred income taxes	313	848	449
Loss on sale of fixed assets	12	21	6
Changes in operating assets and liabilities (net)	5,218	12,008	(29,104)
Net cash provided by (used in) operations	$12,056	$14,630	$(18,407)

During 1994 Tuesday Morning entered into a new lease to obtain additional store locations. As a result of the lease, the firm made an entry to increase the "Property, plant, and equipment" account by $2,642,000.

TUESDAY MORNING CORPORATION AND SUBSIDIARIES

Consolidated Statements of Operations

	Years ended December 31		
($ in thousands)	1994	1993	1992
Net sales	$190,081	$175,790	$160,075
Cost of sales	126,931	123,148	104,581
Gross profit	63,150	52,642	55,494
Selling, general, and administrative expenses	57,523	54,895	45,315
Operating income (loss)	5,627	(2,253)	10,179
Other income (expenses)			
Interest income	198	311	367
Interest expense	(2,458)	(1,689)	(771)
Other, net	649	1,059	440
	(1,611)	(319)	36
Earnings (loss) before income taxes and cumulative effect of changes in accounting principles	4,016	(2,572)	10,215
Income tax benefit (expense)	(1,365)	956	(3,643)
Earnings (loss) before cumulative effect of changes in accounting principles	2,651	(1,616)	6,572
Cumulative effect to December 31, 1992 of change in accounting for income taxes	–	564	–
Cumulative effect to December 31, 1991 of change in accounting for inventories (net of tax)	–	–	1,599
Net earnings (loss)	$ 2,651	$ (1,052)	$ 8,171

(continued)

TUESDAY MORNING CORPORATION AND SUBSIDIARIES

Consolidated Statements of Cash Flows

($ in thousands)	1994	1993	1992
	Years ended December 31		
Cash flows from operating activities:			
Cash received from customers	$190,081	$175,790	$160,075
Cash paid to suppliers and employees	(177,676)	(157,295)	(175,732)
Interest received	198	311	366
Interest paid	(2,458)	(1,689)	(771)
Income taxes (paid) refunded	1,911	(2,487)	(2,345)
Net cash provided by (used in) operating activities	12,056	14,630	(18,407)
Cash flows from investing activities:			
Sale of marketable equity securities	–	–	1,791
Capital expenditures	(5,693)	(4,850)	(5,087)
Advances/loans to officer	(2,398)	(2,067)	(1,884)
Proceeds from sale of property, plant, and equipment	99	420	14
Net cash used in investing activities	(7,992)	(6,497)	(5,166)
Cash flows from financing activities:			
Net increase (decrease) in notes payable	–	(3,500)	3,500
Principal payments on mortgages	(1,298)	(1,194)	(1,453)
Principal payments under capital lease obligation	(214)	–	–
Proceeds from common stock offering	–	–	2,419
Proceeds from exercise of common stock options/stock purchase plan	255	145	319
Repurchase of common stock	–	(3,383)	(1,390)
Net cash provided by (used in) financing activities	(1,257)	(7,932)	3,395
Net increase (decrease) in cash and cash equivalents	2,807	201	(20,178)
Cash and cash equivalents at beginning of year	1,728	1,527	21,705
Cash and cash equivalents at end of year	$ 4,535	$ 1,728	$ 1,527

REQUIRED:

1. How much cash was expended on new property, plant, and equipment during fiscal 1994?
2. Make the journal entry for requirement (1).
3. What is the total amount of depreciation and amortization reported by Tuesday Morning in fiscal 1994?
4. Where do you think the depreciation and amortization is accounted for on Tuesday Morning's 1994 Consolidated Statement of Operations?
5. Make the journal entry for requirement (4).
6. What was the gain/loss recognized by Tuesday Morning on the sale of property, plant, and equipment in fiscal 1994?
7. What was the original cost of property, plant, and equipment sold in fiscal 1994?
8. Make the journal entry to record the sale of property, plant, and equipment during fiscal 1994.
9. Where do you think the gain/loss from requirement (8) is reported on Tuesday Morning's 1994 Consolidated Statement of Operations?

10. What impact, if any, did the gain/loss on the sale of property, plant, and equipment in 1994 have on the firm's 1994 Consolidated Statement of Cash Flows?
11. Assume that on January 1, 1995 Tuesday Morning acquired some new property, plant, and equipment at a total cost of $100,000. Of the total, $50,000 was for buildings, $30,000 was for furniture and fixtures, and $20,000 was for equipment. Assume that all the assets are expected to have a zero salvage value and that the buildings have a useful life of 30 years, the furniture and fixtures seven years, and the equipment three years. Tuesday Morning has decided to use the straight-line method to depreciate the buildings, the sum-of-the-years' digits method to depreciate the furniture and fixtures, and the double-declining balance method to depreciate the equipment. Calculate the depreciation expense to be recorded on the buildings, furniture and fixtures, and equipment in 1995.

11

Financial Instruments as Liabilities

LEARNING OBJECTIVES:

After studying this chapter, you will understand:

1. How to compute a bond's issue price from its effective yield to investors.
2. How to construct an amortization table for calculating bond interest expense and net carrying value of the debt.
3. Why and how bond interest expense and net carrying value change over time.
4. How and when floating-rate debt protects lenders.
5. How debt extinguishment gains and losses arise, and what they mean.
6. How to find the future cash payments for a company's debt.
7. Why off-balance sheet financing and loss contingencies are important concerns for statement readers.
8. How futures, swaps, and options contracts are used to hedge financial risk.
9. When hedge accounting can be used, and how it reduces earnings volatility.

The Financial Accounting Standards Board (FASB) says:

> Liabilities are probable future sacrifices of economic benefits arising from present obligations of a particular entity to transfer assets or provide services to other entities in the future as a result of past transactions or events.[1]

Simply, this means a financial statement liability is

1. an existing obligation arising from past events, which calls for . . .
2. . . . payment of cash or provision of goods and services (say, delivery of a product for which a deposit has already been received) to some other entity at some future date.

Liabilities help businesses conduct their affairs by permitting delay—delay in payment or performance. But since "time is money," **interest** is a common feature of delayed payment liabilities. Interest is the price charged for the privilege of delaying payment.

---

[1] "Elements of Financial Statements," *Statement of Financial Accounting Concepts No. 6* (Stamford, CT: FASB, 1985), para. 35. In October 2000, the FASB proposed modifying this definition to include as liabilities certain obligations settled by the issuance of equity shares (see "Proposed Amendment to FASB Concepts Statement No. 6 to Revise the Definition of Liabilities," *Financial Accounting Series Exposure Draft* [Stamford, CT: FASB, 2000]).

Here's an example. Suppose a start-up Internet company, Yellowbird.com, buys $100,000 of computers from a manufacturer, say Dell Computers. Instead of paying cash, Yellowbird promises to pay Dell $100,000 worth of Yellowbird stock once the company goes public (in about six months). Yellowbird is using its stock as "currency" for the transaction because it lacks cash.

Notice that a fixed amount of value ($100,000) must be conveyed to Dell, not a fixed number of Yellowbird shares. The FASB says that this makes the relationship look more like a debtor-creditor relationship—unlike an owner, Dell cannot benefit from increases or suffer from decreases in share value—so Yellowbird should record a "liability" for the $100,000.

Most liabilities are **monetary liabilities** because they are payable in a fixed future amount of cash. There are **nonmonetary liabilities** that are satisfied by the delivery of things other than cash, such as merchandise or services. An example is a product warranty. If the product fails during the warranty period, the warranty liability is satisfied by either repairing or replacing the product. The liability is paid by providing nonmonetary assets—labor and replacement parts from inventory or a new product—but not cash.

Conceptually, monetary liabilities should be shown in the financial statements at the *discounted present value* of the future cash outflows required to satisfy the obligation. This allows interest to accumulate over time through accounting entries that assign interest expense—the cost of delay—to the time period(s) over which payment is delayed. In practice, this is what is done with long-term monetary liabilities.

However, **current liabilities**—obligations due within a year or within the company's operating cycle, whichever is longer—are rarely discounted. This is because the short maturity of current liabilities makes the difference between the amount due at maturity and present value immaterial. So current liabilities are shown at the undiscounted amount due (an exception is the current portion of long-term debt). This treatment of current liabilities departs from the conceptual "ideal" solely on pragmatic grounds.

Noncurrent monetary liabilities, however, are initially recorded at their present value when incurred. There are occasional exceptions. One is the deferred tax liability account, which is reported at an undiscounted amount for reasons explained in Chapter 13. But the general rule is that noncurrent monetary liabilities are first recorded at their present value. The next section explains why.

> **Debentures,** the most common type of corporate bond, are backed only by the general credit of the company. **Mortgage bonds** have real estate as collateral for the repayment of the loan. **Serial bonds** specify periodic payment of interest and a portion of the principal (e.g., an equal amount each year to maturity). Despite these and other differences, the accounting for these financial instruments follows the general approach described here.

Bonds Payable

Firms issue bonds to raise cash. A **bond** is a financial instrument that represents a formal promise to repay both the amount borrowed as well as interest. The precise terms of the borrowing are specified in the **bond indenture agreement**—the contract between the issuer and investors. In this section we look at how companies account for this debt instrument and how to interpret debt disclosures in financial statements.

Characteristics of Bond Cash Flows

Bond certificates are usually issued with a **principal amount** of $1,000. The principal amount—also called the **par value, maturity value,** or **face value**—represents the amount that will be repaid to the investor at the maturity date specified in the indenture agreement. The bond certificate also displays the **stated interest rate**—sometimes called the **coupon** or **nominal rate.**

The annual cash interest payments on the bond are computed by multiplying the principal amount by the stated interest rate. A bond with $1,000 principal and a 9% per year stated interest rate will have annual cash interest payments of $90. Typically, the total annual cash interest is paid in installments, either quarterly or semiannually.

> Investors must be careful to read the details of a bond's interest payment terms. For example, a bond that pays "9% interest annually" yields a single payment of $90 (per $1,000 of face value) each year. A bond that pays "9% interest semiannually" yields two payments of $45 each year (9% ÷ 2 = 4.5% each payment period). Although the total dollar interest payment is $90 per year in both cases, the semiannual bond is slightly more valuable because investors receive half of the cash earlier than in the case of the annual payment bond.

While the face value is typically $1,000 per bond, the price at which it is issued can be equal to, below, or above the face value.

- When the issue price exactly equals the face value, the bond is sold at **par.**
- If the issue price is below face value, the bond is sold at a **discount.**
- If the issue price is greater than the face value, the bond is sold at a **premium.**

Market conditions dictate the relationship between what investors are willing to pay—the issue price—and the bond's face value.

Bonds Issued at Par

A bond's issue price determines its **effective yield**—or true rate of return. When the issue price of the bond equals its par value, the yield to investors is exactly equal to the coupon (or stated) rate. Consider this example:

> On January 1, 2001 Huff Corporation issued $1,000,000 face value of 10% per year bonds at par—that is, Huff got $1,000,000 cash from investors and promised to make interest and principal payments in the future. Since the cash interest payments on the bonds are always equal to the stated interest rate (10%) times the bond principal amount ($1,000,000), cash interest will total $100,000 per year. The bonds mature in 10 years (on December 31, 2010), and interest is paid annually on December 31 of each year.

The accounting entry to record issuance of these bonds on Huff's books is:

DR Cash	$1,000,000	
CR Bonds payable		$1,000,000

The bond is recorded at its issue price—the $1,000,000 cash received by Huff.

When bonds are sold at par (or face value), their effective yield to the investor is exactly equal to the coupon interest rate, which is 10% in this example. To show this, we list the cash payments and compute their present value as of the issue date—January 1, 2001—in Table 11.1. The effective yield is precisely 10% since the present value of the ten annual interest payments ($614,456) plus the present value of the principal repayment ($385,544) is equal to the issue proceeds received on January 1, 2001 ($1,000,000) when discounted at a 10% rate.

For bonds issued at par, the coupon rate on the bond is equal to the effective yield earned by bond investors. Furthermore, recording the bonds at par on the issuer's books automatically records them at their discounted present value.

In the example, the amount received for the bonds ($1,000,000) is precisely equal to the present value of the future debt-related cash outflows (interest and principal payments) discounted at the 10% effective yield on the bonds.

The cash interest payments on the Huff bonds are an **annuity,** which just means a series of payments in the same amount made at equally spaced time intervals. If the first payment is made at the start of period 1, then it's an **annuity due.** Apartment leases often have this feature—the first month's payment is due when the lease is signed. The cash interest payments on Huff's bonds are an **ordinary annuity** (in arrears) because the first payment is due at the end of period 1 (December 31, 2001).

Table 11.1 ■ HUFF CORPORATION

Demonstration that the Yield on Bonds Issued at Par Is Equal to the Coupon Rate (here 10%)

Date of Payment	Type of Payment	Amount of Payment	10% Present Value Factor	Discounted Present Value
12/31/01	Interest	$ 100,000	.90909	$ 90,909
12/31/02	Interest	100,000	.82645	82,645
12/31/03	Interest	100,000	.75131	75,131
12/31/04	Interest	100,000	.68301	68,301
12/31/05	Interest	100,000	.62092	62,092
12/31/06	Interest	100,000	.56447	56,447
12/31/07	Interest	100,000	.51316	51,316
12/31/08	Interest	100,000	.46651	46,651
12/31/09	Interest	100,000	.42410	42,410
12/31/10	Interest	100,000	.38554	38,554
Total present value of interest payments				**$ 614,456**
12/31/10	Principal	$1,000,000	.38554	**385,544**
Total issue price on January 1, 2001				**$1,000,000**

Subsequent accounting for bonds issued at par is straightforward. Let's say Huff prepares monthly financial statements; the *monthly* journal entry for the accrual of interest is:

DR Interest expense	$8,333.33	
CR Accrued interest payable		$8,333.33

This (rounded) amount represents 1/12 of the $100,000 annual interest. At the end of the year, the accrued interest would total $100,000; upon payment of the interest by Huff, the entry would be:

DR Accrued interest payable	$100,000.00	
CR Cash		$100,000.00

Bonds are seldom sold directly to investors by the issuing company. Instead, the bonds are sold through a financial intermediary—an **investment banker.** In most cases the investment banker purchases the bonds and resells them to institutional investors (e.g., pension funds) at whatever price the market will bear. The investment banker's profit (or loss) is the difference between the price it pays to buy the bonds from the issuing company and the price at which it sells them to investors, plus any fees paid by the company.

Bonds Issued at a Discount

Arranging for the sale of bonds can take considerable time. The terms of the indenture—the bond contract—must be drafted and printed, an investment banker must be found, and the bond certificates themselves must be engraved. Market interest rates may change during the time it takes to do this and before the bonds are ready to be issued.

Assume the Huff bonds are printed during late 2000 and carry a 10% coupon interest rate. That rate immediately establishes the yearly cash interest payout of $100,000 (10% multiplied by the $1,000,000 face amount of the bonds).

But let's say there's a sudden increase in the anticipated rate of inflation, causing investors to demand an 11% return on the January 1, 2001 issue date. To provide the 11% return that investors demand, the Huff bonds must be sold at a *discount* relative to face value. Here's why. Since the annual cash interest payments are fixed at $100,000, the bond issue price must be lower than the $1,000,000 face amount to attract purchasers. How much lower than $1,000,000 must the issue price be? It must be reduced to a level that gives prospective investors exactly the 11% return they require. ***The price is determined by discounting the contractual cash flows at 11%,*** as shown in Table 11.2. Lowering the issue price gives investors the higher return they demand.

The price that yields the required 11% return, given the stipulated $100,000 annual contractual interest payments, is $941,108. Investors seeking an 11% return will not be willing to pay more than $941,108 for 10-year bonds with a face value of $1,000,000 and a coupon rate of 10%. Why? Because if they pay more than this amount, they will earn less than 11% on the bond's fixed cash flow stream. And Huff will not be willing to issue the bonds for less than $941,108 because to do so would mean paying more than 11% to investors. Thus, market forces will set the issue price at $941,108.

The accounting entry made on issuance of the bonds under these terms is:

DR Cash	$941,108	
DR Bond discount	58,892	
CR Bonds payable–par		$1,000,000

The bond discount is a **liability valuation account** that is deducted from the bonds payable account for financial reporting purposes. The net balance sheet value for the bonds when they are issued will be $941,108 ($1,000,000 − $58,892)—the amount of cash Huff received. This again illustrates the basic principle that newly issued bonds are recorded at the present value of the contractual cash outflows for interest and principal repayment—where ***the discount rate is the effective yield on the bonds at the issuance date*** (here 11%).

Table 11.2 ■ HUFF CORPORATION

Determining the Issue Price for 10% Coupon Bonds When the Market Rate Is 11%

Date of Payment	Type of Payment	Amount of Payment	11% Present Value Factor	Discounted Present Value
12/31/01	Interest	$ 100,000	.90090	$ 90,090
12/31/02	Interest	100,000	.81162	81,162
12/31/03	Interest	100,000	.73119	73,119
12/31/04	Interest	100,000	.65873	65,873
12/31/05	Interest	100,000	.59345	59,345
12/31/06	Interest	100,000	.53464	53,464
12/31/07	Interest	100,000	.48166	48,166
12/31/08	Interest	100,000	.43393	43,393
12/31/09	Interest	100,000	.39093	39,093
12/31/10	Interest	100,000	.35218	35,218
Total present value of interest payments				**$588,923**
12/31/10	Principal	$1,000,000	.35218	**352,185**
Total issue price on January 1, 2001				**$941,108**

Equivalently

December 31	2000	2001	2002	2003	2004	2005	2006	2007	2008	2009	2010
Cash interest payments	●	$100k	$100k	$100k	$100k	$100k	$100k	$100k	$100k	$100k	$100k
Cash principal payment	●	•	•	•	•	•	•	•	•	•	$1 m

→ Present value of single payment at 11%: $1 million × 0.352185 = $352,185

→ Present value of 10-period ordinary annuity at 11%: $100 thousand × 5.88923 = $588,923

When bonds are not sold at par, the calculation of annual interest expense and the accounting entry that records that expense are slightly more complicated. Consider the nature of the bond discount of $58,892. The discount amount is the difference between the cash Huff received and the amount Huff promised to repay on December 31, 2010. This $58,892 is really just additional interest—over and above the stated cash interest of $100,000 per year—that will be *earned* over the term of the loan, but it will not be *paid* until maturity. Cumulative interest expense over the 10 years will total $1,058,892—the coupon interest of $1,000,000 paid out over the life of the bond plus the issue discount of $58,892 paid at maturity.

Cumulative interest expense can also be thought of as follows: The investor will ultimately receive total debt-related cash flows of $2,000,000 in principal plus cash interest. Huff received only $941,108 when the bonds were issued. The difference ($2,000,000 minus $941,108) is $1,058,892, which must be the cumulative total interest expense over the life of the bond.

How should this "extra" interest of $58,892 be allocated across the 10 years? Generally accepted accounting principles (GAAP) require that the bond discount be allocated to interest expense on an **effective interest basis.** This requires the use of an amortization schedule, as shown in Table 11.3 on the next page. In column (a) Huff received $941,108 on January 1, 2001 in exchange for issuing the bond certificates. Bondholders require an 11% return on the amount invested. Therefore, their interest income—and Huff's interest expense—in 2001 must be 11% of $941,108 or $103,521.88, as shown in column (b). The difference between $103,521.88 and the cash interest of $100,000 is the portion of "extra" interest allocated to 2001 and, consequently, reduces the bond discount amount. If interest is recorded annually, the entry is:

DR Interest expense	$103,521.88	
CR Accrued interest payable		$100,000.00
CR Bond discount		3,521.88

Table 11.3 ■ HUFF CORPORATION

Bond Discount Amortization Schedule

Year	(a) Bond Net Carrying Amount at Start of Year	(b) Interest Expense (Column a × 11%)	(c) Bond Discount Amortized (Column b − $100,000)	(d) Bond Discount Balance at End of Year	(e) Bond Net Carrying Amount at End of Year (Column a + Column c)
2001	$941,108.00	$ 103,521.88	$ 3,521.88	$55,370.12	$ 944,629.88
2002	944,629.88	103,909.29	3,909.29	51,460.83	948,539.17
2003	948,539.17	104,339.31	4,339.31	47,121.52	952,878.48
2004	952,878.48	104,816.63	4,816.63	42,304.89	957,695.11
2005	957,695.11	105,346.46	5,346.46	36,958.43	963,041.57
2006	963,041.57	105,934.57	5,934.57	31,023.86	968,976.14
2007	968,976.14	106,587.38	6,587.38	24,436.48	975,563.52
2008	975,563.52	107,311.98	7,311.98	17,124.50	982,875.50
2009	982,875.50	108,116.30	8,116.30	9,008.20	990,991.80*
2010	990,991.80*	109,008.20*	9,008.20	—	$1,000,000.00
		$1,058,892.00	$58,892.00		

*Rounded.

The process of "spreading" the discount on bonds to increase interest expense over the life of the bonds is called **discount amortization.** The yearly amortization amount is shown in column (c) of Table 11.3. After the amortization is recorded, the year-end balance in the bond discount account—shown in column (d)—will be $55,370.12 (the original discount of $58,892 minus the 2001 amortization of $3,521.88). Notice that the smaller the balance in the bond discount account, shown in column (d), the higher the **net carrying value** of the bond liability in column (e). The balance sheet value of the bond increases as the discount is amortized.

The bond amortization schedule illustrates that annual interest expense, column (b), always equals the effective interest rate (here 11%) multiplied by the start of the year borrowing balance, column (a). The difference between the accrual accounting interest expense, column (b), and the $100,000 cash interest paid each year is the discount amortization, column (c). This amortization process is represented in Exhibit 11.1.

Bonds Issued at a Premium

Recording bonds that are issued at a premium is similar to the accounting for bonds issued at a discount. Assume that after the Huff Corporation bonds were printed late in 2000, interest rates *fell* to 9%. If the bonds were sold at par, Huff would be paying investors 10%—the coupon rate as printed—when investors are willing to accept 9% interest. Instead, Huff will issue the bonds at a *premium*—that is, at an amount sufficiently higher than the $1,000,000 face value so that investors will get only a 9% return. The exact amount is determined, as in the discount example, by taking the bond-related cash flows and discounting them at the effective yield rate (here 9%), as shown in Table 11.4.

The bonds would be issued for $1,064,177—the present value of the contractual principal and interest payments at a discount rate of 9%. Buying the bonds at this price will give investors a 9% effective yield.

Exhibit 11.1 ■ DETERMINING THE AMORTIZATION AMOUNT

Interest expense − Cash interest payment = Amortization amount

[Beginning of period carrying amount of bond × Effective yield at issuance] − [Principal amount of bond × Stated (coupon) rate] = Amortization amount

Table 11.4 ■ HUFF CORPORATION

Determining the Issue Price for 10% Coupon Bonds When the Market Rate Is 9%

Date of Payment	Type of Payment	Amount of Payment	9% Present Value Factor	Discounted Present Value
12/31/01	Interest	$ 100,000	.91743	$ 91,743
12/31/02	Interest	100,000	.84168	84,168
12/31/03	Interest	100,000	.77218	77,218
12/31/04	Interest	100,000	.70843	70,843
12/31/05	Interest	100,000	.64993	64,993
12/31/06	Interest	100,000	.59627	59,627
12/31/07	Interest	100,000	.54703	54,703
12/31/08	Interest	100,000	.50187	50,187
12/31/09	Interest	100,000	.46043	46,043
12/31/10	Interest	100,000	.42241	42,241
Total present value of interest payments				**$ 641,766**
12/31/10	Principal	$1,000,000	.42241	422,411
Total issue price on January 1, 2001				**$1,064,177**

Equivalently

December 31	2000	2001	2002	2003	2004	2005	2006	2007	2008	2009	2010
Cash interest payments	●	$100k	$100k	$100k	$100k	$100k	$100k	$100k	$100k	$100k	$100k
Cash principal payment	●	•	•	•	•	•	•	•	•	•	$1 m

→ Present value of single payment at 9%: $1 million × 0.422411 = $422,411

→ Present value of 10-period ordinary annuity at 9%: $100 thousand × 6.41766 = $641,766

The entry to record the bond issuance is:

DR Cash	$1,064,177	
CR Bond premium		$ 64,177
CR Bonds payable–par		1,000,000

The bond premium (like the bond discount) is also a liability valuation account; the premium balance is added to the bonds payable account to increase the balance sheet carrying value of the bonds. The Huff bonds will initially have a carrying value of $1,064,177. ***When bonds are sold at a premium, interest expense will always be less than the cash interest payment.*** The extra cash paid represents the amount of the premium being returned to bondholders. Table 11.5 on the next page shows the amortization schedule. For example, the 2001 interest expense entry shows interest expense (from column [b]) equal to the $100,000 cash interest payment minus the premium amortization (from column [c])—that is:

DR Interest expense	$95,775.93	
DR Bond premium	4,224.07	
CR Cash		$100,000.00

Interest expense each year is less than the $100,000 annual cash interest payment. To see why, notice that Huff initially received more cash than it promised to pay back at the end of 10 years ($1,064,177 versus $1,000,000). The difference—or premium—is returned to bondholders gradually over the entire period of the borrowing. For example, $4,224.07 of

Table 11.5 ■ HUFF CORPORATION

Bond Premium Amortization Schedule

Year	(a) Bond Net Carrying Amount at Start of Year	(b) Interest Expense (Column a × 9%)	(c) Bond Premium Amortized ($100,000 − Column b)	(d) Bond Premium Balance at End of Year	(e) Bond Net Carrying Amount at End of Year (Column a − Column c)
2001	$1,064,177.00	$ 95,775.93	$ 4,224.07	$59,952.93	$1,059,952.93
2002	1,059,952.93	95,395.76	4,604.24	55,348.69	1,055,348.69
2003	1,055,348.69	94,981.38	5,018.62	50,330.08	1,050,330.08
2004	1,050,330.08	94,529.71	5,470.29	44,859.78	1,044,859.78
2005	1,044,859.78	94,037.38	5,962.62	38,897.16	1,038,897.16
2006	1,038,897.16	93,500.74	6,499.26	32,397.91	1,032,397.91
2007	1,032,397.91	92,915.81	7,084.19	25,313.72	1,025,313.72
2008	1,025,313.72	92,278.23	7,721.77	17,591.95	1,017,591.95
2009	1,017,591.95	91,583.28	8,416.72	9,175.22	1,009,175.22*
2010	1,009,175.22*	90,824.78*	9,175.22	–	1,000,000.00
		$935,823.00	$64,177.00		

*Rounded.

the premium is returned in 2001 (as shown in column [c]), and another $4,604.24 is returned in 2002.

Looking at Bonds Graphically

The bar graphs in Figure 11.1 depict the components of issue price for Huff bonds when the interest rate is 10% (from Table 11.1), 11% (from Table 11.2), and 9% (from Table 11.4). These bar graphs illustrate that ***the issue price is determined by discounting the contractual principal and interest flows at the market yield rate.***

Figure 11.2 is based on the numbers from Table 11.3, where the Huff bonds were sold at a discount because the market interest rate was 11%. Figure 11.2(a) shows interest expense

Figure 11.1

ILLUSTRATION OF SELLING PRICES OF 10% COUPON BONDS AT DIFFERENT MARKET (EFFECTIVE) YIELDS

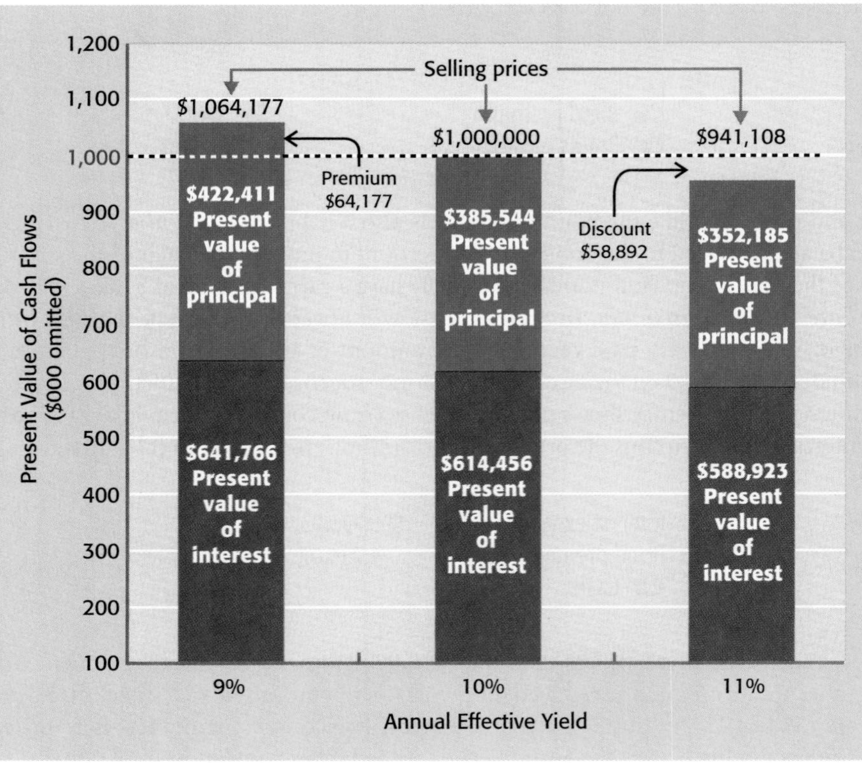

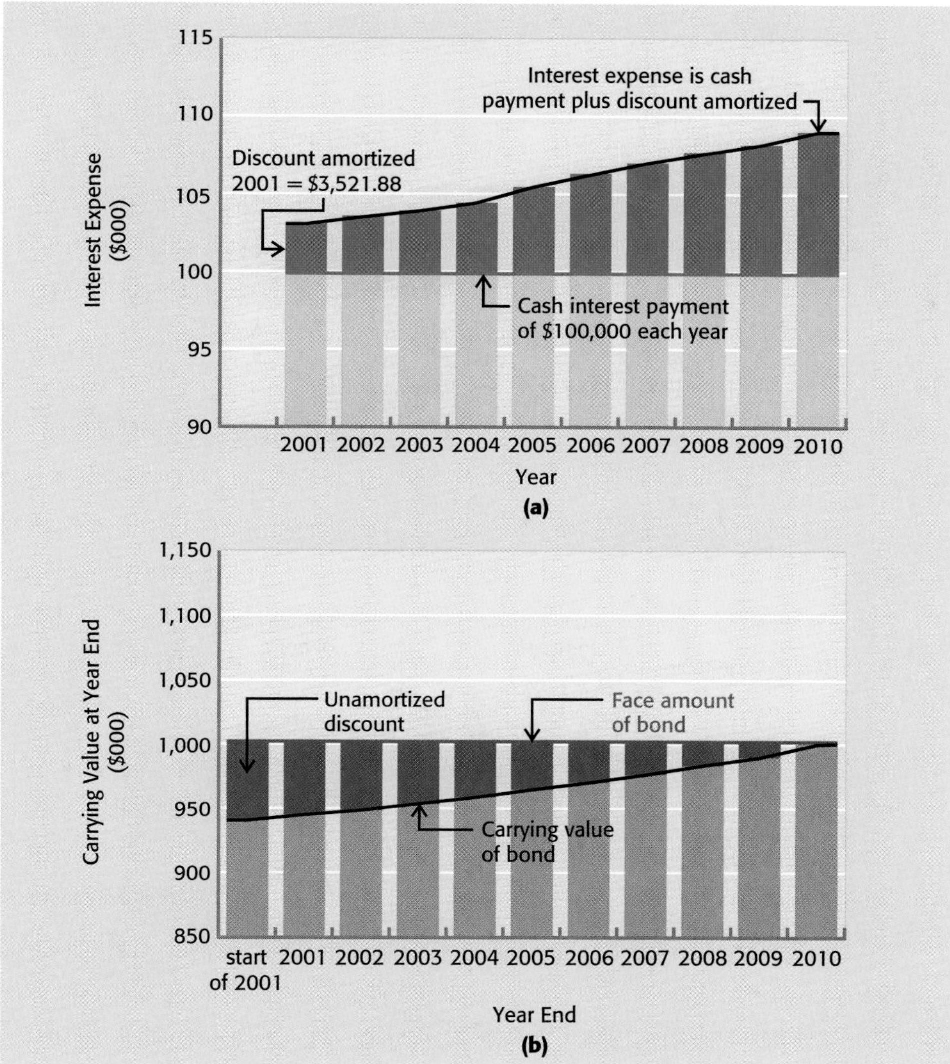

Figure 11.2

ILLUSTRATION OF (a) CASH INTEREST PAYMENT, INTEREST EXPENSE AND (b) CARRYING VALUE FOR 10% BONDS SOLD AT DISCOUNT

Market yield 11%

and cash interest payments, and the difference between the two is the discount amortization. For example, $3,521.88, the discount amortized in 2001, is the amount from column (c) of Table 11.3. Figure 11.2(b) shows that the carrying value of the bonds increases as the discount is amortized each year.

Figure 11.3 on the next page depicts the bond sold at a premium due to a 9% market interest rate. Figure 11.3(a) shows that interest expense is less than the coupon cash payment of $100,000. Figure 11.3(b) shows that the carrying value of the bond falls as the premium is amortized.

RECAP

The cash interest and principal payments on a bond are set before the bond is issued, but market forces determine the issue price and thus the effective yield to investors. All bonds are first recorded on the issuer's books at the issue price. The effective interest rate is then used to compute interest expense and the net carrying value of the bond in subsequent periods.

When bonds are sold at a discount, the effective interest rate is above the coupon rate. Amortization of the discount increases interest expense and adds to the bond's net carrying value. When bonds are sold at a premium, the effective interest rate is below the coupon rate. Amortization of the premium decreases interest expense and reduces the bond's net carrying value.

Figure 11.3

ILLUSTRATION OF (a) CASH INTEREST PAYMENT, INTEREST EXPENSE AND (b) CARRYING VALUE FOR 10% BONDS SOLD AT PREMIUM

Market yield 9%.

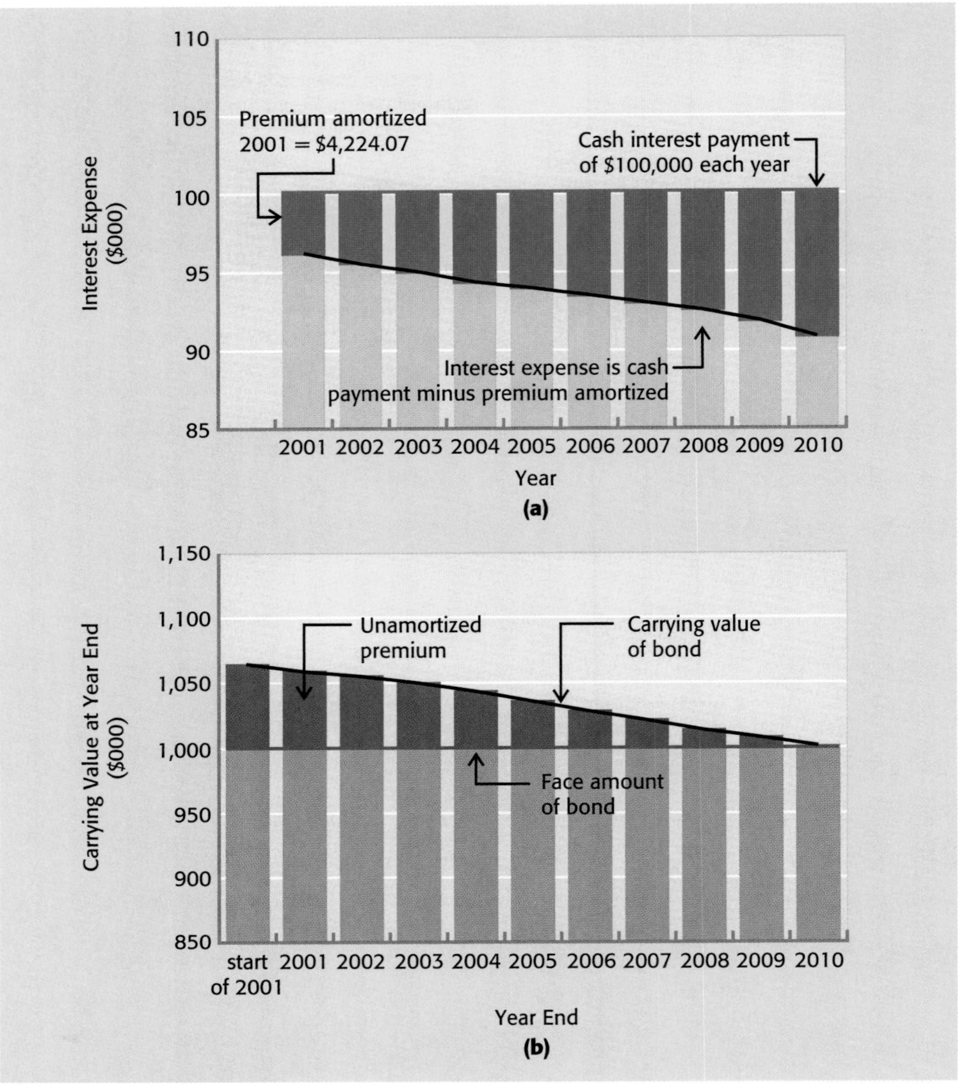

Book Value Versus Market Value After Issuance

Although bonds payable are shown at their market value (meaning their present value) when they are first issued, their balance sheet value will not necessarily equal their market value later. That's because GAAP requires bonds payable to be carried on the books at **amortized historical cost.** Since market interest rates often change, bond prices also often change. ***Thus, after issuance, the reported book value of bonds payable and their market value will frequently differ.***

To see this, let's return to the Huff Corporation example where 10% coupon bonds were issued at par on January 1, 2001. Because the bonds were issued at par, there is no discount or premium to amortize. Hence, the book value of the bonds will always equal the principal amount of $1,000,000 each year the bonds are outstanding. Bonds payable would be shown on the balance sheet at $1,000,000 at December 31, 2001, one year after being issued.

Now it's January 1, 2002, and market interest rates suddenly jump to 11%. Remember, prevailing interest rates "set" the price at which bonds are originally issued. It's no different after bonds have been issued—the market price is still set by prevailing interest rates. So the market price of Huff bonds after interest rates jump on January 1, 2002 is the remaining cash payments for interest and principal discounted at the new 11% effective yield that investors now require. The market price on January 1, 2002 would be $944,630, as shown in

Table 11.6 ■ HUFF CORPORATION

Calculation of Bond Price After an Interest Rate Increase from 10% to 11%

Date of Payment	Type of Payment	Amount of Payment	11% Present Value Factor	Discounted Present Value
12/31/02	Interest	$ 100,000	.90090	$ 90,090
12/31/03	Interest	100,000	.81162	81,162
12/31/04	Interest	100,000	.73119	73,119
12/31/05	Interest	100,000	.65873	65,873
12/31/06	Interest	100,000	.59345	59,345
12/31/07	Interest	100,000	.53464	53,464
12/31/08	Interest	100,000	.48166	48,166
12/31/09	Interest	100,000	.43393	43,393
12/31/10	Interest	100,000	.39093	39,093
Total present value of interest payments				**$553,705**
12/31/10	Principal	$1,000,000	.39093	**390,925**
Total market price on January 1, 2002				**$944,630**

Table 11.6. However, under GAAP, the bond payable would still be shown on the books at the original $1,000,000 amount. In general then, ***reported book values after issuance will not necessarily equal the market value of the bonds, since market interest rates fluctuate over time.***

Floating-Rate Debt Table 11.6 illustrates another point—fluctuations in market interest rates change the value of financial instruments like Huff's 10% coupon bond. In our example, a one percentage point increase in the market rate of interest (from 10% to 11%) at the end of 2001 would cause the value of Huff's bond to fall by $55,370 (from $1,000,000 to $944,630). Investors who buy Huff bonds are exposed to market value losses because the coupon (stated) interest rate is fixed at 10% for the life of the bonds. When market interest rates increase, Huff bonds continue to pay only the fixed-rate of 10% even though investors could do better elsewhere.

There are several ways investors can protect themselves from such losses; the most common is investing in **floating-rate debt.** In contrast to the Huff Corporation bond, floating-rate debt has a stated interest rate that fluctuates in tandem with some interest rate benchmark like the **London Interbank Offered Rate (LIBOR).** This widely used benchmark for floating-rate debt is the base interest rate paid on deposits between European banks.

Suppose that the contractual interest rate on Huff's bonds was "LIBOR plus 4%, reset annually" and that the bonds were issued on January 1, 2001 when the LIBOR was 6%. Investors would receive a cash interest payment of $100,000 during 2001 because the contractual interest rate is 10% (LIBOR of 6% plus another 4%). If the LIBOR increased to 7% by January 1, 2002, investors would receive a cash interest payment of $110,000 (or 11%) that year because of the annual "reset" provision. The new rate equals the LIBOR of 7% plus another 4% by contract. The additional $10,000 cash payment, if maintained over the life of the bond, would exactly offset in present value terms the $55,370 value decline ($1,000,000 − $944,630) we computed from Table 11.6. ***The market value of Huff's floating-rate debt would remain $1,000,000 and investors would be protected from losses like those associated with Huff's fixed-rate debt.***

Floating-rate debt can also benefit the issuing company. If the LIBOR falls to 5%, Huff would be able to reduce its cash interest payments to $90,000, since the contractual interest rate would be reset to 9% (LIBOR of 5% plus another 4% by contract).

Investors benefit from floating-rate debt when market interest rates increase, and issuing corporations benefit when market rates fall. Floating-rate debt allows investors and issuing companies to share in the risks and rewards of changing market interest rates. Risk sharing lowers the company's overall borrowing costs, and this translates into floating-rate debt that has a lower (expected) interest rate than would be charged on comparable fixed-rate debt.

Since virtually all floating-rate debt is issued at par, the accounting entries required are simple. Interest expense and accrued interest payable are recorded using the contractual rate in effect during the period. The entries made by Huff if it had issued the "LIBOR plus 4%, reset annually" bonds on January 1, 2001 are:

1/1/01:	**DR** Cash	$1,000,000	
	CR Bonds payable		$1,000,000
12/31/01:	**DR** Interest expense	$100,000	
	CR Accrued interest payable		$100,000
	2001 interest rate set at 10% (LIBOR of 6% plus another 4%)		
12/31/02:	**DR** Interest expense	$110,000	
	CR Accrued interest payable		$110,000
	2002 interest rate reset to 11% (LIBOR of 7% plus another 4%)		

The balance sheet would continue to show bonds payable at $1,000,000, which also equals the market value of the floating-rate debt.

Book value equals **market value** on the maturity date because the principal payment is then due immediately and, consequently, is not discounted for time or risk.

Extinguishment of Debt Interest rates constantly adjust to changes in levels of economic activity and changes in expected inflation rates, among many other factors. When interest rates change, the market price of fixed-rate debt changes—as interest rates rise, the market price falls; as interest rates fall, the price rises. However, as we just saw, GAAP accounting for debt is at the original transaction price. Subsequent market price changes are not recorded on the financial statements. This means that there will be differences (nearly always) between the book carrying amount of debt and its market value. This divergence creates no accounting gain or loss for debt that is not retired before maturity, since book value and debt market value are equal on the maturity date.

However, when debt is retired before maturity, book value and market value are not typically equal at the retirement date, generating an accounting gain or loss.

To see this, let's go back to Huff's $1,000,000 of 10% fixed-rate debt. On January 1, 2002, immediately after interest rates jump to 11%, Huff repurchases the 10% coupon bonds issued one year earlier. At the repurchase date, the market value of the bonds is $944,630, as we saw from Table 11.6. The book value is $1,000,000. The entry to record the repurchase (ignoring possible income taxes) is:

DR Bonds payable	$1,000,000	
CR Cash		$944,630
CR Extraordinary gain on debt extinguishment		55,370

When bonds are initially sold at a premium or discount, the book value is equal to the face value plus the premium or minus the discount. The premium or discount account must also be closed when debt is retired. Remember that interest expense and accrued interest payable may need to be brought up to date before recording the extinguishment itself.

The accounting gain (or loss) at retirement—more commonly called **extinguishment**—is the difference between the cash paid to extinguish the debt and the book value of the debt. Any extinguishment gain or loss is treated as an *extraordinary* item on the income statement even though extinguishments do *not* meet the criteria for extraordinary items discussed in Chapter 2.[2] The FASB chose to ignore the usual criteria for extraordinary items as a stopgap measure "until such time as the broader issues involved can be addressed."[3]

[2] "Reporting Gains and Losses from Extinguishment of Debt," *Statement of Financial Accounting Standards (SFAS) No. 4* (Stamford, CT: FASB, 1975). From Chapter 2, remember that to qualify as an extraordinary item, an event must be both *unusual* and *infrequent;* but debt extinguishment is neither unusual nor infrequent.

[3] Ibid., para. 15.

The "broader issues" appear to include the fact that historical cost accounting for debt ignores market value changes as they occur. Instead, the full cumulative past price impact is recognized as a gain or loss on extinguishment in the single period when early retirement occurs. Apparently, the FASB believed that including this full cumulative effect in the computation of income from continuing operations is potentially misleading to statement users. Items included "above the line" in income from continuing operations are presumed to represent recurring events that are likely to affect both current and future performance. Since gains and losses on debt extinguishment are unlikely to satisfy this criterion, separate (extraordinary) line item disclosure was required in *Statement of Financial Accounting Standards (SFAS) No. 4.*

RECAP

When interest rates change after a bond has been issued, the bond's reported book value and market value will no longer be the same. That's because GAAP requires bonds to be carried on the issuer's books at amortized historical cost using the effective yield to investors when the bonds were first issued. So when interest rates have increased and bonds are retired before maturity, market value is below book value and this generates an accounting gain. If interest rates have fallen, market value is above book value and an accounting loss results. Gains and losses from early debt retirement are treated as extraordinary items on the income statement.

Managerial Incentives and Financial Reporting for Debt

CONTRACTING

In Chapters 1 and 7 we explained that accounting numbers are widely used to enforce contracts. One example is debt covenants, which could motivate managers to manipulate accounting numbers to evade contract restrictions. Critics suggest that GAAP accounting for long-term debt makes it possible to "manage" accounting numbers to achieve this evasion.

Debt Carried at Amortized Historical Cost

Some analysts contend that reporting debt at amortized historical cost—rather than at current market value—makes it easier to manipulate accounting numbers. **Debt-for-debt swaps** and **debt-for-equity swaps** illustrate the kinds of transactions that may be driven more by the financial statement effects they elicit than by any underlying economic benefits. In a debt-for-debt swap, investors are offered the opportunity to exchange existing (old) debt for new debt issued by the company. Debt-for-equity swaps give investors the opportunity to exchange old debt for the company's common stock.

To illustrate, consider a highly simplified version of a debt-for-debt swap. Shifty Corporation has $1 million of outstanding 10% coupon debt originally issued at par. This debt will mature in exactly one year. Interest is paid annually. Since the debt was sold at par, its book value is $1 million. Assume that the current market rate for bonds of this risk class is 12%; therefore, the market price of the bonds is $982,146. Shifty induces the holders of the bonds to swap them for new bonds—also maturing in exactly one year—with a coupon rate of 12%. For simplicity, assume that the face value of the 12% bonds given to investors is exactly $982,146; this would also be the market value of the bonds, since the coupon rate of 12% equals the prevailing market rate. This debt-for-debt swap is illustrated in Figure 11.4.

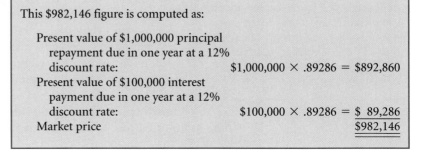

This $982,146 figure is computed as:

Present value of $1,000,000 principal repayment due in one year at a 12% discount rate:	$1,000,000 × .89286 = $892,860
Present value of $100,000 interest payment due in one year at a 12% discount rate:	$100,000 × .89286 = $ 89,286
Market price	$982,146

The holders of the bonds will be indifferent between the old bonds and the new bonds because the market values are identical. (To induce the bondholders to exchange

Figure 11.4

SHIFTY CORPORATION
Debt-for-Debt Swap

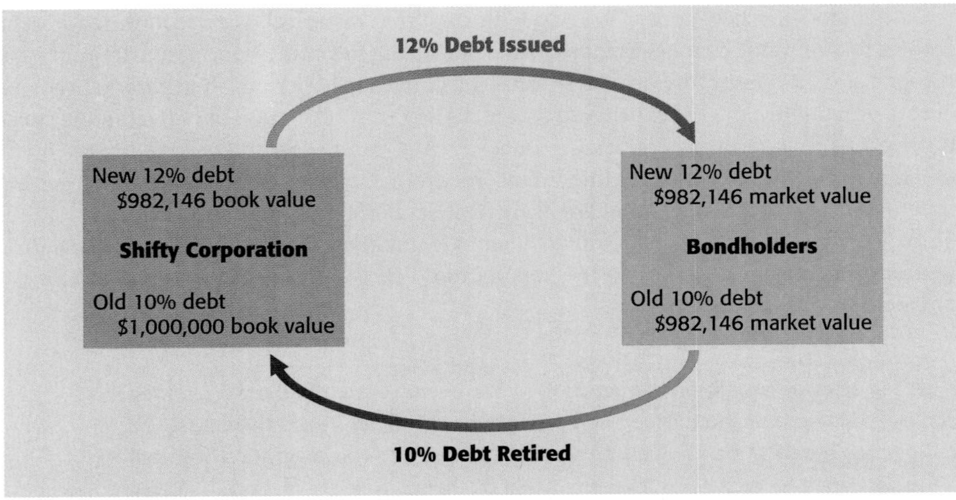

the 10% bonds for 12% bonds, some "sweetener" would have to be provided in the real world.) The market values are identical precisely because the present values of the two cash flow streams are identical when discounted at the prevailing 12% market interest rate:

Old 10% Bonds		New 12% Bonds	
Principal Repayment		**Principal Repayment**	
$1,000,000 × .89286 =	$892,860	$ 982,146 × .89286 =	$876,919*
Interest Payment		**Interest Payment**	
$ 100,000 × .89286 =	$ 89,286	$ 117,854* × .89286 =	$105,227*
$1,100,000	$982,146	$1,100,000	$982,146
Interest Computation		**Interest Computation**	
$1,000,000 × 10% =	$100,000	$ 982,146 × 12% =	$ 117,854*

Note: The present value of $1 due in one year at 12% is .89286.
*Rounded

As the computation reveals, even the *undiscounted* cash flows are identical (principal payment plus interest payment is $1,100,000). Ignoring tax effects, we find that a debt-for-debt swap like this has no real economic benefit to Shifty. However, if the swap was consummated, the entry on Shifty's books would be:

DR Bonds payable (old)	$1,000,000	
CR Bonds payable (new)		$982,146
CR Extraordinary gain on debt extinguishment		17,854

The wealth transfer gain from bondholders to stockholders gets reflected obliquely in historical cost statements, since historical cost interest expense is lower than interest expense at current market rates. Accordingly, ***net income is higher than it would have been at current interest rates.***

Despite the absence of real economic substance, an accounting "gain" would be reported. The gain really arose in prior periods as unanticipated inflation or other factors caused the market rate on the bonds to rise above the coupon rate. Because Shifty was paying interest at 10% when prevailing rates were higher, a year-by-year wealth transfer out of the pockets of the original bondholders and into the pockets of Shifty's shareholders was taking place. Historical cost accounting ignores this wealth transfer until the "artificial" swap transaction triggers recognition of the gain.

This example is designed to demonstrate the potential incentive for managerial opportunism that is introduced by historical cost accounting for debt. Critics of historical cost accounting raise the possibility that managers whose bonuses are tied to reported earnings might use swap gains to boost earnings (and bonuses) in years of poor operating performance. Also, a reduction in the book value of debt ($1,000,000 versus $982,146 in our example) would improve the debt-to-equity ratio—thus providing "opportunistic" motivations for companies in danger of violating covenant restrictions tied to this ratio.

This simple example makes it easy for us to help you visualize the problem. But we must now complicate the example so it corresponds to real-world swaps.

To induce holders of the old bonds to swap, some sweeteners must be provided because the transaction costs them time and energy. Since the market value of the old bonds is $982,146, one inducement is to offer a higher principal amount of new bonds—say, $990,000. ***This change makes the net present value of the swap negative for Shifty because it is retiring debt with a market value of $982,146 by giving bondholders something worth $990,000.*** Despite this real loss, if the swap went through on these altered terms, there would be a reported accounting *gain* of $10,000 for Shifty—the difference between the $1 million book value of the old bonds and the $990,000 market value of the new bonds. Extinguishment gains are generally taxable, and there are fees that must be paid to investment bankers or others who orchestrate the transaction. These added costs further increase the potential disparity between the reported accounting gain and the economic effects of the transaction.

On the other hand, there are sometimes real economic benefits associated with debt-for-debt exchanges. In contrast to our simple example, debt-for-debt swaps are rarely designed to be a "wash," one involving debt instruments with identical maturities and market values. Typical swaps are structured to extend debt maturity, to postpone cash outflows by altering the mix of interest and principal payments and to take advantage of operating loss carryforwards (making the swap tax free). On balance, therefore, it is entirely possible that some debt-for-debt exchanges generate real economic benefits even after factoring in the costs of doing the transaction.

This is precisely what a study of debt swaps in the airline industry found. Analyzing the economic effects of swaps structured by American Airlines, Eastern Airlines, and TWA revealed economic benefits for each company in the range of $4.6 million to $5.0 million.[4] However, ***the reported book gain (net of tax) for each airline was substantially higher***—for example, it was $24.65 million for Eastern, $47.1 million for TWA, and $48.4 million for American. Therefore, a large disparity exists between the reported historical cost book gains and the estimated real economic benefits. If the economic benefits of debt-for-debt exchanges are small (on average), stock prices should change little when swaps are announced. In fact, that is the case.[5]

Differences between book profits and real profits have aroused curiosity about the motives underlying another—somewhat similar—debt extinguishment transaction: debt-for-equity swaps.

The conditions for a debt-for-equity swap exist when a company has low coupon rate debt outstanding (say, 4½%) and market rates are much higher (say, 12%). ***The market value of that debt is much lower than its book value.*** As Figure 11.5 on the next page shows, Company X retires its low coupon debt by issuing common stock of equal market value. The difference between the book value of the debt and the market value of the stock that is issued is recorded as an accounting gain. The convoluted nature of the transaction, as well as the investment banker's involvement as an intermediary, is required to make the gain on debt extinguishment tax free.

---

[4] J. R. Dietrich and J. W. Deitrick, "Bond Exchanges in the Airline Industry: Analyzing Public Disclosures," *The Accounting Review* (January 1985), pp. 109–26.

[5] See J. R. Dietrich, "Effects of Early Bond Refundings: An Empirical Investigation of Security Returns," *Journal of Accounting and Economics* (April 1984), pp. 67-96; and W. B. Johnson, "Debt Refunding and Shareholder Wealth: The Price Effects of Debt-for-Debt Exchange Offer Announcements," *The Financial Review* (February 1988), pp. 1–23.

Figure 11.5

THE SEQUENCE OF EVENTS IN A DEBT-FOR-EQUITY SWAP

Source: From J. R. M. Hand, "Did Firms Undertake Debt-Equity Swaps for an Accounting Paper Profit or True Financial Gain?" *The Accounting Review,* October 1989 (page 587–634). Reprinted with permission.

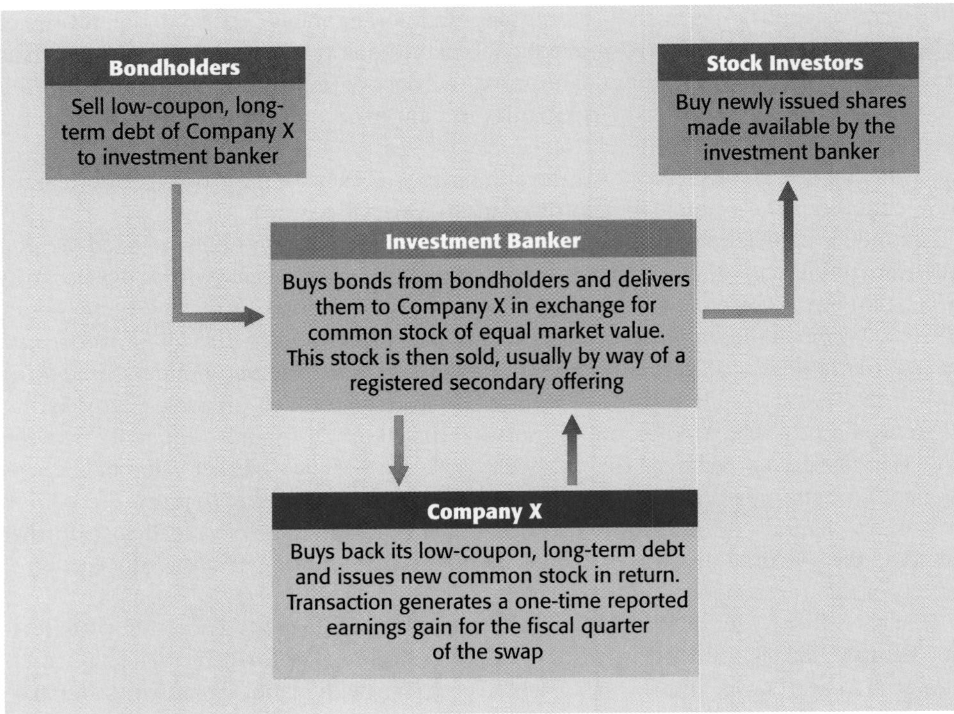

The accounting entry on the books of Company X is:

DR Bonds payable	$ Book value	
CR Common stock		$ Market value
CR Extraordinary gain on debt extinguishment		Difference

Debt book value is greater than the market value of stock issued because the debt has a low coupon rate but the market interest rate is high.

Debt-for-equity swaps alter the company's capital structure and undoubtedly precipitate real economic effects. One study found that debt-for-equity swaps were associated with a 9.9% share price decline (on average) at the transaction's announcement.[6] That price decline is especially interesting since most debt-for-equity transactions result in extinguishment gains rather than losses. This prevalence of gains (and negative market reaction) raises the suspicion that earnings enhancement—rather than capital structure alteration—may be the motivation behind these transactions. Companies can use debt-for-equity swaps to smooth otherwise unexpected and transitory decreases in quarterly earnings per share or to relax otherwise binding covenant constraints.[7]

Debt-for-debt swaps, debt-for-equity swaps, and other similar transactions may serve valid economic purposes in certain instances. Nevertheless, the belief persists that the dominant motivation for these transactions is to increase reported income. This income effect results from the difference between the book value and market value of the liabilities.

[6] See R. Masulis, "The Impact of Capital Structure Changes on Firm Value: Some Estimates," *Journal of Finance* (March 1983), pp. 107–26. Interestingly, this same study found that share prices *increase* by 14% (on average) when firms announce their willingness to retire common stock in exchange for new debt.

[7] J. R. M. Hand, "Did Firms Undertake Debt–Equity Swaps for an Accounting Paper Profit or True Financial Gain?" *The Accounting Review* (October 1989), pp. 587–623.

In response to this and other criticisms of accounting for liabilities, the FASB issued *SFAS No. 107,* which requires footnote disclosure of the market value of all financial instruments—both financial liabilities and assets.[8] However, the FASB response is unlikely to eliminate "accounting-driven" liability transactions. Since the *SFAS No. 107* market value disclosures appear in a footnote to the financial statements, the carrying amount of liabilities on the balance sheet itself is not altered. Consequently, the swap transactions described in this section still generate income statement gains and favorable financial ratio effects. Managers can still use these transactions as mechanisms for altering bonus payouts, as well as for evading loan covenant restrictions or other contracting effects whenever the contracts are tied to the financial numbers reported in the body of the statement. Only if the contract ratios and income measures are computed using the fair value footnote data would *SFAS No. 107* be effective in reducing this avenue for managerial opportunism.

GAAP for long-term debt creates opportunities for managing reported earnings and balance sheet numbers using debt-for-debt or debt-for-equity swaps. So statement readers must be alert to the possibility that reported swap gains (and losses) are just window dressing. How can you tell? Look behind the accounting numbers and see if there are real economic benefits from the swap.

RECAP

Extracting Analytical Insights: Future Cash Flow Effects of Debt

Exhibit 11.2 on the next page contains excerpts from Maytag Corporation's financial statement footnote for long-term debt. This example illustrates the type of information about a company's long-term debt that is currently available in corporate annual reports.

Maytag provides details about interest rates and maturity dates for each major class of debt. However, the company provides no information about the covenants contained in its various borrowing agreements. This nondisclosure is typical and imposes a burden on the financial analyst who must search through the lending agreements themselves to discover covenant details.

Maytag's footnote disclosure provides a wealth of information useful for determining the future cash flow implications of the company's long-term debt. For example, the table reveals current maturities of \$170.473 million at the end of 1999 (see highlighted figures next to ①). This is the principal amount that Maytag must repay in 2000.

We also learn from the footnote text next to ② that Maytag paid \$63.1 million in interest during 1999. Dividing this interest payment by the average book value of outstanding long-term debt [(\$508.237 + \$586.681)/2] suggests that the company's "cash" interest rate for 1999 was about 11.5%. Using this rate as the basis for forecasting 2000 interest payments, we discover that Maytag will have to spend about \$58.4 million (11.5% multiplied by \$508.237 million debt outstanding) for 2000 interest. This cash outflow is in addition to the \$107.473 million of scheduled principal repayment for 2000.

Cash flow forecasts of this sort can be constructed for each year from 2000 through 2004, because Maytag, like all U.S. companies today, is required to disclose scheduled debt repayments for each of the five years after the balance sheet date. From the paragraph adjacent to ③, we can see that these repayments are particularly large in 2000 (\$107.473 million) and 2002 (\$133.542 million). Analysts studying the company will want to estimate whether Maytag's operating cash flows for 2000 and 2002 will be sufficient to meet its scheduled debt interest and principal payments. Any anticipated shortfalls will necessitate asset sales or additional financing.

[8] "Disclosures About Fair Value of Financial Instruments," *SFAS No. 107* (Norwalk, CT: FASB, 1991).

Exhibit 11.2 ■ MAYTAG CORPORATION

Long-Term Debt

Long-term debt consisted of the following:

($ in thousands)		December 31 1999	1998
Notes payable with interest payable semiannually:			
Due May 15, 2002 at 9.75%		$125,358	$125,358
Due July 15, 1999 at 8.875%			116,820
Medium-term notes, maturing from 2000 to 2010, from 5.30% to 9.03% with interest payable semiannually		149,230	125,230
Medium-term notes, maturing from 2000 to 2001, with interest adjusted each quarter based on LIBOR and payable quarterly		185,000	160,000
Employee stock ownership plan notes payable semiannually through July 2, 2004 at 5.13%		35,300	42,360
Other		13,349	16,913
		508,237	586,681
Less current portion of long-term debt	①	170,473	140,176
Long-term debt		$337,764	$446,505

The $125.4 million of notes payable and $84.2 million of the medium-term notes grant the holders the right to require the Company to repurchase all or any portion of their notes at 100 percent of the principal amount thereof, together with accrued interest, following the occurrence of both a change of Company control and a credit rating decline to below investment grade.

② Interest paid during 1999, 1998 and 1997 was $63.1 million, $64 million and $65.1 million, respectively. When applicable, the Company capitalizes interest incurred on funds used to construct property, plant and equipment. Interest capitalized during 1997 was $4.2 million. Interest capitalized during 1999 and 1998 was not significant.

③ The aggregate maturities of long-term debt in each of the next five years and thereafter are as follows (in thousands): 2000–$170,473; 2001–$64,534; 2002–$133,542; 2003–$43,276; 2004–$25,327; thereafter–$71,085.

In 1999, the Company issued a $24 million medium-term note with a fixed interest rate of 6 percent due January 26, 2009 . . . The Company also issued a $40 million medium-term note with a floating interest rate based on LIBOR with the interest rate reset quarterly due September 17, 2001. As of December 31, 1999, the floating interest rates based on LIBOR for the $185 million medium-term notes ranged from 6.20 percent to 6.81 percent . . .

In 1998, the Company made early retirements of debt totalling $71.1 million at an after-tax cost of $5.9 million (net of income tax benefit of $3.5 million). Included in this amount was $22.1 million of the 9.75 percent notes due May 15, 2002, $31.7 million of the 8.875 percent notes due July 15, 1999 and $17.3 million of medium-term notes . . . The 1998 . . . charge for the early retirement of debt have been reflected in the Consolidated Statements of Income as extraordinary items.

Source: Maytag Corporation 1999 annual report

In another footnote, Maytag tells us about the fair market value of its long-term debt.

Exhibit 11.2 ■ MAYTAG CORPORATION (*continued*)

The fair values of long-term debt were estimated based on quoted market prices, if available, or quoted market prices of comparable instruments . . . The carrying amounts and fair values of the Company's financial instruments, consisted of the following:

	December 31, 1999		December 31, 1998	
	Carrying Amount	Fair Value	Carrying Amount	Fair Value
Long-term debt	$508,237	$516,942	$586,681	$620,230

The fair market value of Maytag's debt is greater than its balance sheet carrying amount in both years. There are two reasons why this might happen. One reason may be that Maytag is a better credit risk today than it was several years ago when the debt was first issued. As a company's creditworthiness improves, the market value of its debt increases even though the book value of the debt is unchanged. A second reason may be that interest rates have fallen for reasons unrelated to the company itself (e.g., lower inflation or a stronger economy). From our earlier discussion, you know that a decline in interest rates—whether due to company-specific factors or to macroeconomic forces—will cause the market value of fixed-rate debt to increase.

Maytag has been a financially strong company for many years. So, a falling interest rate is the most plausible explanation for why Maytag's debt has a fair market value greater than its carrying amount.

Incentives for Off-Balance Sheet Liabilities

In Chapters 1 and 7 we described modern business contracts linked to (among other things) the amount of liabilities on a company's balance sheet. Examples include loan covenants and bond indentures. These kinds of contracts usually contain terms and conditions designed to protect the lender against loss. The protection is in the form of contract terms tied to the borrower's debt-to-equity ratio, or debt-to-tangible-asset ratio or to some other financial ratio that includes reported liabilities. Accounting-related covenants typically contain language like "if the debt-to-equity ratio exceeds 1.7 in any quarter, the loan must immediately be repaid." The intent of these covenants is to provide an early warning signal regarding deteriorating creditworthiness. In principle, the early warning allows the lender to require repayment of the loan before the borrower's condition deteriorates further.

CONTRACTING ANALYSIS

These kinds of terms in loan contracts create incentives for managers of borrowing companies to minimize *reported* financial statement liabilities. Reducing the total amount of reportable liabilities in the contractual ratio makes covenant violations less likely.

Consider one example of the way these incentives influence business behavior: **Unconsolidated subsidiaries** are sometimes established to finance specialized projects or **joint ventures.** Critics say these separately incorporated entities have been used to evade loan covenants linked to reported liabilities and to misrepresent the firm's total liabilities. This strategy exploits a loophole in the rules governing when subsidiaries need to be consolidated.

> As will be explained in Chapter 16, **consolidation** essentially means that the financial statements of the parent and subsidiary are added together line-by-line. For example, the consolidated statements would report as cash the sum of the parent's cash plus the subsidiary's cash. Similarly, total consolidated liabilities would consist of the sum of the parent's liabilities plus those of the subsidiary.

When one company owns *more* than 50% of the stock of another company, the owner (parent) is deemed to "control" the subsidiary. The financial statements of subsidiaries that are under the control of a parent must be consolidated. But when one company owns 50% or *less* of another company's stock, consolidation is not required (except under special circumstances described in Chapter 16). Instead, the owner's *net investment* in the affiliated company is reported as an asset in the owner's balance sheet using what is called the **equity method** of accounting.

The equity method is described in Chapter 16. Here's all we need to know about it now. Assume Blue Company and Yellow Company both use an identically manufactured input called T-spanners in their respective production processes. Manufacturing T-spanners requires a large investment in plant and equipment that must be financed by borrowing. Both Blue Company and Yellow Company wish to avoid adding further debt to their balance sheets, so they agree to form a separate jointly owned venture called Green Company.

Each venture partner contributes $25 million cash to establish Green Company and receives common stock representing a 50% ownership interest in it. A bank then loans Green $300 million to purchase the plant and equipment needed to produce T-spanners. This loan is collateralized by Green's factory, and guaranteed by both Blue Company and Yellow Company. Immediately after these transactions take place, the balance sheet of Green Company would appear as shown in Figure 11.6.

In real-world joint ventures, the debt is often guaranteed by the parent companies, since the joint venture (e.g., Green Company) is usually thinly capitalized and lenders accordingly look to the parents for added assurance that the loan will be repaid.

The balance sheets of Blue Company and Yellow Company would each show their $25 million investment in an asset account called "Investment in joint venture." Under the equity method, this account balance would grow if further investments were made in the joint venture or if Green earned a profit. Since Green is equally owned by Blue and Yellow, each would add 50% of Green's profit to the balance in its "Investment in joint venture" account.

The partners' balance sheets do not report any of the joint venture's $300 million bank loan! Neither Blue nor Yellow owns more than 50% of Green, so neither needs to consolidate it. Consequently, the borrowing necessary to fund the venture appears on neither partner's financial statements under the equity method. The "Investment in joint ven-

The "Investment in joint venture" account is unchanged because each partner's investment in the net assets (i.e., assets minus liabilities) of the joint venture is unchanged by the borrowing. Green Company's assets increased by $300 million but so did liabilities. Consequently, Green's *net* assets remained at $50 million after the borrowing.

Prior to the issuance of "Consolidation of All Majority-Owned Subsidiaries," *SFAS No. 94* (Stamford, CT: FASB, 1987), even 100% wholly owned subsidiaries were accounted for in many cases under the equity method. This kept the subsidiaries' debt off the balance sheet in much the same manner as joint-venture debt. Here's how: In many industries, companies help customers finance the purchase of their products. One example is the automobile industry. If no financing subsidiary were formed, the cash necessary to finance the credit extended to dealers and customers would come from bank loans or other borrowing by the parent. As a consequence, the parent's debt-to-equity ratio would be worsened. However, if a separate finance subsidiary were formed and this subsidiary borrowed the funds directly in its own name, the borrowing was effectively kept off the parent's balance sheet. The trick here was accomplished by using the equity method of accounting for subsidiaries, as discussed in Chapter 16. This is no longer permitted.

Figure 11.6

JOINT VENTURE FINANCING
($ in millions)

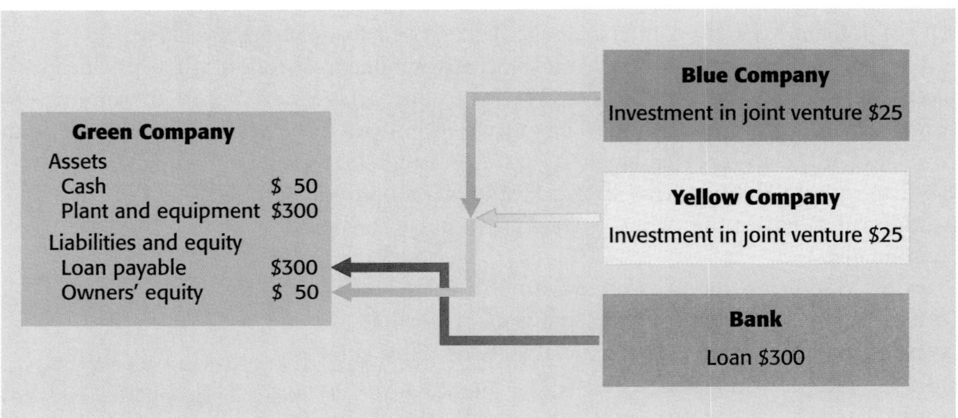

ture" account on each company's books would continue to show $25 million. Blue and Yellow have effectively each borrowed $150 million "off balance sheet."

The motivation for off-balance sheet financing transactions is strong. Managers continue to develop innovative strategies to understate reported liabilities and to ensure that certain items remain "off the balance sheet." Financial analysts and auditors must remember the motivations behind off-balance sheet financing, know how to identify peculiar and contorted borrowing arrangements, and adjust the reported financial statement numbers to better reflect economic reality.

RECAP

Hedging[9]

Businesses are exposed to **market risks** from many sources—changes in interest rates, foreign currency exchange rates, and commodity prices. Suppose a bank makes numerous five-year term loans at an annual interest rate of 8%. The earnings from those loans generate the cash needed to pay interest to "money-market" account depositors. The bank is exposed to interest rate risk: If money-market interest rates rise, the 8% fixed return from the loans may not be adequate to pay the new higher rates promised to depositors.

Similar risks confront manufacturers. Consider Ridge Development, a real estate development company that simultaneously constructs many single-family homes. Buyers make a down payment and agree to a fixed contract price to be paid upon completion of the home. The typical home is completed in four months or less, and lumber comprises the bulk of construction costs. Since lumber prices are volatile, the developer is at risk that profits could erode (or disappear) if lumber prices were to soar during the four-month construction cycle.

Managing market risk is essential to the overall business strategies of most companies today. This trend has been driven by the need to reduce cash flow volatility that arises from factors beyond management's control—the exchange rate of U.S. dollars to Japanese yen, the LIBOR interest rate (the benchmark interbank interest rate for European banks), or the price of natural gas to run a factory. In response to these and other market risks, many companies engage in **hedging**—business transactions designed to insulate them from commodity price, interest rate, or exchange rate risk. **Derivative securities** are often used to accomplish this insulation.

> Businesses are also exposed to **operating risks** from severe weather conditions, industrial accidents, raw material shortages, labor strikes, and so on. Insurance contracts, financial guarantees, and other business arrangements are used to hedge operating risks—but these risks do not qualify for the special hedge accounting rules described later in this section. Only certain financial risks qualify for hedge accounting.

Typical Derivative Securities and the Benefits of Hedging

Derivative securities get their name from the fact that they have no inherent value but instead represent a claim against some other asset—their value is *derived* from the value of the asset underlying that claim.[10]

A **forward contract** is an example of a derivative security. In a forward contract, two parties agree to the sale of some asset or commodity on some *future* date—called the settlement date—at a price specified today. You have been dealing with forward contracts your whole life, perhaps without knowing it. Suppose you walk into a bookstore on October 5 to buy the bestseller *Seven Unbeatable Strategies for e-Commerce.* The book is sold out, but the

[9] We gratefully acknowledge the substantial contribution of Professor Thomas Linsmeier to the material in this section.

[10] For an overview of the characteristics and uses of derivative securities, see S. A. Ross, R. W. Westerfield, and B. D. Jordan, *Fundamentals of Corporate Finance,* 2nd ed. (Homewood, IL: Irwin, 1993), Ch. 24; and C. W. Smithson, C. W. Smith, and D. S. Wilford, *Managing Financial Risk* (Homewood, IL: Irwin, 1995).

clerk will reorder it for you and call you when it arrives. The clerk says that the book should arrive in about 15 days and will cost $39.95. If you agree on October 5 to pick up and pay for the book when called, you and the clerk have agreed to a forward contract. Three elements of this contract are key: the agreed upon price ($39.95) to be paid in the future; the delivery date ("in about 15 days"); and that you will "take delivery" by paying for the book and picking it up when notified. The clerk has "sold" you a forward contract for the bestseller.

What happens if you pay for the book on October 5? Then it's a simple cash sales transaction (with a promised future delivery date) but there is no forward contract involved. As long as both parties are *obligated* to perform under the agreement, it's a forward contract. Here that means the clerk is required to obtain a copy of the bestseller and deliver it to you within the specified time. And you are required to pay the agreed upon price and to take delivery.

Futures Contracts A variation of a forward contract takes place on financial exchanges like the New York Mercantile Exchange (COMEX) where **futures contracts** are traded daily in a market with many buyers and sellers. Futures contracts exist for commodities like corn, wheat, live hogs and cattle, cotton, copper, crude oil, lumber, and even electricity. Here is how they work.

Suppose on October 5 you "write" (meaning sell) a futures contract for 10 million pounds of February copper at 95 cents per pound—we'll show why you might want to do so in just a moment. By selling the contract, you are obligated to deliver the copper at the agreed-upon price in February. The buyer (or contract counterparty) is obliged to pay the fixed price per pound and take delivery of the copper. So far this looks like a forward contract because both parties have an obligation to perform in the future (February).

But there's more! Futures contracts do not have a predetermined settlement date—you (the seller) can choose to deliver the copper on any day during the delivery month (February). This gives sellers additional flexibility in settling the contract. When you decide to deliver the copper, you notify the COMEX clearinghouse, which then notifies an individual—let's call her Anne Smythe—who bought February copper contracts. (The clearinghouse selected Anne at random from all individuals who bought February copper contracts.) Anne is then told to be ready to accept delivery within the next several days. But what if she bought the contract as a speculative investment, has no real use for the copper and doesn't want delivery? Futures contracts have an added advantage over forward contracts because futures are actively traded on an exchange. This means Symthe can avoid delivery by selling a February copper contract for 10 million pounds thus creating a zero net position. The first contract obligates Smythe to accept delivery of 10 million pounds of copper, but the second contract obligates her to turn over 10 million pounds to someone else. One contract cancels the other, and Smythe avoids the embarrassment of having all of that copper dumped on the floor of her garage.

How can you (the seller) avoid having to deliver the copper? Form a zero net position of your own by purchasing a February copper contract from someone else—perhaps even from Anne Smythe.

Now that you understand how futures contracts work, let's see how they can be used to hedge financial risk. Consider the opportunities confronting Rombauer Metals, a copper mining company. On October 1, 2001, Rombauer has 10 million pounds of copper inventory on hand at an average cost of 65 cents per pound. The "spot" (current delivery) price for copper on October 1 is 90 cents a pound. Rombauer could receive $9 million (10 million pounds times $0.90 per pound) by selling the entire copper inventory today. Selling the copper on October 1 would yield a $2.5 million gross profit ($0.90 selling price minus $0.65 average cost per pound, multiplied by 10 million pounds). However, Rombauer has decided to hold on to its copper until February 2002 when management believes the price will return to a normal level of 95 cents a pound. The commodities market seems to agree since February copper futures are priced as though copper will sell for 95 cents in February. The decision not to sell copper in October exposes Rombauer to **commodity price risk** from a possible future decline in copper prices.

Figure 11.7(a) illustrates the company's commodity price risk exposure. If copper prices increase to 95 cents by February as expected, Rombauer will receive $9.5 million for its copper and earn a gross profit of $3 million ($0.95 selling price minus $0.65 average cost per pound, multiplied by 10 million pounds). That's $0.5 million more gross profit than Rombauer would earn by selling the copper on October 1. But what if the February price of copper falls to 85 cents? The cash received from selling copper would then be only

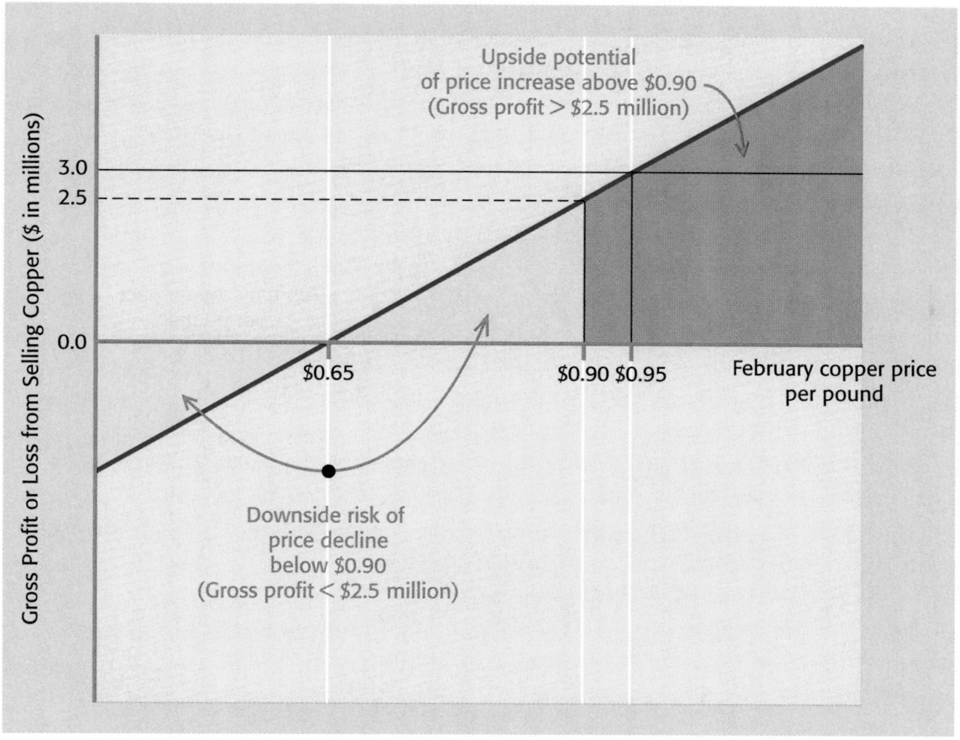

Figure 11.7 (a)

ROMBAUER METALS

Using Futures Contracts to Hedge Copper Inventory

Potential gross profit and loss from the sale of copper in February

$8.5 million, and the gross profit would be only $2 million. Each 10-cent decline in the February copper price lowers the company's cash flows and expected gross profits by $1 million. At 65 cents per pound, Rombauer just breaks even (zero gross profit) and, at any price below 65 cents, the company has a loss. These potential cash flow and gross profit declines represent the *downside risk* associated with the February price of copper. There is *upside potential* as well. Each 10-cent increase in the February copper price will produce a $1 million increase in the company's cash flows and gross profits.

One way Rombauer can protect itself from a decline in the price of copper is to hedge its position with futures contracts. Suppose Rombauer sells 400 copper contracts—each contract is for 25,000 pounds—at 95 cents a pound for February delivery. The delivery month is chosen to coincide with the company's expected physical sale of the copper. The ultimate value of these contracts depends on the February price of copper as shown in Figure 11.7(b) on the next page. For example, if the February copper price is 85 cents, the contracts will have provided $1 million of cash flow and profit protection ($0.95 contract price minus $0.85 February spot market price, multiplied by the 10 million pounds of copper). If the February spot price is 65 cents, the contracts will have provided $3 million of protection.

The futures contracts "lock in" a February price of 95 cents and eliminate the company's downside exposure to a decline in copper prices. February cash receipts will be $9.5 million, and profits will total $3.0 million, no matter what the February spot price for copper turns out to be. Of course, there is another side to the story. By hedging its original exposure to commodity price risk with futures contracts, Rombauer has given up the cash flow and gross profit increases that could result if the February spot price is above $0.95. Figure 11.7(c) on the next page shows how the company's hedging strategy eliminates downside risk (and upside potential) and results in predictable cash flows and gross profits.

Indeed, the futures contracts provide an immediate 5 cent benefit (ignoring present value considerations, inventory holding costs, and fees and commissions on the contracts) since the October 1 price of copper is only 90 cents.

Swap Contract Another common derivative security is a **swap contract.** These contracts are a popular way to hedge interest rate or foreign currency exchange rate risk. Let's say Kistler Manufacturing has issued $100 million of long-term 8% fixed-rate debt and

Figure 11.7 (b)

ROMBAURER METALS
Using Futures Contracts to Hedge Copper Inventory

Potential value of forward contract for February copper

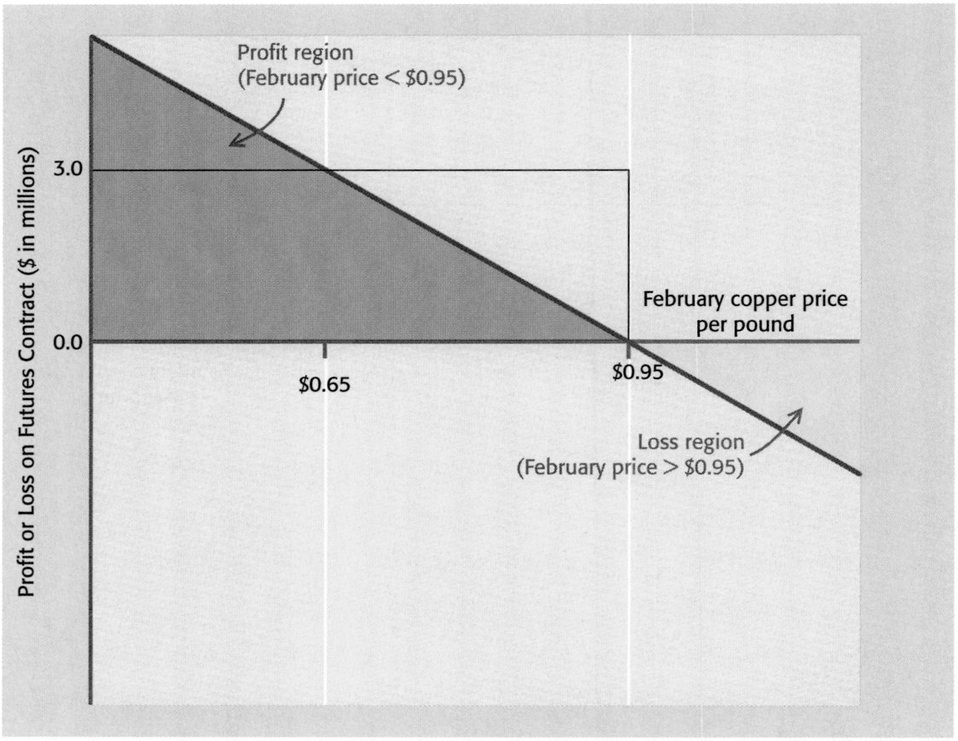

Figure 11.7 (c)

ROMBAURER METALS
Using Futures Contracts to Hedge Copper Inventory

Gross profit from hedged position: Combination of unhedged copper inventory and forward contract

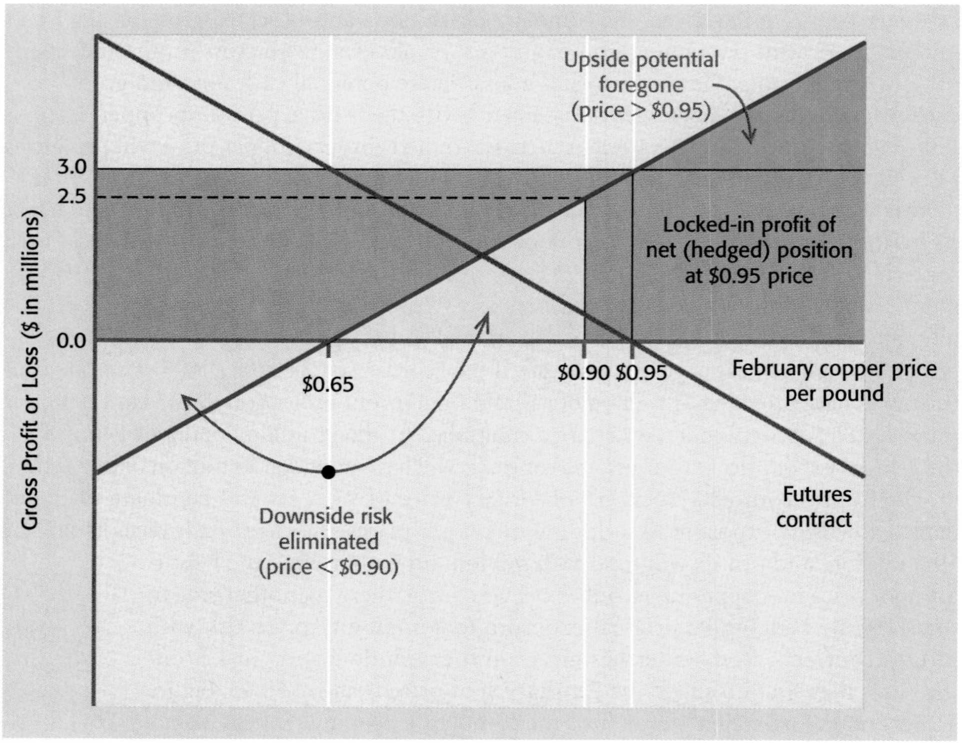

wants to protect itself against a *decline* in market interest rates. There are several ways the company could reduce its exposure. We already discussed one earlier in this chapter, using a debt-for-debt exchange offer to replace the fixed-rate debt with a floating-rate loan. A second—and perhaps less costly—way is to create *synthetic* floating-rate debt using an interest rate swap.

One reason protection might be needed is that Kistler's operating cash flows are positively correlated with interest rates. In this case a decline in market rates would be accompanied by a decrease in operating cash flows, and the company may lack the cash flow needed to meet its payment obligations under the 8% fixed-rate loan.

This form of hedging is accomplished with a "swap dealer." Swap dealers are typically banks who locate someone—a counterparty—who would like to make fixed-rate interest *payments* in exchange for floating-rate interest *receipts*. The swap transaction in Figure 11.8 includes a counterparty with outstanding floating-rate debt where interest payments are linked to the one-year U.S. Treasury bill rate. This is exactly the kind of interest payment Kistler seeks. Kistler and the counterparty agree to swap interest payments on $100 million of debt for the next three years, with settlement every year. At the settlement date the counterparty gives Kistler the fixed-rate payment of $8 million, which is then passed on to Kistler's lender. At the same time Kistler gives the counterparty cash equal to the floating-rate payment (say $7 million based on a Treasury rate of 7%), and this too is passed on to the floating-rate lender. In reality only the $1 million difference in interest payments would be exchanged between the two parties to the swap.

What's in it for the counterparty? By replacing floating-rate interest payments with synthetic fixed-rate payments, the counterparty has reduced its exposure to cash flow volatility from interest rate changes.

The swap transforms Kistler's debt into floating rate, because receipts from the counterparty offset the fixed payment it is obligated to make. Figure 11.9 shows how the swap transaction eliminates Kistler's downside exposure to interest rate risk. If the Treasury rate falls to 7%, Kistler will receive a net cash inflow of $1 million from the swap counterparty. This net cash inflow is the $8 million fixed-rate payment minus the $7 million floating-rate payment. Kistler then pays its lender $8 million as required, with $1 million of the payment coming from the swap counterparty. Kistler's out-of-pocket interest cost is just $7 million, the amount it would have been required to pay if it had issued floating-rate debt in the first place.[11]

Kistler ends up with floating-rate debt that it could perhaps not otherwise obtain at attractive rates. The counterparty ends up with fixed interest payments, and the bank gets a fee for arranging the swap transaction. Everybody wins—as long as all parties fulfill their payment obligations.

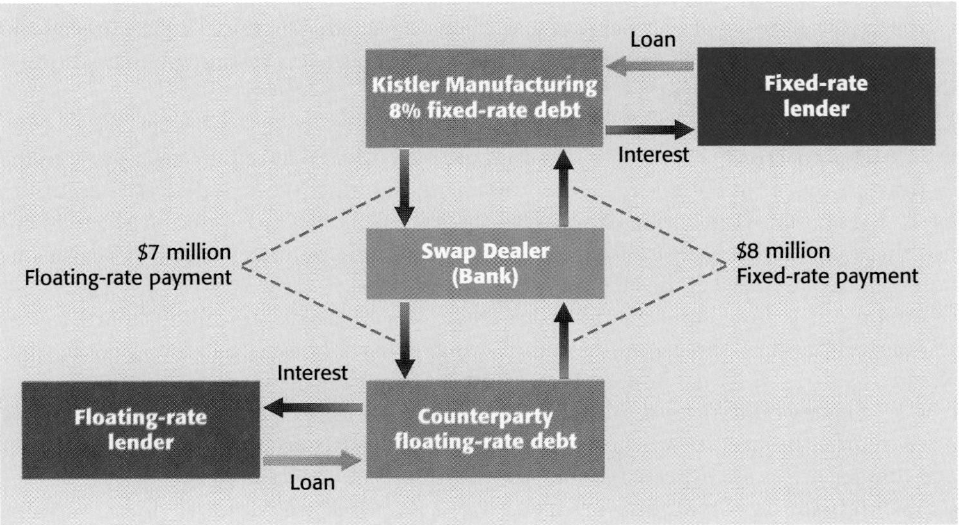

Figure 11.8

KISTLER MANUFACTURING
An Interest Rate Swap that Creates Synthetic Floating-Rate Debt

[11] An **interest rate "collar"** may be part of the swap agreement as well—for example, the two parties could agree that the swap remains in force as long as the Treasury rate is less than 8.5% and greater than 6%.

Figure 11.9

KISTLER MANUFACTURING
Using a Swap to Hedge Interest Rate Risk

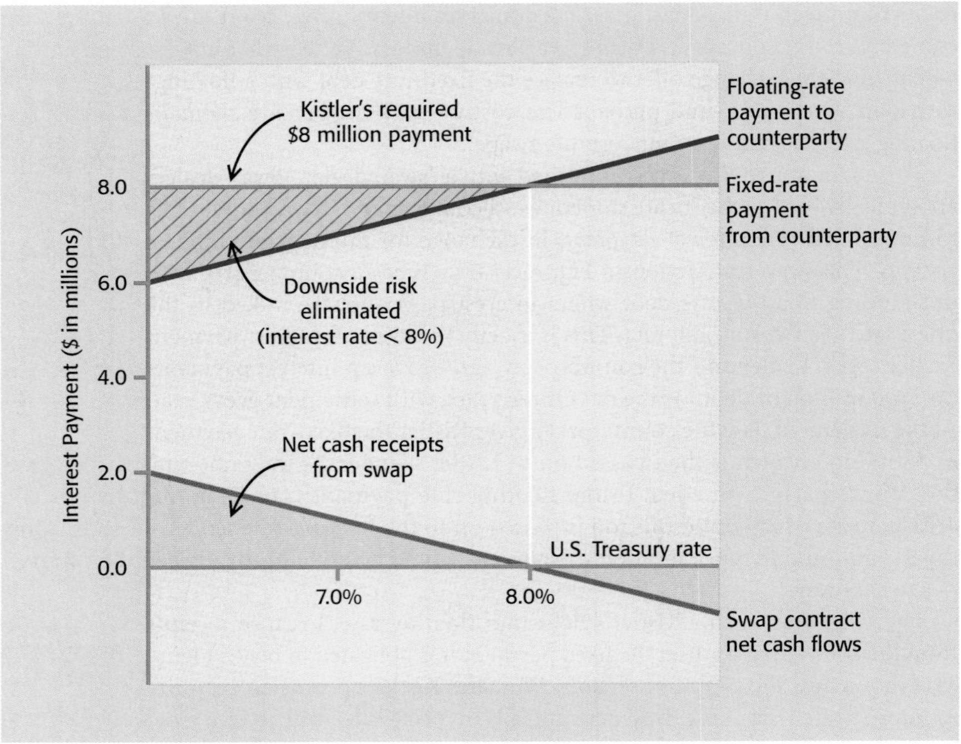

A foreign exchange (currency) swap has the same structural features as those outlined in Figures 11.8 and 11.9 except that the loans are denominated in different currencies. Suppose St. Jean Inc. manufactures products in France but sells exclusively in the United States. The company borrows francs to finance construction of a manufacturing plant in France, and it wants to hedge its foreign exchange exposure on the loan. The company's exposure arises because its operating cash flows are in U.S. dollars but its loan payments are in francs. With the aid of a swap dealer, the company can identify a counterparty willing to exchange franc-denominated payments for dollar-denominated payments. The pattern of swapped cash flows would be identical to the flows depicted in Figure 11.8. St. Jean ends up with synthetic U.S. dollar-denominated debt and eliminates its exposure to fluctuations in the franc-dollar exchange rate.

Options Contract Futures and swaps are derivatives that require each party to the contract to engage in the agreed-upon transaction. But other types of derivative securities exist. One example is an option contract, which gives the holder an "option"—the right but not the obligation—to do something. To illustrate how options work, let's revisit our homebuilder discussed at the beginning of this section.

Suppose it is now January and Ridge Development needs 10 million board feet of lumber on hand in three months (April) to construct homes that the company has already sold to residential homebuyers. Lumber currently sells for $250 per 1,000 board feet, so Ridge would have to purchase $2.5 million of lumber at the current (January) price in order to meet its April commitment. But Ridge has no place to store the lumber and lumber prices are expected to increase over the next few months. How can the company eliminate its commodity price risk from its *anticipated* lumber purchase three months from now?

One approach is to buy a futures contract for April lumber. Ridge can "lock in" the profit margin on unbuilt homes it has sold by agreeing to pay a set price now (in January) for lumber delivered in April. But if lumber prices fall during the next three months, the builder—now locked into higher lumber prices by the futures contract—would forego the increased profits from lower lumber prices.

By using options instead of futures, the builder can protect against lumber cost increases without sacrificing potential gains if lumber prices decline. This can be done by purchasing a call option on lumber—an option to buy lumber at a specified price over the option period. The call option protects the builder against lumber cost increases. But because it is an option, Ridge is not obligated to exercise the option should lumber prices fall. Options enable Ridge to hedge unfavorable price movements and still participate in the upside possibility of increased margins if lumber prices fall. Figure 11.10 shows how.

Some option contracts give the holder the right to *buy* a specific underlying asset at a specified price during a specified time. These are termed **call options.** Other option contracts give the holder the option to *sell* an asset at a specified price during a specified time period. These are called **put options.**

Without hedging its anticipated lumber purchase, Ridge is exposed to commodity price risk if lumber prices rise above the current $250 level over the next three months. To eliminate this exposure, Ridge buys a call option for 10 million board feet of April lumber at $250 per 1,000 board feet. If the April price of lumber is more than $250 per 1,000 board feet, Ridge will exercise the option and pay just the $250 contract price. But if the April price is, say, $200, Ridge will let the option expire and instead buy lumber in the open market—saving $500,000 in lumber costs ($50 per 1,000 board feet). The net result of the option hedge is a "hockey stick" shape (see Figure 11.10)— the *downside risk* of a lumber price increase is eliminated but the *upside potential* of a lumber price decrease is retained.

When options are used in this way, they do not necessarily "lock in" a specified profit margin or price. Instead, they provide a hedge that resembles insurance. Options allow companies to hedge against downside risk—value losses—while retaining the opportunity to benefit from favorable price movements.

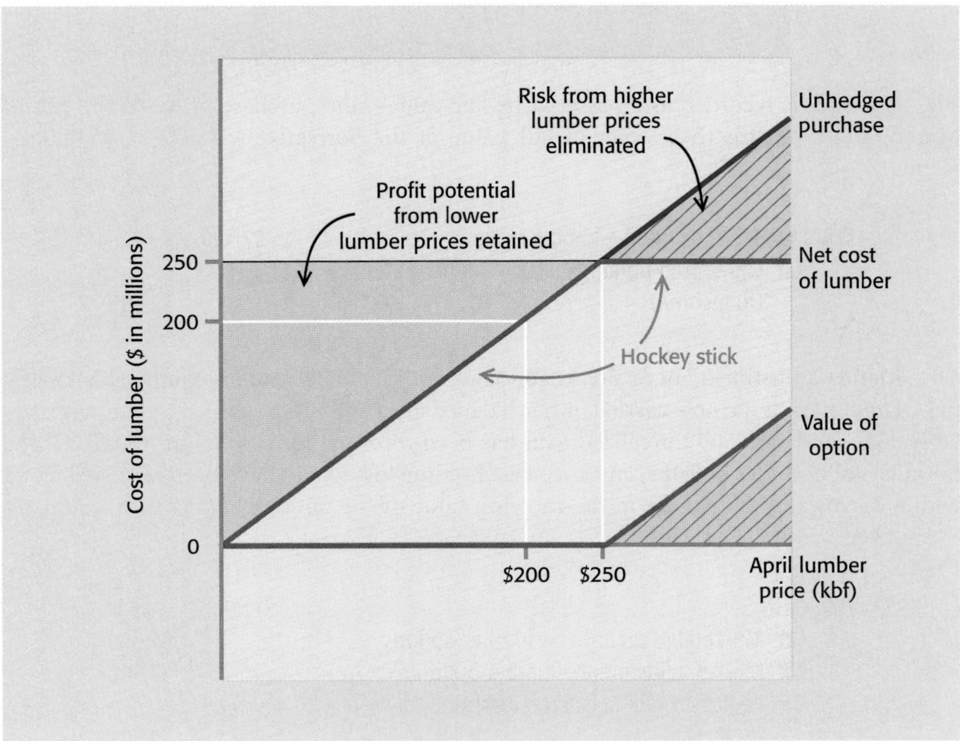

Figure 11.10

RIDGE DEVELOPMENT COMPANY

Using an Option to Hedge Commodity Price Risk

Financial Reporting for Derivative Securities

Before we turn our attention to hedge accounting, let's consider first how GAAP treats stand alone derivative securities in the absence of a hedging transaction. Here's a quick synopsis:

- All derivatives must be carried on the balance sheet at fair value—no exceptions.
- Generally, changes in the fair value of derivatives must be recognized in income when they occur. The only exception is for derivatives that qualify as hedges (explained below) according to GAAP.

Here's an example that illustrates the basic accounting treatment for derivatives that do not qualify for special "hedge accounting" rules:

> On March 1, 2001 Heitz Metals buys call options (i.e., options to purchase) for 10 million board feet of June lumber. Each call option gives Heitz the opportunity to purchase 1,000 board feet of lumber, so the firm bought a total of 10,000 option contracts (10 million board feet/1,000 per contract). Heitz has no use for the lumber nor is the company hedging a financial risk. ***Instead, Heitz is just speculating that lumber prices will increase during the next several months.*** The settlement price is $240 per 1,000 board feet, the current spot price is $240, and Heitz pays $5,000 for the contracts.
>
> Over the next 30 days, a series of winter storms dump several feet of snow in the mountains of the Pacific Northwest. This late snowfall delays the timber-harvesting season and creates a lumber shortage. By March 31, the spot price for lumber is $245 and June contracts are trading for $7,500 at the commodities exchange. Lumber prices have increased to $245 but Heitz owns an option to buy lumber at $240, so the value of the option has increased along with lumber prices. On April 15, Heitz decides to liquidate its position. The June lumber contracts are sold for $12,000 when the spot price for lumber is $252.

The accounting entry to record Heitz Metals' *speculative* purchase—remember, Heitz has no real use for the lumber—of June lumber contracts is:

DR Marketable securities—lumber options	$5,000	
CR Cash		$5,000

The derivative is recorded as an asset at its fair value—the purchase price. At the end of March, Heitz records the *change* in fair value of the derivative ($7,500 − $5,000, or $2,500):

DR Market adjustment—lumber options	$2,500	
CR Unrealized holding gain on lumber options (to income)		$2,500

The unrealized gain (or loss) would be included in "Income from continuing operations" on the Heitz income statement.

The "Market adjustment" of $2,500 is added to the $5,000 balance in "Marketable securities." The contracts are now carried on the balance sheet at $7,500—which is their fair market value—and a $2,500 unrealized gain has been recorded in income for March. (If the options had declined in value, an unrealized holding loss would have been recorded along with a downward adjustment in the carrying value of the options.) Heitz then liquidates the options contracts on April 15:

DR Cash	$12,000	
CR Marketable securities—lumber options		$5,000
CR Market adjustment—lumber options		$2,500
CR Realized holding gain on lumber options (to income)		4,500

A final entry reclassifies the unrealized holding gain:

DR Unrealized holding gain on lumber options	$2,500	
CR Realized holding gain on lumber options		$2,500

These accounting entries are used for all types of derivatives—forwards, futures, swaps and options—unless the special "hedge accounting" rules described next apply. Three key points should be remembered:

1. Derivative contracts represent balance sheet assets and liabilities.
2. The carrying value of the derivative is adjusted to fair value at each balance sheet date.
3. The amount of the adjustment—the change in fair value—flows to the income statement as a holding gain (or loss).

As a result, speculative investments in derivative contracts can increase the volatility of reported earnings. But the earnings volatility that results from this accounting treatment perfectly reflects the derivative's inherent economic risk.

Hedge Accounting

When a company successfully hedges its exposure to market risk, any economic loss on the hedged item (e.g., copper inventory) will be offset by an economic gain on the derivative security (e.g., copper futures contracts). ***To accurately reflect the underlying economics of the hedge, the company should match the loss on the hedged item with the derivative's offsetting gain in the income statement of the same period.*** This matching is what the rules governing hedge accounting try to accomplish.[12] These special hedge accounting rules eliminate or reduce the earnings volatility that would otherwise result from reporting the change in the derivative's fair value in income. The type of hedge accounting to be applied varies depending on the nature of the exposure that is being hedged. In some cases, changes in the fair value of the derivative are reported in income as they occur, but the earnings impact is then offset by a corresponding charge (or credit) from adjusting the carrying value of the asset or liability being hedged. In other cases, earnings volatility is avoided by recording changes in the fair value of the derivative directly in "Other comprehensive income."

> The matching process works like this. If an economic gain (or loss) on the *hedged item* flows to accounting income in the current period, so does the offsetting loss (or gain) on the derivative. But if the hedged item's economic gain (or loss) flows to accounting income some time later—for example, when the copper inventory is sold—then income statement recognition of the derivative's offsetting loss (or gain) is also postponed to that later period.

> You may want to review Chapter 2 for a discussion of **other comprehensive income** and the income statement.

When can hedge accounting be used? The answer depends on four considerations:

- Hedged item
- Hedging instrument
- Risk being hedged
- Effectiveness of hedge.

Stringent GAAP criteria must be met to qualify for hedge accounting. Management must designate the derivative security as a hedging instrument, describe the hedging strategy, and document its effectiveness in eliminating a specific market risk for a specific hedged item. The details are voluminous and complex, so we cannot possibly cover all the bases here. What we can do is provide an overview of the most common hedging situations and how hedge accounting works. The basics are outlined in Figure 11.11 on the next page.

The **hedged item** can be (1) an existing asset or liability on the company's books, (2) a firm commitment, or (3) an anticipated (forecasted) transaction. Inventories of commodities like copper and lumber, receivables and loans, and debt obligations are examples of *existing assets and liabilities* that qualify as hedged items. If Hess Company agrees in June to buy network storage equipment from another company at a specific price with delivery in

[12] "Accounting for Derivative Instruments and Hedging Activities," *SFAS No. 133* (Norwalk, CT: FASB, 1998); "Accounting for Certain Derivative Instruments and Certain Hedging Activities," *SFAS No. 138* (Norwalk, CT: FASB, 2000). These statements are summarized and interpreted in the 540-page implementation guide *Accounting for Derivative Instruments and Hedging Activities* (Norwalk, CT: FASB, 2000).

Figure 11.11

FINANCIAL REPORTING FOR DERIVATIVE SECURITIES

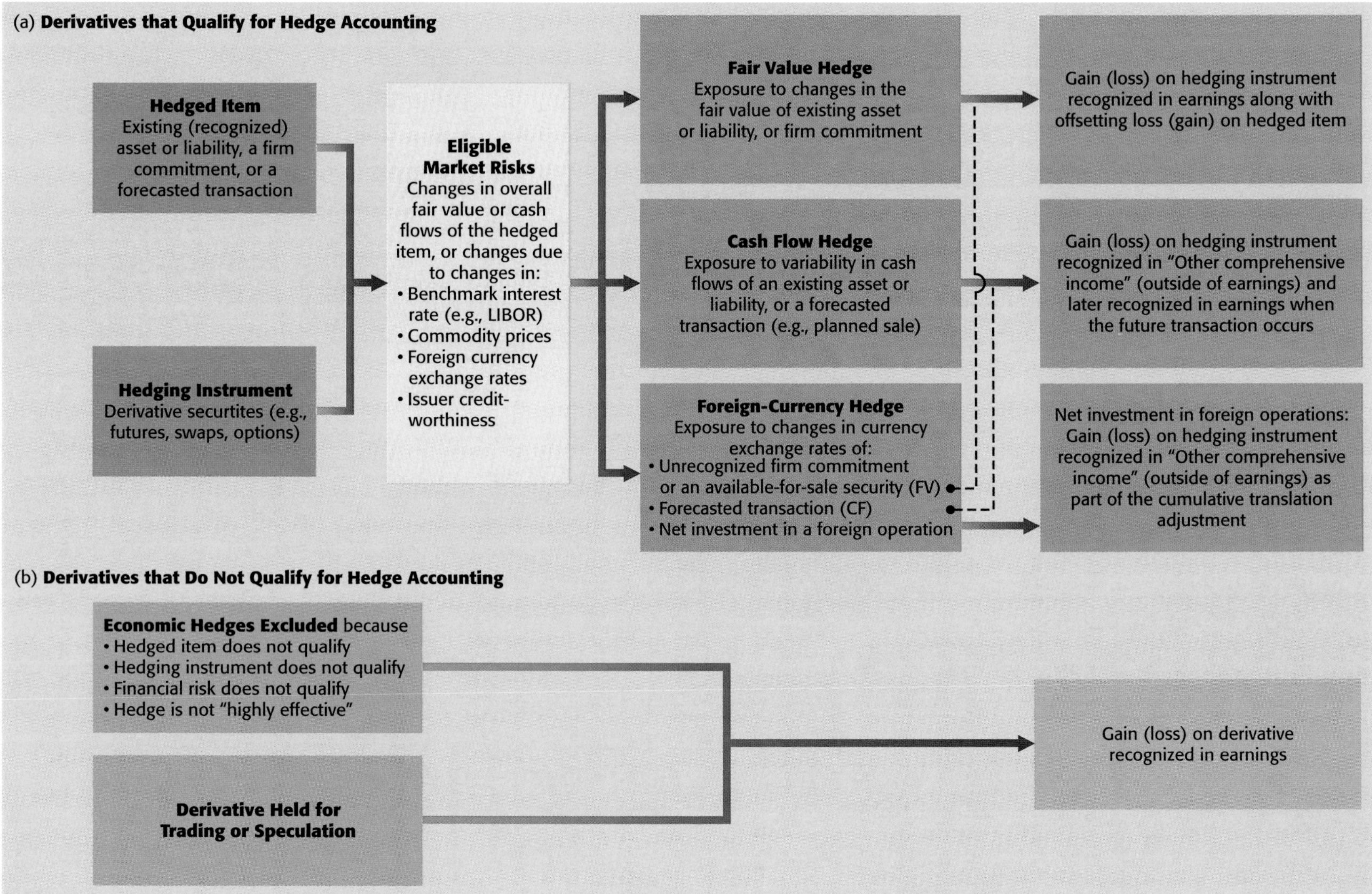
(a) Derivatives that Qualify for Hedge Accounting
Hedged Item
Existing (recognized) asset or liability, a firm commitment, or a forecasted transaction
Hedging Instrument
Derivative securtites (e.g., futures, swaps, options)
Eligible Market Risks
Changes in overall fair value or cash flows of the hedged item, or changes due to changes in:
• Benchmark interest rate (e.g., LIBOR)
• Commodity prices
• Foreign currency exchange rates
• Issuer credit-worthiness
Fair Value Hedge
Exposure to changes in the fair value of existing asset or liability, or firm commitment
Cash Flow Hedge
Exposure to variability in cash flows of an existing asset or liability, or a forecasted transaction (e.g., planned sale)
Foreign-Currency Hedge
Exposure to changes in currency exchange rates of:
• Unrecognized firm commitment or an available-for-sale security (FV)
• Forecasted transaction (CF)
• Net investment in a foreign operation
Gain (loss) on hedging instrument recognized in earnings along with offsetting loss (gain) on hedged item
Gain (loss) on hedging instrument recognized in "Other comprehensive income" (outside of earnings) and later recognized in earnings when the future transaction occurs
Net investment in foreign operations: Gain (loss) on hedging instrument recognized in "Other comprehensive income" (outside of earnings) as part of the cumulative translation adjustment
(b) Derivatives that Do Not Qualify for Hedge Accounting
Economic Hedges Excluded because
• Hedged item does not qualify
• Hedging instrument does not qualify
• Financial risk does not qualify
• Hedge is not "highly effective"
Derivative Held for Trading or Speculation
Gain (loss) on derivative recognized in earnings

the future (say, August), that's a *firm commitment.* If, on the other hand, Hess just knows in June that it must buy the equipment by August but no purchase agreement has been signed, then it's a *forecasted transaction.*

The **hedging instrument** is most often a derivative security, although not all derivatives meet the GAAP rules and some qualifying hedges do not involve derivatives. Qualifying hedging instruments include options to purchase or sell an exchange-traded security, futures and forward contracts, and interest-rate and currency swaps. ***Insurance contracts, options to purchase real estate, equity and debt securities, and financial guarantee contracts do not qualify as hedging instruments.***

The **risk being hedged** must meet certain GAAP criteria. The eligible market risks are limited to those arising from overall changes in the fair value or cash flow of the hedged item, or from changes in benchmark interest rates (e.g., LIBOR), commodity prices (e.g., copper), foreign-currency exchange rates (e.g., Japanese yen to U.S. dollar), and the creditworthiness of the party (a company, institution, or government agency) that issued a financial security. Other sorts of financial and operating risks (e.g., risks from weather conditions, industrial accidents, or labor strikes) do not qualify for hedge accounting. (We will discuss the effectiveness of the hedge later.)

> Derivatives that fail to meet the GAAP rules for hedge accounting—because either the hedged item, the derivative itself, or the hedged risk doesn't qualify—are treated as though they were speculative investments.

GAAP groups the risks being hedged into three general categories:

1. **A fair value hedge** is a hedge of the exposure to changes in the fair market value of:
   - an *existing* asset or liability (e.g., the interest-rate risk exposure of a company's existing fixed-rate debt), or
   - a *firm commitment* (e.g., the price risk exposure of a gold mining company that has agreed to sell refined gold to a jewelry manufacturer next year at a fixed price).
2. **A cash flow hedge** is a hedge of the exposure to changes in cash flows of:
   - an *existing* asset or liability (e.g., the interest-rate risk exposure of a company's existing floating-rate debt), or
   - an *anticipated transaction* (e.g., a building contractor's exposure to the price risk of future lumber purchases).
3. **A foreign currency exposure hedge** is a hedge of the exposure to changes in currency exchange rates of an existing asset or liability, a firm commitment, a forecasted transaction, or a multinational company's net investment in a foreign operation. Here GAAP applies the fair value and cash flow hedge accounting rules to foreign currency exchange exposure. The one unique element of this exposure is a net investment in foreign operations. In Chapter 16 we describe the accounting and reporting issues unique to foreign subsidiaries.

Figure 11.11 describes the accounting procedures for (a) derivatives that qualify for hedge accounting, and (b) derivatives that do not qualify for hedge accounting. GAAP requires all derivative securities—whether held for trading and speculation or as financial hedges—to be **marked-to-market,** meaning that they are carried at fair value on the balance sheet as assets or liabilities. The offsetting debit or credit that results from mark-to-market accounting then flows either to current income (for fair value hedges, certain foreign currency hedges, and derivatives that do not qualify for hedge accounting) or to "Other comprehensive income" (for cash flow hedges and most other foreign currency hedges).

Hedge accounting makes it possible for companies engaged in financial risk management to recognize the gain (or loss) on the hedged item in the same period as the offsetting loss (or gain) on the derivative security. To see how this is done, let's return to Rombauer Metals and its copper inventory hedge:

ANALYSIS

> On October 1, 2001 Rombauer has 10 million pounds of copper inventory on hand at an average cost of $0.65 a pound. The spot price for copper is $0.90 a pound. Instead of selling copper now, Rombauer decides to hold on to the inventory until February

2002 when management believes the price will return to a normal level of $0.95 a pound. To hedge its position, Rombauer sells futures contracts for 10 million pounds at $0.95 for February delivery. The margin deposit on the contracts is $280,000. This is the amount the commodities broker requires as a good-faith cash deposit on the contracts. Spot and futures prices over the next several months are:

	COMEX Copper Prices	
	Spot Price	**February 2002 Futures Price**
October 1, 2001	$0.90	$0.95
December 31, 2001	0.85	0.91
February 26, 2002	0.94	0.94

Rombauer has successfully hedged its exposure to commodity price risk—and the fair value of its copper inventory—by selling the futures contracts. Then, for GAAP purposes, Rombauer designates the futures contracts (the hedging instrument) as a **fair value hedge** of its exposure to market price fluctuations (the hedged risk) for existing copper inventory (the hedged item). As long as the futures contracts pass the GAAP test for hedge effectiveness—and they do, as we will see later—Rombauer can use the special **fair value hedge accounting** rules. Here are the accounting entries.

On October 1, 2001 Rombauer records the initial margin deposit on its fair value hedge:

DR Amount due from broker (a receivable)	$280,000	
CR Cash		$280,000

No entry is made that day for the futures contracts themselves because they have zero value at inception—the February contract price ($0.95) equals the current $0.95 market price of February copper.

The spot price and the February futures price of copper both decline over the next several months. Rombauer makes two journal entries at year-end, December 31. The first entry records the fair value increase for the hedging instrument:

DR Amount due from broker	$400,000	
CR Gain on hedge activity (to income)		$400,000

The futures contracts are worth $400,000 on December 31, 2001. This amount is the difference between the copper price guaranteed by the contracts ($0.95) and the current futures price of February copper ($0.91), multiplied by the 10 million pounds of copper being hedged. Copper prices have fallen, but the hedge has provided $400,000 of commodity price protection.

The second year-end entry adjusts the carrying value of the hedged item—copper inventory—for the change in fair value ($0.91 minus $0.95, a $0.04 loss, multiplied by 10 million pounds):

DR Loss on hedge activity (to income)	$400,000	
CR Copper inventory		$400,000

The carrying value of the copper inventory is now $6.1 million, that's the inventory's $6.5 million historical cost *minus* the $400,000 decline in the February fair value since October 1, 2001. (Note that GAAP measures this fair value decline using the $0.95 futures contract price as the benchmark. The October 1 spot price of $0.90 does not enter into the GAAP calculation of the fair value decline.)

In the first entry, the derivative is marked-to-market and a gain on the hedging instrument is recorded to income. But the gain from the futures contracts is fully offset by Rombaurer's loss on copper inventory in the second entry. (In practice only one "Gain or loss on hedge activity" account is used to record the gain and the loss.) These offsetting gains and losses eliminate earnings volatility.

On February 26, 2002 Rombaurer sells the copper on the spot market for $0.94 a pound and cancels the futures contracts. Rombaurer makes three journal entries at this time. The first entry records the fair value change for the hedging instrument ($0.91 minus $0.94, a $0.03 loss, multiplied by 10 million pounds), the cash returned from the broker, and eliminates the broker receivable:

DR Cash	$380,000	
DR Loss on hedge activity (to income)	300,000	
CR Amount due from broker		$680,000

February copper prices have increased $0.03 a pound since December and the futures contracts are now worth only $100,000 ($0.95 minus $0.94, multiplied by 10 million pounds). Rombaurer receives $380,000 from the broker. This amount is the sum of the returned margin deposit ($280,000) and the settlement value of the contracts ($100,000).

The second entry adjusts the carrying value of the hedged copper inventory for the fair value change ($0.94 minus $0.91, multiplied by 10 million pounds):

The $6.4 million adjusted carrying value ($0.64 per pound) is determined as:

10/5/01	cost at $0.65 per pound	$6.5 million
12/31/01	adjustment for $0.04 decline	(.4) million
2/26/02	adjustment for $0.03 increase	.3 million
2/26/02	adjusted carrying value	$6.4 million

DR Copper inventory	$300,000	
CR Gain on hedge activity (to income)		$300,000

In this case, the loss from the futures contracts (the first entry) is offset by a gain on copper inventory (the second entry). The final entry records the credit sale of copper inventory at the spot market price:

DR Accounts receivable	$9,400,000	
DR Cost of goods sold	6,400,000	
CR Sales revenue		$9,400,000
CR Copper inventory		6,400,000

Rombaurer's gross profit from selling copper is $3 million (the $9.4 million selling price minus the $6.4 million adjusted carrying value of the inventory sold). This is exactly the gross profit Rombaurer would have reported if the inventory—originally carried on the books at $6.5 million—had been sold at the anticipated February price of $0.95 a pound, or $9.5 million. By selling futures contracts, Rombaurer "locked in" the February price of $0.95 a pound and eliminated its exposure to commodity price risk. That's the economics behind Rombaurer's hedging activities and that's what the accounting statements report.

What if Rombaurer did not (or could not) use hedge accounting rules for the copper futures contracts. In that case, GAAP still requires the derivative security to be marked-to-market. So Rombaurer would record a $400,000 gain on December 31, 2001 followed by a $300,000 loss on February 26, 2002—the change in fair value of the futures contracts. But GAAP would not allow an offsetting loss (on December 31, 2001) or gain (on February 26, 2002) to be recorded on the copper inventory itself. Instead, the inventory would continue to be carried at its historical cost of $6,500,000 until sold. The net result is increased earnings volatility: net income for 2001 would include a $400,000 gain, while net income for 2002 would include a $300,000 loss and a $100,000 gross margin reduction due to the higher carrying value of inventory ($0.65 per pound original cost rather than $0.64 per pound adjusted carrying value).

Exhibit 11.3 illustrates the accounting for a **cash flow hedge.** Chalk Hill Inc. issues a $10 million three-year floating-rate note with interest equal to the LIBOR rate, reset annually. To hedge its exposure to cash flow variability from changes in the LIBOR, Chalk Hill enters into an interest-rate swap with a bank. The bank agrees to make the required floating-rate interest payments and Chalk Hill agrees to pay the bank 7.5% fixed-rate interest annually for the entire three years. The interest-rate swap allows Chalk Hill to "lock in" the 7.5% fixed-rate cash payment for interest even though the actual interest rate charged on the note will rise or fall with changes in the LIBOR rate.

Exhibit 11.3 ■ CHALK HILL'S CASH FLOW HEDGE

Using an Interest-Rate Swap to Hedge Variable-Rate Debt

On January 1, 2001 Chalk Hill borrows $10 million signing a three-year note with interest equal to the LIBOR (currently at 7.5%), reset annually on December 31. To hedge its exposure to the variability in cash flows associated with the floating-rate note, Chalk Hill enters into a three-year interest-rate swap with Beringer Bank. Under the swap contract, Chalk Hill pays interest to the bank at the fixed rate of 7.5% and receives interest payments from the bank at a variable rate equal to the LIBOR, based on a notional amount of $10 million. Both the note and swap require that payments be made or received annually on December 31 of each year.

Chalk Hill designates the swap (hedging instrument) as a ***cash flow hedge*** of its exposure to variability in the cash flows of the floating-rate note (hedged item), with the specific risk being changes in cash flows due to changes in the LIBOR rate. This hedge is fully effective because the key terms of the note and swap are identical. The LIBOR rates, cash payments made and received, and the fair value of the swap contract (based on dealer quotes) are:

		Gross Cash Flow			
	LIBOR Rate	**To Beringer Bank**	**From Beringer Bank**	**Net Cash Flow**	**Swap Fair Value Asset (Liability) from Dealer Quotes**
January 1, 2001	7.50%	$750,000	$750,000	—	—
December 31, 2001	8.50	750,000	850,000	$100,000	$323,000
December 31, 2002	7.00	750,000	700,000	(50,000)	(55,000)

Swap contracts are not traded in an organized exchange (like the New York Mercantile Exchange where copper futures contracts are traded), so contract fair values can be difficult to determine. Chalk Hill's fair value estimates ("quotes") are from knowledgable "dealers" (usually investment bankers) who are actively involved in structuring swap transactions. Chalk Hill makes the following entries over the life of the swap contract and note:

January 1, 2001:

DR Cash	$10,000,000	
CR Note payable		$10,000,000

(To record the initial borrowing by the company. There is no entry for the swap contract because it has no initial value—the "pay" and "receive" rates for both parties are the same, 7.5% times $10 million.)

December 31, 2001:

DR Interest expense	$750,000	
CR Interest payable		$750,000

(To accrue annual interest at a variable rate of 7.5%—the LIBOR rate on January 1, 2001.)

DR Interest payable	$750,000	
CR Cash		$750,000

(To record the annual interest payment on the note. There is no entry for the swap settlement this year because the "pay" and "receive" amounts are the same, $750,000.)

DR Swap contract	$323,000	
CR Other comprehensive income		$323,000

(To record the change in fair value of the swap based on dealer quotes.)

Exhibit 11.3 ■ *(continued)*

December 31, 2002:

DR Interest expense	$850,000	
CR Interest payable		$850,000
(To accrue annual interest at a variable rate of 8.5%—the LIBOR rate on December 31, 2001.)		
DR Interest payable	$850,000	
CR Cash		$850,000
(To record the annual interest payment on the note.)		
DR Cash	$100,000	
CR Interest expense		$100,000
(To record the swap settlement net receipt from Beringer Bank.)		
DR Other comprehensive income	$378,000	
CR Swap contract		$378,000
(To record the change in fair value of the swap based on dealer quotes. The swap contract account now has a $55,000 credit balance.)		

December 31, 2003:

DR Interest expense	$700,000	
CR Interest payable		$700,000
(To accrue annual interest at a variable rate of 7.0%—the LIBOR rate on December 31, 2002.)		
DR Interest payable	$700,000	
CR Cash		$700,000
(To record the annual interest payment on the note.)		
DR Interest expense	$50,000	
CR Cash		$50,000
(To record the swap settlement net payment to Beringer Bank.)		
DR Swap contract	$55,000	
CR Other comprehensive income		$55,000
(To record the change in fair value of the swap. The swap agreement has now been concluded, and the contract has no further value to either party.)		
DR Note payable	$10,000,000	
CR Cash		$10,000,000
(To record payment of the note principal.)		

As you work through the journal entries in Exhibit 11.3, notice that the hedging instrument (swap contract) shows up as a balance sheet asset or liability. (If the account has a debit balance, it's an asset; if the balance is a credit, it's a liability.) The carrying value of the swap is its fair value at each balance sheet date. This means that changes in the swap's fair value are recorded when they occur—***but they do not flow directly to the income statement.*** Instead, gains and losses on the swap contract flow to "Other comprehensive income" and shareholders' equity, as indicated in Figure 11.11. What's the reason for this accounting treatment? Changes in the LIBOR rate do not affect the underlying economic value of the floating-rate note—as interest rates on a floating-rate liability change, the market price of the liability remains constant. So, we are unable to offset fair value changes in the hedging instrument with changes in the fair value of the hedged item. The only way earnings volatility can be avoided is to keep swap gains and losses off the income statement by allowing them to flow to "Other comprehensive income."

Problem 11.8 looks at the accounting for Chalk Hill's swap when it does not qualify for hedge accounting.

There is one more feature of the Chalk Hill example you should notice. Interest expense is $750,000 each year, or the 7.5% fixed-rate of interest multiplied by the $10 million note principal amount. This may at first seem surprising because Chalk Hill makes a floating-rate interest payment each year, and the amount paid varies from $700,000 to $850,000 over the three years. But the interest-rate swap insulates Chalk Hill from this cash flow volatility. For example, in 2002 Chalk Hill pays $850,000 in interest on the note but receives $100,000 from the swap counterparty. The company's net cash payment for interest that year is $750,000, which is also the amount of interest expense reported.

Now let's see how hedge accounting works for a **forecasted transaction.** In this example, Vintage Construction uses lumber options contracts as a cash flow hedge for its projected lumber needs during the year:

> Vintage Construction Corporation builds houses in the far northern United States from April through November. No homes are built on speculation. Building begins only after a firm contract is signed. Construction on average takes four months. Since contract prices with home purchasers are fixed at the inception of the sale, Vintage is vulnerable to lumber price increases. To protect its margins during the 2001 construction season, Vintage buys 20 lumber futures contracts on April 1, 2001. The expiration dates on these contracts are staggered over the April through November season to approximate the monthly level of construction activity.
>
> Lumber prices rise during the 2001 construction season. Because of these unanticipated higher costs, gross profits from home construction are reduced by $600,000. However, Vintage realized a gain of $580,000 on the futures contracts due to the lumber price increase. How was this gain reflected on the company's financial statements?
>
> Vintage designates the lumber contracts as a ***cash flow hedge*** of forecasted lumber purchases, with commodity price volatility being the source of market risk. At inception, the futures contracts are recorded as an asset at the purchase price. At each monthly balance sheet date, the contracts are marked-to-market with the change in fair value flowing to "Other comprehensive income" and then shareholders' equity. As homes are completed each month, Vintage records the revenues and expenses from the construction business. At the same time, the cumulative gain and loss on the lumber contracts for completed homes is transferred out of "Other comprehensive income" to the income statement.
>
> ***This accounting treatment offsets changes in the gross profit from construction due to lumber price fluctuations (the hedged item) with realized gains and losses from lumber futures contracts (the hedging instrument).*** Earnings volatility is avoided by allowing the futures contracts gains and losses to initially flow to shareholders' equity. These gains and losses eventually flow to earnings, but only when the forecasted transaction is completed ***and affects earnings.*** For Vintage Construction, that means when the homes are finished and sold—not earlier when lumber is purchased.

Because all of the options contracts were realized in 2001, the $580,000 gain would be included in income and would largely offset the $600,000 gross margin reduction that is reflected in the same period. This income statement result corresponds to the almost perfect hedging strategy followed by Vintage Construction. A "perfect" hedge would have exactly offset the $600,000 margin shortfall.

For interest-rate swaps like the one described in Exhibit 11.3, the critical terms include the notional and principal amounts, contract term and loan maturity date, "pay" and "receive" rates on the benchmark interest rate, and the interest rate reset dates.

Few hedges are perfect. When they are not—as here—notice that reported income corresponds to the underlying economics. That is, while Vintage insulated itself from most of the lumber price increase, it did experience a $20,000 earnings reduction. This is precisely the reported income statement effect (i.e., a $580,000 gain on the options and a $600,000 gross margin reduction).

Hedge effectiveness—the derivative's ability to generate offsetting changes in the fair value or cash flows of the hedged item—is a key qualifying criterion for hedge accounting. If critical terms of the hedging instrument and hedged item are the same, changes in the fair value or cash flow of the derivative will completely offset changes in the fair value or cash flow of the hedged item. In this case, the hedge will be "fully effective." Except for Vantage Construction, all of our examples have involved fully effective hedges.

But what if the hedge is not fully effective? Does that disqualify the derivative from special hedge accounting rules? Not necessarily, because GAAP only requires the hedge to be "highly effective" in offsetting changes in those fair values or cash flows that are due to the hedged risk. This requirement must be met both at the inception of the hedge and on an ongoing basis. SFAS No. 133 provides general guidelines but does not say exactly how effectiveness should be determined.

How effective is "highly effective"? The hedging instrument should offset somewhere between 80% and 125% of the hedged item's fair value or cash flow changes attributable to the hedged risk. For Vintage Construction, this means that the company must purchase enough staggered lumber futures contracts to hedge at least 80% of its exposure to lumber price fluctuations. Purchase less than this amount and the futures contracts are an "ineffective" hedge according to GAAP. On the other hand, if Vintage buys too many contracts, the hedge is also considered ineffective. That's because the futures contracts are excessive and more like a speculative investment than a true hedge of underlying market risk.

SFAS No. 133 and *No. 138* do not provide a bright line that define "highly effective" and therefore the interpretation of this phrase will often be a matter of judgment. The range of 80% to 125% is becoming an accepted threshold for high effectiveness, but it has not been sanctioned by the FASB.

The GAAP distinction between *highly effective* and *ineffective* hedges determines when gains and losses on the hedging instrument flow to current income. A highly effective hedge qualifies for special hedge accounting treatment; an ineffective hedge does not. Even if the highly effective test is met, some ineffectiveness may occur. And when it does, the ineffective portion of the hedge must flow directly to income. So, if Vintage Construction buys futures contracts to hedge just 50% of its exposure, all of the gains and losses from this *ineffective* hedge flow directly to current income. That's because the contracts are ineffective and do not qualify for hedge accounting. And if the company buys futures contracts to hedge 110% of its exposure, the gains and losses on the *ineffective* portion of the hedge (the portion over 100% coverage) also flow directly to current income. Gains and losses on the effective portion of the hedge flow to other comprehensive income.

Critics of hedge accounting claim that additional income statement and balance sheet volatility is created when the gains and losses on the hedging instrument exceed the losses and gains on the hedged item. ***This may force managers to choose between achieving sound economic results—meaning hedges that effectively address real financial risks—or minimizing accounting volatility using risk management approaches that are less efficient or simply not prudent.***

In a letter to the FASB, Al Wargo of Eastman Chemical said that hedge accounting could cause his company's quarterly earnings per share (EPS) to fluctuate by roughly 100% in either direction—from a $0.12 loss to a $2.24 profit based on Eastman's $1.12 EPS for the second quarter of 2000. The only way Eastman can eliminate this EPS volatility is to change how it hedges financial risk. But this means replacing a sound economic hedging transaction with a less effective hedge. EPS would then be less volatile but the company may be more exposed to financial risks. See P. A. McKay and J. Niedzielski, "New Accounting Standard Gets Mixed Reviews," the *Wall Street Journal* (October 23, 2000).

RECAP

Derivatives, when used properly, allow companies to stabilize their operating cash flows by eliminating specific sources of volatility such as fluctuations in interest rates, exchange rates and commodity prices. The GAAP rules for derivatives are detailed and complex, but the essential points are simple. Derivative contracts represent balance sheet assets and liabilities that must be marked-to-market at each balance sheet date. The resulting mark-to-market adjustment—the change in fair value—then flows either to current earnings (for fair value hedges, certain foreign currency hedges, and derivatives held for trading and speculation) or to "Other comprehensive income" (for cash flow hedges and most other foreign currency hedges). Other aspects of hedge accounting then match gains (or losses) on the derivative with offsetting losses (or gains) on the hedged item. This allows the financial statements to reflect accurately the underlying economics of the hedge.

Loss Contingencies

A **loss contingency** occurs when there is an event that raises the possibility of future loss. These contingencies arise from factors like litigation, industrial accidents, debt guarantees, and product warranties. For financial reporting purposes, two questions arise: (1) When do loss contingencies need to be measured and recognized in the financial statements? and (2) Under what circumstances do these contingencies need to be disclosed in footnotes, even when no liability is recorded on the balance sheet itself?

Measuring and Recognizing Loss Contingencies

The rules for measuring and recognizing loss contingencies in the financial statements are virtually identical to the rules governing revenue recognition. *SFAS No. 5* states that a loss contingency shall be accrued by a charge to income if *both* of the following conditions exist:

1. It is *probable* that an asset has been impaired or a liability has been incurred at the date of the financial statements.
2. The amount of loss can be *reasonably estimated.*[13]

The FASB established a range representing the likelihood of losses occurring, which is depicted in Figure 11.12, where "probable" indicates the highest likelihood. Notice that the two loss contingency recognition conditions correspond to the two income recognition conditions—"critical event" and "measurability"—discussed in Chapter 2. Specifically, the critical event for loss recognition is that it is probable that a loss has or will occur; similarly, the measurability criterion corresponds closely to how well the loss can be estimated. In this sense, the criteria that trigger income and loss recognition are roughly parallel.

For certain categories of events, applying the loss contingency rules has become routine. One example of a routine loss contingency is the expense for **estimated uncollectible receivables** described in Chapter 8. Uncollectibles are a normal cost of business when companies sell goods or services on credit, but the amount of the uncollectible loss is unknown at the time of sale. Since some loss is probable, and since the amount can be estimated, an expense (estimated loss) is recorded in the same period that the sale occurs.

In other situations the issue of whether to recognize a loss contingency is highly subjective and complicated by the fact that recognizing and disclosing the loss could itself cause further harm. Consider a company that is being sued for actions that allegedly harmed others.

> Wren Corporation manufactures a wide range of chemical food additives sold to numerous food processors throughout the country. Due to a serious production error, a highly toxic batch of a flavor enhancer was produced by Wren and sold in October 2001. Thousands of consumers were made seriously ill; some died. A class-action lawsuit seeking $10 billion in damages has been filed.

The fictitious Wren scenario illustrates a setting in which a straightforward application of the *SFAS No. 5* loss contingency rules could prove harmful to the company. Let's say Wren's management was indeed negligent and expects to negotiate an out-of-court settlement that is approximately $2 billion. If Wren accrued a charge for this expected payout, its negotiating position could be seriously weakened by a disclosure to the plaintiffs that it is

Figure 11.12

SFAS NO. 5 LOSS PROBABILITY CONTINUUM

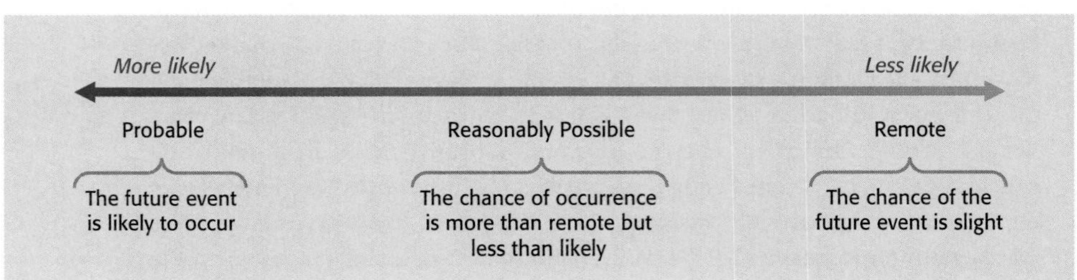
More likely
Less likely
Probable
Reasonably Possible
Remote
The future event is likely to occur
The chance of occurrence is more than remote but less than likely
The chance of the future event is slight

[13] "Accounting for Contingencies," *SFAS No. 5* (Stamford, CT: FASB, 1975), para. 8.

prepared to pay at least \$2 billion. Because the plaintiffs might be willing to settle for less than \$2 billion, candid disclosure of the minimum estimated loss by Wren could raise the ultimate loss payout. Companies like Wren have strong incentives to either (1) accrue a loss that is significantly *smaller* than the real estimated loss or (2) disclose that while a loss may have occurred, its amount is not yet measurable. Consequently, the *SFAS No. 5* rules for loss contingencies arising from litigation are difficult to enforce. ***Statement readers must be aware of the potential understatement of litigation losses and liabilities.***

Loss Contingency Disclosures

When a loss contingency is accrued, companies also frequently disclose other information regarding the loss separately in footnotes to the financial statements. *SFAS No. 5* requires this disclosure when a failure to provide additional supplemental data could lead to misleading inferences.

Loss contingency disclosures are also sometimes made even when no loss has been recognized in the income statement itself. For example, if the loss probability is only "reasonably possible" or "remote" (refer to Figure 11.12), then no loss accrual needs to be made in the financial statements. ***Nevertheless, footnote disclosure of loss contingencies is necessary when the loss is both reasonably possible and can be estimated.*** Furthermore, even contingencies arising from remote possibilities must be disclosed in certain circumstances, such as when one company guarantees another company's debt—that is, it agrees to repay a loan if the borrower cannot.

SUMMARY

An astounding variety of financial instruments, derivatives, and nontraditional financing arrangements are now used to fund corporate activities and to manage risk. Statement readers face a daunting task when trying to grasp the economic implications of some financial innovations. Off-balance sheet obligations and loss contingencies are difficult to evaluate because the information needed is often not disclosed. Derivatives—whether used for hedging or speculation—pose special problems because of both their complexity and the involved details of hedge accounting.

For many companies, however, the single most important long-term obligation is still traditional debt financing. GAAP in this area is quite clear. Noncurrent monetary liabilities are initially recorded at the discounted present value of the contractual cash flows—that is, the issue price. The effective interest method is then used to compute interest expense and net carrying value in each period. Interest rate changes occurring after the debt has been issued are ignored.

GAAP accounting for long-term debt makes it possible to "manage" reported income statement and balance sheet numbers when debt is retired before maturity. The opportunity to do so comes from the difference between debt book value and market value when interest rates have changed. The incentives for "managing" income statement and balance sheet numbers may be related to debt covenants, compensation, regulation, or just the desire to paint a favorable picture of the company's performance and health.

Extinguishment gains and losses from early debt retirement and swaps require careful scrutiny. Statement readers need to know whether real economic benefits for the company and its shareholders are produced—or if the gains or losses are just window dressing.

Self-Study Problem: Mallard Corporation

Mallard Corporation constructs and operates private waterfowl hunting facilities throughout the western United States. On July 1, 2001 the company issued \$5 million of par value 10-year bonds to finance construction of a guest lodge at its newest site in Klamath, Oregon. The bonds pay interest semiannually (on December 31 and June 30) at an annual rate of 8% and are callable by Mallard at 102% of par value. The bonds were issued at a price that yields 10% annually to maturity.

(*continued*)

1. Compute the issue price of the bonds.

The bond cash flows include a semiannual interest payment of $200,000 (or $5 million at 4%) plus the principal payment of $5 million at maturity. With an effective (market) interest rate of 5% for each six-month interval, the present value factors are:

20-period ordinary annuity at 5% = 12.46221
20-period single payment = .37689

Multiplying each factor by the corresponding cash flow gives the issue price as:

$ 200,000 ×	12.46221	=	$2,492,442
+ $5,000,000 ×	.37689	=	1,884,450
			$4,376,892

The bonds were thus issued at a discount of $623,108 (or $5,000,000 − $4,376,892).

2. Compute the amount of interest expense on the bonds for 2001. Mallard Corporation uses the effective interest method for amortizing bond discounts and premiums.

Because the bonds were issued on July 1, 2001, only six months of interest needs to be recorded for the year. Interest expense is computed at the effective interest rate of 5%. This rate is multiplied by the amount borrowed (opening book value) to get interest expense:

$4,376,892 × 5% = $218,845 (rounded)

Computed interest expense is more than the required $200,000 cash payment. The $18,845 difference represents amortization of the bond discount—that is, an increase to the book value of the bond. The year-end financial statements of Mallard Corporation would show the bond at $4,395,737 ($4,376,892 + $18,845).

3. Mallard uses the indirect method of computing cash flows from operations on its cash flow statement. Indicate how much will be added to (or subtracted from) the 2001 accrual basis net income figure that is related to the bonds to obtain cash flows from operations.

The accrual income figure contains interest expense of $218,845, but the cash interest payment is only $200,000. The additional interest expense of $18,845 does not represent an operating cash outflow for the year, and so it is added back to net income to arrive at cash flows from operations. Notice that this amount equals the discount amortization for the year.

4. Assume that the market yield on the bonds had fallen to 9% by July 1, 2003 and that Mallard decided to retire the debt on that date either by purchasing the bonds on the open market or by exercising its 102% call option. Which method of debt retirement is the least expensive for Mallard?

Under the terms of the call option, Mallard can retire the debt by paying bond holders 102% of par value or:

$5,000,000 × 102% = $5,100,000

However, the current market value of the bonds at an annual yield of 9% is:

$ 200,000 ×	11.23402	=	$2,246,804
+ $5,000,000 ×	.49447	=	2,472,350
			$4,719,154

The open-market purchase is the less expensive way for Mallard to retire its debt. (Notice that the present value factors used to compute the current market price are based on a 4.5% semiannual yield and 16 six-month periods to July 1, 2010.)

5. Produce the journal entry that Mallard Corporation would record on July 1, 2003 when it retired the bonds through an open market purchase.

Assume that all interest expense and cash interest payments have been recorded. Then the book value of the bonds on July 1, 2003 is $4,458,115, as shown on the next page in the amortization table.

	Period (Six-month Interval)	Liability at Start of Period	Effective Interest: 5% per Period	Coupon Rate: 4% of Par	Increase in Recorded Book Value	Liability at End of Period
7/1/01	0					$4,376,892
1/1/02	1	$4,376,892	$218,845	$200,000	$18,845	4,395,737
7/1/02	2	4,395,737	219,787	200,000	19,787	4,415,524
1/1/03	3	4,415,523	220,776	200,000	20,776	4,436,300
7/1/03	4	4,436,300	221,815	200,000	21,815	4,458,115

Based on our previous calculation, we find that Mallard would pay $4,719,154 to retire the bonds on that date, so the entry is:

DR Bonds payable	$5,000,000	
DR Extraordinary loss on retirement	261,039	
CR Discount on bonds		$ 541,885
CR Cash		4,719,154

where $541,885 represents the remaining (unamortized) balance of the original issue discount ($5,000,000 face value minus $4,458,115 book value).

Self-Study Problem: MEDIQ, Inc.

Exhibit 11.4 is taken from the 1995 Shareholder Report of MEDIQ, Inc., a medical equipment and nuclear imaging services company. This exhibit typifies the required disclosures for long-term liabilities. The various categories of debt are identified and key characteristics of major debt instruments—such as required sinking fund payments—are described. An enumeration of scheduled principal repayments over the ensuing five years is also provided. The intent of the disclosures is to provide data on future cash outflows and credit risk; these data help analysts and others generate cash flow forecasts.

Some bond indenture agreements specify that periodic cash payments will be made to a trust to ensure that the principal amount of the bond liability will be repaid. These are called **sinking fund payments.**

Exhibit 11.4 ■ MEDIQ, INC.

1995 Long-Term Debt Footnote

Long-Term Debt and Other Obligations

Senior debt consisted of the following: ($ in thousands)	**September 30 1995**	**1994**
Corporate debt		
Revolving credit facility	$ 567	$ 11,147
Term loans payable in varying installments through 2005 at rates from prime (8.75% at September 30, 1995) to 12%	1,815	1,862
Mortgage payable	—	3,917
Subsidiary debt		
Senior secured notes due 1999	100,000	100,000
Term loan payable monthly through 2000 at prime plus 2%	37,493	43,000
Term loans payable in varying installments through 1999 at rates from prime plus 1% to 13%	2,828	13,114
Capital lease obligations payable in varying installments through 1999 at fixed rates from 8% to 21%	9,046	12,833
	151,749	185,873
Less current portion	14,800	23,437
	$136,949	$162,436

(continued)

Subordinated debt consisted of the following: ($ in thousands)	**September 30 1995**	**1994**
Corporate debt		
7.5% Exchangeable subordinated debentures due 2003	$ 34,500	$ 34,500
7.25% Convertible subordinated debentures due 2006	51,729	51,729
Subsidiary debt		
10% Subordinated notes due 2004	8,664	8,547
10% Subordinated notes due 1999	9,514	8,612
	104,407	103,388
Less current portion	22,500	—
	$ 81,907	$103,388

In September 1994 in connection with the acquisition of the rental equipment inventory of KCI, the Company obtained financing consisting of a $43.0 million term loan, $8.5 million of senior subordinated notes, $8.6 million of subordinated notes payable to KCI, and two term loans aggregating $8.5 million payable to KCI. The $43.0 million term loan is payable in equal monthly payments through December 2000 of approximately $600,000 plus interest at the prime rate plus 2%, or, at the Company's option, a rate equal to the adjusted Eurodollar rate plus 4.25% and is collateralized by all of the acquired equipment. The $8.5 million of senior subordinated notes, which have a face value of $10 million, include warrants which allow the holders to purchase, in the aggregate, up to 10% of the common stock of MEDIQ/PRN for a nominal amount. Interest on the notes of 10% is payable semiannually on April 1 and October 1. Annual principal payments on the notes of $1.0 million commence April 1, 2000, with the remaining principal balance payable on October 1, 2004. . . .

In October 1993 the Company entered into an agreement with a commercial bank for a $7.5 million revolving credit facility, which was increased to $13.4 million in August 1994. In December 1995 this credit facility, which bears interest at prime plus 1% and was originally scheduled to expire in October 1995, extended to December 1996. In connection with the extension to December 1996, the facility was increased to $15 million and the interest rate was reduced to prime plus .5%. In addition, as amended, the facility will be reduced by an amount equal to 50% of the net cash proceeds from the sale of discontinued operations and certain other assets. At September 30, 1995 the Company had $.6 million outstanding and $2.2 million of letters of credit under this facility. The facility is secured by a portion of the shares of common stock of NutraMax and PCI, owned by the Company.

In September 1994 in connection with the acquisition of equipment from KCI, MEDIQ/PRN amended the indenture related to its outstanding $100 million of 11.125% senior secured notes to obtain approval for the transaction. The amendment also provided for an increase in the interest rate on the notes to 12.125% effective September 30, 1995. . . . The Company's ability to obtain cash from MEDIQ/PRN is limited by provisions in certain of MEDIQ/PRN's debt agreements. For 1995 and 1994, such provisions did not permit MEDIQ/PRN to pay any dividends to the Company.

The 7.5% subordinated debentures are exchangeable for an aggregate 2,225,000 shares of NutraMax common stock owned by the Company, or an equivalent of $15.30 per share, and are redeemable in whole or in part at the option of the Company after July 1996. Interest is payable semiannually on January 15 and July 15.

The 7.25% subordinated debentures are convertible at any time prior to maturity into shares of the common stock of the Company at $7.50 per share.

. . . Annual sinking fund payments equal to 10% of the principal commence in June 1997. The Company is also required to offer to repurchase a portion of the debentures if stockholders' equity is $40 million or less at the end of two consecutive fiscal quarters. Since June 30, 1994 the Company's stockholders' equity has been less than $40 million.

The requirements to repurchase debentures at December 31, 1994 and June 30, 1995 were satisfied through the Company's previous acquisition of $23.3 million principal amount of debentures. As of September 30, 1995, $22.5 million of the debentures was classified as current obligations pursuant to the terms of the indenture. In October and November 1995 the Company repurchased an aggregate of $11.25 million of its debentures at a discount in the open market and through a private transaction resulting in a pre-tax gain of approximately $1.5 million. This gain will be recorded in the first quarter of fiscal 1996 as an extraordinary item. The Company is required to either repurchase or redeem $11.25 million of debentures prior to June 30, 1996 and semiannually thereafter until all of the debentures are repurchased or stockholders' equity is more than $40 million.

Certain of the Company's loan agreements require the maintenance of specified financial ratios and impose financial and dividend limitations. The terms of one of the Company's indentures currently limits the payment of future dividends or the purchase of the Company's stock to approximately $5 million in the aggregate as of September 30, 1995. As of September 30, 1995 the Company and one of its subsidiaries did not comply with certain financial ratios, principally working capital and tangible net worth. Subsequent to September 30, 1995 the Company and its subsidiary obtained the necessary waivers/amendments from its lenders regarding these ratios. Restricted net assets of consolidated subsidiaries and unconsolidated affiliates aggregated approximately $38.4 million at September 30, 1995.

Maturities of long-term debt are as follows:

	Year Ending September 30		
($ in thousands)	Senior	Subordinated	Total
1996	$ 14,800	$ 22,500	$ 37,300
1997	10,243	22,500	32,743
1998	9,294	6,729	16,023
1999	108,667	—	108,667
2000	6,931	9,514	16,445
Thereafter	1,814	43,164	44,978
	$151,749	$104,407	$256,156

Source: MEDIQ Inc. 1995 Shareholder Report.

1. **The first paragraph of the footnote describes debt instruments issued in connection with MEDIQ's acquisition of rental equipment inventory from another company. Included among these securities are $8.5 million of senior subordinated notes. Sketch the contractual cash payments required under the terms of these notes.**

Interest is paid semiannually on April 1 and October 1, the contractual interest rate is 10%, and the notes have a face value of $10 million. Consequently, MEDIQ is obligated to pay note holders $500,000 every six months ($10 million × 5% semiannual interest) beginning April 1, 1995. However, required principal payments of $1 million annually begin on April 1, 2000, and each principal payment reduces the interest burden by $50,000. The final payment on October 1, 2004 will consist of $5 million principal and $250,000 for interest.

2. **How much cash did MEDIQ receive when the company issued these senior subordinated notes?**

The notes have a face value of $10 million, but they are described in the footnote as totaling $8.5 million. The September 30, 1994 book value of the notes is $8,547,000, as shown in the subordinated debt table. Apparently, MEDIQ issued these notes at a discount and received a little more than $8.5 million cash.

3. **Verify that the effective interest rate on these senior subordinated notes is about 6.42% semiannually.**

This involves finding the interest rate (6.42%) that equates the present value of the cash payment stream with the $8.547 million loan proceeds. Computer spreadsheets provide an efficient way of solving this problem. The accompanying table lists the scheduled payments, net cash flows, present value factor, and present value amount for the notes based on the 6.42% effective interest rate. This rate is a reasonable approximation of the true effective interest rate (yield to maturity) for these notes, because the sum of all cash-flow present value amounts ($8.548 million) nearly equals the loan proceeds ($8.547 million).

Date	Face Amount Outstanding	Interest Payment	Principal Repayment	Net Cash Flows	Present Value Factor at 6.42%	Present Value Amount
10/1/94	$10.0					
4/1/95	10.0	$0.500	—	$0.500	0.93967	$0.470
10/1/95	10.0	0.500	—	0.500	.88299	0.441
4/1/96	10.0	0.500	—	0.500	.82972	0.415
10/1/96	10.0	0.500	—	0.500	.77966	0.390
4/1/97	10.0	0.500	—	0.500	.73263	0.366
10/1/97	10.0	0.500	—	0.500	.68843	0.344
4/1/98	10.0	0.500	—	0.500	.64690	0.323
10/1/98	10.0	0.500	—	0.500	.60787	0.304
4/1/99	10.0	0.500	—	0.500	.57120	0.286
10/1/99	10.0	0.500	—	0.500	.53674	0.268
4/1/00	9.0	0.500	$1.000	1.500	.50436	0.757
10/1/00	9.0	0.450	—	0.450	.47394	0.213
4/1/01	8.0	0.450	1.000	1.450	.44535	0.646
10/1/01	8.0	0.400	—	0.400	.41848	0.167
4/1/02	7.0	0.400	1.000	1.400	.39323	0.551
10/1/02	7.0	0.350	—	0.350	.36951	0.129
4/1/03	6.0	0.350	1.000	1.350	.34722	0.469
10/1/03	6.0	0.300	—	0.300	.32627	0.098
4/1/04	5.0	0.300	1.000	1.300	.30659	0.399
10/1/04	0.0	0.250	5.000	5.250	.28809	1.512
						$8.548

Note: $ in millions.

4. **How much interest expense did MEDIQ record when it made the first $500,000 interest payment on April 1, 1995?**

Interest expense is computed at the "effective" interest rate (6.42%) using the outstanding book value of the note ($8.547 million). In other words, the April 1, 1995 interest expense figure is:

$$\$8.547 \text{ million} \times 6.42\% = \$548{,}717$$

The difference between this amount and the $500,000 cash payment ($48,717) is recorded as amortization of the note discount.

5. **According to the footnote, the senior subordinated notes were issued with warrants which allow the holders to purchase up to 10% of the common stock of MEDIQ's subsidiary at a nominal price. How do these warrants affect the interest rate on the notes?**

The warrants represent a valuable option that gives note holders the opportunity to purchase stock at below market prices sometime in the future. Although it may be difficult to measure the exact value of the warrants, MEDIQ attached them to the subordinated notes so that the company would receive more cash at issuance than otherwise. Presumably, MEDIQ would have received less than $8.547 million for the notes had the warrants not been included. The company would still have been obligated to make the scheduled cash principal payments but at a higher effective interest rate. The net result is that by including the warrants, MEDIQ was able to reduce its effective interest rate to 6.42% from some higher amount.

6. **Does the company face any near-term cash flow problems as a consequence of its current borrowing?**

From the maturities table, we see the company is scheduled to repay $108.667 million of long-term debt in 1999. This amount is substantially higher than the scheduled debt payments for 1996 through 1998, so 1999 could be a critical cash flow year. The footnote also refers to covenant defaults and accelerated debt repayment, suggesting that MEDIQ may be experiencing cash flow problems in 1995.

Indeed, 1999 proved to be a difficult year for MEDIQ. The company defaulted on its long-term debt, and lenders accelerated the principal repayment dates. MEDIQ's 1999 annual report painted a bleak picture: "The company has incurred recurring losses from operations, has negative working capital, and a significant shareholders' deficiency. These conditions plus the [loan default] raise substantial doubt about the company's ability to continue as a going concern."

7. **In December 1995 the company renegotiated its revolving credit facility, extending the expiration date to December 1996, increasing the borrowing limit to $15 million, and reducing the interest rate by .5%. However, in September 1994 the company had to pay an additional 1% interest on its $100 million senior secured notes to obtain lender approval for a major equipment acquisition. Why did the company obtain a lower interest rate in one case but not in the other?**

There are several explanations for this difference in interest rate charges. The most obvious is that the company agreed to dedicate specific anticipated cash flows to repayment of the revolving credit facility. The footnote indicates that 50% of the net cash proceeds from the sale of discontinued operations and certain other assets would be used to reduce the revolver. This feature lowers the lender's credit risk exposure and, in return, the lender has lowered the company's interest rate on the debt. The senior secured notes do not contain this sort of cash "carve out" provision.

EXERCISES

E11–1 Finding the issue price

AICPA adapted

Akers Company sold bonds on July 1, 2001, with a face value of $100,000. These bonds are due in 10 years. The stated annual interest rate is 6% per year, payable semiannually on June 30 and December 31. These bonds were sold to yield 8%.

REQUIRED:

How much did these bonds sell for on July 1, 2001?

E11–2 Market price following a change in interest rates

By July 1, 2002 the market yield on the Akers Company bonds described in E11–1 had risen to 10%.

REQUIRED:

What was the market price of the bonds on July 1, 2002?

E11–3 Finding the discount at issuance

AICPA adapted

On January 1, 2001, when the market interest rate was 14%, Luba Corporation issued bonds in the face amount of $500,000, with interest at 12% payable semiannually. The bonds mature on December 31, 2010.

REQUIRED:

Calculate the bond discount at issuance. How much of the discount should be amortized by the effective interest method on July 1, 2001?

E11–4

Balance sheet value of a bond

AICPA adapted

On January 2, 2001 West Company issued 9% bonds in the amount of $500,000, which mature on December 31, 2010. The bonds were issued for $469,500 to yield 10%. Interest is payable annually on December 31. West uses the effective interest method of amortizing bond discounts.

REQUIRED:

In its June 30, 2001 balance sheet, what net amount should West report as bonds payable?

E11–5

Gain or loss at early retirement

AICPA adapted

On February 1, 1998 Davis Corporation issued 12%, $1,000,000 par, 10-year bonds for $1,117,000. Davis reacquired all of these bonds at 102% of par, plus accrued interest, on May 1, 2001 and retired them. The unamortized bond premium on that date was $78,000.

REQUIRED:

Before income taxes, what was Davis' gain or loss on the bond retirement?

E11–6

Amortizing a premium

AICPA adapted

Webb Company has outstanding a 7% annual, 10-year, $100,000 face-value bond that was issued by the company several years ago. The bond was originally sold to yield 6% annual interest. Webb uses the effective interest rate method to amortize the bond premium. On June 30, 2001 the carrying amount of the outstanding bond was $105,000.

REQUIRED:

What amount of unamortized premium on the bond should Webb report in its June 30, 2002 balance sheet?

E11–7

Loss contingencies

AICPA adapted

Brower Corporation owns a manufacturing plant in the country of Oust. On December 31, 2001 the plant had a book value of $5,000,000 and an estimated fair market value of $8,000,000. The government of Oust has clearly indicated that it will expropriate the plant during the coming year and will reimburse Brower for only 40% of the plant's estimated fair market value.

REQUIRED:

What journal entry should Brower make on December 31, 2001 to record the intended expropriation?

E11–8

Bonds sold at par

On January 1, 2001 Buckingham Corporation issued $10 million of 8% coupon bonds. The bonds pay interest semiannually on June 30 and December 31, and they mature in 10 years. They were issued to yield a market interest rate of 8%.

REQUIRED:

Compute the issue price of the bonds on January 1, 2001. Why is there no discount or premium to record?

E11–9

Debt-for-equity swap

On January 1, 2001 Tusk Corporation issued $100 million of 10% coupon bonds at par value. Interest is paid semiannually on June 30 and December 31 of each year. The bonds mature in 10 years. On January 1, 2004 the market yield on Tusk bonds is 14%.

REQUIRED:

1. What is the market value of the bonds on January 1, 2004?
2. Suppose Tusk retired the bonds on January 1, 2004 by exchanging common stock of equal value with bondholders. What journal entry would Tusk record to retire the bonds?

E11–10

Zero coupon bonds

Zero coupon bonds pay no interest—the only cash investors receive is the lump-sum principal payment at maturity. On January 1, 2001 The Ledge Inc. issued $250 million of zero coupon bonds at a market yield rate of 12%. The bonds mature in 20 years.

REQUIRED:

1. What was the January 1, 2001 issue price of these zero coupon bonds?
2. How much interest expense will The Ledge record on the bonds in 2001?

E11–11

Floating rate debt

On January 1, 2001 3Way Energy issued $200 million of 15-year floating rate debentures at par value. The debentures pay interest on June 30 and December 31 of each year. The floating interest rate is set equal to "LIBOR plus 6%" on January 1 of each year. The LIBOR was 6% when the bonds were issued and 8% on January 1, 2002.

REQUIRED:

1. How much cash interest did 3Way Energy pay on the debentures in 2001? How much will it pay in 2002?
2. How much interest expense did the company record on the debentures in 2001? How much will it record in 2002?

E11–12

Incentives for early debt retirement

On January 1, 2000 Roland Inc. issued $125 million of 8% coupon bonds at par. The bonds pay interest semiannually on June 30 and December 31 of each year, and they mature in 15 years. On December 31, 2001 (one day before the next interest payment is made), the bonds are trading at a market yield of 12% plus accrued interest.

REQUIRED:

1. Suppose Roland Inc. repurchased the entire $125 million bonds for cash at the market price on December 31, 2001. Using a 40% corporate tax rate, how much of a gain or loss would the company record on this transaction?
2. Why might the company want to retire the debt early?

E11–13

Off-balance sheet debt

Wood Company and Willie Inc. form a joint venture—Woodly Partners—to manufacture and distribute agricultural pesticides. Wood and Willie each contribute $20 million cash and receive 50% of Woodly's common stock. Woodly then borrows $200 million from a consortium of banks and uses the money to build its manufacturing and distribution facilities. The loan is made on December 31, 2001 and is fully guaranteed by both Wood and Willie.

REQUIRED:

How much of the $200 million debt shows up on the December 31, 2001 balance sheet of Wood Company? Why?

E11–14

Non–interest-bearing loan

McClelland Corporation agreed to purchase some landscaping equipment from Agri-Products for a cash price of $500,000. Before accepting delivery of the equipment, McClelland learned that the same equipment could be purchased from another dealer for $460,000. To avoid losing the sale, Agri-Products has offered McClelland a "no interest" payment plan—McClelland would pay $100,000 at delivery, $200,000 one year later, and the final $200,000 in two years.

REQUIRED:

1. McClelland would usually pay annual interest of 9% on a loan of this type. What is the present value of the Agri-Products loan at the delivery date?
2. What journal entry would McClelland make if it accepts the deal and buys from Agri-Products?
3. What should McClelland do?

E11–15

Understanding GAAP hedges

REQUIRED:

1. Which of the following qualifies as a hedged item?

   a. A company's work-in-process inventory of unfinished washers, dryers, and refrigerators.
   b. Credit card receivables at Sears, Roebuck and Company.
   c. Bushels of corn owned by the Farmers' Cooperative.
   d. Salaries payable to employees of Ford Motor Company.
   e. A three-year note issued by General Motors and payable in U.S. dollars.
   f. A three-year note issued by Daimler-Chrysler and payable in Euros.

2. Which of the following qualifies as a hedging instrument?

   a. An electricity futures contract purchased by Alliant Energy, an electrical power company.

b. A crop insurance contract purchased by Farmers' Cooperative that pays the co-op for crop losses from drought or flood.
c. An option to buy shares of common stock in Ford Motor Company.
d. An option to sell shares of common stock in General Motors.
e. A four-year lease for office space in downtown Toronto.

3. Which of the following qualifies as an eligible risk for hedge accounting?

   a. Alliant Energy's risk that summer demand for electricity may exceed the company's power generating capacity.
   b. Ford Motor Company's risk that not enough steel will be available in six months when the company must purchase steel to produce a new sports utility vehicle.
   c. The risk to American Express that its members won't pay their credit card bills.
   d. The risk to Farmers' Cooperative that corn mold will destroy its inventory of corn held in silos for sale next year.
   e. The possibility of changes in the exchange rate of U.S. dollars for Mexican pesos for Coca Cola Company, which has a major foreign investment in Mexico.

Problems/Discussion Questions

P11–1

Bonds issued at a discount

On July 1, 2001 McVay Corporation issued $15,000,000 of 10-year bonds with a coupon interest rate of 8%. The bonds pay interest semiannually on June 30 and December 31 of each year. The market rate of interest on July 1, 2001 for bonds of this type was 10%. McVay closes its books on December 31.

Required:

1. At what price were the bonds issued?
2. Using the effective interest method, prepare an amortization schedule showing interest expense, discount or premium amortization, and bond carrying value for each of the first four semiannual interest payment periods.
3. Prepare journal entries to record the first four semiannual interest payments.
4. How should the bonds be shown on McVay's December 31, 2001 balance sheet, and on its December 31, 2002 balance sheet?

P11–2

Bonds issued at a premium

On January 1, 2002 Fleetwood Inc. issued bonds with a face amount of $25 million and a coupon interest rate of 8%. The bonds mature in 10 years and pay interest semiannually on June 30 and December 31 of each year. The market rate of interest on January 1, 2002 for bonds of this type was 6%. Fleetwood closes its books on December 31.

Required:

1. At what price were the bonds issued?
2. Using the effective interest method, prepare an amortization schedule showing interest expense, amortization, and bond carrying value for each of the first four semiannual interest payment periods.
3. Prepare journal entries to record the first four semiannual interest payments.
4. How would the bonds be shown on Fleetwood's December 31, 2002 balance sheet, and on its December 31, 2003 balance sheet?

P11–3

Understanding the numbers

Cory Company needs to raise about $500,000 to finance the expansion of its office building. Three alternative loan arrangements are being considered:

- *Alternative A:* Issue a $500,000, 20-year bond with an interest rate of 10%.
- *Alternative B:* Issue a $700,000, 20-year bond with an interest rate of 6%.
- *Alternative C:* Issue a $400,000, 20-year bond with an interest rate of 12%.

Each bond pays interest annually. The market interest rate for bonds of this risk and duration is 9%, and the company needs to raise the money on January 1, 2002.

Required:

1. What is the issue price of each bond?
2. How much cash would the company have to pay out in 2002 for each bond?

3. For each alternative, how much interest expense would be recorded in 2003 and in 2008?
4. For each alternative, how much interest expense would Cory Company record over the entire 20-year life of the loan?
5. For each alternative, how much cash would Cory Company pay to bondholders over the entire 20-year life of the loan?
6. If Cory Company's marginal tax rate is 40%, which alternative do you recommend? Why?

P11–4

Call options as investments

On July 1, 2001 Stan Getz, Inc. bought call option contracts for 500 shares of Selmer Manufacturing common stock. The contracts cost $200, expire in 90 days, and have an exercise price of $40 per share. The market price of Selmer's stock that day was also $40 a share. On July 31, 2001 Selmer shares were trading at $38 a share and the fair value of the option contracts was $125—meaning that Getz could buy the identical $40 strike price contracts on July 31 for $125. On August 31, 2001 the market price of Selmer stock was $44 a share and the fair value of the options contracts was $2,075.

REQUIRED:

1. Prepare the journal entry to record Getz's purchase of call option contracts on July 1, 2001.
2. Prepare the journal entry to record the change in fair value of the option contracts on July 31, 2001.
3. Prepare the journal entry to record the change in fair value of the option contracts on August 31, 2001.
4. Why are the option contracts worth so much more on August 31 ($2,075) than they were worth on July 31 ($125)?
5. What entry would Getz make to record exercising the options on September 15, 2001 when Selmer's shares were trading at $46?
6. Suppose instead that Getz allowed the option contracts to expire on September 15, 2001 without exercising them. What entry would Getz then make?

P11–5

Put options as investments

On March 1, 2001 Kenton Company bought put option contracts for 500 shares of Rugolo Manufacturing common stock. The contracts cost $300, expire in 90 days, and have an exercise price of $50 per share. The market price of Rugolo's stock that day was also $50 a share. On March 31, 2001 Rugolo shares were trading at $52 a share and the fair value of the option contracts was $200—meaning that Kenton could buy the identical $50 strike price contracts on March 31 for $200. On April 30, 2001 the market price of Rugolo stock was $46 a share and the fair value of the options contracts was $2,100.

REQUIRED:

1. Prepare the journal entry to record Kenton's purchase of put option contracts on March 1, 2001.
2. Prepare the journal entry to record the change in fair value of the option contracts on March 31, 2001.
3. Prepare the journal entry to record the change in fair value of the option contracts on April 30, 2001.
4. Why are the option contracts worth so much more on April 30 ($2,100) than they were worth on March 31 ($200)?
5. What entry would Kenton make to record exercising the options on May 15, 2001 when Rugolo's shares were trading at $42?
6. Suppose instead that Kenton allowed the option contracts to expire on May 15, 2001 without exercising them. What entry would Kenton then make?

P11–6

Early debt retirement

On January 1, 2001 Tango-In-The-Night, Inc. issued $75,000,000 of bonds with a coupon interest rate of 9%. The bonds mature in 10 years and pay interest semiannually on June 30 and December 31 of each year. The market rate of interest on January 1, 2001 for bonds of this type was 11%. The company closes its books on December 31.

REQUIRED:

1. At what price were the bonds issued?
2. What is the book value of the bonds on January 1, 2003?

(continued)

3. On January 1, 2003 the market interest rate for bonds of this type is 10%. What is the market value of the bonds on this date?
4. Suppose the bonds were repurchased for cash on January 1, 2003 at the market price. If you ignore taxes, what journal entry would the company make to record the debt retirement?

P11–7

Partial debt retirement

On July 1, 2002 Mirage Company issued $250 million of bonds with a coupon interest rate of 8.5%. The bonds mature in 10 years and pay interest semiannually on June 30 and December 31 of each year. The market rate of interest on July 1, 2002 for bonds of this risk class was 7%. Mirage closes its books on December 31.

REQUIRED:

1. At what price were the bonds issued?
2. Using the effective interest method, prepare an amortization schedule showing interest expense, amortization, and bond carrying value for each of the first four semiannual payment periods.
3. Prepare journal entries to record the first four semiannual interest payments and related interest accruals.
4. On July 1, 2004 the market interest rate for bonds of this risk class is 8.0%. What is the market value of the bonds on this date?
5. Suppose 50% of the bonds were repurchased for cash on July 1, 2004 at the market price. If you ignore taxes, what journal entry would the company make to record this partial retirement?

P11–8

Chalk Hill: Interest-rate swap as a speculative investment

Exhibit 11.3 describes Chalk Hill's use of an interest-rate swap to hedge its cash flow exposure to interest rate risk from variable rate debt. The journal entries shown in the exhibit illustrate how special "hedge accounting" rules apply to the swap. Suppose instead that the swap *did not qualify* for special hedge accounting—but that all other aspects of the transaction remain as described in the exhibit. Prepare the journal entries needed to account for the variable-rate debt and swap transaction for January 1, 2001 through December 31, 2003.

P11–9

Sears: Reading the financials

Information taken from a recent Sears, Roebuck and Company annual report is shown below.

REQUIRED:

1. How much interest expense did the company record during 1992 on the 7% debentures? How much of the original issue discount was amortized during 1992?
2. How much interest expense did the company record during 1992 on the zero coupon bonds?
3. Suppose that interest payments on the participating mortgages are made on December 31 of each year. What journal entry did the company make in 1992 to recognize interest expense on this debt?
4. How much cash interest did the company pay out during 1992 on the 7% debentures and the zero coupon bonds?

	December 31	
Long-Term Debt ($ in millions)	**1992**	**1991**
7% Debentures, $300 million face value, due 2001, effective rate $14.6%	$ 188.6	$ 182.7
Zero coupon bonds, $500 million face value, due 1998, effective rate 12.0%	267.9	239.2
Participating mortgages, $850 million face value, due 2005, effective rate 8.7%, collateralized by Sears Tower and related properties	834.5	833.9
Various other long-term debt	12,444.2	16,329.2
Total long-term debt	$13,735.2	$17,585.0

Information taken from the Mead Corporation annual report is shown below.

P11–10

Reading the financials

STRETCH

REQUIRED:

1. How much interest expense did the company record during 1999 on the 8⅛% debentures? How much of the original issue discount was amortized during 1999?
2. How much interest expense did the company record during 1999 on the 6.60% notes? How much of the original issue discount was amortized during 1999?
3. What is the "weighted-average" effective interest rate on long-term debt at December 31, 1999?
4. If Mead calls the 8⅛% debentures at the beginning of 2003, how much cash will the company pay to debt holders?
5. If debt holders "put" the 6.84% debentures back to the company, how much cash will Mead pay out?

Long-Term Debt **December 31** ($ in millions)	**1999**	**1998**
Capital lease obligations	$ 287.4	$ 288.3
Variable-rate Industrial Development Revenue Bonds, due from 2001 through 2023, average effective rate 3.2%	165.4	165.4
8⅛% debentures, face amount of $150.0, due 2023 (effective rate 8.4%)	148.0	147.9
7⅛% debentures, face amount of $150.0, due 2025 (effective rate 7.4%)	147.3	147.2
7.35% debentures, face amount of $150.0, due 2017 (effective rate 7.4%)	148.6	148.5
6.84% debentures, face amount of $150.0, due 2037 (effective rate 7.0%)	148.4	148.2
7.55% debentures, face amount of $150.0, due 2047 (effective rate 7.7%)	143.7	143.6
6.60% notes, face amount of $100.0, due 2002 (effective rate 6.9%)	99.3	99.0
Medium-term notes, 7.3% to 9.8%, face amount of $78.5, due from 2000 through 2020 (effective rate 10.0%)	76.8	75.9
Other	3.9	11.3
	1,368.8	1,375.3
Less current portion	35.1	7.9
	$1,333.7	$1,367.4

The 8⅛% and 7⅛% debentures are callable by the company at approximately 103% beginning in 2003. The 6.84% debentures can be put to the company at par value in 2007. Maturities of long-term debt for the next five years are $35.1 million in 2000, $12.6 million in 2001, $135.3 million in 2002, $.7 million in 2003 and $6.7 million in 2004.

The following excerpts were taken from the 1996 annual report of Quaker Oats Company:

P11–11

Hedging

STRETCH

FOREIGN CURRENCY SWAPS.

In 1988 the Company swapped $15.0 million of long-term debt for 27.9 million in deutsche mark (DM) denominated long-term debt, effectively hedging part of the German net investment. . . . Due to the sale of the European pet food business in 1995, the net investment in Germany was reduced to the point where the DM swap was no longer effective as a net investment hedge, requiring any subsequent revaluation adjustments to be charged or credited to the consolidated income statement. To offset this charge or credit, the Company entered into a foreign exchange forward contract and the net effect on the consolidated income statements for 1996 and 1995 was not material. . . .

Commodity Options and Futures.

The Company uses commodity options and futures contracts to reduce its exposure to commodity price changes. The Company regularly hedges purchases of oats, corn, corn sweetener, wheat, coffee beans, and orange juice concentrate. Of the $2.81 billion in cost of goods sold, approximately $275 million to $325 million is in commodities that may be hedged. The Company's strategy is typically to hedge certain production requirements for various periods up to 12 months. As of December 31, 1996 and 1995, approximately 32% and 54%, respectively, of hedgeable production requirements for the next 12 months were hedged. . . .

Interest Rate Hedges.

The Company actively monitors its interest rate exposure. In 1995 the Company entered into interest rate swap agreements with a notional value of $150.0 million. The swap agreements were used to hedge fixed interest rate risk related to anticipated issuance of long-term debt. The swap agreements were subsequently terminated at a cost of $11.9 million as long-term debt was issued. Included in the consolidated balance sheets as of December 31, 1996 and 1995 were $8.9 million and $10.8 million, respectively, of prepaid interest expense as settlement of all the interest rate swap agreements. . . . In 1994 the Company entered into interest rate cap agreements with a notional value of $600.0 million to hedge floating interest rate risk. . . .

Required:

1. What did Quaker accomplish by swapping $15.0 million of its long-term debt for 27.9 million in deutsche mark (DM) denominated long-term debt?
2. Why was the DM swap "no longer effective" after Quaker sold its European pet food business?
3. What is a foreign exchange forward contract, and how can it be used to hedge a company's foreign currency exposure?
4. What are commodity options and futures contracts, and how do they reduce Quaker's exposure to commodity price changes?
5. What is an interest rate swap, and how can it reduce a company's exposure to interest rate risk?
6. What is an interest rate cap, and how is it used to reduce a company's exposure to interest rate changes?

P11–12
Callable bonds

On January 1, 2001 Merrill Corporation issued $2 million of par value 10-year bonds. The bonds pay interest semiannually on January 1 and July 1 at an annual rate of 10% and are callable at 102% of par. The bonds were issued to yield 8% annually.

Required:

1. Compute the issue price of the bonds.
2. Compute the amount of interest expense on the bonds for 2001, assuming the effective interest method is used.
3. Merrill uses the **indirect method** of computing cash flows from operations on its cash flow statement (see Chapter 4). How much will be added to or subtracted from reported net income in 2001 for these bonds to obtain cash flows from operations?
4. On January 1, 2002 the market yield on the bonds increased to 9%, and Merrill decided to retire the debt early. Indicate how much Merrill would save by exercising the call option rather than by purchasing the debt in the open market.
5. What entry would Merrill make on January 1, 2002 to record the bond retirement, assuming it exercises the call option?

P11–13

Working backward from an amortization table

Clovis Company recently issued $500,000 (face value) bonds to finance a new construction project. The company's chief accountant prepared the following bond amortization schedule:

Date	Interest Expense	Semiannual Payment	Premium Amortization	Net Liability
7/1/01				$540,554
12/31/01	$21,622	$25,000	($3,378)	537,176
6/30/02	21,487	25,000	(3,513)	533,663
12/31/02	21,347	25,000	(3,653)	530,010
6/30/03	21,200	25,000	(3,800)	526,210
12/31/03	21,048	25,000	(3,952)	522,258
6/30/04	20,890	25,000	(4,110)	518,148
12/31/04	20,726	25,000	(4,274)	513,874
6/30/05	20,555	25,000	(4,445)	509,429
12/31/05	20,377	25,000	(4,623)	504,806
6/30/06	20,194	25,000	(4,806)	500,000

REQUIRED:

1. Compute the discount or premium on the sale of the bonds, the semiannual coupon interest rate, and the semiannual effective interest rate.
2. The company's vice president of finance wants any discount (or premium) at issuance of the bonds to be recorded immediately as a loss (or gain) at the issue date. Do you agree with this approach? Why or why not?
3. On December 31, 2003 the net carrying value of the bonds is $522,258. In present value terms, what does this amount represent?
4. Suppose market interest rates were 6% semiannually on January 1, 2004, or 12.36% annually. (This 12.36% annual rate of interest is equal to the 6% semiannual rate, compounded: $0.1236 = [1.06 \times 1.06] - 1$.) What is the market price of the bond on that date? Is the company better off or worse off because of the interest rate change? Explain.

P11–14

How notes affect cash flows

On January 1, 2001 Prism Corporation issued $5 million of two-year, 10% per year notes. The market interest rate at issuance was 14%. Interest is payable semiannually on June 30 and December 31 of each year.

REQUIRED:

1. How much cash did the company receive by issuing the notes?
2. Prepare an amortization schedule showing interest expense, semiannual cash payments, amortization, and carrying value of the notes at each payment date to maturity.
3. Prepare journal entries to record issuance of notes; accrual and payment of interest on December 31, 2001; and payment of face value on maturity.
4. Describe how each of the following affects the company's cash flow statement: issuance of notes; payment of interest on December 31, 2001; and payment of face value on maturity.
5. Suppose the annual market interest rate falls to 10% on December 31, 2001. What is the market price of the notes on that date? Is the company better off or worse off because of the change in interest rates? Explain.

P11–15

Serial bonds

AICPA adapted

On January 1, 2001 MyKoo Corporation issued $1 million in five-year, 5% serial bonds to be repaid in the amount of $200,000 on January 1 of 2002, 2003, 2004, 2005 and 2006. Interest on the unpaid balance of the bonds is due at the end of each year. The bonds were sold to yield 6%.

REQUIRED:

1. Prepare a schedule showing the computation of the total amount received from the issuance of the serial bonds.
2. Prepare a schedule of amortization of the bond discount through 2006 using the effective interest rate method.

P11–16 **Discount and premium amortization**

The following information appeared in the 1999 annual report of Rumours, Inc.:

LONG-TERM DEBT:

$10 million 10% coupon bonds issued on January 1, 1996 and due on December 31, 2000. The prevailing market interest rate on January 1, 1996 was 12%, and the bonds pay interest on June 30 and December 31 of each year.

$10 million 10% coupon bonds issued January 1, 1997 and due on December 31, 2001. The prevailing market interest rate on January 1, 1997 was 8%, and the bonds pay interest on June 30 and December 31 of each year.

REQUIRED:

1. The carrying value of each bond is shown in the following (incomplete) table. Calculate the missing values.

	Carrying Value	
	December 31, 1998	December 31, 1999
10% bonds due in 2000	$9,653,550	?
10% bonds due in 2001	?	$10,362,950

2. How much interest expense did Rumours record in 1999 on the bond due in 2000?
3. How much interest expense did Rumours record in 1999 on the bond due in 2001?

P11–17 **Loss contingencies**

The following information appeared in the annual reports of Apparel America, Borden, Inc., and Exxon Corporation.

APPAREL AMERICA, INC.

In December 1994 the Company entered into an agreement to pay $460,000 to a former executive in settlement of certain litigation. According to the terms of the agreement, an initial payment of $150,000 was made in December 1994, with the balance payable in five semiannual installments of $50,000 commencing June 30, 1995 and a final payment of $60,000 on December 31, 1997. The settlement has been discounted at an annual effective interest rate of 9% to reflect its present value at July 31, 1996.

BORDEN, INC.

The Company and Combined Companies, like others in similar businesses, is subject to extensive Federal, state and local environmental laws and regulations. Although Company and Combined Companies environmental policies and practices are designed to ensure compliance with these laws and regulations, future developments and increasingly stringent regulation could require the Company and Combined Companies to make additional unforeseen environmental expenditures.

Accruals for environmental matters are recorded when it is probable that a liability has been incurred and the amount of the liability can be reasonably estimated. Environmental accruals are routinely reviewed on an interim basis as events and developments warrant and are subjected to a comprehensive review annually during the fiscal fourth quarter. The Company and the Combined Companies have each accrued approximately $22 at December 31, 1999, for probable environmental remediation and restoration liabilities. These liabilities at December 31, 1998, totaled approximately $20. This is management's best estimate of these liabilities. Based on currently available information and analysis, the Company believes that it is reasonably possible that costs associated with such liabilities may exceed current reserves by amounts that may prove insignificant, or by amounts, in the aggregate, of up to approximately $13.

EXXON CORPORATION.
A number of lawsuits, including class actions, have been brought in various courts against Exxon Corporation and certain of its subsidiaries relating to the release of crude oil from the tanker Exxon Valdez in 1989. Most of these lawsuits seek unspecified compensatory and punitive damages; several lawsuits seek damages in varying specified amounts. Certain of the lawsuits seek injunctive relief. The claims of many individuals have been dismissed or settled. Most of the remaining actions are scheduled for trial in federal court commencing May 2, 1994. Other actions will likely be tried in state court later in 1994. The cost to the corporation from these lawsuits is not possible to predict; however, it is believed that the final outcome will not have a materially adverse effect upon the corporation's operations or financial condition.

REQUIRED:

1. What is a loss contingency, and why is it disclosed in financial statements? Which of the preceding examples represents a loss contingency?
2. What was the December 1994 present value of Apparel America's settlement with its former executive? What is the July 31, 1996 present value, and where is it shown in the financial statements?
3. Borden has a $22 million liability on its 1999 balance sheet for "probable environmental remediation and restoration." But the company says actual remediation and restoration costs could be up to $13 million more than this amount. Why doesn't Borden's balance sheet liability include the additional $13 million?
4. Why doesn't Exxon report a dollar amount for its litigation case like the one reported by Apparel America?
5. Does the lack of a specific dollar amount in Exxon's case mean that stock analysts will just ignore the litigation when valuing the company? Why or why not?

P11–18

Floating-rate debt

On January 1, 2001 Nicks Corporation issued $250 million of floating rate debt. The debt carries a contractual interest rate of "LIBOR plus 5.5%" and this rate is reset annually on January 1 of each year. The LIBOR rates on January 1, 2001, January 1, 2002, and January 1, 2003 were 6.5%, 7.0%, and 5.5%, respectively.

REQUIRED:

1. Prepare a journal entry to record the issuance of the bonds on January 1, 2001 at par. What was the effective (or market) interest rate when the bonds were issued?
2. Prepare a journal entry to record interest expense for 2001, 2002, and 2003. Assume that interest is paid annually on December 31.
3. What is the market value of the debt at December 31, 2003 assuming there has been no change in the credit risk of Nicks Corporation.

P11–19

Unconditional purchase obligations

STRETCH

The following information appeared in the 1996 annual report of Lyondell Petrochemical Company, a manufacturer of petrochemicals and refined petroleum products such as gasoline, heating oil, jet fuel, aromatics, and lubricants:

The Company is party to various unconditional purchase obligation contracts as a purchaser for products and services. At December 31, 1996, future minimum payments under these contracts with noncancelable contract terms in excess of one year were as follows ($ in millions):

1997	$ 35
1998	34
1999	33
2000	33
2001	31
Thereafter	155
Total minimum payments	$321

REQUIRED:

1. Suppose the company was obligated to purchase $31 million per year in 2002 and each of the next four years. If Lyondell's normal rate of interest for a 10-year loan is 9%, what is the present value of the company's purchase commitments?
2. The company's 1996 balance sheet shows long-term debt of $1,194 million and shareholders' equity of $431 million. The unconditional purchase obligation is not shown on the balance sheet. What impact would including the present value of unconditional purchase obligations as part of long-term debt have on the company's 1996 ratio of long-term debt to shareholders' equity?
3. Why are unconditional purchase obligations an "off-balance sheet" liability? Why might some companies prefer to keep the purchase commitment off the balance sheet?

P11–20

Debt-for-debt swaps

STRETCH

On January 1, 1991 Chain Corporation issued $5 million of 7% coupon bonds at par. The bonds mature in 20 years and pay interest semiannually on June 30 and December 31 of each year. On December 31, 2001 the market interest rate for bonds of similar risk was 14%, and the market value of Chain Corporation bonds (after the December 31 interest payment) was $3,146,052.

Although the company's books are not yet closed for the year, a preliminary estimate shows net income to be $500,000. This amount is substantially below the $3 million management had expected the company to earn. The company has long-term debt totaling $7.5 million (including the $5 million bond issue) and shareholders' equity of $12.5 million (including the $500,000 of estimated net income). This means the company's long-term debt-to-equity ratio is 60%.

Unfortunately, a covenant in one of the company's loan agreements requires a long-term debt-to-equity ratio of 55% or less. Violating this covenant gives lenders the right to demand immediate repayment of the loan principal. Worse yet, a "cross default" provision in the $5 million bond makes it immediately due and payable if the company violates any of its lending agreements.

Since the company does not have the cash needed to repurchase the bonds, management is considering a debt-for-debt exchange in which the outstanding 7% bonds would be replaced by new 14% bonds with a face amount of $3.2 million. The interest rate on the new bonds is equal to the market interest rate.

REQUIRED:

1. Prepare a journal entry to record the swap on December 31, 2001. (Any gain or loss to the company would be taxed at 35%, and the tax should be included in your entry.)
2. What would the company's debt-to-equity ratio be after the swap?
3. What impact would the transaction have on net income for the year?
4. How else could management have avoided violation of the loan covenant?

P11–21

Zero coupon bonds

STRETCH

The following information was taken from the financial statements of ALZA Corporation.

NOTE 2: DEBT OBLIGATIONS AND OTHER LIABILITIES

In December 1990, ALZA completed a public offering of zero coupon convertible subordinated debentures. The 20-year debentures, due December 2010, will have a principal amount at maturity of $862.5 million. The debentures were issued at a price of $229.34 per $1,000 principal amount at maturity, resulting in an initial obligation to ALZA of $197.806 million. The yield to maturity is 7½% per annum, computed on a semiannual basis, and the notes have no periodic interest payments. Each debenture is convertible, at the option of the holder, into 4.326 shares of ALZA Class A Common Stock. The debentures will be purchased by ALZA, at the option of the holder, on December 21, 1995, December 21, 2000, or December 21, 2005 at purchase prices equal to the issue price plus accreted original issue discount to such purchase date. ALZA, at its option, may elect to deliver either stock or cash in the event of any conversion or purchase of the debentures. The debentures are listed for trading on the American Stock Exchange. In connection with the offering, ALZA incurred underwriting fees and other costs of $5.934 million, which are included in other assets and are being amortized over the term of the debentures.

REQUIRED:

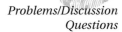

1. ALZA issued zero coupon debentures with a total maturity value of $862.5 million for a total price of $197.806 million. The company had debt issuance costs of $5.934 million. Show how the issue price was calculated.
2. If you purchased these debentures at the issue date, what is your annualized expected rate of return?
3. Reproduce the journal entries on ALZA's book for these debentures over the 1990–1993 period. For each *cash entry,* identify whether the cash increase or decrease represents an operating, investing, or financing activity. Do you agree with ALZA's classification of these cash entries in the cash flow statement shown below?
4. ALZA had debt issuance costs of $5.934 million dollars. According to *FASB Concept Statement No. 6* ("Elements of Financial Statements"), "[d]ebt issuance cost in effect reduces the proceeds of borrowing and increases the effective interest rate and thus may be accounted for the same as debt discount" (para. 237). Does the way in which ALZA accounts for debt issue costs achieve this result?

ALZA CORPORATION

Consolidated Statement of Cash Flows

	Years Ended December 31			
($ in thousands)	1993	1992	1991	1990
Cash flows from operating activities				
Net income (loss)	$45,612	$72,170	$(62,076)	$ 24,654
Noncash adjustments				
Depreciation and Amortization	(amounts not reproduced)			
Interest on 7½% zero coupon convertible subordinated debentures	14,912	15,746	15,002	412
....				
Total adjustments	30,623	24,395	81,667	(1,395)
Net cash provided by operating activities	$76,235	$96,565	$ 19,591	$ 23,259
Cash flows from financing activities				
Redemption of 7½% zero coupon convertible subordinated debentures	$(243,878)	-0-	-0-	$191,872

P11–22

Comprehensive problem on bond premium

On July 1, 2001 LekTech Corporation issued $20 million of 12%, 20-year bonds. Interest on the bonds is paid semiannually on December 31 and June 30 of each year, and the bonds were issued at a market interest rate of 8%.

REQUIRED:

1. Compute the issue price of the bonds on July 1, 2001.
2. Prepare an amortization schedule that shows interest expense, premium or discount amortization, bond carrying value, and cash interest payment for each interest payment period through December 31, 2006.
3. Prepare the journal entries to record all interest expense and all cash interest payments for 2002.
4. A new employee in the accounting group at LekTech has asked you to explain why interest expense on the bond changes each year. Write a two-paragraph memo that helps the employee understand interest recognition for this bond.
5. LekTech used the proceeds of the bond to construct a new manufacturing facility near Waterloo, Iowa. The company will make taillight lenses for tractors manufactured by Deere & Company at its Waterloo plant. In fact, Deere has signed a letter guaranteeing payment of the LekTech bonds. How is the guarantee shown in Deere's financial statements?

6. On January 1, 2007 the company exercised a call provision in the debenture agreement and redeemed 40% of the bonds at 105% of par. What journal entry did the company make to record this partial redemption?
7. The market yield for the bonds on January 1, 2007 was 10%. How much less did the company pay to retire bonds using the call provision than it would have paid using an open market purchase?

P11–23
Hedging a Purchase Commitment (TL)

Silverado Inc. buys titanium from a supplier who requires a six-month firm commitment on all purchases. On January 1, 2001 Silverado signs a contract with the supplier to purchase 10,000 pounds of titanium at the current forward rate of $310 per pound with settlement on June 30, 2001. However, Silverado wants to actually pay the June 30 market price for titanium. To achieve this goal, the company enters into a forward contract to sell 10,000 pounds of titanium at the current forward price of $310 per unit. The firm commitment contract and the forward contract both have zero value at inception. Titanium spot prices and the contract fair values are:

			Contract Fair Value	
	Spot Price	Forward Price (June 30)	Forward	Firm Commitment
January 1, 2001	$300	$310	0	0
March 31, 2001	292	297	$128,079	($128,079)
June 30, 2001	285	n.a.	250,000	(250,000)

REQUIRED:

1. Why did Silverado hedge its firm commitment with the supplier? After the fact, was it a good idea to do so?
2. What journal entries are made when the two contracts are signed on January 1, 2001?
3. Silverado designates the forward contract as a fair value hedge of its future titanium purchase. What journal entries are made on March 31, 2001?
4. What journal entries are made on June 30, 2001 when the contracts are settled and Silverado pays for the titanium?

P11–24
Hedging a Planned Sale (TL)

Newton Grains plans to sell 100,000 bushels of corn from its current inventory in March 2002. The company paid $1 million for the corn during the fall 2001 harvest season. On October 1, 2001 Newton writes a forward contract to sell 100,000 bushels of corn on March 15, 2002 for $1,100,000. The forward contract has zero value at inception. On December 31, 2001 the March forward price for corn is $1,050,000 and the forward contract has a fair value of $95,000. On March 15, 2002 Newton sells the corn for $1,075,000 and settles the forward contract (now valued at $25,000).

REQUIRED:

1. Why did Newton hedge its planned sale of corn? Was it a good idea to do so?
2. Newton designates the forward contract as a cash flow hedge of its exposure to corn price fluctuations. What journal entries are made when the forward contract is signed on October 1, 2001?
3. What journal entries are made on December 31, 2001?
4. What journal entries are made on March 15, 2002 when the forward contract is settled and Newton sells the corn?
5. How would your original journal entries change if the forward contract covered only 50,000 bushels of corn? (Contract fair values would then have been $47,500 on December 31, 2001 and $12,500 on March 15, 2002.)

P11–25
Interest-rate swap as a cash flow hedge
STRETCH

Basie Business Forms borrowed $5 million on July 1, 2001 from First Kansas City Bank. The loan required annual interest payments at the LIBOR rate, reset annually each June 30. The loan principal is due in five years. The LIBOR rate for the first year is 6.0%.

Basie decided to swap its variable-interest payments for fixed-interest payments of 6.0%. Basie will pay 6.0% interest to the swap counterparty—Quincy Bank & Trust—and receive LIBOR payments based on a $5 million notional amount for the entire five-year term of the original loan. The swap has no value at its inception on July 1, 2001.

Basie designates the swap as a hedge of its cash flow exposure to interest rate risk on its variable-rate debt. The hedge is fully effective because the key terms of the loan and swap are identical. The variable rate was reset to 6.25% on June 30, 2002 and to 5.75% on June 30, 2003. Basie uses a June 30 fiscal year-end and records interest expense annually.

REQUIRED:

1. How much is the net cash settlement that Basie will pay to (or receive from) Quincy Bank & Trust on July 1, 2002? On July 1, 2003?
2. How much cash will Basie pay to First Kansas City Bank on July 1, 2002? On July 1, 2003?
3. On June 30, 2002 the swap had a fair value of $40,000 based on dealer quotes. Prepare journal entries to record Basie's cash interest payments and receipts, and interest expense for the year ended June 30, 2002.
4. On June 30, 2003 the swap had a fair value of ($28,000), a negative amount. Prepare journal entries to record Basie's cash interest payments and receipts, and interest expense for the year ended June 30, 2003.

P11–26

Interest-rate swap as a fair value hedge

STRETCH

On January 1, 2001 Four Brothers Manufacturing borrowed $10 million from Guiffrie Bank by signing a three-year 8.0% fixed-rate note. The note calls for interest to be paid annually on December 31. The company then entered into an interest-rate swap agreement with Herman Bank. The agreement is that Four Brothers will receive from Herman a fixed-rate interest payment of 8.0% based on a $10 million notional amount each December 31 for three years. Four Brothers will pay Herman a variable LIBOR rate reset every December 31. The LIBOR rate for the first year is 8.0%.

Four Brothers designates the swap as a hedge of its fair value exposure to interest rate risk on its fixed-rate note. The hedge is fully effective because the key terms of the note and swap are identical. The variable rate was reset to 8.25% on December 31, 2001 and to 7.75% on December 31, 2002. Four Brothers uses a December 31 year-end and records interest expense annually.

REQUIRED:

1. How much is the net cash settlement that Four Brothers will pay to (or receive from) Herman Bank on December 31, 2001? On December 31, 2002?
2. How much cash will Four Brothers pay to Guiffrie Bank December 31, 2001? On December 31, 2002?
3. On December 31, 2001 the swap had a fair value of ($45,000), a negative amount, and the fair value of the $10 million note was $9,955,000. Prepare journal entries to record Four Brothers' cash interest payments and receipts, and interest expense for the year ended December 31, 2001.
4. On December 31, 2002 the swap had a fair value of $23,000, and the fair value of the $10 million note was $10,023,000. Prepare journal entries to record Four Brothers' cash interest payments and receipts, and interest expense for the year ended December 31, 2002.

P11–27

Hedge effectiveness

STRETCH

Recall the Rombaurer Metals example described in the chapter: On October 5, 2001 Rombaurer has 10 million pounds of copper inventory on hand at an average cost of $0.65 a pound. The spot price for copper is $0.90 a pound. Instead of selling copper now, Rombaurer decides to hold on to the inventory until February 2002 when management believes the price will return to a normal level of $0.95 a pound. To hedge its position, Rombaurer sells futures contracts at $0.95 for February delivery. Spot and futures prices over the next several months are as follows:

COMEX Copper Prices

	Spot Price	February 2002 Futures Price
October 5, 2001	$0.90	$0.95
December 31, 2001	0.85	0.91
February 26, 2002	0.94	0.94

On February 26, 2002 Rombaurer sells its copper on the spot market for $0.94 a pound and cancels the futures contracts.

The chapter described how "hedge accounting" rules are used when Rombaurer hedges its entire 10 million pounds of copper inventory.

REQUIRED:

1. Suppose Rombaurer sells futures contracts for only 5 million pounds of copper. (Management had decided that it is prudent to only hedge half of the company's economic exposure.) The margin requirement on these contracts is $140,000. Because the futures contracts are now "ineffective" in hedging the company's entire fair value exposure to copper price fluctuations, Rombaurer cannot use "hedge accounting." Prepare all journal entries needed to account for the futures contracts and sale of copper from October 5, 2001 through February 26, 2002.
2. Now assume that Rombaurer designates these futures contracts as a "fully effective" hedge of its risk exposure for 5 million pounds of copper inventory. (The remaining 5 million pounds of inventory is not being hedged.) Rombaurer can now use "hedge accounting" for the futures contracts. Prepare all journal entries needed to account for the futures contracts and sale of copper from October 5, 2001 through February 26, 2002.
3. What impact does changing the definition of the hedged item (10 million pounds of copper inventory versus 5 million pounds) have on the company's financial statements for 2001 and 2002?

CASES

C11–1

Risk management

The following information was taken from the 2000 annual report of H.J. Heinz Company:

INTEREST RATE SWAP AGREEMENTS

The company may utilize interest rate swap agreements to lower funding costs or to alter interest rate exposure. Amounts paid or received on interest rate swap agreements are deferred and recognized as adjustments to interest expense. Gains and losses realized upon the settlement of such contracts are deferred and amortized to interest expense over the remaining term of the debt instrument or are recognized immediately if the underlying instrument is settled.

FOREIGN CURRENCY CONTRACTS

The company enters into forward, purchased option and swap contracts to hedge transactions denominated in foreign currencies in order to reduce the currency risk associated with fluctuating exchange rates. Such contracts are used primarily to hedge certain intercompany cash flows, purchases and sales of certain raw materials and finished goods and for payments arising from certain foreign currency denominated obligations. Realized and unrealized gains and losses from instruments qualifying as hedges are deferred as part of the cost basis of the underlying transaction. Realized and unrealized gains and losses from foreign currency contracts used as economic hedges but not qualifying for hedge accounting are recognized currently in miscellaneous income and expense.

COMMODITY CONTRACTS

In connection with purchasing certain commodities for future manufacturing requirements, the company enters into commodities futures and option contracts, as deemed appropriate, to reduce the effect of price fluctuations. Such contracts are accounted for as hedges, with gains and losses recognized as part of cost of products sold, and generally have a term of less than one year.

REQUIRED:

1. How does an interest-rate swap reduce market risk?
2. Suppose Heinz only has fixed-rate debt. Is the company's interest-rate swap a cash flow hedge or a fair value hedge? Explain.
3. Why are gains and losses on settlement of the interest-rate swaps recognized immediately when the underlying instrument is settled?
4. How does a foreign currency forward contract reduce market risk from the sale of finished goods?
5. Why are some foreign currency hedge gains and losses "deferred" while others are "recognized currently" in income?
6. Explain the advantage of an option over a futures contract for reducing the market risk of a future commodity purchase.
7. Is the company's commodities futures contract a cash flow hedge or a fair value hedge? Explain.

C11–2

Tuesday Morning Corporation (CW): Interpreting long-term debt disclosures

Tuesday Morning Corporation operates a chain of 246 discount retail stores in 32 states. The company purchases close-out merchandise at prices generally ranging from 10% to 50% of the normal wholesale price and sells the merchandise at prices that are 50% to 80% lower than retail prices generally charged by department and specialty stores.

Appearing next is information taken from Tuesday Morning's 1994 annual report.

Note 5: Mortgages on Property, Plant, and Equipment

($ in thousands)	1994	1993
Industrial development bond, payable in quarterly installments of $108 plus interest at 91.656% of prime (not to exceed 15%), maturing March 31, 1998;	$1,401	$1,834
Payable to bank, payable in quarterly installments of $104 plus interest at LIBOR plus 2.50%, maturing September 30, 1997, with remaining principal due at that time;	4,504	4,920
Payable to bank, payable in quarterly installments of $112 plus interest at LIBOR plus 2.50% through October 15, 1994, with the remaining principal and interest due April 30, 1995;	1,794	2,243

In connection with these mortgages, the Company is required to maintain minimum net worth and comply with other financial covenants, including a restriction limiting loans to officers to less than $2,000,000. At December 31,1994 the Company is in compliance with these covenants.

The $1,794,000 note payable to bank due on April 30, 1995 is classified as a current liability at December 31, 1994. The aggregate maturities of mortgages are as follows ($ in thousands):

Year	Amount
1995	$2,747
1996	849
1997	4,003
1998	100

Consolidated Balance Sheet ($ in thousands)	**1994**	**1993**
Current liabilities:		
Current installments on mortgages	$ 2,747	$ 1,402
Current installments on capital lease obligation	607	-0-
Accounts payable	12,916	15,859
Accrued sales tax	1,574	1,760
Other accrued expenses	1,945	3,118
Deferred income taxes	303	146
Due to officer	-0-	599
Income taxes payable	988	-0-
Total current liabilities	$21,080	$22,884

Consolidated Statement of Cash Flows ($ in thousands)	**1994**	**1993**
Cash flows from financing activities:		
Net increase (decrease) in notes payable	-0-	($3,500)
Principal payments on mortgages	($1,298)	(1,194)
Principal payments under capital lease obligation	(214)	-0-
Proceeds from common stock offering	-0-	-0-
Proceeds from exercise of common stock options	255	145
Repurchase of common stock	-0-	(3,383)
Net cash provided by (used in) financing activities	($1,257)	($7,932)

REQUIRED:

1. What was the *current portion* of Tuesday Morning's mortgage payable at the end of fiscal 1993?
2. How much did Tuesday Morning pay in cash to reduce its mortgage payable during 1994?
3. Explain the difference between your answer to (1) and your answer to (2).
4. What are the components of the current portion of the mortgage payable as of the end of fiscal 1994?
5. Assume the next quarterly installment on the industrial development bond is due on March 31, 1995. Prepare a journal entry to record the installment payment and any interest. Assume the effective interest rate for the bond is 14% per year.
6. The company has a mortgage note payable for $1,794,000 that comes due on April 30, 1995. Suppose that this note is paid by the signing of a new 14% note for the amount due. Prepare the April 30, 1995 journal entry to record this refinancing of the old note.
7. Instead of refinancing the note, suppose the company pays the principal along with any remaining interest on April 30, 1995. Prepare a journal entry to record this cash payment.

C11–3

Delhaize American, Inc. (CW): Fair value disclosure of long-term debt

Delhaize American, Inc. operates retail supermarkets in the Southeastern and Mid-Atlantic regions of the United States. The company's stores sell a wide variety of groceries, produce, meats, dairy products, seafood, frozen food, and deli/bakery items; and nonfood articles such as health and beauty aids and other household and personal products. The company offers nationally and regionally advertised brand name merchandise as well as products manufactured and packaged for the company under the private label of "Food Lion" and "Kash n' Karry."

The following information appeared as a footnote to the company's 1999 annual report:

6. Long-Term Debt

Long-term debt consists of the following:

($ in thousands)	1999	1998
Medium-term notes, due from 2000 to 2006 Interest ranges from 8.40% to 8.73%	$123,300	$150,300
Debt securities, 7.55%, due 2007	150,000	150,000
Debt securities, 8.05%, due 2027	150,000	150,000
Mortgage payables due from 2000 through 2011 Interest ranges from 7.50% to 9.30%	5,148	19,029
Other	1,316	2,952
	429,764	472,281
Less current portion	2,834	42,518
	$426,930	$429,763

At January 1, 2000, $10.7 million (net book value) in property was pledged as collateral for mortgage payables. At January 1, 2000 and January 2, 1999, the Company estimated that the fair value of its long-term debt was approximately $413.6 million and $522.0 million, respectively. The fair value of the Company's long-term debt is estimated based on the current rates offered to the Company for debt with the same remaining maturities.

REQUIRED:

1. How much would Delhaize American have to pay to retire all of its long-term debt at the end of 1999 by purchasing the debt in the market?
2. Prepare a journal entry to record the open market purchase and retirement of the company's long-term debt at the end of 1999.
3. How would the gain or loss on retirement be shown on the company's 1999 income statement? What impact would the retirement have on net income for 2000?
4. At the end of 1996, the company had $495 million of long-term debt outstanding. The fair market value of the debt was $536 million. Prepare a journal entry to record the open market purchase and retirement of the company's long-term debt at the end of 1996.
5. Suppose the company could instead retire all of its 1996 long-term debt at 103% of par using a call provision. How would this approach affect the company's 1996 income statement?
6. Some of the company's debt is collateralized by property, plant, and equipment (PP&E). What does this mean? Why might bondholders prefer such an arrangement? Why might management agree? In what industries are you likely to see "collateralized" loans?

C11–4

ShopKo Stores Inc. (CW): Comprehensive case on long-term debt

ShopKo Stores Inc. is a leading regional discount store chain operating 109 retail stores in 13 states. ShopKo stores carry a wide selection of branded and private label nondurable "hardline" goods—housewares, music/videos, health and beauty aids, toys, and sporting goods—and "softline" goods such as home textiles, men's, women's, and children's apparel, shoes, jewelry, cosmetics, and accessories. In addition, 106 of the company's stores include pharmacy departments and 99 include optical departments.

Appearing next is information taken from ShopKo's 1993 annual report.

C. Long-term obligations and leases

($ in thousands)	February 27, 1993	February 29, 1992
Senior unsecured notes, 8.50% due March 15, 2002, less unamortized discount of $332	$ 99,668	$ –
Senior unsecured notes, 9.25% due March 15, 2022, less unamortized discount of $556	99,444	–
Industrial revenue bond, 6.40% due May 1, 2008	1,000	1,000
Capital lease obligations	9,632	10,417
	209,744	11,417
Less current portion	822	786
Long-term obligations	$208,922	$10,631

On March 12, 1992, the Company issued $100 million 8.50% senior unsecured notes due March 15, 2002 and $100 million 9.25% senior unsecured notes due March 15, 2022 in the public bond market. The notes provide for semiannual interest payments payable on June 15 and December 15 of each year. There is no sinking fund requirement and the notes are not redeemable prior to maturity.

The notes contain certain covenants which, among other things, restrict the ability of the Company to consolidate, merge or convey, transfer or lease its properties and assets . . . to create liens or to enter into sale and leaseback transactions.

The net proceeds of $197.1 million, after underwriting and issuance costs, were used to repay the outstanding borrowings under the Company's credit agreement with SUPERVALU of $181.2 million, with the remainder being used for working capital and other general corporate purposes. The underwriting and issuance costs are being amortized over the terms of the related notes, using the straight-line method. At February 27, 1993, $1.8 million remained to be amortized over future periods. Amortized expense for these costs for fiscal 1993 was $.1 million.

H. Fair values of financial instruments

The following disclosure is made in accordance with the requirements of SFAS No. 107, "Disclosures about Fair Value of Financial Instruments." The following methods and assumptions were used by the Company in estimating its fair value disclosures for financial instruments.

Cash, accounts receivable and accounts payable: The carrying amounts of these items are a reasonable estimate of their fair value.

Short-term debt and long-term obligations: The carrying amounts of the Company's borrowings under its short-term revolving credit agreements approximate their fair value. The fair values of the Company's long-term obligations are estimated using discounted cash flow analysis based on interest rates that are currently available to the Company for issuance of debt with similar terms and remaining maturities.

The carrying amounts and fair values of the Company's financial instruments at February 27, 1993 are as follows:

($ in thousands)	Carrying Amount	Fair Value
Short-term debt	$15,025	$15,025
Long-term obligations		
Senior unsecured notes, due March 15, 2002	99,668	105,757
Senior unsecured notes, due March 15, 2022	99,444	107,341
Industrial revenue bond, due May 1, 2005	1,000	1,000

REQUIRED:

1. How much long-term debt was issued during the year ended February 27, 1993?
2. Prepare a journal entry to record the long-term debt issued during that year.
3. How much of the discount or premium (state which) on long-term debt was amortized during that year?
4. What did the company do with the cash it received from the long-term debt it issued during the year ended February 27, 1993?
5. How much would ShopKo have to pay to retire all of its 9.25% senior unsecured notes as of February 27, 1993 by purchasing the notes in the open market? Prepare a journal entry to record the purchase and retirement of the notes on that date.

C11–5

Coca-Cola Company (CW): Using long-term debt footnotes

The following information is from Coca-Cola Company's 1997 annual report:

6. Long-term Debt ($ in millions)	**1996**	**1995**
7¾% U.S. dollar notes due 1996	$ 0	$ 250
5¾% Japanese yen notes due 1996	0	292
5¾% German mark notes due 1998	161	175
7⅞% U.S. dollar notes due 1998	250	250
6% U.S. dollar notes due 2000	251	252
6⅝% U.S. dollar notes due 2002	150	149
6% U.S. dollar notes due 2003	150	150
7⅜% U.S. dollar notes due 2093	116	116
Other, due 1997 to 2013	47	59
	1,125	1,693
Less current portion	9	552
	$1,116	$1,141

Interest paid was approximately $100 million, $25 million, and $97 million, in 1996, 1995, and 1994, respectively. Maturities of long-term debt for the five years after 1996 (i.e., 1997–2001) are as follows ($ in millions): $9, $422, $16, $257, and $2.

REQUIRED:

1. How much of Coca-Cola's long-term debt is due in 1997?
2. How much of Coca-Cola's long-term debt is due in each of the next five years (1997–2001)?
3. Why might financial analysts be interested in these scheduled debt payments? What options does the company have with regard to making its payments?
4. Compute the company's effective interest rate for 1996.
5. What will the company's interest expense be for 1997?
6. Why does Coca-Cola have loans in U.S. dollars, Japanese yen, and German marks?

The company's 1999 annual report contained the following information about long-term debt:

Note 6: Long-Term Debt (in millions)	**1999**	**1998**
6% U.S. dollar notes due 2000	$ 250	$251
$6\frac{5}{8}$% U.S. dollar notes due 2002	150	150
6% U.S. dollar notes due 2003	150	150
$5\frac{3}{4}$% U.S. dollar notes due 2009	399	0
$7\frac{3}{8}$% U.S. dollar notes due 2093	116	116
Other, due 2000 to 2013	50	23
	1,115	690
Less current portion	261	3
	$ 854	$687

Total interest paid was approximately $314 million, $298 million and $264 million in 1999, 1998 and 1997, respectively. Maturities of long-term debt for the five years succeeding December 31, 1999, are as follows (in millions):

2000	**2001**	**2002**	**2003**	**2004**
$261	$22	$154	$153	$1

7. Has the company's weighted-average interest rate increased or decreased since 1996? Why?
8. The company no longer has any Japanese yen or German mark borrowing. Why might the company have decided to eliminate these types of borrowings?
9. Approximately $261 million of long-term debt is due in 2000. Describe how the company might obtain the cash needed to make this payment.

12

Financial Reporting for Leases

Humans have three basic needs: (1) food, (2) shelter, and (3) keeping debt off the balance sheet.

—Author unknown

LEARNING OBJECTIVES:

After studying this chapter, you will understand:

1. The difference between capital leases and operating leases.
2. The incentives lessees have to keep leases off the balance sheet.
3. The criteria used to classify leases on the books of the lessee.
4. The treatment of executory costs, residual values, and other aspects of lease contracts.
5. The effects of capital lease versus operating lease treatment on lessees' financial statements.
6. How analysts can adjust for ratio distortions from off-balance sheet leases when comparing firms.
7. That lessors also classify leases as capital leases or operating leases but that their reporting incentives are very different from those of lessees.
8. The difference between sales-type, direct financing, and operating lease treatment by lessors and the criteria for choosing the accounting treatment.
9. How the different lessor accounting treatments can affect income and net asset balances.
10. Sale/leaseback arrangements and other special leasing situations.
11. How to use footnote disclosures to estimate the increase in assets and liabilities that would ensue if operating leases had been capitalized instead.

A lease is a contract in which the owner of an asset (the **lessor**) conveys to another party (the **lessee**) the right to use that asset. This right is granted in exchange for a fee (the **lease payment**) that is usually paid in installments. Legal title to the asset typically remains with the lessor. The duration of a lease may be short (e.g., a one-week car rental agreement) or long (a 20-year lease for retail space in a shopping center).

At its inception, a lease is what is called a **mutually unperformed contract.** This means neither party to the lease arrangement has yet performed all of the duties called for in the contract. For example, the lessor has an obligation to provide the lessee with the right to use the asset for the entire duration of the lease; in exchange, the lessee has an obligation to pay the stipulated periodic fee to the lessor during the lease term.

Evolution of Lease Accounting

Statement of Financial Accounting Standards (SFAS) No. 13 spells out the current generally accepted accounting principles (GAAP) for leases.[1] Before it was issued in 1976, virtually all leases were accounted for using the **operating lease approach.** Here, the accounting conforms to the legal structure of lease arrangements. Since lease contracts typically do not convey title, the asset remains on the books of the lessor. Further, under the operating lease approach, the lessee does not immediately record as a liability the stream of future payments called for in the contract. No liability is recorded because the lessee is not legally obligated to make the payments until the lessor per-

[1] "Accounting for Leases," *SFAS No. 13* (Stamford, CT: Financial Accounting Standards Board [FASB], 1976).

forms the duties specified in the contract. Because these are mutually unperformed (sometimes called **executory**) contracts, accounting entries are made over time in piecemeal fashion only as partial performance under the contract takes place. ***As each party performs its respective duties, that portion of the contract that has been performed is no longer considered executory and is accordingly recognized in the financial records.***

The following example illustrates the operating lease approach.

> Crest Company owns a building with a book value of $200,000. This building is leased to Iris Company under a five-year lease for a monthly rental of $2,000, which is to be paid at the end of each month.

Upon signing the lease, Iris Company, the lessee, makes no entry on its books. Each month, as Crest performs its part of the agreement by making the premises available to Iris Company, Iris accrues a liability:

DR Rent expense	$2,000	
CR Lease liability		$2,000

Upon payment of the stipulated rental at the end of the month, Iris makes the following entry:

DR Lease liability	$2,000	
CR Cash		$2,000

In practice, the accrual for the lease liability is seldom made. Instead, only one entry is made at the time of cash payment:

DR Rent expense	$2,000	
CR Cash		$2,000

Iris does not record any liability on its books for *future* rental payments—neither at the time of signing the lease nor afterward. The reason is that these future rental payments are contingent upon future performance by Crest, the lessor. The stipulated payments do not become a liability to Iris under the operating lease approach until time passes and performance takes place. As each party to the mutually unperformed contract performs its duties specified in the contract, the "performed" portion is no longer considered executory. The stipulated rental for the period over which performance took place is accrued as a liability; the liability is reduced when payment is made.

Similarly, no entry would be made on the books of Crest, the lessor, at the time this operating lease was signed. However, as piecemeal performance takes place and payment is received, the following entry is made on Crest's books:

DR Cash	$2,000	
CR Rental revenue		$2,000

Because the building remains an asset on the books of Crest Company, periodic depreciation is also recorded:

DR Depreciation expense—leased building	$ XXX	
CR Accumulated depreciation—leased building		$ XXX

The operating lease approach conforms to the legal structure of lease arrangements. Journal entries are made piecemeal over time as partial performance takes place.

RECAP

Popularity of the Operating Lease Method

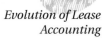

Lessees like the operating lease method for lease accounting. One obvious reason is that the operating lease method never reflects the cumulative liability for all future lease payments on the balance sheet of the lessee. Instead, only a portion of the obligation gets accrued piecemeal as partial performance takes place under the lease. The phrase **off-balance sheet financing** means the lessee has financed the acquisition of asset services without recognizing a liability on the financial statement.

CONTRACTING

As we will see, GAAP requires *footnote* disclosure of the future cash outflows arising from operating leases. And because reasonably informed financial decision makers do read statement footnotes, the liability isn't really "hidden." Nevertheless, it is easy to envision circumstances in which lessees will be made better off by using the operating lease method. To see how, recall that many contracts are linked to financial statement numbers. One example is bank lending agreements that contain covenants—safety measures to protect banks against financial deterioration of the borrower. Since most covenants are based on financial statement numbers—not on footnote numbers—keeping liabilities off the balance sheet may convey benefits to borrowers even if the liabilities aren't hidden in a real sense. For example, the numerator of the lessee's debt-to-equity ratio is unaffected at the inception of an operating lease, since no liability is recorded on signing. Keeping the liability off the balance sheet strengthens the debt-to-equity ratio. The off-balance sheet liability reduces the likelihood that the lessee-borrower will violate a debt-to-equity loan covenant.

Furthermore, some lessees believe that omitting the lease liability improves their ability to obtain *future* credit. Here's why. Lenders use leverage ratios as a rule of thumb in assessing borrowing capacity. Keeping the lease liability off the books lowers reported leverage. The lower is the firm's reported leverage, the greater is that firm's perceived borrowing capacity. (But if lenders read footnotes, the off-balance sheet liabilities are disclosed and this perception by lessees may be incorrect.)

Lessees also like the operating lease accounting method because it keeps the leased *asset* off the balance sheet. Certain long-term leases give lessees the *exclusive* right to use assets for the preponderance of their economic life. Nevertheless, despite the "ownership-like" property rights conveyed to the lessee, no balance sheet asset is recorded with operating leases.

ANALYSIS

Keeping leased assets off the books produces a favorable impact on lessee's financial statements that is just as substantial as the benefit that arises from omitting lease liabilities. Consider an airline that leases a portion of its aircraft fleet and accounts for the leases using the operating lease method. The leased aircraft generate gross revenues and net profits just as the owned aircraft do. However, not reporting the leased aircraft as assets under the operating lease approach raises the return-on-assets (ROA) ratio:

$$\text{ROA} = \frac{\text{NOPAT}}{\text{Average assets}}$$

Income generated by the leased assets will appear in the numerator, net operating profit after taxes (NOPAT); however, the leased assets will not appear in the denominator. The net effect increases the return on reported average assets.

Investors and others use ratios like return on assets to evaluate a firm's performance. The operating lease method makes the ROA for companies that lease a significant portion of their assets *appear* to be higher than the corresponding return for companies that own their assets outright. (See the example illustrated in the Appendix to this chapter.)

While lessees have been reluctant to treat leases as a transfer of ownership interest, lessors have not. When a lease is treated as a transfer of ownership interest on the books of the lessor, the timing of the recognition of leasing income is accelerated—thus creating favorable financial statement effects for the lessor, as we'll show later in the chapter.

The Securities and Exchange Commission's Initiative

Throughout the 1960s and early 1970s, leasing became an important financing vehicle. The virtually exclusive use of the operating lease approach was criticized, especially by the Securities and Exchange Commission (SEC), since it felt that this approach did not portray the economics of many leasing transactions.

The SEC issued *Accounting Series Release (ASR) No. 147* in 1973 to improve financial reporting for leases.[2] The SEC took what is called a **property rights** approach to lease accounting. Under this approach, leases are viewed as conveying property rights in the asset to the lessee, and the payment stream represents the lessee's liability. However, *ASR No. 147* emphasized footnote *disclosure* and thus stopped short of requiring balance sheet *recognition* of leases that conveyed property rights. But the FASB soon extended and embellished the SEC property rights approach, as we discuss next.

Lessee Accounting

SFAS No. 13 ***adopted a compromise position concerning capitalization of leases on lessees' books.*** Leases meeting certain specified criteria *must* be capitalized by the lessee (i.e., recorded as assets). These types of leases are called **capital leases.** Leases not meeting the *SFAS No. 13* criteria *cannot* be capitalized. Noncapitalized leases are called **operating leases** and are accounted for using the procedures illustrated previously.

Criteria for Capital Lease Treatment

If, at its inception, a lease satisfies *any one or more* of the following criteria, it must be treated as a capital lease on the books of the lessee:

1. The lease transfers ownership of the asset to the lessee by the end of the lease term.
2. The lease contains a bargain purchase option.
3. The noncancelable lease term is 75% or more of the estimated economic life of the leased asset.
4. The present value of the minimum lease payments equals or exceeds 90% of the fair value of the leased asset.

Each criterion represents a condition under which property rights in the leased asset have been transferred to the lessee. This property rights transfer is easily seen in criterion (1). If a lease transfers ownership, title to the asset will eventually pass to the lessee, and the FASB requires that the accounting method conform to the substance of the transaction (an installment purchase) rather than to its form (a long-term lease). Similarly, in lease arrangements where a **bargain purchase option** exists—criterion (2)—there is a strong probability the lessee will exercise the option and obtain ownership. These two criteria represent instances in which ownership will likely transfer, thus conveying significant property rights in the leased asset. This is the reason *SFAS No. 13* requires that such leases be treated as capital leases.

> International Accounting Standards (IAS) also differentiate between operating leases and capital leases. (The latter are called "finance leases.") Classification is based on which party has the risks and rewards of ownership. Criteria that are similar to (but less precise than) the four *SFAS No. 13* criteria are cited as examples of situations where a lease should be classified as a finance lease. See "Accounting for Leases," *IAS 17* (London: International Accounting Standards Committee [IASC], 1997).

The philosophy underlying the third criterion—economic life—is different since legal ownership of the asset does not pass to the lessee. Nevertheless, *SFAS No. 13* indicates that criterion (3) also conveys significant property rights. The reason is that the *right to use* a leased asset for 75% or more of its expected economic life is *itself* an asset—a valuable property right representing an exclusive claim to the asset's services for the preponderance of its benefit period.

Criterion (4), sometimes called the **recovery of investment criterion,** is the most technically complicated, but it is still easy to understand in principle. A good indication that

---

[2] "Notice of Adoption of Amendments to Regulations S-X Requiring Improved Disclosure of Leases," *ASR No. 147* (Washington, D.C.: SEC, 1973).

the lessor is recovering virtually all of the investment in the asset occurs when the present value of the minimum lease payments is equal to or greater than 90% of the fair market value of the asset itself. The relative magnitude of the payment schedule and the willingness of the lessee to engage in the transaction are both considered evidence that substantial property rights have been transferred to the lessee.

These four criteria for capital leases suggest the FASB has moved part of the way toward the property rights approach. But it's not a "pure" property rights approach, since these criteria do not consider *all* leases to convey property rights. Only leases that satisfy certain arbitrary conditions (e.g., the 75% rule or the 90% rule) qualify. ***So SFAS No. 13 is a compromise between the operating lease approach, where no leases appear on the lessee's balance sheet, and a strict property rights approach, where all leases would be shown as assets and liabilities.***

Leases that satisfy at least one of the four criteria are treated as capital leases, and the following entry is made on the books of the lessee at the inception of the lease:

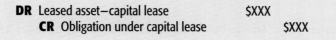

DR Leased asset—capital lease	$XXX	
CR Obligation under capital lease		$XXX

Leases that do not satisfy *any* of the previously discussed criteria must be accounted for as operating leases.

Capital Lease Treatment Illustrated

To illustrate the accounting for leases that qualify as capital leases, suppose Lessee Company signs a five-year noncancelable lease with Lessor Company on January 1, 2001 when the lease begins. Several other facts pertain to the lease:

1. The lease calls for five payments of $79,139.18 to be made at the end of each year.
2. The leased asset has a fair market value of $315,000 on January 1, 2001.
3. The lease has no renewal option and possession of the asset reverts to the lessor on January 1, 2006.
4. Lessee Company regularly uses the straight-line method to depreciate owned assets of this type.
5. The leased asset has an expected economic life of six years.

Since the lease term covers more than 75% of the asset's expected economic life (5/6 = 83.3%), this lease must be treated as a capital lease, following criterion (3). That means Lessee Company must recognize both an asset and a liability on its books.

But what is the asset and liability dollar amount that should be recorded? *SFAS No. 13* requires that the dollar amount be equal to the discounted present value of the **minimum lease payments** specified in the lease. Contingent payments are ignored. The discount rate that is used to determine the present value is the *lower* of the lessee's incremental borrowing rate[3] or the lessor's rate of return that is implicit to the lease.[4] But if the lessee can't determine the lessor's rate of return, the lessee uses the incremental borrowing rate.

> Minimum lease payments are defined as follows: If the payment schedule called for a fixed fee of $79,139.18 per year plus an additional fee of five cents per unit for each unit manufactured using the leased asset, only the $79,139.18 would be included in the computation of minimum lease payments. The five cents per unit for each unit manufactured is *the contingency that is ignored in the calculation.* In more complicated leases, the minimum lease payments also include the amount of any **residual value guarantee** by the lessee (as discussed later), any penalties that must be paid if the lessee chooses not to renew the lease and, if the lease contains a bargain purchase option, the amount of the bargain purchase option payment.

[3] The FASB defines the **lessee's incremental borrowing rate** as the rate that the lessee "would have incurred to borrow the funds necessary to buy the leased asset on a secured loan with repayment terms similar to the payment schedule called for in the lease" (*SFAS No. 13,* para. 5 [1]).

[4] The **lessor's rate of return** is the pre-tax internal yield on the lease contract (i.e., that rate which equates the fair value of the asset and the present value of the payments accruing to the lessor). Ibid., para. 5(k).

Assume Lessee Company's incremental borrowing rate is 10% and the lessee can't determine the lessor's implicit rate of return on the lease. The discount rate is accordingly 10%, and the present value of the minimum lease payments is:

Present value of minimum lease payments		Minimum lease payment		Present value factor for an ordinary annuity for five years at 10%
$300,000	=	$79,139.18	×	3.79079 (from Appendix I, Table 2)

The lease also meets criterion (4) since $300,000 is greater than 90% of the $315,000 fair market value of the asset.

Lessee Company makes the following entry on January 1, 2001 at the inception of the lease:

DR Leased asset–capital lease	$300,000	
CR Obligation under capital lease		$300,000

If a lease meets either the first or second capital lease criterion on p. 578, the leased asset is depreciated over the life of the *asset* since legal title to the asset ultimately passes to the lessee. If the lease is a capital lease because it meets either the third or fourth criterion, it is depreciated over the life of the *lease* since the asset reverts to the lessor at lease-end. In Table 12.1, the asset is depreciated over 5 years since it qualified under the third criterion.

It is important to understand that the amount shown for the asset and the amount shown for the related liability ($300,000) are equal only at the inception of the lease. Thereafter, as the term of the lease progresses, the amount in the asset account will equal the amount in the liability account only by sheer coincidence. The reason is that the asset account is reduced in accordance with Lessee Company's depreciation schedule for assets of this type, whereas the liability account is reduced in accordance with the payment schedule contained in the lease. The asset and liability accounts are reduced at independent—and usually different—rates over the life of the lease. These different rates are illustrated in the Appendix to this chapter.

Each lease payment of $79,139.18 comprises two elements. One represents interest on the amount of the obligation that was outstanding during the year. The other represents a repayment of a portion of the principal amount of the obligation. *SFAS No. 13* requires that the interest portion and principal repayment of each $79,139.18 outflow be measured using the **effective interest method.** The amortization schedule in Table 12.1 shows this breakdown in columns (b) and (c).

On December 31, 2001 Lessee Company records both the cash payment of $79,139.18 (column a) and the amortization of the capitalized leased asset (column e). Based upon the figures in Table 12.1, the entries are:

Table 12.1 ■ LESSEE COMPANY

Amortization Schedule–Effective Interest Method

Date	(a) Total Payment	(b) Interest Expense[1]	(c) Principal Payment[2]	(d) Lease Obligation Balance	(e) Amortization of Asset	(f) Total Annual Capital Lease Expense [Col. (b) + Col. (e)]
1/1/01				$300,000.00		
12/31/01	$ 79,139.18	$30,000.00	$ 49,139.18	250,860.82	$ 60,000.00	$ 90,000.00
12/31/02	79,139.18	25,086.08	54,053.10	196,807.72	60,000.00	85,086.08
12/31/03	79,139.18	19,680.77	59,458.41	137,349.31	60,000.00	79,680.77
12/31/04	79,139.18	13,734.93	65,404.25	71,945.06	60,000.00	73,734.93
12/31/05	79,139.18	7,194.12[3]	71,945.06	—	60,000.00	67,194.12
	$395,695.90	$95,695.90	$300,000.00	$ –0–	$300,000.00	$395,695.90

[1]Column (d) for preceding year times 10%.
[2]Column (a) minus column (b).
[3]Rounded.

DR Obligation under capital lease	$49,139.18	
DR Interest expense	30,000.00	
CR Cash		$79,139.18
DR Depreciation expense–capital lease	$60,000.00	
CR Accumulated depreciation–capital lease		$60,000.00

The amount of interest expense recognized each year is equal to 10% (the discount rate) times the principal amount of the obligation outstanding at the start of the year. Since the principal amount at the start of the lease on January 1, 2001 was $300,000 (column d), the interest expense for 2001 is $300,000 times 10%, or $30,000. The difference between the cash payment of $79,139.18 and the interest expense of $30,000 represents repayment of principal. This 2001 difference—$49,139.18 (column c)—reduces the remaining principal balance at December 31, 2001 to $250,860.82 ($300,000 − $49,139.18), as shown in column d. Interest expense for 2002 would then be $250,860.82 times 10%, or $25,086.08. The 2002 journal entry for the cash payment is:

DR Obligation under capital lease	$54,053.10	
DR Interest expense	25,086.08	
CR Cash		$79,139.18

Notice that the entry to record depreciation expense would be the same in all years of the lease, since Lessee Company uses the straight-line depreciation method.

Executory Costs

Executory costs represent costs of *using* assets, such as maintenance, taxes, and insurance. Often, these costs are paid directly by the lessee. Sometimes they are paid by the lessor and passed along to the lessee as an additional lease payment. For example, if executory costs paid by Lessor Company total $2,000 per year, Lessor would include an added yearly charge of $2,000 in the lease, in addition to the basic $79,139.18 rental fee.

Since executory costs represent a cost of using assets—rather than a cost of the assets themselves—these costs are omitted when determining minimum lease payments, and thus they are not a component of the capitalized amount shown in the "Leased asset—capital leases" account. Consider this illustration. If Lessee Company's annual rental fee was $81,139.18—including $2,000 of executory costs—the minimum lease payments to be capitalized would be $79,139.18 (i.e., $81,139.18 − $2,000). Under this assumption, the capitalized amount would still total $300,000 and the amortization schedule would be identical to Table 12.1. The $2,000 of executory costs would be treated as a period cost by Lessee Company and charged to expense when paid. For example, the payment of $81,139.18 on December 31, 2001 would trigger this entry:

DR Obligation under capital lease	$49,139.18	
DR Interest expense	30,000.00	
DR Miscellaneous lease expense	2,000.00	
CR Cash		$81,139.18

Residual Value Guarantees

Lease contracts sometimes contain a provision under which the lessee guarantees that the leased asset will have a certain value at the end of the lease. If the actual market value of the asset is less than this **residual value guarantee,** the lessee must pay the difference to the lessor. Let's now assume that the lease required Lessee Company to guarantee that the asset's residual value would be no lower than $20,000 when the lease ends on January 1, 2006. If the asset's fair market value on that date is $20,000 or higher, Lessee Company would simply return it to the lessor, since the residual value guarantee is satisfied. But if the fair market value is only $15,000 on January 1, 2006, Lessee Company would return the asset and pay $5,000 cash to Lessor Company.

Leased assets often revert to the lessor at the end of the lease term. Residual value guarantees protect the lessor against several types of losses. Unforeseen technological or marketplace changes erode residual value; the residual value guarantee insulates the lessor from these unanticipated changes. Similarly, the lessor is vulnerable to losses if the lessee does not take proper care of the asset over the lease period. The residual value guarantee gives lessors protection against lessees who abuse leased assets.

The lessee must include the amount specified as the residual value guarantee in the computation of minimum lease payments. The reason is that the lessee potentially owes the full amount of the guarantee to the lessor. To illustrate the accounting, return to Lessee Company data on page 579 and now assume there is a $20,000 residual value guarantee. The present value of the minimum lease payments is:

Present value of minimum lease payments		Minimum lease payment		Present value factor at 10%
$300,000.00	=	$79,139.18	×	3.79079 (Present value factor for five-year ordinary annuity)
12,418.40	=	$20,000.00	×	.62092 (Present value factor for $1 due in five years, from Appendix I, Table 1)
$312,418.40				

With the residual value guarantee, Lessee Company makes the following entry on January 1, 2001 at the inception of the lease:

DR Leased asset—capital lease	$312,418.40	
CR Obligation under capital lease		$312,418.40

Table 12.2 shows the amortization schedule that Lessee Company uses when this residual value guarantee is included in the lease. After making the December 31, 2005 cash payment of $79,139.18, the lease obligation balance (column d) and the lease asset balance (column f) both are $20,000. We're assuming that the asset's value at the end of the lease on January 1, 2006 equals or exceeds $20,000—the amount of the residual value guarantee. When Lessee Company returns the asset on that date, its obligation to Lessor Company is satisfied and the following entry results:

DR Obligation under capital lease	$20,000.00	
CR Leased asset—capital lease		$20,000.00

Now let's alter the example and assume that the asset has a fair market value of only $15,000 at December 31, 2005. Lessee Company would have to pay $5,000 in addition to relinquishing the asset. The entry is:

DR Obligation under capital lease	$20,000.00	
DR Loss on residual value guarantee	5,000.00	
CR Leased asset—capital lease		$20,000.00
CR Cash		5,000.00

Table 12.2 ■ LESSEE COMPANY

Amortization Schedule—Effective Interest Method With Guaranteed Residual Value

Date	(a) Total Cash Payment	(b) Interest Expense[1]	(c) Principal Payment[2]	(d) Lease Obligation Balance	(e) Amortization of Asset; Residual Value Return	(f) Lease Asset Balance	(g) Total Annual Capital Lease Expense (b) + (e)
1/1/01	—	—	—	$312,418.40	—	$312,418.40	—
12/31/01	$ 79,139.18	$ 31,241.84	$ 47,897.34	264,521.06	$ 58,483.68[(3)]	253,934.72	$ 89,725.52
12/31/02	79,139.18	26,452.11	52,687.07	211,834.00	58,483.68	195,451.04	84,935.79
12/31/03	79,139.18	21,183.40	57,955.78	153,878.22	58,483.68	136,967.36	79,667.08
12/31/04	79,139.18	15,387.82	63,751.36	90,126.86	58,483.68	78,483.68	73,871.50
12/31/05	79,139.18	9,012.32[(4)]	70,126.86	20,000.00	58,483.68	20,000.00	67,496.01
1/1/06[5]			20,000.00	—	20,000.00	—	
	$395,695.90	$103,277.50	$312,418.40	$ -0-	$312,418.40	$ -0-	$395,695.90

[1]Column (d) for preceding year times 10%.
[2]Column (a) minus column (b).
[3]($312,418.40 − $20,000) ÷ 5
[4]Rounded.
[5]Asset returned.

Payments in Advance

When lease payments are due at the *start* of each lease period, the journal entries and amortization tables differ slightly. We'll use the original Lessee Company example on page 579 to illustrate this. Assume that the annual payment is due at the start of each year and, because the payments are received earlier, the lessor lowers the required annual payment to $71,945. Under these slightly altered conditions, the present value of the minimum lease payments is:

Present value of minimum lease payments	=	Minimum lease payment	×	Present value factor for an annuity in advance for five years at 10%
$300,000	=	$71,945	×	4.16987 (from Appendix I, Table 2)

Table 12.3 shows the amortization schedule for this lease with up-front payments. Lessee Company records the following two entries on January 1, 2001 upon signing the lease and making the required lease payment:

DR Leased asset—capital lease	$300,000	
CR Obligation under capital lease		$300,000
DR Obligation under capital lease	$ 71,945	
CR Cash		$ 71,945

Notice from both the second journal entry and from Table 12.3 that no portion of the January 1, 2001 payment represents interest expense; instead, all of the $71,945 payment reduces the principal balance. The reason is that interest expense ensues only as times passes, not at the inception of the lease.

Table 12.3 ■ LESSEE COMPANY

Amortization Schedule—Effective Interest Method With Payments at the Start of Each Period

Date	(a) Total Payment	(b) Interest Expense[1]	(c) Principal Payment[2]	(d) Lease Obligation Balance	(e) Amortization of Asset	(f) Total Annual Capital Lease Expense (b) + (e)
1/1/01				$300,000.00		
1/1/01	$ 71,945.00	—	$ 71,945.00	228,055.00	$ 60,000.00	$ 60,000.00
1/1/02	71,945.00	$22,805.50	49,139.50	178,915.50	60,000.00	82,805.50
1/1/03	71,945.00	17,891.55	54,053.45	124,862.05	60,000.00	77,891.55
1/1/04	71,945.00	12,486.21	59,458.79	65,403.26	60,000.00	72,486.21
1/1/05	71,945.00	6,541.74[3]	65,403.26	—	60,000.00	66,541.74
	$359,725.00	$59,725.00	$300,000.00	$ -0-	$300,000.00	$359,725.00

[1]Column (d) for preceding year times 10%.
[2]Column (a) minus column (b).
[3]Rounded.

Financial Statement Effects of Capital Versus Operating Lease Treatment

To understand the financial statement effects of lease capitalization, we need to compare the numbers that result from the capital lease approach with the numbers that would have resulted had the operating lease method been used instead.

Let's return to the beginning of Lessee Company example (p. 579) where we assumed that lease payments were due at the end of the year, executory costs were zero, and there was no residual value guarantee. If that lease had been accounted for as an operating lease, the following journal entry would have been made in each of the five years of the lease:

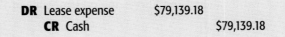

DR Lease expense	$79,139.18	
CR Cash		$79,139.18

This is equivalent to assuming that the executory costs are paid directly by the lessee and are not included in the payments due to the lessor.

Under the operating lease method, the total lease expense over the life of the lease is equal to the total cash outflow. This total expense number under the operating lease method is $395,695.90 and is shown at the bottom of column (a) of Table 12.1.

Under the capital lease method, the total lease expense over the life of the lease comprises both (1) the interest payments, and (2) the amortization of the capitalized asset amount. The sum of these two elements is shown at the bottom of column (f) of the amortization schedule in Table 12.1. This total is also $395,695.90.

A comparison of the Table 12.1 column (a) total (lifetime expense under the operating lease method) and the column (f) total (lifetime expense under the capital lease method) demonstrates that ***the two methods give rise to identical cumulative total lifetime charges to expense.*** Over the life of a lease, total income is unaffected by the choice of lease accounting method. However, a comparison of the year-by-year numbers in columns (a) and (f) demonstrates that the *timing* of the expense charge differs between the two methods. The capital lease approach leads to higher expense in the earlier years of the lease and lower lease expense in the later years, as shown in Figure 12.1. From the graphical representation, you can see that in the early lease years expenses under the capital lease approach exceed lease expenses that would be recognized under the operating lease approach. Ultimately, capital lease expense drops below operating lease expense.

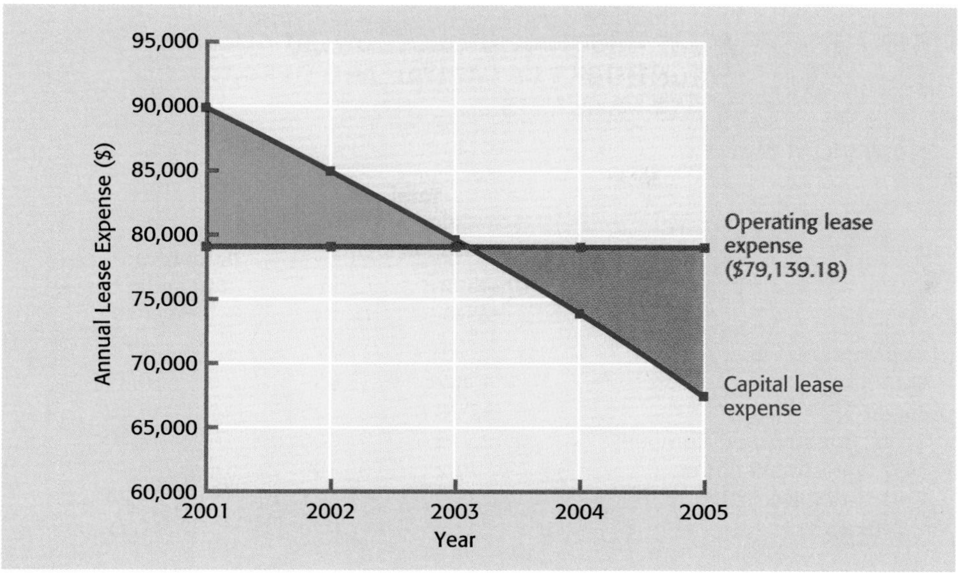

Figure 12.1

LESSEE COMPANY

Pattern of Expense Recognition: Capital Versus Operating Lease Method

CONTRACTING

This accelerated recognition of lease expenses under the capital lease approach provides yet another reason why many lessees prefer the operating lease method. Consider the incentives of a manager whose performance evaluations and bonuses are tied to financial numbers. A lease accounting method that front-end loads expenses lowers near-term income and thus also reduces the discounted present value of expected bonuses. Worse yet, if managers' accomplishments are evaluated "strictly by the numbers," the higher expenses and lower profitability may jeopardize their continuing employment and advancement. So managers have a strong incentive to structure lease contracts in ways that circumvent the capitalization rules.

Table 12.4 shows the total amount of scheduled capital versus operating lease payments for the five largest firms in each of five industries that use leases extensively. Notice that the dollar amount of the minimum lease payments arising from operating leases is, on average, almost 23 times larger than the capital lease payments for supermarket companies and 88 times larger for airlines. This demonstrates that capital leases are used infrequently even in industries that utilize leasing heavily.

One possible explanation for this is that the criteria for capitalizing lease commitments in *SFAS No. 13* can be readily circumvented. For example, a lessee can simply refuse to sign a lease contract that transfers legal title or contains a bargain purchase option. This avoids triggering the first and second capitalization criteria. Criterion 3—the 75% rule—can also be circumvented by bargaining with the lessor to shorten the lease term until it is less than 75% of the expected economic life of the asset. However, criterion 4—the 90% rule (or recovery of investment criterion)—is the most difficult to circumvent and undoubtedly accounts for many of the capital leases that ultimately appear on financial statements. Because the first three criteria are easy to evade and because the fourth is not, U.K. accounting standards for leases—which were heavily influenced by the U.S. experience with *SFAS No. 13*—use only the fourth criterion for differentiating between operating and capital leases.[5]

We can only infer why companies in these five industries that extensively use leases have so few capital leases. A reasonable conjecture is that they have chosen to keep these leases "off the balance sheet" to improve ratios like debt-to-equity and return-on-assets.

[5] See "Accounting For Leases and Hire Purchase Contracts," *Statement of Standard Accounting Practice (SSAP) No. 21* (Institute of Chartered Accountants in England and Wales, 1984), para. 15.

Table 12.4 ■ COMPARISON OF UNDISCOUNTED DOLLAR MAGNITUDES OF CAPITAL AND OPERATING LEASE PAYMENTS

(1999 Fiscal Year)

	Total Scheduled Minimum Lease Payments		
($ in millions)	Operating Leases	Capital Leases	Ratio of Operating to Capital Lease Payments
Department/Variety Stores			
Wal-Mart	$ 4,962	$5,609	0.88
Target	1,098	225	4.88
Sears, Roebuck and Company	2,419	1,006	2.40
May Department Stores	482	128	3.77
Costco Wholesale	929	21	44.24
Average			**11.23**
Supermarkets			
Safeway	$ 3,971	$ 877	4.53
Kroger	8,518	903	9.43
Albertson's Inc.	3,427	461	7.43
Publix Supermarkets	2,543	—	*
Winn-Dixie	5,072	73	69.48
Average			**22.72**
Railroads			
Burlington Northern Santa Fe	$ 1,062	$ 60	17.70
Norfolk Southern Corporation	8,711	478	18.22
Union Pacific	3,435	2,187	1.57
Florida East Coast Industries, Inc.	187	—	*
RailAmerica, Inc.	11,916	1,171	10.18
Average			**11.92**
Airlines			
Delta Airlines	$14,530	$ 297	48.92
AMR	17,061	2,484	6.87
Southwest Airlines	3,005	190	15.82
US Airways	9,407	26	361.81
UAL	22,093	3,668	6.02
Average			**87.89**
Communications			
AT&T Corporation	$ 3,284	$ —	*
MCI WorldCom	12,850	705	18.23
SBC Communications	1,838	—	*
BellSouth Corporation	1,447	—	*
Bell Atlantic Corporation	1,575	157	10.03
Average			**14.13**

*Ratio cannot be calculated due to lack of capitalized leases.

Source: Company SEC filings and annual reports.

Lessees have incentives to keep leases off the balance sheet. Criteria exist for identifying capital leases. However, the terms of a lease can easily be designed to evade these criteria. So operating leases far outnumber capital leases for most firms.

RECAP

Lessee Accounting

Lessees' Footnote Disclosures

ANALYSIS

The ratio of operating lease to capital lease cash flows in Table 12.4 is fairly typical of other industries as well. Operating leases predominate by a wide margin. However, capital leases *do* exist, and their frequency does differ across companies, even within the same industry. For this reason, analysts try to adjust financial statements to include the effects of off-balance sheet operating leases in order to enhance comparisons between firms in an industry. The footnote disclosures required by *SFAS No. 13* make these adjustments possible. Exhibit 12.1 shows portions of the leases footnote from Sears, Roebuck and Company's 1999 annual report.

Exhibit 12.1 contains the disclosures required of all lessees. Notice that a schedule of future minimum lease payments must be reported for both capital leases and operating leases. (We used these schedules to develop the data in Table 12.4.) Payments for each of the ensuing five years must be separately disclosed, as Sears has done for 2000 through 2004. Minimum lease payments for all later years may be aggregated (e.g., $714 million for capital leases and $1,092 million for operating leases). ***These scheduled payments on operating leases make it possible for analysts to estimate the discounted present value of the off-balance sheet leases.*** In the Appendix to this chapter, we use the Sears disclosures to illustrate this computation step-by-step. Once the present value of the off-balance sheet leases is determined, dollar amounts can be added to both assets and liabilities. This adjustment allows analysts to compensate for distortions that can arise from off-balance sheet leases when making interfirm comparisons.

Exhibit 12.1 ■ SEARS, ROEBUCK AND COMPANY

Excerpts from Lease and Service Agreements Footnote
January 1, 2000

Minimum lease obligations, excluding taxes, insurance and other expenses payable directly by the Company, for leases in effect as of January 1, 2000, are as follows:

($ in millions)	Capital Leases	Operating Leases
2000	$ 66	$ 352
2001	60	303
2002	56	253
2003	56	224
2004	54	195
After 2004	714	1,092
Total minimum payments	$1,006	$2,419
Less imputed interest	589	
Present value of minimum lease payments	417	
Less current maturities	16	
Long-term obligations	$ 401	

Adjusting Income

ANALYSIS

If one company has structured its lease contracts to keep these commitments off the balance sheet while a competitor has not, how do analysts make the two companies' income numbers comparable? It is not difficult to make such adjustments for companies whose average lease is approximately 50% expired. Figure 12.1 shows that halfway through the life of the lease (December 31, 2003), Lessee Company's lease expense under the operating lease approach will be very close to the lease expense under the capital lease approach. Table 12.1 indicates that operating lease expense in year 2003 is $79,139.18 while capital lease expense is virtually the same—$79,680.77.

The intuition behind the intersecting operating lease and capital lease curves in Figure 12.1 can be extended to financial analysis by reference to Exhibit 12.2. This is an excerpt

Exhibit 12.2 ■ KMART CORPORATION

Excerpts from Leases Footnote
January 25, 1995

Reconciliation of capital lease information: The impact of recording amortization and interest expense versus rent expense on capital leases follows:

($ in millions)	1994	1993	1992
Amortization of capital lease property	$119	$117	$113
Interest expense related to obligations under capital leases	196	192	185
Amounts charged to earnings	315	309	298
Related minimum lease payments net of executory costs	(312)	(306)	(294)
Excess of amounts charged over related minimum lease payments	$ 3	$ 3	$ 4

Related minimum lease payments above exclude executory costs for 1994, 1993, and 1992 in the amounts of $97, $91, and $96, respectively.

from Kmart's 1995 annual report lease footnote. In it, Kmart voluntarily disclosed the difference between its *reported* capital lease expense and the expense that would have been reported if those capital leases had, instead, been treated as operating leases.[6] These expense differences for 1992 through 1994 (highlighted in Exhibit 12.2) are $4 million in 1992 and $3 million in 1993 and 1994. What is important to see is that the $3 million expense difference is less than 1% of 1994 capital lease expense of $315 million. This small difference reflects the fact that Kmart was a mature company with a stable portfolio of leases that were, on average, close to the midpoint of their contractual life.

We can extend this intuition to comparisons between companies. Assume that two competitors in the same industry have capitalized different percentages of their leases and that both companies have a stable portfolio of leases. Then, generalizing from the Kmart illustration, despite these different capitalization policies, the two firms will, nevertheless, have comparable lease expense numbers. ***For mature firms, the income statement effects of capital versus operating lease treatment will often not be significantly different.***

We will show in the next subsection that this is not true for balance sheet effects. On the contrary, capital versus operating lease treatment can significantly alter balance sheet numbers and resulting ratios.

Balance Sheet and Ratio Effects

Accounting for leases using the capital lease approach invariably worsens certain key ratios on the lessee's balance sheet—thus providing yet another explanation for lessees' resistance to lease capitalization.[7]

One ratio that deteriorates under capital lease accounting is the current ratio. Using numbers in the Lessee Company example from Table 12.1, ***we will demonstrate that the current ratio over the term of the lease will be lower under the capital lease approach than it would be under the operating lease approach.*** To see this, assume Lessee Company is preparing a balance sheet on January 1, 2001 immediately after signing the lease. Under the operating lease approach, the first cash payment of $79,139.18 due on December 31, 2001 is not considered to be a liability; it will become a liability only as time passes and as the lessor performs its duties under the lease. Since no part of the year-end 2001 payment

[6] Kmart abandoned this disclosure in its 1996 annual report. This information was useful and explains why we continue to use the 1995 report even though more recent reports are now available.

[7] See E. A. Imhoff, Jr., R. C. Lipe, and D. W. Wright, "Operating Leases: Impact of Constructive Capitalization," *Accounting Horizons* (March 1991), pp. 51–63.

of $79,139.18 is recognized as a liability at January 1, 2001 under the operating lease approach, the current ratio would be unaffected if Lessee Company were somehow able to avoid capitalization and were allowed to treat this as an operating lease.

By contrast, at the inception of the lease, the capital lease approach *does* recognize a liability—called "Obligation under capital lease." As shown in Table 12.1, the balance in this liability account at January 1, 2001 is $300,000.00. Furthermore, *SFAS No. 13* requires that a portion of this $300,000.00 balance be classified as a current liability. The current portion of the "Obligation under capital lease" is the reduction in the principal balance that will take place over the ensuing 12 months of 2001. Table 12.1 shows the current portion to be $49,139.18, since this is the expected 2001 reduction in the principal balance. Thus, treating the lease as a capital lease rather than as an operating lease will increase Lessee Company's current liabilities by $49,139.18 and thereby lower its January 1, 2001 current ratio. Table 12.1 illustrates that this negative effect on the current ratio *increases* as the lease grows older, since the portion of each $79,139.18 cash outflow that represents principal repayment grows over time.

To protect the lender, many loan agreements require borrowers to maintain a certain prespecified current ratio level. It is not surprising, therefore, that lessees resist lease capitalization. As the preceding discussion illustrates, treating a lease as a capital lease lowers the current ratio; therefore, capitalization could push financially struggling lessees into technical violation of their existing loan agreements by lowering their current ratio below the prespecified limit.

CONTRACTING

Two far more obvious cases of ratio deterioration under capital lease accounting relate to the leverage ratio and the return-on-assets ratio. These effects were discussed at the start of the chapter and will not be repeated here.

> When lease payments must be paid in *advance,* there is also a current ratio *numerator* effect under the capital lease approach. The advance payment reduces cash as well as the liability account "Obligation under capital lease," as shown in the journal entry on page 583. The net effect is to lower the numerator of the current ratio. By contrast, if the same lease were treated as an operating lease, when cash is credited the offsetting debit is to "Prepaid expense"—a current asset account. Accordingly, the current ratio numerator is unchanged.

There are also cash flow statement implications arising from lease treatment. To see this, refer back to Table 12.1, which shows the amortization schedule for a capital lease. On the cash flow statement, the interest expense component—column (b)—of each yearly payment would be classified as an *operating* cash flow while the principal payment component—column (c)—would be classified as a *financing* cash flow. In contrast, if the lease had been treated as an operating lease, the entire annual payment of $79,139.18 would be classified as an operating cash flow. So when lessees successfully keep leases off the balance sheet, reported cash flow from operations is lowered.

We have seen that lease capitalization affects balance sheet ratios and that the *SFAS No. 13* capitalization criteria can be circumvented. Since different firms can conceivably treat virtually identical leases dissimilarly, financial statements may not be immediately comparable across firms. To make comparisons, statement users need to adjust for these differences. The Appendix to this chapter outlines procedures for capitalizing off-balance sheet (operating leases) and thereby increasing interfirm statement comparability.

RECAP

Lessor Accounting

In addition to outlining rules for lessees, *SFAS No. 13* specifies the treatment of leases on the books of lessors.

Sales-type and Direct Financing Leases

From the perspective of the lessor, if a lease arrangement (1) transfers property rights in the leased asset to the lessee *and* (2) allows reasonably accurate estimates regarding the amount and collectibility of the eventual net cash flows to the lessor, the lease is treated as a capital lease by the lessor. In a capital lease, the leased asset is considered to be "sold" and is removed from the lessor's books. For lessors, there are two types of capital leases:

1. A **sales-type lease,** which exists when the lessor is a manufacturer or dealer.
2. A **direct financing lease,** which exists when the lessor is a financial institution (e.g., an insurance firm, bank, or financing company).

When both conditions—the transfer of property rights *and* reasonably accurate estimates of net cash flows—are *not simultaneously* met, the lease must be treated as an operating lease.

Figure 12.2 diagrams the various possibilities for lessor accounting, which we are about to explain in detail.

Sales-type Leases Leases can serve as a marketing vehicle since leasing arrangements generate "sales" from potential customers who are unwilling or unable to buy the assets outright for cash. For example, Deere & Company manufactures farm equipment for sale and also leases farm equipment through its wholly owned subsidiary, John Deere Credit. A lessor who uses leasing as a means for marketing products earns a profit from two sources:

1. One component of the total return on the lease is called the **manufacturer's or dealer's profit**—the difference between the fair market value (*cash* sales price) of the asset and its cost to the manufacturer or dealer.
2. Another component of the lessor's return is called **financing profit**—the difference between the total (undiscounted) minimum lease payments plus unguaranteed residual value and the fair market value of the leased asset.

The following sales-type lease example illustrates these components.

> ABC Company manufactures tractors. Each tractor has a total production cost of \$36,000 and a cash sales price of \$50,000. ABC Company "sells" some of these tractors under five-year sales-type leases, which call for annual lease payments of \$15,000. At the end of the fifth year, legal ownership of the tractor transfers to the lessee.

Figure 12.2

DECISION TREE FOR LESSOR'S TREATMENT OF LEASES

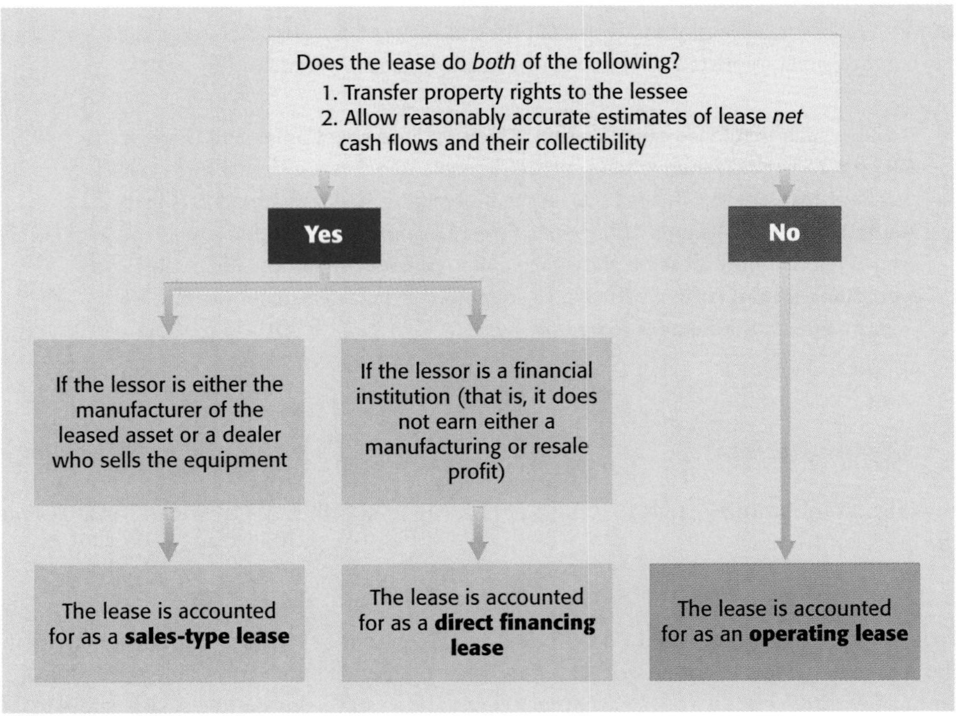

ABC Company's total profit over the five years of the lease is $39,000—that is, the lessee's payments of $75,000 ($15,000 per year times five years) minus the production cost of $36,000. This total profit is comprised of two components:

Manufacturer's profit: Cash sales price of $50,000 minus production cost of $36,000	$14,000
Financing profit: The difference between the cash sales price of the tractor ($50,000) and the gross inflows from the lessee ($15,000 × 5 years = $75,000)	25,000
Total profit	$39,000

Direct Financing Leases Some lessors are not manufacturers or dealers; instead, they are organizations like banks, insurance firms, or financing companies that provide lessees with a means for financing asset acquisitions. These organizations acquire assets from manufacturers by paying the fair market value and then leasing the asset to lessees. Lessors who are neither manufacturers nor dealers earn their profit from a single source—the finance fee that they charge the lessee for financing the asset acquisition. A direct financing lease example illustrates this single profit dimension.

The Pleasant City National Bank leases tractors to local farmers. Tractors are purchased from ABC Company, the manufacturer, at their fair market value of $50,000. The tractors are then leased under five-year direct financing leases, which call for annual lease payments of $15,000. At the end of the fifth year, legal ownership of the tractor transfers to the lessee.

The Bank's total profit on this lease is $25,000, which represents the difference between the cost of the tractor to the bank ($50,000) and the gross inflows from the lessee ($75,000).

Lessors' Operating Leases

Some lease arrangements do not transfer property rights in the asset to the lessee; or if they do transfer property rights, there may be great uncertainty about the ultimate profit or its collectibility. In either case, the leased asset is not considered to be "sold" and remains on the books of the lessor. Such leases are called operating leases.

Distinguishing Between Capital and Operating Leases

SFAS No. 13 identifies two types of characteristics that must be met for a lease to be treated as a capital lease (either a sales-type or a direct financing lease) on the books of the lessor. For ease of reference, these will be called Type I and Type II characteristics. A lease meeting *at least one* of the Type I characteristics and *both* of the Type II characteristics is a capital lease. The Type I characteristics are identical to the lessee's criteria for capital lease treatment.

Type I Characteristics

1. The lease transfers ownership of the asset to the lessee by the end of the lease term.
2. The lease contains a bargain purchase option.
3. The noncancelable lease term is 75% or more of the estimated economic life of the leased asset.
4. The present value of the minimum lease payments equals or exceeds 90% of the fair market value of the leased asset.

Type II Characteristics

1. The collectibility of the minimum lease payments is reasonably predictable.
2. There are no important uncertainties surrounding the amount of unreimbursable costs yet to be incurred by the lessor under the lease.

The purpose of these characteristics is to establish the appropriate time for recognizing income on the lessor's books. We already know from Chapter 2 that revenue should be recognized when both of the following conditions exist:

1. The "critical event" in the process of earning the revenue has taken place.
2. The amount of the revenue that has been earned is measurable with a reasonable degree of assurance.

Accounting rules for the lessor in *SFAS No. 13* are directly linked to these two revenue recognition criteria. The Type I characteristics dealing with transfer of property rights identify the critical event in determining whether a lease is in substance a "sale of assets." The Type II characteristics in *SFAS No. 13* relate to the riskiness of cash flows and thus to the measurability of revenue.

When at least one of the Type I characteristics and both of the Type II characteristics are satisfied by a lease, then the criteria for revenue recognition are met. This means that manufacturers or dealers can immediately recognize the sale, match costs, and reflect manufacturer's or dealer's profit. (By contrast, under the operating lease treatment, this profit recognition occurs over the life of the lease as each party performs its duties.) Furthermore, lessors can begin to recognize financing profit as a function of time when the Type I and Type II characteristics exist in a lease. (Under the operating lease treatment, the recognition of financing profit is related to performance. As we will see, the recognition of financing profit is accelerated when it is recognized as a pure function of time rather than as a function of performance.)

When a lease does not meet any of the Type I characteristics, or when it meets at least one of the Type I characteristics but not *both* of the Type II characteristics, then that lease must be accounted for as an operating lease on the lessor's books. Under the operating lease approach, the lessor's recognition of income takes place piecemeal as contractual performance by the lessor and the lessee progresses.

SFAS No. 13 tries to establish symmetry in the accounting for leases by lessors and lessees. If a lease qualifies as a "sale" from the perspective of the lessor, then the property rights inherent in the lease require asset recognition by the lessee. Of course, this symmetry is not perfect, since a particular lease may meet at least one of the Type I characteristics but not both of the Type II characteristics. In such cases, the asset would appear on *both* the lessor's and the lessee's books. Another factor that inhibits symmetry is that the discount rate used by the lessor and the lessee may differ. The lessor is required to use the rate of return that is implicit to the lease. If this rate is *higher* than the lessee's incremental borrowing rate, then the lessor and the lessee will use different discount rates when accounting for the lease.

Direct-Financing Lease Treatment Illustrated

To illustrate the accounting for leases that qualify as direct financing leases, we will use a variation of our earlier lease example. Assume that Lessee Company signs a noncancelable five-year lease on January 1, 2001 with Lessor Company. The lease begins on January 1, 2001 and has the following terms:

1. The lease calls for five payments of $79,139.18 to be made at the end of each year.
2. The leased asset has a fair market value of $304,359.49 on January 1, 2001.[8]
3. The lease has no renewal option and possession of the asset reverts to Lessor Company on January 1, 2006.
4. The leased asset has an expected economic life of six years.
5. The collectibility of the lease payments is reasonably predictable.

[8] This unusual amount was chosen to arrive at a round number (exactly 11%) for the rate of return implicit to the lease. In the previous residual value guarantee example on pages 581–3, Lessee Company capitalized $312,418.40 using a discount rate of 10%. Here in this altered example, we see that the market value of the asset is only $304,359.49. If this market value also applied to the example on pages 581–3, then Lessee Company would only capitalize $304,359.49 and use an 11% amortization rate.

6. There are no important uncertainties regarding unreimbursable costs yet to be incurred by Lessor Company.
7. The lease contract requires the lessee to guarantee a residual value of $20,000 at the end of the fifth year of the lease.

These lease terms satisfy both the third and the fourth Type I characteristics. We'll assume the lease also satisfies both Type II characteristics. Therefore, this is a capital lease. Assume Lessor Company is not a manufacturer or dealer, so this lease is a direct financing capital lease. Table 12.5 shows that the rate of return implicit to this lease from the perspective of the Lessor Company is 11%.[9] Therefore, Lessor Company must use an 11% interest factor in accounting for this lease.

Table 12.5 ■ LESSOR COMPANY

Computation of Implicit Rate of Return on Lease

Rate of return implicit to the lease is the rate that equates the present value of lease inflows and outflows.

Present value of outflows at 1/1/01		
Fair market value of the leased asset		$304,359.49
Present value of inflows at 1/1/01		
Five annual payments times 11% ordinary annuity factor:		
$79,139.18 × 3.69590* =	$292,490.49	
Guaranteed residual times 11% five-year single payment factor:		
$20,000.00 × .59345† =	$ 11,869.00	
		$304,359.49

Present value of inflows exactly equals present value of outflows at a discount rate of 11%. Hence, Lessor Company's rate of return is 11%.

*Present value factor for a five-year ordinary annuity at 11%.
†Present value factor for $1 due in five years at 11%.

Lessor Company's amortization schedule for this lease is shown in Table 12.6 on the following page.

At the inception of the lease, Lessor Company creates an account called "Gross investment in leased asset"—the sum of the minimum rental payments plus the guaranteed residual value of the asset at the end of the lease term.

Minimum rental payments over the life of the lease ($79,139.18 × 5)	$395,695.90
Guaranteed residual value at 12/31/05	20,000.00
Gross investment in leased asset	$415,695.90

The journal entry on January 1, 2001 is:

DR Gross investment in leased asset	$415,695.90	
CR Equipment		$304,359.49
CR Unearned financing income—leases		111,336.41

[9] Table 12.5 merely "proves" that the internal rate of return on this lease is 11%. When the rate is unknown and must be determined, standard procedures for computing the internal rate of return on an investment project must be used.

Table 12.6 ■ LESSOR COMPANY

Amortization Schedule—Effective Interest Method

Date	(a) Total Receipts	(b) Interest Income[1]	(c) Principal Reduction[2]	(d) Remaining Principal Amount
1/1/01				$304,359.49
12/31/01	$ 79,139.18	$ 33,479.54	$ 45,659.64	258,699.85
12/31/02	79,139.18	28,456.98	50,682.20	208,017.65
12/31/03	79,139.18	22,881.94	56,257.24	151,760.41
12/31/04	79,139.18	16,693.65	62,445.53	89,314.88
12/31/05	79,139.18	9,824.30(3)	69,314.88	20,000.00
	$395,695.90	$111,336.41	$284,359.49	

[1]Column (d) for preceding year times 11%.
[2]Column (a) minus column (b).
[3]Rounded.

The credit to unearned financing income is the difference between the gross investment in leased asset and the $304,359.49 Lessor paid to purchase the asset. "Unearned financing income," a contra-account to "Gross investment in leased asset," is used to arrive at "Net investment in leased asset." Only the "Net investment in leased asset" would appear on the balance sheet but the lessor's footnote disclosure for leases would show:

Gross investment in leased asset	$415,695.90
Less: Unearned financing income—leases	(111,336.41)
Net investment in leased asset	$304,359.49

The effect of this entry is to remove the asset account representing the equipment being leased and to replace it with two accounts which together reflect the net investment in the lease. The dollar amount for the asset removed ($304,359.49) is equal to the dollar amount for the net investment in leased asset ($415,695.90 − $111,336.41).

At December 31, 2001 Lessor Company makes the following journal entries:

DR Cash	$79,139.18	
CR Gross investment in leased asset		$79,139.18
DR Unearned financing income—leases	$33,479.54	
CR Financing income—leases		$33,479.54

The amount of financing income recognized in each subsequent year would be equal to the amounts shown in column (b) of Table 12.6, Lessor Company's amortization schedule. Lessor Company records no depreciation since the equipment itself is not being carried on its books.

After the last payment is made at the end of the lease term on December 31, 2005, the balance in the "Gross investment in leased asset" account will be $20,000.00, shown in column (d) of the amortization schedule. This amount represents the guaranteed residual value of the asset on the date that possession of the asset reverts to Lessor Company. Assume that the fair market value of the asset equals or exceeds $20,000; then the following entry would be made on December 31, 2005 to reflect the end of the lease and physical repossession of the asset.

DR Equipment—residual value	$20,000.00	
CR Gross investment in leased asset		$20,000.00

Financial Statement Effects of Direct Financing Versus Operating Leases

Comparing the financial statement effects of direct financing versus operating lease treatment allows a more complete understanding of lessor accounting.

Had the previous lease been accounted for by Lessor Company as an operating lease, the following journal entry would have been made each year:

DR Cash	$79,139.18	
CR Rental revenue		$79,139.18

Since the leased asset remains on the lessor's books under the operating method, annual depreciation must be recognized. Assume the asset is depreciated down to a $20,000 residual value on a straight-line basis; then the annual depreciation expense is $56,871.90 ([$304,359.49 − $20,000.00] ÷ 5), and the entry each year would be:

DR Depreciation expense	$56,871.90	
CR Accumulated depreciation		$56,871.90

Table 12.7 shows operating method amounts in columns (a) through (c) and (f) and contrasts these numbers with direct financing amounts. Income on the operating method totals $111,336.41 over the life of the lease, as shown in column (c) of Table 12.7. This total is identical to the income recognized under the direct financing method, as the total in column (d) reflects. ***So income over the life of the lease is unaffected by which accounting method is used. However, the timing of income does differ between the two methods,*** as indicated in the highlighted column (e) of Table 12.7. The direct financing method recognizes income sooner. Notice that the income timing difference would widen if an accelerated depreciation method were used in conjunction with the operating method, as opposed to the straight-line method employed in the example.

The "front-ending" of income under the direct financing method may explain why lessors—unlike lessees—have never seriously opposed the property rights approach to

Table 12.7 ■ LESSOR COMPANY

Operating Method Versus Direct Financing Method Income and Asset Balance Comparison

	Operating Method					Net Asset Balance at End of Year		
Year	(a) Lease Payment Received	(b) Depreciation	(c) Operating Method Income[1]	(d) Direct Financing Method Income[2]	(e) Income Difference Between Methods	(f) Operating Method[3]	(g) Direct Financing Method[4]	(h) Asset Balance Difference Between Methods
2001	$ 79,139.18	$ 56,871.90	$ 22,267.28	$ 33,479.54	+$11,212.26	$247,487.59	$258,699.85	+$11,212.26
2002	79,139.18	56,871.90	22,267.28	28,456.98	+ 6,189.70	190,615.69	208,017.65	+ 17,401.96
2003	79,139.18	56,871.90	22,267.28	22,881.94	+ 614.66	133,743.79	151,760.41	+ 18,016.62
2004	79,139.18	56,871.90	22,267.28	16,693.65	− 5,573.63	76,871.89	89,314.88	+ 12,442.99
2005	79,139.18	56,871.89	22,267.29	9,824.30	− 12,442.99	$ 20,000.00	$ 20,000.00	$ –0–
	$395,695.90	$284,359.49	$111,336.41	$111,336.41	$ –0–			

[1]Column (a) minus column (b).
[2]From column (b) of Table 12.6.
[3]$304,359.49 minus the period-to-date cumulative amount in column (b).
[4]From column (d) of Table 12.6.

lease accounting. Furthermore, the direct financing method results in other favorable financial statement effects. For example, the lessor's rate of return on assets ratio is usually improved under the direct financing method in the early years of a lease. Highlighted columns (e) and (h) in Table 12.7 illustrate this effect. Income and the end of year asset balance are both $11,212.26 higher under the direct financing method in 2001. An equal dollar increase in the numerator and denominator of a ratio will increase the ratio value as long as the initial value of the ratio is under 100%. Since reported rates of return on assets are almost always far less than 100%, the adoption of the direct financing method will almost always increase the lessor's reported rate of return in the early years of the lease.

CONTRACTING ANALYSIS

Of course, Table 12.7 also illustrates that this effect reverses as the lease grows older. In 2005, for example, income is $12,442.99 lower under the direct financing method while the end-of-year asset value is equal to what it would have been under the operating lease treatment. This would make the 2005 return on the direct financing method lower than the return that would have been reported on the operating lease approach.[10]

The current ratio of a lessor who uses the direct financing method will also be improved. Consider the current ratio at December 31, 2001. Under the operating lease method, the 2002 lease cash receipt of $79,139.18 would not be shown as an asset on Lessor Company's books on December 31, 2001, since performance under the lease contract has not yet taken place and will not take place until 2002. Under the direct financing method, however, the 2002 lease payment would be included as a component of the "Net investment in leased assets" account. Returning to Table 12.6, look at the December 31, 2001 balance in this account (column d), which is $258,699.85; of this amount, $50,682.20 (the principal reduction in the next 12 months) is classified as a current asset. This amount is shown in column (c) of Table 12.6 and represents the difference between the gross 2002 cash receipt of $79,139.18 from the lessee and the interest income of $28,456.98 that will be recognized in 2002. Thus, current assets on the direct financing basis would be higher than they would have been under the operating lease approach—and the current ratio is accordingly improved.

Sales-type Lease Treatment Illustrated

Accounting for sales-type leases is a simple extension of the direct financing method. A sales-type lease includes a manufacturer's or dealer's profit *in addition to* financing profit; a direct financing lease doesn't.

To illustrate the accounting for sales-type leases, we'll now assume Lessor Company is the *manufacturer* of the leased equipment. Prior to the start of the lease on January 1, 2001, the equipment was carried on Lessor Company's books at its manufactured cost of $240,000. All other facts in the original example (pages 592–593) remain unchanged.

Lessor Company would record the transaction on January 1, 2001 as:

DR Gross investment in leased asset	$415,695.90	
CR Sales revenue		$304,359.49
CR Unearned financing income–leases		111,336.41
DR Cost of goods sold	$240,000.00	
CR Inventory		$240,000.00

The net effect of these entries is to recognize $64,359.49 of manufacturing profit ($304,359.49 − $240,000.00) immediately. The $111,336.41 of financing profit will be recog-

[10] The ratio effect described here holds for each lease in isolation. However, most lessors have many leases of various ages outstanding. In these situations, the number of leases outstanding over time determines the effect on the return ratio. Assume Lessor Company's total number of leases is constant over time. Initially, when Lessor Company uses the direct financing method for new leases, its reported rate of return will increase. However, with a constant volume of leases, the average age of the leases accounted for on the direct financing method will eventually stabilize. When this happens, the return-on-assets ratio under the direct financing method will essentially be equal to what it would have been under the operating approach. If Lessor Company's leasing business is expanding over time, then there will be a constant infusion of new leases, and the average age of the leases in place will be falling. When this situation exists, the rate of return on assets will be higher under the direct financing method.

nized over the life of the lease, as shown in column (b) of the amortization schedule in Table 12.6. The entries for recording this financing profit are absolutely identical to the entries for the direct financing method on page 594.

The capital lease/operating lease dichotomy also exists for lessors. The criteria for classifying these leases include the same four criteria that apply to lessees plus two additional criteria. Lessors' incentives regarding how to classify leases are very different from those of lessees, since capital lease treatment accelerates the timing of income recognition for lessors. In addition, capital lease treatment improves many ratios for lessors in contrast to operating lease treatment.

RECAP

Additional Leasing Aspects

Sale and Leaseback

A sale and leaseback occurs when one company sells an asset to another company and immediately leases it back. This is done as a way to finance asset acquisition and/or for tax reasons. For example:

> First Company sells a manufacturing plant (excluding land) with a book value of $800,000 to Second Company for $1,000,000. First Company immediately leases the plant from Second Company for 20 years at an annual rental of $120,000.

First Company can treat the entire annual rental of $120,000 as a deductible expense for tax purposes; if it had continued to own the asset, it could deduct depreciation only for the building itself but not for the land on which the building is located. Thus, total tax deductions may be higher under sale and leaseback arrangements. Also, the cash infusion of $1,000,000 may help meet cash flow needs.

No new *lease* accounting issues arise in sale and leaseback transactions. If the lease satisfies any of the four lessees' criteria on page 578, First Company must account for the lease as a capital lease; if none of the criteria are met, it is treated as an operating lease. If the lease satisfies at least one of the lessors' Type I characteristics and both of the Type II characteristics (page 591), Second Company treats the lease as a direct financing lease; otherwise, it is an operating lease on Second Company's books.

The only complication in sale and leaseback arrangements is the treatment of the difference between the sale price of $1,000,000 and the $800,000 carrying value of the manufacturing plant on First Company's books. Typically, when assets are sold, this $200,000 would be recognized immediately on First Company's books as a gain on sale.

But this is not the way gains are treated in sale and leaseback transactions. Instead, First Company must record the $200,000 as a balance sheet credit, called a **deferred gain.** If the lease is a capital lease to First Company, this gain is then amortized into income using the same rate and life used to amortize the asset itself. If the lease is an operating lease to First Company, the gain is amortized in proportion to the rental payments.

Assume that the lease qualifies as a capital lease; then First Company's entries would initially be:

DR Cash (or receivable)	$1,000,000	
CR Property		$ 800,000
CR Deferred gain		200,000
DR Leased asset-capital lease	$1,000,000	
CR Obligation under capital lease		$1,000,000

(This assumes that the discounted present value of the minimum lease payments is equal to $1,000,000.)

The rationale for deferring the gain is simple. Notice that at the time of "sale," the sales price of $1,000,000 and the annual lease payment schedule of $120,000 are simultaneously set, and the transaction will continue for 20 years. It may be that the property is only "worth" $800,000 and that Second Company is effectively loaning $200,000 to First Company, which will be recovered over time through the $120,000 annual payments on the lease. Recognizing a gain in such circumstances would allow First Company to initially overstate its income by $200,000; this would be offset in later years by overstating its expenses by an identical amount. Thus, the GAAP requirement of deferring the gain protects against income manipulation possibilities. However, the conservatism inherent to GAAP requires that losses in sale and leaseback transactions be recognized immediately on the seller's books.

Other Special Lease Accounting Rules

SFAS No. 13 also covers a number of highly specialized leasing situations and outlines in detail the rules for handling these situations. Real estate leases are an example of situations requiring specialized rules in *SFAS No. 13.*[11] Leveraged leases represent another example. In a **leveraged lease,** the lessor obtains nonrecourse financing for the leased asset from a third party, such as a bank. The lease is "leveraged" because the lessor borrows to finance the transaction. A leveraged lease does not affect the lessee's accounting. For these leases, lessees use the same procedures outlined earlier. However, the lessor must account for leveraged leases using the direct financing approach, and there are special details—outlined at length in *SFAS No. 13*—which apply.

Financial Reporting versus Tax Accounting for Leases

The U.S. income tax rules also distinguish between operating leases and capital leases. However, the tax criteria for differentiating between them are not the same as the *SFAS No. 13* criteria. Further, the parties' incentives are reversed for tax purposes. *Lessees* prefer the capital lease approach because it accelerates recognition of expenses and thereby lowers the discounted present value of their tax liability. *Lessors* prefer the operating lease approach on the tax return because it delays recognition of revenue and lowers the present value of the tax liability. So book versus tax differences are frequent for both lessors and lessees.

The divergence between book accounting and tax accounting for lessees has widened in recent years with the invention of **synthetic leases.** Synthetic leases result from complicated arrangements that include a lender, outside investors, a special purpose entity and the lessee. We'll skip the gory details of the legal arrangement and give you the punchline. A synthetic lease is structured to achieve the best of both worlds from the lessee's perspective: operating lease treatment on the books and capital lease treatment on the tax return. The lease contract is structured to avoid triggering any of the four *SFAS No. 13* criteria, so it's an operating lease for financial reporting purposes. But for tax purposes, the lessee is considered the owner of the asset because the contractual arrangement gives the lessee the proceeds of any appreciation in the asset value at the end of the lease term. There will seldom be disclosure that the lessee has engaged in a synthetic lease arrangement. The synthetic lease(s) will be included without special designation along with other operating leases in the footnote disclosure.

We encountered special purpose entities in Chapter 8, pages 360–361, when examining securitization transactions.

Lessors' Disclosures

Exhibit 12.3 is taken from the notes to the December 31, 1999 financial statements of Boeing Corporation, the aircraft manufacturer. The exhibit illustrates *SFAS No. 13* disclosure requirements for lessors. Capital and operating leases must be disclosed separately, and a minimum lease payment schedule must be provided—just as lessees do. Furthermore, the components of the net investment in capital leases (minimum lease payments, estimated residual values, etc.) are delineated, as are the cost and accumulated depreciation of assets under operating leases. The proportion of capital to operating leases for lessors is frequently greater than one—a stark contrast with lessees. Exhibit 12.3 illustrates this understandably lower resistance to capital lease treatment by lessors.

---

[11] Op. cit., para. 24–27.

Exhibit 12.3 ■ BOEING CORPORATION

Illustration of Lessor's Financial Statement Note Disclosures December 31, 1999

Note 10 **Customer and Commercial Financing**

Customer and commercial financing at December 31 consisted of the following:

		1999		1998
Investment in Sales-type/Financing Leases				
Aircraft financing		$1,497		$1,325
Commercial equipment financing		506		548
Total		$2,003		$1,873
Operating Leases				
Operating lease equipment cost:				
Aircraft financing	$2,661		$2,396	
Commercial equipment financing	500		639	
Cost		$3,161		$3,035
Less: Accumulated depreciation:				
Aircraft financing	(304)		(195)	
Commercial equipment financing	(92)		(129)	
		(396)		(324)
Net investment		$2,765		$2,711

Customer and commercial financing assets that are leased by the Company under capital leases and have been subleased to others totaled $502 and $333 as of December 31, 1999 and 1998. Commercial equipment financing under operating lease consists principally of real property, highway vehicles, machine tools, and production equipment.

Scheduled payments on customer and commercial financing are as follows:

Year	Sales-type/ Financing Lease Payments Receivable	Operating Lease Payments Receivable
2000	$ 587	$ 294
2001	416	267
2002	212	249
2003	195	236
2004	175	216
Beyond 2004	797	2,045
Total	$2,382	$3,307

The components of investment in sales-type/financing leases at December 31 were as follows:

	1999	1998
Minimum lease payments receivable	$2,382	$2,362
Estimated residual value of leased assets	479	438
Unearned income	(858)	(927)
Total	$2,003	$1,873

Authors' note: This financial statement note has been edited and a portion of the disclosure format has been modified slightly. The unedited footnote also includes notes receivable from customers. There is a December 31, 1999 valuation allowance of $275 deducted from the investment in leases and notes receivable combined.

SUMMARY

The treatment of leases in *SFAS No. 13* represents a compromise between the unperformed-contracts and property-rights approaches. *SFAS No. 13* adopted a middle-of-the-road position that neither capitalized all leases nor prohibited capitalization. Instead, the FASB developed criteria for determining the precise intermediate circumstances under which leases would be capitalized.

Several of the lease capitalization criteria that the FASB decided on are essentially arbitrary; examples are the 75% economic life rule and the 90% recovery of investment rule. Since lease capitalization adversely affects lessees' financial statements, many lessees have tried to circumvent the *SFAS No. 13* rules and thus avoid lease capitalization. Unfortunately, some of these arbitrary rules are easy to circumvent in a way that cannot be prevented. For example, a lessee who wants to avoid lease capitalization could simply negotiate lease terms that span only 74% of the estimated economic life of the property rather than 75%. As a result, the number of leases capitalized on lessees' books pursuant to *SFAS No. 13* has been small. But the proportion of operating lease payments to capital lease payments can vary greatly even between firms in the same industry. This complicates financial analysis because keeping leases off the balance sheet improves various ratios like return on assets, debt-to-equity, and the current ratio. Consequently, analysts must constructively capitalize operating leases to make valid comparisons between firms with different proportions of capitalized leases.

The FASB has been compelled to issue 10 statements on leases subsequent to *SFAS No. 13* and numerous interpretations of the original statement in an effort to close loopholes for keeping leases off the balance sheet as soon as those loopholes are perceived. But this process demonstrates the inherent weakness of a compromise approach that must rely on essentially arbitrary criteria for implementation.

The ingenuity of lessees who wish to keep leases off the balance sheet suggests that new loopholes will continue to be invented and that new rules designed to plug these loopholes will be forthcoming.

When lessors use the capital lease approach, income recognition is accelerated, in contrast to the timing of income recognition under the operating lease approach. Lessors' financial statement ratios are also improved. It is perhaps not surprising, therefore, that capital leases appear frequently on lessors' financial statements.

APPENDIX Making Balance Sheet Data Comparable by Adjusting for Off-Balance Sheet Leases

ANALYSIS

Some lessees deliberately structure leases to evade capital lease criteria, thereby keeping most of their leases off the balance sheet. Other companies are less aggressive and have a larger proportion of capital leases. This complicates comparisons between any two companies, because each may have similar lease contract terms but very dissimilar lease balance sheet numbers.

The most straightforward method for making lessees' balance sheet data comparable is to treat *all* leases as if they were capital leases. That is, analysts should use the disclosed minimum *operating* lease payment schedule as a basis for approximating what the balance sheet numbers would have been had those operating leases been treated instead as capital leases. This is called **constructive capitalization.** We use the Sears, Roebuck data from Exhibit 12.1 to illustrate how this is done. For convenience, these numbers for Sears are reproduced in the following exhibit.

The liability that would appear on the balance sheet if these operating leases were instead treated as capital leases is the *discounted present value* of the stream of minimum operating lease payments. This payment stream totals $2,419. Two items must be estimated in order to compute this present value. First, a discount rate must be selected. Second, each year's payments beyond 2004 must be estimated, since lease payments for all years after 2004 are aggregated.

SEARS, ROEBUCK AND COMPANY

Operating Lease Payments from Lease Footnote
January 1, 2000 Annual Report

($ in millions)

Fiscal Year	Minimum Operating Lease Payments
2000	$ 352
2001	303
2002	253
2003	224
2004	195
After 2004	1,092
Total minimum lease payments	$2,419

Selecting a Discount Rate: In some cases a company will disclose in its lease footnote the weighted average discount rate used for all its capital lease commitments. This rate would be appropriate to use for capitalizing operating leases. Alternatively, an estimate of the discount rate can be derived from the lessee's financial statement footnote for long-term debt. The interest rate paid on each debt issue is disclosed in this footnote. The weighted average rate on outstanding long-term debt provides a reasonable estimate of the lease discount rate. Another way to estimate the average long-term debt rate is to compute the ratio of interest expense to average debt outstanding. Doing this using data from Sears' debt footnote yields an estimated rate of 8%.

Sears discloses interest paid in 1999 was $1.2 billion. Long-term debt at the beginning of 1999 was $15.045 billion and at the end of 1999 was $15.049 billion. So a simple estimate of average debt outstanding is $15.047 billion. The estimate of the long-term debt rate is:

$$\frac{\$1.2 \text{ billion}}{\$15.047 \text{ billion}} \cong 8\%$$

Estimating Payments Beyond Five Years: Procedures for estimating annual operating lease payments for periods after 2004 can also be developed. One approach is as follows. Notice that the annual *decline* in minimum operating lease payments between 2002 and 2004 is $29 million per year. This suggests that the undisclosed minimum operating lease payment for 2005 is probably in the vicinity of $166 million—the $195 million 2004 payment minus approximately $29 million of estimated yearly decline. The simplest approach for estimating a schedule of annual payments for 2005 and beyond is to assume that all subsequent payments are also somewhere near $166 million per year. Dividing the total later years' minimum operating lease payments ($1,092 million, the highlighted figure) by $166 million yields an initial estimate of how many years beyond 2004 the existing operating leases run. The computation is:

$$\frac{\text{Minimum operating lease payments for years after 2004}}{\text{Estimated yearly lease payment (assumed to be the same for all years)}} = \frac{\$1{,}092 \text{ million}}{\$166 \text{ million per year}} = 6.578 \text{ years}$$

The initial estimate is 6.578 years, which we round to 7 years. Based on this estimate, the net minimum lease payments will be discounted over a 12-year period—that is, 2000 through 2004 (5 years) plus the estimated 7 years we just computed.

Our estimate of the amount of additional liability that would appear on Sears' balance sheet at January 1, 2000 if all operating leases were capitalized is the highlighted amount shown in Table 12.8. This number is an additional liability of approximately $1,672.0 million. A small portion ($218.2 million) would be a current liability and $1,672 million − $218.2 million, or $1,453.8 million, would be a long-term liability.

The current liability of $218.2 million is determined as follows. Interest expense in fiscal year 2000 on these capitalized operating leases would approximate $1,672.0 × 8%, or $133.8. The 2000 minimum operating lease payment is $352 in Table 12.8. Since interest is a liability that accrues over time, only the difference between the total 2000 payment of $352 and the as-yet unaccrued interest of $133.8 (i.e., $218.2) is a current liability as of January 1, 2000.

Once the capitalized operating lease liability has been estimated, the next task is to estimate the capitalized operating lease *asset* amount. One approach is to assume that

Table 12.8 ■ SEARS, ROEBUCK AND COMPANY

Estimate of Capitalized Operating Lease Liability as of January 1, 2000

($ in millions)

Fiscal Year	Minimum Operating Lease Payment	Present Value Factor at 8%	Discounted Present Value
2000	$352	.92593	$ 325.9
2001	303	.85734	259.8
2002	253	.79383	200.8
2003	224	.73503	164.6
2004	195	.68058	132.7
2005–2011	166	3.54337[(1)]	588.2
Total			$1,672.0

[1]Present value of an ordinary annuity for 12 years at 8% minus present value of an ordinary annuity for 5 years at 8%, or 7.53608 minus 3.99271.

the amount of the asset equals the amount of the computed operating lease liability. Since the asset and liability amounts are equal at the inception of a capital lease, this approach assumes that this initial equality is maintained over the entire life of the lease. But a more precise estimate can easily be made, as shown in Figure 12.3.

Figure 12.3(a) graphically represents data from the Lessee Company illustration from Table 12.1 where lease payments are due at the end of each period. The year-end book value of the capitalized asset (the blue line in the graph) starts at $300,000 and declines yearly by $60,000—the straight-line amortization amount from column (e) in Table 12.1—until it reaches zero at the end of 2005. The red line depicts the year-end lease obligation balance from column (d) in Table 12.1. While the two balances are obviously equal at the beginning and end of the lease, ***for all intermediate periods, the asset amount is lower than the liability.*** This relationship holds in general, since early-year payments do not reduce the liability by as much as later-year payments do (compare columns [c] and [e] of Table 12.1). Notice that Figure 12.3(a) includes the percentage relationship between the capitalized asset and liability balances for all intermediate lease years. For example, at December 31, 2001, the asset balance is 95.7% of the obligation balance for the five-year lease.

Figure 12.3

LESSEE COMPANY
General Relationship Between Capital Lease Asset and Liability When Payments Are at *End* of Period (a) 5-Year Lease; (b) 10-Year Lease; (c) 20-Year Lease

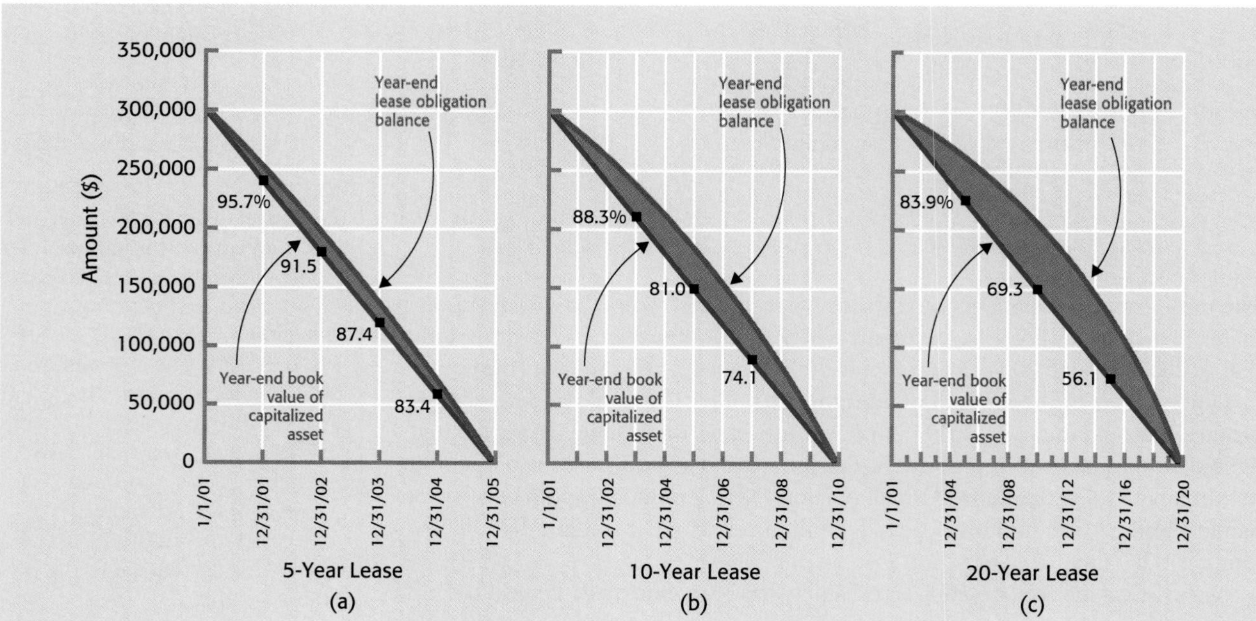

Parts (b) and (c) in the figure show the relationship between the lease asset and lease liability balances for the same basic facts as in (a), but here the lease period is for 10 years and 20 years, respectively. The *difference* between the asset and liability balances *increases* the longer the life of the lease. The reason is that the lease liability balance decreases at a lower rate when lease payments are spread over longer periods—that is, a greater portion of each early lease payment is for interest and a correspondingly smaller portion goes toward reducing the lease obligation the longer the term of the lease.

Lessee Company's interest expense for 2001 would be 10% times $228,055 or $22,805.50.

Lease Payments in Advance Leases frequently require the lessee to make an up-front payment when the lease is signed. Advance payments in a capital lease mean that at the inception of the lease the amount of the recorded asset will exceed the liability. Using the Table 12.3 example (p. 584), we assume a 10% discount rate and that Lessee Company makes its five annual payments in advance. Each payment is $71,945. The journal entry on January 1, 2001 is:

DR Capital lease asset	$300,000.00	
CR Cash		$ 71,945
CR Obligation under capital lease		228,055

Figure 12.4 depicts the general relationship between the lease asset and lease liability for a five-, ten- and twenty-year lease at a 10% discount rate where the contract calls for payments at the beginning of each lease period.

In contrast to the situation depicted in Figure 12.3 where payments are at the end of each lease period, the up-front payment means that the asset carrying amount initially *exceeds* the liability amount, as shown in both the journal entry and in Figure 12.4. With payments in advance, in periods subsequent to the lease signing, the relationship between the leased asset and liability carrying amounts depends on the length of the lease term. With five- and ten-year leases and a 10% discount rate, the carrying value of the lease

The relationship also will depend on the discount rate. With higher discount rates, the lease liability balance will decrease at a slower rate. Accordingly, the curvature of the lease liability book value line depicted in Figure 12.4 will be more pronounced.

Figure 12.4

LESSEE COMPANY
General Relationship Between Capital Lease Asset and Liability When *Up-Front* Payments Are Made for a (a) 5-Year Lease; (b) 10-Year Lease; (c) 20-Year Lease.

With a $300,000 present value at 10%, the annual payments for a 5-year, 10-year, and 20-year lease are $71,945.00, $44,385.11, and $32,034.44, respectively. The vertical distance between the lease asset and obligation lines on 1/1/01 represent these initial payments.

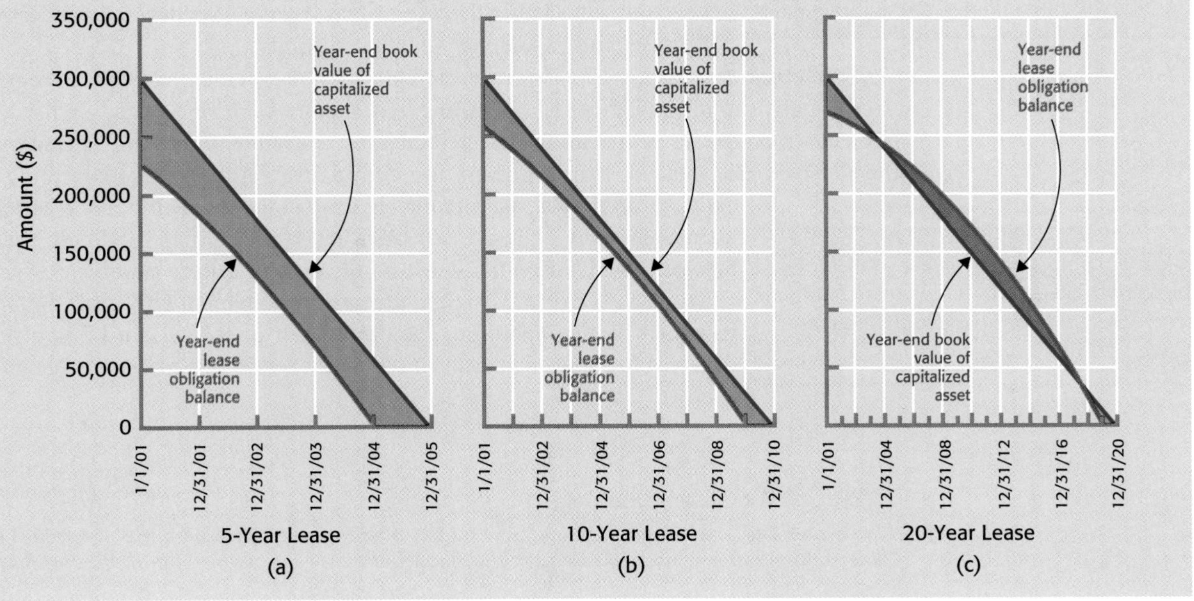

liability is always less than the asset book value throughout the lease term. However, as shown for a 20-year lease, the liability amount quickly exceeds the asset amount, and this relationship is maintained until the last two years of the lease. This excess is the red area in Figure 12.4(c). The liability quickly "overtakes" the asset because early year payments on an amortization schedule do not reduce the liability by as much as later year payments do. For a given lease length, the higher the interest rate, the quicker the liability exceeds the asset.

Most companies have a portfolio of operating leases with different ages, interest rates, and payment timing. Therefore, on average across the entire portfolio, many companies' asset-to-liability ratio will be somewhere in the red area of Figure 12.4(c). ***The capital lease liability will often exceed the asset as illustrated in both Figures 12.3 and 12.4(c).*** However, there are exceptions. When most of a firm's leases have up-front payments, the interest rate is low, and/or the life of the average lease is relatively short, then the asset amount *can* exceed the liability amount. As you will see, this is true for Sears at January 1, 2000.

The percentage relationship between the asset and the liability is a function of payment timing, the interest rate, and the length of the lease.[12] Furthermore, the precise relationship *at any specific date* depends upon the average age of existing leases. Rather than attempting to estimate the percentage relationship between the asset and liability for capitalized operating leases, we can use the disclosure the company makes for capital leases. For example, at January 1, 2000 Sears disclosed that its net capital lease assets totaled $496 million and its net capital lease obligations were $417 million. This results in an asset-to-liability ratio for capital leases of 119%. It may be reasonable to use this same percentage to estimate the operating lease asset to be capitalized. Our estimate of the balance sheet asset that would arise from capitalized operating leases is therefore the computed liability from Table 12.8—$1,672.0 million—times 119%, or $1,989.7 million.

SFAS No. 13 (para. 16) requires that lessees disclose the net capital lease asset and liability.

Table 12.9 illustrates the estimated ratio effects for fiscal year 1999 that result from capitalizing operating leases for Sears. Table 12.9(a) column (1) shows financial statement numbers as reported in Sears' 1999 statements. Column (2) shows the adjustments for operating lease capitalization. Notice, in addition to the capital lease asset and liability adjustments, there is a "net credit to balance" of $318—simply the difference between the $1,990 estimated asset amount minus the $1,672 liability amount. The credit of $318 is the net of two items, (1) a debt to a deferred tax asset and (2) a credit to owners' equity.

Of course, this is only a rough approximation. The higher the proportion of leases with up-front payments, the shorter the lease life, and/or the lower the interest rate, the higher the asset-to-liability ratio. So, if operating leases differ along these dimensions from capital leases, using the disclosed capital leases asset-to-liability ratio will tend to misstate the asset carrying value after capitalizing operating leases.

A deferred tax asset arises because capitalization accelerates expense recognition. Accordingly, capitalizing these leases means that expenses are recognized earlier on the books than on the tax return and a deferred tax asset consequently results. The amount of the deferred tax asset is determined by the cumulative capital versus operating lease expense difference. Unfortunately, this cumulative difference cannot be estimated easily or accurately. As a result we cannot subdivide the $318 between the deferred tax asset and the owners' equity credit.

This paragraph assumes you are comfortable with deferred tax concepts. If you are not, you can safely skip this paragraph and return to Table 12.9 after reading Chapter 13.

As discussed in the chapter, the income statement effects of capital lease treatment versus operating lease treatment often will not be significantly different for mature firms. Consequently, we do not adjust income in Table 12.9(a).

[12] See Imhoff, Lipe, and Wright, op. cit., pp. 51–63. A table in this article computes the asset-to-liability ratio for leases of various duration and interest rates. The table presumes that lease payments are made at the *end* of each period.

Table 12.9 ■ SEARS, ROEBUCK AND COMPANY

Effect on Selected Ratios of Capitalizing Operating Leases
January 1, 2000

(a)
Financial Statement Data

($ in millions) **Statement Item**	**(1) January 1, 2000 Financial Statements**	**(2) Adjustments for Capitalization**		**(3) Total, After Capitalization**
Total assets	$36,954	Capital lease asset	+ $1,990	$38,944
		Current portion lease obligation	+ 218	218
Total long-term obligations	16,414	Long-term lease obligation	+ 1,454	17,868
Owners' equity	6,839	Net credit to balance	+ 318	7,157
Operating income before taxes and other charges	2,413		0	$ 2,413

(b)
Adjusted Ratios After Capitalization

Ratio	**(1) As Reported in 1/01/00 Financial Statements**	**(2) Ratio After Capitalization**
Total long-term obligations to equity ratio	2.40	2.50#
Pre-tax return on total assets	6.530	6.196*

#Computed by adding $1,454 to column (1) obligations and $318 to column (1) equity. This ignores the unknown deferred tax effect and distorts the adjusted column (3) ratio slightly.

*Computed by adding $1,990 to column (1) total assets. This ignores the unknown deferred tax effect and distorts the adjusted column (3) ratio slightly.

The adjusted ratios after capitalization are shown in Table 12.9(b). Notice that the adjustments from capitalizing operating leases do not change Sears' ratios significantly. Pre-tax return on assets is lowered by approximately 5.1% and the total long-term obligations to equity ratio is increased by approximately 4.2%. Nevertheless, it is important to make adjustments like these if you're making financial comparisons *across* firms. While the effect on Sears is small, some of Sears' competitors may be more aggressive in keeping leases off the balance sheet. So interfirm comparisons may be misleading unless adjustments are also made to the competitors' statements. The underlying real economic differences appear only when the adjusted statements for all firms are compared. The easiest way to overcome these capitalization differences between firms is to treat all leases that convey significant property rights as though they were capital leases.

> Table 12.4 shows that three of the other firms in the "Department/Variety Stores" industry have a higher ratio of operating to capital lease payments than Sears. This difference underscores the importance of making adjustments to Sears' competitors before undertaking financial comparisons.

A movement to do this in the financial statements themselves is emerging internationally. The FASB recently published a special report formulated by a working group comprising standard-setters from Australia, Canada, the International Accounting Standards Committee (IASC), New Zealand, the United Kingdom, and the United States. This report proposed that many leases that are now treated as operating leases should be treated as capital leases.[13]

[13] See W. McGregor (Principal Author), *Accounting for Leases: A New Approach*, Financial Accounting Series, Special Report No. 163–A (Norwalk, CT: FASB, 1996).

EXERCISES

E12–1

Lessee and lessor accounting

AICPA adapted

Fox Company, a dealer in machinery and equipment, leased equipment to Tiger, Inc. on July 1, 2001. The lease is appropriately accounted for as a sale by Fox and as a purchase by Tiger. The lease is for a 10-year period (the useful life of the asset), expiring June 30, 2011. The first of 10 equal payments of $500,000 was made on July 1, 2001. Fox had purchased the equipment for $2,675,000 on January 1, 2001 and established a list selling price of $3,375,000 on the equipment. Assume that the present value at July 1, 2001 of the rent payments over the lease term discounted at 12% (the appropriate interest rate) was $3,165,000.

REQUIRED:

1. What is the amount of profit on the sale and the amount of interest income that Fox should record for the year ended December 31, 2001? How much interest income should Fox record in 2002?
2. Assume that Tiger uses straight-line depreciation and a 12% discount rate. What is the amount of depreciation and interest expense that Tiger should record for the year ended December 31, 2001 and for the year ended December 31, 2002?

E12–2

Lessee accounting

AICPA adapted

On January 2, 2001 Lafayette Machine Shops, Inc. signed a 10-year noncancelable lease for a heavy-duty drill press, stipulating annual payments of $15,000 starting at the end of the first year, with title passing to Lafayette at the expiration of the lease. Lafayette treated this transaction as a capital lease. The drill press has an estimated useful life of 15 years, with no salvage value. Lafayette uses straight-line depreciation for all its fixed assets. Aggregate lease payments were determined to have a present value of $92,170, based on implicit interest of 10%.

REQUIRED:

What amount should Lafayette record for interest expense and depreciation expense for 2001?

E12–3

Lessee accounting: Purchase option

AICPA adapted

East Company leased a new machine from North Company on May 1, 2001 under a lease with the following information:

Lease term	10 years
Annual rental payable at beginning of each lease year	$40,000
Useful life of machine	12 years
Implicit interest rate	14%
Present value of an annuity of $1 paid at the beginning of each of 10 periods at 14%	5.95
Present value of $1 due at the end of 10 periods at 14%	0.27

East has the option to purchase the machine on May 1, 2011 by paying $50,000, which approximates the expected fair market value of the machine on the option exercise date.

REQUIRED:

What is the amount of the capitalized leased asset on May 1, 2001?

E12–4

Lessee accounting and classification

AICPA adapted

On December 31, 2001 Ball Company leased a machine from Cook for a 10-year period, expiring December 30, 2011. Annual payments of $100,000 are due on December 31. The first payment was made on December 31, 2001, and the second payment was made on December 31, 2002. The present value at the inception of the lease for the 10 lease payments discounted at 10% was $676,000. The lease is appropriately accounted for as a capital lease by Ball.

REQUIRED:

1. Compute the December 31, 2002 amount that Ball should report as lease liability.
2. What portion of this total liability should be classified as a current liability?

E12–5

Lessor accounting

AICPA adapted

Grady Company purchased a machine on January 1, 2001 for $720,000. The machine is expected to have a ten-year life, no residual value, and will be depreciated by the straight-line method. On January 1, 2001 the machine was leased to Lesch Company for a three-year period at an annual rental of $125,000. Grady could have sold the machine for $860,000 instead of leasing it. Grady incurred maintenance and other executory costs of $15,000 in 2001 under the terms of the lease.

REQUIRED:

What amount should Grady report as operating profit on this leased asset for the year ended December 31, 2001?

E12–6

Lessor accounting: Sales-type lease

AICPA adapted

Benedict Company leased equipment to Mark Inc. on January 1, 2001. The lease is for an eight-year period, expiring December 31, 2008. The first of eight equal annual payments of $600,000 was made on January 1, 2001. Benedict had purchased the equipment on December 29, 2000 for $3,200,000. The lease is appropriately accounted for as a sales-type lease by Benedict. Assume that the present value at January 1, 2001 of all rental payments over the lease term discounted at a 10% interest rate was $3,520,000.

REQUIRED:

What amount of interest income should Benedict record in 2002 (the second year of the lease period) as a result of the lease?

E12–7

Lessor accounting: Direct financing leases

AICPA adapted

Glade Company leases computer equipment to customers under direct financing leases. The equipment has no residual value at the end of the lease term, and the leases do not contain bargain purchase options. Glade wishes to earn 8% interest on a five-year lease of equipment with a fair value of $323,400. The present value of an annuity of $1 paid at the start of each period for five years at 8% is 4.312.

REQUIRED:

Compute the total amount of interest revenue that Glade will earn over the life of the lease.

E12–8

Lessor accounting: Sales-type lease

AICPA adapted

Peg Company leased equipment from Howe Corporation on July 1, 2001 for an eight-year period, expiring June 30, 2009. Equal payments under the lease are $600,000 and are due on July 1 of each year. The first payment was made on July 1, 2001. The rate of interest contemplated by Peg and Howe is 10%. The cash selling price of the equipment is $3,520,000, and the cost of the equipment on Howe's accounting records is $2,800,000. The lease is appropriately recorded as a sales-type lease.

REQUIRED:

Determine the amount of profit on the sale and interest revenue that Howe should record for the year ended December 31, 2001.

E12–9

Lessee accounting: Discount rate

AICPA adapted

On December 31, 2001 Day Company leased a new machine from Parr with the following pertinent information:

Lease term	6 years
Annual rental payable at beginning of each year	$50,000
Useful life of machine	8 years
Day's incremental borrowing rate	15%
Implicit interest rate in lease (this rate was known by Day)	12%
Present value of annuity of $1 paid at the start of each of six periods at	
12%	4.61
15%	4.35

The lease is not renewable, and the machine reverts to Parr at the termination of the lease. The cost of the machine on Parr's accounting records is $375,500.

REQUIRED:

Compute the amount of Day's lease liability at the beginning of the lease term.

E12–10

Lessee accounting: Purchase option

AICPA adapted

Robbins, Inc. leased a machine from Ready Leasing Company. The lease qualifies as a capital lease and requires 10 annual payments of $10,000, beginning immediately. The lease specifies an interest rate of 12% (the lessor's return) and a purchase option of $10,000 at the end of the tenth year even though the machine's estimated value on that date is $20,000. Robbins' incremental borrowing rate is 14%.

The present value of an annuity paid at the start of each period at:

12% for 10 years is 6.328
14% for 10 years is 5.946

The present value of $1 at:

12% for 10 years is 0.322
14% for 10 years is 0.270

REQUIRED:

Compute the amount that Robbins should record as the lease liability at the beginning of the lease term.

E12–11

Lessee accounting
AICPA adapted

On January 1, 2001 Babson, Inc. leased two automobiles for executive use. The lease requires Babson to make five annual payments of $13,000, beginning January 1, 2001. At the end of the lease term, on December 31, 2005, Babson guarantees the residual value of the automobiles will total $10,000. The lease qualifies as a capital lease. The interest rate implicit in the lease is 9%. Present value factors for the 9% rate implicit in the lease are as follows:

For a five-period annuity paid at the start of each period	4.240
For a five-period annuity paid at the end of each period	3.890
Present value of $1 due in five periods	0.650

REQUIRED:

Compute Babson's recorded capital lease liability immediately after the first required payment.

E12–12

Lessee reporting: Executory costs
AICPA adapted

On December 31, 2001 Roe Company leased a machine from Colt for a five-year period. Equal annual payments under the lease are $105,000 (including $5,000 annual executory costs) and are due on December 31 of each year. The first payment was made on December 31, 2001, and the second payment was made on December 31, 2002. The five lease payments are discounted at 10% over the lease term. The present value of minimum lease payments at the inception of the lease and before the first annual payment was $417,000. The lease is appropriately accounted for as a capital lease by Roe.

REQUIRED:

What is the lease liability that Roe should report in its December 31, 2002 balance sheet?

E12–13

Sale and leaseback
AICPA adapted

On December 31, 2001 Lane, Inc. sold equipment to Noll and simultaneously leased it back for 12 years. Pertinent information at this date is as follows:

Sales price	$480,000
Carrying amount	360,000
Estimated remaining economic life	15 years

REQUIRED:

1. At December 31, 2001 should Lane report a gain from the sale of the equipment?
2. If not, how should the sale and leaseback be accounted for?

PROBLEMS/DISCUSSION QUESTIONS

P12–1

Lease accounting overview: Lessors and lessees

Lessor Company has a machine with a cost and fair market value of $100,000 that it leases for a 10-year period to Lessee Company. The machine has a 12-year expected economic life. Payments are received at the beginning of each year. The machine is expected to have a $10,000 residual value at the end of the lease term. (The residual value is not guaranteed by the Lessee.)

REQUIRED:

1. What would the lease payments be if Lessor Company wants to earn a 10% return on its net investment?
2. What would be the lease obligation reported by Lessee Company when the lease is signed?
3. What would be the interest revenue reported by Lessor Company and the interest expense reported by Lessee Company in the first year assuming they both use the 10% discount rate?
4. How would the answers to (2) and (3) change for Lessee Company if the residual value is guaranteed by Lessee Company?

P12–2

Lessees' accounting for capital leases

On January 1, 2001 Seven Wonders Inc. signed a five-year noncancelable lease with Moss Company. The lease calls for five payments of $277,409.44 to be made at the end of each year. The leased asset has a fair market value of $1,200,000 on January 1, 2001. Seven Wonders cannot renew the lease, there is no bargain purchase option, and ownership of the leased asset reverts to Moss at the end of the lease. The leased asset has an expected useful life of six years, and Seven Wonders uses straight-line depreciation for financial reporting purposes. Seven Wonders' incremental borrowing rate is 12%. Moss' implicit rate of return on the lease is unknown. Seven Wonders uses a calendar year for financial reporting purposes.

REQUIRED:

1. Why must Seven Wonders account for the lease as a capital lease?
2. Prepare a schedule for the amortization of the lease liability. Round the amount of the initial lease liability at January 1, 2001 to the nearest dollar. Round all amounts in the amortization table to the nearest cent.
3. Make the journal entry to record (a) the lease as a capital lease on January 1, 2001, (b) the lease payments on December 31, 2001 and 2002, and (c) the depreciation of the leased asset in 2001 and 2002.
4. What is the total amount of expense reported on Seven Wonders' 2001 income statement from the lease? Is this amount the same as, more than, or less than the amount that would have been reported if the lease had been classified as an operating lease? Why?

P12–3

Lessees' accounting for capital leases

REQUIRED:

1. Repeat requirement (2) of P12–2. Assume that the lease payments are due at the beginning of the year rather than at the end of the year. In this case the first payment of $277,409.44 would be made on January 1, 2001. Round the amount of the initial lease liability at January 1, 2001 to the nearest dollar. Round all amounts in the amortization table to the nearest cent.
2. Make the journal entry to record the lease as a capital lease on January 1, 2001. In addition, prepare the lessee's adjusting entries for December 31, 2001 and 2002 as well as the entries to record the lease payments on January 1, 2002 and 2003, and the depreciation of the leased asset in 2001 and 2002.

P12–4

Lessees' accounting for capital leases including executory costs and residual value guarantee

On January 1, 2001 Bare Trees Company signed a three-year noncancelable lease with Dreams Inc. The lease calls for three payments of $62,258.09 to be made at the end of each year. The lease payments include $3,000 of executory costs. The lease is nonrenewable, and there is no bargain purchase option. Ownership of the leased asset reverts to Dreams at the end of the lease period, at which time Bare Trees has guaranteed that the leased asset will be worth at least $15,000. The leased asset has an expected useful life of four years, and Bare Trees uses straight-line depreciation for financial reporting purposes. Bare Trees' incremental borrowing rate is 9%, which is less than Dreams' implicit rate of return on the lease.

REQUIRED:

1. Prepare a schedule for the amortization of the lease liability. Round the amount of the initial lease liability at January 1, 2001 to the nearest dollar. Round all amounts in the amortization table to the nearest cent.

2. Make the journal entry to record (a) the lease on January 1, 2001, (b) the lease payments on December 31, 2001 and 2002, and (c) the depreciation of the leased asset in 2001 and 2002.
3. Assume that at the end of the lease term the leased asset is worth $16,000. Make the journal entry to account for the residual value guarantee.
4. Repeat (3), but assume that the leased asset is worth only $12,000 at the end of the lease term.

P12–5

Capital lease effects on ratios and income

On December 31, 2001 Thomas Henley, financial vice president of Kingston Corporation, signed a noncancelable three-year lease for an item of manufacturing equipment. The lease called for annual payments of $41,635 per year due at the *end* of each of the next three years. The expected economic life of the leased equipment was four years. No cash changed hands since the first payment wasn't due until December 31, 2002.

Mr. Henley was talking with his auditor that afternoon and was surprised to learn that the lease qualified as a capital lease and would have to be put on the balance sheet. Although his intuition told him that capitalization adversely affected certain ratios, the size of these adverse effects was unclear to him. Because similar leases on other equipment were up for renewal in 2002, he wanted a precise measure of the ratio deterioration. "If these effects are excessive," he said, "I'll try to get similar leases on the other machinery to qualify as operating leases when they come up for renewal next year."

Assume that the appropriate rate for discounting the minimum lease payments is 12%. (The present value of an ordinary annuity of $1 per period for three periods at 12% is 2.40183.) Also assume that the asset "Leased equipment under capital leases" will be depreciated on a straight-line basis.

REQUIRED:

1. Prepare an amortization schedule for the lease.
2. The effect of lease capitalization on the current ratio worried Mr. Henley. *Before factoring in the capital lease signed on December 31, 2001,* Kingston Corporation's current ratio at December 31, 2001 was:

$$\frac{\text{Current assets } \$500{,}000}{\text{Current liabilities } \$294{,}118} = 1.7$$

Once this lease is capitalized on December 31, 2001, what is the adjusted December 31, 2001 current ratio?

3. Mr. Henley was also concerned about the effect that lease capitalization would have on net income. He estimated that if the lease previously described were treated as an *operating* lease, 2002 pre-tax income would be $225,000. Determine the 2002 pre-tax income on a capital lease basis if this lease were treated as a capital lease and if the leased equipment were depreciated on a straight-line basis over the life of the lease.

P12–6

Lessors' direct financing lease

AICPA adapted

Rankin Corporation, a lessor of office machines, purchased a new machine for $725,000 on December 31, 2001, which was delivered the same day (by prior arrangement) to Liska Company, the lessee. The following information relating to the lease transaction is available:

- The leased asset has an estimated useful life of five years, which coincides with the lease term.
- At the end of the lease term, the machine will revert to Rankin, at which time it is expected to have a salvage value of $60,000 (which is not guaranteed by Liska).
- Rankin's implicit rate of return on its net lease investment is 8%, which is known by Liska.
- Liska's incremental borrowing rate is 12% at December 31, 2001.
- Lease rentals consist of five equal annual payments, the first of which was paid on December 31, 2001.
- The lease is appropriately accounted for as a direct financing lease by Rankin and as a capital lease by Liska. Both lessor and lessee are calendar-year corporations and depreciate all fixed assets on the straight-line basis.

REQUIRED:

Round all amounts to the nearest dollar.

1. Compute the annual rental under the lease.
2. Compute the amounts of the "Gross rentals receivable" and the "Unearned interest revenue" that Rankin should disclose at the inception of the lease on December 31, 2001.
3. What expense should Liska record for the year ended December 31, 2002?

P12–7

Lessors' direct financing lease

On January 1, 2001 Railcar Leasing Inc. (the lessor) purchased 10 used boxcars from Railroad Equipment Consolidators at a price of $8,345,640. Railcar Leasing Inc. immediately leased the boxcars to the Reading Railroad Company (the lessee) on the same date. The lease calls for eight annual payments of $1,500,000 to be made at the beginning of each year (i.e., the first payment is due at the inception of the lease on January 1, 2001). The boxcars have a remaining useful life of eight years, the lease contains no renewal or bargain purchase option, and possession of the boxcars reverts to the lessor at the end of the lease. The lease does not require the lessee to guarantee any residual value for the boxcars. The collectibility of the payments is reasonably certain, and there are no important uncertainties regarding unreimbursable costs to be incurred by the lessor. The lessor has structured the lease to earn a rate of return of 12.0%.

REQUIRED:

1. What method must Railcar Leasing Inc. use to account for the lease?
2. Prepare an amortization schedule for the lease for Railcar Leasing Inc. (Round all amounts to the nearest cent.)
3. Make all journal entries for Railcar Leasing Inc. for 2001 and 2002. Assume that the company reports on a calendar-year basis.

P12–8

Lessor accounting

Refer to the information contained in P12–7. Assume that collectibility of the payments is *not* reasonably certain and that the lessor uses the straight-line depreciation method.

REQUIRED:

1. Make the necessary journal entries for Railcar Leasing Inc. for 2001 and 2002 under the lease.
2. How much income before tax does the firm expect to recognize in total over the life of the lease in these altered circumstances?
3. Is the amount in (2) the same as, more than, or less than the total amount of income before tax that is recognized in P12–7?

P12–9

Lessor accounting for sales-type leases

On January 1, 2001 ABC Builders Inc. (the lessor) entered into a lease with Winged Foot Company (the lessee) for an asset that ABC Builders had manufactured at a cost of $15,000,000. The fair market value of the asset on January 1, 2001 is $19,354,730. The lease calls for six annual payments of $5,000,000 to be made at the end of each year. The asset has a useful life of six years. The lease contains no renewal or bargain purchase option, and possession of the asset reverts to ABC Builders at the end of the lease. The lease requires that Winged Foot Company guarantee that the residual value of the asset will be at least $1,000,000 at the end of the lease. The collectibility of the payments is reasonably certain, and there are no important uncertainties regarding unreimbursable costs to be incurred by the lessor. ABC Builders has structured the lease so as to earn a rate of return of 15.0%.

REQUIRED:

1. Why must ABC Builders account for the lease as a sales-type lease?
2. Prepare an amortization schedule for the lease for ABC Builders. (Round all amounts to the nearest cent.)
3. Make the journal entries for ABC Builders at the inception of the lease and for the payments received in 2001 and 2002.
4. Make the journal entry for ABC Builders at the expiration of the lease. Assume the leased asset's residual value is $0.

P12–10

Financial statement effects for lessees: Capital versus operating leases

Assume that on January 1, 2001 Trans Global Airlines leases two used Boeing 727s from Aircraft Lessors Inc. The eight-year lease calls for payments of $10,000,000 at the end of each year. On January 1, 2001 the Boeing 727s have a total fair market value of $55,000,000 and a remaining useful life of 10 years. Assume that Trans Global's incremental borrowing rate is 12% and that it uses straight-line depreciation for financial reporting purposes. The lease is noncancelable, and it cannot be renewed by Trans Global. In addition, there is no bargain purchase option, and ownership of the leased asset reverts to Aircraft Lessors at the end of the lease. Aircraft Lessors' implicit rate of return on the lease is unknown.

REQUIRED:

1. Should Trans Global account for the lease as a capital or an operating lease? Why?
2. Based on your answer to question (1), make all the journal entries that Trans Global would make related to the lease for 2001, 2002, 2003, and 2008. Round all amounts to the nearest cent.
3. Assume that Trans Global accounts for the lease using whichever method (capital or operating) that you did not select in question (1). Make all journal entries related to the lease for 2001, 2002, 2003, and 2008.
4. Prepare a schedule of the year-to-year and total (before tax) income differences that would result from accounting for the lease as a capital lease versus an operating lease. Round all amounts to the nearest cent.
5. Why might Trans Global's managers prefer the lease to be accounted for as an operating lease rather than as a capital lease?

P12–11

Direct financing versus operating leases: Lessors' income statement and balance sheet effects

On January 1, 2001 Overseas Leasing Inc. (the lessor) purchased five used oil tankers from Seven Seas Shipping Company at a price of $99,817,750. Overseas Leasing immediately leased the oil tankers to Pacific Ocean Oil Company (the lessee) on the same date. The lease calls for five annual payments of $25,000,000 to be made at the end of each year. The tankers have a remaining useful life of five years with no salvage value, and the lease does not require the lessee to guarantee any residual value for the tankers. The lessor has structured the lease to earn a rate of return of 8.0%.

REQUIRED:

Prepare a schedule like the one appearing in Table 12.7 of the text. This schedule should contain the year-to-year income statement and balance sheet differences that would arise depending on whether this lease is accounted for as a direct financing lease or as an operating lease.

P12–12

Asset acquisition: Cash purchase versus lease versus note payable

On January 1, 2001 Corporal Motors Corporation needs to acquire a vehicle painting machine. The company is considering three alternative methods for acquiring the machine.

Option 1: Issue a $125,000 noninterest-bearing note to the seller on January 1, 2001 (due date: December 31, 2005).

Option 2: Lease the machine from the seller. The lease would require five equal annual payments of $22,000 to be made on December 31 each year from 2001 to 2005.

Option 3: Purchase the machine outright by paying $90,000 in cash on January 1, 2001.

OTHER INFORMATION:

- Corporal Motors uses straight-line depreciation for financial reporting purposes.
- The machine has a five-year useful life with no salvage value.
- Round all amounts to the nearest whole dollar.
- Corporal Motors incremental borrowing rate is 8% (compounded annually).
- Corporal Motors reports on a calendar-year basis.

REQUIRED:

1. Which of the three alternatives should be selected and why?
2. What will be the total expense (and components making up the total expense) for the first year if Option 1 is adopted?

3. What will be the total expense (and components making up the total expense) for all five years together if Option 1 is adopted?
4. What will be the total expense (and components making up the total expense) for the first year if Option 2 is adopted and if the lease is accounted for as an operating lease?
5. What will be the total expense (and components making up the total expense) for all five years together if Option 2 is adopted and if the lease is accounted for as an operating lease?
6. What will be the total expense (and components making up the total expense) for the first year if Option 2 is adopted and if the lease is accounted for as a capital lease?
7. What will be the total expense (and components making up the total expense) for all five years together if Option 2 is adopted and if the lease is accounted for as a capital lease?
8. What will be the total expense (and components making up the total expense) for the first year if Option 3 is adopted?
9. What will be the total expense (and components making up the total expense) for all five years together if Option 3 is adopted?

P12–13

Constructive capitalization of operating leases

The following lease footnote disclosure is provided by Penguin Corporation:

5. LEASE COMMITMENTS

The Company leases certain of its facilities and equipment under various operating and capital leases. The lease agreements frequently include renewal and purchase provisions and require the Company to pay taxes, insurance, and maintenance costs.

Total rental expense under operating leases was $11,243,000, $9,985,000, and $8,853,000 in 1997, 1996, and 1995, respectively.

The following is a schedule of future minimum lease payments under capital leases and rental payments required under long-term operating leases at the end of the 1997 fiscal year:

Fiscal Years	Operating Leases	Capital Leases
1998	$ 8,494	$77
1999	6,835	-0-
2000	4,952	-0-
2001	4,740	-0-
2002	4,023	-0-
Later years	12,979	-0-
Total	$42,023	$77
Less: amount representing interest		(7)
Present value of minimum lease payments		$70

Assume that all lease payments are made at the end of the year.

REQUIRED:

1. Estimate the interest rate implicit in the firm's capital lease obligation.
2. Based on the rate in (1), make the journal entry to record the 1998 capital lease payment.
3. Use the interest rate in (1) to estimate the present value of the operating leases as of the end of the 1997 fiscal year. When doing so, assume that the payments due after 2002 are equal and will be made over a four-year period.
4. Prepare a 1997 end-of-year journal entry that would capitalize (i.e., convert from operating to capital) the present value of Penguin's 1997 end-of-year operating leases computed in (3).

5. Make the journal entry for the 1998 operating lease payment. Assume that the operating leases are being accounted for as capital leases.
6. Describe the impact on the firm's interest coverage ratio in the 1998 fiscal year if the operating leases were instead accounted for as capital leases at the end of 1997.
7. Describe the impact on the firm's leverage ratios (e.g., total debt to stockholders' equity and long-term debt to stockholders' equity) at the end of 1997 if the operating leases were instead being accounted for as capital leases.
8. If the operating leases were instead being accounted for as capital leases, how would the 1998 payment affect the firm's 1998 statement of cash flows?
9. Is the answer to (8) the same as or different from what the effect on the statement of cash flows would be if the leases were to be accounted for as operating leases?
10. Describe the rationale for treating some leases as capital leases and others as operating leases.

P12–14

Capital leases: Visualizing the asset-liability relationship over time

This problem is designed to allow you to see how different lease durations and interest rates affect the relationship between the capitalized lease asset and lease liability. Of course, these same asset–liability relationships apply if one wishes to constructively capitalize a lease that the lessee has treated as an operating lease.

Assume that Cambria Corporation signs a noncancelable lease that obliges it to make annual payments of $10,000. This amount excludes all executory costs, and there is no residual value guarantee included in the lease terms. The lease will be treated as a capital lease and Cambria uses straight-line depreciation for the leased asset.

REQUIRED:

1. Assume that the lease payments are made at the *beginning* of each period.
   a. If the discount rate is 8% and the lease runs for 20 years, approximately when—if at all—does the capitalized lease liability first exceed the depreciated net carrying value of the leased asset?
   b. Repeat this calculation using a 12% discount rate for 20 years.
   c. Repeat this calculation using a 12% discount rate for 12 years.
2. Assume that the lease payments are made at the *end* of each period.
   a. If the discount rate is 8% and the lease runs for 20 years, does the depreciated carrying value of the leased asset ever exceed the capitalized lease liability?
   b. Will this result change if you raise the interest rate and/or shorten the duration of the lease?

CASES

C12–1

Arcadia Financial Ltd.: Lessee accounting and constructive capitalization

In its 10-K, Arcadia Financial Ltd., a company based in Minneapolis, describes its business as follows:

> The Company purchases, sells and services consumer automobile loans originated primarily by car dealers affiliated with major foreign and domestic manufacturers. Loans are purchased through 17 regional buying centers ("hubs") located in 14 states. . . .
>
> The Company's lending programs are designed to serve consumers who have limited access to traditional automobile financing, typically because they have prior credit difficulties or limited credit histories. Because the Company serves consumers who are unable to meet the credit standards imposed by most traditional automobile financing sources, it generally charges interest at rates higher than those charged by traditional sources. The Company also expects to sustain a higher level of credit losses than traditional sources because it provides financing to relatively high-risk borrowers.

Arcadia finances a portion of its assets through the use of capital leases. In addition, the company has substantial operating lease commitments. Details on both capital and operating leases for Arcadia are included in two footnotes to its 1999 annual report, which follow. Arcadia's income statement and balance sheet for 1999 are also shown.

NOTE 6. FURNITURE, FIXTURES AND EQUIPMENT

Furniture, fixtures and equipment, as of December 31, consists of the following:

($ in thousands)	1999	1998
Owned:		
Furniture, fixtures and leasehold improvements	$ 10,161	$ 10,351
Automobiles	212	194
Computer equipment	3,608	3,894
Software	15,066	9,278
Total	29,047	23,717
Capitalized Leases:		
Furniture and fixtures	4,493	4,376
Computer equipment	5,046	4,918
Software	387	386
	9,926	9,680
Total furniture, fixtures and equipment	$38,973	$33,397
Less: Accumulated depreciation and amortization	(22,607)	(15,886)
Furniture, fixtures and equipment, net	$16,366	$17,511

Depreciation expense including amortization of assets under capital lease obligations for the years ended December 31, 1999, and 1998, was $8.2 million and $6.9 million, respectively.

NOTE 10. COMMITMENTS AND CONTINGENCIES

The Company leases furniture, fixtures, and equipment under capital and operating leases with terms in excess of one year. Additionally, the Company leases its office space under operating leases. Total rent expense on operating leases was $8.3 million, $13.4 million and $13.5 million for the years ended December 31, 1999, 1998, and 1997, respectively.

Future minimum lease payments required under capital and non-cancelable operating leases with terms of one year or more, at December 31, 1999 were:

($ in thousands) **Year ending:**	**Capital Leases**	**Operating Leases**
2000	$ 1,978	$ 9,369
2001	946	6,427
2002	89	3,033
2003	11	1,369
2004	–0–	423
2005 and thereafter	–0–	366
Total	$3,024	$20,987
Less amounts representing interest	(250)	
Present value of net minimum lease payments	$2,774	

ARCADIA FINANCIAL LTD.

Edited and Condensed Consolidated Balance Sheets

($ in thousands)	1999	1998
Assets		
Cash	$ 17,562	$ 10,827
Due from securitization trust	–0–	62,081
Auto loans held for sale	239,323	17,899
Retained interest in securitized assets	557,372	587,946
Furniture, fixtures and equipment	16,366	17,511
Other assets	34,692	31,419
Total assets	$865,315	$727,683
Liabilities and Shareholders' Equity		
Amounts due under sale agreement	$192,886	$ –0–
Senior notes	367,674	366,657
Subordinated notes	92,556	51,898
Capital lease obligations	2,774	3,384
Interest payable	15,102	11,344
Accounts payable and accrued liabilities	22,239	25,591
Total liabilities	693,231	458,874
Shareholders' equity:		
Capital stock	394	392
Additional paid-in capital	326,471	324,565
Accumulated other comprehensive income	12,372	18,550
Accumulated deficit	(167,153)	(74,698)
Total shareholders' equity	172,084	268,809
Total liabilities and shareholders' equity	$865,315	$727,683

ARCADIA FINANCIAL LTD.

Edited and Condensed Consolidated Statements of Operations Year Ended December 31

($ in thousands)	1999	1998
Total revenues	$140,605	$146,383
Expenses:		
Salaries, general, administrative and other operating expenses	(173,929)	(187,187)
Interest expense	(55,155)	(51,672)
	(229,084)	(238,859)
Operating loss before income taxes and cumulative effect of accounting change	(88,479)	(92,476)
Income tax benefit	–0–	9,235
Loss before cumulative effect of accounting change	(88,479)	(83,241)
Cumulative effect of accounting change net of tax	(3,976)	–0–
Net loss	$ (92,455)	$ (83,241)

REQUIRED:

1. Prepare summary journal entries that Arcadia Financial Ltd. would make in 2000 pertaining to its capital and operating leases. Assume that assets financed by capital leases are depreciated over a four-year period with no salvage value and that no lease commitments were entered into subsequent to December 31, 1999.

2. Suppose that all operating leases were capitalized on December 31, 1998. Using the procedures set forth in the Appendix to this chapter, quantify the effect of capitalizing Arcadia's operating lease commitments on its debt-to-equity ratio, interest coverage ratio, and ROA for 1999.
   In making the calculations, assume the following:
   a. Lease commitments after 2004 are spread evenly over the next three years.
   b. All scheduled lease payments are made at the *end* of each year.
   c. Arcadia's incremental borrowing rate is 12%.
   d. The average total lease period for operating leases is eight years, and 50% of the original lease life has expired on average.
   e. Income taxes can be ignored.
3. What is your conjecture regarding how Arcadia's bond rating might be affected if a new accounting policy came out that required all operating leases to be capitalized?

C12–2

May Department Stores (CW): Constructive capitalization of operating leases

http://www

May Department Stores operates department stores in 34 states and the District of Columbia. The company's department stores operate under the following names: Lord & Taylor, Hecht's, Strawbridge's, Foley's, Robinsons-May, Filene's, Kaufmann's, Famous-Barr, L. S. Ayres, The Jones Store, Meier & Frank, ZCMI, and David's Bridal.

The following information is taken from a recent annual report of the company.

LEASE OBLIGATIONS

The company owns approximately 77% of its stores. Rental expense for the company's operating leases consisted of:

($ in millions)	1999	1998	1997
Minimum rentals	$48	$49	$47
Contingent rentals based on sales	18	18	17
Real property rentals	66	67	64
Equipment rentals	3	3	4
Total	$69	$70	$68

Future minimum lease payments at January 29, 2000, were as follows:

($ in millions)	Capital Leases	Operating Leases	Total
2000	$ 7	$ 51	$ 58
2001	7	46	53
2002	7	43	50
2003	7	40	47
2004	7	38	45
After 2004	93	264	357
Minimum lease payments	128	$482	$610
Less imputed interest component	71		
Present value of net minimum lease payments, of which $1 million is included in current liabilities	$ 57		

The present value of operating leases was $291 million at January 29, 2000.

OTHER INFORMATION/ASSUMPTIONS:

- Assume that the amount of May's operating lease payments due each year after 2004 are equal and that these leases all terminate in the year 2014.

(continued)

- Excerpted balance sheet data

	January 29, 2000	January 30, 1999
Long-term debt	$3,560	$3,825
Total shareowners' equity	4,077	3,836

- Assume that all operating lease payments are made at the end of May Department Store's fiscal year.

REQUIRED:

1. Make the journal entry to record May's operating leases as if they were being treated as capital leases as of January 29, 2000.
2. Calculate May's ratio of long-term debt to stockholders' equity as of January 29, 2000 using the information reported in the balance sheet. Ignore income tax effects.
3. Repeat (2) after capitalizing the firm's operating leases as in question (1). Comment on the difference between the two ratio results.
4. Demonstrate that the rate of return implicit in the present value of May's operating leases at January 29, 2000 is closer to 8% than to 9%.
5. Assume that the interest rate implicit in the present value of May's operating leases is 8%. Make the journal entry for the operating lease payment of $51 million in 2000 assuming that the leases had been treated as capital leases rather than as operating leases.
6. Repeat requirements (1) through (3) using data from May Department Stores' most recent financial statements.

C12–3

Tuesday Morning Corporation (CW): Comprehensive lessee reporting

Tuesday Morning Corporation operates a chain of 246 deep discount retail stores in 32 states. As a deep discount retailer, the company purchases close-out merchandise at prices generally ranging from 10% to 50% of normal wholesale prices and sells the merchandise at prices that are 50% to 80% lower than the retail prices that are generally charged by department and specialty stores.

Appearing next is information taken from Tuesday Morning's 1994 annual report. Tuesday Morning's financial statements appear in C10-8.

NOTE 6: CAPITAL LEASE

During September 1994, the Company entered into a capital lease with a financial institution to finance part of the acquisition of Point of Sale registers and Electronic Article Surveillance equipment. The amount purchased under the capital lease totaled $2,642,000. Depreciation expense during 1994 was $264,000.

This lease is for five years and contains a bargain purchase option that the Company would be expected to exercise. This lease bears an implicit interest rate of approximately 12.5%.

The following is a schedule of future minimum lease payments under the capital lease, together with the present value of the net minimum lease payments as of December 31, 1994 ($ in thousands):

Year	Amount
1995	$ 933
1996	933
1997	707
1998	255
1999	170
Total	A
Less: Amount representing interest	B
Present value of minimum lease payments	C
Less: Current installments	$ 607
Long-term capital lease obligation	$1,821

NOTE 10: OPERATING LEASES

The Company leases substantially all store locations under noncancelable operating leases. Future minimum rental payments under leases are as follows ($ in thousands):

Year	Amount
1995	$12,437
1996	10,487
1997	8,211
1998	6,239
1999	3,106
Later years	1,985
Total minimum rental payments	$42,465

In the normal course of business, management expects to renew or replace leases for store locations as they expire. Rental expense for 1994, 1993, and 1992 was $12,323,000, $11,239,000, and $8,375,000, respectively.

REQUIRED:

1. Did Tuesday Morning have any leases that were being accounted for as capital leases in 1993?
2. Why did the lease Tuesday Morning entered into in 1994 qualify as a capital lease?
3. What was the amount of the capital lease obligation incurred in 1994?
4. Solve for the unknowns (A, B, and C) in Note 6.
5. Assume that payment on all capital leases is made on September 30 of each year. Based on the interest rate reported in Note 6, make the journal entry to account for Tuesday Morning's 1995 capital lease payment.
6. Assume that all operating leases will be fully amortized by the end of the year 2000. Using an interest rate of 12%, calculate the present value of the operating lease payments at December 31, 1994.
7. Make the journal entry that would be necessary at December 31, 1994 to account for the operating leases as if they were being treated as capital leases. (Ignore income taxes and assume that the amount of the capitalized asset equals the capitalized liability.)
8. Assume that payment on all operating leases is made on the last day of the fiscal year (December 31). Based on your answer to (6), make the journal entry at December 31, 1995 to account for the operating lease payment assuming operating leases are being accounted for as capital leases.
9. Tuesday Morning's December 31, 1994 balance sheet lists the following long-term debt items ($ in thousands):

Mortgages payable	$4,952
Long-term capital lease obligations	1,821
Deferred taxes	2,920

   In addition, total shareholders' equity was $58,630. This gives a long-term debt-to-shareholders'-equity ratio of 16.5%. Calculate Tuesday Morning's total long-term debt-to-shareholders'-equity ratio after treating its operating leases as if they were capital leases. (Ignore tax effects.)
10. Comment on the differences in the unadjusted and adjusted ratios.

C12–4

Delta Air Lines, Inc. (CW): Constructive capitalization of operating leases

Delta Air Lines is a major air carrier providing scheduled air transportation for passengers, freight, and mail over a network of routes throughout the United States and abroad. Delta is one of the largest U.S. airlines when measured by aircraft departures and passengers enplaned and by revenues and revenue passenger miles flown. The company serves approximately 184 domestic cities in 44 states, the District of Columbia, Puerto Rico, and the U.S. Virgin Islands, as well as 42 cities in 29 foreign countries.

(continued)

OTHER INFORMATION CONDENSED FROM THE FINANCIAL STATEMENTS:

($ in millions)	June 30 1999	1998
Current Liabilities		
Current maturities of long-term debt	$ 660	$ 67
Current obligations under capital leases	39	63
Accounts payable and miscellaneous accrued liabilities	2,144	2,025
Air traffic liability	1,819	1,667
Accrued rent	195	202
Accrued salaries and vacation pay	470	553
Total current liabilities	$ 5,327	$ 4,577
Noncurrent Liabilities		
Long-term debt	$ 1,756	$ 1,533
Postretirement benefits	1,894	1,873
Accrued rent	720	651
Capital leases	196	249
Deferred taxes and other	1,290	773
Total noncurrent liabilities	$ 5,856	$ 5,079
Deferred credits and other	913	924
Total shareholders' equity	$ 4,448	$ 4,023
Total liabilities and shareholders' equity	$16,544	$14,603

NOTES TO CONSOLIDATED FINANCIAL STATEMENTS

NOTE 6. LEASE OBLIGATIONS

Our Company leases aircraft, airport terminal and maintenance facilities, ticket offices, and other property and equipment. We record rent expense on a straight-line basis over the life of the lease. Rental expense for operating leases totaled $1.1 billion in fiscal 1999, $0.9 billion in fiscal 1998 and $0.9 billion in fiscal 1997. Amounts due under capital leases are recorded as liabilities, and our interest in assets acquired under capital leases are shown as assets on our Consolidated Balance Sheets.

The following table summarizes our minimum rental commitments under capital leases and operating leases with initial or remaining terms of more than one year as of June 30, 1999:

Years Ending June 30 ($ in millions)	**Capital Leases**	**Operating Leases**
2000	$63	$1,020
2001	57	1,030
2002	57	1,040
2003	48	1,020
2004	32	980
After 2004	40	9,440
Total minimum lease payments	A	$14,530
Less: Amounts of lease payments which represent interest	B	
Present value of future minimum capital lease payments	C	
Less: Current obligations under capital leases	D	
Long-term capital lease obligations	E	

ASSUMPTIONS:

- All lease payments are made on June 30 of each year (the end of Delta's fiscal year).
- The operating lease obligation will be fully accounted for in 15 years, and the amounts due annually after 2004 are equal.
- The capital lease obligation will be fully accounted for in seven years, and the amounts due annually after 2004 are equal.
- Ignore depreciation.

REQUIRED:

1. Refer to Note 6 on leases. Solve for the unknowns A through E.
2. Calculate the amount of the annual payments under capital leases for 2005 and 2006.
3. The ratio of interest expense to average debt outstanding for 1999 is approximately 10%. Use this rate to calculate the present value of the capital lease payments as of June 30, 1999. Compare this amount to what you computed in (1). What does this comparison tell you about the 10.0% interest rate relative to the interest rate implicit in the reported capital lease obligation?
4. Using the 10.0% discount rate, make the journal entry at June 30, 2000 to account for the capital lease payment.
5. Refer to Note 6 on leases. Calculate the amount of the annual payments under operating leases from 2005 through 2014.
6. Using the 10.0% discount rate, calculate the present value of the operating lease payments as of June 30, 1999.
7. Make the journal entry that would be required at June 30, 1999 to recognize the operating leases as capital leases. (Ignore taxes and assume that the capitalized asset equals the capitalized liability.)
8. Make the journal entry at June 30, 2000, to account for the operating lease payment assuming the operating leases were being accounted for as capital leases.
9. Calculate the ratio of long-term debt to shareholders' equity and the ratio of total liabilities to total assets at June 30, 1999 using the reported balance sheet data appearing earlier. Recalculate these ratios assuming the operating leases are instead accounted for as capital leases. Comment on the differences. (Ignore tax effects.)
10. It is often alleged that managers prefer leases to be accounted for as operating leases rather than as capital leases. Why do you think this is the case?

C12–5

Nationsbank (KR): Lease classification and the times interest earned ratio

In a recent lending agreement (dated March 3, 1997), Nationsbank of Texas, N.A., included the following definitions for terms used in its loan covenants with a borrower:

> "Fixed Charges" means the sum of, for Borrower and its Subsidiaries, determined in accordance with GAAP on a consolidated basis, (a) interest expense (including interest expense pursuant to Capital Leases), plus (b) lease expense payable for Operating Leases, determined for the four fiscal quarters preceding the date of calculation.
>
> "Net Earnings Available for Fixed Charges" means, for Borrower and its Subsidiaries, determined in accordance with GAAP on a consolidated basis, (a) Net Income before Taxes, plus (b) extraordinary noncash charges, plus (c) interest expense (including interest expense pursuant to Capital Leases), plus (d) lease expense pursuant to Operating Leases, determined for the fiscal quarter preceding the date of calculation.
>
> "Fixed Charges Coverage Ratio" means the ratio of Net Earnings Available for Fixed Charges to Fixed Charges.
>
> Borrower shall not permit the Fixed Charges Coverage Ratio to be less than the following ratios for the fiscal quarters ending as follows:

December 31, 1996	0.70 to 1.00
March 31, 1997	1.00 to 1.00
June 30, 1997	1.20 to 1.00
September 30, 1997	1.50 to 1.00
December 31, 1997	1.75 to 1.00

Notice that the definitions of "Fixed charges" and "Net earnings available for fixed charges" *both* add back lease expenses under operating leases. The objective of this case is to allow you to see why astute lenders carefully design covenants to protect themselves against borrowers who might use the latitude in GAAP lease accounting rules to circumvent covenant restrictions.

Assume the following initial conditions for the borrower on June 30, 1997:

Income before interest and taxes	$120,000
Interest on capital lease	$ 60,000
Interest on other borrowings	$ 40,000
Fixed charges	$100,000
Fixed charges coverage ratio	1.20

Notice that the fixed charges coverage ratio equals the covenant constraint at June 30, 1997; even minor adversity might cause a covenant violation in the next quarter. In addition, the borrower is required to increase the ratio to 1.50 by September 30, 1997.

REQUIRED:

1. Assume that the borrower "somehow" restructures the existing lease to have it qualify as an operating lease. What effect will this change in lease classification have on the times interest earned ratio as typically defined? (See Chapter 5.) What effect will this change have on the fixed charges coverage ratio as defined in the lending agreement? What does your answer to this part tell you about the vigilance that credit analysts must exert in designing and monitoring financial contractual restrictions?
2. Now assume that the initial times interest earned ratio was less than 1.00 to 1.00. Would changing the capital lease to an operating lease benefit the borrower's compliance with lending covenants?

Note: In answering both parts, make assumptions when sufficient information is not available.

C12-6 The Retail Industry (CW): Comparative effects of constructive capitalization

The following information is drawn from recent annual reports of three firms in the retail industry: Sears, Roebuck and Company, Dillard Department Stores, Inc., and Federated Department Stores, Inc.

A. Sears, Roebuck and Company is a multiline retailer that provides a wide array of merchandise and services. The company is among the largest retailers in the world on the basis of sales of merchandise and services.

($ in millions)	December 28 1996	December 30 1995
Long-term debt	$12,170	$10,044
Total shareholders' equity	4,945	4,385
Total liabilities and shareholders' equity	$36,167	$33,130

Excerpts from its leases footnote follow.

The company leases certain stores, office facilities, warehouses, computers, and transportation equipment. Minimum lease obligations as of December 28, 1996, were:

($ in millions)	Capital Leases	Operating Leases
1997	$ 56	$ 279
1998	52	259
1999	49	231
2000	47	207
2001	44	189
After 2001	600	1,050
Minimum payments	$848	
Imputed interest	515	
Present value of minimum lease payments	$333	

B. Dillard Department Stores, Inc. is a company that operates retail department stores located primarily in the Southwest, Southeast, and Midwest.

($ in thousands)	February 1, 1997	February 3, 1996
Long-term debt	$1,186,708	$1,178,025
Total shareholders' equity	2,717,178	2,478,327
Total liabilities and shareholders' equity	5,059,726	4,778,535

Excerpts from its leases footnote follow.

CAPITAL LEASES

Future minimum payments under capital leases as of February 1, 1997 are as follows (in thousands of dollars):

Fiscal Year	Amount
1997	$ 2,987
1998	2,987
1999	2,710
2000	2,627
2001	2,371
After 2001	13,800
Total minimum lease payments	27,482
Less amount representing interest	(11,926)
Present value of net minimum lease payments	$15,556

(continued)

OPERATING LEASES

The future minimum rental commitments as of February 1, 1997 for all non-cancelable operating leases are as follows ($ in thousands):

Fiscal Year	Amount
1997	$ 29,444
1998	26,241
1999	24,746
2000	24,093
2001	22,857
After 2001	147,000

C. Federated Department Stores Inc. is one of the leading operators of full-line department stores in the United States, with 411 department stores in 33 states. The company's department stores are located at urban or suburban sites, principally in densely populated areas across the United States.

($ in thousands)	February 1, 1997	February 3, 1996
Long-term debt	$ 4,605,916	$ 5,632,232
Shareholders' equity	4,669,154	4,273,686
Total liabilities and shareholders' equity	$14,264,143	$14,295,050

Excerpts from its lease footnote follow.

Minimum rental commitments at February 1, 1997 for noncancelable leases are:

($ in millions)	Capital Leases	Operating Leases
Fiscal year		
1997	$ 13.6	$ 174.6
1998	13.1	151.4
1999	12.6	139.0
2000	12.6	132.8
2001	12.1	128.7
After 2001	84.0	1,250.0
Total minimum lease payments	148.0	
Less amount representing interest	72.0	
Present value of net minimum capitalized lease payments	$ 76.0	

ADDITIONAL INFORMATION:

1. For Sears, assume that the capital lease payments due after 2001 are equal and are to be made over a 15-year period. For the operating lease payments, assume that the amounts due after 2001 are equal and will be made over a six-year period.
2. For Dillard's, assume that the operating lease payments due after 2001 are equal and will be made over a seven-year period.
3. For Federated, assume that the operating lease payments due after 2001 are equal and will be made over a 10-year period.

REQUIRED:

1. Show that the interest rate implicit in the capital lease obligations of Sears is closer to 12% than to 13%.
2. Using the 12% rate from (1), calculate the present value of the operating lease obligations of Sears.
3. Using the approach followed in (1), we can determine that the interest rate implicit in the capital lease obligations of Dillard's is close to 12%. Use this rate to calculate the present value of the firm's operating lease payments.
4. The approach in (1) allows us to determine that the interest rate implicit in the capital lease obligations of Federated is close to 11%. Use this rate to calculate the present value of the firm's operating lease payments.
5. Using the balance sheet information reported earlier, calculate the long-term debt-to-shareholders'-equity ratio and the long-term debt-to-total-assets ratio of the three firms for the most recent fiscal year.
6. Repeat (5) after treating the operating leases as if they are being accounted for as capital leases. How do the results compare with those in (5)? (Ignore taxes and assume that the capitalized asset equals the capitalized liability.)

COLLABORATIVE LEARNING CASE

C12–7

United Airlines: Capital lease criteria and reporting incentives (The case of the curious speech)

Along with others in the industry, United Airlines faced a dramatically altered operating environment in the early 1980s. The primary cause was the Airline Deregulation Act of 1978, which permitted airlines to make unilateral decisions about domestic routes and fares—decisions which previously required regulatory approval. Just as airlines began to adapt to these changed circumstances, a severe recession struck the U.S. economy in 1980. The combination of recession-induced excess capacity and competitive price cutting led to widespread industry operating losses during 1981 and 1982.

The recession ended in 1983, and for the first time since 1978, UAL, Inc. (the parent of United Airlines) reported an operating profit from airline activities. However, UAL's 1983 annual report received a qualified opinion from its auditor, Arthur Andersen & Co.; the qualification was due to liability arising from class action litigation because of United's "no-marriage rule" for stewardesses. (In September 1984 the trial court awarded the plaintiffs $37,973,000 in back pay, and Andersen removed the qualification from the 1984 annual report.)

Late in 1984 Richard J. Ferris, who was then chief executive officer (CEO) of UAL, Inc., gave a speech to the Society of Airline Analysts in New York City. A transcript of this speech was printed and circulated by UAL; excerpts from that document follow.

Richard J. Ferris, Chairman, President, and Chief Executive Officer, UAL, Inc. and Chairman and Chief Executive Officer, United Airlines, Before the Society of Airline Analysts, New York, November 28, 1984.

. . .

I know many airline analysts believe that continuing progress in the industry depends on the airlines' ability to focus on lower labor costs; to assure competitive market positioning; and to distribute their product effectively.

A PROFITABLE YEAR

United—and all of UAL, Inc.—is on target in these areas. In addition, we've made advances in our financial position and in our asset use. . . .

I'd like to address each of these four areas today.

First, our financial position.

As you know, the third quarter was good. At the operating level, it was much better than a year ago. But because of higher nonoperating expenses, our net was about the same as last year.

IMPROVED DEBT : EQUITY RATIO

. . .

Although our net profit margin for 1984 will be the best in six years, it still will not meet our goal of 5 percent. On the other hand, our balance sheet is in excellent condition.

At the end of 1982, UAL, Inc. 's consolidated debt:equity ratio stood at 59 percent debt and 41 percent equity. So we set out to reverse it. And reverse it we did. In 1983, we raised more than $300 million of equity by selling UAL, Inc. stock and by exchanging new preferred stock for some high-cost debt. At the end of 1983, our debt:equity ratio was 44:56.

This year, we further improved the debt:equity ratio by realizing profits, by selling additional stock, by paying off all outstanding revolving credit notes and by defeasance of debt and a long-term facility lease obligation. At the end of September, UAL Inc.'s debt:equity ratio was 34 percent debt and 66 percent equity—one of the strongest ratios in the industry.

In addition:

- We recently extended to 1994 the 20-member, $1.5 billion bank line of credit available to us on three days' notice.
- Standard & Poor's and Moody's both raised our senior debt ratings two notches.
- Currently all our senior debt is rated investment grade.
- Arthur Andersen & Co. removed its qualification from our financial statements following the court's award in the *McDonald* lawsuit.
- We resumed payment of dividends to our shareholders.
- And we have begun to use off-balance-sheet financing.

Off-Balance-Sheet Financing

We used off-balance-sheet financing for the three DC-10-30 aircraft we recently acquired from the EX/IM Bank, after the bank repossessed them from Laker Airways.

Almost all the money to finance the planes came in yen. We can finance in long-term yen, without cross-currency exposure, because our Pacific operations are generating yen sales at a rate close to the equivalent of $50 million a year.

The Industrial Bank of Japan put up the yen for the Security Pacific Bank at the long-term prime rate of 7.9 percent. Security Pacific Bank, the owner of the DC-10s—and the beneficiary of the accelerated depreciation and interest on the yen borrowing—rents them to United. We pay rent for 15¼ years at an effective interest rate of 4.9 percent annually.

At the end of the lease, United can buy the planes back for the fair market value at that time or for 50 percent of the original amount of financing, whichever is less. We believe this might be the first time a long-term aircraft operating lease has accompanied a fixed-price buyout.

The groundwork has been laid for similar transactions in the future without putting debt on our balance sheet. . . .

1985: A Challenge

How does 1985 look to us? . . .

What we can count on are the strengths I mentioned earlier—a healthy balance sheet, better use of assets, improved cost control (especially labor costs), and marketing superiority.

Our advances in all these areas this year prepare us well for the unexpected twists and turns that next year is sure to bring.

REQUIRED:

1. A lease that contains a bargain purchase option must be treated as a capital lease by the lessee. What is the justification for not treating the lease of the three DC-10s described in the speech as a capital lease?
2. Consider the job function of members of the Society of Airline Analysts. What was Mr. Ferris' motivation for boasting to this group about UAL's "aggressive" accounting for the lease transaction?

13

Income Tax Reporting

LEARNING OBJECTIVES:

After studying this chapter, you will understand:

1. The different objectives underlying income determination for financial reporting (book) purposes versus tax purposes.
2. The distinction between a temporary (timing) and a permanent difference and the items that give rise to each of these differences between book income and taxable income.
3. The distortions created when the deferred tax effects of temporary differences are ignored.
4. How tax expense is determined with interperiod tax allocation.
5. How changes in tax rates are measured and recorded.
6. The reporting rules for net operating loss carrybacks and carryforwards.
7. How to read and interpret tax footnote disclosures and how these footnotes can be used to enhance interfirm comparability.
8. How tax footnotes can be used to evaluate the degree of conservatism in firms' book (GAAP) accounting choices.

"I'm proud to be paying taxes to the United States. The only thing is . . . I could be just as proud for half the money."

—Arthur Godfrey, television host
1940's–1970's

In the United States and many other industrialized countries, the rules for computing income for financial reporting purposes—known as **book income**—do not correspond to the rules for computing income for taxation purposes—referred to as **taxable income.** This divergence is allowable and makes sense because of the different objectives underlying book income versus taxable income.[1]

Book income is intended to reflect increases in a firm's "well-offness"; it includes all increases in net assets that meet the GAAP criteria for revenue recognition (critical event and measurable) and for costs that have expired according to the expense matching principle outlined in Chapter 2. ***Book income includes all earned inflows of net assets, even inflows not immediately convertible into cash; and it reflects expenses as they accrue, not just when they are paid.***

Determining income for tax purposes does not always focus on changes in well-offness. Instead, taxable income is governed by the "constructive receipt/ability to pay" doctrine. This means the timing of taxation usually (but not always) follows the inflow of cash or cash equivalents; when liquid assets enter the firm, they are frequently taxed, since it is easiest to collect money at that time. For example, rent received in advance is taxed when received even though it is not yet earned from an accounting standpoint. Similarly, tax deductions generally are allowed only when expenditures are made or when a loss occurs. ***Because of different underlying objectives, the rules for determining book income (according to GAAP) diverge from the rules for determining taxable income (according to the Internal Revenue Service or IRS). This divergence complicates the way that income taxes are reflected in financial reports.***

[1] Countries where the rules for determining accounting (book) income and taxable income for parent companies are essentially the same include, for example, Germany, Japan and Switzerland.

This chapter describes the major differences between U.S. book income and taxable income and how these differences complicate the reporting of tax expense and tax obligations. First we outline the major categories of differences between book income and taxable income, and we illustrate the distortions that would result on GAAP income statements if tax expense were to be set equal to taxes owed the IRS. Next, we explain and illustrate the GAAP solution for avoiding these distortions—referred to as **deferred income tax accounting** or **interperiod tax allocation.** We also explore what happens from an accounting standpoint when income tax rates are changed by Congress, and we discuss how the accounting works for special U.S. tax laws that apply to unprofitable firms.

Interperiod tax allocation refers to the allocation of income tax expense *across periods* when book and tax income differ. **Intraperiod tax allocation,** introduced in Chapter 2, refers to the allocation of the tax cost (benefit) across various components of book income *within a given period.* For example, the current tax provision (expense) is related to (pre-tax) income from continuing operations, while extraordinary items and cumulative effects of accounting changes are reported *net of tax* on the income statement.

The second part of the chapter guides you through an analysis of typical income tax footnote disclosures. Our purpose is to explain the wealth of information that can be extracted from these disclosures. We demonstrate how analysts can use tax footnotes to glean information not provided elsewhere in the financial statements to better understand a firm's performance and future prospects.

Understanding Income Tax Reporting

Temporary and Permanent Differences Between Book Income and Taxable Income

The differences that result from determining income reported in external financial statements on the one hand and determining taxable income for tax purposes on the other fall into two broad categories:

1. **Temporary** or **timing differences**
2. **Permanent differences.**

In this chapter we use the terms "temporary" and "timing" differences interchangeably. They mean the same thing. *Accounting Principles Board (APB) Opinion No. 11,* "Accounting for Income Taxes," used the term "timing difference," while *Statement of Financial Accounting Standards (SFAS) No. 109,* "Accounting for Income Taxes," which superseded *APB Opinion No. 11,* uses the term "temporary differences." The same term should have been used in both standards but, unfortunately, it wasn't.

A timing difference results when a revenue (gain) or expense (loss) enters into the determination of book income in one period but affects taxable income in a different (earlier or later) period. A brief summary of common temporary differences is provided in Table 13.1. Timing differences are considered "temporary" because they eventually reverse. That is, a revenue (or expense) item that causes book income to be greater than (less than) taxable income when it is initially recorded (called an ***originating* timing difference**) will eventually reverse. These reversals cause book income to be less than (greater than) taxable income in future periods and are called ***reversing* timing differences.**

Temporary differences that will cause taxable income to be *higher* than book income in future periods give rise to a **deferred tax liability.** Conversely, temporary differences that will cause taxable income to be *lower* than book income in future periods when those differences reverse give rise to a **deferred tax asset.** Deferred tax liabilities and assets are explained in the following sections.

A **permanent difference** between taxable income and book income is caused by income items that:

1. Enter into the determination of accounting income but *never* affect taxable income. For example, interest income received on municipal bonds is included in accounting income but is not included in taxable income under current tax rules.
2. Enter into the determination of taxable income but *never* affect accounting income. For example, the **dividends-received deduction** in the U.S. tax laws

This special treatment of dividend income was put into the tax code largely to avoid double taxation of corporate profits. For ownership interests of less than 20%, U.S. corporations are permitted to deduct 70% of dividends received from other U.S. companies. For ownership interests between 20% and 80%, the deduction is 80%; and for interests of 80% or greater, corporations are allowed to deduct 100% of the dividends received from their U.S. subsidiaries.

Table 13.1 ■ EXAMPLES OF TEMPORARY (TIMING) DIFFERENCES BETWEEN BOOK INCOME AND TAXABLE INCOME

Depreciation Expense
Accelerated depreciation is used for taxable income; straight line is used for book income. Modified Accelerated Cost Recovery System (MACRS) useful lives are used for taxable income and useful economic lives are used for book income. Both of these items result in larger depreciation deductions for tax purposes than for book purposes in the early years of an asset's life, and the opposite effect occurs in later years.

Bad Debts Expense
Bad debts are accrued and recognized under the allowance method for book purposes, but tax rules follow the direct write-off method, allowing a deduction only when a particular account is deemed to be uncollectible and written off.

Warranty Expense
Warranty expenses are accrued and recorded in the year the product is sold for book purposes, but for tax purposes the deduction is allowed when the actual warranty expenditures are made to correct the defect.

Prepaid Expenses
Some business expenses, like insurance premiums and rent, are paid in advance. For book purposes these expenditures are initially recorded as assets—"prepaid insurance," or "prepaid rent"—but later they are expensed over the periods when the benefits are received. Tax rules allow the deduction in the period the payment is made.

Pension and Other Post Retirement Benefits (OPEB) Expenses
For book purposes the deduction is based on the amount of pension or OPEB expense accrued. For pensions, a tax deduction is allowed for the amounts funded (i.e., contributed to the pension fund) each period, and for OPEB costs a deduction is allowed for amounts actually paid during the period.

Purchased Goodwill
The Revenue Reconciliation Act of 1993 allows firms a deduction for goodwill amortization on a 15-year straight-line basis under certain special conditions. But in most situations goodwill is *not* deductible. For book purposes, purchased goodwill is amortized over varying periods up to 40 years. As this book goes to press, the FASB is considering nonamortization of goodwill with periodic impairment tests (see Chapter 16).

Installment Sales
Sales are generally recognized for book purposes when the goods are delivered to the customer regardless of when collections are made. If collections are made over an extended period, tax rules record the sales revenue as payments are received.

Long-Term Construction Contracts
For long-term construction contracts (Chapter 3), firms may elect to use either the percentage-of-completion or the completed-contract method of revenue recognition for book purposes. In general, taxpayers may only use the percentage-of-completion method to account for long-term contracts entered into after July 11, 1989.

Revenues Received in Advance
Revenues received in advance (e.g., rent revenue or subscription revenue) are initially recorded as a liability for book purposes and are transferred to income as those revenues are "earned." For tax purposes, these amounts are taxed when received.

Equity in Undistributed Earnings of Investees
If a company (Investor) owns 20% or more of the outstanding voting stock of another corporation (Investee), the equity method of accounting is used for book purposes (Chapter 16). Under the equity method, the Investor records as income its share of Investee profits for the period. For tax purposes, income is recognized when Investee dividends are received, but this recognition is subject to special dividends-received deduction rules discussed below under permanent differences.

allows one U.S. corporation to deduct from taxable income a portion of the dividends received from another U.S. corporation.

Because permanent differences between book income and taxable income do not reverse and are not offset by corresponding differences in subsequent periods, they do *not* give rise to deferred tax assets or liabilities. Table 13.2 provides examples of permanent differences.

Table 13.2 ■ EXAMPLES OF PERMANENT DIFFERENCES BETWEEN BOOK INCOME AND TAXABLE INCOME

Items Recognized for Book Purposes but *Not* for Tax Purposes

- Interest received on state and municipal bonds is not subject to federal or state tax but is included in book income.
- If a company pays fines or expenses resulting from violations of the law (e.g., environmental damages), these payments are not deductible for tax purposes but would be deducted from book income.
- Goodwill write-offs generally are not deductible for tax purposes unless they meet certain special conditions.* Goodwill amortization is subtracted in determining book income (but see Chapter 16 for pending new rules).
- Premiums for life insurance on executives paid for by a company that is the designated beneficiary on these policies are not deductible for tax purposes. Similarly, any benefits collected are not taxed. For book purposes, both the premiums paid and proceeds received on such policies are used in determining income.
- Compensation expense associated with certain employee stock options is not deductible for tax purposes but is deductible in determining book income.

Items Recognized for Tax Purposes but *Not* for Book Purposes

- Tax laws allow a statutory depletion deduction on certain natural resources that may be in excess of the cost-based depletion recorded for book purposes. This excess statutory depletion is a permanent difference between book and taxable income.
- U.S. corporations that own stock in other U.S. companies are allowed to deduct a portion of the dividends received from these Investees from taxable income according to the following schedule:

Ownership	Deductible Portion of Dividends
Less than 20%	70%
Equal to or greater than 20%, but less than 80%	80%
Equal to or greater than 80%	100%

*See P. McConnell, "Goodwill: The Facts," *Accounting Issues* (New York: Bear, Stearns & Co., August 26, 1994); and sections 1060 and 338 of the Internal Revenue Code.

RECAP

Temporary differences occur when a revenue (gain) or expense (loss) enters into the determination of book (GAAP) income and taxable income in different periods. Temporary differences that cause taxable income to be higher (lower) than book income in future periods give rise to a deferred tax liability (asset). Permanent differences are revenue or expense items that are recognized as part of book income but are *never* recognized as part of taxable income, or vice versa. Permanent differences do *not* give rise to deferred tax assets or liabilities.

Problems Caused by Temporary Differences

To illustrate the issues related to interperiod tax allocation, consider the most prevalent temporary book/tax timing difference: depreciation expense. For tax purposes, profit-maximizing firms try to *minimize* the discounted present value of their future tax payments. Each dollar of tax deduction today is more valuable than a dollar of tax deduction in the future. This time-value-of-money principle is why most firms use accelerated depreciation for tax purposes. But many of these same firms use straight-line depreciation for financial reporting purposes. This creates a temporary difference between book income and taxable income.

Technically, firms are required to use Modified Accelerated Cost Recovery System depreciation schedules for tax purposes, and these differ by type of asset and useful life. We use SOYD here to simplify the illustration of depreciation temporary differences.

Consider this illustration. Assume Mitchell Corporation buys new equipment for $10,000 on January 1, 2001. The asset has a five-year life and no salvage value. It will be depreciated using the straight-line method for book purposes, but for tax purposes the sum-of-the-years'-digits (SOYD) method will be used. Table 13.3 and Figure 13.1(a) show the two depreciation schedules.

Table 13.3 ■ MITCHELL CORPORATION

Book Versus Tax Depreciation

Year	(a) Book Depreciation	(b) Tax Return Depreciation	(c) Excess of Tax Over Book Depreciation	
2001	$ 2,000	$ 3,333	$1,333	Originating timing differences
2002	2,000	2,667	667	
2003	2,000	2,000	—	
2004	2,000	1,333	(667)	Reversing timing differences
2005	2,000	667	(1,333)	
	$10,000	$10,000	–0–	

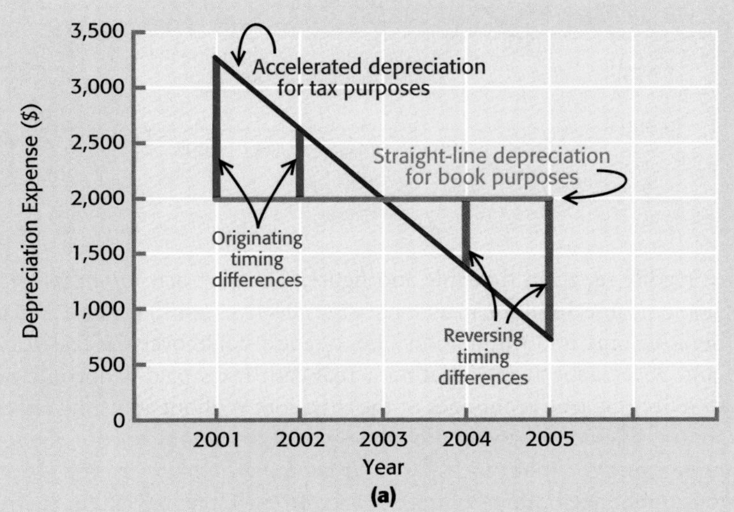

Figure 13.1(a)

MITCHELL CORPORATION

Comparison of Book Versus Tax Depreciation Expense

Let's assume for Mitchell Corporation that depreciation constitutes the only book versus tax difference; income before depreciation is expected to be $22,000 each year over the next five years; and the statutory tax rate is 35%. Pre-tax book income, taxable income per Mitchell's tax return, and taxes payable are reflected in Table 13.4 on the following page. Figure 13.1(b) displays graphically the relation between taxable income and pre-tax book income over the five-year period.

The **statutory tax rate** is the rate set by law—in this case, 35%.

The easiest way to reflect book income tax expense here would be to simply treat the actual taxes payable each year (column [c] of Table 13.4) as the reported *book* income tax expense. Table 13.5 and Figure 13.2 on p. 635 show what would happen if this were done.

Table 13.4 ■ MITCHELL CORPORATION

Income and Income Tax Payable

Year	(a) Pre-Tax Book Income ($22,000 − Book Depreciation)	(b) Taxable Income per Tax Return ($22,000 − Tax Depreciation)	(c) Income Tax Payable (35% of Col. [b])
2001	$ 20,000	$ 18,667*	$ 6,533
2002	20,000	19,333	6,767
2003	20,000	20,000	7,000
2004	20,000	20,667	7,233
2005	20,000	21,333	7,467
Total	$100,000	$100,000	$35,000

*For example, in 2001, $22,000 − $3,333 (Table 13.3, column [b]) = $18,667.

Figure 13.1(b)

MITCHELL CORPORATION

Pre-tax Book Income and Taxable Income

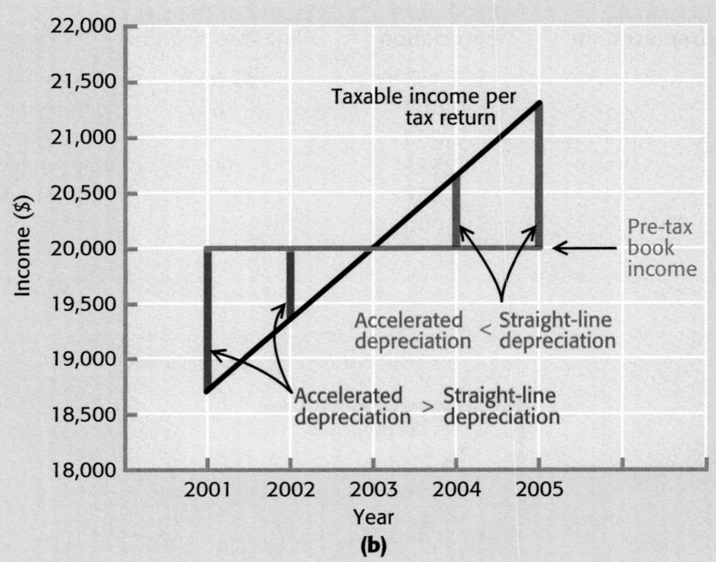

The **effective** (book) **tax rate** is the tax expense divided by pre-tax income that is reported on the GAAP income statement.

As you can readily see from the table and figure, this approach *mismatches* tax expense with pre-tax book income, resulting in an increasing effective (book) tax rate even though the pre-tax book income and the statutory tax rate are stable over the five-year period at $20,000 and 35%, respectively. Treating actual cash taxes paid as income tax expense would *not* reflect the true economics of the situation. Without adjusting tax expense for the temporary differences between book and tax depreciation expense, the results show an *increasing* effective (book) tax rate—and *declining* after-tax income—over the five-year period, as reflected both in columns (c) and (d) of Table 13.5 and in Figure 13.2. The effective (book) tax rate would range from 32.7% in 2001 to 37.3% in 2005, and the after-tax earnings would decline from $13,467 in 2001 to $12,533 in 2005. Clearly, this approach leads to an inappropriate matching between pre-tax book income and income tax expense.

Besides leading to a mismatch on the income statement, treating actual cash taxes paid as income tax expense introduces a reporting distortion on the balance sheet. This distortion occurs because total tax depreciation deductions on an asset cannot exceed the asset's cost minus its salvage value. Accordingly, "extra" tax depreciation in early years will be offset by lower allowable tax depreciation in later years. As shown in column (c) of Table 13.3, during 2001 tax depreciation ($3,333) exceeds book depreciation ($2,000). The "extra" tax depreciation of $1,333 means that future years' *tax* depreciation must be $1,333 lower than future years' *book* depreciation. Thus, the extra tax depreciation taken in 2001 generates a liability for future taxes of $1,333 times 35%, or $467.

Table 13.5 ■ MITCHELL CORPORATION

Result from Treating Actual Taxes Paid as Income Tax Expense

Year	(a) Pre-Tax Book Income	(b) Tax Expense = Income Tax Payable	(c) Reported Tax Rate (b ÷ a)	(d) After-Tax Book Income
2001	$20,000	$6,533	32.7%	$13,467
2002	20,000	6,767	33.8	13,233
2003	20,000	7,000	35.0	13,000
2004	20,000	7,233	36.2	12,767
2005	20,000	7,467	37.3	12,533

There is another way to visualize how the extra tax depreciation creates a liability for future taxes. The Financial Accounting Standards Board (FASB) states that GAAP assumes "... the reported amounts of assets ... will be recovered.... Based on that assumption, a difference between the tax basis of an asset ... and its reported amount ... will result in taxable ... amounts ... when the reported amounts ... are recovered...."[2] In our example, at the end of 2001, the reported (book) amount of the asset is $8,000 (i.e., $10,000 minus book depreciation of $2,000), while the tax basis is $6,667 (i.e., $10,000 minus tax depreciation of $3,333). Notice that if the asset was sold for its net book value of $8,000, a taxable gain of $1,333 would ensue, measured as the difference between the $8,000 cash received and the asset's $6,667 *tax* basis. Thus, given the GAAP assumption that reported amounts of assets will be recovered, the extra depreciation in 2001 would generate a liability for future taxes of $1,333 times 35%, or $467.

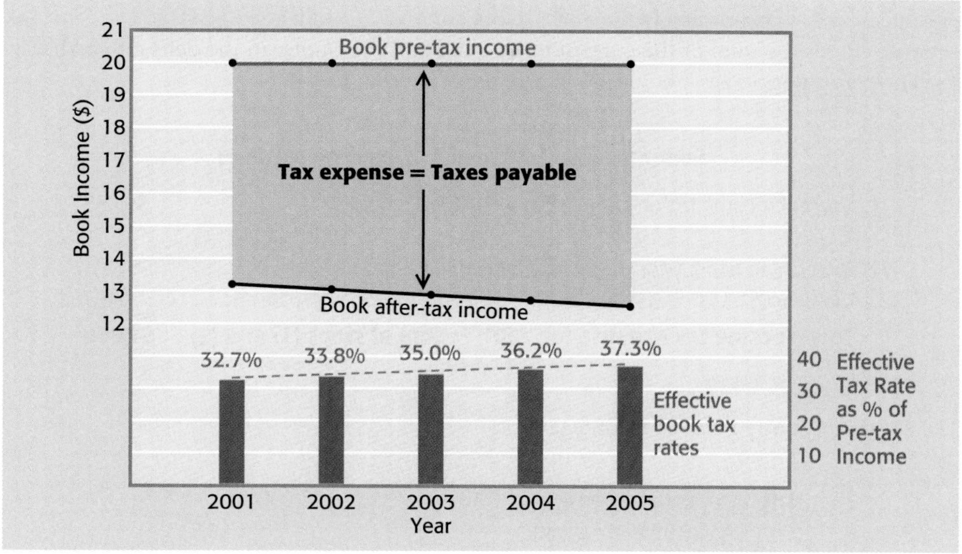

Figure 13.2

MITCHELL CORPORATION

Tax Expense *Without* Interperiod Tax Allocation

RECAP

Setting tax expense equal to current taxes payable (as in column [b] of Table 13.5) ignores the future tax liability that results from temporary (timing) differences between book and taxable income, and it results in a mismatching of tax expense with the related revenue and expense items reported on the GAAP income statement.

[2] "Accounting for Income Taxes," *Statement of Financial Accounting Standards (SFAS) No. 109* (Norwalk, CT: FASB, 1992), para. 11.

Table 13.6 ■ MITCHELL CORPORATION

Computation of Income Tax Expense With Interperiod Tax Allocation

Year	(a) Current Income Tax Payable (Table 13.4, Col. [c])	(b) Excess (Deficiency) of Tax Depreciation Relative to Book Depreciation (Table 13.3, Col. [c])	(c) Increase (Decrease) in Deferred Income Tax Liability (Col. [b] × 35%)	(d) Total Income Tax Expense (Col. [a] + Col. [c])	(e) Cumulative Balance in Deferred Income Tax Payable at Year-End
2001	$ 6,533	$1,333	$467	$ 7,000	$467
2002	6,767	667	233	7,000	700
2003	7,000	–0–	–0–	7,000	700
2004	7,233	(667)	(233)	7,000	467
2005	7,467	(1,333)	(467)	7,000	–0–
	$35,000	–0–	–0–	$35,000	

Deferred Income Tax Accounting: Interperiod Tax Allocation

To avoid the drawbacks just illustrated, income tax accounting does not simply equate tax expense with current taxes paid (or payable). Instead, the journal entry for income taxes reflects both taxes currently due as well as any liability for future taxes arising from current period book-versus-tax temporary differences that will reverse in later periods. The GAAP rules are specified in *SFAS No. 109*.[3] To illustrate them we continue the Mitchell Corporation example in Table 13.6 above.

Column (c) shows that for 2001 the *change* in the liability for future taxes is an increase of $467 (35% tax rate × $1,333 depreciation timing difference). Income tax currently payable is 35% of tax return income of $18,667, or $6,533. Under *SFAS No. 109*, income tax expense equals the total of the current taxes owed and the *change* in the deferred tax liability. The computation is:

Computation of Income Tax Expense for 2001

1. Current income tax payable (35% × $18,667)	$6,533
plus	
2. *Increase* in liability for future taxes arising during the year ($1,333 × 35%)	467
Total income tax expense for 2001 = sum of steps (1) and (2)	**$7,000**

In any year Congress changes U.S. tax rates, this matching disappears under *SFAS No. 109*. The reason is that *SFAS No. 109* focuses on the liability for future taxes, which changes as tax rates change.

The accounting entry for 2001 income taxes is:

DR Income tax expense	$7,000	
CR Income tax payable		$6,533
CR Deferred income taxes payable		467

When tax rates do not change from year to year, this entry simultaneously overcomes both of the drawbacks that would exist if we simply measured tax expense as cash taxes paid—the liability for future taxes is explicitly recognized, and the reported tax expense is exactly 35% of pre-tax book income of $20,000 (i.e., $7,000/$20,000 equals 35%). Thus, tax expense is also "matched" with book income. (This is true provided there are no permanent book/tax differences. When there are permanent differences between book and

[3] Ibid.

taxable income, then tax expense will *not* equal the tax rate times the pre-tax book income—a point demonstrated later in the chapter.)

You can readily see what this entry simultaneously accomplishes by carefully analyzing how each of the debits and credits of the entry are computed:

DR Income tax expense (Equal to the sum of taxes payable and the increase in deferred taxes payable. However, when tax rates are constant and there are no permanent book/tax differences, this debit will equal the tax rate [35%] times pre-tax book income [$20,000])	$7,000	
CR Income tax payable (35% times taxable income per tax return of $18,667)		$6,533
CR Deferred income taxes payable (35% times the depreciation temporary difference of $1,333 in 2001—Table 13.6, column [b] "excess" depreciation)		467

As illustrated here, the debit to income tax expense is a "plug" number that represents the combination of current taxes payable and any *change* in the deferred tax balance (in this case a deferred tax liability) that arises from timing differences during the year. When the deferred income tax liability increases, the increase is *added* to current income tax payable to arrive at income tax expense. When the deferred income tax liability decreases, the decrease is *subtracted* from current income tax payable in order to determine income tax expense. This relation is summarized in Figure 13.3.

In any year that the tax rate remains constant (say, at 35%) and there are no permanent book/tax differences, the debit to tax expense will automatically equal pre-tax book income times the 35% tax rate.

Sometimes the originating timing differences generate deferred income tax *assets* because taxable income will be lower than book income in future periods when those differences reverse. In that circumstance the debit to income tax expense represents the sum of current taxes payable plus the decrease (minus the increase) in the deferred tax *asset* account for the period.

Column (b) of Table 13.6 shows that the *original* book-versus-tax depreciation differences—called *originating timing differences,* and shown as the bars shaded blue in Figure 13.1(a)—increase the liability for future taxes (the deferred tax liability) in 2001 and 2002 (column [c] of Table 13.6). But all originating differences ultimately reverse. This occurs in the Mitchell Corporation illustration when tax depreciation drops below book depreciation in 2004 and 2005. The reversals of originating differences are called *reversing timing differences* and are shown as the bars shaded magenta in Figure 13.1(a).

To show what happens when book-versus-tax temporary differences reverse, let's consider the income tax entry in 2004. From Figure 13.3, the formula for computing income tax expense is as shown on next page.

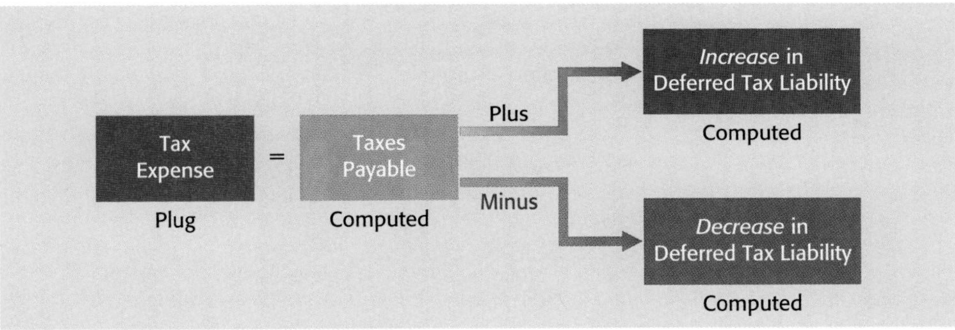

Figure 13.3

RELATION BETWEEN TAX EXPENSE, TAXES PAYABLE, AND CHANGES IN DEFERRED TAX LIABILITIES

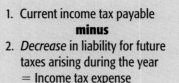

1. Current income tax payable
minus
2. *Decrease* in liability for future taxes arising during the year
= Income tax expense

Since book depreciation exceeds tax depreciation in 2004 by $667, the liability for future taxes *decreases* by $667 times 35%, or $233. Therefore, tax expense for 2004 is:

Computation of Income Tax Expense for 2004

1. Current income tax payable:	
$20,667 × 35%	$7,233
minus	
2. *Decrease* in liability for future taxes:	
$667 × 35%	(233)
Total income tax expense for 2004	**$7,000**

The journal entry for 2004 taxes is:

DR Income tax expense	$7,000	
DR Deferred income taxes payable	233	
CR Income tax payable		$7,233

Column (d) of Table 13.6 as well as Figure 13.4 show the computation of income tax expense for Mitchell Corporation for the entire five-year period (2001–2005) using interperiod tax allocation. Notice that in 2001 and 2002 the deferred tax liability *increases* and these increases are *added* to taxes payable to arrive at the tax expense reported on the income statement for those years. In 2004 and 2005 the depreciation timing differences reverse, resulting in *decreases* in the deferred tax liability (since the additional taxes are now being paid), and these decreases are *subtracted* from taxes payable to arrive at tax expense for those years. By the end of 2005 the depreciation book-versus-tax timing differences have totally reversed, and the balance in deferred income tax payable is zero. With constant

Figure 13.4

MITCHELL CORPORATION
Tax Expense *With* Interperiod Tax Allocation

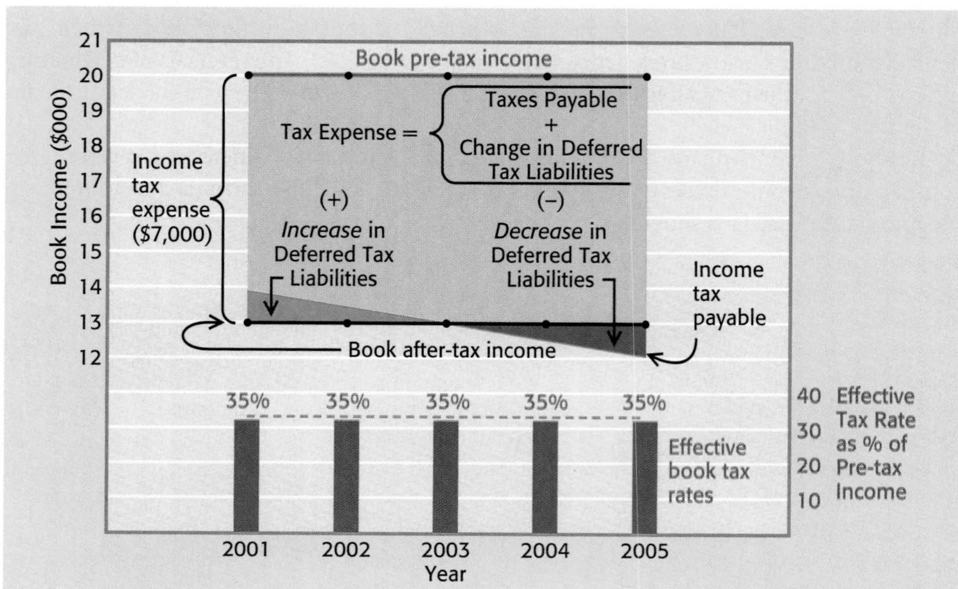

tax rates of 35% over the entire period, income tax expense (column [d] in Table 13.6) is always 35% times pre-tax book income of $20,000, and the pattern of tax expense matches the pattern of pre-tax book income.

RECAP

With interperiod tax allocation, tax expense equals current taxes payable to the IRS plus (minus) the increase (decrease) in deferred tax liabilities. This results in a tax expense number that is matched with the revenue and expense amounts that are recognized for book purposes.

Deferred Income Tax Accounting When Tax Rates Change

Tax rates periodically get changed by Congress. When that happens, the tax effects of the reversals change as well. To measure deferred income taxes, *SFAS No. 109* adopts the so-called **"liability approach"—*in any year current or future tax rates are changed, the income tax expense number absorbs the full effect of the change, and the relationship between that year's tax expense and book income is destroyed.***

Returning to the Mitchell Corporation example, let's assume that on December 31, 2003, a new income tax law raises the income tax rate from 35% to 38% beginning January 1, 2004. Reference to column (e) of Table 13.6 shows that just prior to the tax law change on December 31, 2003 the amount of deferred income tax payable for Mitchell was $700. That number represents the cumulative excess of tax over book depreciation in 2001 and 2002 (the dollar amount of temporary depreciation differences = $1,333 + $667, or $2000) times the initial tax rate of 35%. But because future tax rates have been increased, the liability for future taxes is actually larger than the $700 amount currently reported. At the new, higher income tax rate that will be in effect in 2004 and 2005, the liability for future taxes becomes $760, not $700. This future liability represents the cumulative excess of tax over book depreciation ($2,000) multiplied by the new 38% tax rate that will be in effect beginning January 1, 2004.

Under the liability approach of SFAS No. 109, the full change in the amount of future liability for income taxes (in this case, $60) is recognized as an increase or decrease in income tax expense in the year that the tax rate change becomes known. Accordingly, income tax expense for 2003 is computed as:

1. Current 2003 income tax payable (35% × $20,000 [see Table 13.4])	$ 7,000
plus	
2. *Increase* in the liability for future taxes arising during 2003	
($1,333 + $667) × (.38 − .35)	60
Total income tax expense for 2003	**$7,060**

The accounting entry for 2003 income taxes is:

DR Income tax expense	$7,060	
CR Income tax payable		$7,000
CR Deferred income taxes payable		60

After this entry is made, the balance in deferred income taxes payable will total $760, which is the liability for future taxes at the new 38% rate. Also, because tax rates for future years were changed in 2003, the debit to income tax expense does not equal the $20,000 pre-tax book income times the 2003 tax rate of 35%.

Table 13.7 on the following page shows the revised computation of income tax expense and deferred taxes payable for Mitchell Corporation for 2003 through 2005 after reflecting the income tax rate increase. The journal entry for income taxes in 2004 is shown at the top of page 640.

DR Income tax expense	$7,600	
DR Deferred income tax payable	253	
CR Income tax payable		$7,853

Similarly, the 2005 entry is:

DR Income tax expense	$7,600	
DR Deferred income tax payable	507	
CR Income tax payable		$8,107

As shown in column (f) of Table 13.7, the balance in the deferred income tax payable account will be zero after the year 2005 entry is made.

Table 13.7 ■ MITCHELL CORPORATION

Revised Computation of Income Tax Expense

Year	(a) Taxable Income (Table 13.4, Col. [b])	(b) Current Income Tax Payable = 38% of Col. (a)	(c) Difference Between Tax and Book Depreciation (Table 13.3, Col. [c])	(d) Increase (Decrease) in Liability for Future Taxes = Col. (c) = 38%	(e) Total Income Tax Expense = Col. (b) + Col. (d)	(f) Cumulative Balance in Deferred Income Tax Payable at Year-End
2003	$20,000	$7,000[1]	—	$ 60[2]	$7,060	$760
2004	20,667	7,853	(667)	(253)	7,600	507
2005	21,333	8,107	(1,333)	(507)	7,600	-0-

[1]Tax rate is still 35% in 2003 so this is $20,000 × 35%.
[2]This is the increase that arose in 2003 when the rate went from 35% to 38%—i.e., 3% × $2,000 cumulative depreciation differences in column (b) of Table 13.6.

A change in tax rates of this magnitude is not that uncommon. For example, the 1986 Tax Reform Act lowered the marginal corporate tax rate for large firms from 46% to 34%.

Because of the oblique way accounting rules recognize the effects of tax rate changes—through an adjustment to the tax expense number—analysts must be alert to recognize how these tax changes can inject one-shot (transitory) adjustments to earnings in the year Congress passes the new tax rates. Moreover, it is important to recognize that the effect of a tax rate change on bottom-line earnings can vary considerably across companies depending on three factors:

1. Whether the tax rates are increased or decreased
2. Whether the firm has net deferred tax assets or net deferred tax liabilities
3. The magnitude of the deferred tax balance.

Consider how differently a tax rate change can affect firms' bottom-line earnings: Suppose Congress passes a new tax law in 2002, one that raises the marginal statutory corporate tax rate from 35% to 45% effective in 2004. Further assume that Companies A, B, and C have the following net deferred tax asset (liability) balances on their books when the new tax law is passed:

($ in millions)	Company A	Company B	Company C
Net deferred tax asset (liability) balance in year 2002	$100	$0	($100)

Table 13.8 shows how the change in tax rate will affect the after-tax earnings of these three companies in 2002—the year the new tax rate is passed. We first divide the net deferred tax asset (liability) balance by the old marginal tax rate to get the dollar magnitude of the timing differences that gave rise to the balances in these accounts. (Recall that the balances in the deferred tax asset [liability] accounts equal the cumulative dollar amount of the timing differences giving rise to future deductible [taxable] amounts times the marginal corporate tax rate when those timing differences originated. Therefore, to derive the dollar amount of the timing differences, we simply divide the deferred tax asset or liability balance by the relevant tax rate.)

Company A has $285.71 ($100/.35) million of future *deductible* amounts, Company C has $285.71 of future *taxable* amounts, and Company B has neither future deductible nor taxable amounts. These timing differences are then multiplied by the *difference* between the new tax rate and the old tax rate (i.e., 10%) to obtain the increase in the deferred tax asset (liability) balance and the corresponding increase (decrease) in reported after-tax earnings.

ANALYSIS

As shown, Company A's 2002 earnings will *increase* by $28.571 million. This is because each dollar of future deductible amounts will yield an additional $0.10 in tax savings under the newly enacted tax rates (i.e., when these timing differences reverse). Company C, on the other hand, will report a $28.571 million *decrease* to its after-tax earnings number, since each dollar of future taxable amounts will generate $0.10 of additional taxes as these timing differences reverse in future years (i.e., when the tax rates will be higher). Company B's 2002 after-tax earnings are unaffected by the tax rate change because there are no temporary differences.

Table 13.8 ■ COMPUTATION OF HOW CHANGE IN TAX RATE AFFECTS EARNINGS IN YEAR THAT RATE CHANGE IS PASSED

($ in millions)	Company A		Company B	Company C	
Net deferred tax asset (liability) balance in 2002	$ 100		$0	($ 100)	
Divide by old marginal tax rate	÷ 35%		÷ 35%	÷ 35%	
Dollar amount of timing difference	$285.71 ←	Future Deductible Amount	$0	($285.71) ←	Future Taxable Amount
Multiply by difference between old and new tax rates (45% − 35%)	× 10%		× 10%	× 10%	
Increase (decrease) to after-tax earnings in year of rate change	$28.571		$0	($28.571)	

If the tax rates had been reduced from 35% to 25%, the earnings impacts reported above for Companies A and C would be reversed. As this example demonstrates, tax rate changes can have very different effects on firms' reported earnings depending on their deferred tax status and the direction of the tax rate change.

Under *SFAS No. 109,* when tax rates change, the additional tax benefits or costs are recognized as an adjustment to tax expense in the year that the tax rate changes are *passed*, not when they *become effective*. These one-shot earnings effects are often difficult to detect, since they are reported as part of the tax expense line on the income statement. However, a careful reading of the tax footnote that reconciles the book-effective tax rate with the marginal statutory tax rate (described in greater detail later in this chapter) can reveal the magnitude of earnings increases or decreases due to tax rate changes.

RECAP

SFAS No. 109 calls temporary differences that result in deferred tax liabilities **future taxable amounts,** since future tax return income will be higher than future book income; temporary differences that result in deferred tax assets are called **future deductible amounts,** since future tax return income —all other factors being equal—will be lower than future book income.

Deferred Income Tax Assets

The Mitchell Corporation example illustrated a situation in which pre-tax book income initially exceeded taxable income, creating a deferred income tax liability. Because this temporary difference later reverses, the liability ultimately is eliminated. But temporary differences can go in the opposite direction as well. In certain circumstances taxable income can initially exceed pre-tax book income, thereby giving rise to deferred income tax assets.

To illustrate how a deferred income tax asset comes about, let's assume that in December 2001 Paul Corporation owns an office building that it leases to another company for $100,000. The lease covers all of 2002 and specifies that the tenant pays the $100,000 to Paul Corporation immediately on signing the lease in 2001. On an accrual basis, rental income will be earned only in 2002. Accordingly, Paul Corporation makes the following entry on receiving the cash:

DR Cash	$100,000	
CR Rent received in advance		$100,000

The account "Rent received in advance" is a liability account that will be reduced monthly by $8,333 (with an offsetting credit to the "Earned lease revenue" account) in 2002 as Paul provides the tenant with the use of the facility and earns the lease revenue. For tax purposes, the entire $100,000 rent prepayment by the tenant is included in Paul Corporation's taxable income in 2001 when it is received. Assume that the lease receipt represents the only book/tax temporary difference for Paul and that 2001 pre-tax book income totals $1,500,000. Taxable income in the tax return will accordingly total $1,600,000 in 2001—$1,500,000 plus the immediately taxable advance rental payment of $100,000. If book income is also $1,500,000 in 2002, then book income will exceed taxable income by $100,000 in 2002 when this temporary difference reverses. These relationships are summarized in Table 13.9.

Table 13.9 ■ PAUL CORPORATION

Book Versus Tax Timing Differences That Give Rise to a Deferred Tax Asset

		2001 Lease Receipt of $100,000		
	Book Income	Included in Book Income?	Included in Tax Return Income?	Tax Return Income
2001	$1,500,000	No	Yes	$1,600,000
2002	1,500,000	Yes	No	1,400,000

Table 13.10 shows that when the rent is earned in 2002 for book purposes, accounting income will exceed taxable income by $100,000—but no tax will be due on this difference because the tax has already been paid in 2001. Thus, the temporary difference that originates in 2001 because of book/tax differences in lease revenue represents a deferred income tax asset at the end of 2001. If we assume the income tax rate is 35%, then the computation of 2001 tax expense is composed of the current taxes payable *minus* the increase in the deferred tax asset account computed as follows:

Computation of Income Tax Expense for 2001

1. Current income tax payable (Taxable income × 35% = $1,600,000 × 35%)	$ 560,000
minus	
2. *Increase* in deferred tax asset ($100,000 × 35%)	(35,000)
Total income tax expense for 2001	**$525,000**

Table 13.10 ■ PAUL CORPORATION

Computation of Tax Expense *With* Interperiod Tax Allocation

Year	(a) Taxable Income per Tax Return	(b) Book Income	(c) Excess (Deficiency) of Tax Lease Revenue over Book Lease Revenue	(d) Taxes Payable (35% of Col. [a])	(e) Increase (Decrease) in Deferred Tax Asset (Col. [c] × 35%)	(f) Total Income Tax Expense (Col. [d] – Col. [e])
2001	$1,600,000	$1,500,000	$100,000	$560,000	$35,000	$525,000
2002	1,400,000	1,500,000	(100,000)	490,000	(35,000)	525,000

Paul Corporation makes the following 2001 entry for income taxes:

DR Income tax expense	$525,000	
DR Deferred income tax asset	35,000	
CR Income tax payable		$560,000

In column (b) of Table 13.10, book income is $1,500,000 in 2002 after the $100,000 of rent revenue *earned* during the year is included. If we assume that there are no other book/tax temporary differences, then taxable income in the tax return will be $1,400,000, since the $100,000 advance rental receipt was included in taxable income in 2001—the previous year—when the rent revenue was *collected.* The $100,000 temporary difference in lease revenue that originated in 2001 reverses in 2002. The related deferred tax asset of $35,000 that was created in 2001 (column [e]) is decreased and eliminated in 2002. As shown in column (f), the decrease in the deferred tax asset of $35,000 is added to the taxes payable for that year to arrive at the tax expense number of $525,000. Paul will record the following income tax expense entry in 2002 when the timing difference reverses:

> Notice that income tax expense in both 2001 and 2002 is 35% of each year's book income—(i.e., $525,000 ÷ $1,500,000). Thus, income tax expense is properly matched with pre-tax income.

DR Income tax expense	$525,000	
CR Deferred income tax asset		$ 35,000
CR Income tax payable		490,000

Figure 13.5 on the following page depicts the relationships for computing *SFAS No. 109* income tax expense by adjusting taxes payable for changes in deferred income tax assets and liabilities.

Deferred Income Tax Asset Valuation Allowances

If Paul Corporation experienced adversity in 2002 and had no taxable income in that year, the $35,000 deferred income tax asset would generate no benefit—that is, if 2002 taxes were zero, the "benefits" arising from the $35,000 tax payment on the 2001 advance rental receipt would be lost. Thus, it is always possible that a firm that has recognized deferred income tax assets may not receive tax payment reductions in future years. For this reason the FASB requires firms with deferred income tax assets to assess the likelihood that these assets may not be fully realized in future periods.

> Later in this chapter, we'll see that the U.S. Income Tax Code allows unprofitable companies to recapture previously paid taxes. We temporarily ignore this provision in the tax code in order to sharpen your understanding of the possibility that deferred income tax assets may not generate future benefits.

The realization of tax benefits from existing deferred income tax assets depends on whether or not the firm has future taxable income. If management believes that the probability of future taxable income is greater than 50%, deferred income tax assets can be

Figure 13.5

RELATION BETWEEN TAX EXPENSE, TAXES PAYABLE, AND CHANGES IN DEFERRED TAX ASSETS AND LIABILITIES

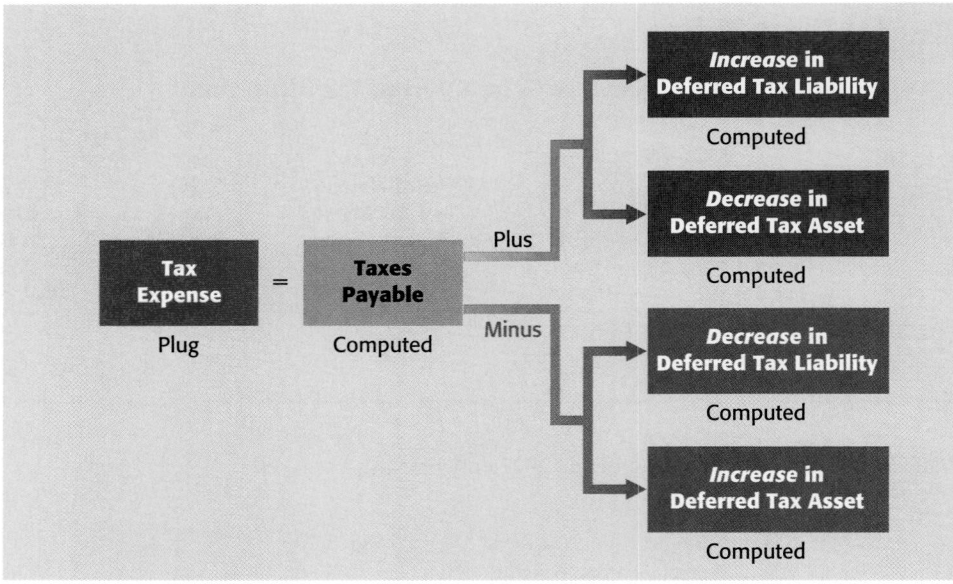

recognized (without adjustment) in their entirety. However, if management's assessment indicates that *it is more likely than not* that some portion of the benefit will not be realized in its entirety, a **deferred tax asset valuation allowance** is required. The FASB stated that this valuation allowance ***"should be sufficient to reduce the deferred tax asset to the amount that is more likely than not to be realized."***[4]

To illustrate the procedure for establishing a valuation allowance for deferred tax assets, let's assume (1) that for book purposes Norman Corporation accrued $900,000 of estimated warranty expenses associated with product sales in 2001, and (2) the actual warranty parts and services from these sales are provided in 2002 and beyond. Since the U.S. Income Tax Code only allows companies to deduct warranty expense when the warranty services are provided, this timing difference gives rise to a deferred tax asset of $315,000 (35% tax rate × $900,000 timing difference) that would be recorded in 2001. If we assume Norman's pre-tax book income is $600,000, taxable income is $1,500,000 and the 2001 entry for tax expense is:

DR Income tax expense ($600,000 × .35)	$210,000	
DR Deferred income tax asset ($900,000 × .35)	315,000	
CR Income tax payable ($1,500,000 × .35)		$525,000

Now assume that early in 2002 Norman Corporation determines that it is unlikely to earn enough taxable income in future years to realize more than $200,000 of the deferred tax asset. The entry made in 2002 is:

DR Income tax expense ($315,000 − $200,000)	$115,000	
CR Allowance to reduce deferred tax asset to expected realizable value		$115,000

The credit to the allowance account reduces the net carrying amount of the deferred tax asset from $315,000 to $200,000—its estimated realizable value. This occurs because the allowance account is shown on the balance sheet as a contra-account to the deferred tax

[4] Ibid., para. 17. Operationally, "more likely than not" means greater than a 50% probability of happening.

asset. Notice that income tax expense is increased in the year during which it is determined that a portion of the income tax asset is unlikely to be recovered. Accordingly, income tax expense will exceed pre-tax book income multiplied by the tax rate in years when allowance accounts are established or increased. If Norman Corporation's future prospects improve and if in 2003 it is determined that an allowance account is no longer needed, the allowance account is reduced to zero and a *credit* to income tax expense is made.

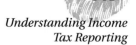

When circumstances indicate that it is "more likely than not" that some portion of the future tax benefit from a deferred tax asset will not be realized, then a deferred tax asset valuation allowance must be established to reduce the deferred tax asset book value to the amount expected to be realized.

RECAP

Net Operating Losses: Carrybacks and Carryforwards

Since firms pay taxes during profitable years, it would be inequitable to deny them some form of tax relief in unprofitable years. Therefore, the U.S. Income Tax Code provides an opportunity for firms reporting operating losses to offset those losses against either past or future tax payments—that is, when an operating loss occurs (e.g., when deductible expenses exceed taxable revenues), firms can elect one of two options described in the following sections:

1. *Both* carryback and carryforward incurred losses.
2. *Only* carryforward incurred losses.

Prior to 1998, the loss carryback period was three years and the carryforward period was 15 years.

Carryback and Carryforward Assume that Unfortunato Corporation experienced a $1,000,000 pre-tax operating loss in 2002. Under the U.S. Income Tax Code, Unfortunato can elect to carry back the operating loss and offset it against taxable income in the previous two years—2000 and 2001. The loss must be offset against the earliest year first—in this case, 2000. If the loss exceeds the total taxable income for the 2000–2001 period, then the remaining portion of the loss can be carried forward and offset against *future* taxable income in the ensuing 20 years—2003 through 2022—as shown in Figure 13.6.

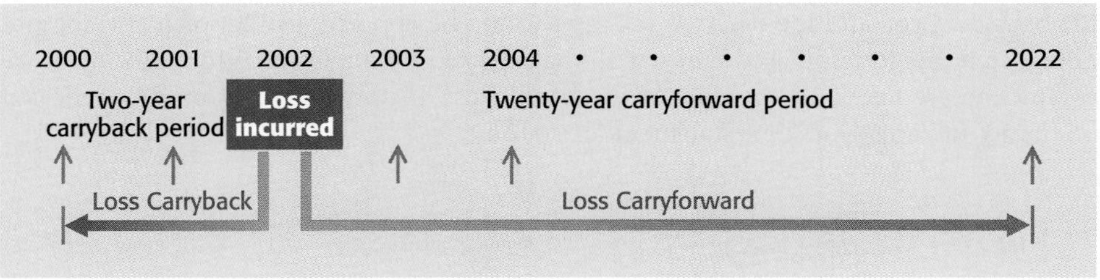

Figure 13.6

UNFORTUNATO CORPORATION
Illustration of Tax Loss Carryback/Carryforward Provision

Carryforward Only Another alternative is available to Unfortunato Corporation. Rather than first carrying the loss back and then carrying forward any unused amounts, Unfortunato could elect *only* to carry the loss forward against taxable profits in the next 20 years, as shown in Figure 13.7 on the following page.

To illustrate how the two options work, let's assume that the tax rate in effect from 1999 through 2002 was 35% and that Unfortunato had the following operating profits in those years:

Year	Taxable Profit (Loss)	Tax (at 35%)
1999	$ 300,000	$105,000
2000	400,000	140,000
2001	350,000	122,500
2002	(1,000,000)	–

Why would firms elect the carryforward-only option, thereby foregoing an immediate income tax refund? Most companies *do* elect to carryback first, since this strategy usually maximizes the discounted present value of the benefit. In unusual situations—for example, where a firm expects to be profitable in the future and expects future tax rates to be much higher than past rates—the carryforward-only option may be preferred.

Figure 13.7

UNFORTUNATO CORPORATION

Illustration of Tax Loss Carryforward

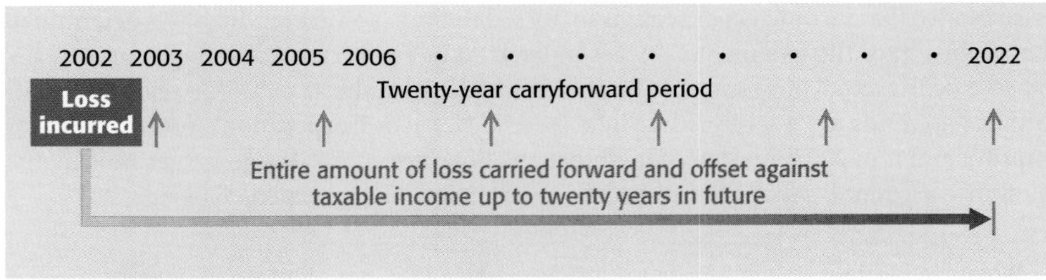

If Unfortunato Corporation elects to use the combined carryback/carryforward option, losses must first be offset against 2000 income ($400,000), the earliest year in the two-year carryback time frame, and then against 2001 income ($350,000). This offsets $750,000 of the 2002 loss and generates a tax refund of $262,500 ($750,000 × 35%). Unfortunato makes the following entry in 2002 to reflect the refund due:

DR Income tax refund receivable	$262,500	
CR Income tax expense (*carryback* benefit)		$262,500

The loss in excess of the combined prior two-years' profits ($1,000,000 − $400,000 − $350,000 = $250,000) will result in future tax benefits—if Unfortunato becomes profitable again before 2022. If we assume that future tax rates remained at 35%, these potential future benefits would total $87,500 ($250,000 × 35%). If Unfortunato expects that pre-tax income in the ensuing 20 years will exceed $250,000, then an additional entry would be made in 2002:

DR Deferred income tax asset	$87,500	
CR Income tax expense (*carryforward* benefit)		$87,500

The "Income tax refund receivable" asset account would be shown among current assets on the balance sheet, and the deferred tax asset would be apportioned between current and noncurrent categories in accordance with the expected timing of the future income. If we assume the pre-tax book loss equaled the taxable loss, then the credits would be reflected on the accompanying income statement for 2002 as:

Pre-tax operating loss	($1,000,000)
Income tax benefit due to operating loss *carryback*	262,500
Income tax benefit due to operating loss *carryforward*	87,500
After-tax operating loss	($ 650,000)

Deferred income tax assets that result from operating loss carryforwards will generate future benefits only if the firm earns profits in the ensuing 20 years. Because future profits are never assured, the probability of realizing deferred income tax assets arising from operating loss carryforwards must be carefully evaluated. The criterion here for deciding whether a valuation allowance is needed is identical to the criterion applied to deferred tax assets arising from book-versus tax-timing differences—if ***it is more likely than not*** that the benefit will not be realized in its entirety, a valuation allowance is required. This allowance should reduce the asset to a net amount that is more likely than not to be realized.

U.S. tax rules allow firms to offset operating losses against taxable income. Firms can elect to carry back losses up to two years, with any unused loss carried forward up to 20 years; or they can elect to only carry forward the loss up to 20 years. The tax benefit associated with the loss carryback or carryforward is recorded as an adjustment to tax expense in the year of the loss.

RECAP

Illustration of Footnote Disclosure for Valuation Allowances

Exhibit 13.1 contains an excerpt from Bethlehem Steel Corporation's 1999 income tax footnote. Bethlehem experienced operating losses in the 1991–1993 period and again in 1996 and 1999. These losses raise questions regarding the recoverability of the gross deferred income tax asset of $1.3 billion on the company's December 31, 1999 balance sheet. In this excerpt, Bethlehem discusses the need for a valuation allowance and explains how the size of the allowance was computed. Notice that this disclosure provides information regarding expected future earnings. Consequently, it can be used by analysts to develop or refine estimates of the company's future performance.

ANALYSIS

On the other hand, the determination of whether a valuation allowance is necessary requires subjective assessments. Similarly, the amount of the allowance is also not based on

Exhibit 13.1 ■ BETHLEHEM STEEL CORPORATION

Excerpt from 1999 Annual Report Income Tax Footnote

At December 31, 1999, we had regular tax net operating loss carryforwards of about $1.4 billion and alternative minimum tax loss carryforwards of about $600 million. A regular net operating loss of about $65 million is expected to expire when we file our 1999 federal tax return later in 2000. Regular federal tax net operating loss carryforwards of about $145 million and $220 million will expire in 2000 and 2001, with the balance expiring in varying amounts from 2005 through 2019, if we are unable to use the amounts in related federal income tax returns. Under certain conditions involving future changes in Bethlehem's ownership, Section 382 of the Internal Revenue Code could substantially reduce and limit the annual utilization of our net operating loss carryforwards.

FASB Statement No. 109, *Accounting for Income Taxes,* requires that we record a valuation allowance when it is "more likely than not that some portion or all of the deferred tax assets will not be realized." It further states, "forming a conclusion that a valuation allowance is not needed is difficult when there is negative evidence such as cumulative losses in recent years." The ultimate realization of this deferred tax asset depends on our ability to generate sufficient taxable income in the future. Excluding estimated (losses) gains on exiting businesses, Bethlehem has reported net income for five out of the past six years, and has undergone substantial restructuring and made strategic capital expenditures during the last several years. Also, we have tax planning opportunities that could affect taxable income including selection of depreciation methods and lives, sales of assets and timing of distributions to our pension trust fund.

Based on our current outlook for 2000, 2001 and beyond, we believe that our deferred tax asset will be realized by future operating results together with tax planning opportunities. However, our significant net operating loss carryforwards and future tax deductions from temporary differences make it appropriate to record a valuation allowance. Accordingly, we have provided a valuation allowance equal to 50% of the deferred tax asset related to our operating loss carryforward and certain temporary differences. We have provided a valuation allowance for other postretirement benefits, except for the temporary differences of $1,555 million as of January 1, 1992, and of $195 million assumed in connection with the acquisition of Lukens. If we have a tax loss in any year in which our tax deduction for other postretirement benefits exceeds our financial statement expense, the tax law currently provides for a 20-year carryforward of that loss against future taxable income. Because we should have sufficient time to realize these future tax benefits, we believe a valuation allowance is not appropriate for the deferred tax assets related to these temporary differences for other postretirement benefits.

If we are unable to generate sufficient taxable income in the future through operating results or tax planning opportunities, we will be required to reduce our net deferred tax asset through a charge to income tax expense (reducing our stockholders' equity). On the other hand, if we achieve sufficient profitability to use all of our deferred income tax asset, we will reduce the valuation allowance through a reduction in income tax expense (increasing our stockholders' equity).

readily observable criteria. When a valuation allowance is established, the offsetting debit is to income tax expense, which reduces income; similarly, when a previously existing allowance is lowered, the offsetting credit to income tax expense increases income. Because of the subjective judgments used when determining the need for (and the amount of) valuation allowances, the possibility of income manipulation exists. Specifically, valuation allowances could be used to smooth year-to-year earnings fluctuations. For example, in a "good" earnings year management might decide to establish an allowance account, assuming the offsetting charge to earnings is relatively small.

Once the allowance is established, it can be diminished or even eliminated in subsequent "bad" earnings years. Notice that the credit arising from the allowance reversal increases income, thereby partially offsetting the bad earnings. The result is that income fluctuations are smoothed across years. One recent study investigated whether managers use the valuation allowance to manage earnings.[5] Two types of earnings management are considered: (1) income smoothing (as just described), and (2) "big bath" charge-offs in bad years. While there is anecdotal evidence that the valuation allowance may be used by some firms to manage earnings, the general conclusion is that this is not a pervasive practice. Nevertheless, statement readers must be careful to analyze whether reported changes in valuation allowance amounts seem reasonable in the context of the firm's known prospects.

Using Footnote Disclosures to Improve Financial Analysis

Understanding Footnote Disclosures

Typical income tax footnote disclosures provide financial statement users with a wealth of data. If you understand these disclosures, you'll be able to extract useful insights about a firm's performance and prospects. To illustrate, let's look at the income tax footnote from the 1999 annual report of Merck & Co., Inc., shown in Exhibit 13.2 on pages 649 and 650. To make things easy to refer to, we have subdivided the footnote into panels (a) through (d) and numbered key lines or sections in these schedules.

Exhibit 13.2(a) shows the components of Merck's tax expense provision for the years 1997 through 1999. Notice how Merck differentiates between the portion of tax expense that is currently payable (denoted Item ①) and the portion that is deferred taxes (Item ②). Within each category, separate amounts for U.S. Federal, foreign and state taxes are disclosed. In the aggregate, the 1999 entry for taxes ($ in millions) was:

DR Income tax expense (Item ③)	$2,729.0	
DR Deferred tax liability or asset (Item ②)	682.9	
CR Income tax currently payable (Item ①)		$3,411.9

The $682.9 million debit to deferred taxes arises because of temporary differences in revenue and expense items reported on Merck's GAAP income statement versus what was reported on its tax return in 1999. In aggregate, these temporary differences caused book income to be smaller than taxable income in 1999. The result was either a decrease in deferred tax liabilities or an increase in deferred tax assets (both debits).

Exhibit 13.2(b) explains why the debit to tax expense in the 1997–1999 period is greater or less than the U.S. statutory corporate tax rate of 35% times pre-tax book income. For example, the $2,729 million debit to tax expense in the previous entry is 31.7% of $8,619.5 million, Merck's reported pre-tax income in 1999. The reconciliation in this portion of Exhibit 13.2(b) (Item ④) explains what caused the divergence between Merck's effective tax rate of 31.7% and the 35% statutory rate (Item ⑤).

---

[5] G. Miller and D. J. Skinner, "Determinants of the Valuation Allowance for Deferred Tax Assets Under SFAS-109," *The Accounting Review* (April 1998), pp. 213–234.

Exhibit 13.2 ■ MERCK & CO., INC.

1999 Annual Report Footnote on Income Taxes

Taxes on income consist of:

($ in millions)		Years Ended December 31 1999	1998	1997
Current Provision				
Federal	①	**$2,674.9**	$1,750.5	$1,322.2
Foreign	①	**439.9**	699.5	476.8
State	①	**297.1**	264.7	90.5
		3,411.9	2,714.7	1,889.5
Deferred Provision				
Federal	②	**(718.9)**	226.2	(48.1)
Foreign	②	**21.9**	(21.0)	(6.4)
State	②	**14.1**	(35.0)	13.2
		(682.9)	170.2	(41.3)
[Current period tax expense*]	←③→	**$2,729.0**	$2,884.9	$1,848.2

(a)

A reconciliation between the Company's effective tax rate and the U.S. statutory rate is as follows:

($ in millions)		1999 Amount	Tax Rate 1999	1998	1997
U.S. statutory rate applied to pre-tax income		**$3,016.8**	**35.0%**	35.0%	35.0%
Differential arising from					
Foreign earnings	④	**(245.1)**	**(2.8)**	0.6	(0.8)
Tax exemption for Puerto Rico operations	④	**(133.2)**	**(1.5)**	(1.6)	(1.9)
Equity income from affiliates	④	**8.8**	**0.1**	(1.7)	(2.4)
Acquired research	④	**17.9**	**0.2**	4.5	–
State taxes	④	**169.6**	**2.0**	1.6	1.0
Other	④	**(105.8)**	**(1.3)**	(2.9)	(2.3)
[Reported tax expense*]		**$2,729.0**	**31.7%**** ⑤	35.5%	28.6%

(b)

*Description added by authors for clarity.
**Reported 1999 pre-tax income of Merck was $8,619.5 million, so $2,729.0 ÷ $8,619.5 = 31.7%.

(continued)

The reconciliation in Exhibit 13.2(b) is required under SFAS 109.[6] It is potentially useful to analysts because it provides information about the firm's tax policy. Specifically, the divergence between the **statutory tax rate** (the tax rate set forth in federal tax laws) and **effective tax rate** (measured by book tax expense divided by book pre-tax income) arises from two types of tax policy decisions:

1. The tax jurisdictions in which the firm chooses to operate
2. Special characteristics of the income tax law.

One frequent cause for differences between effective and statutory rates is that tax rates differ across countries. For example, to attract investment, certain countries levy extremely low (or no) taxes on income earned within their boundaries. And other countries' tax rates may exceed U.S. rates. Furthermore, many U.S. states impose income taxes on income earned within the state, which causes a firm's effective tax rate to exceed the 35% federal statutory rate. One important element of a firm's tax planning strategy is choosing to operate subsidiaries

[6] SFAS 109, para. 47.

Exhibit 13.2 ■ MERCK & CO., INC. (*continued*)

Deferred income taxes at December 31 consisted of:

($ in millions)		1999 Assets	1999 Liabilities		1998 Assets	1998 Liabilities
Other intangibles	⑥	**$ 198.3**	**$1,372.1**	⑦	$ 6.7	$1,434.6
Inventory related		**799.1**	**316.3**		546.6	210.5
Accelerated depreciation		**–**	**642.2**		–	606.6
Advanced payment		**338.6**	**–**		–	–
Investment related		**–**	**216.1**		–	210.0
Equity investments		**57.8**	**201.6**		57.8	91.7
Pensions and OPEB		**185.5**	**192.5**		176.9	140.1
Compensation related		**129.3**	**–**		118.9	–
Environmental related		**115.6**	**–**		131.0	–
Restructuring charge		**71.3**	**–**		107.9	–
Other		**897.1**	**424.3**		758.0	413.3
Subtotal		**2,792.6**	**3,365.1**		1,903.8	3,106.8
Valuation allowance ← ⑧ →		**(4.1)**	**–**		(9.1)	–
Total deferred taxes		**$2,788.5**	**$3,365.1**		$1,894.7	$3,106.8
Net deferred tax liabilities ← ⑨ →		**$576.6**			$1,212.1	

(c)

		1999	1998
Recognized as:			
Prepaid expenses and taxes	⑩	($ 869.2)	($ 666.3)
Other assets		(50.3)	(48.2)
Income taxes payable		151.9	163.5
Deferred income taxes and non-current liabilities		1,344.2	1,763.1
		$ 576.6	$1,212.1

(d)

within lower marginal tax rate jurisdictions. This lowers the firm's overall tax burden, thereby increasing after-tax returns to shareholders.[7] Merck apparently did this in 1999.

> Exhibit 13.2(b) reveals that Merck saved $133.2 million in taxes for 1999 because it had earnings from Puerto Rico operations that were tax exempt. We can determine the dollar amount of these tax-exempt earnings by dividing the tax savings by the U.S. statutory tax rate ($133.2 ÷ .35 = $380.6 million).

Another reason for differences between effective and statutory rates is due to special tax law characteristics that treat certain GAAP revenue items as non-taxable and certain GAAP expenses as non-deductible for tax purposes. Remember, book versus tax differences that never reverse are referred to as *permanent differences.* Permanent difference items that cause book income to be *higher* but are not taxed (e.g., interest on municipal bonds) will cause the effective tax rate per books to be *lower* than the statutory tax rate. Conversely, permanent differences that cause book income to be *lower* but are not deductible for tax purposes (e.g., most types of goodwill amortization or fines levied for law violations) will cause the effective tax rate per books to be *higher* than the statutory rate.

The reconciliation between effective and statutory tax rates, like that shown in Exhibit 13.2 (b) (Item ④), can reflect important elements of a firm's tax policy decisions. Effective tax rates that are far lower than statutory tax rates might indicate aggressive tax postures. This could benefit shareholders. But, aggressive tax positions might also generate future tax audits and additional tax assessments.[8]

[7] For an expanded discussion of this point, see M. Scholes and M. Wolfson, *Tax and Corporate Financial Strategy: A Global Planning Approach* (Upper Saddle River, N.J.: Prentice Hall, 1991).

[8] For an analysis of tax footnote disclosures from the perspective of tax aggressiveness and future tax audit risk, see R. Weber and J. Wheeler, "Using Income Tax Disclosures to Explore Significant Economic Transactions," *Accounting Horizons* (September 1992), pp. 14–29.

Items ⑥ and ⑦ of Exhibit 13.2(c) show year-end balances in deferred tax asset and deferred tax liability accounts and the source of those amounts. After deducting the valuation allowance of $4.1 million on deferred tax assets (Item ⑧), Merck had a *net* deferred tax liability balance at December 31, 1999 of $576.6 million (Item ⑨), or $3,365.1 million of deferred tax liabilities minus $2,788.5 million of deferred tax assets. One year earlier, Merck had a *net* deferred tax liability balance (after allowance) of $1,212.1 million ($3,106.8 million liability minus $1,894.7 million asset). Thus, the year-to-year change in *net* deferred tax liabilities was $1,212.1 − $576.6 = $635.5 million.

Notice the $635.5 million decrease in Merck's net deferred tax liability on its balance sheet in Exhibit 13.2(c) does *not* equal the $682.9 million journal entry debit to deferred taxes shown earlier. The $47.4 million difference is partially explained by reference to **intraperiod income tax allocation** discussed briefly in Chapter 2. Recall that all income statement items shown below income from continuing operations and direct charges or credits to stockholders' equity *are shown net of any related income tax effects.* Accordingly, tax effects (including deferred tax effects) that arose from discontinued operations, extraordinary items, cumulative effects of accounting changes, or direct charges or credits to stockholders' equity for prior period adjustments or other comprehensive income items are not included in Merck's tax journal entry on page 648. This journal entry is limited to income tax effects that relate to income from continuing operations.

Merck has no discontinued operations, no extraordinary items, and no accounting changes reported in its 1999 income statement. However, scrutiny of Merck's Statement of Comprehensive Income (not shown) reveals two "Other comprehensive income" items—market value adjustments on available for sale securities and pension liability adjustments—that increased stockholders' equity by $29.4 million net of tax effects. The deferred tax liability associated with these two items would be approximately $15.8 million.

> This amount is determined in two steps. First, we divide the after-tax amount of $29.4 million by one minus the statutory tax rate [$29.4 ÷ (1 − .35) = $45.2 million]. This gives the before-tax amount of other comprehensive income components. Next, taking the difference between the before-tax amount of $45.2 million and the after-tax amount of $29.4 million gives the *increase* in deferred tax liabilities ($15.8 million) related to these other comprehensive income components.

This $15.8 million is included in deferred tax liabilities on the balance sheet, but is not included in the 1999 journal entry for taxes. Thus, it provides a partial explanation for why the $682.9 debit to deferred taxes in Merck's 1999 tax expense entry (see p. 648) exceeds the decrease in net deferred tax liabilities of $635.5 million reflected on its balance sheet ($1,212.1 − $576.6 in Exhibit 13.2[c]). But this still leaves an unexplained difference of $31.6 million—that is, the original difference of $47.4 million minus the $15.8 million. The most likely source of this remaining difference is various acquisitions and divestitures made during the year, which are discussed elsewhere in Merck's 1999 annual report. When the acquired or divested subsidiary holds assets having a tax basis that differs from their financial accounting basis, changes occur in deferred tax accounts on the consolidated balance sheet. These deferred tax changes are not reflected in the deferred portion of the current period's tax provision. Unfortunately, Merck's disclosures do not allow us to determine this amount directly. The lesson here is that certain events (e.g., acquisitions or divestitures of subsidiaries) can complicate full reconciliation of the deferred tax accounts.

Exhibit 13.2(c) also shows the specific items that collectively comprise the deferred tax asset (Item ⑥) and deferred tax liability (Item ⑦) balances at December 31, 1999. The major items giving rise to deferred tax assets are inventory and advance payments, while the major items giving rise to deferred tax liabilities are other intangibles and depreciation differences. Finally, Exhibit 13.2(d) shows in which specific accounts the net deferred tax asset and liability amounts of $576.6 million are reported on Merck's December 31, 1999 balance sheet (Item ⑩).

Overview of Tax Journal Entry Components

Figure 13.8 on the following page provides a flow diagram of the elements that give rise to the debits and credits in the income tax journal entry. The diagram depicts how temporary book versus tax differences, permanent differences, and loss carryforwards affect the vari-

Figure 13.8

ELEMENTS COMPRISING INCOME TAXES JOURNAL ENTRY

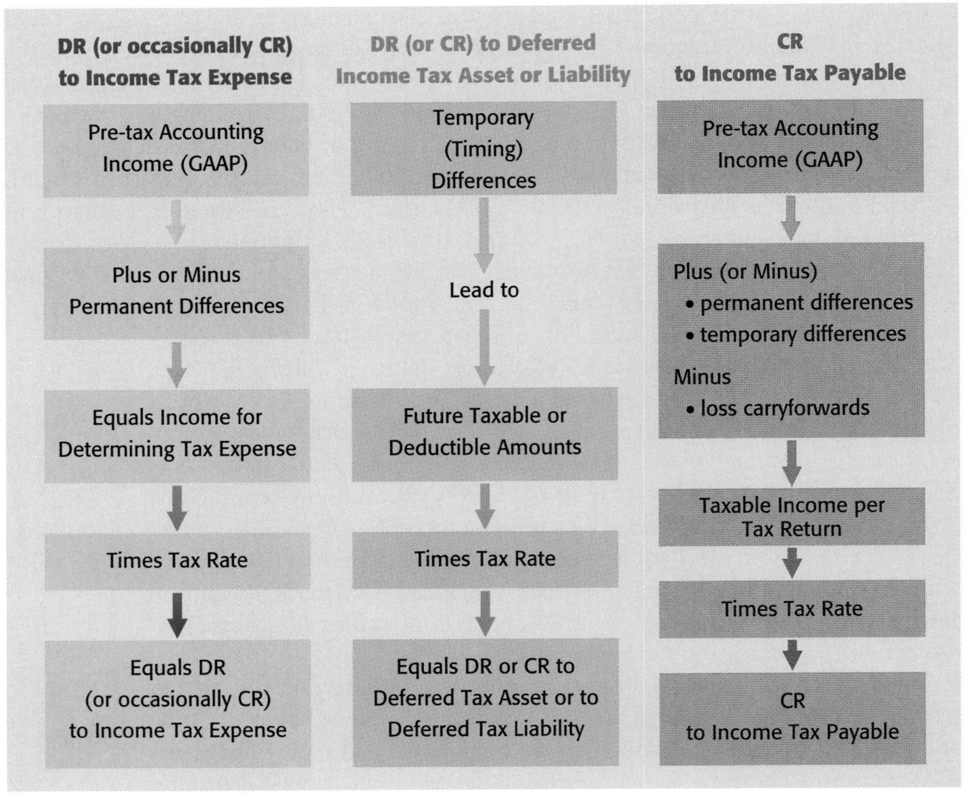

ous entry components, and it provides a graphic overview of the preceding sections under the assumption of no changes in statutory tax rates.

Extracting Analytical Insights from Footnote Disclosures

ANALYSIS

Scrutiny of the detail comprising deferred taxes can reveal much to the astute analyst. To illustrate, refer to Exhibit 13.3, which contains a portion of the 1999 income tax footnote of Winn-Dixie Stores, Inc.. This portion identifies elements of deferred tax balances. Notice that the deferred income tax liability attributable to book versus tax depreciation differences (highlighted area) increased by \$19.140 million between 1998 and 1999 (\$31,098 − \$11,958). Some portion of this increase is attributable to growth in fixed assets (e.g., June 30, 1999 net property, plant and equipment exceeded the year-earlier amount by \$52.785 million). Again, however, fixed asset growth explains only a part of the increase in this segment of the deferred income tax liability. What factor explains the rest of the increase? In another note in its 1999 annual report, Winn-Dixie states:

> During the second quarter of fiscal 1999, the Company increased the estimated useful lives used to compute depreciation for certain assets, principally store equipment (5 to 8 years) and leaseholds (8 to 15 years). Store equipment and leaseholds associated with larger, full-service store formats are expected to have a longer life because of the types of equipment and the expected timing of store remodels. In addition, the change resulted in useful lives more consistent with the predominant industry practices for these types of assets. The change has been accounted for as a change in estimate and resulted in a reduction in operating and administrative expenses of . . . \$45.8 million for the 53 weeks ended June 30, 1999.

The \$16.03 million figure is derived as follows. The company discloses that the change in estimated useful lives increased before-tax income by \$45.8 million. If we assume that the fixed assets are domiciled in the U. S. and subject to U. S. corporate tax rates of 35%, then the increase in deferred taxes payable is .35 × \$45.8 = \$16.03 million.

By extending the useful lives of fixed assets, Winn-Dixie lowered book depreciation and widened the excess of 1999 book income over tax return income. This increased the deferred tax liability related to depreciation timing differences by \$16.03 million, which is nearly 84% of the \$19.140 million increase from the prior year.

Exhibit 13.3 ■ **WINN-DIXIE STORES INC.**

Excerpt from 1999 Annual Report Income Tax Footnote

The tax effects of temporary differences that give rise to significant portions of the deferred tax assets and deferred liabilities at June 30, 1999, June 24, 1998 and June 25, 1997 are presented below:

($ in thousands)	1999	1998	1997
Deferred tax assets:			
Reserve for insurance claims and self-insurance	$ 62,429	$ 61,160	$ 57,169
Reserve for vacant store leases	20,511	20,137	14,521
Unearned promotional allowance	3,143	6,844	12,520
Reserve for accrued vacations	14,225	14,172	10,145
State net operating loss carry forwards	12,929	9,249	7,410
Excess of book over tax depreciation	12,196	10,985	11,033
Excess of book over tax rent expense	1,084	1,058	1,482
Excess of book over tax retirement expense	17,009	14,757	12,565
Uniform capitalization of inventory	9,684	7,796	6,797
Other, net	43,213	38,066	31,366
Total gross deferred tax assets	196,423	184,224	165,008
Less: Valuation allowance	12,401	9,154	7,314
Net deferred tax assets	184,022	175,070	157,694
Deferred tax liabilities:			
Excess of tax over book depreciation	(31,098)	(11,958)	(16,312)
Undistributed earnings of the Bahamas subsidiary	(14,347)	(12,616)	(10,680)
Other comprehensive income	(1,921)	(1,656)	(1,105)
Other, net	(26,397)	(20,632)	(17,879)
Total gross deferred tax liabilities	(73,763)	(46,862)	(45,976)
Net deferred tax assets	$110,259	$128,208	$111,718

A financial statement reader can glean important information from changes in deferred tax balances, as demonstrated in Exhibit 13.3. It was possible to infer that depreciable lives were extended because of the relatively large increase in deferred taxes arising from book versus tax depreciation differences. As we saw, Winn-Dixie clearly disclosed this change in estimated useful lives. *APB Opinion No. 20* requires disclosure of a change in an accounting estimate only if the impact of the change is material.[9]

Regrettably, widely accepted guidelines for assessing materiality do not exist. Consequently, firms that are not as candid as Winn-Dixie could conceivably decide to extend asset lives and not disclose the change. Their motive could be to manipulate or smooth income, and they would justify nondisclosure by contending that the impact of the change is immaterial. Since materiality guidelines are subjective, careful scrutiny of the income tax footnote provides analysts with a way of detecting subtle changes in accounting estimates that affect bottom-line earnings but are not separately disclosed. This avenue is especially useful to auditors. A detailed examination of deferred income tax balances provides auditors with evidence for evaluating management's candor.[10]

[9] "Accounting Changes," *APB Opinion No. 20* (New York: American Institute of CPAs [AICPA], 1971), para. 38.

[10] For readers who are neither auditors nor studying to be auditors, some elaboration is necessary. At the start of an audit, the auditor discusses significant issues with the client's managers in order to identify potential problem areas. When managers do not voluntarily disclose things like income-increasing changes in accounting estimates, auditors consider this to be a potential danger signal that warrants an expansion in the scope of the audit. Scrutiny of the tax footnote provides auditors with another tool for identifying problem areas.

Increases in deferred income tax liability balances result from a widening excess of book income over taxable income. These increases represent a potential danger signal that should be investigated, because an increase in a deferred tax liability might be an indication of deteriorating earnings quality. One way to uncover such subtle deterioration in earnings quality is to investigate all large, sudden changes in deferred tax balances. The analyst should try to understand *why* the deferred tax liability balance increased.

RECAP

Using Deferred Tax Footnotes to Assess Earnings Quality

To illustrate how deferred tax footnotes can be used to assess earnings quality, consider the relatively large increase in the deferred tax liability related to depreciation—from $11.958 million to $31.098 million-that was highlighted in Exhibit 13.3. We know that if a company lengthens the estimated useful lives of its fixed assets, book depreciation will be lowered and the excess of book income over taxable income will be widened, causing an increase in deferred tax liabilities. Other depreciation-related explanations for the increase in the deferred tax liability include growth in capital expenditures and tax law changes which permit more accelerated depreciation. If investigation reveals that the deferral increased without either a corresponding increase in capital expenditures or a change in tax depreciation schedules, then the analyst should try to determine whether an undisclosed change in useful lives has been made to raise income. Similar investigations should be undertaken for any sudden increase in other types of deferred income tax liabilities.

ANALYSIS

Sudden decreases in deferred income tax assets are also a potential sign of deteriorating earnings quality. Using warranty expense as an example, we will explain why a sudden decrease in a deferred tax asset may be a danger signal.

We saw earlier that accruals for product warranties generate deferred tax assets. The reason is that GAAP requires warranty expenses to be matched against the revenues of the products to which the warranty applies. But income tax rules do not allow deductions for warranty expenses until the costs of providing the warranty services are actually incurred. This is often later than the period in which the revenues have been recognized. Accordingly, for growing companies, GAAP warranty expenses exceed tax return warranty expenses, giving rise to a deferred tax asset.

Assume that on January 1, 2001 Carson Company begins offering a one-year warranty on all sales. Its 2001 sales were $20,000,000, and Carson estimates that warranty expenses will be 1% of sales; therefore, $200,000 of warranty expense is deducted on Carson's books in 2001.

Assume that tax deductions for warranties in 2001 were zero. If tax rates in 2001 are 35%, Carson will have a deferred tax asset of $70,000 for warranties at December 31, 2001—the $200,000 book-versus-tax warranty difference times 35%. If the *actual* warranty costs incurred in 2002 that are associated with 2001 sales were precisely $200,000, this would indicate that Carson's warranty estimate was accurate and should be maintained in 2002.

Table 13.11(a) shows what will happen if Carson Company uses the same warranty expense estimate of 1% of sales in 2002. Here it is assumed that sales in 2002 are again $20,000,000 and that actual warranty costs on 2002 sales are not incurred until 2003. Using these assumptions, notice that Carson's December 31, 2002 deferred tax asset balance will still be $70,000. That is, the 2001 book versus tax timing difference reversed in 2002 (see arrow in Table), but a new $200,000 timing difference on warranties associated with 2002 sales originated. ***The example in Table 13.11(a) is designed to demonstrate that the deferred income tax asset balance will remain stable if the warranty estimate is accurate and if sales volume is unchanged.***

To illustrate why it is also important to scrutinize deferred tax asset balances, let us now assume that instead of maintaining the warranty expense estimate at 1% of sales, Carson lowers the estimate to 0.5% of sales in 2002. Carson does this because its managers wish to increase 2002 income despite the fact that the 1% number reflects actual warranty

Table 13.11 ■ CARSON COMPANY

Illustration of Decline in Deferred Tax Assets

Warranty Percentage Unchanged

	2002	2001
Sales revenues	$20,000,000	$20,000,000
Estimated warranty cost percentage	.01	.01
Warranty expense per books	200,000	200,000
Warranty expense per tax return		
Attributable to 2001 sales	200,000 ← 2002 Reversal	–
Attributable to 2002 sales	–	–
Excess of book over tax expense		
Arising from 2001 sales	–	200,000
Arising from 2002 sales	200,000	–
Tax rate	.35	.35
December 31 deferred tax asset balance	$ 70,000	$ 70,000

(a)

Warranty Percentage Lowered in 2002

	2002	2001
Sales revenues	$20,000,000	$20,000,000
Estimated warranty cost percentage	.005	.01
Warranty expense per books	100,000	200,000
Warranty expense per tax return		
Attributable to 2001 sales	200,000 ← 2002 Reversal	–
Attributable to 2002 sales	–	–
Excess of book over tax expense		
Arising from 2001 sales	–	200,000
Arising from 2002 sales	100,000	–
Tax rate	.35	.35
December 31 deferred tax asset balance	$ 35,000	$ 70,000

(b)

experience. Notice that since the 1% estimate accurately reflects estimated warranty costs in 2001, this change of an accounting estimate in 2002 represents a deterioration in earnings quality.

Table 13.11(b) shows that the deferred tax asset balance will decrease from $70,000 to $35,000 under these circumstances. The reason for the decrease in the deferred income tax asset balance is that the book versus tax difference narrowed from $200,000 in 2001 to $100,000 in 2002 as a consequence of the reduction in estimated warranty expense from 1% to 0.5% of sales.

RECAP

This example demonstrates why shrinkage in a deferred tax asset balance should be investigated. Year-to-year changes in warranty expense estimates are just like other changes in accounting estimates in that they need to be disclosed only if they are material. Since materiality guidelines are subjective, companies can conceivably use undisclosed estimate changes as a way to artificially increase earnings. Decreases in deferred tax asset balances can provide clues of such possibilities to statement readers.[11]

[11] Changes in deferred balances can also provide evidence regarding aggressive tax behavior that could result in subsequent additional assessments; see Weber and Wheeler, op. cit.

ANALYSIS

Using Tax Footnotes to Improve Interfirm Comparability

The deferred tax portion of the income tax footnote can be used to undo differences in financial reporting choices across firms and thus to improve interfirm comparisons.

Here's a specific illustration. Lubrizol and Cambrex are both classified in the same Standard Industrial Classification (SIC) code and compete in many product categories. But each uses different depreciation methods. Lubrizol's 1999 10-K states the following:

> Accelerated depreciation methods are used in computing depreciation on certain machinery and equipment, which comprise approximately 21% of the depreciable assets. The remaining assets are depreciated using the straight-line method. The estimated useful lives are 10 to 40 years for buildings and land improvements and range from 3 to 20 years for machinery and equipment.

SIC is a system maintained by the Office of Federal Statistical Policy and Standards in the Department of Commerce to classify firms by the nature of their operations. Lubrizol and Cambrex are both in SIC Code 2860—Industrial Organic Chemicals.

So Lubrizol is using accelerated depreciation for some of its assets. By contrast, Cambrex's 1999 report says:

> Property, plant and equipment is stated at cost, net of accumulated depreciation. Plant and equipment are depreciated on a straight-line basis over the estimated useful lives for each applicable asset group as follows:

Buildings and improvements	15 to 20 years
Machinery and equipment	5 to 10 years
Furniture and fixtures	3 to 5 years

Table 13.12 gives several key financial statement figures for each company from their respective 1999 10-Ks and excerpts from their income tax footnotes. It's possible that the different depreciation choices of each firm conform perfectly to differences in the service-potential of each firm's assets. But what if they don't? How can an analyst adjust the numbers to improve interfirm comparisons?

Let's begin by looking at Table 13.12(a), which shows the balances in the subcomponents of the deferred tax liability account for Lubrizol. The highlighted depreciation item reflects the $99.9 million cumulative deferred tax liability arising from book versus tax depreciation expense at December 31, 1999.

Companies like Lubrizol have an incentive to use the most accelerated depreciation method that the tax law allows and to depreciate the assets over the shortest allowable tax life. This minimizes the discounted present value of their tax liability by accelerating deductions to the fullest legal extent. These *tax* depreciation rate and useful life deductions exceed the *book* accelerated method and useful lives chosen by Lubrizol, so a deferred liability results. The liability declined by $1.7 million during 1999 ($99.9 million minus $101.6 million).

A reduction in the deferred tax liability related to depreciation timing differences probably arises because either: (1) accelerated methods used for books gives higher depreciation than allowed for tax purposes, or (2) assets for which Lubrizol uses straight-line depreciation for books have reached a point in their useful lives where the straight-line depreciation exceeds the accelerated depreciation per tax return (see again Figure 13.1).

The change in the deferred income tax liability arising from depreciation is:

$$\text{Change} = (\text{Tax depreciation} - \text{Book depreciation}) \times \text{Statutory tax rate}$$

Lubrizol's statutory tax rate is 35%, and the depreciation deferred tax *change* was −$1.7 million (a decrease), as shown in Table 13.12(a). Substituting these values into the preceding equation, we get:

$$-\$1.7 \text{ million} = (\text{Tax depreciation} - \text{Book depreciation}) \times .35$$

Dividing both sides by .35 yields:

$$-\$4.9 \text{ million} = (\text{Tax depreciation} - \text{Book depreciation})$$

Since Table 13.12(a) shows that Lubrizol's book depreciation was $88.3 million, tax depreciation must have been $88.3 million − $4.9 million = $83.4 million, which was 5.5% lower.

Table 13.12 ■ SELECTED FINANCIAL STATEMENT DISCLOSURES FROM THE 1999 10-K REPORTS OF LUBRIZOL AND CAMBREX

Lubrizol: ($ in thousands)	**December 31 1999**	**1998**
Book depreciation	$ 88,300	$ 79,700
Income before income taxes	195,350	118,814
Property, plant & equipment, net of accumulated depreciation (at year-end)	670,512	718,850
Significant deferred tax liabilities	**1999**	**1998**
Depreciation and other basis differences	$ 99,938	$101,658
Undistributed foreign equity income	5,566	3,894
Inventory basis difference	1,497	3,706
Other	3,977	2,986

(a)

Cambrex: ($ in thousands)	**December 31 1999**	**1998**
Book depreciation	$ 33,118	$ 30,547
Income before income taxes	58,901	61,695
Property, plant, and equipment, net of accumulated depreciation (at year-end)	280,163	255,016
Significant deferred tax liabilities	**1999**	**1998**
Depreciation	$ 30,967	$ 29,591
Environmental reserves	796	—
Intangibles	14,963	14,839
Italian intangibles	4,581	6,086
Other benefits	2,143	—
Other	1,722	1,667

(b)

We can now perform the same analysis on Cambrex and determine what its tax depreciation was in 1999. The highlighted portion of Table 13.12(b) shows that Cambrex's depreciation-related deferred income tax liability was slightly less than $31.0 million in 1999—an increase of $1.4 million over the previous year. Repeating the analytical approach we used for Lubrizol yields:

$$\text{Change} = (\text{Tax depreciation} - \text{Book depreciation}) \times \text{Statutory tax rate}$$

or:

$$\$1.4 \text{ million} = (\text{Tax depreciation} - \text{Book depreciation}) \times .35$$

or:

$$\$4 \text{ million} = (\text{Tax depreciation} - \text{Book depreciation})$$

Cambrex's book depreciation was $33.1 million (Table 13.12[b]), so tax depreciation must have been $33.1 million + $4 million = $37.1 million, an increase of 12.1%.

We have now approximated the tax return depreciation taken by each firm and established a "common denominator" for interfirm analysis. While we do not have enough information to put Cambrex on Lubrizol's book depreciation basis, we do have enough information to put each firm on an identical tax depreciation basis, thereby facilitating comparisons.

Adjusting each firm's financial reporting to the same rate as well as the useful lives used for tax purposes increases Lubrizol's pre-tax income by 2.5% ($4.9 million ÷ $195.4 million). Cambrex's pre-tax income is lowered by 6.8% ($4 million ÷ $58.9 million). In any setting, the difference may—or may not—be significant. But making interfirm comparisons using comparable data is better than basing the analysis on diverse financial reporting choices.

It is important to note that the preceding analysis works only in those situations where firms have not had major asset disposals during the year. When depreciable assets are sold, the deferred tax amounts for these assets are eliminated from the deferred tax liability account. Moreover, the amount eliminated due to asset sales is rarely disclosed. So the year-to-year change in the deferred tax liability balance for depreciation no longer reflects only current period book versus tax depreciation differences. We can determine if the firm sold assets during the period by looking in the "Investing activity" section of the cash flow statement to see if cash was generated from asset sales. In this illustration, neither Lubrizol nor Cambrex reported major asset sales in their 1999 cash flow statement.

Using Income Tax Footnotes to Assess the Degree of Conservatism in Firms' Accounting Choices

ANALYSIS

Determining the degree of conservatism in a firm's set of accounting choices is an important part of assessing the earnings quality for that company. Conservative choices, like accelerated depreciation, decrease earnings and asset values relative to more liberal techniques, like straight-line depreciation. Ceteris paribus, the more conservative the set of accounting choices, the higher the quality of earnings.

Useful information for assessing the degree of conservatism in a firm's portfolio of accounting choices can be extracted from the income tax footnote by comparing the ratio of pre-tax book income to taxable income. While this is admittedly a relatively coarse way of assessing accounting conservatism, it can be useful in selected settings. The ratio is computed as

$$EC = \frac{\text{Pre-tax book income (adjusted for permanent differences)}}{\text{Taxable income per tax return}}$$

where EC is the current period's **earnings conservatism** ratio.

Consider the denominator, "Taxable income per tax return." In most instances firms seek to minimize tax return income. Because of this income minimization incentive, the denominator represents a very conservative income benchmark. Usually, it is the lowest permissible—meaning "legal"—taxable income number for the period.

> The only exceptions will arise where firms either (1) have unused operating loss carryforwards that are about to expire, or (2) expect future tax rates to rise sharply.

The numerator—pre-tax GAAP income—incorporates the latitude available to firms in selecting accounting method choices, accounting estimates for things like bad debts expense and asset useful lives, and discretionary expenses such as advertising and research and development (R&D) that we have outlined elsewhere in the book. Consequently, the numerator can range from a highly aggressive (income increasing) number to a highly conservative (income decreasing) number.

To illustrate how this ratio is used, we will compute the EC ratio for Merck & Co. for 1999 (EC_{99}). Exhibit 13.2(b) on page 649 indicates that 1999 income before income taxes was \$8,619.5 million. ***This number needs adjustment for net permanent difference items that do not enter into the computation of taxable income and, therefore, would distort the comparison between book and taxable income made below.*** From Exhibit 13.2(b), Merck reported the tax effects of net permanent difference items to be \$287.8 million (\$3,016.8 − \$2,729.0). We divide this amount by the 35% statutory tax rate to get the before-tax amount of permanent differences (\$287.8 ÷ 0.35 = \$822.3). Since Merck's effective tax rate of 31.7% is lower than the statutory rate, this \$822.3 million of permanent differences represents income reported on Merck's books that will never be taxed. For comparability, we need to subtract this amount from Merck's reported pre-tax book income of \$8,619.5 million. This yields \$7,797.2 million as the company's adjusted pre-tax book income. This is the numerator of EC_{99}.

Since most companies do not disclose details of their income tax returns, we need to estimate the denominator, "Taxable income per tax return." This is easily done. We saw in

Exhibit 13.2(a) that income taxes currently payable in 1999 totaled \$3,411.9 million. Taxable income can then be computed as

$$\text{1999 Income taxes currently payable} = \text{1999 Taxable income per tax return} \times \text{1999 Statutory tax rate}$$

Substituting the two pieces of data from Merck's tax footnote, we get

$$\text{1999 Income taxes currently payable} = \text{1999 Taxable income per tax return} \times \text{1999 Statutory tax rate}$$

$$\$3{,}411.9\text{ million} = \ ? \times .35$$

Rearranging, in order to isolate the unknown taxable income per tax return on the left side, we get:

$$\text{1999 Taxable income} = \$3{,}411.9\text{ million} \div .35 = \$9{,}748.3\text{ million}$$

Thus, EC_{99} for Merck is (\$ in millions):

$$EC_{99} = \frac{\text{1999 Pre-tax book income (adjusted)}}{\text{1999 Taxable income}}$$

$$EC_{99} = \frac{\$7{,}797.2}{\$9{,}748.3}$$

$$EC_{99} = 0.80$$

In general, an EC ratio close to 1.0 indicates relatively conservative financial reporting choices. (Remember, companies have an incentive to minimize the denominator, "Taxable income per tax return." When the numerator—pre-tax book income—is even smaller, this suggests that earnings conservatism is high.)

Analysts can also compare EC ratios for a single company over time to monitor overall earnings conservatism. For example, using Exhibit 13.2, we can compute Merck's 1998 taxable income—the denominator of its EC_{98} ratio as follows:

$$\text{1998 Taxable income} = \text{1998 Income taxes currently payable} \div \text{1998 Statutory tax rate}$$

$$\text{1998 Taxable income} = \$2{,}714.7\text{ million} \div .35$$

$$\text{1998 Taxable income} = \$7{,}756.3\text{ million}$$

Merck's 1998 pre-tax book income was $8,133.1. Accordingly, EC_{98} is computed as follows:

> We make no adjustment to pre-tax book income in 1998 for permanent difference items because Merck's effective tax rate was only **0.5%** higher than the statutory rate.

$$EC_{98} = \frac{\text{1998 Pre-tax book income}}{\text{1998 Taxable income}}$$

$$EC_{98} = \frac{\$8,133.1}{\$7,756.3}$$

$$EC_{98} = 1.05$$

The decrease from EC_{98} (1.05) to EC_{99} (0.80) suggests that Merck may have been somewhat less aggressive in its financial reporting choices for 1999 relative to 1998. However, year-to-year changes in EC ratios must be interpreted with caution when dramatic changes in economic conditions or the tax law occur.

The earnings conservatism ratio can also be used to compare reporting choices across companies. For example, Merck's EC_{99} might be compared with the EC_{99} ratio of a competitor, like Pfizer, to assess whether each has similar earnings conservatism.

Having introduced the EC ratio, we now need to emphasize its three primary limitations.

1. EC ratio comparisons for a single company over time (e.g., EC_{99} versus EC_{98}) can be misleading if the tax law has changed over the period of comparison. For example, if the U.S. Congress allows more accelerated tax depreciation schedules, this will cause the EC ratio to rise (i.e., showing *lower* earnings conservatism) even though the firm's real earnings conservatism has remained constant.
2. Comparisons across companies in different industries should be made cautiously. Specifically, tax burdens can vary because of differences in capital intensity or specific tax rules (like the oil depletion allowance) which affect only certain industries.
3. One category of deterioration in earnings conservatism is not captured by the EC ratio. Whenever companies dip into old LIFO layers, the impact of the earnings increase affects both the numerator and the denominator of the ratio because of the LIFO conformity rule discussed in Chapter 9. That's why earnings conservatism deterioration arising from LIFO dipping is not reliably captured in EC.

Tax footnotes provide information that allows the analyst to estimate firms' taxable income. By comparing pre-tax accounting income with the estimate of taxable income, analysts can develop a rough index (subject to the limitations noted above) of the overall degree of conservatism in a firm's set of GAAP accounting choices. The degree of conservatism in a firm's set of accounting choices is an important part of assessing the earnings quality of that company.

RECAP

SUMMARY

The rules for computing income for financial reporting purposes—book income—differ from the rules for computing income for tax purposes. The differences between book income and taxable income are caused by both permanent and temporary (timing) differences in the revenue and expense items reported on a company's books versus its tax return. Temporary differences give rise to both deferred tax assets and deferred tax liabilities. Deferred tax accounting generally allows firms to report tax costs or benefits on the income statement in the period in which the related revenue and expense items are recognized for book purposes irrespective of when these amounts are recorded on the tax return.

The income tax footnote provides useful information for understanding how much of the current period's tax provision (expense) is actually payable to the federal and state governments, and how much is deferred. Tax footnotes also allow users to understand why firms' effective tax rates may differ from the statutory rate. Finally, tax footnotes provide a wealth of information that can be exploited to improve interfirm comparability and evaluate firms' earnings quality.

Appendix A Comprehensive Interperiod Tax Allocation Problem

The following example for Hawkeye Corporation combines the various aspects of accounting for income taxes discussed in this chapter to demonstrate the interrelation between pre-tax accounting income, taxable income, taxes payable, deferred taxes, and tax expense. Working through this example will demonstrate the following points:

1. How to convert a pre-tax accounting income number to a taxable income number
2. How taxes payable are determined
3. How the change in deferred tax assets and deferred tax liabilities are determined
4. How tax expense is determined
5. How to reconcile the total tax costs (benefits) reported in the income statement with the total taxes payable according to the tax return for the period.

Before working through the Hawkeye Corporation example, look at Figure 13.9 (it expands on Figure 13.8, covering things discussed since that figure appeared), which provides a more complete road map for understanding how the various book and taxable income numbers and tax amounts relate to one another.

Computation of Taxable Income and Taxes Payable

Reading from left to right across the top of Figure 13.9, we see three categories of items that cause differences between pre-tax book income and taxable income on the tax return:

1. Permanent differences
2. Operating loss carryforwards
3. Temporary differences.

Technically, operating loss carryforwards are treated as a temporary difference under *SFAS No. 109*. Although a deferred tax asset will be reported on the company's books, the operating losses themselves are not carried over from previous periods and, thus, are not included as part of the current period's book income computation. Therefore, to reconcile pre-tax book income to taxable income requires an adjustment for the dollar amount of the loss carryforward. We have chosen to discuss the loss carryforward separately from the other temporary differences which are discussed later.

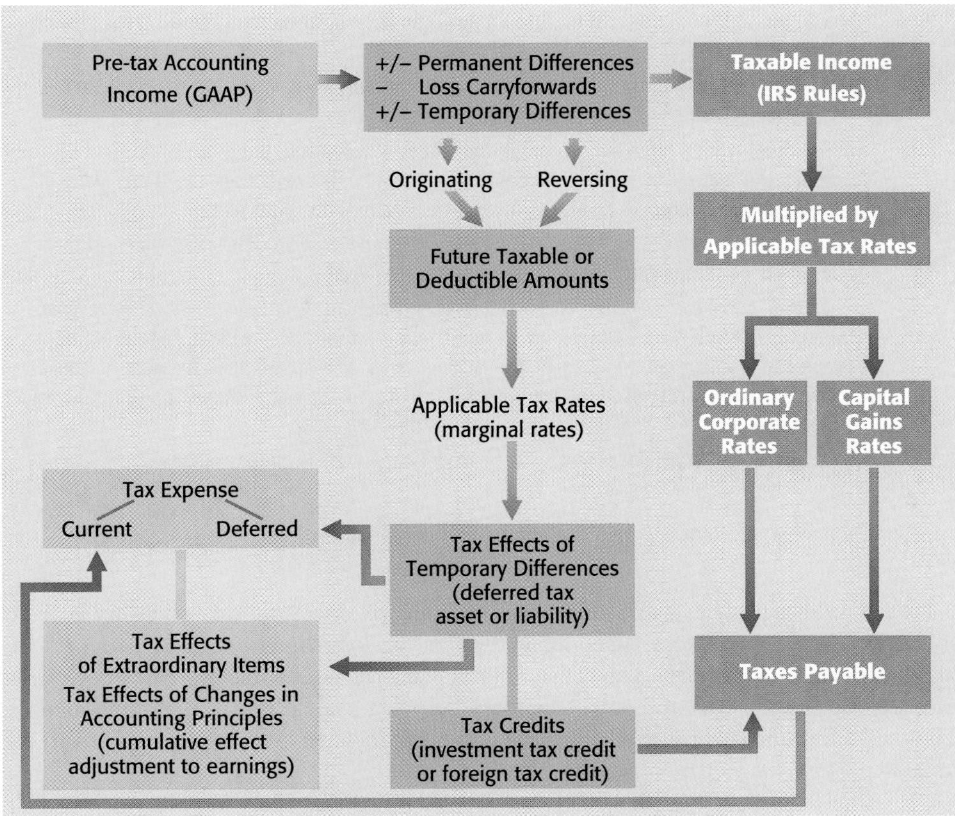

Figure 13.9

OVERVIEW OF INTERPERIOD TAX ALLOCATION

Taxable income is determined by making adjustments to the reported pre-tax book income numbers for each of these items.

The first category of reconciling items is permanent differences. We know these are revenue or expense items that the tax rules treat differently—on a permanent basis—than the GAAP (book) rules treat them for income determination purposes. As shown below, Hawkeye Corporation has two permanent difference items—Item ①, "Interest earned on municipal bonds"; and Item ⑥, "Executive life insurance premiums paid by the company."

To arrive at taxable income, the municipal bond interest must be *subtracted* from the reported pre-tax book income number, since it is not taxable but has been included in book income. In addition, the executive life insurance premiums that were subtracted in arriving at pre-tax book income must be *added back* since they are not deductible for tax purposes when the company is the named beneficiary.

Example: Interperiod Tax Allocation

Hawkeye Corporation starts the current year, 2001, with a deferred tax asset balance of $20,000 and a deferred tax liability balance of $30,000. The current tax rate is 40% and is projected to be in effect when all temporary differences reverse. The reported pre-tax accounting income is $500,000. Analyze the following items to determine taxable income, the *change* in deferred taxes payable (future taxable and deductible amounts), and the tax expense to be reported on the income statement for 2001. Assume that there is no need for a valuation allowance provision for deferred tax assets.

Item	**Description**
①	Book income includes $12,000 of interest revenue from municipal bonds.
②	Straight-line depreciation for book purposes is $100,000 in the current year, and $140,000 is deductible for tax purposes under the Modified Accelerated Cost Recovery System (MACRS).
③	Hawkeye collected $60,000 of rent for a warehouse it leases to a local manufacturer. Of this amount, $40,000 is deferred for accounting purposes and will be recognized in 2002 when it is earned.
④	Hawkeye accrued $50,000 for estimated future warranty costs in 2001 and paid $35,000 in warranty expenses in the current period.
⑤	Bad debts written off in the current period totaled $20,000, and the provision for bad debts under the allowance method amounted to $15,000. Hawkeye uses the direct write-off method for tax purposes and the allowance method for book purposes.
⑥	Book income includes an $18,000 deduction for premiums paid on executive life insurance in which the company is the named beneficiary.
⑦	In 2001 Hawkeye collected $15,000 on an installment land sale made several years earlier. The profit on the sale, all of which was recorded at the time of sale for book purposes, amounted to 30% of the selling price. The installment method of recognizing profit is being used for tax purposes. Ignore any imputed interest on the deferred payments.
⑧	Hawkeye has $35,000 of operating loss carryforward at the beginning of 2001.

The second general category of reconciling items is operating loss carryforwards. As shown in Item ⑧, Hawkeye has a $35,000 operating loss carryforward. This represents losses reported on previous years' tax returns (i.e., tax deductible expenses and losses exceeded taxable income and gains) that can be offset against the 2001 taxable income. Thus, this amount is subtracted from pre-tax book income to arrive at taxable income in 2001.

The last category of reconciling items is temporary differences. These are revenue and expense items that enter into the determination of book income in one period and taxable income in a different period. There are several temporary differences for Hawkeye:

- Item ②: *Depreciation expense.* Hawkeye's pre-tax book income includes a deduction for $100,000 of straight-line depreciation expense. But for tax purposes, Hawkeye is using an accelerated depreciation method, which produces a deduction of $140,000 in the current period. To arrive at taxable income, this $40,000 dollar originating timing difference must be subtracted from pre-tax book income because it represents an additional amount that is deductible on the 2001 tax return that was not deducted in arriving at pre-tax book income.
- Item ③: *Rent collections.* In 2001, Hawkeye collected $60,000 of lease rent, and all of this amount is taxable when received. However, for book purposes, $40,000 of this amount is deferred and will be recognized in future periods when it is earned. This leaves $20,000 that was included in the $500,000 of pre-tax book income. Therefore, this $40,000 originating timing difference must be added to the pre-tax income number to arrive at 2001 taxable income.
- Item ④: *Warranty expenses.* Hawkeye accrued $50,000 for estimated warranty costs that were subtracted in arriving at the pre-tax book income number. For tax purposes, Hawkeye is allowed to deduct only the $35,000 of warranty costs that were actually paid. The $15,000 difference represents an originating timing difference that must be added back to the pre-tax book income number to yield taxable income.
- Item ⑤: *Bad debt provisions.* For book income purposes, Hawkeye uses the allowance method (described in Chapter 8) to determine the $15,000 bad debts deduction in 2001. For tax purposes, Hawkeye is allowed to take a deduction only when accounts are actually written off; this is the direct write-off method. As shown, Hawkeye wrote off $20,000 of accounts receivable in 2001. Note that all or a portion of the accounts written off in 2001 would have been deducted as an expense to arrive at GAAP/book income in prior accounting periods. Accordingly, the additional $5,000 that is deductible for tax purposes, an amount which represents a reversing timing difference, must be subtracted from pre-tax book income to arrive at taxable income for 2001.
- Item ⑦: *Profit on installment sale.* Hawkeye is using the installment method for tax purposes (Chapter 3) to record profit on a land sale made in a previous period. All of this profit was recorded in a previous period's book income number. Thus, the gross profit on the amounts collected in 2001 (30% × $15,000 collected = $4,500) represents a reversing timing difference that must be added to the pre-tax book income number to arrive at taxable income.

After adjustments for the operating loss carryforward and the temporary difference items, Hawkeye's taxable income for 2001 is determined to be $485,500, as shown in Schedule 13.1 on the following page. To arrive at taxes payable, the taxable income number must be multiplied by the applicable tax rates, as illustrated in the right-hand column of Figure 13.9. If some of the components of taxable income are subject to special tax rates (e.g., capital gains rates), then these amounts would need to be isolated and multiplied by the appropriate special rates. For simplicity, we have assumed that a flat tax rate of 40% applies to all components of taxable income, yielding taxes payable to the IRS in 2001 of $194,200 (as shown in Schedule 13.1 on the next page).

Schedule 13.1 ■ HAWKEYE CORPORATION

Calculation of Taxable Income and Taxes Payable

Computation of taxable income	
Pre-tax accounting Income (given)	$500,000
Adjustments for permanent differences	
− Interest on municipal bonds (Item ①)	(12,000)
+ Premium on executive life insurance (Item ⑥)	18,000
Income before adjustment for temporary differences	$506,000
Adjustment for operating loss carryforward (Item ⑧)	(35,000)
Adjustments for temporary differences	
− Excess of accelerated over straight-line depreciation (Item ②) ($140,000 − $100,000)	(40,000)
+ Rent received in excess of rent earned (Item ③) ($60,000 − $20,000)	40,000
+ Excess of accrued warranty costs over actual costs incurred on warranties (Item ④) ($50,000 − $35,000)	15,000
− Excess of accounts written off over current provision for bad debts (Item ⑤) ($20,000 − $15,000)	(5,000)
+ Installment profit recognized for tax purposes in 2001 but recognized in earlier periods for book purposes (Item ⑦) (30% × $15,000)	4,500
Taxable income	$485,500
Tax rate	× 40%
Taxes payable for 2001	$194,200

Calculation of Change in Deferred Tax Asset and Liability Accounts

The next step in determining the tax provision (expense) that will be reported on Hawkeye's GAAP (book) income statement for 2001 is to determine the *change* in the deferred tax asset and deferred tax liability accounts. These calculations are represented in the center column of Figure 13.9 and the details are provided in Schedule 13.2. For each temporary difference (including operating loss carryforwards), we must determine three things:

1. Whether an item is an originating or reversing temporary difference
2. Whether it affects a deferred tax asset or a deferred tax liability balance
3. What the applicable tax rate is for determining the tax effect of the temporary difference.

Originating temporary differences are "new" differences between book and taxable income that cause *increases* in either the deferred tax asset or the deferred tax liability balance. Reversing temporary differences are realizations or reversals of "old" temporary differences that gave rise to deferred tax assets or liabilities in previous accounting periods. Because they represent reversals of previously recorded temporary differences, reversing temporary differences are recorded as *decreases* in either the deferred tax asset or the deferred tax liability accounts.

Determining whether a particular temporary difference affects a deferred tax asset or liability balance hinges on whether the item causes taxable income to be higher or lower than book income in the current period and whether it is an originating or reversing temporary difference.

Schedule 13.2 ■ HAWKEYE CORPORATION

Calculation of Changes in Deferred Tax Accounts

	Deferred Tax Asset	Deferred Tax Liability
Operating loss carryforward (Item ⑧)		
Realization of Future Deductible Amount		
40% × $35,000	($14,000) **CR**	
Depreciation (Item ②)		
Future Taxable Amount		
($140,000 – $100,000 = $40,000) × 40%		($16,000) **CR**
Rent received in advance of rent earned (Item ③)		
Future Deductible Amount		
($60,000 – $20,000 = $40,000) × 40%	16,000 **DR**	
Excess of accrued warranty costs over cash warranty expenses (Item ④)		
Future Deductible Amount		
($50,000 – $35,000 = $15,000) × 40%	6,000 **DR**	
Bad debts written off (Item ⑤)		
Realization of Future Deductible Amount		
$20,000 × 40%	(8,000) **CR**	
New bad debt provisions in 2001 (Item ⑤)		
Future Deductible Amount		
$15,000 × 40%	6,000 **DR**	
Installment profit recognized for tax (Item ⑦)		
Realization of Future Taxable Amount		
(30% × $15,000 = $4,500) × 40% (30% = Gross profit rate; 40% = Tax rate)		1,800 **DR**
Change in Deferred Tax Asset/Liability	6,000 **DR**	(14,200) **CR**
Beginning balance	20,000 **DR**	(30,000) **CR**
Ending balance	$ 26,000 **DR**	($44,200) **CR**

Hawkeye has one originating temporary difference that causes taxable income to be *lower* than book income in the *current* period:

- Item ②. Accelerated depreciation expense deductions for tax purposes ($140,000) exceed the straight-line depreciation deductions for book purposes ($100,000). This temporary difference gives rise to a future taxable amount—that is, taxable income will be *higher* than book income in future periods when this temporary difference reverses. Therefore, this temporary difference causes an increase (credit) to deferred tax liabilities of $16,000, as shown in Schedule 13.2.

Hawkeye has two reversing temporary differences that cause taxable income to be *lower* than book income in the *current* period:

- Item ⑧. The operating loss carryforward is $35,000.
- Item ⑤. The bad debts write-off is $20,000.

Both of these items represent realizations of future deductible amounts and result in a decrease (credit) to the deferred tax asset account, as we see in Schedule 13.2.

Hawkeye has three originating temporary differences that cause taxable income to be *higher* than book income in the *current* period:

- Item ③. Rent received ($60,000) is in excess of rent earned for book purposes ($20,000).
- Item ④. Accrued warranty expenses for book purposes ($50,000) is in excess of warranty expenditures for tax purposes ($35,000).

- Item ⑤. Bad debts expense of $15,000 that is accrued under the allowance method for book purposes will not be deductible for tax purposes until specific accounts are written off in future periods.

Each of these items gives rise to a future deductible amount and accordingly causes increases (debits) to the deferred tax asset account, as shown in Schedule 13.2.

The one remaining temporary difference for Hawkeye is the profit on the land sale that is recognized under the installment method for tax purposes.

- Item ⑦. This $4,500 amount represents a reversing temporary difference that causes taxable income to be higher than book income in 2001. Since a deferred tax liability would have been set up in a previous period (when the land was sold and the entire profit was recognized for book purposes), the deferred tax liability account is being reduced (debited) now because the tax will be paid in the current period.

The assumed marginal corporate tax rate of 40% is applied to all temporary differences to determine the dollar amount of the change in the deferred tax asset or liability accounts. This is appropriate when there are no enacted changes in the tax rates scheduled to go into effect in future periods. Using the 40% rate, the net effect of the temporary differences for Hawkeye is to increase deferred tax assets by $6,000 and increase deferred tax liabilities by $14,200, as shown in Schedule 13.2.

Calculation of Tax Expense

The calculation of tax expense that Hawkeye will report on its 2001 GAAP income statement (assuming a 40% tax rate for all periods) follows the formulas presented in Figure 13.5 and is reproduced below in Figure 13.10. The numbers appearing in magenta below the appropriate boxes are taken from Schedules 13.1 and 13.2.

When tax rates are *not* scheduled to change in the future, the tax expense reported for book purposes can be computed directly by multiplying the pre-tax book income number that is adjusted for permanent difference items by the current tax rate. The pre-tax book income number of Hawkeye adjusted for permanent differences is $506,000 (Schedule 13.1); and the current tax rate is 40%, thus yielding a tax expense of $202,400, which is the same number arrived at under the indirect approach shown in Figure 13.10. When tax rates are scheduled to change, then tax expense must be determined using the indirect approach, which adjusts taxes payable for changes in the deferred tax asset and liability accounts, as shown in Figure 13.10.

Figure 13.10

CALCULATION OF TAX EXPENSE: INDIRECT APPROACH

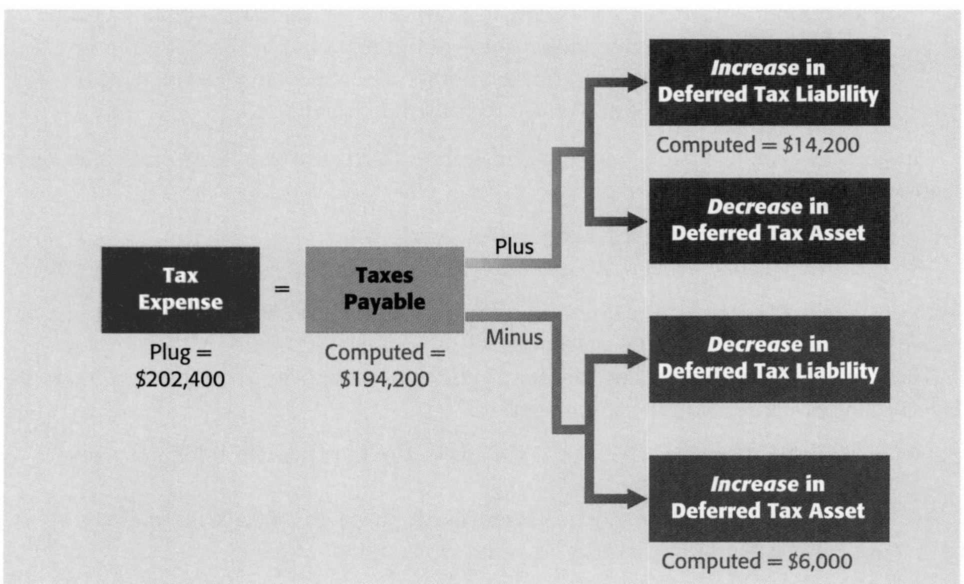

EXERCISES

E13-1

Determining current taxes payable

AICPA adapted

On January 2, 2000 Allen Company purchased a machine for $70,000. This machine has a five-year useful life, a residual value of $10,000, and it is depreciated using the straight-line method for financial statement purposes. For tax purposes, depreciation expense was $25,000 for 2000 and $20,000 for 2001. Allen's 2001 book income, before income taxes and depreciation expense, was $100,000, and its tax rate was 30%.

REQUIRED:

If Allen had made *no* estimated tax payments during 2001, what amount of current income tax liability would Allen report in its December 31, 2001 balance sheet?

E13-2

Determining deferred tax liability

AICPA adapted

Huff Corporation began operations on January 1, 2001. Huff recognizes revenues from all sales under the accrual method for financial reporting purposes and appropriately uses the installment method for income tax purposes. Huff's gross margin on installment sales under each method was as follows:

Year	Accrual Method	Installment Method
2001	$ 800,000	$300,000
2002	1,300,000	700,000

Enacted income tax rates are 30% for 2001 and 2002 and 25% thereafter. There are no other temporary differences.

REQUIRED:

In Huff's December 31, 2002 balance sheet, the deferred income tax liability should be how much?

E13-3

Determining deferred tax liability

AICPA adapted

In its 2001 income statement, Tow, Inc. reported proceeds from an officer's life insurance policy of $90,000 and depreciation of $250,000. Tow was the owner and beneficiary of the life insurance on its officer. Tow deducted depreciation of $370,000 in its 2001 income tax return when the tax rate was 30%. Data related to the reversal of the excess tax deduction for depreciation follow:

Year	Reversal of Excess Tax Deduction for Depreciation	Enacted Tax Rates
2002	$50,000	35%
2003	40,000	35
2004	20,000	25
2005	10,000	25

There are no other temporary differences.

REQUIRED:

In its December 31, 2001 balance sheet, what amount should Tow report as a deferred income tax liability?

E13-4

Deferred tax effects on balance sheet

AICPA adapted

As a result of differences between depreciation for financial reporting purposes and tax purposes, the financial reporting basis of Noor Company's sole depreciable asset, acquired in 2001, exceeded its tax basis by $250,000 at December 31, 2001. This difference will reverse in future years. The enacted tax rate is 30% for 2001, and 40% for future years. Noor has no other temporary differences.

REQUIRED:

In its December 31, 2001, balance sheet, how much should Noor report as the deferred tax effect of this difference? Indicate the amount and whether it is an asset or a liability.

E13–5

Deferred tax effects on long-term contracts

AICPA adapted

Mill Company began operations on January 1, 2001 and recognized income from construction-type contracts under the percentage-of-completion method for tax purposes and the completed-contract method for financial reporting purposes. Information concerning income recognition under each method is as follows:

Year	Percentage-of-Completion (Tax Purposes)	Completed Contract (Book Purposes)
2001	$400,000	$ 0
2002	625,000	375,000
2003	750,000	850,000

REQUIRED:

For all years, assume that the income tax rate is 40% and that there are no other timing differences. In its December 31, 2003 balance sheet, Mill should report deferred income taxes of how much? Indicate whether the amount is an asset or a liability.

E13–6

Determining current portion of tax expense

AICPA adapted

For the year ended December 31, 2001 Tyre Company reported pre-tax financial statement income of $750,000. Its taxable income was $650,000. The difference is due to accelerated depreciation for income tax purposes. Tyre's income tax rate is 30%, and Tyre made estimated tax payments during 2001 of $90,000.

REQUIRED:

1. What amount should Tyre report as the current portion of income tax expense for 2001?
2. What amount should Tyre report as the deferred portion of income tax expense for 2001?
3. Give the journal entry Tyre would make to record 2001 taxes.

E13–7

Determining current taxes payable

AICPA adapted

Dunn Company's 2001 income statement reported $90,000 income before provision for income taxes. To aid in the computation of the provision for federal income taxes, the following 2001 data are provided:

Rent received in advance	$16,000
Income from exempt municipal bonds	20,000
Depreciation deducted for income tax purposes in excess of depreciation reported for financial statement purposes	10,000
Enacted corporate income tax rate	35%

REQUIRED:

What amount of current federal income tax liability should be reported in Dunn's December 31, 2001 balance sheet?

E13–8

Determining deferred tax liability and current portion of tax expense

AICPA adapted

Kent, Inc.'s reconciliation between financial statement and taxable income for 2001 follows:

Pre-tax financial income	$150,000
Permanent difference	(12,000)
	138,000
Temporary difference—depreciation	(9,000)
Taxable income	$129,000

ADDITIONAL INFORMATION:

	At December 31 2000	2001
Cumulative temporary difference (future taxable amounts)	$11,000	$20,000

The enacted tax rate was 35% for 2000 and 40% for 2001 and years thereafter.

REQUIRED:

1. In its December 31, 2001 balance sheet, what amount should Kent report as its deferred income tax liability?
2. In its 2001 income statement, what amount should Kent report as the current portion of income tax expense?

E13–9

Determining deferred tax asset amounts

AICPA adapted

West Corporation leased a building and received the $36,000 annual rental payment on June 15, 2001. The beginning of the lease was July 1, 2001. Rental income is taxable when received. West's tax rates are 30% for 2001 and 40% thereafter. West had no other permanent or temporary differences. West determined that no valuation allowance was needed.

REQUIRED:

What amount of deferred tax asset should West report in its December 31, 2001 balance sheet?

E13–10

Determining deferred tax asset amounts

AICPA adapted

Black Company, organized on January 2, 2001, had pre-tax accounting income of $500,000 and taxable income of $800,000 for the year ended December 31, 2001. The only temporary difference is accrued product warranty costs, which are expected to be paid as follows:

2002	$100,000
2003	50,000
2004	50,000
2005	100,000

Circumstances indicate that it is highly likely that Black will have taxable income in the future. There were no temporary differences in prior years. The enacted income tax rates are 35% for 2001, 30% for 2002 through 2004, and 25% for 2005.

REQUIRED:

In Black's December 31, 2001 balance sheet, the deferred income tax asset should be how much?

E13–11

Deferred portion of tax expense

AICPA adapted

Quinn Company reported a net deferred tax asset of $9,000 in its December 31, 2001 balance sheet. For 2002 Quinn reported pre-tax financial statement income of $300,000. Temporary differences of $100,000 resulted in taxable income of $200,000 for 2002. At December 31, 2002 Quinn had cumulative taxable differences of $70,000. The income tax rate is 30%.

REQUIRED:

In its December 31, 2002 income statement, what should Quinn report as the deferred portion of income tax expense?

E13–12

Temporary and permanent differences

AICPA adapted

Note: Students may want to review the material on the equity method of accounting in Chapter 16 before beginning work on this exercise.

Tara Corporation uses the equity method of accounting for its 40% investment in Flax's common stock. During 2001 Flax reported earnings of $750,000 and paid dividends of $250,000. Assume that:

- All the undistributed earnings of Flax will be distributed as dividends in future periods.
- The dividends received from Flax are eligible for the 80% dividends received deduction.
- There are no other temporary differences.
- Tara's 2001 income tax rate is 30%.
- Enacted income tax rates after 2001 are 25%.

REQUIRED:

In Tara's December 31, 2001 balance sheet, the increase in the deferred income tax liability from the preceding transactions would be how much?

E13–13

Loss carrybacks and carryforwards

AICPA adapted

Town, a calendar-year corporation that was incorporated in January 2000, experienced a $600,000 net operating loss (NOL) in 2002. For the years 2000 and 2001, Town reported taxable income in each year and a total of $450,000 for the two years combined. Assume that (1) there are no differences between pre-tax book income and taxable income for all years; (2) the income tax rate is 40% for all years; (3) the NOL will be carried back to the profit years (2000–2001) to the extent of $450,000, and $150,000 will be carried forward to future periods; and (4) Town expects to report taxable income for the foreseeable future.

REQUIRED:

1. What amounts should Town report as "Tax benefit due to NOL carryback and carryforward" in its 2002 income statement?
2. How much will Town report as a deferred tax asset on its December 31, 2002 balance sheet?

E13–14

Tax effects of loss carryback and carryforward

AICPA adapted

Dix Company reported operating income/loss before income tax in its first three years of operations as follows:

2000	$ 100,000
2001	(200,000)
2002	400,000

There are no permanent or temporary differences between book income and taxable income in these years. Dix elected to use the loss carryback in 2001 and to apply unused losses against future taxable income. Assume a 40% tax rate for all years.

REQUIRED:

1. What amount should Dix report as a tax benefit on its 2001 income statement?
2. What amount of deferred tax asset should Dix report on its December 31, 2001 balance sheet?
3. What amount should Dix report as current taxes payable on December 31, 2002 (the year after the loss)?

E13–15

Accounting for loss carryforwards

AICPA adapted

For the year ended December 31, 2001 Colt Corporation had a loss carryforward of $180,000 available to offset future taxable income. At December 31, 2001 the company believes that realization of the tax benefit related to the loss carryforward is probable. The tax rate is 30%.

REQUIRED:

1. What amount of the tax benefit should be reported in Colt's 2001 income statement?
2. What additional account(s) would be affected when the loss carryforward is recognized?

E13–16

Accounting for loss carrybacks and carryforwards

AICPA adapted

Operating income in Mobe's first three years of operations were as follows:

2000	$ 300,000
2001	(700,000)
2002	1,200,000

There were no other deferred income taxes in any year, and Mobe's income tax rate is 30%. In 2001 Mobe elected to carryback the maximum amount of loss possible and expected to have sufficient taxable income in future years to take full advantage of the loss carryforward tax benefits.

REQUIRED:

1. What would be the amount of tax benefit reported in Mobe's 2001 income statement? Give the entry to record this tax benefit.
2. In 2002 what amount should Mobe report as its current income tax liability after taking into account the loss carryforward?

In Figland Company's first year of operations (2001), the company had pre-tax book income of $500,000 and taxable income of $800,000 at the December year-end. Figland expected to maintain this level of taxable income in future years. Figland's only temporary difference is for accrued product warranty costs, which are expected to be paid as follows:

E13–17

Deferred tax asset and valuation allowance

AICPA adapted

2002	$100,000
2003	$200,000

The enacted income tax rate for these years is 30%. Figland believes there is a high likelihood that one third of the tax benefit associated with this future deductible amount will not be realized.

REQUIRED:

Compute the amount of deferred tax asset and related valuation allowance that would be reported in Figland's 2001 tax footnote.

Note: Students may want to review the material on the equity method of accounting in Chapter 16 before beginning work on this exercise.

E13–18

Deferred tax asset and valuation allowance

AICPA adapted

Taft Corporation uses the equity method to account for its 25% investment in Flame, Inc. During 2001 Taft received dividends of $30,000 from Flame and recorded $180,000 as its equity in the earnings of Flame. Additional information follows:

- All the undistributed earnings of Flame will be distributed as dividends in future periods.
- The dividends received from Flame are eligible for the 80% dividends received deduction.
- There are no other temporary differences.
- Enacted income tax rates are 30% for 2001 and thereafter.

REQUIRED:

In its December 31, 2001 balance sheet, what amount should Taft report for deferred income tax liability?

The following information is provided for Lally Corporation for 2001 and 2002:

E13–19

Determining tax expense, taxes payable, and deferred taxes

CMA adapted

	2001	2002
Book income before income taxes	$4,000,000	$5,000,000
Interest income included above that was not subject to income taxes	100,000	100,000

- Income before income taxes in 2001 included accrued rent revenue of $80,000 that was not subject to income taxes until its receipt in 2002.
- Lally was subject to an income tax rate of 40% in 2001 and 2002.

REQUIRED:

1. What was Lally's taxable income for 2001?
2. Lally Corporation's taxes payable for 2001 was how much?
3. What was the change in Lally's deferred tax asset (liability) balance for 2001?
4. What amount of income tax expense would Lally report on its 2001 income statement?
5. Repeat requirements (1) through (4) for 2002.

Problems/Discussion Questions

P13–1

Deferred tax amounts with different tax rates

AICPA adapted

Moss, Inc. uses the accrual method of accounting for financial reporting purposes and appropriately uses the installment method of accounting for income tax purposes. Installment income of $250,000 will be collected in the following years when the enacted tax rates are as indicated.

	Collection of Income	Enacted Tax Rates
2000	$ 25,000	35%
2001	50,000	30
2002	75,000	30
2003	100,000	25

The installment income is Moss's only temporary difference.

Required:

What amount should be included as the deferred income tax liability in Moss's December 31, 2000 balance sheet?

P13–2

Temporary and permanent differences and tax entry

The following information pertains to Ramesh Company for the current year:

Book income before income taxes	$106,000
Income tax expense	52,000
Income taxes payable for this year	32,000
Statutory income tax rate	40%

The company has both a permanent and a temporary difference between book and taxable income. The permanent difference relates to goodwill (i.e., assume that amortization of goodwill is not allowed as an expense for tax purposes) and the temporary difference relates to depreciation expense.

Required:

1. Calculate the amount of temporary difference for the year and indicate whether it causes the book income to be larger or smaller than the taxable income.
2. Calculate the amount of permanent difference for the year and indicate whether it causes the book income to be larger or smaller than the taxable income.
3. Provide the journal entry to record the income tax expense for the year.
4. Compute the effective tax rate (i.e., income tax expense divided by book income before taxes). Explain why this rate is different from the statutory tax rate of 40%.

P13–3

Deferred tax amount on income statement

AICPA adapted

For financial statement reporting, the Lexington Corporation recognizes royalty income in the period earned. For income tax reporting, royalties are taxed when collected. At December 31, 2000 unearned royalties of $400,000 were included in Lexington's balance sheet. All these royalties had been collected in 2000. During 2001 royalties of $600,000 were collected. Unearned royalties in Lexington's December 31, 2001 balance sheet amounted to $350,000. Assume that the income tax rate was 50%.

Required:

What amount should be reported as the provision for deferred income taxes in Lexington's income statement for the year ended December 31, 2001?

P13–4

Current and deferred portion of tax expense

AICPA adapted

Joy Corporation prepared the following reconciliation of income per books with income per tax return for the year ended December 31, 2001:

Book income before income taxes	$750,000
Add temporary difference:	
Construction contract revenue which will reverse in 2002	100,000
Deduct temporary difference:	
Depreciation expense which will reverse in equal amounts in each of the next four years	(400,000)
Taxable income	$450,000

Joy's income tax rate is 35% for 2001.

REQUIRED:

1. What amount should Joy report in its 2001 income statement as the current provision for income taxes?
2. How much should Joy report as deferred income taxes on the income statement in 2001?

P13–5

Tax expense and deferred tax calculations

Nelson Inc. purchased machinery at the beginning of 2001 for $90,000. Management used the straight-line method to depreciate the cost for financial reporting purposes and the sum-of-the-years'-digits method to depreciate the cost for tax purposes. The life of the machinery was estimated to be two years, and the salvage value was estimated at zero. Revenues less expenses other than depreciation expense and amortization of goodwill equaled $500,000 for 2001 and 2002. Nelson pays income tax at the rate of 20% of taxable income. The amortization of goodwill equaled $50,000 for 2001 and 2002.

REQUIRED:

1. Compute the taxable income and the financial reporting income (before tax) for the years 2001 and 2002.
2. What are the permanent and timing differences? Give an example of each for Nelson Inc.
3. Complete the following table on your answer to (1).

Year	Ending Balance in Tax Liability	Tax Expense	Ending Balance in Deferred Income Taxes
2001			
2002			

[**Note:** Be sure to identify whether it is a debit or credit balance for deferred income taxes.]

4. Assume that the tax rate was changed by the federal government to 30% at the beginning of 2002. Compute the following:

   Increase/decrease in deferred income taxes
   Income tax liability for 2002
   Income tax expense for 2002

P13–6

Determining current and deferred portion of tax expense and reconciling statutory and effective tax rates

Metge Corporation's worksheet for calculating taxable income for 2001 is as follows:

($ in thousands)	2001
Pre-tax income	$1,000
Permanent differences	
Goodwill amortization	400
Interest on municipal bonds	(200)
Temporary differences	
Depreciation	(800)
Warranty costs	400
Rent received in advance	600
Taxable income	$1,400

The enacted tax rate for 2001 is 35%, but it is scheduled to increase to 40% in 2002 and subsequent years. All temporary differences are originating differences.

REQUIRED:

1. Determine Metge's 2001 taxes payable.
2. What is the change in deferred tax assets (liabilities) for 2001?
3. Determine tax expense for 2001.
4. Provide a schedule that reconciles Metge's statutory and effective tax rates (both in percentages and dollar amounts).

P13–7 **Entries for loss carrybacks and carryforwards**

Smith Corporation started doing business in 2000. The following table summarizes the taxable income (loss) of the company over the 2000–2012 period, along with the statutory tax rate effective in each of the years:

Year	Taxable Income (Loss)	Enacted Tax Rate
2000	$100,000	40%
2001	200,000	40
2002	250,000	35
2003	400,000	32
2004	(350,000)	30
2005	(275,000)	30
2006	125,000	30
2007	175,000	30
2008	275,000	30
2009	300,000	35
2010	(800,000)	35
2011	(250,000)	35
2012	150,000	35

Since the company had no permanent or timing differences during this period, its pre-tax financial reporting income was identical to its taxable income in each of these years. During the 2009–2012 period, the company expected the current and future tax rates to be 35%. Whenever possible, the company took advantage of the loss carryback provision of the tax law. When recording the tax benefits of the loss carryforward provision, the company felt it was more likely than not that the tax benefits will be fully realized.

REQUIRED:

1. Provide journal entries to record income tax expense for the years 2004, 2005, 2010, 2011, and 2012.
2. In answering this requirement, make the following assumptions. During 2010 and 2011, Smith Corporation felt it was more likely than not that only 40% of the tax benefits will be realized through a loss carryforward. However, during 2012 the company revised its expectation and felt that it was more likely than not that 100% of the tax benefits will be fully realized through a loss carryforward. Provide journal entries to record income tax expense for the years 2010, 2011, and 2012. Also show how the deferred tax asset will be reported as of the end of 2010, 2011, and 2012.

P13–8 **Entries for loss carrybacks and carryforwards**

Barron Corporation started doing business in 2000. The following table summarizes the taxable income (loss) of the company over the period 2000–2008:

Year	Taxable Income (Loss)
2000	$200,000
2001	150,000
2002	125,000
2003	90,000
2004	200,000
2005	(150,000)
2006	(180,000)
2007	125,000
2008	(120,000)

Since the company had no permanent or timing differences during this period, its pre-tax financial reporting income was identical to its taxable income in each of the preceding years. During the entire period, the company's current as well as its expected future tax rate was 40%. Whenever possible, the company took advantage of the loss carryback provision of the tax law. When recording the tax benefits of the loss carryforward provision, the company felt it was more likely than not that the tax benefits will be fully realized.

REQUIRED:

Provide journal entries to record income tax expense for the years 2005 through 2008.

P13–9

Reconciling statutory and effective tax rates

The following information pertains to Enis Corporation for the year ended December 31, 2001. The company reported a loss before taxes of $1,500,000 in its GAAP income statement, which included the effects of the following items:

- On January 1, 2001 Enis Corporation acquired Hansen Technology Group for $5,000,000 in cash. The breakdown for the acquisition cost is:

Marketable securities	$1,800,000
Other current assets	200,000
Value of in-process technology	2,000,000
Goodwill	1,000,000
	$5,000,000

Under GAAP, if a portion of the acquisition price can be allocated to the value of "in-process technology" (i.e., technology under development), that portion should be expensed as a part of the R&D expense of the acquiring company (i.e., Enis Corporation) in the year of the acquisition. However, the value of the in-process technology is not considered as an expense for tax purposes.

In its GAAP income statement, Enis Corporation amortizes its goodwill over a 20-year period using a straight-line approach. However, none of the goodwill amortization qualifies for a deduction in the tax statement of Enis Corporation.

- The bad debts written off during the year was $75,000 more than the provision for uncollectibles (or bad debt expense) recorded during the year.
- Enis Corporation earned $80,000 during 2001 from income on municipal bonds. The company has hired an investment management company to manage its portfolio of municipal bonds. Enis Corporation paid a $10,000 fee to the management company during 2001. This fee is nondeductible for tax purposes, since the income is nontaxable.
- Enis Corporation recorded a straight-line depreciation expense of $140,000 in its GAAP income statement. The corresponding accelerated tax depreciation was $210,000.
- Enis Corporation incurred an insurance expense of $15,000 during 2001; this expense was the premium on the life insurance policies of its senior executives. Enis Corporation is the beneficiary on these policies. During 2001 one of the senior executives passed away and Enis Corporation received $250,000 from the insurance company as death benefits.

REQUIRED:

1. Determine the taxable income and taxes payable for Enis in 2001. Assume a 35% statutory tax rate.
2. Determine the change in deferred tax assets (liabilities) for 2001.
3. Calculate the income tax expense of Enis Corporation for the year 2001.
4. Determine the effective book tax rate for Enis in 2001, and prepare a schedule to explain why the effective tax rate is different from the statutory tax rate.
5. Provide the journal entry to record the income tax expense, taxes payable, and deferred taxes for the year 2001.

P13–10

Analytical insights from deferred tax account

STRETCH

Weber Manufacturing Company started doing business on January 1, 2001. The company's current business plan predicts significant growth in sales over the next several years. To respond to this predicted growth, Weber is planning to buy annually new factory equipment at a cost of $60,000 during the first six years of its operations (2001 through 2006). The first piece of equipment was purchased on January 1, 2001. The company plans to use the straight-line method to depreciate the equipment cost for financial reporting purposes and the sum-of-the-years'-digits method for tax purposes. The useful life of the factory equipment was estimated to be three years, with no salvage value for both tax and financial reporting purposes. Weber expects to pay income taxes at the rate of 35% of its taxable income. Apart from the depreciation expense, Weber expects no other temporary or timing differences.

REQUIRED:

1. Calculate the balance in the deferred income tax liability account as of the end of years 2001 through 2006.
2. In answering this part, assume that Weber purchased the factory equipment at the beginning of each year (starting from 2001) for six years. However, the equipment costs $60,000 in 2001, which is expected to increase by $6,000 each year over the following five years ($66,000 in 2002, $72,000 in 2003, and so on). Calculate the balance in the deferred income tax liability as of the end of 2001 through 2006.
3. Consider the facts given in (2). Due to expected changes in business technology, the company expects the demand for its current products to start falling in 2007. Consequently, it plans to cut down substantially its production after 2007. In fact, Weber expects to purchase no more machinery after 2006. With this new information, compute the balance in the deferred income tax liability account for 2007 and 2008.
4. Based both on your answers to parts (1) through (3), and on changes in its deferred tax liability account, what conclusions might you draw about the financial condition of Weber?

P13–11

Comprehensive tax allocation problem

STRETCH

Bush Inc. started its retail business on January 1, 2001. The following information is extracted from the financial reporting income statement of the company for the years 2001 and 2002:

BUSH INCORPORATED

Income Statements for the Years Ended December 31

	2001	2002
Sales revenue	$1,000,000	$1,200,000
Income from municipal bonds	60,000	75,000
Cost of goods sold	(400,000)	(504,000)
Depreciation expense	?	?
Warranty expense	(100,000)	(110,000)
Provision for uncollectibles	?	?
Life insurance premium for senior executives	(30,000)	(30,000)
Other operating expenses	(300,000)	(350,000)
Income before income taxes	?	?
Income tax expense	?	?
Net income	?	?

REQUIRED:

1. Using the following additional information, complete the income statements for 2001 and 2002:

   a. The company purchased a piece of computer equipment on January 1, 2001 for $330,000. The equipment has a useful life of five years and an estimated salvage value of $30,000. The company uses the straight-line method of depreciation for financial reporting purposes.

b. The company estimates bad debt expense (or provision for uncollectibles) at 8% of sales revenue.
c. Bush Inc. is the beneficiary on the life insurance policies of its senior executives.
d. The income tax rate is 35%.

2. Using the following additional information, calculate taxable income and the income tax liability for the years 2001 and 2002:

   a. The company uses the sum-of-the-years'-digit method of depreciation for tax.
   b. The warranty liability account had balances of $15,000 and $25,000 at the end of 2001 and 2002, respectively.
   c. The allowance for uncollectibles had balances of $50,000 and $21,000 at the end of 2001 and 2002, respectively.

3. Provide a schedule showing why the effective tax rates for the company during 2001 and 2002 are different from the statutory tax rate of 35%.
4. Calculate the balances in the deferred tax accounts at the end of 2001 and 2002.
5. Provide a schedule reconciling the income tax expense with the income tax liability for both 2001 and 2002.
6. Provide journal entries to record income tax expense for 2001 and 2002.

P13–12

Determination of taxes payable, deferred taxes, and tax expense

STRETCH

[**Note:** Students may want to review the material on the equity method of accounting in Chapter 16 before beginning work on this problem.] In the current year, 2001, Reality Corporation reported $200,000 of pre-tax earnings on its income statement. The corporate tax rate is 40% in the current year and next year, and it is scheduled to remain at this level for the foreseeable future. Additional information relevant to figuring taxes is as follows:

a. Reality acquired $500,000 of machinery in 2000. The machinery is being depreciated on a straight-line basis over five years (zero salvage) for accounting purposes and on a modified accelerated cost recovery system (MACRS) for tax purposes. A comparison of depreciation charges under these two methods is as follows:

	2000	2001	2002	2003	2004
Straight line	$100,000	$100,000	$100,000	$100,000	$100,000
MACRS	165,000	225,000	75,000	35,000	–0–

b. Investment income from a 30% ownership of an investee company carried under the equity method is shown on the income statement as $80,000 (after amortization of $10,000 of implicit goodwill). The investee paid dividends to Reality in the amount of $30,000 in the current year. The remaining undistributed earnings for 2001 are expected to be received in equal amounts over the next two years in the form of dividends. All dividends are subject to the 80% dividend exclusion rule.
c. During the year, Reality recognized $4,000 of rental income that had been collected and taxed in 2000. In addition, $10,000 of rent revenue was received in advance in the current year. This amount was deferred for accounting purposes and will be recognized as income in 2002.
d. Reality received $5,000 of interest on State of North Carolina bonds in the current year, which is included in pre-tax income.
e. Reality sold land in the current year for $50,000 that had a $20,000 book value and tax basis. The entire gain (*not* considered extraordinary) was recognized for accounting purposes in 2001. However, since collections are to be received in three equal installments, Reality elected to use the installment sales method for tax purposes and picked up one-third of the gain on its tax return in 2001. The remaining amount of the gain will be recognized equally in 2002 and 2003.
f. Reality provided for future product warranty costs in the amount of $50,000 in the current year for book purposes. For tax purposes, such costs are deductible when paid. Actual warranty costs paid in 2001 were $15,000. It is expected that the remainder of the accrued warranty costs will be paid in 2002.
g. Included in pre-tax accounting income is a deduction for $3,000 for insurance premiums paid on Mr. Reality's life.

h. Reality made charges to bad debts expense in the current year of $15,000. The beginning balance in the "Allowance for bad debts" account was $12,000, and $6,000 of accounts was written off in the current year. It is expected that the 2001 year-end balance in the allowance account will be written off in 2002.
i. Reality has a $10,000 operating loss carryforward that can be used to offset the current period's taxable income.
j. The balance in the deferred tax asset (liability) account was $40,000 ($50,000) at the beginning of 2001.
k. Assume that it is estimated that it is more likely than not that 20% of the deferred tax asset at the end of 2001 will not be realized.

REQUIRED:

1. Starting with pre-tax accounting income, compute taxable income and taxes payable for 2001. Clearly label all amounts used in arriving at taxable income.
2. Using the following schedule, compute the change in the deferred tax asset (liability) account for 2001. The depreciation temporary difference has been completed as an example.

Temporary difference item	Deferred tax asset	Deferred tax liability
Depreciation ($225,000 − $100,000) × 40%		$50,000 **CR**

3. Determine the tax expense for 2001.

P13–13

Leasing and deferred taxes

The following information pertains to Crum International Corporation.

The company entered into the following lease agreement with Capital Leases, Inc. as of January 1, 2001. In accordance with the agreement, Crum leased a piece of computer equipment with a fair market value of $24,869 for its entire useful life of three years. In return, Crum promised to pay $10,000 per year *payable at the end of each year,* with the first payment to be made on December 31, 2001. At the end of the lease agreement, the estimated salvage value of the asset is zero.

For both tax and financial reporting purposes, Crum has *annual* income of $100,000 before taxes and before recording any expense on this lease transaction during each of the years 2001, 2002, and 2003. The tax rate is 40%.

REQUIRED:

1. Assuming that Crum treats the lease transaction as an *operating lease for tax purposes,* compute the taxable income for 2001–2003. Also calculate the amount of tax liability in each of the three years.
2. Assume Crum treats the lease transaction as a *capital lease for financial reporting purposes.* (The implicit interest rate in the lease contract is 10%.) Prepare a lease amortization schedule allocating the annual payments between interest expense and repayment of lease obligation. Clearly indicate the outstanding lease liability at the end of each period. Assuming further that Crum uses the straight-line method of depreciation for financial reporting purposes, prepare *income statements for financial reporting purposes,* clearly indicating the amount of tax expense for each of the three years.
3. Using all the assumptions up to this point, prepare journal entries to record the tax expense for each of the three years.

C13–1

Baldwin Piano and Organ Company (KR): Analysis of tax footnote

The following is adapted from the 1999 financial statements of Baldwin Piano and Organ Company. The components of income tax expense (benefit) are as follows:

($ in thousands)	1999	1998	1997
Current			
Federal	($ 1,464)	($ 104)	($ 407)
State	10	167	(242)
Foreign	1,509	118	113
	55	181	(536)
Deferred			
Federal	(6,181)	(1,605)	1,014
State	(1,095)	(415)	374
	(7,276)	(2,020)	1,388
Total	**($7,221)**	**($1,839)**	**$ 852**

The significant components of deferred income tax expense (benefit) are as follows:

($ in thousands)	1999	1998	1997
Reserves for inventories	–	($ 154)	$ 597
Allowance for doubtful accounts	($ 52)	134	894
Nondeductible accruals	514	304	555
LIFO inventory decrease	(737)	(384)	(539)
Investments in affiliated companies	–	(783)	–
Net operating loss carryforwards	(7,448)	–	–
Other	447	(1,137)	(119)
Deferred tax expense (benefit)	**($7,276)**	**($2,020)**	**$1,388**

Components of deferred tax balances as of December 31, 1999 and 1998 are as follows:

($ in thousands)	1999	1998
Deferred tax assets		
Accounts receivable, principally due to allowance for doubtful accounts	$ 242	$ 190
Inventories, principally inventory reserves and LIFO differences	1,084	347
Nondeductible accruals, principally due to accrual for financial reporting purposes	1,734	2,248
Foreign tax credit carryforwards	806	403
Valuation allowance	(806)	(232)
Net operating loss carryforwards	8,178	730
Other	849	586
Total gross deferred tax assets	**$12,087**	**$4,272**
Deferred tax liabilities		
Property, plant and equipment, principally due to differences in depreciation	($ 814)	($ 641)
State income taxes	(561)	(195)
Total gross deferred tax liabilities	**(1,375)**	**(836)**
Net deferred tax assets	**$ 10,712**	**$3,436**

The following are selected items included under "Accrued and other liabilities" in the balance sheet as of December 31, 1999.

Accrued and Other Liabilities ($ in thousands)	
Compensation and Benefits	$1,147
Postretirement and postemployment	195

REQUIRED:

1. Provide journal entries to record the income tax expense for the years 1997 through 1999. You may indicate the sum of the changes in the various deferred tax assets/liabilities by a single debit or credit to the "Net deferred tax asset/liability" account.
2. During 1999, there are several accounting items that cause the income tax expense of Baldwin Piano to be different from taxes currently payable. Using available information, explain how each one of these items are accounted for in Baldwin's tax versus financial reporting books. Explain whether these items reflect originating or reversing differences. With respect to each of the timing differences, clearly discuss whether it is indicative of a higher or lower financial reporting revenue or expense relative to the amount reported on the 1999 tax return.

C13–2 Edited excerpts from Sara Lee Corporation's 1999 tax footnote follow.

Sara Lee Corporation: Analysis of tax footnotes

SARA LEE CORPORATION

Excerpts from Tax Footnote

($ in millions)	1999	1998
Effective Income Tax Rates		
Tax expense (benefit) at U.S. statutory rate*	$ 585	($155)
State taxes, net of federal benefit	16	9
Difference between U.S. and foreign rates	(106)	(76)
Nondeductible amortization	49	351
Other, net	(64)	(49)
Taxes at effective worldwide tax rates	$ 480	$ 80

Current and deferred tax provisions (benefits) were:

	1999		1998	
	Current	Deferred	Current	Deferred
United States	$147	$ 51	$ 142	($286)
Foreign	237	20	329	(118)
State	62	(37)	14	(1)
	$446	$ 34	$ 485	($405)

The following are components of the deferred tax (benefit) provisions occuring as a result of transactions being reported in different years for financial and tax reporting:

($ in millions)	1999	1998
Depreciation	($ 72)	($ 3)
Inventory valuation methods	(27)	6
Nondeductible reserves	105	(405)
Other, net	28	(3)
Net deferred tax (benefit) provision	$ 34	($405)
Cash payments for income taxes	$321	$288

* Assume a statutory tax rate of 35%.

REQUIRED:

1. Prepare the book journal entry for income tax expense for 1999 (combine U.S., foreign, and state income taxes). Clearly indicate both the account title and whether the account is being debited or credited.
2. Using information given in the segment "Effective Income Tax Rates" regarding the statutory marginal tax rate for 1999, estimate Sara Lee Corporation's pre-tax book income for 1999. Show your work!
3. What was the 1999 effective overall tax rate for Sara Lee Corporation after taking into account differences arising from state and foreign income taxes, nondeductible amortization, etc? Show your work!
4. Estimate Sara Lee Corporation's taxable income. (**Note**: You do not have enough information to do this by category; therefore, combine U.S., foreign, and state taxes.) Show and clearly label all work.

C13–3

Motorola vs. Intel: Adjusting for depreciation differences

Motorola and Intel are both in the semiconductor industry and compete in many of the same product sectors. But each uses different depreciation methods. Motorola's 1996 10-K states the following:

> Depreciation is recorded principally using the declining-balance method based on the estimated useful lives of the assets (buildings and building equipment, 5–50 years; machinery and equipment, 2–12 years).

So Motorola is using accelerated depreciation for most of its assets. By contrast, Intel's 1996 report says:

> Depreciation is computed for financial reporting purposes principally by use of the straight-line method over the following estimated useful lives: machinery and equipment, 2 to 4 years; land and buildings, 4 to 45 years.

The table below gives several key financial statement figures for each company from their respective 1996 10-Ks and excerpts from their income tax footnote.

FROM THE 1996 10-Ks OF MOTOROLA AND INTEL

Selected, Edited Financial Statement Disclosures

Motorola

($ in millions)	1996	1995
Book depreciation	$2,308	$1,919
Income before income taxes	1,775	3,225
Property, plant & equipment, net of accumulated depreciation (at year-end)	9,768	9,356

	December 31	
Significant deferred tax assets (liabilities)	1996	1995
Inventory reserves	$ 440	$ 345
Contract accounting methods	231	157
Employee benefits	291	286
Capitalized items	138	89
Tax basis differences on investments	(199)	(176)
Depreciation	(213)	(197)
Deferred taxes on non-U.S. earnings	(545)	(382)
Other deferred income taxes	329	132
Net deferred tax asset	$ 472	$ 254

FROM THE 1996 10-Ks OF MOTOROLA AND INTEL

Selected, Edited Financial Statement Disclosures *(continued)*

Intel

($ in millions)	1996	1995
Book depreciation	$1,888	$1,371
Income before income taxes	7,934	5,638
Property, plant & equipment, less accumulated depreciation (at year-end)	8,487	7,471

	December 31	
Significant deferred tax assets (liabilities)	1996	1995
Deferred tax assets:		
Accrued compensation and benefits	$ 71	$ 61
Deferred income	147	127
Inventory valuation and related reserves	187	104
Interest and taxes	54	61
Other, net	111	55
	$570	$408
Deferred tax liabilities:		
Depreciation	(573)	(475)
Unremitted earnings of certain subsidiaries	(359)	(116)
Other, net	(65)	(29)
	($997)	($620)

Assume a statutory tax rate of 35% for all years.

REQUIRED:

1. Using the information provided and the analytical techniques illustrated in the chapter, determine the tax depreciation for Motorola and Intel for 1996.
2. Adjust each firm's pre-tax income to reflect the same depreciation method and useful lives used for tax purposes.
3. Explain why the adjusted numbers provide a better basis for comparing the operating performance of the two companies.

C13–4

Circuit City Stores Inc. (KR): Analysis of tax footnotes

The following information is from the annual reports of Circuit City Stores Inc. The components of the provision for income taxes (i.e., income tax expense) are as follows:

Tax Footnote:	Years Ended		
	February 29	February 28	
($ in thousands)	2000	1999	1998
Current			
Federal	$ 140,119	$ 99,228	$ 58,453
State	17,756	13,148	3,076
	157,875	112,376	61,529
Deferred			
Federal	41,762	16,718	12,801
State	1,291	517	2,251
	43,053	17,235	15,052
Provision for income taxes	**$200,928**	**$129,611**	**$76,581**

The components of deferred income taxes are as follows:

($ in thousands)	February 29 2000	February 28 1999
Deferred tax asset		
Deferred revenue	$ 1,146	$ 8,332
Inventory capitalization	2,609	2,578
Accrued expenses	33,484	27,080
Other	6,330	5,430
Total gross deferred tax asset	43,569	43,420
Deferred tax liabilities		
Depreciation and amortization	$ 51,035	$ 48,035
Deferred revenue	29,656	6,903
Gain on sale of receivables	18,988	14,990
Other prepaid expenses	26,111	20,210
Other	6,651	707
Total gross deferred tax liabilities	132,441	90,845
Net deferred tax liability	**$88,872**	**$47,425**

The following excerpt is from the financial statements of the company.

DEFERRED REVENUE

The Circuit City Group sells its own extended warranty contracts and extended warranty contracts on behalf of unrelated third parties. The contracts extend beyond the normal manufacturer's warranty period, usually with terms (including the manufacturer's warranty period) between 12 and 60 months. Inasmuch as the company is the primary obligor on these contracts, revenue from the sale of the Circuit City Group's own extended warranty contracts is deferred and amortized on a straight line basis over the life of the contracts. . . . Commission revenue for the unrelated third-party extended warranty contracts is recognized at the time of sale.

When necessary, assume a statutory tax rate of 35%.

REQUIRED:

1. Provide journal entries to record the income tax expense for 1998 through 2000. You may indicate the sum of the changes in the various deferred tax assets/liabilities by a single debit or credit to the "Net deferred tax asset/liability" account.
2. Provide possible explanations for why the deferred portion of the tax provision in 2000 does not equal the change in the net deferred tax liability from 1999 to 2000 on Circuit City's balance sheet.
3. What source of Circuit City's revenue gives rise to the deferred tax asset entitled "Deferred revenue"? With respect to that revenue source, explain how Circuit City's financial reporting revenue recognition method is different from its tax accounting method? During the year ended February 29, 2000, how much more revenue did Circuit City report in taxable income than in its financial reporting income statement?
4. Estimate and comment on the Circuit City's earnings conservatism ratio for 1999 and 2000.

C13-5

ABC Inc. (KR): Interpreting tax footnotes and reconciling statutory and effective rates

The following information is adapted from the 2001 financial statements of ABC Inc.

ABC Inc. is in the business of airframe maintenance, modification and retrofit services, avionics and aircraft interior installations, the overhaul and repair of aircraft engines, and other related services.

The following are excerpted from its income statement for the year ended December 31, 2001. ***(All figures are in thousands of dollars.)***

($ in thousands)	2001
Earnings (loss) before income taxes	$10,891
Income tax benefit (provision)	(3,267)
Net earnings (loss)	$ 7,624

The details for the income tax expense or provision are provided next.

Income Tax Expense	2001
Current	$1,756
Deferred	1,511
Income tax expense	$3,267

Due to the nondeductibility of amortization of goodwill, the company's tax expense was higher by $1,076 than would be expected based on the statutory tax rate of 35%. State taxes further added another $927 to the tax expense. However, the reduction in the valuation allowance decreased the accounting income tax expense. In addition, several other items caused the tax expense to deviate from the tax liability. Since these items by themselves are immaterial, no separate breakdowns are available.

The following breakdowns are available for the balance sheet values of deferred tax assets and liabilities:

	December 31	
($ in thousands)	2001	2000
Deferred Tax Assets		
Accounts receivable	$ 977	$ 1,070
Inventories, principally due to additional costs inventoried for tax purposes and financial statement allowances	3,523	1,679
Employee benefits, principally due to accrual for financial reporting purposes	9,814	13,510
Accrual for costs of restructuring	5,392	8,750
Accrual for disposal of discontinued operations	4,312	5,020
Others	23,634	19,257
Gross deferred tax assets	$47,652	$49,286
Less: Valuation allowance	(13,588)	(15,710)
Total deferred tax asset	$34,064	$33,576
Deferred Tax Liability		
Plant and equipment	($ 7,770)	($ 8,993)
Others	(5,187)	(1,964)
Total deferred tax liability	(12,957)	(10,957)
Net deferred tax asset	$ 21,107	$22,619

The book value of the company's inventories increased from $91,130 at the end of 2000 to $127,777 at the end of 2001.

REQUIRED:

1. Prepare a schedule reconciling the statutory and effective tax rates of ABC Inc. for the year ended 2001.
2. Provide the journal entry to record the income tax expense for 2001, showing separately the effects on deferred tax asset, valuation allowance, and deferred tax liability.
3. For each component of deferred tax asset/liability, provide possible reasons for the change in its values from 2000 to 2001.

COLLABORATIVE LEARNING CASE

C13-6

Waste Management: Analysis of tax footnotes

Waste Management is one of the largest trash haulers in the United States. In the late 1980s, the firm was widely viewed as a growth company. In an article about the company written 10 years later, *Fortune* stated that Waste Management "used improper, overly aggressive accounting tactics in an effort to boost sagging earnings . . . to retain its status as a Wall Street highflier . . . ."[1] In early 1998, the firm announced they would take a $3.54 billion pre-tax charge to correct these "accounting irregularities." The two largest charge-offs resulted from aggressive extensions of the expected depreciable lives of trucks and dumpsters and understated reserves for federal environmental liabilities. One magazine article reported that the earnings "hit" taken by Waste Management "stunned the investment community." Reproduced below are selected excerpts from Waste Management's financial statements over the period 1993–1996. Using your understanding of financial reporting and your ability to make inferences from these pre–1998 disclosures, should knowledgeable investors have been "stunned" by the early 1998 write-off? More explicit questions to guide your analysis follow the statement excerpts.

WASTE MANAGEMENT

Consolidated Condensed Income Statement Data (Before Correction)

	Years Ended December 31			
($ in thousands)	1993	1994	1995	1996
Revenue	$7,827,280	$ 8,482,718	$9,053,018	$ 9,186,970
Costs and expenses	6,361,233	6,824,806	7,225,747	7,352,037
Special charges	550,000	–	335,193	471,635
Gains from stock transactions of subsidiaries And exchange of Exchangeable LYONs	(15,109)	–	–	–
Other expense	193,272	363,000	390,165	320,460
Income from continuing operations before income taxes	737,884	1,294,912	1,101,913	1,042,838
Provision for income taxes	319,798	552,606	483,670	565,047
Income from continuing operations	418,086	742,306	618,243	477,791
Income (loss) from discontinued operations	34,690	42,075	(14,344)	(285,706)
Net income	$ 452,776	$ 784,381	$ 603,899	$ 192,085

[1] Peter Elkind, "Garbage In; Garbage Out," *Fortune*, May 25, 1998.

Consolidated Condensed Balance Sheets (Before Correction)—*continued*

($ in thousands)	1993	As of December 31 1994	1995	1996
Total Current Assets	$ 2,777,520	$ 3,088,844	$ 2,608,085	$ 3,093,224
Property and Equipment, at cost				
Land, primarily disposal sites	3,625,412	4,162,418	4,553,717	5,019,065
Buildings	1,223,139	1,372,782	1,532,305	1,495,252
Vehicles and equipment	6,856,044	7,162,217	7,164,767	7,520,902
Leasehold improvements	100,262	91,554	84,587	85,998
	11,804,857	12,788,971	13,335,376	14,121,217
Less—Accumulated depreciation and amortization	(3,035,398)	(3,503,219)	(3,829,658)	(4,399,508)
Total Property and Equipment, Net	8,769,459	9,285,752	9,505,718	9,721,709
Total Other Assets	4,717,497	5,164,318	6,250,471	5,551,659
Total Assets	$16,264,476	$17,538,914	$18,364,274	$18,366,592
Total Current Liabilities	$ 2,677,562	$ 3,179,731	$ 3,192,484	$ 3,038,708
Total Deferred Items	1,933,319	1,985,298	2,192,150	2,197,234
Long-Term Debt, less portion payable within one year	6,145,584	6,044,411	6,390,041	6,971,607
Minority Interest in Subsidiaries	1,348,559	1,536,165	1,385,301	1,186,955
Put Options	–	252,328	261,959	95,789
Total Stockholders' Equity	4,159,452	4,540,981	4,942,339	4,876,299
Total Liabilities and Stockholders' Equity	$16,264,476	$17,538,914	$18,364,274	$18,366,592

Additional Financial Disclosures (Before Correction)

($ in thousands)	1993	1994	1995	1996
From the Consolidated Statement of Cash Flows:				
Depreciation and amortization	$796,691	$880,466	$885,384	$920,685

From Management's Discussion and Analysis*: (Before Correction)

Acquisitions and Capital Expenditures Capital expenditures, including [$443.5 million,] $56.8 million, $154.1 million and $91.8 million for property and equipment of purchased businesses in [1993,] 1994, 1995 and 1996, respectively, are shown in the following table:

($ in millions)	1993	1994	1995	1996
Land (primarily disposal sites)	$ 660.2	$ 582.3	$ 517.2	$ 467.7
Buildings and leasehold improvements	195.5	141.2	148.8	109.3
Vehicles	373.0	226.0	345.8	204.9
Containers	231.6	167.9	181.2	115.8
Other equipment	702.4	395.0	348.1	319.2
Total	$2,162.7	$1,512.4	$1,541.1	$1,216.9

From the summary of Accounting Policies Footnote: (Before Correction)

Property and Equipment Property and equipment (including major repairs and improvements) are capitalized and stated at cost. Items of an ordinary maintenance or repair nature are charged directly to operations. Disposal sites are carried at cost and to the extent this exceeds end use realizable value, such excess is amortized over the estimated life of the disposal site. Disposal site improvement costs are capitalized and

* The text is from the 1996 Annual Report and is edited to include 1993 data.

charged to operations over the shorter of the estimated usable life of the site or the improvement.

. . .

Depreciation and Amortization The cost, less estimated salvage value, of property and equipment is depreciated over the estimated useful lives on the straight-line method as follows: buildings—10 to 40 years; vehicles and equipment—3 to 20 years; leasehold improvements—over the life of the applicable lease.

Annual Report Condensed Note on Income Taxes (Before Correction)*

($ in thousands)	1993	1994	1995	1996
Deferred tax assets				
Reserves not deductible until paid	($ 538,062)	($ 494,549)	($ 503,074)	($ 495,940)
Deferred revenue	(27,714)	(25,708)	(37,284)	(16,158)
Net operating losses and tax credit carryforwards	(43,028)	(110,073)	(266,916)	(233,008)
Other	(104,059)	(70,281)	(78,474)	(73,229)
Subtotal	($ 712,863)	($ 700,611)	($ 885,748)	($ 818,335)
Deferred tax liabilities				
Depreciation and amortization	$ 948,024	$1,106,155	$1,335,559	$1,384,164
Other	183,655	233,178	374,084	359,035
Subtotal	1,131,679	1,339,333	1,709,643	1,743,199
Valuation allowance	29,890	26,955	98,605	86,729
Net deferred tax liabilities	$ 448,706	$ 665,677	$ 922,500	$1,011,593

**Note:* In the notes accompanying its pre-correction 1996 Annual Report, the Company says: "Certain amounts in previously issued financial statements have been restated to conform to 1996 classifications." Similar statements were made in the 1994 and 1995 annual reports relating to those reporting years. Since only two years of comparative data were given in each report, the 1994 data are not strictly classified in conformity with the 1996 classifications. The differences from year to year appear to be minor. However, the reader should be aware that adjacent years' data are not always perfectly comparable.

ANNUAL REPORT NOTE ON ENVIRONMENTAL COSTS AND LIABILITIES (TEXT FROM 1996 ANNUAL REPORT, BEFORE CORRECTION)

The continuing business in which the Company is engaged is intrinsically connected with the protection of the environment. As such, a significant portion of the Company's operating costs and capital expenditures could be characterized as costs of environmental protection . . .

Estimates of the extent of the Company's degree of responsibility for remediation of a particular site and the method and ultimate cost of remediation require a number of assumptions and are inherently difficult, and the ultimate outcome may differ from current estimates. However, the Company believes that its extensive experience in the environmental services business, as well as its involvement with a large number of sites, provides a reasonable basis for estimating its aggregate liability. As additional information becomes available, estimates are adjusted as necessary. While the Company does not anticipate that any such adjustment would be material to its financial statements, it is reasonably possible that technological, regulatory, or enforcement developments, the results of environmental studies, or other factors could necessitate the recording of additional liabilities, which could be material.

Where the Company believes that both the amount of a particular environmental liability and the timing of the payments are reliably determinable, the cost in current dollars is inflated at 3% until expected time of payment and then discounted to present value at 7%. Had the Company not discounted any portion of its liability, the amount recorded would have been increased by approximately $160 million at December 31, 1996.

The Company's active landfill sites have estimated remaining lives ranging from 1 to over 100 years based upon current site plans and annual volumes of waste. During this remaining site life, the Company will provide for an additional $1.03 billion of closure and post-closure costs, including accretion for the discount recognized to date.

As of December 31, the Company's liabilities for closure, post-closure monitoring and environmental remediation costs were as follows:

($ in thousands)	1993	1994	1995	1996
Current portion, included in accrued expenses	$ 130,863	$ 108,750	$ 138,533	$ 122,209
Non-current portion	745,637	704,015	621,186	543,723
Total recorded	876,500	812,765	759,719	665,932
Amount to be provided over remaining life of active sites,				
including discount of $154 million in 1993 and $169 million in 1994	987,000	1,149,617		
including discount of $171 million in 1995 and $160 million in 1996			1,118,739	1,028,437
Expected aggregate undiscounted environmental liabilities	$1,863,500	$1,962,382	$1,878,458	$1,694,369

Anticipated payments of environmental liabilities at December 31, 1996, are as follows:

($ in thousands)	
1997	$ 122,209
1998	56,000
1999	47,450
2000	33,571
2001	38,429
Thereafter	1,396,710
	$1,694,369

REQUIRED:

What elements in the Waste Management financial data and footnote excerpts included in the case might have given analysts an inkling of the excessive depreciable lives estimates and understated environmental reserves? (Hints: (1) Explain why the deferred tax liability for depreciation and amortization is increasing. Is this increasing CR balance consistent with year-to-year capital expenditure patterns? (2) Carefully compare recorded environmental liabilities with asset amounts.)

14

Pensions and Postretirement Benefits

LEARNING OBJECTIVES:
After studying this chapter, you will understand:

1. The difference between defined contribution and defined benefit pension plans.
2. What the components of pension expense are and their relation to pension assets and the pension liability.
3. The requirements for funding pension plans, computing the return on plan assets, and the role of the plan trustee.
4. How GAAP smoothes the volatility inherent in pension estimates and forecasts.
5. The determinants of the pension funding decision.
6. How to analyze the funded status footnote and reconciliation of pension asset and liability accounts and how to use this information.
7. When a minimum balance sheet pension liability must be recognized.
8. The financial reporting rules for other postretirement benefits.
9. What research tells us about the usefulness of the detailed pension and other postretirement benefits disclosures.

A **pension plan** is an agreement by an organization to provide a series of payments—called a **pension**—to employees when they retire. In most instances these company pension payments supplement payments from government sponsored pension plans in the United States—such as Social Security. A pension plan represents a valuable benefit to employees. Employers create these plans as a way of attracting a qualified work force. Firms derive benefits from pension plans, since they help them retain a more capable work force with higher morale. For this reason, the cost of a worker's pension plan is treated as an expense over that worker's period of employment.

Pension plans can be divided into two categories—**defined contribution** plans and **defined benefit** plans—based on the nature of the promise embedded in the plan.

Defined contribution plans specify the amount of cash that the employer puts *into* the plan for the benefit of the employee. In a defined contribution plan, no explicit promise is made about the size of the periodic payments the employee will receive on retirement. The amount that will ultimately be paid out to the employee is determined by the accumulated value at retirement of the amounts contributed to the plan over the period of employment. In defined contribution plans, the employee bears the risk that the ultimate pension payments will be large enough to sustain a comfortable retirement income. Accounting for such plans is straightforward, as shown in the following example.

Defined Contribution Plan

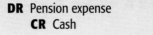

XYZ Company sponsors a defined contribution pension plan under which it makes an annual contribution equal to 10% of employees' salaries into a fund ***whose accumulated proceeds will be paid to the employees at retirement.*** Employees' salaries in 2001 total $10 million. Accordingly, XYZ records pension expense equal to the amount of cash contributed to the plan ($10,000,000 × 10%) as follows:

DR Pension expense	$1,000,000	
CR Cash		$1,000,000

A defined benefit plan is quite different. These agreements specify the formula for determining the amount that will be paid *out* to the employee after retirement rather than the amount that will be put into the plan. To illustrate:

Defined Benefit Plan

ABC Company sponsors a pension plan in which employees qualify for a pension equal to ***3% of their salary at retirement for each year of service.*** Thus, an employee with 25 years of service and with an annual salary at retirement of $60,000 would receive an annual pension benefit of $45,000 (25 years of service times 3% for each year—75%—multiplied by the ending salary of $60,000).

A defined contribution plan specifies the initial level of pay-*in* to the plan. A defined benefit plan specifies the formula for determining pension pay-*outs*.

In defined contribution pension plans, employees are sometimes also required to contribute to the plan. For example, a plan might specify that the employer is to contribute 10% of the employee's salary to the plan and that the employee is to contribute 5%, for a total of 15%. The employees' 5% contributions are typically deducted from their paychecks and directly transferred to the plan trustee, whose role is discussed later.

Table 14.1 shows the total dollar amount of assets in each type of pension plan over the years from 1985 to 1999. The proportion of assets in defined benefit plans has declined over this period. Nevertheless, 47.4% of all pension plan assets were still in defined benefit plans at the end of 1999.

A defined benefit pension plan raises many financial reporting complications. The main one is how much should be charged to pension expense in each year while covered employees are working.

Financial reporting for defined benefit plans is further complicated because only the benefit *formula* is specified, not the benefit *amount.* In the ABC Company example, at the time the plan was adopted it was known that retiring employees with 25 years of service would receive a pension equal to 75% of their annual salary at the time of retirement. However, to determine what the periodic pension expense should be over the span of the employees' working careers, the following factors must be estimated:

1. What proportion of the workforce will remain with the company long enough to qualify for benefits under the plan? Qualifying for benefits is called **vesting.** A forecast of the length of employee service requires actuarial assumptions regarding personnel turnover, mortality rates, and disability.
2. At what rate will salaries rise over the period until eventual retirement?
3. What is the anticipated life span of covered employees after retirement—that is, over what length of time will the pension benefits be paid?
4. What rate of return will be earned on the investments made with the cash contributed by the employer to fund the plan?
5. What is the appropriate discount rate that should be used to reflect the present value of the future benefits earned by employees in the current period?

Statement of Financial Accounting Standards (SFAS) No. 87, which was issued in December 1985, specifies measurement and disclosure requirements for defined benefit

Table 14.1 ■ ASSETS BY TYPE OF PENSION PLAN

($ in billions)

End of Year	Defined Benefit	Defined Contribution	Defined Benefit	Defined Contribution
1985	$ 814	$ 417	66.1%	33.9%
1986	885	478	64.9	35.1
1987	883	523	62.8	37.2
1988	883	549	61.7	38.3
1989	942	672	58.4	41.6
1990	896	676	57.0	43.0
1991	1,048	829	55.8	44.2
1992	1,043	892	53.9	46.1
1993	1,170	1,014	53.6	46.4
1994	1,193	1,076	52.6	47.4
1995	1,444	1,301	52.6	47.4
1996	1,542	1,505	50.6	49.4
1997	1,783	1,911	48.3	51.7
1998	1,988	2,210	47.4	52.6
1999	2,206	2,450	47.4	52.6

Source: Employee Benefit Research Institute, Washington, D.C.

pension plans.[1] The disclosure aspects of *SFAS No. 87* were amended by *SFAS No. 132* in 1998.[2] *SFAS No. 87* was designed to avoid volatility in pension expense. This objective was achieved by using numerous smoothing devices and deferrals in computing pension expense. The result is arguably the most technically complicated financial reporting pronouncement ever issued. Consequently, analysts and other external users have experienced considerable difficulty in comprehending the concepts underlying the reported numbers. We try to clarify the topic by providing a less technical, more intuitive overview of the financial reporting rules for defined benefit pension plans.[3]

Financial Reporting for Pensions

Under current GAAP, pension expense is comprised of six separate components. These components are (+ indicates increase in expense and − indicates decrease in expense):[4]

1. Service cost (+)
2. Interest cost (+)
3. Expected return on plan assets (−)
4. Recognized gains or losses (− or +)

---

[1] Entitled "Employers' Accounting for Pensions," *SFAS No. 87* replaced both *Accounting Principles Board (APB) Opinion No. 8* ("Accounting for the Cost of Pension Plans," 1966) and *SFAS No. 36* ("Disclosure of Pension Information," 1980), which previously governed pension accounting and disclosure.

[2] "Employers' Disclosures About Pensions and Other Postretirement Benefits," *SFAS No. 132* (Norwalk, CT: Financial Accounting Standards Board [FASB], 1998).

[3] The material on pp. 691–704, 711–713, and 716–718 is adapted from L. Revsine, "Understanding Financial Accounting Standard 87," *Financial Analysts Journal* (January–February 1989), pp. 61–8, and is presented here with permission from the publisher.

[4] If a company either (1) curtails a plan, or (2) settles a plan's liabilities by purchasing an annuity contract and generates a gain or loss from either event, that gain or loss would also be included in pension expense as a seventh element. Measuring the gain or loss on plan settlements or curtailments is outlined in "Employers' Accounting for Settlements and Curtailments of Defined Benefit Pension Plans and for Termination Benefits," *SFAS No. 88* (Stamford, CT: FASB, 1985).

5. Amortization of unrecognized transition asset or obligation (− or +)
6. Recognized prior service cost (− or +).

We use a simple example to illustrate how pension expense is computed and disclosed under the *SFAS Nos. 87* and *132* rules. The example assumes an environment characterized by *complete certainty.* This assumption simplifies the setting and clarifies the relationship between the various pension expense components. The complete certainty assumption makes it easy to see that there would be no need for components 4 through 6 in an environment with no surprises. Later, we will show how components 4 through 6 come into play in a world of uncertainty, one where expectations are often not realized and where changes in assumptions occur frequently.

A Simple Example in a Certainty Setting

Consider the following example:[5]

> On January 1, 2001, Wildcat Corporation decides to provide a lump-sum pension payment equal to $10,000 for each year of service to its sole employee, Ed Cate. No previous pension plan existed. Wildcat expects Cate to retire on December 31, 2002 and desires to pay the pension in one lump sum on December 31, 2003.
>
> Further assume that Wildcat operates in an environment of complete certainty where the interest rate and the rate of return on investments are both equal and known. Furthermore, Cate's life expectancy and the duration of his employment service are also known in advance. Wildcat's discount rate is 7%, and the pension trust will also earn exactly 7% on all contributions to the pension fund, which are funded fully as soon as Cate qualifies for benefits.

Component 1—Service Cost In a typical defined benefit pension plan, the pension pay-out increases for each additional year of service. This increase in the expected pay-out results in an increase in the discounted present value of the liability. This increase is **service cost.** Stated more rigorously, ***service cost is the increase in the discounted present value of the pension benefits ultimately payable that is attributable to an additional year's employment.***

Most pension plans create a trust—a legal entity which takes custody of assets contributed by the employer and manages them for the benefit of the employees. Contributing assets to the plan is termed **funding.** When the employer funds the plan, these assets are transferred to the trustee.

In the simplified example, Cate worked throughout 2001 and according to the terms of the pension benefit formula became eligible for a $10,000 pension payable on December 31, 2003. The discounted present value of this obligation on December 31, 2001 (at a 7% discount rate) is $8,734. Because no obligation existed at the start of the year, the *increase* in the discounted present value of the obligation during the year is $8,734—this is the service cost element of pension expense on Wildcat's books for 2001 and the pension obligation at the end of the year. Because Wildcat fully funds the pension expense, the economic status of the pension plan at December 31, 2001 is:

Wildcat Corporation

Pension expense = pension obligation $= \dfrac{\$10{,}000}{(1.07)^2} = \$8{,}734$ = Service cost

Pension funding $8,734 = Cash transferred to trust

Wildcat Employees' Pension Trust

Pension fund assets and obligation $8,734 = Cash received from Wildcat Corporation

[5] This example is adapted from a pre-*SFAS No. 87* illustration that was prepared by Professor Norman Bartczak.

Ed Cate's continued employment throughout 2002 qualifies him for a $20,000 pension payable on December 31, 2003. The service cost element of pension expense for the year 2002 is the increase in the present value of the amount ultimately payable that is attributable to an additional year's employment. Table 14.2 shows the computation.

Table 14.2 ■ WILDCAT CORPORATION

Computation of Service Cost for 2002

Pension payout to Cate with two years of service (2001 and 2002)		$20,000
Less: Pension payout to Cate with one year of service (2001)	−	10,000
Undiscounted increase attributable to 2002 service	=	10,000
Discount factor at 7% for one year (this increase is discounted since the additional payout is one year away)	×	.9346
Service cost for 2002	=	$ 9,346

The ultimate pension payout has grown by $10,000, since Cate earned additional benefits by working in 2002. As shown in Table 14.2, the discounted present value of this increase is $10,000 × .9346—or $9,346. By definition, this is service cost.

In addition to service cost, the 2002 *total* pension expense for Wildcat Corporation includes two other items—interest cost and return on plan assets.

Component 2—Interest Cost Service cost for 2001 was initially recorded at $8,734, the discounted present value of the pension payment due on December 31, 2003. Because the payment of this liability drew one year closer by the end of 2002, its present value has increased by $611 ($8,734 × 7%). Therefore, in addition to service cost, there is interest cost in 2002. The **interest cost** component of pension expense (and the increase in the liability) arises from the passage of time. (By contrast, the service cost element arises because the pension liability grows as workers accumulate additional years of service.) Interest cost is computed by taking the pension liability at the beginning of the period ($8,734) and multiplying it by the 7% interest rate factor.

Component 3—Expected Return on Plan Assets At December 31, 2001 the pension fund assets (held by the trustee) also had a balance of $8,734. During 2002 these assets earned a return of $611 ($8,734 × 7%). (Because our example is set in a world of complete certainty, the expected return and the actual return on plan assets are equal.) The **expected return on plan assets** reduces pension expense. As a consequence of all of these events, total pension expense for 2002 is $9,346 ($9,346 + $611 − $611). Table 14.3 on page 694 gives the 2002 pension expense components and pension fund asset balance at December 31, 2002.

If Cate retires at the end of 2002, there will be no service cost component of pension expense in 2003. There will be interest cost because the present value of the amount owed at the pension payout date increases as time passes. There will also be a return on plan assets in 2003. Table 14.4 shows that the interest cost and return on plan assets offset so 2003 pension expense is zero. Notice that the December 31, 2003 accumulated asset balance of $20,000 is exactly equal to the required pension payment.

In this example perfect certainty meant:

1. The exact ***date of retirement was known*** at the time the plan was initiated. In technical terms, the precise service life of employees was known with certainty.
2. The ultimate ***amount of the pension was also known in advance.*** No unexpected salary increases raised the amount of the final payment, nor were there unforeseen actuarial events such as turnover or death.
3. ***Discount rates and earnings rates were equal and could be perfectly forecast over the entire period.***

Table 14.3 ■ WILDCAT PENSION PLAN

Pension Expense and Assets for 2002

Wildcat Corporation			
Pension Expense			
Service cost ($10,000)/1.07	=		$ 9,346
Interest cost ($8,734 × 7%)	=		611
Expected return on plan assets ($8,734 × 7%)	=		(611)
2002 pension expense	=		$ 9,346
Pension funding	=		$ 9,346
Wildcat Employees' Pension Trust			
Pension Fund Assets and Obligations			
Accumulated balance of 12/31/01 pension assets as of 12/31/02: ($8,734 × 1.07)	=		$ 9,346*
2002 pension funding (equal to 2002 service cost)	=		9,346
Balance of pension assets at 12/31/02	=		$18,692
Present value of pension obligation at 12/31/02	=	$\frac{\$20{,}000}{1.07}$ =	$18,692

*Rounded

Table 14.4 ■ WILDCAT PENSION PLAN

Pension Expense and Assets for 2003

Wildcat Corporation		
Pension Expense		
Interest cost (i.e., present value of pension obligation at 12/31/02 × discount rate: $18,692 × 7%)	=	$ 1,308
Expected return on plan assets ($18,692 × 7%)	=	(1,308)
2003 pension expense	=	–0–
Pension funding	=	–0–
Wildcat Employees' Pension Trust		
Pension Fund Assets and Obligations		
Accumulated balance of 12/31/02 pension assets as of 12/31/03: ($18,692 × 1.07)	=	$20,000
Less: 12/31/03 payment to Cate	=	(20,000)
Balance of pension assets at 12/31/03	=	–0–
Present value of pension obligation as of 12/31/03	=	$20,000
Less: 12/31/03 payment to Cate	=	(20,000)
Balance of pension obligation at 12/31/03	=	–0–

With these simple (and unrealistic) circumstances, pension expense is equal to service cost in every period over which the pension plan is in effect, as shown next:

Year	Service Cost	Total Pension Expense
2001	$8,734	$8,734
2002	9,346	9,346
2003	–0–	–0–

Pension expense equals service cost when there is complete certainty because interest cost is exactly offset by the return on plan assets. With full funding of service cost, this also means that the accumulated amount of pension assets is exactly sufficient to pay the liability. Relaxing these certainty assumptions complicates pension financial reporting considerably.

We use perfect certainty in this example to help you see the relationship between the components comprising pension expense. There is no perfect certainty in the real pension world. On the contrary, unforeseen pension events arise continuously, like higher or lower than anticipated employee turnover and unusually high or low preretirement mortality. In addition, the return earned on pension plan assets could differ significantly from expectations. Furthermore, changes in social and economic conditions may prompt companies to retroactively alter the level of benefits promised upon retirement or to alter the discount rate assumptions.

The reason that pension expense does not equal service cost when unexpected events occur is that past funding (which was based on the original actuarial and earnings assumptions) generates returns that are larger or smaller than interest cost (which is based on the revised actuarial assumptions).

All these factors explain why, in the real world, there is no simple equality between plan assets and liabilities and why pension expense does not equal service cost. Depending on the age distribution of the workforce and the amount of retroactive plan alterations, interest cost—not service cost—could be the dominant part of pension expense.

Our example does capture one real-world characteristic of pension plans. Wildcat Corporation (the plan sponsor) recognized on its books only the pension expense and the cash payout when funding the pension. For example, Wildcat made the following entry to record pension expense and funding in 2002:

DR Pension expense	$9,346	
CR Cash		$9,346

The assets and liabilities of the pension plan are not included in Wildcat's financial statements. Instead, the assets and liabilities are reflected on the statements of the **plan trustee.** The plan trustee receives the payments and disburses pension benefits. The relationship between the firm that establishes the pension plan (the plan sponsor), the plan trustee, and the plan beneficiaries (the eventual retirees) is shown in Figure 14.1.

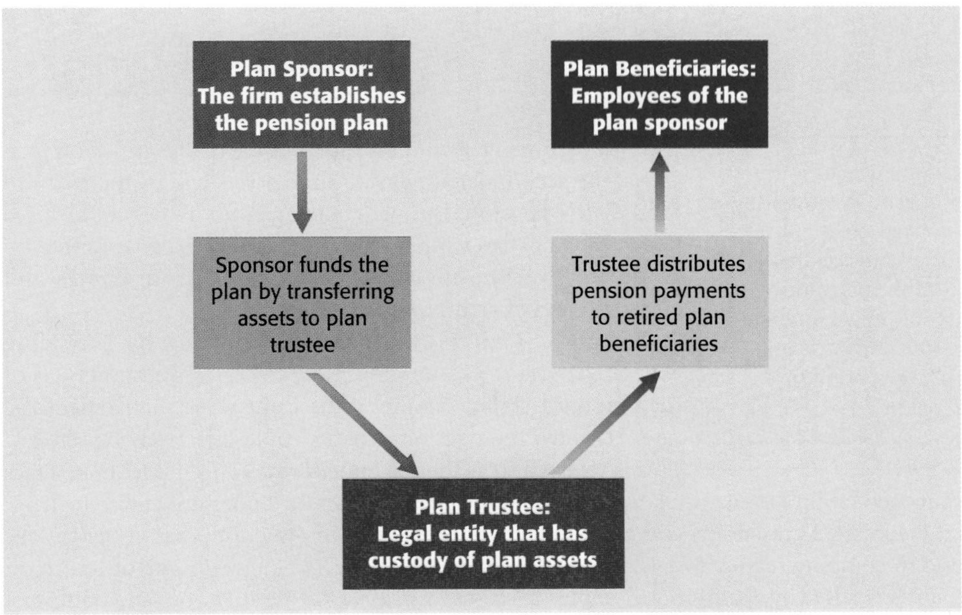

Figure 14.1

PENSION PLAN ENTITIES AND RELATIONSHIPS

If the future were known with certainty, pension expense would always equal service cost and pension plan assets would always equal plan liabilities. Starting with this simple setting will help you understand the complications that uncertainty introduces.

RECAP

Uncertainty Introduces Deferrals and Amortizations

Uncertainty requires estimates of future discount rates, expected return on plan assets, and numerous other future events like employee turnover and longevity beyond retirement. *SFAS No. 87* requires that the same interest rate be used for computing both the service cost *and* the interest cost components of pension expense. However, companies are free to choose some other interest rate for computing the *expected* rate of return on pension plan assets and many do.

The simplified complete certainty example suggests that the higher the interest rate initially chosen for computing service cost, the lower the reported service cost component of pension expense. This reduction in service cost is offset by an increase in the interest cost component of pension expense, which is due to the higher interest rate. In our Wildcat Corporation example, if the same higher rate is *also* used for computing the expected return on plan assets, then pension expense is reduced. Table 14.5 illustrates the decrease in pension expense that results from using an 8% rate rather than 7% in the Wildcat Corporation example.

Table 14.5 ■ WILDCAT CORPORATION

Pension Expense at Two Different Interest Rates

			Interest Rate 8%	Interest Rate 7%
2001 Pension Expense				
2001 Service cost	$10,000 / (1.08)^2$	=	$8,573	
	$10,000 / (1.07)^2$	=		$8,734
2002 Pension Expense				
2002 Service cost	($20,000 − $10,000) / 1.08	=	$9,259	
	($20,000 − $10,000) / 1.07	=		$9,346
Interest cost	$8,573 × 8%	=	686	
	$8,734 × 7%	=		611
Return on plan assets	$8,573 × 8%	=	(686)	
	$8,734 × 7%	=		(611)
			$9,259	$9,346

> The FASB provides the following guidance for estimating the settlement rate: "It is appropriate in estimating those rates to look to available information about rates implicit in current prices of annuity contracts that could be used to effect settlement of the obligation. . . . [E]mployers may also look to rates of return on high-quality fixed-income investments currently available and expected to be available during the period to maturity of the pension benefits" (para. 44).

If the assumed 8% interest rate is not actually *earned* on plan assets, the accumulated pension fund assets will be too small to fund Cate's pension. But generalizing from Table 14.5, we see that companies can temporarily alter pension expense (either up or down) by choosing higher or lower discount rates and expected rates of return on plan assets.

SFAS No. 87 improves pension reporting by providing explicit criteria for estimating discount rates. Paragraph 44 of the Standard states, "assumed discount rates shall reflect the rates at which the pension benefits could effectively be settled." This is referred to as the **settlement rate.** This guideline reduces managers' ability to manipulate pension expense; unfortunately it does not eliminate it.

Figure 14.2 graphically compares settlement rates (used to discount pension obligations and to compute service cost and interest cost) and the expected long-run rate of return on plan assets used by a sample of Compustat® firms from 1994 to 1998.[6] The top and bottom of

[6] Compustat® is a computerized financial database for over 7,000 firms listed on the New York Stock Exchange (NYSE), American Stock Exchange (AMEX), and National Association of Securities Dealers Automated Quotations (NASDAQ) exchanges, which is developed and distributed by Standard & Poor's Corporation. The sample excludes American Depositary Receipts (ADRs), which are non-U.S. common stock listings on these exchanges.

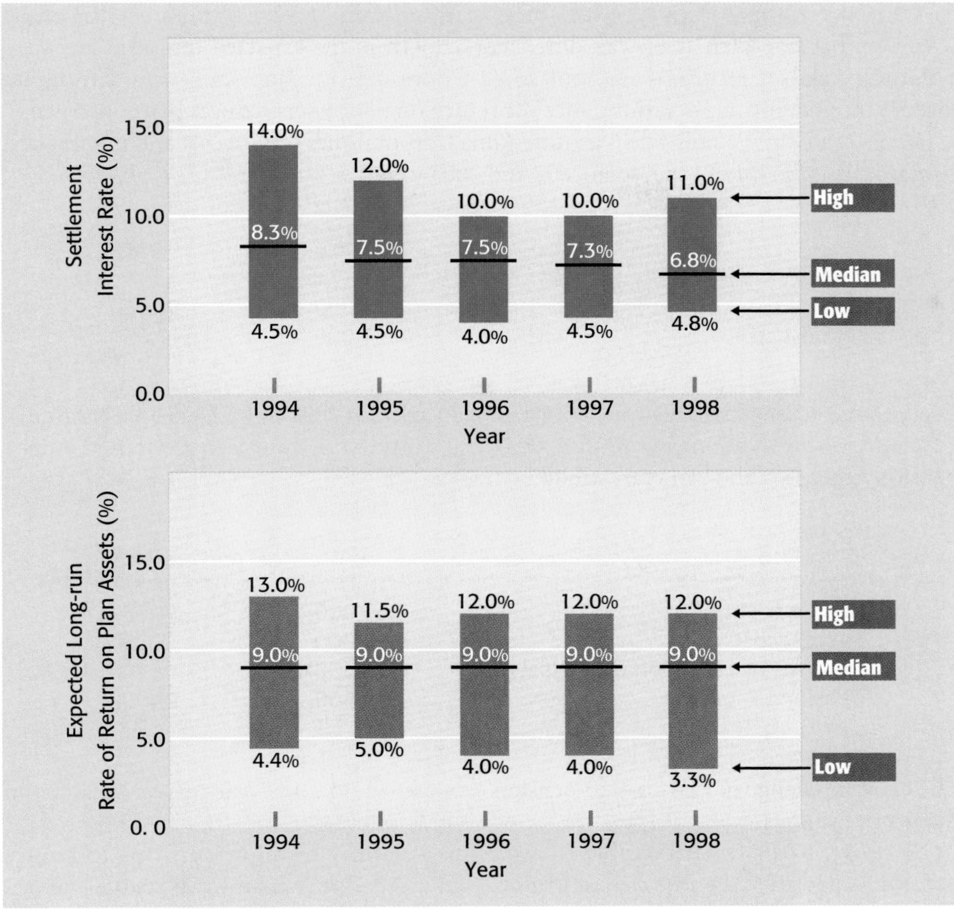

Figure 14.2

PENSION SETTLEMENT RATE AND EXPECTED LONG-RUN RATE OF RETURN ON PLAN ASSETS 1994–1998

Sample consists of all AMEX and NYSE firms with defined benefit plans.

Source: Standard & Poor's Research Insight(SM) as data source; methodology not verified or controlled by Standard & Poor's.

each bar represent the high and low rates used by firms in that year; the line crossing each bar represents the median rate. As you can see, there is considerable variation in both rates across firms within a given year. For example, the settlement rates in 1994 range from 4.5% to 14%, with a median of 8.3%; the expected long-run rate of return on plan assets in 1994 ranges from 4.4% to 13%, with a median of 9%. Throughout this five-year period the median expected rate of return on plan assets remained at 9%, while the median settlement rate varied from 6.8% in 1998 to 8.3% in 1994. Since interest costs can comprise a large portion of total pension charges (see Figure 14.4 on p. 704), even small changes in the discount rate can have a material impact on pension expense. Changes in interest rate assumptions can have an even more dramatic effect on the estimated present value of pension obligations.[7]

Components 4 through 6—Smoothing Devices Uncertainty not only complicates the measurement of service cost and interest cost, it also means realizations will likely differ from expectations. For example, the actual return on pension plan assets will differ from the expected return, and actual turnover and pay increases will differ from actuarial assumptions. These deviations between expected and actual events—if recognized immediately—would inject volatility into the periodic measure of pension expense. Managers abhor earnings volatility, and, not surprisingly, strong sentiments for reducing this volatility emerged early in the exposure draft stage of *SFAS No. 87*. Components 4 through 6 of the annual pension expense calculation are designed to smooth this volatility.

Our discussion now turns to each of these components of pension expense.

[7] An article in *Forbes* estimates that a 1% decrease in the discount rate can boost the estimated pension liability by as much as 10% to 15% for the typical firm. See "The Surplus Vanishes," *Forbes* (November 17, 1986), p. 94. The reason for this large multiplier effect is discussed more fully later in the chapter.

COMPONENT 4—RECOGNIZED GAINS OR LOSSES In an uncertain environment, the actual return on pension plan assets can differ markedly from the expected return in any year. Volatility in asset returns—without some smoothing mechanism—would translate directly into net income volatility since the return on plan assets reduces pension expense.

To illustrate this volatility, let's assume Anna Corporation's service cost and interest cost components of pension expense in 2002 and 2003 were:

	2002	2003
Service cost	$1,000	$1,050
Interest cost	1,000	1,050

In addition, assume that the *actual* return on plan assets in 2002 was $1,500 but (because of adverse market conditions) was only $100 in 2003. If no smoothing were permitted, Anna's pension expense in the two years would be:

	2002	2003
Service cost	$1,000	$1,050
Interest cost	1,000	1,050
Less: Actual return on plan assets	(1,500)	(100)
Pension expense	$ 500	$2,000

The extreme change in year-to-year pension expense would cause year-to-year volatility in the firm's earnings.

SFAS No. 87 makes it possible to avert this volatility by allowing firms to reduce pension expense by the *expected* return on plan assets rather than by the actual return. This result is accomplished in two steps. First, firms select a target return that they *expect* to earn on plan assets in the long run. Second, any difference between this expected return and the actual return that is earned in a given year is kept track of "off the balance sheet" and the cumulative balance of these unrecognized gains (losses) is monitored periodically for possible inclusion in pension expense at a later time.

To show how the smoothing mechanism works, assume that Anna's pension plan assets were $10,000 and $11,500 at the start of 2002 and 2003, respectively. Further assume that given the riskiness of the investment strategy selected, Anna expects to earn a return of 9% on average each year. Under the *SFAS No. 87* smoothing approach, Anna's pension expense would be reduced by the *expected* return in each year—$900 in 2002 ($10,000 × 9%) and $1,035 in 2003 ($11,500 × 9%). This is pension expense Component 3, discussed earlier. The difference between the expected and actual return in each year is deferred using an off-balance sheet smoothing device called the **unrecognized gain or loss.** Specifically:

		2002		2003
Service cost		$1,000		$1,050
Interest cost		1,000		1,050
Less:				
Actual return on plan assets	($1,500)		($100)	
Unrecognized gain (loss)	600		(935)	
Expected return on plan assets		(900)		(1,035)
Pension expense		$1,100		$1,065

In years like 2002 when the actual return ($1,500) exceeds the expected return ($900), there is an unrecognized gain. In years like 2003, there is an unrecognized loss of $935 since the actual return ($100) is less than the expected return ($1,035). By using the ***expected*** return to compute pension expense and deferring the unrecognized gain or loss, the year-to-year change in Anna Corporation's pension expense was only $35 ($1,100 − $1,065). This is much smaller than the $1,500 year-to-year change in pension expense if ***actual*** return on plan assets had been subtracted ($2,000 − $500, on the previous page).

Figure 14.3 graphically shows how large the differences between the actual and expected return on pension plan assets can be. The data in Figure 14.3 come from the pension footnotes for General Electric Company (GE) for the years 1991 through 1999, excerpts of which follow the figure. While GE's long-run expected rate of return on plan assets was 9.5% over the entire period, the actual rate of return ranged from a high of 20.8% in 1995 to a low of 1.2% in 1994. Figure 14.3 depicts the actual and expected dollar return on plan

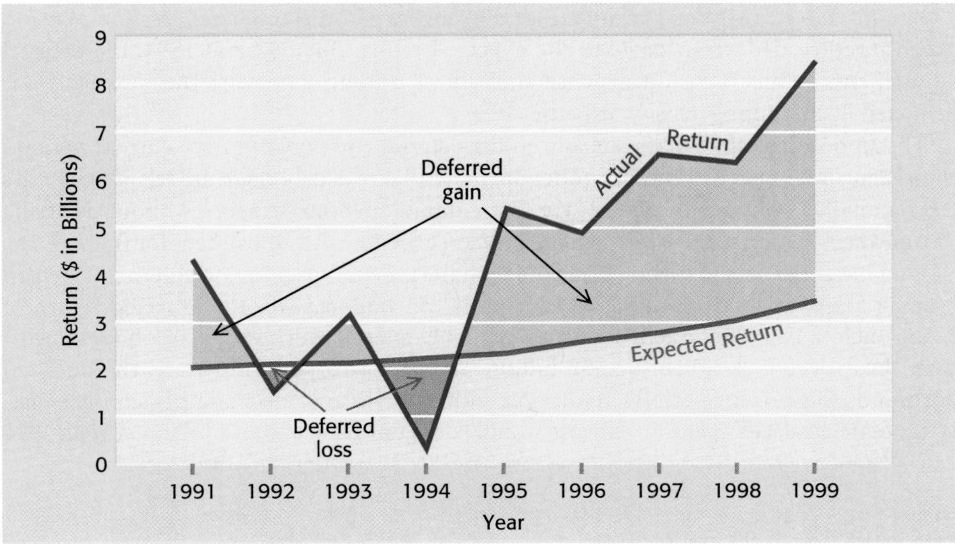

Figure 14.3

GENERAL ELECTRIC COMPANY COMPARISON OF ACTUAL AND EXPECTED RETURN ON PENSION PLAN ASSETS

Excerpts from General Electric Company Footnotes Underlying Figure 14.3 Data

($ in billions)	1991	1992	1993	1994	1995	1996	1997	1998	1999
Actual dollar return on pension plan assets	$ 4.331	$ 1.562	$ 3.221	$ 0.316	$ 5.439	$ 4.916	$ 6.587	$ 6.363	$ 8.472
Market value of plan assets[1]	$22.933	$26.133	$26.466	$27.193	$26.166	$30.200	$33.686	$38.742	$43.447
Actual return on plan assets	18.9%	6.0%	12.2%	1.2%	20.8%	16.3%	19.6%	16.4%	19.5%
Long-run expected return	9.5%	9.5%	9.5%	9.5%	9.5%	9.5%	9.5%	9.5%	9.5%
Expected dollar return on plan assets[2]	$2.059	$2.146	$2.155	$2.267	$2.352	$2.587	$2.721	$3.024	$3.407
Unrecognized gains or losses (actual minus expected return)	$2.272	($0.584)	$1.066	($1.951)	$3.087	$2.329	$3.866	$3.339	$5.065

[1]This is the value of the plan assets at the *start* of each year.

[2]You may notice that the expected dollar return for any year is not equal to the beginning market value of plan assets times the expected return rate. To illustrate using 1999, we get:

Market value of plan assets ($43.447) × expected return (.095) = $4.127 Expected dollar return

This amount differs from the $3.407 reported by GE. Why? The reason is that firms are allowed to compute the expected return on a moving-average of the market value of plan assets over a period not exceeding the preceding five years. GE apparently did this, so the 9.5% expected return was applied to some measure of late 1990s average plan assets. We do not have enough information to compute the $3.407 directly.

Source: General Electric Company Annual Reports, 1991–99.

assets by year. The actual return displays considerable variability from year to year; the expected dollar return gradually increases, reflecting a stable expected return rate (9.5%) times an increasing pension asset base. For the 1993–1995 period, the actual dollar return on GE's plan assets goes from $3.221 billion in 1993 to $316 million in 1994 to $5.439 billion in 1995. GE's earnings before taxes and accounting charges for the 1993–1995 period were ($ in billions) $6.136, $8.661, and $9.737, respectively. Clearly, without some mechanism to smooth out the big swings in the yearly returns on pension assets, considerable volatility would be introduced into GE's bottom line.

The data highlighted in the bottom row of the table following Figure 14.3 on the previous page is the deferred portion of each year's actual return. This is the unrecognized gain or loss, and it is represented by the vertical distance between the actual and expected return lines in Figure 14.3. Note that in seven of the years (1991, 1993, 1995, 1996, 1997, 1998, and 1999), this deferral increases pension expense since it *reduces* the pension expense return deduction *down* to the expected return. In 1992 and 1994, the deferral adjustments reduce pension expense since these amounts *increase* the return that is deducted in computing pension expense.

The smoothing effect that results from the deferral component of the current period's actual return on plan assets is illustrated in Table 14.6 (the data there are taken from GE's 1994 and 1995 pension footnotes). We first compute pension expense without deferring the unexpected return, then we calculate pension expense with adjustment for the deferral.

Looking at the data following Figure 14.3 on the previous page, in 1994 the actual return on plan assets was $316 million, which was $1.951 billion *below* the expected return of $2.267 billion. In 1995 the actual return was $5.439 billion, which was $3.087 billion *higher* than the expected return of $2.352 billion. As these two years illustrate, the deferred portion of the current period's return can either increase or decrease pension expense. Without deferral, GE's pension expense would have gone from a $1.671 billion *debit* in 1994

Table 14.6 ■ GENERAL ELECTRIC COMPANY

Smoothing Effect of Deferring Unexpected Gains or Losses

($ in millions)		1994		1995
Without Deferral				
Component 1: Service cost		$ 496		$ 469
Component 2: Interest cost		1,491		1,580
Actual return on plan assets		(316)		(5,439)
Pension expense *without deferral* of unexpected gain or loss		$1,671 **DR**		($3,390) **CR**
		Year-to-year "swing" of $5,061		
With Deferral				
Component 1: Service cost		$ 496		$ 469
Component 2: Interest cost		1,491		1,580
Actual return on plan assets	(316)		(5,439)	
Deferral of unexpected gain (or loss)	(1,951)		3,087	
Component 3: Expected return on plan assets		(2,267)		(2,352)
Pension expense *with deferral* of unexpected return		($ 280) **CR**		($ 303) **CR**
		Year-to-year "swing" of $23		

to a \$3.390 billion *credit* in 1995, a swing of \$5.061 billion.[8] By deferring the unexpected gain or loss, the year-to-year change is reduced to only \$23 million, as shown in Table 14.6.

Companies are free to use a rate for computing the *expected* return on plan assets that differs from the discount rate used for service and interest cost. That makes it possible to lower pension expense in the short-run by using an expected asset return rate that is higher than the discount rate. Large disparities between the two rates affect the pension expense calculation and should be carefully monitored by analysts since these disparities represent a possible earnings management vehicle.

HOW COMPONENT 4 IS MEASURED If gains and losses do not offset one another over time, the cumulative off-balance sheet deferred amounts continue to grow. When this happens, some adjustment is needed to correct for the past smoothing. This is the role of component 4—recognized gains or losses.

Cumulative off-balance sheet net gains or losses can arise from three causes:

1. Cumulative differences between actual and expected returns on pension plan assets—as illustrated previously
2. Cumulative differences between actuarial assumptions and actual experience—for example, employee turnover, pay increases, and longevity beyond retirement
3. Changes in assumptions—for example, a change in the discount rate used for computing service cost and interest cost.

Because pension accounting requires numerous estimates of future events, differences between forecasted amounts and subsequent occurrences should be expected. These differences mean that *past* measures of pension expense were misstated:

- Cumulative asset return differences mean that the difference between actual return on plan assets and expected return on plan assets did not offset one another over time.
- Cumulative actuarial assumption differences mean that service cost (component 1) was either over- or understated.
- Changes in the assumed discount rate mean both service cost (component 1) and interest cost (component 2) were misstated in some previous years.

These misstatements of *past* pension expense exist because the FASB responded to corporate managers' dislike for income volatility and opted to smooth period-to-period fluctuations. *SFAS No. 87* does not require each year's results to correspond perfectly to market returns or actuarial experience. ***However, if the smoothing adjustments do not offset one another over time, the periodic differences will ultimately accumulate and exceed some threshold level. The FASB believes these past errors must be corrected once this threshold is exceeded.*** Rather than requiring the total correction be made at one time, the FASB again opted for a smoothing approach and allowed the correction for cumulative *past* errors to be spread over a series of *future* years.

Here's how the component 4 adjustment mechanism works. At the *start* of each reporting year, the cumulative unrecognized off-balance sheet gain (or loss) is computed. A portion of this cumulative gain or loss will be amortized over current and future years if it exceeds a certain materiality threshold called the **corridor.** This threshold is defined as 10% of the *larger* of the following two numbers, which are measured at the *beginning* of the year: (1) The present value of pension obligations based on assumed future compensation levels (called the **projected benefit obligation**), or (2) The **market-related value** of pension plan assets. If

> In *SFAS No. 87*, "market-related value" of pension plan assets is a technical term. It can be either (1) the fair market value of the assets, or (2) some moving-average type smoothed value that recognizes changes in value more slowly (over not more than five years).

[8] These numbers ignore any additional amortization due to components 4, 5, or 6. GE's earnings before taxes and accounting changes were \$8.661 billion and \$9.737 billion in 1994 and 1995, respectively. So reducing the pension expense "swing" by \$5.038 billion (i.e., \$5.061 billion versus \$23 million) is significant in relation to pre-tax earnings.

the 10% threshold is exceeded, the excess cumulative gain or loss is amortized straight-line over the estimated **average remaining service period** of active employees. To illustrate:

The average remaining service period is an actuarial computation—it's an estimate of the average number of years over which existing employees are expected to continue on the job.

On January 1, 2001 Dore Corporation had a cumulative unrecognized gain of $1,600,000 arising from (1) differences between actual and expected returns on plan assets, (2) differences between actuarial assumptions and actual experience, and (3) changes in interest rate assumptions. The market-related value of pension plan assets on that date was $10,000,000, and the projected benefit obligation was $8,500,000. The estimated average remaining service period of active employees is 15 years.

The 10% threshold is $1,000,000, which is 10% of $10,000,000 (the larger of the $8,500,000 obligation and the $10,000,000 asset totals). Because the cumulative unrecognized gain of $1,600,000 is larger than the $1,000,000 threshold, component 4 is triggered. The $600,000 amount in excess of the threshold will be amortized over 15 years. This means that pension expense component 4 will be *credited* for $40,000 of the unrecognized gain ($600,000 ÷ 15), thereby *reducing* pension expense. ($40,000 is the minimum gain that must be recognized. A systematic method consistently applied to both gains and losses that results in a larger amount is permissible.)[9]

If there were no future misestimates, the $560,000 unamortized excess—$600,000 minus the $40,000 of 2001 amortization—would be totally taken into income over the ensuing 14 years. Realistically, pension accounting requires many estimates of uncertain future events. Uncertainty means that further misestimates are likely. Consequently, *SFAS No. 87* requires that the computation illustrated in the example be redone at the start of each subsequent year to determine that year's pension expense component 4.

Let's assume that one year later—on January 1, 2002—Dore Corporation's cumulative unrecognized gain has fallen to $250,000, plan assets are $11,000,000, and the projected benefit obligation is $9,000,000. The 10% threshold is now $1,100,000 (i.e., $11,000,000 × 10%). This is larger than the unrecognized gain. The threshold is not triggered, and no amortization would be required in 2002.

It is easy to understand why the FASB chose the projected benefit obligation and the market–related value of pension plan assets as the two benchmarks that potentially trigger the component 4 amortization. Measures of projected benefit obligations and plan assets constitute the "critical 10% corridor" because the factors giving rise to the cumulative gain or loss represent misestimates of the "real" pension plan obligations and assets.

In other words, **cumulative asset gains or losses** occur because the rate chosen for the expected return on plan assets in the computation of pension expense either understated or overstated the actual increase in pension assets. Similarly, **cumulative obligation gains or losses** occur because the amount of service cost and/or interest cost included in pension expense either understated or overstated the actual increase in pension obligations. Thus, obligations and assets constitute the appropriate benchmarks for assessing when the cumulative error is "excessive." The 10% threshold is simply an arbitrary measure of this "excessiveness."

COMPONENT 5—AMORTIZATION OF UNRECOGNIZED TRANSITION ASSET OR OBLIGATION Before *SFAS No. 87* was issued, there was usually a disparity between the value of pension plan assets and the present value of the pension obligation. Some plans were overfunded (i.e., assets exceeded obligations), while others were underfunded (obligations exceeded assets). The FASB sought to reduce future periods' pension expense charges for overfunded plans and to increase future pension expense for underfunded plans.

The following example illustrates the approach:

Rett Corporation adopted *SFAS No. 87* on January 1, 1987. On that date the fair value of the pension plan assets was $238,000,000, and the projected benefit obligation was $202,000,000. The actuarial estimate of the average remaining service period of employees who are expected to receive benefits under the plan was 18 years.

9 *SFAS No. 87,* para. 33.

The FASB required that the amount of overfunding or underfunding be computed at the time *SFAS No. 87* was first adopted. To determine the funding status, a firm must compare the amount of the pension liability and the pension plan assets. The difference—the **transition asset or liability**—is amortized over the average remaining service period of employees who are expected to receive benefits under the plan. Rett's $202,000,000 projected benefit obligation (PBO) is the discounted present value of the expected pension payments, which takes into account expected pay raises over future years. This PBO is then compared to the fair value of plan assets—here $238,000,000. The funded status of the plan at adoption was an *overfunding* of $36,000,000. This transition asset amount will be amortized as component 5 over 18 years on a straight-line basis. Therefore, component 5 for Rett Corporation will be a $2,000,000 *credit* (reduction) to pension expense for each of the years 1987 through 2004. (Amortization of a transition liability results in a debit—addition—to pension expense.)

When *SFAS No. 87* was adopted, if a firm's balance sheet included either a "Prepaid pension cost" or "Accrued pension cost" account (as described on pp. 705–706), the transition asset or liability is adjusted for these amounts. See *SFAS No. 87*, para. 77.

However, if the average remaining service period is less than 15 years, the firm may still elect to use a 15-year amortization period.

Components 5 and 4 both represent a smoothing approach for correcting *past* errors in the computation of pension expense. In the case of component 5, the pension expense errors arose prior to the adoption of *SFAS No. 87*—that is, a plan that was overfunded at transition presumably used asset earnings rate assumptions that were too low, or service cost estimates that were too high, or both. In the case of component 4, similar errors arose *after* the adoption of *SFAS No. 87*. In either case the effect is the same: Past errors in computing pension expense are corrected in a smoothed fashion over current and *future* years.

COMPONENT 6—RECOGNIZED PRIOR SERVICE COST Pension plans are frequently amended to provide increased benefits to employees. A firm may do this because increases in retirees' living costs warrant an increase in pension benefits. When a firm retroactively enhances the benefits provided by its pension plan, it means past pension expense and pension funding—which were both based on the "old" pension plan terms—were too low. This also means that when a firm enhances its pension plan, it immediately increases its projected benefit obligation under the plan. The dollar amount of the increase in the projected benefit obligation due to plan enhancements is called **prior service cost.**

Pension plan amendments sometimes reduce benefits—for instance, when unions "give-back" previously obtained benefits to help the firm avoid bankruptcy and preserve jobs.

Here's how prior service cost arises:

> Schiller Corporation's pension plan granted employees a pension of 2% of ending salary at retirement for each year of service to a maximum of 30 years. Therefore, an employee with 30 years of service at Schiller could retire with a pension equal to 60% of his or her salary at retirement.
>
> Management at Schiller Corporation now believes that the 60% pension maximum is inadequate given existing general economic conditions. The pension plan is retroactively changed on January 1, 2001. Under the revised plan, employees qualify for a pension of 2.25% of ending salary at retirement for each year of service, again to a maximum of 30 years. Under the revised plan, the maximum pension is 67.5% of the employee's salary at retirement (2.25% × 30 years).

Firms retroactively enhance—or "sweeten"—pension plans for various reasons. One is to generate employee goodwill and loyalty to the organization; firms do this to retain a quality workforce. Another reason for retroactive pension enhancement arises as a result of union demands in labor negotiations.

Even though these sweeteners are computed on the basis of services rendered in prior periods, the benefits to the firm will be realized in future periods. The benefits of retroactive plan enhancements are realized by the firm in future periods because of decreased employee turnover or better labor relations. Accordingly, *SFAS No. 87* allows these prior service costs to be amortized into pension expense on a straight-line basis over the expected service lives of employees who are expected to receive benefits under the plan.

If Schiller's plan enhancement increased the projected benefit obligation by $14,000,000 and if the average remaining service period of employees expected to receive benefits under the plan is 10 years, then $1,400,000 would be added to pension expense over each of the next 10 years. This is the role of component 6.

Relative Magnitude of Pension Expense Components

Figure 14.4 shows the relative magnitude of the various components of pension expense for a sample of firms over the 1987–1990 period.[10] The bars above the zero line represent debits that *increased* pension expense; the bars below the line depict credits that *decreased* pension expense. The bar at the end of each year's data (PENX)—represents that portion of the total charges to pension expense that remain after offsetting the credit items against the debit items (the **net pension expense** reported on the income statement).

Three items shown in Figure 14.4 are noteworthy. First, for the average firm, the service cost (SVC) and interest cost (INT) components are fairly stable through time. The interest component is more than twice as large as the service cost component (an average of $0.69 per share versus $0.28 per share, respectively, over the four years), which means the cumulative pension obligation from past years of service far exceeds the obligation that arises from the current period employee service. One potential explanation for this is the prevalence of retroactive plan enhancements; another is an aging workforce.

Second, in contrast to the stable service and interest cost components, the actual return on plan assets (RPA) varies considerably over this four-year period, ranging from a high of $1.44 per share in 1989 to a low of −$0.02 per share in 1990. This variability reflects the general fortunes of stocks during this period, which comprise a major portion of many pension fund portfolios. Without the smoothing effects that result from deferring the unexpected return on

Figure 14.4

PENSION EXPENSE COMPONENTS (1987–1990)

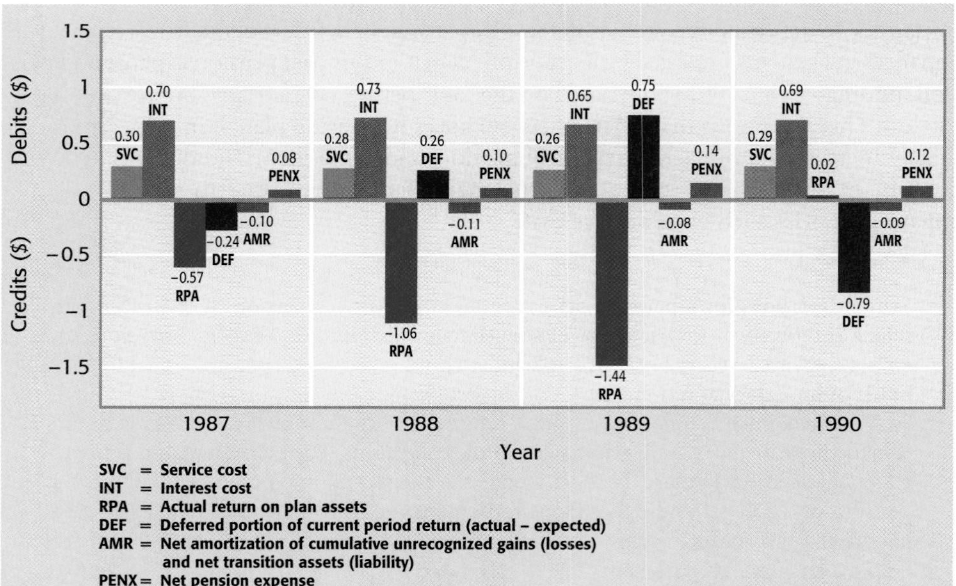

All amounts are shown in dollars per share.
Source: From Barth, Beaver, and Landsman, op cit. (see footnote 10 on this page). Copyright 1993, Association for Investment Management and Research. Reproduced and republished from Financial Analysts Journal with permission from the Association for Investment Management and Research. All Rights Reserved. CFA(R) and Chartered Financial Analysis™ are trademarks owned by the Association for Investment Management and Research (AIMR(R)). The AIMR does not endorse, promote, review, or warrant the accuracy of the products or services offered by Prentice Hall.

[10] The average values for the 1987–1990 period are based on a sample of 300 firms representing a broad cross section of industries. See M. E. Barth, W. H. Beaver, and W. R. Landsman, "A Structural Analysis of Pension Disclosures Under SFAS 87 and Their Relation to Share Prices," *Financial Analysts Journal* (January–February, 1993), pp. 18–26.

plan assets (as *SFAS No. 87* allows), pension expense would have been quite volatile over this period. With the deferral (DEF) of unrecognized gains or losses (note in some years this increases pension expense while in other years it decreases pension expense), the volatility in actual return is offset, leaving a relatively stable credit adjustment to pension expense for the *expected* return on plan assets.

Third, the net amortization of components 4 through 6 (AMR) is a credit to pension expense of roughly $0.09 per share. This suggests that the average firm's pension plan was overfunded at transition and/or that there are cumulative unrecognized gains being amortized as a reduction to pension expense.

The net effect of the various smoothing procedures allowed under *SFAS No. 87* is apparent in the pattern of *net* pension expense amounts—the PENX bar—in Figure 14.4. Although individual components of pension expense are relatively large and actual return on plan assets is quite volatile, the net pension expense amount is relatively stable, averaging about $0.11 per share over the period.

RECAP

Estimates pervade pension accounting. When these estimates need to be adjusted, the adjustment could conceivably be recorded all at once. Doing this would make pension expense volatile from year to year. The FASB chose a different approach for adjusting pension estimates and plan changes. Components 4 through 6 are designed to be smoothing devices. When an adjustment is made, its effect is initially deferred and brought into pension expense slowly over a series of future years.

The Journal Entry to Record Pension Expense and Funding

To illustrate the journal entry for pension expense, let's assume that Northern Corporation disclosed the following components in its pension footnote at December 31, 2001:

Service cost	$23,000
Interest cost	42,500
Expected return on plan assets	(38,250)
Components 4–6	22,750
2001 Pension expense	$50,000

In years in which the entire amount of pension expense—$50,000 in this example—is funded by payments to the plan trustee, the entry is straightforward:

DR Pension expense	$50,000	
CR Cash		$50,000

However, a firm is not required to fund the full amount of the pension expense provision each period. (Factors that affect firms' funding policies are discussed in the next section.) When the amount of funding differs from the recognized expense, an additional balancing debit or credit must be established. If Northern Corporation chose to fund $53,000 in 2001, the entry would be:

DR Pension expense	$50,000	
DR Prepaid pension cost	3,000	
CR Cash		$53,000

The "Prepaid pension cost" account would be shown as an *asset* on the December 31, 2001 balance sheet.

If Northern had chosen to make a funding payment of only $44,000 in 2001, the entry would be:

DR Pension expense	$50,000	
CR Cash		$44,000
CR Unfunded accrued pension cost		6,000

The "Unfunded accrued pension cost" account in this entry would appear on the balance sheet as a *liability*.

The Pension Funding Decision

Legislation and income tax rules have a strong impact on pension plan funding. We first explain why. Then we outline the factors that firms with defined benefit pension plans use to determine the amount of annual pension funding.

The U.S. Congress enacted legislation to regulate private U.S. pension plans in 1974. The Employees Retirement Income Security Act (ERISA) was designed to protect workers covered by company- or industry-sponsored pension plans. This legislation was deemed necessary because some companies with largely unfunded pension plans went out of business. When Studebaker Corporation—once a major automobile manufacturer—experienced severe economic hardship and declared bankruptcy in 1964, its pension liabilities greatly exceeded its plan assets. The Studebaker retirees were unprotected and consequently lost most of their promised pension. Such hardships ultimately motivated legislation designed to prevent recurrences. ERISA established minimum funding guidelines. A pension plan sponsor is obliged to fund at least the annual service cost computed under the plan. The requirement to fund service cost is suspended if the plan is *over*funded at the start of the plan year.

> In addition, when pension plans have been retroactively "sweetened," the prior service costs generated by the sweetening must be funded over 30 to 40 years. Furthermore, shortfalls arising from changes in assumptions and actuarial gains and losses must be funded over periods ranging from 5 to 30 years. For details, see H. E. Winklevoss, *Pension Mathematics With Numerical Illustrations,* 2nd ed. (Philadelphia: University of Pennsylvania Press, 1993.)

> ERISA has its own guidelines for determining whether a plan is overfunded or underfunded. These guidelines differ from those in *SFAS No. 87* because ERISA allows plan sponsors to use a broader range of actuarial and other assumptions.

The U.S. tax law also influences pension plan funding. Because plan contributions are tax deductible—subject to a constraint discussed later—and plan earnings are nontaxable to the plan sponsor, there is a tax incentive to overfund pension plans. Because of this incentive, the tax law places limits on the deductibility of contributions to already overfunded pension plans. Consequently, firms with overfunded plans limit subsequent funding to that amount which is deductible for tax purposes.

Finally, firms with pension plans have a wide range of other uses for cash flows generated by operating activities. Examples include plant expansion, corporate acquisitions, debt retirement, and dividend increases. So firms sometimes reduce or even forego funding of the current period's pension expense—provided minimum ERISA funding guidelines are satisfied—to meet competing investment or financing cash needs.

The longer term pension funding strategy that a firm chooses to follow is determined not only by its internal cash flow needs but also by many complex economic forces. Two studies seek to explain variation in firms' funding strategies by examining the relationship between *funding ratios*—plan assets divided by accrued pension obligations—and a variety of variables that represent the economic incentives (and costs) associated with pension funding.[11] These economic incentives can be broadly classified as (1) tax in-

---

[11] See J. R. Francis and S. A. Reiter, "Determinants of Corporate Pension Funding Strategy," *Journal of Accounting and Economics* (April 1987), pp. 35–60; and J. K. Thomas, "Corporate Taxes and Defined Benefit Pension Plans," *Journal of Accounting and Economics* (July 1988), pp. 199–238.

centives, (2) finance incentives, (3) labor incentives, and (4) contracting/political cost incentives.[12]

The findings were:

- Firms with high marginal tax rates tend to have higher funding ratios—higher marginal tax rates provide an incentive to overfund.
- Firms with less stringent capital constraints and larger union membership tend to have higher funding ratios.
- Firms with more "precarious" debt/equity ratios (that is, firms close to violating debt covenant restrictions) tend to fund a lower proportion of their pension obligations.

In general, variables designed to measure political costs were not found to be significant determinants of pension funding ratios.

While economic incentives appear to influence long-run corporate pension funding strategies, our understanding of this multidimensional decision is far from complete. **RECAP**

The Pension Footnote

Exhibit 14.1 on the following two pages reproduces the pension footnote from the 1999 Annual Report of General Electric Company. We will use this disclosure to discuss several elements of pension reporting.

The actuarial assumptions portion of G.E.'s footnote in Exhibit 14.1 (page 709) provides information about the discount rate (7.75%) used in measuring components 1 and 2 of pension expense, the assumed rate of increase in salary levels built into the projected benefit obligation computation (5%), and the expected return on plan assets (9.5%).

In the next section, we discuss other information contained in Exhibit 14.1 and explain how one determines the funded status of the pension plans.

Funded Status Disclosure

We explained earlier that neither pension plan assets nor liabilities appear on the balance sheet of the plan sponsor but are instead shown on the separate statements of the plan trustee. The Wildcat Corporation example (Tables 14.2 through 14.4) showed that when the future was known with certainty the (off-balance sheet) pension assets are exactly equal to the (off-balance sheet) pension liability. In the more complex real world, where future events are uncertain and changes in pension assumptions occur, ***the off-balance sheet pension assets and liabilities will usually differ.*** When pension assets exceed liabilities, a plan is **overfunded.** If pension liabilities exceed plan assets, a plan is **underfunded.** Since both the pension plan assets and liabilities are off the plan sponsor's balance sheet, the **funded status** of the plan can only be determined from footnote disclosures. This funded status disclosure is important to statement readers, since the plan sponsor—the reporting entity—is ultimately responsible for underfunded pension plans. Moreover, sometimes the reporting entity can reclaim a portion of the excess in overfunded plans. So, information about the funded status helps analysts assess the financial condition of the sponsor. In this section we illustrate and interpret the funded status footnote disclosure.

---

[12] The reader is referred to the articles cited in footnote 11 for a more complete discussion of each of these incentives and their hypothesized effect on firms' pension funding strategy.

Exhibit 14.1 ■ GENERAL ELECTRIC COMPANY

Edited, Condensed 1999 Annual Report Pension Benefits Footnote

Principal pension plans are the GE Pension Plan and the GE Supplementary Pension Plan.

The GE Pension Plan provides benefits to certain U.S. employees based on the greater of a formula recognizing career earnings or a formula recognizing length of service and final average earnings. Benefit provisions are subject to collective bargaining. At the end of 1999, the GE Pension Plan covered approximately 470,000 participants. . . .

The GE Supplementary Pension Plan is a pay-as-you-go plan providing supplementary retirement benefits primarily to higher-level, longer-service U.S. employees.

The effect on operations of principal pension plans is as follows:

Effect on Operations

($ in millions)	1999	1998
Service cost for benefits earned[(a)]	$ (693)	$ (625)
Interest cost on benefit obligation	(1,804)	(1,749)
Expected return on plan assets	3,407	3,024
Net actuarial gain recognized	467	365
SFAS No. 87 transition gain	154	154
Prior service cost	(151)	(153)
Total pension plan income	$1,380	$1,016

[(a)]Net of participant contributions.

Funding policy for the GE Pension Plan is to contribute amounts sufficient to meet minimum funding requirements as set forth in employee benefit and tax laws plus such additional amounts as GE may determine to be appropriate. GE has not made contributions since 1987 because the fully funded status of the GE Pension Plan precludes current tax deduction and because any GE contribution would require payment of excise taxes.

Changes in the projected benefit obligation for principal pension plans follow.

Projected Benefit Obligation

($ in millions)	1999	1998
Balance at January 1	$27,572	$25,874
Service cost for benefits earned[(a)]	693	625
Interest cost on benefit obligation	1,804	1,749
Participant contributions	122	112
Actuarial (gain)/loss[(b)]	(2,790)	1,050
Benefits paid	(1,879)	(1,838)
Balance at December 31	$25,522	$27,572

[(a)]Net of participant contributions.
[(b)]Principally associated with discount rate changes.

To understand the funded status of a plan, we must first understand what factors cause the pension plan assets and liabilities to change over time. Figure 14.5 on page 710 displays the causes for increases and decreases in plan assets. *SFAS No. 132* requires that plan sponsors disclose these increases and decreases in the pension footnote.[13] Using G.E.'s fair

[13] In addition to the items shown in Figure 14.5, *SFAS No. 132* (para. 5) requires—if applicable—disclosure of (1) changes in plan assets arising from exchange rate changes for pension plans of certain foreign subsidiaries, and (2) changes in plan assets arising from business combinations, divestitures, and plan settlements.

Exhibit 14.1 ■ *(continued)*

Changes in the fair value of assets for principal pension plans follow.

Fair Value of Assets

($ in millions)	1999	1998
Balance at January 1	$43,447	$38,742
Actual return on plan assets	8,472	6,363
Employer contributions	81	68
Participant contributions	122	112
Benefits paid	(1,879)	(1,838)
Balance at December 31	$50,243	$43,447

Plan assets are held in trust and consist mainly of common stock and fixed-income investments. GE common stock represented 9.8% and 7.5% of trust assets at year-end 1999 and 1998, respectively.

GE recorded assets and liabilities for principal pension plans as follows:

Prepaid Pension Asset

December 31 ($ in millions)	1999	1998
Fair value of plan assets	$50,243	$43,447
Add (deduct) unrecognized balances:		
Prior service cost	699	850
SFAS No. 87 transition asset	(154)	(308)
Net actuarial gain	(16,850)	(9,462)
Projected benefit obligation	(25,522)	(27,572)
→ Accrued pension liability	981	797
→ Prepaid pension asset	$ 9,397	$ 7,752

Actuarial assumptions used to determine costs and benefit obligations for principal pension plans follow.

Actuarial Assumptions

December 31	1999	1998
Discount rate	7.75%	6.75%
Compensation increases	5.0	5.0
Return on assets for the year	9.5	9.5

Experience gains and losses, as well as the effects of changes in actuarial assumptions and plan provisions, are amortized over the average future service period of employees.

value of assets disclosures on this page in Exhibit 14.1 as a concrete example, we discuss the separate elements of Figure 14.5:

- Item A represents the beginning-of-period market value of the pension plan assets. For G.E., the January 1, 1999 amount totaled $43,447 million.
- The dollar value of plan assets is increased by Item B, the actual return on plan assets. In very bad investment years, Item B can be negative, thereby reducing plan assets. G.E.'s 1999 actual return on plan assets was a positive $8,472 million.
- Plan assets are further increased by Item C, the amount that the plan sponsor funds during the period. G.E.'s 1999 contributions were $81 million.[14]

[14] The contributions were made to the GE Supplementary Pension Plan, which is a pay-as-you-go plan. The other plan—the GE Pension Plan—is fully funded. We are told in Exhibit 14.1 that G.E. has not contributed to this plan since 1987 because doing so yields no tax deduction and triggers payment of excise taxes.

Figure 14.5

CAUSES OF INCREASES AND DECREASES IN PLAN ASSETS

Plan Assets

DR	CR
A. Beginning balance of plan assets at market value	E. Plan trustee's distribution of plan assets (i.e., pension payments) to plan retirees
B. Actual return on plan assets during the period (dividends, interest, and change in market value)	
C. Contribution of additional plan assets during the period by the plan sponsor	
D. Contribution of additional plan assets during the period by the plan participants	
F. Ending balance of plan assets at market value ($A \pm B + C + D - E = F$)	

> Another measure of the pension liability is called the **accumulated benefit obligation,** or **ABO.** The ABO differs from the PBO because the ABO does not include projected salary increases between the statement date and the expected retirement date of employees. The PBO does.

- Plan assets are also increased by Item D, contributions by plan participants. During 1999, contributions by G.E. plan participants totaled $122 million.
- Retirees receive benefits during the period; these benefits are disbursed by the plan trustee and reduce plan assets, as indicated by Item E. Benefits paid to participants by the plan trustee in 1999 were $1,879 million.
- The end-of-period market value of plan assets is Item F. This amount totaled $50,243 million for the G.E. plans.

Figure 14.6 shows changes in the pension plan liability—the PBO. *SFAS No. 132* also requires that plan sponsors disclose these increases and decreases in the pension footnote.[15] We use G.E.'s projected benefit obligation disclosures in Exhibit 14.1 (p. 708) to explain the elements in Figure 14.6:

- Item G is the start-of-period present value of expected future benefits that will ultimately be paid both to active and already retired employees. The 1999 G.E. beginning amount is $27,572 million.
- Item H represents the increase in benefits that active employees continue to earn from additional years of work. This increase in the projected benefit obligation is service cost. G.E.'s service cost in 1999 was $693 million.
- As time passes, the present value of future pension benefit payouts becomes larger because the number of discount periods is getting smaller. This increase in the discounted present value of the liability represents interest cost, which increases the PBO (as shown in Item I). G.E.'s 1999 interest cost was $1,804 million.
- Changes in economic and other social conditions cause firms to adjust promised benefits, as indicated by Item J. These prior service cost adjustments either raise

[15] In addition to the items shown in Figure 14.6, *SFAS No. 132* (para. 5) requires—if applicable—disclosure of (1) changes in the PBO arising from exchange rate changes for pension plans of certain foreign subsidiaries, and (2) changes in the PBO arising from business combinations, divestitures, plan settlements, and special termination benefits.

Figure 14.6

CAUSES OF INCREASES AND DECREASES IN PROJECTED BENEFIT OBLIGATION (PBO)

Projected Benefit Obligation

DR	CR
M. Plan trustee's distribution of plan assets (i.e., pension payments) to plan retirees	G. Beginning balance. Start-of-period discounted present value of expected pension benefits that will ultimately be paid
	H. Service cost during the period
	I. Interest cost during the period
	J. Change in promised benefits arising from plan amendments or curtailments during period
	K. Contribution of additional plan assets during the period by plan participants
	L. Actuarial gains or losses during period from changes in assumptions (i.e., mortality and turnover rates, interest rates, and so on.)
	N. Ending balance. End-of-period discounted present value of expected pension benefits (G + H + I ± J + K ± L − M = N)

the PBO (when the plan is sweetened) or reduce the PBO (when benefits are curtailed). G.E. did not alter promised benefits in 1999. Consequently, this amount is zero.

- The projected benefit obligation is also increased by Item K, contributions by plan participants. During 1999, such contributions totaled $122 million.
- The assumptions used in estimating the pension liability lead to gains or losses due to changing medical, lifestyle, and economic conditions. Denoted by Item L, these increases (or decreases) in the PBO can also arise from revised interest rate assumptions. Because of discount rate increases, this gain totaled $2,790 million in 1999.
- Item M represents the payout of retirement benefits to participants. This is the offsetting debit to the Item E credit in Figure 14.5. The 1999 amount for G.E. was $1,879 million.
- Finally, the ending PBO balance (Item N) is the net result of each of the preceding items. This amount totaled $25,522 million for the G.E. plans.

Because the pension assets and liabilities do not appear on the sponsor's balance sheet and because the plan can be either over- or underfunded, disclosure of the funded status of the plan is required under GAAP. Next, we examine this disclosure.

Reconciling Funded Status to Balance Sheet Amounts The smoothing objective that pervades *SFAS No. 87* keeps numerous gains and losses that have already occurred off the balance sheet and income statement. These deferred gains and losses are brought into income slowly over current and future years through components 4 through

6. Until these past gains and losses are totally amortized, the balance sheet will not reflect the current *funded status* of the pension plan. ***The current funded status of a pension plan at a given date is the difference between the fair value of the plan assets at that date and the discounted present value of the expected liability.*** This liability is computed using projected future compensation levels—this is the projected benefit obligation (PBO) previously discussed in conjunction with component 4. Exhibit 14.1 shows the current economic status of General Electric Company's pension plan at December 31, 1999. Plan assets totaled $50,243 million (p. 709) while the projected benefit obligation was only $25,522 million (p. 708). Therefore, the G.E. plan was overfunded by the excess of plan assets over plan liabilities—$24,721 million. ***This $24,721 million represents the current funded status of the pension plan at December 31, 1999.***

Because of the recognition delays that pervade *SFAS No. 87*, this $24,721 million does not correspond to the pension amounts shown on the December 31, 1999 balance sheet. The FASB believes the current funded status of the pension plan at the balance sheet date constitutes the benchmark against which companies' balance sheet pension accounts ought to be compared. For this reason, the FASB requires a footnote disclosure that reconciles—explains the difference between—the *current* funded status of the pension plan and the *recorded* balance sheet amounts. The table labeled "Prepaid pension asset" in Exhibit 14.1 (p. 709) is designed to provide this reconciliation.[16] Scrutiny of this table confirms that the plan is overfunded by $24,721 million, that is, assets of $50,243 million minus PBO of $25,522 million. Despite this, there is an accrued pension *liability* of $981 million on the balance sheet as well as a prepaid pension asset (see arrows in Exhibit 14.1, p. 709). The purpose of this footnote section is to provide a reconciliation between the $24,721 million current overfunded status of the plan and the $8,416 million net pension asset shown on the balance sheet (i.e., the net of the two arrows: $9,397 − $981 = $8,416). G.E.'s Exhibit 14.1 "Prepaid pension asset" disclosure is rearranged into a somewhat easier-to-understand format for December 31, 1999 in Exhibit 14.2 ($ in millions):

Exhibit 14.2 ■ GENERAL ELECTRIC COMPANY

Understanding the Funded Status Disclosure

Funded Status of Plans		Recognized / Unrecognized Amounts	
Plan assets at fair value	$50,243 **DR**	**Recognized amounts**	
Projected benefit obligation	(25,522) **CR**	1. Prepaid pension asset included in consolidated balance sheet	$ 9,397 **DR**
		2. Accrued pension liability included in consolidated balance sheet	(981) **CR**
		Unrecognized amounts	
		3. Unrecognized prior service cost	(699) **CR**
		4. Unrecognized transition asset	154 **DR**
		5. Unrecognized actuarial gain	16,850 **DR**
Plan assets in excess of projected benefit obligation	$24,721 **DR**	Plan assets in excess of projected benefit obligation	$24,721 **DR**

We now discuss each of the numbered items on the right side of the reconciliation in Exhibit 14.2. Items 1 and 2 represent amounts that are already recognized on the December 31, 1999 balance sheet, while Items 3 through 5 represent amounts that are not yet recognized on the December 31, 1999 balance sheet.

1. *Prepaid pension asset included in consolidated balance sheet.* This is the debit that is made to balance the journal entry when pension expense is less than pension fund-

[16] Typically, the terminology "funded status" is used by companies to identify this reconciliation in the footnote. G.E. is in the minority in not using this terminology.

ing. The cumulative amount of this excess of funding over expense in past years is $9,397 million at December 31, 1999.

2. *Accrued pension liability included in consolidated balance sheet.* This item represents the credit that arises when pension *expense* exceeds the amount of pension *funding.* The cumulative amount of this excess of expense over funding which occurred in past years totals $981 million at December 31, 1999.

This account is also called "unfunded accrued pension cost" and was illustrated in the final journal entry on page 706. G.E. has both a prepaid pension asset and an accrued pension liability because cumulative funding exceeded cumulative pension expense on some plans and expense exceeded funding on others. *SFAS No. 132* (para 6) requires separate disclosure of both the prepaid pension asset and the accrued pension liability.

3. *Unrecognized prior service cost.* General Electric enhanced the benefits provided to employees subsequent to adopting *SFAS No. 87.* This item is being amortized into pension expense over time in component 6—recognized prior service cost. Consequently, the as-yet unrecognized portion ($699 million) at December 31, 1999 is an off-balance sheet liability.
4. *Unrecognized transition asset.* At the time General Electric adopted *SFAS No. 87,* its pension plans were in a net overfunded position. This initially unrecognized asset gets amortized into pension expense (and thus into the financial statements) through component 5—amortization of the unrecognized transition asset or liability. The $154 million figure represents the amortization amount that will reduce pension expense over future years.
5. *Unrecognized actuarial gain.* This $16,850 million number represents the cumulative amount of three elements: (1) the difference between the expected return on plan assets and the actual return; (2) the difference between actuarial assumptions and actual experience regarding mortality, turnover, etc.; and (3) the effects of changes in discount rate and other assumptions. Since the total is outside the 10% corridor on December 31, 1999, some of this item will be amortized into income during 2000. Because the cumulative amount is an unrecognized gain, it represents an off-balance sheet asset.

At December 31, 1999, the fair value of plan assets is larger than the PBO. The corridor is therefore $5,024.3 million—i.e., 10% of the assets of $50,243 million. The unrecognized actuarial gain of $16,850 million is larger than this, so some portion of the gain will be amortized in 2000. Notice that the 10% corridor threshold was also exceeded in 1999 so amortization took place in that year too.

By focusing on the funded status of the plan, the funded status portion of the pension footnote overcomes some of the confusing smoothing-driven complexities that pervade pension accounting. For example, General Electric's December 31, 1999 balance sheet reflects a net pension asset of $8,416 million (i.e., a prepaid pension asset of $9,397 million minus an accrued pension liability of $981 million) although the pension plan was overfunded by a larger amount—$24,721 million—on that date. The net on-balance sheet pension asset of $8,416 million exists because cash funding in certain past years was greater than the amount of those years' pension expense by $8,416 million. The reconciliation directs attention to the more important *current* funded status of the plan rather than to *past* funding decisions.

A thorough understanding of pension reporting rules and disclosures allows analysts to reconstruct the pension journal entry that General Electric made in 1999. The entry ($ in millions) was:

DR Prepaid pension asset	$1,645	
CR Pension plan income		$1,380
CR Accrued pension liability		184
CR Cash		81

The amount of the debit to the prepaid pension asset account ($1,645 million) is the change in this account balance between the beginning and end of 1999—i.e., $9,397 million minus $7,752 million (see the purple arrow in Exhibit 14.1). Similarly, the credit to accrued pension liability is the 1999 change in that account, $981 million minus $797 million (see the orange arrow in Exhibit 14.1).[17] The credit to pension income is the total shown in the "Effect on operations" portion of the footnote on p. 708, while the credit to cash is the amount of employer contributions reported in the "Fair value of assets" section on p. 709.[18]

Extracting Analytic Insights From the Footnote Disclosures

The funded status reconciliation in Exhibit 14.2 provides insights regarding expected *future* pension-related cash flows. Firms with greatly overfunded pension plans have been tempting takeover targets in the past.[19] After such takeovers, acquirers could terminate the overfunded plan, set up a new plan whose funding just equaled the liability, and use the excess funds from the terminated plan to help finance the takeover. To prevent this from happening, many potential takeover targets with overfunded pension plans voluntarily terminated the overfunded plans themselves and redeployed the excess cash proceeds. After doing this, they were no longer a tempting target. The Tax Reform Act of 1986 increased the tax on the gains from plan termination; consequently, terminations of overfunded plans are somewhat less attractive to both acquirers and targets, but they still constitute a potential source of cash.[20]

ANALYSIS

By scrutinizing the causes for increases and decreases in plan assets in the pension footnote (see Figure 14.5), analysts can often make more refined estimates of future cash flows. For example, let's assume the plan assets disclosure shows that a firm did not contribute additional funding during the reporting period. Further assume that the funded status reconciliation shows that the market value of plan assets barely exceeds the PBO at the end of the year. Because the plan was overfunded, the firm could *temporarily* suspend funding. But can it continue to not fund? Depending upon the extent of the overfunding and future asset returns, the answer may be "no." If its funded status were to change in future periods, the firm would be compelled to fund the plan in future years, ***thereby decreasing future net operating cash flows.*** Lenders and others who forecast future cash flows to estimate "safety cushions" must consider these factors when preparing their forecasts. Merely extrapolating the most recent net operating cash flow into future years would overlook the possibly unsustainable "boost" provided by the absence of current pension funding. But companies with greatly overfunded plans can suspend funding for long periods and use the cash for other operating purposes. On the other hand, underfunded plans may reflect past and continuing cash flow difficulties. If a plan is seriously underfunded and if there are insufficient funds to pay retirees, the Pension Benefit Guarantee Corporation (PBGC)—an agency set up under ERISA—pays the promised benefits. But the PBGC tries to recover the pension payments from the pension plan sponsor. The PBGC claim ranks on an equal footing alongside those of unsecured creditors; accordingly, the funded status reconciliation could serve as an early warning device for signaling other cash demands on the firm.

> In 1977 International Harvester Company (now Navistar International Corporation) sold its Wisconsin Steel division to a subsidiary of Envirodyne Industries. At the time of the sale, Wisconsin Steel's pension plans were underfunded. The Envirodyne subsidiary declared bankruptcy in 1980, and the PBGC terminated and assumed responsibility for the Wisconsin Steel pension plans. The PBGC subsequently sued Navistar, contending that the sale of Wisconsin Steel was motivated by a desire to evade its responsibility for the pension plans. Navistar was found to be liable and agreed to a $65 million settlement to be paid to the PBGC. See "Navistar Will Pay $65 Million to Settle Pension Fund Claims," the *Wall Street Journal* (August 21, 1992).

---

[17] There is a separate debit to a prepaid asset account and credit to an accrued liability account because General Electric maintains several pension plans. For some plan(s), the amount of the plan pension expense apparently exceeded the amount of G.E.'s funding.

[18] Sometimes the journal entry for a particular firm won't balance using this change in statement amounts approach. The two most frequent explanations for the failure to balance are (1) foreign currency exchange rate changes and (2) acquisitions accounted for using the purchase method (discussed in chapter 16).

[19] L. Asinof, "Excess Pension Assets Lure Corporate Raiders," the *Wall Street Journal* (September 11, 1985).

[20] Empirical studies investigate what factors underlie firms' decisions to remove excess pension assets from overfunded pension plans. See J. K. Thomas, "Why Do Firms Terminate Their Overfunded Pension Plans?" *Journal of Accounting and Economics* (November 1989), pp. 361–98; and H. F. Mittelstaedt, "An Empirical Analysis of the Factors Underlying the Decision to Remove Excess Assets from Overfunded Pension Plans," *Journal of Accounting and Economics* (November 1989), pp. 399–418.

Because pension funding status is important for assessing current and future cash flows of a firm, we need to stress how sensitive the asset and liability measures are to changes in interest rates. A 1% decrease in the discount rate will typically boost the estimated pension obligation by 10% to 15%.[21] For firms with a relatively young workforce where the pension commitments will be paid 20 to 30 years in the future, small changes in interest (settlement) rate assumptions can cause large increases in the present value of these estimated obligations. Why is there this relatively large multiplier effect from small changes in interest rates? This effect is due to the impact of duration—the further into the future the cash flows are to be paid out, the greater the impact of a change in interest rates on the present value of those cash flows.

The effect of a 1% change in interest rates on the asset side is typically much smaller since fixed income investments generally represent only a fraction of the pension asset portfolio and the maturity of those investments is typically much shorter. Therefore, even modest declines in interest rates can easily shift firms from being in an overfunded position in one year to an underfunded position in the next year.

Table 14.7 provides data on the proportion of firms with defined benefit pension plans falling into each of three funded status categories for the 1991–1995 period:[22]

1. *Overfunded plans*: The fair value of plan assets (FVPA) exceeds the projected benefit obligation (PBO) (i.e., FVPA > PBO).
2. *Underfunded plans*: PBO > FVPA > ABO (accumulated benefit obligation).[23]
3. *Severely underfunded plans*: ABO > FVPA.[24]

Over the five-year period, 38.3% of the firms were in a net overfunded position, 32.6% were underfunded but still had pension assets whose value exceeded the ABO, and 29.1% were in a severely underfunded position where the ABO exceeded the fair value of plan assets. Note that the proportion of overfunded plans dropped from 46.0% in 1991 to 33.0% in 1995. This shift in funded status probably resulted from an increase in PBOs caused by a decline in settlement rates (the median settlement rate declined from 8.5% in 1991 to 7.5% in 1995). These results highlight how sensitive pension funded status is to changes in inter-

Table 14.7 ■ FUNDED STATUS OF PENSION PLANS (1991–1995)

	Proportion Overfunded (FVPA > PBO)	Proportion Underfunded (PBO > FVPA > ABO)	Proportion Severely Underfunded (ABO > FVPA)
1991	46.0%	29.2%	24.8%
1992	42.7	32.9	24.4
1993	33.6	32.6	33.8
1994	36.0	33.2	30.8
1995	33.0	35.3	31.7
Average	38.3	32.6	29.1

Source: Standard & Poor's Research Insight(SM) as data source; methodology not verified or controlled by Standard & Poor's.

[21] See the articles by L. Jeresky, "Tapping the Golden Pool," *Forbes* (April 21, 1986), pp. 35–6; and "The Surplus Vanishes," *Forbes* (November 17, 1986), p. 94.

[22] These summary statistics are based on all AMEX/NYSE firms on Standard & Poor's Compustat® PC Plus with funded status data required under *SFAS No. 87*.

[23] The ABO is the discounted present value of the pension liability computed *without* considering future pay raises. *SFAS No. 132* severely curtailed disclosure of this pension liability measure. As a consequence, it is not possible to group firms into three funded status categories today. Only two categories are possible: overfunded plans and all others.

[24] Severely underfunded plans get special treatment under *SFAS No. 87*, as described on pages 716–718 in the section entitled "Minimum Balance Sheet Liability."

This assumes that the discount rate (settlement rate) is higher than the assumed rate of compensation increase, which is the typical relationship.

est rate assumptions. The return performance of pension assets from year to year can also quickly alter funded status.

Changes in various pension rate assumptions also affect pension expense. An increase in the discount rate lowers service cost and raises interest cost. Whether pension expense goes up or down depends upon the number of years to retirement (i.e., average age of the workforce) and other factors. If the assumed rate of compensation increase used in determining the PBO is lowered, then service cost is reduced too. Also, an increase (decrease) in the *spread* between the discount rate and the assumed rate of compensation increase will lower (raise) service cost. Finally, an increase (decrease) in the expected return on plan assets will decrease (increase) pension expense.

The pension footnote provides information about the current economic status of the pension plan. This allows insight regarding expected future pension-related cash flows.

RECAP

Cash-Balance Plans

Toward the end of the 1990s, more than 400 U.S. companies with defined benefit pension plans modified their existing plan and adopted a new method for determining the rate at which pension benefits accumulate. These modified plans are called **cash-balance plans.** Here, employers contribute a fixed amount per year (say 5% of annual pay) to the account of individual employees. Interest is earned at approximately the rate on long-term U.S. Treasury bonds. Cash-balance plans are defined benefit plans "because the employer [still ultimately] bears the investment risks and rewards and the mortality risk if the employee elects to receive benefits in the form of an annuity". [25] However, should employees leave the firm prior to retirement, the accumulated vested balance belongs to them and can be rolled-over into another pension plan.

Cash-balance pension plans are attractive to firms because, after switching, service cost usually decreases for firms with older employees. Here's why. In traditional defined benefit pension plans, the largest benefits accrue in the later years of employment. But when older workers are switched to a cash-balance plan, they usually receive the same benefit accumulation percent as do younger workers.

While popular with firms, these plans have been challenged as discriminating against older employees. Bills have been introduced in Congress to require firms to give older affected employees a choice between the pre-existing plan and the new cash-balance plan. Simultaneously, the Internal Revenue Service is reviewing the tax status of these plans. With this uncertain legal and tax status, the move to cash-balance plans will assuredly slow down until the issues are resolved.

Minimum Balance Sheet Liability

While the funded status footnote explains the differences between balance sheet disclosures and the funded status of the plan, it does not introduce any amounts into the balance sheet itself. The FASB believed that footnote disclosure alone was inadequate for *severely* underfunded plans. The FASB defined a severely underfunded plan as one in which the liability *without* considering future pay raises—the previously defined ABO—exceeds the fair value of plan assets (FVPA). The Board mandated a **minimum balance sheet liability** for severely underfunded plans equal to the difference between the ABO and the FVPA.

[25] A. T. Arcady and F. Mellors, "Cash Balance Conversions," *Journal of Accountancy* (February 2000), pp. 22–28.

To illustrate the computation of the minimum liability provision, assume that at December 31, 2001 Nguyen Corporation's defined benefit pension plan had the following component values:

Fair value of plan assets (FVPA)	$10,000,000
Accumulated benefit obligation (ABO)	12,000,000
Projected benefit obligation (PBO)	17,000,000
Unrecognized prior service cost	3,000,000

Further assume that in all prior years the amount of pension plan funding was equal to the amount of recorded pension plan expense. Therefore, there was no prepaid pension asset or accrued pension liability on Nguyen's books at December 31, 2001.

The minimum balance sheet liability provision would be triggered here. *SFAS No. 87* requires that a liability of at least $2,000,000 (the difference between the ABO and the FVPA) appear on Nguyen's books to "flag" the serious underfunding. Because there is currently no liability on the books, an entry must be made to put one there. The accounting entry would be:

DR Intangible asset	$2,000,000	
CR Minimum pension liability		$2,000,000

The presumption is that the serious underfunding exists because Nguyen retroactively "sweetened" benefits (thereby increasing both the ABO and PBO) to maintain employee morale. So the intangible asset account represents the benefits conveyed to the firm by happy employees.[26]

Neither the minimum liability nor the offsetting asset are amortized over future years. Instead, the entry for each year is reversed after the financial statements are prepared and the computation is redone for the ensuing year. Plans with continuing, serious underfunding problems would therefore again display asset and liability amounts based on the ensuing year's computations.

The rationale for not carrying the intangible asset forward for amortization is related to the reasons why seriously underfunded plans exist. The two primary reasons are (1) cumulative unrecorded losses and (2) unrecognized prior service cost. Cumulative unrecorded losses are already being amortized under component 4, while unrecognized prior service cost is being amortized under either component 5 or component 6 (depending on when the sweetener was adopted). Thus, to amortize the asset that arises as an offset to the minimum balance sheet liability would result in double counting.

If Nguyen had an "Accrued pension liability" of, say, $400,000 on its books at December 31, 2001, the entry would be different since *SFAS No. 87* requires a *total* liability of $2,000,000—and $400,000 is already on the books. So an additional liability of only $1,600,000 (i.e., $2,000,000 − $400,000) need be recorded. The entry is:

DR Intangible asset	$1,600,000	
CR Minimum pension liability		$1,600,000

On the other hand, if Nguyen had a "Prepaid pension asset" of $400,000 on its books at December 31, 2001, the entry to get to a total *net* liability of $2,000,000 is:

DR Intangible asset	$2,400,000	
CR Minimum pension liability		$2,400,000

The credit of $2,400,000, when offset against the "Prepaid pension asset" of $400,000, yields the required $2,000,000 minimum liability balance.

[26] The debit to the intangible asset account is limited to the sum of the unrecognized prior service cost at the balance sheet date plus any unrecognized transition liability at the date of initial adoption of *SFAS No. 87* (para. 37). The debit to the intangible asset is limited to this sum because the remainder of the underfunding must be attributable to cumulative unrecorded losses and cannot be the result of plan "sweeteners" that generated employee goodwill (i.e., the intangible asset). To illustrate, if Nguyen's prior service cost is $1,500,000 rather than $3,000,000, then the minimum liability of $2,000,000 exceeds prior service costs by $500,000. In these altered circumstances, the entry to recognize the minimum liability would be:

DR Intangible asset	$1,500,000	
DR Comprehensive income (charge)	500,000	
CR Minimum pension liability		$2,000,000

The intangible asset is limited to the amount of prior service cost ($1,500,000) and the $500,000 excess would be shown as an element of comprehensive income.

The highlighted portion of Exhibit 14.3 illustrates the disclosures under *SFAS No. 132* for severely underfunded plans.

Exhibit 14.3 ■ USX CORPORATION

Edited Excerpt from Pension Footnote, 1999 Annual Report

($ in millions)	Pension Benefits 1999	1998
Benefit obligations at December 31	($ 7,584)	($ 8,629)
Fair value of plan assets at December 31	11,305	11,574
Funded status of plans at December 31	$ 3,721[(a)]	$ 2,945[(a)]

[(a)]Includes several plans that have accumulated benefit obligations in excess of plan assets:		
Aggregate accumulated benefit obligations	($53)	($98)
Aggregate projected benefit obligations	(76)	(120)
Aggregate plan assets	–	–

International financial reporting rules for pensions are specified by "Employee Benefits," *IAS 19* (London, U.K.: International Accounting Standards Committee, 1998). These rules roughly parallel those of *SFAS No. 87*. The primary differences are that *IAS 19* contains fewer smoothing provisions than *SFAS No. 87* and does not require recognition of a minimum liability. Required financial statement disclosures are also similar.

Notice that the ABO is reported *only* for severely underfunded plans. The amount of the minimum liability (if any) that USX included in the balance sheet is not separately reported under *SFAS No. 132*.

Funded Status and Operating Cash Flows

The funded status of a pension plan appears to be an indicator of potential cash flow problems. Figure 14.7 provides evidence that firms with underfunded plans are not only experiencing lower *current* cash flows but are also likely to experience lower *future* cash flows than firms with overfunded plans. To demonstrate this, we form two portfolios based on firms' funded status at the end of 1994: (1) firms in an overfunded position (FVPA > PBO) and (2) firms in an underfunded position (PBO > FVPA).[27] The bar graph in Figure 14.7 displays the median cash flow from operations (on a per-share basis) for the year of the portfolio formation (1994) and for the subsequent four years.

Firms whose pension plans were underfunded in 1994 experienced lower operating cash flows in that year ($1.88 per share) in comparison to firms with overfunded plans ($2.28

Figure 14.7

OPERATING CASH FLOWS BY FUNDED STATUS GROUP 1994–1998

Source: Standard & Poor's Research Insight[(SM)] as data source; methodology not verified or controlled by Standard & Poor's.

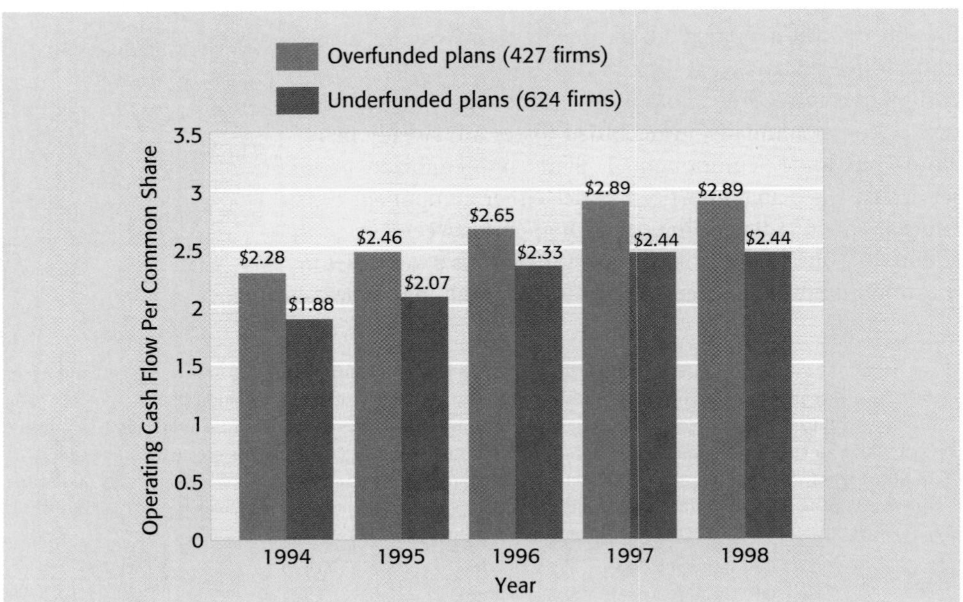

[27] All firms listed on either the AMEX or NYSE with valid data for computing pension funded status in 1994 are included.

per share). Moreover, the operating cash flows of the underfunded firms continued to lag behind those of the overfunded firms in the subsequent four years. This suggests that pension funded status is a potentially useful indicator of the level of future cash flows.[28]

Postretirement Benefits Other than Pensions

Many companies promise to provide health care and life insurance to employees and their spouses during retirement. Analyzing these promises indicates that—like pensions—the intent of these benefits is to attract and retain a highly qualified workforce. Under the matching principle of accrual accounting, an expense should be recognized over the period of employment as employees qualify for these **other postretirement benefits (OPEB).** Historically, however, few companies with postretirement benefit plans made expense accruals. Instead, "pay-as-you-go" accounting was employed—that is, as cash payments were made to provide the health-care benefit coverage to retired employees, the amount of the cash outflow was charged to expense. No liability appeared on the books. Worse yet, few companies funded the plans as benefits were earned. There are two reasons for this lack of funding. First, in contrast to pension plans, there is no ERISA requirement that says these benefits have to be funded. Second, even if firms voluntarily do fund their plans, these payments are not deductible for U.S. income tax purposes. As a result of these circumstances, by the mid-1980s enormous unrecorded (off-balance sheet) liabilities for postretirement benefits existed, but no periodic debits to expense nor credits to a liability account were made to reflect the continued growth of these obligations. To give some idea of the size of these previously unrecorded postretirement benefit liabilities, when General Motors adopted *SFAS No. 106* in 1992, the liability totaled $33.116 billion and the after-tax charge to the income statement was $20.838 billion. (The pre-tax loss *before* the cumulative effect of the change in accounting principle was $3.333 billion in 1992.)

To correct this situation, the FASB issued *SFAS No. 106* in December 1990.[29] This standard became effective in 1993, although earlier application was permitted. Exhibit 14.4 contains excerpts from the postretirement benefit plans footnote in the 1999 annual report of General Electric Company.

Exhibit 14.4 ■ GENERAL ELECTRIC COMPANY

Edited, Condensed 1999 Annual Report Health and Life Benefits Footnote

Principal retiree benefit plans generally provide health and life insurance benefits to employees who retire under the GE Pension Plan . . . with 10 or more years of service. Retirees share in the cost of health care benefits. Benefit provisions are subject to collective bargaining. At the end of 1999, these plans covered approximately 250,000 retirees and dependents.

The effect on operations of principal retiree benefit plans is shown in the following table.

(continued)

[28] Prior to the issuance of *SFAS No. 132*, it was possible to form three portfolios: (1) firms in an overfunded position, (2) firms in a moderately underfunded position (PBO > FVPA > ABO), and (3) firms in a severely underfunded position (ABO > FVPA). But *SFAS No. 132* reduced the minimum liability disclosure so it is no longer possible to identify firms that are severely underfunded in the aggregate. Consequently, the accuracy of cash flow forecasting using pension funded status has declined. See M. Cipriano, D. W. Collins, and L. Revsine, "*SFAS No.* 132 and Disclosure Effectiveness: An Examination," Unpublished manuscript (February 2000), for a detailed analysis of the deterioration in the accuracy of operating cash flow forecasts as a result of the disclosure cutbacks in *SFAS No. 132*.

[29] "Employers' Accounting for Postretirement Benefits Other Than Pensions," *SFAS No. 106* (Norwalk, CT: FASB, 1990).

Exhibit 14.4 ■ *(continued)*

Effect on operations

($ in millions)	1999	1998
Retiree health plans		
Service cost for benefits earned	$ 88	$ 79
Interest cost on benefit obligation	206	205
Prior service cost	14	14
Net actuarial loss recognized	38	28
Retiree health plan cost	346	326
Retiree life plans		
Service cost for benefits earned	19	17
Interest cost on benefit obligation	117	114
Expected return on plan assets	(165)	(149)
Prior service cost	(6)	(6)
Net actuarial loss recognized	7	11
Retiree life plan cost (income)	(28)	(13)
Total cost	$318	$313

Funding policy for retiree health benefits is generally to pay covered expenses as they are incurred. GE funds retiree life insurance benefits at its discretion.

Changes in the accumulated postretirement benefit obligation for retiree benefit plans follow.

Accumulated postretirement benefit obligation

	Health plans		Life plans	
December 31 ($ in millions)	**1999**	**1998**	**1999**	**1998**
Balance at January 1	$3,220	$3,098	$1,787	$1,677
Service cost for benefits earned	88	79	19	17
Interest cost on benefit obligation	206	205	117	114
Participant contributions	24	24	–	–
Actuarial (gain)/loss	103	177	(165)	91
Benefits paid	(392)	(363)	(107)	(112)
Other	26	–	–	–
Balance at December 31	$3,275	$3,220	$1,651	$1,787

Changes in the fair value of assets for retiree benefit plans follow.

Fair value of assets

	Health plans		Life plans	
December 31 ($ in millions)	**1999**	**1998**	**1999**	**1998**
Balance at January 1	$ –	$ –	$2,121	$1,917
Actual return on plan assets	–	–	355	316
Employer contributions	368	339	–	–
Participant contributions	24	24	–	–
Benefits paid	(392)	$(363)	(107)	(112)
Balance at December 31	$ –	$ –	$2,369	$2,121

Plan assets are held in trust and consist mainly of common stock and fixed-income investments. GE common stock represented 6.2% and 4.5% of trust assets at year-end 1999 and 1998, respectively.

Exhibit 14.4 ■ *(continued)*

GE recorded assets and liabilities for retiree benefit plans as follows:

Retiree benefit liability/asset

	Health plans		Life plans	
December 31 ($ in millions)	**1999**	**1998**	**1999**	**1998**
Accumulated postretirement benefit obligation	$3,275	$3,220	$1,651	$1,787
Add (deduct) unrecognized balances:				
Prior service cost	(143)	(157)	43	49
Net actuarial gain/(loss)	(637)	(572)	576	214
Fair value of plan assets	—	—	(2,369)	(2,121)
Retiree benefit liability/(asset)	$2,495	$2,491	$ (99)	$ (71)

Actuarial assumptions used to determine costs and benefit obligations for principal retiree benefit plans are shown below.

Actuarial assumptions

December 31	**1999**	**1998**
Discount rate	7.75%	6.75%
Compensation increases	5.0	5.0
Health care cost trend[(a)]	9.0	7.8
Return on assets for the year	9.5	9.5

(a) For 1999, gradually declining to 5% after 2004.

Increasing or decreasing the health care cost trend rates by one percentage point would have had an insignificant effect on the December 31, 1999, accumulated postretirement benefit obligation and the annual cost of retiree health plans.

Experience gains and losses, as well as the effects of changes in actuarial assumptions and plan provisions, are amortized over the average future service period of employees.

The computations for postretirement benefits expense and measures of the liability generally parallel the format for pension expense and liability. Notice in Exhibit 14.4 that G.E. maintains both retiree health and life insurance benefit plans. The life plans are funded while the health plans are on a "pay-as-you-go" basis. The net postretirement benefit cost of $318 million for 1999 (as shown in the "Effect on operations" section of Exhibit 14.4 on p. 720), includes service cost plus interest cost components and, for the life plans, expected return on plan assets.

Further scrutiny of this section shows that *SFAS No. 106* also incorporates smoothing devices that are virtually identical to components 4 through 6 in pension accounting. Specifically, when plans are funded, postretirement benefit expense is reduced by the *expected* return on plan assets; to accomplish this, asset gains or losses are deferred off-balance sheet. Similarly, these gains and losses are accumulated and amortized as component 4 if they exceed a 10% corridor, just as they are in pension accounting. Pension component 5—amortization of transition liability—also exists in postretirement benefits accounting if the firm adopting *SFAS No. 106* chose to recognize the liability over a period of future years rather than all at once, as we'll see next. Finally, a counterpart to pension component 6—amortization of prior service costs—exists as well in instances in which firms enhance or reduce the level of postretirement benefits subsequent to adopting *SFAS No. 106.*

One difference between accounting for pensions and accounting for other postretirement benefits (OPEB) is that postretirement benefits are rarely tied to salary at retirement. Consequently, *SFAS No. 106* contains no projected benefit obligation calculation. The typical postretirement benefit plan promises employees full coverage (e.g., comprehensive postretirement health insurance) after a certain period of employment—say, 10 years. In such circumstances, the actuarially determined service cost of the plan will also be accrued over the first 10 years of the employee's service. The liability attributed to service to date is called the **accumulated postretirement benefit obligation (APBO)**.

> The actuarial and other assumptions required encompass factors such as (1) what proportion of employees will work for at least 10 years and thereby qualify for benefits, (2) how long after retirement will the employee live to receive benefits, and (3) what will be the annual cost of providing the benefit over the retirement years.

The FASB permitted companies to adopt the provisions of *SFAS No. 106* in one of two ways: (1) recognize the transition obligation or transition asset (the difference between the accumulated postretirement benefit obligation and the fair value of plan assets) immediately in net income of the period in which *SFAS No. 106* is adopted; or (2) amortize the transition obligation or asset as a component of OPEB expense on a straight-line basis over the *longer* of (a) the average remaining service period of active plan participants, or (b) 20 years.

CONTRACTING

Like most U.S. firms, G.E. chose to recognize the *SFAS No. 106* transition obligation immediately. Why did most firms choose to take the earnings "hit" all at once, rather than amortizing it over a period of future years?[30] The best explanation is that firms wanted to avoid the "drag" on future earnings that would result from amortizing the usually very large unrecorded liability over, say, the ensuing 15 years. One reason for taking the "hit" all at once is that future years' bonuses tied to earnings would be reduced by the "drag". Another is that firms may have feared that investors would soon forget the source of the earnings "drag" and bid share prices lower. Those few firms that chose not to recognize the liability all at once now have an expense charge that is a counterpart to pension component 6, as mentioned above. Exhibit 14.5 contains a 1991 footnote excerpt that describes how G.E. recognized the full *SFAS No. 106* liability immediately. It made the following entry retroactive to the start of 1991:

> Case C14–4 covers G.E.'s initial adoption of *SFAS No. 106*.

DR Cumulative effect of a change in accounting principle	$1,799,000,000	
DR Deferred income tax asset	911,000,000	
CR Accumulated postretirement benefit obligation		$2,710,000,000

Exhibit 14.5 ■ GENERAL ELECTRIC COMPANY

Excerpt from 1991 Annual Report

1991 Accounting Change. Statement of Financial Accounting Standards *(SFAS) No. 106*—"Employers' Accounting for Postretirement Benefits Other Than Pensions"—was implemented using the immediate recognition transition option, effective as of January 1, 1991.

SFAS No. 106 requires recognition during employees' service with the Company, of the cost of their retiree health and life insurance benefits. At January 1, 1991, the accumulated postretirement benefit obligation was $4,287 million; however, $1,577 million of this obligation had been provided through the fair market value of related trust assets ($1,037 million) and recorded liabilities ($540 million), thus resulting in a pre-tax adjustment (i.e., transition obligation) of $2,710 million. The effect on net earnings and share owners' equity was $1,799 million ($2.07 per share) after [a] deferred tax benefit of $911 million. Aside from the one-time effect of the adjustment, adoption of *SFAS No. 106* was not material to 1991 financial results.

[30] For example, see E. Amir and J. Livnat, "Adoption Choices of *SFAS No. 106:* Implications for Financial Analysis," *The Journal of Financial Statement Analysis* (Winter, 1997) pp. 51–60; and K. Ramesh and L. Revsine, "The Effects of Regulatory and Contracting Costs on Banks' Choice of Accounting Method for Other Postretirement Employee Benefits," *Journal of Accounting and Economics* (October, 2000) pp. 159–86.

The cumulative effect of this accounting change ($1,799 million) was shown as a charge on the 1991 income statement. Deferred taxes are debited because the U.S. income tax law does not permit a tax deduction for postretirement benefits until the benefit premiums are paid. Consequently, a timing difference exists because book income for 1991 is lower than taxable income as a consequence of this item.

Exhibit 14.4 in the section "Retiree benefit liability/asset" on p. 721 also shows General Electric's disclosure of the plans' status at the end of 1999. Reformulating the reconciliation of the life insurance benefit plans using the approach we used for pensions in Exhibit 14.2 shows:

Funded Status of Plans		Recognized and Unrecognized Amounts	
Accumulated postretirement benefit obligation	($1,651) **CR**	**Recognized amount**	
Fair value of plan assets	2,369 **DR**	Retiree benefit asset	$ 99 **DR**
		Unrecognized amounts	
		Prior service cost	43 **DR**
		Unrecognized actuarial gain	576 **DR**
Excess of plan assets over accumulated postretirement benefit obligation	$ 718 **DR**	Excess of plan assets over accumulated postretirement benefit obligation	$718 **DR**

The financial reporting and disclosures for postretirement benefit plans are similar to pension reporting and disclosures. However, most postretirement benefit plans are unfunded. Consequently, statement readers must be mindful of future cash outflows that these unfunded plans might precipitate.

RECAP

Are Pension and Other Postretirement Benefits (OPEB) Disclosures Useful? The Research Evidence

Pension and other postretirement benefits (OPEB) disclosures and measurement rules are not simple. Detailed breakdowns of expense components abound (service cost, interest cost, etc.). But, are the detailed components of pension and postretirement benefits expense, as well as footnote disclosures of asset and liability amounts, useful to statement readers in equity valuation? This section describes research evidence regarding the value relevance of the rules in *SFAS No. 87, No. 106,* and *No. 132.*

Do the Components of Net Periodic Pension Cost Have Different Equity Pricing Implications?

VALUATION

The decision of the FASB to require separate disclosure of the various components of net periodic pension expense, as detailed earlier in this chapter, raises an interesting question: Is the distinction between these pension expense components important to investors and other statement users? In valuing a company's stock, does the market assign different multiples to the various components of net periodic pension cost? For example, does a dollar of service cost have the same impact on share price as a dollar of amortization of unrecognized transition asset or obligation? If not, why not?

These questions were addressed in a study that used the simple earnings capitalization equity valuation model presented in Chapter 6—that is, equation (6.7), which expresses the market value of equity as the capitalized value of a firm's "permanent" or sustainable earnings.[31] The study conjectures that the various components of net periodic pension

[31] M. E. Barth, W. H. Beaver, and W. R. Landsman, "The Market Valuation Implication of Net Periodic Pension Cost Components," *Journal of Accounting and Economics* (March 1992), pp. 27–62.

expense (service cost, interest cost, expected return on plan assets, and so on) convey different information regarding the firm's permanent earnings potential, and, therefore, each will have a different multiple applied to it. Specifically, service cost, interest cost, and *expected* return on plan assets are relatively permanent components of earnings that are likely to persist into the future. Consequently, these components are expected to have multiples approximating $1/r$, where r is the firm's cost of equity capital. Thus, if r is 8%, the multiple applied to these earnings components would be $1/.08$, or 12.5—that is, each dollar of these expenses would lower permanent earnings and thus lower market value by $12.50, while each dollar of expected return would raise market value by $12.50.

Other components of pension expense are viewed as more transitory, and, therefore, they are expected to have a lower multiple. This lower multiple reflects the presumably less sustainable nature of these items. For example, a lower multiple would be expected for the deferred portion of the current period's actual return on plan assets. The deferred portion reflects the difference between the actual and expected return in the current period (the unexpected return), ***which is expected to net to zero in the long run.*** Because the unexpected gain or loss in a given year is *not* expected to recur in the future, the multiple for this component of pension expense is expected to be approximately 1. A multiple of 1—which is far below 12.5—would reflect the one-time transitory effect of this item on the market value of equity.

The researchers hypothesize that components 4, 5, and 6 provide no incremental information about future permanent earnings that is not already reflected in other pension expense components. For example, the recognition of total net deferrals of gains and losses from previous periods (component 4) and the amortization of the net transition asset or liability (component 5) are viewed as "stale" numbers, since they derive from past gains and losses. Accordingly, these components of pension expense are viewed as irrelevant to the pricing of a firm's stock, so the multiple applied to these amounts is expected to be zero.

To see whether different multiples are applied to different components of pension cost in the determination of security prices, the researchers express market value of equity as a function of various nonpension and pension-related components of net income, as depicted in Figure 14.8. Overall, the variables depicted in the figure (including the nonpension variables) explain roughly 55% to 65% of the variation in year-end share prices across firms in the sample. The study found that the multiples applied to the pension variables in Figure 14.8 are ***significantly different from one another.***[32] This difference in multiples implies that the various components of pension expense affect share price differently. In particular, the multiple on the amortization of the transition amount

Figure 14.8

RESEARCH DESIGN ON THE RELATIONSHIP BETWEEN STOCK PRICES AND COMPONENTS OF PENSION EXPENSE

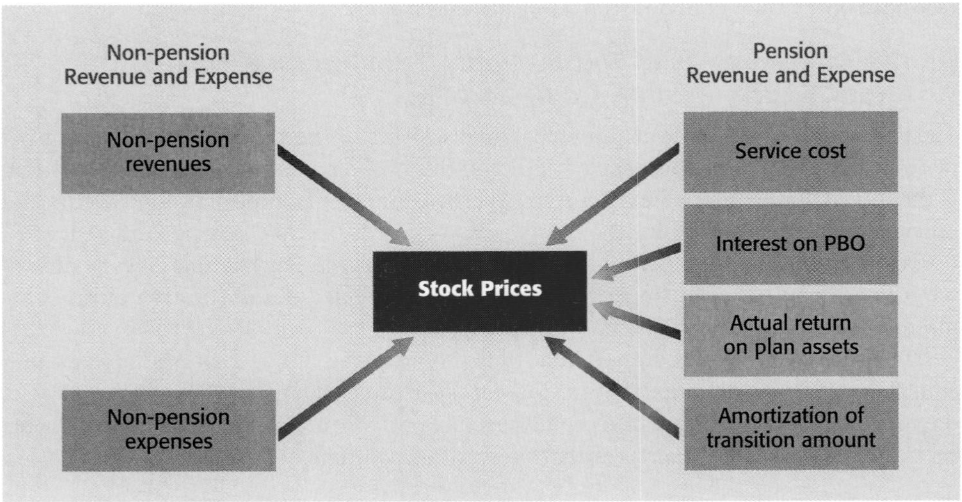

[32] Ibid.

(component 5) is essentially zero, thus suggesting that this item is viewed by the market as a low-quality component of earnings that is price-irrelevant. This finding is noteworthy because many of the firms that adopted *SFAS No. 87* early (in 1986) were in large overfunded positions—the fair market value of plan assets exceeded the projected benefit obligation. This overfunding resulted in a large and significant reduction in reported pension expense in the adoption year and in subsequent periods (as this transition asset was amortized).[33] Research findings suggest that the market views this earnings boost to be largely transitory and not a significant determinant of equity prices. Further evidence shows that the multiples applied to the service cost, interest, and return on plan assets components of pension expense generally have the predicted sign and magnitude.[34]

Research results suggest that the breakdown of the components of pension expense—as called for under *SFAS No. 87* and *SFAS No. 132*—is useful to investors, since these components appear to have different share price implications.

RECAP

Equity Pricing Implications of Pension Cost: An Alternative View

VALUATION

The research just described tells us how the stock market appears to use pension disclosures in valuing firms. More recent articles have argued for a different approach.[35]

During the "bull market" of the late 1990s, "pension expense" gradually became "pension income" for some firms with greatly overfunded pension plans. This happened because rising equity values raised the base on which the expected return on plan assets is computed.[36] Consequently, the expected return—*which lowers pension expense*—ultimately exceeded charges to pension expense like service cost and interest cost. For example, in Exhibit 14.1 (p. 708) we see that G.E. had pension *income* of $1,380 million in 1999. Pension income grew so large that, for many firms, it had a discernible positive effect on operating income. Table 14.8 on p. 726 shows pension income as a percentage of pre-tax operating income in 1998 for several firms with a very high ratio of pension income to operating income.

Some analysts and financial writers have argued that deducting pension expense or adding pension income in the operating section of the income statement misstates *operating* income. They maintain that only service cost is a true current period *operating* item since service cost represents the present value of the increased pension payout arising from current services. Interest cost (component 2 of pension expense) is thought to be a financing cost and not an element of operating income. Similarly, these critics feel that the expected return on plan assets (component 3) should be shown in other income, just like the return on investment securities firms may hold.[37] Consistent with the research result in the

These proponents further contend that OPEB items—other than service cost—also should not be included in operating income. Since OPEB obligations are seldom funded, return on assets is not a significant issue here; only interest cost is. Consequently, critics contend that the OPEB effect in isolation tends to *understate* operating income

[33] One study reports that 92% of 192 firms that adopted *SFAS No. 87* in 1986 sponsored at least one overfunded pension plan. For this set of firms, the fair value of plan assets exceeded the projected benefit obligation at transition by an average of $165.6 million. This transition asset typically is amortized over 15 years, thus resulting in an average reduction of pension expense of slightly over $11 million. See M. Stone and R. W. Ingram, "The Effect of *Statement No. 87* on the Financial Reports of Early Adopters," *Accounting Horizons* (September 1988), pp. 48–61.

[34] Barth, et. al., op. cit.

[35] For example, see R. McGough and E. E. Schultz, "How Pension Surpluses Lift Profits," *Wall Street Journal,* September 20, 1999, and G. Morgenson, "What's Hiding in Big Blue's Small Print," *New York Times,* June 4, 2000.

[36] Recall, this pension plan asset base is termed the market-related asset value. Firms can compute this in either of two ways. One is to use the fair market value (FMV) of the plan assets at the start of the reporting period. The other is to use some sort of moving average (not to exceed five years) which smoothes out the year-to-year volatility inherent in a point estimate like FMV on a specific date.

[37] See Bear Stearns, "Retirement Benefits Impact Operating Income," *Accounting Issues* (Bear, Stearns & Co. Inc.: September 17, 1999) for a thorough exposition of this position.

Table 14.8 ■ RATIO OF 1998 PENSION INCOME TO 1998 PRE-TAX OPERATING INCOME FOR SELECTED FIRMS

Firm	Ratio
Boeing Company	8%
Crown Cork & Seal Company	12
Eaton Corporation	10
General Electric Company	7
GTE Corporation	8
International Business Machines Corporation	6
International Paper Company	8
Lucent Technologies Incorporated	15
Nicor Incorporated	10
PG&E Corporation	11
Tenneco Incorporated	10
Unocal Corporation	38

Source: Bear Stearns *Accounting Issues,* September 17, 1999.

previous section, amortization components 4 through 6 are considered valuation irrelevant. In these critics' view, only service cost is related to core operations and, accordingly, should receive a different valuation multiple than interest cost and return on plan assets.

Table 14.9 shows how the adjustments just described for pensions and OPEB would alter the year-to-year percentage decline in Bethlehem Steel's 1997 and 1998 operating income. Rather than a 6% decline in continuing, core operating income, the adjusted decline is 16%.

This view of pension/OPEB expense (income) as being comprised of several non-operating elements is controversial. Here's why. At the start of this chapter we showed that in a world of certainty the return on plan assets would exactly offset interest cost. Pension expense would consist exclusively of service cost. In the real world, this offset won't be precise. Sometimes there will be a return shortfall. If this persists, pension expense will grow. In words, this growing charge to pension expense means the firm will have to make up the shortfall by expending cash in later periods to adequately fund pension payouts. In this scenario, it seems that the entirety of pension expense (i.e., service cost, interest cost and the reduction for return on plan assets) should be included as an expense in determining operating income. A growing year-to-year charge to pension expense means that events of the current and recent past periods point to the need for increased *future* pension funding to deliver the promised benefits.

Table 14.9 ■ BETHLEHEM STEEL'S GROWTH RATE COMPARISON

($ in millions)	1998	1997	Year-over-Year Growth Rate
Reported operating income	$190	$374	
Add (deduct) loss (gain) on exiting a business	35	(135)	
Recurring *reported* operating income	225	239	−6%
Add back:			
Net pension cost	85	155	
Net other retirement benefit cost	165	150	
Deduct:			
Service cost—pensions	(55)	(48)	
Service cost—other retirement benefits	(9)	(7)	
Recurring *adjusted* operating income	$411	$489	−16%

Source: Bear Stearns *Accounting Issues,* September 17, 1999.

At the other extreme, sometimes return on plan assets will exceed interest. When this persists, pension expense may reverse and become pension income and even grow over time, as happened in the late 1990s for some firms. This growing excess means that the firm's need to use additional resources in the future to fund benefits currently earned is shrinking. Again, in this scenario of rising returns, it seems appropriate to treat the entirety of pension income as an increase in operating income.

How to treat interest cost and return on pension plan assets in equity valuations is an unsettled issue. We expect continuing debate among financial observers.

Reliability and the Valuation Relevance of Alternative Pension Asset and Liability Measures

Among the several alternative pension asset and liability measures we have discussed, some are reported on the balance sheet while others appear in the pension footnote. For example, the cumulative difference between asset funding and the amounts charged to pension expense each year is included directly on the balance sheet. If cumulative past pension expense exceeds cumulative past funding, an accrued pension liability is shown on the balance sheet. Alternatively, if cumulative past pension funding exceeds cumulative past expense, the balance sheet will reflect a prepaid pension asset.

Footnote disclosures under *SFAS No. 87* include, as part of the funded status reconciliation, the accumulated benefit obligation, the projected benefit obligation, and the vested benefit obligation as measures of pension obligations, and they also include the fair value of plan assets as the relevant measure of plan assets.

From an accounting measurement perspective, an important question is this: Which of these alternative liability and asset measures best captures the true pension obligations and resources of the firm and which are measured with the greatest reliability? From a user perspective, do the net pension amounts reported in the balance sheet or the amounts reported in the footnotes more closely reflect the asset and liability measures that investors implicitly use when they value the firm? Both sets of questions are addressed in a research study.[38]

Overall, the results suggest that the pension asset and liability measures in the pension *footnotes* are more closely associated with security prices than are the measures recognized in the balance sheet. These results underscore the fact that footnotes to the financial statements often contain useful information for investors' valuation decisions—and, therefore, they should be carefully scrutinized.

Reliability and Valuation Relevance of Postretirement Benefit Obligations

Accumulated postretirement benefit obligations (APBOs) represent significant off-balance sheet obligations for many firms. Several questions can be raised about estimated APBO amounts, both from an accounting measurement perspective and from a user perspective. Are APBO amounts sufficiently reliable to be useful in assessing share prices? Are APBO amounts less reliable than pension ABO amounts? Do APBO amounts provide incremental information over and above ABO amounts when assessing share prices? These questions are addressed in several studies.[39] Before summarizing the results of these studies, we briefly consider objections that were raised about reporting postretirement benefit obligations.

> These studies were done before the FASB reduced pension ABO disclosures in *SFAS No. 132.*

[38] M. E. Barth, "Relative Measurement Errors Among Alternative Pension Asset and Liability Measures," *The Accounting Review* (July 1991), pp. 433–63. Some of the measures tested in the study—for example the ABO and vested benefit obligation—are no longer reported under *SFAS No. 132.*

[39] H. F. Mittelstaedt and M. J. Warshawsky, "The Impact of Liabilities for Retiree Health Benefits on Share Prices," *Journal of Risk and Insurance,* Vol. 60, No. 1 (1993), pp. 13–35; E. Amir, "The Market Valuation of Accounting Information: The Case of Postretirement Benefits Other Than Pensions," *The Accounting Review* (October 1993), pp. 703–24; and B. Choi, D. W. Collins, and W. B. Johnson, "Valuation Implications of Reliability Differences: The Case of Non-pension Postretirement Obligations," *The Accounting Review* (July 1997), pp. 351–83.

While there is general agreement that postretirement obligations are an economic liability of a firm promising them, questions have been raised about the reliability of the accounting estimates of this liability. This concern about reliability of APBO estimates arises from difficulties encountered in measuring future health-care benefits granted to employees. Unlike employee pension obligations, which are contractually defined in terms of dollar payments (e.g., 60% of salary at retirement), employee health-care benefits are typically defined in terms of future services to be provided in kind. While both ABO and APBO estimates require numerous actuarial assumptions, there are more uncertainties associated with measuring the costs of future health-care benefits. The three most important factors contributing to uncertainty in estimating APBO amounts are (1) per-capita claims cost by age, (2) future health-care cost trend rates, and (3) future medicare reimbursement rates.[40]

Escalating health-care costs and the new *SFAS No. 106* reporting requirements have caused some firms to alter or terminate their contractual obligations under existing postretirement health-care benefit plans. One compensation consulting firm estimated that as many as 80% of the employers surveyed were likely to reduce or terminate health-care benefits in the future.[41] These contemplated changes in benefits contribute another source of uncertainty about reported APBO amounts. Corporate decisions to reduce or terminate health-care benefits are reflected in accounting estimates of APBO only after the cutback occurs, but the possibility of such actions makes the original APBO figures reported by firms less reliable as a measure of their expected ultimate liability for health-care benefits.

Opponents of *SFAS No. 106* argue that the additional assumptions required to estimate future health-care benefits and the possibility that these benefits will be curtailed in the future lower the precision of the resulting APBO estimates. Thus, concern is raised about the reliability of APBO amounts both in absolute terms and in comparison to the reliability of employee pension obligations. Clearly, by issuing *SFAS No. 106,* the FASB felt that including estimates of employee post-retirement benefit obligations in the financial statements would be useful and informative. Which of these opposing positions is most consistent with empirical evidence is the subject of the studies to which we now turn our attention.

RECAP

Empirical Evidence Two studies use a variant of the earnings and book value valuation model equation (6.11) introduced in Chapter 6 to determine whether investors were adjusting share prices for estimates of APBO amounts even before firms began disclosing their own estimates of APBO amounts under *SFAS No. 106*.[42] The results of both studies suggest that estimated APBO amounts are valuation relevant and were apparently being impounded into share prices prior to the *SFAS No. 106* disclosures. However, these studies find that a dollar of the estimated OPEB obligation reduces the market value of equity by only $0.40 to $0.60. One explanation for why these reductions are smaller than the theoretical (expected) reduction of one dollar is that these estimated obligations contain substantial measurement error and, therefore, lack the necessary reliability to affect share values dollar for dollar.

---

[40] *SFAS No. 106*, para. 30, op. cit.

[41] UNYSIS announced it would curtail all payments of retiree benefits within three years, thereby reducing the APBO obligation it would have otherwise reported by approximately $700 million. See "UNYSIS Corp. Says It Will Stop Paying Retiree Medical Benefits In Three Years," the *Wall Street Journal* (November 4, 1992).

[42] H. F. Mittelstaedt and M. J. Warshawsky, op. cit., and E. Amir, op. cit. The researcher-derived estimates of APBO amounts used in these studies were based on firm-specific annual pay-as-you-go costs and other publicly available information about discount rates, health-care cost trend rates, and employee age profiles.

Another study used actual APBO amounts that were computed by firms themselves to investigate whether these obligations contain greater measurement error (less reliability) than pension ABO amounts and whether these OPEB obligations are helpful in explaining share prices.

The study finds that postretirement APBO amounts are negatively and significantly correlated with equity market values.[43] However, the multiple applied to these OPEB obligations appears to be roughly half as large as the multiple associated with the pension ABO amounts. The study concludes that *SFAS No. 106* APBO amounts are significantly less reliable than are pension ABO measures and are less reliable for firms with relatively few retirees. This is consistent with the conjecture that it is more difficult to reliably estimate health-care benefits that are to be provided farther into the future. Thus, the results of this study suggest that the APBO measures reported under *SFAS No. 106* do not have the same reliability that *SFAS No. 87* pension disclosures have in valuing equity securities.

SUMMARY

Under *SFAS Nos. 87* and *132*, pension expense consists of service cost, interest cost, expected return on plan assets, and three other components. The three latter components are smoothing mechanisms that avoid year to year volatility in pension expense but make pension accounting exceedingly complex, since many pension-related items are "off-balance sheet."

Because some pension items are "off-balance sheet," the FASB requires firms to disclose the funded status of the plan—the difference between the market value of plan assets and the projected benefit obligation—and to reconcile funded status to reported balance sheet amounts. An understanding of the funded status disclosure provides readers with an improved basis for assessing future operating cash flow.

The reporting rules for postretirement benefit plans closely parallel the pension accounting rules. Prior to the issuance of *SFAS No. 106*, only a few companies funded postretirement benefits other than pensions. Consequently, significant amounts of off-balance sheet liabilities exist for many firms. Careful scrutiny of the *SFAS No. 106* footnote disclosures provides analysts with an improved basis for assessing the future cash outflows that are associated with existing promises to provide postretirement benefits. However, the research evidence suggests that the equity valuation impact of these estimated obligations is less than dollar-for-dollar due to the considerable uncertainty and measurement error associated with these estimates.

Statement readers should view the following circumstances as potential warning signals or indicators of earnings management.

1. A significant divergence between any of the various pension and OPEB rates selected by a firm (i.e., the discount rate, the expected rate of return on plan assets, or the rate of increase in future compensation levels or health care costs) and the rates chosen by other firms in its industry.
2. A very large difference between the chosen expected rate of return on plan assets and the discount rate used.
3. An increase in the year-to-year expected rate of return on plan assets that seems unrelated to changes in market conditions.
4. A decrease in the assumed rate of increase in future compensation levels (or—for OPEB—future health cost trends) that cannot be explained by changing industry or labor market conditions.

Each of these items can change reported income. Furthermore, they also affect the reported PBO or APBO.

[43] Choi, et al., op. cit.

EXERCISES

E14–1 **Determining projected benefit obligation** AICPA adapted

The following information pertains to Seda Company's pension plan:

Actuarial estimate of projected benefit obligation at 1/1/01	$72,000
Assumed discount rate	10%
Service cost for 2001	18,000
Pension benefits paid during 2001	15,000

REQUIRED:

If no change in actuarial estimates occurred during 2001, how much would Seda's projected benefit obligation be at December 31, 2001?

E14–2 **Pension liability on balance sheet** AICPA adapted

At December 31, 2001 the following information was provided by Kerr Corporation's pension plan administrator:

Fair value of plan assets	$3,450,000
Accumulated benefit obligation	4,300,000
Projected benefit obligation	5,700,000

REQUIRED:

What is the amount of the pension liability that should be shown on Kerr's December 31, 2001 balance sheet?

E14–3 **Determining prepaid pension cost** AICPA adapted

On January 2, 2001 Loch Company established a noncontributory defined benefit plan covering all employees, and it contributed $1,000,000 to the plan. At December 31, 2001 Loch determined that the 2001 service and interest costs on the plan were $620,000. The expected and the actual rate of return on plan assets for 2001 was 10%. There are no other components of Loch's pension expense.

REQUIRED:

What amount should Loch report in its December 31, 2001 balance sheet as prepaid pension cost?

E14–4 **Determining employer's pension contribution** AICPA adapted

Webb Company implemented a defined benefit pension plan for its employees on January 1, 1998. During 1998 and 1999, Webb's contributions fully funded the plan. The following data are provided for 2000 and 2001:

	2001 Estimated	2000 Actual
Projected benefit obligation, December 31	$750,000	$700,000
Plan assets at fair value, December 31	675,000	600,000
Projected benefit obligation in excess of plan assets	75,000	100,000
Pension expense	90,000	75,000
Employer's contribution	?	50,000

REQUIRED:

What amount should Webb contribute in order to report an accrued pension liability of $15,000 in its December 31, 2001 balance sheet?

E14–5 **Required additional pension liability** AICPA adapted

Nome Company sponsors a defined benefit plan covering all employees. Benefits are based on years of service and compensation levels at the time of retirement. Nome determined that as of September 30, 2001 its accumulated benefit obligation was $380,000 and its plan assets had a $290,000 fair value. Nome's September 30, 2001 trial balance showed a prepaid pension cost of $20,000.

REQUIRED:

In its September 30, 2001 balance sheet, what amount should Nome report as *additional* pension liability?

E14–6

Determining actual return on plan assets

AICPA adapted

The following information pertains to Gali Company's defined benefit pension plan for 2001:

Fair value of plan assets, beginning of year	$350,000
Fair value of plan assets, end of year	525,000
Employer contributions	110,000
Benefits paid	85,000

REQUIRED:

What was the dollar amount of actual return on plan assets for Gali Company in 2001?

E14–7

Determining accrued pension liability on balance sheet

AICPA adapted

The following information pertains to Kane Company's defined benefit pension plan:

Prepaid pension cost, 1/1/01	$ 2,000
Service cost	19,000
Interest cost	38,000
Expected return on plan assets	22,000
Amortization of unrecognized prior service cost	52,000
Employer contributions	40,000

The fair value of plan assets exceeds the accumulated benefit obligation.

REQUIRED:

In its December 31, 2001 balance sheet, what amount should Kane report as unfunded accrued pension cost?

E14–8

Prepaid pension cost on balance sheet

AICPA adapted

Dell Company adopted a defined benefit pension plan on January 1, 2001. Dell amortizes the prior service cost over 16 years and funds prior service cost by making equal payments to the fund trustee at the end of each of the first 10 years. The service cost is fully funded at the end of each year. The following data are available for 2001:

Service cost for 2001	$220,000
Prior service cost	
Amortized	83,400
Funded	114,400

REQUIRED:

How much is Dell's prepaid pension cost at December 31, 2001?

E14–9

Prepaid pension cost on balance sheet

AICPA adapted

On January 2, 2001 East Corporation adopted a defined benefit pension plan. The plan's service cost of $150,000 was fully funded at the end of 2001. Prior service cost was funded by a contribution of $60,000 in 2001. Amortization of prior service cost was $24,000 for 2001.

REQUIRED:

At December 31, 2001 what amount should East report as prepaid pension cost?

E14–10

Minimum pension liability

AICPA adapted

Payne, Inc. implemented a defined benefit pension plan for its employees on January 2, 2001. The following data are provided for 2001, as of December 31, 2001:

Accumulated benefit obligation	$103,000
Plan assets at fair value	78,000
Net periodic pension cost	90,000
Employer's contribution	70,000

REQUIRED:

What amount should Payne record as additional minimum pension liability at December 31, 2001?

E14–11

Determining postretirement expense

AICPA adapted

Hukle Company has provided the following information pertaining to its postretirement plan for 2001:

Service cost	$240,000
Benefit payment	110,000
Interest on accumulated postretirement benefit obligation	40,000
Unrecognized transition obligation (amortized over 20 years)	200,000

REQUIRED:

Calculate Hukle Company's 2001 net periodic postretirement benefit cost.

E14–12 **Determining pension expense** AICPA adapted

The following information pertains to Lee Corporation's defined benefit pension plan for 2001:

Service cost	$160,000
Actual and expected return on plan assets	35,000
Unexpected loss on plan assets due to 2001 disposal of a subsidiary	40,000
Amortization of unrecognized prior service costs	5,000
Annual interest on pension obligation	50,000

REQUIRED:

Determine Lee Corporation's pension expense that would be reported on its 2001 income statement.

E14–13 **Determining pension expense, actual and deferred return on plan assets**

Bostonian Company provided the following information related to its defined benefit pension plan for 2001:

Projected benefit obligation (PBO) on 1/1/01	$2,500,000
Fair value of plan assets on 1/1/01	2,000,000
Interest rate for discounting pension obligations	10%
Service cost	120,000
Fair value of plan assets on 12/31/01	2,300,000
Payments made to retirees during the year	100,000
Amortization of transition asset	40,000
Recognized actuarial losses	50,000
Expected return on plan assets	12%
Contributions made to plan during 2001	80,000

REQUIRED:

1. What amount of pension expense should Bostonian report for 2001?
2. What is the actual dollar return on plan assets for 2001?
3. What was the dollar amount of return on plan assets that was deferred in 2001?

E14–14 **Funded status reconciliation**

On December 31, 2001 Nelson Corporation reported the following balances related to its defined benefit pension plan:

Accumulated benefit obligation	$825,000
Projected benefit obligation	900,000
Accrued pension cost	112,500
Plan assets (fair value)	307,500
Market-related asset value	301,250
Unrecognized prior service cost	190,000
Unamortized transition obligation	160,000
Unrecognized net (gain) loss	?

REQUIRED:

Prepare a funded status reconciliation and determine the missing amount for the "Unrecognized net (gain) loss."

E14–15 **Determining postretirement (health-care) benefits expense and obligation**

Jones Company has a postretirement benefit (health-care) plan for its employees. On January 1, 1998 the balance in the "Accumulated postretirement benefit obligation" account was $300 million. The assumed discount rate—for purposes of determining postretirement obligations and expenses—is 8%. Jones does not prefund postretirement benefits, so there are no plan assets. The unrecognized transition obligation that existed on January 1, 1996 (when *SFAS No. 106, "Employer's Accounting for Postretirement Benefits Other than Pensions,"* was adopted) was $240 million; this amount is being amortized over 20 years. A prior service cost *credit* of $45 million was created in 1997 when Jones modified the health-care plan to reduce the maximum benefits paid to each employee. This amount is being amortized over 15 years. The service cost component of postretirement benefits for 1998 is $35 million.

REQUIRED:

1. Determine the amount of postretirement benefits cost for 1998.
2. If benefits paid out to retirees totaled $64 million in 1998, determine the balance in the "Accumulated postretirement benefit obligation" account on December 31, 1998.

E14–16

Postretirement health-care expenses and liability balance

Zeff Manufacturing provides the following information about its postretirement health-care plan for 2001:

Accumulated benefit obligation on 1/1/01	$300,000
Fair value of plan assets on 1/1/01	30,000
Fair value of plan assets on 12/31/01	40,000
Service cost for 2001	20,000
Discount rate	8%
Expected long-run rate of return on plan assets	10%
Recognized prior service cost *credit*	5,000
Recognized loss	7,000
Amortization of transition net liability (loss)	15,000
Actual return on plan assets	4,500
Contributions to the plan	12,000

REQUIRED:

1. Determine the postretirement health-care expense for Zeff in 2001.
2. Determine the amount of benefits paid out to employees in 2001.
3. Determine the amount of accumulated benefit obligation at December 31, 2001.

PROBLEMS/DISCUSSION QUESTIONS

P14–1

Determining components of pension expense

AICPA adapted

The following information pertains to Sparta Company's defined benefit pension plan:

Discount rate	8%
Expected rate of return on plan assets	10%
Average service life	12 years
At 1/1/01	
Projected benefit obligation	$600,000
Fair value of pension plan assets	720,000
Unrecognized prior service cost	240,000
Unrecognized prior pension gain	96,000
At 12/31/01	
Projected benefit obligation	910,000
Fair value of pension plan assets	825,000

Service cost for 2001 was $90,000. There were no contributions made or benefits paid during the year. Sparta's unfunded accrued pension liability was $8,000 at January 1, 2001. Sparta uses the straight-line method of amortization over the maximum period permitted.

REQUIRED:

Determine the amount for each of the following items:

1. Interest cost
2. Expected dollar return on plan assets
3. Actual return on plan assets
4. Balance in "Unrecognized prior pension gain" account on December 31, 2001
5. Recognized prior service costs
6. Recognized pension gain (minimum amortization)

P14–2 **Comprehensive pension reporting computations**

Turner Inc. provides a defined benefit pension plan to its employees. The company has 150 employees. The average remaining service life of employees is 10 years. Prior to 2001, the net pension expense recognized has always equaled the company's contributions to the plan. However, in 2001 the company changed its funding policy to make at least the minimum annual contribution required by applicable regulations. The cumulative unrecognized net gain or loss was zero at December 31, 2000. Additional information follows:

Description	December 31 2001	2000
Projected benefit obligation	$1,450,000	$1,377,000
Accumulated benefit obligation	1,425,000	1,350,000
Fair value of plan assets	1,395,000	1,085,000
Moving average (smoothed) value of plan assets	1,180,000	1,085,000
Unrecognized prior service cost	?	292,000
Service cost	117,400	
Contribution	169,000	
Settlement rate	10%	10%
Expected rate of return	10%	10%
Benefit payments made	None	None

REQUIRED:

Round all amounts to nearest dollar:

1. Compute unrecognized prior service cost that would be amortized as a component of pension expense for 2001 and 2002.
2. Compute the actual return on plan assets for 2001.
3. Compute the unexpected net gain or loss for 2001.
4. Compute pension expense for 2001.
5. Prepare the company's required pension journal entries for 2001.
6. Compute the 2001 increase/decrease in unrecognized net gains or losses and the amount to be amortized in 2001 and 2002. (Assume Turner uses the moving average value of plan assets in computing the 10% corridor.)
7. Reconcile the funded status of the plan with the pension amounts reported in the financial statements as of December 31, 2001.

P14–3 **Comprehensive pension reporting computations**

Puhlman Inc. provides a defined benefit pension plan to its employees. Prior to 2001, the net pension expense recognized has always equaled the company's contributions to the plan. However, in 2001 the company changed its funding policy to make at least the minimum annual contribution required by applicable regulations. Additional information follows.

Description	December 31 2001	2000
Projected benefit obligation	$2,700,000	$2,500,000
Accumulated benefit obligation	2,335,000	2,150,000
Fair value of plan assets	?	2,100,000
Moving average (smoothed) value of plan assets	2,140,000	2,100,000
Benefit payments made	?	231,000
Unrecognized net loss	114,000	-0-
Unrecognized prior service cost	?	400,000
Average remaining service life of employees	15 years	15 years
Service cost	214,000	
Contribution	321,000	
Settlement rate	9%	10%
Expected rate of return	10%	10%

During 2001 the PBO increased by $33,000 due to a decrease in the settlement rate from the previous year. Assume for 2002 that the expected rate of return remains at 10% and the expected return is $227,800.

REQUIRED:

Round all amounts to nearest dollar:

1. Compute the fair value of plan assets at December 31, 2001.
2. Compute unrecognized prior service cost that would be amortized as a component of pension expense for 2001 and 2002.
3. Compute the actual return on plan assets for 2001.
4. Compute the benefit payments made in 2001.
5. Compute pension expense for 2001.
6. Prepare the company's required pension journal entries for 2001.
7. Compute the 2001 increase/decrease in unrecognized net gains or losses and the amount to be amortized in 2001 and 2002. (Assume Puhlman uses the moving average value of plan assets in computing the 10% corridor.)
8. Reconcile the funded status of the plan with the pension amounts reported in the financial statements as of December 31, 2001.

P14–4

Determining PBO and ABO

Mary Abbott is a long-time employee of Love Enterprises, a manufacturer and distributor of farm implements. Mary plans to retire on her sixty-fifth birthday (January 1, 2006), five years from today. Mary's current salary is $48,000 per year and her projected salary for her last year of employment is $60,000.

Love Enterprises sponsors a defined benefit pension plan. The plan provides for an annual pension benefit equal to 60% of the employee's annual salary immediately prior to retirement. Payments commence on the employees sixty-sixth birthday or one year after the anniversary date of their retirement. The discount ("settlement") and earnings rate on plan assets is 8%. The average life expectancy for female employees is 80 and for males is 76.

REQUIRED:

1. Compute the projected benefit obligation related to Ms. Abbott's pension benefits as of January 1, 2001.
2. Compute the accumulated benefit obligation related to Ms. Abbott's pension benefits as of January 1, 2001.
3. Repeat requirement (1), assuming the discount and earnings rate are 11%.

P14–5

PBO, ABO, and pension expense

Assume the pension benefit formula of ABC Corporation calls for paying a pension benefit of $250/year for each year of service with the company plus 50% of the projected last year's salary just prior to retirement. Payments begin one year after the employee attains the age of 65 and are paid annually thereafter. The average life expectancy of employees is 76.

The pension plan is adopted on January 1, 2001. One of the company's employees, Ima Workaholic, is granted credit for 10 years of prior service. He is 50 years old at the date the plan is adopted. His current annual salary is $20,000, but his salary level when he retires in 15 years is expected to be $30,000.

Assume a 10% rate of interest for both the discounting ("settlement rate") and earnings rate on plan assets.

REQUIRED:

1. Determine the projected benefit obligation and accumulated benefit obligation related to Mr. Workaholic's pension benefits as of January 1, 2001.
2. What would the projected benefit obligation be on January 1, 2002?
3. How much pension expense should ABC Corporation recognize in 2001 for Workaholic? Show the components of pension expense.

P14–6

PBO, ABO, and pension expense

STRETCH

Assume the same facts for ABC Corporation that were cited in P14–5, with the following exceptions:

- Assume both that ABC Corporation fully funds the estimated PBO on January 1, 2001 and that invested funds earn an actual return of 12% in 2001.
- Suppose that in addition to funding the estimated PBO on January 1, 2001, ABC Corporation follows a policy of contributing to the pension

fund (at the end of each year) an amount equal to the estimated pension expense less the prior service cost component, which was prefunded. On January 1, 2002 the settlement rate drops from 10% to 9%, while the expected return on plan assets remains at 10% for 2002.

REQUIRED:

1. How much pension expense should ABC Corporation recognize in 2001? Show the components of pension expense. Explain how this differs from your answer in requirement (3) of P14–5.
2. Compute the pension expense and amount funded in 2002. (Assume the actual return on plan assets was 10% in 2002.) Compare the funded status of the plans at the end of 2002 and 2001. Explain the change.

P14–7

Effect of funding and discount rate assumption on pension expense

On January 1, 2001 Magee Corporation started doing business by hiring R. Walker as an employee at an annual salary of $50,000, with an annual salary increment of $10,000. Based on his current age and the company's retirement program, Mr. Walker is required to retire at the end of the year in 2004. However, at his option, Mr. Walker could retire any time after completing one full year of service. Regardless of when he retires, the company will pay a lump-sum pension at the end of the year in 2005. The lump-sum payment is calculated to be 25% of the cumulative lifetime salary earned by Mr. Walker. Magee's annual discount rate is 10%. Assume that Mr. Walker retires at the end of the year in 2004.

REQUIRED:

1. Assuming that Magee Corporation does not fund its pension expense, calculate the pension expense for the years 2001–2004. Clearly identify the service and interest cost components. Based on your calculations, provide journal entries both to record the pension expense during the 2001–2004 period as well as to record the lump-sum payment of Mr. Walker's pension at the end of the year in 2005.
2. Assume that Magee Corporation fully funds its pension cost as soon as it vests and that the contributions to the pension fund earn exactly a 10% rate of return annually. Based on these revised assumptions, redo requirement (1).
3. Explain why the total pension expense in requirement (1) is different from that in requirement (2).
4. Assume that Magee Corporation does not fund its pension expense. Discuss how different assumptions regarding the discount rate affect the pension expense. You may compare the pension expense with discount rates of 5%, 10%, and 15%.

P14–8

Determining effect of discount rate assumption on pension expense and PBO

STRETCH

Use the same set of facts as in problem P14–7. In addition, assume that based on ERISA rules, Magee Corporation must contribute the following amounts to the pension fund:

	2001	2002	2003	2004
Contributions	$8,475	$11,000	$15,000	$18,000

Magee Corporation intends to fund the pension plan only to the extent required by the ERISA rules. Assume that the contributions to the pension fund earn exactly a 10% rate of return annually.

REQUIRED:

1. The CEO of the company, Mr. R. Magee, is considering three possible discount rates (8%, 10%, and 12%) for calculating the annual pension expense. Provide schedules showing how much pension expense will be reported under each of the three scenarios during the 2001–2005 period.
2. Provide schedules showing the funded status of the pension plan during the 2001–2004 period.
3. Mr. Magee is wondering which of the three discount rate assumptions would be considered the most and least conservative for the purposes of determining net income. Prepare a schedule that shows how total pension expense compares across the three discount rate assumptions. Explain your results.

P14–9

Components of pension liability and pension expense

The following is the funded status of the pension plan of Saddington, Inc. as of December 31, 2001:

	End of Year 2001
Projected benefit obligation	($1,000,000)
Fair value of plan assets	1,000,000
Fair value in excess of PBO	-0-
Unrecognized gain	-0-
Accrued pension liability	-0-

The following information is provided for the years 2002–2005:

	2002	2003	2004	2005
Actual rate of return on plan assets	22%	20%	12%	10%
Contribution to pension fund	$220,000	$260,000	$300,000	$340,000
Pension payments	200,000	260,000	320,000	380,000
Service cost	300,000	350,000	400,000	450,000
Average remaining service period of active employees (in years)	10	10	10	10

The "Contribution to pension fund" component represents the cash flows from the company to the pension fund. The "Pension payments" component represents the payments made by the pension fund to the retired employees. The income earned by the pension fund in a given year is found by multiplying the fair value of the plan assets at the beginning of the year by the actual rate of return on plan assets for that year. The discount rate is 10% and the expected rate of return is 12% during each year from 2002 to 2005. Assume that the pension fund is not considered to be severely underfunded in any of the years over the 2002–2005 period.

REQUIRED:

1. Prepare schedules showing the changes in the following pension components over the 2002–2005 period:

   a. Projected benefit obligation
   b. Fair value of plan assets
   c. Unrecognized gain

2. Based on your answer to requirement (1), show the funded status of the plan at the end of years 2002 through 2005.
3. Calculate pension expense for the years 2002 through 2005 and provide breakdowns for service cost, interest cost, actual return on plan assets, unrecognized portion of return, and recognized gain or loss amounts.
4. Prepare all necessary journal entries pertaining to the accrued pension liability for the years 2002–2005. On the basis of the journal entries, construct the T-account for accrued pension liability over the same period.

P14–10

Effect of actual versus expected return on pension funded status and pension expense

On December 31, 2001 Muller Corporation eliminated its employee pension plan. The company has currently funded its pension plan for $100,000 (which is the value of the pension plan assets and PBO as of December 31, 2001). The expected return on plan assets and the settlement rate are both 10%. As part of the agreement with the current employees, the company expects to pay a lump sum of $133,100 on January 1, 2005 for pension obligations existing under the canceled pension plan. While the annual expected rate of return is 10%, the realized rates of return on pension assets depend on the state of the U.S. economy over the next three years. Assume that depending on whether the economy is stable, growing, or declining, the pension assets earn the following rates of return over the next three years:

State of the Economy	Actual Rates of Return for 2002	2003	2004
Scenario 1: Stable economy	10.00%	10.00%	10.00%
Scenario 2: Growth	5.00%	10.00%	15.24%
Scenario 3: Decline	15.00%	10.00%	5.22%

REQUIRED:

1. Show for each state of the economy over the next three years that the pension plan will have sufficient funds to meet the pension obligation at the end of the year 2004. Indicate the value of the pension plan assets at the end of the years 2002–2004. Over the three-year period, what is the difference between the actual and expected annual rates of return under each state of the economy?
2. Ignoring the deferral of unexpected gains or losses, calculate the pension expense of Muller Corporation over the next three years under each of the three states of the economy.
3. Recalculate the pension expense of Muller Corporation over the next three years under each of the three states of the economy after incorporating the deferral of unexpected gains or losses. Also show the funded status of the pension plan at the end of 2002, 2003, and 2004.
4. Based on your answers so far, discuss the potential benefit of deferring unexpected gains or losses in the calculation of pension expense.

P14–11

Components of OPEB and journal entries

Excerpts from Unicom Corporation's footnotes for the year ended December 31, 1999 follow:

> ComEd and certain of Unicom's subsidiaries provide certain postretirement medical, dental and vision care, and life insurance for retirees and their dependents and for the surviving dependents of eligible employees and retirees. Generally, the employees become eligible for postretirement benefits if they retire no earlier than age 55 with ten years of service. The liability for postretirement benefits is funded through trust funds based upon actuarially determined contributions that take into account the amount deductible for income tax purposes. The health care plans are contributory, funded jointly by the companies and the participating retirees. The December 31, 1999 and 1998 postretirement benefit liabilities and related data were determined using the January 1, 1999 actuarial valuations.
>
> Reconciliation of the beginning and ending balances of the accumulated postretirement benefit obligation, and the funded status of the plan for the years 1999 and 1998 follows:

($ in thousands)	Year ended December 31 1999	1998
Change in benefit obligation		
Benefit obligation at beginning of period	$1,236,000	$1,139,000
Service cost	41,000	38,000
Interest cost	82,000	78,000
Plan participants' contributions	4,000	3,000
Actuarial loss (gain)	(188,000)	25,000
Benefits paid	(51,000)	(47,000)
Special termination benefits	27,000	–
Benefit obligation at end of period	1,151,000	1,236,000
Change in plan assets		
Fair value of plan assets at beginning of period	865,000	767,000
Actual return on plan assets	105,000	122,000
Employer contributions	24,000	20,000
Plan participants' contributions	4,000	3,000
Benefits paid	(51,000)	(47,000)
Fair value of plan assets at end of period	947,000	865,000
Plan assets less than benefit obligations	(204,000)	(371,000)
Unrecognized net actuarial gain	(555,000)	(371,000)
Unrecognized prior service cost	41,000	48,000
Unrecognized transition obligation	276,000	323,000
Accrued liability for benefits	($442,000)	($371,000)

The assumed discount rate used to determine the benefit obligation as of December 31, 1999 and 1998 was 7.75% and 6.75%, respectively. The fair value of plan assets excludes $9 million and $7 million held in a grantor trust as of December 31, 1999 and 1998, respectively, for the payment of postretirement medical benefits.

The components of other postretirement benefit costs, portions of which were recorded as components of construction costs for the years 1999, 1998 and 1997 were as follows:

($ in thousands)	1999	1998	1997
Service cost	$?	$?	$34,000
Interest cost on accumulated benefit obligation	?	?	76,000
Expected return on plan assets	?	?	(61,000)
Amortization of transition obligation	22,000	22,000	22,000
Amortization of prior service costs	4,000	4,000	4,000
Recognized gain	(14,000)	(14,000)	(13,000)
Severance plan costs	1,000	6,000	8,000
Curtailment loss	35,000	–0–	–0–
Net periodic benefit cost	$?	$?	$ 70,000

The other postretirement benefit curtailment losses in December 1999 represent the recognition of prior service costs and transition obligations, and an increase in the benefit obligations resulting from special termination benefits, related to the reduction in the number of employees due to ComEd's sale of the fossil stations.

The health care cost trend rates used to measure the expected cost of the postretirement medical benefits are assumed to be 8.0% for pre-Medicare recipients and 6.0% for Medicare recipients for 1999. Those rates are assumed to decrease in 0.5% annual increments to 5% for the years 2005 and 2001, respectively, and to remain level thereafter. The health-care cost trend rates, used to measure the expected cost of postretirement dental and vision benefits, are a level 3.5% and 2.0% per year, respectively. Assumed health care cost trend rates have a significant effect on the amounts reported for the health care plans. A one-percentage point change in the assumed health care cost trend rates would have the following effects:

	1 Percentage Point	
($ in thousands)	Increase	Decrease
Effect on total 1999 service and interest cost components	$ 26,000	($20,000)
Effect on postretirement benefit obligation as of 12/31/1999	190,000	151,000

REQUIRED:

1. Assuming an expected rate of return on plan assets for 1999 and 1998 of 8.8% and 9%, compute the missing amounts in the above table and determine the "Net periodic benefit cost" for years 1999 and 1998. (Round amounts to nearest million.)
2. Assuming that the $4,000,000 of participant contributions were submitted directly to the trustee by the employees, show the journal entry that Unicom would make to record the 1999 company (employer) contribution and its related "Net periodic benefit cost."
3. What amount (if any) would appear on Unicom's 1999 balance sheet relating to its OPEB plans and how would it be classified?

P14–12

Amortization of actuarial gains (losses) and minimum pension liability

The following information pertains to the pension plan of Beatty Business Group:

	Beginning of the Year		
Year (1)	Projected Benefit Obligation (2)	Fair Value of Pension Plan Assets (3)	Gain (Loss) for the Year (4)
2002	$ 400,000	$ 390,000	
2003	450,000	410,000	$ (60,000)
2004	570,000	500,000	(120,000)
2005	840,000	800,000	120,000
2006	1,000,000	1,100,000	175,000
2007	1,200,000	1,280,000	250,000
2008	1,450,000	1,310,000	80,000

Note that the information in columns (2) and (3) are as of the beginning of the year, whereas the information in column (4) is measured *over* the year.

The cumulative unrecognized *loss* at the end of 2002 was $70,000. The "Gain (loss) for the year" represents the excess of the realized return on pension plan assets over the expected return for the specific year. When a gain (loss) was reported, then the realized return was higher (lower) than the expected return during that year. The estimated remaining service period of active employees is five years for each of the calendar years.

REQUIRED:

1. Provide a schedule showing how the gain (or loss) is amortized over the 2003–2008 period. Clearly indicate whether the amortization increases or decreases the pension expense in each year.
2. Based on available information, prepare a schedule showing the funded status of the plan at the end of the years 2002 through 2007.
3. In answering this requirement, assume that the *accumulated* benefit obligation is 95% of the *projected* benefit obligation in each year. Using this additional information, prepare a schedule showing the funded status of the plan at the end of the years 2002 through 2007. (*Note*: You may have to calculate the minimum pension liability.) Also provide journal entries to reflect the minimum pension liability over the 2002 through 2007 period.

P14–13

Pension expense and funded status

The following is the funded status of the pension plan of McKeown Consulting Company at December 31, 2001:

	2001
Projected benefit obligation	($900,000)
Fair value of plan assets	1,000,000
Fair value in excess of PBO	100,000
Unrecognized prior service cost	–0–
Unrecognized (gain) loss	–0–
Accrued pension asset (liability)	$ 100,000

The following information is available for the years 2002 and 2003:

	Years Ended December 31	
	2002	2003
Discount rate	10%	10%
Expected rate of return on plan assets	9%	11%

The service cost for 2002 and 2003 are $125,000 and $145,000, respectively. The interest cost for a given year is estimated by multiplying the PBO at the beginning of the year by the discount rate for the year. Similarly, the expected return on plan assets is computed by multiplying the fair value of plan assets at the beginning of the year by the assumed expected rate of return for the year. During the years 2002 and 2003 the pension fund's actual earnings are $100,000 and $64,740, respectively.

At the end of 2002, McKeown Consulting Company retroactively enhanced the benefits provided under its pension plan, and this increased the projected benefit obligation by $110,000. The average remaining service period of employees expected to receive these retroactive benefits under the plan was 10 years.

During 2002 and 2003 the company made contributions of $99,000 and $123,000, respectively, to the pension fund. In turn, the pension fund made payments of $120,000 and $85,000 to the retired employees during the same periods.

REQUIRED:

1. Compute pension expense for the years 2002 and 2003. Show the funded status of the pension plan and the funded status reconciliation as of the end of each of these years. (*Hint*: You will need to calculate the ending balances for PBO, fair value of plan assets, unrecognized prior service costs, and the unrecognized gain or loss at the end of the year.)
2. Provide necessary journal entries in the books of McKeown Consulting Company for the years 2002 and 2003 to record all transactions relating to its pension plan. Also, explain the changes in the accrued pension asset (liability) over the same period.
3. Explain the cause(s) for the difference between the funded status of the pension plan and the reported balance sheet status as of the end of the years 2001 through 2003.

P14–14 **Solving for pension cost and funded status components**

The following information pertains to Kothari Manufacturing Company:

	As of December 31		
	2001	2002	2003
Projected benefit obligation	($550,000)	($684,000)	($768,720)
Less: Fair value of plan assets	550,000	595,000	686,400
Fair value in excess of PBO	-0-	(89,000)	(82,320)
Unrecognized prior service cost	-0-	80,000	64,000
Unrecognized gain	-0-	-0-	(11,900)
Accrued pension asset (liability)	-0-	($ 9,000)	($ 30,220)

	Years Ended December 31	
	2002	2003
Discount rate	8%	8%
Expected rate of return on plan assets	10%	10%
Actual rate of return on plan assets	10%	12%

The following additional information is available on the annual pension cost:

	Years Ended December 31	
	2002	2003
Service cost	$110,000	$130,000
Interest cost	?	?
− Actual return on plan assets	?	?
+/− Deferral of unrecognized gain/loss	?	?
+ Recognized prior service cost	-0-	16,000
Annual pension cost	?	?

Breakdown of the annual pension cost	2002	2003
Manufacturing employees	$63,000	$85,000
Administrative employees	?	?
Annual pension cost	?	?

At the end of 2002 Kothari Manufacturing Company retroactively enhanced the benefits provided under its pension plan. The average remaining service period of employees expected to receive these retroactive benefits under the plan was five years.

REQUIRED:

1. Calculate the missing information required to solve for the annual pension cost for the years 2002 and 2003. Based on this information, complete the breakdown of the annual pension cost between manufacturing and administrative employees.
2. Provide schedules reconciling the changes in the components of the funded status of the pension plan over the years 2002 and 2003 (PBO, fair value of plan assets, unrecognized prior service cost, and unrecognized gain). (*Hint*: You need to prepare the schedule to reconcile beginning and ending PBO before preparing the schedule for the fair value of plan assets.)
3. Provide necessary journal entries in the books of Kothari Manufacturing Company for the years 2002 and 2003 to record all transactions relating to its pension plan. (*Hint*: The annual pension cost for the manufacturing employees is a product cost.)

P14–15

OPEB expense and journal entries

On January 1, 1993 Eccher Retail Stores adopted the provisions of *SFAS No. 106*, "Employers' Accounting for Postretirement Benefits Other Than Pensions." At that time, the company estimated its accumulated benefit obligation for postretirement medical expenses to be $2,000,000. The company elected to amortize this transition obligation over a 20-year period. The service and interest costs during 1993 were $210,000 and $175,000, respectively. The company made cash payments of $245,000 to retired employees for medical expenses.

REQUIRED:

1. Calculate the OPEB expense for the year 1993. Provide appropriate disclosures for the components of accrued OPEB liability as of the end of 1993.
2. Provide journal entries to record transactions pertaining to postretirement benefits during the year 1993.
3. Repeat requirements (1) and (2), but assume that the company had elected to immediately recognize the entire transition obligation as of January 1, 1993. Assume a tax rate of 35%.

P14–16

Reconciling accumulated postretirement benefit obligations and preparing journal entries

The following information on postretirement benefit obligations is excerpted from Ordonez Corporation's Form 10-K for the fiscal year ending June 30, 1999. (This is a real company whose name has been disguised.)

	As of June 30	
	1999	1998
Accumulated benefit obligation (ABO)	($21,743,000)	($20,494,000)
Unrecognized transition obligation	12,577,000	13,475,000
Unrecognized net gain	(699,000)	(1,192,000)
Accrued cost (OPEB liability)	($9,865,000)	($8,211,000)
Assumptions	**1999**	**1998**
Discount rate used to determine (ABO)	7.00%	7.25%

	Year Ended June 30, 1999
Service cost	$ 467,000
Interest cost	1,444,000
Amortization of transition obligation	898,000
Amortization of unrecognized net gain	0
Net periodic benefit (OPEB) cost	$2,809,000

Benefit payments in 1999 totaled $1,155,000.

REQUIRED:

1. Using the format in the chapter on pages 712 and 723, reconcile the funded status of the plan with the amounts that are recognized/unrecognized on the balance sheet.
2. Assume that only administrative employees are eligible for postretirement benefits. Provide the journal entry to record all transactions pertaining to the OPEB liability during fiscal 1999.
3. Prepare a schedule showing the changes in the accumulated postretirement benefit obligation from 1998 to 1999.
4. What would have been the OPEB expense had the company used the cash basis approach?
5. Prepare a schedule showing the changes in the accrued OPEB liability from 1998 to 1999.

CASES

C14–1

OPEB reconciliation of funded status and expense components

The following is based on information obtained from the 1996–1999 annual reports of the E. L. Baer Company. (These numbers have been slightly modified but are based on the activities of a real company whose name has been disguised.)

	Years Ended December 31			
($ in thousands)	1999	1998	1997	1996
Accumulated postretirement benefit obligation	$15,894	$16,675	$ 17,815	$15,502
Unrecognized net gain	5,082	3,477	2,789	3,913
Prior service cost (plan curtailments)	2,314	3,070	3,826	4,582
Accrued OPEB liability	$23,290	$23,222	$24,430	$23,997

Other information	Years Ended December 31		
($ in thousands)	1999	1998	1997
Net periodic OPEB cost	$ 883	$ 791	$1,308
Service cost	681	642	998
Interest cost	1,140	1,113	1,199

At the end of years 1996 through 1999, the company had made the following assumptions in measuring the accumulated benefit obligation:

	Years Ended December 31			
Assumptions	1999	1998	1997	1996
Discount rate	7.50%	7.25%	7.25%	7.50%
Health-care cost trend rate (near-term)	6.5–7.0%	7.0–8.5%	8.0–9.5%	8.5–10%

The discount rate is used to find the present value of the expected future payments to employees under the company's OPEB Plan. The health-care cost trend rate is used to forecast the expected growth in the future medical payments due to inflation in medical costs. Assume there have been no amendments to the plan after 1995 and that the plan is totally unfunded.

REQUIRED:

1. Prepare a schedule like the one on page 723 which reconciles the funded status of the OPEB plans with the recognized and unrecognized amounts at December 31, 1999.
2. Complete the following schedule to determine net periodic OPEB cost for 1997, 1998 and 1999.

Net periodic OPEB cost	1999	1998	1997
Service cost	$	$	$
Interest cost			
Amortization of prior service cost			
Recognized net actuarial (gain) loss			
Net periodic OPEB cost	$	$	$

3. Complete the following schedule to explain changes in the accumulated benefit obligation over the period 1997 through 1999.

Accumulated postretirement benefit obligation ($ in thousands)	1999	1998	1997
APBO at beginning of year	$	$	$
Service cost			
Interest cost			
Actuarial losses (gains)			
Benefits paid			
APBO at end of year	$	$	$

4. Prepare journal entries to record transactions pertaining to the accrued OPEB liability for the period 1997 through 1999. Based on the journal entries, prepare a schedule that shows the changes in the accrued OPEB liability from the beginning to the end of the year for 1997 through 1999.
5. In each of the years 1997 through 1999, the company experienced some unrecognized gain (or loss) from changes in assumptions. Explain the year-to-year changes in unrecognized gain (or loss) by relating them to specific changes in the assumptions made by the company.

C14–2

Interpreting pension footnote disclosures

Selected pension information extracted from the retirement benefits footnote that appeared in Aeromed's 1999 annual report follows. The entity's name has been disguised.

All employees of Aeromed and employees of certain other subsidiaries are eligible to participate in the company's pension plans. The defined benefit plans provide benefits for participating employees based on years of service and average compensation for a specified period of time before retirement.

The following table provides a reconciliation of the changes in the plans' benefit obligations and fair value of assets for the years ended December 31, 1999 and 1998:

Reconciliation of projected benefit obligation ($ in millions)	**1999**	**1998**
Obligation at January 1	$ 6,117	$5,666
Service cost	236	213
Interest cost	433	418
Actuarial loss (gain)	?	300
Plan amendments	?	-0-
Benefit payments	?	(480)
Obligation at December 31	$5,624	$ 6,117

Reconciliation of fair value of plan assets ($ in millions)	**1999**	**1998**
Fair value of plan assets at January 1	$5,564	$ 5,127
Actual return on plan assets	7	847
Employer contributions	?	70
Benefit payments	?	(480)
Fair value of plan assets at December 31	?	$5,564

The following table provides a statement of funded status of the plans as of December 31, 1999 and 1998:

Funded status ($ in millions)	**1999**	**1998**
Projected benefit obligation	$5,624	$6,117
Fair value of assets	?	5,564
Funded status at December 31:	(341)	(553)
Unrecognized loss	288	651
Unrecognized prior service costs	138	68
Unrecognized transition asset	(7)	(11)
Prepaid pension cost	$ 78	$ 155

The following table provides the components of net periodic pension cost for the years ended December 31, 1999, 1998 and 1997:

Components of net periodic pension cost ($ in millions)	**1999**	**1998**	**1997**
Defined benefit plans:			
Service cost	$ 236	$ 213	$ 179
Interest cost	433	418	393
Expected return on assets	(514)	(472)	(421)
Amortization of:			
Transition asset	(4)	(11)	(12)
Prior service cost	5	4	4
Unrecognized loss	21	22	26
Net periodic benefit cost	$ 177	$ 174	$ 169

The following assumptions were used by the Company in the measurement of the benefit obligation as of December 31:

Weighted-average assumptions	1999	1998
Discount rate	8.25%	7.00%
Salary growth rate	4.26%	4.26%
Expected return on plan assets	9.50%	9.50%

REQUIRED:

Show supporting computations with clear labels for all calculations.

1. What is the journal entry to record the amount of cash contributed to the pension plan in 1999?
2. What was the amount of benefit payments distributed to retirees in 1999?
3. Determine the amount of increase (decrease) in the projected benefit obligation (PBO) as a result of amendments to the plan during 1999 and reconcile it with unrecognized prior service costs.
4. Determine the effect of the actuarial loss (gain) on the PBO in 1999. Reconcile the unrecognized loss at December 31, 1998 to the balance at December 31, 1999.
5. What was the effect of increasing the discount rate from 7.00% in 1998 to 8.25% in 1999?
6. Reconcile the funded status of the plan as of December 31, 1999 with the amounts that are recognized/unrecognized on the balance sheet, using the format illustrated on page 712 of the chapter.

C14–3

Interpreting pension footnote disclosures

The retirement benefit footnote that appeared in Shileny & Cribbs' 1999 annual report follows. The entity's name has been disguised. The firm is primarily engaged in the exploration, production, and sale of crude oil and natural gas and in contract drilling of oil and gas wells for others.

All employees of Shileny & Cribbs are eligible to participate in the company's pension plan. The defined benefit plan provides benefits for participating employees based on years of service and average compensation for a specified period of time before retirement.

The following tables provide information about the pension plan:

Projected benefit obligation ($ in thousands)	Years Ended September 30 1999	1998
PBO at beginning of year	$36,954	$33,913
Service cost	3,700	2,836
Interest cost	2,468	2,430
Actuarial (gain) loss	(4,468)	231
Benefit paid	?	(2,456)
PBO at end of year	?	$36,954

Fair value of plan assets and funded status ($ in thousands)	Years Ended September 30 1999	1998
Fair value of plan assets at beginning of year	$51,572	$53,834
Actual return on plan assets	?	194
Benefits paid	?	(2,456)
Fair value of plan assets at end of year	$58,517	$51,572
Funded status of the plan (FVPA > PBO)	21,522	14,618
Unrecognized net actuarial gain	(10,127)	(1,647)
Unrecognized prior service cost	1,025	1,263
Unrecognized net transition asset	(1,619)	(2,159)
Prepaid pension cost	$10,801	$ 12,075

Pension plan assumptions	Years Ended September 30 1999	1998	1997
Discount rate	7.50%	6.75%	7.25%
Expected return on plan assets	9.00%	8.50%	9.00%
Rate of compensation increase	5.00%	5.00%	5.50%

Components of net pension expense ($ in thousands)	Years Ended September 30 1999	1998	1997
Service cost	$3,700	$2,836	$2,114
Interest cost	2,468	2,430	1,797
Expected return on assets	(4,606)	(4,542)	(3,592)
Amortization of prior service cost	238	238	239
Amortization of transition asset	(540)	(540)	(540)
Recognized net actuarial loss (gain)	14	(65)	(66)
Net pension expense (income)	$1,274	$ 357	$ (48)

REQUIRED:

Show supporting computations with clear labels for all calculations.

1. What is the required journal entry to record the 1999 net pension expense? What is the primary reason for the $917,000 increase from 1998?
2. You determined the 1999 cash funding of the plan in answering requirement (1). Explain why the company chose to contribute this amount.
3. Compute the PBO at September 30, 1999.
4. Prepare a schedule like the one on page 712, which reconciles the funded status of the pension plan with the recognized and unrecognized amounts at September 30, 1999.
5. Assuming the firm had an unexpected gain of $3,998,000, what was 1999's actual return on plan assets in both dollars and as a percentage?
6. What was the amount of benefit payments distributed to retirees in 1999?
7. Prepare a schedule that reconciles the beginning and ending balances of the unrecognized net actuarial gain number between 1998 and 1999.

Excerpts from General Electric's 1991 Annual Report footnote for retiree insurance benefits follow:

C14–4

General Electric–Interpreting OPEB footnote disclosures

GE and its affiliates sponsor a number of . . . retiree health and life insurance plans. Principal plans are discussed below; other plans are not significant individually or in the aggregate.

1991 Accounting Change. Statement of Financial Accounting Standards *(SFAS) No. 106*—"Employers' Accounting for Postretirement Benefits Other Than Pensions"—was implemented using the immediate recognition transition option, effective as of January 1, 1991.

SFAS No. 106 requires recognition during employees' service with the Company, of the cost of their retiree health and life insurance benefits. At January 1, 1991, the accumulated postretirement benefit obligation was $4,287 million; however, $1,577 million of this obligation had been provided through the fair market value of related trust assets ($1,037 million) and recorded liabilities ($540 million), thus resulting in a pre-tax adjustment (i.e., transition obligation) of $2,710 million. The effect on net earnings and share owners' equity was $1,799 million ($2.07 per share) after [a] deferred tax benefit of $911 million. Aside from the one-time effect of the adjustment, adoption of *SFAS No. 106* was not material to 1991 financial results.

Prior to 1991, GE health benefits for eligible retirees under age 65 and eligible dependents were generally included in costs as covered expenses were actually incurred. For eligible retirees and spouses over age 65, the present value of future health benefits was included in costs in the year the retiree became eligible for benefits. The present value of future life insurance benefits for each eligible retiree was included in costs in the year of retirement.

Principal retiree insurance plans generally provide health and life insurance benefits to employees who retire under the GE Pension Plan with 10 or more years of service. Benefit provisions are subject to collective bargaining. At the end of 1991, the plans covered approximately 237,000 retirees and dependents.

Employer costs for principal retiree insurance plans follow.

Cost (income) for retiree insurance plans ($ in millions)	**Total**	**For the year 1991 Health**	**Life**
Benefit cost for service during the year—net of retiree contributions	$ 88	$ 65	$ 23
Interest cost on benefit obligations	318	214	104
Actual return on plan assets	(138)	(9)	(129)
Unrecognized portion of return	44	5	39
Amortization	(33)	(33)	-0-
Retiree insurance cost	$279[1]	$242	$ 37

[1]Retiree insurance cost was $249 million in 1990 and $283 million in 1989.

Actuarial assumptions used to determine 1991 costs and benefit obligations for principal plans include a discount rate of 9.0% (8.5% in 1990 and 1989). . . . Recognized return on plan assets for 1991 was determined by applying the expected long-term rate of return of 9.5% (8.5% in 1990 and 1989) to the market-related value of assets. The assumed rate of future increases in per capita cost of health-care benefits (the health-care cost trend rate) was 13.0% for 1991, decreasing gradually to 6.6% by the year 2050. These trend rates reflect GE's prior experience and management's expectation that future rates will decline. Increasing the health-care cost trend rates by one percentage point would increase the accumulated postretirement benefit obligation by $50 million and would increase annual aggregate service and interest costs by $5 million. In connection with its 1992 annual funding review, GE may revise certain actuarial assumptions effective January 1, 1992; however, it is anticipated that any such revision would increase benefit obligations by no more than 5%.

Pension gains and losses that occur because actual experience differs from that assumed are amortized over the average future service period of employees. Amounts allocable to prior service for amendments to . . . retiree insurance plans are amortized in a similar manner.

Funding policy . . . The present value of future life insurance benefits for each eligible retiree is funded in the year of retirement. In general, retiree health benefits are paid as covered expenses are incurred.

The following table compares the market-related value of assets with the value of benefit obligations, recognizing the effects of future . . . service. The market-related value of assets is based on cost plus recognition of market appreciation and depreciation in the portfolio over five years, a method that reduces the impact of short-term market fluctuations.

Funded status for principal plans ($ in millions)	**December 31** **1991**	**1990**
Retiree insurance plans		
Market-related value of assets	$1,124	$1,037
Accumulated postretirement benefit obligation	3,675	4,110

Schedules reconciling the benefit obligations for principal plans with GE's recorded liabilities in the Statement of Financial Position follow.

Reconciliation of benefit obligation with recorded liability ($ in millions)	**Retiree Insurance Plans December 31** **1991**	**1990**[1]
Benefit obligation	$3,675	$4,110
Fair value of trust assets	(1,171)	(1,037)
Unamortized balances		
Experience gains (losses)	(351)	-0-
Plan amendments	829	
Recorded liability	$2,982	$3,073

[1] 1990 amounts include the pro forma effects of adopting *SFAS No. 106* as of January 1, 1991.

Unamortized balances for amendments include the effects of changes in retiree insurance plan provisions during 1991.

REQUIRED:

1. Explain the nature of the "plan amendments" element in the funded status portion of General Electric's footnote disclosure.
2. Discuss some possible explanations for why a company would initiate changes in plan benefits immediately *after* adopting *SFAS No. 106*.

The following information is excerpted from the footnotes to the 1990 financial statements of Square D:

C14–5

Groupe Schneider (KR): Effect of postretirement benefits on company valuation

Note P: Post-Retirement Benefits ($ in 000)
The company provides health-plan coverage and life insurance benefits for retired employees of substantially all of its domestic operations. Substantially all of the company's employees may become eligible for these benefits when they retire from active employment with the company. The cost of retiree health coverage is recognized as an expense when claims are paid. The cost of life insurance benefits is recognized as an expense as premiums are paid. These costs totaled $6,165 in 1990, $5,075 in 1989, and $3,982 in 1988.

The Financial Accounting Standards Board has issued Statement of Financial Accounting Standards No. 106, "Employers' Accounting for Postretirement Benefits Other Than Pensions." This Statement will require accrual of postretirement benefits during the years an employee provides services. While the impact of this new standard has not been fully determined, the change will result in significantly greater expense being recognized for these benefits. The company plans to adopt this Statement in 1993.

The company had also provided similar footnote disclosures during the previous three years. An article related to Groupe Schneider's investment in Square D appears below.

REQUIRED:

What does the article consider as one main reason for the fall in the stock price of Groupe Schneider? What might have been the economic impact if the accounting standard for postretirement benefits *(SFAS No. 106)* were in place when Groupe Schneider acquired Square D Company?

SQUARE D OWNER'S STOCK FALLS BY JACQUES NEHER
The stock of Groupe Schneider, which acquired Palatine-based Square D Co. last summer, dropped sharply last week on the Paris stock exchange. Market sources said that, among other things, Schneider failed to assess correctly the impact of retiree health-benefit liabilities facing Square D.

Under new rules adopted by the Financial Accounting Standards Board, U.S. companies are required by 1993 to record their liability for retiree health benefits on their balance sheets, either as a one-time charge to earnings or spread out over 20 years.

Although it is based in France, Schneider will have to follow U.S. accounting rules, at least for its operations here, if it plans to borrow money or otherwise raise capital in the United States, accounting sources said.

Groupe Schneider, a giant French electrical-equipment and construction firm, acquired Square D this summer for $1.3 billion. At one point last week Schneider stock was off 10 percent in Paris, about twice the decline of the overall market.

The stock closed Monday in Paris at 639.5 French francs, up 2.5 francs from Friday but off from a recent high of 703 earlier this month.

Ian Furnivall, an analyst with UBS/Phillips & Drew in Paris, recently wrote a negative report on the company, saying that Schneider was going to have to increase its so-called goodwill write-offs (reflecting the premium over market value that Schneider paid for Square D) "principally [because of] an unforeseen exceptional charge for staff postretirement health benefits."

The report came about the same time Schneider's finance director, Alain Bommelaer, was replaced.

Jean de Courcel, who took the post of finance director, downplayed the market reports and said the accounting rule change was known to the company when it bought Square D. A Schneider spokesman added that replacing Bommelaer, who is still with the company awaiting a new assignment, had nothing to do with a miscalculation of the Square D purchase price.

Another Schneider financial source, who asked not to be named, described the effect of the accounting change as "a big problem. We've been considering it for three months, like other French companies with operations in the United States, and we still haven't decided what to do."

A spokesman for Square D in Palatine confirmed that the treatment of the accounting rule remains under consideration. One question, he said, is whether to account for the charge on the books of the French company or of Schneider North America, the U.S. subsidiary that includes Square D.

(continued)

But the Square D spokesman said, "I would not tie [Schneider] stock being down to retiree health benefits." He said a more likely problem is the economic slump in France and the United States. On the other hand, he acknowledged that France's system of socialized health care creates a gulf between company operations in that country and in the United States. "They're not used to doing what we do," he said.

"The acquisition of Square D strategically is a good move, but unfortunately it's going to cost Schneider a lot of money," said Andrew Haskins, an analyst with James Capel, a London brokerage firm. "We predict a very significant dilution of earnings this year and next and maybe even in 1993."

Source: *Chicago Tribune* (November 26, 1991).

C14–6

Understanding postretirement footnote disclosures

Selected information from Houston Marine Corporation's 1999 postretirement benefits footnote follows. (This is a real company, whose name has been disguised.)

Other postretirement benefits, including certain health care and life insurance benefits, are provided to retired employees. The amount of health care benefits is limited to lifetime maximums as outlined in the plan. Substantially all employees of Houston Marine may become eligible for these benefits if they satisfy eligibility requirements during their working lives.

The following table provides a reconciliation of the changes in the plan's benefit obligations and fair value of assets for the years ended December 31, 1999 and 1998:

Accumulated postretirement benefit obligation ($ in millions)	**1999**	**1998**
APBO at beginning of year	$1,523	$1,353
Service cost	?	52
Interest cost	?	99
Actuarial loss (gain)	?	84
Benefit payments	?	(65)
APBO at end of year	$?	$1,523

Fair value of plan assets ($ in millions)	**1999**	**1998**
Fair value of plan assets at beginning of year	$62	$49
Actual return on plan assets	1	4
Employer contributions	?	74
Benefit payments	?	(65)
Fair value of plan assets at end of year	$72	$62

The following table provides a statement of funded status of the plan as of December 31, 1999 and 1998:

Funded status ($ in millions)	**1999**	**1998**
Accumulated postretirement benefit obligation	$?	$ 1,523
Fair value of assets	72	62
Funded status at December 31	?	(1,461)
Unrecognized gain	(395)	(89)
Unrecognized prior service cost	?	(45)
Accrued OPEB liability	$(1,669)	$(1,595)

The following table provides the components of net periodic OPEB cost for the years ended December 31, 1999, 1998, and 1997:

Net periodic OPEB cost ($ in millions)	**1999**	**1998**	**1997**
Service cost	$?	$ 52	$ 44
Interest cost	?	99	92
Expected return on assets	?	(5)	(4)
Amortization of prior service cost	(5)	(5)	(5)
Amortization of unrecognized net gain	?	(2)	(9)
Net periodic OPEB cost	$153	$139	$118

The following assumptions were used by the Company in the measurement of the benefit obligation as of December 31:

OPEB plan assumptions	**1999**
Discount rate	7.10%
Expected return on plan assets	9.50%

REQUIRED:

Round all calculations to nearest million.

1. Compute 1999 interest cost.
2. Compute 1999 expected return on assets.
3. What was the employer contribution for 1999?
4. Determine 1999 benefit payments.
5. Assuming there were no plan amendments, compute the unrecognized prior service cost at December 31, 1999.
6. Determine the accumulated postretirement benefit obligation at December 31, 1999.
7. Compute 1999 actuarial gain or loss.
8. Assuming an average remaining service life of ten years, determine the 1999 amortization of unrecognized gain.
9. What was the service cost for 1999?
10. Prepare a schedule like the one on page 723, which reconciles the funded status of the postretirement benefit plan with the recognized and unrecognized amounts at December 31, 1999.
11. Redo Houston Marine's postretirement benefits footnote (in good form), filling in all missing 1999 components.

COLLABORATIVE LEARNING CASE

C14–7

Chrysler Corporation (KR): OPEB expense and management incentive compensation

The following text is excerpted from the 1993 proxy statement of Chrysler Corporation. A proxy is a document prepared by management to obtain authorization from shareholders to act on their behalf. In the following passage, the management of Chrysler Corporation is requesting its shareholders' permission to modify the method of computing the incentive compensation awarded to its officers and executives.

> Under a resolution adopted by the stockholders in 1929, and since amended from time to time, it has been a continuing practice of the Corporation to provide incentive compensation awards to officers and executives of the Corporation and its subsidiaries whenever permitted by the formula in the stockholders' resolution as then in effect. The authority to award incentive compensation under the stockholders' resolution as last amended extended through the fiscal year ended December 31, 1992. Stockholder action is required at this time to permit the Corporation to continue its practice with respect to awards of incentive compensation for fiscal years commencing on and after January 1, 1993, subject to certain modifications in the resolution which would eliminate the effect of a mandated change in accounting for certain postretirement benefits. . . . .
>
> The formula in the resolution as most recently amended on June 7, 1984 (the "Stockholders' Resolution") provides that awards may be made only for those years in which the consolidated net earnings of the Corporation and consolidated subsidiaries (as reported in the annual report to the stockholders) plus the provision for incentive compensation exceed earnings of $0.4444 per share (adjusted from $1.00 per share for two three-for-two stock splits since 1984) on the average number of shares of Common Stock outstanding during the year. The total provision for any year is limited to 8% of such excess. The Board may set aside such total provision or any lesser amount for incentive compensation. Any part of the amount set aside for any year that is not awarded for that year, as well as any amount awarded that is subsequently forfeited, may be carried forward to and awarded in a subsequent year.
>
> **Amendment for New Accounting Standard**
>
> The ability of the Corporation to award incentive compensation has been a significant factor in attracting, retaining, and motivating competent and experienced executive personnel; and in competing for their services with the Corporation's larger competitors and other companies that are able to offer comparable total compensation, including bonuses and other incentive based compensation.
>
> As stated above, under the Stockholders' Resolution, incentive compensation may be awarded only out of consolidated net earnings of the Corporation and its consolidated subsidiaries (as reported in the annual report to the stockholders). However, the Financial Accounting Standards Board has issued a new accounting standard (SFAS No. 106), "Employers' Accounting for Postretirement Benefits Other Than Pensions" ("OPEB"), that will significantly reduce or eliminate the Corporation's ability to award incentive compensation unless its effect is excluded by an amendment to the Stockholders' Resolution.
>
> The Corporation provides health and life insurance benefits to its eligible employees and retirees. The costs of these benefits are currently accounted for as expenses in the Corporation's financial statements in the periods in which they are paid, except that the cost of life insurance provided to retirees after age 65 is accrued. The new OPEB accounting standard will instead require accrual of retiree benefits for both U.S. and Canadian employees during the years the employees provide services. SFAS No. 106 is effective for fiscal years beginning after December 15, 1992.
>
> Implementation of the new standard will result in the Corporation's recognition of a transition obligation that can either be taken as a one-time charge in determining net income for the period in which the new standard is adopted or be recognized as an expense on a straight-line basis over a 20-year period. The transition obligation is the aggregate amount that would have been accrued in the years prior to adoption of SFAS No. 106 had the OPEB standard been in effect for those years. The Corporation will adopt the new standard in both the United States and Canada effective in the first quarter of 1993.

The Corporation estimates that the transition obligation was approximately $7.5 billion at January 1, 1993. If, when the OPEB standard is adopted effective in the first quarter of 1993, the transition obligation is recognized as a one-time charge, the Corporation estimates that there would be a $4.7 billion reduction (after applicable income taxes) in the Corporation's net earnings and shareholders' equity.

The Corporation estimates that its annual expense for postretirement health and life insurance benefits after adoption of the OPEB standard will increase by $380 million per year on a pre-tax basis, or by $240 million per year on an after-tax basis, assuming that the entire transition obligation is recognized as a one-time charge in 1993. If the transition obligation is accrued over a 20-year period, the Corporation's annual expense is estimated to increase by $750 million per year on a pre-tax basis, or by $470 million per year on an after-tax basis.

The Corporation has announced that it intends to recognize the transition obligation as a one-time charge that will result in an approximately $4.7 billion (after applicable income taxes) reduction in its shareholders' equity and in its 1993 first quarter and annual net results. Although implementation of the new standard will result in Chrysler reporting a net loss in the first quarter and for [all of] 1993 after the effects of this accounting adjustment, it will have no cash impact and Chrysler does not anticipate that it will adversely affect Chrysler's payment of dividends or compliance with its debt covenants.

The Board of Directors deems it essential to be able to award incentive compensation in the future on the basis of consolidated net earnings (losses) adjusted to exclude the effect of SFAS No. 106, in order to avoid a significant reduction or elimination of funds available for incentive compensation as a result of this mandated new accounting standard. Accordingly, the Board of Directors recommends that the stockholders adopt a resolution... to continue the authority to award incentive compensation on the same basis (except as further provided below) as in the recent past, by adjusting consolidated net earnings (losses) to exclude any amounts accrued to recognize postretirement benefit obligations, other than pensions, prior to the period in which such benefits are paid by the Corporation and its subsidiaries. The adjustment to exclude the OPEB accrual will be made in 1993 and each year thereafter to the extent that the amount accrued is different than the amount paid. The incentive compensation formula would continue to limit the incentive compensation fund for any year to 8% of the sum of (1) consolidated net earnings (losses) of the Corporation and consolidated subsidiaries (provided that such net earnings [losses] would be adjusted as described above), and (2) the provision for incentive compensation, after deducting from such sum an amount equal to $0.4444 per share times the average number of shares of Common Stock outstanding during the year.

REQUIRED:

If you were a stockholder of Chrysler Corporation, would you have agreed to the management's proposal? What factor(s) did you consider in making your decision?

Financial Reporting for Owners' Equity

15

LEARNING OBJECTIVES:
After studying this chapter, you will understand:

1. Why some financing transactions—like debt repurchases—generate reported gains and losses, while others—like stock repurchases—do not.
2. Why companies buy back their stock, and how they do it.
3. Why some preferred stock resembles debt, and how it gets reported.
4. How and when retained earnings limits a company's distributions to common stockholders.
5. How to calculate basic and fully diluted earnings per share (EPS), and whether EPS is a meaningful number.
6. What GAAP says about employee stock options, and why this accounting treatment has been so controversial.
7. How and why GAAP understates the true cost of convertible debt, and what to do about this understatement.
8. Why employee stock ownership plans (ESOPs) have become so popular, and what they mean for statement readers.

Statement readers must understand the accounting procedures and reporting conventions for owners' equity for these reasons:

1. *Appropriate income measurement.* Differentiating between owners' equity changes that do increase or decrease income and changes that don't will help answer: "Why are bond interest payments an expense that reduces income, while dividend payments on common and preferred stock are not?" "Why do certain financing transactions—like early debt retirements—generate accounting gains and losses while others—like stock repurchases—do not?"
2. *Compliance with contract terms and restrictions.* Many "exotic" securities having characteristics of both debt and equity have been developed by investment bankers. How should these hybrid securities be classified for monitoring compliance with contractual restrictions (like maximum allowable debt-to-equity ratios)?
3. *Legality of corporate distributions to owners.* Owners' equity is generally regarded as a financial "cushion" protecting corporate creditors. Cash distributions to shareholders—dividends and stock repurchases—reduce this cushion. How much of this cushion can legally be distributed as dividends? In case of corporate liquidation, in what order can cash payouts be made to various claimants?
4. *Linkage to equity valuation.* Analyzing the true worth of equity shares requires an understanding of the amount of earnings which accrue to each share. Equity valuation thus depends on how a company's options, warrants, and convertible instruments affect its earnings per share.

After discussing each of these issues, we will look at existing GAAP for stock options granted to employees and the controversy surrounding current reporting practice.

Appropriate Income Measurement

Some increases (decreases) in owners' equity are considered to be income (loss), while other increases (decreases) are not income (loss). To see why, we must understand the modern GAAP definition of the "firm."

What Constitutes the "Firm"? Entity Versus Proprietary Views

Recall the basic accounting equation:

Entity view of the firm:

$$\underbrace{\text{Assets}}_{\text{Capital Deployed}} = \underbrace{\text{Liabilities} + \text{Owners' Equity}}_{\text{Capital Sources}}$$

This perspective—called the **entity view** of the firm—focuses on the firm's *assets.* Capital sources (debt and shareholder financing) are lumped together. The firm's assets are considered to drive economic performance, so the *firm* is considered to be the capital deployed—the assets themselves. Who provided those assets (creditors versus shareholders) is of secondary importance.

Prevailing GAAP is based on a different perspective—called the **proprietary view** of the firm—where the focus of the basic accounting equation is on shareholders. The proprietary view sharply differentiates between capital provided by owners and capital provided by creditors.

Proprietary view of the firm:

$$\underbrace{\text{Assets} - \text{Liabilities}}_{\text{Net Capital Deployed}} = \underbrace{\text{Owners' Equity}}_{\text{Owners' Capital}}$$

The proprietary view isolates the capital provided by owners. In this perspective, the firm and its owners are inseparable—the *firm* is considered to be the owner's equity investment.

The prevalence of the proprietary view in GAAP greatly influences income measurement. To see why, consider the basic accounting principle that income can be earned (or expenses incurred) *only* through transactions between the firm and "outsiders." But who is "inside" the firm and who are the outsiders? ***Under the proprietary view, the firm and its owners are the same.*** Consequently, no income (or loss) can arise from transactions between the firm and its owners, because owners are *not* outsiders. This perspective explains why interest payments to banks or bondholders are expenses that reduce income, while dividend payments to common and preferred shareholders are *not* expenses that reduce income. Banks and bondholders are outsiders—hence, interest costs are expenses. Shareholders are not outsiders—thus, dividends are a *distribution of earnings* to owners, not an expense of the company.

The proprietary view helps us understand why certain financing transactions generate income (or losses), while other transactions do not.

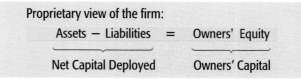

> Investors who buy debt instruments do not participate in the company's future profitability. Instead, debtholders gain only a specified fixed (or variable) rate of return—for example, "7% interest per annum," or in the case of variable rate debt, "prime plus ½%."

Financing Transactions One way corporations raise capital is by selling equity shares to investors. Called **common stock,** these shares provide the opportunity for purchasers to participate in the company's future profitability. In addition to conveying ownership rights, common stock has **limited liability.** As long as each share is sold for more than an arbitrary per-share dollar amount—called **par value**—the shareholder's potential future loss is limited to the original purchase price of the common share. Limited liability makes investing in common stock attractive because although potential gains from ownership are unlimited, downside risk of loss is limited to the share purchase price.

To see how the accounting for common stock works, assume that at its creation Nahigian Corporation sells 5,000 shares of common stock at $50 per share and that the shares have a par value of $1 each. Nahigian records the stock issuance as:

DR Cash	$250,000	
CR Common stock–$1 par value		$ 5,000
CR Paid-in capital in excess of par		245,000

The $1 par value per share bears no necessary relationship to the *market value* of the shares. The difference between the issue price of $50 and the par value of $1 is credited to a separate owners' equity account called "Paid-in capital in excess of par"—sometimes also called "Additional paid-in capital."

> The term *par value* refers to the **nominal** or **face value** of a security. With common stock, par value is set by the company issuing the stock. At one time, par value represented the original investment behind each share of stock in cash, goods, or services. Today, it is an assigned amount (such as $1 per share) used to compute the dollar accounting value of the common shares on the company's balance sheet. ***Par value has no relation to market value.***

Suppose that several years later, Nahigian Corporation reacquires 200 of these shares at a cost of $48 each. When a corporation buys back its own shares, the repurchased shares are called **treasury stock** because the shares are held in the corporate treasury for later use. The accounting entry is:

DR Treasury stock	$9,600	
CR Cash		$9,600

Notice that no gain or loss is recorded for the difference between the $50 per-share price at which the shares were first issued and the $48 repurchase price. ***The reason stock repurchases do not involve accounting gains and losses is that they are transactions between the company and its owners.***

When treasury stock is acquired, it is not considered a corporate asset. Treasury stock is debited, as shown earlier, and it is treated as a **contra-equity** account on the balance sheet.

NAHIGIAN CORPORATION	
Owners' Equity	
Common stock, $1 par value, 5,000 shares issued	$ 5,000
Paid-in capital in excess of par	245,000
Retained earnings (assumed for illustration)	700,000
Total paid-in capital and retained earnings	$950,000
Less: Treasury stock (at cost)	(9,600)
Total owners' equity	$940,400

Now let's say Nahigian decides to raise more equity capital by reselling all 200 treasury shares several months later at $53 per share. The entry would be:

DR Cash	$10,600	
CR Treasury stock		$9,600
CR Paid-in capital in excess of par		1,000

This entry eliminates the contra-equity account called "Treasury stock." The per-share selling price of $53 is $5 per share higher than the $48 paid to reacquire the shares. Despite this "excess," ***no income is recognized on the transaction.*** Instead, the difference of $1,000 (200 shares × [$53 − 48]) is added to the "Paid-in capital in excess of par" account.

RECAP

No income (or expense) arises from treasury stock transactions—not in the proprietary view, which equates the firm with its owners. Since treasury stock transactions are between the company and its shareholders (owners) and not outsiders, no income is recognized—not even when the successive stock transactions are favorable, like those in the Nahigian Corporation illustration.

But if Nahigian had reacquired outstanding *debt* at a price lower than its book value, then a gain *would* be recorded, as described in Chapter 11. Debt repurchases generate gains (and losses) while stock repurchases do not, because debtholders are outsiders under the GAAP proprietary view while shareholders are insiders.

Why Companies Repurchase Their Stock

Firms reacquire their own common stock for many reasons. Sometimes a company needs a supply of shares for employee stock options. Sometimes management may conclude that the company's shares are undervalued at the prevailing market price and that the best use of corporate funds is to invest in the firm's own shares. Other times, perhaps management just wants to distribute surplus cash to shareholders rather than to keep it inside the company.

A company's *surplus* cash—the amount over and above what is needed for day-to-day operating activities—can be a problem for management and for shareholders. Management worries that another company or investor group might launch a hostile takeover of the business, using the company's own cash surplus to partially finance the takeover. If a hostile takeover is successful, some managers will inevitably lose their jobs. Shareholders on the other hand worry that management might spend the company's surplus cash on unprofitable—negative net present value—projects and on lavish "perks" such as corporate speedboats or race cars. So, it is better to give the money to shareholders—after all, it is their money.

Stock repurchases have one other advantage: Shareholders who take the cash are taxed at capital gain rates. If the cash is paid out as dividends, shareholders would be taxed at ordinary income rates, which are usually higher than capital gain rates.

The popularity of stock repurchases has varied over time as a result of changes in the economic climate, stock market price levels, and the availability of surplus corporate cash. Only 87 U.S. companies announced stock buyback plans in 1980, with the dollar value totaling $1.4 billion. In 1998, stock repurchases were announced by 1,570 U.S. companies and totaled $222.0 billion.[1] Figure 15.1 shows the (a) number of stock repurchase announcements each year, and (b) the total dollar value of the buybacks, for 1980 through 1999.

There are a number of ways a company can repurchase its shares. The most common is an **open market repurchase**—the company buys back its stock a little at a time over a period, sometimes two to three years. Open market repurchase programs are approved by company boards and formally announced to the public. However, companies do not announce each stock repurchase transaction so it is difficult for analysts and investors to track completion of the buyback.

Another common way is the **fixed-price tender offer**—the company announces both the number of shares it wants to repurchase and the price it will pay for those shares. The offer is typically valid for a limited time and may be withdrawn if not enough shares are

[1] G. Grullon and D. Ikenberry, "What Do We Know About Stock Repurchases?" *Journal of Applied Corporate Finance* (Spring 2000), pp. 31–51.

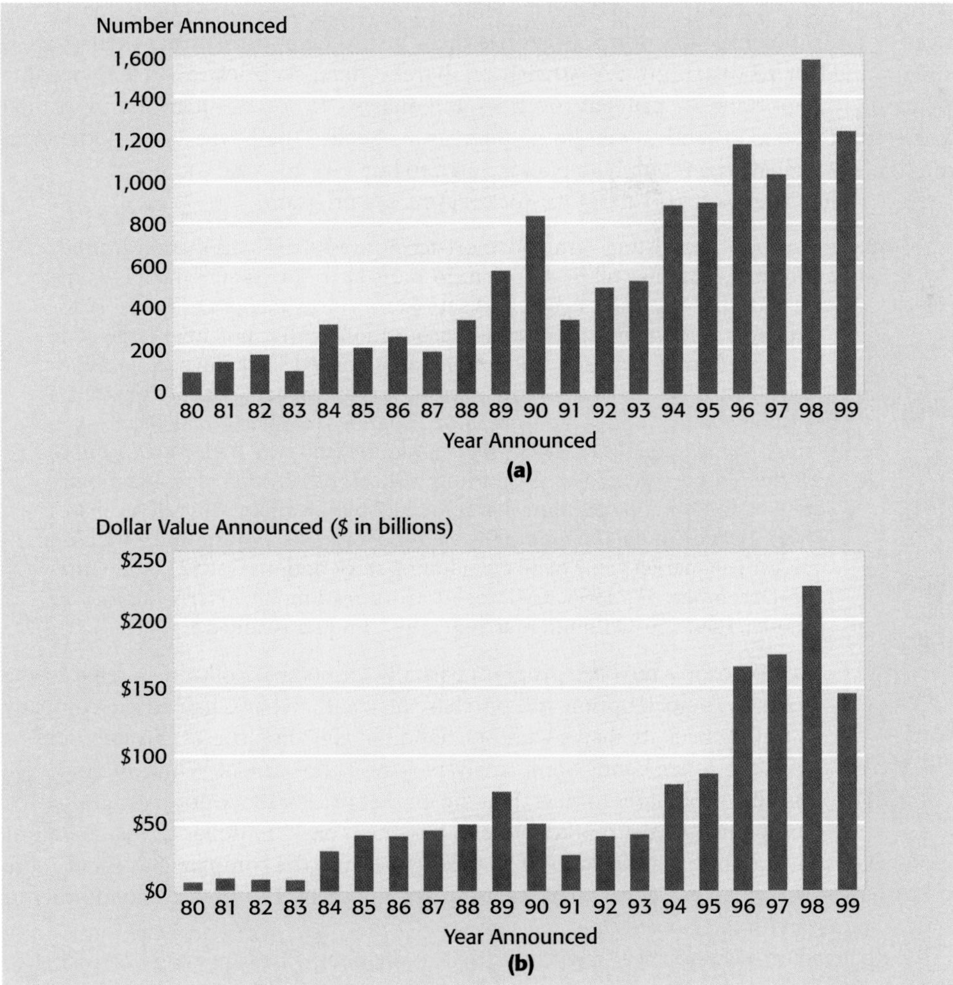

Figure 15.1

THE NUMBER AND DOLLAR VALUE OF STOCK REPURCHASES ANNOUNCED BY U.S. COMPANIES FROM 1980 THROUGH 1999

The charts do not include stock repurchases announced in the last quarter of 1987 because so many U.S. companies announced repurchases that quarter as a response to the October 1987 stock market crash.

Source: From G. Grullon & D. Ikenberry, "What Do We Know About Stock Repurchases?" *Journal of Applied Corporate Finance* (Spring 2000). Reprinted with permission.

tendered. If the offer is oversubscribed—meaning too many shares are tendered—management has the option to increase the size of the repurchase.

In the 1980s a technique called the **Dutch auction** became popular. Here, the company announces the total number of shares it will repurchase and sets a range of prices within which it is willing to buy back stock. Shareholders responding to the offer must specify how many shares they are willing to sell and at what price within the range. The company then determines the lowest offered price that allows it to repurchase the number of shares it seeks. All the shares are purchased at this single price.[2]

The Dutch auction looks like the most satisfactory way to treat shareholders fairly. If a shareholder names too high a price, that shareholder may have no shares accepted. Naming too low a price simply increases the likelihood that the price paid will be low. Consequently, this approach encourages shareholders to be truthful and to name a price that reflects their personal valuation of the stock.

The typical share repurchase is at a price about 23% greater than the stock's market value just before the repurchase offer is announced.[3] Those shareholders who sell their stock back to the company capture this price premium. But what about the shareholders who don't sell? According to perhaps the best known study on the subject, the stock of the average corporation that repurchases its shares outperforms the rest of the market by 12% over the four years following the announcement of the repurchase program. Even better, high book-to-market price stocks that are repurchased beat the market by 45% over the next four years.[4]

[2] See D. B. Hausch, D. E. Logue, and J. K. Seward, "Dutch Auction Share Repurchases: Theory and Evidence," *Journal of Applied Corporate Finance* (Spring 1992), pp. 44–49.

[3] D. Ikenberry, J. Lakonishok, and T. Vermaelen, "Market Underreaction to Open Market Share Repurchases," *Journal of Financial Economics* (October 1995), pp. 181–208.

[4] Ibid.

ANALYSIS

But not all buybacks are created equal. While share repurchases as a whole help to boost investor returns, companies don't always use them just to demonstrate that their stock is undervalued or to distribute excess cash to shareholders, skeptics say. It has become increasingly important for prudent investors and analysts to sort through the individual share repurchase plans and to determine the reasons behind the buyback. Only then can you figure out whether a repurchase plan is a sign to buy—or to avoid the stock.

Here's what Microsoft said about its stock repurchase program:

> Management believes existing cash and short-term investments together with funds generated from operations will be sufficient to meet operating requirements for the next twelve months. Microsoft's cash and short-term investments are available for strategic investments, mergers and acquisitions, other potential large-scale cash needs that may arise, and to fund an increased stock buyback program over historical levels to reduce the dilutive impact of the Company's employee stock option and purchase programs. *Despite recent increases in stock repurchases, the buyback program has not kept pace with employee stock option grants or exercises.* Beginning in fiscal 1990, Microsoft has repurchased 134 million common shares for $4.2 billion while 336 million shares were issued under the Company's employee stock option and purchase plans. The market value of all outstanding stock options was $21.8 billion as of December 31, 1996. (Microsoft Corporation, Quarterly Report to Shareholders [10-Q filing], March 31, 1997. Emphasis added.)

Intel's experience highlights the issue. Every year since 1992 the semiconductor manufacturer has bought back stock. But in 1999, for example, while it issued only $543 million of stock and bought back a whopping $4.6 billion of stock under its share repurchase plan, its **common shares outstanding actually grew** to 3,334 million from 3,315 million. What is the reason? The company paid $64.95 a share for the stock it repurchased—but it received only $9.70 for each share issued through options. (Intel also issued 34 million shares in connection with an acquisition.)

Microsoft's buyback program partially offsets share dilution caused by the company's stock option and purchase plans. But what is gained if a company is buying back its shares with one hand but is issuing shares through options with the other hand? Some analysts answer: not much. While an employee usually buys shares for less than the market price under option programs, the company pays the market price to buy them back. In dollar terms, the number of shares outstanding may seem to be shrinking, because the company has spent more to buy back shares than employees have spent to acquire them. But in fact, the number of shares could remain unchanged or even grow.

Another factor of concern to analysts is that many companies are now borrowing to finance their stock repurchase programs. While such moves might have tax or other advantages, they simply replace equity with debt, so shareholders get the buyback's benefits only at the expense of owning a more leveraged company. They also face the risk that an economic downturn could make it harder to service debt.

Microsoft terminated its stock buyback program in January 2000. Before doing so, the company sold "put" warrants for 157 million shares. The warrants—an off-balance-sheet liability—entitle the holders to sell shares of Microsoft back to the company at a price of about $74 per share on certain dates before December 2002. If Microsoft shares are trading at $54 when the warrants are exercised, and the average purchase price is $74, the company will have to come up with $20 a share—or $3.14 billion—to settle the warrants. That's a lot of cash!

Even more worrisome is that ***some stock buybacks are motivated solely by a desire to boost earnings per share (EPS).*** Consider Rocket Software. The company just completed a successful third quarter with earnings of $220,000 and EPS of $1.00. This is the ninth consecutive quarter that Rocket Software's EPS has grown by 10% or more. But it looks like this string of EPS increases is about to be broken—fourth quarter earnings are projected to be only $220,000, unchanged from the third quarter.

How can the company keep its EPS record intact? Management could increase earnings (as well as EPS) by finding ways to grow sales revenues or reduce expenses. Or, Rocket Software could buy back some of its common stock:

	Without Buyback	With Buyback
Projected fourth quarter earnings	$220,000	$220,000
÷ Common shares outstanding	220,000	200,000
Projected EPS	$ 1.00	$ 1.10

If the buyback reduces total shares outstanding from 220,000 to 200,000, fourth quarter EPS will be $1.10 and the company can claim another quarter of 10% EPS growth.

Sounds simple, but it's not—there is a hidden assumption. Stock buybacks consume cash. Where did Rocket Software get the cash needed for its buyback? Suppose the company had to borrow the cash. The (after-tax) interest expense on the loan—let's say it's $5,500—would reduce projected fourth quarter earnings to $214,500. The company would then have to buy back 25,000 shares—or 5,000 more than originally anticipated—to reach its $1.10 EPS goal ($1.10 EPS = $214,500/195,000 shares outstanding after the expanded buyback). Instead of borrowing the cash, Rocket Software could sell some of its marketable securities, investments, or other productive assets. But asset sales may also have a dampening effect on future earnings.

As long as earnings fall by less (in percentage terms) than the buyback percentage reduction in shares outstanding, EPS will indeed go up! But this EPS increase may actually mask deteriorating business fundamentals. When it comes to stock buybacks and EPS growth, it pays to look behind the numbers.

Stock repurchases don't produce accounting gains or losses, but they can produce above-market returns for investors. Still, it's important to look behind the numbers and determine why a company is buying back its stock and how.

RECAP

Compliance with Contract Terms

Owners' equity is used in many contracts with lenders, suppliers, and others (Chapter 7). For example, lending agreements usually include covenants which restrict maximum allowable debt-to-equity levels, where equity refers to the book value amount disclosed on the company's balance sheet. Firms have incentives to use financial reporting latitude to circumvent these restrictions. Consequently, financial statement analysts must understand how owners' equity is reported to determine whether companies are in compliance with their contract terms.

For example, the 1992 Annual Report of Sears Roebuck and Company contained the following statement:

CONTRACTING

> The Illinois Insurance Holding Company Systems Act permits Allstate Insurance Company to pay, without regulatory approval, dividends to Sears Roebuck and Co. during any 12-month period in an amount up to the greater of 10% of surplus (as regards policyholders) or its net income (as defined) as of the preceding Dec. 31. Approximately $477 million of Allstate's **retained income** at Dec. 31, 1992 had no restriction relating to distribution during 1993 which would require prior approval. As of Dec. 31, 1992, subsidiary companies could remit to Sears Roebuck and Co. in the form of dividends approximately $5.6 billion, after payment of all related taxes, without prior approval of regulatory bodies or violation of contractual restrictions. (Sears Roebuck and Company, 1992 Annual Report. Allstate was a wholly owned subsidiary of Sears in 1992 but was sold by the company in 1995.)

In this case, insurance regulators are using an owners' equity item—retained earnings—to restrict Allstate's ability to distribute cash to stockholders (in this case, the parent, Sears Roebuck and Company, is affected). This restriction was intended to ensure that Allstate maintains a cash cushion for payment of insurance claims. Monitoring compliance with the form and substance of this regulation requires an understanding of accounting for owners' equity.

Some financial experts suggest that certain equity instruments, like **preferred stock,** are popular because they can be used to avoid various contractual restrictions. Preferred stock gets its name because relative to common stock, it confers on investors certain *preferences* to dividend payments and the distribution of corporate assets. Preferred shareholders must be paid their dividends in full before *any*

Preferred stock does not ordinarily carry voting rights. *Participating* preferred stock entitles its holders to share in profits above the declared dividend, along with common shareholders. Most preferred stock is *nonparticipating* meaning that holders are entitled to receive only the stipulated dividends.

cash distribution can be made to common shareholders; and if the company is liquidated, preferred stockholders must receive cash or other assets at least equal to the **stated value** of their shares before any assets are distributed to common shareholders.

The stated value of preferred stock is typically \$100 per share. The dividend is often expressed as a percentage of the stated value. A typical 8% preferred issue would promise a dividend of \$8 per share (\$100 stated value × 8%). Unlike bond interest expense, however, preferred stock dividends are not contractual obligations which, if unpaid, could precipitate bankruptcy proceedings. Instead, preferred dividends are declared quarterly by the company's board of directors and can be omitted even in profitable years.

An alternative to the 8% fixed-rate preferred stock is an **adjustable-rate preferred**, which pays a dividend that is adjusted, usually quarterly, based on changes in the Treasury bill rate or other money market rates.

However, preferred shares are usually *cumulative*. This means that if for any reason a particular quarter's preferred dividend is not paid, then no dividends on common shares can be paid until all unpaid past and current preferred dividends are paid. This feature protects purchasers of preferred shares from excessive cash distributions to common stockholders. Also because it's okay to "skip" a preferred dividend, preferred shares are less risky than debt to issuing corporations.

Figure 15.2 shows the dollar value of preferred stock issued by U.S. companies each year from 1980 through 1997. Sixty-nine companies issued \$3.1 billion of preferred stock in 1980, compared to \$55.4 billion issued by 386 companies in 1997.

The widespread use of preferred stock by companies is a curious phenomenon. Preferred dividends—unlike bond interest expense—are not a deductible corporate expense for tax purposes. Why do companies choose to raise capital this way rather than through debt where tax deductible interest payments reduce financing costs relative to preferred stock issues?

There are lots of conjectures about the popularity of preferred stock. Preferred stock is attractive to *corporate investors* because 70% to 80% of dividends that corporations receive from their stock investments can be tax free (Chapter 13), whereas the interest income corporations receive from debt investments is fully taxable.

Corporations that *issue* preferred stock do so because:

1. Preferred stock is less risky than debt since missing a preferred dividend payment, unlike missing an interest payment, will not trigger bankruptcy. This appeals to financially weak companies.
2. Companies with a history of operating losses usually don't pay income taxes because of their operating loss carryforwards. For these companies, debt no longer has a tax advantage, and thus preferred stock becomes more attractive.

Figure 15.2

THE DOLLAR VALUE OF PREFERRED STOCK ISSUED BY U.S. COMPANIES FROM 1980 THROUGH 1997

Source: From K. A. Carow, G. R. Erwin, and J. J. McConnell, "A Survey of U.S. Corporate Financing Innovations: 1970–1997," *Journal of Applied Corporate Finance* (Spring 1999). Reprinted with permission.

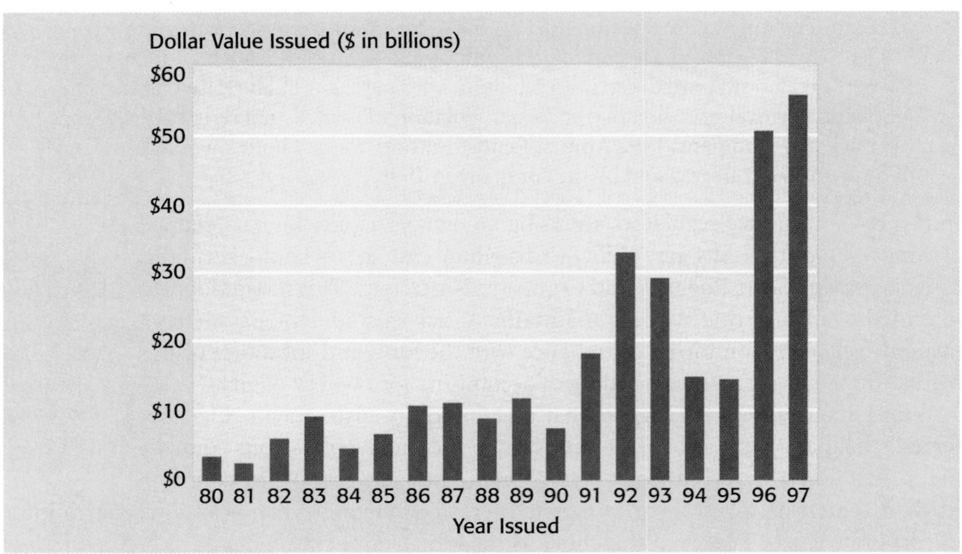

3. Preferred stock is treated as equity rather than debt on financial statements. Companies precluded from issuing more debt because of covenant restrictions can issue preferred stock instead and side-step these restrictions.

The distinction between preferred stock and debt is often murky, since preferred stock (like debt) usually does not grant its holders voting rights, and preferred shareholders have no direct control over the affairs of the company. The distinction between debt and preferred stock has been further blurred recently as companies began issuing **mandatorily redeemable preferred stock.** Although called preferred *stock,* these financial instruments *require* the issuing company to retire them (just like debt) at some future date—usually in five or ten years. This kind of preferred stock represents what many consider to be debt "disguised" as equity.

Exhibit 15.1 shows excerpts from Starship Cruise Line's footnote disclosure for mandatorily redeemable preferred stock.

The Securities and Exchange Commission (SEC) does not consider mandatorily redeemable preferred stock to be equity. So it prohibits firms who issue such securities from including them under the caption "Owners' equity" on the balance sheet.[5] This means that amounts for redeemable preferred stock cannot be combined with true owners' equity items like nonredeemable preferred stock and common stock in financial statements that are filed with the SEC. Exhibit 15.2 on the next page illustrates the required SEC treatment in Starship Cruise Line's condensed balance sheet. Notice that the $1.5 million of mandatorily redeemable preferred stock is shown on a separate line *between* liabilities and shareholders' equity.

SEC rules further require companies to differentiate clearly between common stock and any type of preferred stock, whether redeemable or not. Finally, *Statement of Financial Accounting Standards (SFAS) No. 47* requires companies to disclose the dollar amount of preferred stock redemption requirements for each of the five years following the balance sheet date.[6] Accordingly, future cash flow commitments for redeemable preferred stock are clearly highlighted for statement users.

Exhibit 15.1 ■ STARSHIP CRUISE LINE, INC.

Footnote Disclosure of Mandatorily Redeemable Preferred Stock

The Company issued 15,000 shares of mandatorily redeemable convertible preferred stock in November 1998. The Preferred Stock bears annual dividends of $10.00 per share payable quarterly in arrears. Each preferred share is convertible into one share of common stock at the option of the holder. The Company has the option to redeem the preferred shares in whole or in part at a price of $100.00 plus accrued dividends as of December 31, 2001 and the **obligation to redeem all shares at a price of $100.00 on December 31, 2004, plus accrued dividends.** The holder of the preferred shares has no voting rights except at any time when the equivalent of three quarterly dividends are unpaid or the Company fails to make any mandatory redemption of the preferred shares at which time the number of directors of the Company will be increased by two and elected by the preferred shareholder. No dividends on the Preferred Stock have been paid since issuance; the amount of dividends payable at March 31, 2000 is $204,760 and is included within current liabilities in the accompanying balance sheet. The holder of the Preferred Shares has taken no action as a result of the nonpayment of the dividends.

Source: Starship Cruise Line, Inc., 1999 Annual Report. Emphasis added.

[5] *Accounting Series Release No. 268* (Washington, D.C.: Securities and Exchange Commission [SEC], 1979).

[6] "Disclosure of Long-Term Obligations," *SFAS No. 47* (Stamford, CT: Financial Accounting Standards Board [FASB], 1981).

Exhibit 15.2 ■ STARSHIP CRUISE LINE, INC.

Balance Sheet Excerpts

Current Liabilities:	
Current portion of notes payable	$ 455,985
Revolving line of credit	443,198
Accounts payable	116,463
Preferred stock dividends payable	204,760
Accrued liabilities	93,061
Unearned revenue	106,628
Total current liabilities	1,420,095
Long-term notes payable, less current portion	6,204,015
Mandatorily redeemable preferred stock $1.00 par value, 2,000,000 shares authorized; 15,000 shares subscribed, issued and outstanding	1,500,000
Stockholders' Equity:	
Common stock, $1.00 par value; 20,000,000 shares authorized; 54,900 issued and outstanding	54,900
Additional paid-in capital	379,431
Accumulated deficit	(1,818,122)
Total stockholders' equity	(1,383,791)
Total liabilities and stockholders' equity	$7,740,319

Here's what Art Technology Group (ATG) said about its preferred stock redemption schedule:

> The Series B Preferred Stock is subject to mandatory redemption provisions that require ATG to redeem 25% on December 31, 2001, increasing by 25% annually thereafter, at $7.05 per share (subject to certain dilutive effects, as defined), plus any dividends accrued but unpaid thereon. In addition, the holders of Series D Preferred Stock can individually request redemption of all, but not less than all, of the shares of Series D Preferred Stock held at any time after August 18, 2003. (Art Technology Group Inc., 1998 Annual Report.)

The company has about $8 million of mandatorily redeemable preferred stock outstanding. The redemption provision requires Art Technology Group to redeem 25% of the outstanding shares each year beginning in 2001. So the company is obligated to spend $2 million each year—plus unpaid dividends—to redeem its preferred stock.

The SEC's classification criterion excludes mandatorily redeemable preferred stock from the owners' equity section of the balance sheet. However, this classification may not capture the real economic characteristics of these securities. The reason is that many companies—including Starship Cruise Line—have issued mandatorily redeemable preferred shares that are convertible into common stock. It's possible that preferred shares with this convertibility feature may never be redeemed by the company—and thus their SEC status as nonequity may be arguable.[7]

Investors seem to be aware of this possibility. One study confirmed that the stock price behavior of companies whose redeemable preferred shares had clear debt-like characteristics was different from the behavior of companies whose shares had equity-like character-

[7] See P. Kimmel and T. D. Warfield, "Variation in Attributes of Redeemable Preferred Stock: Implications for Accounting Standards," *Accounting Horizons* (June 1993), pp. 30–40. These authors report that almost 69% of the mandatorily redeemable preferred stock issued in 1989 and included in their sample was convertible into common stock.

istics.[8] Investors apparently use disclosures about redeemable preferred shares to assess whether a particular issue should be regarded as debt or equity for valuation purposes.

A new form of mandatorily redeemable preferred stock has become popular in recent years, and it's called a **trust preferred security.** Here's what Motorola said about its newly issued trust preferred securities:

> In February 1999, Motorola Capital Trust I, a . . . wholly-owned subsidiary of Motorola, sold 20 million Trust Originated Preferred Securities ("TOPrS") to the public at an aggregate offering price of $500 million. The Trust used the proceeds from this sale . . . to buy . . . Subordinated Debentures from Motorola with the same payment terms as the TOPrS. Motorola, in turn, used the $484 million of net proceeds from the sale of the Subordinated Debentures to reduce short-term indebtedness. (Motorola 1999 Annual report.)

Motorola formed a wholly owned subsidiary—Motorola Capital Trust—which sold $500 million of trust preferred stock to the public. The trust then transfered $484 million of cash (the $500 million proceeds minus $16 million in investment banking fees and other transaction costs) to Motorola in exchange for the company's subordinated debentures. Motorola has the cash, its wholly owned subsidiary has the debentures, and outside investors have trust preferred stock. Sounds complicated, but it's really quite simple. And here's the final piece of the puzzle—the interest and principal payments on the loan are matched to the dividend and mandatory redemption payments on the preferred stock. So, when Motorola makes an interest (or principal) payment to the trust, the trust then makes a dividend (or redemption) payment to outside investors.[9]

The benefit to Motorola should now be clear—interest expense is tax deductible but preferred dividends are not. By issuing trust preferred securities instead of traditional preferred stock, Motorola has transformed what would otherwise be a nondeductible dividend payment into an interest expense tax deduction.

> Motorola's debt held by the wholly owned trust is eliminated when the company prepares its consolidated financial statements (Chapter 16 tells you why). That leaves only the redeemable preferred stock sold to outside investors on the consolidated balance sheet.

How are trust preferred securities shown on the balance sheet? Despite having the characteristics of debt—a required payment each period (called a "dividend" instead of "interest") and a final payment at the end (called a "mandatory redemption payment" instead of a "principal payment")—these hybrid securities are *not* classified as debt on the balance sheet. Instead, they are listed in the "mezzanine" section between debt and equity along with all other mandatorily preferred stock. The FASB is currently developing reporting standards for trust preferred securities that may help resolve the classification issue.

Equity or debt? When it comes to mandatorily redeemable preferred stock, the answer isn't obvious. That's why the SEC requires preferred stock with a mandatory redemption feature to be shown on a separate line between liabilities and shareholders' equity.

RECAP

Legality of Corporate Distributions

State laws govern corporate distributions to shareholders and these laws vary from state to state. The intent of these laws is to prohibit companies from distributing "excessive" assets to owners and thereby making themselves insolvent—that is, incapable of paying creditor claims. In some states, distributions to owners are limited to the amount of retained earn-

> Remember the repayment problem described in Chapter 7? Managers have incentives to borrow money and then pay all the cash out to shareholders, leaving the company insolvent and the bank with a loan receivable that will never be repaid!

[8] P. Kimmel and T. D. Warfield, "The Usefulness of Hybrid Security Classifications: Evidence from Redeemable Preferred Stock," *The Accounting Review* (January 1995), pp. 151–67.

[9] The key features of trust preferred securities are described in P. J. Frischmann, P. D. Kimmel, and T. D. Warfield, "Innovation in Preferred Stock: Current Developments and Implications for Financial Reporting," *Accounting Horizons* (September 1999), pp. 201–18.

ings; in others, the limit is retained earnings plus paid-in capital in excess of par. These laws protect creditors by ensuring that only solvent companies distribute cash to owners.

Assume Delores Corporation's balance sheet owners' equity section appears on December 31, 2001 as:

Common stock, $1 par value	$20,000,000
Paid-in capital in excess of par	35,000,000
Retained earnings	43,000,000
Owners' equity	$98,000,000

In some states, Delores Corporation could only distribute up to $43,000,000 of assets—the retained earnings amount—to owners. The distribution could be in the form of cash dividends and stock repurchases, or other assets such as inventory, equipment, or even land. In other states the maximum might be $78,000,000—retained earnings plus paid-in capital. (Many states would require corporations to give public notice if their dividends were "paid" from paid-in capital.)

Existing GAAP disclosures focus on the *source* of owners' equity—*contributed* capital (par plus capital in excess of par) versus *earned* capital (retained earnings)—under the often erroneous presumption that this distinction informs analysts about legally permitted asset distributions. But many states have now adopted the **1984 Revised Model Business Corporation Act** as a guide to the legality of distributions. This act redefined solvency. Under this act, as long as the *fair value of assets* exceeds the *fair value of liabilities* after the distribution, the company is considered to be solvent. In extreme cases this means that an asset distribution would be legal even if the *book value* of net assets is *negative* after the distribution. If Delores Corporation's fair value of assets minus fair value of liabilities totaled $200 million, then $200 million (rather than $43 million or $78 million) would be the maximum legal asset distribution. Notice that a $200 million distribution would result in negative owners' equity of $102 million. ***The point is that the book value of owners' equity may not give an accurate picture of potentially legal distributions in states which have adopted the 1984 Act.***

The potential irrelevance of traditional equity disclosures is forcefully made in an article by Michael Roberts, William Samson, and Michael Dugan.

> As an example of the inadequacies of existing accounting disclosures, consider the 1987 and 1988 stockholders' equity balance sheet sections of Holiday Corporation, the parent corporation of Holiday Inns of America [see Exhibit 15.3]. The January 2, 1987 stockholders' equity section reports the traditional segregation of stockholders' equity items: par value of common stock, additional paid-in capital, and retained earnings, less treasury stock at cost, and foreign currency adjustments. Total stockholders' equity is $639 million. However, the January 1, 1988 stockholders' equity section reveals a $770 million deficit in Holiday's total stockholders' equity. How did this deficit occur? The explanation lies in the $65 per share dividend that Holiday distributed in 1987 to prevent a hostile takeover. This aggregate $1.55 billion dividend, financed with borrowed funds, not only exceeded the corporation's retained earnings but total stockholders' equity as well by more than three quarters of a billion dollars.
>
> Holiday was able to borrow a large portion of the amount required for the dividend by using the fair value (i.e., appraised value) of its real estate assets as collateral. Holiday was able to distribute the dividend (legally, according to Delaware law) because the fair value of its assets exceeded its liabilities after the distribution, and therefore it has positive equity on a fair value basis. ***However, the traditional accounting disclosures of par value, additional paid-in capital, and retained earnings do not contain any information (either before or after the dividend distribution) enabling financial statement users to assess the corporation's capacity for making such distributions.*** While stockholders and other interested parties may have had notice of Holiday's intent to leverage its assets to make the massive dividend, only Holiday's management had information about the fair values of the assets involved.

Exhibit 15.3 ■ HOLIDAY CORPORATION AND CONSOLIDATED SUBSIDIARIES

Balance Sheet

($ in thousands, except share amounts)	January 1, 1988	January 2, 1987
Stockholders' equity		
Preferred stock, $100.00 par value, authorized—150,000 shares, none issued		
Special stock, authorized—5,000,000 shares	—	—
Series A—$1.125 par value, redeemable at $105.00, convertible into 1.5 shares of common stock, outstanding—none and 170,171 shares (excluding none and 98,072 shares held in treasury)	—	$ 191
Series B—$1.25 par value, none issued	—	—
Common stock, $1.50 par value, authorized—120,000,000 shares, outstanding—26,225,980 and 23,592,569 shares (excluding 14,613,417 and 17,246,828 shares held in treasury)	$ 39,339	35,389
Capital surplus	12,625	205,717
Retained earnings (deficit)	(791,021)	404,655
Cumulative foreign currency translation adjustment	7,972	(63)
Restricted stock	(38,861)	(7,156)
Total stockholders' equity	($769,946)	$638,733

The point of the Holiday example is that state laws governing a corporation's ability to make distributions to stockholders have continued to evolve from the time when minimum legal capital was considered to be equivalent to the par value of the corporation's stock. Thus, the traditional stockholders' equity presentation of par value, additional paid-in capital, and retained earnings is obsolete because it implies that some amount, represented by a portion of stockholders' equity, exists to protect creditors.[10]

As the Holiday Corporation example illustrates, existing disclosure rules for owners' equity ***"focus attention on the source of capital, but ignore the capacity of the corporation for making distributions to stockholders."***[11] To ascertain the amount of potential distributions, statement analysts would need to know two things: (1) The distribution law in the state where the firm is incorporated, and (2) Fair value information if state law permits distributions based on the excess fair value of net assets. Unfortunately, this fair value information may be difficult to obtain since GAAP does not require its disclosure except for marketable securities and certain investments (Chapter 16) and limited other items.

> Under current GAAP, stock *dividends* reduce retained earnings but stock *splits* may not. Small stock distributions (less than 25% of shares outstanding) are required to be recorded as stock dividends: The market value of the distributed shares is transferred from retained earnings to the par value and paid-in capital account. Distributions that equal or exceed 25% of shares outstanding—commonly called stock splits—can be treated in either of two ways: (1) like a true split, which reduces the per-share par value and increases the number of shares proportionately; or (2) like a stock dividend. Consequently, stock dividends—and stock splits recorded as stock dividends—reduce the company's future cash dividend paying ability in states where cash dividends are limited by retained earnings. Peterson, Millar, and Rimbey (1996) report that 83% of the 285 "stock split" companies in their study actually accounted for the distribution as stock dividends.[12] They also found that the stock market does indeed recognize that retained earnings reductions may restrict future dividends in some states but *not* in others.

Certain limited disclosures regarding potential distributions are required by GAAP. We saw earlier that when mandatorily redeemable preferred stock has been issued, the dollar amount of the redemption requirement for each of the ensuing five years after the balance

[10] M. L. Roberts, W. D. Samson, and M. T. Dugan, "The Stockholders' Equity Section: Form Without Substance?" *Accounting Horizons* (December 1990), pp. 36–37. Emphasis added.

[11] *Ibid.*, p. 35. Seventeen U.S. companies paid cash dividends in 1999 despite having negative stockholders' equity.

[12] C. A. Peterson, J. A. Millar, and J. N. Rimbey, "The Economic Consequences of Accounting for Stock Splits and Large Stock Dividends," *The Accounting Review* (April 1996), pp. 241–53.

sheet date must be disclosed. Similarly, preferred stock dividend and liquidation preferences must be disclosed, along with significant differences between the liquidation amount and the par or stated value of the underlying shares.[13] Nevertheless, these disclosures still do not allow interested readers to compute the *total* potential distribution to owners.

RECAP

GAAP reporting rules are often not sufficient to allow analysts to ascertain the maximum legal distribution available to common stockholders. Analysts must be aware that other data may have to be gathered to ascertain the dollar amount that can be distributed.

Earnings Per Share

The amount of future income and cash flow that a company is expected to generate is a major determinant of firm value (Chapter 6). Valuing the firm *as a whole* is crucial during merger negotiations, during buyouts, and in similar settings—relatively rare events in the ongoing life of a company. For day-to-day valuations, many analysts prefer to focus on the value of *individual* common shares. For this purpose it is helpful to know how much of the company's total earnings accrue to each share. This is why **earnings per share (EPS)** is computed.

Computing EPS is straightforward when the company has a simple capital structure. We first describe these procedures, and then we extend the analysis to situations involving more complicated capital structures.

Simple Capital Structure

A simple capital structure exists when a company has no convertible securities (either convertible debt or convertible preferred stock) and no stock options or warrants outstanding. In these circumstances a straightforward formula is used to compute **basic earnings per common share:**[14]

Basic earnings per common share:

$$\text{EPS} = \frac{\text{Net income} - \text{Preferred dividends}}{\text{Weighted average number of common shares outstanding}}$$

To illustrate, let us assume Solomon Corporation had the following capital structure in 2001:

	January 1	December 31
Preferred stock, $100 par value, 7%,		
10,000 shares issued and outstanding	$ 1,000,000	$ 1,000,000
Common stock, $1 par value		
160,000 shares issued and outstanding	160,000	
200,000 shares issued and outstanding		200,000
Paid-in capital in excess of par	12,000,000	16,000,000
Retained earnings	1,100,000	1,800,000
Total stockholders' equity	$14,260,000	$19,000,000

[13] "Disclosure of Information about Capital Structure," *SFAS No. 129* (Norwalk, CT: FASB, 1997).

[14] The guidelines for computing EPS are contained in "Earnings per Share," *SFAS No. 128* (Norwalk, CT: FASB, 1997).

The 40,000 additional common shares were issued on September 1 and thus were outstanding for the last third of the year. The change in retained earnings during 2001 is:

Retained earnings, January 1	$ 1,100,000
Net income for the year	1,257,331
Preferred stock dividends	(70,000)
Common stock dividends	(487,331)
Retained earnings, December 31	$1,800,000

The denominator of the basic EPS formula uses the **weighted average** number of common shares outstanding. Since additional shares were issued during the year, this weighted average number of outstanding shares is computed as:

Time Span	(a) Shares Outstanding	(b) Portion of Year	(c) Weighted Shares (Col. a × Col. b)
January 1–August 31	160,000	2/3	106,667
September 1–December 31	200,000	1/3	66,667
			173,334

Solomon Corporation's basic EPS for the year 2001 is:

$$\text{Basic EPS} = \frac{\text{Net income} - \text{Preferred dividends}}{\text{Weighted average number of common shares outstanding}}$$

$$= \frac{\$1{,}257{,}331 - \$70{,}000}{173{,}334 \text{ shares}} = \$6.85 \text{ per share}$$

Complex Capital Structure

A firm has a **complex capital structure** when its financing includes either securities that are convertible into common stock, or options and warrants that entitle holders to obtain common stock under specified conditions. These financial instruments increase the likelihood that additional common shares will be issued in the future. This possible increase in the number of shares is called potential **dilution.**

Convertibles are corporate securities—usually preferred shares or bonds—that are exchangeable for a set number of other securities—usually common shares—at a prestated price. From the issuer's standpoint the convertible feature "sweetens" the marketability of the bond or preferred stock. A **call option** gives the holder the right to buy shares (typically 100) of the underlying stock at a fixed price before a specified date in the future—usually three, six, or nine months. **Employee stock options** are often of three to five years in duration. If the stock option is not exercised, the right to buy common shares expires. A **subscription warrant** is a security usually issued together with a bond or preferred stock that entitles the holder to buy a proportionate amount of common stock at a specified price—usually higher than market price at the time of issuance—for a period of years or in perpetuity.

Suppose Jackson Products Company has 30,000 shares of common stock outstanding along with $100,000 of convertible debentures—that is, bonds that can be converted into common stock. According to the terms of the debenture agreement, each $1,000 face value bond can be exchanged for 300 shares of common stock. If all debentures were exchanged, bondholders would receive 30,000 new shares of common stock. The effect on current common shareholders would be to *dilute* their claim to earnings from 100%—when they own all the common stock—to 50%—when they own only half of all outstanding shares.

Computed basic EPS ignores this potential dilution of current shareholders' ownership interest in the company. To recognize the increase in outstanding shares that would ensue from conversion or options exercise, *SFAS No. 128* requires companies with complex capital structures to compute another measure, one called **diluted EPS.**

> Remember Microsoft's stock repurchase program cited earlier? Between 1990 and 1996 the company bought back 134 million shares of common stock for $4.2 billion, while 336 million shares were issued under the company's employee stock option and purchases plan. But there's more! At the end of 1996 Microsoft employees owned stock options worth $21.8 billion, so the potential future dilution was even greater.

The diluted EPS figure is a conservative measure of the earnings flow to each share of stock. It's conservative because the diluted EPS measure presumes the *maximum* possible new share creation—and thus the *minimum* earnings flow to each share. The computation of diluted EPS requires that certain reasonable assumptions be made. For example, consider the potential conversion of convertible debentures into common shares. Obviously, once the bonds are converted to common stock, the company does not need to make further debt principal and interest payments. Consequently, the diluted EPS computation recognizes (1) the new shares issued upon conversion (a denominator effect), and (2) the increase in after-tax net income that follows from the elimination of debt interest payments after conversion (a numerator effect).

Assumptions must also be made for options or warrants when computing diluted EPS. When holders of options or warrants exercise them, they receive common shares; but at the same time, the company receives cash in an amount representing the exercise price of the options or warrants. In the computation of diluted EPS, this cash is assumed to be used to acquire already outstanding common shares in the market. Because of adjustments like these, the diluted EPS formula is slightly more complicated, as shown here:

Diluted earnings per share:

$$\text{Diluted EPS} = \frac{\text{Net income} - \text{Preferred dividends} + \begin{matrix}\text{Income adjustments due to}\\ \text{dilutive financial instruments}\end{matrix}}{\begin{matrix}\text{Weighted average number of}\\ \text{common shares outstanding}\end{matrix} + \begin{matrix}\text{Newly issuable shares due to}\\ \text{dilutive financial instruments}\end{matrix}}$$

To illustrate how the diluted EPS computation works, we will extend the Solomon Corporation example. Assume that as of January 1, 2001 Solomon also had the following financial instruments outstanding:

- $1,000,000 of 5% convertible debenture bonds due in 15 years, which were sold at par ($1,000 per bond). Each $1,000 bond pays interest of $50 per year and is convertible into 10 shares of common stock.
- Options to buy 20,000 shares of common stock at $100 per share. These options were issued on February 9, 1999 and expire on February 9, 2002.

> There were 1,000 bonds outstanding ($1,000,000 ÷ $1,000 par = 1,000 bonds), each convertible into 10 shares of common stock. Conversion of all bonds results in 1,000 bonds × 10 shares per bond 10,000 new shares.

Let's say the tax rate is 35% and Solomon stock sold for an average market price of $114 during 2001. Each financial instrument is potentially dilutive and must be incorporated into the diluted EPS computation as shown on the next page.

The convertible debentures are included in diluted EPS by assuming conversion on the first day of the reporting period (here, January 1, 2001). The after-tax effect of interest payments on the debt is *added back* in the EPS numerator, and the additional shares that would be issued on conversion are added to the denominator. *SFAS No. 128* calls this the **"if-converted" method.** We now illustrate the computation of diluted EPS in the presence of convertible debt.

The convertible debentures are presumed to have been converted into 10,000 additional shares of stock at the beginning of the year (January 1, 2001). Accordingly, 10,000 new common shares are added to the diluted EPS denominator. Under the if-converted method, no interest would have been paid on the debentures this year because all bonds are assumed to be converted as of January 1. This means that interest of \$50,000 would not have been paid on the presumptively converted bonds. With a 35% tax rate, net income would increase by \$32,500 (i.e., \$50,000 × [1 − 0.35]), and this amount is added to the diluted EPS numerator.

$$\text{Diluted EPS} = \frac{\text{Net income} - \text{Preferred dividends} + \text{Income adjustments due to dilutive financial instruments}}{\text{Weighted average number of common shares outstanding} + \text{Newly issuable shares due to dilutive financial instruments}}$$

$$\text{Diluted EPS} = \frac{\$1{,}257{,}331 - \$70{,}000 + \text{Income adjustments due to dilutive financial instruments}}{173{,}334 + \text{Newly issuable shares due to dilutive financial instruments}}$$

Basic EPS

$$\text{Diluted EPS} = \frac{\$1{,}257{,}331 - \$70{,}000 + \$32{,}500}{173{,}334 + 10{,}000} = \$6.65 \text{ per share}$$

"As-if" conversion of debt

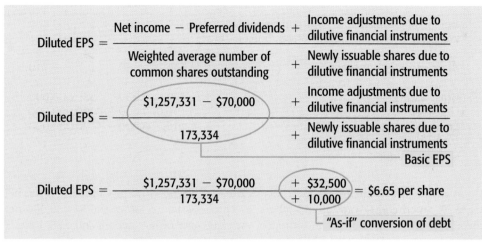

In our example, the outstanding stock options will affect only the denominator of the diluted EPS computation. This adjustment reflects the difference between the option **exercise price** (\$100 per common share) and the **average market price** (\$114 per common share) during the period. *SFAS No. 128* assumes that any proceeds received on exercise of the options (\$100 per share) are used to buy back already outstanding common shares at the average market price for the period. This is called the **treasury stock method.** We now illustrate the adjustment to compute diluted EPS under the treasury stock method.

> This is not always the case. If the options are issued as employee compensation, then the after-tax portion already charged to expense during the period (described later in this chapter) must be reversed in the EPS numerator.

Stock options are dilutive when they are "in the money"—that is, when the average market price (\$114) exceeds the option price (\$100). Using the treasury stock method, we assume that the \$2,000,000 proceeds to the company from presumptive exercise of the options (i.e., 20,000 shares at \$100 per share) are used to repurchase previously issued common shares at the \$114 average market price. The cash from the options is sufficient to acquire 17,544 shares (i.e., \$2,000,000 ÷ \$114 per share = 17,544 shares). Since 20,000 shares are presumed issued and 17,544 are presumed acquired, the difference (2,456 net new common shares) is added to the diluted EPS denominator:

> In-the-money options are dilutive because the number of shares that can be repurchased with the proceeds from the options is smaller than the number of new shares issued on exercise of the options.

$$\text{Diluted EPS} = \frac{\$1{,}257{,}331 - \$70{,}000 + \$32{,}500}{173{,}334 + 10{,}000 + 2{,}456} = \$6.57 \text{ per share}$$

Treasury stock conversion of options

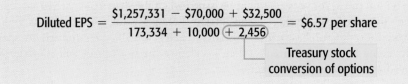

Notice that diluted EPS equals \$6.57, an amount lower than the basic EPS number \$6.85. It is this potential decrease in the computed earnings flow to each common share that motivates the diluted EPS computation.

Is Earnings Per Share a Meaningful Number?

EPS data are reported in the financial news and are prominent in corporate annual reports even though EPS suffers as a financial performance measure.

EPS ignores the amount of *capital* required to generate the reported earnings. This is easy to show. Consider the 2001 financial performance of two companies:

	Company A	Company B
Net income available to common shareholders	$ 1,000,000	$ 1,000,000
Weighted-average common shares outstanding	100,000	100,000
Basic earnings per share	$ 10	$ 10
Gross assets	$20,000,000	$30,000,000
Liabilities	10,000,000	10,000,000
Equity capital (assets − liabilities)	10,000,000	20,000,000
Return on equity	10%	5%

Company A and Company B report identical basic EPS of $10. But Company B needed twice as much equity capital and 50% more gross assets to attain the $1,000,000 net income. Even though both A and B report the same *level* of net income and EPS, B has a return on equity of only 5%, while A's figure is 10%. Company A generates more earnings from existing resources—that is, equity capital.

Because EPS ignores capital commitments, problems can arise when trying to interpret it. The narrow focus of the EPS ratio clouds comparisons between companies as well as year-to-year EPS changes for a single company. For example, even if year-to-year earnings' levels are the same, a company can "improve" its reported EPS by simply repurchasing some previously outstanding common shares.

Earnings per share (EPS) is a popular and useful summary measure of a company's profit performance. It tells you how much profit (or loss) each share of common stock has earned after adjustments for potential dilution from options, warrants, and convertible securities are factored in. But EPS has its limitations.

RECAP

Accounting for Stock-Based Compensation

Many U.S. companies compensate managers and other salaried employees with a combination of cash and stock options—that is, options to purchase equity shares in the company. A typical employee stock option gives the employee the right to purchase a specified number of common shares at a specified price over some specified time period. The specified price—called the **exercise price**—is usually equal to or higher than the market price of the underlying shares at the time the options are issued. An option to buy 100 shares at $50 per share at any time within the next five years might be issued when the shares themselves are selling for $30. When the exercise price exceeds the current share price, the stock option is "out of the money." An option to purchase common shares at $50 is valuable even though the shares are currently selling for only $30 because there's a chance the stock price will climb above $50 sometime during the ensuing five years.

Companies use stock options to augment cash compensation for several reasons:

- Options help align employees' interests with those of owners (stockholders). Employees with stock options have an incentive to make decisions that ultimately cause the share price to exceed the option exercise price.

- Many "start-up" high-growth companies are "cash starved" and cannot afford to pay competitive cash salaries. Stock options provide a way for them to attract talented employees while conserving cash.
- As long as the exercise price is equal to or greater than the stock price when the option is issued, this compensation is not taxable to the employee until the option is exercised. This is an attractive feature, because it allows employees to accumulate wealth while postponing taxes.

> Granting employee stock options with an exercise price that is *below* the current market price of the firm's common stock imposes a tax cost on employees. This is because the excess of market price over exercise price must be included in employees' taxable income when the options are issued.

Financial reporting for employee stock options granted as compensation is governed by *SFAS No. 123*.[15] The controversy that raged during the evolution of this FASB document is unprecedented in the history of U.S. accounting standard setting. Companies that issued employee stock options, their auditors, the SEC, and ultimately, the U.S. Senate lobbied the FASB to influence the final reporting rules. The fight over stock options presents an opportunity to discuss financial reporting incentives (Chapters 1 and 7) in a concrete setting and to illustrate how politics often enters the standard-setting process.

Historical Perspective

Suppose an employee agrees to work this year in exchange for a small current salary and the promise of additional cash compensation five years later. No one disputes the notion that the employee's salary should be recorded on the company's books as an expense of the current year. But what about promised compensation? Should it be recorded as a current year expense, or should the expense be postponed five years until the employee actually receives the cash? This question is at the heart of the employee stock options debate.

Before *SFAS No. 123* was adopted in 1995, accounting for stock-based compensation was governed by *Accounting Principles Board (APB) Opinion No. 25*.[16] This pronouncement was issued in 1972, one year prior to publication of what is now the universally accepted approach for valuing traditional stock options—the Black–Scholes method.[17] Because *APB No. 25* preceded modern option pricing theory, it offered no mechanism for establishing the value of stock options granted as compensation to employees. Options issued with an exercise price equal to or above the market price of the underlying common shares ***were assumed to have no value*** for compensation expense purposes. Under *APB No. 25*, if Ramos Corporation issued on June 28, 1972 10-year options to employees that entitled each one of them to buy 100 shares at $10 per share when the existing share price was also $10, ***no compensation expense would be recognized because these options were deemed to be valueless.***

Obviously, options with terms like those in the Ramos Corporation example are valuable; the price of the company's common stock could easily rise above the $10 exercise price sometime during the 10-year life of the option. Over the 1970s and early 1980s, option pricing *theory* evolved into option pricing *practice* using the Black–Scholes model as the standard device for valuing traded options. Despite this *post-APB No. 25* breakthrough, options issued as compensation were generally treated as being valueless at the grant date. Compensation expense *was* recognized in rare instances.

During the 1980s U.S. companies increasingly adopted employee compensation packages designed to link employee pay to company performance. Stock option plans proliferated as an element of employee compensation. Many auditors and other financial experts

---

[15] "Accounting for Stock-Based Compensation," *SFAS No. 123* (Norwalk, CT: FASB, 1995).

[16] "Accounting for Stock Issued to Employees," *APB Opinion No. 25* (New York: American Institute of Certified Public Accountants [AICPA], 1972).

[17] F. Black and M. Scholes, "The Pricing of Options and Corporate Liabilities," *Journal of Political Economy* (May–June, 1973), pp. 637–54. Corporate finance books explore the derivation of the Black–Scholes method and other option valuation techniques in detail; for example, see R. A. Brealey and S. C. Meyers, *Principles of Corporate Finance*, 4th ed. (New York: McGraw-Hill, 1991), pp. 483–504.

considered the *APB No. 25* presumption that options were valueless to be simply incorrect. Because these beliefs were widespread, the FASB began reconsidering the accounting for stock options in 1984.[18]

Sentiment in the business community soon shifted considerably. Strong and widespread opposition to the FASB initiative surfaced as it became clear that the new proposal would result in expenses being recognized on the income statement when stock options were granted. Those opposed to the FASB's proposal raised arguments against expense recognition that roughly parallel the themes of this chapter. Their criticisms cited four issues: (1) appropriate income measurement, (2) compliance with contract terms and restrictions, (3) legality of corporate distributions to owners, and (4) linkage to equity valuation.

Next, we survey these objections to the FASB's stock options approach.

Opposition to the FASB

Some opponents of the FASB's proposal questioned whether providing stock options to employees constituted an accounting expense. These opponents said that treating stock options as an expense would violate ***appropriate income measurement*** because stock options do not involve a cash outflow. On the contrary, they argued, when—and if—the options were eventually exercised, cash would flow *into* the company, not *out*. Supporters of the FASB counterargued that cash was not the issue. Expenses often arise independently of cash outflows. One prominent advocate of this position was Warren Buffett, Chairman of Berkshire Hathaway, Inc., who said:

> [Some contend] that options should not be viewed as a cost because they "aren't dollars out of a company's coffers." I see this line of reasoning as offering exciting possibilities to American corporations for instantly improving their reported profits. For example, they could eliminate the cost of insurance by paying for it with options. So if you're a CEO and subscribe to this "no cash–no cost" theory of accounting, I'll make you an offer you can't refuse: Give us a call at Berkshire and we will happily sell you insurance in exchange for a bundle of long-term options on your company's stock.
>
> Shareholders should understand that companies incur costs when they deliver something of value to another party and not just when cash changes hands. (Warren Buffett, Letter to Shareholders, Berkshire Hathaway, Inc., 1992 Annual Report.)

Buffett's position that expenses arise when stock options are issued is consistent with how we account for issued stock. When stock is issued, shareholders give up something of value—a portion of their ownership interest—in exchange for something else of value—usually cash from new investors. The value given up and the value received both get recorded. Buffett argues that the same accounting rules should apply for employee stock options. Shareholders are giving up a portion of their ownership interest by having the company issue additional stock—or options for stock—to employees. In exchange, shareholders receive valuable services from the employees—services that are paid for in stock options rather than in cash. From this perspective, issuing stock options to employees represents an expense to the company.

CONTRACTING

Another argument raised by opponents to the FASB's proposal was that treating employee stock options as an expense could jeopardize ***compliance with contract terms and conditions.*** Companies with large employee stock option awards might, under the FASB's proposal, violate loan covenants tied to reported earnings. For example, the "times-interest-earned" ratio would deteriorate if option grants were expensed.

Impartial observers who understand contracting incentives can see why companies with significant employee options would raise this objection. Their interests would be harmed by the FASB proposal, and economic intuition tells us that companies would resist such initiatives. But one can appreciate the FASB's mission to "do the right thing"—to draft rules

---

[18] *SFAS No. 123,* para. 5.

that closely mirror underlying economic circumstances. If a particular accounting approach correctly captures these economic effects, it presumably should be used even though some companies may be harmed. Furthermore, many of the FASB's most vocal opponents were companies whose employee stock options—if expensed—would have decreased earnings by a trivial amount. Since the potential impact of the FASB proposal on these firms' covenants was insignificant, what was really motivating their opposition?

The compensation paid to top corporate executives was under intense scrutiny in the early 1990s. Corporate restructurings and layoffs were widespread, a recession was in progress, and many companies demonstrated lackluster financial performance. In this climate some critics questioned whether top corporate executives should continue to enjoy increasingly large salaries and bonuses while their employees were experiencing financial hardship. The issue quickly became political.

In 1993 the U.S. Congress limited the tax deductibility of executive compensation to $1,000,000 per employee—any excess could not be claimed as a deduction on the corporate tax return except when compensation was tied to the achievement of explicit and preset performance goals. (See Reebok International's discussion of the tax limitation on executive pay in Exhibit 7.1.) The passage of this law clearly illustrates public sentiment on this issue. Corporate leaders, sensitive to the growing scrutiny of executive compensation levels, may have felt that the FASB's plan would draw unwanted attention to executive pay.

The ***legality of corporate distributions to owners*** was never at issue regarding executive compensation. Political considerations aside, companies are free under the law to pay corporate executives whatever amounts are deemed appropriate by their board of directors. However, an issue did arise—whether large executive salaries were *proper.* Some companies were perceived to oppose the FASB's proposal because it would add the value of options to cash compensation and thus make it easier for critics of "excessive" pay to spotlight certain companies and executives.

VALUATION

Opponents to the FASB's proposal also invoked an argument based on the ***linkage to equity valuation.*** They believed that a simple "price–earnings multiple" relationship exists between reported earnings and common stock values. Under the FASB's plan, they argued, employee stock option grants would increase compensation expense and lower earnings—and thus lower stock price. (Our discussion of the earnings capitalization model in Chapter 6 suggests that the relationship between earnings and share price is more complicated than this.) They argued that as stock prices fell, small companies who were heavy users of stock options would have difficulty raising new equity capital. This position was voiced by Senator Dianne Feinstein (Democrat, California) when she introduced legislation designed to block the FASB's plan. She said:

> [The Bill] will also require the Financial Accounting Standards Board (FASB) to reexamine [its] recent decision to impose huge new accounting charges on the use of employee stock options. I am seriously concerned that if FASB's rule is adopted, tens of thousands of desperately needed jobs in California and the Nation will never be created. (Congressional Record—Senate, June 29, 1993, S8252.)

Senator Feinstein believed that the FASB plan would make it more difficult for high-technology companies to raise new equity capital, thereby inhibiting expansion and job creation.

Despite growing business opposition, the FASB persisted and continued to move toward expense treatment of stock-based compensation. Congress later initiated legislation which would have eliminated the FASB's independence by requiring the SEC to approve of all new FASB standards.[19] Faced with this threat, the FASB was compelled to abandon its proposal and implement a compromise treatment.

---

[19] Called the Accounting Standards Reform Act of 1994, this bill was introduced by Senator Joe Lieberman (Democrat, Connecticut). Congressional Record—Senate, October 6, 1994, S14510.

The Compromise–*SFAS No. 123*

The widespread, powerful opposition to recognizing stock-based compensation as an expense caused the FASB to allow a choice of accounting methods:

1. Companies could choose to continue using the *APB Opinion No. 25* approach, under which compensation expense was rarely recognized.
2. Alternatively, companies could measure the **fair value** of the stock option and charge this amount to expense.[20]

The fair value of a stock option is measured using standard option-pricing models, with adjustments for factors unique to employee stock options. The FASB encouraged companies to adopt the fair value approach rather than to continue using *APB Opinion No. 25,* since it considered the fair value approach to be preferable. Companies that chose to continue using *APB Opinion No. 25* accounting were also required to disclose in a footnote what net income would have been if compensation expense had been recognized under the fair value approach. The stock option reporting alternatives are represented graphically in Figure 15.3.

Implementing the fair value approach of *SFAS No. 123* is not difficult. However, the standard contains many detailed guidelines for measuring compensation expense. We describe these procedures tersely using a "big-picture" approach—that's all you need to grasp the overall impact on financial numbers.

Assume that Guyton Corporation grants 100 common stock options to each of its top 300 managers on January 1, 2001. At that date, both the exercise price of the options and the market price of Guyton's stock is $30. To provide managers with an incentive to remain at Guyton, the options cannot be exercised before January 1, 2004. This time span between the grant date and the first available exercise date is called the **vesting period.** Guyton's options do not expire until January 1, 2011, giving the options a ten-year legal life. But *SFAS No. 123* requires that we estimate the **expected life of the options**—meaning we must forecast when the options are likely to be exercised by employees. Factors to consider in estimating the expected life include the average length of time similar grants have remained outstanding in the past and the expected volatility of the company's common stock price. Let's assume Guyton's options have an expected life of five years.

For most companies today, the expected life of employee stock options is somewhere between three and ten years.

Figure 15.3

EMPLOYEE STOCK OPTION REPORTING ALTERNATIVES UNDER *SFAS NO. 123*

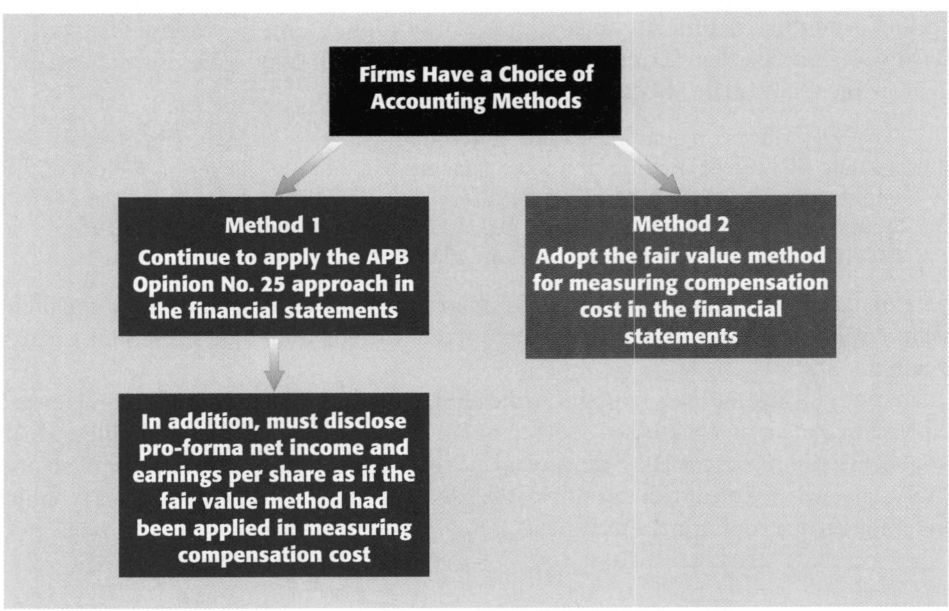
Firms Have a Choice of Accounting Methods
Method 1
Continue to apply the APB Opinion No. 25 approach in the financial statements
Method 2
Adopt the fair value method for measuring compensation cost in the financial statements
In addition, must disclose pro-forma net income and earnings per share as if the fair value method had been applied in measuring compensation cost

[20] *SFAS No. 123,* para. 11.

SFAS No. 123 specifies that the fair value of the stock options is to be measured at the **grant date**—the date when both the terms are mutually agreed upon and the stock options are awarded to individual employees. Here's how the fair value of stock option should be determined:

> The fair value of a stock option . . . shall be estimated using an option-pricing model (for example, the Black–Scholes or a binomial model) that takes into account as of the grant date the exercise price and expected life of the option, the current price of the underlying stock and its expected volatility, expected dividends on the stock . . . and the risk-free interest rate for the expected term of the option. (*SFAS No. 123*, para. 19.)

It is not necessary to understand the theory behind option pricing models to understand the financial reporting for employee stock options. As the preceding excerpt indicates, the measurement of fair value requires estimates of several other variables that we have not yet specified in the Guyton example. We will assume that the risk-free interest rate is 6.75%, that no dividends are forecasted for the company's common stock, and that the expected volatility of Guyton's common stock is 20%. These facts are summarized in Table 15.1.

Volatility in option pricing models is measured using a benchmark of one standard deviation of a stock's return over a specified time period. Assume Guyton stock has experienced a return of 10%. Since one standard deviation is roughly 66% of a normal distribution, the 20% expected volatility means there is a 66% probability that the return on Guyton's stock will be 10% ± 20% in any one year—that is, there is a two thirds chance that the return in any one year will range between a low of −10% to a high of +30%.

Inserting the numbers in Table 15.1 into the Black–Scholes option pricing model indicates that each option has a fair value of \$10.05 at the grant date.[21] The total compensation cost of all employee stock option awards is \$301,500 (\$10.05 × 30,000 options). Let's assume that all 300 managers will meet the vesting requirements and ultimately exercise all 30,000 options.

SFAS No. 123 (para. 28) requires firms to estimate what proportion of the options originally granted will never vest due to employee turnover. Compensation expense includes only those options that are not forfeited. For example, if Guyton Corporation estimated that only 29,000 options would ultimately vest, total compensation cost would be \$291,450 (i.e., \$10.05 × 29,000) rather than \$301,500.

Stock-based compensation is intended to increase the employees' stake in the firm, creating an incentive for employees to work in the best interests of all the other owners. The

Table 15.1 ■ GUYTON CORPORATION

Variables Used in Determining the Value of Employee Stock Options

Options granted (100 shares × 300 employees)	30,000
Exercise price (E)	\$30
Stock price at grant date (S)	\$30
Expected life of options (t)	5 years
Risk-free interest rate (r)	6.75%
Expected volatility of common stock (σ)	20%
Expected dividends on common stock	–0–

Black-Scholes Option Valuation (V) Formula

$$V = SN(d_1) - Ee^{-rt}N(d_2)$$

where $N(d)$ is the value of the cumulative standard normal function,

$$d_1 = [\log(S/E) + (r + 0.5\sigma^{2)}t]/\sigma t^{1/2} \text{ and}$$

$$d_2 = d_1 - \sigma t^{1/2}$$

Using the formula, the fair market value of each Guyton option is estimated to be \$10.05 at the grant date.

[21] The Black–Scholes formula in Table 15.1 can be used only when there are no dividends paid on the common stock. If the stock pays dividends, then a modified version of the Black–Scholes option valuation model should be used. The current stock price (S) is replaced with the stock price adjusted for continuous dividends. To illustrate, suppose the common stock described in Table 15.1 will pay a \$1 quarterly dividend in 90 days (and every subsequent quarter). This dividend stream implies a continuous dividend rate of 13.75%. So we replace the current stock price (S = \$30) with the stock price adjusted for the continuous dividend ($Se^{-\delta t}$ = \$30 $e^{-13.75\% \times 5 \text{ years}}$) and then solve the Black–Scholes formula.

vesting requirements provide an extra incentive to stay with the company long enough to benefit from the anticipated value of the options. For these reasons *SFAS No. 123* charges total compensation cost of $301,500 to expense on a ***straight-line basis over the vesting period.*** Guyton Corporation would recognize $100,500 ($301,500 ÷ 3) as compensation expense in each of the years 2001 through 2003:

DR Compensation expense	$100,500	
CR Paid-in capital–stock options		$100,500

We ignore deferred income tax considerations (discussed in Chapter 13) for simplicity. Deferred taxes arise because compensation expense is recognized in the financial statements and for income tax purposes at different amounts and in different periods. For income tax purposes, employers can deduct the *tax cost* of options—calculated as the difference between the exercise price and the stock price on the day the employee exercises the option—from taxable income.

This same entry is made each year even though the market value of the company's stock—and therefore the value of outstanding employee stock options—will undoubtedly change over time. ***SFAS No. 123 specifies that compensation cost—option fair value—is measured only once (i.e., at the grant date).***

Let's say Guyton's share price rises above the $30 exercise price after the vesting period and all 30,000 options are exercised by managers on the same day. The entry to record the exercise of employee stock options is (assuming $20 par value stock):

DR Cash (30,000 × $30)	$900,000	
DR Paid-in capital–stock options ($100,500 × 3 years)	301,500	
CR Common stock–par ($20 × 30,000)		$600,000
CR Paid-in capital in excess of par		601,500

In evaluating the financial statement effect of these two entries, notice that: (1) compensation expense is recognized in the same amount each year over the vesting period; and (2) if the options are exercised, the total amount added to the common stock and capital in excess of par is $1,201,500—the sum of the cash received when the options are exercised plus the calculated fair value of the options at the grant date.

If we assume that Guyton's share price never rises above the exercise price, then the options will never be exercised. No cash will flow in. The offset to cumulative three-year compensation expense ($301,500) will remain in the "Paid-in capital—stock options" account. This dollar figure represents the estimated value of employee productivity (measured at the option grant date) that in effect was "donated" to the company without any corresponding ownership claim being given up to Guyton's employees.

RECAP

SFAS No. 123 **is a political compromise. The FASB was unanimous in its belief that expenses are incurred when companies grant stock options to employees as a part of a compensation package. Nevertheless, companies are not required to record this expense in the financial statements. Instead, the compromise requires firms to disclose the fair value amount of stock-based compensation in a footnote to the statements.**

Stock Option Disclosures

A recent survey of 1999 annual reports shows that most companies are still accounting for employee stock options as they have in the past.[22] This means that no compensation

[22] P. McConnell, J. Pegg, and D. Zion, "Employee Stock Option Expense," *Accounting Issues* (New York: Bear, Stearns & Co., August 17, 2000).

expense is recorded unless the option exercise price is *below* the stock price on the grant date.

SFAS No. 123 requires companies to provide ***pro forma***—"as if"—disclosures of net income and EPS that are calculated with a charge to compensation expense for options granted. Table 15.2 shows the impact on 1999 EPS for selected companies included in the survey. Aggregate EPS for companies in the S&P 500 drops by about 6% when the fair value of employee stock options is charged to 1999 earnings. There are 122 companies where the EPS decline is 10% or more, and 42 of those are technology companies.

> Under *APB No. 25*, compensation expense for employee stock option plans was measured by the *difference* between the exercise price and the stock price on the grant date that is, the date when the company's board of directors award the stock options to employees. If the exercise price is $47 and the share price is $50 on the grant date, compensation expense of $3 per stock option would be recorded. This feature of *APB No. 25* was retained in *SFAS No. 123.*

The 1999 pro forma information in Table 15.2 reflects the full impact of a company's stock compensation program. ***But pro forma results reported prior to 1999 may not reflect the full impact of a company's stock compensation program.*** This is because:

- the compensation charge is calculated by valuing employee stock options at the grant date and then spreading the expense over the option's vesting period—the time it takes employees to earn them fully (often three or more years).
- for the pro forma disclosures, companies only need to include the effects of options granted in fiscal years beginning after December 15, 1994. Unexpired options granted in earlier years are not included in the calculations.

For example, if the vesting period is five years, the 1996 pro forma EPS adjustment would include only one fifth of the value of stock options granted that year plus one fifth of the

Table 15.2 ■ EARNINGS PER SHARE (EPS) IMPACT OF EXPENSING THE VALUE OF EMPLOYEE STOCK OPTION GRANTS FOR SELECTED COMPANIES

	EPS as Reported	EPS Adjusted for Compensation Expense	EPS Decrease in $	Percent Decrease
Adaptec	$1.56	$0.83	$0.73	47%
America Online	0.60	0.39	0.21	35
Autodesk	0.16	(0.74)	0.90	563
BellSouth	1.80	1.76	0.04	2
Biogen	1.40	1.25	0.15	11
Bristol Meyers	2.06	1.96	0.10	5
Citrix Systems	0.61	0.33	0.28	46
Compaq Computer	0.34	0.23	0.11	32
First Data	2.76	2.64	0.12	4
Fluor	1.37	1.26	0.11	8
Intel	2.11	1.98	0.13	6
Kroger	0.74	0.70	0.04	5
Lucent	1.10	0.89	0.21	19
Microsoft	1.42	1.30	0.12	8
Pepsico	1.37	1.27	0.10	7
Quaker Oats	3.23	3.12	0.09	3
Schering Plough	1.42	1.38	0.04	3
Texas Instruments	1.68	1.52	0.16	10
United Technologies	1.65	1.50	0.15	9
Williams Companies	0.36	0.23	0.13	36

Source: From P. McConnell, "Employee Stock Option Expense," *Accounting Issues* (August 17, 2000). Reprinted with permission of Bear, Stearns & Co.

value of stock options granted in 1995. In this case the pro forma compensation expense adjustment could be understated by a substantial amount—one-fifth of the value of stock options granted in 1992, 1993, and 1994. Analysts must be aware of this problem when comparing pro forma EPS figures across time.

Here's what Cisco Systems says about its employee stock options:

The Company is required under Statement of Financial Accounting Standards No. 123, "Accounting for Stock Based Compensations" ("SFAS 123"), to disclose pro forma information regarding option grants made to its employees based on specified valuation techniques that produce estimated compensation charges. These amounts have not been reflected in the Company's Consolidated Statements of Operations because no compensation charge arises when the price of the employees' stock options equals the market value of the underlying stock at the grant date, as is the case of options granted to the Company's employees. Pro forma information under SFAS 123 is as follows (in millions, except per share amounts):

Year Ended	July 29, 2000	July 31, 1999	July 25, 1998
Net income–as reported	$2,668	$2,023	$1,331
Net income–pro forma	1,549	1,487	1,074
Basic net income per common share–as reported	$0.39	$0.30	$0.21
Diluted net income per common share–as reported	0.36	0.29	0.20
Basic net income per common share–pro forma	0.22	0.22	0.17
Diluted net income per common share–pro forma	0.21	0.21	0.16

The fair value of stock option grants is estimated on the date of grant using the Black–Scholes option pricing model with the following weighted average assumptions:

	Employee Stock Option Plan			Employee Stock Purchase Plan		
	July 29, 2000	July 31, 1999	July 25, 1998	July 29, 2000	July 31, 1999	July 25, 1998
Expected dividend yield	0.0%	0.0%	0.0%	0.0%	0.0%	0.0%
Risk-free interest rate	6.4%	5.1%	5.7%	5.3%	4.9%	5.4%
Expected volatility	33.9%	40.2%	36.5%	43.3%	47.2%	44.8%
Expected life (in years)	3.1	4.1	5.1	0.5	0.5	0.5

The Black–Scholes options pricing model was developed for use in estimating the fair value of traded options that have no vesting restrictions and are fully transferable. In addition, options pricing models require the input of highly subjective assumptions including the expected stock price volatility. The Company uses projected volatility rates which are based upon historical volatility rates trended into future years. Because the Company's employee stock options have characteristics significantly different from those of traded options, and because changes in the subjective input assumptions can materially affect the fair value estimate, in management's opinion, the existing models do not necessarily provide a reliable single measure of the fair value of the Company's options. The weighted average estimated fair values of employee stock options granted during fiscal 2000, 1999 and 1998 were $19.44, $8.40, and $3.57, respectively.

The above pro forma disclosures under SFAS 123 are also not likely to be representative of the effects on net income and net income per common share in future years, because they do not take into consideration pro forma compensation expense related to grants made prior to fiscal 1996. (Cisco Systems, Inc., 2000 Annual Report.)

The dollar impact of stock compensation expense can be staggering. For example, Cisco Systems' 2000 basic EPS would have been reduced from $0.39 to $0.22, or $0.17 per share. This 43% decline represents $1,119 million of Cisco's earnings that year. Of course, for many companies the dollar impact is much smaller.

Stock options are an important part of employee pay at many companies today—and for good reason. They save cash, they motivate employees, and companies are not currently required to record compensation expense for employee stock options except in a footnote to the financial statements.

RECAP

Convertible Debt

On September 27, 1999 VerticalNet offered investors the opportunity to purchase up to $100 million of convertible subordinated debentures. These bonds paid a stated interest rate of 5.25% annually, matured in 5 years, and could be exchanged at any time for VerticalNet stock at a conversion price of $20 per common share. Because the debentures were issued in units of $1,000 face value, the conversion price meant investors could exchange each bond for 50 shares of stock ($1,000 ÷ $20 = 50 shares).

What price do you suppose VerticalNet received for each $1,000 face value debenture?

To put this question in context, the yield to maturity—the effective interest rate—on risk-free U.S. government bonds of a similar duration was 5.9% in September 1999, and the average yield on newly issued high-grade industrial debt that month was about 8%. Given the economic climate of the time, it may surprise you to learn that VerticalNet was able to sell its 5.25% bonds at a price of 100%, receiving $1,000 in cash for each $1,000 face value issued. By contrast, the promised cash flows associated with each bond—$52.50 each year plus another $1,000 at maturity in the year 2004—have a discounted present value at 8% of only $890.20. ***Investors were willing to pay $109.80 more than the present value of each VerticalNet bond because of the conversion feature attached to the debt.***

We now explain the financial reporting for convertible debt and its implications for those who use financial statements.

Background

The VerticalNet example illustrates that convertible bonds give investors the opportunity—but not the obligation—to exchange a company's debt for common stock in accordance with terms in the bond indenture. The **conversion price**—the dollar value at which the debt can be converted into common stock—is typically above the prevailing market price of the company's common shares at the time the debt is issued. The option to convert is solely at the discretion of the investor, and it will only be exercised when and if the investor finds the exchange desirable. Shares of VerticalNet were trading around $16 in September 1999—or about $4 below the conversion price. Investors had little incentive to exchange their bonds for stock immediately. The real value of the conversion feature to investors was the possibility that the stock price might climb above $20 sometime over the next 5 years.

Convertible bonds are typically **subordinated debentures.** This means that in the event of insolvency or bankruptcy the claims of "senior" creditors must be settled in full before any payment will be made to holders of subordinated debentures. Senior creditors typically encompass all other long-term debt issues and bank loans. However, subordinated debentures do have priority over common and preferred stock.

Figure 15.4 on the next page reports the dollar value of new convertible debt issues in the United States between 1980 and 1997. Industrial corporations have been the primary issuers of convertible debt.

Convertible debt offerings increase during periods of rising stock prices, which explains much of the year-to-year variation in Figure 15.4. The opportunity to share in future stock price increases is more attractive during a period of bullish market expectations for common stocks. This sentiment allows companies to issue convertibles on favorable terms.

Convertible bonds are also usually **callable,** or redeemable, by the issuer at a specified price before maturity. When convertible bonds are called, investors must either convert or have the debt redeemed for a cash price that is generally less than the value of the common

Figure 15.4

THE DOLLAR VALUE OF CONVERTIBLE DEBT ISSUED BY U.S. COMPANIES FROM 1980 THROUGH 1997

Source: From K. A. Carow, G. R. Erwin, and J. J. McConnell, "A Survey of U.S. Corporate Financing Innovations: 1970–1997," *Journal of Applied Corporate Finance* (Spring 1999). Reprinted with permission.

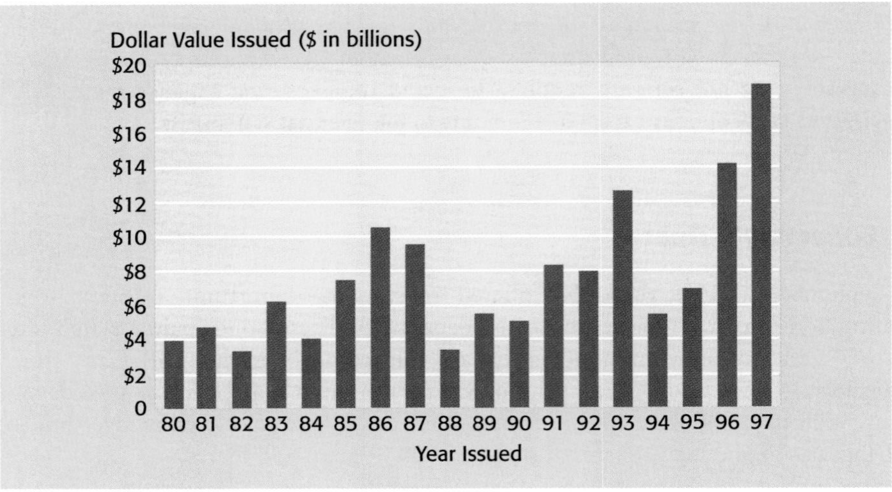

stock into which the debt can be converted. Call provisions protect the company against extreme price increases by forcing investor action. Otherwise, investors would simply continue holding the debt in anticipation of further share price increases.

To illustrate, suppose that VerticalNet's stock price reached $25 per share in 2000. Each $1,000 par-value convertible bond would then represent a claim to $1,250 in common stock (50 shares × $25 per share). Suppose that VerticalNet's bonds were callable at a price of $1,027.50 each. VerticalNet could force conversion by "calling" the debt—investors would then take the more valuable common stock rather than the less valuable cash payment.

Financial Reporting Issues

Convertible debt poses this financial reporting dilemma: Should a value be assigned to the debt's conversion feature? Clearly, conversion features are valuable to both the issuing company and investors. The conversion option enabled VerticalNet to borrow $100 million at 5.25% interest when other more established companies were paying 8% interest. Moreover, the availability of Black–Scholes and other option pricing models means that we now have well-established methods for assigning values to option features—like the VerticalNet conversion privilege. However, GAAP for convertible debt is outlined in *APB Opinion No. 14,* which predates the development of modern option pricing theory.[23]

APB No. 14 specifies that convertible bonds must be recorded as *debt only,* with no value assigned to the conversion privilege. Two reasons for this treatment are cited: (1) the inseparability of the conversion feature from the debt component of the convertible security; and (2) the practical problems of determining separate values for the debt and the conversion option in the absence of separability.

On this last point, the APB concluded:

> In the absence of separate transferability, values are not established in the marketplace, and accordingly, the value assigned to each feature is necessarily subjective. A determination of the value of the conversion feature poses problems because of the uncertain duration of the right to obtain the stock and the uncertainty as to the future value of the stock obtainable upon conversion. Furthermore, issuers often claim that a subjective valuation of a debt security without the conversion option but with identical other terms . . . is difficult because such a security could not be sold at a price which the issuer would regard as producing an acceptable cost of financing. (*APB No. 14,* para. 8.)

Given modern option pricing methods, it is unlikely that accounting standard setters would reach the same conclusion today. Nevertheless, APB No. 14 continues to be GAAP for convertible debt.

[23] "Accounting for Convertible Debt and Debt Issued with Stock Purchase Warrants," *APB Opinion No. 14* (New York: AICPA, 1969).

Here's how VerticalNet records the issuance of all $100 million of its convertible subordinate debentures at par value:

DR Cash	$100,000,000	
CR Convertible subordinated debentures		$100,000,000

This entry assigns the entire $100 million to the convertible debt liability. One year later, VerticalNet records an interest payment of $5,250,000 (or 5.25% times $100 million):

DR Interest expense	$5,250,000	
CR Cash		$5,250,000

(This entry ignores the real-world complication that arises when companies accrue interest throughout the year.)

Thus far, the accounting for convertible debt parallels that for the straight-debt securities described in Chapter 11. VerticalNet will continue to record interest expense at the rate of 5.25% annually until the debt is retired or converted. Let's move several years forward to see what happens at conversion.

Suppose it is 2001, and some (but not all) investors have chosen to exercise their conversion privilege by exchanging $50 million of the debentures. Furthermore, the company's stock has a current market value of $30 per share, which is above the $20 conversion price. This means that investors will surrender bonds with a face value (and book value) of $50 million in exchange for common stock with a market value of $75 million. *APB No. 14* permits companies to record debt conversion in either of two ways:

> At the stated conversion price, investors will receive 2,500,000 common shares for their $50 million of debentures ($50 million divided by $20 price per share). Since each share has a market value of $30, investors receive stock worth $75 million.

1. The **book value method** records the newly issued stock at the book value of debt retired.

DR Convertible subordinated debentures	$50,000,000	
CR Common stock ($1 par)		$ 2,500,000
CR Paid-in capital in excess of par		47,500,000

2. The **market value method** records the newly issued shares at their current market value. Any difference between that market value and the conversion price is recognized as a loss (or gain) on conversion.

DR Convertible subordinated debentures	$50,000,000	
DR Loss on debt conversion	25,000,000	
CR Common stock ($1 par)		$ 2,500,000
CR Paid-in capital in excess of par		72,500,000

The conversion loss is not classified as an extraordinary item because it is neither *unusual in nature* nor *infrequent in occurrence.* Of course, VerticalNet would continue to record interest expense on the remaining $50 million of outstanding convertible debentures.

Under the book value approach, no accounting gain or loss is recognized at retirement, because the debt book value is just transferred to the common stock accounts. Under the market value approach, however, common stock is credited at full market value *as if* the shares issued were sold for cash on the conversion date. It is easy to see why the book value method is more popular. Almost all debt conversions occur when the company's stock price is above the conversion price, and this situation triggers recognition of an accounting loss under the market value method. Managers can avoid recording this loss by instead selecting the book value approach.

Analytical Insights

There are two messages in this discussion of convertible debt for financial statement readers.

First, ***estimating the future cash flow implications of convertible debt is difficult.*** This is because it is necessary to consider both the scheduled interest and principal payments for the debt, as well as the likelihood of conversion prior to maturity. Option pricing methods can be used to evaluate the probability of conversion over long time intervals. For near-term projections, however, a simple comparison of the conversion price with the current market price of common stock can prove informative—that is, if the exercise price is considerably above the current share price and the options are close to expiration, it is unlikely they will be exercised. The bond indenture agreement should also be examined for call provision details.

Second, ***recorded interest expense may seriously understate the true cost of debt financing for companies that issue convertible bonds or notes.*** Few people would argue that VerticalNet is more creditworthy than the U.S. government. Yet the company borrowed money at 5.25% when investors were charging the federal government 5.9% for loans of similar duration. By ignoring the value of conversion features, current GAAP understates interest expense.

Convertible debt gives investors the upside potential of common stock and the safety net of debt. That's why the interest rate on convertible debt is so low—the option value of the conversion feature compensates for the lower interest paid to investors. Because GAAP ignores the conversion option, interest expense may be understated and cash flow forecasting may be impeded.

RECAP

SUMMARY

Many aspects of financial reporting for owners' equity transactions are built on technical rules and procedures that have evolved over time. Other aspects of owners' equity accounting have not changed despite changing economic and legal environments. Still other aspects of owners' equity accounting involve complicated pronouncements that reflect political compromise. Financial statement readers must recognize these influences and avoid unwarranted inferences based on the reported figures.

Here's some of what we've learned. Stock buybacks don't produce accounting gains and losses, but they can boost the returns to stock market investors. Preferred stock looks a lot like debt when it has a mandatory redemption feature. Some companies can pay dividends in excess of their retained earnings' balance, but their ability to do so depends on state law. Earnings-per-share (EPS) numbers are adjusted for potential dilution from stock options, warrants, and convertible securities. GAAP doesn't require companies to record compensation expense when stock options are given to employees and GAAP ignores the option value in convertible debt.

While some rules for owners' equity accounting may seem arbitrary—and therefore insignificant—you must remember that these financial statement items have a profound impact on lending agreements, regulation, and the cost of equity capital.

APPENDIX Employee Stock Ownership Plans

An **employee stock ownership plan (ESOP)** is an employee pension plan that invests primarily in the common stock of the employer company. To establish an ESOP, the company first sets up a trust to hold the ESOP assets and makes contributions of up to 25% of pay-

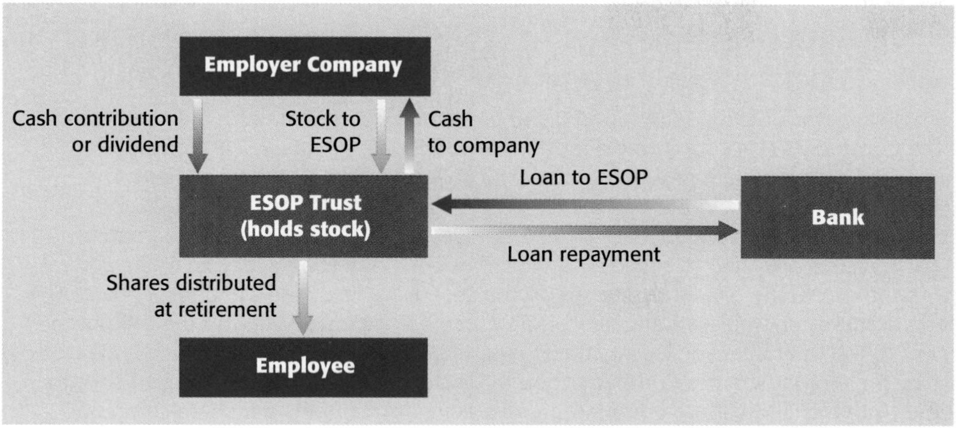

Figure 15.5

RELATIONSHIP BETWEEN THE ESOP, EMPLOYER COMPANY, EMPLOYEES, AND EXTERNAL FUNDING SOURCES

Cash contributions and dividends paid by employer company to trust are deductible for income tax purposes, within certain limits. Hence the sponsor company can use ESOP to lower the cost of debt financing.

roll for employees in the plan. Stock contributed to (or purchased by) the trust is allocated to the accounts of employees who have met certain eligibility requirements—like having worked at the company for at least three years. ESOPs are subject to vesting like other pensions. Plan enrollees are not taxed on the income earned by the plan, on contributions to the plan, or on other amounts added to their accounts, until the time of distribution. So ESOPs enable employees to gain a tax-free ownership stake in their company. Figure 15.5 illustrates the relationship between the ESOP, employer company, employees, and external funding sources like banks.

ESOPs are attractive to employer companies for three reasons:

1. ESOPs have considerable tax advantages.
2. ESOPs can provide a source of low-cost debt financing for firms.
3. ESOPs have been used to finance management buyouts and as part of a takeover defense.

Company payments into the ESOP trust are tax deductible within certain limits. The employer company can contribute its own stock to the ESOP and take a tax deduction for the fair value of the stock contributed. In addition, as the company makes payments to the trust to repay principal and interest on trust borrowing, *both* payments are tax deductible. Similarly, dividend payments on shares held by the trust are also tax deductible—to the extent that the trust uses the dividend payments to repay the loan. The money borrowed by the ESOP trust goes to the company as payment for the shares issued to the trust.

In a **leveraged ESOP,** the trust borrows funds from a financial institution to purchase the securities of the employer company. The employer in turn makes annual or quarterly—tax deductible—cash contributions to the trust which it then uses to make the interest and principal payments on the loan. Loan proceeds flow directly to the company as ESOP shares are purchased, and loan repayment occurs over time with the ESOP shares serving as collateral for the loan. Employee ownership of the shares accrues according to the rate at which the loan principal is repaid.

Apart from their tax advantages, ESOPs have been used to take companies private, to acquire divested subsidiaries or divisions, to provide takeover defenses, and to save failed companies. ESOPs were widely used as takeover defenses since ESOP shares are impervious to buyout by a hostile acquirer.

The financial statement implications of ESOPs are described in Exhibit 15.4 on the next page, which reprints the footnote from Maytag Company's 1999 annual report.

In addition to this footnote, Maytag Company's 1999 balance sheet included \$35.3 million of ESOP debt as part of long-term liabilities and a corresponding \$35.3 million owners' equity *reduction* labeled "Employee stock plans." The following example illustrates how these two balance sheet items arise, and it also illustrates how employers account for ESOPs.[24]

[24] The accounting standards for ESOPs are described in "Accounting Practices for Certain Employee Stock Ownership Plans," *Statement of Position No. 76–3* (New York: AICPA, 1976).

Exhibit 15.4 ■ MAYTAG COMPANY

Footnote Disclosure for Employee Stock Ownership Plan (ESOP)

The Company established an Employee Stock Option Plan (ESOP), and a related trust issued debt and used the proceeds to acquire shares of the Company's stock for future allocation to ESOP participants. ESOP participants generally consist of all U.S. employees except certain groups covered by a collective bargaining agreement. The Company guarantees the ESOP debt and reflects it in the Consolidated Balance Sheets as Long-term debt with a related amount shown in the Shareowners' equity section as part of Employee stock plans. Dividends earned on the allocated and unallocated ESOP shares are used to service the debt. The Company is obligated to make annual contributions to the ESOP trust to the extent the dividends earned on the shares are less than the debt service requirements. As the debt is repaid, shares are released and allocated to plan participants based on the ratio of the current year debt service payment to the total debt service payments over the life of the loan. If the shares released are less than the shares earned by the employees, the Company contributes additional shares to the ESOP trust to meet the shortfall. All shares held by the ESOP trust are considered outstanding for earnings per share computations and dividends earned on the shares are recorded as a reduction of retained earnings.

The ESOP shares held in trust consisted of the following:

	December 31	
	1999	1998
Original shares held in trust:		
Released and allocated	1,932,055	1,700,757
Unreleased shares (fair value; 1999–$44,404,224, 1998–$71,985,029)	925,088	1,156,386
	2,857,143	2,857,143
Additional shares contributed and allocated	666,295	666,295
Shares withdrawn	(597,530)	(514,211)
Total shares held in trust	2,925,908	3,009,227

The components of the total contribution to the ESOP trust consisted of the following:

	Year Ended December 31		
($ in thousands)	1999	1998	1997
Debt service requirement	$8,963	$9,325	$9,831
Dividends earned on ESOP shares	(2,150)	(2,086)	(1,960)
Cash contribution to ESOP trust	6,813	7,239	7,871
Fair market value of additional shares contributed	–0–	6	726
Total contribution to ESOP trust	$6,813	$7,245	$8,597

The components of expense recognized by the Company for the ESOP contribution consisted of the following:

	Year Ended December 31		
($ in thousands)	1999	1998	1997
Contribution classified as interest expense	$1,903	$2,265	$4,636
Contribution classified as compensation expense	4,910	4,980	3,961
Total expense for the ESOP contribution	$6,813	$7,245	$8,597

Source: Maytag Company 1999 annual report.

Assume Chittendon Manufacturing established an ESOP for hourly employees on January 1, 2001. The following transactions summarize the activities of the ESOP over its first year:

1. On January 1 the ESOP borrowed $20 million from a large regional bank, signing a ten-year installment note with annual interest payments equal to 9% of the outstanding balance. The note is guaranteed by the company.
2. That same day, the ESOP purchased 400,000 unissued shares of $10 par common stock from Chittendon Manufacturing at the current market price of $50 per share. These shares of stock are collateral for the bank loan.

3. During 2001 Chittendon Manufacturing declared and paid common dividends of $3 per share. The company also contributed $2.6 million in cash to the ESOP.
4. At the end of 2001 the ESOP "released and allocated" 40,000 shares to employees of the company.

> These shares actually remain in the ESOP trust until distributed to employees at retirement or when they leave the company.

Keep in mind that the following accounting entries are made on the books of Chittendon Manufacturing—they are not those made by the ESOP trust itself.

The first two transactions are recorded by Chittendon as:

1. **DR** Employee stock plan	$20,000,000	
CR ESOP note payable		$20,000,000
2. **DR** Cash	$20,000,000	
CR Common stock–$10 par		$ 4,000,000
CR Paid-in capital in excess of par		16,000,000

Entry 1 records the ESOP borrowing. The debit is to a balance sheet contra-equity account called "Employee stock plan" (the same account title used by Maytag). It tracks the cost ($50 multiplied by 400,000 common shares) of unreleased ESOP shares, as we will see. Entry 2 records the sale of 400,000 shares of common stock to the ESOP.

Chittendon declared and paid cash dividends of $3 per share during the year. Entry 3 that follows reflects this transfer of $1.2 million ($3 per share multiplied by 40,000 ESOP shares) to the ESOP trust. However, the trust is required to make a $2.0 million principal payment on the note ($20 million ÷ 10 years) and to pay $1.8 million in interest ($20 million outstanding multiplied by 9%) at year-end. Consequently, the company must contribute $2.6 million in cash to the ESOP in addition to the $1.2 million in cash already in the trust. Entry 4 records this contribution.

3. **DR** Dividends	$1,200,000	
CR Cash (to ESOP trust)		$1,200,000
4. **DR** Interest expense	$1,800,000	
DR Compensation expense	800,000	
CR Cash (to ESOP trust)		$2,600,000

When the trust makes the $3.8 million payment to the bank and allocates shares to employees, Chittendon reduces the carrying value of the ESOP debt and the contra-equity account by the amount of the loan *principal* payment and shares allocated:

DR ESOP Note payable	$2,000,000	
CR Employee stock plan		$2,000,000

At this point the balance sheet of Chittendon Manufacturing shows an $18 million liability for the unpaid ESOP note and a corresponding $18 million contra-equity item labeled "Employee stock plan." The income statement shows $800,000 of compensation expense and $1.8 million of interest expense, but the other $1.2 million paid out by Chittendon is shown as a dividend distribution.

There are three points financial statement readers must keep in mind when examining ESOPs.

First, ***ESOP debt is not hidden in financial statement footnotes as an off-balance sheet item.*** Instead, the debt is carried on the books of the employer like any other long-term liability. Consequently, the future cash flow implications of ESOP debt are no more difficult to assess than for other long-term debt obligations of the company.

Second, ***ESOP accounting produces an unusual balance sheet item, which is called "Employee stock plan" in our example.*** This account tracks the cost of ESOP shares not yet allocated to employees but still held by the trust. All common shares purchased by the ESOP—whether allocated to employees or not—are included in the "Common stock par" and "Paid-in capital in excess of par" accounts as outstanding stock.

Third, ***some analysts argue that ESOP accounting understates the company's true cost of employee compensation.*** To see why, notice that Chittendon employees "earned"—that is, they were allocated—40,000 ESOP shares during 2001 for a total cost of $2 million at $50 per share. This $2 million equals the ESOP debt principal repayment made during the year. Since the only source of ESOP cash is the employer company, Chittendon effectively made the $2 million debt payment using $1.2 million of cash labeled "dividends" and another $800,000 labeled "compensation expense." Chittendon's total cash outlay for stock-based compensation was $2 million—excluding ESOP debt interest—even though only $800,000 is recorded as an expense. This treatment *understates* employee compensation expense, and it *overstates* the company's gross margin and net income for the year. Analysts must be aware of this possibility when evaluating companies that have large ESOPs.

EXERCISES

E15–1
Issuing common stock

Spridget Company has 1,000,000 shares of common stock authorized with a par value of $3 per share, of which 600,000 shares are outstanding. The company received $7 per share when it issued shares to the public.

REQUIRED:

What is the book value of the common stock par account and the additional paid-in capital account?

E15–2
Stockholders' equity
AICPA adapted

The stockholders' equity section of Peter Corporation's balance sheet at December 31, 2001 was as follows:

Common stock ($10 par value); authorized 1,000,000 shares, issued and outstanding 900,000 shares	$ 9,000,000
Additional paid-in capital	2,700,000
Retained earnings	1,300,000
Total stockholders' equity	$13,000,000

On January 2, 2002 Peter purchased and retired 100,000 shares of its stock for $1,800,000.

REQUIRED:

What was the balance in additional paid-in capital *and* in retained earnings immediately after retirement of the shares?

E15–3
Entity and proprietary views

ForeEver Yours, Inc., a manufacturer of wedding rings, issued two financial instruments at the beginning of 2001: a $10 million, forty-year bond that pays interest at the rate of 11% annually, and 10,000 shares of $100 preferred stock that pays a dividend of 7.5% annually. The preferred stock has a mandatory redemption feature that requires the company to repurchase all outstanding shares at par ($100 per share) in 40 years.

REQUIRED:

1. Describe how each financial instrument will affect the company's balance sheet and income statement in 2001.
2. Why does GAAP treat preferred stock differently from the bond?

E15–4
Various stock transactions
AICPA adapted

Warren Corporation was organized on January 1, 2001 with an authorization of 500,000 shares of common stock ($5 par value per share). During 2001 the company had the following capital transactions:

January 5	Issued 100,000 shares at $5 per share
April 6	Issued 50,000 shares at $7 per share
June 8	Issued 15,000 shares at $10 per share
July 28	Purchased 25,000 shares at $4 per share
December 31	Sold 25,000 shares held in treasury at $8 per share

REQUIRED:

What should be the balance in the additional paid-in capital account at December 31, 2001?

E15–5

Return on common equity
AICPA adapted

Selected information for Irvington Company is as follows:

	December 31	
	2000	2001
Preferred stock, 8%, par $100	$125,000	$125,000
Common stock	300,000	400,000
Retained earnings	75,000	185,000
Dividends paid on preferred stock	10,000	10,000
Net income	60,000	120,000

REQUIRED:

What is Irvington's return on common stockholders' equity for 2001, rounded to the nearest percentage point?

E15–6

How many shares?
AICPA adapted

Munn Corporation's records included the following stockholders' equity accounts:

Preferred stock, par value $15, authorized 20,000 shares	$255,000
Additional paid-in capital–preferred stock	15,000
Common stock, no par, $5 stated value, 100,000 shares authorized	300,000

REQUIRED:

How many shares of preferred stock and how many shares of common stock have been issued?

E15–7

Stockholders' equity after a stock repurchase
AICPA adapted

Newton Corporation was organized on January 1, 2001. On that date, it issued 200,000 shares of its $10 par-value common stock at $15 per share (400,000 shares were authorized). During the period from January 1, 2001 through December 31, 2003, Newton reported net income of $750,000 and paid cash dividends of $380,000. On January 5, 2003 Newton purchased 12,000 shares of its common stock at $12 per share. On December 31, 2003 the company sold 8,000 treasury shares at $8 per share.

REQUIRED:

What is the book value of total shareholders' equity as of December 31, 2003?

E15–8

Stock dividends and retained earnings
AICPA adapted

On December 31, 2001 the stockholders' equity section of Mercedes Corporation was as follows:

Common stock, par value $5; authorized 30,000 shares; issued and outstanding, 9,000 shares	$ 45,000
Additional paid-in capital	58,000
Retained earnings	73,000
Total stockholders' equity	$176,000

On March 1, 2002 the board of directors declared a 10% stock dividend—and accordingly, 900 additional shares were issued. The fair value of the stock at that time was $8 per share. For the three months ended March 31, 2002 Mercedes sustained a net loss of $16,000.

REQUIRED:

What amount should the company report as retained earnings on its quarterly financial statement dated March 31, 2002?

E15–9

Stock dividends and market prices

AICPA adapted

On June 30, 2001 the stockholders' equity section of Comet Corporation's balance sheet was as follows:

Common stock, par value $25; authorized 500,000 shares; issued and outstanding 300,000 shares	$ 7,500,000
Additional paid-in capital	1,400,000
Retained earnings	1,890,000

On July 1, 2001 the board of directors of Comet declared a 5% stock dividend on common stock, to be distributed on August 10, 2001 to shareholders of record on July 31, 2001. The market price of Comet's common stock on each of these dates was as follows:

July 1	$30 per share
July 31	$31 per share
August 10	$32 per share

REQUIRED:

Prepare the general journal entry to record the stock dividend on Comet's books.

E15–10

Stockholders' equity after a stock split

AICPA adapted

Effective April 27, 2001 the stockholders of Dorr Corporation approved a two-for-one split of the company's common stock and an increase in authorized common shares from 100,000 shares (par value of $20 per share) to 200,000 shares (par value of $10 per share). The stock split shares were issued on June 30, 2001. Dorr's stockholders' equity accounts immediately before issuance of the stock split shares were:

Common stock, par value $20; 100,000 shares authorized; 50,000 shares outstanding	$1,000,000
Additional paid-in capital	150,000
Retained earnings	1,350,000

REQUIRED:

After issuing the stock split shares, what are the balances of additional paid-in capital and retained earnings in Dorr's June 30, 2001 statement of stockholders' equity?

E15–11

Employee stock options

AICPA adapted

On July 1, 2001 Austin Company granted Harry Ross, an employee, an option to buy 500 shares of Austin common stock at $30 per share. The option was exercisable for five years from the date of the grant. Ross exercised his option on October 1, 2001 and sold his shares on December 2, 2001. The quoted market prices for Austin common stock during the year were:

July 1	$30 per share
October 1	$35 per share
December 2	$37 per share

REQUIRED:

How much compensation expense should Austin recognize in 2001 as a result of the option granted to Ross? (*Note*: Austin has elected to follow *APB No. 25.*)

E15–12

Computing basic EPS

AICPA adapted

The Tam Company's net income for the year ending December 31, 2001 was $10,000. During the year, Tam declared and paid $1,000 cash dividends on preferred stock and $1,750 cash dividends on common stock. At December 31, 2001 the company had 12,000 shares of common stock issued and outstanding—10,000 had been issued and outstanding throughout the year and 2,000 were issued on July 1, 2001. There were no other common stock transactions during the year, and the 5,000 shares of preferred stock are not convertible into common shares.

REQUIRED:

What should be the 2001 earnings per common share of Tam Company, rounded to the nearest penny?

E15–13

Finding the number of shares for EPS

AICPA adapted

Fountain Inc. has 5,000,000 shares of common stock outstanding on January 1, 2001. An additional 1,000,000 shares of common stock were issued on April 1, 2001, and 500,000 more were issued on July 1, 2001. On October 1, 2001 Fountain issued 10,000 convertible bonds; each one had a face value of $1,000 and paid 7% interest. Each bond is convertible into 40 shares of common stock. No bonds were converted into common stock during 2001.

REQUIRED:

What is the number of shares that is to be used in computing basic EPS and diluted EPS, respectively?

E15–14

Earnings per share

AICPA adapted

Information concerning the capital structure of the Petrock Corporation is as follows:

	December 31	
	2000	2001
Common stock	90,000 shares	90,000 shares
Convertible preferred stock	10,000 shares	10,000 shares
8% convertible bonds	$1,000,000	$1,000,000

During 2001 Petrock paid dividends of $1 per share on its common stock and $2.40 per share on its preferred stock. The preferred stock is convertible into 20,000 shares of common stock. The 8% convertible bonds are convertible into 30,000 shares of common stock. The net income for the year ending December 31, 2001 was $285,000, and the company's income tax rate was 40%.

REQUIRED:

1. What was basic EPS for 2001, rounded to the nearest penny?
2. What was diluted EPS for 2001, rounded to the nearest penny?

E15–15

Employee stock options

AICPA adapted

On July 18, 2001 the Amos Corporation granted nontransferable options to certain key employees as additional compensation. The options permitted the purchase of 20,000 shares of Amos' common stock at a price of $30 per share. On the grant date, the market value of the stock was $42 per share. The options are exercisable beginning January 1, 2002 and expire on December 31, 2010. On February 3, 2002 when the stock was selling for $45 per share, all the options were exercised.

REQUIRED:

How much compensation expense should Amos record from the issuance of these options in 2001 and in 2002? (*Note*: Amos has chosen to follow *APB No. 25.*)

E15–16

Incentives for stock repurchases

Keystone Enterprises just announced record 2001 EPS of $5.00, up $0.25 from last year. This makes the tenth consecutive year the company has increased its EPS, an enviable record to be sure. Unfortunately, it looks to management like this string of EPS increases is about to be broken. Keystone is forecasting net income for 2002 and 2003 at $10 million each year, the same level earned in 2001. The company has 2,000,000 shares of common stock outstanding, no preferred stock, and no convertible debt.

REQUIRED:

1. How many common shares does Keystone need to buy back at the beginning of 2002 *and* 2003 to maintain EPS growth of $0.25 per share each year? (*Note:* Keystone will use cash from operations to pay for the stock.)
2. Explain why your answer to (1) would change if the buybacks were to occur in the middle of each year.
3. Why do you think Keystone's management would be concerned about maintaining the company's record of EPS growth?

E15–17

ESOPs

The 2000 annual report of Procter & Gamble Company contained the following information:

> The ESOP borrowed $1,000 in 1989, which has been guaranteed by the Company. The proceeds were used to purchase Series A ESOP Convertible Class A Preferred Stock. . . . Principal and interest requirements are $117 per year, paid by the trust from dividends on the preferred shares and from cash contributions by the Company. . . . In 1991 the ESOP borrowed an additional $1,000, also guaranteed by the Company. The proceeds were used to purchase Series B ESOP Convertible Class A Preferred Stock. . . . Debt service requirements are $94 per year, funded by preferred stock dividends and cash contributions from the Company.

REQUIRED:

1. What journal entry is made on the books of Procter & Gamble when its ESOP trust borrows money?
2. How will the ESOP affect Procter & Gamble's cash flows?
3. How will the ESOP affect Procter & Gamble's income statement?

PROBLEMS/DISCUSSION QUESTIONS

P15–1

Cash and stock dividends

The stockholders' equity section of Warm Ways Inc.'s balance sheet at January 1, 2001 shows:

Preferred stock, $100 par value, 10% dividend, 50,000 shares issued and outstanding	$ 5,000,000
Common stock, $6 par value, 1 million shares issued and outstanding	6,000,000
Paid-in capital in excess of par	119,000,000
Retained earnings	50,000,000
Total stockholders' equity	$180,000,000

Warm Ways reported net income of $9,250,000 for 2001, declared and paid the preferred stock cash dividend, and declared and paid a $0.25 per-share cash dividend on 1 million shares of common stock. The company also declared and paid a 10% stock dividend on its common shares. There were 1 million common shares outstanding when the stock dividend was declared, and the market price of common stock at that time was $135 per share.

REQUIRED:

1. Prepare journal entries to record the three dividend "events" that took place during 2001.
2. If the company's common stock was valued at $135 per share when the stock dividend was declared, what would the stock price be just after the dividend shares were distributed?

P15–2

Splits, dividends, and retained earnings

It's July 1, 2002, and the market price of Warm Ways' common stock is $175 per share. There are 1.1 million common shares outstanding, and the retained earnings account shows a balance of $45,000,000. Management wants to declare and pay a 20% common stock dividend, but this would mean halting the company's cash dividend payments. That's because a 20% stock dividend would cause retained earnings to fall by $38,500,000 (i.e., 20% × 1.1 million shares × $175 per share). This would leave a balance of only $6,500,000, far below the $25,000,000 minimum required for cash dividends as specified in the company's loan agreement. It would take several years to build up retained earnings to the point where Warm Ways could again pay cash dividends.

The company's chief financial officer (CFO) has proposed two ways the company could distribute common shares and still manage to pay cash dividends:

- Option A: Split the stock 12 for 10.
- Option B: Increase the size of the stock dividend from 20% to 30%, and record the share distribution as a stock split.

REQUIRED:

1. How will these two approaches affect the company's retained earnings?
2. As a common stockholder, would you prefer a 20% stock dividend, a 12-for-10 stock split, or a 30% stock dividend? Why?

P15–3

Convertible debt

AICPA adapted

On January 1, 1999 when its $30 par-value common stock was selling for $80 per share, Hershey Corporation issued $10 million of 4% convertible debentures that were due in 10 years. The conversion option allowed the holder of each $1,000 bond to convert the bond into five shares of the company's $30 par-value common stock. The debentures were issued for $10 million. Without the conversion feature, the bonds would have been issued for $8.5 million.

On January 1, 2001 the company's $30 par-value common stock was split three for one. On January 1, 2002 when the company's $10 par value common stock was selling for $90 per share, holders of 40% of the convertible debentures exercised their conversion options.

REQUIRED:

1. Prepare a journal entry to record the original issuance of the convertible debentures.
2. How much interest expense would the company recognize on the convertible debentures in 1999?
3. Prepare a journal entry to record the exercise of the conversion option.
4. Why do many companies use the book value method to record debt conversions?

P15–4

EPS computations

The shareholders' equity section of the balance sheet for Holiday Roads Company shows:

	January 1 2001	December 31 2001
Preferred stock, $200 par value, 5% dividend, 20,000 shares issued and outstanding	$ 4,000,000	$ 4,000,000
Common stock, $2 par value	400,000	520,000
Paid-in capital in excess of par	19,600,000	26,800,000
Retained earnings	3,000,000	4,000,000
Total stockholders' equity	$27,000,000	$35,320,000

Net income for 2001 was $1,700,000, preferred stock dividends were $200,000, and common stock dividends were $500,000. The company issued 60,000 shares of common stock on July 1, 2001.

REQUIRED:

1. What is the company's basic EPS for 2001?
2. Suppose Holiday Road also had $500,000 of 10% convertible subordinated debentures outstanding at the beginning and end of 2001. Each $1,000 bond is convertible into 100 shares of common stock, and the company's income tax rate is 34%. What is the company's diluted EPS for 2001?
3. What other types of securities—in addition to convertible debt—can affect the calculation of diluted EPS?

P15–5

Limits on dividends

Tredegar Industries Inc. makes plastic films and molded plastic products, produces soft alloy aluminum extrusions, distributes business applications software, and provides proprietary chemistry services. A footnote to the company's 1996 annual report stated:

> While certain of the Company's subsidiaries' debt facilities are outstanding, the Company's subsidiaries must meet specific financial tests on an ongoing basis, which are customary for these types of facilities. Except as provided by applicable corporate law, there are no restrictions on the Company's ability to pay dividends from retained earnings. However, the payment of cash dividends by the Company's subsidiaries to the Company are subject to certain restrictions under the terms of various agreements covering the Company's subsidiaries' long-term debt. Toledo, PDI, and Balcrank [three of Tredegar's subsidiaries] are not permitted under each subsidiary's respective debt agreements to pay cash dividends. Assuming certain financial covenants are met, General Chemical [another subsidiary] is permitted to pay cash dividends of up to 50 percent of the net income (subject to certain adjustments) of General Chemical for the applicable period. Consequently, the Company's ability to pay cash dividends on Common Stock may effectively be limited by such agreements. At December 31, 1996 approximately $51,000 was available for dividend payments in accordance with these covenants.

The company's 1996 financial statements showed net income of $45,035, dividends of $3,176, and year-end retained earnings of $99,027. (All dollar amounts here and in the footnote are in thousands.)

REQUIRED:

1. Explain why and how lenders restrict a subsidiary's ability to pay dividends to the parent corporation.
2. What was Tredegar Industries' dividend payout ratio for 1996?
3. What is the maximum amount of dividends the company could have paid to common stockholders that year without violating the terms of its lending agreements?
4. Suppose Tredegar Industries' loan agreements contained no restrictions on dividend payments by subsidiaries or the parent company. What is the maximum legal amount of dividends the company could have paid to common stockholders in 1996?
5. Do contractual or legal restrictions on dividend payments seem to be influencing the company's dividend policy?

P15–6

Stock options

Schlumberger Ltd. provides exploration and production services to the petroleum industry. The following footnote appeared in the company's 1996 annual report:

> As of December 31, 1996, the Company has two types of stock-based compensation plans. . . . The Company applies APB Opinion 25 and related Interpretations in accounting for its plans. Accordingly, no compensation cost has been recognized for its stock option plans and its stock purchase plan. Had compensation cost for the Company's stock-based plans been determined based on the fair value at the grant dates for awards under those plans, consistent with the method of FASB Statement 123, the Company's net income and earnings per share would have been the pro forma amounts indicated below:

($ in millions except per share amounts)	1996	1995
Net income as reported	$851	$649
Pro forma net income	$809	$641
Earnings per share as reported	$3.47	$2.69
Pro forma EPS	$3.30	$2.65

> As required by FASB Statement 123, the above pro forma data reflect the effect of stock option grants during 1996 and 1995.

Stock Option Plans

During 1996, 1995, and in prior years, officers and key employees were granted stock options under the Company's stock option plans. The exercise price of each option equals the market price of the company's stock on the date of grant, an option's maximum life is ten years, and options generally vest in 20% increments over five years. . . . As required by FASB Statement 123, the fair value of each grant is estimated on the date of grant using the multiple option Black–Scholes option-pricing model. . . . The weighted-average fair value of options granted during 1996 and 1995 is $21.07 and $17.04, respectively. . . . A summary of the status of the Company's stock option plans [follows]:

	Number of Shares	Weighted-Average Exercise Price
Outstanding 12/31/95	11,070,480	$58
Granted	4,131,000	79
Exercised	(2,758,242)	54
Lapsed or canceled	(244,840)	64
Outstanding 12/31/96	12,198,398	$65

REQUIRED:

1. Why doesn't Schlumberger Ltd. grant stock options with a shorter term (say, three years) and vesting period (say, one year)?
2. How much compensation expense would the company have recorded in 1996 if the stock options granted that year had an exercise price $2 below the market price at the grant date?
3. What costs would Schlumberger employees have incurred if stock options granted in 1996 had an exercise price $2 below the market price at the grant date?
4. What journal entry would the company have made to record compensation expense for options granted in 1996 if it had used the fair value method of *FASB No. 123?*
5. Describe how the company's 1996 pro forma EPS amount gives an incomplete picture of the full impact of Schlumberger's stock option compensation program.

P15–7

Equity management

Abbott Stores must raise $100 million on January 1, 2002 to finance its expansion into the lucrative Boston metropolitan market. The money will be used to finance construction of five retail stores and a distribution center. The stores are expected to open later this year. Three alternatives for raising the money are being considered:

1. Issue $100 million of 8% nonconvertible debt due in 20 years.
2. Issue $100 million of 6% nonconvertible preferred stock (100,000 shares).
3. Issue $100 million of common stock (1 million shares).

The company's internal forecasts indicate the following 2002 year-end amounts (before the impact of the $100 million of new financing is considered):

($ in millions)	
Total debt	$425
Total shareholders' equity	250
Net income for the year	10

Abbott has no preferred stock outstanding. There are 10 million shares of common stock outstanding, and EPS has been declining for the past several years. Earnings in 2001 were $1 per share, down from $1.10 the year before, and management wants to avoid another decline this year. One of the company's existing loan agreements requires its debt-to-equity ratio to be less than two. Abbott pays taxes at a 40% rate.

REQUIRED:

1. Assess the impact of each financing alternative on 2002 EPS and the year-end debt-to-equity ratio.
2. Which financing alternative would you recommend?

P15–8

Stock repurchases and EPS

Central Sprinkler Corporation manufactures and sells automatic fire sprinkler heads and valves, and it distributes components for automatic sprinkler systems. The company's 2001 financial statements show:

	Year Ended October 31			
($ in thousands except per share amounts)	1998	1999	2000	2001
Earnings available to common	$2,376	$4,018	$8,458	$3,763
Average common shares outstanding	4,752	5,023	3,383	3,330
Earnings per share (EPS)	$ 0.50	$ 0.80	$ 2.50	$ 1.13

In late December 1999 Central Sprinkler bought back 1,237,000 shares of common stock for $11,750,000.

REQUIRED:

1. What would EPS have been in 2000 and 2001 had the company not repurchased its common shares? (Assume the stock buyback occurred on December 31, 1999, and notice the company has an October 31 fiscal year-end.)
2. Compare the company's profit performance in 2000 to earlier years, and comment on this comparison.
3. The stock buyback isn't the only reason average common shares declined from 1999 to 2000. What else do you think might have contributed to this decline in average common shares?

P15–9

Earnings management

STRETCH

General Electric (GE) Company has two major parts: an industrial conglomerate and a financial-services conglomerate. In the past decade, GE's EPS have risen almost every year. How does GE do it? One reason is the real growth in earnings of its business units. But another way is what the *Wall Street Journal* calls "earnings management, the orchestrated timing of gains and losses to smooth out bumps." Shown next is information taken from the company's annual reports to shareholders.

($ in millions except per share amounts)	1999	1998	1997	1996	1995	1994	1993
Earnings available for common shares	$10,717	$9,296	$8,203	$7,280	$6,573	$5,905	$4,424
Restructuring charges	(265)	–0–	(2,322)	–0–	–0–	(1,189)	(1,101)
Special gains	653	–0–	1,538	–0–	–0–	–0–	1,430
Average common shares outstanding	9,834	9,807	9,824	9,922	10,102	10,252	10,240
Earnings per share	$ 1.07	$ 0.93	$ 0.82	$ 0.72	$ 0.64	$ 0.57	$ 0.42

($ in millions except per share amounts)	1992	1991	1990	1989	1988	1987	1986
Earnings available for common shares	$4,305	$4,435	$4,303	$3,939	$3,386	$ 2,119	$2,492
Restructuring charges	–0–	–0–	–0–	–0–	–0–	(1,027)	(311)
Special gains	–0–	–0–	–0–	–0–	–0–	850	50
Average common shares outstanding	10,282	10,426	10,659	10,833	10,797	10,953	10,905
Earnings per share	$ 0.41	$ 0.42	$ 0.40	$ 0.36	$ 0.31	$ 0.19	$ 0.22

Restructuring charges include such items as the costs of employee severance packages and plant closings, as well as losses sustained on shuttered business units like Kidder Peabody, GE's discontinued securities broker–dealer. Special gains include profits from the sale of business units, properties, or investments. Restructuring charges and special gains are both included in earnings available for common shares.

REQUIRED:

1. Suppose GE had not recorded any of the special gains shown in the table. What would its EPS have been each year?
2. Suppose GE had not recorded any of the restructuring charges shown in the table. What would its EPS have been each year?

3. How do the EPS amounts from (1) and (2) compare to the company's reported EPS amounts? Why might an analyst conclude that GE has engaged in earnings management?
4. Companies can smooth their reported EPS in several ways. One approach is to orchestrate the timing of gains and losses. What other ways can EPS be managed?
5. What was GE's EPS for 2000? Were restructuring charges or special gains reported that year? What impact (if any) did they have on the pattern of EPS increases?

P15–10

Stock buyback incentives

Hershey Foods Corporation manufactures and sells consumer food products including chocolate bars, chocolate drink mixes, refrigerated puddings, beverages, pasta, cough drops, and jelly beans. In August 1995 the company repurchased 9,049,773 shares of common stock from a single stockholder—Milton Hershey School Trust—for $500 million. This stock buyback, plus other repurchases that year, reduced shareholders' equity by 25%.

Excerpts from Hershey Foods' 1995 annual report follow:

As of December 31, 1995, the Corporation had 530,000,000 authorized shares of capital stock. Of this total, 450,000,000 shares were designated as Common Stock, 75,000,000 shares as Class B Common Stock (Class B Stock), and 5,000,000 shares as Preferred Stock, each class having a par value of one dollar per share. As of December 31, 1995, a combined total of 89,975,436 shares of both classes of common stock had been issued, of which 77,265,883 shares were outstanding. No shares of the Preferred Stock were issued or outstanding during the three-year period ended December 31, 1995.

Holders of the Common Stock and the Class B Stock generally vote together without regard to class on matters submitted to stockholders, including the election of directors, with the Common Stock having one vote per share and the Class B stock having ten votes per share. However, the Common Stock, voting separately as a class, is entitled to elect one-sixth of the Board of Directors. With respect to dividend rights, the Common Stock is entitled to cash dividends 10% higher than those declared and paid on the Class B Stock . . . Class B Stock can be converted into Common Stock on a share-for-share basis at any time.

Hershey Trust Company, as Trustee for the benefit of Milton Hershey School . . . and as direct owner of investment shares . . . was entitled to cast approximately 76% of the total votes of both classes of the Corporation's common stock [as of December 31, 1995]. The Milton Hershey School Trust must approve the issuance of shares of Common Stock or any other action which would result in the Milton Hershey School Trust not continuing to have voting control of the Corporation.

In August 1995, the Corporation purchased an additional 9,049,773 shares of its Common Stock to be held as Treasury Stock from the Milton Hershey School Trust for $500.0 million. In connection with the share repurchase program begun in 1993, a total of 2,000,000 shares were also acquired from the Milton Hershey School Trust in 1993 for approximately $103.1 million.

($ in thousands)	Year Ended December 31 1995	1994
Cash flows from operating activities	$494,929	$337,306
Common stock book value	$137,707	139,802
Treasury stock book value	$685,076	158,711
Common shares outstanding	74,733.9	74,679.4
Class B shares outstanding	15,241.4	15,242.9
	89,975.3	89,922.3
Treasury shares held	12,709.5	3,187.1

(continued)

REQUIRED:

1. Why has Hershey Food Corporation issued two classes of common stock? Both types of common stock have a $1 par value. Do they have the same market price?
2. On the basis of the 1995 year-end balance sheet amounts, compute the average price per share that Hershey Food received for its common and Class B shares.
3. Compute the average price Hershey Food paid for treasury stock held at the end of 1994. How does this price compare to the average price paid for treasury shares held at the end of 1995?
4. What was the per-share price Hershey Food paid for the shares it bought back from Milton Hershey School Trust in 1995 and in 1993?
5. Why did the company buy back its shares? What are some other reasons companies repurchase their common stock?
6. As a credit analyst, how would you react to the company's announcement of its 1995 stock buyback?

P15–11

Preferred stock and credit analysis

Time Warner, Inc. is a holding company with subsidiaries that produce and distribute theatrical motion pictures, cartoons, television series, films, and recorded music. The company also operates a television network and theme parks, and its retail stores feature consumer products based on the company's characters and brands.

Information taken from Time Warner's 1996 annual report to shareholders follows:

($ in millions)	December 31 1996	1995
Long-term debt	$13,201	$9,907
Preferred stock	2,625	979
Common stockholders' equity	9,498	3,637
Total stockholders' equity	$12,123	$4,616
Net income before interest and taxes	$ 1,178	$ 879
Interest expense	$ 1,174	$ 877
Long-term debt/total equity	1.09	2.15
Times interest earned	1.00	1.00

The company's preferred stock pays dividends at the rate of 8% annually.

REQUIRED:

1. Suppose the increase in the preferred stock account was due to the issuance of new preferred shares at par on January 1, 1996. What journal entry would the company make on January 1, 1996 to record the new preferred stock?
2. What journal entry would the company make to record preferred dividends for 1996 and for 1995?
3. Suppose Time Warner had issued 8% debt (at par) rather than *any* preferred stock. What general journal entry would the company make to record interest on the debt for 1996 and for 1995?
4. Compute the company's long-term debt-to-total-equity ratio and its interest coverage ratio for 1996 and 1995 *as if* Time Warner had issued 8% debt rather than preferred stock.
5. Lenders generally do not restrict a company's ability to raise more equity capital. That's because the dollars raised from selling stock provide a cash cushion that protects the lender's debt claim. Under what conditions might lenders want to limit a company's ability to issue preferred stock?

P15–12

Comprehensive EPS calculations

Kadri Corporation reported basic EPS of $3.00 and diluted EPS of $2.40 for 2001. The company's EPS calculations are shown next:

	EPS Calculation for 2001 Numerator	Denominator
Net income	$3,500,000	
Less dividend on 10% convertible preferred stock	(500,000)	
Weighted-average common shares outstanding		1,000,000
Basic EPS = $3.00	$3,000,000	1,000,000
Stock option dilution	—	33,334
Series A convertible debt dilution	240,000	250,000
Series B convertible debt dilution	300,000	200,000
10% Convertible preferred stock dilution	500,000	200,000
Diluted EPS = $2.40	$4,040,000	1,683,334

The convertible preferred stock was issued at the beginning of 2001. The Series A and Series B convertible debt was issued at par in late 2000. No stock options were granted or exercised in 2001.

REQUIRED:

1. The convertible preferred stock has a $100 par value per share. How many preferred shares were issued, and what is the common stock conversion rate for each preferred share?
2. The Series B convertible debt pays interest at 10% annually, and Kadri's marginal income tax rate for 2001 was 40%. How much Series B debt was outstanding, and what is the common stock conversion rate for each $1,000 face Series B bond?
3. What is the interest rate and common stock conversion rate for the $5 million par of Series A debt?
4. There were 50,000 shares under option during the year, and the average exercise price was $20 per share. What was the average market price of the company's common stock during 2001?
5. Explain why Series A debt carries a lower interest rate than Series B debt even though both were issued at par on the same day in 2000.

P15–13

Stockholders' equity

AICPA adapted

Trask Corporation, a public company whose shares are traded in the over-the-counter market, had the following stockholders' equity account balances at December 31, 2000:

Common stock	$ 7,875,000
Additional paid-in capital	15,750,000
Retained earnings	16,445,000
Treasury common stock	750,000

Transactions during 2001 and other information relating to the stockholders' equity accounts were as follows:

- Trask had 4,000,000 authorized shares of $5 par-value common stock; 1,575,000 shares were issued, of which 75,000 were held in treasury.
- On January 21, 2001 Trask issued 50,000 shares of $100 par value, 6% cumulative preferred stock in exchange for all of Rover Company's assets and liabilities. On that date the net carrying amount of Rover Company's assets and liabilities equaled their fair values. On January 22, 2001 Rover distributed the Trask shares to its stockholders in a complete liquidation and dissolution of Rover. Trask had 150,000 authorized shares of preferred stock.
- On February 17, 2001 Trask formally retired 25,000 of 75,000 treasury common stock shares. The shares were originally issued at $15 per share and had been acquired on September 25, 2000 for $10 per share.
- Trask owned 15,000 shares of Harbor, Inc. common stock, which was purchased in 1995 for $600,000. The shares of Harbor stock were trading securities. On March 5, 2001 Trask declared a property dividend of one share of Harbor common stock for every 100 shares of Trask common stock that were

held by a stockholder of record on April 16, 2001. The market price of Harbor stock on March 5, 2001 was $60 per share. The property dividend was distributed on April 29, 2001.

- On January 2, 1999 Trask granted stock options to employees to purchase 200,000 shares of the company's common stock at $12 per share, which was also the market price on that date. The options are exercisable within a three-year period, beginning January 2, 2001. On June 1, 2001 employees exercised 150,000 options when the market value of the stock was $25 per share. Trask issued new shares to settle the transaction.
- On October 27, 2001 Trask declared a two-for-one stock split on its common stock and reduced the per-share par value accordingly. Trask stockholders of record on August 2, 2001 received one additional share of Trask common stock for each share of Trask common stock held. The laws of Trask's state of incorporation protect treasury stock from dilution.
- On December 12, 2001 Trask declared the yearly cash dividend on preferred stock, payable on January 11, 2002 to stockholders of record on December 31, 2001.
- On January 16, 2002 before the accounting records were closed for 2001, Trask became aware of the fact that depreciation expense was understated by $350,000 for the year ended December 31, 2000. The after-tax effect on 2000 net income was $245,000. The appropriate correcting entry was recorded on the same day.

Net income for 2001 was $2,400,000.

REQUIRED:

1. Prepare Trask's statement of retained earnings for the year ended December 31, 2001.
2. Prepare the stockholders' equity section of Trask's balance sheet at December 31, 2001.
3. Compute the book value per share of common stock at December 31, 2001.

P15–14

Valuing stock option grants

STRETCH

Texas Instruments manufactures and sells electrical and electronic products, including semiconductor integrated circuits and subassemblies, electronic control devices, notebook computers, electronic calculators, and learning aids. The company also manufactures metallurgical materials. Two types of stock option plans are used at Texas Instruments:

- *Long-term incentive plans.* Options granted under this plan have a 10-year term and cannot be exercised for 8 years, although exercisability may be accelerated to the extent that EPS goals are achieved. The exercise price per share cannot be less than 100% of the fair market value of common stock on the date of grant.
- *Employee stock option purchase plan.* This plan provides for options to be offered to all eligible employees in amounts based on a percentage of the employee's prior year's compensation. These options become exercisable in 14 months—and expire not more than 27 months—from the date of grant.

The following footnote appeared in the company's 1996 annual report:

> In accordance with the terms of APB No. 25, the company records no compensation expense of its stock option awards. As required by SFAS No. 123, the company provides the following disclosure of hypothetical values for these awards. The weighted-average grant-date value of options granted during 1996 was estimated to be $18.47 under the Long-Term Incentive Plans and $12.10 under the Employee Stock Option Purchase Plan. These values were estimated using the Black–Scholes option pricing model with the following weighted-average assumptions: expected dividend yield of 1.48% (Long-Term Plans) and 1.21% (Employees' Plan), expected volatility of 39%, risk-free interest rates of 5.42% (Long-Term Plans), and 6.15% (Employees' Plan), and expected lives of 6 years (Long-Term Plans) and 1.5 years (Employees' Plan).

Had compensation expense been recorded based on these hypothetical values, the company's 1996 net income would have been $40 million, or $0.21 per share. A similar computation for 1995 would have resulted in net income of $1,078 million, or $5.57 per share. Because options vest over several years and additional option grants are expected, the effects of these hypothetical calculations are not likely to be representative of similar future calculations.

	Number of Shares	Weighted Average Exercise Price
Long-term incentive plans		
Outstanding 12/31/95	7,882,572	$29.24
Granted	2,663,375	45.84
Exercised	(434,660)	25.80
Lapsed or canceled	(198,739)	26.16
Outstanding 12/31/96	9,912,548	33.91
Employees' stock option plan		
Outstanding 12/31/95	1,133,709	$56.13
Granted	848,546	56.25
Exercised	(386,162)	50.86
Lapsed or canceled	(399,909)	58.43
Outstanding 12/31/96	1,196,184	57.31

The company reported net income of $63 million in 1996 and $1,088 million in 1995.

REQUIRED:

1. Why does the company use a higher risk-free rate for its long-term incentive plans than it does for its employees' plan?
2. Using the Black–Scholes option pricing model and the company's weighted-average assumptions, verify the $18.47 valuation for long-term incentive plans and the $12.10 valuation for the employees' plan. Assume all options granted had an exercise price equal to the fair value of the stock at the grant date.
3. Using the Black–Scholes option pricing model, compute per-share valuations for long-term incentive plans and the employees' plan using the following weighted-average assumptions:

	Long-term Incentive Plans	Employees' Plans	All Other Black–Scholes Variables
1. Expected dividend yield	0%	0%	Use the company's original estimates
2. Expected dividend yield	5	5	Use the company's original estimates
3. Expected volatility	29	29	Use the company's original estimates
4. Expected volatility	49	49	Use the company's original estimates
5. Risk-free interest rate	4.92	5.65	Use the company's original estimates
6. Risk-free interest rate	5.92	6.65	Use the company's original estimates
7. Expected life	4 years	0.5 years	Use the company's original estimates
8. Expected life	8 years	2.5 years	Use the company's original estimates

Assume all options granted had an exercise price equal to the fair value of the stock at the grant date. You will be computing eight valuation estimates for each stock option plan.

4. Which variable—dividend yield, expected volatility, risk-free interest rate, or expected life—has the greatest impact on the option valuation estimates?
5. Using the valuation estimates from (3), compute the maximum and minimum *SFAS No. 123* compensation expense for Texas Instruments' 1996 stock option grants. Assume that long-term options vest over eight years and that employee-plan options vest over two years.

P15–15

Stockholders' equity

ShopKo Stores, Inc. (ShopKo) is a leading regional discount store chain that operates 109 discount retail stores in 13 states. ShopKo stores carry a wide selection of branded and private label nondurable "hardline" goods such as housewares, music and videos, health and beauty aids, and toys and sporting goods. They also carry "softline" goods such as home textiles; men's, women's, and children's apparel; shoes; jewelry; cosmetics; and accessories. In addition, 106 of the company's stores include pharmacy departments, and 99 include optical departments.

Appearing next is information taken from ShopKo's 1993 annual report.

E. Preferred and Common Stock

The Company has 20,000 shares of $0.01 preferred stock authorized but unissued. There are 75,000,000 shares of $0.01 par value common stock authorized, with 32,000,000 issued and outstanding at February 27, 1993 and February 29, 1992, respectively.

	Fiscal Years Ended		
($ in thousands)	February 27 1993	February 29 1992	February 23 1991
Cash Flows from Operating Activities:			
Net earnings	$50,059	$ 49,589	$45,080
Adjustments	25,198	26,863	34,551
Net cash provided by operating activities	$75,257	$ 76,452	$79,631
Cash Flows from Investing Activities:	($90,652)	($ 52,064)	($57,759)
Cash Flows from Financing Activities:			
Payments to related parties	($181,167)	($ 22,867)	($ 19,417)
Net proceeds from long-term debt	197,112	–0–	–0–
Proceeds from short-term debt	15,025	–0–	–0–
Net proceeds from sale of common stock	–0–	240,830	–0–
Dividends paid	(14,080)	(240,830)	–0–
Reduction in capital lease obligation	(784)	(1,446)	(2,263)
Net cash provided by (used in) financing activities	$ 16,106	($ 24,313)	($ 21,680)

Required: Part A

1. How many shares of preferred stock were outstanding on February 27, 1993? What is the par value of each share of preferred stock?
2. Suppose ShopKo sold 10,000 shares of preferred stock for $25 per share on March 1, 1993. Prepare the journal entry to record this sale of preferred stock.
3. Assume the preferred stock pays a $1 per share annual dividend, on February 13 of each year. Prepare the journal entry to record the dividend payment on February 13, 1994.
4. How many shares of common stock were issued and outstanding on February 27, 1993?
5. Explain why the number of shares issued might be different from the number of shares outstanding.

Required: Part B

Ignore all of Part A, and instead assume the following:

- ShopKo had 14,750,000 shares outstanding at the end of February 1990. On this date the balance in (a) the common stock account was $1; (b) the additional-paid-in capital account was $2,282,000; and (c) the retained earnings account was $226,069,000.
- All cash dividends are paid in the year they are declared.
- During the year ended February 29, 1992, the company issued 17,250,000 common shares to the public as a stock dividend.

Determine the fiscal year-end balances of common stock; additional paid-in capital; and retained earnings accounts for 1991, 1992, and 1993.

C15–1

Amazon.com: Stock options at a dot.com

Amazon.com, Inc. is the world's leading online retailer with over 17 million customer accounts in over 150 countries. The company sells books, music, DVDs, videos, toys, electronics, software, video games and home improvement products. Amazon.com also offers several e-commerce auction sites. The following footnote appeared in the company's 1999 annual report:

The Company follows the intrinsic value method in accounting for its stock options. Had compensation cost been recognized based on the fair value at the date of grant for options granted in 1999, 1998 and 1997, the pro forma amounts of the Company's net loss and net loss per share for the years ended December 31, 1999, 1998 and 1997 would have been as follows:

	For the Years Ended December 31,		
($ in thousands, except per share data)	**1999**	**1998**	**1997**
Net loss–as reported	($719,968)	($124,546)	($31,020)
Net loss–pro forma	(1,031,925)	(194,269)	(35,983)
Basic and diluted loss per share–as reported	($2.20)	($0.84)	($0.24)
Basic and diluted loss per share–pro forma	(3.16)	(1.31)	(0.28)

The fair value for each option granted was estimated at the date of grant using a Black-Scholes option pricing model, assuming no expected dividends and the following weighted average assumptions:

	For the Years Ended December 31,		
	1999	**1998**	**1997**
Average risk-free interest rates	5.5%	4.7%	6.3%
Average expected life (in years)	3.5	3.0	3.0
Volatility	84.9%	81.6%	50.0%

The weighted average fair value of options granted during 1999, 1998 and 1997 was $43.36, $19.07 and $2.07, respectively, for options granted with exercise prices at the current fair value of the underlying stock. During 1998 and 1997, some options were granted with exercise prices that were below the current fair value of the underlying stock. The weighted average fair value of options granted with exercise prices below the current fair value of the underlying stock during 1998 and 1997 was $4.61 and $0.55, respectively. Compensation expense that is recognized in providing pro forma disclosures might not be representative of the effects on pro forma earnings for future years because SFAS No. 123 does not apply to stock option grants made prior to 1995.

REQUIRED:

1. The average exercise price for employee stock options granted in 1999 was $63.60. Suppose that Amazon.com's stock now trades at only $30 per share. Are the options worthless?
2. Some companies "reprice" their stock options when the exercise price gets too high. As a shareholder, do you favor repricing the Amazon.com options so that the exercise price is $30? Why or why not?
3. Why do you think Amazon.com uses the "intrinsic value" (*APB No. 25*) method of accounting for employee stock options rather than the fair value method allowed in *SFAS No. 123*?

C15–2

A study in political processes—Financial reporting for executive stock options

In March 1984 dissatisfaction with the accounting treatment of incentive stock option plans prompted the FASB to place reexamination of this topic on its agenda. As discussed earlier in this chapter, GAAP at that time was based on *APB No. 25,* which ignored the inherent value of "out of the money" options. After being placed on the agenda in 1984, no new FASB Statement or Exposure Draft emerged. The adverse publicity surrounding allegedly excessive executive compensation prompted the U.S. Senate Subcommittee on Oversight of Government Management (chaired by Senator Carl Levin, Democrat, Michigan) to hold hearings on stock compensation plans in January 1992. The vice chairman of the FASB, James J. Leisenring, testified at that hearing. In the FASB's written submission that was prepared for the hearing, the slow progress that the FASB was making in addressing accounting for stock options was explained as follows:

> Existing models are designed for tradeable, usually short-term, options. Employee stock options are nontransferable, usually long-term, and generally are subject to other conditions like continued employment of the holder. The existing models, therefore, may not be directly applicable to employee stock options.
>
> The problems of applying existing pricing models are especially acute in nonpublic companies, since their stock is not publicly traded. Nonpublic companies, in particular emerging growth companies and "start-up" companies, frequently use stock options to attract skilled employees.
>
> The issues proved to be complex and highly controversial. Still, each time the issue was raised, board members voted unanimously that employee stock options result in compensation expense that should be recognized in the employer corporation's financial statements. Deciding just how and when to measure the compensation expense—the measurement method and measurement date—always has been the hard part.

Perhaps because of these hearings, the FASB accelerated its consideration of new rules for accounting for employee stock options. Opposition to the FASB's renewed initiative quickly emerged. Since all FASB meetings are open to the public, it is easy for interested parties to follow (and to try to influence) the board's deliberations. With this in mind, those opposed to expense recognition for options argued that since no cash is expended when options are issued, no expense exists. Taking a contrary view in his 1992 letter to shareholders of Berkshire Hathaway, Inc., CEO Warren Buffett argued that options *are* an expense even though no cash is paid to employees:

> [Some contend] that options should not be viewed as a cost because they "aren't dollars out of a company's coffers." I see this line of reasoning as offering exciting possibilities to American corporations for instantly improving their reported profits. For example, they could eliminate the cost of insurance by paying for it with options. So if you're a CEO and subscribe to this "no cash–no cost" theory of accounting, I'll make you an offer you can't refuse: Give us a call at Berkshire and we will happily sell you insurance in exchange for a bundle of long-term options on your company's stock.
>
> Shareholders should understand that companies incur costs when they deliver something of value to another party and not just when cash changes hands.
>
> Source: Berkshire Hathaway 1992 Annual Report.

While the FASB concurred with the view expressed by Mr. Buffett, progress continued to be slow on the employee stock option project. Because of the political visibility of the "excess" executive compensation issue, the SEC on October 15, 1992 issued rules for disclosure of option grants in the proxy mailed to shareholders. These SEC rules do *not* affect reported income; instead, companies are required to disclose the potential realizable value of the options at two assumed rates of stock price appreciation—that is, at 5% and 10%. However, the SEC also provided an alternative disclosure avenue. Rather than computing potential value at the 5% and 10% appreciation rates, companies could alternatively disclose the estimated value of the options at the grant date using some options pricing model such as Black–Scholes.

The SEC rules represent what is termed a "disclosure" approach. Under a disclosure approach, the financial statements themselves are unaffected. Only footnotes and supplemental schedules include the required data. By contrast, once the FASB resumed work on the options project, its approach concentrated on "measurement"—that is, the development of numbers that would appear in the financial statements and result in a charge to earnings for compensation expense. To this end, in early 1992 the FASB began exploring the range of estimates that would arise from attempting to measure the value inherent in various option scenarios. To gather such information, the FASB asked five compensation consulting firms to provide option value estimates for *artificial* scenarios it had developed. Then the FASB used the dispersion of these estimates to assess whether a measurement-based approach was feasible. As the FASB deliberated and publicized this continuing effort to change the accounting for stock options, influential sectors of the business community expressed strong opposition to expense recognition.

THE BUSINESS COMMUNITY'S RESPONSE

In an article that appeared in August 1992, the *New York Times* reported that consulting firms that participated in the FASB valuation scenarios in March 1992 experienced subtle negative feedback from their clients. It said,

"The Business Roundtable let a number of consultants know in no uncertain terms that they would not view this as responsive to clients' needs, which is a buzzword," said Michael J. Halloran, the head of the Wyatt Company's executive compensation practice, referring to the help consultants have given to reporters or regulators. . . . Compensation consultants say Arthur Andersen, the accounting and consulting firm, was the target of some of the most pointed letters, perhaps because the valuations it had supplied to the accounting standards board in March came in on the high side. Some of the letter writers reportedly went so far as to threaten to drop Andersen as their auditor unless the firm cooperated more on the options issue, the consultants said.

Source: A. L. Cowan, "Executives Are Fuming Over Data on Their Pay," *New York Times* (August 25, 1992).

Once the SEC proxy disclosure rules were issued in October 1992, the Business Roundtable endorsed the SEC's disclosure approach. Disclosure was viewed as preferable to the FASB's measurement initiative, which would cause an expense to appear in the income statement. The Business Roundtable sent a memo to its members and other interested parties on January 18, 1993 regarding strategies for complying with the SEC disclosure rules. The opening sentence of this document set the tone. It said:

> In light of the efforts by FASB to require that companies value stock options as a basis for a charge to earnings for options granted, it is important that proxy statements be structured to reinforce the fact that the present value of an option at the time of grant is not accurately determinable and that future options [sic] values are not predictable.
>
> Source: Business Roundtable memorandum, January 18, 1993.

The Roundtable memo outlined a strategy for conveying the message that the FASB's approach was flawed. It juxtaposed the 5% and 10% stock price appreciation rates approach proposed by the SEC with the alternative point-estimate valuation model approach favored by the FASB, and then stated:

> **Even though this valuation model may produce a smaller reportable dollar amount, we urge caution in adopting this approach.** [Emphasis in original.]

The Roundtable memo communicates a preference for supplemental disclosures over income statement compensation expense deductions. Members are urged to avoid point estimates of option value—*even if lower than the 5% and 10% range esti-*

mates—as part of a long-run strategy to forestall the FASB initiative. The Roundtable memo further contends:

> To use the Black–Scholes model could place the company in the position of predicting a future stock price that would almost certainly be wrong and potentially misleading to investors.

Weeks later, the American Compensation Association (ACA) circulated a copy of the Business Roundtable memo to its members along with a cover memo which supported the Roundtable position. The ACA memo cautioned firms:

> Clearly, the more companies that "endorse" the notion of a definitive stock option value [i.e., "measurement approach"] that can be calculated at grant, the easier it will be for [the] FASB to conclude that such a value is appropriate for accounting purposes.
>
> Source: American Compensation Association memorandum, January 29, 1993.

These efforts by the Roundtable and ACA appear to have been persuasive. As reported in the *New York Times* on March 26, 1993, Sibson & Company found that 56% of large clients which it surveyed intended to use the higher range-based numbers urged by the Roundtable and ACA. The *New York Times* article further said:

> At least five large companies also borrow heavily from the Roundtable's playbook in their willingness to use their proxy statements to hammer home the Roundtable's contention that options are almost impossible to value accurately: Ameritech, B.F. Goodrich, Pfizer, PPG, and Anheuser-Busch.
>
> All five proxy statements dutifully recite verbatim the Roundtable's assertion that no known model values options "with reasonable accuracy." They also remind shareholders that the options may be duds if their stocks fail to appreciate, and they include tables that claim to show how trivial the options are compared with how much shareholders stand to gain from a [5% and 10%] rise in their stock price.
>
> Source: "Methods in Stock Options Madness," *New York Times* (March 26, 1993).

Taking an opposite position to the Roundtable, Buffett also commented on the accuracy of options valuation in his 1992 letter to shareholders:

> Moreover, it is both silly and cynical to say that an important item of cost should not be recognized simply because it can't be quantified with pinpoint precision. Right now, accounting abounds with imprecision. After all, no manager or auditor knows how long a 747 is going to last, which means he also does not know what the yearly depreciation charge for the plane should be. No one knows with any certainty what a bank's annual loan loss charge ought to be. And the estimates of losses that property-casualty companies make are notoriously inaccurate.
>
> Does this mean that these important items of cost should be ignored simply because they can't be quantified with absolute accuracy? Of course not. Rather, these costs should be estimated by honest and experienced people and then recorded. When you get right down to it, what other item of major but hard-to-precisely-calculate cost—other, that is, than stock options—does the accounting profession say should be ignored in the calculation of earnings?
>
> Source: Berkshire Hathaway 1992 Annual Report.

The FASB also received two letters on the employee stock options issue dated February 17, 1993. One was from a group of preparers and users of financial statements. Signatories included, among others, the Council of Institutional Investors, General Mills, General Electric, B.F. Goodrich, the United Shareholders Association, and the National Association of Corporate Directors. The letter included a six-page listing of recommended disclosure requirements for traditional fixed stock options. In the letter, the group wrote:

> Our proposal calls for complete, clear, and accurate disclosure of information that investors of all types need to protect and evaluate their investments. *This disclosure is in lieu of, not in addition to, any new charge to earnings for stock options.* [Emphasis added.]

The second letter was signed by all of the Big Six public accounting firms. This letter endorsed the views expressed by the group of preparers and users in its February 17 letter and urged the FASB to "leave the current accounting standards in place."

Even the U.S. Congress joined the fray. In the first six months of 1993, three resolutions and bills were introduced regarding the accounting for stock options. One bill, S.259, which was sponsored by Senator Carl Levin (Democrat, Michigan), required that stock options be treated as compensation expense in financial reports filed with the SEC. Senator Levin was a long-time opponent of the failure to recognize the value of options as an expense; he called this "stealth compensation." However, his was a clear minority sentiment.

Two proposals against expense treatment were introduced. One of these, H.C.R 98, which was sponsored by Congresswoman Anna Eshoo (Democrat, California), was designed to send a message to the FASB regarding the opposition of Congress to its stock option accounting initiative. The other legislation opposing expense treatment, S.259, was co-sponsored by Senators Lieberman (Democrat, Connecticut), Mack (Republican, Florida), Feinstein (Democrat, California), and Boxer (Democrat, California). In introducing the bill, Senator Lieberman said:

> . . . estimating the value of an option to purchase stock in the future requires predicting the company's future earnings, cash flow, market share, capital spending, as well as future Government policy. A high degree of subjectivity is simply unavoidable. Yet the FASB proposes to force such guesses about the future onto the company's income statement as a reduction of its hard-won earnings.
>
> Source: Congressional Record – Senate, June 29, 1993, S8250.

Notwithstanding H.C.R 98 and S.259, on June 30, 1993, the FASB issued an exposure draft entitled "Accounting for Stock-Based Compensation," which proposed that the estimated value of stock options issued to employees be recognized as an expense in the income statement.

The FASB scheduled a public hearing on the Exposure Draft in San Jose, California, in the heart of Silicon Valley, home of many high-tech, start-up firms that use stock options as an important part of total employee compensation. These firms organized a rally—which included a high school marching band—to coincide with the hearings in order to show opposition to the FASB proposal. Numerous employees were given time off and encouraged to attend the rally.

Despite this widespread, persistent opposition, the FASB pressed ahead with the stock option project. Opponents then "raised the stakes" considerably. First, a sense of the Senate resolution was introduced and passed by a vote of 88 to 9 (with 3 not voting). Sixteen senators—ten Democrats and six Republicans—co-sponsored the legislation, which was orchestrated by Senator Joe Lieberman of Connecticut. In speaking in favor of the resolution, he stated:

> . . . accurately estimating the present value of an employee stock option at the date on which it is granted is, as I have said, simply not possible. The option is granted on a given day. It is only later that it is determined by market forces whether the option is worth anything and what it is worth. How can we possibly have a system which values that option on the day on which it is granted before there is any clear understanding of its value?
>
> Source: Congressional Record – Senate, May 3, 1994, S5033.

Another proponent, Senator Dianne Feinstein (Democrat, California) contended:

> I am concerned that if FASB's rule is adopted, tens of thousands of desperately needed jobs in California and the Nation will never, in fact, be created.
>
> Source: Congressional Record—Senate, May 3, 1994, S5036.

Despite the passage of the resolution, the FASB continued to move toward issuing a final statement that would require stock options to be recognized as an expense. To prevent this, Senator Lieberman introduced another bill on October 6, 1994, called the Accounting Standards Reform Act of 1994. This bill would require that any new FASB standard "shall become effective only following an affirmative vote of a majority of a quorum of the members of the [Securities and Exchange] Commission." If enacted, this bill would have effectively destroyed private sector accounting standard-setting. The FASB understood that if it persisted, this legislation would likely be enacted. Consequently, in December 1994 the FASB said it was relenting to pursue a footnote disclosure approach despite the fact that

> . . . [t]he Board remains convinced that employee options have value and are compensation.
>
> Source: *Status Report No. 259* (Norwalk, CT: FASB, 1994), p. 1.

In October 1995 *SFAS No. 123,* a disclosure approach described earlier in this chapter, was issued.

REQUIRED:

1. Analyze the reaction of business executives and their membership associations to the FASB initiative regarding accounting for executive stock options. What factors motivated the strong opposition? Were the methods used surprising?
2. What motivations appear to underlie the position of the Big Six accounting firms and sponsors of the various bills introduced in the U.S. Congress?
3. In *Statement of Financial Accounting Concepts No. 2* ("Qualitative Characteristics of Accounting Information"), **representational faithfulness** is identified as an important element in financial reporting. The FASB defined representational faithfulness as "correspondence or agreement between a measure or description and the phenomenon it purports to represent." Evaluate the various parties' adherence to this objective in the context of the debate over accounting for stock options.

C15–3

Tuesday Morning Corporation (CW): Shareholders' equity

Tuesday Morning operates a chain of 246 deep discount retail stores in 32 states. As a deep discount retailer, the company purchases close-out merchandise at prices generally ranging from 10% to 50% of normal wholesale prices, and it sells the merchandise at prices that are 50% to 80% lower than retail prices generally charged by department and specialty stores.

Appearing next is information taken from Tuesday Morning's 1994 annual report. Please refer to Tuesday Morning's financial statements in C10–8.

> NOTE 7: SHAREHOLDERS' EQUITY
>
> On January 13, 1992, the Company sold 195,000 shares of its common stock, receiving net proceeds of $2,419,000. This offering was completed in conjunction with the exercise of an overallotment option associated with a December 18, 1991 public offering. On May 5, 1992, the Board of Directors of the Company approved the purchase of the Company's stock in open market purchases to be effected from time to time. During 1992, 160,000 shares were purchased and retired by the Company. . . .

- At the beginning of fiscal 1992 Tuesday Morning had 8,515,000 common shares outstanding. On this date the balance in (a) the common stock account was $85,150; (b) the additional paid-in capital account was $22,185,000; (c) the retained earnings account was $32,775,000; and (d) treasury stock was $0.
- Cash dividends are paid in the year they are declared.
- During fiscal 1992 the company sold 195,000 common shares to the public.
- During fiscal 1992 Tuesday Morning's managers exercised options on 91,000 shares of stock. The company issued new common shares (as opposed to shares from treasury) to the managers.
- During fiscal 1992 Tuesday Morning repurchased and retired 160,000 shares in the open market. The shares were retired.

REQUIRED:

1. Derive the balances in the common stock, additional paid-in capital, retained earnings, and treasury stock accounts at the end of fiscal 1992.
2. How many shares of preferred stock did Tuesday Morning have outstanding at the end of fiscal 1994?
3. What is the par value of each share of preferred stock?
4. Assume that Tuesday Morning sold 100,000 shares of preferred stock on March 1, 1995 for $25.00 per share. Each share pays an annual dividend of $2.50 on March 1, starting in 1996. Prepare all journal entries for the preferred stock issue from March 1, 1995 to March 1, 1996.

C15–4

RN Nabisco Group: Dividends and agency costs

On June 1, 1993 RJR Nabisco Holdings Corporation (Holdings) offered for sale 93 million shares of its subsidiary RN-Nabisco Group. According to the prospectus, the estimated initial public offering price for RN-Nabisco common stock would be in the range of $17 to $19 per share. Holdings hoped to raise about $1.7 billion from the stock offering and to use the proceeds to reduce its debt burden. But investors weren't buying—at least not at the prospectus price—and Holdings scuttled the stock offer on June 23.

At the time the Nabisco Group was one of the world's leading packaged foods businesses, with 1992 sales of over $6.7 billion. The Group's Nabisco Biscuit Division was the largest cookie and cracker manufacturer and marketer in the United States, with eight of the nine top selling brands.

Holdings was comprised of the Nabisco Group and the Reynolds Group, which included the R.J. Reynolds Tobacco Company, the second largest manufacturer of cigarettes. The Reynolds Group's net sales as a percentage of Holdings' total consolidated net sales were 57% in 1992 and 1991. Holdings was formed in 1989 when its predecessor company—RJR Nabisco, Inc. (RJRN)—was taken private in a leveraged buyout transaction. Holdings was taken public again in 1991 with the buyout group retaining 49% of Holdings' stock.

The plan at the time was to split off Nabisco Group from Reynolds Group and thereby improve the company's share price. Holdings had seen its stock price fall 36% since January 1993 for two reasons: R.J. Reynolds' earnings had been hurt by a brutal cigarette price war that began in early April, and investors had become increasingly concerned about the uncertainty over tobacco liability.

The Proposal: The Nabisco Stock offered to the public would initially represent 25% of the equity of the Nabisco Group. The Reynolds Group would retain the balance of the equity of Nabisco. Each outstanding share of common stock of Holdings would be redesignated into a common share of Reynolds Stock, which was intended to reflect separately the performance of the Reynolds Group as well as the retained interest of the Reynolds Group in the Nabisco Group.

The offering prospectus described the company's dividend policy as:

> The Board of Directors of Holdings currently intends to pay regular quarterly dividends on the Nabisco Stock in an aggregate annual amount equal to approximately 45% of the prior year's earnings of Holdings attributable to the outstanding Nabisco Stock. Consistent with this policy, Holdings currently intends to pay in the fourth quarter of 1993 an initial regular quarterly dividend of $0.13 per share of Nabisco Stock. While the Board of Directors does not currently intend to change such initial quarterly dividend rate or dividend policy, it reserves the right to do so at any time and from time to time. Under the Certificate of Incorporation and Delaware law, the Board of Directors is not required to pay dividends in accordance with such policy.
>
> Dividends on the Nabisco Stock are limited by the Certificate of Incorporation and will be payable when, as and if declared by the Board of Directors out of the lessor of (i) the Available Nabisco Dividend Amount and (ii) funds of Holdings legally available therefor. Payment of dividends on the Nabisco Stock is also subject to the prior payment of dividends on the outstanding shares of Preferred Stock of Holdings (and any new class or series of capital stock of Holdings with similar preferential dividend provisions) and to restrictions contained in the Credit Agreements and certain other debt instruments of RJRN. . . . The "Available Nabisco Dividend Amount" is similar to that amount that would be legally available for the payment of dividends on Nabisco Stock under Delaware law if the Nabisco Group were a separate company, and will be increased or decreased as appropriate by, among other things, Holdings Earnings Attributable to the Nabisco Group. "Holdings Earnings Attributable to the Nabisco Group," for any period, means the net income or loss of the Nabisco Group during such period determined in accordance with generally accepted accounting principles (including income and expenses of Holdings allocated to the Nabisco Group on a substantially consistent basis). . . .
>
> Holdings has never paid any cash dividends on shares of Common Stock. . . . The Board of Directors currently intends to pay future quarterly "pass-through" dividends on the Reynolds Stock with respect to the Reynolds Group's Retained Interest in the Nabisco Group. Holdings currently intends to pay in the fourth quarter of 1993 an initial quarterly pass-through dividend of approximately $0.03 per share of Reynolds Stock. . . . Subject to [certain limitations], the Board of Directors would be able, in its sole discretion, to declare and pay dividends exclusively on the Nabisco Stock or exclusively on the Reynolds Stock, or on both, in equal or unequal amounts, notwithstanding the respective amount of funds available for dividends on each series, the amount of prior dividends declared on each series or any other factor.

REQUIRED:

As a potential investor in Nabisco Group stock, what agency problems do you face that are not present when you buy common stock in most other companies?

COLLABORATIVE LEARNING CASE

C15–5

Time Warner Inc.: Is it equity or debt?

Your boss, Barbara Wallace, has asked you to review the "Time Warner situation." It's only your second day on the job as a credit analyst at the bank, and Time Warner is your first real assignment.

"What do you mean, the Time Warner *situation?*" you ask. Wallace explains that the bank has a $200 million credit facility with Time Warner that is undergoing a renewal review. The loan agreement states that Time Warner must maintain a long-term debt-to-total-equity ratio of no more than 2.0; otherwise the interest rate on the facility gets increased by 25 basis points (0.25%). The company must also maintain a times-interest-earned ratio of at least 1.0 or the interest rate is raised another 25 basis points. The loan agreement specifies both that total equity includes the book value of any preferred stock issued and outstanding, and that preferred dividends are not counted in the computation of the times-interest-earned ratio.

Wallace goes on to clarify your task. "The situation is this—Time Warner now has about $2.6 billion of preferred stock, far more than we thought possible when we negotiated the credit facility; and although it's called preferred stock, it looks a lot like debt. I want you to dig into the details of the company's preferred stock and decide how it should be classified—as debt or equity?—from the bank's perspective. Then see if the company is still in compliance with its covenants. I'll need a memo outlining your reasoning for debt or equity treatment of each type of preferred. I'd also like you to suggest some new covenant language so that we can avoid situations like this in the future."

Background: Time Warner Inc. is a holding company with subsidiaries that produce and distribute theatrical motion pictures, cartoons, television series, films, and recorded music. The company also operates a television network and theme parks. Its retail stores feature consumer products based on the company's characters and brands.

During 1995 and 1996 the company issued several types of preferred stock as part of the company's debt reduction program. This program was described in the company's 1996 annual report to shareholders as:

DEBT REDUCTION PROGRAM

As part of a continuing strategy to enhance the financial position and credit statistics of Time Warner and the Entertainment Group, a \$2–\$3 billion debt reduction program was initiated in 1995. Including the sale of 51% of TWE's interest in Six Flags in June 1995, the sale of an interest in QVC, Inc. in February 1995, the sale of certain unclustered cable systems, the proceeds raised from the monetization of Time Warner's investment in Hasbro in August 1995 (through the issuance of mandatorily redeemable preferred securities of a subsidiary) and a portion of its interest in TWE in April 1996 (through the issuance of Series M preferred stock), and the expected 1997 sale of TWE's interest in E Entertainment Television, Inc., Time Warner and the Entertainment Group on a combined basis have exceeded their initial goals under this program.

TWE is Time Warner Entertainment, a subsidiary of Time Warner Inc. The parent company has a substantial investment in the common stock of Hasbro, a toy manufacturer. Time Warner Inc. goes on to describe its financial condition and its preferred stock as:

1996 FINANCIAL CONDITION

At December 31, 1996, Time Warner had \$12.7 billion of debt, \$452 million of available cash and equivalents (net debt of \$12.2 billion), \$488 million of borrowings against future stock option proceeds, \$949 million of mandatorily redeemable preferred securities of subsidiaries, \$1.7 billion of Series M Preferred Stock, and \$9.5 billion of shareholders' equity, compared to \$9.9 billion of debt, \$1.2 billion of available cash and equivalents (net debt of \$8.7 billion), \$949 million of mandatorily redeemable preferred securities of subsidiaries, and \$3.7 billion of shareholders' equity at December 31, 1995. At December 31, 1996, Time Warner also had \$62 million of noncurrent cash and equivalents held in escrow for purposes of funding certain preferred dividend requirements.

The increase in net debt principally reflects the assumption or incurrence of approximately \$4.8 billion of debt related to the TBS [Turner Broadcasting System] Transaction and the CVI Acquisition, offset in part by the use of approximately \$1.55 billion of net proceeds from the issuance of the Series M Preferred Stock for debt reduction. The increase in shareholders' equity principally reflects the issuance in 1996 of approximately 173.4 million shares of common stock in connection with the TBS Transaction and approximately 2.9 million shares of common stock and 6.3 million shares of preferred stock in connection with the CVI Acquisition. The effect from such issuances was offset in part by an increase in dividend requirements and the repurchase of approximately 11.4 million shares of Time Warner common stock at an aggregate cost of \$456 million.

9. MANDATORILY REDEEMABLE PREFERRED SECURITIES

In August 1995, Time Warner issued approximately 12.1 million Company-obligated mandatorily redeemable preferred securities of a wholly owned subsidiary ("PERCS") for aggregate gross proceeds of $374 million. The sole assets of the subsidiary that is the obligor on the PERCS are $385 million principal amount of 4% subordinated notes of Old Time Warner [the predecessor company] due December 23, 1997. Cumulative cash distributions are payable on the PERCS at an annual rate of 4%. The PERCS are mandatorily redeemable on December 23, 1997, for an amount per PERCS equal to the lesser of $54.41, and the market value of 1.5 shares of common stock of Hasbro on December 17, 1997 (as adjusted for the Hasbro Stock Split), payable in cash or, at Time Warner's option, Hasbro common stock. Time Warner has the right to redeem the PERCS at any time prior to December 23, 1997, at an amount per PERCS equal to $54.41 (or in certain limited circumstances the lesser of such amount and the market value of 1.5 shares of Hasbro common stock at the time of redemption) plus accrued and unpaid distributions thereon and a declining premium, payable in cash or, at Time Warner's option, Hasbro common stock.

In December 1995, Time Warner issued approximately 23 million Company-obligated mandatorily redeemable preferred securities of a wholly owned subsidiary ("Preferred Trust Securities") for aggregate gross proceeds of $575 million. The sole assets of the subsidiary that is the obligor on the Preferred Trust Securities are $592 million principal amount of 8⅞% subordinated debentures of Old Time Warner due December 31, 2025. Cumulative cash distributions are payable on the Preferred Trust Securities at an annual rate of 8⅞%. The Preferred Trust Securities are mandatorily redeemable for cash on December 31, 2025, and Time Warner has the right to redeem the Preferred Trust Securities, in whole or in part, on or after December 31, 2000, or in other certain circumstances, in each case at an amount per Preferred Trust Security equal to $25 plus accrued and unpaid distributions thereon.

10. SERIES M EXCHANGEABLE PREFERRED STOCK

In April 1996, Time Warner raised approximately $1.55 billion of net proceeds in a private placement of 1.6 million shares of 10¼% exchangeable preferred stock. This issuance allowed the Company to realize cash proceeds through a security whose payment terms are principally linked (until a reorganization of TWE occurs, if any) to a portion of Time Warner's currently noncash-generating interest in the Series B Capital of TWE. The proceeds raised from this transaction were used by Time Warner to reduce debt. As part of the TBS Transaction, these preferred shares were converted into registered shares of Series M exchangeable preferred stock with substantially identical terms ("Series M Preferred Stock").

Each share of Series M Preferred Stock is entitled to a liquidation preference of $1,000 and entitles the holder thereof to receive cumulative dividends at the rate of 10¼% per annum, payable quarterly (1) in cash, to the extent of an amount equal to the Pro Rata Percentage (as defined below) multiplied by the amount of cash distributions received by Time Warner from TWE with respect to its interests in the Series B Capital and Residual Capital of TWE, excluding stock option related distributions and certain tax related distributions (collectively, "Eligible TWE Cash Distributions"), or (2) to the extent of any balance, at Time Warner's option, (i) in cash or (ii) in-kind, through the issuance of additional shares of Series M Preferred Stock with an aggregate liquidation preference equal to the amount of such dividends. The "Pro Rata Percentage" is equal to the ratio of (1) the aggregate liquidation preference of the outstanding shares of Series M Preferred Stock, including any accumulated and unpaid dividends thereon, to (2) Time Warner's total interest in the Series B Capital of TWE, including any undistributed priority capital return thereon. Because cash distributions to Time Warner with respect to its interests in the Series B Capital and Residual Capital of TWE are generally restricted until June 30, 1998 and are subject to additional limitations thereafter under the TWE partnership agreement, Time Warner does not expect to pay cash dividends in the foreseeable future.

The Series M Preferred Stock may be redeemed at the option of Time Warner, in whole or in part, on or after July 1, 2006, subject to certain conditions, at an amount per share equal to its liquidation preference plus accumulated and accrued and unpaid dividends thereon, and a declining premium through July 1, 2010 (the "Optional Redemption Price"). Time Warner is required to redeem shares of Series M Preferred Stock representing up to 20%, 25%, 33 1/3%, and 50% of the then-outstanding liquidation preference of the Series M Preferred Stock on July 1 of 2012, 2013, 2014, and 2015, respectively, at an amount equal to the aggregate liquidation preference of the number of shares to be redeemed plus accumulated and accrued and unpaid dividends thereon (the "Mandatory Redemption Price"). Total payments in respect of such mandatory redemption obligations on any redemption date are limited to an amount equal to the Pro Rata Percentage of any cash distributions received by Time Warner from TWE in the preceding year in connection with the redemption of Time Warner's interest in the Series B Capital of TWE and in connection with certain cash distributions related to Time Warner's interest in the Residual Capital of TWE. The redemption of the Series B Capital of TWE is scheduled to occur ratably over a five-year period commencing on June 30, 2011. Time Warner is required to redeem any remaining outstanding shares of Series M Preferred Stock on July 1, 2016 at the Mandatory Redemption Price; however, in the event that Time Warner's interest in the Series B Capital of TWE has not been redeemed in full prior to such final mandatory redemption date, payments in respect of the final mandatory redemption obligation of the Series M Preferred Stock in 2016 will be limited to an amount equal to the lesser of the Mandatory Redemption Price and an amount equal to the Pro Rata Percentage of the fair market value of TWE (net of taxes) attributable to Time Warner's interests in the Series B Capital and Residual Capital of TWE.

Upon a reorganization of TWE, as defined in the related certificate of designation, Time Warner must elect either to (1) exchange each outstanding share of Series M Preferred Stock for shares of a new series of 10 1/4% exchangeable preferred stock ("Series L Preferred Stock") or (2) subject to certain conditions, redeem the outstanding shares of Series M Preferred Stock at an amount per share equal to 110% of the liquidation preference thereof, plus accumulated and accrued and unpaid dividends thereon or, after July 1, 2006, at the Optional Redemption Price. The Series L Preferred Stock has terms similar to those of the Series M Preferred Stock, except that (i) Time Warner may only pay dividends in-kind until June 30, 2006, (ii) Time Warner is required to redeem the outstanding shares of Series L Preferred Stock on July 1, 2011 at an amount per share equal to the liquidation preference thereof, plus accumulated and accrued and unpaid dividends thereon and (iii) Time Warner has the option to exchange, in whole but not in part, subject to certain conditions, the outstanding shares of Series L Preferred Stock for Time Warner 10 1/4% Senior Subordinated Debentures due July 1, 2011 (the "Senior Subordinated Debentures") having a principal amount equal to the liquidation preference of the Series L Preferred Stock plus accrued and unpaid dividends thereon. Interest on the Senior Subordinated Debentures is payable in cash or, at Time Warner's option through June 30, 2006, in-kind through the issuance of additional Senior Subordinated Debentures with a principal amount equal to such interest. The Senior Subordinated Debentures may be redeemed at the option of Time Warner, in whole or in part, on or after July 1, 2006, subject to certain conditions, at an amount per debenture equal to its principal amount plus accrued and unpaid interest, and a declining premium through July 1, 2010.

Source: Time Warner Inc. 1996 Annual Report.

Information taken from Time Warner's 1996 annual report to shareholders follows:

($ in millions)	December 31 1996	1995
Long-term debt	$13,201	$9,907
Preferred stock	2,625	979
Common stockholders' equity	9,498	3,637
Total stockholders' equity	$12,123	$4,616
Net income before interest and taxes	$ 1,178	$ 879
Interest expense	$ 1,174	$ 877
Long-term debt/total equity	1.09	2.15
Times interest earned	1.00	1.00

REQUIRED:

1. Should Time Warner's preferred stock be classified as debt or equity from the bank's perspective? Draft a brief memo outlining your reasoning.
2. Based on your classification of the company's preferred stock, is Time Warner still in compliance with its debt covenants?
3. What new covenant language would you suggest the bank add to its loan agreement?

16

Intercorporate Equity Investments

LEARNING OBJECTIVES:
After studying this chapter, you will understand:

1. How a company benefits from owning another company's common stock.
2. How an investor's ownership share is used to determine the accounting treatment of equity investments, and why.
3. How the accounting for short-term speculative investments differs from the accounting for long-term investments.
4. The equity method and when to use it.
5. What consolidated financial statements are, and how they are compiled.
6. What goodwill is, and when it is shown on the financial statements.
7. How business acquisitions and mergers are recorded and why the recording method matters to statement readers.
8. How foreign subsidiaries are treated when financial statements in U.S. dollars are prepared.

One company will buy equity shares in another company to earn an investment return or to improve its competitive position. When a company buys equity shares for investment purposes, its return comes from share price increases and dividends. But when a company buys shares to improve its competitive position, its return comes from increased operating profits and growth. A company that owns shares in another company that is a supplier or customer gains influence over that company, as well as access to new markets or greater production capacity.

Under existing GAAP, the method of accounting for intercorporate investments depends on the size of the ownership share of the investor corporation. Does the investor own 10% or 40% of the other company? As we will see, the ownership proportion is used to infer the purpose of the investment.

We first discuss minority ownership, cases in which the corporate investor owns less than 50% of the voting shares of another company. Then we analyze majority (more than 50%) ownership, and we'll look at the special reporting problems created by subsidiaries in foreign countries. Figure 16.1 (next page) depicts the financial reporting methods that are used under different percentage ownership conditions.

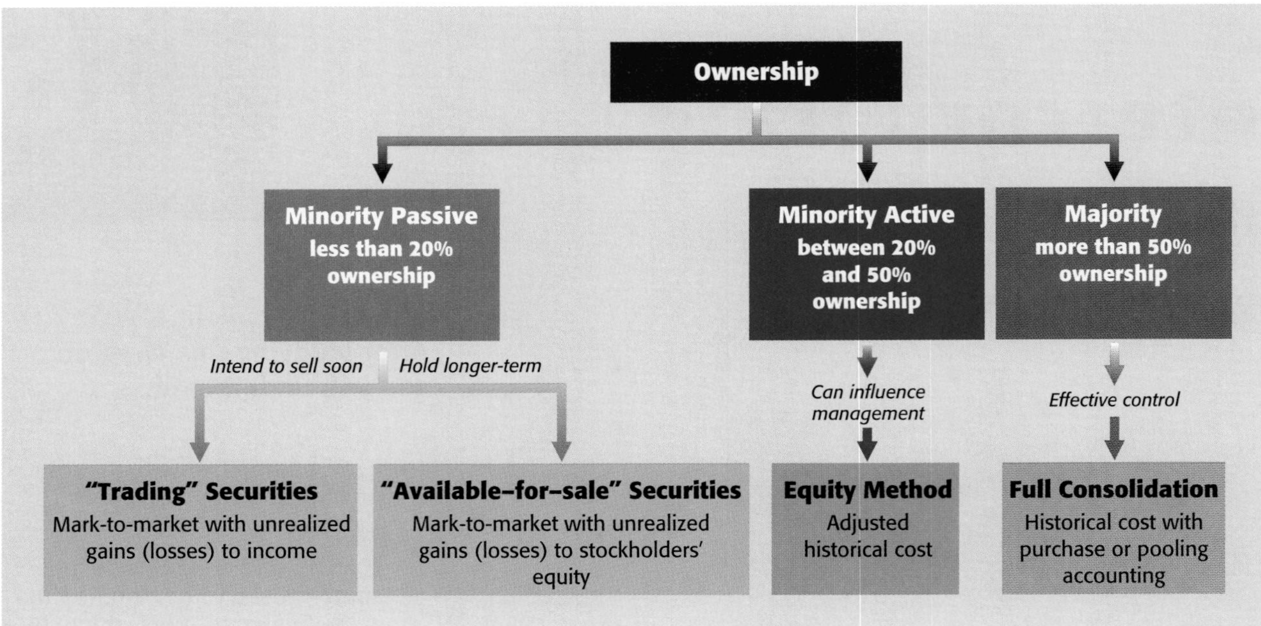

Figure 16.1

FINANCIAL REPORTING ALTERNATIVES FOR INTERCORPORATE EQUITY INVESTMENTS

Minority Ownership

Share ownership usually entitles the shareholder (the corporate investor) to vote at the company's shareholder meetings. Shareholders vote to elect company directors and to approve or reject proposals put forth by management or by shareholders. Management will ask shareholders to approve the company's outside auditor, proposed mergers and buyouts, compensation plan changes, and corporate charter amendments. Shareholder proposals often address environmental, social, and political issues such as prohibiting the company from doing business in unfavored countries.

A "one share, one vote" rule governs shareholder voting procedures in most companies. This means that each shareholder's influence over the company is proportional to the shares (votes) owned. A majority shareholder—one who owns more than 50% of the votes—can often dictate the company's business strategy and its major operating, investment, and financing decisions. A minority investor—one who owns less than 50% of the votes—has less influence over the company but still may be able to elect a corporate director or gain the ear of management.

> Each share of **common stock** usually entitles the owner to one vote, while those who own **preferred stock** usually have no voting rights. There are exceptions. Some companies issue dual-class common stock (often denoted Common A and Common B), in which one class has voting rights and the other does not. In addition, some companies do issue voting preferred stock.

For financial reporting purposes, minority investments fall into one of two categories: **minority passive** investments, those in which the shareholder has no ability to influence the company; or **minority active** investments, in which the ownership percentage is large enough for shareholder influence. Consider these examples: Owning a single share of stock is a minority passive investment, but owning 49.9% of the company's voting shares is a minority active investment. Deciding where to draw the line between passive and active minority investments can be difficult, as we shall see.

Minority Passive Investments: Mark-to-Market Accounting

When one company owns a small proportion of the voting shares of another company, it's safe to presume the investment was made for speculation—that is, the investor hopes to earn a return from dividends and share price increases. We may presume this because small proportionate ownership of a public company does not convey the power to elect directors or influence the company's operating policies. What the investor company hopes is to earn a return on cash not currently needed in its own business. Existing GAAP presumes that ownership of less than 20% of another company's voting shares constitutes a passive investment because ownership of less than 20% seldom provides the investor with an opportunity to exert significant influence over a company's activities.

As Figure 16.1 shows, minority passive investments are classified on the investor's books in one of two ways, depending upon the expected duration of the investment.[1]

Equity securities designated by the investor as intended to be held for a short time are classified as **trading securities,** typically purchased to generate profits on short-term differences in price.[2] All trading securities are shown on the balance sheet as current assets. Equity investments of less than 20% that are not trading securities are **available-for-sale securities.** These are usually shown as noncurrent on the balance sheet. Both trading securities and available-for-sale securities are reported at fair value—current market price—not at historical cost.

Trading Securities Trading securities are actively managed in order to achieve trading gains. Under the guidelines of Statement of Financial Accounting Standards *(SFAS) No. 115*, trading securities are reported at **fair value**—or **marked-to-market**—at each balance sheet date. Market price increases are debited to a **market adjustment account** which is *added* to the trading securities asset account (reported at original cost). Market price decreases are credited to the same market adjustment account, which (for price decreases) is *deducted* from the trading securities asset account. The offsetting credit for market price increases is made to the unrealized gain on trading securities account on the income statement; market price decreases are offset as a debit to the unrealized loss on trading securities account. Here's an example of securities that were purchased by Principal Financial Corporation for **short-term speculation:**

Purchases and Sales of Trading Securities by Principal Financial Corporation

Security	Date Acquired	Acquisition Cost	Market Value December 31 2001	2002	2003	2004
A Company common	1/1/01	$10,000	$11,000	$13,000	$ 14,000	$12,000
B Company preferred	1/1/01	20,000	18,000	17,000	18,000	*
C Company common	7/1/02	30,000	—	26,000	33,000	34,000
D Company options	7/1/02	40,000	—	41,000	37,000	30,000
			$29,000	$97,000	$102,000	$76,000

* B Company preferred stock was sold on January 1, 2004 for $18,500.

Let's first consider the entry to record the purchase of Company A common shares and Company B preferred shares on January 1, 2001:

DR Trading securities–A Company common	$10,000	
DR Trading securities–B Company preferred	20,000	
CR Cash		$30,000

[1] The reporting rules for minority passive investments are contained in "The Equity Method of Accounting for Investments in Common Stock," *Accounting Principles Board (APB) Opinion No. 18* (New York: APB, 1971); and "Accounting for Certain Investments in Debt and Equity Securities," *Statement of Financial Accounting Standards (SFAS) No. 115* (Norwalk, CT: Financial Accounting Standards Board [FASB], 1993).

[2] *SFAS No. 115*, para. 12. Bond investments made to generate short-run trading gains are also classified as trading securities, and they are accounted for in a manner identical to equity securities in the trading portfolio.

Dividends on these securities are recorded as income when declared—if dividends of $1,000 were declared by Company A on December 15, 2001, the entry would be:

DR Dividends receivable	$1,000	
CR Dividend income		$1,000

When Principal Financial receives the cash dividend in January 2002, cash for $1,000 will be debited and the dividends receivable account will be credited for $1,000.

The 2001 year-end mark-to-market adjustment entry requires two steps:

Step 1. The total market value of all trading securities is compared to the total cost of the securities. Any difference becomes the **target balance** for the market adjustment account.

Step 2. The market adjustment account must be increased (or decreased) to equal its target balance, and then an unrealized gain (or loss) for the same amount must be recorded.

The 2001 year-end adjustment by Principal Financial would be:

Step 1		**Step 2**	
Trading Securities Portfolio		**Market Adjustment Account**	
Total market value	$29,000	($1,000)	Target balance (CR)
− Total cost	(30,000)	− 0	Current balance
= Difference	($ 1,000)	($1,000)	Adjustment needed (CR)

DR Unrealized holding loss on trading securities (income statement)	$1,000	
CR Market adjustment–trading securities		$1,000

Once this entry is recorded the balance sheet section for trading securities appears as:

Trading securities (at cost)	$30,000
Less: Market adjustment–trading securities	(1,000)
Trading securities at market	$29,000

Now let's look at the entry to record the purchase of Company C common shares and Company D stock options on July 1, 2002:

DR Trading securities–Company C common stock	$30,000	
DR Trading securities–Company D stock options	40,000	
CR Cash		$70,000

Following the two-step process, Principal Financial's 2002 year-end mark-to-market adjustment is:

Step 1		**Step 2**	
Trading Securities Portfolio		**Market Adjustment Account**	
Total market value	$ 97,000	($3,000)	Target balance (CR)
− Total cost	(100,000)	− (1,000)	Current balance (CR)
= Difference	($ 3,000)	($2,000)	Adjustment needed (CR)

DR Unrealized holding loss on trading securities (income statement)	$2,000	
CR Market adjustment–trading securities		$2,000

This entry highlights why it is necessary to use the two-step procedure. Comparing the portfolio market value to the *cost* of the underlying shares at each valuation date (as shown in Step 1), rather than comparing the total portfolio market value at two successive dates, corrects for changes in the number of shares at successive valuation dates.

The mark-to-market adjustment for 2003 is:

Step 1		Step 2	
Trading Securities Portfolio		**Market Adjustment Account**	
Total market value	$102,000	$2,000	Target balance (DR)
− Total cost	(100,000)	− (3,000)	Current balance (CR)
= Difference	$ 2,000)	$5,000	Adjustment needed (DR)

DR Market adjustment–trading securities	$5,000	
CR Unrealized holding gain on trading securities–(income statement)		$5,000

When trading securities are sold, the *realized* gain or loss is recorded. The amount of the realized gain or loss is the sale price of the securities *minus* the most recent mark-to-market price. The original cost of the securities sold and the related portion of the market adjustment account are removed from the accounts. This is illustrated for the sale of Company B preferred stock on January 1, 2004 as follows:

Using the most recent mark-to-market price in computing the realized gain or loss avoids double counting any unrealized gain or loss recorded in previous periods' income statements.

Computation of Realized Gain or Loss

Sale price of Company B preferred stock	$18,500
Mark-to-market value at 12/31/03 balance sheet date	(18,000)
Realized gain	$ 500

Entry to Record the Sale of Company B Common Stock

DR Cash	$18,500	
DR Market adjustment–trading securities	2,000[1]	
CR Realized gain on sale of trading securities		$ 500
CR Trading securities–Company B preferred		20,000

[1] $20,000 cost − $18,000 market value at 12/31/03 = $2,000.

After this entry is recorded, the balance in the "Trading securities" account and the "Market adjustment" account is:

Trading securities account at cost ($100,000 − $20,000)	$80,000
Market adjustment account ($2,000 **DR** balance on 12/31/03 + $2,000 **DR** from sale)	4,000
Trading securities at market	$84,000

The mark-to-market adjustment entry at the end of 2004 compares the target balance for the market adjustment account to the balance that will appear in this account after the sale of the Company B preferred stock, as in the following computation:

Step 1		**Step 2**	
Trading Securities Portfolio		**Market Adjustment Account**	
Total market value	$ 76,000	($4,000)	Target balance (CR)
− Total cost	(80,000)	− 4,000	Current balance (DR)
= Difference	($ 4,000)	($8,000)	Adjustment needed (CR)

DR Unrealized holding loss on trading securities (income statement)	$8,000	
CR Market adjustment–trading securities		$8,000

After this entry is recorded, the trading securities section of Principal Financial's balance sheet on December 31, 2004 would show:

Trading securities (at cost)	$80,000
Less: Market adjustment–trading securities	(4,000)
Trading securities (at market)	$76,000

Available-for-Sale Securities Now assume Principal Financial bought the equity securities described earlier because of their perceived **longer-term investment potential**—not for short-term speculation purposes. In this case the securities would be "available for sale" and shown (usually) as noncurrent investments on the balance sheet. The entries to record the purchase, dividend, and mark-to-market adjustment for available-for-sale securities are very similar to the entries for these same items as trading securities.

The only significant difference between treating investment securities as "available for sale" rather than "trading" is that the ***mark-to-market adjustment is not included in income. Instead, the upward or downward adjustment to reflect fair value for available-for-sale securities is a direct (net of tax) credit or debit to a special owners' equity account.*** These unrealized gains or losses on available-for-sale securities are one of the "Other comprehensive income" components described in Chapter 2.

Returning to our example, we find that the 2001 year-end downward market adjustment for Principal Financial's available-for-sale portfolio is:

DR Unrealized change in value of available-for-sale securities (owners' equity)	$650	
DR Deferred income taxes (assumed 35%)	350	
CR Market adjustment–available-for-sale-securities		$1,000

As before, a credit balance in the "Market adjustment" account is treated as a contra-asset so that the net book value of the available-for-sale portfolio on the December 31, 2001 balance sheet is $29,000 ($30,000 cost minus the $1,000 market adjustment).

If market prices rise as they did in 2003, the upward adjustment at December 31, 2003 would be:

DR Market adjustment–available-for-sale securities	$5,000	
CR Unrealized change in value of available-for-sale securities (owners' equity)		$3,250
CR Deferred income taxes (assumed 35%)		1,750

The FASB excluded unrealized gains and losses on available-for-sale securities from earnings because the securities are not held for active trading. Running the debit or credit directly into owners' equity—rather than through income—alleviates the potential for earnings volatility unrelated to eventual investment performance. When available-for-sale securities are later sold, then the cumulative unrealized gain or loss is realized and gets included in income.

RECAP

Trading securities and available-for-sale securities—the two types of minority passive investments—are carried at fair value on the balance sheet. The unrealized holding gain or loss on trading securities is run through income in the period of the security price change. Unrealized gains and losses on available-for-sale securities do not affect income in the period of the price change; instead these gains and losses go directly to a special owners' equity account and are reported as a component of other comprehensive income.

Minority Active Investments: Equity Method

GM Agrees to Buy 20% of Fuji Heavy Industries

– General Motors Corp. was to announce today in Japan the signing of an agreement to acquire a 20% stake in Japan's Fuji Heavy Industries Ltd. for $1.4 billion.

The transaction, which was expected, includes plans to form a broad strategic alliance. This would allow GM to tap certain small-vehicle technologies in which Fuji is a leader and will help GM to quickly add a new small sport-utility vehicle for Europe, officials said. Fuji, which makes Subaru cars, will get access to GM's global marketing reach and to expensive propulsion technologies that GM is developing.

GM's alliance with Fuji nails down another plank in the No. 1 auto maker's platform for expanding in Asia. GM has linkups with Japan's Isuzu Motors Ltd., in which it holds a 49% stake, and Suzuki Motor Corp., in which it holds a 10% stake. . . .

Fuji brings experience in building small cars with all-wheel-drive – such as its popular Forester and Outback models. In addition, GM wants to use Fuji's advanced continuously variable transmissions and ability to integrate controls for all of a modern vehicle's elements into a single system. . . .

The first fruit of this technology sharing is expected to be the development of a small SUV GM would aim mainly at Europe, although it may appear in North America. . . . [T]he alliance is expected to significantly speed GM's ability to develop vehicles that combine car and truck features for the U.S.

Fuji Heavy is expected to use the partnership to expand its lineup of Subaru vehicles. The company sells 550,000 to 600,000 vehicles a year world-wide and has a limited presence in Europe and South America.

Source: The *Wall Street Journal* (December 10, 1999).

When the ownership percentage equals or exceeds 20%, GAAP presumes two elements:

1. A significant ownership position like 20% implies that the investor has the capability to exert influence over the company. This influence could encompass operating decisions, such as which research and development projects should be undertaken, and financing decisions, such as dividend payouts.
2. A substantial ownership percentage also implies a continuing relationship between the two companies, since investments of this magnitude are usually entered into in order to achieve some long-run strategic objective.

Both elements are present in GM's ownership stake in Fuji Heavy Industries (hereafter Fuji).

The 20% threshold is only a guideline. It is possible that ownership of less than 20% would, under certain circumstances, allow the investor to influence the company's activities. This could happen when share ownership is widely distributed across a large number of individual investors. An investor who owns, say, 18% of a widely held company could still influence management's decisions. Accordingly, judgment must be used to categorize minority investments between passive and active in certain situations.

Once the ownership percentage becomes large enough for investor influence, the simple accounting system introduced for passive investments is no longer suitable. To see why, recall that the entry made on a minority passive investor's books when dividends are declared is:

DR Dividends receivable	$1,000	
CR Dividend income		$1,000

When the investor can influence the company's dividend policy, the minority passive accounting treatment would allow the investor to augment its own reported income. Suppose GM wants to increase reported earnings during the period. It owns enough Fuji stock to influence the company's dividend policy, and it uses that influence to raise Fuji's dividend. This higher dividend would immediately run through GM's income statement.

To preclude this avenue for income distortion, minority active investments are accounted for through the **equity method,** as shown earlier in Figure 16.1. Under the equity method, GM records its initial investment in Fuji at cost. Subsequently, however, the investment account is increased for the pro rata share of Fuji's income, and there is a corresponding credit to the investment income account—or, in the case of a loss, GM's investment account decreases and there's a corresponding debit to the investment loss account.

Since GM's earnings are increased for its share of Fuji's earnings each period, it would be inappropriate to record dividend distributions received from Fuji as income too. This would "double-count" Fuji's earnings on GM's books. Under the equity method, dividends from Fuji are recorded as an increase (debit) to cash—or dividends receivable—and a decrease (credit) to the investment account. ***Thus, the investment account is increased for GM's share of Fuji's earnings and decreased when those earnings are received in the form of dividends.***

The following example illustrates the entries under the equity method:

> On January 1, 2001 Willis Company purchases 30% of the outstanding common shares of Planet Burbank, Inc. for $9,000,000. The book value and market value of Planet Burbank's net assets (assets minus liabilities) is $30,000,000. During 2001 Planet Burbank earns a net profit of $10,000,000, and the company declares a dividend of $500,000 on December 31, 2001. Using the equity method, the entries made by Willis are:

January 1, 2001

DR Investment in Planet Burbank	$9,000,000	
CR Cash		$9,000,000

December 31, 2001

DR Investment in Planet Burbank	$3,000,000	
CR Income from affiliate		$3,000,000

(To recognize 30% of Planet Burbank's total reported income of $10,000,000)

December 31, 2001

DR Dividend receivable from affiliate	$150,000	
CR Investment in Planet Burbank		$150,000

(To reduce the investment account for dividends declared–30% of $500,000)

The example shows how the equity method reduces possibilities for income distortion. Willis Company's income statement is affected only by its pro rata share of Planet Burbank's income. ***The dividend declaration—and subsequent payment—by Planet Bur-***

bank has no effect on Willis' income. Thus, while Willis could conceivably use the influence arising from its 30% ownership share to increase Planet Burbank's dividend declaration, doing so would leave its income unchanged ***when the equity method is used.*** Under the equity method, the carrying amount in the investment account at any point in time is comprised of the following items:

Initial investment amount	$ 9,000,000
Plus: Willis' cumulative pro rata share of Planet Burbank's income	3,000,000
Minus: Willis' cumulative pro rata share of dividends declared by Planet Burbank	(150,000)
Investment account carrying amount	$11,850,000

In contrast to balance sheet amounts for minority passive investments, the carrying amount under equity method accounting is *not* marked-to-market. Why? A substantial ownership percentage—equal to or greater than 20%—signals an intended continuing relationship between investor and investee. Since ownership of this magnitude implies some long-term strategic intent, sale of the investment is not imminent, and fair value is presumably less important to statement readers.

This is the *rationale* for not reporting fair values under the equity method. Whether, in fact, statement readers are uninterested in the fair value of minority active investments is an empirical issue for which limited evidence is available.

When Cost and Book Value Differ In contrast to our Planet Burbank example, investors rarely buy shares at a price exactly equal to the book value of those shares, and when the investor's cost differs from book value, a new issue surfaces.

To illustrate, let's return to the Willis Company purchase of Planet Burbank stock. Here book value is $30,000,000, but let's say Willis paid $24,000,000 for its 30% stake. Why would Willis pay $24,000,000 when the book value of the shares purchased is only $9,000,000 (30% of $30,000,000)? Why would an informed buyer pay $15,000,000 ($24,000,000 minus $9,000,000) more than book value?

There are two reasons. First, Planet Burbank's books are prepared using GAAP, which reflects balance sheet items at historical cost rather than at current value. As shown in Exhibit 16.1(a) on the next page, the fair market value of Planet Burbank's *net* assets is $70,000,000, or $40,000,000 above the $30,000,000 book value (see highlighted area). Sellers of Planet Burbank stock presumably know that the company's *net* assets are worth $70,000,000 rather than the lower $30,000,000 book value. On the basis of this knowledge, the asking price for the shares acquired by Willis Company will be higher than book value. But how much higher?

Willis decided to pay $24,000,000, or $15,000,000 more than book value. Exhibit 16.1(b) on the next page shows that $12,000,000 of the $15,000,000 excess of cost over book value is explained by the difference between fair value and book value of inventories and fixed assets (see highlighted area). This still leaves $3,000,000 of the disparity unexplained. The remaining difference brings us to the second reason why an informed buyer would knowingly pay a premium to acquire influence over another company.

This second potential explanation relates to **goodwill.** Goodwill exists because thriving, successful companies are frequently worth more than the sum of their individual net assets. Planet Burbank has developed a reputation for product quality, prompt service, and fair treatment of both employees and customers. Consequently, employees like to work for the company, and customers actively seek out its products. The result is that Planet Burbank is exceptionally profitable—it earns a very large return on its investment base. The capitalized value of this earning potential is what gives rise to the remaining $3,000,000 difference. This "extraordinary" earnings potential is called goodwill.

Exhibit 16.1 ■ WILLIS COMPANY

Investment with Goodwill

On January 1, 2001 Willis Company purchases 30% of the outstanding shares of common stock of Planet Burbank for $24,000,000. The book value and fair value of Planet Burbank's net assets on this date are as follows:

($ in millions)	Book Value	Fair Value	Difference	Investor's Share (30%)
Cash and Receivables	$10	$10	$ 0	$ 0
Inventories (FIFO cost flow)	15	25	10	3
Depreciable assets (net of depreciation)*	25	55	30	9
Total assets	50	90	40	12
Minus liabilities	(20)	(20)	0	0
Net assets	$30	$70	$40	$12

*Average remaining useful life of 10 years.

During 2001 Planet Burbank reported net profit of $10,000,000, and the company declared a dividend of $4,000,000 on December 31, 2001.

(a)

	($ in millions)
Analysis of Willis' investment cost over book value	
Cost of 30% investment	$24
30% of Planet Burbank's net asset book value (30% × $30)	(9)
Excess of cost over book value of Willis' shares	$15
Amount of excess attributable to	
Inventories—30% × ($25 − $15)	$ 3
Depreciable assets—30% × ($55 − $25)	9
Remainder attributable to implicit goodwill**(plug figure)	3
	$15

** To be amortized over 20 years.

(b)

A summary of the factors comprising the $24,000,000 purchase price for 30% of Planet Burbank is ($ in millions):

Recorded historical book value of the company's net assets ($50 − $20) × 30%	$ 9
Difference between fair value and cost of net assets ($40 × 30%)	12
Amount attributable to goodwill (plug figure)	3
Purchase price	$24

When the cost of the shares exceeds the underlying book value at the acquisition date, the investor is required to amortize any excess that is attributable to (1) inventory, (2) depreciable assets, or (3) goodwill.[3] Amortization is recorded as a reduction (debit) to invest-

[3] As this book goes to press, the FASB has issued a revision to their Exposure Draft, *Business Combinations and Intangible Assets—Accounting for Goodwill,* that would dramatically alter the accounting for the implicit goodwill in equity method transactions. Paragraph 25 of the revised Exposure Draft states: "The portion of the difference between the cost of an investment and the amount of underlying equity in net assets of an investee that represents goodwill (equity method goodwill) shall *not* be amortized." [Emphasis added]. In addition, equity method goodwill will *not* be tested for impairment as would be required under the Exposure Draft for goodwill arising from purchase accounting for business combinations. "Business Combinations and Intangible Assets—Accounting for Goodwill," *FASB Exposure Draft (Revised)* (Norwalk, CT: FASB, February 14, 2001).

ment income and a reduction (credit) to the investment account. The rationale for amortizing the excess of the investor's cost over book value is based on the matching principle. Since Willis is picking up its share of Planet Burbank's reported earnings each period as investment income, it follows that Willis should write off any amount paid in excess of Planet Burbank's book value as a cost of gaining access to those earnings.

Using the equity method, the entries based on the preceding set of facts are:

January 1, 2001: Initial investment in Planet Burbank

DR Investment in Planet Burbank	$24,000,000	
CR Cash		$24,000,000

December 31, 2001: Investor's share of earnings

DR Investment in Planet Burbank	$3,000,000	
CR Investment income		$3,000,000

(To recognize 30% of Planet Burbank's total reported income of $10,000,000)

December 31, 2001: Investor's share of dividends declared

DR Dividend receivable from Planet Burbank	$1,200,000	
CR Investment in Planet Burbank		$1,200,000

(To reduce the investment account for dividend declared–30% of $4,000,000)

December 31, 2001: Amortization of excess cost over book value attributable to inventory, depreciable assets, and implicit goodwill

DR Investment income	$4,050,000	
CR Investment in Planet Burbank		$4,050,000

Amortization is computed as:	Amount	Amortization
Attributed to inventory (all sold during the year)	$3,000,000	$3,000,000
Attributed to depreciable assets (over 10 years)	9,000,000	900,000
Attributed to goodwill (over 20 years)	3,000,000	150,000
		$4,050,000

The excess investment cost over book value attributable to inventory is assigned to inventory items on hand on January 1, 2001, when Willis purchased Planet Burbank's stock. This inventory is presumed to have been sold during 2001 under the FIFO cost flow assumption (see Chapter 9). The amount attributed to depreciable assets is amortized over the average remaining 10-year life of those assets. The amount attributed to goodwill is amortized over 20 years.

The December 31, 2001: balance in the investment in Planet Burbank's account is $21,750,000 ($24,000,000 + $3,000,000 − $1,200,000 − $4,050,000).

RECAP

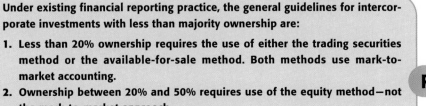

Under existing financial reporting practice, the general guidelines for intercorporate investments with less than majority ownership are:

1. **Less than 20% ownership requires the use of either the trading securities method or the available-for-sale method. Both methods use mark-to-market accounting.**
2. **Ownership between 20% and 50% requires use of the equity method—not the mark-to-market approach.**
3. **Under the equity method, the excess cost of purchased shares over their book value is amortized as a charge to income and a reduction to the investment account.**

Majority Ownership

Following current GAAP, when a **parent** company owns more than 50% of the voting shares of another company (**subsidiary**), the subsidiary is controlled by the parent. Under these circumstances the financial statements of the subsidiary are combined—line by line—with those of the parent using a process called **consolidation.**

Currently, consolidated statements are required only when the parent company owns *more than 50%* of the outstanding voting stock of the subsidiary. If exactly 50% of the voting shares are owned, the equity method is used and no line-by-line consolidation is necessary. In February 1999, the FASB issued an Exposure Draft that would change the existing definition of control.[4] **Control** was defined as the "ability of one entity to direct the policies and management that guide the ongoing activities of another entity." The Exposure Draft presumes control exists if any of the following conditions are met:[5]

> When two companies form a **joint venture** and each company owns exactly 50% of the joint-venture entity, neither "parent" consolidates the joint venture. Chapter 11 described how this allows the joint-venture entity to incur debt—usually guaranteed by the "parents"—***but the debt does not appear on either parent's balance sheet*** because consolidation is not required. Intercorporate investment reporting rules can be skillfully used to create "off-balance sheet" assets and liabilities.

- An entity has a majority voting interest in the election of a corporation's board of directors or the right to appoint a majority of the board.
- An entity has a large minority voting interest (i.e., more than 50% of the votes typically cast in electing directors) and no other significant voting interest exists.
- An entity owns convertible securities which, if exercised, would give it the right to obtain a majority in board elections or the right to appoint a majority of the board.

This proposed new broader definition of control means companies owning less than 50% of the voting stock of another corporation will sometimes be required to consolidate that entity. However, consolidation is not required if the parent's control is "temporary." As we go to press, this proposal is still being deliberated.

> Control of a newly acquired subsidiary is considered temporary if at the date of acquisition the parent (1) has committed to a plan to relinquish control of the subsidiary, or (2) is obligated to do so and it is likely that the loss of control will occur within one year.

When control exists (more than 50% ownership under current rules), the parent and subsidiary are really one in an economic sense. **Consolidated financial statements** are designed to cut across artificial corporate boundaries to portray the economic activities of the parent and subsidiary as if it were one entity. Let's see how this happens using the following example. On December 31, 2001 the balance sheet of Alphonse Corporation looks as follows:

Assets	
Current assets	$ 5,000,000
Fixed assets minus accumulated depreciation	20,000,000
Total assets	$25,000,000
Liabilities and equity	
Current liabilities	$ 1,000,000
Common stock ($1 par)	24,000,000
Total liabilities and equity	$25,000,000

[4] "Consolidated Financial Statements: Purpose and Policy," *FASB Exposure Draft, Revised* (Norwalk, CT: FASB, February 23, 1999).

[5] Ibid., para. 18.

On January 1, 2002 Alphonse issues 8,000,000 additional shares of its stock to new outside investors for $10,000,000 cash. Immediately after the stock issue, the balance sheet of Alphonse Corporation is:

Assets	
Current assets	$15,000,000
Fixed assets minus accumulated depreciation	20,000,000
Total assets	$35,000,000
Liabilities and equity	
Current liabilities	$ 1,000,000
Common stock ($1 par)	32,000,000
Capital in excess of par	2,000,000
Total liabilities and equity	$35,000,000

Alphonse immediately uses the cash to buy all of the outstanding shares of Gaston Corporation for $10,000,000. Since Alphonse has used its cash to make an investment, after buying Gaston's shares Alphonse's current assets will be $10,000,000 lower than before and an investment account of $10,000,000 will exist. Alphonse's balance sheet after the stock purchase, as well as Gaston's, are shown in Exhibit 16.2.

The steps that follow describe the procedures for preparing the consolidated balance sheet for Alphonse and Gaston in Exhibit 16.2. The individual balance sheets of the two companies are *not* simply added together; doing that would result in double-counting, as we'll see.

Step 1. Analysis of the "Investment in Gaston" Account Alphonse paid $10,000,000 for Gaston, a company whose *net* assets total only $8,000,000 (assets of $8,500,000 minus $500,000 of liabilities). Why did Alphonse pay more than $8,000,000? There are two reasons why an informed buyer would pay more than book value: (1) the fair market value of Gaston's individual assets is greater than their combined book value (we assume this excess is $1,500,000 here and is attributable to the fixed assets); and (2) goodwill, which is the remaining $500,000.

Exhibit 16.2 ■ ALPHONSE AND GASTON

Preparation of Consolidated Balance Sheet (Purchase Method)

	After the Acquisition			
	Alphonse	**Gaston**	**Adjustments**	**Consolidated Balance Sheet**
Assets				
Current assets	$ 5,000,000	$2,000,000		$ 7,000,000
Fixed assets minus accumulated depreciation	20,000,000	6,500,000	$1,500,000 B	28,000,000
Investment in Gaston	10,000,000	—	(8,000,000) A (1,500,000) B (500,000) C	—
Goodwill			500,000 C	500,000
	$35,000,000	$8,500,000		$35,500,000
Liabilities and Equity				
Current liabilities	$ 1,000,000	$ 500,000		$ 1,500,000
Common stock	32,000,000	8,000,000	(8,000,000) D	32,000,000
Capital in excess of par	2,000,000	—		2,000,000
	$35,000,000	$8,500,000		$35,500,000

The factors comprising the $10,000,000 purchase price for Gaston are:

Recorded book value of Gaston's *net* assets	$ 8,000,000
Unrecorded difference between fair value and book value of Gaston's fixed assets ($8,000,000 − $6,500,000)	1,500,000
Unrecorded value of Gaston's goodwill	500,000
Purchase price	$10,000,000

This purchase price breakdown explains why we do not add the two balance sheets together to get the consolidated balance sheet. Adding the two balance sheets together would double-count the $8,000,000 book value of Gaston's net assets. To see why, notice that the full purchase price of $10,000,000 is already on Alphonse's balance sheet (under "Investment in Gaston" in Exhibit 16.2); but as we have just seen, $8,000,000 of this purchase price represents the book value of Gaston's net assets. Since this $8,000,000 already appears on Gaston's balance sheet (assets of $8,500,000 minus $500,000 of liabilities), simply adding the two balance sheets together would double-count the $8,000,000. To avoid doing this, we have to remove $8,000,000 from Alphonse's "Investment in Gaston" account, leaving a balance of $2,000,000. Notice that this is done in Exhibit 16.2 in the "Adjustments" column (next to notation "A").

Step 2. Elimination of the "Investment in Gaston" Account The remaining balance in the "Investment in Gaston" account represents the amount of the purchase price that is *not* reflected in Gaston's balance sheet book values. As shown in the purchase price breakdown, this $2,000,000 remaining balance represents unrecorded fixed asset appreciation of $1,500,000 and goodwill of $500,000. These amounts must stay on the consolidated balance sheet, since Alphonse paid for them. However, they must be assigned to the items they actually represent: (1) an increase to fixed assets, and (2) the acquisition of goodwill. This is done in Exhibit 16.2 in the "Adjustments" column (next to the notations "B" and "C"). After these adjustments are made, notice that the "Investment in Gaston" account has been eliminated and thus does not appear in the consolidated column of Exhibit 16.2. Also, consolidated fixed assets have been increased by $1,500,000, and goodwill of $500,000 is separately reported.

Step 3. Analysis of the Common Stock Account To consolidate both balance sheets, we need to eliminate one more element of potential double-counting. Consider the $32,000,000 common stock account on the books of Alphonse. Since Alphonse owns Gaston, Alphonse's common stock account shows the ownership of *both* companies.

Now consider the $8,000,000 balance in the common stock account of Gaston. These shares represent ownership of Gaston. ***If the two common stock accounts were simply added together, ownership of Gaston would be counted twice***—once as a part of the $32,000,000 on Alphonse's books and once again in the $8,000,000 on Gaston's books.

To avoid this double-counting, the equity of Gaston is eliminated when the consolidated balance sheet is prepared. This is done opposite notation "D" in the "Adjustments" column in Exhibit 16.2. After this is done, consolidated owners' equity is comprised only of Alphonse's common stock, since this alone represents ownership of the entire consolidated entity.

The adjustment process described here can also be expressed in journal entry form. For example, the entry to avoid double-counting both the book value of Gaston's net assets and its owners' equity (Adjustments notations "A" and "D" in Exhibit 16.2) is:

DR Common stock	$8,000,000	
CR Investment in Gaston		$8,000,000

(To avoid double-counting Gaston's net assets [Adjustments notation "A"] and its owners' equity [Adjustments notation "D"].)

Similarly, reclassification of the remaining $2,000,000 in the "Investment in Gaston" account can also be expressed in journal entry form:

DR Fixed assets	$1,500,000	
DR Goodwill	500,000	
CR Investment in Gaston		$2,000,000
(Elimination of the remaining investment account balance [Adjustments notations "B" and "C"].)		

The acquisition of Gaston by Alphonse was accomplished using cash. The accounting for cash buyouts using the procedures outlined here is called **purchase accounting.** Later in the chapter, we describe another method for reflecting mergers—the **pooling of interests** method.

Other Consolidation Adjustments Suppose that several months prior to the Gaston acquisition, Alphonse had borrowed $300,000 from Gaston; this borrowing had not been repaid at the time of the acquisition on January 1, 2002. Under these circumstances, another adjustment is needed to consolidate the financial statements.

This adjustment is necessary because Alphonse and Gaston are now part of the same economic unit. The ***Alphonse loan receivable*** on Gaston's books and the ***Gaston loan payable*** on Alphonse's books are not owed to outsiders. To include the intercompany receivable and payable in the consolidated balance sheet would overstate assets and overstate liabilities, each by $300,000. That's why the following adjustment is made in preparing the consolidated statements:

DR Loan payable–Gaston (on Alphonse's books)	$300,000	
CR Loan receivable–Alphonse (on Gaston's books)		$300,000
(To eliminate intercompany loan from Gaston to Alphonse.)		

Another frequently encountered consolidation adjustment arises when Gaston and Alphonse make sales to one another. Suppose Alphonse sold goods to Gaston on March 15, 2002 after the January 1, 2002 acquisition, and then Gaston resold all these goods to outside customers. The facts are as follows:

Intercompany Sale

	Alphonse's Sale to Gaston	Gaston's Resale to "Outsiders"	Total
Selling price	$25,000	$34,000	$59,000
Cost of goods sold	20,000	25,000	45,000
Profit	$ 5,000	$ 9,000	$14,000

If Alphonse's and Gaston's income statements were merely added together to form the consolidated income statement, double-counting would result. This happens because neither Alphonse's $25,000 sale to Gaston nor the $25,000 of cost of goods sold on Gaston's income statement represents a transaction with outsiders. This means that the intercompany sales transaction must be eliminated in preparing the consolidated income statement, as follows:

Eliminate $25,000 Intercompany Sale

	Income Statement Totals		Sale	
	Alphonse	Gaston	Elimination	Consolidated
Sales	$250,000,000	$150,000,000	($25,000)	$399,975,000
Cost of goods sold	(200,000,000)	(109,000,000)	25,000	(308,975,000)
Gross margin	$ 50,000,000	$ 41,000,000	—	$ 91,000,000

After this elimination, all that remains of the intercompany sale and Gaston's subsequent resale of the goods to outsiders is the following:

	Alphonse's Sale to Gaston	Gaston's Resale to "Outsiders"	Sale Elimination	Net
Selling price	$25,000	$34,000	($25,000)	$34,000
Cost of goods sold	(20,000)	(25,000)	25,000	(20,000)
Profit	$ 5,000	$ 9,000	—	$14,000

Notice that the consolidated income statement now only reflects revenues realized from outsiders ($34,000) and costs paid to outsiders ($20,000). The double-counting of the intercompany sales and cost of goods sold has been eliminated.

Consolidated financial statements portray the parent company and its majority-owned subsidiaries as a single economic unit. But the individual balance sheets (and income statements) of each subsidiary and the parent are not simply added together. Instead, consolidation adjustments are made to avoid double-counting internal business transactions as well as various balance sheet items.

RECAP

Pooling of Interests

Instead of paying cash to acquire another company, mergers are sometimes accomplished using a "stock-for-stock" exchange. In these transactions one company exchanges equity shares with the stockholders of another company. The accounting for these mergers follows a procedure called **pooling of interests.** Let's see how Alphonse and Gaston would pool their interests.

Recall that Alphonse Corporation issued 8,000,000 new shares of stock for $10,000,000 cash and then used the cash to buy all of the outstanding shares of Gaston Corporation. To illustrate how pooling of interests works, let's assume Alphonse does not issue new shares for cash. Instead, on January 1, 2002, Gaston's shareholders agree to relinquish all of their shares in exchange for 8,000,000 newly issued shares of Alphonse stock. After the transaction is completed, Alphonse shareholders own both companies—that is, the merger has been accomplished by an exchange of shares rather than by an outright cash buyout.

In a stock-for-stock exchange, the owners of *both* Alphonse and Gaston continue as equity investors in the newly merged corporation. This continuation of ownership interests in poolings is in sharp contrast to what happens in a cash buyout, one in which the acquired company's shareholders accept cash and—after the buyout—have no further equity interest in the combined enterprise.

Existing reporting rules treat pooling of interests as though two formerly independent companies have decided to join resources and "keep house together." Since both original ownership interests survive, ***no buyout is considered to have taken place.*** In the consolidation of Alphonse's and Gaston's financial statements, the *book values* of the two entities are combined. As in purchase accounting, however, intercompany transactions and double-counted items must be eliminated, as shown in Exhibit 16.3.

The entry to record the acquisition on Alphonse's books would use the *book value* of Gaston's net assets ($2,000,000 + $6,500,000 − $500,000) as the carrying amount in the investment account—that is,

DR Investment in Gaston	$8,000,000	
CR Common Stock		$8,000,000

The only adjustment needed here is the elimination of the potential double-counting of Gaston's net assets and equity. This entry is identical to the purchase accounting (or cash buyout) adjustment illustrated in Exhibit 16.2 (see notations "A" and "D"). No other adjustments or reclassifications are needed, since Alphonse's "Investment in Gaston" account equals the net book value shown on Gaston's books. This means that under a pooling of

Exhibit 16.3 ■ ALPHONSE AND GASTON

Preparation of Consolidated Balance Sheet (Pooling of Interests Method)

	After the Merger			
	Alphonse	Gaston	Adjustments	Consolidated Balance Sheet
Assets				
Current assets	$ 5,000,000	$2,000,000		$ 7,000,000
Fixed assets minus accumulated depreciation	20,000,000	6,500,000		26,500,000
Investment in Gaston	8,000,000	—	(8,000,000)	—
	$33,000,000	$8,500,000		$33,500,000
Liabilities and Equity				
Current liabilities	$ 1,000,000	$ 500,000		$ 1,500,000
Common stock	32,000,000	8,000,000	(8,000,000)	32,000,000
	$33,000,000	$8,500,000		$33,500,000

interests there will never be a write-up of assets to a new, higher carrying value. Similarly, there will never be any goodwill recognized.

In poolings of interests, the owners of previously separate companies now own the merged organization. No buyout has occurred and therefore no new accounting basis—no asset "write-up" to fair value—is recognized in the consolidated statements. Instead, the book values of the previously separate companies are carried forward to the consolidated financial statements.

RECAP

Purchase, Pooling, and Financial Analysis

The pooling of interests method has been widely criticized. To help understand why, consider Exhibit 16.4 on the following page, which highlights the differences in consolidated balance sheets that would result for Alphonse & Gaston Company—the combined organization—under purchase versus pooling of interests accounting.

This comparison makes the financial statement differences under purchase versus pooling of interests accounting easy to see. Prior to the acquisition, Gaston had a fair value of $10,000,000—the amount of cash Alphonse was willing to pay to gain control. Purchase accounting brings Gaston into the consolidated statement at its fair value of $10,000,000; under pooling of interests accounting, Gaston is shown in the consolidated statement at its net book value of $8,000,000. The $2,000,000 difference is shown in the "Difference" column in Exhibit 16.4.

Critics argue that pooling permits acquiring companies to record acquisitions at artificially low amounts. In our example Gaston is *worth* $10,000,000, and this is presumably the value that the sellers demanded. Therefore, the value of Alphonse stock that Gaston's shareholders received must have been close to $10,000,000. ***Despite this economic reality, the transaction is booked at $8,000,000 under the pooling of interests method.*** Critics charge that this understatement distorts the balance sheet as well as subsequent income statements. The income in future years is affected since fixed assets are $1,500,000 lower—the unrecorded difference between fair value and book value—under pooling than under purchase accounting, thereby lowering future depreciation expense. Similarly, since there is no goodwill under pooling, there is no goodwill amortization to reduce future earnings. Both of these effects make income under pooling higher.

By contrast, under purchase accounting, goodwill must be amortized over a period *not longer than* 40 years. Not surprisingly, most companies choose the longest allowable amortization period and write goodwill off over 40 years.

Critics further charge that the lower pooling balance sheet numbers for gross assets and equity make rate-of-return ratios appear higher. That's because, under pooling, the

Exhibit 16.4 ■ ALPHONSE AND GASTON

Purchase Versus Pooling of Interests Methods: Comparative Consolidated Balance Sheets

	Purchase Accounting	Pooling of Interests Accounting	Difference
Assets			
Current assets	$ 7,000,000	$ 7,000,000	–
Fixed assets minus accumulated depreciation	28,000,000	26,500,000	$1,500,000
Goodwill	500,000	–	500,000
	$35,500,000	$33,500,000	$2,000,000
Liabilities and Equity			
Current liabilities	$ 1,500,000	$ 1,500,000	–
Common stock	32,000,000	32,000,000	–
Capital in excess of par	2,000,000	–	$2,000,000
	$35,500,000	$33,500,000	$2,000,000

denominator of both the return-on-assets and return-on-equity ratios is lower. Some critics go so far as to suggest that these distortions are not accidental. They argue that the *cosmetic* statement effects of pooling explain its popularity among takeover-minded executives. Pooling provides an opportunity—critics contend—to buy companies and then record the acquisition on the books at artificially low numbers, thereby improving the appearance of subsequent financial statements.

Because it carries the potential for statement distortion, pooling is allowed only if certain conditions are met. These conditions, which were set out in *APB No. 16,* are listed in Exhibit 16.5.[6] The conditions are designed to preclude the use of pooling where the separate ownership groups—owners of Gaston and those of Alphonse—do not continue to

Exhibit 16.5 ■ CONDITIONS FOR POOLING OF INTERESTS METHOD

1. Each of the combining companies is autonomous and has not been a subsidiary or division of another corporation within two years before the plan of combination is initiated.
2. Each of the combining companies is independent of the other combining companies.
3. The combination is effected in a single transaction or is completed in accordance with a specific plan within one year after the plan is initiated.
4. A corporation offers and issues only common stock with rights identical to those of the majority of its outstanding voting common stock in exchange for substantially all the voting common stock interests of another company at the date the plan of combination is consummated.
5. None of the combining companies changes the equity interest of the voting common stock in contemplation of effecting the combination either within two years before the plan of combination is initiated or between the dates the combination is initiated and consummated; changes in contemplation of effecting the combination may include distributions to stockholders and additional issuances, exchanges, and retirements of securities.

[6] "Business Combinations," *APB Opinion No. 16* (New York: Accounting Principles Board [APB], 1970).

Exhibit 16.5 ■ (continued)

6. Each of the combining companies reacquires shares of voting common stock only for purposes other than business combinations, and no company reacquires more than a normal number of shares between the dates the plan of combination is initiated and consummated.
7. The ratio of the interest of an individual common stockholder to those of other common stockholders in a combining company remains the same as a result of the exchange of stock to effect the combination.
8. The voting rights to which the common stock ownership interests in the resulting combined corporation are entitled are exercisable by the stockholders; the stockholders are neither deprived of nor restricted in exercising those rights for a period.
9. The combination is resolved at the date the plan is consummated, and no provisions of the plan relating to the issue of securities or other consideration are pending.
10. The combined corporation does not agree directly or indirectly to retire or reacquire all or part of the common stock issued to effect the combination.
11. The combined corporation does not enter into other financial arrangements for the benefit of the former stockholders of a combining company, such as a guaranty of loans secured by stock issued in the combination, which in effect negates the exchange of equity securities.
12. The combined corporation does not intend or plan to dispose of a significant part of the assets of the combining companies within two years after the combination other than to dispose of assets in the ordinary course of business of the formerly separate companies and to eliminate duplicate facilities or excess capacity.

maintain ownership of the merged organization. This is easily seen in Condition 10 in Exhibit 16.5. This condition disqualifies an acquisition for pooling if there is an agreement to buy back some of the stock issued in the transaction. If this happens, Gaston shareholders who are bought out would no longer have a part ownership of the merged companies, and thus the buy back effectively makes the transaction equivalent to a cash takeover.

Financial press articles will often report the price paid in pooling transactions.

Another problem with pooling is that it is impossible to tell what exactly the buyer paid for the acquired company by merely looking at the financial statements—analysts and investors typically must seek other sources for that information—and it's difficult (if not impossible) to judge performance unless you know the price paid for the acquired company.

Figure 16.2 on the following page demonstrates that companies clearly prefer to use pooling rather than the purchase method for large deals. For deals larger than $100 million, both the dollar value (panel [a]) and the number of deals (panel [b]) was much greater for transactions accounted for as poolings rather than purchases throughout most of the 1990–2000 period. The reason that pooling is so popular for high dollar-value deals is obvious—pooling avoids the drain on the post-combination earnings that would otherwise result under purchase accounting. But as noted previously, many believe pooling artificially inflates the post-combination earnings of the combined entity and understates the asset base used to generate those earnings.

FASB Seeks to Eliminate Pooling

Concern about distortions caused by pooling prompted the FASB to issue an Exposure Draft in September 1999 proposing to eliminate pooling.[7] The Board also proposed shortening the maximum write-off period for goodwill from 40 to 20 years. These proposals

[7] "Business Combinations and Intangible Assets—Accounting for Goodwill," *FASB Exposure Draft* (Norwalk, CT: FASB, September 7, 1999).

Figure 16.2

LARGE U.S. ACQUISITIONS ACCOUNTED FOR AS PURCHASE VERSUS POOLING OF INTERESTS.

(a) Dollar value of Large U.S. Acquisitions (Deal Size > $100 million) Using Purchase Versus Pooling of Interest Accounting

(b) Number of Large U.S. Acquisitions (Deal Size > $100 Million) Using Purchase Versus Pooling of Interest Accounting

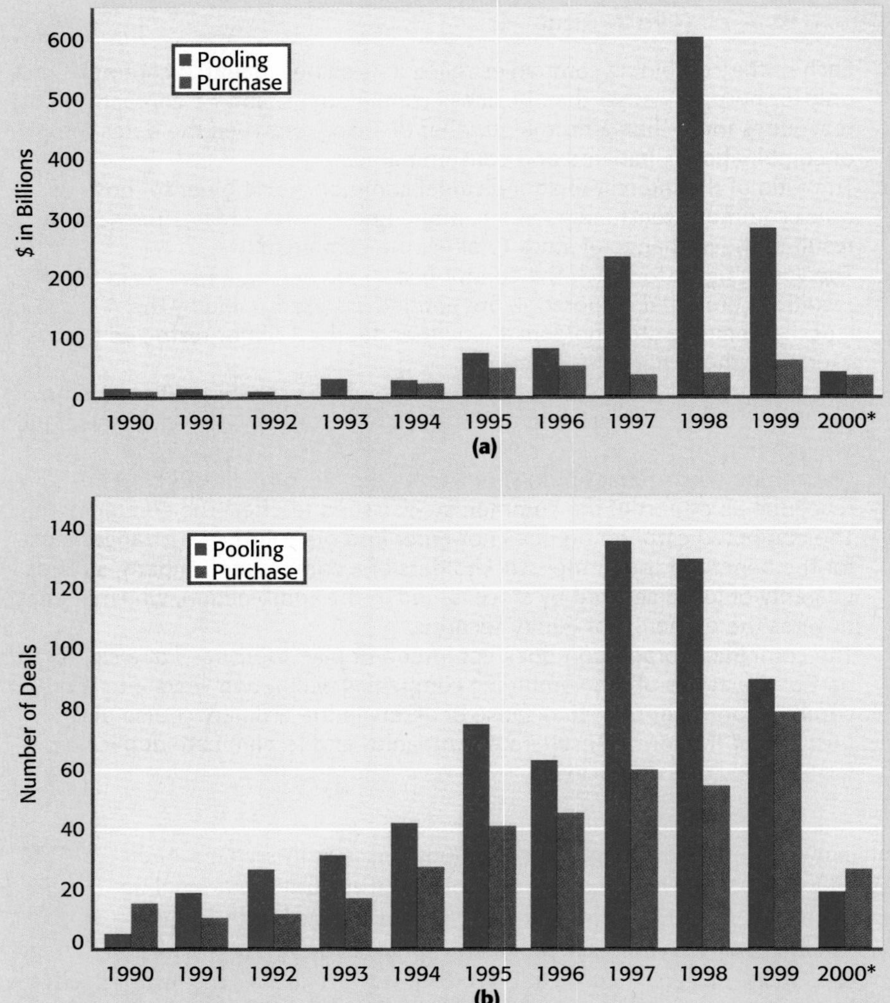

*2000 data through November 1, 2000 only
Source: Securities Data Corporation.

generated substantial resistance and intense lobbying pressure.[8] Internet and technology companies that used their inflated share values in the late 1990s to acquire smaller companies at huge premiums over book value led the resistence. These companies insist they need pooling because accounting standards fail to measure the assets that are the main value-drivers of the companies they acquire—technological savvy, employee skills, and customer loyalty.[9] If pooling were abolished, the acquired "intangibles" show up as goodwill on the consolidated statements. But many of these things continue to enhance shareholder value long after the combination is complete. Therefore, they argue, writing off these intangibles (goodwill) over an arbitrarily short period as the Board proposed, is misleading and would hinder their acquisition-oriented growth strategies.

The FASB Relents

The lobbying efforts made by the technology industries caused the Board to reconsider its position that goodwill be amortized over periods up to 20 years. In December 2000, the Board reached a tentative conclusion to require use of a **nonamortization approach** to

[8] T. Bridis, "Congress Is Seeking Delay in Change on Merger Rules," the *Wall Street Journal* (October 4, 2000).
[9] M. McNamee, "What Could Burst the Net's Bubble," *Business Week* (March 1, 1999), p. 98.

account for purchased goodwill.[10] Under the nonamortization approach, goodwill would be reviewed for impairment annually. It would be written down and expensed against earnings only when the recorded value exceeds its fair value (see Chapter 10 for further discussion of impairment criteria). In 2001, the Board will redeliberate the related issue of whether pooling accounting will be retained. As this book goes to press, no final pronouncement has been issued.

It seems likely that the pooling method of accounting for business combinations will be prohibited by the FASB in the near future. It also appears that accounting for past poolings will not be retroactively altered. Furthermore, the nonamortization approach for goodwill is likely to be approved by the Board.[11]

Disclosures Subsequent to a Business Combination

Although pooling of interests is preferred by U.S. companies for *large* business combinations, the overwhelming majority of all business combinations are accounted for as purchases. The American Institute of Certified Public Accountants (AICPA) publishes an annual survey of accounting practices that are followed by U.S. companies, based on a sample of 600 company annual reports. Table 16.1 summarizes the number of business combinations as well as the accounting method used over the 1990–1999 period for companies included in the survey. ***Roughly 90% of all business combinations use purchase accounting.***

ANALYSIS

The disclosure rules for business combinations accounted for as purchases complicate financial analysis. Trend analysis becomes difficult because comparative financial statements are not retroactively adjusted to include data for the acquired company for periods prior to the acquisition. To illustrate, study Exhibit 16.6(a) on the next page, which presents comparative income statements from ShopKo Stores' 1999 annual report. On July 6, 1999, ShopKo acquired Pamida Holdings Corporation, a discount retailer, in an acquisition accounted for as a purchase. Accordingly, ShopKo's 1999 consolidated income statement numbers include the revenues and expenses of Pamida from the acquisition date (July 6) through January 29, 2000, ShopKo's fiscal year end. However, under the rules for purchase accounting,[12] the 1998 numbers (fiscal year ended January 30, 1999) presented in ShopKo's 1999 comparative income statement do not include any of Pamida's results for that fiscal year. But Pamida's *full-year* revenues and expenses will be included in ShopKo's 2000 consolidated income statement numbers (not yet published when we went to press). ***Thus, the income statements over the three years are noncomparable—ShopKo's 2000 statements include Pamida's results for 12 months, 1999 statements reflect Pamida's performance for seven months, and 1998 statements exclude Pamida's results entirely!***

To aid inter-period comparisons, existing disclosure rules require a **pro forma**—meaning *as if*—footnote like the one ShopKo provided in its 1999 annual report, as shown in Exhibit 16.6(b). The footnote gives information for key income statement items *as if* the acquisition had taken place on the first day of the earliest year for which

Table 16.1 ■ BUSINESS COMBINATIONS IN SURVEY OF 600 COMPANIES

	1999	1998	1997	1996	1995	1994	1993	1992	1991	1990
Total number of combinations	397	344	316	288	276	234	221	199	176	200
Number using purchase accounting	343	317	278	256	244	215	200	182	160	190
Percentage of total	86.4	92.2	88.0	88.9	88.4	91.9	90.5	91.5	90.9	95.0

Sources: A. Mrakovcic, ed. *Accounting Trends and Techniques* (New York: AICPA, 2000); G. Yarnell and R. Rikert, eds. *Accounting Trends and Techniques* (New York: AICPA, 1997, 1993).

[10] "FASB Reaches Tentative Decision on Accounting for Purchased Goodwill," *News Release* (Norwalk, CT: FASB, December 6, 2000).

[11] "Business Combinations: Project Summary," (Norwalk, CT: FASB, April 5, 2001).

[12] *APB Opinion 16*, op. cit.

Exhibit 16.6 ■ SHOPKO STORES, INC. AND SUBSIDIARIES

Disclosures Subsequent to a Business Combination: Purchase Accounting

Consolidated Statement of Earnings ($ in thousands)	**Fiscal Years Ended** January 29 2000	January 30 1999
Revenues:		
Net sales	$3,898,090	$2,958,557
Licensed department rentals and other income	13,856	12,325
	3,911,946	2,970,882
Costs and Expenses:		
Cost of sales	3,047,930	2,296,085
Selling, general and administrative expenses	601,157	471,546
Special charges	8,068	5,723
Depreciation and amortization expenses	84,438	67,590
	3,741,593	2,840,944
Income from operations	170,353	129,938
Interest expense—net	(46,894)	(38,311)
Gain on sale of ProVantage stock	56,760	—
Earnings before income taxes, minority interest and extraordinary item	180,219	91,627
Provision for income taxes	71,800	35,991
Earnings before minority interest and extraordinary item	108,419	55,636
Minority interest	(2,463)	—
Earnings before extraordinary item	105,956	55,636
Extraordinary (loss) on retirement of debt, net of income taxes of $2,443	(3,776)	—
Net earnings	$ 102,180	$ 55,636

(a)

Excerpts from Annual Report Footnote

On July 6, 1999, the Company acquired all of the outstanding voting and nonvoting common stock of Pamida for $94.0 million in cash, $285.8 million in assumed debt and $138.6 million in assumed trade and other accrued liabilities. Pamida is a retail chain headquartered in Omaha, Nebraska, operating Pamida retail stores in 15 Midwest, North Central and Rocky Mountain states. In connection with the Pamida acquisition, the Company incurred special charges of $8.1 million for employee retention programs, elimination of administrative functions and various integration initiatives. The allocation of the purchase price of Pamida was based on estimated fair values at the date of acquisition.

This acquisition was accounted for under the purchase method of accounting and the allocation of the purchase price was based on fair values at the date of acquisition. Goodwill associated with the Pamida acquisition of approximately $186.6 million is being amortized on a straight-line basis over 40 years. The results of operations since the dates of acquisition have been included in the consolidated statements of earnings.

The following presents selected unaudited pro forma consolidated statement of earnings information that has been prepared assuming the Pamida acquisition occurred on January 31, 1999 and February 1, 1998, respectively:

($ in thousands, except per share data—unaudited)	**Fiscal Years Ended** January 29 2000	January 30 1999
Net sales	$4,181,567	$3,630,951
Earnings before extraordinary item	101,190	56,678
Diluted earnings per share before extraordinary item	3.54	2.14

(b)

Source: ShopKo 1999 Annual Report.

comparative data are shown—in this case February 1, 1998. Therefore, these pro-forma numbers reflect full-year results for Pamida both in 1998 and 1999. Notice, however, that these pro forma data do *not* encompass all income statement items and do not include periods prior to 1998. Consequently, even with the supplemental disclosure, it is usually not possible for analysts to make comparisons of *complete* income statements adjusted for the acquisition. This is a serious deficiency that destroys the comparability of time-series financial statement data used by lenders and other financial analysts. Indeed, if the acquired company is large in relation to the size of the acquirer, serious distortions can exist in trends and other comparative data derived from the consolidated financial statements.

To illustrate the problem of trying to perform time-series comparisons for a business combination accounted for as a purchase, we concentrate on the net sales disclosures in Exhibit 16.6(a). The two-year sales data from ShopKo's consolidated statement of income, along with a computation of year-to-year sales growth from 1998 to 1999 are:

($ in thousands)	1999	1998
Net sales as reported in consolidated financial statements	$3,898,090	$2,958,557
Rate of growth in sales compared to prior year	31.8%	–

The computed sales growth rate of 31.8% is misleading because the basic sales data—and all other items in the income statement—are noncomparable between 1999 and 1998 fiscal years. The reason is that ShopKo's 1999 data include Pamida's results for seven months, while the 1998 data exclude it altogether. To perform a valid comparison of sales growth, the 1999 and 1998 sales numbers must be restated "as if" the combination had occurred at the start of the 1998 fiscal year. These pro-forma numbers are reported in Exhibit 16.6(b) and reproduced below:

($ in thousands)	1999	1998
Net sales from consolidated statements	$3,898,090	$2,958,557
Net sales from pro-forma disclosure	4,181,567	3,630,951
Rate of growth in sales compared to prior year (pro-forma disclosure)	15.2%	–

The actual rate of growth in sales assuming the combination occurred at the beginning of the 1998 fiscal year—15.2%—is *less than half* the rate computed from the sales numbers in the financial statements—31.8%. Also notice from Exhibit 16.6(b) how the sparseness of pro-forma disclosures makes it possible to perform valid comparisons for only two other income statement lines besides sales: earnings before extraordinary items and diluted earnings per share before extraordinary items. The only way to overcome this problem is to gather past financial statement data for Pamida and consolidate its past results with those of ShopKo (using appropriate assumptions about intercompany sales and loans, of course). It's easy to obtain these data when the acquired company is publicly held. However, if the acquired company is not publicly held, these data may be difficult or even impossible to obtain.

When a business combination is accounted for as a pooling of interests, this comparability problem does not arise. That's because all past financial statement data are retroactively consolidated to include both parties to the combination. Keep in mind, however, that while the pooling of interests approach overcomes problems of comparability, the reported financial data are still fraught with the deficiencies that come with pooling of interests accounting.

Pooling permits companies to record business acquisitions at artificially low amounts—at book value rather than at fair market value. This makes rate-of-return ratios and other financial performance measures appear higher than they should. That's why pooling is allowed only when certain conditions are met. Purchase accounting avoids this distortion by recording business acquisitions at fair market value. However, time-series comparisons are difficult because purchase acquisitions produce a "blip" in the reported financial data.

RECAP

Foreign Subsidiaries

All majority-owned subsidiaries—foreign and domestic—must be consolidated using the methods we've just described. Regrettably, there's an additional complication when consolidating foreign subsidiaries—that is, the financial records of the subsidiary will be expressed in foreign currency units. The subsidiary's numbers must first be *transformed* into the parent's currency units—into dollars, if it's a U.S. parent—before the consolidation process begins.

The transformation under U.S. GAAP (*SFAS No. 52*) specifies one of two procedures, depending on the operating characteristics of the foreign subsidiary:[13]

1. Foreign subsidiaries that are mere extensions of the parent with no self-sufficiency are **remeasured** using the **temporal method.** For example, in the case of a European sales subsidiary of a U.S. seed company, the subsidiary sells seed produced by the U.S. parent to European farmers and sends the cash proceeds back to the U.S.
2. Foreign subsidiaries that are essentially free-standing units with self-contained foreign operations are **translated** using the **current rate method.** For example, in the case of a European manufacturing and sales subsidiary of a U.S. computer company, the subsidiary buys parts in Europe, assembles the final product, and sells it to European businesses, retaining the cash proceeds for growth and expansion.

The procedure selected to transform subsidiary statements expressed in foreign currency units into the parent's currency units is called the **functional currency choice.** What guides this choice is subtle;[14] foreign subsidiaries whose operations are not self-sufficient are considered to be engaging in a continuing series of **foreign currency transactions.** The consolidation process accordingly treats the financial results of these subsidiaries in the same way foreign currency transactions are treated. To illustrate, we must digress briefly to explain the accounting for foreign currency transactions.

Foreign Currency Transactions

Foreign currency transactions are simply business transactions denominated in units of a foreign currency. Examples include a U.S. company taking out a bank loan denominated in Norwegian kroner or purchasing inventory on credit for a price expressed in Dutch guilder. The accounting for foreign currency transactions depends on the type of asset acquired or liability incurred. Let's consider a foreign currency transaction that involves the acquisition of a **monetary asset**—that is, an asset like cash or accounts receivable whose value is derived from the number of monetary units into which it is convertible.

Assume that on January 1, 2001 Yankee Corporation (a U.S. company) sells 100 units of its product to a U.K. customer. The selling price is £10 per unit, or £1,000 total. Payment is

[13] "Foreign Currency Translation," *SFAS No. 52* (Stamford, CT: FASB, 1981). Although our discussion centers on *consolidation* of a foreign subsidiary, the rules described here must also be used in conjunction with the *equity method* when the parent owns between 20% and 50% of a foreign company.

[14] See L. Revsine, "The Rationale Underlying the Functional Currency Choice," *The Accounting Review* (July 1984), pp. 504–14.

due on April 1, 2001. On January 1, 2001 let's say that one British pound is worth $2 U.S., and that the per-unit cost of production incurred by Yankee is $8.00. Given this information, we would record the foreign currency transaction on Yankee's books in this way:

DR Accounts receivable	$2,000	
CR Sales revenue		$2,000
(To record the receivable of £1,000 at its 1/1/01 U.S. dollar equivalent of $2,000.)		

DR Cost of goods sold	$800	
CR Inventory		$800

The receivable is denominated in pounds—which is what makes this a foreign currency transaction. Since Yankee keeps its books in dollars, the receivable must be reexpressed in home-currency units when preparing financial statements. This is done using the exchange rate in effect at the transaction date—£1 = $2 U.S. It is important to understand that while the receivable is initially reflected on the books at $2,000, in reality what's owed by the customer is £1,000.

By the end of the quarter, the pound has fallen relative to the dollar, so that on March 31, 2001 the exchange rate is £1 = $1.80 U.S. This means that at current exchange rates the receivable is worth only $1,800, and so Yankee would book the following entry when preparing its quarterly statements:

DR Foreign currency transaction loss	$200	
CR Accounts receivable		$200
(To reflect the £1,000 receivable at its end-of-quarter dollar equivalent of $1,800.)		

Yankee has a loss because it was owed pounds but the pound has fallen in value. This loss is reflected in the income statement of the period in which the loss occurs. Monetary assets (like accounts receivable) that arise from foreign currency transactions are shown in the financial statements at their dollar equivalent using ***the exchange rate in effect at the financial statement date.*** Monetary liabilities (like accounts or bonds payable) are similarly translated using the exchange rate in effect at the statement date. The statement date exchange rate is referred to as the **current rate.**

Most liabilities are monetary since they are expressed in units of currency (e.g., a Japanese yen account payable of ¥9,000,000) and will be settled using foreign currency monetary assets. However, there are a few liabilities that are settled by using *nonmonetary* assets; this small class of liabilities is considered to be nonmonetary. Examples include estimated product warranty liabilities and customer deposits for products to be produced and delivered in future periods.

Suppose the exchange rate on April 1, 2001, when the receivable is paid, is still £1 = $1.80 U.S. The customer remits £1,000, which Yankee then converts into dollars. The entry on Yankee's books is:

DR Cash	$1,800	
CR Accounts receivable		$1,800
(To remove the receivable from the books. The initial $2,000 minus the 3/31/01 write-down of $200 equals the carrying amount of $1,800.)		

We next illustrate the accounting for a foreign currency transaction that involves a nonmonetary asset. Nonmonetary assets are items like inventory, equipment, land, buildings, and trucks whose value is determined by supply and demand.

Suppose Yankee—because of its growing volume of sales to U.K. customers—decides to purchase a warehouse in London to store inventory awaiting shipment to customers. A building is purchased on June 30, 2001 for £300,000; on that date the exchange rate is £1 = $1.75 U.S. The building is recorded on Yankee's books at the U.S. dollar equivalent of the foreign currency transaction price at the purchase date:

DR Warehouse building	$525,000	
CR Cash		$525,000

(To record the acquisition of the London warehouse at the U.S. dollar equivalent of the foreign currency transaction price: £300,000 × 1.75 = $525,000.)

The subsequent accounting for nonmonetary assets acquired in a foreign currency transaction is identical to the accounting for nonmonetary assets acquired in the domestic currency. Specifically, the historical cost of the fixed asset in dollars is used as the measurement basis in subsequent financial statements throughout the asset's life. Even if the value of the pound falls to £1 = $1.60 U.S. by year-end 2001, the London warehouse would still be shown on Yankee's books at $525,000—that is, at its acquisition cost in dollars (minus depreciation, of course). Thus, to reflect the gross carrying amount of nonmonetary assets acquired in a foreign currency transaction, Yankee would use the exchange rate in effect at the time of the transaction. This rate is called the **historical exchange rate.**

The accounting for assets and liabilities arising from foreign currency transactions depends on the nature of the item—that is,

1. **Foreign currency monetary assets and liabilities are remeasured using the current rate of exchange in effect at the balance sheet date.**
2. **Foreign currency nonmonetary assets (and liabilities) are remeasured using the historical rate of exchange that was in effect at the time the item was acquired or incurred.**

RECAP

Accounting for Non–Free-Standing Subsidiaries

Now that we've outlined the accounting for foreign currency transactions, we can return to our main theme—that is, accounting for foreign subsidiaries. In introducing this topic, we said the method used to transform the foreign currency accounts of foreign subsidiaries depends on the nature of the subsidiary. Subsidiaries that are not free-standing—that is, subsidiaries whose operations are simply an extension of the parent—are remeasured using the temporal method. We now explain why.

To see what it means when we say a foreign subsidiary is not free-standing, let us consider a U.S. company, Doodle Corporation, with a U.K. subsidiary called Dandy Ltd. The role of Dandy is to serve as the U.K. marketing arm of Doodle. Doodle manufactures a product in the United States using U.S. sourced materials and labor. Some of the production is shipped from the United States to the United Kingdom where it is sold to U.K. customers at a price denominated in pounds sterling. The distribution of the product and collection of the receivables are coordinated by two U.K. employees of Dandy Ltd. Upon collection of the receivables, the pounds are remitted to the United States. This cycle is repeated as the pounds are converted into dollars, the dollars are used in the United States to manufacture more inventory, and some portion of the inventory is again shipped to the United Kingdom for sale to customers there. Dandy's only U.K. assets are (1) a small amount of cash to pay expenses, (2) inventory from Doodle that has not yet been shipped to customers, and (3) a building that serves as both a warehouse and an office for the two employees.

The situation described here is a classic illustration of a foreign subsidiary that is merely an extension of the parent. Dandy Ltd. is a marketing arm of Doodle rather than a viable, free-standing company. It is a conduit for administering foreign sales, and it has no independent life of its own.

Under *SFAS No. 52,* subsidiaries like Dandy Ltd. are treated as if they were created for the sole purpose of facilitating foreign currency transactions. Because such subsidiaries are a conduit for foreign transactions, upon consolidation they are treated as if the parent company had engaged in the foreign transactions directly. That is, ***the numbers included when consolidating a non–free-standing subsidiary are identical to the numbers that would have been included had the subsidiary not existed and instead the parent had engaged in the foreign currency transactions directly.***

To achieve this effect in the financial statements, the temporal method is used to translate the subsidiary's foreign currency statements into dollars.[15] The exchange rates for translating various accounts under the temporal method are shown in Table 16.2.

Table 16.2 ■ TRANSLATION EXCHANGE RATES UNDER THE TEMPORAL METHOD

Account Category	Rate Used
Balance Sheet	
Monetary assets and liabilities	Current rate
Nonmonetary assets and liabilities	Historical rate
Income Statement	
All revenue and expense accounts except those listed below	Rate at time of transaction
Cost of goods sold and depreciation	Historical rate

To illustrate the temporal method, consider the following transactions for Dandy Ltd. during 2001:

1. On January 1, 2001 it received inventory costing $800 from Doodle when 1£ = $2 U.S, and sold these goods on credit for £1,000.
2. The pound falls to 1£ = $1.80 U.S. on March 31, 2001. Receivables of £1,000 were collected on April 1, 2001, when 1£ = $1.80 U.S.
3. The company purchased a building in London for £300,000 on June 30, 2001 when 1£ = $1.75 U.S.

These transactions are identical to the foreign currency transactions entered into by Yankee Corporation earlier in this section. In Table 16.3 on the next page we show the result of using the temporal method to translate Dandy Ltd.'s statements. The results under GAAP for Yankee's foreign currency transactions is displayed in the shaded column for comparison.

Comparing the Dandy statement numbers with those of Yankee in Table 16.3 demonstrates the point of the example. Using the temporal method results in Dandy statements whose dollar figures are equal to those of Yankee. This is no coincidence. ***Both Dandy and Yankee are considered to have engaged in identical foreign currency transactions, so the two sets of results should be equal.*** Notice how the translation rules under the temporal method help achieve this result.

---

[15] *SFAS No. 52* uses the term **remeasure** when describing the conversion from foreign currency units to home currency units under the temporal method. For simplicity, we ignore this nuance and refer to the process as translation.

Table 16.3 ■ COMPARISON OF TEMPORAL METHOD RESULTS WITH ACCOUNTING FOR FOREIGN CURRENCY TRANSACTIONS

	Temporal Method Translation			Foreign Currency Transactions
	Dandy Ltd. in £s	Exchange Rate	Dandy Ltd in $s	Yankee Corporation
Income Statement				
Sales	£ 1,000	1£ = $2	$ 2,000	$ 2,000
Cost of sales	400	1£ = $2	800	800
Gross margin	£ 600		$ 1,200	$ 1,200
Loss on receivables*	—		200	200
Gross income	£ 600		$ 1,000	$ 1,000
Selected Balance Sheet Accounts				
At 3/31/01				
Account receivable	£ 1,000	1£ = $1.80	$ 1,800	$ 1,800
At 4/1/01				
Cash	£ 1,000	1£ = $1.80	$ 1,800	$ 1,800
At 6/30/01				
Building	£300,000	1£ = $1.75	$525,000	$525,000

* Computed as:

Monetary asset on acquisition,	£1,000 when 1£ = $2.00 =	$2,000
Monetary asset at March 31, 2001,	£1,000 when 1£ = $1.80 =	1,800
Loss on receivables		$ 200

Accounting for Self-Contained Foreign Subsidiaries

When the majority-owned foreign subsidiary and its parent operate independently, the translation of the subsidiary's financial statements into dollars uses the current rate method. To understand why, let us consider a self-contained subsidiary whose operations do not rely extensively on the parent.

A U.S. food company has a Swiss subsidiary that was formed by a capital infusion from the U.S. parent. Once the equity cushion was in place, the remainder of the Swiss subsidiary's long-term capital was raised using Swiss franc borrowing. The subsidiary engages in no transactions with the parent. Operations are entirely contained in Switzerland, where the company hires employees, buys inventory, manufactures its product line, and sells to Swiss and other European customers. Operating profits are plowed back into the Swiss operation to expand into new product lines and to increase production capacity. While the parent may periodically receive dividends from the subsidiary, its investment will remain until the subsidiary is either sold or liquidated.

For self-contained foreign subsidiaries, the effect of exchange rate changes on future dollar cash flows is uncertain. Consider a rise in the Swiss franc. One possible effect of the rise is that it will make the subsidiary's products more expensive to foreign purchasers and could adversely affect profits. But, the rise in the Swiss franc also means that input purchases in other currencies are cheaper, so a favorable profit effect could ensue. The possibilities are many and depend on the individual characteristics of the subsidiary and on the characteristics of the markets in which it operates. These include:

1. Does the subsidiary price its product sales in countries outside Switzerland in Swiss francs or in units of the foreign currencies?
2. Does the subsidiary adjust its Swiss franc selling price when the value of the franc rises or falls?
3. What proportion of the product input is purchased locally in Switzerland in francs?
4. Does the Swiss franc borrowing have a floating rate of interest which would be sensitive to exchange rate changes?

These are only a few of the many possibilities that could influence the magnitude and direction of the effect of the exchange rate change on ultimate dollar cash flows from the subsidiary. ***Because the ultimate exchange rate effects on U.S. dollar cash flows are uncertain, the FASB decided that such subsidiaries should be translated using the current rate method and that any debit or credit arising from translation "gains" or "losses" should be put directly into an owners' equity account and not run through the income statement.*** Under the current rate method, *all* balance sheet accounts are translated at the current exchange rate in effect at the balance sheet date and *all* income statement accounts are translated at the weighted average rate of exchange that was in effect over the period covered by the statement.

This is another example of an element of **comprehensive income** discussed in Chapter 2.

If *all* accounts in a statement are translated at the *same* rate—which is what happens under the current rate method—then the translated statements have the same proportionality as the untranslated statements expressed in foreign currency units. In other words, the quick ratio of the Swiss subsidiary derived from its pretranslated Swiss franc statements will be identical to the quick ratio once the statements are translated into dollars using the current rate method. The current rate method provides a practical way to get from foreign currency units to dollars while still maintaining or very closely approximating the subsidiary's financial ratios. ***Furthermore, by denying income statement recognition to the balancing debit or credit that arises from translation, the uncertain ultimate effect of exchange rate changes is explicitly carried forward.*** Figure 16.3 is a diagram of the *SFAS No. 52* translation approach.

Ratio proportionality between foreign currency and translated dollar numbers is maintained *precisely* for any ratio for which the numerator and denominator are confined to a single statement. Examples include the current ratio—both balance sheet accounts—and gross margin ratio—both income statement accounts. This is true because the current rate method translates all accounts within a single statement at the same rate—weighted average rate for income statement items and end-of-year rate for balance sheet items. For ratios that use numbers from both statements—e.g., rate of return on assets—the current rate method does not maintain perfect proportionality. However, the difference between the "mixed-statement ratio" expressed in foreign currency and the translated ratio expressed in U.S. dollars is usually very small.

The figure shows that *SFAS No. 52* requires firms to categorize their foreign subsidiaries into

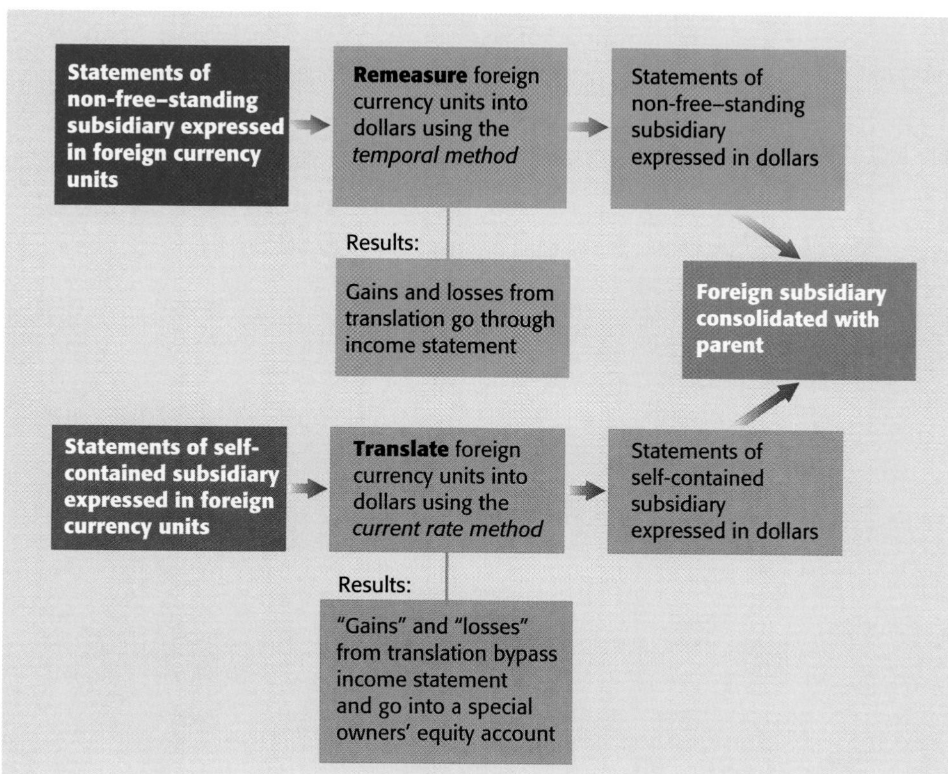

Figure 16.3

TRANSLATION APPROACH USED IN *SFAS NO. 52*

Exhibit 16.7 ■ PFIZER, INC.

Excerpts from 1999 Annual Report

For most international operations, local currencies are considered their functional currencies. We translate assets and liabilities to their U.S. dollar equivalents at rates in effect at the balance sheet date and record translation adjustments in Shareholders' Equity. We translate Statement of Income accounts at average rates for the period. Transaction adjustments are recorded in Other Deductions—Net.

For operations in highly inflationary economies, we translate the balance sheet items as follows:

- Monetary items (that is, assets and liabilities that will be settled for cash) at rates in effect at the balance sheet date, with translation adjustments recorded in Other Deductions—Net
- Non-monetary items at historical rates (that is, those rates in effect when the items were first recorded).

(a)

Consolidated Statement of Shareholders' Equity

Year Ended December 31	Common Stock		Additional Paid-In	Employee Benefit Trusts		Treasury Stock		Retained	Accum. Other Comprehensive	
($ in millions)	Shares	Par Value	Capital	Shares	Fair Value	Shares	Cost	Earnings	Income/(Exp.)	Total
Balance December 31, 1997	4,165	$207	$3,101	(107)	($2,646)	(283)	($1,993)	$ 9,349	($ 85)	$7,933
Comprehensive income:										
Net income								3,351		3,351
Other comprehensive expense—net of tax										
Currency translation adjustment									(74)	(74)
Net unrealized loss on available-for-sale securities									(2)	(2)
Minimum pension liability									(73)	(73)
Total Other Comprehensive Expense									(149)	(149)
Total comprehensive income										3,202
Cash dividends declared								(1,261)		(1,261)
Stock options transaction	55	3	745			—	(18)			730
Purchases of common stock						(58)	(1,912)			(1,912)
Employee benefit trusts transactions—net			1,633	5	(1,554)	2	12			91
Other	2	–	27							27
Balance December 31, 1998	4,222	$210	$5,506	(102)	($4,200)	(339)	($3,911)	$11,439	($234)	$8,810
Comprehensive income:										
Net income								3,179		3,179
Other comprehensive expense—net of tax										
Currency translation adjustment									(222)	(222)
Net unrealized gain on available-for-sale securities									81	81
Minimum pension liability									(24)	(24)
Total Other Comprehensive Expense									(165)	(165)
Total comprehensive income										3,014
Cash dividends declared								(1,222)		(1,222)
Stock options transactions	35	3	526			—	(16)			513
Purchases of common stock						(66)	(2,500)			(2,500)
Employee benefit trusts transactions—net			(735)	13	1,312	(8)	(424)			153
Other	3	–	119							119
Balance December 31, 1999	4,260	$213	$5,416	(89)	($2,888)	(413)	($6,851)	$13,396	($399)	$8,887

(b)

one of two groups: (1) *nonfree-standing subsidiaries,* whose activities are so closely integrated with the parent that they are considered to be engaging in foreign currency transactions on behalf of the parent; or (2) *self-contained subsidiaries* with an independent or virtually independent operating existence of their own. For subsidiaries in the first group, exchange rate movements have an immediately determinable effect on dollar cash flows; for this reason, translation gains or losses are run through the income statement. By contrast, subsidiaries in the second group are put into an income "holding pattern," because exchange rate movements have an indeterminate impact on the parent's ultimate dollar cash flows. Consequently, a *neutral* translation mechanism—the current rate method—is used for these subsidiaries, and the resulting equity debits or credits are simply treated as balancing items rather than as elements of income.

Illustrative Disclosure Exhibit 16.7 on the previous page contains excerpts from the Pfizer Inc. 1999 Annual Report. Exhibit 16.7(a) shows a portion of the footnote disclosure regarding foreign subsidiaries. Most of Pfizer's foreign subsidiaries are translated using the current rate method, which means that translation adjustments go to a currency translation adjustment account in the "Shareholders' equity" section of the balance sheet. This section is reproduced in Exhibit 16.7(b).

Note that the highlighted currency translation adjustment loss is shown as part of Comprehensive income in the "Shareholders' equity" section of the balance sheet in Exhibit 16.7(b). Here we learn that the translation adjustment loss was $222 million (net of tax) in 1999, compared to a $74 million loss in 1998. Several factors may have contributed to this decline—falling exchange rates, operating losses at foreign subsidiaries, or a real reduction in the company's net foreign investment. Analysts would have to dig deeper to understand exactly why the translation losses increased and what it means.

SUMMARY

Financial reporting for intercorporate equity investments depends on the size of the parent's ownership share. Proportionate share size is used to infer the purpose of the investment.

When the ownership share is less than 20%, it is presumed that the investor cannot exert influence on the decisions of the investee. These *minority passive investments* are shown at market value on the balance sheet. Unrealized gains or losses on the *trading portfolio* go through the income statement, while all others go to a special owners' equity account via comprehensive income. *Minority active investments* involve between 20% and 50% ownership. Investment at this level presumably conveys both permanency and the ability to influence decisions—and thus, the equity method is used. Full consolidation is required when ownership exceeds 50%. Business acquisitions arising from a cash buyout use purchase accounting, while those accomplished by a stock-for-stock exchange use the pooling of interests method. Accounting goodwill is recorded under the purchase method but not the pooling method. That's because with pooling, book values—not fair market values—form the basis for the consolidated statements.

Majority-owned foreign subsidiaries also need to be consolidated. Doing so requires that foreign currency amounts be re-expressed in dollars. Foreign subsidiaries that are mere extensions of the U.S. parent and have no self-sufficiency are remeasured using the *temporal method.* The temporal method treats the subsidiaries' business transactions as if they had been undertaken by the parent—but in the foreign currency. Foreign subsidiaries that are free-standing economic units are remeasured using the *current rate method.* This method provides an easy way to re-express foreign currency amounts in dollars while still maintaining the subsidiary's financial ratios.

EXERCISES

E16–1

Mark-to-market for trading and available-for-sale securities

AICPA adapted

The following data pertain to Tyne Company's investments in marketable equity securities. (Assume all securities were held throughout 2001 and 2002.)

	Cost	Market Value 12/31/02	Market Value 12/31/01
Trading	$150,000	$155,000	$100,000
Available for sale	150,000	130,000	120,000

(continued)

REQUIRED:

1. What amount should Tyne report as unrealized holding gain (loss) in its 2002 income statement?
2. What amount should Tyne report as net unrealized gain (loss) on available-for-sale securities at December 31, 2002 in its statement of stockholders' equity? Ignore tax effects.

E16–2
Mark-to-market for available-for-sale securities
AICPA adapted

During 2001 Rex Company purchased marketable equity securities as a short-term investment. These securities are classified as available-for-sale. The cost and market values at December 31, 2001 were as follows:

Security	Cost	Market Value
Company A– 100 shares	$ 2,800	$ 3,400
Company B–1,000 shares	17,000	15,300
Company C–2,000 shares	31,500	29,500
	$51,300	$48,200

Rex sold 1,000 shares of Company B stock on January 31, 2002 for $15 per share, incurring $1,500 in brokerage commission and taxes.

REQUIRED:

1. Ignoring taxes, how much should Rex report as unrealized gain or loss on its available-for-sale securities at December 31, 2001 in the statement of stockholders' equity?
2. On the sale, Rex should report a realized loss of how much?

E16–3
Mark-to-market for trading securities

Information related to Jones Company's portfolio of trading securities for December 31, 2002 is provided next:

Aggregate cost of securities	$340,000
Gross unrealized gains	8,000
Gross unrealized losses	52,000

Jones reported a $10,000 credit balance in its "Market adjustment—Trading securities" account in its December 31, 2001 (prior year) balance sheet. Assume no trading securities were sold during 2001 or 2002.

REQUIRED:

1. How much should Jones report as unrealized gain or loss on its 2002 income statement?
2. Give the journal entry that Jones would make to record the mark-to-market adjustment to its trading portfolio.

E16–4
Equity method
AICPA adapted

In January 2001 the Harold Corporation acquired 20% of the outstanding common stock of Otis Company for $400,000. This investment gave Harold the ability to exercise significant influence over Otis. The book value of these shares was $300,000. The excess of cost over book value was attributed to an identifiable intangible asset which was undervalued on Otis' balance sheet and which had a remaining useful life of 10 years.

For the year ended December 31, 2001 Otis reported net income of $90,000 and paid cash dividends of $20,000 on its common stock.

REQUIRED:

1. How much would Harold Corporation's income increase in 2001 as a result of its investment in Otis?
2. What is the carrying value of Harold's investment in Otis Company at December 31, 2001?

E16–5
Equity method
AICPA adapted

Sage, Inc. bought 40% of Adams Corporation's outstanding common stock on January 2, 2001 for $400,000. The carrying amount of Adams' net assets at the purchase date totaled $900,000. Fair values and carrying amounts were the same for all items except for plant and inventory, for which fair values exceeded the carrying amounts by $90,000 and $10,000, respectively. The plant has an 18-year life. All inventory was sold during 2001. Goodwill, if any, is to be amortized over 40 years. During 2001 Adams reported net income of $120,000 and paid a $20,000 cash dividend.

REQUIRED:

1. What amount should Sage report in its income statement from its investment in Adams for the year ended December 31, 2001?
2. What would be the December 31, 2001 balance in the "Investment in Adams" account?

E16–6

Equity versus cost method for long-term investments
CMA adapted

On January 1, 2001 Boggs, Inc. paid $700,000 for 100,000 shares of Mattly Corporation, which represented 30% of Mattly's outstanding common stock. The following computation was made by Boggs:

Purchase price	$700,000
30% equity in book value of Mattly's net assets	500,000
Excess of cost over book value	$200,000

The excess cost over book value was attributed to goodwill and will be amortized over 20 years. Mattly reported net income for the year ended December 31, 2001 of $300,000. Mattly Corporation paid cash dividends of $100,000 on July 1, 2001.

REQUIRED:

1. If Boggs, Inc. exercised significant influence over Mattly Corporation and properly accounted for the long-term investment under the equity method, the amount of net investment revenue Boggs should report from its investment in Mattly would be how much?
2. If Boggs, Inc. did not exercise significant influence over Mattly Corporation and properly accounted for the long-term investment under the cost method, the amount of net investment revenue Boggs should report from its investment in Mattly would be how much?

E16–7

Goodwill—purchase method
AICPA adapted

On April 1, 2001 Dart Company paid $620,000 for all the issued and outstanding common stock of Wall Corporation in a transaction properly accounted for as a purchase. The recorded assets and liabilities of Wall Corporation on April 1, 2001 follow:

Cash	$ 60,000
Inventory	180,000
Property and equipment (net of accumulated depreciation of $220,000)	320,000
Goodwill (net of accumulated amortization of $50,000)	100,000
Liabilities	(120,000)
Net assets	$540,000

On April 1, 2001 Wall's inventory had a fair value of $150,000, and its property and equipment (net) had a fair value of $380,000.

REQUIRED:

What is the amount of goodwill resulting from the business combination?

E16–8

Consolidated financial statements
AICPA adapted

On January 1, 2001 Pitt Company purchased an 80% investment in Saxe Company. The acquisition cost was equal to Pitt's equity in Saxe's net assets at that date. On January 1, 2001 Pitt and Saxe had retained earnings of $500,000 and $100,000, respectively. During 2001 (1) Pitt had net income of $200,000, which included its equity in Saxe's earnings, and declared dividends of $50,000; (2) Saxe had net income of $40,000 and declared dividends of $20,000; and (3) there were no other intercompany transactions between the parent and subsidiary.

REQUIRED:

What should the consolidated retained earnings be on December 31, 2001?

E16–9

Consolidated balance sheet

CMA adapted

Immediately after the purchase of 60% ownership of the Island Company by the Sea Company, the separate condensed balance sheets of the two companies are as follows:

	Sea Company	Island Company
Other assets	$750,000	$320,000
Investment in Island Company	187,500	—
	$937,500	$320,000
Liabilities	$250,000	$ 70,000
Common stock	450,000	200,000
Retained earnings	237,500	50,000
	$937,500	$320,000

REQUIRED:

What would be the dollar amount of the total assets in the consolidated balance sheet immediately after the acquisition?

E16–10

Transaction foreign exchange gain/loss

AICPA adapted

On September 1, 2001 Cano & Company, a U.S. corporation, sold merchandise to a foreign firm for 250,000 francs. Terms of the sale require payment in francs on February 1, 2002. On September 1, 2001 the spot exchange rate was $0.20 per franc. At Cano's year-end on December 31, 2001, the spot rate was $0.19, but the rate increased to $0.22 by February 1, 2002, when payment was received.

REQUIRED:

1. What would be the foreign currency transaction gain or loss recorded in 2001?
2. What would be the foreign currency transaction gain or loss recorded in 2002?

E16–11

Mark-to-market for available-for-sale securities

AICPA adapted

Stone has provided the following information on its available-for-sale securities:

Aggregate cost as of 12/31/01	$170,000
Unrealized gain as of 12/31/01	4,000
Unrealized losses as of 12/31/01	26,000
Net realized gains during 2001	30,000

Stone reported $1,500 in the contra-asset valuation account to reduce these securities to their market value at December 31, 2000.

REQUIRED:

What amount should be debited as an unrealized loss to the stockholders' equity section of Stone's December 31, 2001 balance sheet as a result of 2001 market value changes related to its available-for-sale securities? (Ignore taxes.)

E16–12

Mark-to-market for trading securities

Gehl Company founded on January 1, 2001 had the following short-term investments in securities at the end of 2001 and 2002 (all were held in the "trading" portfolio):

Equity Security	Cost	2002 Market Value
A	$ 96,000	$ 94,000
B	184,000	162,000
C	126,000	136,000

REQUIRED:

If the company recorded a $4,000 debit to its "Market adjustment—trading securities" account at the end of 2002 as its mark-to-market adjustment, what must have been the unrealized gain or loss recorded at the end of 2001?

E16–13

Purchase versus pooling

CMA adapted

On July 1, 2001 Pushway Corporation issued 200,000 shares of $5-par value common stock in exchange for all of Stroker Company's common stock. This stock had a fair market value that was $200,000 in excess of the stockholders' equity of Stroker Company on the date of exchange. This difference was attributed to the fact that the fair value of Stroker Company's equipment was higher than book value. The equipment has an estimated remaining life of 10 years. Pushway Corporation and Stroker Company reported depreciation expense in 2001 of $400,000 and $100,000, respectively, before consolidation and before any adjustment for the exchange. For financial reporting purposes, both companies use a calendar year and the straight-line depreciation method, with depreciation calculated on a monthly basis beginning with the month of acquisition.

REQUIRED:

1. Assume the business combination is appropriately accounted for as a purchase. Consolidated depreciation expense reported in 2001 would be how much?
2. Assume the business combination is appropriately accounted for as a pooling of interests. Consolidated depreciation expense reported in 2001 would be how much?

E16–14

Foreign currency translation

AICPA adapted

A wholly owned subsidiary of Ward, Inc. has certain expense accounts for the year ended December 31, 2001, stated in local currency units (LCU) as follows:

	LCU
Depreciation of equipment (related assets were purchased January 1, 1999)	120,000
Provision for doubtful accounts	80,000
Rent	200,000

The exchange rates at various dates are as follows:

	Dollar Equivalent of LCU
12/31/01	$0.40
Average for year ended 12/31/01	0.44
1/1/99	0.50

Assume that the LCU is the subsidiary's functional currency and that the charges to the expense accounts occurred approximately evenly during the year.

REQUIRED:

What total dollar amount should be included in Ward's 2001 consolidated income statement to reflect these expenses?

E16–15

Transaction foreign exchange gain/loss

AICPA adapted

Lindy, a calendar-year U.S. corporation, bought inventory items from a supplier in Germany on November 5, 2001 for 100,000 marks, when the spot rate was $0.4295. At Lindy's December 31, 2001 year-end, the spot rate was $0.4245. On January 15, 2002 Lindy bought 100,000 marks at the spot rate of $0.4345 and paid the invoice.

REQUIRED:

How much should Lindy report in its income statements of 2001 and 2002 as foreign exchange gain or (loss)?

E16–16

Intercompany eliminations on consolidated statements

AICPA adapted

Scroll, Inc., a wholly owned subsidiary of Pirn, Inc., began operations on January 1, 1998. The following information is from the condensed 2001 income statements of Pirn and Scroll:

	Pirn	Scroll
Sales to Scroll	$100,000	$ –
Sales to others	400,000	300,000
	500,000	300,000
Cost of goods sold		
Acquired from Pirn	–	(80,000)
Acquired from others	(350,000)	(190,000)
Gross profit	150,000	30,000
Depreciation	(40,000)	(10,000)
Other expenses	(60,000)	(15,000)
Income from operations	50,000	5,000
Gain on sale of equipment to Scroll	12,000	–
Income before income taxes	$ 62,000	$ 5,000

Additional Information:

- Sales by Pirn to Scroll are made on the same terms as those made to third parties.
- Equipment purchased by Scroll from Pirn for $36,000 on January 1, 2001 is depreciated using the straight-line method over four years.

Required:

1. In Pirn's December 31, 2001 consolidated worksheet, how much intercompany profit should be eliminated from Scroll's inventory?
2. What amount should be reported as depreciation expense in Pirn's 2001 consolidated income statement?

E16–17

Intercompany eliminations—Purchase versus pooling

AICPA adapted

On June 30, 2001 Purl Corporation issued 150,000 shares of its $20 par common stock for which it received all of Scott Corporation's common stock. The fair value of the common stock issued is equal to the book value of Scott Corporation's net assets. Both corporations continued to operate as separate businesses, maintaining accounting records with years ending December 31. Net income from *separate* company operations (which excludes equity method earnings and dividend income) and dividends paid were as follows:

	Purl	Scott
Net income		
Six months ended 6/30/01	$750,000	$225,000
Six months ended 12/31/01	825,000	375,000
Dividends paid		
3/25/01	950,000	–
11/15/01	–	300,000

On December 31, 2001 Scott held in its inventory merchandise that had been acquired from Purl on December 1, 2001 for $150,000, which included a $45,000 markup.

Required:

1. Assume that the business combination qualifies for treatment as a purchase. In the 2001 consolidated income statement, net income should be reported at what amount?
2. Assume that the business combination qualifies for treatment as a pooling of interests. In the 2001 consolidated income statement, net income should be reported at what amount?

Problems/Discussion Questions

P16–1

Intercorporate investments—Balance sheet

The balance sheets of Herb Corporation and Aside Chemical Company at December 31, 2000 were as follows:

($ in thousands)	Herb	Aside
Assets	$850	$400
Liabilities	$275	$100
Common stock (par value, $1)	200	100
Other equity (paid-in capital plus Retained earnings)	375	200
	$850	$400

Required:

1. Assume that on January 1, 2001 Herb Corporation sold an additional 100,000 shares of its stock to its existing shareholders for $425,000. The entire proceeds of the stock issue were then used to buy all the shares of Aside. Prepare a consolidated balance sheet after the acquisition.
2. Assume the preceding facts except that Herb acquired only 80% of the stock for a cash payment of $425,000. How would the consolidated balance sheet differ from that in (1)?
3. Now assume a slightly altered set of initial conditions. While the respective December 31, 2000 balance sheets for the two companies were identical to those shown above, the 100,000 shares of Herb stock were not sold to existing Herb Corporation shareholders. Instead, assume that these 100,000 shares (which had a January 1, 2001 market value of $425,000) were issued to Aside's shareholders in exchange for all 100,000 shares of Aside's stock. Prepare a consolidated balance sheet after the acquisition.

P16–2

Equity method

On January 1, 2001 the Figland Company purchased for cash 40% of the 300,000 shares of voting common stock of the Irene Company for $1,800,000. At the time, 40% of the book value of the underlying equity in the net assets of Irene was $1,400,000; $50,000 of the excess was attributed to the excess of fair market value over book value of inventory, which Irene accounts for using the First-In, First-Out (FIFO) inventory method; and $150,000 is attributed to undervaluation of depreciable assets with an average remaining life of 10 years. The remainder is attributed to implicit goodwill.

Figland amortizes goodwill over a forty-year period, with a full year's amortization taken in the year of the purchase. As a result of this transaction, Figland has the ability to exercise significant influence over the operating and financial policies of Irene. Irene's net income for the year ended December 31, 2001 was $600,000. During 2001 Irene paid $325,000 in dividends to its stockholders.

Required:

1. How much income would Figland report on its 2001 income statement for its investment in Irene?
2. What would be the balance in the "Investment in Irene Company" account on December 31, 2001?

P16–3

Mark-to-market accounting

Consider the following information:

1. Giant Motors purchases 5% of Crane Tire Company's common stock (one of its suppliers) for $30 million on January 1, 2001.
2. Crane Tire Company earned $25 million in net income for 2001.
3. Crane Tire Company pays total dividends of $15 million during 2001.
4. The market value of Giant Motors' 5% investment in Crane Tire is $25 million on December 31, 2001.

(continued)

REQUIRED:

1. Assume the investment in Crane Tire is considered as a trading security by Giant Motors management. At what amount should Giant Motors report its investment in Crane Tire Company in its 2001 balance sheet?
2. How would Giant Motors' investment in Crane Tire Company affect its 2001 income statement?
3. In contrast to (1), assume that the investment in Crane Tire is considered as an available-for-sale security by Giant Motors' management. At what amount should Giant Motors report its investment in Crane Tire Company in its 2001 balance sheet?
4. Using the facts presented in (3), determine how, if at all, Giant Motors' investment in Crane Tire Company would affect its 2001 income statement.

P16–4

Mark-to-market for trading securities

Second National Insurance Company provided the information shown below for its trading securities portfolio:

Security	Acquisition Date	Cost	Market Values 12/31/00	12/31/01	12/31/02
Company A Common	1/15/00	$50,000	$60,000	$55,000	$58,000
Company B Common	6/30/00	30,000	25,000	13,000[1]	10,000
Company C Preferred	2/1/01	20,000	–	25,000	18,000
Company D Warrants	5/1/02	10,000	–	–	12,000

[1]Second National sold 50% of the Company B common shares for $14,000 on July 1, 2001. Market values for December 31, 2001 and December 31, 2002 are for the Company B shares remaining in the trading portfolio.

REQUIRED:

1. Provide the journal entries to record the mark-to-market adjustment on December 31, 2000. Assume Second National uses an account entitled "Market adjustment—trading securities" to adjust the cost of the trading portfolio to year-end market values. Show supporting calculations in good form.
2. Provide the entry to record the sale of Company B common shares on July 1, 2001. Assume the last market adjustment for these shares was on December 31, 2000.
3. Provide the journal entry and supporting calculations for the mark-to-market adjustment on December 31, 2001.
4. Provide the journal entry and mark-to-market adjustment on December 31, 2002.
5. What would the entry to record the sale of Company B common on July 1, 2001 have been if this security had been considered an available-for-sale security? Ignore tax effects.

P16–5

Comprehensive intercorporate investments problem

AICPA adapted

At December 31, 2000 Poe Corporation properly reported as available-for-sale securities the following marketable securities. All these securities were acquired in 2000.

	Cost	Fair Value
Axe Corporation, 1,000 shares, $2.40 convertible preferred stock	$ 40,000	$ 42,000
Purl, Inc., 6,000 shares of common stock	60,000	66,000
Day Company, 2,000 shares of common stock	55,000	40,000
Total available-for-sale securities	$155,000	$148,000

On January 2, 2001 Poe purchased 100,000 shares of Scott Corporation common stock for $1,700,000, representing 30% of Scott's outstanding common stock and an underlying equity of $1,400,000 in Scott's net assets on that date. Poe, which had no other financial transactions with Scott during 2001, amortizes goodwill over a forty-year period. As a result of Poe's 30% ownership of Scott, Poe has the ability to exercise significant influence over Scott's financial and operating policies.

During 2001 Poe disposed of the following securities:

- January 18—sold 2,500 shares of Purl for $13 per share.
- June 1—sold 500 shares of Day for $21 per share.

The following 2001 dividend information pertains to stock owned by Poe:

- April 5 and October 5—Axe paid dividends of $1.20 per share on its $2.40 preferred stock to stockholders of record on March 9 and September 9, respectively.
- June 30—Purl paid a $1.00 per-share dividend on its common stock.
- March 1, June 1, September 1, and December 1—Scott paid quarterly dividends of $0.50 per share on each of these dates. Scott's net income for the year ended December 31, 2001 was $1,200,000.

At December 31, 2001 Poe's management intended to hold Scott's stock on a long-term basis, with the remaining investments considered available-for-sale securities. Market prices per share of these securities were as follows:

	Market Value at December 31, 2001
Axe Corporation—preferred	$56
Purl, Inc.—common	11
Day Company—common	22
Scott Corporation—common	16

REQUIRED:

1. Determine the unrealized gain or loss on Poe's available-for-sale securities for 2000, and provide the journal entry to record the mark-to-market adjustment on December 31, 2000. Ignore tax effects.
2. Prepare the journal entries to record the realized gains or losses on Poe's sales of securities for 2001.
3. Prepare the entries to record Poe's receipt of dividends on all securities in 2001 and all entries related to Poe's equity investment in Scott Corporation.
4. Determine the unrealized gain or loss on Poe's available-for-sale securities for 2001, and provide the journal entry to record the mark-to-market adjustment on December 31, 2001. Ignore tax effects.

P16–6

Intercorporate investments—Equity method

Consider the following sequence of events:

- On January 1, 2001 Big Time Motors purchases 25% of Cooper Tire Company's common stock (one of its suppliers) for $150 million. The book value of Cooper Tire Company's net assets on this date was $400 million. All of the excess is attributed to goodwill that is to be amortized over 20 years.
- Cooper Tire Company earned $25 million in net income for 2001.
- Cooper Tire Company declares and pays total dividends of $15 million during 2001.
- On January 1, 2002 Big Time Motors purchases an additional 15% of Cooper Tire Company common stock for $100 million. The excess of cost over book value is attributed to goodwill, which is to be amortized over 20 years.
- Cooper Tire Company had a net loss of $40 million for 2002.
- Cooper Tire Company pays total dividends of $18 million during 2002.

REQUIRED:

1. What amount of investment income should Big Time Motors report on its 2001 income statement as a result of its investment in Cooper Tire? At what amount would Big Time Motors report its investment in Cooper Tire Company in its December 31, 2001 balance sheet?
2. At what amount should Big Time Motors report its investment in Cooper Tire Company in its December 31, 2002 balance sheet?

P16–7

Purchase method with goodwill

On January 1, 2001 Delta Inc. acquired all the outstanding stock of Sigma Company for $80,000 cash. Following are the balance sheets for Delta and Sigma immediately before the acquisition, as well as fair market value information regarding Sigma Company:

	Delta Inc.	Sigma Company Book Value	Sigma Company Fair Value
Assets			
Cash	$ 91,000	$ 8,000	$ 8,000
Accounts receivable	19,000	15,000	9,000
Inventory	47,000	31,000	43,000
Land	12,000	5,000	12,000
Plant and equipment, net	66,000	35,000	51,000
Total	$235,000	$94,000	$123,000
Liabilities and shareholders' equity			
Accounts payable	$ 52,000	$35,000	$ 35,000
Long-term debt	66,000	15,000	15,000
Common stock			
Delta—5,000 shares, $1.00 par	5,000	—	
Sigma—4,000 shares, $0.50 par	—	2,000	
Additional paid-in capital	30,000	12,000	
Retained earnings	82,000	30,000	
Total	$235,000	$94,000	

REQUIRED:

1. Give the journal entry Delta would make to record the acquisition of Sigma.
2. Calculate the amount of goodwill that Delta will record as a result of acquiring Sigma.
3. Provide the elimination entry Delta would make to prepare the consolidated balance sheet immediately after the acquisition.
4. Prepare Delta Inc.'s balance sheet immediately after its acquisition of Sigma Company.

P16–8

Purchase method versus pooling and effect on ratios

STRETCH

On January 1, 2001 DGA, Inc. acquired all the outstanding stock of CLH Systems in exchange for DGA's common stock which had a market value of $100,000. The acquisition is accounted for as a purchase. Below are the balance sheets for DGA and CLH Systems immediately before the acquisition, as well as fair market value information regarding CLH Systems:

	DGA Inc.	CLH Systems Book Value	CLH Systems Fair Value
Assets			
Cash	$166,000	$ –	$ –
Accounts receivable	25,000	15,000	15,000
Inventory	49,500	13,000	13,000
Land	12,000	7,000	7,000
Plant and equipment, net	76,000	25,000	36,000
Patents	2,500	6,500	10,500
Total	$331,000	$66,500	$81,500
Liabilities and shareholders' equity			
Accounts payable	$ 64,000	$29,000	$29,000
Other liabilities	35,000	—	
Common stock, no par	80,000	5,000	
Retain earnings	152,000	32,500	
Total	$331,000	$66,500	

REQUIRED:

1. Give the journal entry DGA, Inc. would make to record the acquisition of CLH Systems.
2. Calculate the amount of goodwill that DGA, Inc. will record as a result of acquiring CLH Systems.
3. Provide the elimination entry DGA, Inc. would make to prepare the consolidated balance sheet immediately after the acquisition.
4. Prepare DGA, Inc.'s balance sheet immediately after its acquisition of CLH Systems.
5. Assume that DGA and CLH reported net income of $145,000 (before equity in CLH earnings) and $25,000, respectively in 2001. Also, consolidated total assets (before adjustments for goodwill amortization and stepped up-basis depreciation) at December 31, 2001 were identical to the consolidated total assets at acquisition (determined in Requirement 4).

   Goodwill is being amortized over 40 years in accordance with APB 16. Assume the remaining useful life for the Plant and Equipment and the Patents is five (5) years. Determine the following (ignore income taxes):

   - Consolidated net income for the year ended December 31, 2001.
   - ROA at December 31, 2001 (Net Income/Total assets).
6. Recently the FASB proposed that purchased goodwill not be amortized, but be carried on the balance sheet at its historical value unless impaired. How would your answer to Requirement 5 change if the FASB proposal were adopted assuming the following (ignore all income tax considerations):
   - No impairment of goodwill.
   - 90% of the goodwill was impaired.
7. Repeat Requirements 1, 2, 3, 4 and 5 assuming all of the same facts above except that DGA, Inc. acquired CLH Systems by issuing 2,000 shares of its no par common stock and accounted for the transaction as a pooling of interests. At that time DGA's shares were trading for $50.00 per share.

P16–9

Business combination—Purchase versus pooling

CFA adapted

STRETCH

Aspen Pharmaceuticals is a major producer of prescription drugs with an outstanding record of sales and earnings growth. During the past 18 months, however, the company's profit growth has slowed and its stock price has underperformed market averages. Two factors have been advanced to explain these developments: increasing price discounts to large managed-care buyers and concern about possible "reforms" that the U.S. Congress may mandate later this year.

Aspen has just announced its plan to acquire 100% of the common stock of Pharmacy Services, Inc. (PSI). PSI is much smaller than Aspen but is a leading player in the mail-order delivery of pharmaceuticals and also provides related cost-containment services. Aspen's stock is currently selling at $30 per share, and PSI's stock is selling at $25 per share. Both companies are U.S.-based, and their shares are traded on the New York Stock Exchange (NYSE).

Financial data for Aspen and PSI follow.

ASPEN PHARMACEUTICALS

Balance Sheet
December 31, 2001
($ in millions)

Assets	
Current assets	$4,500
Property, plant, and equipment	5,000
Total assets	$9,500
Liabilities and stockholders' equity	
Current liabilities	$3,500
Long-term debt	1,000
Deferred taxes	1,000
Stockholders' equity[1]	4,000
Total liabilities and equity	$9,500

[1] One billion shares outstanding.

(continued)

ASPEN PHARMACEUTICALS

Income Statement
Years Ended December 31

($ in millions except per-share data)	2001 Actual	2002 Estimated
Sales	$10,000	$10,500
Cost of goods sold	(2,000)	(2,500)
Marketing and administration	(2,700)	(2,700)
Depreciation	(200)	(200)
Interest	(100)	(100)
Research	(1,000)	(1,000)
Pre-tax income	4,000	4,000
Income tax expense	(1,600)	(1,600)
Net income	$ 2,400	$ 2,400
Earnings per share[1]	$ 2.40	$ 2.40
Dividends per share	$ 1.10	$ 1.14

[1] One billion shares outstanding.

PHARMACY SERVICES, INC. (PSI)

Balance Sheet
December 31, 2001

($ in millions)	
Assets	
Current assets	$1,000
Property, plant, and equipment	200
Total assets	$1,200
Liabilities and stockholders' equity	
Current liabilities	$ 300
Long-term debt	300
Stockholders' equity[1]	600
Total liabilities and equity	$1,200

[1] 100 million shares outstanding.

PHARMACY SERVICES, INC. (PSI)

Income Statement
Years Ended December 31, 2001

($ in millions except per-share data)	2001 Actual	2002 Estimated
Sales	$2,500	$3,360
Cost of goods sold	(2,130)	(2,880)
Marketing and administration	(80)	(110)
Depreciation	(20)	(20)
Interest	(20)	(20)
Pre-tax income	250	330
Income tax expense	(100)	(130)
Net income	$ 150	$ 200
Earnings per share[1]	$1.50	$2.00
Dividends per share	None	None

[1] 100 million shares outstanding.

Additional Information:

Aspen is considering two alternative approaches to making the acquisition of PSI: share-for-share exchange or cash purchase. Assume the following:

- The $3 billion cost of purchasing PSI at $30 per share would be financed by debt with a 10% interest rate.
- All assets and liabilities of PSI have fair market values equal to their balance sheet values except property, plant, and equipment, which has a fair market value of $1.2 billion. PSI depreciates its property, plant, and equipment over 10 years using the straight-line method.
- Any acquisition goodwill would be amortized over 20 years.
- The marginal tax rate is 40%.

Required:

1. Assume Aspen uses a share-for-share exchange to acquire PSI and accounts for the transaction as a *pooling of interests*.
   a. Prepare a pro forma December 31, 2001 balance sheet for Aspen that reflects the acquisition, and calculate the resulting book value per share.
   b. Prepare a pro forma estimated 2002 income statement for Aspen that reflects the acquisition, and calculate the resulting earnings per share.
2. Assume Aspen pays $30 cash per share to acquire 100% of the common stock of PSI and accounts for the transaction as a *purchase*.
   a. Prepare a pro forma December 31, 2001 balance sheet for Aspen that reflects the acquisition, and calculate the resulting book value per share.
   b. Prepare a pro forma estimated 2002 income statement for Aspen that reflects the acquisition, and calculate the resulting earning per share.
3. Briefly discuss three reasons Aspen would prefer to use a share-for-share exchange and pooling of interests accounting to acquire PSI.
4. Briefly discuss three criticisms of pooling of interests accounting that many financial analysts cite.

P16–10

Business acquisitions and ratio analysis

CFA adapted

Company B, an auto parts company, has made several acquisitions with newly issued stock over the past five years, using the purchase method of accounting. In each case the purchase price exceeded the fair value of the net assets of the acquired company. AutoParts Heaven, a competitor, has made no acquisitions. Wholesale prices of auto parts have been rising over the last five years. Both Company B and AutoParts Heaven account for inventories using the FIFO method.

Required:

1. Briefly explain why Company B's acquisition history makes it difficult to analyze the *trend* of Company B's financial data and ratios.
2. Briefly explain why Company B's acquisition history makes it difficult to compare the *ratios* of Company B with those for AutoParts Heaven.
3. For each of the following financial measures, compare the effect (higher, lower, or no effect) of the purchase method on the financial measure of Company B with the effect of the pooling method. Briefly explain why each effect occurs:
   a. Gross profit margin percentage
   b. Long-term debt-to-equity ratio
   c. Pre-tax earnings

P16–11

Translation effect on ratios

CFA adapted

AutoParts Heaven is a U.S. company whose operations include a large, 100% owned foreign subsidiary. The subsidiary's functional currency is the dollar. The local currency in the country where the foreign subsidiary operates is appreciating against the U.S. dollar. The subsidiary accounts for inventories using the FIFO method.

Required:

Compare each of the following ratios for the foreign subsidiary *in its functional currency after remeasurement* to the same ratios *in the local currency before remeasurement*. Briefly explain why each ratio differs.

1. Gross profit margin percentage
2. Operating profit margin
3. Net profit margin

P16–12 **Business acquisitions and ratio analysis**

STRETCH

The balance sheets of ABD, Inc. and C Corporation on December 31, 2001 are given next. (Unless otherwise noted, all amounts are in millions.)

	ABD, Inc.	C Corporation
Assets		
Cash	$200	$ –
Accounts receivable	–	600
Inventory	300	–
Current assets	500	600
Plant and equipment, net	–	800
Total	$500	$1,400
Liabilities and shareholders' equity		
Accounts payable	$250	$ –
Long-term debt	–	1,050
Total liabilities	$250	$1,050
Common stock ($1 par per share)	100	200
Additional paid-in capital	50	–
Retained earnings	100	150
Total	$500	$1,400

1. Immediately following the preparation of the preceding balance sheets, ABD issues 250 shares of common stock and receives $350 in cash proceeds. ABD immediately uses these cash proceeds to purchase 100% of the common stock of C Corporation. Provide the balance sheet for ABD, Inc. after these two transactions. (*Note:* On its own financial statements, ABD accounts for its investment in C Corporation using the equity method.)
2. Provide the *consolidated* balance sheet that ABD, Inc. would report immediately following the investment in C Corporation. How do these two methods of reporting the acquisition, in (1) and (2), differ in their description of what ABD bought? What are some key ratios that are affected by the accounting method?
3. For this question only, suppose that C Corporation's "Plant and equipment, net" account had been $5,800 and its "Long-term debt" account had been $6,050. How would your answers to (1) and (2) have changed? (A qualitative answer, rather than a whole balance sheet, will do here.)
4. For this question only, suppose that at the time of the acquisition, ABD owed $20 to C Corporation for services it had provided in the preceding year. How would your answer to (2) change? (Again, a qualitative answer will do.)
5. For this question, suppose that ABD, Inc. issued 250 shares of common stock, received $400 in proceeds, and used the entire proceeds to purchase 100% of the outstanding common shares of C Corporation. Provide the *consolidated* balance sheet that ABD, Inc. would report immediately following the investment in C Corporation.
6. Start with the information in (5). Now suppose that ABD only acquired 80% of the outstanding common stock of C Corporation. Provide the *consolidated* balance sheet that ABD, Inc. would report immediately following the investment in C Corporation.
7. Start with the information in (5). Now suppose that ABD *exchanged* its 250 common shares (which had a market value of $400) for the 200 outstanding common shares of C Corporation. What method would ABD use to account for the acquisition? Provide the *consolidated* balance sheet that ABD, Inc. would report immediately following the investment in C Corporation. Why might the management of ABD prefer to structure the acquisition and consolidation in this fashion?

C16–1

The Seagram Company Ltd.: Equity method

STRETCH

Seagram Company Ltd. is a Canadian corporation whose shares trade on the NYSE and on the major Canadian exchanges. Seagram is principally engaged in the production and worldwide marketing of distilled spirits, wines, fruit juices, and other beverages.

E.I. du Pont de Nemours and Company (Du Pont), the largest U.S. chemical producer and one of the leading chemical producers worldwide, concentrates in industrial chemicals, fibers, and polymers, as well as various petroleum products.

In 1981 Seagram became involved in a bidding war with Du Pont for controlling interest in Conoco, a major oil company. Du Pont eventually gained control of Conoco but had to swap slightly over 20% of its own shares to get the Conoco shares Seagram had already accumulated at an investment of nearly $3 billion. As part of the exchange agreement (subsequently amended in 1986), Du Pont has the right to designate two nominees to the Seagram's board of directors, and Seagram has the right to designate 25% of the members of the Du Pont board. Other details about the agreement appear in footnote 1 of the Seagram 1988 Annual Report reproduced next.

Note 1: Equity in Du Pont

The Company owns 54.7 million shares (approximately 22.9%) of the outstanding common stock of E.I. du Pont de Nemours and Company (Du Pont). The Company and Du Pont have entered into an agreement providing for mutual board representation and other matters concerning their future relationship. Subject to certain conditions, the Company will not as a general matter exceed a 25% holding of Du Pont voting stock, and Du Pont will have a right of first refusal if the Company offers its Du Pont shares for sale or transfer during the term of the agreement. The Company may terminate the agreement upon the occurrence of specified events, including dilution of the Company's stock position.

The Company accounts for its interest in Du Pont using the equity method whereby its proportionate share of Du Pont earnings is included in income. The $401 million excess at acquisition of the Company's carrying value above the equity in Du Pont net assets was allocated primarily to Du Pont LIFO inventory. The portion allocated to property, plant, and equipment and long-term borrowings is being amortized over varying periods, none exceeding fifteen years.

Summarized financial information for Du Pont, based upon its publicly reported financial statements, follows:

($ in millions)	Year Ended December 31 1987	1986	1985
Sales	$30,468	$27,148	$29,483
Cost of goods sold and other expenses	27,132	24,436	26,670
Net income	$ 1,786	$ 1,538	$ 1,118

($ in millions)	December 31, 1987	1986
Current assets	$ 9,953	$ 8,960
Noncurrent assets	18,256	17,773
	$28,209	$26,733
Current liabilities	$ 6,140	$ 5,636
Noncurrent liabilities	7,825	7,723
Stockholders' equity	14,244	13,374
	$28,209	$26,733

(continued)

Information regarding dividends from Du Pont and the Company's accounting for unremitted Du Pont earnings follows:

	Ended January 31		
($ in thousands)	1988	1987	1986
Dividends received from Du Pont	$179,481	$165,511	$162,017
Income tax provided	14,114	11,420	11,179
	$165,367	$154,091	$150,838
Interest expense allocated against unremitted Du Pont earnings	$ 11,192	$ 10,662	$ 11,557
Income tax benefit	4,415	4,853	4,111
	$ 6,777	$ 5,809	$ 7,446

Cumulative unremitted Du Pont earnings of $778.8 million are included in consolidated retained earnings at January 31, 1988; no provision for taxes has been made in view of available options for realization.

The following financial statements for Seagram and Du Pont will be used to answer the questions posed at the end of the case.

THE SEAGRAM COMPANY LTD.

(Incorporated under the Canada Business Corporations Act)
and Subsidiary Companies
Consolidated Statement of Income

	Twelve Months Ended January 31		
(U.S. $ in thousands)	1988	1987	1986
Sales and other income	$3,815,480	$3,344,820	$2,970,669
Cost of goods	2,436,640	2,189,628	1,940,993
	1,378,840	1,155,192	1,029,676
Selling, general, and administrative expenses	1,093,127	927,360	815,021
Restructuring costs		35,000	
Operating income	285,713	192,832	214,655
Interest expense	80,397	84,294	82,013
Income before income taxes	205,316	108,538	132,642
Provision for income taxes	60,801	5,715	33,417
Income from spirits and wine operations	144,515	102,823	99,225
Interest expense related to share repurchase, after income taxes		(2,513)	(6,683)
Dividend income from E.I. du Pont de Nemours and Company, after income taxes	165,367	154,091	150,838
Equity in unremitted earnings of E.I. du Pont de Nemours and Company	211,206	169,057	75,694
Net income	$ 521,088	$ 423,458	$ 319,074

THE SEAGRAM COMPANY LTD. AND SUBSIDIARIES

Consolidated Balance Sheet

(U.S. $ in thousands)	January 31 1988	1987
Assets		
Current assets		
Cash and short-term investments at cost, which approximates market	$ 633,748	$ 593,590
Receivables	713,917	590,155
Inventories	1,535,464	1,250,029
Prepaid expenses	67,226	48,110
Wine company assets held for sale	—	220,000
Total current assets	2,950,355	2,701,884
Common stock of E.I. du Pont de Nemours and Company	3,587,455	3,329,727
Note receivable from Sun Company, Inc.	20,250	51,000
Property, plant, and equipment, at cost	1,006,673	842,593
Accumulated depreciation	(404,305)	(343,634)
	602,368	498,959
Investments and advances—spirits and wine companies	155,610	76,686
Sundry assets, including excess of cost over net assets of companies acquired	227,427	228,206
Total assets	$7,543,465	$6,886,462
Liabilities and shareholders' equity		
Current liabilities		
Short-term borrowings	$ 522,310	$ 460,410
United States excise taxes	62,558	61,047
Payables and accrued liabilities	587,915	450,780
Income and other taxes	154,127	57,637
Indebtedness payable within one year	66,774	72,420
Total current liabilities	1,393,684	1,102,294
Long-term indebtedness	1,057,981	911,764
Deferred income taxes and other credits	601,775	882,040
Minority interest	32,510	34,804
Shareholders' equity		
Shares without par value 1988—94,786,225 shares; 1987—95,494,856 shares	276,417	257,368
Share purchase warrants	27,275	27,679
Cumulative currency translation adjustments	(105,922)	(228,456)
Retained earnings	4,259,745	3,898,969
Total shareholders' equity	4,457,515	3,955,560
Total liabilities and shareholders' equity	$7,543,465	$6,886,462

(continued)

E.I. DU PONT

Consolidated Income Statement

($ in millions, except per share)	1987	1986	1985
Sales	$30,468	$27,148	$29,483
Other income	324	273	382
Total	30,792	27,421	29,865
Cost of goods sold and other operating charges	17,150	15,129	17,898
Selling, general and administrative expenses	2,716	2,350	2,077
Depreciation, depletion, and amortization	2,225	2,119	1,796
Exploration expenses, including dry hole costs and impairment of unproved properties	459	550	561
Research and development expense	1,223	1,156	1,144
Interest and debt expense	435	438	513
Taxes other than on income	3,085	2,656	2,282
Gains from sales of businesses	(161)	(140)	(27)
Loss on restructuring of investments	—	178	226
Early retirement program expense	—	—	200
Total	27,132	24,436	26,670
Earnings before income taxes	3,660	2,985	3,195
Provision for income taxes	1,874	1,447	2,077
Net income	$ 1,786	$ 1,538	$ 1,118

REQUIRED:

1. Explain the basis or rationale for Seagram's use of the equity method to account for its investment in Du Pont.
2. Given that Seagram uses the equity method to account for its investment in Du Pont, how do you explain the dividend income from Du Pont shown on Seagram's income statement? Is this consistent with the way Seagram recorded its share of Du Pont earnings? Explain.
3. Note 1 indicates that Seagram effectively paid $401 million in excess of net book value of the Du Pont shares at the time of acquisition. How much of this excess was amortized to earnings by Seagram in 1988? (Show the details.)
4. Reconcile the beginning and ending balances of Seagram's investment in Du Pont that appears on Seagram's balance sheet (i.e., explain the change in this account balance) for 1988.
5. Evaluate the return on assets that Seagram is earning on its own wine and spirits operation against the return on its investment in Du Pont. Which appears most profitable?

C16–2

Tyler Corporation (1): Business acquisitions and analysis of sales growth (Continued in C18–1.)

The narrative portions of corporate annual financial reports (including footnote explanations and other qualitative disclosures) represent an important source of information for understanding the past operations and for evaluating the future prospects of publicly held companies. Corporate managers consider these disclosures to be an important vehicle for informing present and prospective investors about managerial performance, strategies, and plans.

This emphasis is typified in the 1979 Annual Report of Tyler Corporation, then a Fortune 500 company headquartered in Dallas. In the president's letter included in the 1979 report, Joseph P. McKinney made the following observations on the company's performance in that year:

> For Tyler Corporation, 1979 was another year of growth, marking—on a historically reported basis—the ninth consecutive year of record sales, net income, and earnings per share.

At the close of 1979, Tyler's operations encompassed four separate divisions: (1) Tyler Pipe, a leading manufacturer of pipe, fittings, and related applications in commercial, industrial, and residential construction; (2) C&H Transportation, the nation's largest carrier of heavy and cumbersome items; (3) Atlas Powder, ranked second in sales among domestic manufacturers of commercial and industrial explosives; and (4) Thurston Motor Lines, a leading general commodity carrier that was acquired in April of 1979 for a cash payment of $45.5 million.

The acquisition of Thurston was accounted for using the purchase method of accounting. Certain data relating to the acquisition were reported in the following note to the consolidated financial statements.

Acquisition of General Commodity Carrier

On April 6, 1979 the Company acquired all the business and assets of Thurston, Inc. for approximately $45,500,000 cash. The acquisition is being accounted for by the purchase method of accounting. The consolidated statement of income includes sales of $74,234,000 and income before taxes of $2,438,000 of the general commodity carrier since April 6, 1979. Since acquisition, the operating results of the general commodity carrier, after deduction for interest expense on funds borrowed at the prime rate and invested in the operation, reduced earnings per share by $0.10. The excess of the purchase price over the fair value of the assets acquired was approximately $9,300,000 and is being amortized by the straight-line method over 40 years.

The following information summarizes the combined operating results of the acquired business and the Company for the years ended December 31, 1978 and 1979 on a pro forma basis as though the business was acquired January 1, 1978.

	1978	1979
Net sales	$480,048,000	$540,327,000
Net income	25,069,000	23,012,000
Earnings per common share	$2.33	$2.29

Sales growth received heavy attention in three separate sections of the narrative in Tyler's annual report. First, the third paragraph of the president's letter included the following information:

> Net income gained 2% to $23.5 million and total sales were 33% higher at $519.2 million.

Second, the "Highlights" section of the report prominently emphasized the 33% sales increase over 1978 as follows:

> Among the significant events and achievements of 1979 were:
>
> - ninth consecutive year of record sales and profits;
> - increase of 33% in net sales, which for the first time exceeded one-half billion dollars.

Third, the "Operations review" included the following comments:

> Sales jumped 33% in 1979, of which $74 million was contributed by the addition of Thurston and the remaining $54 million by the other three operations. Over the last nine years, sales have increased at a compounded annual rate of 17% and operating profits at a compounded rate of 19%.

(continued)

Tyler's consolidated statements of income for 1978 and 1979 follow:

TYLER CORPORATION

Consolidated Statements of Income

	Years Ended December 31	
	1978	**1979**
Net sales	$390,873,000	$519,242,000
Costs and expenses		
Cost of sales	308,164,000	423,946,000
Selling, administrative, and general expenses	35,412,000	41,754,000
Interest expense	4,986,000	11,212,000
	348,562,000	476,912,000
Income before income tax	42,311,000	42,330,000
Income tax	19,252,000	18,873,000
Net income	$ 23,059,000	$ 23,457,000
Earnings per common share	$2.14	$2.34
Average shares outstanding	10,764,000	10,040,000

REQUIRED:

1. As a lending officer at Gotham National Bank, you have been asked to prepare a cash flow forecast for Tyler Corporation for 1980. You begin with a sales forecast, believing that this is one of the key drivers of cash flow forecast accuracy. Given available data, what is your best estimate of the sustainable growth in sales between 1978 and 1979?
2. If Tyler had acquired Thurston in a stock-for-stock exchange, would the comparative income statement sales and other numbers be different from those shown earlier? Explain how.
3. Comment on Tyler's repeated reference to 33% sales growth.

C16–3

City Holding Company: Mark-to-market accounting for available-for-sale securities

City Holding Company is a multibank holding company headquartered in West Virginia, which is comprised of multiple facilities located in West Virginia, Ohio, and California. The banking subsidiaries provide a full range of banking services and make investments in debt and equity securities under limitations and restrictions imposed by regulations of the Comptroller of the Currency.

Appearing on the following pages are the consolidated balance sheet and cash flow statement of City Holding Company, as well as selected footnote information pertaining to the available-for-sale securities in 1999 and 1998.

Using the information provided, determine responses to the questions that follow. Provide detailed support where appropriate.

Note: Unrealized gains (losses) on available-for-sale securities are not recognized for tax purposes until the securities are sold. Accordingly the tax effects of these unrealized gains (losses) are recognized as adjustments to the deferred tax liability (asset) accounts. Unrealized gains (losses) on available-for-sale securities are shown net of related tax effects as an adjustment to stockholders' equity. Assume the realized gains and losses reported in the footnote on page 869 all relate to available-for-sale securities. Transfers of securities from the held-to-maturity to available-for-sale category are recorded at market with the unrealized gain/loss recorded in stockholders' equity.

REQUIRED:

STRETCH

1. Determine the net before-tax unrealized holding gain (loss) on available-for-sale securities that City Holding recognized in 1999. Assume no adjustments are made to the unrealized holding gain (loss) account when securities are sold.
2. Assuming a 35% tax rate, determine the deferred tax amounts related to the net unrealized holding gains (losses) that were recorded in 1999. Indicate whether the deferred tax amounts were a liability or an asset.

3. Give the entry that City Holding made at December 31,1999 to record the unrealized gain (loss) on available-for-sale securities and to adjust the related stockholders' equity account.
4. Give the entry that City Holding made to record sales on available-for-sale securities in 1999.
5. To the extent possible, explain the year-to-year change in the cost basis of the available-for-sale securities (from $358,382,000 on December 31, 1998 to $387,969,000 on December 31, 1999).

CITY HOLDING COMPANY AND SUBSIDIARIES

Consolidated Balance Sheets

($ in thousands)	December 31 1999	1998
Assets		
Cash and due from banks	$ 120,122	$ 87,866
Federal funds sold	1,990	31,911
Cash and Cash Equivalents	122,112	119,777
Securities available for sale, at fair value	381,112	356,659
Securities held-to-maturity (approximate fair value $40,539)	—	39,063
Loans		
Gross loans	1,886,114	1,715,929
Allowance for possible loan losses	(27,113)	(17,610)
Net Loans	1,859,001	1,698,319
Loans held for sale	118,025	246,287
Retained interests	76,963	65,623
Premises and equipment	66,119	71,094
Accrued interest receivable	18,149	19,358
Other assets	151,009	89,824
Total assets	$2,792,490	$2,706,004
Liabilities		
Deposits		
Noninterest-bearing	$ 246,555	$ 303,421
Interest-bearing	1,709,215	1,760,994
Total deposits	1,955,770	2,064,415
Short-term borrowings	386,719	183,418
Long-term debt	116,000	102,719
Corporation-obligated mandatorily redeemable capital securities of subsidiary trusts holding solely subordinated debentures of City Holding Company	87,500	87,500
Other liabilities	47,959	47,893
Total liabilities	2,593,948	2,485,945
Stockholders' equity		
Preferred stock, par value $25 per share; authorized—500,000 shares: none issued	—	—
Common stock, par value $2.50 per share; authorized—50,000,000 shares; issued and outstanding at December 31, 1999 and 1998: 16,879,815 and 16,820,276 shares, including 9,646 and 10,000 shares in treasury, respectively	42,199	42,051
Capital surplus	59,164	58,365
Retained earnings	112,951	120,209
Cost of common stock in treasury	(285)	(274)
Accumulated other comprehensive loss	(15,487)	(292)
Total stockholders' equity	198,542	220,059
Total liabilities and stockholders' equity	$2,792,490	$2,706,004

(continued)

CITY HOLDING COMPANY AND SUBSIDIARIES

Consolidated Statements of Cash Flows

($ in thousands)	1999	Year Ended December 31 1998	1997
Operating Activities			
Net income	$ 6,213	$ 5,234	$ 26,291
Adjustments to reconcile net income to net cash provided by (used in) operating activities:			
Net amortization	5,674	2,647	1,776
Provision for depreciation	11,822	10,313	6,599
Provision for probable loan losses	19,286	8,481	4,064
Deferred income tax benefit	(9,198)	(3,011)	(909)
Loans originated for sale	(343,755)	(695,576)	(97,465)
Purchases of loans held for sale	(229,148)	(754,703)	(797,537)
Proceeds from loans sold	707,765	1,364,657	850,742
Realized gains on loans sold	(6,600)	(14,238)	(4,392)
Increase in retained interests	(11,340)	(61,260)	(4,360)
Realized investment securities losses (gains)	9,897	(7)	(8)
Decrease (increase) in accrued interest receivable	1,310	(3,515)	(1,763)
(Increase) decrease in other assets	(56,483)	3,230	(27,565)
Increase in other liabilities	145	6,547	9,193
Net cash provided by (used in) operating activities	105,588	(131,201)	(35,334)
Investing Activities			
Proceeds from maturities and calls of securities held-to-maturity	27	3,390	4,565
Purchases of securities held-to-maturity	–	(898)	–
Proceeds from sales of securities available for sale	83,185	33,930	87,139
Proceeds from maturities and calls of securities available for sale	24,304	146,140	79,912
Purchases of securities available for sale	(105,785)	(201,487)	(102,523)
Net increase in loans	(175,061)	(119,225)	(128,169)
Net cash paid in branch sales	(56,104)	–	–
Realized gain on branch sales	(8,883)	–	–
Net cash acquired (paid) in acquisitions	7,409	2,584	(4,516)
Purchases of premises and equipment	(7,944)	(26,446)	(11,840)
Net cash used in investing activities	(238,852)	(162,012)	(75,432)
Financing Activities			
Net (decrease) increase in noninterest-bearing deposits	(22,178)	52,960	(3,262)
Net (decrease) increase in interest-bearing deposits	(30,323)	129,083	79,733
Net increase in short-term borrowings	191,168	10,529	52,940
Proceeds from long-term debt	57,999	87,917	41,252
Repayment of long-term debt	(47,719)	(65,700)	–
Net proceeds from issuance of trust preferred securities	–	84,148	–
Purchases of treasury stock	(398)	(6,987)	(2,840)
Proceeds from sales of treasury stock	–	–	80
Exercise of stock options	521	675	94
Cash dividends paid	(13,471)	(12,167)	(11,421)
Net cash provided by financing activities	135,599	280,458	156,576
Increase (decrease) in cash and cash equivalents	2,335	(12,755)	45,810
Cash and cash equivalents at beginning of year	119,777	132,532	86,722
Cash and cash equivalents at end of year	$122,112	$ 119,777	$132,532

Notes to Consolidated Financial Statements City Holding Company and Subsidiaries Note Five Investments

During the fourth quarter of 1999, the Company recognized a pre-tax charge of $10 million as a result of a determination that the Company's investment in Altiva Financial Corporation ("Altiva") could no longer be supported as "other than temporary." Factors that were considered that resulted in this charge to earnings included the significant changes that have occurred within the specialty finance industry in recent months and the dilution in the Company's ownership position of Altiva as a result of a second recapitalization completed by Altiva in December 1999. The $10 million pre-tax charge is included in Investment securities (losses) gains in the Consolidated Statements of Income.

Horizon (a subsidiary of City Holding) maintained selected debt securities in a held-to-maturity classification based on its management's intent and Horizon's ability to hold such securities to maturity. On April 1, 1999, the Company reclassified those securities from held-to-maturity to available for sale. This transfer was consistent with the Company's investment portfolio accounting policies and provides management with additional liquidity alternatives and more flexibility in managing the Company's interest rate risk. At the date of transfer, the amortized cost of those securities was $39.04 million and the unrealized gain on those securities was $1.26 million.

Included in the Company's investment portfolio are structured notes with an estimated fair value of $1.2 million and $1.4 million at December 31, 1999 and 1998, respectively. Such investments are used by management to enhance yields, diversify the investment portfolio, and manage the Company's exposure to interest rate fluctuations. These securities consist of federal agency securities with an average maturity of approximately two years. Management periodically performs sensitivity analyses to determine the Company's exposure to fluctuation in interest rates of 3% and has determined that the structured notes meet regulatory price sensitivity guidelines.

The aggregate carrying and approximate market values of securities follow. Fair values are based on quoted market prices, where available. If quoted market prices are not available, fair values are based on quoted market prices of comparable instruments.

December 31, 1999 ($ in thousands)	Available-for-Sale Securities Cost	Gross Unrealized Gains	Gross Unrealized Losses	Estimated Fair Value
U.S. Treasury securities and obligations of U.S. government corporations and agencies	$235,451	$ 48	($5,968)	$229,531
Obligations of states and political subdivisions	100,002	807	(1,666)	99,143
Mortgage-backed securities	5,732	37	(70)	5,699
Other debt securities	5,605	34	(44)	5,595
Total debt securities	346,790	926	(7,748)	339,968
Equity securities	41,179	108	(143)	41,144
	$387,969	$1,034	($7,891)	$ 381,112

December 31, 1998 ($ in thousands)	Available-for-Sale Securities Cost	Gross Unrealized Gains	Gross Unrealized Losses	Estimated Fair Value
U.S. Treasury securities and obligations of U.S. government corporations and agencies	$244,706	$2,508	($ 413)	$246,801
Obligations of states and political subdivisions	66,926	2,179	(103)	69,002
Mortgage-backed securities	11,102	199	(7)	11,294
Other debt securities	8,565	292	–	8,857
Total debt securities	331,299	5,178	(523)	335,954
Equity securities	27,083	357	(6,735)	20,705
	$358,382	$5,535	($7,258)	$356,659

Gross gains of $113,000, $47,000, and $431,000, and gross losses of $10.01 million, $40,000, and $423,000, were realized on sales and calls of securities during 1999, 1998, and 1997, respectively.

The book value of securities pledged to secure public deposits and for other purposes as required or permitted by law approximated $252 million and $161 million at December 31, 1999 and 1998, respectively.

C16-4

Acquisitive, Inc.[1]: Purchase versus pooling

Acquisitive, Inc., a pharmaceuticals manufacturer, is based in the United States and is a Securities and Exchange Commission (SEC) registrant. Acquisitive's capital structure includes an authorized 500 million shares of $2.50 par-value common stock, of which 300 million shares are issued and outstanding.

Patents associated with certain of Acquisitive's more profitable products are set to expire in the near future, and the company's recent research and development efforts in these areas have not been particularly successful. As a result, management has been in search of a compatible merger candidate to bolster its future cash flows and profits.

Approximately one year ago, Acquisitive identified Target Pharmaceuticals Corporation as a likely merger candidate. Target is closely held and is headquartered in the United States. Its capital structure includes an authorized 1.5 million shares of $10 par-value common stock, of which 1 million shares are issued and outstanding. Martin Johnson, Target's founder and chair of its board of directors, controls 800,000 of these shares through MJ, Inc., a personal holding company; the remaining shares are held by various Johnson family members.

Shortly after identifying Target as a merger candidate, when Acquisitive's stock was trading at approximately $75 per share, Acquisitive's management approached Target's board of directors with a tentative offer to exchange 40 new shares of Acquisitive stock for each share of Target stock. Johnson's response was extremely negative. Boasting that he would liquidate Target before he'd see it merge with Acquisitive, he had the board of directors declare a special $100 per share cash dividend on its common stock.

Recently, Acquisitive's management learned that Johnson had softened his stance on the proposed merger, and merger discussions resumed. Johnson expressed his willingness to enter into a merger at an exchange rate of 60 shares of Acquisitive stock for each Target share.

Acquisitive had appraisal and audit work performed which indicated that unrecorded patents owned by Target have an estimated value of $4 billion.These patents have an average expected economic life of eight years. Upon receiving these estimates, Acquisitive's management agreed to issue 60 shares for each Target share—but only if the business combination could be accounted for as a pooling of interests. Acquisitive's stock is currently trading at approximately $80 per share.

Acquisitive has asked its independent auditor to evaluate the potential combination and express an opinion as to whether the transaction meets the pooling criteria of *APB No. 16*.

Recent condensed balance sheets of the two companies are as follows (all dollar amounts are in millions):

	Acquisitive	Target
Cash	$ 117	$ 150
Noncash assets	22,083	4,875
Total	$22,200	$5,025
Liabilities	$11,800	$4,825
Common stock, $2.50 par value	750	
Common stock, $10 par value		10
Paid-in capital in excess of par value	650	117
Retained earnings	9,000	73
Total	$22,200	$5,025

REQUIRED:

1. Using the condensed balance sheets of the two companies and the other facts and circumstances of the case, prepare pro-forma balance sheets for the merged firm. First, do so under the assumption that the combination is accounted for as a purchase; and second, do so under the assumption that the combination is accounted

for as a pooling of interests. Document any assumptions which you believe are necessary to complete the balance sheets.
2. Why, in your opinion, is Acquisitive insistent that the business combination be accounted for as a pooling of interests? Using the facts and circumstances of the case, attempt to provide hard evidence to support your opinion.
3. In your opinion and based on your answers to (1) and (2), is Acquisitive's management's insistence on accounting for the combination as a pooling of interest rational or irrational? In what circumstances might it be rational? In what circumstances might it be irrational?
4. Based on the facts and circumstances of the case, in your opinion, can the merger of Acquisitive and Target be accounted for as a pooling of interests? Why or why not? Attempt to respond to this question on two levels: First, irrespective of the specific pooling criteria of *APB No. 16,* does the combination appear to be in substance a pooling of interests? Second, have specific pooling criteria of *APB No. 16* been violated?
5. If you concluded in your answer to (4) that the combination could not be accounted for as a pooling of interests, could anything be done by either of the companies to remedy the violation(s) and allow the combination to be accounted for as a pooling of interests?

C16–5

Air Products: Joint ventures and off-balance sheet effects

Excerpts from the 1999 annual report of Air Products and Chemicals, Inc. are shown next. The income statement and balance sheet are condensed but the footnote entitled "Summarized Financial Information of Equity Affiliates" is shown in its entirety.

The footnote provides information on several joint ventures that Air Products has entered into—primarily to incinerate municipal solid waste and generate electricity.

REQUIRED:

1. What are some of the reasons companies give to justify entering into joint ventures?
2. Using the information provided, estimate what the effect on Air Products' return-on-assets ratio and debt-to-equity ratio would have been if its proportionate share of the joint ventures had been included as individual assets and liabilities on the consolidated balance sheet. For this purpose use a tax rate of 35% and assume that Air Products' proportionate ownership in these equity affiliates averaged 37%.

AIR PRODUCTS AND CHEMICALS, INC. AND SUBSIDIARIES

Consolidated Income Statement (Modified)

($ in millions)	Year Ended September 30 1999	1998
Sales and other income		
Sales	$5,020.1	$4,919.0
Other income, net	19.7	15.5
	5,039.8	4,934.5
Costs and expenses		
Cost of sales	3,501.4	3,317.0
Selling and administrative	690.6	659.8
Research and development	123.1	112.0
Operating income	724.7	845.7
Income from equity affiliates, net of related expenses	61.5	38.0
Gain on asset sales and settlements	34.9	103.5
Gain on currency options	7.0	—
Interest expense	(159.1)	(162.8)
Income before taxes and minority interest	669.0	824.4
Income taxes	(203.4)	(276.9)
Minority interest in earnings of subsidiary companies	(15.1)	(0.7)
Net income	$ 450.5	$ 546.8

AIR PRODUCTS AND CHEMICALS, INC. AND SUBSIDIARIES

Consolidated Balance Sheets (Modified)

	September 30	
($ in millions)	**1999**	**1998**
Assets		
Total current assets	$1,782.4	$1,641.7
Investments		
Investment in net assets of and advances to equity affiliates	521.4	362.0
Other investments and advances	38.4	18.4
Total investments	559.8	380.4
Plant and equipment, at cost	10,187.9	9,489.5
Less—accumulated depreciation	(4,995.0)	(4,703.4)
Plant and equipment, net	5,192.9	4,786.1
Goodwill	350.4	324.9
Other noncurrent assets	350.0	356.5
Total assets	$8,235.5	$7,489.6
Liabilities and shareholders' equity		
Total current liabilities	$1,857.8	$1,265.6
Long-term debt	1,961.6	2,274.3
Deferred income and other noncurrent liabilities	596.1	570.9
Deferred income taxes	731.1	703.0
Total liabilities	5,146.6	4,813.8
Minority interest in subsidiary companies	127.3	8.5
Total shareholders' equity	2,961.6	2,667.3
Total liabilities and shareholders' equity	$8,235.5	$7,489.6

Summarized Financial Information of Equity Affiliates

The following table presents summarized financial information on a combined 100% basis of the principal companies accounted for by the equity method. Amounts presented include the accounts of the following equity affiliates: Cambria CoGen Company (50%); Stockton CoGen Company (50%); Orlando CoGen Limited, L.P. (50%); Pure Air on the Lake, L.P. (50%); Bangkok Cogeneration Company Limited (48.9%); Sankyo Air Products Co., Ltd. (50%); San-Apro Ltd. (50%); Sapio Produzione Idrogeno Ossigeno S.R.L. (49%); INFRA Group (40%); San Fu Chemicals (48.1%); ProCal (50%); Korea Industrial Gases (48.9%); Air Products South Africa (50%); Bangkok Industrial Gases Company Ltd. (49%); INOX Air Products Limited (48.9%); APP GmbH in WPS GmbH & CoKG (20%); and principally other industrial gas producers.

($ in millions)	**1999**	**1998**
Current assets	$ 648.3	$ 458.8
Noncurrent assets	1,659.4	1,416.8
Current liabilities	483.5	372.4
Noncurrent liabilities	790.5	813.0
Net sales	1,436.0	1,168.1
Sales less cost of sales	487.8	416.7
Net income	221.3	110.0

The company's share of income of all equity affiliates for 1999, 1998, and 1997 was $83.7 million, $48.4 million, and $84.3 million, respectively. These amounts exclude $22.2 million, $10.4 million, and $18.0 million of related net expenses incurred by the company. Dividends received from equity affiliates were $36.1 million, $44.6 million, and $61.5 million in 1999, 1998, and 1997, respectively.

The investment in net assets of and advances to equity affiliates at September 30, 1999 and 1998 included investment in foreign affiliates of $478.9 million and $315.3 million, respectively.

As of September 30, 1999 and 1998, the amount of investment in companies accounted for by the equity method included goodwill in the amount of $75.4 million and $45.7 million, respectively. The goodwill is being amortized into income over periods not exceeding 40 years.

C16–6

Texaco and Exxon: Functional currency choices

The oil industry in the early 1980s was undergoing significant change. In the late 1970s international crude oil prices were predominately determined by Organization of Petroleum Exporting Countries (OPEC) posted prices that were stated in U.S. dollars. While OPEC prices continued to exert a powerful influence on market prices in the early 1980s, a combination of factors led to excess crude oil supply. These factors included a widespread recession which began in late 1981, an increase in non-OPEC oil output, and a sustained rise in European oil prices attributable to the strength of the U.S. dollar.

As a consequence of these factors, after peaking in 1981 at an average of $34.50 per barrel, official OPEC sales prices in U.S. dollars began a slow but steady decline. (The real extent of the decline is difficult to assess since "unofficial" price cutting was widely practiced by 1985 and may have been practiced by some countries even earlier.) The trade-weighted value of the U.S. dollar, however, rose consistently over the 1980–83 period. This latter effect more than offset the OPEC price decline, which explains why oil prices in most European currencies continued to rise even after 1981. Summary data regarding these effects are provided in Exhibit 1.

Earnings for 1982 were generally depressed throughout the oil industry as a consequence of the severe recession. Exxon's 1982 income decreased slightly despite $1.9 billion of inventory profits attributable to depletion of old LIFO layers. The pattern of oil price declines that began in late 1981 was widely expected by analysts at the time to continue into 1983 and beyond. As a consequence, oil industry profit forecasts were generally pessimistic.

Both Texaco and Exxon adopted the FASB's *SFAS No. 52* on Foreign Currency Translation in 1982. Selected excerpts from Texaco's 1982 annual report are shown in Exhibit 2; corresponding excerpts from Exxon's 1982 annual report are reproduced in Exhibit 3. Notice that Texaco chose the dollar as the functional currency for *all* of its foreign subsidiaries, while Exxon chose the local currency as the functional currency for most of its foreign subsidiaries.

A majority of the other multinational oil companies followed Texaco's approach and chose the U.S. dollar as the functional currency for virtually all foreign subsidiaries. (However, many of these firms did use the Canadian dollar as the functional currency for their Canadian oil subsidiaries.) While the U.S. dollar actually strengthened against most foreign currencies well into 1985, in early 1983 (when Texaco and Exxon were finalizing their 1982 reporting choices), the general consensus among economic experts was that the U.S. dollar was "overvalued" and therefore due for a substantial fall.

(*continued*)

Exhibit 1 ■ SUMMARY DATA REGARDING OIL PRICES AND EXCHANGE RATES

	Crude Oil Official Sales Price (U.S. $ per Barrel)					
	1978	**1979**	**1980**	**1981**	**1982**	**1983**
OPEC average	$12.93	$18.67	$30.87	$34.50	$33.63	$29.31

Trade-Weighted Value of the U.S. Dollar			
1980	**1981**	**1982**	**1983**
90.7	99.5	109.8	114.2

Index numbers, 1980–82 average = 100. Each number shows the U.S. dollar's trade-weighted appreciation or depreciation measured against 15 other major currencies,* using averages of daily noon spot exchange rates in New York and bilateral trade weights based on 1980 trade in manufactured goods. Figures are calendar-year averages.

* Canada, Japan, Australia, France, Germany, Italy, the United Kingdom, Austria, Belgium, the Netherlands, Spain, Switzerland, Denmark, Norway, and Sweden.

Source: World Financial Markets, Morgan Guaranty Trust Company of New York.

Exhibit 2 ■ CONDENSED, SELECTED EXCERPTS FROM TEXACO'S 1982 ANNUAL REPORT

Statements of Consolidated Income, Balance Sheet, and Retained Earnings

Income Statement ($ in millions)	For the Years Ended December 31 **1982**	**1981**
Revenues	$48,019	$59,297
Deductions		
Costs and operating expenses	(39,890)	(49,334)
All other deductions	(5,492)	(5,798)
	(45,382)	(55,132)
Provision for income taxes	(1,356)	(1,855)
Net income	$ 1,281	$ 2,310
Balance Sheet		
Assets		
Total current assets	$ 9,343	$11,947
Investments and advances	2,162	2,193
Net properties, plant, and equipment	14,086	12,753
Deferred charges	1,523	596
Total assets	$27,114	$27,489
Liabilities and stockholders' equity		
Total current liabilities	$ 6,243	$ 7,025
Long-term debt	1,731	2,112
Capital lease obligations	696	748
Deferred credits—Income taxes	2,205	2,159
Other deferred credits and noncurrent liabilities	1,845	1,540
Minority interest in subsidiary companies	168	153
Total stockholders' equity	14,226	13,752
Total liabilities and stockholders' equity	$27,114	$27,489

Exhibit 2 ■ CONDENSED, SELECTED EXCERPTS FROM TEXACO'S 1982 ANNUAL REPORT (*continued*)

Statements of Consolidated Income, Balance Sheet, and Retained Earnings

Retained earnings		
Balance at beginning of year	$11,915	$10,345
Add: Net income for the year	1,281	2,310
Deduct: Cash dividends	780	740
Balance at end of year	$12,416	$11,915

Notes to Consolidated Financial Statements

Note 1. Revision in Accounting Policy

In accordance with Financial Accounting Standards Board Statement No. 52, Texaco revised its accounting policy for the translation of amounts recorded in foreign currencies into U.S. dollars effective January 1, 1982.

The Company determined that the U.S. dollar is the functional currency for its foreign operations, which resulted in a minor revision in its previous accounting procedures. Under this revised policy, deferred income tax accounts are translated at current exchange rates rather than the combination of current and historic rates. The cumulative effect of this accounting change was recorded in the fourth quarter of 1982, and prior periods were not restated because the effect of this change was immaterial.

Under the provisions of Statement No. 52, the functional currency for each company operating abroad is either the U.S. dollar or the local currency. In the judgment of Texaco's management, the U.S. dollar represents the functional currency for all operations abroad because: (1) international pricing in the petroleum business is dominated by OPEC crude prices based on U.S. dollars, and (2) there exists an extensive interrelationship between the operations of the Company's foreign entities and the parent company because of the high level of intercompany transactions, which are generally denominated in U.S. dollars.

Note 11. Foreign Currency Translation

Currency gains and losses resulted in gains of $38 million in 1982, losses of $36 million in 1981, and gains of $4 million in 1980, before applicable income taxes. The effects after applicable income taxes were gains of $62 million and $57 million in 1982 and 1981, respectively, and losses of $69 million in 1980. These amounts include Texaco's equity in such gains and losses of the Japanese and South Korean affiliates of the Caltex group of companies, which are accounted for by Caltex on the equity method.

(*continued*)

Exhibit 3 ■ CONDENSED EXCERPTS FROM EXXON'S 1982 ANNUAL REPORT

Consolidated Statement of Income and Earnings Reinvested

Income Statement ($ in thousands)	**1982**	**1981**
Revenue	$103,558,545	$114,922,561
Costs and other deductions		
Purchases, operating, and other deductions	(77,929,543)	(86,753,601)
Income, excise, and other taxes	(21,443,070)	(23,342,745)
Net income	$ 4,185,932	$ 4,826,215
Earnings reinvested		
Balance at beginning of year	$ 25,629,781	$ 23,397,835
Net income	4,185,932	4,826,215
Dividends	(2,604,456)	(2,594,269)
Balance at end of year	$ 27,211,257	$ 25,629,781

Balance Sheet ($ in thousands)	**December 31** **1982**	**1981**
Assets		
Total current assets	$ 19,792,686	$ 23,242,248
Investments and advances	1,714,484	1,643,229
Property, plant, and equipment, net	38,981,829	35,285,519
Other assets, including intangibles	1,799,551	1,403,961
Total assets	$ 62,288,550	$ 61,574,957
Liabilities		
Total current liabilities	$ 16,464,740	$ 17,741,855
Long-term debt	4,555,580	5,153,444
Annuity reserves and accrued liabilities	2,697,771	2,041,182
Deferred income tax credits	8,676,170	7,490,551
Deferred income	268,170	178,694
Equity of minority shareholders in affiliated companies	1,185,928	1,226,365
Total liabilities	33,848,359	33,832,091
Shareholders' equity		
Capital stock	1,760,554	1,826,023
Earnings reinvested	27,211,257	25,629,781
Cumulative foreign exchange translation adjustments	(531,620)	287,062
Total shareholders' equity	28,440,191	27,742,866
Total liabilities and shareholders' equity	$ 62,288,550	$ 61,574,957

Analysis of Change in Cumulative Foreign Exchange Translation Adjustments	**December 31** **1982**	**1981**
Balance at beginning of year	$ 287,062	$ 1,534,582
Adjustments for the year	(818,682)	(1,247,520)
Balance at end of year	$ (531,620)	$ 287,062

Exhibit 3 ■ *(continued)*

2. Accounting change

The method of accounting for foreign currency translation was changed in 1982 by implementation of Financial Accounting Standards Board Standard No. 52—Foreign Currency Translation. The statement was given initial application as of January 1, 1980; all 1980 and 1981 financial data have been restated for comparability.

FAS-52 was implemented by using the local currency of the country of operation as the "functional currency" for translating the accounts of the majority of foreign operations. These operations include essentially all foreign petroleum refining and marketing as well as chemical operations, except for those located in highly inflationary economies; also included are exploration and production operations where the production is consumed locally, such as in Australia, Canada, the United Kingdom, and continental Europe. For other foreign operations, principally exploration and production operations in Norway, Malaysia, and the Middle East, together with operations in highly inflationary economies, the U.S. dollar is used as the functional currency.

FAS-52 provides that asset and liability accounts which are fixed in terms of currencies other than the functional currency be remeasured and stated in the functional currency using the applicable exchange rate at the balance sheet date. Adjustments arising from such remeasurement are included in current net income.

For those operations for which the local currency was adopted as the functional currency, translation of all asset and liability accounts is required to convert the functional currency amounts into U.S. dollars, using exchange rates at the balance sheet date. Adjustments resulting from this translation process are accumulated in a separate component of shareholders' equity entitled "Cumulative foreign exchange translation adjustments," and are not included in determining net income. The initial cumulative adjustment, effective as of January 1, 1980, was an increase in shareholders' equity of $1,752 million.

The effect of implementing these procedures was to decrease net income for 1980, 1981, and 1982 by $300 million ($ 0.34 per share), $741 million ($ 0.86 per share), and $130 million ($ 0.15 per share), respectively. Earnings reinvested at January 1, 1980, December 31, 1980, and December 31, 1981 were reduced from amounts previously reported by $20 million, $320 million, and $1,061 million, respectively.

REQUIRED:

1. *SFAS No. 8*—which was replaced by *SFAS No. 52*—required companies to use the temporal method exclusively. Using the disclosures in the case, one can infer that Exxon had a relatively higher exposed net liability position under the *SFAS No. 8* temporal method than its liability exposure under the current rate method which it dominantly adopted for *SFAS No. 52*. Demonstrate this point using the data reported in the case.
2. Given that most other multinational oil firms did not concur with Exxon's functional currency choice in adopting *SFAS No. 52*, try to construct a "story" which could explain Exxon's selection.

COLLABORATIVE LEARNING CASE

C16-7

The Tribune Company—Financial statement effects of consolidating versus not consolidating a subsidiary

The Tribune Company is engaged in the businesses of publishing and entertainment. Operations include newspapers such as the *Chicago Tribune*, television and radio stations, and the Chicago Cubs National League baseball team. In February 1993 a previously wholly owned, consolidated newsprint subsidiary, QUNO Corporation, issued shares to outsiders in an initial public offering. After the stock offering, the Tribune Company owned 49% of outstanding *voting* common shares and 59% of total common shares. Beginning with the 1993 annual report, the Tribune Company accounted for QUNO using the equity method of accounting. Prior years' financial statements in which QUNO was consolidated were not restated.

Exhibit 1 contains a note from the 1992 Tribune annual report, which describes the QUNO initial public offering and provides pro-forma data. (These pro-forma data were not repeated in the 1993 annual report.) Exhibit 2 contains the financial statements from the 1993 Tribune Company annual report. Exhibit 3 shows selected excerpts from the notes to the 1993 financial statements relating to the QUNO deconsolidation as well as a small section taken from the management discussion and analysis portion of the annual report relating to QUNO.

Exhibit 1 ■ 1992 ANNUAL REPORT DISCLOSURE OF SUBSEQUENT EVENT

QUNO Initial Public Offering

QUNO INITIAL PUBLIC OFFERING On February 17, 1993 the Company's newsprint subsidiary, QUNO Corporation, sold 9 million shares of common stock in an initial public offering. At the conclusion of the offering, the Company holds 8.8 million, or 49%, of the voting common shares and 4.2 million nonvoting common shares for a combined total of 59% of QUNO's total 22 million outstanding common shares. The Company also holds a $138.8 million subordinated debenture, convertible into 11.7 million voting common shares of QUNO. As the Company's voting interest is now less than 50%, the Company will account for its investment in QUNO using the equity method of accounting beginning in 1993.

At closing, QUNO used the net proceeds of approximately $100 million from the stock offering plus proceeds of approximately $80 million from QUNO's new bank financing agreement to repay a portion of its intercompany borrowings owed the Company. The net price per share realized from the offering was approximately the same as the Company's carrying value per share of its investment in QUNO. In April 1993 QUNO plans to use additional proceeds of approximately $80 million from its new bank financing agreement to repay its New Zealand dollar notes which are guaranteed by the Company.

The following unaudited pro forma consolidated financial position data assumes [that] the QUNO common share offering had occurred on December 27, 1992 and that the proceeds of the share offering and related debt transactions had been used to reduce debt:

	December 27, 1992	
($ in thousands)	As Reported	Pro Forma (Unaudited)
Assets		
Investment in QUNO	$ —	$ 277,466
Net properties	1,073,943	606,061
All other assets	1,677,627	1,532,985
Total assets	$2,751,570	$2,416,512
Liabilities and stockholders' investment		
Total debt	$ 840,971	$ 580,971
All other liabilities	998,710	923,652
Stockholders' investment	911,889	911,889
Total liabilities and stockholders' investment	$2,751,570	$2,416,512

Exhibit 2 ■ TRIBUNE COMPANY AND SUBSIDIARIES

1993 Financial Statements
Consolidated Statements of Income

($ in thousands)		December 26, 1993	Year Ended December 27, 1992	December 29, 1991
Operating Revenues	Publishing			
	Advertising	$ 892,524	$ 868,051	$ 854,526
	Circulation	246,093	238,302	234,720
	Other	90,785	69,827	61,636
	Total	1,229,402	1,176,180	1,150,882
	Broadcasting and entertainment	727,213	684,051	617,514
	Newsprint operations (Canada)	—	366,269	422,128
	Intercompany	(4,105)	(121,556)	(146,551)
	Total operating revenues	1,952,510	2,104,944	2,043,973
Operating Expenses	Cost of sales (exclusive of items shown below)	998,345	1,150,956	1,121,334
	Selling, general, and administrative	495,000	546,046	497,616
	Depreciation and amortization of intangible assets	102,762	139,579	137,048
	Total operating expenses	1,596,107	1,836,581	1,755,998
Operating Profit		356,403	268,363	287,975
Equity in QUNO net loss		(18,355)	—	—
Interest income		19,039	13,782	16,983
Interest expense		(24,660)	(49,254)	(63,083)
Income Before Income Taxes		332,427	232,891	241,875
Income taxes		(143,821)	(96,266)	(99,894)
Income Before Cumulative Effects of Changes in Accounting Principles		188,606	136,625	141,981
Cumulative effects of changes in accounting principles, net of tax		—	(16,800)	—
Net Income		188,606	119,825	141,981
Preferred dividends, net of tax		(18,439)	(18,168)	(16,900)
Net Income Attributable to Common Shares		$ 170,167	$ 101,657	$ 125,081

See Notes to Consolidated Financial Statements.

1993 Financial Statements
Consolidated Statements of Financial Position

($ in thousands)

Assets		December 26, 1993	December 27, 1992
Current Assets	Cash and short-term investments	$ 18,524	$ 16,768
	Accounts receivable (less allowances of $25,432 and $23,411)	284,110	295,742
	Inventories	26,290	82,124
	Broadcast rights	144,233	160,703
	Prepaid expenses and other	18,102	19,001
	Total current assets	491,259	574,338

(continued)

Exhibit 2 ■ TRIBUNE COMPANY AND SUBSIDIARIES *(continued)*

1993 Financial Statements
Consolidated Statements of Financial Position

($ in thousands)		December 26, 1993	December 27, 1992
Investment in and Advances to QUNO		250,923	—
Properties	Machinery, equipment, and furniture	792,642	1,327,533
	Buildings and leasehold improvements	307,266	459,367
	Timber limits and leases, and land improvements	7,687	53,556
		1,107,595	1,840,456
	Accumulated depreciation	(599,552)	(913,522)
		508,043	926,934
	Land	54,471	51,724
	Construction in progress	39,101	95,285
	Net properties	601,615	1,073,943
Other Assets	Broadcast rights	217,229	226,981
	Intangible assets (less accumulated amortization of $156,372 and $135,664)	719,965	645,385
	Mortgage notes receivable from affiliates	119,437	84,486
	Other	135,982	146,437
	Total other assets	1,192,613	1,103,289
	Total assets	$2,536,410	$2,751,570

Liabilities and Stockholders' Investment		December 26, 1993	December 27, 1992
Current Liabilities	Long-term debt due within one year	$ 25,817	$ 99,992
	Employee compensation	77,335	76,691
	Accounts payable	85,334	106,703
	Contracts payable for broadcast rights	142,686	152,605
	Accrued liabilities	135,497	163,463
	Income taxes	38,358	33,545
	Total current liabilities	505,027	632,999
Long-Term Debt	(less portions due within one year)	510,838	740,979
Other Noncurrent Liabilities	Deferred income taxes	87,605	85,018
	Contracts payable for broadcast rights	194,846	182,190
	Compensation and other obligations	141,716	192,462
	Total other noncurrent liabilities	424,167	459,670
Stockholders' Investment	Series B Convertible preferred stock (without par value) Authorized: 1,600,000 shares Issued and outstanding: 1,531,084 shares in 1993 and 1,554,352 shares in 1992 (liquidation value $220 per share)	335,532	340,634
	Common stock (without par value) Authorized: 400,000,000 shares; 81,771,658 shares issued	1,018	1,018
	Additional paid-in capital	105,819	100,445
	Retained earnings	1,589,695	1,483,016
	Treasury stock (at cost) 14,791,114 shares in 1993 and 16,292,181 shares in 1992	(607,332)	(667,668)
	Unearned compensation related to ESOP	(298,969)	(321,690)
	Cumulative translation adjustment	(30,136)	(23,866)
	Total stockholders' investment	1,095,627	911,889
	Total liabilities and stockholders' investment	$2,536,410	$2,751,570

Exhibit 3 ■ TRIBUNE COMPANY AND SUBSIDIARIES

Excerpts from Notes to 1993 Financial Statements and Management Discussion and Analysis

Note 2: Investment in QUNO Corporation

On February 17, 1993 the Company's previously wholly owned newsprint subsidiary, QUNO Corporation ("QUNO"), completed an initial public offering of 9 million shares of common stock. The Company now holds 8.8 million, or 49%, of the voting common shares and 4.2 million nonvoting common shares for a combined total of 59% of QUNO's total 22 million outstanding common shares. The Company also holds a $138.8 million subordinated debenture, convertible at the option of the company into 11.7 million voting common shares of QUNO. The debenture is callable by QUNO after December 27, 1997, matures in 2002 and bears interest at an effective rate of 2.77%. As the Company's voting interest is less than 50%, the Company is using the equity method of accounting for its investment in QUNO beginning in 1993. Prior year financial statements have not been restated. At closing, QUNO used the net proceeds of approximately $100 million from the stock offering plus proceeds of approximately $80 million from QUNO's new stand-alone bank financing agreement to repay a portion of its intercompany borrowings owed the Company. The net price per share realized from the offering was approximately the same as the Company's carrying value per share of its investment in QUNO. Summarized 1993 financial information for QUNO was as follows:

($ in thousands)

Revenues	$386,646	Current assets	$130,989
Operating loss	(31,110)	Noncurrent assets	458,649
Net loss	(28,881)	Current liabilities	82,213
		Noncurrent liabilities	309,346

The financial statements and transactions of QUNO are maintained in its functional currency (Canadian dollars) and translated into U.S. dollars. Translation adjustments are accumulated in a separate component of stockholders' investment. QUNO separately issues its financial statements in accordance with Canadian accounting principles. The financial information included herein has been adjusted to reflect U.S. accounting principles.

QUNO manufactures newsprint for sale to the Company's newspapers and other North American and overseas customers. The Company is party to a contract with QUNO expiring in 2007 to supply newsprint based on market prices. Under the contract, the Company has agreed to purchase specified minimum amounts of newsprint each year subject to certain limitations. The specified minimum annual volume is 250,000 metric tons in years 1994 to 1999, 225,000, 200,000, and 175,000 metric tons in years 2000 to 2002, respectively, and 150,000 metric tons in each of years 2003 to 2007. In 1993, 33% of QUNO's sales, or $127.2 million, were to the Company's newspapers, which represented 74% of their consumption.

During the period that QUNO was a wholly owned subsidiary, provision was made for U.S. income taxes on undistributed earnings of QUNO that were expected to be remitted to the Company. No provision for U.S. income taxes, however, was made on undistributed earnings that were intended to be reinvested in facilities and other assets in Canada for an indefinite period of time. The cumulative amount of unremitted earnings that has been reinvested indefinitely and other book/tax bases differences totaled approximately $75.0 million as of December 26, 1993. Determination of the taxes due on this amount is not practicable. No U.S. tax benefit has been provided on the Company's 1993 equity in QUNO net loss.

(*continued*)

Exhibit 3 ■ *(continued)*

Note 6: Long-Term Debt

Long-term Debt Consists of ($ in thousands)	**December 26 1993**	**December 27 1992**
Promissory notes, weighted-average interest rate of 3.3%	$ 41,829	$200,387
Medium-term notes, weighted-average interest rates of 7.3% and 8.7%, due 1993–2003	163,200	107,900
New Zealand dollar notes, U.S. dollar interest rate of 8.6%, paid 1993	–	77,427
8.0% notes, paid 1993	–	100,000
8.40% guaranteed ESOP notes, due 1993–2003	280,999	300,913
8.19% guaranteed ESOP notes, due 1993–98	17,970	20,777
Other notes and obligations	32,657	33,567
Total debt	536,655	840,971
Less portions due within one year	(25,817)	(99,992)
Long-term debt	$510,838	$740,979

In 1990 the Company began offering up to $200.0 million of its Series B medium-term notes, which have maturities from two to ten years and may not be redeemed by the Company prior to maturity. The proceeds from the sale of the notes have been used for general corporate purposes. The final $78 million of these notes were issued during 1993. The Company redeemed its $100 million 8% notes prior to their scheduled maturity. These notes, which were originally due in 1996, were redeemed in July 1993 at par. The Company financed this redemption with commercial paper. QUNO's New Zealand dollar notes were repaid by QUNO in April 1993 with proceeds from its new stand-alone bank financing agreement.

(EXCERPT FROM MANAGEMENT DISCUSSION AND ANALYSIS)

Equity in QUNO Net Loss

The Company's 1993 equity in QUNO's net loss, after interest expense and taxes, was $18.4 million. This amount represents 100% of QUNO's net loss prior to February 17, 1993, the date of QUNO's stock offering, and 59% of QUNO's net loss thereafter. QUNO reported an operating loss of $31 million in 1993, $23 million less than the $54 million operating loss incurred in 1992. This was the result of higher average newsprint selling prices and lower operating expenses, partially offset by a 4% decrease in newsprint shipments. Though average newsprint selling prices began to soften in the second half of 1993, they averaged 5% higher in 1993 than in 1992 due to the implementation of transaction price increases in August 1992 and March 1993.

Required:

1. Do you agree with the Tribune Company's decision not to consolidate QUNO Corporation in 1993?
2. What factors do you think prompted the decision?
3. Suggest some reasons that might explain why the Tribune Company decided not to deconsolidate QUNO in the 1992 comparative financial statements. Is this decision consistent with GAAP?

17

Statement of Cash Flows

LEARNING OBJECTIVES:
After studying this chapter, you will understand:

1. The major sources and uses of cash reported in the operating, investing, and financing sections of the statement of cash flows.
2. Why accrual net income and operating cash flow differ and the factors that explain this difference.
3. The difference between the direct and indirect method of determining cash flow from operations.
4. How to prepare a statement of cash flows from comparative balance sheet data, an income statement, and other financial information.
5. Why changes in balance sheet accounts over a year may not reconcile to the corresponding account changes included in the statement of cash flows.
6. What "cash burn rates" are and how they can be used to evaluate the financial viability of Internet companies.

Ode to Cash Flow

Though my bottom line is black, I am flat upon my back,
My cash flows out and my customers pay slow,
The growth of my receivables is almost unbelievable;
The result is certain—unremitting woe!
And I hear the banker utter an ominous low mutter,
"Watch cash flow!"[1]

As this poem suggests, accrual earnings may not always provide a reliable measure of enterprise performance and financial health. There are several reasons for this. Accrual accounting is often based upon subjective judgments that can introduce measurement error and uncertainty into reported earnings. Examples include estimates of uncollectible receivables, useful lives of assets, and future pension and health-care benefits. One-time write-offs and restructuring charges require subjective judgments that can adversely affect the quality of the reported earnings number as a reliable indicator of the long-run performance of a company. Moreover, managers can readily manipulate accrual income by postponing discretionary expenditures for research and development or advertising or by purposeful Last-In, First-Out (LIFO) dipping.

For these reasons, analysts must scrutinize a firm's cash flows—not just its accrual earnings—to evaluate its performance and creditworthiness. A significant difference between accrual earnings and operating cash flow may be a "red flag" that signals distortions of reported profits or impending financial difficulties.

Equity analysts are interested in operating cash flows because a firm's value ultimately depends upon the discounted present value of its expected future cash flows. Recent operating cash flows are sometimes used in conjunction with current earnings as a jumping-off point for generating fore-

[1] H. S. Bailey, Jr., cited in R. Green, "Are More Chryslers in the Offing?" *Forbes* (February 2, 1981), p. 69.

casts of expected future operating cash flows. Thus, cash flows can provide useful information for assessing equity values.[2]

Commercial lenders monitor a firm's operating cash flows because such cash flows provide the resources for periodic interest payments and the eventual repayment of principal. Low or negative operating cash flows signal poor credit risks.

Investment bankers scrutinize operating cash flows before deciding whether to underwrite a debt or equity issue. They know that the ultimate purchasers of the securities will assess the attractiveness of the securities based, in part, upon the firms' expected operating cash flows.

Statement Format

Some form of **funds flow statement** has been required under GAAP since the early 1970s.[3] The purpose of this statement is to provide users with a clear explanation of what caused the liquid assets of the company to increase or decrease during the reporting period. The format of this statement was originally designed to explain changes in **working capital**—current assets minus current liabilities. But since 1988, the Financial Accounting Standards Board (FASB) has mandated that firms provide a **cash flow statement** that explains the sources and uses of cash.[4] Firms are required to disclose cash-flows generated (or used) from three distinct types of activities:

> "Funds" is a generic term used to describe liquid assets—those readily convertible into cash or cash equivalents. The two most common definitions of funds are *working capital* and *cash*. A funds flow statement shows the inflows and outflows of funds as defined for that statement.

1. **Operating cash flows** result from events or transactions that enter into the determination of net income—that is, transactions related to the production and delivery of goods and services to customers. In effect, operating cash flows are the cash-basis revenues and expenses of a company.
2. **Investing cash flows** result from the purchase or sale of productive assets like plant and equipment, from the purchase or sale of marketable securities (government bonds or stocks and bonds issued by other companies), and from the acquisitions of other companies or divestitures.
3. **Financing cash flows** result when a company sells its own stocks or bonds, pays dividends or buys back its own shares (treasury stock), or borrows money and repays the amounts borrowed.

SFAS No. 95 allows firms the option of choosing between two alternative formats for presenting cash flows from *operating* activities: (1) the **direct approach,** and (2) the **indirect approach.** Each of these alternative formats is illustrated on the following pages.

> The International Accounting Standard (IAS) format for cash flow statements is similar to the U.S. GAAP format. See "Cash Flow Statements," *IAS No. 7* (revised 1992, London: International Accounting Standards Committee, 1992). Cash flows are classified by operating, investing and financing activities. Operating cash flows can be reported using either the direct method or the indirect method, but the direct method is preferred (paras. 18–20). One difference in the IAS approach is that firms have latitude in classifying cash flows from interest and dividends received or paid. Interest paid can be classified either as operating or financing cash flows; interest and dividends received can be classified either as operating or investing cash flows (para. 33).

---

[2] Research evidence which supports this assertion includes J. Rayburn, "The Association of Operating Cash Flow and Accruals with Security Returns," *Journal of Accounting Research* (Supplement, 1986), pp. 112–33; P. Wilson, "The Relative Information Content of Accruals and Cash Flows: Combined Evidence at the Earnings Announcement and Annual Report Release Date," *Journal of Accounting Research* (Supplement, 1986), pp. 165–200; P. Wilson, "The Relative Information Content of Accrual and Funds Components of Earnings After Controlling for Earnings," *The Accounting Review* (April 1987), pp. 293–322; M. Johnson and D. Lee, "Financing Constraints and the Role of Cash Flow from Operations in the Prediction of Future Profitability," *Journal of Accounting, Auditing and Finance* (Fall 1994), pp. 619–52.

[3] "Reporting Changes in Financial Position," *Accounting Principles Board (APB) Opinion No. 19* (New York: American Institute of Certified Public Accountants [AICPA], 1971).

[4] "Statement of Cash Flows," *Statement of Financial Accounting Standards (SFAS) No. 95* (Stamford, CT: Financial Accounting Standards Board [FASB], 1987).

The Direct Approach

Exhibit 17.1 presents the 1999 statement of cash flows for ABM Industries broken down into operating, investing, and financing activities. Operating activities generated a positive cash flow of $35.305 million. Investing activities resulted in a net cash outflow of $31.394 million, and most of this total was due to capital expenditures for property and equipment and purchases of intangible assets. The company paid out $3.616 million of cash for financing activities, principally for debt repayments, dividend distributions, and stock repurchases, while raising funds from stock issuance and long-term borrowing. Thus, ABM's overall cash position increased by $295 thousand in 1999 ($35.305 − $31.394 − $3.616), highlighted in Exhibit 17.1.

ABM is the largest facility services contractor listed on the New York Stock Exchange, performing mechanical and engineering services for commercial and industrial facilities throughout North America.

ABM follows the direct approach to presenting cash flows from operations. The direct approach requires that firms report major classes of gross cash receipts (cash revenues) and gross cash payments (cash expenses). Note that "Interest paid" and "Interest received" are shown as com-

The specific categories included by the FASB in para. 27 of *SFAS No. 95* are:

(a) cash collected from customers (including lessees and licensees)
(b) interest and dividends received
(c) other operating cash receipts
(d) cash paid to employees and other suppliers of goods and services
(e) interest paid
(f) income taxes paid
(g) other operating cash payments

Exhibit 17.1 ■ ABM INDUSTRIES INCORPORATED

Statement of Cash Flows
"Direct" Approach

	Year Ended October 31		
($ in millions)	1997	1998	1999
Cash flows from operating activities			
Cash received from customers	$1,203.314	$1,463.918	$1,589.775
Other operating cash receipts	1.126	1.331	1.491
Interest received	0.552	0.682	0.870
Cash paid to suppliers and employees	(1,154.572)	(1,406.600)	(1,522.495)
Interest paid	(2.685)	(3.334)	(2.025)
Income taxes paid	(19.988)	(23.936)	(32.311)
Net cash provided by operating activities	27.747	32.061	35.305
Cash flows from investing activities			
Additions to property, plant and equipment	(13.272)	(11.715)	(19.451)
Proceeds from sale of assets	0.660	0.497	0.922
Decrease (increase) in investments and long-term receivables	3.041	0.495	(1.885)
Intangible assets acquired	(28.606)	(10.010)	(10.980)
Net cash used in investing activities	(38.177)	(20.733)	(31.394)
Cash flows from financing activities			
Common stock issued, including tax benefit	8.778	15.151	17.178
Common stock repurchased	—	—	(5.448)
Dividends paid	(8.597)	(10.708)	(13.055)
Increase (decrease) in bank overdraft	8.035	(10.500)	2.492
Long-term borrowings	116.145	93.204	57.064
Repayment of long-term borrowings	(113.715)	(98.414)	(61.847)
Net cash provided by (used in) financing activities	10.646	(11.267)	(3.616)
Net increase in cash and cash equivalents	0.216	0.061	0.295
Cash and cash equivalents beginning of year	1.567	1.783	1.844
Cash and cash equivalents end of year	$ 1.783	$ 1.844	$ 2.139

ponents of cash flows from operating activities. This treatment is in accordance with *SFAS No. 95*. Many financial analysts and other statement users believe that interest paid should be included as part of cash flows from financing activities while interest received should be included with cash flows from investing activities. The FASB classified these two items as elements of cash flows from operating activities because "in general, cash flows from operating activities should reflect the cash effects of transactions and other events that enter into the determination of net income."[5]

ABM discloses "Cash received from customers" of $1,589.775 million on its 1999 cash flow statement. This number differs from the accrual accounting revenue number of $1,629.716 million which is reported on ABM's 1999 income statement and shown in Exhibit 17.2. There are several reasons for this difference:

1. Some 1999 credit sales made late in the year had not been collected in cash by year-end.
2. Some 1999 credit sales were made to customers who ultimately were unable to pay their balance due.
3. During 1999, cash was received for payment on accounts receivable generated from sales in prior years.

For analogous reasons, the "Cash paid to suppliers and employees" of $1,522.495 million on ABM's 1999 cash flow statement (Exhibit 17.1) differs from the "Operating expenses and cost of goods sold" ($1,413.541 million) and from "Selling, general and administrative" expenses ($146.984 million), which total $1,560.525 million and are reported on ABM's accrual-basis income statement (Exhibit 17.2). Similarly, "Income taxes paid" ($32.311 million) and "Interest paid" ($2.025 million) from the cash flow statement differ from the "Income taxes" ($27.565 million) and "Interest" ($1.959 million) reported on ABM's income statement (Exhibit 17.2).

Overall, Exhibits 17.1 and 17.2 show that ABM generated positive operating cash flows of $35.305 million in 1999, while its accrual-basis income was somewhat larger—that is,

Exhibit 17.2 ■ ABM INDUSTRIES INCORPORATED

Income Statement

	Year Ended October 31		
($ in millions, except per share amounts)	**1997**	**1998**	**1999**
Revenues and other income	$1,252.472	$1,501.827	$1,629.716
Expenses			
Operating expenses and cost of goods sold	1,076.078	1,298.423	1,413.541
Selling, general and administrative	126.755	142.431	146.984
Interest	2.675	3.465	1.959
	1,205.508	1,444.319	1,562.484
Income before income taxes	46.964	57.508	67.232
Income taxes	19.725	23.578	27.565
Net income	$ 27.239	$ 33.930	$ 39.667
Net income per common share			
Basic	$ 1.33	$ 1.58	$ 1.77
Diluted	1.22	1.44	1.65
Common and common equivalent shares			
Basic	20.143	21.110	22.067
Diluted	21.872	23.161	23.748

[5] *SFAS No. 95*, para. 88.

Exhibit 17.3 ■ ABM INDUSTRIES INCORPORATED

Reconciliation of Net Income to Cash from Operating Activities
"Indirect" Approach for Presenting Cash Flows from Operating Activities
Excerpts from Statement of Cash Flows

($ in millions)	1997	Year Ended October 31 1998	1999
Net income	$27.239	$33.930	$39.667
Adjustments:			
① Depreciation and amortization	16.118	19.593	20.698
Impairment of long-lived assets	2.700	—	—
② Provision for bad debt expense	2.988	2.821	2.257
③ Gain on sale of assets	(0.257)	(0.202)	(0.160)
④ Increase in deferred income taxes	(1.777)	(4.521)	(6.537)
⑤ Increase in accounts receivable	(50.312)	(28.907)	(39.304)
⑥ Increase in inventories	(4.069)	(1.768)	(0.331)
⑦ Increase in prepaid expenses and other current assets	(5.628)	(2.440)	(1.950)
⑧ Decrease (increase) in other assets	1.580	0.454	(3.295)
⑨ Increase in income taxes payable	1.514	4.163	1.791
⑩ Increase in retirement plans accrual	3.273	2.561	3.320
⑪ Increase (decrease) in insurance claims liability	5.212	(0.778)	4.500
⑫ Increase in trade accounts payable and other accrued liabilities	29.166	7.155	14.649
Total adjustments to net income	0.508	(1.869)	(4.362)
Net cash provided by operating activities	$27.747	$32.061	$35.305

$39.667 million. What are the major reasons for the discrepancy between ABM's net income and operating cash flows? The answer is found in the reconciliation of net income to cash from operations, the alternative indirect approach allowed in *SFAS No. 95* for presenting cash flows from operating activities. This other statement format from ABM's 1999 cash flow statement is shown in Exhibit 17.3 above.[6]

The Indirect Approach

The indirect approach begins with the accrual-basis net income (before extraordinary items) and adjusts for the following:

- Items *included* in accrual-basis net income that *did not* affect cash in the current period, such as
  1. noncash revenues or gains (e.g., revenues earned but not received in cash, and gains on disposal of fixed assets);
  2. noncash expenses or losses (e.g., depreciation and amortization, provision for bad debt expense, and expenses accrued but not paid in cash).
- Items *excluded* from accrual-basis income that *did* affect operating cash flows in the current period, such as
  3. cash inflows (revenues) received but not recognized as earned in the current period (e.g., rent received in advance and collections on account);
  4. cash outflows (expenses) paid but not recognized for accrual purposes in the current period (e.g., prepaid insurance and payments on account).

[6] This reconciliation schedule is required of all firms that use the direct method of presenting operating cash flows. "Statement of Cash Flows," *SFAS No. 95* (Stamford, CT: FASB, 1987), para. 28.

The indirect approach is used by the overwhelming majority of public companies. Of the 600 companies included in the AICPA's annual financial reporting survey, 593—or 98.8%—used the indirect approach for reporting cash generated by operating activities.[7] There are two reasons why firms favor the indirect approach:

1. The indirect approach is easier for firms to implement because it relies exclusively on data already available in the accrual accounts.
2. The indirect approach is more familiar to many accountants because this format was widely used in the changes in working capital statement that preceded *SFAS No. 95.*

We'll use Exhibit 17.3 to show how the indirect approach reconciles accrual accounting net income ($39.667 million in Exhibit 17.2) with cash flow from operations ($35.305 million in Exhibit 17.1). Each one of the reconciling items is discussed individually.

Items ① through ③ represent amounts included in the $39.667 million net income figure *that did not have a cash flow effect*—that is, they did not cause cash to increase or decrease during the year. Since they did not have a cash flow effect, the accrual-basis net income must be adjusted for these items to arrive at cash flows from operations.

① DEPRECIATION AND AMORTIZATION. This is the most common example of an indirect method adjustment. During 1999, ABM made the following entry for depreciation and amortization expense ($ in millions):

DR Depreciation and amortization	$20.698	
CR Accumulated depreciation and amortization		$20.698

While the debit reduced income, the credit did not represent a cash outflow. Hence, this typical noncash expense causes "Net income" to diverge from "Cash provided by operating activities." That's why depreciation must be added back to income in the indirect method statement as a reconciling item.

② PROVISION FOR BAD DEBT EXPENSE. ABM uses the "allowance method" to record bad debt expense (Chapter 8). During 1999, ABM made the following entry ($ in millions):

DR Bad debt expense	$2.257	
CR Allowance for doubtful accounts		$2.257

Although this entry reduced accrual-basis net income, it did not cause a corresponding decrease in cash. Therefore, this amount must be added to accrual income to arrive at cash flows from operations.

③ GAIN ON SALE OF ASSETS. This represents the difference between the selling price and book value of assets sold during the period. For 1999, ABM sold assets for a gain of $0.160 million. The proceeds from the asset sales shown in the "Investing activities" section of ABM's cash flow statement totaled $0.922 million. Thus, the gain ($0.160 million) that increased accrual income does *not* reflect the increase in cash related to this transaction ($0.922 million). Since the gain is a non-cash addition to accrual income, it must be subtracted from this amount to arrive at cash flows from operations.

We can infer that the assets sold had a net book value of $0.762 million by subtracting the gain of $0.160 million from the cash proceeds received from the sale of $0.922. So the entry to record the sale of assets was ($ in millions):

DR Cash	$0.922	
CR Assets (net of accumulated depreciation)		$0.762
CR Gain on sale		0.160

Items ④ through ⑫ represent amounts that were included in the $39.667 million net income for which the income effect either exceeds or falls

[7] A. Mrakovcic (ed.), *Accounting Trends and Techniques* (New York, NY: AICPA, 2000).

below the cash flow effect. Because the income effect and the cash flow effect differ, the following adjustments must appear in the reconciliation.

④ **Increase in Deferred Income Taxes (Asset).** ABM showed an increase in its net deferred tax assets for 1999 of $6.537 million. Thus, ABM's taxable income exceeded its book income in 1999 due to a variety of temporary differences (Chapter 13). When this happens, the debit to income tax expense falls below the taxes owed and paid in the current period. This increase in net deferred tax assets must be subtracted from accrual-basis net income, because the tax expense *understates* the cash outflow for taxes.

The entry to record ABM's taxes for 1999 is shown below ($ in millions). Adjustment ⑨ below corrects for the current portion of tax expense not paid in cash and for previous years' taxes paid in the current year.

DR Tax expense	$27.565	
DR Deferred tax asset	6.537	
CR Cash or taxes payable		$34.102

⑤ **Increase in Accounts Receivable.** During 1999, ABM's accounts receivable increased by $39.304 million. This means sales on account (accrual-basis revenue) exceeded cash collections on account (cash-basis revenue) in 1999. Accordingly, a subtraction must be made from accrual-basis income to arrive at cash provided by operating activities.

⑥ **Increase in Inventories.** During 1999, ABM's inventories increased by $0.331 million. So ending inventory was higher than beginning inventory, which means that inventory purchased was greater than the cost of inventory sold during the year. Let's temporarily assume that all inventory purchases were paid for in cash. (Adjustment ⑫ discussed below for changes in accounts payable and other accrued liabilities corrects for non-cash inventory purchases.) The inventory buildup means the cash outflow for inventory exceeded accrual-basis cost of goods sold. Thus, the increase in inventories must be subtracted from accrual-basis income to obtain cash flows from operations because the cash outflow for inventory exceeded the amount charged to expense under accrual accounting.

⑦ **Increase in Prepaid Expenses and Other Current Assets and ⑧ Increase in Other Assets.** These increases of $1.950 million and $3.295 million, respectively, represent cash outflows that were charged to asset accounts rather than expense accounts. As a result, these amounts represent a decrease in cash that did not cause a decrease in accrual earnings. ABM subtracts these increases from accrual earnings to obtain cash flows from operations because these asset increases represent operating cash outflows for the period.

⑨ **Through ⑫ Increase in Taxes Payable, Retirement Plans Accrual, Insurance Claims Liability, Trade Accounts Payable and Other Liabilities.** Because all of these liability accounts increased, we discuss their effect on the cash flow statement together. In each case, the off-setting debits to these increases in accrued liability accounts were to various expense accounts that decreased accrual earnings. But because these expenses did not result in cash outflows, the increases in these liability accounts are added to accrual earnings to obtain operating cash flows.

Both the direct and indirect approaches for computing net cash provided by operating activities will obviously report the same number—$35.305 million in ABM's 1999 annual report. Those who prefer the direct approach justify their preference by claiming that this method discloses operating cash flows by category—inflows from customers, outflows to suppliers, etc. They contend that this categorization facilitates cash flow predictions. For example, assume that an analyst expects product selling prices to increase by 6% in the ensuing year. The direct method's disclosure of cash received from customers could then be multiplied by 106% to construct next year's cash forecast. (There is no similarly easy way to incorporate the expectation of a 6% price increase in the indirect method approach.)

ANALYSIS

Analysts who prefer the indirect approach do so because the size and direction of the items reconciling income to operating cash flow provide a rough yardstick for evaluating the quality of earnings. When a company reports high accounting income but simultaneously has low or negative cash flow from operations, this situation is considered a sign of low-quality earnings that are not sustainable. For example, if the excess of income over cash flow is accompanied by a large buildup in accounts receivable, this increase could indicate that the company is aggressively recognizing revenue (Chapters 3 and 8)—that is, the receivables buildup may have occurred because the recorded amounts reflect a policy of shipping unwanted merchandise to distributors. Or the buildup could result from sales to customers with marginal creditworthiness that may never be collected.

Although the FASB allowed a choice between the direct and indirect approaches when calculating cash flow from operating activities, it anticipated that the vast majority of firms would use the indirect approach. Since few firms were expected to use the direct approach, the FASB feared that users might find it difficult to compare the operating cash flows of these "direct approach" firms with the operating cash flows of those firms choosing the indirect approach. To address this comparability concern, the FASB requires firms using the direct approach to *also* provide a reconciliation between accrual earnings and operating cash flows like the one that is presented by those firms using the indirect approach. Since ABM chose the direct approach, this explains why we have operating cash flow information for them under both methods.

Firms using the indirect approach are required to separately disclose the amount of interest paid. Consequently, those who believe interest expense represents a cash flow from financing activities will always have sufficient information available to reclassify this item out of cash flows from operating activities for firms using the indirect approach. The FASB did *not* require a separate disclosure of dividends and interest income *received*. Therefore, analysts who believe that these items should be classified as cash flows from investing activities will not have sufficient information to make this reclassification for firms who opt for the indirect approach.

SFAS No. 95 also requires firms using the indirect approach to separately disclose income taxes paid.

One additional difficulty confronting analysts using *SFAS No. 95* disclosures relates to the treatment of income taxes. Recollect from Chapter 2 that intraperiod income tax allocation is followed in constructing the income statement—that is, the income tax expense associated with income from continuing operations is separately disclosed. Items not included in the computation of income from continuing operations (such as extraordinary items and the cumulative effects of changes in accounting principles) are reflected *net* of their associated income tax effects. This is done to facilitate predictions by statement users. The tax expense associated with the presumably recurring income from continuing operations is reported separately from the tax expense associated with items appearing below income from continuing operations. Regrettably, *SFAS No. 95* does not treat *cash* outflows for income taxes in the same way. The entire amount of taxes paid in cash is included in the "Cash flows from operating activities" computation even though some of the taxes relate, for example, to gains on sales of assets whose gross cash flows are included in the "Cash flows from investing activities" section of the statement. The failure to differentiate tax cash flows by type (those pertaining to income from continuing operations versus other items) complicates forecasts of future cash flows. The FASB justified this treatment as follows:

> The Board decided that allocation of income taxes paid to operating, investing, and financing activities would be so complex and arbitrary that the benefits, if any, would not justify the costs involved. (*SFAS No. 95*, para. 92.)

While this cost–benefit justification may be correct, *SFAS No. 95* provides no evidence to support this assertion.

RECAP

The statement of cash flows provides a summary of a firm's operating, investing, and financing activities that explain its change in cash position for the period. Operating cash flows can be presented using either the direct or indirect approach. The direct approach details major sources of cash receipts and major categories of cash expenditures. The indirect approach begins with accrual earnings and adjusts for (1) items included in accrual-basis income that did not affect cash, and (2) items excluded from accrual earnings that did affect operating cash flows.

Other Elements of the Cash Flow Statement

Let's return to Exhibit 17.1. ABM's cash flow statement illustrates the typical range of items included in the "Investing activities" and "Financing activities" sections of the statement. The items included are relatively straightforward, and there should be no difficulties in interpreting these disclosures. For example, ABM shows investing cash outflows in 1999 for purchases of property and equipment ($19.451 million), purchase of investments and long-term receivables ($1.885 million), and acquisition of intangible assets ($10.980 million). Direct cash inflows from investing activities resulted from the sale of assets ($0.922 million).

Financing cash inflows resulted from the issuance of common stock ($17.178 million), bank overdrafts ($2.492 million), and long-term borrowings ($57.064 million). Major financing cash outflows occurred for purchase of treasury stock ($5.448 million), dividends paid ($13.055 million), and repayment of long-term borrowings ($61.847 million).

The net result of ABM's operating, investing, and financing activities for the year was an increase in cash and cash equivalents of $295,000.

Preparing the Cash Flow Statement

This section illustrates the procedures used to prepare a cash flow statement. Exhibits 17.4 (a) and (b) on the following page provide comparative 2000–2001 balance sheet data, a 2001 income statement, and selected additional information for Burris Products Corporation.

Reviewing the comparative balance sheets in Exhibit 17.4(a) shows that the cash balance decreased by $8,000 during 2001. The purpose of a cash flow statement is to explain the underlying *causes* for this $8,000 change in the cash balance. Recall that the causes for change arise from operating, investing, and financing activities.

Constructing a cash flow statement requires the preparer to gather information like that in Exhibit 17.4. The three-step process that follows is then used to build the components of the statement.

Step 1. Identify the journal entry or entries that led to the reported change in each balance sheet account.

Step 2. Determine the net cash flow effect of the journal entry (or entries) identified in Step 1.

Step 3. Compare the financial statement effect of the entry (Step 1) with its cash flow effect (Step 2) to determine what cash flow statement treatment is necessary for each item.

This three-step approach is used to develop Burris' cash flow statement in Exhibit 17.5 on page 893 using the indirect method of determining cash flow from operations.

Cash Flows from Operations

The operating cash flow section of the statement in Exhibit 17.5 begins with net income of $182,000. Under the indirect approach, net income represents an initial rough approximation of the cash generated by operations. Starting the statement with net income presumes that revenues are ultimately collected in cash and that expenses represent cash outflows. In the long run this approximation is basically correct. However, in any single period accrual accounting net income will not equal that same period's cash flow from operations. The reason is that cash flows for some revenue and expense items occur either before or after accrual accounting revenue and expenses are recognized. The adjustment for these differences between the timing of revenue/expense recognition and cash flow impact appear as the eight numbered items below the net income figure in Exhibit 17.5. We now explain each of these items.

Exhibit 17.4 ■ BURRIS PRODUCTS CORPORATION

Comparative Balance Sheets, 2001 Income Statement and Additional Information

Comparative Balance Sheets	December 31 2001	2000	Increase or Decrease
Cash	$ 25,000	$ 33,000	$ 8,000 Decrease
Accounts receivable	171,000	180,000	9,000 Decrease
Inventory	307,000	295,000	12,000 Increase
Land	336,000	250,000	86,000 Increase
Buildings and equipment	1,628,000	1,430,000	198,000 Increase
Accumulated depreciation	(653,000)	(518,000)	135,000 Increase
	$1,814,000	$1,670,000	
Accounts payable	$ 163,000	$ 160,000	$ 3,000 Increase
Customer advance deposits	99,000	110,000	11,000 Decrease
Bonds payable	500,000	500,000	–0– —
Discount on bonds payable	(66,000)	(70,000)	4,000 Decrease
Deferred income tax payable	100,000	94,000	6,000 Increase
Common stock	850,000	800,000	50,000 Increase
Retained earnings	168,000	76,000	92,000 Increase
	$1,814,000	$1,670,000	

(a)

2001 Income Statement	
Sales revenues	$3,030,000
Cost of goods sold	(2,526,625)
Depreciation expense	(158,000)
Sales commissions (all cash)	(34,000)
Interest expense	(44,000)
Gain on sale of equipment	17,000
Income before taxes	284,375
Income tax expense	(102,375)
Net income	$ 182,000

(b)

Additional information

1. Equipment with a cost of $63,000 and a book value of $40,000 was sold for $57,000.
2. Cash dividends of $90,000 were paid in 2001.

① **Depreciation** The income statement in Exhibit 17.4(b) indicates that depreciation expense recognized during 2001 was $158,000. We use the three-step analytic approach, as follows:

Step 1. The journal entry that generated the account change was:

DR Depreciation expense	$158,000	
CR Accumulated depreciation		$158,000

Step 2. Neither of the two accounts that appear in the Step 1 journal entry involve cash. Indeed, depreciation is unlike most other expenses, since the cash outflow often occurs *before* the expense recognition—that is, when the asset is initially purchased.

Step 3. Depreciation expense was included as an element in the determination of net income (Step 1) as if it were a cash outflow. But depreciation expense does not represent a cash outflow (Step 2). Consequently, depreciation expense must be added back to net income.

Exhibit 17.5 ■ BURRIS PRODUCTS CORPORATION

2001 Statement of Cash Flows

Operating Activities		
Net income		$182,000
Adjustments to reconcile net income to cash provided by operating activities		
① Depreciation	$158,000	
② Gain on equipment sale	(17,000)	
③ Amortization of bond discount	4,000	
④ Deferred income taxes increase	6,000	
⑤ Accounts receivable decrease	9,000	
⑥ Customer advance deposits decrease	(11,000)	
⑦ Inventory increase	(12,000)	
⑧ Accounts payable increase	3,000	
		140,000
Cash provided by operating activities		322,000
Investing Activities		
② Equipment sale		$ 57,000
⑨ Land purchase		(86,000)
⑩ Buildings and equipment purchase		(261,000)
Cash used for investing activities		(290,000)
Financing Activities		
⑪ Common stock issued		$ 50,000
⑫ Dividend paid		(90,000)
Cash used for financing activities		(40,000)
Net decrease in cash during 2001		$ (8,000)

In short, depreciation expense is added back to accrual basis income to obtain operating cash flows because it was included in the determination of net income even though—unlike most other expenses—it does not represent a cash outflow of the current period.

② Gain on Equipment Sale The net income number includes a gain on equipment sale of $17,000, as shown in Exhibit 17.4(b). Using the same three-step approach, we arrive at the following:

Notice that if the equipment originally cost $63,000 and its book value was $40,000, the accumulated depreciation must have been $23,000.

Step 1. With the additional information disclosed beneath the income statement in Exhibit 17.4(b), we can develop the following journal entry for the gain:

DR Accumulated depreciation	$23,000	
DR Cash	57,000	
CR Equipment		$63,000
CR Gain on sale		17,000

Step 2. Scrutiny of the journal entry reveals that the sale resulted in a cash inflow of $57,000. This cash inflow is the result of investment activities.

Step 3. Comparing the accrual accounting effect (Step 1) to the cash flow effect (Step 2) reveals three problems: (1) the recognized accrual gain ($17,000) does not correspond to the cash inflow ($57,000); (2) the $17,000 gain is included in income, and thus would be categorized as an operating cash inflow unless adjustments are made; and (3) the $57,000 cash inflow from investing activities must be separately reflected in the statement.

The cash flow statement in Exhibit 17.5 reflects the information uncovered in Step 3. The gain of $17,000 is subtracted from net income to arrive at cash flow from operations, and the total cash received of $57,000 is correctly categorized and shown as a cash inflow from investing activities.

③ **Amortization of Bond Discount** Exhibit 17.4(a) discloses that the discount on bonds payable account decreased by $4,000 during 2001. The three-step approach shows the following:

Step 1. Since the income statement reports interest expense as $44,000, the journal entry that led to the balance sheet change for discount on bonds payable was:

DR Interest expense	$44,000	
CR Discount on bonds payable		$ 4,000
CR Cash		40,000

Step 2. An examination of the journal entry reveals that interest expense of $44,000 was deducted in computing net income, although the cash outflow for the payment of interest in 2001 was only $40,000.

Step 3. Since the accrual accounting income statement charge for interest expense ($44,000) exceeds the cash outflow ($40,000), the difference of $4,000 must be added back to net income in the operating section of the cash flow statement.

④ **Deferred Income Taxes Increase** Deferred income taxes payable increased by $6,000, as shown in Exhibit 17.4(a). The three-step approach shows the following:

Step 1. Since income tax expense for 2001 was $102,375, the journal entry for taxes in 2001 was:

DR Income tax expense	$102,375	
CR Deferred income payable		$ 6,000
CR Cash		96,375

Step 2. Again, there is a disparity between the amount of the expense included in the determination of net income ($102,375) and the cash outflow to pay taxes ($96,375).

Step 3. Because the income statement expense charge is larger than the cash outflow by $6,000, this $6,000 must be added back in the operating activities section of the cash flow statement in Exhibit 17.5.

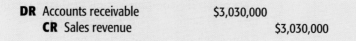

⑤ **Accounts Receivable Decrease** During 2001, Exhibit 17.4(a) shows that accounts receivable decreased by $9,000. Following the three-step approach at top of next page:

Step 1. If we assume that all 2001 sales were initially credit sales, the aggregate entry to record these sales would be:

DR Accounts receivable	$3,030,000	
CR Sales revenue		$3,030,000

If we assume the only transaction causing a decrease in accounts receivable is collections on account, then the $9,000 decrease during 2001 implies the following entry for cash collections:

DR Cash	$3,039,000	
CR Accounts receivable		$3,039,000

Step 2. Examination of the entries in Step 1 reveals that when the total in accounts receivable decreased, the amount of cash collections during the year ($3,039,000) exceeded the amount of accrual revenues included in income ($3,030,000).

Step 3. The $9,000 excess of cash collections over accrual revenues must be added back to net income in Exhibit 17.5 in order to obtain cash from operations.

⑥ **Customer Advance Deposits Decrease** Burris Products Corporation requires cash payments from customers prior to the sale of special order custom merchandise. This advance payment represents a liability on the balance sheet. As the custom products are delivered to customers, the liability is reduced and revenue is recognized. During 2001, the amount of the liability decreased by $11,000, as shown in Exhibit 17.4(a).

Step 1. The accounting entry that reflects the reduction in the advance payment liability during 2001 was:

DR Customer advance deposits	$11,000	
CR Sales revenues		$11,000

Step 2. Scrutinizing the entry in Step 1 indicates that accrual sales revenues increased by $11,000. However, there was no corresponding cash flow effect this year since the cash flow originated in 2000 when the liability was initially recorded.

Step 3. Because revenues included in the computation of 2001 net income exceeded 2001 cash inflows by $11,000, this amount must be deducted in the operating section of the cash flow statement.

⑦ **Increase in Inventory** When inventory increases during a period, the dollar amount of new inventory purchases exceeds the cost of goods that were sold.

Step 1. If we initially assume that all inventory is purchased for cash (we will relax this assumption in adjustment ⑧ discussed next), then the two accounting entries giving rise to a $12,000 increase in inventory (see Exhibit 17.4[a]) are:

DR Inventory	$2,538,625	
CR Cash		$2,538,625
($2,526,625 C of GS + $307,000 E.I. − $295,000 B.I.)		
		(continued)

and

DR Cost of goods sold	$2,526,625	
CR Inventory		$2,526,625

Notice that the combined result of these two entries increases inventory by $12,000.

Step 2. Comparing the two journal entries in Step 1 indicates that the cost-of-goods-sold number that is deducted in the computation of net income ($2,526,625) is $12,000 *lower* than the cash outflow to buy inventory.

Step 3. Since net income understates the cash outflow to acquire inventory, $12,000 must be deducted from income in Exhibit 17.5.

⑧ **Increase in Accounts Payable** Adjustment ⑦ for the increase in inventory was computed under the assumption that all inventory was purchased for cash. We assumed this because it makes it easier to see why an increase in inventory must be adjusted for when preparing a cash flow statement. We now relax this assumption since scrutiny of Exhibit 17.4(a) shows that accounts payable increased by $3,000 during 2001. A $3,000 increase in accounts payable means that $3,000 of the $12,000 inventory increase during the year was not paid for in cash. Therefore, $3,000 is added to net income in the cash flow statement.

There is another way to look at adjustments ⑦ and ⑧ which may make it easier for you to understand the accrual-to-cash adjustment. Together, adjustments ⑦ and ⑧ are designed to isolate the difference between accrual accounting's cost-of-goods-sold measure and cash inventory purchases. Specifically:

Accrual accounting cost-of-goods-sold deduction included in determining income	$2,526,625
Add: Adjustment ⑦ (inventory increase)	12,000
Equals: 2001 *total* inventory purchases	$2,538,625
Subtract: Adjustment ⑧ (payables increase)	(3,000)
Equals: 2001 *cash* inventory purchases	$2,535,625

In combination, adjustments ⑦ and ⑧ subtract $9,000 from income, an amount which is equal to the difference between cost of goods sold ($2,526,625) and cash inventory purchases ($2,535,625).

Cash Flows from Investment Activities

Turning to the investing activities section of Burris' cash flow statement (Exhibit 17.5), we see there are three transactions that affected cash—one that resulted in a cash inflow and two that reduced cash.

② **Equipment Sale** This transaction was analyzed earlier when we adjusted accrual net income for the gain on sale of equipment. The $57,000 cash received when this equipment was sold represents an investing source of cash.

⑨ **Land** Exhibit 17.4(a) indicates that the land account increased by $86,000. The analysis here is straightforward.

Step 1. The journal entry that reflects this increase is

DR Land	$86,000	
CR Cash		$86,000

Step 2. This transaction represents an outflow of cash of $86,000.

Step 3. The cash outflow is categorized as a $86,000 investment outflow.

⑩ **Buildings and Equipment Purchase** The "Buildings and equipment" account increased by $198,000 during 2001 (see Exhibit 17.4[a]). However, in computing the cash outflow that was incurred to acquire these fixed assets, we cannot simply use the $198,000 net account change. The reason is that some equipment was also sold during 2001 (see preceding Item ②). It is therefore necessary to adjust the change in the buildings and equipment account for the cost of the equipment sold in order to deduce the amount of buildings and equipment purchased.

Step 1. When several items affect a particular account, it is useful to begin by reconstructing the account over the period being analyzed.

Buildings and Equipment

12/31/00 balance	$1,430,000		
"Plug" figure necessary to balance the account	261,000	Reduction in account arising from sale of equipment (see discussion of Item ②)	$63,000
12/31/01 balance	$1,628,000		

The analysis reveals that the gross increase in buildings and equipment was $261,000 and resulted in the following journal entry:

DR Buildings and equipment	$261,000	
CR Cash		$261,000

Step 2. This transaction represents a cash outflow of $261,000.

Step 3. The outflow is categorized as a $261,000 investment cash outflow.

This adjustment illustrates that when constructing a cash flow statement, the analyst must be careful to look beyond just the net change in the account—he or she must also consider other known items that were added to or subtracted from the account during the period.

Cash Flows from Financing Activities

The financing section of Burris' cash flow statement in Exhibit 17.5 shows two other account changes during the period that had cash flow implications.

⑪ and ⑫ Stock Sale and Dividend Paid The increase in the common stock account indicates that additional capital was raised when new shares were sold. Furthermore, the additional information lists a cash dividend of $90,000 (see Exhibit 17.5). The analysis of these items is straightforward:

Step 1. The stock sale journal entry was:

DR Cash	$50,000	
CR Common stock		$50,000

The dividend generated the following entry:

DR Retained earnings	$90,000	
CR Cash		$90,000

Step 2. The cash effects of these items are unambiguously indicated in the entries—that is, a $50,000 inflow for the new financing and a $90,000 dividend outflow.

Step 3. Both the cash inflow of $50,000 as well as the cash outflow of $90,000 should be categorized as cash flows from financing activities.

To prepare a cash flow statement: (1) Recreate the accounting entries that explain the changes in all noncash balance sheet accounts, (2) determine the net cash flow effect of the entry and the type of activity that generated or used the cash, and (3) compare the accrual accounting effect of the entry with the cash flow effect to determine what adjustments, if any, are needed to convert accrual earnings to cash flow from operations.

RECAP

Reconciling Between Statements: Some Complexities

Users of financial statements will frequently encounter situations in which changes in balance sheet accounts over the year will *not* reconcile to the corresponding account changes in the statement of cash flows. We'll demonstrate this discrepancy and explain why it happens using data from the H.J. Heinz Company 2000 annual report. Exhibit 17.6 shows Heinz' statement of cash flows for the fiscal year ended May 3, 2000 and the previous fiscal year. The operating section of Heinz' cash flow statement is prepared using the indirect approach, and starts with fiscal 2000 accrual-basis net income of $890,553,000. Adjustments to reconcile net income to cash provided by operations are presented next. We'll refer to these as **net accrual adjustments** because these are the items that cause accrual income to differ from operating cash flows. These adjustments total $347,478,000 (highlighted in Exhibit 17.6), resulting in $543,075,000 cash provided by operating activities. Notice that Heinz' net accrual adjustments cause net income to exceed cash from operations. We will call these **income-increasing accrual adjustments.**

Exhibit 17.7 on page 900 compares the working capital accrual adjustments from the statement of cash flows to the changes in non-cash working capital accounts taken from Heinz' comparative balance sheets for fiscal years 1999 and 2000. This exhibit shows that *changes in balance sheet working capital account balances are not necessarily equal to the net accrual adjustments in the operating section of the cash flow statement.* We'll explain why shortly.

Column 1 of Exhibit 17.7 shows that Heinz reported income increasing net working capital accrual adjustments of $659,300,000 (highlighted). Column 3 shows the corresponding changes in working capital accounts taken directly from Heinz' comparative balance sheets for fiscal 1999–2000 (Exhibit 17.8 on page 901), which imply income increasing accrual adjustments of only $162,701,000. Thus, the change in non-cash working capital accounts from the balance sheet understates Heinz' income increasing accrual adjustments by nearly *half a billion dollars* ($659,300,000 − $162,701,000 = $496,599,000).

A similar discrepancy exists when trying to reconcile changes in Heinz' property, plant and equipment balance sheet account with information presented on its cash flow statement. Exhibit 17.8 also shows comparative balance sheet data for Heinz' property, plant and equipment account. The year-to-year increase in this account (before accumulated depreciation) is $273,772,000 (highlighted). However, the "Investing activities" section of Heinz' statement of cash flows (Exhibit 17.6) shows fiscal year 2000 capital expenditures of $452,444,000—a difference of nearly $178,672,000. What accounts for these differences in working capital and fixed asset accounts? There are at least four reasons for these differences:

> Note the $217,127,000 change in the inventory balance (excluding the effects of acquisitions and divestitures) is *subtracted* from accrual-basis net income to arrive at cash provided by operations. This means that inventory *increased* during the period after adjusting for the effects of acquisitions and divestitures.

1. Asset write-offs due to impairment, corporate restructuring, or retirement
2. Translation adjustments on assets and liabilities held by foreign subsidiaries
3. Acquisitions and divestitures of other companies
4. Simultaneous investing and financing activities not directly affecting cash.

Discrepancies in Current Accruals

We'll use the inventory account to illustrate reasons for the discrepancy between working capital components of net accrual adjustments on the cash flow statement and changes in these accounts on the balance sheet. From Exhibit 17.7, the change in inventories from the balance sheet is +$190,255,000 (column [3]), while the inventory increase reflected in the cash flow statement is +$217,127,000 (column [1]). Although a precise reconciliation is not possible, the primary factors causing the $26,872,000 difference arise for the reasons explained next.

Exhibit 17.6 ■ H.J. HEINZ COMPANY AND SUBSIDIARIES

Consolidated Statement of Cash Flows

($ in thousands)	May 3, 2000 (53 Weeks)	Fiscal Year Ended April 28, 1999 (52 Weeks)
Operating Activities:		
Net income	$ 890,553	$ 474,341
Adjustments to reconcile net income to cash provided by operating activities:		
Depreciation	219,255	207,852
Amortization	87,228	94,360
Deferred tax provision	28,331	23,564
① Gain on sale of Weight Watchers	(464,617)	—
Gain on sale of bakery products unit	—	(5,717)
Gain on sale of Ore-Ida frozen food-service business	—	—
② Provision for restructuring	392,720	527,107
Other items, net	48,905	(43,147)
Changes in current assets and liabilities, excluding effects of acquisitions and divestitures:		
Receivables	(123,994)	(88,742)
③ Inventories	(217,127)	(115,743)
Prepaid expenses and other current assets	(23,296)	2,604
Accounts payable	111,976	3,410
Accrued liabilities	(372,999)	(150,533)
Income taxes	(33,860)	(19,220)
Net accrual adjustments*	(347,478)	435,795
Cash provided by operating activities	543,075	910,136
Investing Activities:		
④ Capital expenditures	(452,444)	(316,723)
⑤ Acquisitions, net of cash acquired	(394,418)	(268,951)
⑥ Proceeds from divestitures	726,493	180,400
Purchases of short-term investments	(1,175,538)	(915,596)
Sales and maturities of short-term investments	1,119,809	883,945
Investments in The Hain Celestial Group, Inc.	(99,764)	—
Other items, net	7,188	46,396
Cash (used for) provided by investing activities	(268,674)	(390,529)
Financing Activities:		
Proceeds from long-term debt	834,328	259,593
Payments on long-term debt	(627,498)	(65,744)
Proceeds from (payments on) commercial paper and short term borrowings, net	532,305	74,464
Dividends	(513,782)	(484,847)
Purchase of treasury stock	(511,480)	(410,103)
Exercise of stock options	20,027	77,158
Other items, net	6,937	33,989
Cash used for financing activities	(259,163)	(515,490)
Effect of exchange rate changes on cash and cash equivalents	6,397	15,565
Net increase (decrease) in cash and cash equivalents	21,635	19,682
Cash and cash equivalents at beginning of year	115,982	96,300
Cash and cash equivalents at end of year	$ 137,617	$ 115,982

*This line added by authors for clarity.

Exhibit 17.7 ■ H.J. HEINZ COMPANY

Comparison of Implied Accruals from Change in Balance Sheet Accounts Versus Actual Accruals from Cash Flow Statement Fiscal Year Ending May 3, 2000

($ in thousands)	(1) Statement of Cash Flows	(2) *Actual* Effect of Accrual on Income*	(3) Adjustments to Arrive at Cash Flow from Operations Based on Changes in Balance Sheet Accounts	(4) *Implied* Effect of Balance Sheet Working Capital Changes on Income*
Operating Activities:				
Net income	$ 890,553			
Adjustments to reconcile net income to cash provided by operating activities:				
Depreciation	219,255	−		
Amortization	87,228	−		
Deferred tax provision	28,331	−		
Gain on sale of Weight Watchers	(464,617)	+		
Provision for restructuring	392,720	−		
Other items, net	48,905	−		
	311,822			
Changes in current assets and liabilities:				
Receivables	(123,994)	+	(73,889)	+
Inventories	(217,127)	+	(190,255)	+
Prepaid expenses and other current assets	(23,296)	+	11,981[a]	−
Accounts payable	111,976	−	81,472	−
Accrued liabilities	(372,999)	+	(20,586)[b]	+
Income taxes	(33,860)	+	28,576	−
Working capital accruals	(659,300)	+	(162,701)	+
Cash provided by operating activities	$ 543,075			

*A plus (+) indicates an income increasing accrual adjustment; a minus (−) indicates an income decreasing accrual adjustment. Remember, income increasing accrual adjustments are *subtracted* from net income to arrive at cash provided by operating activities.

[a]This amount is the net change in two current asset accounts on Heinz' balance sheet ($ in thousands): $16,980 increase in "Prepaid expenses" minus the $28,961 decrease in "Other current assets" (see Exhibit 17.8).

[b]This amount is the net change in three current liability (payable) accounts on Heinz' balance sheet ($ in thousands): $18,751 increase in "Accrued marketing" minus the $25,452 decrease in "Salaries and wages" minus the $13,885 decrease in "Other accrued liabilities" (see Exhibit 17.8).

Write-offs Due to Restructuring The following excerpt from Heinz' footnote 4 describing its 2000 "Operation Excel" reorganization and restructuring program reveals that a portion of the restructuring charge (highlighted) relates to inventory write-offs:

> During Fiscal 2000, the company recognized net restructuring charges and implementation costs totaling $392.7 million pre-tax. . . . Non-cash asset write-downs totaled $61.6 million in Fiscal 2000 and related to property, plant and equipment ($48.7 million) and current assets ($12.9 million). . . . Current asset write-downs included inventory and packaging material, prepaids and other current assets and were determined based on management's estimate of net realizable value.

Exhibit 17.8 ■ H.J. HEINZ COMPANY AND SUBSIDIARIES

Selected Accounts from Comparative Balance Sheets

($ in thousands)	May 3, 2000	April 28, 1999	Changes in Selected Account Balances*	*Implied* Effect on Income
Selected Current Asset Accounts:				
Receivables (net of allowances: 2000–$18,697 and 1999–$21,633)	$1,237,804	$1,163,915	$ 73,889	+
Inventories:				
Finished goods and work-in-process	1,270,329	1,064,015		
Packaging material and ingredients	329,577	345,636		
Total inventories	1,599,906	1,409,651	190,255	+
Prepaid expenses	171,599	154,619	16,980	+
Other current assets	6,511	35,472	(28,961)	–
Selected Current Liability Accounts:				
Accounts payable	1,026,960	945,488	81,472	–
Salaries and wages	48,646	74,098	(25,452)	+
Accrued marketing	200,775	182,024	18,751	–
Accrued restructuring costs	125,704	147,786		
Other accrued liabilities	358,738	372,623	(13,885)	+
Income taxes	188,672	160,096	28,576	–
Property, Plant, and Equipment Accounts:				
Land	45,959	48,649	(2,690)	
Buildings and leasehold improvements	860,873	798,307	62,566	
Equipment, furniture and other	3,440,915	3,227,019	213,896	
	4,347,747	4,073,975	273,772	
Less: Accumulated depreciation	–1,988,994	–1,902,951	–86,043	
Total property, plant, and equipment, net	$2,358,753	$2,171,024	$187,729 ←	

*Amounts without parentheses represent increases in accounts from 1999 to 2000, while amounts with parentheses represent decreases in accounts.

This write-off resulted in a decrease of an undisclosed amount to the inventory accounts unrelated to the sales of merchandise. It is part of the $392.7 million **"Provision for restructuring"** that is added back to accrual basis net income shown in the "Operating activities" section of Heinz' 2000 statement of cash flows (Item ② in Exhibit 17.6). So this write-down in inventory on the balance sheet is not part of the $217,127,000 inventory accrual adjustment shown in the cash flow statement (item ③ in Exhibit 17.6).

Translation Adjustments Heinz has numerous foreign subsidiaries whose statements are translated using the current rate approach described in Chapter 16. This method of measuring the increase or decrease in inventories of foreign subsidiaries generates a potential discrepancy between the balance sheet inventory change figure and the statement of cash flows inventory change figure. Here's why. On the cash flow statement, inventory change is computed by comparing purchases with cost of goods sold. If purchases exceed cost of goods sold, an inventory increase is indicated. To determine the direction of the inventory change for *foreign* subsidiaries, *translated* purchases and cost of goods sold are compared. Inventory purchases and cost of goods sold are translated into dollars using the exchange rate in effect at the time of the transaction. In contrast, the inventory change on the balance sheet is computed differently. Foreign subsidiaries' beginning inventories are translated at the beginning-of-period rate of exchange while ending inventories are translated at the end-of-period rate of exchange. The difference corresponds to the different nature of the two statements: the balance sheet reflects an *instant in time* (and thus uses the *exchange rate at that instant*); the cash flow statement uses a *series of exchange rates*. It

For simplicity, the translation may also be done using the weighted-average rate of exchange in effect over the period.

should not be surprising therefore that the measures of inventory change on the two statements will differ.

> This difference will usually not arise when *all* foreign subsidiaries are accounted for using the temporal method (Chapter 16). The reason is that the method for computing inventory change for temporal method subsidiaries on the cash flow statement translates both beginning and ending inventory at the *historical* rate of exchange. The historical rate is also used on the balance sheet. For firms whose subsidiaries all utilize the temporal approach, inventory change differences between the two statements will usually not arise.

Acquisitions and Divestitures Another reason why the inventory change on the two statements differs is because of acquisitions and divestitures. Companies bought and sold usually possess inventories. The ending inventory number reported on the consolidated balance sheet includes the inventory of subsidiary companies purchased and excludes the inventories of subsidiaries or divisions sold during the year. But on the statement of cash flows, the inventory of companies acquired is reported as a component of "Acquisitions, net of cash acquired" and the inventory of companies sold is part of the "Proceeds from divestitures" reported in the "Investing activities" section of Exhibit 17.6. ***Therefore, the inventory change figure on the cash flow statement is limited to inventory changes for those segments of the firm that were owned at both the start and end of the reporting period.***

> Changes in inventories due to acquisitions or divestitures do not create a corresponding accrual adjustment to cost of goods sold on the income statement. Therefore, changes due to these events would *not* be included as part of the inventory adjustment to accrual basis income (item ③ in Exhibit 17.6) to arrive at operating cash flows.

The same factors will explain discrepancies between changes in other working capital accounts on the balance sheet and accrual adjustments shown on the statement of cash flows.

Discrepancies Related to Property, Plant and Equipment

A portion of the discrepancy between the change in property, plant and equipment on the balance sheet and capital expenditures on the cash flow statement can be explained by asset write-downs taken in conjunction with Heinz' "Operation Excel" reorganization and restructuring program described earlier. As shown above in the excerpt from footnote 4 in Heinz' 2000 10-K report, $48.7 million of the $61.6 million asset write-down related to property, plant and equipment which explains some of the change in this account on the balance sheet. Without this write-down, the year-to-year change in property, plant and equipment net of depreciation would have been a $236,429,000 increase [$187,729,000 increase from Exhibit 17.8 (see arrow) + $48,700,000 write-down]—still far short of the $452,444,000 increase shown for capital expenditures in the "Investing Activities" section on Heinz' cash flow statement in Exhibit 17.6.

Three additional events are likely to have contributed to the reported balance sheet change:

Retirements During the year, Heinz may have retired fixed assets (not related to the restructuring) that were not fully depreciated. Recall from Chapter 10 that the entry to record the retirement would take the following form:

DR Accumulated depreciation—plant and equipment	XXX	
DR Loss on retirement	XXX	
CR Plant and equipment (for cost of assets retired)		XXX

Prior to 1995 it was possible to determine the cost of assets retired from Schedule V, Property, Plant and Equipment—a required schedule in firms' 10-K reports filed with the SEC—that reconciled the beginning and ending balances of the property, plant and equipment account reported in firms' balance sheets. Unfortunately, this schedule is no longer required. Therefore, it is generally not possible for external users to determine the exact dollar amount of the year-to-year change in fixed asset accounts due to retirements.

Foreign Currency Translation Adjustment As noted already, Heinz translates the accounts of most of its foreign subsidiaries using the current rate approach. Accordingly, the property, plant and equipment accounts of these subsidiaries are translated using the current rate of exchange—at the balance sheet date—between the dollar and the foreign currency. If the dollar falls (rises) in relation to the functional currencies of these subsidiaries, this would result in an increase (decrease) in the balance of property, plant and equipment account that would not be reflected on the cash flow statement. Again, these adjustments were recorded in Schedule V of the 10-K report prior to 1995 but are no longer disclosed, making it difficult to ascertain the impact of translation adjustments on individual changes in balance sheet accounts.

Acquisitions and Divestitures Heinz acquired and sold companies during the year. These companies all owned property, plant and equipment. This immediately raises a classification dilemma on Heinz' statement of cash flows: Should that portion of cash flow related to the cost of properties acquired be classified as "Capital expenditures" or should it be included as a part of "Acquisitions, net of cash acquired"? Under the *SFAS 95* classification criteria, "Capital expenditures" contain only cash outflows made to acquire property directly. Cash outflows for property acquired as part of a business acquisition are classified under "Acquisitions," following *SFAS 95* guidelines. You can see from examining the "Investing activities" section of the statement of cash flow in Exhibit 17.6 that Heinz paid $394,418,000 for acquisitions, net of cash acquired (Item ⑤). Part of this purchase price would contribute to an increase in property, plant and equipment because the acquired firms' assets are included in Heinz' consolidated reports if Heinz' ownership exceeds 50%.

The "Investing activities" section of Exhibit 17.6 also shows cash proceeds from divestitures of $726,493,000 (Item ⑥). When business units included as part of a consolidated entity are sold, the property, plant and equipment account is reduced by the book value—cost minus accumulated depreciation—of the fixed assets in the business unit sold. Before it was eliminated by the SEC, Schedule V of the 10-K report provided detailed information on increases and decreases in the property, plant and equipment account due to acquisitions and divestitures. Now that this schedule is no longer required, analysts and other statement users must rely on fragmented and somewhat incomplete information provided elsewhere in the statements to deduce the book value of assets sold.

To illustrate how this is done, recall from Chapter 10 that the gain or loss on asset disposal is the difference between the sales price and the book value of the assets sold. Heinz' statement of cash flow (Exhibit 17.6) shows "Proceeds from divestitures" of $726,493,000 (Item ⑥) in the "Investing activities" section and a "Gain on sale of Weight Watchers" of $464,617,000 (Item ①) as a non-cash adjustment to income in the "Operating activities" section. Combining these two pieces of information, we can deduce the book value of assets sold or divested in this transaction as follows:

> This calculation assumes that the cash proceeds from divestiture represents the entire sales price of the assets sold. If non-cash consideration was received (e.g., a promissory note), then the sales price and the cash proceeds would differ and the amount of the note would need to be considered in calculating the book value of assets sold.

	($ in thousands)
Proceeds from divestiture	$726,493
Less: Gain on assets sold	(464,617)
Book value of assets sold	$261,876

Unfortunately, it is not possible to determine from the information given what portion of this $261,876,000 book value relates to property, plant and equipment versus current assets like inventory or receivables held by the business unit that was sold.

Simultaneous Non-Cash Financing and Investing Activities

Occasionally firms will engage in investing and financing activities that cause changes in balance sheet asset and liability accounts even though they do not affect cash receipts or cash payments. Examples include (1) purchasing a building by incurring a mortgage to the seller; (2) acquiring an asset by entering into a capital lease; or (3) issuing stock for non-cash assets in connection with a business acquisition. *SFAS No. 95* requires firms to disclose these non-cash simultaneous financing and investing activities either in a narrative or in a schedule, which is sometimes included as a separate section of the statement of cash flows. Although there is no evidence in Heinz' 2000 annual report that any of the balance sheet changes in property, plant and equipment were acquired with non-cash consideration, this is fairly common, especially for Internet and start-up companies that are typically short on cash.

Exhibit 17.9 shows Amazon.com's 1999 cash flow statement. Note the supplemental schedule (at the bottom of this statement) summarizing each of the three types of simultaneous financing and investing activities we just discussed. Each of these transactions resulted in increases in fixed asset accounts on Amazon's balance sheet but did not have a direct effect on cash flows. Also note that Amazon received non-cash revenues in the form of equity securities of other companies for advertising and promotional services. The latter is a common form of transaction among Internet companies.

RECAP

The year-to-year changes in comparative balance sheet accounts may not coincide with the changes implied from amounts reported on the statement of cash flows. The factors contributing to these differences include (1) asset write-downs due to impairment or restructuring, (2) the translation of foreign subsidiary accounts using the year-end current exchange rate between the dollar and the foreign currency, (3) acquisitions and divestitures of other companies, and (4) simultaneous non-cash financing and investing transactions. Footnote disclosures, along with information in the income statement and in the operating section of the cash flow statement, are often helpful in reconciling some of these differences.

Analytical Insights: Cash Burn Rate of Internet Stocks

The ability to generate positive operating cash flows is critical to the survival and success of any company. This is particularly true for Internet companies. Expenditures for managerial talent, employees with technical expertise, computer hardware, physical plant, research and development, and advertising create heavy cash flow demands on start-up Internet companies while they await cash inflows from new products or services they are developing. As a result, many Internet companies generate negative operating cash flows while at the same time investing large amounts of cash in business infrastructure and operating assets.

> A recent survey conducted by Pegasus Research International, an Internet stock evaluation firm, reports that 74% of the 371 publicly traded Internet companies in the United States had negative operating cash flows as of the fourth quarter of 1999. See J. Willoughby, "Burning Up," *Barron's* (March 20, 2000), p. 29.

The **"cash burn rate"** has become a popular metric for assessing how quickly Internet firms are using up their cash reserves.[8] The related measure of **"months to burnout"** provides an estimate of how much longer a company can survive without an infusion of external capital (via debt or equity financing).

> These metrics were compiled by Pegasus Research International, an Internet stock evaluation firm as part of an exclusive study conducted for *Barron's*.

The "cash burn rate" is typically calculated in one of two ways:

Method (1). Cash used for operations plus cash used for capital expenditures and purchases of on-going businesses (net of cash received) divided by number of months covered by cash flow statement (i.e., 12 for annual and 3 for quarterly statements).

Method (2). Earnings before interest, taxes, depreciation and amortization (EBITDA) excluding nonrecurring gains and losses divided by number of months covered by income statement.

[8] Ibid.; J. Willoughby, "Up in Smoke," *Barron's* (June 19, 2000), p. 31; J. Willoughby, "Smoldering," *Barron's* (October 2, 2000), p. 38; M. Krantz, "E-retailers Run Low on Fuel," *USA Today* (April 26, 2000), p. 1B; S. Pulliam and P. Beckett, "Goldman's E-Commerce List Reduces Nonclients to Low Tiers," the *Wall Street Journal* (June 20, 2000).

Exhibit 17.9 ■ AMAZON.COM, INC.

Consolidated Statement of Cash Flows

($ in thousands)	December 31 1999	Fiscal Year Ended December 31 1998	December 31 1997
Operating Activities:			
Net loss	($ 719,968)	($124,546)	($ 31,020)
Adjustments to reconcile net loss to net cash provided (used) in operating activities:			
Depreciation and amortization of fixed assets	36,806	9,421	3,442
Amortization of deferred stock-based compensation	30,618	2,386	1,354
Equity in losses of equity-method investees	76,769	2,905	—
Amortization of goodwill and other intangibles	214,694	42,599	—
Non-cash merger, acquisition, and investment costs	8,072	1,561	—
Non-cash revenue for advertising and promotional services	(5,837)	—	—
Loss on sale of marketable securities	8,688	271	—
Non-cash interest expense	29,171	23,970	64
Changes in operating assets and liabilities, net of effects from acquisitions:			
Inventories	(172,069)	(20,513)	(8,400)
Prepaid expenses and other current assets	(60,628)	(16,758)	(3,055)
Accounts payable	330,166	78,674	30,172
Accrued expenses and other current liabilities	65,121	21,615	5,274
Accrued advertising	42,382	9,617	2,856
Deferred revenue	262	—	—
Interest payable	24,878	(167)	—
Net cash provided (used) in operating activities	(90,875)	31,035	687
Investing Activities:			
Sales and maturities of marketable securities	2,064,101	227,789	5,198
Purchases of marketable securities	(2,359,398)	(504,435)	(20,454)
Purchases of fixed assets	(287,055)	(28,333)	(7,603)
Acquisitions and investments in businesses, net of cash acquired	(369,607)	(19,019)	—
Net cash used in investing activities	(951,959)	(323,998)	(22,859)
Financing Activities:			
Proceeds from issuance of capital stock and exercise of stock options	64,469	14,366	53,358
Proceeds from long-term debt	1,263,639	325,987	75,000
Repayment of long-term debt	(188,886)	(78,108)	(47)
Financing costs	(35,151)	(7,783)	(2,309)
Net cash provided by financing activities	1,104,071	254,462	126,002
Effect of exchange rate changes	489	(35)	—
Net increase (decrease) in cash and cash equivalents	61,726	(38,536)	103,830
Cash and cash equivalents at beginning of period	71,583	110,119	6,289
Cash and cash equivalents at end of period	$ 133,309	$ 71,583	$110,119
Supplemental Cash Flow Information:			
Fixed assets acquired under capital leases	$ 25,850	—	$ 3,463
Fixed assets acquired under financing agreements	5,608	—	1,500
Stock issued in connection with business acquisitions	774,409	$217,241	—
Equity securities of other companies received for non-cash revenue for advertising and promotional services	54,402	—	—
Cash paid for interest, net of amounts capitalized	59,688	26,629	326

The "months to burnout" is calculated as:

$$\frac{\text{Cash} + \text{Cash equivalents} + \text{Short-term marketable securities}}{\text{Cash burn rate}}$$

These amounts are taken from the balance sheet at the end of the quarter or year.

We'll illustrate these measures using data from Amazon.com's 1999 annual cash flow statement given in Exhibit 17.9 along with earnings and other balance sheet information (not shown). In Exhibit 17.9, Amazon's net cash used in operations was $90,875,000. In the "Investing activities" section, Amazon used additional cash of $287,055,000 to buy fixed assets and another $369,607,000 to acquire other existing businesses. Thus, the cash burn rate computed using Method (1) is −($90,875,000 + $287,055,000 + $369,607,000)/12 months = −$747,537,000/12 months = −$62,294,750 per month. Amazon's cash, cash equivalents and short-term marketable securities totaled $706,188,000 on December 31, 1999. Dividing this number by the cash burn rate yields 11.3 "months to burnout."

The EBITDA cash burn rate [Method (2)] is computed from data reported in Amazon's 1999 10-K as follows:

	($ in thousands)
Loss from operations before interest and other income	($605,755)
Add back –	
Depreciation and amortization of fixed assets	36,806
Amortization of deferred stock-based compensation	30,618
Amortization of goodwill and other intangibles	214,694
Loss on sale of marketable securities	8,688
Adjusted EBITDA for 1999	($314,949)

Dividing this number by 12 months yields an EBITDA cash burn rate of −$26,245,750 per month. Dividing this amount into the cash, cash equivalents and marketable securities amount of $706,188,000 yields 26.9 "months to burnout."

Using EBITDA generally yields a lower cash burn rate and longer time to burnout because it ignores working capital cash flows and cash used to acquire fixed assets (capital expenditures) and cash used to acquire other businesses. These expenditures are often necessary to carry out a firm's business plan and to continue to build market share. Therefore, some suggest that cash burn rate Method (1) is a better metric for evaluating the financial viability of Internet stocks.[9]

Table 17.1 presents cash burn rates and months to burnout based on data for the second quarter 2000 for a selected group of Internet stocks. As can be seen, many of these companies were perilously close to running out of funds to support their operations without a significant infusion of additional debt or equity financing. This may well account for why many of these stocks saw a large decline in their stock values in the latter half of 2000.

[9] Recall from Chapter 5 that EBITDA is a "flawed" measure of operating cash flow, although some analysts mistakenly use it for that purpose. The same point could be made here—if you want to measure the *cash* burn rate, look to cash flows [Method (1)], not EBITDA [Method (2)].

Table 17.1 ■ ESTIMATED CASH BURN RATES FOR SELECTED INTERNET COMPANIES

($ in millions)		Cash Flow Method		EBITDA Method	
Company	Ending Cash Balance[1] as of 6/30/00	Burn Rate(1)[2] (CFO + Capital Expenditures)[3]	Months Until Burnout(1)	Burn Rate(2)[1] (EBITDA)*	Months Until Burnout(2)
GenesisIntermedia.com	$ 0.4	−$10.20	0.12	−$ 4.97	0.24
Onemain.com	1.4	−24.90	0.17	−3.58	1.17
drkoop.com	2.0	−23.50	0.26	−22.65	0.26
Choice One	8.1	−55.40	0.44	−13.89	1.75
Streamline.com	4.8	−12.80	1.13	−8.90	1.62
Medium4.com	1.4	−2.50	1.68	−1.70	2.47
Bluefly	3.9	−6.00	1.95	−4.99	2.34
Medinex Systems	3.8	−5.70	2.00	−5.54	2.06
LendingTree	19.0	−27.90	2.04	−18.76	3.04
Audiohighway.com	3.5	−4.90	2.14	−4.81	2.18
Streamedia Comm	1.8	−2.50	2.16	−1.91	2.83
Pacific Softworks	0.7	−0.90	2.33	−0.98	2.14
Cavion Tech	2.0	−2.50	2.40	−2.28	2.63
Quokka Sports	19.6	−24.00	2.45	−15.43	3.81
RMI.net	2.5	−3.00	2.50	−3.65	2.05
BiznessOnline.com	2.7	−2.60	3.12	−2.08	3.89
TriZetto Group	8.4	−7.70	3.27	−5.27	4.78
Pets.com	37.2	−31.30	3.57	−21.91	5.09
ZipLink	6.6	−5.10	3.88	−3.96	5.00
Claimsnet.com	3.4	−2.50	4.08	−2.73	3.74
eGain Comms[4]	30.2	−18.30	4.95	−18.00	5.03
Netzee	5.4	−2.90	5.59	−3.18	5.09
Intraware[5]	18.1	−8.50	6.39	−8.81	6.16
US SearchCorp.com	9.0	−2.90	9.31	−8.84	3.05
RoweCom	10.1	34.70	—	−11.34	2.67

[1]Includes cash, cash equivalents and short-term marketable securities at end of second quarter 2000.
[2]Calculated from data for second quarter 2000. Numbers in these columns are divided by 3 before calculating months to burnout.
[3]Cash from operations + capital expenditures + purchases of going businesses.
[4]Calculated from data for year ended June 30, 2000.
[5]Calculated for second quarter ended August 31, 2000.

*Source: Pegasus Research International as reported in *Barron's* (October 2, 2000, p. 38) and company quarterly reports filed with SEC.

SUMMARY

The statement of cash flows provides information for assessing the ability of a firm to generate sufficient cash to pay for operating expenses, capital improvements and currently maturing obligations. Firms able to generate consistently strong positive cash flows from operations are considered better credit risks and benefit from a lower cost of capital.

The two alternative methods for presenting the operating section of a cash flow statement are the direct and indirect approach. Most firms use the indirect approach that begins with accrual-basis earnings and adjusts for depreciation, amortization, non-cash gains and losses, and changes in non-cash working capital accounts—for example, inventories, receivables, payables—that cause earnings to differ from operating cash flows for the period.

Frequently, you will encounter situations where the changes in non-cash accounts shown on comparative balance sheets will not reconcile with the adjustments shown on the cash flow statement. These discrepancies are due to one or more of the following causes:

1. Asset write-offs due to impairment, corporate restructuring, or retirement.
2. Translation adjustments on assets and liabilities held by foreign subsidiaries.
3. Acquisitions and divestitures of other companies or operating units.
4. Simultaneous investing and financing activities not directly affecting cash.

Failure to understand how these events cause balance sheet account changes to differ from changes in account balances shown on the cash flow statement can lead to incorrect interpretation of both statements.

Knowing how to prepare and interpret cash flow statements is critical to conducting sound credit analysis and making informed investment and lending decisions. This is particularly true for start-up companies and Internet stocks that often have negative operating cash flows. Cash burn rates and months to burnout are measures that can be helpful in evaluating the financial viability of these companies.

EXERCISES

E17–1 Determining cash flow from operations

Information for ABC Company is as follows ($ in thousands):

Net income	$280
Equity in investee loss	20
Decrease in prepaid expenses	7
Cash paid for new plant equipment	30
Amortization of premium on bonds payable	10
Decrease in accounts payable	2
Increase in inventory	21
Depreciation expense	13
Increase in salaries payable	8
Increase in accounts receivable	15
Dividends paid to stockholders	5

REQUIRED:

What is the net cash provided by operating activities?

E17–2 Determining cash flow from operations

AICPA adapted

Lino Company's worksheet for the preparation of its 2001 statement of cash flows included the following information:

	December 31	January 1
Accounts receivable	$29,000	$23,000
Allowance for uncollectible accounts	1,000	800
Prepaid rent expense	8,200	12,400
Accounts payable	22,400	19,400

Lino's 2001 net income is $150,000.

REQUIRED:

What amount should Lino include as net cash that is provided by operating activities in the statement of cash flows?

E17–3 Cash flow from operations

AICPA adapted

Patsy Corporation has estimated its activity for December 2001. Selected data from these estimated amounts are as follows:

Sales	$350,000
Gross profit (based on sales)	30%
Increase in gross trade accounts receivable during month	10,500
Change in accounts payable during month	–0–
Increase in inventory during month	5,000
Variable selling, general, and administrative (SG&A) expenses include a charge for uncollectible accounts of 1% of sales; Accounts receivable write-offs were $3,000	
Total SG&A expenses are $35,000 per month plus 15% of sales	
Depreciation expense of $20,000 per month is included in fixed SG&A	

REQUIRED:

1. Calculate accrual-basis net income for December.
2. On the basis of the preceding data, what is the net cash flow provided from operating activities for December?

E17–4

Analysis of changes in balance sheet accounts
AICPA adapted

Roe Company is preparing a statement of cash flows for the year ended December 31, 2001. It has the following account balances:

	December 31 2000	December 31 2001
Machinery	$250,000	$320,000
Accumulated depreciation—machinery	102,000	120,000
Loss on sale of machinery		4,000

During 2001, Roe sold for $26,000 a machine that cost $40,000, and purchased several items of machinery.

REQUIRED:

1. How much depreciation expense was recorded on machinery for 2001?
2. What was the amount of machinery purchased in 2001?

E17–5

Cash flows from investing and operating activities
AICPA adapted

Karr, Inc. reported net income of $300,000 for 2001. Changes occurred in several balance sheet accounts as follows:

Equipment	$25,000 increase
Accumulated depreciation	40,000 increase
Note payable	30,000 increase

ADDITIONAL INFORMATION:

1. During 2001 Karr sold equipment that cost $25,000 and had accumulated depreciation of $12,000, for a gain of $5,000.
2. In December 2001 Karr purchased equipment costing $50,000 with $20,000 cash and a 12% note payable of $30,000.
3. Depreciation expense for the year was $52,000.

REQUIRED:

1. In Karr's 2001 statement of cash flows, what should be the net cash from operating activities?
2. In Karr's 2001 statement of cash flows, what should be the net cash used in investing activities?

E17–6

Cash flows from investing and financing activities
AICPA adapted

In preparing its cash flow statement for the year ended December 31, 2001, Reve Company collected the following data:

Gain on sale of equipment	($ 6,000)
Proceeds from sale of equipment	10,000
Purchase of A.S., Inc. bonds (par-value $200,000)	(180,000)
Amortization of bond discount	2,000
Dividends declared	(45,000)
Dividends paid	(38,000)
Proceeds from the sale of treasury stock (carrying amount $65,000)	75,000

REQUIRED:

Determine the following amounts that should be reported in Reve's 2001 statement of cash flows.

1. What amount should Reve report as net cash used in investing activities?
2. What amount should Reve report as net cash provided by financing activities?

E17–7

Cash flow from investing activities
AICPA adapted

Alp, Inc. had the following activities during 2001:

- Acquired 2,000 shares of stock in Maybel, Inc. for $26,000.
- Sold an investment in Rate Motors for $35,000 when the carrying value was $33,000.
- Acquired a $50,000, four-year certificate of deposit from a bank. (During the year, interest of $3,750 was paid to Alp.)
- Collected dividends of $1,200 on stock investments.

REQUIRED:

In Alp's 2001 statement of cash flows, what amount would be shown for net cash used in investing activities?

E17–8

Cash flows from investing and financing activities

AICPA adapted

Kollar Corporation's transactions for the year ended December 31, 2001 included the following:

1. Purchased real estate for $550,000 using cash borrowed from a bank.
2. Sold investment securities for $500,000.
3. Paid dividends of $600,000.
4. Issued 500 shares of common stock for $250,000.
5. Purchased machinery and equipment for $125,000 cash.
6. Paid $450,000 toward a bank loan.
7. Reduced accounts receivable by $100,000.
8. Increased accounts payable by $200,000.

REQUIRED:

1. Determine Kollar's net cash used in investing activities for 2001.
2. Determine Kollar's net cash used in financing activities for 2001.

E17–9

Determining operating cash flow

AICPA adapted

Metro, Inc. reported net income of $150,000 for 2001. Changes occurred in several balance sheet accounts during 2001 as follows:

Investment in Videogold, Inc. stock, carried on the equity basis	$ 5,500 increase
Accumulated depreciation, caused by major repair to projection equipment	2,100 decrease
Premium on bonds payable	1,400 decrease
Deferred income tax liability (long term)	1,800 increase

REQUIRED:

Determine the reported net cash provided by operating activities for Metro in 2001.

E17–10

Determining operating, investing, and financing cash flows

AICPA adapted

The differences in Beal Inc.'s balance sheet accounts at December 31, 2001 and 2000 are presented next:

	Increase (Decrease)
Assets	
Cash and cash equivalents	$ 120,000
Short-term investments	300,000
Accounts receivable, net	–0–
Inventory	80,000
Long-term investments	(100,000)
Plant assets	700,000
Accumulated depreciation	–0–
	$1,100,000
Liabilities and Stockholders' Equity	
Accounts payable and accrued liabilities	$ (5,000)
Dividends payable	160,000
Short-term bank debt	325,000
Long-term debt	110,000
Common stock, $10 par	100,000
Additional paid-in capital	120,000
Retained earnings	290,000
	$1,100,000

The following information is related to 2001:

- Net income was $790,000.
- Cash dividends of $500,000 were declared.

- A building costing $600,000 and having a carrying amount of $350,000 was sold for $350,000.
- Equipment costing $110,000 was acquired through the issuance of long-term debt.
- A long-term investment was sold for $135,000. There were no other transactions affecting long-term investments.
- Ten thousand shares of common stock were issued for $22 a share.

REQUIRED:

In Beal's 2001 statement of cash flows, determine:

1. Net cash provided by operating activities.
2. Net cash used in investing activities.
3. Net cash provided by financing activities.

PROBLEMS/DISCUSSION QUESTIONS

P17–1

Determining cash provided (used) by operating, investing, and financing activities

AICPA adapted

Dice Corporation's balance sheet accounts as of December 31, 2001 and 2000 and information relating to 2001 activities are presented next.

DICE CORPORATION

Balance Sheet

	2001	2000
Assets		
Cash	$ 230,000	$ 100,000
Short-term investments	300,000	–0–
Accounts receivable—net	510,000	510,000
Inventory	680,000	600,000
Long-term investments	200,000	300,000
Plant assets	1,700,000	1,000,000
Accumulated depreciation	(450,000)	(450,000)
Goodwill	90,000	100,000
Total assets	$3,260,000	$2,160,000
Liabilities and Stockholders' Equity		
Accounts payable and accrued liabilities	$ 825,000	$ 720,000
Short-term debt	325,000	–0–
Common stock ($10 par)	800,000	700,000
Additional paid-in capital	370,000	250,000
Retained earnings	940,000	490,000
Total liabilities and stockholders' equity	$3,260,000	$2,160,000

Information relating to 2001 activities follows:

- Net income for 2001 was $690,000.
- Cash dividends of $240,000 were declared and paid in 2001.
- Equipment costing $400,000 and having a carrying value of $150,000 was sold in 2001 for $150,000.
- A long-term investment was sold in 2001 for $135,000. There were no other transactions affecting long-term investments in that year.
- Ten thousand shares of common stock were issued in 2001 for $22 per share.
- Short-term investments consist of Treasury bills maturing on June 30, 2002.

REQUIRED:

1. What was the amount of net cash provided by Dice's 2001 operating activities?
2. What was the amount of net cash used in Dice's 2001 investing activities?
3. What was the amount of net cash provided by Dice's 2001 financing activities?

P17–2 **Comparing direct and indirect methods of determining cash flows from operations** CMA adapted

The Spoke Company, a major retailer of bicycles and accessories, operates several stores and is a publicly traded company. The comparative statement of financial position and income statement for Spoke as of May 31, 2001 follows. The company is preparing its statement of cash flows to comply with "Statement of Cash Flows," *SFAS No. 95*.

SPOKE COMPANY

Comparative Statement of Financial Position as of May 31, 2001 and May 31, 2000

	May 31 2001	May 31 2000
Assets		
Cash	$ 43,250	$ 20,000
Accounts receivable	70,000	50,000
Merchandise inventory	210,000	250,000
Prepaid expenses	9,000	7,000
Total current assets	332,250	327,000
Plant assets	600,000	510,000
Less: Accumulated depreciation	(150,000)	(125,000)
Net plant assets	450,000	385,000
Total assets	$ 782,250	$ 712,000
Liabilities and Shareholders' Equity		
Accounts payable	$ 123,000	$ 115,000
Salaries payable	47,250	72,000
Interest payable	27,000	25,000
Total current liabilities	197,250	212,000
Long-term debt		
Bonds payable	70,000	100,000
Total liabilities	267,250	312,000
Shareholders' Equity		
Common stock, $10 par	370,000	280,000
Retained earnings	145,000	120,000
Total shareholders' equity	515,000	400,000
Total liabilities and shareholders' equity	$ 782,250	$ 712,000

SPOKE COMPANY

Income Statement for the Year Ended May 31, 2001

Sales	$1,255,250
Cost of merchandise sold	712,000
Gross margin	543,250
Expenses	
Salary expense	252,100
Interest expense	75,000
Other expenses	8,150
Depreciation expense	25,000
Total expenses	360,250
Operating income	183,000
Income tax expense	43,000
Net income	$ 140,000

The following is additional information concerning Spoke's transactions during the year ended May 31, 2001:

- All sales during the year were made on account.
- All merchandise was purchased on account, comprising the total accounts payable account.
- Plant assets costing $90,000 were purchased by paying $40,000 in cash and by issuing 5,000 shares of stock.
- The "Other expenses" are related to prepaid items.
- All income taxes incurred during the year were paid during the year.
- In order to supplement its cash, Spoke issued 4,000 shares of common stock at par value.
- There were no penalties assessed for the retirement of bonds.
- Cash dividends of $115,000 were declared and paid at the end of the fiscal year.

REQUIRED:

1. Prepare a statement of cash flows for Spoke Company for the year ended May 31, 2001 using the direct method. Be sure to support the statement with appropriate calculations. (A reconciliation of net income to net cash is not required.)
2. Using the indirect method, calculate only the net cash flow from operating activities for Spoke Company for the year ended May 31, 2001.
3. Compare and contrast the direct method and the indirect method for reporting cash flows from operating activities, as prescribed by *SFAS No. 95*. What are the advantages and limitations of each approach?

P17–3

Determining amounts reported on statement of cash flows

AICPA adapted

The following are selected balance sheet accounts of Zach Corporation at December 31, 2001 and 2000, as well as the increases or decreases in each account from 2000 to 2001. Also presented is selected income statement information for the year ended December 31, 2001, as well as additional information.

Selected Balance Sheet Accounts	2001	2000	Increase (Decrease)
Assets			
Accounts receivable	$ 34,000	$ 24,000	$10,000
Property, plant, and equipment	277,000	247,000	30,000
Accumulated depreciation	(178,000)	(167,000)	11,000
Liabilities and Stockholders' Equity			
Bonds payable	49,000	46,000	3,000
Dividends payable	8,000	5,000	3,000
Common stock, $1 par	22,000	19,000	3,000
Additional paid-in capital	9,000	3,000	6,000
Retained earnings	104,000	91,000	13,000
Selected Income Statement Information for the Year Ended December 31, 2001			
Sales revenue	$155,000		
Depreciation	33,000		
Gain on sale of equipment	13,000		
Net income	28,000		

ADDITIONAL INFORMATION:

- Accounts receivable relate to sales of merchandise.
- During 2001 equipment that cost $40,000 was sold for cash.
- During 2001 $20,000 of bonds payable were issued in exchange for property, plant, and equipment. There was no amortization of bond discount or premium.

REQUIRED:

Items 1 through 5 which follow represent activities that will be reported in Zach's statement of cash flows for the year ended December 31, 2001. For each item, determine both the amount that should be reported in Zach's 2001 statement of cash flows and the section (operating, investing, or financing) in which the item will appear.

1. Cash collections from customers (direct method)
2. Payments for the purchase of property, plant, and equipment
3. Proceeds from the sale of equipment
4. Cash dividends paid
5. Redemption of bonds payable

P17–4

Determining amounts reported on statement of cash flows

AICPA adapted

The Flax Corporation uses the direct method to prepare its statement of cash flows. Flax's trial balances at December 31, 2001 and 2000 are as follows:

	December 31	
	2001	**2000**
Debits		
Cash	$ 35,000	$ 32,000
Accounts receivable	33,000	30,000
Inventory	31,000	47,000
Property, plant, and equipment	100,000	95,000
Unamortized bond discount	4,500	5,000
Cost of goods sold	250,000	380,000
Selling expenses	141,500	172,000
General and administrative expenses	137,000	151,300
Interest expense	4,300	2,600
Income tax expense	20,400	61,200
	$756,700	$976,100
Credits		
Allowance for uncollectible accounts	$ 1,300	$ 1,100
Accumulated depreciation	16,500	15,000
Trade accounts payable	25,000	17,500
Income taxes payable	21,000	27,100
Deferred income taxes	5,300	4,600
8% callable bonds payable	45,000	20,000
Common stock	50,000	40,000
Additional paid-in capital	9,100	7,500
Retained earnings	44,700	64,600
Sales	538,800	778,700
	$756,700	$976,100

ADDITIONAL INFORMATION:

- Flax purchased $5,000 in equipment during 2001.
- Flax allocated one third of its depreciation expense to selling expenses and the remainder to general and administrative expenses.

Show work for all answers to the following questions:

REQUIRED:

What amount should Flax report in its statement of cash flows for the year ended December 31, 2001 for the following:

1. Cash collected from customers?
2. Cash paid for goods sold?
3. Cash paid for interest?
4. Cash paid for income taxes?
5. Cash paid for selling expenses?

The balance sheets of Global Trading Company follow:

P17–5

Preparation and analysis of cash flow statement

GLOBAL TRADING COMPANY

Balance Sheets
December 31

	2001	2000
Assets		
Cash	$120,000	$108,000
Accounts receivable	50,000	300,000
Less: Allowance for doubtful accounts	(20,000)	(30,000)
Inventory	80,000	250,000
Prepaid insurance	–0–	20,000
Property, plant, and equipment	500,000	500,000
Less: Accumulated depreciation	(450,000)	(400,000)
Goodwill	–0–	70,000
Total Assets	$280,000	$818,000
Liabilities and Owners' Equity		
Accounts payable	$100,000	$ 22,000
Salaries payable	17,000	11,000
Bank loan	82,500	390,000
Capital stock	75,000	75,000
Retained earnings	5,500	320,000
Total liabilities and owners' equity	$280,000	$818,000

The following additional information is also provided: (1) The company reported a net loss of $279,500 during the year 2001, (2) there are no income taxes, (3) goodwill as of December 31, 2000 was part of an acquisition made during 2000, and (4) the company's bank provides a working capital loan to a maximum of 75% of net accounts receivable and inventory.

REQUIRED:

1. Prepare a statement of cash flows using the indirect method for the year ended December 31, 2001.
2. On the basis of available information, provide an assessment of the financial performance of the company during 2001. In answering this part, consider both the net income and cash flows of the company. Also evaluate the future prospects of the company.
3. Assuming that the bad debt expense during 2001 was $55,000, calculate the bad debts written off during the year. Further assume that the company collected $1,250,000 cash from its customers during 2001 and then compute the sales revenue for the year. You may assume that all sales are credit sales.
4. In answering this part, assume that Global uses the First-In, First Out (FIFO) inventory method. On December 31, 2001 the company purchased $35,000 worth of inventory on credit from a supplier. The transaction was inadvertently not recorded since physical possession was not obtained as of December 31, 2001. Discuss the effect of this omission on the financial statements of Global Trading Company.

P17–6 **Preparation of the cash flow statement and balance sheet**

The following is the cash account of JKI Advertising Agencies for the year ended December 31, 2001:

Cash Account	DR	CR
Beginning balance as of 1/1/01	$ 30,000	
Cash collected from clients	215,000	
Cash received from sale of land at book value	150,000	
Rent collected	50,000	
Capital contributions	35,000	
Line of credit borrowing from Town Bank	50,000	
Salaries paid		$130,000
Purchase of office equipment		20,000
Cash paid for insurance		12,000
Building loan repaid		85,000
Cash paid for interest		9,000
Dividends declared and paid		18,000
Cash paid for customer lawsuit		32,000
Cash paid for taxes		31,000
	$530,000	$337,000
Ending balance as of 12/31/01	$193,000	

Provided next are the income statement for the year ended December 31, 2001 and the balance sheet as of December 31, 2001 of JKI Advertising Agencies.

Assume there are no bad debts and no deferred taxes.

JKI ADVERTISING AGENCIES

Income Statement for the Year Ended December 31, 2001

Advertising revenue	$250,000
Rent revenue	36,000
Salaries expense	(126,000)
Employee incentive bonus	(25,200)
Depreciation expense—building	(20,000)
Depreciation expense—office equipment	(8,000)
Insurance expense	(12,000)
Interest expense	(10,000)
Income before taxes	84,800
Income tax expense	(33,920)
Net income	$ 50,880

JKI ADVERTISING AGENCIES

Balance Sheet as of December 31, 2001

Cash	$193,000
Accounts receivable	80,000
Prepaid insurance	3,000
Building	600,000
Less: Accumulated depreciation	(380,000)
Office equipment	80,000
Less: Accumulated depreciation	(39,000)
Total assets	$537,000

(*continued*)

JKI ADVERTISING AGENCIES (*continued*)

Balance Sheet as of December 31, 2001

Salaries payable	$ 7,000
Interest payable	3,500
Rent received in advance	14,000
Bonus payable	25,200
Taxes payable	2,920
Borrowing from Town Bank	50,000
Building loan	35,000
Capital stock	135,000
Retained earnings	264,380
Total of liabilities and equities	$537,000

REQUIRED:

1. Based on the cash account, prepare a statement of cash flows using the direct approach.
2. Prepare the balance sheet as of December 31, 2000.
3. Prepare the operating section of the cash flow statement for the year ended December 31, 2001 under the indirect approach.
4. Evaluate the following statements:

   a. "Since depreciation is added to net income when calculating cash flow from operations, depreciation is a direct source of operating cash flow."

   b. "Over the entire life of a company, its cash flow from operations will equal its net income."

5. JKI has a policy of accruing an employee's incentive bonus at 20% of salary. Instead, if JKI had calculated the bonus at 25% of salary, what would be the revised figure for cash flow from operations under the indirect approach?

P17–7

Reconciliation of changes in balance sheet accounts with amounts reported in the cash flow statement

Excerpts from the financial statements of Briggs & Stratton Corporation and Ramsay Health Care, Inc. are provided next. (**Note:** Year 1 is previous year and Year 2 is current year.)

BRIGGS AND STRATTON CORPORATION

Excerpts from Consolidated Balance Sheets as of July 3, Year 2 and June 27, Year 1

	Year 2	Year 1
Assets		
Current assets		
Cash and cash equivalents	$221,101,000	$39,501,000
Short-term investments	–0–	70,422,000
Receivables, less reserves of $1,678,000 and $754,000, respectively	122,597,000	124,981,000

BRIGGS AND STRATTON CORPORATION

Consolidated Statements of Cash Flows
for the Years Ended July 3, Year 2 and June 27, Year 1

	Year 2	Year 1
Cash Flows from Operating Activities		
Net income	$ 69,923,000	$ 70,345,000
Adjustments to reconcile net income to net cash provided by operating activities:		
Cumulative effect of accounting changes, net of income taxes	32,558,000	–0–
Depreciation	42,950,000	47,222,000
(Gain) loss on disposition of plant and equipment	(96,000)	4,027,000
Loss on foreign subsidiary	–0–	3,500,000
Change in operating assets and liabilities:		
(Increase) decrease in receivables	2,384,000	(21,366,000)
(Increase) in inventories	(11,605,000)	(1,576,000)
(Increase) in other current assets	(10,593,000)	(1,893,000)
Increase in accounts payable, accrued liabilities and income taxes	38,132,000	13,731,000
Other, net	1,420,000	(3,699,000)
Net cash provided by operating activities	$165,073,000	$110,291,000

RAMSAY HEALTH CARE, INC. AND SUBSIDIARIES

Consolidated Statements of Cash Flows
Year Ended June 30

	Year 2	Year 1
Cash Flows from Operating Activities		
Net income (loss)	$ 1,322,000	($ 1,560,000)
Adjustments to reconcile net income (loss) to net cash provided by operating activities:		
Cumulative effect of change in accounting for income taxes	–0–	(2,353,000)
Depreciation and amortization	7,638,000	7,173,000
Loss on early extinguishment of debt	258,000	1,580,000
Write-off of development and other costs	–0–	1,367,000
(Gain) loss on disposal of assets	722,000	(121,000)
Provision for deferred income taxes	(1,188,000)	(696,000)
Provision for doubtful accounts	5,846,000	8,148,000
Provision for loss on sales and closure of facilities	–0–	6,415,000
Minority interests	4,824,000	1,126,000
Adjustments for (increase) decrease in operating assets:		
Patient accounts receivable	(2,169,000)	(8,833,000)
Other current assets	(2,071,000)	1,233,000
Other noncurrent assets	(554,000)	164,000
Adjustments for increase (decrease) in operating liabilities:		
Accounts payable	(2,484,000)	940,000
Accrued salaries, wages and other liabilities	3,150,000	(674,000)
Unpaid self-insurance claims	(1,078,000)	(456,000)
Amounts due to third-party contractual agencies	(1,385,000)	724,000
Total adjustments	11,509,000	15,737,000
Net cash provided by operating activities	$12,831,000	$14,177,000

RAMSAY HEALTH CARE, INC. AND SUBSIDIARIES

Excerpts from Consolidated Balance Sheets

	June 30 Year 2	Year 1
Current Assets		
Patient accounts receivable, less allowances for doubtful accounts of $3,925,000 and $4,955,000 at June 30, Year 2 and Year 1, respectively	$23,019,000	$26,696,000

REQUIRED:

1. Reconcile the difference, if any, between the change in accounts receivable as reported in the statement of cash flows and the change in receivables based on the balance sheet values for each company.
2. Explain the different reporting practices adopted by the two companies with respect to adjustments made in the statement of cash flows for changes in accounts receivable.

P17–8

Preparation of cash flow statement—Indirect method

AICPA adapted

Presented next are the balance sheet accounts of Bergen Corporation as of December 31, 2001 and 2000.

	2001	2000	Increase (Decrease)
Assets			
Current Assets:			
Cash	$ 541,000	$ 308,000	$233,000
Accounts receivable, net	585,000	495,000	90,000
Inventories	895,000	780,000	115,000
Total current assets	2,021,000	1,583,000	438,000
Land	350,000	250,000	100,000
Plant and equipment	1,060,000	720,000	340,000
Accumulated depreciation	(295,000)	(170,000)	(125,000)
Leased equipment under capital lease	158,000	-0-	158,000
Marketable investment securities, at cost	-0-	75,000	(75,000)
Investment in Mason, Inc. at cost	180,000	180,000	-0-
Total assets	$3,474,000	$2,638,000	$836,000
Liabilities and Stockholders' Equity			
Current liabilities:			
Current portion of long-term debt	$ 159,000	$ -0-	$159,000
Accounts payable and accrued expenses	760,000	823,000	(63,000)
Total current liabilities	919,000	823,000	96,000
Note payable, long-term	300,000	-0-	300,000
Liability under capital lease	124,000	-0-	124,000
Bonds payable	500,000	500,000	-0-
Unamortized bond premium	16,000	18,000	(2,000)
Deferred income taxes	60,000	45,000	15,000
Common stock, par-value $20	640,000	600,000	40,000
Additional paid-in capital	304,000	244,000	60,000
Retained earnings	611,000	408,000	203,000
Total liabilities and stockholders' equity	$3,474,000	$2,638,000	$836,000

ADDITIONAL INFORMATION:

- On January 2, 2001 Bergen sold all of its marketable investment securities for $95,000 cash.

(continued)

- On March 10, 2001 Bergen paid a cash dividend of $30,000 on its common stock. No other dividends were paid or declared during 2001.
- On April 15, 2001 Bergen issued 2,000 shares of its common stock for land having a fair value of $100,000.
- On May 25, 2001 Bergen borrowed $450,000 from an insurance company. The underlying promissory note bears interest at 15% and is payable in three equal annual installments of $150,000. The first payment is due on May 25, 2002.
- On June 15, 2001 Bergen purchased equipment for $392,000 cash.
- On July 1, 2001 Bergen sold equipment costing $52,000, with a book value of $28,000 for $33,000 cash.
- On September 1, 2001 Bergen paid a $20,000 additional tax assessment for 2000 due to an error in tax calculation discovered by the Internal Revenue Service. This payment was appropriately recorded by Bergen as a prior period adjustment.
- On December 31, 2001 Bergen leased equipment from Tilden Company, for a ten-year period. Equal payments under the lease are $25,000 and are due on December 31 each year. The first payment was made on December 31, 2001. The present value at December 31, 2001 of the 10 lease payments is $158,000. Bergen appropriately recorded the lease as a capital lease. The $25,000 lease payment due on December 31, 2002 will consist of $9,000 principal and $16,000 interest.
- Bergen's net income for 2001 is $253,000.
- Bergen owns a 10% interest in the voting common stock of Mason, Inc. Mason reported net income of $120,000 for the year ended December 31, 2001 and paid a common stock dividend of $55,000 during 2001.

REQUIRED:

Prepare a cash flow statement for Bergen using the indirect method for 2001.

P17–9

Preparing an income statement from statement of cash flows and comparative balance sheets

STRETCH

The following are balance sheets of Kang-Iyer Financial Consultants:

KANG-IYER FINANCIAL CONSULTANTS

Balance Sheet
December 31, 2001

	December 31 2001	December 31 2000
Cash	$ 30,000	$ 70,000
Accounts receivable	80,000	15,000
Less: Allowance for doubtful accounts	(8,000)	(1,500)
Prepaid rent	–0–	30,000
Land	600,000	400,000
Building	500,000	–0–
Less: Accumulated depreciation	(10,000)	–0–
Total assets	$1,192,000	$513,500
Salaries payable	100,000	20,000
Interest payable	20,000	5,000
Loan from Village Bank	700,000	200,000
Contributed capital	75,000	30,000
Retained earnings	297,000	258,500
Total liabilities and owners' equity	$1,192,000	$513,500

The bad debts total written off during the year 2001 totaled $41,500.

KANG-IYER FINANCIAL CONSULTANTS

Statement of Cash Flows for the Year Ended December 31, 2001

Cash Flow from Operating Activities	
Cash collected from customers	$250,000
Cash paid to employees	(70,000)
Cash paid for interest	(50,000)
Cash flow from operations	130,000
Cash Flow from Investing Activities	??
Cash Flow from Financing Activities	
Dividends paid	(15,000)
Change in cash	(40,000)
Beginning cash balance	70,000
Ending cash balance	$ 30,000

REQUIRED:

Complete the following cash flow statement and prepare an income statement for the year ended December 31, 2001.

Hint: To prepare the income statement, use the information in the balance sheets and the cash flow statement to "solve" for the income statement items. For example, by preparing a T-account for salaries payable and then incorporating in this account the information on cash paid to employees, you can solve for salaries expense.

P17–10

Determining components of cash flow statement

AICPA adapted

Best Corporation's financial statements for 2000 and 2001 and additional information for 2001 are presented next.

BEST CORPORATION

Balance Sheets

	2001	2000
Assets		
Current assets:		
Cash	$ 480,000	$ 220,000
Accounts receivable—net	840,000	560,000
Merchandise inventory	760,000	470,000
Total current assets	2,080,000	1,250,000
Land, buildings, and fixtures	1,330,000	800,000
Less: Accumulated depreciation	210,000	150,000
Total noncurrent assets	1,120,000	650,000
Total assets	$3,200,000	$1,900,000
Liabilities and Stockholders' Equity		
Current liabilities:		
Accounts payable	$ 830,000	$ 440,000
Accrued expenses	300,000	130,000
Dividends payable	40,000	—
Total current liabilities	1,170,000	570,000
Stockholders' equity:		
Common stock ($10 par value)	1,200,000	900,000
Additional paid-in capital	200,000	100,000
Retained earnings	630,000	330,000
Total stockholders' equity	2,030,000	1,330,000
Total liabilities and stockholders' equity	$3,200,000	$1,900,000

BEST CORPORATION

Income Statements
Year Ended December 31

	2001	2000
Credit sales	$6,300,000	$4,000,000
Cost of goods sold	4,900,000	3,200,000
Gross profit	1,400,000	800,000
Expenses (including income taxes)	700,000	630,000
Net income	$ 700,000	$ 170,000

BEST CORPORATION

Changes in Stockholders' Equity
Year Ended December 31

	2001	2000
Common Stock		
Balance 1/1/01	$ 900,000	$900,000
Additional shares sold 4/1/01	100,000	-0-
20% stock dividend 6/1/01	200,000	-0-
Balance 12/31/01	$1,200,000	$900,000
Additional Paid-in Capital		
Balance 1/1/01	$ 100,000	$100,000
Additional shares sold 4/1/01	25,000	-0-
20% stock dividend 6/1/01	75,000	-0-
Balance 12/31/01	$ 200,000	$100,000
Retained Earnings		
Balance 1/1/01	$ 330,000	$250,000
Net income	700,000	170,000
Cash dividends	(125,000)	(90,000)
Stock dividends	(275,000)	-0-
Balance 12/31/01	$ 630,000	$330,000

ADDITIONAL INFORMATION:

- During 2001 Best sold fixtures with a book value of $30,000 ($100,000 cost minus $70,000 accumulated depreciation) at a $10,000 loss. This loss was included in the income statement. Depreciation expense for 2001 was $130,000. Best purchased $630,000 of new fixtures during 2001.
- Common stock issued during 2001 was as follows:

Date	Number of shares
4/1/01	10,000
6/1/01	20,000

REQUIRED:

1. How much cash from operations should be reported in the statement of cash flows for 2001?
2. How much cash was provided by financing activities?
3. How much cash was used by investing activities?

The financial statements of Cavalier Toy Stores (a fictitious merchandising company) follow:

P17–11

Analysis of statement of cash flows

STRETCH

CAVALIER TOY STORES

Income Statements
for the Year Ended December 31, 2001

Sales revenue		$1,500,000
Cost of goods sold		(1,200,000)
Gross margin		300,000
Other expenses:		
Salaries expense	$200,000	
Bad debt expense	100,000	
Insurance expense	30,000	
Office supplies expense	55,000	
Depreciation expense—office building	30,000	
Depreciation expense—office equipment	45,000	
Interest expense	90,000	550,000
Net loss		($ 250,000)

CAVALIER TOY STORES

Statement of Retained Earnings
for the Year Ended December 31, 2001

Retained earnings 1/1/01	$600,000
Net loss for the year	(250,000)
Dividends paid	(300,000)
Retained earnings 12/31/01	$ 50,000

CAVALIER TOY STORES

Balance Sheets

	December 31 2001	2000
Assets		
Current Assets:		
Cash	$ 30,000	$ 180,000
Accounts receivable	100,000	525,000
Less: Allowance for doubtful accounts	(10,000)	(30,000)
Prepaid insurance	5,000	35,000
Inventory	50,000	550,000
Noncurrent Assets:		
Office building	900,000	–0–
Less: Accumulated depreciation	(30,000)	–0–
Office equipment	200,000	200,000
Less: Accumulated depreciation	(85,000)	(40,000)
Total assets	$1,160,000	$1,420,000

(*continued*)

CAVALIER TOY STORES (*continued*)

Balance Sheets

	December 31 2001	2000
Liabilities and Owners' Equity		
Current Liabilities:		
Salaries payable	$ 100,000	$ 80,000
Interest payable	8,000	16,000
Accounts payable for inventory purchases	252,000	64,000
Dividends payable	−0−	50,000
Noncurrent Liabilities:		
Loan from Thrifty Bank	700,000	560,000
Owners' Equity:		
Contributed capital	50,000	50,000
Retained earnings	50,000	600,000
Total Liabilities and Owners' Equity	$1,160,000	$1,420,000

REQUIRED:

1. Prepare a statement of cash flows using the indirect method.
2. Compute the following for the year ended December 31, 2001:
   a. Bad debts written off during the year
   b. Cash collected from customers
   c. Purchases of inventory made during the year
   d. Cash paid to suppliers for inventory purchases
   e. Cash paid for insurance.
3. The following is an excerpt from the chief executive officer's letter to the stockholders that was included in the annual report of Cavalier Toy Stores:

It feels real good to finish 2001 and be thankful that your company achieved its best year ever. I am sure that you are all puzzled by my statement given the net loss we have reported in the income statement. Let me explain. Although our gross margin has declined from last year's because of competitive pressures, we have set a company record in terms of sales revenue. You know quite well how accounting income can be manipulated. We don't play that game. We let cash flows tell our success story. Also, we have very efficiently managed our receivables and inventory, and at the same time, taken advantage of all available credit from our suppliers. More importantly, I am sure all of you are very pleased with the dividends that you have received this year. Let me end this letter by proudly inviting you to visit our new executive office building. While touring the luxurious executive suites, please remember that your top management team did not burden you with one dollar of debt to buy this building.

Assume you are a commercial lending officer at Thrifty Bank. The working capital loan given to Cavalier Toy Stores (balance outstanding as of December 31, 2001 is $700,000) is repayable by April 1, 2002. The CEO has sent a loan proposal to Thrifty Bank requesting renewal of the loan for one more year and an increase in the credit limit to $1,000,000. Your job is to write a report to your boss with a specific recommendation on whether to accept or reject the proposal. Base your recommendation on the information available to you. In your report, please consider all the claims made by the CEO in the letter to stockholders.

P17–12

Preparation of the cash flow statement

AICPA adapted

Presented next are the balance sheets of Farrell Corporation as of December 31, 2001 and 2000, as well as the statement of income and retained earnings for the year ended December 31, 2001.

FARRELL CORPORATION

Balance Sheets
December 31, 2001 and 2000

	2001	2000	Increase (Decrease)
Assets			
Cash	$ 275,000	$ 180,000	$ 95,000
Accounts receivable, net	295,000	305,000	(10,000)
Inventories	549,000	431,000	118,000
Investment in Hall, Inc. (equity method)	73,000	60,000	13,000
Land	350,000	200,000	150,000
Plant and equipment	624,000	606,000	18,000
Less: Accumulated depreciation	(139,000)	(107,000)	(32,000)*
Goodwill	16,000	20,000	(4,000)
Total assets	$2,043,000	$1,695,000	$348,000
Liabilities and Stockholders' Equity			
Accounts payable and accrued expenses	$ 604,000	$ 563,000	$ 41,000
Note payable, long-term	150,000	–0–	150,000
Bonds payable	160,000	210,000	(50,000)
Deferred income taxes	41,000	30,000	11,000
Common stock, par value $10	430,000	400,000	30,000
Additional paid-in capital	226,000	175,000	51,000
Retained earnings	432,000	334,000	98,000
Treasury stock, at cost	–0–	(17,000)	17,000
Total liabilities and stockholders' equity	$2,043,000	$1,695,000	$348,000

*This is an increase, but because Accumulated depreciation is shown as a deduction from Plant and equipment, it is shown with parentheses.

(continued)

FARRELL CORPORATION

Statement of Income and Retained Earnings for the Year Ended December 31, 2001

Net sales		$1,950,000
Operating expenses		
Cost of sales	$1,150,000	
Selling and administrative expenses	505,000	
Depreciation	53,000	
		1,708,000
Operating income		242,000
Other (income) expense		
Interest expense	15,000	
Equity in net income of Hall, Inc.	(13,000)	
Loss on sale of equipment	5,000	
Amortization of goodwill	4,000	11,000
Income before income taxes		231,000
Income taxes		
Current	79,000	
Deferred	11,000	
Provision for income taxes		90,000
Net income		141,000
Retained earnings 1/1/01		334,000
		475,000
Cash dividends, paid 8/14/01		43,000
Retained earnings 12/31/01		$ 432,000

ADDITIONAL INFORMATION:

- On January 2, 2001 Farrell sold equipment that cost $45,000 with a $24,000 book value for $19,000 cash.
- On April 1, 2001 Farrell issued 1,000 shares of common stock for $23,000 cash.
- On May 15, 2001 Farrell sold all of its treasury stock for $25,000 cash.
- On June 1, 2001 individuals holding $50,000 face value of Farrell's bonds exercised their conversion privilege. Each of the 50 bonds was converted into 40 shares of Farrell's common stock.
- On July 1, 2001 Farrell purchased equipment with $63,000 cash.
- On December 31, 2001 land with a fair market value of $150,000 was purchased through the issuance of a long-term note in the amount of $150,000. The note bears interest at the rate of 15% and is due on December 31, 2006.
- Deferred income taxes represent temporary differences relating to the use of accelerated depreciation methods for income tax reporting and the straight-line method for financial statement reporting.

REQUIRED:

Prepare a statement of cash flows (indirect approach) and all necessary related schedules of Farrell Corporation for the year ended December 31, 2001.

P17-13 **Statement of cash flows—Indirect approach** AICPA adapted

Omega Corporation's comparative balance sheet accounts worksheet at December 31, 2001 and 2000 follow, with a column showing the increase (decrease) from 2000 to 2001.

Comparative Balance Sheet Worksheet

	2001	2000	Increase (Decrease)
Cash	$ 800,000	$ 700,000	$100,000
Accounts receivable	1,128,000	1,168,000	(40,000)
Inventories	1,850,000	1,715,000	135,000
Property, plant, and equipment	3,307,000	2,967,000	340,000
Accumulated depreciation	(1,165,000)	(1,040,000)	(125,000)
Investment in Belle Company	305,000	275,000	30,000
Loan receivable	270,000	–0–	270,000
Total assets	$6,495,000	$5,785,000	$710,000
Accounts payable	$1,015,000	$ 955,000	$ 60,000
Income taxes payable	30,000	50,000	(20,000)
Dividends payable	80,000	90,000	(10,000)
Capital lease obligation	400,000	–0–	400,000
Capital stock, common, $1 par	500,000	500,000	–0–
Additional paid-in capital	1,500,000	1,500,000	–0–
Retained earnings	2,970,000	2,690,000	280,000
Total liabilities and stockholders' equity	$6,495,000	$5,785,000	$710,000

ADDITIONAL INFORMATION:

- On December 31, 2000 Omega acquired 25% of Belle Company's common stock for $275,000. On that date, the carrying value of Belle's assets and liabilities, which approximated their fair values, was $1,100,000. Belle reported income of $120,000 for the year ended December 31, 2001. No dividend was paid on Belle's common stock during the year.
- During 2001 Omega loaned $300,000 to Chase Company, an unrelated company. Chase made the first semiannual principal repayment of $30,000, plus interest at 10%, on October 1, 2001.
- On January 2, 2001 Omega sold equipment for $40,000 cash that cost $60,000 and had a carrying amount of $35,000.
- On December 31, 2001 Omega entered into a capital lease for an office building. The present value of the annual rental payments is $400,000, which equals the fair value of the building. Omega made the first rental payment of $60,000, when due, on January 2, 2002.
- Net income for 2001 was $360,000.
- Omega declared and paid cash dividends for 2001 and 2000 as follows:

	2001	2000
Declared	12/15/01	12/15/00
Paid	2/28/02	2/28/01
Amount	$80,000	$90,000

REQUIRED:

Prepare a statement of cash flows for Omega Corporation for the year ended December 31, 2001 using the indirect approach.

CASES

C17–1

Q-Mart Retail Stores, Inc. (KR): Analysis of statement of cash flows

The income statement and comparative balance sheet of Q-Mart Retail Stores, Inc. follow.

Q-MART RETAIL STORES, INC.

Income Statement for the Year Ended December 31, 2001

Sales revenue	$1,500,000
Cost of goods sold	(1,050,000)
Gross profit	450,000
Operating expenses:	
Salaries expense	(80,000)
Insurance expense	(60,000)
Bad debt expense	(50,000)
Depreciation expense—building	(25,000)
Depreciation expense—computer equipment	(35,000)
Interest expense	(55,000)
Other expenses	(20,000)
Net income before income taxes	125,000
Provision for income taxes	(43,750)
Net income	$ 81,250

Note: There are no deferred income taxes for this company.

Q-MART RETAIL STORES, INC.

Comparative Balance Sheet

	December 31 2001	2000
Current Assets		
Cash	$ 120,000	$ 504,750
Accounts receivable	500,000	100,000
Less: Allowance for doubtful accounts	(50,000)	(11,000)
Inventory	350,000	75,000
Prepaid insurance	20,000	–0–
Noncurrent Assets		
Building	1,000,000	750,000
Less: Accumulated depreciation—building	(125,000)	(100,000)
Computer equipment	140,000	–0–
Less: Accumulated depreciation—computer	(35,000)	–0–
Total Assets	$1,920,000	$1,318,750
Current Liabilities		
Salaries payable	$ 10,000	$ 42,000
Accounts payable due to suppliers	12,000	17,000
Income tax currently payable	15,000	8,000
Noncurrent Liabilities		
Loan from Upstate Bank	500,000	300,000
Stockholders' Equity		
Common stock	1,000,000	610,000
Retained earnings	383,000	341,750
Total Liabilities and Stockholders' Equity	$1,920,000	$1,318,750

The CEO of Q-Mart, Mr. Peddler, is quite anxious about the dramatic decline in the cash position. He would like your help in understanding the sources and uses of Q-Mart's cash flows.

REQUIRED:

1. Prepare a statement of cash flows for the year ended December 31, 2001 using the indirect method. (*Hint*: In answering this part, just focus on the change in net accounts receivable when converting from net income to cash flow from operations.)
2. Compute the bad debts written off during 2001.
3. Compute the cash collected from customers during 2001. (Assume all sales are credit sales.)
4. Compute the amount of inventory purchases during 2001.
5. Compute the cash paid to suppliers during 2001. (Assume all purchases are credit purchases.)
6. Prepare a short memo to Mr. Peddler identifying the major reasons for the decline in the cash position. Evaluate whether this decline is an indication of future profitability or impending troubles. What additional information do you need to complete this evaluation?

Mr. Peddler skimmed through your cash flow statement. He is still quite puzzled about the change in his firm's cash position. He needs answers for the following questions.

7. "I see that our buildup in accounts receivable is a major drain on our cash flows. If I had known this, I would have stopped all sales to customers during the end of the year to boost our cash flows. What do you think of this strategy?"
8. "I see that depreciation is a source of cash flows. I think I have found the golden goose. Next year, I will increase the depreciation expense twofold to further boost our cash flows. What do you think of this idea?"
9. "I have heard people say that cash flow is king and earnings don't matter. Aren't investors likely to be concerned about our cash flow performance? Tell me what an investor might gain from jointly examining both the income statement and statement of cash flows."

C17–2

Vulcan Corporation: Understanding cash flow statements

Vulcan Corporation (a real company whose name has been disguised) is a leading worldwide manufacturer and distributor of uncoated and coated rubber-like fiberboard products. The Company's products are marketed to various industries, including footwear, headwear, luggage, leather goods, belt backing, furniture, electronic integrated component packaging, and automotive suppliers.

Information developed using Vulcan Corporation's financial statements for the year ended October 31, 2000 appears below.

VULCAN CORPORATION

Cash Flow from Operating Activities

($ in thousands)	Year Ended October 31, 2000
Cash received from customers	$37,378
Cash paid to suppliers	(26,884)
Cash paid for general and administrative expenses	(8,002)
Cash paid for interest	(810)
Cash paid for income taxes	(74)
Net cash provided by operating activities	$ 1,608

(continued)

VULCAN CORPORATION

Selected Balance Sheet Information

($ in thousands)	October 31 2000	1999
Accounts receivable, net	$14,120	$11,043
Inventories	5,465	5,798
Property, plant and equipment, net	10,707	11,523
Accounts payable	7,756	6,375
Accrued general and administrative expenses	2,559	1,871
Interest payable	130	52
Deferred taxes payable	936	675

ADDITIONAL INFORMATION:

- Total comprehensive income for the year ended October 31, 2000 was $336,000.
- Other comprehensive loss (net of applicable income taxes) consisted of unrealized loss on investments classified as available-for-sale securities of $286,000.
- Equipment purchased during the year totaled $854,000.
- The book value of equipment retired during the year totaled $348,000.

REQUIRED:

1. Compute Vulcan Corporation's net loss for the year ended October 31, 2000. (*Hint*: All components of other comprehensive income or loss have been provided.)
2. Prepare Vulcan Corporation's combined Statement of Income (Loss) and Comprehensive Income (Loss) for the year ended October 31, 2000.
3. Determine Vulcan Corporation's net cash provided by operating activities using the indirect method.

C17–3

Fillio Corporation (KR): Comprehensive statement of cash flows

This problem is based on the financial statements and selected footnotes of Fillio Corporation presented on the next few pages. Fillio is a Delaware corporation that is engaged in the contract manufacturing and testing of products and assemblies for use in the computer, communications, medical, instrumentation, and peripherals industries. The company has two operating facilities in Parma, Ohio, one in Columbus, Ohio, and one in Youngstown, Ohio. This is a real company whose name has been disguised.

REQUIRED:

1. Using the indirect method, prepare the statement of cash flows for the year ended December 31, 2001 in as much detail as possible. For example, borrowing and repayment should be shown separately as financing inflow and outflow, respectively. Similarly, to the extent information is available, separately disclose and explain the changes to each asset and each liability account that affected Fillio Corporation's cash flows in 2001.
2. Redo the operating section of the statement of cash flows using the direct method. *Assumptions*: In preparing the statement of cash flows using the direct method, you may assume that (a) the entire depreciation expense relates to manufacturing operations, (b) prepaid expenses as well as accrued payroll and related expenses relate to marketing, general and administrative expenses, (c) other payables and accruals relate to other expenses, and (d) accrued settlement and restructuring costs as well as accrued settlement costs pertain to litigation settlements and restructuring charges expensed in prior accounting periods.

FILLIO CORPORATION

Balance Sheet

($ in thousands)	December 31 2001	2000
Assets		
Current assets		
Cash	$ 897	$ 48
Trade accounts receivable	19,021	32,803
Less: Allowance for doubtful accounts	(531)	(608)
Income tax refund receivable	229	6,960
Inventories	28,410	50,869
Prepaid expenses	1,195	360
Total current assets	49,221	90,432
Property, plant, and equipment		
Land	295	295
Buildings and improvements	9,850	9,386
Building construction in progress	178	371
Machinery and equipment	45,476	45,522
Less: Accumulated depreciation	(26,327)	(18,630)
Deferred financing costs and other, net	2,230	1,817
Total assets	$80,923	$129,193
Liabilities		
Current liabilities		
Current maturities of long-term debt	$ 2,322	$ 7,451
Trade accounts payable	7,592	30,317
Accrued payroll and related expenses	1,162	2,421
Accrued interest	1,087	1,054
Other payables and accruals	2,254	2,273
Accrued settlement and restructuring costs	1,500	3,932
Total current liabilities	15,917	47,448
Long-term liabilities		
Accrued settlement costs	-0-	1,500
Long-term debt	30,017	36,316
Subordinated convertible debentures	34,500	34,500
Total long-term liabilities	64,517	72,316
Stockholders' Equity		
6% Redeemable convertible preferred stock—no par value; authorized 5,000,000 shares; issued and outstanding 1,243,700 shares in 2001 and 1,050,000 in 2000; stated value is $10.00 per share	12,437	10,500
Common stock—par-value $0.01 per share; authorized 50,000,000 shares; issued and outstanding 11,012,373 and 10,872,024 shares in 2001 and 2000, respectively	110	109
Additional paid-in capital	29,544	29,019
Accumulated deficit	(41,602)	(30,199)
Total stockholders' equity	489	9,429
Total liabilities and stockholders' equity	$80,923	$129,193

(continued)

FILLIO CORPORATION

Income Statement
for the Year Ended December 31, 2001
($ in thousands)

Sales	$184,137
Cost of sales	(181,010)
Gross profit	3,127
Marketing, general, and administrative expenses (including bad debt expense of $238)	(7,227)
Interest expense	(5,417)
Interest income (on income tax refund)	1,048
Settlement with Sitco	(1,837)
Other expense (including amortization of deferred financing costs and loss on write-off of equipment)	(935)
Total expenses (net of interest income)	(14,368)
Net loss	($ 11,241)
Dividend in kind on preferred stock	(162)
Net loss applicable to common shares	($ 11,403)

ADDITIONAL INFORMATION

- *Dividend in kind on preferred stock:* The company has the option of paying a dividend in kind to the preferred shareholders. In 2001 the company exercised this option and issued 16,200 additional preferred shares in lieu of cash dividends (i.e., one share per $10.00 of dividend).
- *Settlement with Sitco:* During the second quarter of 2001, the Company recognized a one-time nonrecurring charge of $1,837,000 related to an agreement with Sitco for the satisfaction of certain payments owing from the Company to Sitco. Under the terms of the agreement, the Company agreed to pay Sitco an aggregate $62,000 in cash and $1,775,000 in Series A Preferred Stock (valued at $10.00 per share). The preferred stock was distributed to Sitco during 2001.
- *Property, Plant, and Equipment:* Depreciation expense for the year 2001 was $8,330,000. Machinery and equipment with a net book value of $227,000 was written off as worthless during 2001. Furthermore, the Company purchased some new machinery and equipment and invested additional money on buildings during 2001.
- *Long-term debt:* A summary of long-term debt follows.

	Balance as of December 31	
	2001	**2000**
Industrial development revenue bonds	$ 1,280	$ 1,600
Revolving line of credit, retired in 2001	-0-	19,973
Revolving equipment line of credit, retired in 2001	-0-	15,762
2001 Revolving line of credit	21,006	-0-
2001 Equipment term loan	6,000	-0-
Senior notes secured by equipment	2,450	6,432
2001 Bank loan secured by real property at prime plus 2% (The original term loan was for $3,000, which was reduced to 1,500 in December 2001 after payment to the lenders of $1,500 from the income tax refund proceeds.)	1,500	-0-
2001 Equipment loan at 9% (original amount borrowed $200)	103	-0-
Total debt	$32,339	$43,767
Less: Current maturities of long-term debt	(2,322)	(7,451)
Long-term debt	$ 30,017	$36,316

- *Deferred financing costs:* As part of its credit agreement restructuring costs in March 2001, the Company issued an aggregate of 50,000 shares of common stock to its former bank lenders and 50,000 shares of common stock to its term lenders. These shares were issued as compensation for the financing costs of $400,000 due to the lenders. These financing costs are included in "Deferred financing costs" and are being amortized over the life of the credit agreements. In addition, the company paid $601,000 cash for other loan initiation/structuring costs, which are also included in "Deferred financing costs."
- *Common Stock:* In addition to the common shares issued to compensate for the financing costs, the Company issued additional shares to its employees under its Employee Incentive Stock Option Plans for $126,000 cash. No other common shares were issued during the year.

C17–4

Lucky Lady, Inc.: Comprehensive statement of cash flows

The income statement for the year ended December 31, 2001 as well as the balance sheets as of December 31, 2001 and December 31, 2000, for Lucky Lady, Inc. follow. This information is taken from the financial statements of a real company whose name has been disguised.

LUCKY LADY, INC.

Income Statement

($ in thousands)	For the Year Ended December 31, 2001
Revenues	
Casino	$ 26,702
Rooms	2,897
Food and beverage	2,351
Other hotel/casino	5,066
Airline	20,784
Total revenues	57,800
Operating Expenses	
Casino	9,341
Rooms	1,016
Food and beverage	2,529
Other hotel/casino	5,777
Airline	20,599
Selling, general, and administrative (including bad debt expense of $3,855)	19,679
Depreciation expense	8,018
Hotel preopening expenses	45,130
Aircraft carrying value adjustment	68,948
Total operating expenses	181,037
Operating income	(123,237)
Nonoperating items:	
Interest income	12,231
Interest expense	(6,596)
Other, net	16
Income before taxes	(117,586)
Provision for income taxes	–0–
Net income (loss)	($117,586)

(continued)

LUCKY LADY, INC.

Balance Sheets

($ in thousands)	December 31 2001	2000
Assets		
Cash	$ 211,305	$ 579,963
Gross accounts receivable	35,249	2,178
Less: Allowance for doubtful accounts	(4,733)	(1,531)
Prepaid expenses	11,755	1,219
Inventories	12,662	154
Total current assets	266,238	581,983
Gross property, plant, and equipment	953,796	471,506
Less: Accumulated depreciation	(86,512)	(21,796)
Pre-opening expenses	–0–	10,677
Other operating assets	26,601	21,116
Total assets	$1,160,123	$1,063,486
Liabilities and Stockholders' Equity		
Accounts payable	$ 14,181	$ 4,322
Accrued salaries and wages	8,194	945
Accrued interest on long-term debt	9,472	9,429
Other accrued liabilities	33,502	9,744
Construction payables	96,844	32,296
Current maturities, capital leases	1,830	289
Current maturities, long-term debt	1,573	–0–
Total current liabilities	165,596	57,025
Deferred revenues	10,784	–0–
Deferred income taxes	6,517	6,517
Long-term obligation, capital leases	14,044	162
Long-term debt	481,427	473,000
Total liabilities	678,368	536,704
Common stock	506	485
Capital in excess of par value	662,365	589,827
Common stock in treasury	(29,490)	(29,490)
Retained earnings (deficit)	(151,626)	(34,040)
Total stockholders' equity	481,755	526,782
Total liabilities and equity	$1,160,123	$1,063,486

ADDITIONAL INFORMATION AND AUTHOR-SUPPLIED EXPLANATIONS:

- *Aircraft valuation adjustment:* The company reduced the book value of its aircraft and related equipment to their expected recoverable values, and recognized an aircraft carrying value adjustment in the 2001 income statement. [*Author Note:* You may treat this item as "extra" depreciation recorded during the year due to abnormal decline in the asset value.]
- *Property, plant, and equipment:* Includes land, buildings, aircraft equipment, furniture and fixtures, equipment under capital lease, etc. During 2001, the company acquired equipment under capital leases for $16,987,000. The company also sold equipment with a net book value of $2,501,000 for $684,000 cash. [*Author Note:* The gain or loss on this sale is combined with some other

item in the income statement. Any other change in the gross book value of PP&E may be attributed to outright purchase of other equipment and building construction costs.]

- *Capital lease and long-term liabilities:* [*Author Note:* When preparing the cash flow statement, you may find it convenient to combine the current and long-term portions of each of these liabilities.]
- *Pre-opening expenses:* Pre-opening expenses include direct project salaries, advertising, and other pre-opening services incurred during the pre-opening period of the Lucky Lady Hotel. Such expenses were expensed upon opening of the facility.
- *Stock offering:* The increases in common stock and capital in excess of par accounts are due to a common stock offering completed on August 17, 2001.
- *Laundry loan:* On June 16, 2001 the company obtained a $10,000,000 loan from a financial institution for a laundry facility in North Las Vegas, Nevada. As of December 31, 2001, $10,000,000 has been drawn down under the loan. Construction of the facility was completed in December 2001. The laundry provides the laundry and dry-cleaning services for the Lucky Lady Hotel.

REQUIRED:

1. Using the indirect method, prepare the statement of cash flows for the year ended December 31, 2001 in as much detail as possible. For example, borrowing and repayment, if any, should be shown separately as financing inflow and outflow, respectively. Similarly, to the extent information is available, separately disclose and explain the changes to each asset and each liability account that affected Lucky Lady's cash flows during 2001.
2. Redo the operating section of the cash flow statement using the direct method.

C17–5

Opus One, Inc. (KR): Preparation and analysis of the cash flow statement

The following information is based on the 2001 annual report of Opus One, Inc. (a real company whose name has been disguised). Opus One operates in a single business segment, the retailing and servicing of home audio, car audio, and video equipment. Its operations are conducted in Texas through 20 stores and two service centers. The information provided in the annual report has been combined and abbreviated.

The following additional information is provided with respect to the year ended June 30, 2001:

- The company did not declare or pay any cash or stock dividends during the year.
- The company reported a loss of $7,377 from scrapping equipment with a book value of the same amount.
- The depreciation expense for the year was $2,265,735.
- The following breakdown is provided for the long-term debt:

	June 30	
($ in thousands)	**2001**	**2000**
Long-Term Debt		
Term loan	$3,420,000	$ -0-
Mortgage note	534,475	555,455
Total	3,954,475	555,455
Less: Current installments	(681,716)	(21,348)
Long-term debt—current installments	$3,272,759	$534,107

(continued)

OPUS ONE, INC.

Balance Sheet
June 30, 2001 and 2000

($ in thousands)	June 30 2001	2000
Current Assets		
Cash	$ 50,885	$ 19,481
Receivables	4,625,920	6,963,195
Less: Allowance for bad debts	(403,000)	(1,200,000)
Inventories	25,986,364	26,801,526
Prepaid expenses	455,875	710,058
Income taxes receivable	1,573,055	3,073,537
Noncurrent Assets		
Property and equipment	22,182,371	20,637,912
Less: Accumulated depreciation	(9,031,181)	(6,822,553)
Deferred tax asset, net	1,043,403	531,803
Pre-opening costs	370,458	877,179
Goodwill	366,750	366,750
Less: Accumulated amortization	(122,509)	(98,059)
Total assets	$47,098,391	$51,860,829
Current Liabilities		
Revolving credit agreements	$ 4,810,398	$18,743,407
Accounts payable	11,054,418	7,951,545
Accrued liabilities	4,025,816	3,257,672
Current installments of long-term debt	681,716	21,348
Long-Term Liabilities		
Long-term debt minus current installments	3,272,759	534,107
Other liabilities and deferred credits	4,072,586	3,308,714
Total liabilities	27,917,693	33,816,793
Shareholders' Equity		
Common stock and additional paid-in capital	10,126,944	10,117,946
Retained earnings	9,053,754	7,926,090
Total shareholders' equity	19,180,698	18,044,036
Total liabilities and shareholders' equity	$47,098,391	$51,860,829

On February 26, 2001 the company obtained a term loan of $3,600,000 from a bank, due February 28, 2005.

REQUIRED:

1. Prepare a statement of cash flows for the year ended June 30, 2001 using the indirect approach.
2. On the basis of the cash flow statement, analyze the financial performance of Opus One during the fiscal year 2001.

COLLABORATIVE LEARNING CASE

C17–6

Best Buy Company, Inc.: Analysis of financial performance from the cash flow statement and other information

What follows are the consolidated statements of cash flows of Best Buy Company, Inc. The information provided in the annual report has been combined and abbreviated.

BEST BUY COMPANY, INC.

Consolidated Statements of Cash Flows

($ in thousands)	February 26, 2000	For the Fiscal Years Ended February 27, 1999	February 28, 1998
Operating Activities			
Net earnings	$347,070	$216,282	$ 81,938
Depreciation, amortization and other non-cash charges	109,541	78,367	71,584
	456,611	294,649	153,522
Changes in operating assets and liabilities:			
Receivables	(56,900)	(36,699)	(16,121)
Merchandise inventories	(137,315)	14,422	71,271
Other assets	(11,005)	(4,251)	(3,278)
Accounts payable	302,194	249,094	147,340
Other liabilities	108,829	82,544	63,950
Accrued income taxes	97,814	62,672	33,759
Total cash provided by operating activities	760,228	662,431	450,443
Investing Activities			
Additions to property and equipment	(361,024)	(165,698)	(72,063)
(Increase) decrease in recoverable costs from developed properties	(21,009)	(65,741)	45,270
(Increase) decrease in other assets	(18,081)	(18,128)	4,494
Total cash used in investing activities	(400,114)	(249,567)	(22,299)
Financing Activities			
Long-term debt payments	(29,946)	(165,396)	(22,694)
Long-term debt borrowings	–0–	–0–	10,000
Issuance of common stock	32,229	20,644	14,869
Repurchase of common stock	(397,451)	(2,462)	–0–
Total cash (used in) provided by financing activities	(395,168)	(147,214)	2,175
Increase (Decrease) in Cash and Cash Equivalents	($ 35,054)	$265,650	$430,319

The following data is based on information provided by the company in its SEC filings:

Best Buy Co., Inc. is the nation's largest volume specialty retailer of name-brand consumer electronics, home office equipment, entertainment software and appliances. Part of the Company's strategy is to provide a selection of brand name products comparable to retailers that specialize in the Company's principal product categories and seeks to ensure a high level of product availability for customers. The number of stores operated by the company increased from 272 at the end of 1997, to 284, 311 and 357 at the end of 1998, 1999 and 2000, respectively. When entering a major metropolitan market, the Company establishes a district office, service center and major appliance warehouse. Each new store requires working capital of approximately $4 million for merchandise inventory (net of vendor financing), leasehold improvements, fixtures and equipment. Pre-opening costs of approximately $600,000 per store are incurred through hiring, relocating and training new employees, and in merchandising the store. These costs are expensed as incurred.

REQUIRED:

1. Using information provided in the cash flow statement, compare Best Buy's earnings and cash flows from operations for the last three years and provide an explanation for the differences between these two numbers within each year and from

year-to-year. Does earnings or operating cash flows provide a better indication of Best Buy's performance? Explain.

2. How have new store openings affected Best Buy's working capital needs over the last three years? Compare the company's actual changes in working capital to the working capital needed to support new store openings and comment on any differences.
3. Comment on the year-to-year changes in inventories for the last three years and how these changes have been financed.
4. Comment on any insights gained from an analysis of the Investing and Financing section of Best Buy's cash flow statement.

18

Overview of International Financial Reporting Differences and Inflation

LEARNING OBJECTIVES:
After studying this chapter, you will understand:

1. How financial reporting approaches worldwide fall into two categories—(a) those designed to reflect economic performance and (b) those that conform to tax or statutory law.
2. Why financial reporting philosophies differ across countries.
3. The mechanisms that evolved for coping with financial reporting diversity from country to country.
4. How compliance with GAAP is monitored in different countries.
5. That foreign countries with high inflation rates depart from the historical cost reporting model.
6. The two major approaches for adjusting financial reports for rapidly changing prices—current cost accounting and general price-level accounting.

International investment in equity and debt securities has grown considerably in the last decade. For example, the Bank for International Settlements reports growth in cross-border transactions in bonds and equities (expressed as a percentage of each country's gross domestic product) as shown in Table 18.1 on the next page.

What this table shows is that between 1975 and 1979, total cross-border purchases and sales of securities between residents and nonresidents of the United States averaged only 5.9% of that period's U.S. Gross Domestic Product (GDP), but by 1998 such transactions equaled 222.8% of 1998's U.S. GDP. International bond and equity transactions also grew significantly over this period in Japan and Germany. Furthermore, international private sector debt issues in Europe (not shown in the table) increased by almost 400% between 1994 and 1999.[1]

Indications of this high level of international investment are provided by other facts as well. For instance, stock exchanges across the world now have significant numbers of foreign companies listed. (See Table 18.2 on the next page).

Access to global capital as well as to global consumer markets allows companies from many countries to grow large. Table 18.3 (on p. 941) shows the country of origin for the five largest companies in eight selected industries for 1999. Investors who choose to concentrate on a specific industrial or commercial sector are compelled to think globally.

The growth of global investing has been fueled by several factors. For example, many major industrial countries have relaxed their security market regulatory rules. Another example is improvements in telecommunications and computer technology. Finally, investors understand that portfolios based

[1] Bank for International Settlements, *70th Annual Report*, March 31, 2000, Table VI.2.

Table 18.1 ■ CROSS-BORDER TRANSACTIONS IN BONDS AND EQUITIES

Country	1975–79	1980–89	1990–94	1995	1996	1997	1998	1999*
United States	5.9	43.2	108.7	132.6	156.2	207.9	222.8	178.9
Japan	2.8	73.0	84.3	64.8	79.5	95.4	90.6	85.1
Germany	6.9	32.3	102.5	167.3	195.8	256.3	328.9	334.3

*Preliminary.
Source: Table V.2, Bank for International Settlements, *70th Annual Report* (March 31, 2000), available on the Bank's Web site, www.bis.org.

Table 18.2 ■ FOREIGN LISTINGS ON SELECTED STOCK EXCHANGES

Stock Exchange	Total Number of Companies Listed	Number of Domestic Companies Listed	Number of Foreign Companies Listed
New York Stock Exchange	2,592	2,187	405
Toronto Stock Exchange	1,456	1,410	46
Germany	9,017	1,043	7,974
London	2,791	2,292	499
Paris	1,144	968	176
Tokyo	1,932	1,889	43

Source: International Accounting Standards Committee's Web site, www.iasc.org.uk. Data as of December 1999.

on a global investment strategy are less risky than portfolios composed of strictly domestic securities. That's because foreign issuers of securities are often subject to economic conditions that differ from those of domestic companies.

Global investment decisions are complicated by the diversity of financial reporting measurement and disclosure rules in different countries. Even the philosophy and objective of financial reporting differ considerably between countries. Investors reading foreign financial statements are frequently confronted with unfamiliar reporting rules, unique tax-driven financial statement items, and country-specific nuances. An overview of some of these differences in financial reporting approaches is presented next.

An International Financial Reporting Map

There are numerous ways to classify international financial reporting approaches. In keeping with the philosophy of this book, our classification stresses differences between countries in the general nature of their financial reporting rules and how those differences are reflected in statement content and interpretation.

Two broad categories emerge from this perspective. First, there is a group of countries whose financial statements are intended (at least in principle) to capture and reflect the underlying economic performance of the reporting entity. Accounting principles in those countries are designed and selected to help achieve this objective and thereby aid external users' resource allocation decisions. Second, there is a large group of countries whose financial reporting rules do not try to capture "economic reality." Instead, the accounting reports simply conform to mandated laws or detailed tax rules designed to achieve purposes like raising tax revenues to fund government activities, or stimulating capital investment.

> Before 1990, British GAAP was written by a predecessor group called the Accounting Standards Committee. Its pronouncements were known as *Statements of Standard Accounting Practice.*

Disclosures Designed to Reflect Economic Performance

United Kingdom Financial reporting in the United Kingdom influenced accounting in many other countries, such as the United States and British Commonwealth members.

Contemporary accounting principles in the United Kingdom are based on the Companies Act 1985—called "The Act"—as well as on a series of pronouncements—called *Financial Reporting Standards*—issued by the Accounting Standards Board, a private

Table 18.3 ■ LARGEST COMPANIES IN EIGHT SELECTED INDUSTRIES, RANKED BY 1999 REVENUES

($ in millions)	1999 Revenues		1999 Revenues
Airlines		**Food and Drug Stores**	
1. AMR, United States	$20,262	1. Metro Holding, Switzerland	$ 46,664
2. UAL, United States	18,027	2. Kroger, United States	45,352
3. Delta Air Lines, United States	14,711	3. Carrefour, France	39,856
4. British Airways, Britain	14,405	4. Albertson's, United States	37,478
5. Japan Airlines, Japan	14,356	5. Koninklijke Ahold, Netherlands	35,798
Banks: Commercial and Savings		**Insurance: Property Casualty (Stock)**	
1. Deutsche Bank, Germany	$58,585	1. Allianz, Germany	$ 74,178
2. Bank of America Corp., United States	51,392	2. CGNU, Britain	41,974
3. Credit Suisse, Switzerland	49,362	3. American International Group, U.S.	40,656
4. Fortis, Belgium	43,660	4. Zurich Financial Services, Switzerland	39,962
5. BNP Paribas, France	40,099	5. Munich Re Group, Germany	38,400
Electronics, Electrical Equipment		**Petroleum Refining**	
1. Siemens, Germany	$75,337	1. Exxon/Mobil, United States	$163,881
2. Hitachi, Japan	71,858	2. Royal Dutch/Shell Group, Brit./Netherl.	105,366
3. Matsushita Elec. Indl., Japan	65,556	3. BP Amoco, Britain	83,566
4. Sony, Japan	60,053	4. Total Fina Elf, France	44,990
5. Toshiba, Japan	51,635	5. Sinopec, People's Republic of China	41,883
Food		**Telecommunications**	
1. Nestlé, Switzerland	$49,694	1. Nippon Telegraph & Telephone, Japan	$ 93,592
2. Unilever, Britain/Netherlands	43,680	2. AT&T, United States	62,391
3. Conagra, United States	24,594	3. SBC Communications, United States	49,489
4. Sara Lee, United States	20,012	4. Deutsche Telekom, Germany	37,835
5. Archer Daniels Midland, United States	14,283	5. WorldCom, United States	37,120

Source: *Fortune* 2000 Global 500. www.fortune.com/fortune/global500. Reprinted with permission of Fortune.

sector professional organization. The Act requires U.K. companies to distribute audited financial statements. While The Act does not contain detailed reporting rules, it does specify certain principles that companies must follow when preparing financial statements. For example, U.K. statements must be based on the accrual concept, the going concern perspective must be used, and the reporting rules must be consistently applied. Furthermore, the audit must ascertain whether the statements comply with The Act and whether they give a **true and fair view** of the company's state of affairs and profit or loss.[2]

The phrase "true and fair view" is central to financial reporting in the United Kingdom because it expresses the notion that financial statements must reflect the underlying economic conditions experienced by the reporting firm—that is, financial reporting rules in the United Kingdom are intended to do more than merely present an arbitrary, uniform set of numbers that may bear no correspondence to the existing market conditions under which the firm operates. The U.K. perspective that financial statements should capture a firm's underlying economic situation exerted great influence on the reporting philosophy that prevails in the United States and other countries.

Exhibit 18.1 reproduces the auditor's opinion from the 1999 annual report of BP Amoco. We have highlighted the phrases "the accounts give a true and fair view" and "prepared in accordance with the Companies Act 1985."

[2] See BDO Binder, *The Accounting Profession in the United Kingdom,* 2nd ed., revised (New York: American Institute of Certified Public Accountants [AICPA], 1994).

Exhibit 18.1 ■ BP AMOCO P.L.C.

Excerpts from Report of the Auditors (1999 Annual Report)

To the Members of BP Amoco p.l.c.
We have audited the accounts on pages 36 to 66, which have been prepared under the historical cost convention and the accounting policies set out on pages 36 and 37.

Respective responsibilities of directors and auditors
The directors are responsible for preparing the Annual Report as described above, including responsibility for preparing the accounts in accordance with applicable UK law and accounting standards. Our responsibilities, as independent auditors, are established in the UK by statute, the Auditing Practices Board, the Listing Rules of the London Stock Exchange and by our profession's ethical guidance. . . .

Basis of audit opinion
We conducted our audit in accordance with Auditing Standards issued by the Auditing Practices Board. An audit includes examination, on a test basis, of evidence relevant to the amounts and disclosures in the accounts. It also includes an assessment of the significant estimates and judgements made by the directors in the preparation of the accounts, and of whether the accounting policies are appropriate to the group's circumstances, consistently applied and adequately disclosed.

We planned and performed our audit so as to obtain all the information and explanations which we considered necessary in order to provide us with sufficient evidence to give reasonable assurance that the accounts are free from material misstatement, whether caused by fraud or other irregularity or error. In forming our opinion we also evaluated the overall adequacy of the presentation of information in the accounts.

Opinion
In our opinion the accounts give a true and fair view of the state of affairs of the company and of the group as at 31 December 1999 and of the profit of the group for the year then ended and have been properly prepared in accordance with the Companies Act 1985.

Ernst & Young
Registered Auditor
London
15 February 2000

United States Following its Civil War, the United States experienced rapid industrialization and growth. This expansion was financed by a considerable amount of foreign capital—much of it from the United Kingdom. To review the accounts of their U.S. investments, U.K. investors frequently hired British auditors. These auditors came to the United States and exerted a strong influence on late nineteenth century U.S. accounting practices, which explains some of the parallels between modern financial reporting in the United States and the United Kingdom.

The ultimate responsibility for formulating U.S. financial reporting rules resides in the governmental sector—with the Securities and Exchange Commission (SEC).[3]

[3] These powers are given to the SEC in Section 19(a) of The Securities Act of 1933 as Amended: ". . . the Commission shall have authority, for the purposes of this title, to prescribe the form or forms in which required information shall be set forth, the items or details to be shown in the balance sheet and earning statement, and the methods to be followed in the preparation of accounts, in the appraisal or valuation of assets and liabilities, in the determination of depreciation and depletion, in the differentiation of recurring and nonrecurring income, in the differentiation of investment and operating income, and in the preparation, where the Commission deems it necessary or desirable, of consolidated balance sheets or income accounts of any person directly or indirectly controlling or controlled by the issuer, or any person under direct or indirect common control with the issuer. The rules and regulations of the Commission shall be effective upon publication in the manner which the Commission shall prescribe." (U.S. Congress, "Securities Act of 1933 as Amended" [H.R. 5480], 73d Congress.)

However, the SEC relies on the accounting determinations of a private sector body—the Financial Accounting Standards Board (FASB)—for much of the detailed rule making.

Influenced by its British antecedents, U.S. financial reports are also intended to reflect the underlying economic events and activities of the reporting entity. Statements that are prepared in accordance with this objective are said to "present fairly . . . in conformity with generally accepted accounting principles," as shown in the highlighted text in Exhibit 18.2 on p. 944 from the General Electric Company's auditors' report.

Other Countries The United Kingdom also influenced the financial reporting philosophy and standards in Ireland, as well as in British Commonwealth countries. Accounting statements in Australia, New Zealand, and India clearly display similarities to U.K. reporting. Although each of these countries' standards evolved independently after the initial British influence, their resemblance to U.K. accounting procedures is still recognizable today. For example, periodic write-ups of fixed assets to reflect current appraised values—an accepted practice in the United Kingdom—is also permitted in Commonwealth countries like Australia, New Zealand, India, and Zimbabwe. Furthermore, the notion that financial reporting is designed to capture underlying economic circumstances pervades these countries' procedures. Auditors' opinions in these countries also include the phrase "true and fair view."

United States accounting principles have had a wide impact on financial reporting in countries like Mexico, Canada, and the Philippines. For example, Canadian auditors' reports include the phrase "these consolidated financial statements present fairly . . . in accordance with Canadian generally accepted accounting principles."

> By linking the U.K.'s "true and fair view" with the U.S.'s "present fairly," we only intend to show that each country's financial reporting is designed to capture underlying economic events. But there are *significant* differences between the two approaches. In the United States, "presents fairly" simply means that the statements conform to GAAP. Since U.S. GAAP is designed to reflect economic events, it is *presumed* that conformity to GAAP *automatically* means conformity to the economics of the events portrayed. This is not so in the U.K.'s application of the "true and fair view." There, if a firm's *unique* circumstances mean that U.K. GAAP will not reflect its economic position, departures from U.K. GAAP are permitted as long as the departure better reflects the "true and fair view" of the firm's operations. Despite this subtle difference, both approaches share the characteristic that the reports are designed—in principle—to capture the underlying economic events the firm experienced. (See S. A. Zeff, "A Perspective on the U.S. Public/Private-Sector Approach to the Regulation of Financial Reporting," *Accounting Horizons* [March 1995], pp. 52–70.)

The Netherlands[4] Dutch financial statements, like those in the United Kingdom and the United States, are also intended to reflect the underlying economic conditions experienced by the reporting entity. However, this "tell it like it is" goal for financial reporting in the Netherlands evolved independently of the Anglo-American tradition.

The evolution from reporting that was not designed to capture underlying economics to the modern Dutch approach proceeded slowly following World War II. Three factors appear to have shaped this transformation. First, the destruction caused by World War II as well as the prospect for postwar growth generated tremendous capital investment requirements and opportunities for Dutch companies. These enormous investment expenditures could only be undertaken with a large amount of foreign financing. As a result, improvements in financial reporting began to evolve as a way to attract foreign capital. Second, during the 1950s there was widespread debate in the Netherlands regarding whether or not stockholders had the right to receive expanded information about enterprise performance. Ultimately, these demands for improved disclosure emanating from employees, shareholders, and the general public prevailed; various quasi-public commissions over the next decade persistently recommended more realistic financial reporting. This emerging consensus caused leading companies to improve their

---

[4] The material in this section relies heavily on S. A. Zeff, "The Regulation of Financial Reporting: Historical Development and Policy Recommendations," *De Accountant* [The Netherlands] (November 1993), pp. 152–60.

Exhibit 18.2 ■ GENERAL ELECTRIC COMPANY

Independent Auditors' Report (1999 Annual Report)

To Share Owners and Board of Directors of General Electric Company
We have audited the accompanying statement of financial position of General Electric Company and consolidated affiliates as of December 31, 1999 and 1998, and the related statements of earnings, changes in share owners' equity and cash flows for each of the years in the three-year period ended December 31, 1999. These consolidated financial statements are the responsibilities of the Company's management. Our responsibility is to express an opinion on these consolidated financial statements based on our audits.

We conducted our audits in accordance with generally accepted auditing standards. Those standards require that we plan and perform the audit to obtain reasonable assurance about whether the financial statements are free of material misstatement. An audit includes examining, on a test basis, evidence supporting the amounts and disclosures in the financial statements. An audit also includes assessing the accounting principles used and significant estimates made by management, as well as evaluating the overall financial statement presentation. We believe that our audits provide a reasonable basis for our opinion.

In our opinion, the aforementioned financial statements appearing on pages 34–39, 44 and 56–76 present fairly, in all material respects, the financial position of General Electric Company and consolidated affiliates at December 31, 1999 and 1998, and the results of their operations and their cash flows for each of the years in the three-year period ended December 31, 1999, in conformity with generally accepted accounting principles.

KGMG LLP
Stamford, Connecticut
February 4, 2000

financial reports voluntarily. The resulting reforms were ultimately made into law by the Dutch Parliament in 1970. The third influence on Dutch reporting appears to have been driven by the activism of several influential Dutch companies, such as Unilever and Philips. Their financial reports became models that diffused throughout the business sector.

While the philosophy of contemporary Dutch financial reporting is similar to the philosophy that underlies the Anglo-American tradition, there are important differences. The main one is that Dutch GAAP permits more diversity in the financial reporting choices available to companies. Many companies in the Netherlands prepare financial reports which strive to capture the firm's underlying economics. However, due to the pervasive permissiveness of the Dutch environment, there are also some companies whose reports deviate from this philosophy. Accordingly, U.S. readers of Dutch financial statements must be prepared for greater diversity in financial reporting quality than is the norm in the United States.

GAAP in both the United Kingdom and the United States endeavors to capture underlying economic events. Because of the important historical influence of both of these countries, their reporting philosophies have been widely copied. Although numerous financial reporting differences exist among countries whose GAAP tries to capture underlying economics, the similarities in reporting objectives and methods are numerous.

RECAP

Disclosures That Do Not Necessarily Reflect Economic Performance

The British "true and fair view" and the American "presents fairly" philosophy of financial reporting do not prevail everywhere. In many countries, public companies' financial statements are required to conform to tax law and/or to the existing commercial law governing accounting. Financial reports in these countries are not necessarily designed to reflect a firm's underlying economic performance. In France, Italy, and Belgium, financial reporting is heavily influenced by national tax laws; and in Germany, Japan, and Switzerland, financial reporting is influenced by both commercial and tax laws.

Financial reporting in the United States and the United Kingdom is also influenced by law—by the Securities Acts in the United States and The Companies Act in the United Kingdom. However, there is a difference from France, et al., since the U.K. and U.S. also have standard-setting bodies whose role is to develop financial reporting procedures to capture underlying economic conditions, consistent with the philosophy of the law. In other countries, the law simply dictates report content without regard to whether the resulting numbers conform to economic circumstances.

Exhibit 18.3 on p. 946 shows the auditors' report from the 2000 Mazda Motor Corporation Annual Report. In the highlighted portion, the auditors state that the figures are "in conformity with accounting principles generally accepted in Japan. . . ." Just below the audit opinion is a reminder to statement users that Japanese accounting principles could diverge, possibly materially, from GAAP in countries like the United States and United Kingdom. So analysts must be sensitive to a potential divergence between reported statement amounts and underlying economics.

To qualify for tax benefits in many countries, a company that claims deductions on the tax return must also include them in the published financial statements. ***This effectively requires conformity between tax and book amounts and greatly restricts the ability of financial statements to reflect economic performance.*** Regarding German accounting on this point, Frederick Choi and Gerhard Mueller state the following:

> The second pervasive characteristic of accounting in Germany is its complete subordination to tax law. The so-called **determination principle** (Massgeblichkeitsprinzip) basically states that taxable income is determined by whatever is booked in a firm's financial records. Any available tax provisions can only be utilized if they are in fact fully booked. This means, among other things, that if any special or highly accelerated depreciation is to be used for tax purposes, it must be completely and fully booked for financial reporting purposes as well.[5] [Emphasis added.]

An example of the conformity between tax rules and financial reporting in Germany was illustrated in Chapter 10 (p. 485) for Lufthansa. To obtain the extra depreciation allowed by the German tax law, Lufthansa actually had to include the extra tax charge as an expense on its income statement.

These national accounting rules apply to financial statements prepared for distribution within the home country—in France, Germany, Italy, and numerous others. These statements are called **parent company** financial statements. However, the recent trend among European multinationals that have shares listed overseas is to use either International Accounting Standards (IAS) or U.S. GAAP in the consolidated statements that are prepared for foreign investors and others. (IAS standards are discussed later in the chapter.) This trend has begun to narrow the gap between these countries' consolidated reports and underlying economics.

Some elements of the Japanese income tax law are similar to those of Germany—that is, if a company wishes to gain certain tax deductions in Japan, its financial statements must reflect the same charges shown on the tax return. To illustrate, a note in the 1999 Mazda annual report states:

> Allowance for doubtful receivables provides for writing off uncollectible receivables. The maximum amount allowed by the corporate tax law (at the prescribed rate) is recognized while taking . . . into consideration the financial standings of the debtors.

[5] F. D. S. Choi and G. G. Mueller, *International Accounting*, 2nd ed. (Upper Saddle River, NJ: Prentice Hall, 1992), p. 96.

Exhibit 18.3 ■ MAZDA MOTOR CORPORATION

Report of Independent Certified Public Accountants (2000 Annual Report)

To the Shareholders and the Board of Directors of Mazda Motor Corporation:

We have audited the accompanying consolidated balance sheets of Mazda Motor Corporation (a Japanese corporation) and subsidiaries as of March 31, 2000 and 1999, and the related consolidated statements of income, shareholders' equity and cash flows for each of the three years in the period ended March 31, 2000, expressed in Japanese yen. Our audits were made in accordance with generally accepted auditing standards in Japan and, accordingly, included such tests of the accounting records and such other auditing procedures as we considered necessary in the circumstances.

In our opinion, the consolidated financial statements referred to above present fairly the consolidated financial position of Mazda Motor Corporation and subsidiaries as of March 31, 2000 and 1999, and the consolidated results of their operations and their cash flows for each of the three years in the period ended March 31, 2000 in conformity with accounting principles generally accepted in Japan applied on a consistent basis during the periods, except for the new accounting policies and change in accounting policy, with which we concur, as noted in the following paragraph. . . .

Asahi & Co.
(Member Firm of Andersen Worldwide SC)

Hiroshima, Japan
June 23, 2000

Statement on Accounting Principles and Auditing Standards

This statement is to remind users that accounting principles and auditing standards and their application in practice may vary among nations and therefore could affect, possibly materially, the reported financial position and results of operations. The accompanying financial statements are prepared based on accounting principles generally accepted in Japan, and the auditing standards and their application in practice are those generally accepted in Japan. Accordingly, the accompanying consolidated financial statements and the auditors' report presented above are for users familiar with Japanese accounting principles, auditing standards and their application in practice.

But the accounting used to conform the financial reporting numbers and tax numbers in Japanese financial statements differs subtly from the procedures used in Germany. In Japan the debit for the extra tax-driven deduction does not appear on the income statement. Instead, the debit is made to *retained earnings* and a credit is made to a special retained earnings reserve. (This credit can be thought of as a type of deferred income tax payable account, since the extra deductions in Japan reverse in future years.)

In some countries, tax-driven amounts that may not bear any relation to underlying economic costs get reflected in reported financial results. Consequently, the underlying financial statements will not show—in many cases—the reporting firm's real performance during the period.

RECAP

Why Do Reporting Philosophies Differ Across Countries?

What factors explain differences among countries' financial reporting concepts and rules? Why do certain countries' statements try to reflect underlying economics, while the statements in other countries merely conform to arbitrary legal formats?

A country's financial reporting rules represent one aspect of its legal, ethical, institutional, and financial customs, procedures and social objectives. Differences in financial reporting philosophies reflect cross-country differences in underlying social mores and systems. It is difficult to relate specific social differences to individual financial reporting differences between countries, but certain linkages are apparent.

One linkage reflects the source of the financing used by companies. In countries where the bulk of the investment capital is attracted from a broad base of investors, these investors want comprehensive data to help them select appropriate securities. Here, there is a demand for a reporting system that captures underlying economics. The United States and Canada provide examples since an exceedingly large portion of firms' capital requirements are provided by individual debt and equity investors—either directly or indirectly through pension plans and mutual funds. The financial reporting environment in both countries has evolved to meet this demand for information.

Large companies in Japan are often members of an associated corporate group, termed a **keiretsu**. Membership in the keiretsu usually comprises several different industry groups. Members of the group typically purchase inputs from one another and provide each other with equity financing. In addition, a keiretsu typically includes a large bank, which is another source of financing.

By contrast, in countries like Japan and Germany, a small amount of firms' financing is provided by individual investors. The primary capital providers in Germany have been several large banks—and the government itself. The German stock market is small. Similarly, six or eight large banks provide much of the financing in Japan; in addition, firms also raise capital from members of their associated corporate group. As a consequence, external equity financing is also relatively unimportant in Japan. In countries like Japan and Germany, historically there were just a few important capital providers who had great power—such as the ability to acquire information directly from the firm seeking capital. Because of this power and because of the insignificance of the public market, the demand for economically realistic reporting standards has been low, until recently.

Sources of financing do shift over time. When this happens in a country, changes in the financial reporting environment will occur as well. This appears to be taking place in several European countries. As firms in these countries increasingly seek foreign capital, some feel the need to divorce their financial statements from tax rules and to conform more closely to an economic performance perspective. The hope is that by preparing their financial reports using procedures required by the countries in which potential investors reside, these statements will be more understandable to foreign investors. Consequently, a two-tiered financial reporting system is emerging in Europe. The rigid book/tax conformity rules are adhered to only at the parent company level. The parent is a financial (i.e., nonoperating) holding company that is an amalgamation of all the tax-paying entities comprising the firm. Legal rules are satisfied because the parent company statements conform to the tax law. But a second financial reporting tier has evolved in the late 1990s. In this second tier, consolidated financial statements (described in Chapter 16) which encompass the legally separate operating subsidiaries are prepared. These statements—which are directed to potential investors—increasingly use either U.S. GAAP or IASC standards to report performance. This trend is especially evident in Germany, prompted by a 1998 law that allows German companies whose securities are publicly traded to use IAS or U.S. GAAP—rather than German GAAP—in their consolidated financial statements *for domestic reporting purposes.* So there is a clear international movement toward financial reports prepared in the Anglo-American tradition.

"Traditionally, Japanese companies have been managed on behalf of their employees, not shareholders. The majority of a company's shares are likely to be held by banks and other companies for the purpose of maintaining a relationship, so there was little concern about shareholder returns and little fear of hostile takeovers. . . . [A]ccounting rules now under consideration would compel greater disclosure, making it harder for companies to sweep problems under the rug." (A. Pollack, "Japan Considers Opening the Veiled Corporate Ledger," the *New York Times* [August 5, 1997].)

Coping With International Reporting Diversity

How should regulators respond to the diverse financial reporting requirements for publicly traded securities across countries? What information requirements should be imposed by the securities regulatory commission in Country A if a firm from Country B wishes to sell securities in Country A?

There are at least four different approaches that regulatory commissions can use to deal with foreign issuers of securities. They can:

1. Compel foreign issuers to use host country reporting regulations
2. Create bilateral arrangements between a particular host country and a particular foreign country
3. Allow every foreign issuer to use the foreign issuer's own financial reporting rules in a host country
4. Require foreign issuers to use an internationally consistent set of reporting principles and procedures.

We next examine each of these alternatives.

Foreign Issuers Use Host Country Financial Reporting Rules The United States requires foreign companies that wish to have securities traded on U.S. exchanges to reconcile their own reporting methods to U.S. GAAP. This reconciliation is mandated by the SEC on Form 20-F. Diageo—a large British firm formed and renamed after Grand Metropolitan acquired Guinness Group—provided the reconciliation illustrated in Exhibit 18.4. The disclosure is designed for the convenience of U.S. financial statement readers. Form 20-F provides U.S. investors with income, balance sheet, and other statement numbers computed using familiar rules. This allows them to evaluate the performance of foreign issuers relative to U.S. companies using a common reporting basis—U.S. GAAP. However, this reconciliation is controversial from two perspectives.

Exhibit 18.4 ■ DIAGEO P.L.C.

Edited Excerpts from the 1999 Form 20-F Reconciliation to U.S. GAAP

Effect on net income of differences between U.K. and U.S. GAAP
For the year ended June 30, 1999:

	£ million	£ million
Net income in accordance with U.K. GAAP		942
Adjustments in respect of the acquisition of the Guinness Group:		
Brands	(131)	
Goodwill and other intangibles	(93)	
Inventories	(105)	
Disposal of business	(142)	
Merger integration	30	
Deferred taxation		
On above adjustments	51	
Other	18	
		(372)
Other adjustments:		
Brands		(84)
Goodwill and other intangibles		(109)
Restructuring and integration		22
Pensions and other postemployment benefits		(11)
Employee share arrangements		35
Impairment		(74)
Other items		(42)
Deferred taxation		
On above adjustments		–
Other		85
Net income in accordance with U.S. GAAP		392

One controversy relates to the competitive disadvantages that reconciliation may impose on U.S. markets; the other concerns whether the reconciliation really overcomes differences between U.S. and foreign GAAP.

U.S. stock exchanges contend that the Form 20-F reconciliation creates competitive disadvantages. The exchanges say that by imposing what they contend are burdensome disclosure requirements on foreign issuers, these issuers become reluctant to list their securities on U.S. exchanges. The U.S. exchanges believe it is costly for foreign firms to reconcile their statements to U.S. GAAP. To avoid this cost, the exchanges argue that some firms simply refuse to list and sell their securities in the United States. As a consequence, there's a dual loss—U.S. exchanges lose the business of listing foreign issues, and the cost of buying foreign securities is higher for U.S. investors since they must buy them abroad.

There is some evidence to support the exchanges' position. Prior to October 1983 foreign firms could trade their shares on the National Association of Securities Dealers Automated Quotations (NASDAQ) system without registering with the SEC, and they did not have to reconcile their accounting to U.S. GAAP. After this date, registration became mandatory, and the number of foreign securities traded on NASDAQ declined from 294 to 213 over the ensuing eight years.[6] This decline occurred despite the tremendous *increase* in U.S. investors' purchases of foreign securities.

The other problem with the Form 20-F reconciliation is that even after a foreign company reconciles its numbers to U.S. GAAP, the information it provides may still not be truly comparable to the information provided by U.S. firms. The reason is that many U.S. GAAP procedures evolved from business and other institutional relationships which exist in the United States. These same relationships may not exist in the foreign issuer's country. Therefore, reconciliation to U.S. GAAP does not necessarily produce the desired comparability.

Consider the following example. The equity method of accounting for an investment in another company (Chapter 16) is required when the percentage of share ownership is between 20% and 50%. This requirement is based on the fact that in the United States, this large proportionate ownership presumably gives the investor some degree of control over the investee's policies, *including its dividend policy*. Using the cost method in such circumstances would be inappropriate since control over dividend policy would allow the investor to manipulate income by altering dividend levels.

To see the flaw in the Form 20-F reconciliation approach, consider a Japanese company which reconciles its accounting to U.S. GAAP. Most larger Japanese companies are members of a keiretsu, a loosely interconnected corporate group. Members of the keiretsu typically own shares of other members of the keiretsu; this arrangement provides a source of financing and further aligns the group's incentives toward mutual benefits. Cross-ownerships in the 20% to 30% range are not unusual in these situations. But investment by one keiretsu member in another *conveys to the investor no control over the corporate affairs of the investee.* Yet Form 20-F would require the Japanese investor to account for the investee using the equity method. Once we understand the totally different institutional arrangements that govern intercorporate investments in Japan, it is evident that using the equity method to reflect such holdings above 20% will *not* capture underlying economics.

Bilateral Multijurisdictional Agreements Another method for dealing with international financial reporting diversity is "multijurisdictional disclosure," a procedure which is followed to an extent between Canada and the United States. Under this procedure, the U.S. SEC will accept for registration purposes the Canadian GAAP statements of a Canadian firm seeking to issue debt or preferred stock. The agreement does not cover other equity issues like common stock.

The firm issuing financial statements benefits because it avoids the cost of reformulating its statements into another country's GAAP, but statement users must be knowledgeable

[6] F. R. Edwards, "Listing of Foreign Securities on U.S. Exchanges," *Journal of Applied Corporate Finance* (Winter 1993), pp. 28–36.

about the financial reporting standards of *both* Canada and the United States. This cost is tempered by the fact that reporting methods in Canada and the United States are somewhat similar. Indeed, the multijurisdictional disclosure approach seems feasible only between countries with broadly similar accounting measurement and disclosure standards.

Issuer's Reporting Allowed The third approach for coping with international reporting diversity is for a host country to allow foreign firms to use their own financial reporting rules. The host country could allow French firms to report their results using French accounting principles, Indian firms could report their results using Indian accounting principles, and so on. This approach imposes no costs on the reporting firm; however, it does place tremendous burdens on analysts in the host country, who need to be knowledgeable about a wide range of foreign financial reporting practices. Because of the high costs imposed on statement users, this approach for coping with financial reporting diversity is not widely advocated.

> **The SEC's Statement on International Accounting Standards**
> April 1, 1996—The SEC is pleased the IASC has undertaken a plan to accelerate its developmental efforts to complete the requisite core set of standards by March 1998. The commission supports the IASC's objective to develop, as expeditiously as possible, accounting standards that could be used for preparing financial statements used in cross-border offerings. From the commission's perspective, there are three key elements to this program and the commission's acceptance of its results:
>
> - The standards must include a core set of accounting pronouncements that constitutes a comprehensive, generally accepted basis of accounting.
> - The standards must be of high quality—they must result in comparability and transparency, and they must provide for full disclosure.
> - The standards must be rigorously interpreted and applied.
>
> The commission is committed to working with its securities regulatory colleagues, through IOSCO, and with the IASC to provide the necessary input to achieve the goal of establishing a comprehensive set of international accounting standards. As soon as the IASC completes its project, accomplishing each of the noted key elements, it is the commission's intention to consider allowing the utilization of the resulting standards by foreign issuers offering securities in the United States.

Foreign Issuers Use an International Standard Progress is being made toward yet another approach, one in which all foreign firms use an internationally consistent set of reporting principles and procedures developed by the International Accounting Standards Board (IASB), which was called the International Accounting Standards Committee (IASC) prior to April 2001. This group began operation on July 1, 1973, following an agreement by professional accounting organizations in Australia, Canada, France, Germany, Japan, Mexico, the Netherlands, Ireland, the United Kingdom, and the United States. The objectives of the IASC are as follows:

1. To formulate and publish in the public interest accounting standards to be observed in the presentation of financial statements and to promote their worldwide acceptance and observance; and
2. To work generally for the improvement and harmonization of regulations, accounting standards, and procedures relating to the presentation of financial statements.[7]

By 2000 the IASC had 39 accounting standards in effect. While these standards are not binding on participating countries, one of the goals of the IASC is to "persuade governments and standard-setting bodies that published financial statements should comply with International Accounting Standards in all material respects."[8]

A heightened legitimacy for IASC may be emerging. The International Organization of Securities Commissions (IOSCO) stated that it would consider recognizing IASC standards for cross-border registrations if IASC developed a set of acceptable fundamental, or core, financial reporting standards. These core standards were completed in 1998. IOSCO then evaluated their suitability and issued a press release on May 17, 2000. The release recommended that IOSCO members permit use of the core standards "as supplemented by reconciliation, disclosure and interpretation where necessary. . . ." This qualified acceptance gives securities commissions latitude in determining whether IASC standards are acceptable without either reconciliation to local GAAP or supplemental disclosures.

As a member of IOSCO, the U.S. SEC promised to review IASC core standards. If the SEC determines that these standards meet its criteria and are acceptable, it will consider allowing foreign issuers of securities in the United States to use IASC standards in lieu of U.S. GAAP. This review is in process. The SEC is soliciting feedback about the suitability

[7] "Preface to Statements of International Accounting Standards," in *International Accounting Standards* 2000 (London: IASC, 2000), p. 31.
[8] Ibid., p. 32.

of IASC standards in filings with the Commission. If the SEC and other IOSCO members deem the standards to be acceptable, it may make it easier for investors to cope with international reporting diversity.

> The feedback is being elicited through a Securities and Exchange Commission Concept Release, "International Accounting Standards," File No. S7-04-00 which was issued in 2000. The release poses 26 specific questions about the likely impact of allowing foreign registrants to use IASC standards in SEC filings.

Compared to U.S. GAAP, existing IASC standards allow firms much more latitude; this is a natural result of the diversity of IASC's constituencies. As of March 2001, IASC representation included 112 countries and 153 professional organizations. The IASC was restructured effective January 1, 2001. Issuing a new standard now requires approval by eight of the Board's fourteen members. Guidelines for selecting Board members state that the Board should not be dominated by any particular constituency or regional interest. (Before IASC was restructured, 13 different countries were represented on the Board.) Some critics contend that this diversity leads to a "lowest common denominator" approach to IASC standards. To get approval, a standard must be "inoffensive"—that is, broadly acceptable. To these critics, inoffensive standards may also be uninformative.

The extra latitude in IASC standards (compared to U.S. GAAP) provides managers with opportunities to evade covenants, realize bonus goals, or achieve other contracting incentives. In its response letter to the SEC (June 5, 2000), the FASB raised a similar point. Specifically, the FASB is "concerned about the extent to which the core [IASC] standards permit alternative accounting treatments to be used for similar transactions and the ambiguousness of some of the guidance in the core standards." Your authors concur.

RECAP

Several methods exist for coping with diverse international financial reporting standards. Existing U.S. rules require foreign registrants to reconcile their accounting to U.S. GAAP. But the emerging "front-runner" approach for overcoming reporting differences is a movement to an internationally consistent set of reporting principles developed by the IASC. Whether IASC rules will ultimately be permitted by the SEC for foreign issuers offering securities in the United States depends on the SEC's assessment of the quality of the rules that were developed.

Monitoring Compliance

Financial reporting rules differ across countries, and so do the mechanisms for monitoring compliance with these rules. Different countries have different structures for determining whether the stated principles are actually being followed by firms. Of course, industrialized countries require firms to have audited financial statements. The independent auditor provides one mechanism for monitoring compliance with reporting rules. However, there have been instances in which auditors' independence and even adherence to professional standards were challenged. This is why a backup mechanism for monitoring financial reports is needed to provide additional safeguards for statement readers.

In the United States, the SEC has the authority to challenge financial reports which it believes do not conform to GAAP. There have been many cases in which the SEC has objected to the accounting principles used in statements filed with the Commission. The reporting firms were compelled to alter their financial statements to bring them into compliance with the Commission's interpretation of GAAP.

However, the SEC's staff is not very large in relation to the number of statements filed with it. It would be wrong to conclude that each firm's numbers are carefully scrutinized. In the late 1970s in a well-publicized case, *Fortune* magazine contended that Aetna Insurance was violating GAAP in its treatment of income tax loss carryforwards. The SEC acknowledged that due to staffing shortages, it had never read the Aetna filing and was unaware of the issues raised in the *Fortune* article.[9] This understaffing continues. Currently, the SEC scrutinizes the

[9] C. J. Loomis, "Behind the Profits Glow at Aetna," *Fortune* (November 15, 1982), pp. 54–58.

financial statements for *all* new registrants—called initial public offerings (IPOs)—that are filed with the Commission. What little remains of staff time is then used to review—on a sampling basis—the statements of longer established registrants. The SEC compliance "safety net" is not exhaustive.

It can be worse in other countries.[10] For years in Australia, New Zealand, and the United Kingdom, the independent auditor represented the *only* monitoring and compliance force. This situation persists in New Zealand. In Australia a new Australian Securities and Investments Commission has been established to expand monitoring. Similarly, in the United Kingdom a private sector agency called the Financial Reporting Review Panel has recently been formed. The U.K. Parliament has delegated authority to this group to bring actions in civil court for perceived breaches of "true and fair view" reporting.

In the Netherlands a type of "accounting court," which is called the Enterprise Chamber, was created by Parliament in 1970. Interested parties can bring alleged violations of the financial reporting provisions of statute law to this group. However, the cost and inconvenience of this process has led to a decline in the number of actions initiated in recent years. The current effectiveness of the Dutch Enterprise Chamber as a compliance enforcement mechanism is unclear.

RECAP

Users of foreign financial statements need to be cognizant of the mechanisms in place to monitor compliance with reporting rules. Understanding that reporting rules differ across countries is only one part of the story. It is also important to understand that there might be country-by-country differences in the degree of adherence to the reporting rules that are supposed to be in effect.

Inflation Accounting

Inflation—a decline in the purchasing power of a country's currency—complicates analysis of international financial reports. Where inflation is high, historical cost-based financial statements are misleading or totally irrelevant. Financial reporting standards in countries with high rates of inflation mandate some form of **inflation accounting** for both tax and financial statement reporting. Mexico is an example. Two forms of inflation accounting are required by Mexican GAAP: (1) specific price-change adjustments, and (2) general price-level adjustments. Each of these inflation accounting approaches is explained and illustrated in this section.

Introduction: General Versus Specific Price Changes All prices do not change at the same rate. During periods of inflation it is not unusual for the prices of some goods and services to actually fall and move in the opposite direction to prices in general. Let's illustrate using U.S. data. Between 1994 and 1998 the general level of prices as measured by the gross national product (GNP) Implicit Price Deflator *increased* by 7.2%. Over this same period, the average price level for electronic computers *fell* by 57.4%. This illustrates that the *direction* of price change will sometimes differ between economic sectors. Furthermore, the Producer Price Index (PPI) for all finished goods rose from a 1994 level of 125.5 to 130.6 in December 1998, an increase of 4.1%; over the same period, the PPI for "pharmaceuticals (prescription)" went from 250 to 322.3, an increase of 28.9%. Thus, the *rate* of increase for the pharmaceuticals sector was more than seven times the rate of increase for all finished goods.

These examples illustrate that significant differences are likely to arise between *average* rates of inflation for the economy as a whole and *specific* rates of price change for

[10] See S. A. Zeff, "International Accounting Principles and Auditing Standards," *The European Accounting Review* (September 1993), pp. 403–10.

a given firm. Diversity in rates of price changes generates controversy regarding the appropriate method for reflecting economic activity in these circumstances. Some believe that adjustments for changing prices should be based on the specific level of costs and prices experienced by each individual firm. This approach is called **current cost accounting.** The rationale for the current cost approach is that since each firm is unique, its own unique level of costs and prices should be reflected in its accounts.

Others believe that adjustments for changing prices should be based upon the general rate of inflation experienced in the economy as a whole. In this view, inflation adjustments would be derived from broad indices of overall price changes, such as the Consumer Price Index (CPI). This method of adjusting for inflation is called **general price-level accounting.**

We'll first explain and illustrate current cost accounting and then do the same for general price-level accounting.

Remember, current cost accounting for inventories and long-lived assets is a departure from historical costing and is not allowed under U.S. GAAP.

Current Cost Accounting

Current cost refers to the market price that an individual firm would have to pay in order to replace the specific assets it owns. Current cost accounting (discussed briefly in Chapter 9 where Last-In, First-Out [LIFO] and First-In, First-Out [FIFO] were contrasted) is designed to accomplish the following two objectives: (1) to reflect all nonmonetary assets like inventory, buildings, equipment, etc., at their current replacement cost as of the balance sheet date; and (2) to differentiate between (a) current cost income from continuing operations and (b) increases or decreases in current cost amounts (also called "holding gains" or "inventory profits").

These objectives are accomplished by first periodically increasing or decreasing the balance sheet asset carrying amount as current cost changes. Then, as the asset is sold or used up, this current cost carrying amount is written off the books and matched against the revenues from sales. These steps are illustrated in simplified form by the following example.

> A firm purchases a unit of inventory for $100 at the beginning of 2001. The asset's current cost increases by $15 in 2001 and it is sold for $180 on January 1, 2002.

Exhibit 18.5 on the following page illustrates income statements and inventory carrying amounts for this example.

There is controversy about how to treat increases in current cost. Are the increases to be included in net income? Alternatively, are they a direct (nonincome) equity increase?

If the firm wishes to maintain start-of-period equity capital expressed in nominal dollars, then the increase is included in net income. However, if the firm wants to maintain start-of-period equity expressed in dollars of physical productive capacity, then the $15 increase in current cost is not income—that is, it is a direct credit to owners' equity.[11]

In its 1999 annual report, Teléfonos de México SA describes its current cost adjustment process for nonmonetary assets as follows:

> The appraised value of land, buildings and other fixed assets of domestic origin at December 31, 1996, and the cost of subsequent additions to such assets were restated based on the NCPI.

Prior to 1997, Mexican accounting required appraisals of nonmonetary assets. But since January 1, 1997, the previous appraised values can be updated by applying the Mexican National Consumer Price Index (NCPI) to the December 31, 1996 appraisal amounts. *In accordance with Mexican GAAP, the restatement debit or credit offset is not included in income but is taken directly to owners' equity.* Inventory is also a nonmonetary asset. So Mexican GAAP illustrates the direct owners' equity (other comprehensive income) treatment of adjustments for all non-monetary assets in a real-world setting.

Irrespective of whether increases in current cost are treated as income or as a (nonincome) direct credit to owners' equity, the cumulative change in owners' equity under the current cost approach for the two years combined ($80) is equal to the *cumulative* equity change under the historical cost approach. However, although the total equity change is the same, the *timing* of equity-change recognition and the *classification* of the equity change by causes differ between the current and historical cost approaches.

[11] For a simple overview of different capital maintenance concepts, see L. Revsine, "A Capital Maintenance Approach to Income Measurement," *The Accounting Review* (April 1981), pp. 383–389. Current cost is not GAAP in the United States. If it were, the direct credit to owners' equity would be a part of other comprehensive income, which was discussed in Chapter 2.

Exhibit 18.5 ■ CURRENT COST VERSUS HISTORICAL COST

Income Statements and Inventory Carrying Amounts

	2001	2002	Total
Current Cost			
Sales revenues	–	$180	$180
Current cost of goods sold	–	115[1]	115
Current cost income from continuing operations	–	65	65
Unrealized increase in current cost amount (or holding gain)	$ 15	–	15
Change in owners' equity	$ 15	$ 65	$ 80
Inventory carrying amount (end of year)	$115[1]	–	

[1]($100 + $15)

	2001	2002	Total
Historical Cost			
Sales revenues	–	$180	$180
Historical cost of goods sold	–	100	100
Total historical cost income	–	$ 80	$ 80
Inventory carrying amount (end of year)	$100	–	

Current cost income differentiates between operating profits and holding gains. In the example, $15 of the total $80 change in equity is attributable to increases in current cost amounts; these increases are recognized as they occur by increasing the inventory carrying amount. Assuming the increase is considered to be a direct credit to owners' equity, the accounting entry to recognize the inventory carrying amount change is:

DR Inventory	$15	
CR Owners' equity—Unrealized increase in current cost amount		$15

When the sale is made in 2002, the new inventory carrying amount ($115) is matched against the selling price of $180 to yield the $65 current cost income from continuing operations. By contrast, historical cost procedures recognize no equity change as input costs increase. Instead, equity increases are deferred until the sale occurs in 2002. At that time, historical cost accounting reports the equity change as one lump-sum number ($80) and does not break this number into separate operating profit and holding gain components.

The failure of historical cost accounting to differentiate between operating profits and holding gains is a serious limitation of traditional accounting. Proponents of current cost accounting argue that the $80 profit number reported under historical cost accounting provides a misleading picture of current operating efficiency because it seems to imply that the spread between sales price and cost is $80. Statement readers might infer that each *future* sale would also generate a margin of $80. But this is incorrect. Because the current spread between selling price and replacement cost is only $65 ($180 − $115), current cost advocates contend that the $65 figure provides the better measure of existing *operating* efficiency and is also the proper starting point for analysts to use in developing estimates of future per-unit net operating cash inflows. Furthermore, the $15 difference between the current cost operating profit of $65 and total historical cost income of $80 is attributable to cost increases over the period that the inventory was held. These holding gains, it is argued, may or may not be sustainable, so they should be disclosed as a separate item to avoid unwarranted inferences. Since historical cost does not separately disclose operating profits and holding gains, critics claim that it obscures different elements of total profitability which may have different patterns of sustainability.

LIFO inventory accounting represents an attempt to separate operating profits from holding gains within the framework of the historical cost model. As discussed in Chapter 9, this separation is not achieved when LIFO dipping occurs because reported LIFO profit includes both current cost operating profits *and* realized holding gains. Furthermore, during periods of rising input costs, the LIFO inventory carrying amount can be far below the current economic cost of the assets that are tied up in inventory. Consequently, traditionally computed ratios (like return on assets [ROA]) will tend to be overstated because of the understatement of the denominator. A further distortion of return ratios exists when LIFO dipping occurs because the numerator—income—is inflated by the realized holding gains.

Over the 1979–1985 period, U.S. companies with inventories plus property, plant, and equipment totalling more than $125 million were required to disclose certain supplementary information prepared on a current cost basis.[12] Exhibit 18.6 presents a representative current cost disclosure for Union Carbide which was taken from its 1985 annual report. For most companies, 1985 represents the latest disclosure, since these disclosures were made voluntary in 1986.[13]

Exhibit 18.6 ■ UNION CARBIDE CORPORATION (UCC)

1985 Annual Report Supplemental Disclosure
Year Ended December 31, 1985
Data on Changing Prices

($ in millions)	At Historical Cost—Nominal Dollars	Adjusted for Changes in Specific Prices Current Cost—Nominal Dollars
Summary statement of income adjusted for changing prices		
Net sales	$9,003	$9,003
Cost of sales	6,252	6,281
Depreciation	596	711
Other operating expense—net	1,708	1,708
Interest expense	292	292
Provision for income taxes	53	53
Minority share of income	27	29
Net income before unusual charges and extraordinary item	$ 75	$ (71)
Per share	$ 0.36	$ (0.34)
Summary balance sheet data adjusted for changing prices		
Inventories	$1,422	$2,259
Property, plant, and equipment, net of accumulated depreciation	5,780	7,453
UCC stockholders' equity	4,019	6,529

12 "Financial Reporting and Changing Prices," *Statement of Financial Accounting Standards (SFAS) No. 33* (Stamford, CT: FASB, 1979).

13 See "Financial Reporting and Changing Prices," *SFAS No. 89* (Stamford, CT: FASB, 1986). The ostensible reason for altering the disclosure requirement was that because inflation rates had abated, the disclosures were no longer essential. An unexpressed—but more plausible—explanation was that managers of capital-intensive firms opposed the disclosures, since they generated adverse reactions directed against managers by shareholders. For example, it is difficult to justify managerial bonuses tied to reported income when the supplemental disclosure indicated losses were being incurred on a current cost basis. The simplest financial reporting remedy for avoiding this conflict is to dispense with the disclosure altogether. Managers of firms aggressively lobbied the FASB to rescind *SFAS No. 33*. One explanation for why the FASB acquiesces to such efforts is developed in L. Revsine, "The Selective Financial Misrepresentation Hypothesis," *Accounting Horizons* (December 1991), pp. 16–27.

Under the *Statement of Financial Accounting Standards (SFAS) No. 33* current cost rules, the only balance sheet accounts adjusted were the nonmonetary assets such as inventory, buildings, and equipment. (Monetary and nonmonetary items are defined in more detail later in the chapter on p. 961.) Actual market replacement costs were used wherever such data were available. When actual market replacement costs were not available, indices that reflected cost changes for the specific asset category being measured were employed. All monetary assets and liabilities (such as cash, receivables, and accounts payable) were reported at their face value without adjustment. As shown in Exhibit 18.6, Union Carbide (UCC) displayed the current cost amounts for these balance sheet categories as well as their income statement effects on cost of sales and depreciation side-by-side with the historical cost amounts. UCC's historical cost income ($75 million) became a current cost loss ($71 million).

The UCC stockholders' equity number in Exhibit 18.6 was increased as a balancing item that resulted after the inventory and other assets were written up. Specifically,

DR Inventories ($2,259 − $1,422)	$ 837	
DR Property, etc. ($7,453 − $5,780)	1,673	
CR Stockholders' equity ($6,529 − $4,019)		$2,510

In countries like Mexico, where inflation is a continuing problem, current cost data for inventories can be determined from invoices received near the balance sheet date, from suppliers' end-of-period price lists, or from recently updated standard cost amounts. In all cases the objective is to estimate the current cost that would be incurred to *replace* the actual asset in use. ***Input costs that would be paid by the firm are used, not selling prices that would be charged to customers.***

Since inventories are purchased virtually continuously, actual market prices will usually be available at any date, making index adjustments rarely necessary for inventory. Land, buildings, and equipment are purchased sporadically, so actual current market costs will not always be available for these items. When fixed asset market costs *are* available—for example, from used equipment dealers' price lists—these market costs would be used to determine current cost balance sheet amounts. For custom designed buildings and special purpose equipment, actual market replacement costs will seldom be determinable. In these cases, market value **estimation techniques** must be used.

To illustrate the procedure, let us assume that a building constructed in 1990 has the following book value at December 31, 2001:

Historical cost of building	$100,000,000
Accumulated depreciation	30,000,000
Net book value	$ 70,000,000

Further assume that a construction cost index (base period 1980 = 100.0) for this type of building is available and has the following index values:*

Average index value for 1990	246
Index value for December 31, 2001	396

The estimated replacement cost of the building at December 31, 2001 would be:

	Historical Cost Amounts		Index Adjustment		Estimated Current Cost Amounts
Cost of building	$100,000,000	×	$\frac{396}{246}$	=	$160,975,600
Accumulated depreciation	$ 30,000,000	×	$\frac{396}{246}$	=	48,292,680
Net book value	$ 70,000,000				$112,682,920

*The measurement and use of price indices is discussed in full on pp. 959–961.

Market value estimation techniques may take several forms. For example, construction cost price indices by geographical area are widely available. The construction cost index value would be applied to the historical book value of buildings to yield an estimated replacement cost. Special purpose price indices for equipment are also available. These price indices are reported on both an industry basis (e.g., an index specific to equipment used in the automotive industry) and by type of equipment (e.g., an index for general purpose electronics equipment). Again, the index value would be multiplied by the historical book value of the equipment in order to obtain an estimated replacement cost. Market value estimation techniques can also be used to estimate land values. For example, real estate tax assessment data can form the basis for estimating the current cost of land.

Under *SFAS No. 33,* current cost adjustments on the income statement were usually limited to cost of goods sold and to depreciation expense. The current cost expense on the income statement was defined as the cost that prevailed at the time an asset was sold or used up in operations. ***If current costs changed after assets were sold or used up, no retroactive adjustment was made to reflect end-of-year current costs in the income statement.***

Here's an example. Sallas Company had the following sales transactions and associated costs during 2001:

Sales during the year	$3,300,000
Current cost of inventory sold using current cost *at the time of sale*	2,700,000
Current cost of inventory sold using current cost *at year-end*	2,950,000

The reported gross margin using current cost accounting would be:

Sales revenues	$3,300,000
Current cost of goods sold	2,700,000
Current cost gross margin	$ 600,000

The $2,950,000 *year-end* current cost of inventory sold is ignored, since the objective of current costing is to reflect the margin that existed using costs and selling prices that prevailed *at the time of each sale.* Items like sales revenues, salaries, and miscellaneous expenses are presumed to be stated at or near prevailing prices at the time that they appear on the income statement, and therefore they do not require adjustment. ***Thus, the current cost income statement results in a matching of actual sales revenues with the current costs that were in effect at the time of each sale.***

ANALYSIS

By capturing the margin that was in effect at the time of each sale, current costing provides a basis for forecasting future margins and therefore future cash flows. The reasoning is based on the premise that today's *real* margin provides the best basis for estimating tomorrow's margin. The desire to capture the contemporaneous margin—or spread—between selling price and replacement cost explains why the cost-of-goods-sold account is not adjusted "after-the-fact" to year-end replacement cost. If an "after-the-fact" adjustment were made, actual sales prices would be "matched" with subsequent costs that were not even known when sales prices were set.

Exhibit 18.6 shows a $146 million difference ($75 million − (−$71 million)) between historical and current cost net income in 1985 for UCC. Recollect that conventional historical cost income is comprised of two components: (1) current cost income from continuing operations, and (2) realized holding gains. So the $71 million current cost loss means that much more than 100% of UCC's 1985 historical cost income ($75 million) consisted of

This is easily seen by returning to Exhibit 18.5. Conventional historical cost income ($80) can be decomposed as follows:

Current cost income from continuing operations	$65
Plus: Realized holding gains	15
Equals: Historical cost income	$80

realized holding gains. Examining the Exhibit 18.6 income statement disclosure reveals that UCC's realized holding gains arose from three sources:

Cost-of-goods-sold difference	$ 29	($6,281 − $6,252)
Depreciation difference	115	($711 − $596)
Minority share difference[14]	2	($29 − $27)
Realized holding gains in 1985	$146	

Computing realized holding gains allows us to see the various components of UCC's historical cost income number:

Reported current cost loss from continuing operations	$ (71)	(Given)
Realized holding gains	146	***(Computed above)***
Historical cost income	$ 75	(Given)

Over the period that the *SFAS No. 33* disclosures were required, it was not unusual for capital intensive companies like UCC to report historical cost income while simultaneously revealing losses on a current cost basis. The frequency of these disparities fueled the criticisms directed against the traditional income determination approach of historical costing. To give some idea about the relative size of adjusted current cost earnings in relation to reported historical cost earnings, consider the Exhibit 18.7 data from the 1983 *SFAS No. 33* disclosures.

We deliberately focus on 1983 because this was a year of relatively low inflation—3.2% as measured by the CPI. Nevertheless, as shown in Exhibit 18.7, the ratio of current cost profit as a percentage of historical cost profit was only 43% across all industries. That meant that for every dollar of historical cost profit reported during 1983, 57% (1.00 − .43) was attributable to realized holding gains. The eight "worst off" industries (airlines, etc.)

Exhibit 18.7 ■ SUMMARY OF *SFAS NO. 33* DISCLOSURES FOR 1983

Ratio of Current Cost to Historical Cost Income

The Best Off	Current-cost profits as percentage of historical cost	The Worst Off	Current-cost profits as percentage of historical cost
1. Publishing/TV	86%	1. Airline	Loss
2. Office equipment	85	2. General machinery	Loss
3. Aerospace	84	3. Metal and mining	Loss
4. Drugs	84	4. Paper	Loss
5. Retailing (nonfood)	80	5. Rails and trucking	Loss
6. Tobacco	77	6. Special machinery	Loss
7. Services	76	7. Steel	Loss
8. Instruments	76	8. Tire and rubber	Loss
9. Electrical	75	9. Natural resources	38%
10. Textiles	72	10. Building materials	42
11. Appliances	72	11. Real estate	47
All-industry average	43%		

Source: Reprinted from April 30, 1994 issue of *Business Week* by special permission, Copyright © 1994 by The McGraw-Hill Companies, Inc.

[14] The minority share difference arises because the current cost income from those subsidiaries with minority shareholders was apparently *higher* than the historical cost income.

had results comparable to UCC's since they reported *losses* on a current cost basis. Consequently, no meaningful ratio value could be computed for these firms in Exhibit 18.7 since the numerator was negative.

Current Cost Disclosures and Monetary Items During the 1970s and 1980s current cost disclosures centered on nonmonetary assets like inventory and equipment. When the rate of inflation abated in the 1980s, the perceived importance of the effort to adjust nonmonetary assets diminished. With the collapse of the U.S. savings and loan industry in the mid-1980s and the difficulties experienced by many commercial banks, the focus of market value disclosures began to shift to certain types of monetary assets and liabilities. The reason for this shift is that financial institutions are regulated using accounting numbers, particularly owners' equity. These institutions are required to have a certain minimum proportion of equity, which is called **regulatory capital.** Financial assets and liabilities—loans to borrowers, customer deposits, etc.—comprise the bulk of these financial intermediaries' balance sheet amounts. Because savings and loans (S&Ls) and banks used historical cost accounting, the measure of capital used for regulatory purposes was insensitive to changes in the underlying value of these financial institutions' assets and liabilities. Consequently, it was widely believed that inadequate accounting rules were a factor in many of the S&L and bank failures.

In an effort to provide more complete information to the financial community and regulators, the FASB has required footnote disclosure of the current value of financial institutions' items like loans and deposits.[15] The FASB also introduced disclosure requirements for financial instruments like long-term investments and long-term debt obligations.[16] These fair value disclosures are in the footnotes rather than in the body of the financial statements themselves. In addition, current value data for certain investments in debt and equity securities now appear on the balance sheet itself, as illustrated in Chapter 16.[17] The FASB has also issued a statement that requires current value measurements on the balance sheet for derivative instruments, as discussed in Chapter 11.[18]

General Price-Level Accounting

A currency unit such as the U.S. dollar possesses value because of the goods and services that it will buy. The real amount of goods and services that can be acquired at any moment is what determines the **purchasing power** of a currency.

Current costing, as we just discussed, is one way to measure purchasing power. It measures changes in the prices of the specific assets and liabilities of the firm. Current costing thus captures changes in *specific purchasing power.*

General price-level accounting, another way to measure purchasing power, makes no attempt to measure changes in specific prices. Instead, it focuses on changes in *general purchasing power.*

The general purchasing power approach uses a price index. All indices are intended to price a market basket of goods and services at various points of time to determine how the price of the market basket has changed.

Overview of Adjustment Mechanics U.S. GAAP financial statements record the dollar amount expended or incurred at the date of the original transaction. However, because the purchasing power of these dollars changes over time, the amounts stated in original (or "nominal") dollars are not comparable. In other words, historical cost state-

[15] "Disclosures about Fair Value of Financial Instruments," *SFAS No. 107* (Norwalk, CT: FASB, 1991).

[16] "Disclosure of Information about Financial Instruments with Off-Balance Sheet Risk and Financial Instruments with Concentrations of Credit Risk," *SFAS No. 105* (Norwalk, CT: FASB, 1990); and "Disclosure about Derivative Financial Instruments and Fair Value of Financial Instruments," *SFAS No. 119* (Norwalk, CT: FASB, 1994).

[17] "Accounting for Certain Investments in Debt and Equity Securities," *SFAS No. 115* (Norwalk, CT: FASB, 1993).

[18] "Accounting for Certain Derivative Instruments and Certain Hedging Activities," *SFAS No. 138* (Norwalk, CT: FASB, 2000).

ments ignore changes in the purchasing power of the currency. ***The objective of general price-level accounting is to adjust all historical amounts into common purchasing power units using a broad purchasing power index.*** Here's an example. Adess Corporation owns two assets. One was acquired on January 1, 1988 and the other on January 1, 1998:

Date	Original Transaction Amount	General Purchasing Power Index as of January 1
1988 (Asset 1)	$200,000	76
1998 (Asset 2)	200,000	193
2001	—	207
	$400,000	

The gross book value of $200,000 for each asset using historical cost does not reflect the difference in the purchasing power of the *nominal* dollars invested in each asset. That is, the $200,000 of 1988 dollars that were expended on asset 1 did not have the same purchasing power as the $200,000 of 1998 dollars that were expended on asset 2; nor does the sum of these amounts have the same purchasing power as $400,000 of January 1, 2001 dollars. ***In order to reflect changes in the purchasing power of the measuring unit between 1988 and 2001, all amounts must be restated into dollars of uniform purchasing power.*** If all amounts were restated to reflect the purchasing power of the January 1, 2001 dollar, the adjustment would be:

Asset Acquired in	Amount		Restatement Factor		Restated into 2001 Dollars
1988	$200,000	×	$\frac{207}{76}$	=	$544,737
1998	200,000	×	$\frac{207}{193}$	=	214,508
					$759,245

To understand these restated numbers, let's consider the $544,737 amount in 2001 dollars for the asset acquired in 1988. This number indicates that it would take $544,737 dollars on January 1, 2001 to have the same purchasing power that $200,000 had on January 1, 1988. Thus, the $200,000 invested in 1988 has a January 1, 2001 purchasing power equivalent of $544,737. The $200,000 invested on January 1, 1998 has a purchasing power equivalent in January 1, 2001 dollars of $214,508.

Generalizing from the example, to restate historical amounts into current purchasing power units, the nominal dollar amount is multiplied by a **restatement factor,** which is a ratio of price indices. The numerator of the ratio is the price index level of the current period, and the denominator of the ratio is the price index relating to the period of the original transaction amount. To restate 1988 dollars into what those dollars are equivalent to in 2001 purchasing power, we calculate:

$$\begin{array}{c}\text{1988 transaction}\\ \text{amount to be}\\ \text{restated}\end{array} \times \frac{\text{2001 General purchasing power index}}{\text{1988 General purchasing power index}} = \begin{array}{c}\text{2001 purchasing}\\ \text{power equivalent}\end{array}$$

In our example, the 2001 index value is 207 and the 1988 index value is 76, so the restatement factor is 207/76, as shown above.

General price-level accounting is not intended to reflect current market values of assets and liabilities. This is not surprising, since the restatement factor relates to overall average purchasing power changes rather than to changes in the prices of the specific items being adjusted. The intent of general price-level accounting is simply to make historical currency amounts that are expended in different time periods comparable by adjusting all amounts to current purchasing power dollar equivalents. In this sense, general price-level accounting does not abandon the historical cost principle. Instead, nominal dollar historical costs are simply restated into dollars of constant purchasing power.

To apply constant dollar accounting in practice, *SFAS No. 33* required firms to measure purchasing power changes by using the CPI for all urban consumers.[19] This index was selected because it is published monthly, and, unlike most other broad purchasing power indices, it is not retroactively adjusted after initial publication. This meant that the "final" CPI value was always available promptly for use in the preparation of annual constant dollar financial statements. Some critics argued, however, that this practical advantage of using the CPI was negated by the fact that a *consumer* price index is not relevant when considering the purchasing power changes experienced by industrial firms.

After restating financial statements to a current cost basis, Teléfonos de México SA then applies a general price level (constant peso) adjustment described as follows:

> The Company recognizes the effects of inflation on financial information as required by Mexican Accounting Principles Bulletin B-10 ("Accounting Recognition of the Effects of Inflation on Financial Information"), as amended, issued by the Mexican Institute of Public Accountants (MIPA). Consequently, the amounts shown in the accompanying financial statements and in these notes are expressed in thousands of Mexican pesos with purchasing power at December 31, 1999. The December 31, 1999 restatement factor applied to the financial statements at December 31, 1998 was 12.32% (which represents the annual rate of inflation for 1999) based on the Mexican National Consumer Price Index (NCPI) published by Banco de México (the central bank).

This puts all years' comparative statements in pesos of constant purchasing power. Year-to-year comparisons devoid of inflation illusion can then be made.

Overview of the Concepts General price-level accounting requires a clear delineation between monetary items and nonmonetary items, because purchasing power changes affect each category differently. A **monetary item** is money, or a claim to receive or to pay a sum of money, which is fixed in amount. Examples include cash, accounts receivable, accounts payable, and bonds payable. What you should understand about these items is that they are stated in monetary units and that the claim or amount remains fixed even if the price level changes. By contrast, a **nonmonetary item** is not fixed in amount, and its price will likely change as the general level of prices changes. Examples of nonmonetary items include inventories, buildings, manufacturing equipment, and obligations under product warranties.

To illustrate the general concepts of constant dollar accounting, let's consider a firm that is financed entirely with equity. Suppose its only asset is land (a nonmonetary asset), which was purchased for $1,000 on January 1, 2001. Using the basic accounting equation, the firm would appear as follows on this date:

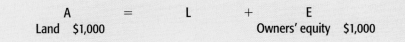

A	=	L	+	E
Land $1,000				Owners' equity $1,000

If we assume that the general level of prices rose by 4% during 2001 and that no transactions occurred during the year, the constant dollar basic accounting equation at the end of 2001 would reflect:

A	=	L	+	E
Land $1,040				Owners' equity $1,040

Notice that both amounts have been restated by the ratio 104/100 to reflect December 31, 2001 general purchasing power. This means that it takes $1,040 on December 31, 2001 to have the same general purchasing power that $1,000 had on January 1, 2001. All other nonmonetary items would be adjusted similarly in preparing general price-level financial statements.

Under constant dollar accounting, the upward restatement of owners' equity is *not* considered to be income. An analogy makes it easy to understand why. Whether you express a temperature at 12° Celsius or at its equivalent of 54° Fahrenheit does not change the underlying real level of the temperature. So too with the purchasing power adjustment from $1,000 January 1, 2001 dollars to $1,040 December 31, 2001 dollars. All that has happened is that the measurement unit has been changed. There is no income or loss.

[19] *SFAS No. 33,* para. 39.

Net monetary assets are the difference between gross monetary assets and gross monetary liabilities. So, if a firm's only monetary items are cash of $35,000 and accounts payable of $15,000, its net monetary assets balance is $20,000. Notice that monetary liabilities generate a *gain* when price-levels rise. The reason is that, by definition, the dollar amount of the liability is fixed and can be paid-off with dollars possessing diminished purchasing power. So it is the *net* monetary asset or liability position of the firm that determines whether purchasing power changes result in a loss or a gain. That is, firms with a net monetary liability position (i.e., an excess of gross monetary liabilities over gross monetary assets) experience purchasing power gains from inflation.

By contrast, when the assets held are monetary, rather than nonmonetary, a gain or loss *does* occur. Let's illustrate this by assuming that the asset held on January 1, 2001 was cash rather than land. Cash, of course, is a monetary item. Since prices, on average, rose by 4% during 2001, to be in the same general purchasing power position at the end of 2001 as it was at the beginning of 2001, the firm would have to possess a cash balance of $1,040. The reasoning is simple—it takes $1,040 end-of-year dollars to buy what $1,000 bought at the start of the year. If, however, there were no transactions during 2001 and if the ending cash balance is still $1,000, then the firm has suffered a real loss of $40 during 2001 because the purchasing power of its cash has declined. This would be reflected in the end-of-period general price-level accounting equation as:

A		=	L	+	E	
Cash	$1,000				Owners' equity	1,040
					Purchasing power loss	(40)

When a firm holds *net* monetary assets during a period of inflation, a loss occurs since the purchasing power of the net monetary assets declines. Put somewhat differently, since monetary items are automatically expressed in end-of-period dollars, no adjustment of these items is necessary in constant dollar balance sheets; however, the implicit gain or loss that results from holding monetary items during a period of general inflation must be recognized. The purchasing power gain or loss account appears on the income statement and is ultimately closed to owners' equity.[20]

Teléfonos de México SA described the gain or loss from holding monetary items as follows in its 1999 annual report:

> The monetary effect represents the impact of inflation on monetary assets and liabilities. The net monetary effect of each year is included in the statements of income as a part of the comprehensive financing (income) cost. . . . The decrease in 1999's monetary position gain was due to lower inflation and a lower net average monetary liabilities.

---

[20] A loss on monetary items that is recognized while the asset carrying value is not changed might cause you to question how the balance sheet can still balance under such circumstances. The issue is best understood by considering the gain or loss on monetary items as a two-step computational process. First, when 4% inflation occurs during 2001 for the all-cash firm in the example, the following entry might be made to put all amounts into end-of-period dollars:

DR Cash	$40	
CR Owners' equity		$40

After this entry is made, the end-of-period general price-level accounting equation is:

A		=	L	+	E	
Cash	$1,040				Owners' equity	$1,040

Cash is now shown as $1,040 when, in reality, the December 31, 2001 balance is only $1,000. The difference, of course, is the purchasing power loss. To adjust cash to the proper year-end balance, the following entry must be made:

DR Owners' equity (purchasing power loss)	$40	
CR Cash		$40

After this entry is made, the basic accounting equation shows:

A		=	L	+	E	
Cash	$1,000				Owners' equity	$1,040
					Purchasing power loss	(40)

Although formal journal entries are seldom employed when historical cost statements are adjusted to a general price-level basis, an understanding of the hypothetical journal entries described here makes it easier to grasp the mechanics of the purchasing power gain or loss on monetary items.

SUMMARY

The objective of financial reporting rules differs across countries. In countries which follow a U.K./U.S. financial reporting tradition, financial reports are designed to reflect underlying economic performance. In countries such as Japan, Germany, and France, financial reporting rules either follow the tax law or are prescribed by statute. Reporting philosophies differ because of underlying differences in capital markets and other societal factors. But as overseas firms seek broader access to world capital markets, the rules requiring conformity to statutory and/or tax law are being relaxed by some governments.

Differences in financial reporting rules complicate international investment analysis. Various mechanisms for coping with cross-country reporting diversity have evolved. In the United States, foreign issuers are required to reconcile their home country reporting rules to U.S. GAAP. Another approach that is gaining significant support is one in which companies are urged to use rules written by the IASC. These standards would then become a type of international accounting language. Mechanisms for monitoring compliance with GAAP also differ significantly from country to country—both in the form of the monitoring and its effectiveness.

Inflation is a serious problem in certain countries. Where this is the case, historical cost reporting becomes less meaningful and inflation accounting is often used. Two methods for reflecting changing prices are current cost accounting and general price-level accounting. Current cost accounting measures changes in the specific purchasing power of the company for which the financial statements are being prepared. By contrast, general price-level accounting strives to reflect overall, average changes in purchasing power.

EXERCISES

E18–1

Why do financial reporting rules differ?

Allocating resources in the most efficient manner maximizes the wealth of any country. It is generally acknowledged that financial information plays an important role in efficient resource allocation.

REQUIRED:

Given that both of the preceding statements are correct, why are the financial reporting rules in some countries designed to be very helpful to external individual investors (e.g., in the United States and Canada) whereas in other countries (e.g., in Japan and Germany), they are less helpful?

E18–2

Overcoming reporting diversity

Some analysts contend that a single, standardized set of uniform financial reporting rules that would be required for all companies in all countries would improve interfirm comparisons and enhance financial analysis.

REQUIRED:

Do you agree that uniform reporting across many countries will always enhance the comparability of financial data and analyses? Why or why not?

E18–3

Alternative return measures

Telefónica S.A. is a Spanish company that is a leading telecommunications operator in Spanish- and Portuguese-speaking countries. Telefónica prepares its annual financial report in accordance with Spanish GAAP. In contrast to U.S. GAAP, Spanish GAAP allows firms to revalue their assets. Since Telefónica's shares trade on the New York Stock Exchange, Telefónica files Form 20-F with the SEC. Selected information from Telefónica's 1999 Form 20-F is as follows (in million pesetas):

Net income for the year reported in the Spanish GAAP Accounts	11,581
Approximate net income in accordance with U.S. GAAP	92,213
Reversal of net effect of revaluation of fixed assets and related accumulated depreciation	(157,475)
Total net fixed and other noncurrent assets (measured in accordance with Spanish GAAP)	8,906,012

(continued)

REQUIRED:

Given that Telefónica's net increase in assets due to asset revaluations totaled 157,475 pesetas, answer the following questions:

1. What is Telefónica's ROA when it reports in accordance with Spanish GAAP?
2. What is Telefónica's ROA under U.S. GAAP?
3. Which ROA measure is preferable? Explain.

E18–4 **Current cost accounting**

Highrate Company's 2001 historical cost income statement is as follows:

Sales	$20,000
Cost of sales	8,000
Gross margin	12,000
Depreciation	2,000
Other operating expenses	8,000
Net income	$ 2,000

Highrate's management is concerned about the increase in inventory costs as well as the increasing costs of property, plant, and equipment. Management believes that the current cost of inventory sold is 25% higher than its historical cost at the time of sale. In addition, if property, plant, and equipment were valued at current costs, an additional $1,000 of depreciation would be recorded.

REQUIRED:

1. Prepare a current cost income statement for Highrate Company.
2. Assume you are a shareholder of Highrate Company. Which net income figure do you think is more useful? Why?

E18–5 **General price-level accounting** AICPA adapted

The following schedule shows the average general purchasing power index of the indicated years:

1999	100
2000	125
2001	150

Carl Corporation's plant and equipment consisted of the following totals at December 31, 2001:

Date Acquired	Percentage Depreciated	Historical Cost
1999	30%	$30,000
2000	20	20,000
2001	10	10,000
		$60,000

Depreciation is calculated at 10% per annum on a straight-line basis. A full year's depreciation is charged in the year of acquisition. There were no disposals in 2001.

REQUIRED:

What amount of depreciation expense should be included in a general price-level accounting income statement?

E18–6 **Distinguishing between monetary and nonmonetary items** AICPA adapted

When computing purchasing power gain or loss on net monetary items, which of the following accounts are classified as nonmonetary?

1. Receivables under capitalized leases
2. Obligations under capitalized leases
3. Minority interest
4. Unamortized discount on bonds payable
5. Long-term receivables
6. Equity investment in unconsolidated subsidiaries

(continued)

7. Obligations under warranties
8. Accumulated depreciation of equipment
9. Advances to unconsolidated subsidiaries
10. Allowance for uncollectible accounts
11. Unamortized premium on bonds payable

E18–7

General price-level accounting
AICPA adapted

Lewis Company was formed on January 1, 2000. Selected balances from the historical cost balance sheet at December 31, 2000 were as follows:

Land (purchased in 2000)	$120,000
Investment in nonconvertible bonds (purchased in 2000 and expected to be held to maturity)	60,000
Long-term debt	80,000

The general purchasing power index was 100 when the debt was issued and the land and bonds were purchased; it was 110 at December 31, 2001.

Required:

In a general price-level accounting balance sheet at December 31, 2001, at what amounts should the land, investment, and long-term debt be shown?

E18–8

Attitude of U.S. companies toward IASC standards

As described in the text, IASC standards allow firms to exercise more latitude than exists in U.S. GAAP.

Required:

1. Taking this latitude difference into account, consider what would happen if the SEC were to allow foreign issuers of securities in the United States to use IASC standards in lieu of U.S. GAAP. What problems would you anticipate? Would there be a "level playing field" for both foreign and U.S. companies when they seek investment capital?
2. In light of your answer in (1), what is your conjecture about how top management of U.S. companies would react to an SEC decision that allows foreign issuers to use IASC standards?

Problems/Discussion Questions

P18–1

Capital sources and disclosure differences

Accounting standards vary across national boundaries. As stated in the chapter, a specific country's financial reporting standards are a function of its legal environment, customs, and social objectives. In addition, the primary source of capital for companies within a country influences the country's financial reporting standards.

Required:

Assume there are two countries in the world. In the first country, Equityland, companies acquire capital through individual investors, who purchase equity shares on public stock exchanges. Companies in the second country, Debtland, acquire their capital from a few large banks. Answer the following questions on the basis of your understanding of the differences in the financial reporting incentives of firms domiciled in Equityland versus Debtland.

1. Who are the primary users of companies' financial reports?
2. What are the users concerned about when assessing companies' financial reports?
3. What financial ratios might financial statement users in the two countries employ when examining companies' economic performances?
4. How are the disclosure demands of financial statement users in Equityland different from those of users in Debtland?

P18–2

Overcoming reporting diversity

Euro Disney S.C.A. began operations on April 12, 1992 by opening the Disneyland Paris Resort. Euro Disney operates the Disneyland Paris Theme Park, six hotels, and several other entertainment establishments. A partial income statement for Euro Disney that was prepared in accordance with French GAAP (measured in millions of French francs) follows:

	Year Ended September 30, 1994
Income (loss) before exceptional items	(1,282)
Exceptional income (loss)	(515)
Net income (loss)	(1,797)

In the footnotes to the financial statements, the "exceptional loss" of 515 million francs is detailed as follows:

Tax reimbursements	8
Provisions for risks and charges	(111)
Costs related to financial restructuring	(406)
Payable forgiveness	1,208
Reduction in carrying value of certain assets	(1,206)
Other	(8)
	(515)

Additional information provided in a footnote explains that the reduction in carrying value of certain assets represents the write-down of certain planning and development costs.

REQUIRED:

1. On the basis of your knowledge of U.S. GAAP, discuss how the "reduction in carrying value of certain assets" would be reported if Euro Disney followed U.S. GAAP.
2. Assume you subscribe to a global data service that provides only summary financial information limited to net income, total assets, and total stockholders' equity. How does this limit your analysis of international companies?
3. What adjustments would you make to approximate Euro Disney's income or loss from continuing operations on a U.S. GAAP basis?

P18–3 Overcoming reporting diversity

Yizheng Chemical Fibre Company Ltd. is a company established in the People's Republic of China. In 1996 Yizheng Chemical prepared two financial reports, one in accordance with standards issued by the IASC and another in accordance with the accounting rules and regulations of the People's Republic of China (PRC). The operating sections of Yizheng's two income statements prepared under the alternate sets of accounting standards are shown next (reported in renminbi):

Consolidated Profit and Loss Prepared under IAS		Consolidated Profit and Loss Prepared under PRC Accounting	
Turnover	6,999,118	Income from principal operations	6,999,118
Profit before tax	243,177	Less: Cost of sales	6,088,427
Tax	(25,232)	Selling expenses	56,323
Profit after tax	217,945	Administrative expenses	386,622
		Financial expenses	233,574
		Business tax and surcharges	30,682
		Profit from principal operations	203,490

REQUIRED:

1. Identify various approaches that regulatory commissions can employ to bring uniformity to foreign issuers' financial reporting.
2. What approach to financial reporting uniformity has Yizheng Chemical taken?

(continued)

3. After examining the partial income statements presented on the previous page, answer the following questions:

   a. What is meant by "turnover"?
   b. Which presentation form do you prefer? Why?
   c. What might contribute to Yizheng Chemical's profit of 217,945 renminbi under IAS and 203,490 renminbi under PRC accounting standards?
   d. As a user of Yizheng's financial reports, which profit figure will you use in your financial statement analysis? Why?

P18–4

Current cost ratio effects

TNT Ltd. is a multinational Australian company whose primary business activity is providing freight transportation services. TNT Ltd. prepares its annual financial report in accordance with Australian GAAP. Australian GAAP allows the revaluation of fixed assets. According to Australian GAAP, the revaluation of fixed assets is recorded by increasing the appropriate fixed-asset accounts and by increasing stockholders' equity by means of a reserve account.

TNT states in its footnotes to the financial statements that "certain assets have been revalued at various times and are shown at their latest valuation. The basis for the revaluations is the recoverable value of the assets to the economic entity as a going concern." TNT also states, "Where assets have been revalued, depreciation is based on the revalued amount."

REQUIRED:

1. Assume you are a user of TNT's financial statements. Explain how the revaluation of fixed assets affects your time-series analysis of TNT's economic performance.
2. How would the revaluation of fixed assets affect (i.e., improve or weaken) the following financial statement ratios?

   a. Total shareholders' equity to total assets
   b. Long-term debt to assets
   c. Current ratio
   d. Return on assets (ROA)

P18–5

Overcoming reporting diversity

Glaxo Wellcome p.l.c. is a U.K. public limited company that is one of the largest pharmaceutical companies in the world. Selected data from its 1999 Form 20-F follows (in millions of pounds sterling):

Net income per U.K. GAAP	1,811
Net income per U.S. GAAP	913
Shareholders' equity per U.K. GAAP	3,142
Shareholders' equity per U.S. GAAP	7,230
Average number of ordinary shares outstanding (in millions)	5,483

REQUIRED:

1. What is Glaxo Wellcome's return on equity (ROE) when it reports in accordance with U.K. GAAP? What is Glaxo Wellcome's ROE under U.S. GAAP?
2. The difference between U.K. GAAP net income and U.S. GAAP net income is due in part to the accounting for goodwill. In accounting for business combinations, U.K. GAAP allows firms to write off the excess of the cost over the market value of assets acquired (i.e., goodwill) directly to shareholders' equity. Glaxo Wellcome did this for all acquisitions prior to January 1, 1998. Goodwill arising from subsequent acquisitions has been accounted for following U.S. GAAP. According to U.S. GAAP in 1999, goodwill must be capitalized and amortized over a period not to exceed 40 years. In its 1999 Form 20-F, Glaxo Wellcome reported a reconciling item between U.K. and U.S. GAAP for goodwill amortization arising from pre-1998 acquisitions totaling 554 million pounds sterling. What impact does the amortization of goodwill have on earnings per share? How does the write-off of goodwill at the time of purchase affect ROE in the current period and in future periods?
3. Assume the entire difference between U.K. GAAP net income and U.S. GAAP net income is due to the pre-1998 accounting for goodwill. Which ROE measure calculated in (1) better reflects the economic performance of Glaxo Wellcome for the year ended 1999? Explain.

P18–6 **Overcoming reporting diversity**

Stork N.V., domiciled in Amsterdam, The Netherlands, is an industrial company with operations worldwide. In a footnote to its Year 2 financial report, Stork disclosed the following current value information (in thousands of guilders):

	Year 2	Year 1
Fixed assets	858,000	825,000
Additional depreciation to be recorded under current value accounting	12,106	12,066

Information from Stork's profit and loss statement and balance sheet includes the following data:

Net income	81,257	55,906
Fixed assets	692,913	657,315
Shareholders' equity	778,364	749,093

REQUIRED:

1. Using the data reported on Stork's profit and loss statement and balance sheet, what is Stork's Year 2 ROE?
2. If Stork N.V. were to book the revaluation of its fixed assets, what is its Year 2 ROE?
3. Which ROE is more relevant when comparing Stork's performance to the performance of an industrial firm domiciled in the United States? Explain.
4. Australian GAAP allows firms the option of revaluing their fixed assets. Which ROE measure is more relevant when comparing Stork's performance to the performance of an industrial firm domiciled in Australia? Explain.

P18–7 **Overcoming reporting diversity**

A recent income statement of Electrolux, a Swedish company that owns the U.S.-based appliance company Frigidaire, reports the following (in millions of Swedish kronor):

Sales	100,121
Operating expense	(92,594)
Share of income in associated companies	(10)
Operating income before depreciation	7,517

A footnote discloses that operating expense included the following items:

Capital gains on sales of real estate	114
Losses on sales of operations	(325)
Capital gains on sale of shares in Email Ltd.	204
Total included in operating expense	(7)

REQUIRED:

Describe how each of the items disclosed in the footnote would be reported if Electrolux prepared its financial statements in accordance with U.S. GAAP.

P18–8 **GAAP differences**

Novo Nordisk, a Danish company, prepared a recent financial report in accordance with Danish GAAP. It reported the following information in a footnote to its financial statements.

> The accounting principles generally accepted in the United States which differ significantly in certain respects from the Company's policies can be summarized as follows:
>
> 1. *Inventories*—It is required that direct labor and appropriate production overheads be included in inventory costs.
> 2. *Intangible assets*—It is required that intangible assets be amortised over the estimated economic life of the asset.

3. *Dividends*—It is required that dividends be recorded in the period in which they are declared.
4. *Capitalisation*—Capitalisation is required of interest costs incurred in connection with the financing of expenditures for the construction of property, plant, and equipment.

REQUIRED:

1. For the preceding four items, discuss how Novo Nordisk's Danish GAAP earnings are different from earnings measured in accordance with U.S. GAAP.
2. Discuss how the four items could potentially change its balance sheet if Novo Nordisk prepared U.S. GAAP financial statements.

P18–9

GAAP differences

Rémy-Cointreau is a French company specializing in cognac, liquors, wine, and spirits. In 1994 Rémy-Cointreau controlled more than one-third of the world market for superior quality cognacs with its Rémy Martin brand. Other popular Rémy-Cointreau brand names include Cointreau, Galliano, and Krug champagne. Rémy-Cointreau's balance sheet contained the following information:

Assets (in thousands of French francs)	
Intangible fixed assets—gross	3,145,544
Less amortization and provisions	(82,739)
Intangible fixed assets	3,062,805
Tangible fixed assets—gross	2,061,156
Less depreciation and provisions	(947,041)
Tangible fixed assets	1,114,115
Investments	765,991
Total fixed assets	4,942,911
Inventories	5,376,018
Trade notes and accounts receivable	1,547,664
Other receivables	648,762
Cash	154,497
Total current assets	7,726,941
Prepaid and deferred charges	289,150
Total assets	12,959,002

REQUIRED:

1. How does Rémy-Cointreau's asset section differ from the asset section of a company preparing its financial statements in accordance with U.S. GAAP?
2. What do you suppose is included in the line classified as "Intangible fixed assets—gross"? How important are these assets to Rémy's economic success?
3. Rémy-Cointreau states in its footnotes to the financial statements that brands are not amortized while they have legal protection. Discuss how this practice differs from the accounting for brand names or trademarks under U.S. GAAP. What specific adjustment would need to be made to Rémy-Cointreau's financial statements in order to compare them to a company preparing U.S. GAAP financial statements?

CASES

C18–1

Tyler Corporation (2): Adjusting reported trend data

(This is a continuation of C16–2.)

In its 1979 annual report, Tyler Corporation repeatedly emphasized a 33% increase in sales between 1978 and 1979. In addition to acquiring Thurston on April 6, Tyler confronted double-digit inflation during 1979. Since Tyler's gross property, plant, and equipment exceeded $150 million, it was required to disclose supplementary inflation adjusted data under *SFAS No. 33,* as described in the chapter. A portion of that (unaudited) disclosure is shown next.

Statement of Income Adjusted for Effects of Changing Prices
Year Ended December 31, 1979

	Historical Financial Statements	Adjusted for General Inflation (Constant Dollar)	Adjusted for Changes in Specific Prices (Current Cost/ Constant Dollar)
Net sales	$519,242,000	$546,992,000	$546,992,000
Costs and expenses			
Cost of sales	411,515,000	435,254,000	435,254,000
Selling, administrative, and general expenses	39,178,000	41,360,000	41,360,000
Depreciation	15,007,000	19,206,000	22,146,000
Interest expense	11,212,000	11,779,000	11,779,000
	476,912,000	507,599,000	510,539,000
Income before income tax and gain from decline in purchasing power of net amounts owed	42,330,000	39,393,000	36,453,000
Income tax	18,873,000	19,879,000	19,879,000
Net income before gain from decline in purchasing power of net amounts owed	23,457,000	19,514,000	16,574,000
Gain from decline in purchasing power of net amounts owed	–0–	8,569,000	8,569,000
Net income including gain from decline in purchasing power of net amounts owed	$ 23,457,000	$ 28,083,000	$ 25,143,000
Per common share			
Net income before gain from decline in purchasing power of net amounts owed	$ 2.34	$ 1.94	$ 1.65
Gain from decline in purchasing power of net amounts owed	–0–	.85	.85
Net income, including gain from decline in purchasing power of net amounts owed	$ 2.34	$ 2.79	$ 2.50
Shareholders' equity at December 31, 1979	$115,535,000	$205,825,000	$240,151,000
Average shares outstanding	10,040,000	10,040,000	10,040,000

Five-Year Summary of Financial Data Adjusted for Effects of Changing Prices

	Year Ended December 31				
	1975	1976	1977	1978	1979
Net sales	$383,302,000	$412,794,000	$447,722,000	$458,952,000	$546,992,000
Cash dividends per common share	0.21	0.32	0.38	0.44	0.48
Market price per common share at year-end	7.08	15.00	15.60	18.41	15.38
Year-end consumer price index	166.3	174.3	186.1	202.9	229.9

REQUIRED:

1. Explain the methodology that Tyler Corporation used to adjust "Net sales" from the historical cost amount of $519,242,000 to the inflation adjusted figure of $546,992,000.
2. There is a "five-year summary" at the bottom of the footnote disclosure. The net sales number for 1978 is $458,952,000. Explain the methodology Tyler used to derive this number.
3. After adjusting for inflation, what was the sales growth between 1978 and 1979?
4. The growth rate that you computed in (3) adjusts the sales growth rate for inflation but not for the acquisition of Thurston (described in C16–2). How can a statement

reader *simultaneously* adjust for *both* the acquisition and inflation? Taking both factors into account, what was the "real" sales growth between the two years? (*Hint*: Utilize the pro forma sales information from C16–2 in conjunction with the inflation information from this case to answer this part.)

C18–2

Tyler Corporation (3): Borrowing strategies under inflationary conditions

In its *SFAS No. 33* footnote disclosure, Tyler described how it managed operations and capital in an inflationary environment. Regarding Tyler's capital management, the footnote stated:

> The Company has also prudently used long-term debt to leverage its capital structure. Long-term debt has been the primary vehicle for financing the acquisition of each of the four operating units. Strong cash flow from the operating units has been used to repay long-term debt with dollars having less purchasing power.
>
> During 1978 and 1979 the capital structure of the Company has changed substantially. At December 31, 1979 the debt-to-equity ratio was 48/52 as compared to the 37/63 ratio at December 31, 1978 and 28/72 at December 31, 1977.

During 1979 Tyler acquired Thurston Motor Lines for approximately $45.5 million in cash. Tyler's annual report contained a footnote entitled Credit Commitments from Banks which is excerpted next:

CREDIT COMMITMENTS FROM BANKS

Under commitments from banks, the Company may borrow at the then effective prime rate of interest up to $25,000,000 on an unsecured short-term basis. The Company is required to be free from borrowings under the commitments for at least 60 consecutive days during the preceding twelve months. There were no borrowings outstanding under these commitments at December 31, 1978 and 1979.

Long-Term Debt	1978	1979
Parent		
8¾% unsecured note due in annual installments of $2,500,000 through 1979, $3,000,000 thereafter	$32,500,000	$30,000,000
Unsecured $50,000,000 revolving line of credit, interest at 106% of prime rate through March 1981, thereafter ½ of 1% above prime rate	-0-	43,000,000
Subsidiaries		
Unsecured $6,000,000 revolving line of credit, interest at prime rate	-0-	4,150,000
5¾% to 8% secured notes	428,000	1,411,000
	32,928,000	78,561,000
Less current maturities	2,636,000	4,366,000
	$30,292,000	$74,195,000

Scheduled repayments of long-term debt during the five years following December 31, 1979 are as follows:

1980–$4,366,000; 1981–$10,679,000; 1982–$12,447,000; 1983–$12,445,000; 1984–$12,445,000.

REQUIRED:

Consider the financing methods Tyler used to acquire companies like Thurston; then evaluate the effectiveness of Tyler's strategy for using debt as a means for protecting shareholders in an inflationary environment.

C18–3

Tyler Corporation (4): Inflation's effect on GAAP ratios

Tyler Corporation sometimes placed ads in the *Wall Street Journal* in order to highlight its financial performance. The following advertisement appeared in the September 22, 1982 edition of the *Wall Street Journal:*

The gross domestic product (GDP) implicit price deflator is a price index that is designed to capture price changes for all items that enter into the computation of GDP. Overall inflation as measured by the year-to-year change in GDP implicit price deflators for the period covered in the ad was:

1981	10.0%	1975	9.6%
1980	9.5	1974	8.7
1979	8.6	1973	6.4
1978	7.9	1972	4.6
1977	6.9	1971	5.4
1976	6.3		

REQUIRED:

1. Carefully explain how continuing, pervasive price increases would affect ROE as computed under GAAP. (*Hint:* How does inflation affect the ROE numerator—income, and the denominator—assets minus liabilities?)
2. Tyler Corporation had a somewhat large proportion of long-lived assets. Specifically, net property, plant, and equipment comprised approximately 30% of total assets. How, if at all, does this capital intensity affect the comparison made between Tyler and other *Fortune 500* companies in the *Wall Street Journal* ad?

C18–4

Robinson Company: General price level and current cost adjustments

The Robinson Company's statement of financial position on January 1, 2001, appeared as follows:

ROBINSON COMPANY

Statement of Financial Position
January 1, 2001

Assets			Equities	
Cash		$ 5,000		
Inventory		8,000		
Fixed asset—cost	$10,000			
Less: Accumulated depreciation	5,000			
		5,000	Common stock	$18,000
		$18,000		$18,000

The inventory consisted of 10 units acquired at an original cost of $800 per unit on November 1, 2000. Robinson Company owns only a single fixed asset that was purchased new on January 1, 1996 for $10,000. The asset has a ten-year life, no salvage value, and experiences a straight-line decline in service potential.

On June 30, 2001 five of the 10 inventory units were sold for $8,600 cash. Robinson Company's pricing strategy was based upon a target return of 20% on the original cost of the assets sold and/or utilized in operations. Dividends equal to total reported historical cost income were also declared and paid on June 30. No other transactions occurred during 2001. Assume, for simplicity, that the only costs incurred were depreciation and cost of goods sold. Historical cost financial results for 2001 were as follows:

ROBINSON COMPANY

Statement of Income and Retained Earnings
Year Ended December 31, 2001

Sales revenues		$8,600
Cost of goods sold	$4,000	
Depreciation	1,000	
		5,000
Operating income		3,600
Plus: Retained earnings, 1/1/01		–0–
Less: Dividend		3,600
Retained earnings, 12/31/01		–0–

ROBINSON COMPANY

Balance Sheet
December 31, 2001

Assets			Equities	
Cash		$10,000		
Inventory		4,000		
Fixed asset—cost	$10,000			
Less: Accumulated depreciation	6,000			
		4,000	Common stock	$18,000
		$18,000		$18,000

Overall inflation as measured by the Consumer Price Index was:

Index value on	1/1/96	100
Index value on	11/1/00	178
Index value on	1/1/01	180
Index value on	6/30/01	190
Index value on	12/31/01	200

At January 1, 2001 the replacement cost of a five-year-old fixed asset that was identical in all respects to the asset owned by Robinson Company was $7,000. A newer, more efficient model of this machine was introduced in early February 1996; the estimated replacement cost of the improved model in a condition equivalent to that of Robinson Company's asset was $8,000 on January 1, 2001. Both used asset prices remained in effect throughout 2001.

The replacement cost of the inventory on January 1, 2001 was $810 per unit. The replacement cost at the date of sale (June 30) was $875. At year-end, the per-unit inventory replacement cost was $890.

REQUIRED:

1. Using the preceding data, compute Robinson Company's historical cost/constant dollar income for 2001 (in year-end dollars) and the December 31, 2001 historical cost/constant dollar balance sheet.

To answer this part, you must compute the gain or loss on net monetary items for 2001. This computation was not illustrated in the chapter but is straightforward. First, the net change in monetary items *in nominal dollars* as well as the causes for the change must be computed. These are:

Net monetary assets, 1/1/01	$ 5,000
Increase in net monetary assets:	
From sales revenues	8,600
Decrease in net monetary assets:	
To pay dividends	(3,600)
Net monetary assets in historical dollars, 12/31/01	$10,000

Next, the timing of the increases and decreases must be established. Here, each took place on June 30. The beginning balance as well as the increases or decreases must be restated to their December 31, 2001 purchasing power equivalent. For example, the January 1 balance would be adjusted by a ratio of 200/180, while sales and dividends would be adjusted by a factor of 200/190. The sum of these three adjusted figures indicates what the net monetary asset balance would have been had all monetary flows been "indexed." Comparing this number to the actual $10,000 amount in nominal dollars results in the gain or loss on monetary items.

Adjusting the income statement also requires you to carefully assess the timing of the income statement flow and to apply the appropriate index adjustment factor.

2. Based upon these data, determine current cost income on a physical capital maintenance basis for 2001—that is, treat holdings gains as a direct owners' equity adjustment (other comprehensive income) rather than as an element of net income. Also prepare the December 31, 2001 current cost balance sheet. Does the current cost income number you derive provide a valid measure of the dividend that can be paid without endangering future productive capacity? Discuss.

C18–5

Differences in reporting philosophies

The excerpt below is from a newspaper article:[1]

> TOKYO, WEDNESDAY, AUGUST 19, 1992— With another steep drop in share prices deepening the sense of crisis in Japan's financial system, the Finance Minister announced a series of measures Tuesday aimed at halting the two-and-a-half-year stock market slide. . . .
>
> In his package . . . the Finance Minister, Tsutomu Hata, sought to put pressure on big investors not to sell shares and said financial institutions would be permitted to withhold negative financial data from the public in the hope of easing worries about the system's fundamental health. He also said steps would be taken to encourage Japanese banks to make more loans. . . .
>
> "This was perhaps the first real admission from the Finance Minister that the situation is severe and that they have to do something," said Richard Koo, a senior economist at the Nomura Research Institute. "But as far as the content goes, I'm not impressed. . . ."

REQUIRED:

1. Evaluate the financial reporting philosophy inherent in the Finance Ministry announcement and compare it to what you understand to be the objective of financial reporting that is designed to enhance efficient investment decisions. What are the differences? What do you think motivated the announcement?
2. What is your conjecture about the nature of the *specific* "negative financial data" that financial institutions would be permitted to withhold?
3. Do you think that the announcement achieved its intended objective?

C18–6

Daimler-Benz (KR): Understanding foreign financial statements

STRETCH

This U.S. GAAP reconciliation is from the 20-F filing of Daimler-Benz, a German company:

(In millions of DM)	For the Years Ended December 31 Year 3	Year 2	Year 1
Net income reported under German GAAP	615	1,451	1,942
(−) Income and losses applicable to minority stockholders	(13)	(33)	(70)
Adjusted net income under German GAAP	602	1,418	1,872
(+) Changes in appropriated retained earnings—provisions, reserves, and valuation differences	(4,262)	774	64
Other adjustments required to conform with U.S. GAAP:			
Long-term contracts	78	(57)	(32)
Goodwill and business acquisitions	(287)	(76)	(270)
Business dispositions	-0-	337	(490)
Pensions and other postretirement benefits	(624)	96	(66)
Foreign currency translation	(40)	(94)	155
Financial instruments	(225)	(438)	86
Earnings of Deutsche Aerospace Airbus	-0-	-0-	636
Other	292	88	57
Deferred taxes	2,627	(646)	(126)
Net income reported under U.S. GAAP before cumulative effects	(1,839)	1,402	1,886
Cumulative effect of change in accounting for postretirement benefits other than pensions as of 1/1/Year 2, net of tax of DM 33	-0-	(52)	-0-
Net income in accordance with U.S. GAAP	(1,839)	1,350	1,886

[1] J. Sterngold, "Japan Announces Series of Steps to Try to Halt Stock Market Slide," *New York Times* (August 19, 1992).

(In millions of DM)	As of December 31 Year 3	Year 2
Stockholders' equity under German GAAP	18,145	19,719
(−) Minority interest	(561)	(1,228)
Adjusted stockholders' equity under German GAAP	17,584	18,491
(+) Appropriated retained earnings—provisions, reserves, and valuation differences	5,770	9,931
	23,354	28,422
Other adjustments required to conform to U.S. GAAP:		
Long-term contracts	207	131
Goodwill and business acquisitions	2,284	1,871
Pensions and other postretirement benefits	(1,821)	(1,212)
Foreign currency translation	85	(342)
Financial instruments	381	580
Other	(698)	(1,708)
Deferred taxes	2,489	(138)
Stockholders' equity in accordance with U.S. GAAP	26,281	27,604

Some of the significant differences between German and United States GAAP are explained in the following excerpts from footnote 2 to the same 20-F filing.

1. "Appropriated Retained Earnings—Provisions, Reserves, and Valuation Differences"

According to German GAAP, accruals or provisions may be recorded for uncertain liabilities and loss contingencies. . . . Application of German GAAP may also lead to higher accrual balances and reserves for possible asset risks than are allowed under U.S. GAAP. To the extent that provisions, reserves and valuations under German GAAP are more conservative than the corresponding U.S. GAAP amounts, such differences can be viewed in a manner similar to appropriated retained earnings. Under U.S. GAAP, in accordance with Statement of Financial Accounting Standards (*"SFAS"*) *No. 5,* "Accounting for Contingencies," an accrual for a loss contingency is recorded by a charge to income if it is both probable that an asset has been impaired or a liability has been incurred and the minimum amount of loss can be reasonably estimated. Unspecified liability reserves for future losses, costs or risks do not meet the conditions for accrual under *SFAS No. 5.*

The adjustments to stockholders' equity of DM 5,770 and DM 9,931 would have reduced other provisions at December 31, Year 3 and Year 2 by DM 4,883 and DM 8,105, respectively. The remainder of the adjustments would have increased property, plant, and equipment, inventories and other receivables under U.S. GAAP.

2. Long-Term Contracts

Daimler-Benz generally accounts for revenues and costs on long-term contracts using the completed contract method, with recognition of performance milestones where practicable. Under U.S. GAAP, revenues and costs on long-term contracts are recognized using the percentage-of-completion method of accounting.

3. Goodwill and Business Acquisitions

In accordance with German GAAP, goodwill may be charged directly to stockholders' equity or capitalized and amortized over its useful life, generally ranging between 5 years and 15 years. . . . Under U.S. GAAP, the difference between the purchase price and fair value of net assets acquired as part of a business combination is capitalized as goodwill and amortized through the income statement over its useful life, which may not exceed 40 years. For the purpose of the reconciliation to U.S. GAAP, goodwill is being amortized through the income statement over estimated useful lives ranging between 15 and 40 years.

4. Business Dispositions

> German GAAP requires the accounting for the disposition of a business [to be] based upon the date of a signed contract. Under U.S. GAAP, a gain on the sale of a business is reflected in the period in which a closing occurs with the exchange of consideration. The gain on the sale of AEG KABEL which was recognized in year 1 for German GAAP purposes is recognized in year 2 under U.S. GAAP. In addition, applying the different accounting principles between German and U.S. GAAP results in differing book values of the underlying businesses. As a result, the German and U.S. GAAP accounting gain or loss on a business disposition may be different.

5. Pensions and Other Postretirement Benefits

> Daimler-Benz provides for pension costs and similar obligations including postretirement benefits based on actuarial studies using the entry age method as defined in the German tax code. U.S. GAAP, as defined by *SFAS No. 87*, "Employers' Accounting for Pensions" is more prescriptive particularly as to the use of actuarial assumptions and requires that a different actuarial method (the projected unit credit method) be used. In addition, the Group adopted *SFAS No. 106* "Employers' Accounting for Postretirement Benefits Other Than Pensions" as of January 1, Year 2. The application of this standard, to provide fully for the transitional liability, is included in the net income reconciliation as a cumulative effect adjustment net of income taxes. . . .

6. Financial Instruments

> The Group enters into contracts using financial instruments to cover certain foreign currency risks related to future transactions. In accordance with the German Commercial Code a reserve is set up for unrealized losses relating to such financial instruments whereas unrealized gains are not recognized until realized. Under U.S. GAAP, there are prescriptive rules that govern the application of hedge accounting. Financial instruments that do not qualify for hedge accounting are marked to market with any resulting unrealized gains or losses recognized in the income statement.

7. Deutsche Aerospace Airbus GmbH

> [U]nder German GAAP Deutsche Aerospace Airbus was not consolidated as part of the Group for periods prior to Year 2. Under U.S. GAAP, Deutsche Aerospace Airbus would have been consolidated to reflect Daimler-Benz' 80% ownership interest during Year 1. The adjustments to net income included in the reconciliation to U.S. GAAP represent the U.S. GAAP earnings of Deutsche Aerospace Airbus.

REQUIRED:

1. How did Daimler-Benz use "hidden reserves" (alternative translation: silent reserves) to smooth its earnings over the Year 1–Year 3 period? How did Daimler-Benz create the hidden reserves? Overall does the approach of hidden reserves lead to more or less conservative financial reporting?
2. Is the German accounting method for long-term contracts more or less conservative than the U.S. accounting method? In answering this part, consider the adjustments made for long-term contract accounting in the 20-F reconciliations.
3. In each of Years 1 through 3, Daimler-Benz *reduced* its German GAAP *income* to conform its income statement to the U.S. accounting standard for goodwill. However, at the end of Year 2 and Year 3, Daimler-Benz *increased* its German GAAP *retained earnings* in order to conform to the U.S. accounting standard for goodwill. Explain these adjustments which appear—at first glance—to be in opposite directions.
4. How does German GAAP differ from U.S. GAAP when reporting the gain or loss on the disposition of businesses (or discontinued operations)? Based on the difference, explain the adjustments made by Daimler-Benz for the gain on the sale of AEG KABEL (included in "business dispositions").
5. How do the German accounting methods for pensions and postretirement benefits differ from U.S. methods? Which of these two GAAP methods leads to a more conservative book value for net worth?

(*continued*)

6. U.S. and German GAAP rules have different recognition criteria for recording gains and losses from derivative instruments that allow firms to manage risk from anticipated (or future) transactions. What is the key difference between the two sets of standards?
7. During Year 1 the consolidation of Deutsche Aerospace Airbus increased the pretax U.S. GAAP income of Daimler-Benz by DM 636 million over its German GAAP income. What accounting method for investment in equity securities of Deutsche Aerospace Airbus was most likely used by Daimler-Benz under German GAAP?

Collaborative Learning Case

C18–7 BP Amoco: Understanding non-U.S. financial statements

The comparative income statements, balance sheets and cash flow statements of BP Amoco p.l.c. follow. The chapter stressed the similarities between the financial reporting approaches in the United Kingdom and the United States. However, significant differences do exist. The purpose of this case is to provide you with an opportunity to utilize your understanding of U.S. GAAP along with logic and intuition to familiarize yourself with some of the differences between the two countries' financial reporting procedures.

Required:

1. Some of BP Amoco's terminology and account titles differ from U.S. usage. Explain the following using U.S. financial reporting terms:

   a. The income and cash flow statements, as well as the left columns of the balance sheet, are labeled *Group* statements. What is the U.S. financial reporting equivalent of the term "group"?

   b. Under U.S. GAAP, what would the following BP Amoco balance sheet accounts be called?

   - Stocks
   - Debtors
   - Creditors
   - Capital and reserves
   - Called up share capital
   - Share premium account
   - Reserves

   c. Under U.S. GAAP, what would the following income and cash flow statement accounts be called?

   - Turnover
   - Exceptional items
   - Investments in associated undertakings

2. The *format* (or *structure*) of the BP Amoco financial statements also differs from that of U.S. statements. Discuss the following differences:

   a. The income statement includes an item termed "stock holding gains (losses)."

      - What are they?
      - Does their inclusion in the statement mean that the "bottom-line" profit number is not measured on an historical cost basis? Explain.
      - Why do you think BP Amoco makes this disclosure?

   b. The income statement includes items labeled "Profit (loss) on sale of businesses" and "Profit (loss) on sale of fixed assets." How, if at all, do the income statement location and treatment of these items differ from U.S. GAAP?

   c. At first glance, the BP Amoco balance sheet appears unfamiliar.

      - What are the primary differences between their format and a "typical" U.S. GAAP balance sheet format?
      - What items "balance" in BP Amoco's balance sheet? Explain the difference in balance sheet format using the basic accounting equation (A = L + E).
      - What balance sheet relationship does the BP Amoco format highlight that must be computed in U.S. statements?

   d. What are the differences in cash flow format between BP Amoco's presentation and U.S. GAAP? Comment on any differences between the U.K. and U.S. treatment of interest received (and paid) as well as dividends received (and paid).

3. The BP Amoco balance sheets include two right-hand columns labeled **parent.**

   a. What is the U.S. financial reporting equivalent of the term "parent"?

   b. Why are parent statements provided only for BP Amoco's balance sheet?

   c. What is your conjecture regarding the following elements in the 1999 parent balance sheet:

      - The £6,588 balance in the "Debtors—amounts falling due within one year" account?
      - The equivalence of the amounts of "Called up share capital" plus "Share premium account" in the "Parent" and "Group" columns? (*Hint*: Understanding this helps you answer [3a]).

   d. In many European countries, taxes are levied at the subsidiary (rather than at the overall corporate) level. European companies frequently provide separate parent data, as BP Amoco has done. What is your conjecture about why separate parent data are provided?

   e. Many countries *require* conformity between book and tax accounting. The BP Amoco report illustrates that individual countries' reporting standards allow companies to differentiate between group and parent statements. Do you think that this differentiation between group and parent statements has implications for harmonization in international financial reporting? Explain.

BP Amoco Annual Report and Accounts 1999

Group Income Statement (£ million)	**For the Year Ended 31 December 1999**	**1998**
Turnover	£101,180	£83,732
Less: Joint ventures	17,614	15,428
Group turnover	83,566	68,304
Replacement cost of sales	68,615	56,270
Production taxes	1,017	604
Gross profit	13,934	11,430
Distribution and administration expenses	6,064	6,044
Exploration expense	548	921
	7,322	4,465
Other income	414	709
Group replacement cost operating profit	7,736	5,174
Share of profits of joint ventures	555	825
Share of profits of associated undertakings	603	522
Total replacement cost operating profit	8,894	6,521
Profit (loss) on sale of businesses	(421)	395
Profit (loss) on sale of fixed assets	84	653
Restructuring costs	(1,943)	–0–
Merger expenses	–0–	(198)
Replacement cost profit before interest and tax	6,614	7,371
Stock holding gains (losses)	1,728	(1,391)
Historical cost profit before interest and tax	8,342	5,980
Interest expense	1,316	1,177
Profit before taxation	7,026	4,803
Taxation	1,880	1,520
Profit after taxation	5,146	3,283
Minority shareholders' interest	138	63
Profit for the year	5,008	3,220
Distribution to shareholders	3,884	4,121
Retained profit (deficit) for the year	£ 1,124	(£ 901)
Earnings per ordinary share—cents		
Basic	25.82	16.77
Diluted	25.68	16.70
Replacement cost results:		
Historical cost profit for the year	£ 5,008	£ 3,220
Stock holding (gains) losses	(1,728)	1,391
Replacement cost profit for the year	3,280	4,611
Exceptional items, net of tax	2,050	(652)
Replacement cost profit before exceptional items	£ 5,330	£ 3,959
Earnings per ordinary share—cents		
On replacement cost profit before exceptional items	27.48	20.62

Balance Sheets

(£ million)		Group 1999		Group At 31 December 1998	Parent 1999	Parent 1998
Fixed assets						
Intangible assets		£ 3,344		£ 3,037	£ –0–	£ –0–
Tangible assets		52,631		54,880	–0–	–0–
Investments						
Joint ventures–Gross assets	9,948		9,053			
–Gross liabilities	4,744		4,048			
Net investment		5,204		5,005	–0–	–0–
Associated undertakings		4,334		4,162	3	3
Other		571		605	8,675	7,508
		10,109		9,772	8,678	7,511
Total fixed assets		66,084		67,689	8,678	7,511
Current assets						
Stocks		5,124		3,642	–0–	–0–
Debtors–amounts falling due:						
Within one year		13,347		9,404	6,588	7,153
After more than one year		3,455		3,305	2,645	2,634
Investments		220		470	–0–	–0–
Cash at bank and in hand		1,331		405	3	1
		23,477		17,226	9,236	9,788
Creditors–amounts falling due within one year						
Finance debt		4,900		4,114	–0–	–0–
Other creditors		18,375		15,329	1,076	1,812
Net current assets (liabilities)		202		(2,217)	8,160	7,976
Total assets less current liabilities		66,286		65,472	16,838	15,487
Creditors–amounts falling due after more than one year						
Finance debt		9,644		9,641	–0–	–0–
Other creditors		2,245		2,047	62	69
Provisions for liabilities and charges						
Deferred taxation		1,783		1,632	–0–	–0–
Other provisions		8,272		8,579	171	85
Net assets		44,342		43,573	16,605	15,333
Minority shareholders' interest–equity		1,061		1,072	–0–	–0–
BP Amoco shareholders' interest		£43,281		£42,501	£16,605	£15,333
Represented by capital and reserves						
Called up share capital		4,892		4,863	4,892	4,863
Share premium account		3,354		3,056	3,354	3,056
Capital redemption reserve		330		330	330	330
Merger reserve		697		697	–0–	–0–
Profit and loss account		34,008		33,555	8,029	7,084
		£43,281		£42,501	£16,605	£15,333

Group Cash Flow Statement

(£ million)	For the Year Ended 31 December 1999	1998
Net cash inflow from operating activities	£10,290	£9,586
Dividends from joint ventures	949	544
Dividends from associated undertakings	219	422
Servicing of finance and returns on investments		
Interest received	179	223
Interest paid	(1,065)	(961)
Dividends received	34	43
Dividends paid to minority shareholders	(151)	(130)
Net cash outflow from servicing of finance and returns on investments	(1,003)	(825)
Taxation		
UK corporation tax	(559)	(391)
Overseas tax	(701)	(1,314)
Tax paid	(1,260)	(1,705)
Capital expenditure and financial investment		
Payments for fixed assets	(6,457)	(8,431)
Purchase of shares for employee share schemes	(77)	(254)
Proceeds from the sale of fixed assets	1,149	1,387
Net cash outflow for capital expenditure and financial investment	(5,385)	(7,298)
Acquisitions and disposals		
Investments in associated undertakings	(197)	(396)
Acquisitions	(102)	(314)
Net investment in joint ventures	(750)	708
Proceeds from the sale of businesses	1,292	780
Net cash inflow (outflow) for acquisitions and disposals	243	778
Equity dividends paid	(4,135)	(2,408)
Net cash outflow	(£ 82)	(£ 906)
Financing	(954)	(377)
Management of liquid resources	(93)	(596)
Increase in cash	965	67
	(£ 82)	(£ 906)

Statement of Total Recognized Gains and Losses

(£ million)	For the Year Ended 31 December 1999	1998
Profit for the year	£5,008	£3,220
Currency translation differences	(921)	55
Total recognized gains and losses relating to the year	4,087	£3,275
Prior year adjustment—change in accounting policy	715	
Total recognized gains and losses	£4,802	

Appendix I

Please visit our internet site (www.prenhall.com/revsine) for a spreadsheet template that can be used to find present value factors for interest rates not shown in this appendix.

Table 1 ■ PRESENT VALUE OF $1

$$p = \frac{1}{(1 + r)^n} = (1 + r)^{-n}$$

(n) Periods	2%	3%	4%	5%	6%	7%	8%	9%	10%	11%	12%	15%	16%	17%
1	0.98039	0.97087	0.96154	0.95238	0.94340	0.93458	0.92593	0.91743	0.90909	0.90090	0.89286	0.86957	0.86207	0.85470
2	0.96117	0.94260	0.92456	0.90703	0.89000	0.87344	0.85734	0.84168	0.82645	0.81162	0.79719	0.75614	0.74316	0.73051
3	0.94232	0.91514	0.88900	0.86384	0.83962	0.81630	0.79383	0.77218	0.75132	0.73119	0.71178	0.65752	0.64066	0.62437
4	0.92385	0.88849	0.85480	0.82270	0.79209	0.76290	0.73503	0.70843	0.68301	0.65873	0.63552	0.57175	0.55229	0.53365
5	0.90573	0.86261	0.82193	0.78353	0.74726	0.71299	0.68058	0.64993	0.62092	0.59345	0.56743	0.49718	0.47611	0.45611
6	0.88797	0.83748	0.79031	0.74622	0.70496	0.66634	0.63017	0.59627	0.56447	0.53464	0.50663	0.43233	0.41044	0.38984
7	0.87056	0.81309	0.75992	0.71068	0.66506	0.62275	0.58349	0.54703	0.51316	0.48166	0.45235	0.37594	0.35383	0.33320
8	0.85349	0.78941	0.73069	0.67684	0.62741	0.58201	0.54027	0.50187	0.46651	0.43393	0.40388	0.32690	0.30503	0.28478
9	0.83676	0.76642	0.70259	0.64461	0.59190	0.54393	0.50025	0.46043	0.42410	0.39092	0.36061	0.28426	0.26295	0.24340
10	0.82035	0.74409	0.67556	0.61391	0.55839	0.50835	0.46319	0.42241	0.38554	0.35218	0.32197	0.24718	0.22668	0.20804
11	0.80426	0.72242	0.64958	0.58468	0.52679	0.47509	0.42888	0.38753	0.35049	0.31728	0.28748	0.21494	0.19542	0.17781
12	0.78849	0.70138	0.62460	0.55684	0.49697	0.44401	0.39711	0.35553	0.31863	0.28584	0.25668	0.18691	0.16846	0.15197
13	0.77303	0.68095	0.60057	0.53032	0.46884	0.41496	0.36770	0.32618	0.28966	0.25751	0.22917	0.16253	0.14523	0.12989
14	0.75788	0.66112	0.57748	0.50507	0.44230	0.38782	0.34046	0.29925	0.26333	0.23199	0.20462	0.14133	0.12520	0.11102
15	0.74301	0.64186	0.55526	0.48102	0.41727	0.36245	0.31524	0.27454	0.23939	0.20900	0.18270	0.12289	0.10793	0.09489
16	0.72845	0.62317	0.53391	0.45811	0.39365	0.33873	0.29189	0.25187	0.21763	0.18829	0.16312	0.10686	0.09304	0.08110
17	0.71416	0.60502	0.51337	0.43630	0.37136	0.31657	0.27027	0.23107	0.19784	0.16963	0.14564	0.09293	0.08021	0.06932
18	0.70016	0.58739	0.49363	0.41552	0.35034	0.29586	0.25025	0.21199	0.17986	0.15282	0.13004	0.08081	0.06914	0.05925
19	0.68643	0.57029	0.47464	0.39573	0.33051	0.27651	0.23171	0.19449	0.16351	0.13768	0.11611	0.07027	0.05961	0.05064
20	0.67297	0.55368	0.45639	0.37689	0.31180	0.25842	0.21455	0.17843	0.14864	0.12403	0.10367	0.06110	0.05139	0.04328
25	0.60953	0.47761	0.37512	0.29530	0.23300	0.18425	0.14602	0.11597	0.09230	0.07361	0.05882	0.03038	0.02447	0.01974
30	0.55207	0.41199	0.30832	0.23138	0.17411	0.13137	0.09938	0.07537	0.05731	0.04368	0.03338	0.01510	0.01165	0.00900
35	0.50003	0.35538	0.25342	0.18129	0.13011	0.09366	0.06763	0.04899	0.03558	0.02592	0.01894	0.00751	0.00555	0.00411
40	0.45289	0.30656	0.20829	0.14205	0.09722	0.06678	0.04603	0.03184	0.02209	0.01538	0.01075	0.00373	0.00264	0.00187

Table 2 ■ PRESENT VALUE OF AN ORDINARY ANNUITY OF $1

$$P_{OA} = \left(1 - \frac{1}{(1 + r)^n}\right)/r$$

(n) Periods	2%	3%	4%	5%	6%	7%	8%	9%	10%	11%	12%	15%	16%	175%
1	0.98039	0.97087	0.96154	0.95238	0.94340	0.93458	0.92593	0.91743	0.90909	0.90090	0.89286	0.86957	0.86207	0.85470
2	1.94156	1.91347	1.88609	1.85941	1.83339	1.80802	1.78326	1.75911	1.73554	1.71252	1.69005	1.62571	1.60523	1.58521
3	2.88388	2.82861	2.77509	2.72325	2.67301	2.62432	2.57710	2.53129	2.48685	2.44371	2.40183	2.28323	2.24589	2.20958
4	3.80773	3.71710	3.62990	3.54595	3.46511	3.38721	3.31213	3.23972	3.16987	3.10245	3.03735	2.85498	2.79818	2.74324
5	4.71346	4.57971	4.45182	4.32948	4.21236	4.10020	3.99271	3.88965	3.79079	3.69590	3.60478	3.35216	3.27429	3.19935
6	5.60143	5.41719	5.24214	5.07569	4.91732	4.76654	4.62288	4.48592	4.35526	4.23054	4.11141	3.78448	3.68474	3.58918
7	6.47199	6.23028	6.00205	5.78637	5.58238	5.38929	5.20637	5.03295	4.86842	4.71220	4.56376	4.16042	4.03857	3.92238
8	7.32548	7.01969	6.73274	6.46321	6.20979	5.97130	5.74664	5.53482	5.33493	5.14612	4.96764	4.48732	4.34359	4.20716
9	8.16224	7.78611	7.43533	7.10782	6.80169	6.51523	6.24689	5.99525	5.75902	5.53705	5.32825	4.77158	4.60654	4.45057
10	8.98259	8.53020	8.11090	7.72173	7.36009	7.02358	6.71008	6.41766	6.14457	5.88923	5.65022	5.01877	4.83323	4.65860
11	9.78685	9.25262	8.76048	8.30641	7.88687	7.49867	7.13896	6.80519	6.49506	6.20652	5.93770	5.23371	5.02864	4.83641
12	10.57534	9.95400	9.38507	8.86325	8.38384	7.94269	7.53608	7.16073	6.81369	6.49236	6.19437	5.42062	5.19711	4.98839
13	11.34837	10.63496	9.98565	9.39357	8.85268	8.35765	7.90378	7.48690	7.10336	6.74987	6.42355	5.58315	5.34233	5.11828
14	12.10625	11.29607	10.56312	9.89864	9.29498	8.74547	8.24424	7.78615	7.36669	6.98187	6.62817	5.72448	5.46753	5.22930
15	12.84926	11.93794	11.11839	10.37966	9.71225	9.10791	8.55948	8.06069	7.60608	7.19087	6.81086	5.84737	5.57546	5.32419
16	13.57771	12.56110	11.65230	10.83777	10.10590	9.44665	8.85137	8.31256	7.82371	7.37916	6.97399	5.95423	5.66850	5.40529
17	14.29187	13.16612	12.16567	11.27407	10.47726	9.76322	9.12164	8.54363	8.02155	7.54879	7.11963	6.04716	5.74870	5.47461
18	14.99203	13.75351	12.65930	11.68959	10.82760	10.05909	9.37189	8.75563	8.20141	7.70162	7.24967	6.12797	5.81785	5.53385
19	15.67846	14.32380	13.13394	12.08532	11.15812	10.33560	9.60360	8.95011	8.36492	7.83929	7.36578	6.19823	5.87746	5.58449
20	16.35143	14.87747	13.59033	12.46221	11.46992	10.59401	9.81815	9.12855	8.51356	7.96333	7.46944	6.25933	5.92884	5.62777
25	19.52346	17.41315	15.62208	14.09394	12.78336	11.65358	10.67478	9.82258	9.07704	8.42174	7.84314	6.46415	6.09709	5.76623
30	22.39646	19.60044	17.29203	15.37245	13.76483	12.40904	11.25778	10.27365	9.42691	8.69379	8.05518	6.56598	6.17720	5.82939
35	24.99862	21.48722	18.66461	16.37419	14.49825	12.94767	11.65457	10.56682	9.64416	8.85524	8.17550	6.61661	6.21534	5.85820
40	27.35548	23.11477	19.79277	17.15909	15.04630	13.33171	11.92461	10.75736	9.77905	8.95105	8.24378	6.64178	6.23350	5.87133

"Please visit our internet site (www.prenhall.com/phlip/revsine) for a spreadsheet template that can be used to find present value factors for interest rates not shown here."

Table 3 ■ PRESENT VALUE OF AN ANNUITY DUE OF $1

$$p_{AD} = 1 + \left(1 - \frac{1}{(1+r)^{n-1}}\right)/r$$

(n) Periods	2%	3%	4%	5%	6%	7%	8%	9%	10%	11%	12%	15%	16%	17%
1	1.00000	1.00000	1.00000	1.00000	1.00000	1.00000	1.00000	1.00000	1.00000	1.00000	1.00000	1.00000	1.00000	1.00000
2	1.98039	1.97087	1.96154	1.95238	1.94340	1.93458	1.92593	1.91743	1.90909	1.90090	1.89286	1.86957	1.86207	1.85470
3	2.94156	2.91347	2.88609	2.85941	2.83339	2.80802	2.78326	2.75911	2.73554	2.71252	2.69005	2.62571	2.60523	2.58521
4	3.88388	3.82861	3.77509	3.72325	3.67301	3.62432	3.57710	3.53129	3.48685	3.44371	3.40183	3.28323	3.24589	3.20958
5	4.80773	4.71710	4.62990	4.54595	4.46511	4.38721	4.31213	4.23972	4.16987	4.10245	4.03735	3.85498	3.79818	3.74324
6	5.71346	5.57971	5.45182	5.32948	5.21236	5.10020	4.99271	4.88965	4.79079	4.69590	4.60478	4.35216	4.27429	4.19935
7	6.60143	6.41719	6.24214	6.07569	5.91732	5.76654	5.62288	5.48592	5.35526	5.23054	5.11141	4.78448	4.68474	4.58918
8	7.47199	7.23028	7.00205	6.78637	6.58238	6.38929	6.20637	6.03295	5.86842	5.71220	5.56376	5.16042	5.03857	4.92238
9	8.32548	8.01969	7.73274	7.46321	7.20979	6.97130	6.74664	6.53482	6.33493	6.14612	5.96764	5.48732	5.34359	5.20716
10	9.16224	8.78611	8.43533	8.10782	7.80169	7.51523	7.24689	6.99525	6.75902	6.53705	6.32825	5.77158	5.60654	5.45057
11	9.98259	9.53020	9.11090	8.72173	8.36009	8.02358	7.71008	7.41766	7.14457	6.88923	6.65022	6.01877	5.83323	5.65860
12	10.78685	10.25262	9.76048	9.30641	8.88687	8.49867	8.13896	7.80519	7.49506	7.20652	6.93770	6.23371	6.02864	5.83641
13	11.57534	10.95400	10.38507	9.86325	9.38384	8.94269	8.53608	8.16073	7.81369	7.49236	7.19437	6.42062	6.19711	5.98839
14	12.34837	11.63496	10.98565	10.39357	9.85268	9.35765	8.90378	8.48690	8.10336	7.74987	7.42355	6.58315	6.34233	6.11828
15	13.10625	12.29607	11.56312	10.89864	10.29498	9.74547	9.24424	8.78615	8.36669	7.98187	7.62817	6.72448	6.46753	6.22930
16	13.84926	12.93794	12.11839	11.37966	10.71225	10.10791	9.55948	9.06069	8.60608	8.19087	7.81086	6.84737	6.57546	6.32419
17	14.57771	13.56110	12.65230	11.83777	11.10590	10.44665	9.85137	9.31256	8.82371	8.37916	7.97399	6.95423	6.66850	6.40529
18	15.29187	14.16612	13.16567	12.27407	11.47726	10.76322	10.12164	9.54363	9.02155	8.54879	8.11963	7.04716	6.74870	6.47461
19	15.99203	14.75351	13.65930	12.68959	11.82760	11.05909	10.37189	9.75563	9.20141	8.70162	8.24967	7.12797	6.81785	6.53385
20	16.67846	15.32380	14.13394	13.08532	12.15812	11.33560	10.60360	9.95011	9.36492	8.83929	8.36578	7.19823	6.87746	6.58449
25	19.91393	17.93554	16.24696	14.79864	13.55036	12.46933	11.52876	10.70661	9.98474	9.34814	8.78432	7.43377	7.07263	6.74649
30	22.84438	20.18845	17.98371	16.14107	14.59072	13.27767	12.15841	11.19828	10.36961	9.65011	9.02181	7.55088	7.16555	6.82039
35	25.49859	22.13184	19.41120	17.19290	15.36814	13.85401	12.58693	11.51784	10.60857	9.82932	9.15656	7.60910	7.20979	6.85409
40	27.90259	23.80822	20.58448	18.01704	15.94907	14.26493	12.87858	11.72552	10.75696	9.93567	9.23303	7.63805	7.23086	6.86946

Appendix II

WWW/Electronic Resources for Financial Information

This appendix describes some of the many www/electronic resources currently available for gathering industry-level and company specific financial information to both to support the text and as your on-going financial accounting information resource. Some of these resources are free, others are only available on a "subscription" basis, and still others charge a fee per unit of time or information.

INTERNET RESOURCES www:prenhall.com/revsine

Prentice Hall's personalized Learning on the Internet Partnership (MyPHLIP): A fully customizable environment that opens up text-specific resources to students and faculty, this site can be accessed through **www.prenhall.com/revsine.**

- **For students,** MyPHLIP provides an online study guide, tied chapter-by-chapter to the text, In the News items, Internet Exercises, lecture notes, downloadable software, Ask the Tutor, and more.
- **For faculty,** MyPHLIP provides a syllabus tool that allows them to manage content, communicate with students, and upload their personal resources.

Accounting Organizations

American Institute of Certified Public Accountants: The AICPA is the national, professional organization for all U.S. Certified Public Accountants. This site describes the organization and answers frequently asked questions about becoming a CPA. Member resources and information about the profession are also provided. **www.aicpa.org**

Financial Accounting Standards Board: The FASB sets the standards of financial accounting and reporting in the U.S. Its Internet site provides information about the structure and workings of the organization, current standards, and emerging issues. **www.fasb.org**

International Accounting Standards Board: The IASB sets global financial accounting and reporting standards, promotes rigorous use of those standards, and works toward the convergence of national accounting standards and International Accounting Standards. This site will help you stay abreast of financial accounting and reporting practices worldwide. **www.iasc.org.uk**

Government Agencies

Department of Commerce: This site provides links to other sites, many of which have important information for business people. **www.doc.gov**

Federal Trade Commission: This site contains a large amount of information about the commission itself as well as the laws and regulations it administers. It also contains good links to other business-oriented sites. **www.ftc.gov**

Internal Revenue Service: This is a surprisingly flashy site, full of free information about the IRS and tax-related issues. **www.irs.ustreas.gov/prod**

Securities and Exchange Commission: This site can be helpful for researching specific industries and companies (see next site). **www.sec.gov**

SEC EDGAR Database: This site contains electronic copies of SEC filings by publicly traded companies. The EDGAR project was launched several years ago on a voluntary basis, so not all public companies have been participating since inception. It is an invaluable source for full text 10-K (annual), 10-Q (quarterly) financial information, and corporate proxy statements. **www.edgar-online.com** and **www.freeedgar.com**

Securities Exchanges

American Stock Exchange: As the nation's second largest floor-based exchange, the AMEX has a significant presence in common stocks, index shares, and equity derivative securities. **www.amex.com**

Chicago Board of Trade: One of Chicago's two major futures and options exchanges, the Board of Trade deals in agricultural products like corn and soybeans and in financial instruments like U.S. Treasury bonds. **www.cbot.com**

Chicago Mercantile Exchange: Chicago's other futures and options exchange, the Merc has plenty of information about futures and options investing, including online courses. There's also information on prices and the products that are traded, from pork bellies to Eurodollars. **www.cme.com**

NASDAQ: The National Association of Securities Dealers Automated Quotation (NASDAQ) exchange Web site has tools that help you track the market, search for stock quotes, research company information, and keep abreast of financial news. **www.nasdaq.com**

New York Stock Exchange: The world's most famous stock exchange. This site provides a history of the exchange and details on the companies that are added each week. You can track the movement of the entire market and there are links to every listed company that has a Web site. **www.nyse.com**

General Business News

Newspapers: For up-to-the-minute business news from around the world and a wealth of information about the economy and specific companies and industries, try the *Financial Times* (**www.financialtimes.com**), the *New York Times* (**www.nyt.com**), or the *Wall Street Journal* Interactive (**www.wsj.com**).

Financial Magazines: *Business Week* (**www.businessweek.com**), the *Economist* (**www.economist.com**), and *Fortune* (**www.fortune.com**) are just three of the many financial magazines that provide business news and analysis on the Internet.

Financial portals: These sites have financial news, stock quotes, earnings projections, and information about companies and industries, plus links to other useful sites. Try

CNBC.com (**www.cnbc.com**), Microsoft's MoneyCentral (**www.moneycentral.com**), SmartMoney's Map of the Market (**www.smartmoney.com**), or the granddaddy of financial portals, Yahoo! (**finance.yahoo.com**). One of the most comprehensive global investing portals on the Internet is WorldlyInvestor (**www.worldlyinvestor.com**).

Industry and Company Information

BestCalls.com: Listen in via phone or Webcast to the CEO of your favorite company explaining recent performance of the business and its future prospects. The site has live broadcasts and recordings of quarterly earnings announcements and management interviews for nearly 2,600 companies. **www.bestcalls.com**

Bloomberg Personal Online: This is the most recent addition to the Bloomberg Media Family. It provides the interactive investor with data and analysis previously available only on the Bloomberg Terminal, as well as industry and company data (some at a fee) with links to other sources. **www.bloomberg.com**

Businesswire: This site contains information, primarily in the form of press releases, about U.S. companies both large and small. **www.businesswire.com**

Dun & Bradstreet: This site has tips about a variety of business-related topics, as well as marketplace information. You can purchase D&B services here, too. **www.dnb.com**

Hoover's Online: This massive site provides information, some of which you must pay for, about thousands of companies. **www.hoovers.com**

Industry Link: This is an excellent compilation of links to sites of interest to those in a number of specific industries. This site, however, does not provide coverage of all industries. **www.industrylink.com**

Multex Investor: A great source for brokerage research online. Search the site by company, industry, research provider, or specific analyst. Registration is free but the research isn't. **www.multexinvestor.com**

PR Newswire: This is an excellent source of current news about companies. Hundreds of companies post their press releases here. **www.prnewswire.com**

Commercial Vendors and Databases

Dow Jones News Retrieval: This service is available by subscription. Started in 1974 to provide only stock market information, it was expanded in 1977 to include summaries of news appearing in the *Wall Street Journal* and *Barron's.* The service has been substantially expanded to include the following databases (incomplete list): DJNEWS, stories from the *Wall Street Journal, Barron's,* and Dow Jones News Service as recent as 90 seconds, and as far back as 90 days; DSCLO, Disclosure Online containing 10-K extracts, company profiles, and other detailed data on over 10,000 publicly held companies compiled by Zacks Investment Research, Inc.; INVEST, full texts of more than 13,000 research reports from top brokers, investment bankers, and other analysts (Investext) including historical, current, and forecasted marketing and financial information; TEXT, all articles that appeared or were scheduled to appear in the *Wall Street Journal* since January 1984, including selected articles back to June 1979.

Global Access: This subscription service of Disclosure Incorporated offers a comprehensive searchable financial database of U.S. and international companies. Includes real-time and historical SEC filings, scanned images of annual reports, full-text articles

Lexis-Nexis: This service is available by subscription. The Accounting Information Library (NAARS) includes the complete financial statement portion of annual reports for more than 4,000 publicly traded companies, plus a vast collection of professional accounting literature.

Standard & Poor's: This service is available by subscription. The COMPUSTAT database consists of fundamental financial and market information on U.S. traded companies with hundreds of financial data items collected from a wide variety of sources including news wire services, news releases, shareholder reports, direct company contracts, and quarterly and annual documents files with the SEC. The GLOBAL Vantage database contains detailed information on 11,000 companies from 70 countries.

Subject Index

A

B

C

D

F

G

H

I

J

L

M

P

S

T

U

V

W

COMMON FINANCIAL RATIOS

Profitability

$$\text{Return on Assets (ROA)} = \frac{\text{Net Income + Interest Expense (1 – Tax Rate)}}{\text{Average Total Assets}}$$

$$\text{Profit Margin for ROA} = \frac{\text{Net Income + Interest Expense (1 – Tax Rate)}}{\text{Sales}}$$

$$\text{Total Asset Turnover} = \frac{\text{Sales}}{\text{Average Total Assets}}$$

$$\text{Common Earnings Leverage} = \frac{\text{Net Income – Preferred Dividends}}{\text{Net Income + Interest Expense (1 – Tax Rate)}}$$

$$\text{Financial Structure Leverage} = \frac{\text{Average Total Assets}}{\text{Average Common Shareholders' Equity}}$$

$$\text{Return on Common Equity (ROCE)} = \frac{\text{Net Income – Preferred Dividends}}{\text{Average Common Shareholders' Equity}}$$

Asset Utilization

$$\text{Accounts Receivable Turnover} = \frac{\text{Net Credit Sales}}{\text{Average Accounts Receivable}}$$

$$\text{Inventory Turnover} = \frac{\text{Cost of Goods Sold}}{\text{Average Inventories}}$$

$$\text{Fixed Asset Turnover} = \frac{\text{Sales}}{\text{Average Fixed Assets}}$$